TEACHER'S EDITION

PRACTICAL BUSINESS MATH PROCEDURES

FOURTH EDITION

JEFFREY SLATER
North Shore Community College
Beverly, Massachusetts

IRWIN
Burr Ridge, Illinois
Boston, Massachusetts
Sydney, Australia

Teacher's Guide

As the author of *Practical Business Math Procedures,* I believe you should put your energy into the classroom. It is my job to provide the best text and supporting package.

In the following pages I will show you many of the key features of my text and package. Be sure to look at the section on how to dissect and solve a word problem. This is a first in business math texts.

I want to hear from you. Here is a toll-free number to my home: 1-800-484-1065 . . . 8980. If you have questions or comments on the book, please call me anytime.

The Slater Text and Supporting Package

The Text

Supplements

For the Instructor

For the Student

Brief Fourth Edition

Highlights of Content Changes

New sections on how to dissect and solve a word problem for Chapters 1–8.

Use of M&M's® Chocolate Candies to illustrate fractions, decimals, and percents.

New section of articles from MONEY Magazine.

New Appendix I, containing a complete set of additional homework assignments by learning unit.

Deletion of aliquot parts.

Expansion of word problems especially for the percent chapter.

Pie charts added for clearer explanation.

Credit card transactions added to the banking chapter.

More realistic bank statements showing ATM, interest, etc.

The annuities chapter now compares compounding and present value to annuities.

Updated Business Math Scrapbooks.

Articles and clippings about real companies are updated and integrated in the text.

Expansion of cumulative reviews.

Chapter openers reflect companies "Then and Now" and how business math relates to them.

Deletion of the quarterly report and tax deposit regulation.

New to This Edition

Blueprint Aid for Dissecting and Solving a Word Problem

The Problem: Students in business math have a terrible time solving word problems.
The Solution: The first eight chapters provide a blueprint on how to dissect and solve a word problem for each learning unit. Below the blueprint are the steps to solve the problem. The answer is highlighted in red.
Classroom Tested: The author has used the blueprint in class for over two years and finds that students become actively involved in the dissecting process. They work them together on the board or on an overhead transparency.

Advantages of the Blueprints (from Student Feedback)

1. Helps the student get started—where do I begin?
2. Builds confidence.
3. Shows visually what has to be done before students start calculating.
4. Gives students a chance to identify their area of weakness (A, B, C, or D).
5. Provides a "structure" to use to provide consistent instruction. We are all learning it one way.

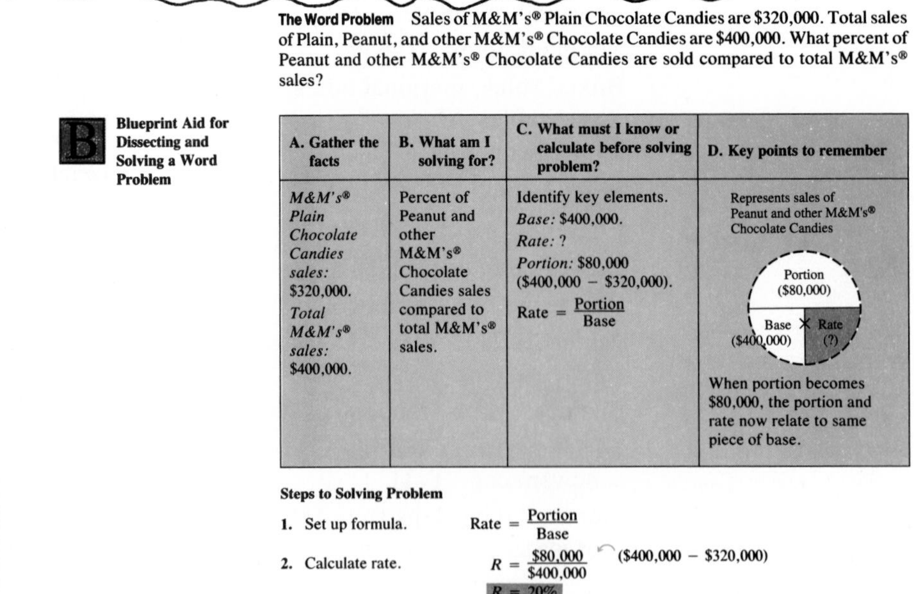

The Word Problem Sales of M&M's® Plain Chocolate Candies are $320,000. Total sales of Plain, Peanut, and other M&M's® Chocolate Candies are $400,000. What percent of Peanut and other M&M's® Chocolate Candies are sold compared to total M&M's® sales?

B Blueprint Aid for Dissecting and Solving a Word Problem

A. Gather the facts	B. What am I solving for?	C. What must I know or calculate before solving problem?	D. Key points to remember
M&M's® Plain Chocolate Candies sales: $320,000. *Total M&M's® sales:* $400,000.	Percent of Peanut and other M&M's® Chocolate Candies sales compared to total M&M's® sales.	Identify key elements. *Base:* $400,000. *Rate:* ? *Portion:* $80,000 ($400,000 − $320,000). Rate = $\frac{\text{Portion}}{\text{Base}}$	Represents sales of Peanut and other M&M's® Chocolate Candies. Portion ($80,000); Base ($400,000) × Rate (?). When portion becomes $80,000, the portion and rate now relate to same piece of base.

Steps to Solving Problem

1. Set up formula. Rate = $\frac{\text{Portion}}{\text{Base}}$
2. Calculate rate. $R = \frac{\$80,000}{\$400,000}$ ($400,000 − $320,000)

$R = 20\%$

The above word problem asks for rate of candy sales that are *not* plain. Thus, $400,000 of total candy sales less sales of M&M's® Plain Chocolate Candies ($320,000) allows us to arrive at sales of Peanut and other M&M's® Chocolate Candies ($80,000).

The functional color key for this edition is:

- Blue: *Movement, cancellations, steps to solve, arrows.*
- Gold: *Formulas, steps, chapter organizer.*
- Green: *Tables, forms, charts.*
- Red: *Key items we are solving for.*
- Magenta: *Worked-out solutions in Teacher's Edition.*

How the Book Is Color Coded

This format was first introduced in the Third Edition. While many books have and will continue to use color, we set out from the beginning to use color to teach.

The author personally color coded each element so that when students see a number in red they know it is a key item they are solving for. Functional color enhances the learning process.

Chapter Opening Photos

At the beginning of each chapter we have interesting photos of real companies in a "That Was Then . . . This Is Now" format. Hopefully you and your students' interest will be piqued by these choices and the vintage photos.

A RING OF CLEANLINESS AROUND THE GLOBE.

Ivory Soap . . . 99 44/100 Per Cent Pure.

THAT WAS THEN . . .
. . . THIS IS NOW

In 1889, a test on Ivory Soap was run to see what impurities it had. The list was .11% uncombined alkali, .28% carbonates, and .17% mineral matter, equaling .56% foreign substances. Thus, 100% − .56% = $99\frac{44}{100}$% pure. The slogan was born and remains today.

Learning Objectives

Learning objectives are included to give students a concise listing of what they need to understand in each learning unit. Each objective is page referenced.

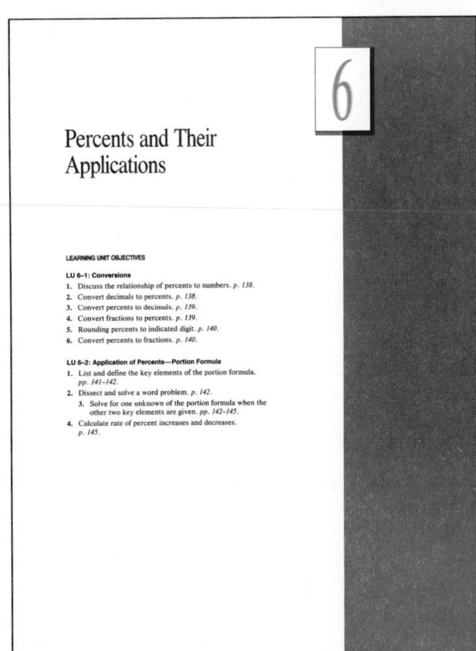

6

Percents and Their Applications

LEARNING UNIT OBJECTIVES

LU 6–1: Conversions

1. Discuss the relationship of percents to numbers. *p. 138.*
2. Convert decimals to percents. *p. 138.*
3. Convert percents to decimals. *p. 139.*
4. Convert fractions to percents. *p. 139.*
5. Rounding percents to indicated digit. *p. 140.*
6. Convert percents to fractions. *p. 140.*

LU 6–2: Application of Percents—Portion Formula

1. List and define the key elements of the portion formula. *pp. 141–142.*
2. Dissect and solve a word problem. *p. 142.*
3. Solve for one unknown of the portion formula when the other two key elements are given. *pp. 142–145.*
4. Calculate rate of percent increases and decreases. *p. 145.*

Marginal Notes

Logos in the page margins inform students when they can use Lotus templates and videotapes, and when instructors have two-color teaching transparencies available.

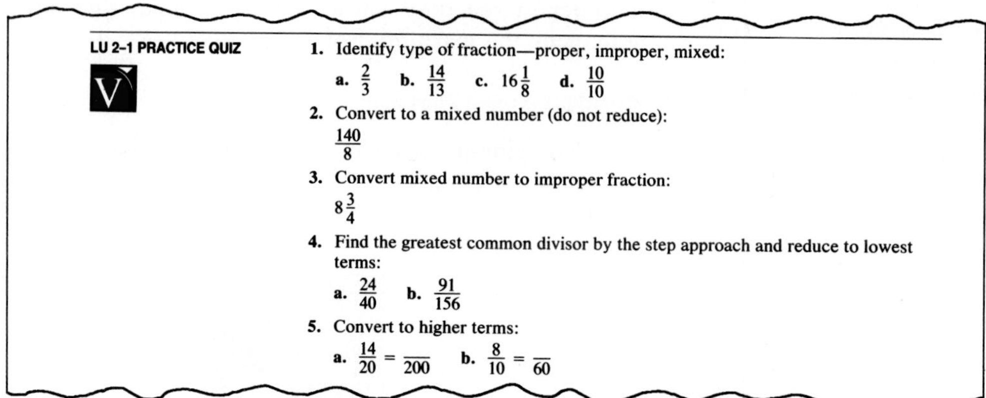

LU 2–1 PRACTICE QUIZ

1. Identify type of fraction—proper, improper, mixed:
   a. $\frac{2}{3}$ **b.** $\frac{14}{13}$ **c.** $16\frac{1}{8}$ **d.** $\frac{10}{10}$
2. Convert to a mixed number (do not reduce):
   $\frac{140}{8}$
3. Convert mixed number to improper fraction:
   $8\frac{3}{4}$
4. Find the greatest common divisor by the step approach and reduce to lowest terms:
   a. $\frac{24}{40}$ **b.** $\frac{91}{156}$
5. Convert to higher terms:
   a. $\frac{14}{20} = \frac{\quad}{200}$ **b.** $\frac{8}{10} = \frac{\quad}{60}$

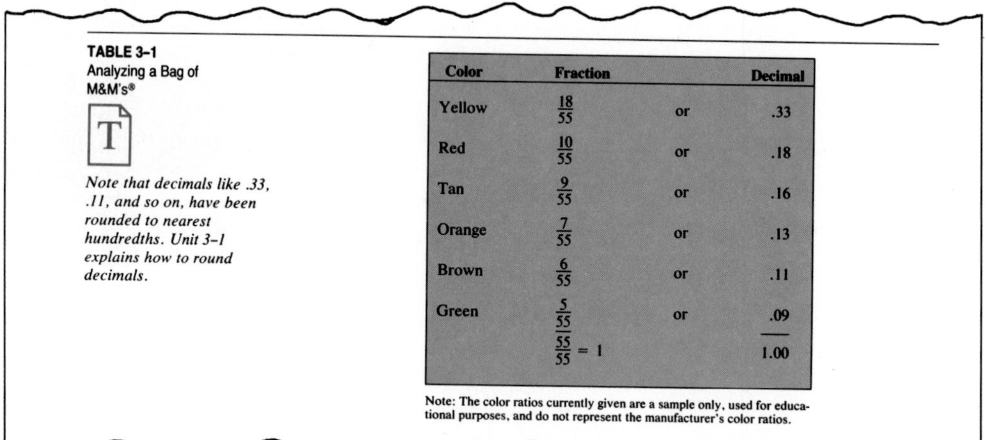

TABLE 3–1
Analyzing a Bag of M&M's®

Note that decimals like .33, .11, and so on, have been rounded to nearest hundredths. Unit 3–1 explains how to round decimals.

Color	Fraction		Decimal
Yellow	$\frac{18}{55}$	or	.33
Red	$\frac{10}{55}$	or	.18
Tan	$\frac{9}{55}$	or	.16
Orange	$\frac{7}{55}$	or	.13
Brown	$\frac{6}{55}$	or	.11
Green	$\frac{5}{55}$	or	.09
	$\frac{55}{55} = 1$		1.00

Note: The color ratios currently given are a sample only, used for educational purposes, and do not represent the manufacturer's color ratios.

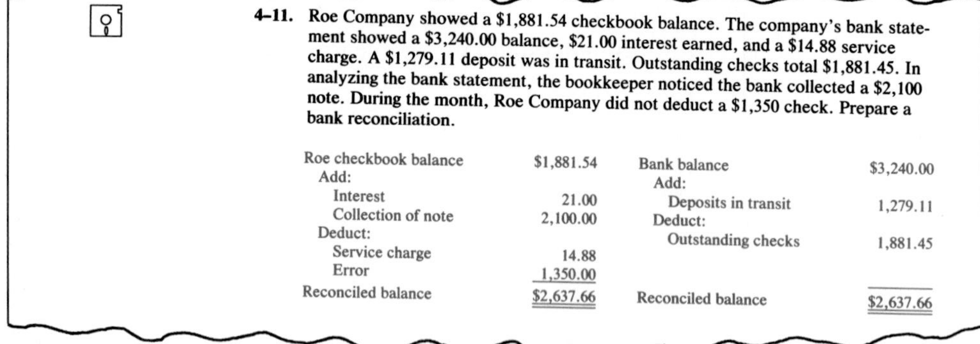

4–11. Roe Company showed a $1,881.54 checkbook balance. The company's bank statement showed a $3,240.00 balance, $21.00 interest earned, and a $14.88 service charge. A $1,279.11 deposit was in transit. Outstanding checks total $1,881.45. In analyzing the bank statement, the bookkeeper noticed the bank collected a $2,100 note. During the month, Roe Company did not deduct a $1,350 check. Prepare a bank reconciliation.

Roe checkbook balance	$1,881.54	Bank balance	$3,240.00
Add:		Add:	
Interest	21.00	Deposits in transit	1,279.11
Collection of note	2,100.00	Deduct:	
Deduct:		Outstanding checks	1,881.45
Service charge	14.88		
Error	1,350.00		
Reconciled balance	$2,637.66	Reconciled balance	$2,637.66

Boxed Definitions and Rules, Marginal Notes, and Tables and Figures

These are used when appropriate to provide emphasis and illustration.

TABLE 6-1
Analyzing a Bag of M&M's®

Sharon Hoogstraten

Color	Fraction	Decimal (hundredth)	Percent (hundredth)
Yellow	$\frac{18}{55}$	.33	32.73%
Red	$\frac{10}{55}$	.18	18.18
Tan	$\frac{9}{55}$	.16	16.36
Orange	$\frac{7}{55}$	.13	12.73
Brown	$\frac{6}{55}$	.11	10.91
Green	$\frac{5}{55}$	.09	9.09
	$\frac{55}{55} = 1$	1.00	100.00%

Note: The color ratios currently given are a sample only, used for educational purposes, and do not represent the manufacturer's color ratios.

Converting Percents to Decimals

Converting percents to decimals first involves learning two basic steps. Then you can learn the conversion steps for percents expressed in fractional form.

Steps for Converting Percents to Decimals

Step 1. Drop percent symbol.
Step 2. Move decimal point two places to the left. You are actually dividing by 100.

Steps for Conversion When Percent Is Expressed in Fractional Form

Step 1. Convert a fraction to a decimal by dividing numerator by denominator.
Step 2. Drop percent symbol.
Step 3. Move decimal point two places to the left.

Note that when a percent is less than 1%, the decimal conversion has at least two leading zeros before the whole number .009.

EXAMPLES

.9% = .009
9% = .09
92% = .92
92.4% = .924
924.4% = 9.244

$8\frac{3}{4}\% = 8.75\% = .0875$
$5\frac{1}{2}\% = 5.5\% = .055$
$\frac{1}{5}\% = .20\% = .0020$
$\frac{1}{4}\% = .25\% = .0025$

Think of $8\frac{3}{4}\%$ as
$8\% = .08$
$+\frac{3}{4}\% = +.0075$
$8\frac{3}{4}\% = .0875$

Real World Applications

Slater integrates real companies into the text presentation. More than 64 companies (such as Nike, Walt Disney, and Liz Claiborne) are included to illustrate chapter concepts and motivate both young and older students.

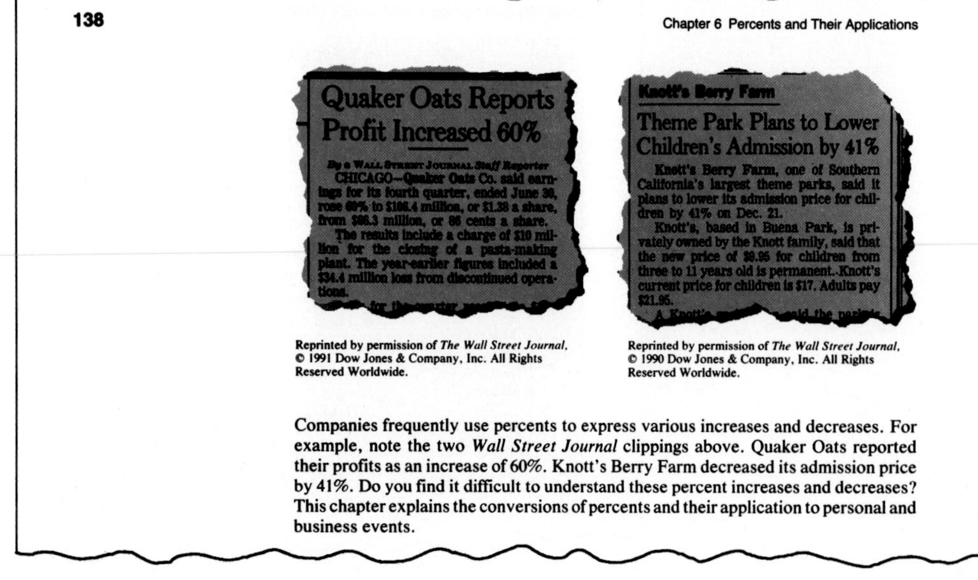
138 Chapter 6 Percents and Their Applications

Quaker Oats Reports Profit Increased 60%

By a WALL STREET JOURNAL Staff Reporter
CHICAGO—Quaker Oats Co. said earnings for its fourth quarter, ended June 30, rose 60% to $106.4 million, or $1.38 a share, from $66.3 million, or 86 cents a share.
The results include a charge of $10 million for the closing of a pasta-making plant. The year-earlier figures included a $34.4 million loss from discontinued operations.

Reprinted by permission of *The Wall Street Journal*, © 1991 Dow Jones & Company, Inc. All Rights Reserved Worldwide.

Knott's Berry Farm

Theme Park Plans to Lower Children's Admission by 41%

Knott's Berry Farm, one of Southern California's largest theme parks, said it plans to lower its admission price for children by 41% on Dec. 21.
Knott's, based in Buena Park, is privately owned by the Knott family, said that the new price of $9.95 for children from three to 11 years old is permanent. Knott's current price for children is $17. Adults pay $21.95.

Reprinted by permission of *The Wall Street Journal*, © 1990 Dow Jones & Company, Inc. All Rights Reserved Worldwide.

Companies frequently use percents to express various increases and decreases. For example, note the two *Wall Street Journal* clippings above. Quaker Oats reported their profits as an increase of 60%. Knott's Berry Farm decreased its admission price by 41%. Do you find it difficult to understand these percent increases and decreases? This chapter explains the conversions of percents and their application to personal and business events.

Practice Quiz

At the end of each learning unit is a sample quiz, followed by worked-out solutions for *immediate* feedback.

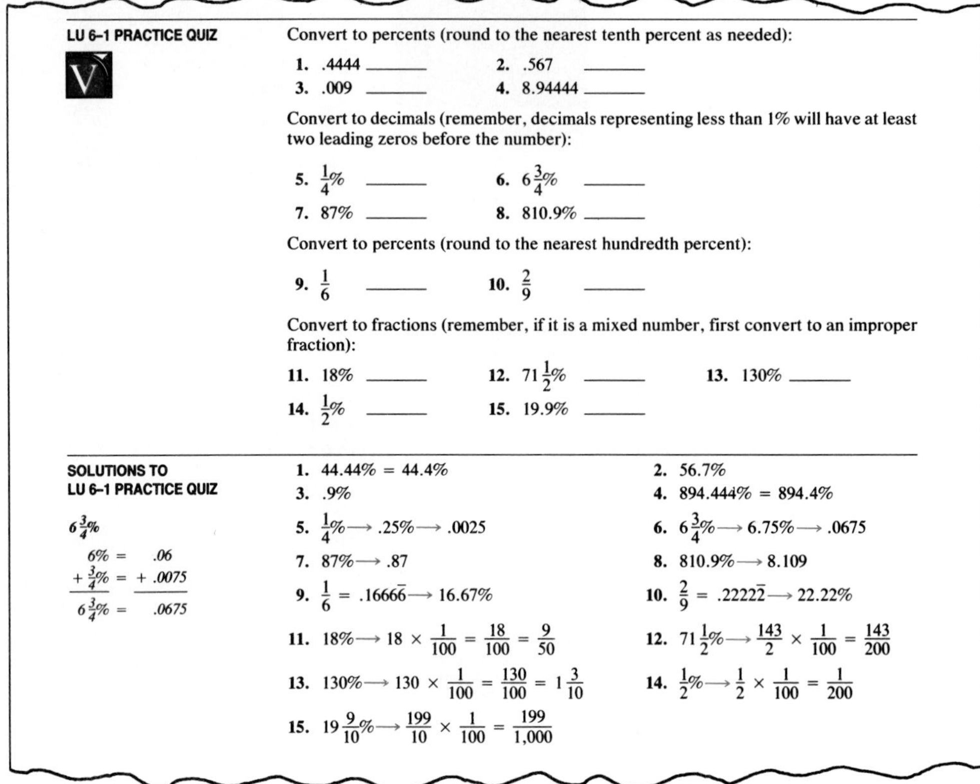

LU 6-1 PRACTICE QUIZ

Convert to percents (round to the nearest tenth percent as needed):

1. .4444 ______ **2.** .567 ______
3. .009 ______ **4.** 8.94444 ______

Convert to decimals (remember, decimals representing less than 1% will have at least two leading zeros before the number):

5. $\frac{1}{4}\%$ ______ **6.** $6\frac{3}{4}\%$ ______
7. 87% ______ **8.** 810.9% ______

Convert to percents (round to the nearest hundredth percent):

9. $\frac{1}{6}$ ______ **10.** $\frac{2}{9}$ ______

Convert to fractions (remember, if it is a mixed number, first convert to an improper fraction):

11. 18% ______ **12.** $71\frac{1}{2}\%$ ______ **13.** 130% ______
14. $\frac{1}{2}\%$ ______ **15.** 19.9% ______

SOLUTIONS TO LU 6-1 PRACTICE QUIZ

$6\frac{3}{4}\%$

$6\% = .06$
$+\frac{3}{4}\% = +.0075$
$6\frac{3}{4}\% = .0675$

1. $44.44\% = 44.4\%$ **2.** 56.7%
3. $.9\%$ **4.** $894.444\% = 894.4\%$
5. $\frac{1}{4}\% \longrightarrow .25\% \longrightarrow .0025$ **6.** $6\frac{3}{4}\% \longrightarrow 6.75\% \longrightarrow .0675$
7. $87\% \longrightarrow .87$ **8.** $810.9\% \longrightarrow 8.109$
9. $\frac{1}{6} = .1666\overline{6} \longrightarrow 16.67\%$ **10.** $\frac{2}{9} = .2222\overline{2} \longrightarrow 22.22\%$
11. $18\% \longrightarrow 18 \times \frac{1}{100} = \frac{18}{100} = \frac{9}{50}$ **12.** $71\frac{1}{2}\% \longrightarrow \frac{143}{2} \times \frac{1}{100} = \frac{143}{200}$
13. $130\% \longrightarrow 130 \times \frac{1}{100} = \frac{130}{100} = 1\frac{3}{10}$ **14.** $\frac{1}{2}\% \longrightarrow \frac{1}{2} \times \frac{1}{100} = \frac{1}{200}$
15. $19\frac{9}{10}\% \longrightarrow \frac{199}{10} \times \frac{1}{100} = \frac{199}{1{,}000}$

Chapter Organizer

A quick reference guide called the chapter organizer is at the end of each chapter. Key points, formulas, examples, and vocabulary are included. All have page references.

CHAPTER ORGANIZER: A REFERENCE GUIDE

Page	Topic	Key point, procedure, formula	Example(s) to illustrate situation
138	Converting decimals to percents	1. Move decimal point two places to right. 2. Place a percent symbol at end of number.	.81 = 81% .008 = .8% 4.15 = 415%
139	Converting percents to decimals	1. Drop percent symbol. 2. Move decimal point two places to left. For fractional form: 1. Convert fraction to a decimal. 2. Drop percent symbol. 3. Move decimal two places to left.	.89% = .0089 $8\frac{3}{4}\%$ = 8.75% = .0875 95% = .95 $\frac{1}{4}\%$ = .25% = .0025 195% = 1.95 $\frac{1}{5}\%$ = .20% = .0020
139	Converting fractions to percents	1. Divide numerator by denominator. 2. Move decimal point two places to right. 3. Add percent symbol.	$\frac{4}{5}$ = 80%
139	Rounding percents	Be sure answer is in percent before rounding. Follow same rounding procedures as for decimals.	Round to nearest hundredth percent. $\frac{3}{7}$ = .4285714 = 42.85714% = 42.86%

End-of-Chapter Problems

Drill problems

END-OF-CHAPTER PROBLEMS

Drill Problems Convert the following decimals to percents:

Additional homework assignments by learning unit are at the end of text in Appendix I (p. I–25). Solutions to odd problems are at the end of text in Appendix II.

6–1. .85 85% **6–2.** .713 71.3% **6–3.** .6 60%
6–4. 6.00 600% **6–5.** 2.145 214.5% **6–6.** 4.006 400.6%

Convert the following percents to decimals:

6–7. 4% .04 **6–8.** 16% .16 **6–9.** $45\frac{9}{10}$% .459
6–10. 86.8% .868 **6–11.** 104% 1.04 **6–12.** 99% .99

Convert the following fractions to percents (to the nearest tenth percent as needed):

6–13. $\frac{1}{15}$ .0666 = 6.7% **6–14.** $\frac{1}{200}$ .005 = .5%
6–15. $\frac{5}{8}$ .625 = 62.5% **6–16.** $\frac{11}{8}$ 1.375 = 137.5%

Word problems

Word Problems (First of Four Sets)

6–52. At a local Dunkin Donuts shop, a survey showed that out of 5,000 customers coming in for breakfast, 4,500 ordered a cup of coffee with their meal. What percent of customers ordered coffee?

$\frac{4,500}{5,000} = 90\%$ Portion and rate must refer to same piece of the base.

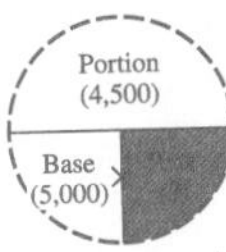

6–53. What percent of customers in Problem 6–52 did not order coffee?

$\frac{500}{5,000} = 10\%$ Portion and rate must refer to same piece of the base.

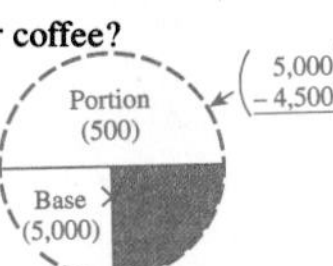

Challenge problems

Challenge Problem
Airfare Special

6–94. Each Tuesday, Ryan Airlines reduces its one-way ticket from Fort Wayne to Chicago from $125 to $40. To receive this special $40 price, the customer must buy a round-trip ticket. Ryan has a nonrefundable 25% penalty fare for cancellation; it estimates that about nine tenths of 1% will cancel their reservations. The airlines also estimates this special price will cause a passenger traffic increase from 400 to 900. Ryan expects revenue for the year to be 55.4% higher than the previous year. Last year, Ryan's sales were $482,000. To receive the special rate, Janice Miller bought two round-trip tickets. On other airlines, Janice has paid $100 round trip (with no cancellation penalty). Calculate the following:

a. Percent discount Ryan is offering. $125 − 40 = $ 85; $\frac{\$85}{\$125} = 68\%$

b. Percent passenger travel will increase. $\frac{500}{400} = 125\%$

c. Sales for new year. 1.554 × $482,000 = $749,028

d. Janice's loss if she cancels one round-trip flight. $80 × .25 = $20

e. Approximately how many more cancellations can Ryan Airlines expect (after Janice's cancellation)?
.009 × 900 = 8.1 people
− 1.0
7.1 people or 7

Summary practice test
Cumulative reviews (after Chapters 3, 8, and 13)
Check figures for the odd-numbered drill and word problems, and the challenge problems are found in Appendix II. Check figures for all problems in summary practice tests and cumulative reviews are in Appendix II.

Summary Practice Test

Solutions are at end of text in Appendix II.
Quick Reference
If you get any wrong answers, study the page numbers given for each problem.
1–4. P. 138.
5–8. P. 139.
9–10. P. 139.

Convert the following decimals to percents:

1. .169 16.9% **2.** .6 60%
3. 16.31 1,631% **4.** 6 600%

Convert the following percents to decimals:

5. 19% .19 **6.** 4.14% .0414
7. 200% 2.0 **8.** $\frac{1}{5}$% .0020

Convert the following fractions to percents (round to nearest tenth percent):

9. $\frac{1}{8}$ 12.5% **10.** $\frac{7}{9}$ 77.8%

Convert the following percents to fractions and reduce to lowest terms as needed:

Business Math Scrapbook

Clippings from *The Wall Street Journal* give students an opportunity to apply theory to real life and see the importance of what they're learning.

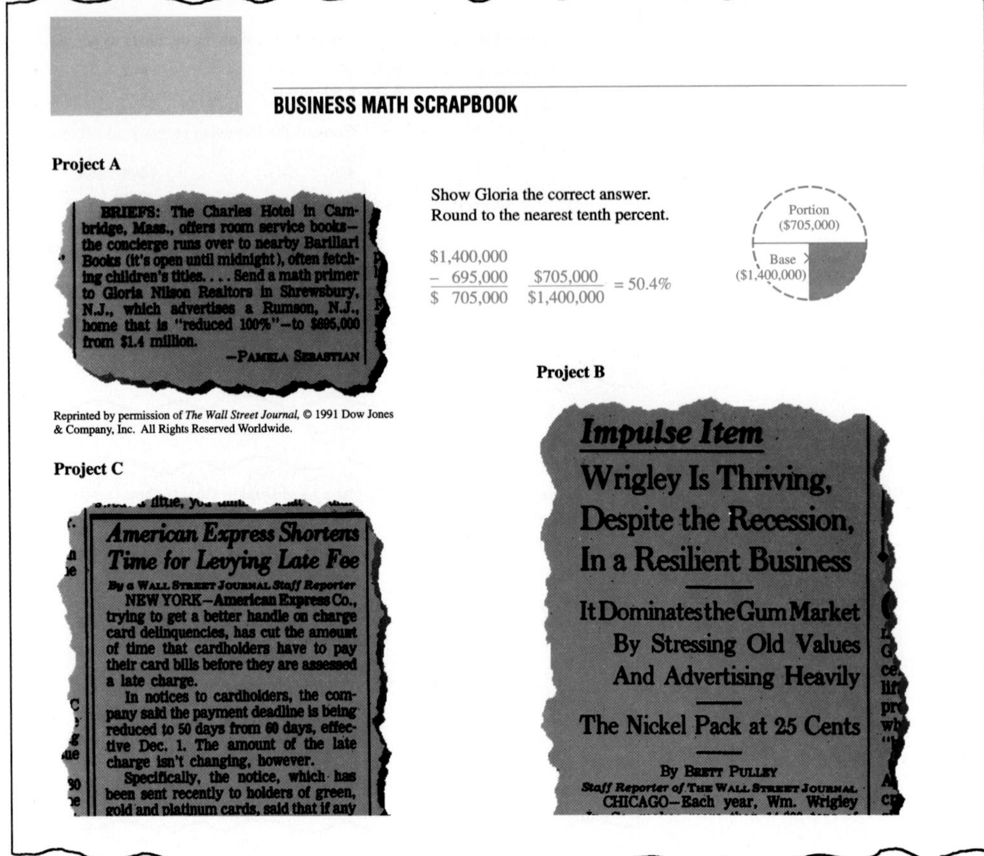

BUSINESS MATH SCRAPBOOK

Project A

BRIEFS: The Charles Hotel in Cambridge, Mass., offers room service books—the concierge runs over to nearby Barillari Books (it's open until midnight), often fetching children's titles. . . . Send a math primer to Gloria Nilson Realtors in Shrewsbury, N.J., which advertises a Rumson, N.J., home that is "reduced 100%"—to $695,000 from $1.4 million.

—PAMELA SEBASTIAN

Show Gloria the correct answer.
Round to the nearest tenth percent.

$$\begin{array}{r} \$1{,}400{,}000 \\ -\ 695{,}000 \\ \hline \$\ 705{,}000 \end{array} \qquad \frac{\$705{,}000}{\$1{,}400{,}000} = 50.4\%$$

Project B

Impulse Item

Wrigley Is Thriving, Despite the Recession, In a Resilient Business

It Dominates the Gum Market By Stressing Old Values And Advertising Heavily

The Nickel Pack at 25 Cents

By BRETT PULLEY
Staff Reporter of THE WALL STREET JOURNAL
CHICAGO—Each year, Wm. Wrigley

Project C

American Express Shortens Time for Levying Late Fee

By a WALL STREET JOURNAL *Staff Reporter*

NEW YORK—American Express Co., trying to get a better handle on charge card delinquencies, has cut the amount of time that cardholders have to pay their card bills before they are assessed a late charge.

In notices to cardholders, the company said the payment deadline is being reduced to 50 days from 60 days, effective Dec. 1. The amount of the late charge isn't changing, however.

Specifically, the notice, which has been sent recently to holders of green, gold and platinum cards, said that if any

Appendix I

Note that at the end of the text in Appendix I we provide a set of additional homework assignments arranged by learning unit. Instructors have the flexibility of assigning homework by learning units in a convenient "tear out" format for Chapters 1–12. Check figures for odd-numbered problems are in Appendix II.

Date ______________ Name ______________________________

LU 1-1: Writing Whole Numbers; Rounding Whole Numbers

Drill Problems

1. Express the following numbers in verbal form:
   a. 3,875 Three thousand, eight hundred seventy-five
   b. 160,501 One hundred sixty thousand, five hundred one
   c. 2,098,767 Two million, ninety-eight thousand, seven hundred sixty-seven
   d. 58,003 Fifty-eight thousand, three
   e. 50,025,212,015 Fifty billion, twenty-five million, two hundred twelve thousand, fifteen
2. Write in numeric form:
   a. Seventy thousand, one hundred eighty-two 70,182
   b. Fifty-eight thousand, three 58,003
   c. Two hundred eighty thousand, five 280,005
   d. Three million, ten 3,000,010
   e. Sixty-seven thousand, seven hundred sixty 67,760
3. Round off the following numbers:
   a. To the nearest ten:
      42 40   379 380   855 860   5,981 5,980   206 210
   b. To the nearest hundred:
      9,664 9,700   2,074 2,100   888 900   271 300   75 100

Business Math Handbook

Inserted in the back cover of every text, this 64-page reference guide contains every table in the text, plus additional reference material. The Business Math Handbook also includes 220 additional word problems (10 per chapter) for extra practice, with check figures for all problems. The back cover of the Business Math Handbook provides a quick reference chart on how to use a pocket calculator. With the Business Math Handbook, instructors don't need to photocopy tables and charts for their students, and students won't need to flip back and forth in the text to use the charts while working problems.

The Wall Street Journal Newspaper (Not Found in Brief Edition)

Located in the front cover, the insert explains how to read *The Wall Street Journal* with an emphasis on business math. It provides an explanation of the Dow Jones Industrial Average and has page references to integrate it to the text.

Money-Saving Tips from MONEY Magazine (Not Found in Brief Edition)

This unique section located at the beginning of the text gives students exposure to advice found in MONEY Magazine. The articles, chosen by business math students, provide motivation and reference material for personal use, as well as support material for specific text chapters.

Who Should Own What?

The Most Important Financial Decision You and Your Spouse Ever Make Is Who Should Legally Own the Assets You Share.

By Jordan E. Goodman If you're married, you and your spouse most likely hold your house and other major possessions in both your names. You figure, correctly, that when one of you dies the other will become sole owner without having to go through a months-long probate proceeding. What could be more loving or more fair? Who could possibly lose in this situation?

Unfortunately, this last question has an unpleasant answer: your children. The ways you and your spouse hold title to major assets can sock your heirs with all sorts of unnecessary taxes. "Few people pay enough attention to estate tax, which can run as high as 55%," says Robert Clarfeld, a financial planner in New York City.

Those taxes can be avoided if you have a lawyer make sure your property is titled correctly. (Typical cost: about $1,000.) This effort can also be important if you are single and share ownership, say, of a house or a car with a relative or friend.

There are three basic forms of co-ownership. With the most common, **joint tenancy with right of survivorship,** each person owns an equal share of the property and can dispose of it without the approval of the others. When an owner dies, his or her share is divided equally among the other owners.

The second method, **tenancy by the entirety,** is similar to joint tenancy, except that neither partner can sell his or her share without permission from the other. This alternative is available in only about 30 states.

Like joint tenancy, the third form, **tenancy in common,** permits co-owners to dispose of their shares independently. When one owner dies, his or her share goes to the heirs named in a will, rather than automatically to the co-owners.

(If you live in one of the nine **community property** states—Arizona, California, Idaho, Louisiana, Nevada, New Mexico, Texas, Washington and Wisconsin—where assets acquired during a marriage are generally considered to be owned equally by both spouses, it would be wise to consult an estate lawyer about co-ownership.)

Which form should you use? The answer ought to be based mostly on estate-tax considerations, not sentiment. Consider the case of an affluent couple who jointly own $800,000 in assets—a $315,000 house, $100,000 in life insurance on the wife and $80,000 on the husband, a $125,000 vacation retreat, $100,000 in investments, two cars worth a total of $50,000, and $30,000 in jewelry and antiques. After both die, they want the property to go to their two children.

If this happily married couple own their property jointly, here's what will happen: When the first spouse dies, his or her half of the property will pass to the survivor tax-free. But when the second one dies, federal estate taxes on the property, even assuming its value has remained flat at $800,000, will run a hefty $52,200. And that doesn't count state death taxes, which can take as much as 6%, or $23,000, in states such as New York, Michigan and Massachusetts.

Those taxes can be avoided if our couple have their lawyer divide the ownership and draw up wills for each of them that include so-called bypass trusts. Then, when the first spouse dies, as much as $600,000 in property can go into his or her trust. The trustee will manage the property and pay out income to the surviving spouse. After the second spouse dies, the principal will go tax-free to the couple's children. Cost of such wills: about $1,000 each.

With that overall scenario in mind, here's a rundown of the best ways to share ownership of six major assets, discussed in terms of the property held by our hypothetical couple:

- **Primary Home.** Set sentiment aside and put the house in one spouse's name. Who should hold the title? Many lawyers and financial planners recommend that it be the spouse with the lower income and the least exposure to lawsuits. "Say the

For the Instructor

Teacher's Edition

This Teacher's Guide is located *only* in the Teacher's Edition. The Teacher's Edition also includes problem answers in red and marginal notes indicating that teaching transparencies are available. The transparencies are found in the Instructor's Resource Package.

END-OF-CHAPTER PROBLEMS

Drill Problems

Additional homework assignments by learning unit are at the end of text in Appendix I (p. I–13). Solutions to odd problems are at the end of text in Appendix II.

Identify the place value:

3–1. 4.938 hundredths **3–2.** 166.481 thousandths

Round as indicated:

		Tenth	Hundredth	Thousandth
3–3.	.4583	.5	.46	.458
3–4.	.4119	.4	.41	.412
3–5.	5.8931	5.9	5.89	5.893
3–6.	6.8415	6.8	6.84	6.842
3–7.	6.5555	6.6	6.56	6.556
3–8.	75.9913	76.0	75.99	75.991

Round to nearest cent:

3–9. $1,822.583 $1,822.58 **3–10.** $6,000.045 $6,000.05

Convert the following types of decimal fractions to decimal forms (round to nearest hundredth as needed):

3–11. $\frac{3}{100}$ .03 **3–12.** $\frac{4}{10}$ .40 **3–13.** $\frac{81}{1,000}$ .08

3–14. $\frac{810}{1,000}$ .81 **3–15.** $\frac{84}{100}$ .84 **3–16.** $\frac{979}{1,000}$ .98

3–17. $16\frac{82}{100}$ 16.82

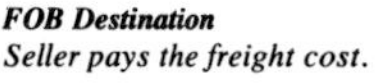
FOB Destination
Seller pays the freight cost.

FOB shipping point means free on board at shipping point; that is, the buyer pays the freight cost of getting the goods to the place of business. This freight term assumes that buyers take title to the goods once they reach the carrier (plane, boat, truck, etc.). For example, assume that IBM in San Diego bought goods from Avon suppliers in Boston. Avon ships the goods FOB Boston by plane. IBM takes title to the goods when the aircraft in Boston receives the goods, so IBM pays the freight from Boston to San Diego. Frequently the seller (Avon in this case) prepays the freight and adds the amount to the buyer's invoice (IBM). When paying the invoice, the buyer takes the cash discount off the net price and adds back the freight cost. FOB shipping point can be illustrated as follows:

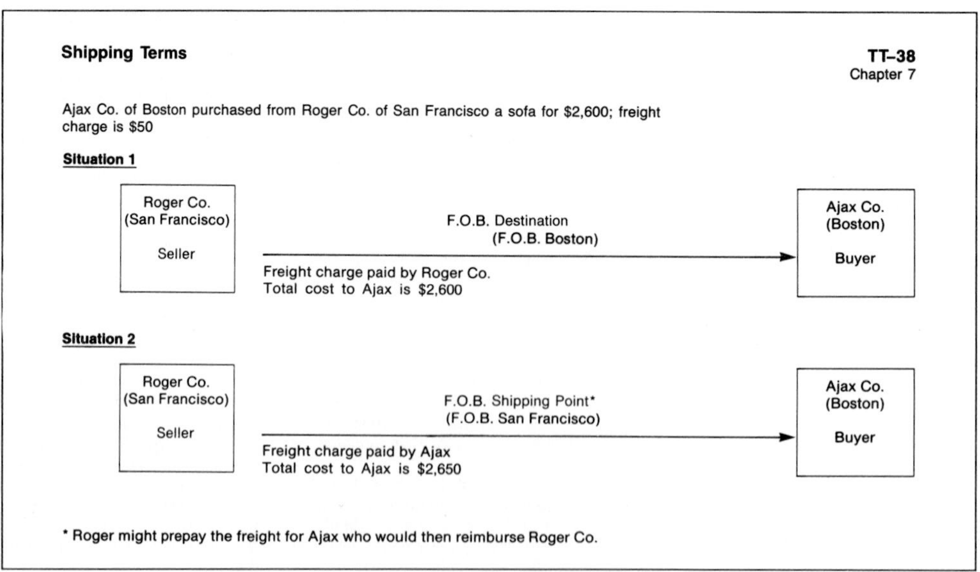

Instructor's Resource Package

New to this edition in each chapter folder are "Tips from Jeff" in which the author talks about his experience in teaching the chapter. These tips reflect 23 years of teaching experience. In the Instructor's Resource Package you will also find:

1. Course preparation folder:
   Chapter objectives by learning unit.
   Syllabus presentation.
   Student progress chart.
   Integrating the electronic calculator.
   Suggestions for using computers and videotapes.
2. Chapter folder (one per chapter):
   Tips from Jeff.
   Lecture outline with points to stress based on typical student misconceptions.
   Pocket calculator workshop.
   Five additional word problems (not in text).
   Worked-out solutions to 10 extra word problems found in the Business Math Handbook.
   Vocabulary crossword puzzles with solutions.
3. Miscellaneous folder:
   Your course versus math anxiety.
   Sample Civil Service Exam with worked-out solutions.
   Aliquot parts and proportions supplement.
   Check figures for even-numbered end-of-chapter drill and word problems (the check figures for odd-numbered problems are in Appendix II of the text).
   Lotus template fact sheet.
   Solutions for the Electronic Calculator Guide.
4. Appendix I solutions (Chapters 13–22).

Teaching and Solution Transparencies

Two-Color Teaching Transparencies are included in the Instructor's Resource Package. Most of these transparencies present additional material not found in the text and are intended to be used for lectures. A set of overlays on How to Dissect and Solve a Word Problem is included in Chapter 6. These transparencies are noted by a logo in the margin.

Solution Transparencies are included for all drill and word problems, as well as the summary practice tests. The type is large and readable from the back of the classroom and exactly follows the format in the Teacher's Edition text.

Sample Table of Decimal Equivalents of Net Cost for Series Discounts

TT–36
Chapter 7

	5%	10%	15%	20%	30%
5	.9025	.855	.8075	.76	.665
10	.855	.81	.765	.72	.63
10/5	.81225	.7695	.72675	.684	.5985
10/10	.7695	.729	.6885	.648	.567
15	.8075	.765	.7225	.68	.595
15/10	.72675	.6885	.65025	.612	.5355
20	.76	.72	.68	.64	.56
25	.7125	.675	.6375	.6	.525
25/20	.57	.54	.51	.48	.42
25/25	.534375	.50625	.478125	.45	.39375

Do not round any of the decimal equivalents.

The calculations we did in text can also be accomplished by use of tables.

Example: 10/5/15

Manually = .9 × .95 × .85 = .72675

By Table = intersection of 10/5 and 15

Teaching Transparency

Word Problems

7-22. A Compaq computer lists for $1,200 with a trade discount of 22%. What is the net price of the computer?
$1,200 × .78 = $936

7-23. Fireside Corporation buys its wood stoves from a wholesaler. The stove has a $400 list price with a 40% trade discount. What is the trade discount? What is the net price of the stove? Freight is FOB destination.
$400 × .40 = $160 trade discount
$400 × .60 = $240 net price

7-24. Pacesetter Furniture buys a living room set with a $4,000 list price and a 55% trade discount. Freight (FOB shipping point) of $50 is not part of the list price. What is the delivered price (including freight) of the living room set assuming a cash discount of 2/10, n/30, ROG? The invoice had an April 8 date. Pacesetter received the goods on April 19 and paid the invoice on April 25.
$4,000 × .55 = $2,200 amount of trade discount
$4,000 − 2,200 = $1,800 × .98 = $1,764 + $50 = $1,814
or ($4,000 × .45 = $1,800)

7-25. McGee of New York sold Jolly of Chicago office equipment with a $6,000 list price. Sale terms were 3/10, n/30 FOB New York. McGee agreed to prepay the $30 freight. Jolly pays the invoice within the discount period. What does Jolly pay McGee?
.97 × $6,000 = $5,820 + $30 freight = $5,850

7-26. Quality Furniture bought a sofa for $900. The sofa had a $1,200 list price. What was the trade discount rate Quality received?
$\frac{(P)\$300}{(B)\$1{,}200} = \frac{1}{4} = 25\%\ (R)$

7-27. Curtis Bookseller paid a $4,500 net price for textbooks. The publisher offered a 25% trade discount. What was the publisher's list price?
$\frac{(P)\$4{,}500}{(R).75} = \$6{,}000\ (B)$

Solution Transparency

Testing Materials

One Test Bank is now included having two parts:

A *Manual of Tests* containing 6 exams for each chapter. New to this edition is a parallel test (Test A) that mirrors the summary practice test in the text. All exams have worked-out solutions.

A *Computest Printout* containing over 1,300 questions; 90% of the questions in the computerized test bank are different from those in the manual test bank.

Irwin's *Computerized Testing Software* is available to allow you to generate, add, and edit questions; save and reload tests; and select questions based on type, level of difficulty, or keyword.

Teletest is a free customized exam preparation service. Simply choose your desired questions from the Computerized Testing printout and call Irwin's Education Software Services for a laser-printed master test with answer key.

Videotapes

There is a complete set of videotapes that review each practice quiz in the text. The author walks students through the review. A brief, real world application introduces each chapter. The author encourages his students to bring in a blank tape and make copies for home use. These video segments are noted with a logo in the margin.

New: Included in the videotapes is a Video Guide to Dissecting and Solving a Word Problem.

Audiocassettes

A complete set of audiocassettes done by Jeff Slater cover all practice quizzes.

Computer Support

The Business Math Tutor, a completely revised tutorial software program, is available free to adopters for student use in a lab or at home. Copying is allowed. This package covers all chapters in the text and was developed at the author's college to be sure it closely matches the text. It is highly visual and user friendly.

Where to Begin

Gather the facts	What am I solving for?	What must I know or calculate before solving the problem?	Key points to remember
Diet Pepsi sales: 60% Total sales: $24,000,000	Sales of Diet Pepsi	Base: $24,000,000 Rate: 60% Portion: ?	Portion = Base x Rate

Press PgUp/PgDn to view, Esc to exit

Lotus Templates are available for selected problems at the end of each chapter (except Chapter 5). These can be run as is or you can enter your own data. The template disk also includes an interest table feature that enables you to input any percentage rate and terms. The program will then generate table values. Adopters have praised them for ease of use and reliability. Problems that can be solved using the template are noted in the text margin by a disk logo.

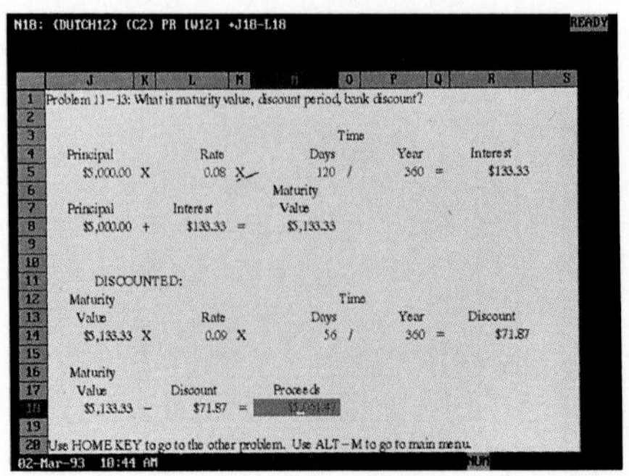

Classroom Presentation Software is an *Authorware*™-based package designed for using computers in lectures. The programs include a lecture outline and display demonstration problems, vocabulary review, and problems to solve in class for each chapter. The package allows instructors to present a highly interactive computerized lecture. (This is tied to the Third Edition of the text.)

Student Solutions Manual

Completely worked-out solutions to selected end-of-chapter drill and word problems, plus additional word problems, are included for student reinforcement.

The Electronic Calculator Guide

This manual coordinates *Practical Business Math Procedures* applications with instruction in the 10-key calculator. It also reviews the touch method, includes speed drills, and helps students apply new skills to business math word problems.

Brief Fourth Edition

Subtract length. Add revised teaching aids. *Practical Business Math Procedures, Brief Fourth Edition* gives you more of what you need for a perfectly balanced, shorter business math course.

This carefully crafted text has been modified, not merely shortened. Chapters were selected according to reviewers' suggestions, then revised to meet your course objectives. It includes Chapters 1–12 from the Fourth Edition, with modifications to Chapter 8.

The Brief Fourth Edition is available with or without the Electronic Calculator Guide shrinkwrapped at no extra charge.

A separate Instructor's Resource Package and Transparencies is available for instructors using the Brief Fourth Edition. The Money-Saving Tips from MONEY Magazine section is included.

PRACTICAL BUSINESS MATH PROCEDURES

FOURTH EDITION

JEFFREY SLATER
North Shore Community College
Beverly, Massachusetts

IRWIN
Burr Ridge, Illinois
Boston, Massachusetts
Sydney, Australia

To Loretta Scholten
who helps untwist those twisted words
"A true one-of-a-kind collectible."

PHOTOS
Cover photo: Sharon Hoogstraten
Chapter 1 *Vintage:* Courtesy of Hershey Foods Corporation. The conical configuration, the attached plume device, and the words HERSHEY'S and HERSHEY'S KISSES are registered trademarks of the Hershey Foods Corporation. *Modern:* Courtesy of Hershey Foods Corporation. HERSHEY'S KISSES and the conical configuration are registered trademarks of Hershey Foods Corporation and used with permission. **Chapter 2** *Vintage:* Courtesy of The Procter & Gamble Company. *Modern:* Sharon Hoogstraten. **Chapter 3** *Vintage:* Reprinted courtesy of the Wm. Wrigley Jr. Company. *Modern:* Reprinted courtesy of the Wm. Wrigley Jr. Company. **Chapter 4** *Vintage:* Courtesy of American Express Company. *Modern:* Sharon Hoogstraten. **Chapter 5** *Vintage:* Coca-Cola and Coke are registered trademarks of The Coca-Cola Company owned and used with permission of The Coca-Cola Company. *Modern:* Kenji Kerin. **Chapter 6** *Vintage:* Courtesy of The Procter & Gamble Company. *Modern:* Sharon Hoogstraten. **Chapter 7** *Vintage:* From the collections of Henry Ford Museum & Greenfield Village. *Modern:* Courtesy of Ford Motor Company. **Chapter 8** *Modern:* Courtesy of JCPenney Company. **Chapter 9** *Vintage:* Courtesy of NCR Corporation. *Modern:* Copyright © Scott Wanner/Nawrocki Stock Photo, Inc. All Rights Reserved. **Chapter 10** *Vintage:* FPG International, Inc. *Modern:* Photo courtesy InterBold. **Chapter 11** *Modern:* Courtesy of Maytag Company. **Chapter 12** *Vintage:* Courtesy of Zenith Electronics Corporation. *Modern:* Courtesy of Zenith Electronics Corporation. **Chapter 13** *Modern:* Sharon Hoogstraten. **Chapter 14** *Vintage:* Courtesy of Sears Roebuck, and Company. *Modern:* Courtesy of Sears Roebuck, and Company. **Chapter 15** *Vintage:* Courtesy of Baird & Warner. *Modern:* Courtesy of Baird & Warner. **Chapter 16** *Vintage:* UPI/Bettmann. *Modern:* Reuters/Bettmann. **Chapter 17** *Vintage:* Courtesy of Fox Theatre. *Modern:* Courtesy of Blockbuster Entertainment Corporation. **Chapter 18** *Vintage:* Photo courtesy of The Hertz Corporation. *Modern:* © 1994 Hertz System, Inc. Hertz is a registered service mark and trademark of Hertz System, Inc. **Chapter 19** *Vintage:* Courtesy of The Goodyear Tire & Rubber Company. *Modern:* Courtesy of The Goodyear Tire & Rubber Company. **Chapter 20** *Vintage:* Reprinted with the permission of The Prudential Insurance Company of America. All Rights Reserved. *Modern:* Reprinted with permission of The Prudential Insurance Company of America. All Rights Reserved. **Chapter 21** *Vintage:* Courtesy of New York Stock Exchange. *Modern:* Courtesy of New York Stock Exchange. **Chapter 22** *Vintage:* Courtesy of Mattel, Inc. *Modern:* Courtesy of Mattel, Inc.

Senior sponsoring editor: *Richard T. Hercher, Jr.*
Developmental editor: *Gail Korosa*
Freelance developmental editor: *Loretta Scholten*
Marketing manager: *Robb Linsky*
Project editor: *Susan Trentacosti*
Production manager: *Bob Lange*
Designer: *Michael Warrell*
Art manager: *Kim Meriwether*
Photo research coordinator: *Patricia A. Seefelt*
Compositor: *Better Graphics, Inc.*
Typeface: *10/12 Times Roman*
Printer: *R. R. Donnelley & Sons Company*

Library of Congress Cataloging-in-Publication Data

Slater, Jeffrey
Practical business math procedures / Jeffrey Slater. — 4th ed.
p. cm.
Includes index.
ISBN 0-256-11217-7. — ISBN 0-256-11791-8 (teacher's ed.)
1. Business mathematics—Problems, exercises, etc. I. Title.
HF5694.S57 1994
650'.01'513—dc20 92-44528

Printed in the United States of America
2 3 4 5 6 7 8 9 0 DOW 0 9 8 7 6 5 4 3

Note to Students

Preview of Special Features

1. **How to Dissect and Solve Word Problems.** The first eight chapters have a blueprint visual, along with steps on how to dissect and solve a word problem, for each learning unit.
2. **MONEY Magazine Articles.** The articles from MONEY Magazine provide tips and resources on saving money. The articles were chosen by students for students.
3. ***The Wall Street Journal* Newspaper.** *The Wall Street Journal* newspaper (inside front cover) explains how to read *The Wall Street Journal* with an emphasis on business math. An explanation of the Dow Jones Industrial Average is also provided.
4. **Business Math Handbook.** The Business Math Handbook is a 64-page reference guide that contains every table found in the text, along with extra word problems and tables not in the text. The back cover provides a quick reference chart on how to use the pocket calculator.

5. **Videotapes.** There is a complete set of videos that review each practice quiz in the text. Also included is a tutorial on how to dissect and solve word problems.
6. **The Business Math Tutor.** The Business Math Tutor is a comprehensive software tutorial that walks you through each part of the text. It is highly visual and user friendly.

7. **Lotus Templates.** Lotus templates are available for selected problems at the end of each chapter (except Chapter 5). You can run these templates as is or enter your own data. The template disk also includes an interest table feature that enables you to input any percentage rate and terms. The program will then generate table values for you.

How to Read and Use the Book

The colors in this text have a purpose. You should read the description below, then look at several pages to see how it works.

Color key

- **Blue:** Movement, cancellations, steps to solve, arrows, blueprints
- **Gold:** Formulas, steps, chapter organizer
- **Green:** Tables, forms, charts
- **Red:** Key items we are solving for

Chapters Each chapter is broken down into learning units. Each learning unit covers a key concept or small group of concepts.

Learning Objectives At the beginning of each chapter you'll find a list of learning objectives. Each is page referenced.

Practice Quizzes At the end of each learning unit is a practice quiz, followed by solutions. These provide you with immediate feedback on your understanding of the unit. These are all solved on videotapes, as well as on audiocasette tapes. Check with your instructor for availability.

Chapter Organizer At the end of each chapter is a quick reference guide called the chapter organizer. Key points, formulas, and examples are provided. A list of key vocabulary terms is also included. All have page references. (A complete glossary is found at the end of the text.) Think of the chapter organizer as your set of notes.

Problems At the end of each chapter is a complete set of drill and word problems. Check figures for the odd-numbered problems are located in Appendix II.

Challenge Problem The last word problem in each chapter tries to let you ''stretch'' your business math skills. These are harder and require more effort.

Additional Homework Assignments by Learning Unit At the end of the text in Appendix I is a complete set of drill and word problems arranged by learning unit. These can be used for additional reinforcement. Your instructor may ask you to turn these in. Check figures for the odd-numbered problems are in Appendix II.

Summary Practice Test This is a test before the test. All questions are page referenced back to the topic so you can check your methods. The test is a combination of drill and word problems. Check figures for *all* practice tests are in Appendix II.

Business Math Scrapbook At the end of each chapter you will find actual clippings from *The Wall Street Journal* and various other publications. These articles will give you a chance to use the theory provided in the chapter to apply to the real world.

Cumulative Reviews At the end of Chapters 3, 8, and 13 are word problems that test your retention of business math concepts and procedures. Check figures for *all* cumulative review problems are in Appendix II.

Jeffrey Slater

Acknowledgments

Academic experts

John Balek
Joyce Caldwell
Charles Chanter
Charles Cheetham
John Farquhar
James Farris
Margaret Gasperoni
Cecil Green
William Harrison
Janice Jenny
Sharon Amos Johnson
Gwendolyn Jones
Linda Leach
Joyce Loudder
Donald Manning
Gary Martin
John McClure
Lee Miller
Marguerite Nagy
Norman Okimoto
Nancy Spillman
Alex Talamantes
Carl Watkins
James Winner
Glen Wood

Business contributors

American Express Company
Apple Computer, Inc.
AT&T Archives
Baird & Warner
Blockbuster Entertainment Corporation
Board of Governors of the Federal Reserve System
Brunswick Corporation
Charles Schwab & Company
Chicago White Sox
Coca-Cola Company
Department of the Treasury
Dunkin Donuts
First National Bank of Chicago
Fleet Bank
Ford Motor Company
Fox Theatre
The Goodyear Tire & Rubber Company
Hershey Foods Corporation
The Hertz Corporation
Hewlett-Packard Company
Illinois Lottery
JCPenney Company
Liz Claiborne, Inc.
M&M/Mars, a division of Mars, Incorporated
Mattel, Inc.
Maytag Company
MONEY Magazine
NCR Corporation
New York Stock Exchange
Nike
The Procter & Gamble Company
The Prudential Insurance Company of America
Sears Roebuck, and Company
The Wall Street Journal, Dow Jones & Company, Inc.
Wm. Wrigley Jr. Company
Zenith Electronics Corporation

Contents

Money-Saving Tips from MONEY Magazine

The following articles from MONEY Magazine were selected by business math students for business math students. These reference articles demonstrate that business math is not static, but dynamic with real-life applications.

"Where to Find Free Financial Advice"

"Who Should Own What?"

"Kiss Your Money Worries Good-Bye in Five Years or Less"

Where to Find Free Financial Advice

By Debra Wishik Englander Free advice is not always worth what you pay for it. And here's the proof: The 29 free or nearly so (top cost: $3) brochures, pamphlets and books listed here can provide valuable information on financial topics ranging from resolving credit-card billing disputes to planning your estate. The publications are especially useful if you do your own financial planning. But they can also save you time and money when dealing with professionals by suggesting the right questions to ask and teaching you enough financial jargon to understand the answers.

One of the most prolific purveyors of free facts is the federal government, which produces around 50 personal-finance brochures (we cite two of the best below). For a rundown of what's available from Uncle Sam, or to get the brochures themselves, write to the Consumer Information Center, Pueblo, Colo. 81002. Since most industry-sponsored handbooks are little more than thinly disguised sales pitches, we included only the publications we judged to be both accurate and reasonably unbiased. When requesting a publication, be sure to enclose a self-addressed, stamped envelope. When organizations appear more than once, we give the address or phone number at the first mention.

BANKING AND CREDIT

- □ *Consumer Credit Handbook* (Consumer Information Center. Item No. 441Y; 50¢). Tells you how to fix errors on your credit report and what you should do if you're turned down for a credit card.
- □ *The Consumer's Almanac* (American Financial Services Association, Consumer Credit Education Foundation, 919 18th St. N.W., Suite 300, Washington, D.C. 20006; $2). Includes worksheets that can help you keep track of your monthly expenses. The association also publishes *What You Should Know Before Declaring Bankruptcy.*
- □ *How to Get Safety Information From Your Financial Institution* (Weiss Research, 2200 N. Florida Mango Rd., West Palm Beach, Fla. 33409; $2). Contains questions to ask your bank, broker or insurer to gauge how much risk they are taking with your money.
- □ *Managing Family Debt* and *Getting Out of Debt* (Bankcard Holders of America, 560 Herndon Pkwy., Suite 120, Herndon, Va. 22070; 703-481-1110; $1 each). Both offer budgeting strategies and tips on using your credit cards.

FINANCIAL PLANNING

- □ *Estate Planning: A Guide for the Days After a Loved One Dies* (Aetna Public Service Library, RWAC, 154 Farmington Ave., Hartford, Conn. 06156; 203-273-2843).
- □ *Money Matters* (AARP-Fulfillment, 60 E St. N.W., Washington, D.C. 20049). Helps you choose a tax preparer, lawyer, financial planner and real estate broker.
- □ *Selecting a Qualified Financial Planning Professional* (The Institute of Certified Financial Planners, 7600 E. Eastman Ave., Suite 301, Denver, Colo. 80231; 800-282-7526).

FRAUD

- □ *Avoiding Travel Problems* (The American Society of Travel Agents, The Fulfillment Center, 1101 King St., Alexandria, Va. 22314).
- □ *Investment Swindles: How They Work and How to Avoid Them* (National Futures Association, 200 W. Madison St., Suite 1600, Chicago, Ill. 60606; 800-621-3570).
- □ *Phone Fraud, We All Pay* (The National Association of Consumer Agency Administrators, 1010 Vermont Ave. N.W., Suite 514, Washington, D.C. 20005; 202-347-7395). Tells you how to guard against such rip-offs as calling-card abuse and phony third-party charges.

INSURANCE

- *A Personal Property Inventory* (Aetna). Provides forms that guide you in listing and describing your valuables to make it easier for you to file insurance claims.
- *Here Today, Gone Tomorrow* (The Insurance Information Institute, 110 William St., New York, N.Y. 10038; 212-669-9218). Includes a glossary of basic insurance terms and points to remember when you buy renter's insurance. Among the institute's other useful brochures: *Auto Insurance Basics, Tenants' Insurance Basics* and *How to File an Insurance Claim.*
- *Shaping Your Financial Fitness* (The National Association of Life Underwriters, 1922 F St. N.W., Washington, D.C. 20006). Explains the ins and outs of annuities, Medigap insurance and other mystifying products.
- *The Consumer's Guide to Health Insurance* (Health Insurance Association of America, P.O. Box 41455, Washington, D.C. 20018). Provides the basics of private health coverage.

INVESTING

- *A Common Sense Guide to Taking Charge of Your Money* (Fidelity Investments; 800-544-4774). Explains how to handle a lump-sum pension distribution.
- *Investors' Bill of Rights* (National Futures Association). Specifies, among other useful facts, the pertinent information a broker must disclose to you before selling you an investment.
- *Nine Tax Tips for Mutual Fund Investors* (GIT Investment Funds, 1655 Fort Myer Dr., Suite 1000, Arlington, Va. 22209; 800-336-3063).

MORTGAGES

- *Home Buyer's Vocabulary* (Consumer Information Center, Item No. 121Y; $1). Helps you master such mortgage jargon as escrow, earnest money and points.
- *How to Shop for a Loan* and *How to Shop for a Home* (Great Western Financial; 800-492-7587).
- *Refinance Kit* (HSH Associates; 1200 Rte. 23, Butler, N.J. 07405; $3). Explains how to calculate the cost of various mortgage refinancing deals.
- *Your Money & Your Home* (Countrywide; 800-669-6064). Discusses all aspects of taking out a mortgage, from application to appraisal to closing.

RETIREMENT

- *A Single Person's Guide to Retirement Planning* (AARP). Serves up guidance on investing, insurance, and other financial topics as well as tips on nutrition, relationships and housing.
- *Can You Afford to Retire?* (Life Insurance Marketing and Research Association, P.O. Box 208, Hartford, Conn. 06141; 800-235-4672; $1.50). Covers various sources of retirement income. Most helpful feature: worksheets to calculate your current and future net worth.

Who Should Own What?

The Most Important Financial Decision You and Your Spouse Ever Make Is Who Should Legally Own the Assets You Share.

By Jordan E. Goodman If you're married, you and your spouse most likely hold your house and other major possessions in both your names. You figure, correctly, that when one of you dies the other will become sole owner without having to go through a months-long probate proceeding. What could be more loving or more fair? Who could possibly lose in this situation?

Unfortunately, this last question has an unpleasant answer: your children. The ways you and your spouse hold title to major assets can sock your heirs with all sorts of unnecessary taxes. "Few people pay enough attention to estate tax, which can run as high as 55%," says Robert Clarfeld, a financial planner in New York City.

Those taxes can be avoided if you have a lawyer make sure your property is titled correctly. (Typical cost: about $1,000.) This effort can also be important if you are single and share ownership, say, of a house or a car with a relative or friend.

There are three basic forms of co-ownership. With the most common, **joint tenancy with right of survivorship,** each person owns an equal share of the property and can dispose of it without the approval of the others. When an owner dies, his or her share is divided equally among the other owners.

The second method, **tenancy by the entirety,** is similar to joint tenancy, except that neither partner can sell his or her share without permission from the other. This alternative is available in only about 30 states.

Like joint tenancy, the third form, **tenancy in common,** permits co-owners to dispose of their shares independently. When one owner dies, his or her share goes to the heirs named in a will, rather than automatically to the co-owners.

(If you live in one of the nine **community property** states—Arizona, California, Idaho, Louisiana, Nevada, New Mexico, Texas, Washington and Wisconsin—where assets acquired during a marriage are generally considered to be owned equally by both spouses, it would be wise to consult an estate lawyer about co-ownership.)

Which form should you use? The answer ought to be based mostly on estate-tax considerations, not sentiment. Consider the case of an affluent couple who jointly own $800,000 in assets—a $315,000 house, $100,000 in life insurance on the wife and $80,000 on the husband, a $125,000 vacation retreat, $100,000 in investments, two cars worth a total of $50,000, and $30,000 in jewelry and antiques. After both die, they want the property to go to their two children.

If this happily married couple own their property jointly, here's what will happen: When the first spouse dies, his or her half of the property will pass to the survivor tax-free. But when the second one dies, federal estate taxes on the property, even assuming its value has remained flat at $800,000, will run a hefty $52,200. And that doesn't count state death taxes, which can take as much as 6%, or $23,000, in states such as New York, Michigan and Massachusetts.

Those taxes can be avoided if our couple have their lawyer divide the ownership and draw up wills for each of them that include so-called bypass trusts. Then, when the first spouse dies, as much as $600,000 in property can go into his or her trust. The trustee will manage the property and pay out income to the surviving spouse. After the second spouse dies, the principal will go tax-free to the couple's children. Cost of such wills: about $1,000 each.

With that overall scenario in mind, here's a rundown of the best ways to share ownership of six major assets, discussed in terms of the property held by our hypothetical couple:

- ☐ **Primary Home.** Set sentiment aside and put the house in one spouse's name. Who should hold the title? Many lawyers and financial planners recommend that it be the spouse with the lower income and the least exposure to lawsuits. "Say the

Reprinted by special permission, MONEY Magazine, August 1992, Time Inc.

wife is a doctor who may get hit with a malpractice suit one day,'' says Edwin Baker, a senior estate attorney for Epstein Becker & Green in New York City.'' If her husband owns title to the house, creditors won't be able to attach it.''

- **Life Insurance.** When either of the spouses in our example dies, the proceeds of his or her life insurance policy will go tax-free to the survivor. But what happens when the second spouse dies and the $180,000 in total benefits is left to the children? You guessed it: The money will be hit with estate taxes. To avoid that, have your lawyer set up an irrevocable life insurance trust. Such a trust cannot be changed after it has been created. When you die, the insurance money will go into the trust, and the trustee will pay income from it to the beneficiaries, including your spouse, for the rest of their lives. When the surviving spouse dies, the money will go to your children or other beneficiaries tax-free. Cost of such a trust: about $1,000.
- **Vacation Home.** The best solution here is the old standby: You and your spouse should hold the property jointly with right of survivorship. If one of you owns the retreat outright and it's in a state other than the one in which you reside, you could be complicating your estate unnecessarily. The reason: If the spouse who is sole owner of vacation property dies first, the property will have to go through probate in the state in which it is located. By contrast, if the property is owned jointly, attorney Edwin Baker explains, ''the surviving spouse inherits it automatically and probate is delayed until that spouse dies.'' There is also a way that you can pass the property to your children while avoiding probate (although not escaping estate taxes). Have your lawyer place the house in a revocable trust, which costs about $1,000 to set up and can be modified later.
- **Securities.** Assets in employee-benefit plans such as 401(k) accounts may be your largest investments, but the only decision you get to make is whom to name as the beneficiary to receive them when you die. For mutual funds, stocks and bonds held outside of such accounts, you can avoid taxes by splitting ownership. Separately titled assets can be readily transferred to a bypass trust to shelter them from estate taxes.
- **Automobiles.** Cars are the only asset that should *never* be owned jointly, even if your estate is so small that it couldn't possibly trigger estate taxes. The reason is legal liability. ''I like to call cars pending lawsuits on wheels,'' says Baker. ''Think of them more as liabilities than as assets.'' If one spouse has an accident and the car is owned jointly, both spouses' assets could be at risk if the driver is sued. Thus automobiles should be held in separate names. If you have a hot-rodding teenager 18 or older, register the car in the child's name and get a separate insurance policy for it. That way, your own assets are not on the line.
- **Valuables.** Here's the best way to bequeath art, antiques, jewelry or collectibles to your heirs with minimum taxes and squabbles: Put each item in either your name or your spouse's. Then, insert letters of instruction in each of your wills and write letters to your executors specifying who should inherit what. Says E. Deane Kanaly, a financial planner and president of the Kanaly Trust Co. in Houston: ''The last thing you want is to have your children bickering over who is going to get which painting or diamond ring.''

Kiss Your Money Worries Good-Bye in Five Years or Less

Wouldn't it be a relief to have all of your big financial concerns under control? If you follow these painless steps, you'll be able to sleep well soon.

By Penelope Wang These days, Americans are more tense about their financial well-being than they've been in years. The most recent MONEY/ABC Consumer Comfort Index sagged near its all-time low in March, as 55% of those surveyed said the condition of their own finances was "not so good" or "poor." Little wonder. The unemployment rate has been hovering at an eight-year high of 7.5%, personal income shrank 0.5% in August, and the cost of living climbed 0.3%. "We live in the Nervous Nineties," notes Irwin Kellner, chief economist at Chemical Bank in New York City. "Despite the election, consumer money worries will continue with the weak economy."

But take heart. You don't have to win the lottery to end your financial jitters. In fact, you can kiss off most of your money problems in just five years or less—or at least get them under control in that time. The key is to follow a disciplined month-by-month savings and investing program that addresses your individual problems. "With a monthly savings plan, you can make the impossible become possible," says financial planner Richard Bergen of Westbury, N.Y. For example, you can build up $10,000 in cash in five years by investing only $133 each month—or less than a typical car payment.

Putting away every cent you'll need to finance college or retirement may of course require a decade or more. But by establishing a plan, you can assure your ultimate success in as little as three years. (The worksheets will help you figure out how much you should be saving each month.) Just knowing that you're on track toward reaching your goals will lower your stress level sharply. (And knowing you are *ahead* of schedule can reduce your stress levels even more.) For example, to amass $100,000 in 15 years for college, you must invest $271 a month, assuming a 9% average annual return. But if you can afford to put aside $350 a month, you can reach your goal in 13 years, or you can lower your monthly payments by about a third, to only $197, after the first five years.

To help make your finances worry-free in five years, MONEY interviewed more than two dozen financial planners, investment advisers and consumer advocates for advice on how to put to rest five of the most common money concerns. We start with solutions for the short-term problems that prey on people's minds and finish with advice for reaching your long-term goals worry-free.

Worry No. 1: *I'm Losing Control of My Credit Cards and Other Debt.* These days, anxiety-ridden consumers are wisely trying to unload their enormous debt burdens with the determination of born-again sinners. Per capita installment debt, for instance, dropped sharply in June to $3,825, vs. $3,939 in 1990, despite inflation. Notes financial planner Ken Shapiro of Garwood, N.J.: "In these uncertain times, reducing your debt should be your first priority."

To find the money to pay down debts, begin by reviewing the past six months of your canceled checks and credit-card receipts to figure out exactly where your funds go each month. Then look for ways to cut back and to sell extra items lying around that can raise cash. Stick with your deficit-reduction program until you clean up your balance sheet. For many families, that can take as long as three years, according to Flora Williams, an associate professor of consumer science at Purdue University. Williams has found that the average middle-class family of four making $40,000 a year can save about $270 a month through some simple economies, such as eating out less often and postponing nonessential purchases.

When you must take out a loan, try your credit union or a 401(k) savings plan at work if you have either, says financial planner Ben Coulter of North Palm Beach, Fla. Both typically offer loans at below-market rates—usually a percentage point or two over the prime rate, now 6%. Credit unions typically don't lend more than $10,000 or so, however. With a 401(k) plan, you can't borrow more than half of the vested balance, and the loan must generally be repaid within five years. But you usually pay the interest to yourself—and that's certainly better than having to give it to a bank.

If your debt problems are at a crisis level now, call the National Foundation for Consumer Credit (800-388-2227), a nonprofit credit counseling service. Usually within a few days, a staffer at one of the service's 750 local offices will negotiate with your creditors and put you on a debt-repayment plan for a nominal fee of $10 or so.

Worry No. 2: *I'm Going to Get a Medical Bill I Can't Handle.* You may well have a group health plan at work that picks up some of your medical expenses. But with health-care costs rising by about 10% a year—more than three times the overall inflation rate—companies everywhere are slashing their employees' coverage. To shield yourself against unreimbursed medical bills and rising insurance co-payments (the percentage of the bill that you pay out of your own pocket), first build an emergency reserve fund of about $2,500. For this and other short-term goals, you can guarantee the money will be there by putting it in a bank money-market account or a money-market mutual fund.

If you're one of the 35 million Americans without any health insurance, however, you need to get coverage before you do anything else. It won't come cheaply. Annual premiums normally run between $80 and $180 a month for an individual, $350 to $750 a month for a family. Boosting your co-payment from the standard 20% to 50% and raising your annual maximum out-of-pocket costs from $1,000 to $2,500 can slash your premiums by 40%, though.

You may also be able to get insurance for 5% to 20% less than a standard policy by buying coverage through a group plan, such as one offered by a college alumni organization or a professional trade association. For instance, Don Porter, 40, got coverage for his Montclair, N.J. family last summer, after rejecting policies costing more than $700 a month, by buying a $610-a-month policy from the American Institute of Architects.

Young, healthy people can frequently buy individual policies for even less than group rates, since insurers know they're good risks. Before purchasing individual coverage, talk to at least three independent agents, and make sure they compare appropriate policies with similar coverage sold by several insurers. If you can't find agents to do the research, you might want to hire Wilkinson Benefit Consultants, of Towson, Md. (800-296-3030). For $270, it will give you an analysis of the coverage and the cost of at least three health policies available to you.

Health maintenance organizations, or HMOs, can also be a money-saving way to relieve your worries about big medical bills. While annual premiums are comparable to private insurance, you usually pay no deductibles and there are rarely co-insurance costs.

If you can't find any insurer or HMO that will accept you because of a medical condition, call your state insurance department. Your state may be one of 24* with a high-risk pool, which provides health coverage for the otherwise uninsurable. Rates can be exorbitant, though; monthly premiums for a family of four sometimes exceed $1,200.

Worry No. 3: *I May Never Be Able to Buy My Own House.* Oh, yes, you will, if you work at it. It's certainly true that thousands of young people are locked out of the housing market these days because they lack the necessary savings for a down payment and closing costs. And banks, burned by their horrendous real estate lending in the 1980s, have grown conservative and are often requiring buyers to put down 10% to 20% of a house's

* California, Colorado, Connecticut, Florida, Georgia, Illinois, Indiana, Iowa, Louisiana, Maine, Minnesota, Missouri, Montana, Nebraska, New Mexico, North Dakota, Oregon, South Carolina, Tennessee, Texas, Utah, Washington, Wisconsin and Wyoming

What to Save for a Five-Year Goal

Use this worksheet to determine how much you need to set aside each month to meet a short-term goal, such as getting out of debt or buying a house. The calculations assume a 4% annual inflation rate and that your savings will earn 4% a year. The amount required for a down payment and closing costs will equal roughly 16% of the price of a house.

1. Amount you will need $______

2. Amount of your ready savings, minus enough to cover three months of your current living expenses $______

3. Amount you must save over five years, before inflation (line 1 minus line 2) $______

4. Amount you must save over five years, taking inflation into account (multiply line 3 by 1.22) $______

5. Amount you must save monthly (divide line 4 by 66.4) $______

price. That amounts to a hefty $8,810 to $17,620 for the $88,100 median home price for first-time buyers, according to the National Association of Realtors. With closing costs, figure you'll really need $10,000 to $20,000 in cash.

You *can* amass that much money over a short period of five years or less, but doing so will demand a full-court-press savings plan. The best, and easiest one to start, is an automatic investing program with a mutual fund. By filling out just one form, you can authorize most fund companies to transfer a regular amount—usually $50 or more a month—straight from your checking account. Since this is money you'll need soon, choose a liquid investment such as a short-term bond fund, which pays yields that are about two percentage points higher than those of money-market funds but carry minimal risks. Financial planner Steven Enright of River Vale, N.J. suggests two no-loads: **Neuberger & Berman Limited Maturity Bond** (currently yielding 4.9%; 800-877-9700), or, if you're in the 28% bracket or higher (taxable income over $21,450 for individuals, $35,800 for married couples), **Dreyfus Short-Intermediate Tax Exempt Bond** (now yielding 4.23%; 800-782-6620).

As you get closer to your goal, explore ways to cut your cash down payment. "By shopping for the right loan, you can sometimes get into a house with a down payment of just 5% to 10%," says Peter Miller, author of *The Common-Sense Mortgage* (Harper-Collins, $10). For example, Joyce Bordley, a computer programmer in Newark, Del., snared a 5%-down, Federal Housing Administration-insured loan and bought her $85,000, three-bedroom townhouse with only $4,250 in cash plus closing costs. FHA loans are available from 10,000 lenders in amounts of up to $67,500 generally, and $151,752 in high-cost areas like Chicago, Los Angeles and New York City. In addition, the Federal National Mortgage Association, known as Fannie Mae, has just launched a program through lenders around the country that lets minorities who want to buy houses in predominantly non-white areas get mortgages with down payments of 3% to 5%.

Another way to buy a house with a down payment of as little as 5% is by buying private mortgage insurance from your lender. With 5% down, you'll pay an up-front fee of 1% of the mortgage, plus an annual charge included in your monthly payment of 0.5% of the mortgage amount—$35 a month on an $85,000 loan.

Worry No. 4: *I Won't Be Able to Pay My Child's College Costs.* Now here's a concern any parent can relate to. After all, average total expenses at public universities soared 10% this year to $5,841, while costs at private colleges climbed 7% to $15,073, according to the College Board. Assuming college costs rise at a 7% annual rate, when today's babes enter college in 2010, the bill for four years at a public school will be $87,654. A private college will cost a stunning $226,196.

Don't panic. Plenty of schools offer top-quality educations for less than the averages today, and others will in the future. At the University of North Carolina–Chapel Hill, for example, in-state costs this year are only $5,246. (For the best college values in America, get the *MONEY Guide: Best College Buys,* P.O. Box 30626, Tampa, Fla. 33630-0626; $4.50.)

Still, the sooner you start putting money aside for tuition bills, the easier it will be for you to cast away this worry. Most advisers say that parents whose children are still 10 years away from college should stash at least 70% of their college-savings portfolios in mutual funds weighted toward growth. That's because over the long term, stocks have offered average returns of 9%, compared with 6% for Treasury bonds. Robert Bingham, an investment adviser with Bingham Osborn & Scarborough in San Francisco, favors steady growth and income funds, such as **American Mutual** (5.75% load; up 54.3% for the five years ended Sept. 30; 800-421-9900) and **Neuberger & Berman Guardian** (no load; up 65.1% over five years). To cushion your college portfolio from stock market drops, invest the balance in stable, high-grade fixed-income funds, such as **Fidelity Intermediate Bond** (no load; now yielding 5.7%; 800-544-8888). As your child reaches age 12 or so, start shifting out of stocks and into bonds. This way, you'll avoid the risks of a market crash just when your child's bill for Wossamotta U. is due. By the time he or she enters college, no more than 20% of your portfolio should be in stocks.

Worry No. 5: *I Won't Be Able to Afford a Comfortable Retirement.* Ah, retirement! A cabana on the beach, an umbrella drink in your hand, and nothing but time to watch the waves roll in. However, to keep a steady income rolling in after you stop working—say,

What to Save For a Long-Term Goal

This worksheet will show you how much you need to save each month to get you on track to cover your kid's college education or your retirement in later years. The calculations assume a higher rate of inflation—5%—than the previous worksheet, since inflation is likely to rise over time. This worksheet also assumes a 9% average annual return because these savings can go into stocks. Figure that a third of your retirement income will come from savings; pensions and Social Security will provide the rest.

1. Amount you think you will need to save, expressed in today's dollars

$_______

2. Amount you should save each month (divide line 1 by the appropriate number from the box below)

$_______

3. How much you will have saved toward your ultimate goal in five years (multiply line 2 by 75.3)

$_______

Years until funds are required	Divisor
15	178
20	243
25	315
30	397
35	492
40	604

$35,000 a year in 20 years, in today's dollars—you'll need (gasp!) $920,000.

You need a plan—and some help. For example, if you work for a mid-size or large company, your employer may be prepared to greatly relieve your retirement worries. "If you've got a company pension and a 401(k) plan, you're sitting on the equivalent of a gold mine," notes Watchung, N.J. retirement planner Paul Westbrook. Take a 40-year-old earning $50,000 a year who plans to retire at age 60 and has a typical defined-benefit pension. When he stops working, he'll get about $12,000 annually in today's dollars. If he's lucky enough to be able also to invest 10% of his salary in a 401(k) and the employer will match 3%, in 20 years his 401(k) balance will have grown tax-free to $411,482—or another $12,300 a year for 30 years—assuming a 9% return. All told, those benefits plus Social Security would give him an annual income of $35,650.

Still, you may be forced by your company to retire sooner than you had planned. Or you may work for one of the 43% of private firms that offer neither a pension nor a 401(k) plan (if that's the case, lobby for one). So you can't afford not to save for retirement on your own. If you have no company retirement program, you can invest—and deduct—as much as $2,000 a year in an Individual Retirement Account. Even if you have a plan, you may be able to deduct some or all of your IRA contribution if your adjusted gross income is under $35,000, or $50,000 for couples filing jointly.

As with college savings, if you have at least 10 years to go before retirement, weight your portfolio toward stocks but boost your bond allocation as you near your goal. For example, a 40-year-old woman might keep 60% of her retirement fund portfolio in stocks, say, while a 55-year-old could shrink that amount to 40%. But you shouldn't ever get out of equities entirely. Bergen warns: "Even in retirement, you should keep at least 30% in stocks to protect your portfolio from inflation."

Are You Worrying Too Much About Money?

When it comes to your personal finances, which are you more like: the Alfred E. Neuman (What, me worry?) type, or the neurotic Scrooge McDuck? To find out whether you're worrying too much, too little or just the right amount, take this quiz:

1. I check my stocks and mutual funds in the financial pages . . .
- a. every day.
- b. every week.
- c. only once a year or so.

2. I'll be able to afford a comfy retirement because . . .
- a. I'm saving to the max right now.
- b. I'm counting on a relative to leave me a pile.
- c. Fat chance! I'm going to end up working till I drop.

3. When I get my bank statement . . .
- a. I throw it in the wastebasket.
- b. I go crazy if it doesn't match my checkbook balance.
- c. I give it a once-over to make sure I know roughly how much is in my account.

4. If I get laid off . . .
- a. I'll get through the following three months on the money in my emergency fund.
- b. I bet I'll find another, similar job fast.
- c. I'll be a wreck.

5. I clip cents-off newspaper coupons . . .
- a. every day.
- b. when I see one for a product I like.
- c. never.

6. If I buy something I have to stretch to pay for . . .
- a. I can't sleep for weeks thinking I overpaid.
- b. I'm pleased that I got my money's worth.
- c. I just put it on plastic and forget about it.

7. When I get cash from a cash machine . . .
- a. I don't bother to get a record slip.
- b. I always enter the withdrawal in my checkbook.
- c. I always get a queasy feeling that I'm taking out money too often, even when I'm not.

Scoring:
Give yourself 5 points for each of these answers: 1c, 2b, 3a, 4b, 5c, 6c and 7a.
Give yourself 10 points for these: 1b, 2a, 3c, 4a, 5b, 6b and 7b.
Give yourself 20 points for these: 1a, 2c, 3b, 4c, 5a, 6a and 7c.
If your score is 20 to 35, get real! You need to worry a little more.
If your score is 40 to 70, you've got a fine grasp of your financial situation.
If your score is 80 or above, get a life! You're worrying way too much.

You'll get the greatest long-term growth potential by investing in stock funds such as **Fidelity Growth Company** (3% load; up 74.3% over five years) or **Janus 20** (no load; up 119.7%; 800-525-8983), which seek out companies with above-average earnings increases. For your bonds, lower the risk of losing principal by sticking with mutual funds that hold primarily issues rated A or better and with maturities of 12 years or less. A top choice: **Vanguard Bond Market** (no load; current yield: 6.6%; 800-662-7447). When your retirement funds have grown to an amount large enough to let you diversify—say, $25,000 or so—shift 10% of your portfolio into a foreign-stock fund, such as **Harbor International** (no load; up 112.8%; 800-422-1050) and another 10% into a small-stock portfolio, such as **SIT New Beginning Growth** (no load; up 62.7%; 800-332-5580).

Once you have your retirement investment program in place, check your portfolio once a year to be sure your funds are meeting your objectives. If they are, leave the stash on cruise control and watch your savings build. With any luck, in five years, your biggest worry may be keeping track of your growing profits.

PRACTICAL BUSINESS MATH PROCEDURES

THAT WAS THEN . . .
. . . THIS IS NOW

In 1893, Milton Hershey introduced the first mass-produced chocolate bar weighing $\frac{9}{16}$ of an ounce. This early poster showed Hershey Kisses wrapped by hand. Today more than 33 million (33,000,000) Kisses are produced daily.

1

Review of Basic Computational Skills; How to Dissect and Solve Word Problems

LEARNING UNIT OBJECTIVES

LU 1-1: Writing Whole Numbers; Rounding Whole Numbers

1. Convert whole numbers into verbal form. *pp. 5–6*
2. Write whole numbers from verbal form. *pp. 5–6.*
3. Identify digits to be rounded. *p. 6*
4. Round whole numbers to indicated position (tens, hundreds, thousands, and so on). *pp. 6–7*
5. Dissect and solve a word problem. *pp. 7–8*

LU 1-2: Whole Numbers—Addition and Subtraction

1. Check addition and subtraction computations. *pp. 9–10*
2. Estimate addition and subtraction computations. *pp. 9–10*
3. Compare and contrast common sense with the process of estimating. *p. 10*
4. Complete horizontal and vertical addition and subtraction. *p. 10*
5. Dissect and solve a word problem. *p. 11*

LU 1-3: Whole Numbers—Multiplication and Division

1. Explain relationship of multiplication to addition. *p. 12*
2. Check and estimate multiplication and division computations. *p. 13*
3. Complete multiplication and division computations with zeros. *pp. 13–14*
4. Complete short and long division. *pp. 14–15*
5. Dissect and solve a word problem. *pp. 15–16*

Business decision making usually involves business math. If you received an allowance as a child, simple business math helped you decide how to spend your money. Adults of all ages use some business math in their daily activities. Companies use business math to make most of their business decisions. From the following *Wall Street Journal* article, you know that Liz Claiborne used business math to decide what the company had to do to sustain the growth of its maturing brand.

Claiborne Unveils Its First Big Campaign

By Teri Agins
Staff Reporter of The Wall Street Journal

NEW YORK—The Liz Claiborne brand, the cherished choice of the working woman, is arguably the most powerful label in retailing.

It isn't enough.

No matter that in some department stores, Claiborne dominates as much as half of the women's-apparel floor space. Or that the double-digit growth rate of the company—Liz Claiborne Inc.—in recent years has been the envy of Seventh Avenue.

It still isn't enough.

As the 15-year-old company prepares to launch its first advertising campaign for Liz Claiborne clothing and accessories in November, it finds itself at a crossroads. Powerhouse or not, Claiborne is grappling with challenges that go well beyond today's sluggish retail environment. To sustain the growth of its maturing brand, Liz Claiborne now must figure out how to recruit new customers and expand into new merchandise areas.

While it focuses on its main label, there are signs that Claiborne is already think-

Liz Claiborne's first ad campaign.

medium-price designer brands including Adrienne Vittadini, Jones New York and Ellen Tracy. And recession-battered department stores have kept a lid on inventories by drastically cutting down on their orders.

In keeping with Claiborne's down-to-earth image—"designer clothes that are aspirational yet accessible," as Ms. Banks puts it—the color ads resemble pages of mail-order catalogs rather than high-style fashion spreads.

How did Liz Claiborne decide to sustain its growth? The complete article stated that to gain substantial growth, Liz Claiborne decided to expand its product line. Since the company is facing increased competition, it is also concerned about losing retail floor space. Using the information from the complete Liz Claiborne article, let's look at how we can apply the following four steps used in business decision making.

Step 1. State the problem(s).	Sustain growth of its maturing brand; facing more competition and potentially less retail floor space.
Step 2. Decide the best method(s) to solve the problem(s).	Promote other Liz Claiborne brands, like Liz Fashion and athletic shoes. Increase advertising to enhance image.
Step 3. Does the solution make sense?	Company expects to receive $100 million in revenue from shoes.
Step 4. Evaluate results.	Has market share increased? Have company earnings increased?

Business math and its applications also affect your business decision making. To make your important business decisions, you can use the same decision-making strategy steps as Liz Claiborne. For example, let's assume you need transportation to get to school and work. To solve this problem, you shop the used-car market and the car-loan market. You realize the importance of finding a used car that will provide years of good service. Also, you know that the interest rate charged for a car loan will add to the price of your car.

You say you have a solution: Your uncle is selling his car and buying a new one, and your older brother will lend you the money at no interest. Therefore, you will borrow money from your brother to buy your uncle's car. That solution makes good sense. Now you can evaluate your results. Your uncle always took good care of his car, so you know the car is in excellent condition. Your brother has lent you money before and has been patient when your cash flow weakened. You should be pleased with your solution to your transportation problem.

Your daily decisions also can be influenced by business math. This is illustrated by using the following "Did you know?" facts.

Did you know?

- □ Starkist tuna has 87% less fat and 46% less cholesterol than skinless roast chicken. (Eating Starkist tuna may help you reduce the fat and cholesterol you eat.)
- □ The United States has over 1 billion credit card users. (You also may find a credit card convenient.)
- □ Weight Watchers has 15.8% of the frozen entree market. (You may decide to try the frozen entrees made by Weight Watchers.)
- □ A $100,000 biweekly mortgage for 30 years at 10% can save you $78,377 and take 9 years off the life of the mortgage. (You may consider a biweekly mortgage when you buy a house.)
- □ A drop of 1% in Coke sales represents 77 million cases of Coke. (You may think about this when you drink a Pepsi.)

From this introduction on business decision making, you can see how important it is to learn more about business math. Before studying the business math topics in this book, however, you should review your basic computational skills for speed and accuracy. You may reply by saying, "But I can use my calculator." Even if you use your calculator (your instructor may allow you to use it in class), you still need to know basic computational skills. Without these skills, you will not know what to calculate, how to interpret your calculations, or how to calculate when you do not have a calculator.

In the United States, we use the decimal numbering system—the most common numbering system. The 10 digits of the decimal system are 0, 1, 2, 3, 4, 5, 6, 7, 8, 9. The decimal point is the center of the system, with **whole numbers** to the left and decimal numbers to the right. In this chapter, we study whole numbers. We study decimal numbers in Chapter 3. Let's first look at how to write whole numbers and then learn how to estimate calculations quickly by rounding.

LEARNING UNIT 1-1 WRITING WHOLE NUMBERS; ROUNDING WHOLE NUMBERS

We often use whole numbers in business situations. For example, the chapter opener states that Hershey Foods Corporation produces approximately 33 million Hershey's Kisses daily. This 33 million is a *whole number*. It also could be a *rounded whole number*.

Writing Whole Numbers

The decimal numbering system has *place* positions. Working from right to left in a number, the place values are units, tens, hundreds, thousands, ten thousands, hundred thousands, millions, and so on.

Using the decimal numbering system, let's write the whole number *6,896* and illustrate place values. We can analyze 6,896 like this:

$$6{,}896 = (6 \times 1{,}000) + (8 \times 100) + (9 \times 10) + (6 \times 1)$$

Now let's write the large number *5,695,695,374* in verbal form using place values.

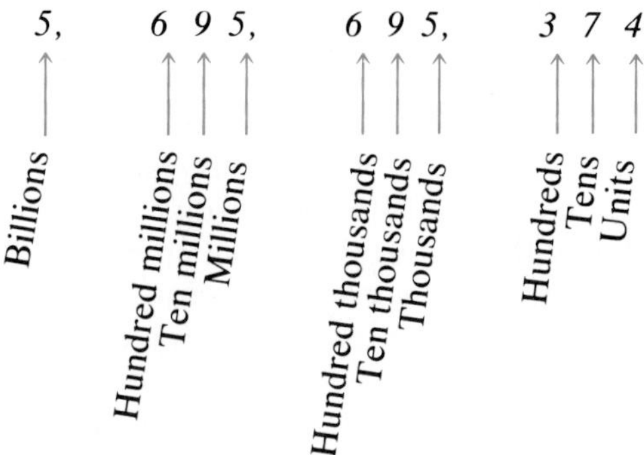

From this diagram, we read the 5,695,695,374 number as five billion, six hundred ninety-five million, six hundred ninety-five thousand, three hundred seventy-four. Note how the diagram positions each number with commas separating every three digits from right to left. You can think of each three digits as a group. Note that when we read the number above, we used commas to separate each group.

When reading (or writing in verbal form) a whole number, do not use the word *and*. In the decimal numbering system, we use *and* to indicate the decimal, which we discuss in Chapter 3. Note also that we use hyphens between any numbers from twenty-one to ninety-nine.

Rounding Whole Numbers

The process of rounding numbers can be an effective tool to quickly estimate arithmetic results and to check actual computations. For example, have you ever shopped in a supermarket and when you reached the cash register, you found you were short of cash? If you had rounded the cost of your items and mentally totaled this cost, you would have avoided this embarrassment.

Whole numbers can be rounded to an identified digit within a number, or the identified digit can be the first digit of a number (rounding all the way). In all rounding, you are approximating the actual answer. As you will see, however, the more rounding you do, the more you are approximating the answer. Use the following three steps for rounding a whole number.

Steps for Rounding Whole Numbers

Step 1. Identify digit you want to round.

Step 2. If digit to right of identified digit in Step 1 is 5 or more, increase identified digit by 1 (round up). If digit to right is less than 5, do not change identified digit.

Step 3. Change all digits to right of identified digit to zeros.

EXAMPLE 1 Round 7,369 to nearest hundred.

Step 1. 7,369 — Identified digit is 3, which is in the hundreds position.

Step 2. — Digit to right of 3 is 5 or more (6). Thus, 3, the identified digit in Step 1, is now rounded to 4. You change identified digit only if digit to right is 5 or more.

7,469

Step 3. 7,400 — Change digits 6 and 9 to zeros, since these digits are to right of 4, the rounded number.

By rounding 7,369 to the nearest hundred, you can see that 7,369 is closer to 7,400 than to 7,300.

EXAMPLE 2 Round 57,950 to nearest thousand.

Step 1. 57,950 — Identified digit is 7, which is in the thousands position.

Step 2. — Digit to right of 7 is 5 or more (9). Thus 7, the identified digit in Step 1, is now rounded to 8.

58,950
↓↓↓
Step 3. 58,000 Change digits 9, 5, and 0 to zeros, since these digits are to right of 8, the rounded number.

By rounding 57,950 to the nearest thousand, we can see that 57,950 is closer to 58,000 than to 57,000.

Now let's look at **rounding all the way.** When you round all the way, you round to the first digit of the number (the left-most digit) and have only one nonzero digit remaining.

EXAMPLE 3 Round 4,698 all the way.

Step 1. 4,698 Identified left-most digit is 4.

Step 2. → Digit to right of 4 is greater than 5 so 4 becomes 5.

5,698
↓↓↓
Step 3. 5,000 Change all other digits to zeros.

4,698 rounded all the way is 5,000.

Remember that rounding to a specific digit depends on what degree of accuracy you want in your estimate. When you round 24,800 all the way, it is 20,000 because the digit to the right of 2 is less than 5. This 20,000 is 4,800 less than the original number, 24,800, and not as accurate as if we rounded 24,800 to the identified digit 4. Before concluding this unit, let's look at how to dissect and solve a word problem.

How to Dissect and Solve a Word Problem

Over the next eight chapters, you will be learning how to dissect and solve word problems. I must admit that as a student, solving word problems was difficult. This difficulty occurred because after reading the word problem, I didn't know where to begin. Not knowing where to begin has also made solving word problems difficult for my students.

The trick to solving word problems is to be *organized* and *persistent*. Like learning to ride a bike or learning to type, you are only successful after much practice. Do not be discouraged. Each person learns at a different speed. Your goal must be to FINISH THE RACE and learn to solve word problems with ease.

To be organized in solving word problems, you need a plan of action that tells you where to begin—a blueprint aid. Like a builder, you will refer to this blueprint aid constantly until you know the procedure. The blueprint aid for dissecting and solving a word problem looks like this:

Blueprint Aid for Dissecting and Solving a Word Problem

A. Gather the facts	B. What am I solving for?	C. What must I know or calculate before solving problem?	D. Key points to remember

Now let's study this blueprint aid. Columns A and B require that you *read* the word problem slowly. By gathering the facts, you are dissecting the word problem. Think of Column C as the basic information you will need to know or calculate before solving the word problem. Many times this column will contain formulas needed to give you the foundation for the step-by-step problem solution. Column D reinforces key points.

It's time now to try your skill at using the blueprint aid for dissecting and solving a word problem.

The Word Problem On the 95th anniversary of Tootsie Roll Industries, the company reported sharply increased sales and profits. Sales reached one hundred ninety-four million dollars and a record profit of twenty-two million, five hundred fifty-six thousand dollars. The president of the company has requested that you round the sales and profit figures all the way.

Study the following blueprint aid and note how we filled in the columns with the information in the word problem. You will find the organization of the blueprint aid most helpful. Be persistent! You *can* dissect and solve word problems! When you are finished with the word problem, make sure the answer seems reasonable.

Blueprint Aid for Dissecting and Solving a Word Problem

A. Gather the facts	B. What am I solving for?	C. What must I know or calculate before solving problem?	D. Key points to remember
Sales: One hundred ninety-four million dollars. *Profit:* Twenty-two million, five hundred fifty-six thousand dollars.	Sales and profit rounded all the way.	Express each verbal form in numeric form. Identify left-most digit in each number.	Rounding all the way means only the left- most digit will remain. All other digits become zeros.

Steps to Solving Problem

1. Convert verbal to numeric.
   One hundred ninety-four million dollars ⟶ $194,000,000
   Twenty-two million, five hundred fifty-six thousand dollars ⟶ $ 22,556,000
2. Identify left-most digit of each number.
   $194,000,000 $22,556,000
3. Round. ↓ ↓
   $200,000,000 $20,000,000

Note that in the final answer, $200,000,000 and $20,000,000 have only one nonzero digit.

Remember that you cannot round numbers expressed in verbal form. These numbers must be converted to numeric form.

Now you should see the importance of the information in Column C of the blueprint aid. When you complete your blueprint aids for word problems, do not be concerned if the order of the information in your boxes does not follow the order given in the text boxes. Often there is more than one way of dissecting a word problem.

LU 1-1 PRACTICE QUIZ

At the end of each unit you can check your progress with a Practice Quiz. If you had difficulty understanding the learning unit, the Practice Quiz will help identify your area of weakness. Work the problems on scrap paper. Check your answers with the solutions that follow the quiz. At the end of the text in Appendix I is an optional worksheet of drill and word problems for this unit. At the end of this chapter (p. 19) is a complete set of drill and word problems. Check with your instructor about specific assignments and the videotapes available for each Practice Quiz in the chapter.

1. Write in verbal form:
   a. 8,696 **b.** 39,865 **c.** 510,846,182
2. Round off the following numbers as indicated:

Nearest ten	Nearest hundred	Nearest thousand	Rounded all the way
a. 77	**b.** 648	**c.** 7,210	**d.** 1,890

3. Kellogg's reported its sales as five million, one hundred eighty-one thousand dollars. The company earned a profit of five hundred two thousand dollars. What would the sales and profit be if each number were rounded all the way? (Hint: You might want to draw the blueprint aid since we show it in the solution.)

SOLUTIONS TO LU 1-1 PRACTICE QUIZ

1. **a.** Eight thousand, six hundred ninety-six
   b. Thirty-nine thousand, eight hundred sixty-five
   c. Five hundred ten million, eight hundred forty-six thousand, one hundred eighty-two

2. a. 80 b. 600 c. 7,000 d. 2,000

3. Kellogg's sales and profit:

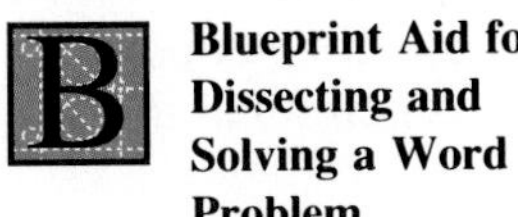

Blueprint Aid for Dissecting and Solving a Word Problem

A. Gather the facts	B. What am I solving for?	C. What must I know or calculate before solving problem?	D. Key points to remember
Sales: Five million, one hundred eighty-one thousand dollars. *Profit:* Five hundred two thousand dollars.	Sales and profit rounded all the way.	Express each verbal form in numeric form. Identify left-most digit in each number.	Rounding all the way means only the left-most digit will remain. All other digits become zeros.

Steps to Solving Problem

1. Convert verbal to numeric.
   Five million, one hundred eighty-one thousand → $5,181,000
   Five hundred two thousand → $ 502,000
2. Identify left-most digit of each number.
   $5,181,000 $502,000
3. Round. ↓ ↓
   $5,000,000 $500,000

LEARNING UNIT 1-2 WHOLE NUMBERS—ADDITION AND SUBTRACTION

When traveling by air, do you find it handy to purchase gifts at the airport shops? The latest trend is to make it possible for customers to order their items from the airplane. The shops have them packaged and ready for you when you arrive. When you pick up your items, you will want to be sure your final bill is accurate. Also, you may later decide not to purchase a certain item(s). If you do not have a calculator, knowing how to add or subtract whole numbers manually will help you estimate the total cost of your bill.

This unit teaches you how to build a solid foundation in business math by manually adding and subtracting whole numbers. When you least expect it, you will catch yourself automatically using this skill.

Addition of Whole Numbers

The numbers that you add in a group of numbers are **addends.** The result of the addition of the numbers or addends is the **sum,** or total.

Columns of numbers are added from top to bottom. The result is checked by reading the columns from bottom to top. Here is an example that will show you how to add a group of numbers and check your sum:

EXAMPLE

```
                 2 1
Checking    ↑   1,541  |  Adding
bottom      |   4,962  |  top to
to top      |   3,821  ↓  bottom
                8,415
               18,739
```

Alternate check

Add each column as a separate total and then combine. The end result is the same.

```
  1,541
  4,962
  3,821
  8,415
      9
    13
   2 6
  16
 18,739
```

How to Quickly Estimate Addition by Rounding All the Way

From Learning Unit 1–1, you know that rounding all the way gives quick arithmetic estimates. Using the "Paying the Pilot" clipping below, note how you can round each number all the way and the total will not be rounded all the way. Remember that rounding all the way doesn't replace actual computations, but it is helpful in making quick commonsense decisions.

EXAMPLE

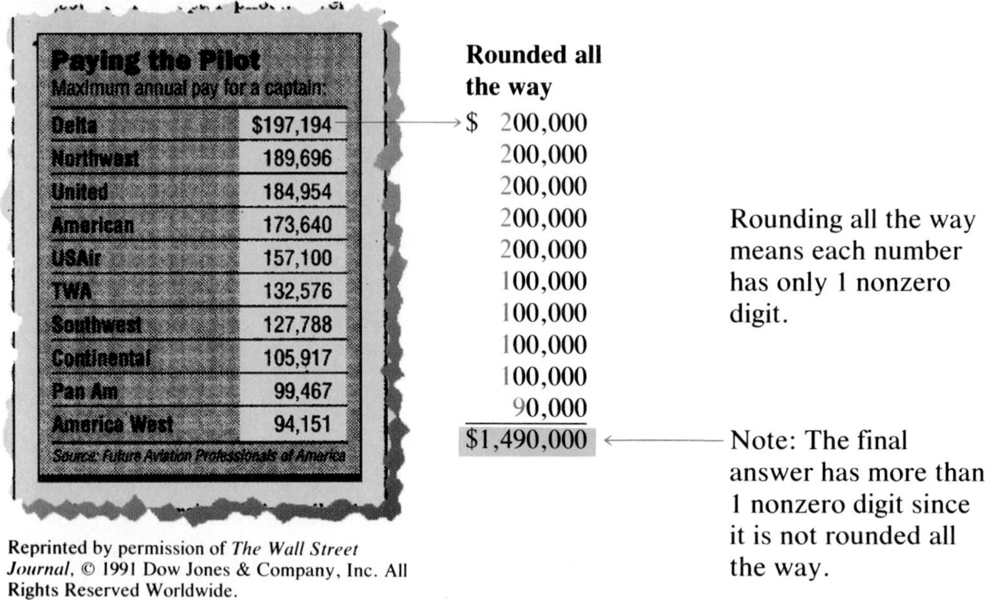

Paying the Pilot

Maximum annual pay for a captain:

Delta	$197,194
Northwest	189,696
United	184,954
American	173,640
USAir	157,100
TWA	132,576
Southwest	127,788
Continental	105,917
Pan Am	99,467
America West	94,151

Source: Future Aviation Professionals of America

Rounded all the way

$ 200,000
200,000
200,000
200,000
200,000
100,000
100,000
100,000
100,000
90,000
$1,490,000

Rounding all the way means each number has only 1 nonzero digit.

Note: The final answer has more than 1 nonzero digit since it is not rounded all the way.

Horizontal and Vertical Addition

Frequently, companies must use both horizontal and vertical additions. For example, manufacturers often need weekly production figures of individual products and a weekly total of all products. Today, many companies use computer spreadsheets for determining various manufacturing figures. In the following example, we show you how to do horizontal and vertical addition manually.

EXAMPLE

Production report: Units produced

	Monday		Tuesday		Wednesday		Thursday		Friday		Total
Sneakers	400	+	300	+	170	+	70	+	450	=	1,390
Boots	650	+	180	+	190	+	210	+	220	=	1,450
Loafers	210	+	55	+	98	+	112	+	310	=	785
Totals	1,260	+	535	+	458	+	392	+	980	=	3,625

Besides production reports, payroll records often require the need for horizontal and vertical addition.

The total of the vertical and the horizontal columns check to the grand total of 3,625.

Subtraction of Whole Numbers

The subtraction of whole numbers is the opposite of the addition of whole numbers. In the following example, note that the top (largest) number is the **minuend.** From the minuend, you subtract the **subtrahend,** which gives you the **difference** between the two numbers.

EXAMPLE

6,815 (borrowing marks: 7 11)	Minuend (the larger number)	**Check**	2,361
−2,361	Subtrahend		+4,454
4,454	Difference		6,815

Starting at the right-hand column of the minuend and subtrahend in the above example, subtract the units 5 − 1 = 4. The 1 to the left of the 5 in the minuend indicates that the number has only 1 ten. Obviously, we cannot subtract the 6 tens in the subtrahend from 1 ten. We need more tens. Looking to the left of the tens—the hundreds—we see that the minuend has 8 hundreds. A hundred is 10 tens. So we take 1 hundred and convert it to tens. We show this by marking out the 8 and writing 7. Then we add the 10 tens to the 1 ten we already have and get 11 tens. Now we can complete the subtraction with 11 − 6 = 5 tens, 7 − 3 = 4 hundreds, and 6 − 2 = 4 thousands.

At the right of the above subtraction example, we show the check indicating that the 4,454 difference is correct. Checking subtraction requires adding the difference (4,454) to the subtrahend (2,361) to arrive at the minuend (6,815).

How to Dissect and Solve a Word Problem

Accurate subtraction is important in many business operations. In Chapter 4, we discuss the importance of keeping accurate subtraction in your checkbook balance. Now let's check your progress by dissecting and solving a word problem.

The Word Problem Hershey's produced 25 million Kisses in one day. The same day, the company shipped 4 million to Japan, 3 million to France, and 6 million throughout the United States. At the end of that day, what is company's inventory of Kisses? What would the inventory balance be if you rounded the number all the way?

Blueprint Aid for Dissecting and Solving a Word Problem

A. Gather the facts	B. What am I solving for?	C. What must I know or calculate before solving problem?	D. Key points to remember
Produced: 25 million. *Shipped:* Japan, 4 million; France, 3 million; United States, 6 million.	Total Kisses left in inventory. Inventory rounded all the way.	Total Kisses produced − Total Kisses shipped = Total Kisses left in inventory.	Minuend − Subtrahend = Difference. Rounding all the way means rounding to last digit on left.

Steps to Solving Problem

1. Calculate total Kisses shipped.

$$\begin{array}{r} 4{,}000{,}000 \\ 3{,}000{,}000 \\ \underline{6{,}000{,}000} \\ 13{,}000{,}000 \end{array}$$

2. Calculate total Kisses left in inventory.

$$\begin{array}{r} 25{,}000{,}000 \\ \underline{-\,13{,}000{,}000} \\ 12{,}000{,}000 \end{array}$$

3. Rounding inventory all the way.

Identified digit is 1. Digit to right of 1 is 2, which is less than 5. Answer: 10,000,000.

LU 1-2 PRACTICE QUIZ

1. Add by totaling each separate column:

$$\begin{array}{r} 7{,}510 \\ 1{,}841 \\ \underline{1{,}399} \end{array}$$

2. Estimate by rounding all the way (do not round total of estimate) and then do the actual computation:

$$\begin{array}{r} 5{,}351 \\ 7{,}682 \\ \underline{2{,}751} \end{array}$$

3. Subtract and check your answer:

$$\begin{array}{r} 9{,}876 \\ \underline{-\,4{,}967} \end{array}$$

4. Jackson Manufacturing Company projected its 1995 furniture sales at $890,000. During 1995, Jackson earned $510,000 in sales from major clients and $369,100 in sales from the remainder of its clients. What is the amount that Jackson over- or underestimated its sales? You might try to use the blueprint aid since the answer will show the completed blueprint aid.

SOLUTIONS TO LU 1–2 PRACTICE QUIZ

1.

```
    10
    14
    16
     9
------
10,750
```

2.

Estimate	Actual
5,000	5,351
8,000	7,682
3,000	2,751
16,000	15,784

3.

```
 8 18 6 16           Check
  9,876  ←            4,909
 −4,967             +4,967
  4,909  ──────────   9,876
```

4. Jackson Manufacturing Company over- or underestimated sales:

Blueprint Aid for Dissecting and Solving a Word Problem

A. Gather the facts	B. What am I solving for?	C. What must I know or calculate before solving problem?	D. Key points to remember
Projected 1995 sales: $890,000. *Major clients:* $510,000. *Other clients:* $369,100.	How much were sales over- or underestimated?	Total projected sales − Total actual sales = Over- or underestimated sales.	Projected sales (minuend) − Actual sales (subtrahend) = Difference.

Steps to Solving Problem

1. Calculate total actual sales. $510,000 + 369,100 = $879,100
2. Calculate over- or underestimated sales. $890,000 − 879,100 = **$ 10,900 (overestimated)**

LEARNING UNIT 1–3 WHOLE NUMBERS—MULTIPLICATION AND DIVISION

Let's assume that you had a financial windfall. After reading the following newspaper clipping, you decided to spend some of your money and take three friends to New York to see a musical.

> **THE PAY'S THE THING on Broadway as musicals tap dance over serious plays.**
> Tickets to the most popular shows like "The Phantom of the Opera" and "Les Miserables" are $60—when they're available. When they're not, "ticket brokers" command as much as $200 for an orchestra seat—even "scalpers," who hawk tickets outside theaters, charge less. Heavy prices for light entertainment give rise to a counter-move. A plan from the Broadway Alliance would help prod[illegible]n of non-musi-

Your friends want to see the musical *Les Miserables*. The article said the tickets were $60 each. By adding $60 four times (tickets for you and your three friends), you could determine that four tickets would cost $240. You also could use a shortcut to find the cost of four tickets and multiply $60 times 4. One of your friends, however, is a math whiz. Before you could add $60 four times or multiply $60 times 4, she said, "The tickets will cost you $240 because $240 divided by 4 is $60."

This unit will sharpen your skills on two important arithmetic operations—multiplication and division. In business decision making, we frequently use these two operations.

Multiplication of Whole Numbers—Shortcut to Addition

From calculating your musical ticket cost for your New York trip, you know that *multiplication is a shortcut to addition*. Here is another example:

$$6 \times 4 = 24 \quad \text{or} \quad 6 + 6 + 6 + 6 = 24$$

Before learning the steps used to multiply whole numbers with two or more digits, you must learn some multiplication terminology. To explain this terminology, let's multiply a larger figure.

Note in the following example that the top number (number we want to multiply) is the **multiplicand.** The bottom number (number doing the multiplying) is the **multiplier.** The final number (answer) is the **product.** The numbers between the multiplier and the product are **partial products.** Also note how we positioned the partial product 2090. This number is the result of multiplying 418 by 50 (the 5 is in the tens position). On each line in the partial products, we placed the first digit directly below the digit we used in the multiplication process.

EXAMPLE

	418	← Top number (multiplicand)		
	× 52	← Bottom number (multiplier)		
Partial	836		2 × 418 =	836
product →	20 90		50 × 418 =	+20,900
	21,736	← Product answer →		21,736

We can now give the following steps for multiplying whole numbers with two or more digits.

Steps for Multiplying Whole Numbers with Two or More Digits

Step 1. Align the multiplicand (top number) and multiplier (bottom number) at the right. Usually, you should make the smaller number the multiplier.

Step 2. Begin by multiplying the right number of the multiplier with the right number of the multiplicand. Keep multiplying as you move left through the multiplicand. Your first partial product aligns at right with the multiplicand and multiplier.

Step 3. Move left through the multiplier and continue multiplying the multiplicand. Your partial product right number or first number is placed directly below the digit in the multiplier that you used to multiply.

Step 4. Continue Steps 2 and 3 until you have completed your multiplication process. Then add the partial products to get the final product.

Checking and Estimating Multiplication

We can check the multiplication process by reversing the multiplicand and multiplier and then multiplying. Let's first estimate 52 × 418 by rounding all the way.

EXAMPLE

50	←	52
× 400	←	× 418
20,000		416
		52
		20 8
		21,736

By estimating before actually working the problem, we know our answer should be about 20,000. When we multiply 52 by 418, we get the same answer as when we multiply 418 × 52—and the answer is about 20,000. Remember, if we didn't round all the way, our estimate would have been closer. If we had used a calculator, the rounded estimate would have helped us check the calculator's answer. Our commonsense estimate tells us our answer is near 20,000—not 200,000.

Before you study the division of whole numbers, you should know (1) the multiplication shortcut involving zeros and (2) how to multiply any number by powers of 10.

Steps for Multiplication Shortcut with Numbers Ending in Zeros

Step 1. When zeros are at the end of the multiplicand or the multiplier, or both, disregard the zeros and multiply.

Step 2. Count the number of zeros in the problem.

Step 3. Add the number of zeros counted in Step 2 to your answer.

No need to multiply rows of zeros.

```
   65,000
    ×420
   00 000
 1 300 00
26 000 0
27,300,000
```

EXAMPLE

```
 65,000        65          3 zeros
 × 420       × 42        + 1 zero
             1 30          4 zeros
            26 0
            27,300,000
```

Steps for Multiplying Any Number by Powers of 10

Step 1. Add the number of zeros to the number you want to multiply based on the power of 10 (10, 100, or 1,000).

Step 2. Insert comma(s) as needed every three digits starting from right to left.

EXAMPLE

$77 \times 10 = 770$ (add 1 zero)
$77 \times 100 = 7,700$ (add 2 zeros)
$77 \times 1,000 = 77,000$ (add 3 zeros)

When a zero is in the center of the multiplier, you can do the following:

EXAMPLE

```
   658          3 × 658 =     1,974
  ×403        400 × 658 =  +263,200
  1 974                     265,174
263 2□
265,174
```

In the above example, remember that the 4 you multiply by is 400, so the partial product is 263,200. You do not have to write the zeros, but leave space for them by writing the last digit of the result below the 4 in the multiplier.

Division of Whole Numbers

Division is the reverse of multiplication and is a timesaving shortcut related to subtraction. For example, $6 \times 4 = 24$ and $24 \div 6 = 4$. (If we subtract 6 four times from 24, we would get zero: $24 - 6$, $18 - 6$, and so on.) When the **divisor** (number used to divide) doesn't divide evenly into the **dividend** (number we are dividing), the result is a partial **quotient,** with the leftover amount the **remainder.** In later chapters, we will see remainders expressed as fractions.

The following example illustrates *even division.*

EXAMPLE

```
                  18 ←—— Quotient
Divisor ——→ 15)270 ←—— Dividend
                 15
                 120
                 120
```

In this example, 15 divides into 27 once with a remainder of 12. We bring the 0 in the dividend down to 12, resulting in 120 divided by 15 equals 8 with no remainder—even division. The example that follows illustrates *uneven division with a remainder.*

EXAMPLE

```
  24 R1 ←—— Remainder
7)169
  14
   29
   28
    1
```

Check

(7 × 24) + 1 = 169
Divisor × Quotient + Remainder = Dividend

Note the check method in the above example. Checking a problem gives assurance that you have calculated correctly.

Because the divisor in the even division example above had more than one digit, we call it *long division.* In the uneven division example, the divisor had only one digit. This is *short division.*

When the divisor has one digit (short division), you can often do the division mentally. Note the following examples:

EXAMPLES

$$9\overline{)981}\ \ \text{quotient } 109 \qquad 7\overline{)118}\ \ \text{quotient } 16\ R6$$

Next, let's look at the value of estimating division.

Estimating Division

Before actually working a division problem, estimate the quotient by rounding. This estimate helps check your answer. The example that follows is rounded all the way. After you make an estimate, work the problem and check your answer by multiplication.

EXAMPLE

```
        36 R111                          50        Check
138 ) 5,079          Estimate  100 ) 5,000          138
      4 14                                        ×  36
        939                                         828
        828                                        4 14
        111                                       4,968
                                                 +  111  Add remainder
                                                  5,079
```

Now let's turn our attention on division shortcuts with zeros.

Division Shortcuts with Zeros

You will find the following steps a great time saver:

Steps for Division Shortcut with Numbers Ending in Zeros

Step 1. When the dividend and divisor have ending zeros, count the number of ending zeros in the divisor.

Step 2. Drop the same number of zeros in the dividend as in the divisor, counting from right to left.

Note the following examples of division shortcut with numbers ending in zeros. Since two of the symbols used for division are ÷ and $\overline{)}$, our first examples show the zero shortcut method with the ÷ symbol.

EXAMPLES

(One ending zero)

Dividend	Divisor		Drop 1 zero in dividend	
75,000 ÷	10	→ 75,00~~0~~ =	7,500	
75,000 ÷	100	→ 75,0~~00~~ =	750	(drop 2 zeros)
75,000 ÷	1,000	→ 75,~~000~~ =	75	(drop 3 zeros)

In a long division problem with the $\overline{)}$ symbol, you again count the number of ending zeros in the divisor. Then drop the same number of ending zeros in the dividend and divide as usual.

EXAMPLE 6,5~~00~~ $\overline{)}$ 88,0~~00~~ (drop 2 zeros) → 65 $\overline{)}$ 880

```
      13 R35
65 ) 880
     65
     230
     195
      35
```

You are now ready to practice what you learned by dissecting and solving a word problem.

How to Dissect and Solve a Word Problem

The blueprint aid that follows will be your guide to dissecting and solving the following word problem.

The Word Problem Dunkin Donuts sells to four different companies a total of $3,500 worth of donuts per week. What is the total annual sales to these companies? What is the yearly sales per company? (Assume each company buys the same amount.) Check your answer to show how multiplication and division are related.

Blueprint Aid for Dissecting and Solving a Word Problem

© Courtesy of Dunkin Donuts/S. J. Barao Photography.

A. Gather the facts	B. What am I solving for?	C. What must I know or calculate before solving problem?	D. Key points to remember
Sales per week: $3,500. *Companies:* 4.	Total annual sales to all these companies. Yearly sales per company.	Sales per week × Weeks in year (52) = Total annual sales. Total annual sales ÷ Total companies = Yearly sales per company.	Division is the reverse of multiplication.

Steps to Solving Problem

1. Calculate total annual sales. $3,500 × 52 weeks = **$182,000**
2. Calculate yearly sales per company. $182,000 ÷ 4 = **$45,500**

Check $45,500 × 4 = $182,000

It's time to try the Practice Quiz.

LU 1-3 PRACTICE QUIZ

1. Estimate actual problem by rounding all the way, work actual problem, and check:

Actual	Estimate	Check
4,692 × 19		

2. Multiply:
66,000
× 1,500
3. Multiply by shortcut method:
75 × 10,000
4. Divide by rounding all the way; complete actual calculation; and check, showing remainder as a whole number.
26)5,325
5. Divide by shortcut method:
2,000)98,000
6. Assume General Motors produces 960 Chevrolets each workday (Monday through Friday). If the cost to produce each car is $6,500, what is General Motors' total cost for the year? Check your answer.

SOLUTIONS TO LU 1-3 PRACTICE QUIZ

1. **Estimate**

   5,000
× 20
100,000

   Actual

   4,692
× 19
42 228
46 92
89,148

   Check

   9 × 4,692 = 42,228
10 × 4,692 = 46,920
89,148

2. 66 × 15 = 990 + 5 zeros = 99,000,000
3. 75 + 4 zeros = 750,000
4. **Rounding**

   166 R20
30)5,000
3 0
2 00
1 80
200
180
20

   Actual

   204 R21
26)5,325
5 2
125
104
21

   Check

   26 × 204 = 5,304
+ 21
5,325

5. Drop 3 zeros = 2)98 = 49

6. General Motors' total cost per year:

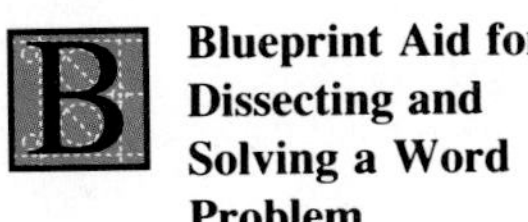

Blueprint Aid for Dissecting and Solving a Word Problem

A. Gather the facts	B. What am I solving for?	C. What must I know or calculate before solving problem?	D. Key points to remember
Cars produced each workday: 960. *Workweek:* 5 days. *Cost per car:* \$6,500.	Total cost per year.	Cars produced per week × 52 = Total cars produced per year. Total cars produced per year × Total cost per car = Total cost per year.	Whenever possible, use multiplication and division shortcuts with zeros. Multiplication can be checked by division.

Steps to Solving Problem

1. Calculate total cars produced per week. — 5 × 960 = 4,800 cars produced per week
2. Calculate total cars produced per year. — 4,800 cars × 52 weeks = 249,600 total cars produced per year
3. Calculate total cost per year. — 249,600 cars × \$6,500 = **\$1,622,400,000** (multiply 2,496 × 65 and add zeros)

Check \$1,622,400,000 ÷ 249,600 = \$6,500 (drop 2 zeros before dividing)

CHAPTER ORGANIZER: A REFERENCE GUIDE

Page	Topic	Key point, procedure, formula	Example(s) to illustrate situation
5	Writing whole numbers	Commas from right to left separate every three digits. Do not use *and;* hyphenate numbers 21 to 99.	462 → Four hundred sixty-two 6,741 → Six thousand, seven hundred forty-one
6	Rounding whole numbers	1. Identify digit. 2. If digit to right is 5 or more, round up; if less than 5, do not change. 3. Change all digits to right of identified digit to zeros.	643 to nearest ten 4 is identified digit. / 3 is not 5 or more. Thus, 643 rounds off to 640.
7	Rounding all the way	One nonzero digit remains. Do not round final answer when total arrived at by rounding all the way. Estimating by rounding all the way is not as exact as other rounding methods.	468,451 → 500,000 The 5 is only nonzero digit remaining.
7	Dissecting and solving problems	Be organized and persistent! Use the blueprint aid for dissecting and solving a word problem.	Moore Company receives 3,500 telephone calls per day (Monday through Friday). How many calls are received in a year?

Blueprint Aid for Dissecting and Solving a Word Problem

A. Gather the facts	B. What am I solving for?	C. What must I know or calculate before solving problem?	D. Key points to remember
Calls per day: 3,500. *Workweek:* 5 days.	Total calls per year.	Total calls per week × 52 weeks in year = Total calls per year.	Use multiplication shortcuts with zeros whenever possible.

Steps to Solving Problem

1. Calculate total calls per week. — 3,500 × 5 = 17,500 → (5 × 35 + 2 zeros)
2. Calculate total calls per year. — 17,500 × 52 = 910,000

Page	Topic	Key point, procedure, formula	Example(s) to illustrate situation
9	Addition	Add from top to bottom. Check by adding bottom to top or by adding each column separately and combining.	↑ 1 ↓ 65 12 Checking the sum of 47 10 each digit 112 112
10	Subtraction	Minuend less subtrahend equals difference.	**Check** 5 18 685 193 − 492 + 492 193 685
12	Multiplication	1. If multiplying by 10, 100, 1,000, and so on, add number of zeros to number multiplied. 2. If zero is in center of multiplier, no need to show row of zeros. In the example, note the 2 × 4 is aligned in the hundreds position.	1. 14 × 10 = 140 (add 1 zero) 14 × 1,000 = 14,000 (add 3 zeros) 2. 524 × 206 3 144 104 8 107,944
14	Division	1. When divisor is divided into the dividend, the remainder is less than divisor. 2. Drop zeros from dividend right to left by number of zeros found in the divisor.	1. 5 R6 14)76 70 6 2. 5,000 ÷ 100 = 50 ÷ 1 = 50 5,000 ÷ 1,000 = 5 ÷ 1 = 5
	Key terms	Addends, p. 9 Difference, p. 10 Dividend, p. 14 Divisor, p. 14 Minuend, p. 10 Multiplicand, p. 13 Multiplier, p. 13 Partial products, p. 13	Product, p. 13 Quotient, p. 14 Remainder, p. 14 Rounding all the way, p. 7 Subtrahend, p. 10 Sum, p. 9 Whole number, p. 5

END-OF-CHAPTER PROBLEMS

Drill Problems

Additional homework assignments by learning unit are at the end of text in Appendix I (p. I-1). Solutions to odd problems are at the end of text in Appendix II.

Add the following:

1–1. 64 + 39 = 103

1–2. 870 + 310 = 1,180

1–3. 97 + 97 = 194

1–4. 58 + 61 = 119

1–5. 9,382 + 4,819 = 14,201

1–6. 59,481 + 51,411 + 70,821 = 181,713

1–7. 69,142 + 14,891 + 17,451 = 101,484

Subtract the following:

1–8. 92 − 18 = 74

1–9. 90 − 38 = 52

1–10. 287 − 199 = 88

1–11. 8,900 − 7,200 = 1,700

1–12. 9,800 − 8,900 = 900

1–13. 1,622 − 548 = 1,074

Multiply the following:

1–14. 27 × 9 = 243

1–15. 510 × 61
510
30 60
31,110

1–16. 800 × 400 = 320,000

1–17. 588 × 302
1 176
176 40
177,576

1–18. 309 × 850
15 450
247 2
262,650

1–19. 450 × 280
36 000
90 0
126,000

Divide by short division:

1–20. 3)369 = 123

1–21. 8)640 = 80

1–22. 4)164 = 41

Divide—show work and remainder:

1–23. 7)316 = 45 R1
28
36
35
1

1–24. 62)8,915 = 143 R49
62
271
248
235
186
49

Add the following without rearranging:

1–25. 97 + 105 = 202

1–26. 1,055 + 88 = 1,143

1–27. 666 + 950 = 1,616

1–28. 1,011 + 17 = 1,028

1–29. Add the following and check by totaling each column individually without carrying numbers:

	Check
6,918	16
8,413	10
9,485	1 7
24,816	23
	24,816

Estimate by rounding all the way and then do actual addition:

		Estimate			Estimate
1–30.	7,800	8,000	**1–31.**	6,980	7,000
	8,400	8,000		3,190	3,000
	3,100	3,000		7,819	8,000
	19,300	19,000		17,989	18,000

Subtract without rearranging:

1–32. 190 − 88 = 102 **1–33.** 950 − 870 = 80

1–34. Subtract and check work:

	8 10 9 9 11	
591,001	591,001	215,045
−375,956	−375,956	+375,956
	215,045	591,001

Multiply horizontally:

1–35. 15 × 7 = 105 **1–36.** 84 × 8 = 672

1–37. 27 × 8 = 216 **1–38.** 17 × 6 = 102

Divide and check by multiplication:

1–39. 45)876 = 19 R21

```
   19 R21
45)876
   45
   426
   405
    21
```

Check 45 × 19 = 855
+21
876

1–40. 46)1,950 = 42 R18

```
     42 R18
46)1,950
   1 84
    110
     92
     18
```

Check 46 × 42 = 1,932
+ 18 (R)
1,950

1–41. Add the following columns both horizontally and vertically:

Production report

	Mon.		Tues.		Wed.		Thurs.		Fri.		
Laser discs	75	+	15	+	19	+	24	+	40	=	173
Videotapes	42	+	68	+	44	+	77	+	30	=	261
Audiotapes	61	+	41	+	22	+	44	+	18	=	186
Chairs	38	+	17	+	51	+	66	+	50	=	222
	216	+	141	+	136	+	211	+	138		842

Using data in Problem 1–41, answer the following:

1–42. What was the total difference in production on Monday versus Friday?
216 − 138 = 78

1–43. If two weeks ago production was 3 times the total of this report, what was total production?
842 × 3 = 2,526

1–44. What was average production of videotapes and chairs for Monday?
42 + 38 = 80 ÷ 2 = 40

Complete:

1–45.
```
  9,200
 -1,510
  7,690
-   700
  6,990
```

1–46.
```
 3,000,000
  -769,459
 2,230,541
-   68,541
 2,162,000
```

1–47. Estimate actual problem by rounding all the way and then do actual multiplication:

Actual	Estimate
940	900
× 71	× 70
940	63,000
65 80	
66,740	

Divide by the shortcut method:

1–48. $1{,}000\overline{)650{,}000}$ = 650

Drop 3 zeros.

1–49. $100\overline{)70{,}000}$ = 700

Drop 2 zeros.

1–50. Estimate actual problem by rounding all the way and do actual division:

Actual
```
       12 R610
695)8,950
    6 95
    2 000
    1 390
      610
```

Estimate
```
       12 R600
700)9,000
    7 00
    2 000
    1 400
      600
```

Word Problems*

1–51. Shannon and Matthew have a dog-walking service. On Monday, they earned $15. They believe that by the end of the week they will earn 4 times as much as they did on Monday. What is their total earnings for the week?
$15
+60 (4 × $15)
$75 for week

1–52. Michelle O'Sullivan went to a rock concert at the Boston Garden. She had $150 in her wallet. Her transportation and ticket cost a total of $65, food cost $12, and a program cost $4. How much did Michelle have left?
$150
−81 ($65 + $12 + $4)
$69

1–53. Jim Cahn called his broker and bought 100 shares of IBM, 300 shares of McDonald's, and 1,650 shares of Apple Computer, Inc. What is the total number of shares Jim bought?
100 shares + 300 shares + 1,650 shares = 2,050 shares

1–54. Members of a local bank plan a family outing. A package of meat will serve 4 people. If the members expect 520 people to attend, how many packages will they need? Each package costs $5. What is the total cost of the meat?
520 ÷ 4 = 130 packages × $5 = $650

* See Appendix IV for blank blueprint aids to help you dissect and solve the word problems.

1–55. Alison Flynn decided to vacation in Mexico. To pay for her trip, she borrowed $1,655 from a friend. Alison promised to pay $85 a month to her friend until she paid back the loan. What is Alison's outstanding loan balance at the end of 7 months?

7 × $85 = $595
$1,655 − $595 = $1,060

1–56. Bruette Catering is supplying the punch for a local wedding reception. Bruette bought 4,800 ounces of punch. If a glass holds 10 ounces, how many glasses can Bruette completely fill? Bruette estimates that 200 people will attend. If each person drinks 2 glasses of punch, will Bruette have enough punch?

4,800 ÷ 10 = 480 glasses   200 × 2 = 400 glasses   Yes.
480 − 400 = 80 glasses left

1–57. Toyo Tires bought 860 tires from a manufacturer for $25 per tire. What is the total cost of Toyo's purchase? If the company can sell all the tires at $48 each, what will be the company's gross profit, or the difference between its sales and costs (Sales − Costs = Gross profit)?

Cost = 860 × $25 = $21,500   Sales = 860 × $48 = $41,280

$41,280	Sales
−21,500	Cost
$19,780	Gross profit

1–58. Amy Hardy loves to ski. She rented a ski chalet for $600 per month for 8 months. What is Amy's rental charge for the 8 months? If Amy spent $5,700 for her entire trip, how much did Amy spend in addition to the ski chalet rent?

$600 × 8 = $4,800 $5,700 − $4,800 = $900

1–59. Pete Gonsales bought 4,800 shares of Gillette Company stock. He held the stock for six months. Then Pete sold 175 shares on Monday, 290 shares on Tuesday and again on Thursday, and 600 shares on Friday. How many shares does Pete still own? The average share of the stock Pete owns is worth $18 per share. What is the total value of Pete's stock?

4,800 (shares bought)
−1,355 (shares sold)   175 + 290 + 290 + 600 = 1,355 shares sold
3,445 ⟶ 3,445 shares × $18 = $62,010

1–60. John Solberg gets 38 miles per gallon on his new Honda. The capacity of the gas tank is 18 gallons. How many miles can John drive on one tank of gas? Check your answer.

18 × 38 = 684 miles

$$\begin{array}{r} 18 \\ 38\overline{)684} \\ \underline{38} \\ 304 \\ \underline{304} \end{array}$$

1–61. Alison Rose received the following grades in her Accounting 101 class: 85, 80, 75, 90, 65, and 90. Alison's instructor, Professor Clark, said he would drop the lowest grade. What is Alison's average?

85 + 80 + 75 + 90 + 90 = 420 ÷ 5 = 84 average

1–62. Jill Curtis, professor of business, has 19 students in Accounting I, 24 in Accounting II, 36 in Data Processing, and 30 in Introduction to Business. What is the total number of students in Professor Curtis's classes? If 15 students withdraw, how many total students will Professor Curtis have?

19 + 24 + 36 + 30 = 109 students   109 − 15 = 94 students

1-63. Ron Alf, owner of Alf's Moving Company, bought a new truck. On Ron's first trip, he drove 1,200 miles and used 80 gallons of gas. How many miles per gallon did Ron get from his new truck? On Ron's second trip, he drove 840 miles and used 60 gallons. What is the difference in miles per gallon between Ron's first trip and his second trip?

1,200 ÷ 80 = 15 miles per gallon
840 ÷ 60 = 14 miles per gallon   Difference = 1 mile per gallon

1-64. Smith Office Equipment reduced its $184 Sharpe calculator by $29. What is the new selling price of the calculator? If Smith sold 1,500 calculators at the new price, what were the store's calculator sales?

$184 − $29 = $155 $155 × 1,500 = $232,500

1-65. Randy's Bookstore has 350 business math texts in inventory. During the month, the bookstore ordered and received an additional 1,950 texts; it also sold 988 texts. What is the bookstore's inventory at the end of the month? If each book costs $44, what is the end-of-month inventory cost?

350 + 1,950 = 2,300   2,300
− 988
1,312 end-of-month inventory

1,312 × $44 = $57,728

1-66. Pete's Diner began the day with an $84 beginning balance in the cash register. During the day, the cashier rang up sales of $9, $14, $6, $5, $15, $25, $6, and $80. What is the ending balance in the cash register? If Pete takes $59 out of the register at the end of the day, what is the new balance in the register?

$84 + $9 + $14 + $6 + $5 + $15 + $25 + $6 + $80 = $244
$244 − $59 = $185

1-67. Wolf Company produced 2,091,000 cans of paint in August. Wolf sold 1,998,000 of these cans. If each can cost $12, what was Wolf's ending inventory of paint cans and its total ending inventory cost?

2,091,000
− 1,998,000
93,000 paint cans × $12 = $1,116,000

1-68. River College has 20 faculty members in the business department, 18 in psychology, 12 in English, and 199 in all other departments. What is the total number of faculty at River College? If each faculty member advises 25 students, how many students attend River College?

20 + 18 + 12 + 199 = 249 faculty
249 × 25 = 6,225 students

1-69. Wong's Buffet had 60 customers on Sunday, 85 on Monday, 25 on Tuesday, and a total of 240 on Wednesday to Saturday. How many customers did Wong's Buffet serve during the week? If each customer spends $7, what were the total sales for the week?

60 + 85 + 25 + 240 = 410 customers
× $7
$2,870

If Wong's Buffet had the same sales each week, what were the sales for the year?

$2,870 × 52 = $149,240

1–70. Jeff estimates the following costs to maintain his home for a year:

Mortgage payments and interest	$ 6,755
Taxes	1,481
Phone	365
Insurance	488
Maintenance	1,200
Heating	1,958
	$12,247

Jeff feels that he can only afford $11,950 per year. By how much is Jeff over or under his estimate?

$12,247
− 11,950
$ 297 over

1–71. Roger Advertising Agency projected its 1996 sales at $891,500. During 1996, the agency earned $475,918 sales from its major clients and $301,582 sales from the remainder of its clients. How much did the agency overestimate its sales?

$475,918 $891,500
+301,582 −777,500
$777,500 $114,000

1–72. Rusty earned $46,000 last year before tax deductions. From Rusty's total earnings, his company subtracted $7,142 federal income taxes and $3,550 social security taxes. What was Rusty's actual or net pay for the year?

Deductions = $7,142 + $3,550 = $10,692

$46,000
− 10,692
$35,308 net pay

1–73. Sears Furniture received the following invoice amounts from suppliers. How much does the company owe?

	Per item	
15 paintings	$125 =	$ 1,875
32 rockers	69 =	2,208
20 desk lamps	55 =	1,100
95 coffee tables	139 =	13,205
		$18,388

1–74. Jole Company produces beach balls and it operates three shifts. It produces 5,000 balls per shift on shifts 1 and 2. On shift 3, the company can produce six times as many balls as on shift 1. Assume a 5-day workweek. How many beach balls does Jole produce per week and per year?

10,000 balls (shifts 1 and 2)
+30,000 balls (shift 3)
40,000 balls per day
× 5
200,000 balls per week

200,000
× 52
10,400,000 balls per year

1–75. Joe's Garage paid the following salaries to its employees: $315, $195, $185, $1,200, and $700. What was the total payroll? What is the average pay per employee?

$315 + $195 + $185 + $1,200 + $700 = $2,595
$2,595 ÷ 5 = $519

1–76. In August, Al's Sports Vehicles sold 25 vans, 34 jeeps, 80 compacts, and 95 trucks. What were Al's total unit sales for August? Total sales were $2,223,000. What was the average selling price of each vehicle?
25 + 34 + 80 + 95 = 234 units
$2,223,000 ÷ 234 units = $9,500

1–77. In planning her theater group's agenda and ticket reservations for the upcoming New York season, Judy Roth calculates that she will need the following:

Show 1: 200 tickets @ $18 =	$ 3,600
Show 2: 180 tickets @ $29 =	5,220
Show 3: 280 tickets @ $26 =	7,280
Show 4: 119 tickets @ $24 =	2,856
Show 5: 190 tickets @ $27 =	5,130
	$24,086

What will be the ticket cost for each show? What is the total cost of tickets for all five shows?

1–78. Mike Rool, a college editor, planned a business trip from New Hampshire (starting point) to New York and Washington D.C. Mike estimated that he would be traveling 1,150 miles *round* trip. When Mike made the trip, the drive from New Hampshire to New York was 310 miles, and from New York to Washington, D.C., 180 miles. How many miles did Mike overestimate his trip?
2 × 310 = 620 1,150 − 980 = 170 miles over
2 × 180 = 360
980

1–79. May Jackson bought a home for $159,800 in Sutton, Georgia. She paid a $21,900 down payment. What is the amount of May's loan?
$159,800 − $21,900 = $137,900

1–80. Joe Chin has a $750 balance in his checkbook. During the week, Joe wrote the following checks: rent, $290; telephone, $58; food, $102; and entertaining, $48. Joe also made a $700 deposit. What is Joe's new checkbook balance?
$290 + $58 + $102 + $48 = $498 $750
− 498
$252 + $700 = $952

1–81. Paul Rey's regular pay is $5 per hour for a 40-hour week. He earns $9 per hour for overtime. Last week Paul worked an 8-hour shift on Saturday in addition to his 40-hour week. What is Paul's overtime pay? What is his total pay for the week?
40 × $5 = $200 regular pay 8 × $9 = $72 overtime
$200 + $72 = $272

1–82. Fleet Street, an athletic sports shop, bought and sold the following merchandise:

	Cost	Selling price
Tennis rackets	$ 2,180	$ 2,910
Tennis balls	60	160
Bowling balls	950	2,151
Sneakers	7,210	12,810
	$10,400	$18,031

What was the total cost of merchandise bought by Fleet Street? If the shop sold all merchandise, what were the sales and the resulting gross profit (Sales − Costs = Gross profit)?

Sales	$18,031
− Costs	− 10,400
= Gross profit	$ 7,631

1-83. John Purcell, the bookkeeper for Roseville Real Estate, and his manager are concerned about the company's telephone bills. Last year the company's average monthly phone bill was $34. John's manager asked him for an average of this year's phone bills. John's records show the following:

January	$ 34	July	$ 28
February	60	August	23
March	20	September	29
April	25	October	25
May	30	November	22
June	59	December	41
	$228		$168

What is the average of this year's phone bills? Did John and his manager have a justifiable concern?
$228 + $168 = $396 ÷ 12 = $33
No justifiable concern.

1-84. Anita Ring borrowed $16,500 to buy a new Mustang. Anita's interest on the loan is $3,000. What will be her monthly payment if she takes 60 months to repay the loan (plus interest)? Assume Anita will repay the loan in equal payments?
$19,500 ÷ 60 = $325

1-85. Jesse Snow wants to buy some tools. He goes to Sears, Roebuck & Co. and finds the following prices: hammer, $5; screwdriver, $3; sander, $22; drill, $15; and workbench, $40. Jesse thinks these prices may be high. So he goes to Jones Supply Company and finds the following prices: hammer, $7; screwdriver, $5; sander, $20; drill, $18; and workbench, $36. Assume Jesse will buy all his tools from one company. Where should Jesse buy his tools?
Sears: $5 + $3 + $22 + $15 + $40 = $85   Buy at Sears.
Jones: $7 + 5 + $20 + $18 + $36 = $86

1-86. On Monday, Wang Hardware sold 15 paint brushes at $3 each, 6 wrenches at $5 each, 7 bags of grass seed at $3 each, 4 lawn mowers at $119 each, and 28 cans of paint at $8 each. What were Wang's total dollar sales on Monday?
$45 + $30 + $21 + $476 + $224 = $796
(15 × $3) + (6 × $5) + (7 × $3) + (4 × $119) + (28 × $8)

1-87. While redecorating, Morris Company used 125 square yards of commercial carpet. The total cost of the carpet was $2,625. How much did Morris pay per square yard?
$2,625 ÷ 125 = $21 per square yard

1-88. Washington Construction built 12 ranch houses for $115,000 each. From the sale of these houses, Washington received $1,980,000. How much gross profit (Sales − Costs = Gross profit) did Washington make on the houses?

$1,980,000	
− 1,380,000	($115,000 × 12)
$ 600,000	

The four partners of Washington Construction split all profits equally. How much will each partner receive?
$600,000 ÷ 4 = $150,000

Challenge Problem
Calculating Net Worth

Net worth = Assets − Liabilities (own) (owe)

1-89. Ellen Swarez is trying to determine her 1995 finances. Ellen's actual 1994 finances were:

Income:		Assets:		
Gross income	$69,000	Checking account	$ 1,950	
Interest income	450	Savings account	8,950	
Total	$69,450	Auto	1,800	
Expenses:		Personal property	14,000	
Living	$24,500	Total	$26,700	
Insurance premium	350	Liabilities:		
Taxes	14,800	Note to bank	4,500	
Medical	585	Net worth	$22,200	($26,700 − $4,500)
Investment	4,000			
Total	$44,235			

Ellen believes her gross income will double in 1995 and her interest income will decrease $150. She plans to reduce her 1995 living expenses in half. Ellen's insurance company wrote a letter announcing that insurance premiums would triple in 1995. Her accountant estimates her taxes will decrease $250 and her medical costs will increase $410. Ellen also hopes to cut her investment expenses by one fourth. Ellen's accountant projects that her savings and checking accounts will each double in value. On January 2, 1995, Ellen sold her auto and began to use public transportation. Ellen forecasts that her personal property will decrease by one seventh. She has sent her bank a $375 check to reduce her bank note. Could you give Ellen an updated list of her 1995 finances? If you round all the way each 1994 and 1995 asset and liability, what would be the difference in Ellen's net worth?

Income:		
Gross income	$138,000	($69,000 × 2)
Interest income	300	($450 − $150)
Total	$138,300	
Expenses:		
Living	$ 12,250	($24,500 ÷ 2)
Insurance premium	1,050	($350 × 3)
Taxes	14,550	($14,800 − $250)
Medical	995	($585 + $410)
Investment	3,000	$\left(\$4{,}000 - \frac{1}{4} \text{ of } \$4{,}000\right)$
Total	$ 31,845	
Assets:		
Checking account	$ 3,900	($1,950 × 2)
Savings account	17,900	($8,950 × 2)
Personal property	12,000	$\left(\$14{,}000 - \frac{1}{7} \text{ of } \$14{,}000\right)$
Total	$ 33,800	
Liabilities:		
Note to bank	4,125	(4,500 − $375)
Net worth	$ 29,675	

	1994	1995	
Checking account	$ 2,000	$ 4,000	
Savings account	9,000	20,000	
Auto	2,000	0	
Personal property	10,000	10,000	
Total	$23,000	$34,000	$30,000 = 1995
Liabilities	5,000	4,000	− 18,000 = 1994
Net worth	$18,000	$30,000	$12,000

Total estimated difference is $12,000 in favor of 1995.

Summary Practice Test

Solutions are at end of text in Appendix II.
Quick Reference
If you get any wrong answers, study the page numbers given for each problem.

1. P. 6.
2. P. 6.
3. P. 6.

1. Translate the following verbal forms into numbers and add:

a.	Seven thousand, three hundred seventy-one	7,371
b.	Eight million, twelve	8,000,012
c.	Fourteen thousand, nine hundred sixty-three	14,963
		8,022,346

2. Express in verbal form:

6,815,569 Six million, eight hundred fifteen thousand, five hundred sixty-nine

3. Round the following numbers:

Nearest ten	Nearest hundred	Nearest thousand	Round all the way
a. 48	**b.** 675	**c.** 8,150	**d.** 14,810
50	700	8,000	10,000

4. P. 9.

4. Estimate actual problem by rounding all the way, work actual problem, and check by adding each column of digits separately:

Actual	Estimate	Check
1,608	2,000	14
4,985	5,000	17
7,891	8,000	2 3
14,484	15,000	12
		14,484

5. P. 13.

5. Estimate actual problem by rounding all the way and then do actual multiplication:

Actual	Estimate
6,315	6,000
× 504	× 500
25 260	3,000,000
3 157 50	
3,182,760	

6. P. 13.

6. Multiply by the shortcut method:
751,810 × 1,000 = 751,810,000

7. P. 15.

7. Divide and check answer by multiplication:

```
      225 R6         225
63)14,181          ×  63
   12 6              675
    1 58           13 50
    1 26           14,175
      321          +    6
      315          14,181
        6
```

8. P. 15.

8. Divide by shortcut method:
700 ÷ 70 = 70~~0~~ ÷ 7~~0~~ = 10

9. P. 10.

9. Evan Shuster bought a $14 calculator that was reduced to $9. Evan gave the clerk a $100 bill. What change does Evan receive?
$100 − $9 = $91

10. Pp. 9, 14.

10. Lynn Shiver plans to buy an $18,000 van with an interest charge of $3,000. Lynn figures she can afford a monthly payment of $850. If Lynn must pay 24 equal monthly payments, can she afford the van?
$18,000 + $3,000 = $21,000 ÷ 24 = $875 No.

11. P. 14.

11. In 1995, Mel Sullivan earned $124,000 in real estate commission. If Mel's average commission was $4,000 per house, how many houses did Mel sell?
$124,000 ÷ $4,000 = 31 houses

12. P. 16.

12. Bev O'Callahan has the oil tank at her home filled 12 times a year. The oil tank has a capacity of 200 gallons. Assume (*a*) the price of home heating fuel is \$2 per gallon and (*b*) the tank is completely empty each time Bev has it filled. What is Bev's average monthly heating bill? Try to complete the following blueprint aid for dissecting and solving a word problem.

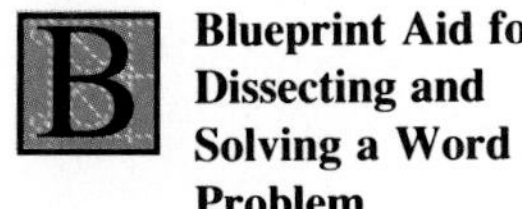

Blueprint Aid for Dissecting and Solving a Word Problem

A. Gather the facts	B. What am I solving for?	C. What must I know or calculate before solving problem?	D. Key points to remember
Oil filled 12 times per year. Tank holds 200 gallons. Cost is \$2 per gallon.	Average monthly heating bill.	Total gallons used × Price per gallon = Total cost of oil.	Average cost is total cost divided by 12 months in year.

Steps to Solving Problem

1. Calculate total number of gallons. 200 × 12 = 2,400 gallons
2. Calculate total cost of oil. 2,400 gallons × \$2 = \$4,800
3. Calculate average monthly bill. \$4,800 ÷ 12 = \$400

Project A

Business Bulletin

A Special Background Report On Trends in Industry And Finance

ROUGH AND TUMBLE magazine selling gets tougher and more expensive.

Magazines generate about $3 billion a year at 200,000 supermarkets and newsstands, but space is at a premium. About 30 titles dominate single-copy sales, all from major publishers. But West Germany's Bauer Publishing manages to make a splash anyway with First for Women magazine, selling about four million copies a month after less than a year. Bauer pays retailers $27 for each checkout-stand display position, plus a $9 quarterly "pocket" fee. Most competitors pay around $5. Another wrinkle: offer the first issue for 25 cents and let the retailer keep it. The push generates prominent newsstand spots.

Other publishers are wary of such spending but take note anyway. Rupert Murdoch's magazine unit will launch Soap Opera Weekly this fall using some of Bauer's tricks, says Joseph Elm, vice president of single-copy sales. Murdoch will pay $10 for checkout position, and a $5 quarterly fee, high compared with the $3.25 the National Enquirer pays.

Murdoch launched fashion magazine Mirabella, normally $3, at $1 a copy and sold out the issue's 600,000 run.

CHINA TOURISM poses moral, practical choices for the travel industry.

Beijing's crackdown turns off American

Assuming Murdoch obtains 7,500 checkout positions (1 per store), how much will he pay out in one year?

$10 × 7,500 =	$ 75,000
$5 × 4 = $20 (per year) × 7,500 =	150,000
Total	$225,000

Project B

VALENTINE'S DAY *is big business. It's the second-biggest day for selling cards, topped only by Christmas, for both Hallmark Cards and the greeting-card industry as a whole. Nationally, 900 million valentines are expected to be exchanged today. Hallmark won't divulge the market share it anticipates, but does say it has 2,000 different valentines from which to choose.*

Write 900 million in numeric form.
900,000,000

Project C

Write the number in verbal.
One hundred sixty-nine billion

THE ONLY ROCK VALUED AT $169,000,000,000.

NOTES

This page is left blank at the end of each chapter for your classroom notes or test review notes. This is a good place for additional work space.

THAT WAS THEN . . .
. . . THIS IS NOW

During the 50s, Procter & Gamble introduced Crest, the first fluoride toothpaste. Today, an assortment of different types of toothpastes are produced with fluoride. Also, 4 out of 5 $(\frac{4}{5})$ of the nation's 50 largest cities use fluoridated water.

2

Fractions

LEARNING UNIT OBJECTIVES

LU 2-1: Types of Fractions and Conversion Procedures

1. Identify proper fractions, improper fractions, and mixed numbers. *p. 35*
2. Convert improper fractions to whole or mixed numbers. *p. 35*
3. Convert mixed numbers to improper fractions. *p. 35*
4. Convert (reduce) fractions to lowest terms. *p. 36*
5. Convert (raise) fractions to highest terms. *p. 37*

LU 2-2: Fractions—Addition and Subtraction

1. Add and subtract proper fractions with same denominators. *p. 39*
2. Add and subtract proper fractions with different denominators. *p. 39*
3. Find least common denominator (LCD) by observation. *p. 39*
4. Find least common denominator by prime numbers. *p. 40*
5. Add and subtract mixed numbers (with same or different denominators). *pp. 41–42*
6. Dissect and solve a word problem. *p. 42*

LU 2-3: Fractions—Multiplication and Division

1. Multiply and divide proper, improper, and mixed numbers. *pp. 45–46*
2. Use the cancellation method in the multiplication and division of fractions. *pp. 45–46*
3. Dissect and solve a word problem. *p. 47*

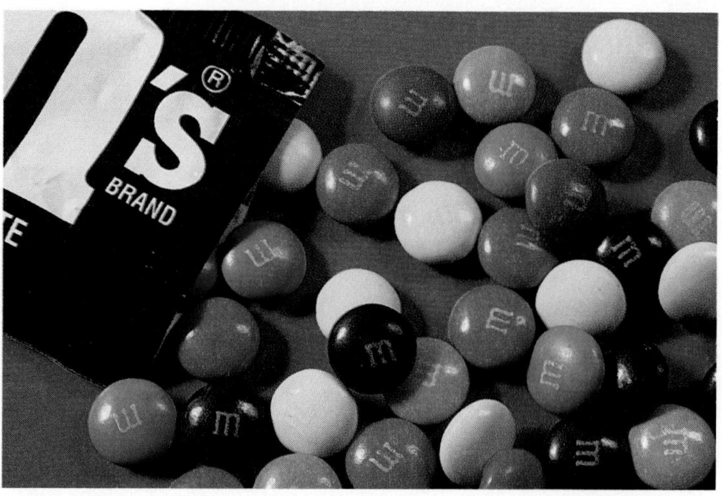

Sharon Hoogstraten

M&M's® Chocolate Candies have been a favorite treat for years. They come in different colors—yellow, brown, tan, green, red, and orange. Did you ever count the number of each color in a bag of M&M's®? You probably have never stopped to sort the colors and count them, but the M&M/Mars company counts them—by machine, of course. Now it tells you on the bag how many of each color the bag contains.

The 1.69-ounce bag of M&M's® shown above contains 55 M&M's®. In this bag, you will find the following:[1]

18 yellow	9 tan	6 brown
10 red	7 orange	5 green

The numbers of different colors might suggest that yellow and red are favorite colors for many people. Since this is a business math text, however, let's look at the 55 M&M's® in terms of fractional arithmetic.

The 1.69-ounce bag contains 55 M&M's®. Since 5 of these M&M's® are green, we can say that 5 parts of 55 represent green candies. We could also say that 1 out of 11 represents green candies. Are you confused?

For many people, fractions are difficult. If you are one of these people, this chapter is for you. First, you will review the types of fractions and the fraction conversion procedures. Then you will gain a clear understanding of the addition, subtraction, multiplication, and division of fractions.

LEARNING UNIT 2–1 TYPES OF FRACTIONS AND CONVERSION PROCEDURES

Sara Martin loves M&M's®. The bag of M&M's® shown at the beginning of this chapter contains 6 brown candies. If Sara eats only the brown M&M's®, she has eaten 6 parts of 55. We can express this in the following **fraction:**

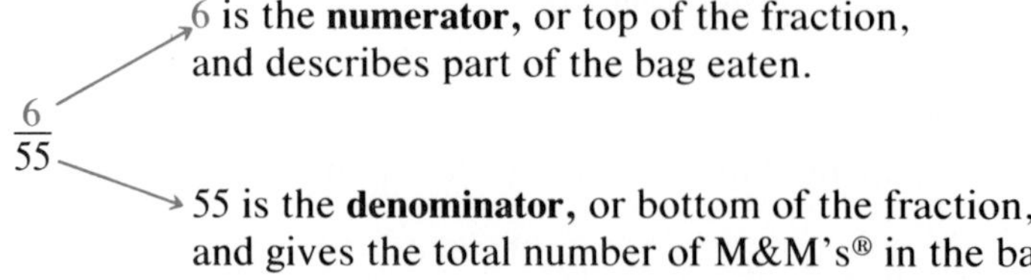

Before reviewing the arithmetic operations of fractions, you must recognize the three types of fractions described in this unit. You must also know how to convert fractions into a workable form.

Types of Fractions

Have you or your child had no cavities in four out of the last five dental checkups? Then you might have made or heard the same statement as the child in the Norman

[1] The color ratios currently given are a sample only, used for educational purposes, and do not represent the manufacturer's color ratios.

Rockwell chapter opener, "Look, Mom—no cavities!" In fractional arithmetic, this says that in $\frac{4}{5}$ of the visits to the dentist, the results were no cavities. The fraction $\frac{4}{5}$ is a proper fraction.

Fractions are classified as proper fractions, improper fractions, and mixed numbers. The definitions of these terms follow.

Proper fractions: A fraction with a numerator that is less than its denominator is a proper fraction.

EXAMPLES $\frac{1}{11}, \frac{1}{4}, \frac{1}{2}, \frac{5}{7}, \frac{8}{9}, \frac{17}{18}, \frac{18}{55}$

Improper fractions: A fraction with a numerator that is equal to or greater than its denominator is an improper fraction.

EXAMPLES $\frac{14}{14}, \frac{9}{8}, \frac{17}{12}, \frac{20}{17}$

Mixed numbers: A number containing a whole number and a proper fraction is a mixed number.

EXAMPLES $3\frac{1}{8}, 4\frac{7}{8}, 8\frac{6}{7}, 55\frac{5}{6}, 111\frac{9}{10}$

Conversion Procedures

In Chapter 1, we worked with two of the division symbols (÷ and $\overline{)\quad}$). The horizontal line (or the diagonal) that separates the numerator and the denominator of a fraction also indicates division. The numerator, like the dividend, is the number we are dividing into. The denominator, like the divisor, is the number we use to divide. In the fraction $\frac{3}{4}$, then, we can say we are dividing 4 into 3, or 3 is divided by 4.

Since it is easiest to work with simple fractions such as $\frac{3}{4}$, we often must convert fractions to their simplest terms. In this unit, we show how to convert improper fractions to whole or mixed numbers, mixed numbers to improper fractions, and fractions to lowest and higher terms.

Converting Improper Fractions to Whole or Mixed Numbers

Let's begin our study of conversion procedures with the following steps:

Steps for Converting Improper Fractions to Whole or Mixed Numbers

Step 1. Divide numerator by denominator.

Step 2. **a.** If you have no remainder, the answer is a whole number.

b. If you have a remainder, the answer is a mixed number with the remainder placed over the old denominator.

EXAMPLES $\frac{13}{6} = 2\frac{1}{6}$

$$\begin{array}{r} 2\text{ R1} \\ 6\overline{)13} \\ \underline{12} \\ 1 \end{array}$$

$\frac{14}{14} = 1$

Converting Mixed Numbers to Improper Fractions

By reversing the procedure of converting improper fractions to mixed numbers, we can change mixed numbers back to improper fractions.

Steps for Converting Mixed Numbers to Improper Fractions

Step 1. Multiply denominator times whole number.

Step 2. Add Step 1 answer to numerator.

Step 3. Place Step 2 answer over old denominator.

EXAMPLE $5\frac{1}{3} = \frac{(3 \times 5) + 1}{3} = \frac{16}{3}$ ← Note denominator stays the same.

Converting (Reducing) Fractions to Lowest Terms

When solving fraction problems, always reduce the fractions to their lowest terms. This reduction does not change the value of the fraction. For example, in the M&M's® bag, 5 out of 55 were green. The fraction for this is $\frac{5}{55}$. You can reduce this fraction to $\frac{1}{11}$ without changing its value by dividing top and bottom by 5. Remember that we said in the chapter introduction that 1 out of 11 M&M's® in the bag of 55 M&M's® represents green candies? Now you should understand why this is true. Let's look at how to reduce a fraction.

To reduce a fraction to its lowest terms, divide the numerator and denominator by the largest possible divisor. This is the **greatest common divisor** (this number cannot be zero). It is the point where we have reduced the fraction to its **lowest terms.** At this point, no number can divide evenly into both parts of the fraction (except 1).

Steps for Reducing Fractions to Lowest Terms

Step 1. Divide numerator and denominator by largest possible divisor (does not change fraction value). Try to do this by observation.

Step 2. Now you have reduced the fraction to lowest terms since no number (except 1) can divide evenly into both numerator and denominator.

EXAMPLE $\frac{20}{25} = \frac{20 \div 5}{25 \div 5} = \frac{4}{5}$

By using observation, you can see that the number 5 in the above example is the largest possible divisor. When you have large numbers, this divisor is not so obvious. For large numbers, you can use the step approach to find the largest possible divisor.

Check with your instructor to see whether the step approach is preferred to the observation method.

Step Approach for Finding the Greatest Common Divisor

Step 1. Divide the smaller number of the fraction into the larger number.

Step 2. Divide the remainder into the divisor of Step 1. Continue this process until you have no remainder.

Step 3. The last divisor you use is the *greatest common divisor.*

EXAMPLES

$\frac{20}{25}$ — Step 1: $20\overline{)25}$ = 1, $25 - 20 = 5$; Step 2: $5\overline{)20}$ = 4, $20 - 20 = 0$; $\frac{20 \div 5}{25 \div 5} = \frac{4}{5}$

$\frac{24}{30}$ — Step 1: $24\overline{)30}$ = 1, $30 - 24 = 6$; Step 2: $6\overline{)24}$ = 4, $24 - 24 = 0$; $\frac{24 \div 6}{30 \div 6} = \frac{4}{5}$

Reducing a fraction by observation can be confusing. Sometimes you are not sure what number you should divide into the top (numerator) and bottom (denominator) of the fraction. The following reference table on divisibility tests will be helpful. Note that to reduce a fraction to lowest terms might result in more than one division.

Will divide evenly into number if:	2	3	4	5	6	10
	Last digit is 0, 2, 4, 6, 8.	Sum of the digits is divisible by 3.	Last two digits can be divided by 4.	Last digit is 5 or 0.	The number is even and 3 will divide into the sum of the digits.	The last digit is a zero.
Examples	$\frac{12}{14} = \frac{6}{7}$	$\frac{36}{69} = \frac{12}{23}$ $3 + 6 = 9 \div 3 = 3$ $6 + 9 = 15 \div 3 = 5$	$\frac{140}{160} = \frac{1(40)}{1(60)} =$ $\frac{35}{40} = \frac{7}{8}$	$\frac{15}{20} = \frac{3}{4}$	$\frac{12}{18} = \frac{2}{3}$	$\frac{90}{100} = \frac{9}{10}$

Converting (Raising) Fractions to Higher Terms

Later in the chapter you will see that it sometimes is necessary to raise fractions to **higher terms** (as in adding fractions). You can do this by multiplying the numerator and the denominator by the same number. For example, if you want to raise the fraction $\frac{1}{3}$, you can multiply the numerator and denominator by 2:

$$\frac{1}{3} \times \frac{2}{2} = \frac{2}{6}$$

Both of these fractions are **equivalent** in value. By raising the value of $\frac{1}{3}$, you only divided it into more parts.

Now let's suppose that you have eaten $\frac{3}{7}$ of a pizza. You decide that instead of expressing the amount you have eaten in 7ths, you want to express it in 28ths. How would you do this?

To find the new numerator when you know the new denominator (28), use the steps that follow.

Steps for Raising Fractions to Higher Terms When Denominator Is Known

Step 1. Divide *new* denominator by *old* denominator.

Step 2. Multiply answer from Step 1 times old numerator and place as numerator over new denominator.

EXAMPLE $\frac{3}{7} = \frac{?}{28}$

Step 1. Divide 28 by 7 = 4.

Step 2. Multiply 4 times the numerator 3 = 12.

Step 3. Result:

$$\frac{3}{7} = \frac{12}{28} \left(\text{Note: This is the same as multiplying } \frac{3}{7} \times \frac{4}{4}.\right)$$

Note that the $\frac{3}{7}$ and $\frac{12}{28}$ are equivalent in value, yet they are different fractions.

Now try the following quiz to check your understanding of this unit.

LU 2-1 PRACTICE QUIZ

1. Identify type of fraction—proper, improper, mixed:

   a. $\frac{2}{3}$ **b.** $\frac{14}{13}$ **c.** $16\frac{1}{8}$ **d.** $\frac{10}{10}$

2. Convert to a mixed number (do not reduce):

   $\frac{140}{8}$

3. Convert mixed number to improper fraction:

   $8\frac{3}{4}$

4. Find the greatest common divisor by the step approach and reduce to lowest terms:

   a. $\frac{24}{40}$ **b.** $\frac{91}{156}$

5. Convert to higher terms:

   a. $\frac{14}{20} = \frac{\quad}{200}$ **b.** $\frac{8}{10} = \frac{\quad}{60}$

SOLUTIONS TO LU 2-1 PRACTICE QUIZ

1. **a.** Proper
   b. Improper
   c. Mixed
   d. Improper

2. $17\frac{4}{8}$

$$\begin{array}{r} 17 \\ 8\overline{)140} \\ \underline{8} \\ 60 \\ \underline{56} \\ 4 \end{array}$$

3. $\frac{(8 \times 4) + 3}{4} = \frac{35}{4}$

4. a.

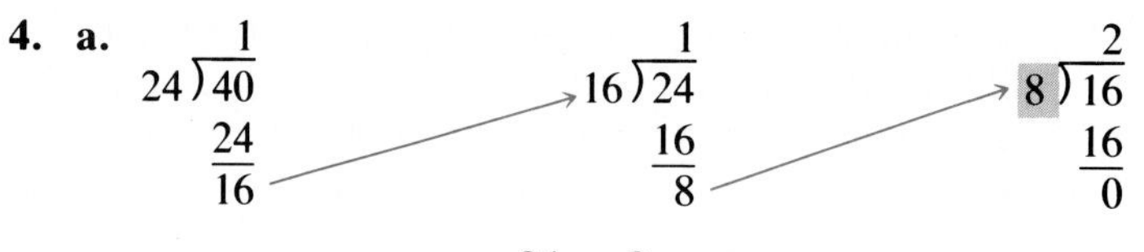

8 is greatest common divisor.

$$\frac{24 \div 8}{40 \div 8} = \frac{3}{5}$$

b.

$91\overline{)156}$ = 1, remainder 65 → $65\overline{)91}$ = 1, remainder 26 → $26\overline{)65}$ = 2, remainder 13 → $13\overline{)26}$ = 2, remainder 0

13 is greatest common divisor.

$$\frac{91 \div 13}{156 \div 13} = \frac{7}{12}$$

5. a. $20\overline{)200}$ = 10 $\qquad 10 \times 14 = 140 \qquad \frac{14}{20} = \frac{140}{200}$

b. $10\overline{)60}$ = 6 $\qquad 6 \times 8 = 48 \qquad \frac{8}{10} = \frac{48}{60}$

LEARNING UNIT 2–2 FRACTIONS—ADDITION AND SUBTRACTION

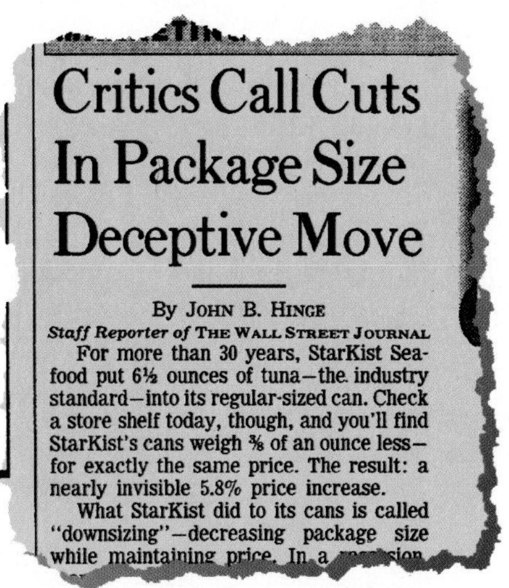

Critics Call Cuts In Package Size Deceptive Move

By John B. Hinge
Staff Reporter of The Wall Street Journal

For more than 30 years, StarKist Seafood put 6½ ounces of tuna—the industry standard—into its regular-sized can. Check a store shelf today, though, and you'll find StarKist's cans weigh ⅜ of an ounce less—for exactly the same price. The result: a nearly invisible 5.8% price increase.

What StarKist did to its cans is called "downsizing"—decreasing package size while maintaining price. In a ...

Reprinted by permission of *The Wall Street Journal*, © 1991 Dow Jones & Company, Inc. All Rights Reserved Worldwide.

The above clipping from *The Wall Street Journal* tells you that StarKist's cans of tuna now weigh $\frac{3}{8}$ of an ounce less for the same price. Can you give the new weight of the tuna in a StarKist can?

By using fractional subtraction, $6\frac{1}{2}$ less $\frac{3}{8}$ of an ounce equals $6\frac{1}{8}$ ounces. So the weight on the new StarKist can of tuna will be $6\frac{1}{8}$ ounces. To check this answer, look at a can of StarKist tuna the next time you go to the supermarket. You can also check this answer by fractional addition. When you add $\frac{3}{8}$ to $6\frac{1}{8}$, you get $6\frac{1}{2}$. In this unit you learn about the addition and subtraction of fractions, which many people find difficult.

Addition of Fractions

When you add two or more quantities, they must have the same name or be of the same denomination. You cannot add six quarts and three pints unless you change the denomination of one or both quantities. You must either make the quarts into pints or the pints into quarts. As you will see, the same principle also applies to fractions.

Adding Proper Fractions with Same Denominators

Adding **like fractions** (proper fractions with the same denominators) is similar to adding whole numbers.

Steps for Adding Proper Fractions with Same Denominators
Step 1. Add numerators.
Step 2. Place total over denominator.
Step 3. Reduce to lowest terms.

EXAMPLE $\frac{2}{9} + \frac{5}{9} = \frac{7}{9}$

The denominator, 9, shows the number of pieces into which some whole was divided. The two numerators, 2 and 5, tell how many of the pieces you have. So if you add 2 and 5, you get 7, or $\frac{7}{9}$.

Adding Proper Fractions with Different Denominators

To add **unlike fractions** (proper fractions with different denominators), you must first change them to *like fractions*. To do this, first find a denominator that is common to all the fractions you want to add. Then look for the **least common denominator (LCD).**[2]

The LCD is the smallest nonzero whole number into which all denominators will divide evenly. You can find the LCD by observation or using prime numbers.

Finding the Least Common Denominator (LCD) by Observation The example that follows shows you how to use observation to find a LCD (this will make all the denominators the same).

EXAMPLE $\frac{3}{7} + \frac{5}{21}$

Inspection of these two fractions shows that the smallest number into which denominators 7 and 21 divide evenly is 21. Thus, 21 is the LCD.

You may know that 21 is the LCD of $\frac{3}{7} + \frac{5}{21}$, but you cannot add these two fractions until you change the denominator of $\frac{3}{7}$ to 21. You do this by raising $\frac{3}{7}$ to higher terms as explained in Learning Unit 2–1. The steps are:

Step 1. Divide new denominator (21) by old denominator (7): $21 \div 7 = 3$.
Step 2. Multiply the 3 in Step 1 times old numerator (3): $3 \times 3 = 9$. The new numerator is 9.
Step 3. Results:

$$\frac{3}{7} = \frac{9}{21}$$

Now that the denominators are the same, you add the numerators.

$$\frac{9}{21} + \frac{5}{21} = \frac{14}{21} = \frac{2}{3}$$

Note that $\frac{14}{21}$ is reduced to its lowest terms $\frac{2}{3}$. Always reduce your answer to its lowest terms.

Now you are ready for the general steps for adding fractions with different denominators. These steps also apply to the following discussion on finding LCD by prime numbers.

Steps for Adding Fractions with Different Denominators
Step 1. Find least common denominator.
Step 2. Change each fraction to a like fraction.
Step 3. Add numerators and place over least common denominator.
Step 4. Reduce to lowest terms.

Finding the Least Common Denominator (LCD) by Prime Numbers When you cannot determine the LCD by observation, you can use the prime number method. The following definition explains prime numbers.

[2] Often referred to as the lowest common denominator.

Prime numbers: Whole numbers that are only divisible by itself and one are prime numbers. The number 1 is not a prime number.

EXAMPLES 2, 3, 5, 7, 11, 13, 17, 19, 23, 29, 31, 37, 41, 43

Note that the number 4 is not a prime number. Not only can you divide 4 by 1 and 4, you can also divide 4 by 2.

Now let's see how to use prime numbers to find the least common denominator.

The lowest prime number is 2.

EXAMPLE $\frac{1}{4} + \frac{1}{8} + \frac{1}{9} + \frac{1}{12}$

Step 1. Copy the denominators and arrange them in a separate row.

4 8 9 12

Step 2. Divide the denominators in Step 1 by prime numbers. Start with the smallest number that will divide into at least two of the denominators. Bring down any number that is not divisible.

2 /	4	8	9	12
	2	4	9	6

Note: The 9 was brought down since it was not divisible by 2.

Step 3. Continue Step 2 until no prime number will divide evenly into at least two numbers.

Note: The 3 is used since 2 can no longer divide evenly into at least two numbers.

2 /	4	8	9	12
2 /	2	4	9	6
3 /	1	2	9	3
	1	2	3	1

Step 4. To find the LCD, multiply all the numbers in the divisors (2, 2, 3) and in the last row (1, 2, 3, 1).

$$\boxed{2 \times 2 \times 3} \times \boxed{1 \times 2 \times 3 \times 1} = 72 \text{ (LCD)}$$

Divisors × Last row

Step 5. Raise each fraction so that each denominator will be 72 and then add fractions.

$$\frac{18}{72} + \frac{9}{72} + \frac{8}{72} + \frac{6}{72} = \frac{41}{72}$$

$\frac{1}{4} = \frac{?}{72}$ $72 \div 4 = 18$; $18 \times 1 = 18$

$\frac{1}{8} = \frac{?}{72}$ $72 \div 8 = 9$; $9 \times 1 = 9$

We have summarized the above steps for finding the LCD by using prime numbers in the following steps for finding the LCD for two or more fractions.

Steps for Finding LCD for Two or More Fractions

Step 1. Copy denominators and arrange in a separate row.

Step 2. Divide denominators by smallest prime number that will divide evenly into at least two numbers.

Step 3. Continue until no prime number divides evenly into at least two numbers.

Step 4. Multiply all numbers in divisor and last row to find LCD.

Step 5. Raise all fractions so each has a common denominator and complete computation.

Adding Mixed Numbers

The following steps will show you how to add mixed numbers.

Steps for Adding Mixed Numbers

Step 1. Add whole numbers.

Step 2. Add fractions (remember that fractions need common denominators, as in the previous section).

Step 3. Combine totals of Steps 1 and 2. Make sure you do not have an improper fraction in your final answer. Convert the improper fraction to a whole or mixed number. Reduce to lowest terms.

Using Prime Numbers to Find LCD of Example

2 /	20	5	4
2 /	10	5	2
5 /	5	5	1
	1	1	1

2 × 2 × 5 = 20 LCD

EXAMPLE

$$\begin{array}{rr} 4\frac{7}{20} & 4\frac{7}{20} \\ 6\frac{3}{5} & 6\frac{12}{20} \\ +\,7\frac{1}{4} & +\,7\frac{5}{20} \\ \hline \end{array}$$

Step 1 ⟶ $17\frac{24}{20} = 17 + 1\frac{4}{20}$

Step 2 $= 18\frac{4}{20}$

Step 3 ⟶ $= 18\frac{1}{5}$

$\frac{3}{5} = \frac{?}{20}$

$20 \div 5 = 4$

$\times 3$

12

Subtraction of Fractions

The subtraction of fractions is not difficult now that you understand the addition of fractions. This section explains how to subtract proper fractions with the same denominators and how to subtract mixed numbers.

Subtracting Proper Fractions with Same Denominators

To subtract proper fractions with the same denominators, use the steps that follow.

Steps for Subtracting Proper Fractions with Same Denominators

Step 1. Subtract numerators and place correct number over common denominator.

Step 2. Reduce to lowest terms.

EXAMPLE $\frac{7}{8} - \frac{1}{8} = \frac{6 \div 2}{8 \div 2} = \frac{3}{4}$

Step 1 **Step 2**

Subtracting Proper Fractions with Different Denominators

Now let's learn the steps for subtracting proper fractions with different denominators.

Steps for Subtracting Proper Fractions with Different Denominators

Step 1. Find least common denominator.

Step 2. Raise fraction to its equivalent value.

Step 3. Subtract numerators and place number over least common denominator.

Step 4. Reduce to lowest terms.

EXAMPLE

$$\begin{array}{rr} \frac{5}{8} & \frac{40}{64} \\ -\frac{2}{64} & -\frac{2}{64} \\ \hline & \frac{38}{64} = \frac{19}{32} \end{array}$$

By observation, we see LCD is 64. Thus: $64 \div 8 = 8 \times 5 = 40$.

Subtracting Mixed Numbers

When you subtract whole numbers, sometimes borrowing is not necessary. At other times, you must borrow. The same is true of subtracting mixed numbers.

Steps for Subtracting Mixed Numbers

When Borrowing Is Not Necessary	*When Borrowing Is Necessary*
Step 1. Subtract fractions, making sure to find LCD.	**Step 1.** Borrow from whole number.
Step 2. Subtract whole numbers.	**Step 2.** Make sure fractions have LCD.
Step 3. Reduce fractions to lowest terms.	**Step 3.** Subtract whole numbers and fractions.
	Step 4. Reduce fractions to lowest terms.

This example is from the StarKist tuna article at the beginning of the unit.

EXAMPLE Where borrowing is not necessary

$$\begin{array}{rl} 6\frac{1}{2} & \text{oz. (weight of original can)} \\ -\frac{3}{8} & \text{(weight being reduced)} \end{array}$$

Find LCD of 2 and 8. LCD is 8.

$$\begin{array}{rl} 6\frac{4}{8} & \text{oz.} \\ -\frac{3}{8} & \\ \hline 6\frac{1}{8} & \text{oz. (new size of StarKist tuna can)} \end{array}$$

EXAMPLE Where borrowing is necessary

$$\begin{array}{rcrcl} 3\frac{1}{2} & = & 3\frac{2}{4} & = & 2\frac{6}{4}\left(\frac{4}{4}+\frac{2}{4}\right) \\ -1\frac{3}{4} & = & -1\frac{3}{4} & = & -1\frac{3}{4} \\ \hline & & & & 1\frac{3}{4} \end{array}$$

Find LCD of 2, 4. LCD is 4.

Since $\frac{3}{4}$ is larger than $\frac{2}{4}$, we must borrow 1 from the 3. This is the same as borrowing $\frac{4}{4}$. A fraction with the same numerator and denominator represents a whole. When we add $\frac{4}{4} + \frac{2}{4}$, we get $\frac{6}{4}$. Note how we subtracted the whole number and fractions, being sure to reduce the final answer if necessary.

How to Dissect and Solve a Word Problem

Let's now look at how to dissect and solve a word problem involving fractions.

The Word Problem The Morton Grocery Store has $550\frac{1}{4}$ total square feet of floor space. Morton's meat department occupies $115\frac{1}{2}$ square feet, and its deli department occupies $145\frac{7}{8}$ square feet. If the remainder of the floor space is for groceries, what square footage remains for groceries.

Blueprint Aid for Dissecting and Solving a Word Problem

A. Gather the facts	B. What am I solving for?	C. What must I know or calculate before solving problem?	D. Key points to remember
Total square footage: $550\frac{1}{4}$ sq. ft. *Meat department:* $115\frac{1}{2}$ sq. ft. *Deli department:* $145\frac{7}{8}$ sq. ft.	Total square footage for groceries.	Total floor space − Total meat and deli floor space = Total grocery floor space.	Denominators must be same before adding or subtracting fractions. $\frac{8}{8} = 1$ Never leave improper fraction as final answer.

Steps to Solving Problem

1. Calculate total square footage of meat and deli departments.

$$\text{Meat: } 115\frac{1}{2} = 115\frac{4}{8}$$
$$\text{Deli: } +145\frac{7}{8} = +145\frac{7}{8}$$
$$260\frac{11}{8} = 261\frac{3}{8} \text{ sq. ft.}$$

2. Calculate total grocery square footage.

$$550\frac{1}{4} = 550\frac{2}{8} = 549\frac{10}{8} \quad \left(\frac{2}{8} + \frac{8}{8}\right)$$
$$-261\frac{3}{8} = -261\frac{3}{8} = -261\frac{3}{8}$$
$$288\frac{7}{8} \text{ sq. ft.}$$

Check

$$261\frac{3}{8}$$
$$+288\frac{7}{8}$$
$$549\frac{10}{8} = 550\frac{2}{8} = 550\frac{1}{4} \text{ sq. ft.}$$

Note how the above blueprint aid helped to gather the facts and identify what we were looking for. To find the total square footage for groceries, we first had to sum the areas for meat and deli. Then we could subtract these areas from the total square footage. Also note that in Step 1 above, we didn't leave the answer as an improper fraction. In Step 2, we borrowed from the 550 so that we could complete the subtraction.

Now let's try the Practice Quiz.

LU 2–2 PRACTICE QUIZ

1. Find LCD by division of prime numbers:
   14, 8, 4, 3
2. Add and reduce to lowest terms if needed:

   a. $\frac{4}{50} + \frac{3}{5}$ **b.** $2\frac{3}{4} + 6\frac{1}{20}$
3. Subtract and reduce to lowest terms:

   a. $\frac{7}{8} - \frac{1}{3}$ **b.** $8\frac{1}{4} - 3\frac{9}{28}$ **c.** $3 - 1\frac{3}{4}$
4. Computerland has $660\frac{1}{4}$ total square feet of floor space. Three departments occupy this floor space: hardware, $201\frac{1}{8}$ square feet; software, $242\frac{1}{4}$ square feet; and customer service, ______ square feet. What is the total square footage of the customer service area? You might want to try a blueprint aid since the solution will show a completed blueprint aid.

SOLUTIONS TO LU 2-2 PRACTICE QUIZ

1.
```
2 / 14   8   4   3
2 /  7   4   2   3
     7   2   1   3
```
LCD $= 2 \times 2 \times 7 \times 2 \times 1 \times 3 = 168$

2. a. $\frac{4}{50} + \frac{30}{50} = \frac{34}{50} = \frac{17}{25}$ $\qquad \frac{3}{5} = \frac{?}{50}$

$50 \div 5 = 10 \times 3 = 30$

b. $2\frac{3}{4} + 6\frac{1}{20}$ $\qquad 2\frac{15}{20} + 6\frac{1}{20} = 8\frac{16}{20} = 8\frac{4}{5}$ $\qquad \frac{3}{4} = \frac{?}{20}$

$20 \div 4 = 5 \times 3 = 15$

3. a. $\frac{7}{8} = \frac{21}{24}$; $-\frac{1}{3} = -\frac{8}{24}$; $\frac{13}{24}$

b. $8\frac{1}{4} = 8\frac{7}{28} = 7\frac{35}{28} \leftarrow \left(\frac{28}{28} + \frac{7}{28}\right)$

$-3\frac{9}{28} = -3\frac{9}{28} \quad -3\frac{9}{28}$

$4\frac{26}{28} = 4\frac{13}{14}$

c. $2\frac{4}{4} - 1\frac{3}{4} = 1\frac{1}{4}$ $\qquad$ Note how we made the 3 as $2\frac{4}{4}$.

4. Computerland's total square footage for customer service:

Blueprint Aid for Dissecting and Solving a Word Problem

A. Gather the facts	B. What am I solving for?	C. What must I know or calculate before solving problem?	D. Key points to remember
Total square footage: $660\frac{1}{4}$ sq. ft. *Hardware:* $201\frac{1}{8}$ sq. ft. *Software:* $242\frac{1}{4}$ sq. ft.	Total square footage for customer service.	Total floor space − Total hardware and software floor space = Total customer floor space.	Denominators must be same before adding or subtracting fractions.

Steps to Solving Problem

1. Calculate total square footage of hardware and software.

$201\frac{1}{8} = 201\frac{1}{8}$ (hardware)

$+\,242\frac{1}{4} = +\,242\frac{2}{8}$ (software)

$443\frac{3}{8}$

2. Calculate total customer service.

$660\frac{1}{4} = 660\frac{2}{8} = 659\frac{10}{8}$ (total square footage)

$-\,443\frac{3}{8} = -\,443\frac{3}{8} = -\,443\frac{3}{8}$ (hardware plus software)

$216\frac{7}{8}$ square feet (customer service)

LEARNING UNIT 2–3 FRACTIONS—MULTIPLICATION AND DIVISION

CHOCOLATE CHIPPER CHAMPS

3/4 cup butter or margarine
1-1/3 cups firmly packed light brown sugar
2 eggs
1 teaspoon vanilla
2-1/4 cups flour
1 teaspoon soda
1/2 teaspoon salt
1 cup "M&M's"® Plain Chocolate Candies
1/2 cup chopped nuts

Beat together butter and sugar until light and fluffy; blend in eggs and vanilla. Gradually add combined flour, soda and salt; mix well. Stir in candies and nuts. Drop dough by heaping tablespoonfuls onto greased cookie sheet about 3 inches apart. Press 3 to 4 additional candies into each cookie, if desired. Bake at 350°F. for 10 to12 minutes or until lightly browned. Cool on cookie sheet about 3 minutes; remove cookies to wire rack to cool thoroughly. **MAKES ABOUT 2 DOZEN 3-1/2 INCH COOKIES.**
VARIATION: For 4 dozen 3-1/2 inch cookies, double ingredients. Proceed as recipe directs.

Following the measurements in a recipe like the one above can be fairly easy until you decide to double or halve the recipe. As stated in the recipe, if you want to make 4 dozen cookies, you double the ingredients. This means you multiply each ingredient by 2. If you want only 1 dozen cookies, you would divide the recipe by 2. In this unit, you learn how to multiply and divide fractions.

Multiplication of Fractions

Multiplying fractions is relatively simple because you do not have to find a common denominator. This section explains the multiplication of proper fractions and the multiplication of mixed numbers.

Steps for Multiplying Proper Fractions[3]
Step 1. Multiply numerators.
Step 2. Multiply denominators.
Step 3. Be sure you reduce to lowest terms.

First let's look at an example that results in an answer that we do not have to reduce.

EXAMPLE $\frac{1}{5} \times \frac{6}{7} = \frac{6}{35}$

In the next example, note how we reduce the answer to lowest terms.

Keep in mind $\frac{5}{1}$ is equal to 5.

EXAMPLE $\frac{5}{1} \times \frac{1}{6} \times \frac{4}{7} = \frac{20}{42} = \boxed{\frac{10}{21}}$

We can reduce $\frac{20}{42}$ by the step approach as follows:

$$20\overline{)42} = 2,\ 40,\ \text{remainder } 2 \qquad 2\overline{)20} = 10,\ 20,\ \text{remainder } 0$$

We could also have found the greatest common divisor by observation.

$$\frac{20 \div 2}{42 \div 2} = \boxed{\frac{10}{21}}$$

As an alternative to reducing fractions to lowest terms, we can use the **cancellation** technique. Let's work the previous example using this technique.

EXAMPLE

$$\frac{5}{1} \times \frac{1}{\cancel{6}_{3}} \times \frac{\cancel{4}^{2}}{7} = \boxed{\frac{10}{21}}$$

2 divides evenly into 4 twice and 6 three times.

[3] You would follow the same procedure to multiply improper fractions.

Note that when we cancel numbers, we are just reducing the answer before multiplying. We know that multiplying or dividing both numerator and denominator by the same number gives an equivalent fraction. So we can divide both numerator and denominator by any number that divides them both evenly. It doesn't matter which we divide first. Note that this division reduces the $\frac{10}{21}$ to its lowest terms.

Multiplying Mixed Numbers

The following steps explain how to multiply mixed numbers.

> **Steps for Multiplying Mixed Numbers**
> **Step 1.** Change mixed numbers to improper fractions.
> **Step 2.** Multiply numerators and denominators.
> **Step 3.** Reduce to lowest terms if you do not use cancellation.

EXAMPLE

$$2\frac{1}{3} \times 1\frac{1}{2} = \frac{7}{\cancel{3}} \times \frac{\overset{1}{\cancel{3}}}{2} = \frac{7}{2} = 3\frac{1}{2}$$

Step 1 **Step 2** **Step 3**

Division of Fractions

When you studied whole numbers in Chapter 1, you saw how multiplication can be checked by division. The multiplication of fractions can also be checked by division, as you will see in this section on dividing proper fractions and mixed numbers.

Dividing Proper Fractions

The division of proper fractions introduces a new term—the **reciprocal.** Note how we use reciprocals in the following steps for dividing proper fractions.

> **Steps for Dividing Proper Fractions**
> **Step 1.** Invert (turn upside down) divisor. Inverted number is the **reciprocal.**
> **Step 2.** Multiply.
> **Step 3.** Use cancellation method or reduce answer to lowest terms.

Do you know why the inverted fraction number is a reciprocal? Reciprocals are two numbers that when multiplied give a product of 1. For example, 2 and $\frac{1}{2}$ are reciprocals because multiplying them gives 1.

EXAMPLE $\frac{1}{5} \div \frac{4}{7}$

$$\frac{1}{5} \times \frac{7}{4} = \frac{7}{20}$$

Dividing Mixed Numbers

Now you are ready to divide mixed numbers by using improper fractions.

> **Steps for Dividing Mixed Numbers**
> **Step 1.** Change all mixed numbers to improper fractions.
> **Step 2.** Invert divisor (take its reciprocal) and multiply. If your final answer is an improper fraction, be sure to reduce it to lowest terms. You can do this by finding the greatest common divisor or by using the cancellation technique.

EXAMPLE $8\frac{3}{4} \div 2\frac{5}{6}$

Step 1. $\frac{35}{4} \div \frac{17}{6}$

Step 2. $\frac{35}{\underset{2}{\cancel{4}}} \times \frac{\overset{3}{\cancel{6}}}{17} = \frac{105}{34} = 3\frac{3}{34}$

Here we used the cancellation technique.

How to Dissect and Solve a Word Problem

The Word Problem Jamie Slater ordered $5\frac{1}{2}$ cords of oak wood. The cost of each cord is \$150. He also ordered $2\frac{1}{4}$ cords of maple at \$120 per cord. Jamie's neighbor, Al, said that he would share the wood and pay him $\frac{1}{5}$ of the total cost. How much did Jamie receive from Al?

Note how we filled in the blueprint aid columns. Column C shows that we first had to find the total cost of all the wood before we could find Al's share—$\frac{1}{5}$ of the total cost.

Blueprint Aid for Dissecting and Solving a Word Problem

A. Gather the facts	B. What am I solving for?	C. What must I know or calculate before solving problem?	D. Key points to remember
Cords ordered: $5\frac{1}{2}$ at \$150 per cord; $2\frac{1}{4}$ at \$120 per cord. *Al's cost share:* $\frac{1}{5}$ total cost.	What will Al pay Jamie?	Total cost of wood $\times \frac{1}{5}$ = Al's cost.	Convert mixed numbers to improper fractions when multiplying. Cancellation is an alternative to reducing fractions.

Steps to Solving Problem

1. Calculate the cost of oak. $5\frac{1}{2} \times \$150 = \frac{11}{\not{2}_1} \times \not{\$150}^{\$75} = \$825$
2. Calculate the cost of maple. $2\frac{1}{4} \times \$120 = \frac{9}{\not{4}_1} \times \not{\$120}^{\$30} = +\ 270$
   \$1,095 (total cost of wood)
3. What Al pays. $\frac{1}{\not{5}_1} \times \not{\$1,095}^{\$219} = \underline{\underline{\$219}}$

It's time to try the Practice Quiz.

LU 2-3 PRACTICE QUIZ

1. Multiply (use cancellation technique):
   a. $\frac{4}{16} \times \frac{4}{5}$ **b.** $21 \times \frac{6}{7}$
2. Multiply (do not use canceling; reduce by finding greatest common divisor):
   $\frac{14}{15} \times \frac{7}{10}$
3. Complete:
   a. $\frac{1}{8} \div \frac{4}{5}$ **b.** $\frac{51}{5} \div \frac{5}{9}$
4. Jill Estes bought a mobile home that was $8\frac{1}{8}$ times as expensive as the home her brother bought. Jill's brother paid \$16,000 for his mobile home. What is the cost of Jill's new home?

SOLUTIONS TO LU 2-3 PRACTICE QUIZ

1. **a.** $\frac{\not{4}^1}{\not{16}_4 {}_1} \times \frac{\not{4}^1}{5} = \frac{1}{5}$ **b.** $\frac{\not{21}^3}{1} \times \frac{6}{\not{7}_1} = 18$
2. $\frac{14}{15} \times \frac{7}{10} = \frac{98 \div 2}{150 \div 2} = \frac{49}{75}$

$$98\overline{)150}\ \text{quotient } 1,\ 98,\ \text{remainder } 52 \quad 52\overline{)98}\ 1,\ 52,\ 46 \quad 46\overline{)52}\ 1,\ 46,\ 6 \quad 6\overline{)46}\ 7,\ 42,\ 4 \quad 4\overline{)6}\ 1,\ 4,\ 2 \quad 2\overline{)4}\ 2,\ 4,\ 0$$

3. a. $\frac{1}{8} \times \frac{5}{4} = \frac{5}{32}$ b. $\frac{51}{5} \times \frac{9}{5} = \frac{459}{25} = 18\frac{9}{25}$

4. Total cost of Jill's new home:

Blueprint Aid for Dissecting and Solving a Word Problem

A. Gather the facts	B. What am I solving for?	C. What must I know or calculate before solving problem?	D. Key points to remember
Jill's mobile home: $8\frac{1}{8}$ as expensive as brother's. *Brother paid:* \$16,000.	Total cost of Jill's new home.	$8\frac{1}{8}$ × Total cost of Jill's brother's mobile home = Total cost of Jill's new home.	Canceling is an alternative to reducing.

Steps to Solving Problem

1. Convert $8\frac{1}{8}$ to a mixed number. $\frac{65}{8}$

2. Calculate total cost of Jill's home. $\frac{65}{\not{8}_1} \times \not{\$16,000}^{\$2,000} = \$130,000$

CHAPTER ORGANIZER: A REFERENCE GUIDE

Page	Topic	Key point, procedure, formula	Example(s) to illustrate situation
35	Types of fractions	*Proper:* Numerator less than denominator. *Improper:* Numerator equal to or greater than denominator. *Mixed:* Whole number and proper fraction.	$\frac{3}{5}, \frac{7}{9}, \frac{8}{15}$ $\frac{14}{14}, \frac{19}{18}$ $6\frac{3}{8}, 9\frac{8}{9}$
35–37	Fraction conversions	*Improper to whole or mixed:* Divide numerator by denominator and place remainder over *old* denominator. *Mixed to improper:* $\frac{\text{Denominator} \times \text{Whole number} + \text{Numerator}}{\text{Old denominator}}$	$\frac{17}{4} = 4\frac{1}{4}$ $4\frac{1}{8} = \frac{32 + 1}{8} = \frac{33}{8}$
36	Reducing fractions to lowest terms	1. Divide numerator and denominator by largest possible divisor (does not change fraction value. 2. When reduced to lowest terms, no number (except 1) will divide evenly into both numerator and denominator.	$\frac{18 \div 2}{46 \div 2} = \frac{9}{23}$
36	Step approach for finding greatest common denominator	1. Divide smaller number of fraction into larger number. 2. Divide remainder into divisor of Step 1. Continue this process until no remainder results. 3. The last divisor used is the greatest common divisor.	$\frac{15}{65}$ → 15)65 = 4, 60, remainder 5; 5)15 = 3, 15, remainder 0 5 is greatest common divisor.
37	Raising fractions to higher terms	Multiply numerator and denominator by same number. Does not change fraction value.	$\frac{15}{41} = \frac{?}{410}$ 410 ÷ 41 = 10 × 15 = 150

Page	Topic	Key point, procedure, formula	Example(s) to illustrate situation
38	Adding and subtracting proper fractions	When denominators are the same (like fractions), add (or subtract) the numerators, place total over common denominator, and reduce to lowest terms. When denominators are different (unlike fractions), you first change them to like fractions by finding LCD using observation or prime numbers. Then add (or subtract) the numerators, place total over common denominator, and reduce to lowest terms.	$\frac{4}{9} + \frac{1}{9} = \frac{5}{9}$ $\frac{4}{9} - \frac{1}{9} = \frac{3}{9} = \frac{1}{3}$ $\frac{4}{5} + \frac{2}{7} = \frac{28}{35} + \frac{10}{35} = \frac{38}{35} = 1\frac{3}{35}$
40	Prime numbers	A whole number greater than one that is divisible only by itself and one.	2, 3, 5, 7, 11
40	LCD by prime numbers	1. Copy denominators and arrange them in a separate row. 2. Divide denominators in Step 1 by prime numbers. Start with the smallest number that will divide into at least two of the denominators. Bring down any number that is not divisible. 3. Continue Step 2 until no prime number will divide evenly into at least two numbers. 4. Multiply all numbers in divisors and in last row.	$\frac{1}{3} + \frac{1}{6} + \frac{1}{8} + \frac{1}{12} + \frac{1}{9}$ 2 /3 6 8 12 9 2 /3 3 4 6 9 3 /3 3 2 3 9 1 1 2 1 3 $2 \times 2 \times 3 \times 1 \times 1 \times 2 \times 1 \times 3 = 72$
41	Adding mixed numbers	1. Add whole numbers. 2. Add fractions. 3. Combine totals of Steps 1 and 2. If denominators are different, a common denominator must be found. Answer cannot be left as an improper fraction.	$1\frac{4}{7} + 1\frac{3}{7}$ Step 1: $1 + 1 = 2$ Step 2: $\frac{4}{7} + \frac{3}{7} = \frac{7}{7}$ Step 3: $2\frac{7}{7} = 3$
42	Subtracting mixed numbers	1. Subtract fractions. 2. Borrow from whole numbers, if necessary. 3. Subtract whole numbers and fractions if borrowing was necessary. 4. Reduce fractions to lowest terms. If denominators are different, a common denominator must be found.	$12\frac{2}{5} - 7\frac{3}{5}$ $11\frac{7}{5} - 7\frac{3}{5}$ $= 4\frac{4}{5}$ Due to borrowing $\frac{5}{5}$ from number 12 $\frac{5}{5} + \frac{2}{5} = \frac{7}{5}$ The whole number is now 11.
45	Multiplying proper fractions	1. Multiply numerators and denominators. 2. If canceling was not done, reduce answer to lowest terms.	$\frac{4}{\not{7}_1} \times \frac{\not{7}^1}{9} = \frac{4}{9}$
46	Multiplying mixed numbers	Change mixed numbers to improper fractions. Multiply as though they were proper fractions. Be sure answer is reduced to lowest terms.	$1\frac{1}{8} \times 2\frac{5}{8}$ $\frac{9}{8} \times \frac{21}{8} = \frac{189}{64} = 2\frac{61}{64}$
46	Dividing proper fractions	Before multiplying, invert divisor and multiply like steps in multiplying proper fractions. (The inverted number is the *reciprocal*).	$\frac{1}{4} \div \frac{1}{8} = \frac{1}{\not{4}_1} \times \frac{\not{8}^2}{1} = 2$

Page	Topic	Key point, procedure, formula	Example(s) to illustrate situation
46	Dividing mixed numbers	Change all mixed numbers to improper fractions; then follow steps in dividing proper fractions.	$1\frac{1}{2} \div 1\frac{5}{8} = \frac{3}{2} \div \frac{13}{8}$ $= \frac{3}{\not{2}_1} \times \frac{\not{8}^4}{13}$ $= \frac{12}{13}$
	Key terms	Cancellation, *p. 45* Denominator, *p. 34* Equivalent (fractional), *p. 37* Fraction, *p. 34* Greatest common divisor, *p. 36* Higher terms, *p. 37* Improper fraction, *p. 35* Least common denominator (LCD), *p. 39*	Like fractions, *p. 39* Lowest terms, *p. 36* Mixed numbers, *p. 35* Numerator, *p. 34* Prime numbers, *p. 40* Proper fractions, *p. 35* Reciprocal, *p. 46* Unlike fractions, *p. 39*

Note: For how to dissect and solve a word problem, see page 43 or page 47.

END-OF-CHAPTER PROBLEMS

Drill Problems

Additional homework assignments by learning unit are at the end of text in Appendix I (p. I–7). Solutions to odd problems are at the end of text in Appendix II.

Identify type of fraction:

2–1. $\frac{4}{5}$ P **2–2.** $9\frac{1}{8}$ M **2–3.** $\frac{11}{4}$ I

Convert to mixed numbers; reduce as necessary:

2–4. $\frac{45}{10} = 4\frac{1}{2}$ **2–5.** $\frac{795}{12} = 66\frac{1}{4}$

Convert to improper fractions:

2–6. $3\frac{7}{8} = \frac{31}{8}$ **2–7.** $14\frac{3}{8} = \frac{115}{8}$

Reduce to lowest terms; show how to calculate greatest common divisor by step approach:

2–8. $\frac{14}{36} = \frac{14 \div 2}{36 \div 2} = \frac{7}{18}$

$$14\overline{)36}=2 \text{ r } 8 \nearrow\; 8\overline{)14}=1 \text{ r } 6 \nearrow\; 6\overline{)8}=1 \text{ r } 2 \nearrow\; 2\overline{)6}=3 \text{ r } 0$$

2–9. $\frac{44}{52} = \frac{44 \div 4}{52 \div 4} = \frac{11}{13}$

$$44\overline{)52}=1 \text{ r } 8 \nearrow\; 8\overline{)44}=5 \text{ r } 4 \nearrow\; 4\overline{)8}=2 \text{ r } 0$$

Convert to higher terms:

2–10. $\frac{7}{15} = \frac{28}{60}$ $60 \div 15 = 4 \times 7 = 28$

Determine LCD by (1) inspection and (2) check by division of prime numbers:

2–11. $\frac{5}{6}, \frac{7}{18}, \frac{5}{9}, \frac{2}{72}$

Inspection 72
$2 \times 3 \times 3 \times 4 = 72$

Check

2 /	6	18	9	72
3 /	3	9	9	36
3 /	1	3	3	12
	1	1	1	4

2–12. $\frac{1}{4}, \frac{3}{32}, \frac{5}{48}, \frac{1}{8}$

Inspection 96
$2 \times 2 \times 2 \times 2 \times 2 \times 3 = 96$

Check

2 /	4	32	48	8
2 /	2	16	24	4
2 /	1	8	12	2
2 /	1	4	6	1
	1	2	3	1

2–13. $\frac{3}{4}, \frac{7}{12}, \frac{5}{6}, \frac{1}{5}$

Inspection 60
$2 \times 2 \times 3 \times 5 = 60$

Check

2 /	4	12	6	5
2 /	2	6	3	5
3 /	1	3	3	5
	1	1	1	5

Add and reduce to lowest terms:

2–14. $\frac{6}{12} + \frac{3}{12} = \frac{9}{12} = \frac{3}{4}$ **2–15.** $\frac{4}{9} + \frac{1}{3} = \frac{4}{9} + \frac{3}{9} = \frac{7}{9}$

2–16. $5\frac{1}{7} + 3\frac{4}{7} = 8\frac{5}{7}$

2–17. $6\frac{3}{8} + 9\frac{1}{24} = 6\frac{9}{24} + 9\frac{1}{24} = 15\frac{10}{24} = 15\frac{5}{12}$

2–18. $9\frac{9}{10} + 6\frac{7}{10} = 15\frac{16}{10} = 16\frac{6}{10} = 16\frac{3}{5}$

Subtract and reduce to lowest terms:

2–19. $\frac{7}{9} - \frac{2}{9} = \frac{5}{9}$

2–20. $14\frac{3}{8} - 10\frac{5}{8}$

$$\begin{array}{r} 13\frac{11}{8} \\ -\ 10\frac{5}{8} \\ \hline 3\frac{6}{8} = 3\frac{3}{4} \end{array}$$

2–21. $12\frac{1}{9} - 4\frac{2}{3}$

$$\begin{array}{rcl} 12\frac{1}{9} & = & 11\frac{10}{9} \quad \left(\frac{9}{9} + \frac{1}{9}\right) \\ -\ 4\frac{6}{9} & = & -\ 4\frac{6}{9} \\ \hline & & 7\frac{4}{9} \end{array}$$

Multiply and reduce (as necessary) all answers to lowest terms; do not use cancellation method for these problems:

2–22. $17 \times \frac{6}{2} = \frac{102}{2} = 51$

2–23. $\frac{5}{6} \times \frac{3}{8} = \frac{15}{48} = \frac{5}{16}$

2–24. $8\frac{7}{8} \times 64 = \frac{71}{8} \times \frac{64}{1} = \frac{4{,}544}{8} = 568$

Multiply (use the cancellation technique):

2–25. $\frac{4}{10} \times \frac{30}{60} \times \frac{6}{10} = \frac{\overset{1}{\cancel{\overset{2}{\cancel{4}}}}}{\underset{5}{\cancel{10}}} \times \frac{\overset{3}{\cancel{30}}}{\underset{5}{\cancel{\underset{10}{\cancel{60}}}}} \times \frac{\overset{1}{\cancel{6}}}{\underset{1}{\cancel{10}}} = \frac{3}{25}$

2–26. $3\frac{3}{4} \times \frac{8}{9} \times 4\frac{9}{12} = \frac{\overset{5}{\cancel{15}}}{\underset{1}{\cancel{4}}} \times \frac{\overset{1}{\cancel{\overset{2}{\cancel{8}}}}}{\underset{1}{\cancel{\underset{3}{\cancel{9}}}}} \times \frac{\overset{19}{\cancel{57}}}{\underset{6}{\cancel{12}}} = \frac{95}{6} = 15\frac{5}{6}$

Divide and reduce to lowest terms (use the cancellation technique as needed):

2–27. $\frac{11}{6} \div 4 = \frac{11}{6} \times \frac{1}{4} = \frac{11}{24}$

2–28. $13 \div \frac{1}{5} = 13 \times \frac{5}{1} = 65$

2–29. $4\frac{2}{3} \div 12 = \frac{\overset{7}{\cancel{14}}}{3} \times \frac{1}{\underset{6}{\cancel{12}}} = \frac{7}{18}$

2–30. $3\frac{5}{6} \div 3\frac{1}{2} = \frac{23}{\underset{3}{\cancel{6}}} \times \frac{\overset{1}{\cancel{2}}}{7} = \frac{23}{21} = 1\frac{2}{21}$

2–31. $12\frac{4}{5} \div 7\frac{6}{7} = \frac{64}{5} \times \frac{7}{55} = \frac{448}{275} = 1\frac{173}{275}$

Word Problems

2–32. The stock of Procter and Gamble, manufacturers of Crest toothpaste, reached a high of $\$89\frac{1}{2}$ per share on Wednesday. At the end of the day, it dropped to $\$79\frac{1}{4}$ per share. How much did the stock drop from its high?

$$\begin{array}{r} \$89\frac{2}{4} \\ -\ 79\frac{1}{4} \\ \hline \$10\frac{1}{4} \end{array}$$

2–33. During the winter, Patrick O'Leary operates an airport shuttle. Patrick thinks he is using too much gas. Last year, he used $1{,}400\frac{3}{4}$ gallons of gas for four months. A summary of this year's usage follows.

December	$510\frac{1}{4}$
January	$490\frac{1}{2}$
February	$480\frac{1}{8}$
March	$220\frac{1}{3}$

Has Patrick used more or less than the previous year? How much more or less?

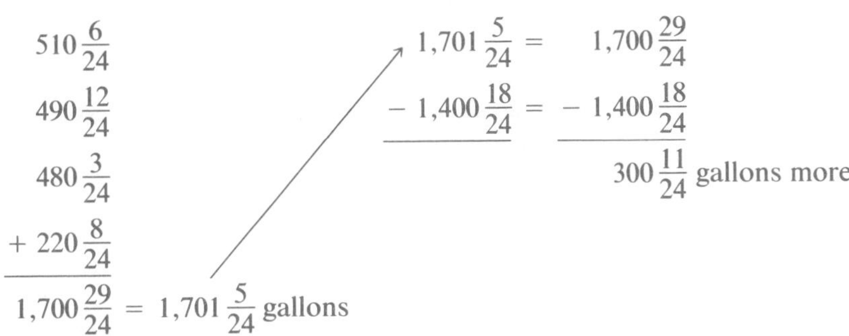

$$510\tfrac{6}{24} + 490\tfrac{12}{24} + 480\tfrac{3}{24} + 220\tfrac{8}{24} = 1{,}700\tfrac{29}{24} = 1{,}701\tfrac{5}{24} \text{ gallons}$$

$$1{,}701\tfrac{5}{24} = 1{,}700\tfrac{29}{24}$$
$$-\,1{,}400\tfrac{18}{24} = -\,1{,}400\tfrac{18}{24}$$
$$300\tfrac{11}{24} \text{ gallons more}$$

2-34. U.S. Air pays John Lutz \$80 per day to clean the airport. John became ill on Monday and went home after $\frac{3}{4}$ of a day. What did he earn on Monday? Assume no work, no pay.

$$\frac{3}{4} \times \$80 = \frac{\$240}{4} = \$60$$

2-35. Brian Summers visited his local health club and lost $1\frac{1}{4}$ pounds in week 1, $2\frac{3}{4}$ pounds in week 2, and $\frac{3}{8}$ pound in week 3. What is the total weight loss for Brian?

$$1\tfrac{2}{8} + 2\tfrac{6}{8} + \tfrac{3}{8} = 3\tfrac{11}{8} = 4\tfrac{3}{8} \text{ pounds}$$

2-36. Ed Mingo received a check for \$1,200. He deposited $\frac{1}{12}$ of the check in his bank account. How much money does Ed have left after the deposit?

$$\frac{11}{\cancel{12}_{1}} \times \cancel{\$1{,}200}^{\$100} = \$1{,}100$$

2-37. Lois Milligan worked the following hours as an operator for MCI: $11\frac{1}{4}$, $5\frac{1}{4}$, $8\frac{1}{2}$, $7\frac{1}{4}$. How many total hours did Lois work?

$$11\tfrac{1}{4} + 5\tfrac{1}{4} + 8\tfrac{2}{4} + 7\tfrac{1}{4} = 31\tfrac{5}{4} = 32\tfrac{1}{4} \text{ hours}$$

2-38. Rachel Spoke has a new Harley-Davidson motorcycle. On her first trip, she drove $7\frac{1}{5}$ hours at a speed of 45 mph. How far did Rachel travel?

$$\cancel{45}^{9} \times \frac{36}{\cancel{5}_{1}} = 324 \text{ miles}$$

2-39. Mrs. Smith loves M&M's® cookies. Using the M&M's® recipe on page 45, how much of each ingredient should she use if she wants to make 1 dozen cookies?

$\frac{1}{2} \times \frac{3}{4} = \frac{3}{8}$ cup margarine

$\frac{1}{2} \times 2 = 1$ egg

$\frac{1}{2} \times 1$ tsp. $= \frac{1}{2}$ tsp. vanilla

$\frac{1}{2} \times \frac{9}{4} = \frac{9}{8} = 1\frac{1}{8}$ cups flour

$\frac{1}{2} \times 1 = \frac{1}{2}$ tsp. soda

$\frac{1}{2} \times \frac{4}{3} = \frac{4}{6} = \frac{2}{3}$ cups of brown sugar

$\frac{1}{2} \times \frac{1}{2} = \frac{1}{4}$ tsp. salt

$\frac{1}{2} \times 1 = \frac{1}{2}$ cup M&M's®

$\frac{1}{2} \times \frac{1}{2} = \frac{1}{4}$ cup chopped nuts

2-40. Antonio's Chevrolet gets $23\frac{1}{5}$ miles per gallon. How far can Antonio travel on 15 gallons of gas?

$$\frac{116}{\cancel{5}_{1}} \times \cancel{15}^{3} = 348 \text{ miles}$$

2-41. Eugene bought a piece of lake property. The sides of the land measured $115\frac{1}{2}$ feet, $66\frac{1}{4}$ feet, $106\frac{1}{8}$ feet, and $110\frac{1}{4}$ feet. Eugene wants to know the perimeter (sum of all sides) of his lake property. Can you calculate the perimeter for Eugene?

$$115\tfrac{4}{8} + 66\tfrac{2}{8} + 106\tfrac{1}{8} + 110\tfrac{2}{8} = 397\tfrac{9}{8} = 398\tfrac{1}{8} \text{ feet}$$

2-42. A $6\frac{7}{9}$-foot piece of tarpaulin consists of three lengths. Two of the three pieces measure $1\frac{1}{3}$ feet and $2\frac{5}{9}$ feet. What is the length of the third piece?

$$1\tfrac{3}{9} + 2\tfrac{5}{9} = 3\tfrac{8}{9}$$

$$6\tfrac{7}{9} - 3\tfrac{8}{9} \qquad 5\tfrac{16}{9} \leftarrow \left(\tfrac{9}{9} + \tfrac{7}{9} = \tfrac{16}{9}\right)$$
$$5\tfrac{16}{9} - 3\tfrac{8}{9} = 2\tfrac{8}{9} \text{ feet}$$

2–43. Dale Severson ordered $\frac{7}{8}$ of a ton of crushed rock to make a patio. If Dale used only $\frac{2}{5}$ of the rock, how much crushed rock remains unused?

$\frac{3}{5} \times \frac{7}{8} = \frac{21}{40}$ of a ton

2–44. A Coke dispenser held $19\frac{1}{4}$ gallons of soda. During working hours, $12\frac{3}{4}$ gallons were dispensed. How many gallons of Coke remain?

$$\begin{array}{r} 19\frac{1}{4} \\ -\ 12\frac{3}{4} \\ \hline \end{array} \qquad \begin{array}{r} 18\frac{5}{4} \swarrow \left(\frac{4}{4} + \frac{1}{4}\right) \\ -\ 12\frac{3}{4} \\ \hline 6\frac{2}{4} = 6\frac{1}{2} \text{ gallons} \end{array}$$

2–45. Mabel Peterson bought a home that is $6\frac{1}{4}$ times as expensive as the home her parents bought. Mabel's parents paid $31,000 for their home. What is the cost of Mabel's new home?

$\frac{25}{4} \times \$31,000 = \$193,750$

2–46. Ajax Company charges $150 per cord of wood. If Bill Ryan orders $3\frac{1}{2}$ cords, what will his total cost be?

$\$150 \times 3\frac{1}{2} = \overset{75}{\cancel{\$150}} \times \frac{7}{\underset{1}{\cancel{2}}} = \$525$

2–47. Raymond served 20 pizzas at his birthday party. Each guest ate $\frac{1}{3}$ of a pizza. How many guests did Raymond have at his party?

$20 \div \frac{1}{3} = 20 \times 3 = 60$ guests

2–48. Marc, Steven, and Daniel entered into a partnership. Marc owns $\frac{1}{9}$ of the company, and Steven owns $\frac{1}{4}$. What part does Daniel own?

$\frac{4}{36} + \frac{9}{36} = \frac{13}{36} \qquad 1 - \frac{13}{36} = \frac{23}{36}$ for Daniel or $\frac{36}{36} - \frac{13}{36} = \frac{23}{36}$

2–49. Aster Jones works for Burger King. She is paid time and a half for Sundays. If Aster works on Sunday for 6 hours at a regular pay of $6, what does she earn on Sunday?

$1\frac{1}{2} \times \$6 = \frac{3}{2} \times \frac{\$6}{1} = \$9 \qquad \$9 \times 6 \text{ hours} = \$54$

2–50. Jane Sanacki went to her local deli and bought the following:

$2\frac{3}{4}$ pounds of roast beef	$2\frac{6}{8}$
$\frac{7}{8}$ pound of ham	$\frac{7}{8}$
$2\frac{1}{2}$ pounds of cole slaw	$2\frac{4}{8}$
$4\frac{1}{4}$ pounds of potato salad	$4\frac{2}{8}$
$2\frac{5}{8}$ pounds of fruit salad	$2\frac{5}{8}$
What was the total weight of Jane's purchases?	$10\frac{24}{8} = 13$ pounds

2–51. Al Davis, an employee at Hertz, is paid $90 per day. He has decided to donate $\frac{2}{3}$ of a day's pay to his local church. How much will Al donate?

$\frac{2}{3} \times \$90 = \$60$

2–52. A trip to New Hampshire from Boston will take you $2\frac{3}{4}$ hours. Assume you have traveled $\frac{1}{11}$ of the way. How much longer will the trip take?

$\frac{\overset{5}{\cancel{10}}}{\underset{1}{\cancel{11}}} \times \frac{\overset{1}{\cancel{11}}}{\underset{2}{\cancel{4}}} = \frac{5}{2} = 2\frac{1}{2}$ hours

2–53 Michael, who loves to cook, makes an apple pie (serves 6) for his family. The recipe calls for $1\frac{1}{2}$ pounds of apples, $3\frac{1}{4}$ cups of flour, $\frac{1}{4}$ cup of margarine, $2\frac{3}{8}$ cups of sugar, and 2 teaspoons of cinnamon. Since guests are coming, Michael wants to

8. P. 40. **8.** Find LCD by using prime numbers—show work:

$$\frac{1}{4}+\frac{1}{5}+\frac{3}{5}+\frac{1}{8} = \begin{array}{r|rrrr} 2 & 4 & 5 & 5 & 8 \\ 2 & 2 & 5 & 5 & 4 \\ 5 & 1 & 5 & 5 & 2 \\ \hline & 1 & 1 & 1 & 2 \end{array}$$

$$2 \times 2 \times 5 \times 1 \times 1 \times 1 \times 2 = 40$$

9. P. 42. **9.** Subtract:

$$\begin{array}{rcrcr} 15\frac{5}{8} & = & 15\frac{10}{16} & = & 14\frac{26}{16} \leftarrow \left(\frac{10}{16}+\frac{16}{16}\right) \\ -\,10\frac{15}{16} & = & -\,10\frac{15}{16} & = & -\,10\frac{15}{16} \\ \hline & & & & 4\frac{11}{16} \end{array}$$

Complete using canceling technique:

10. P. 45. **10.** $\frac{14}{26} \times \frac{4}{7} \times \frac{5}{8} = \frac{\cancel{14}^{\cancel{2}\,1}}{26} \times \frac{\cancel{4}^{1}}{\cancel{7}_{1}} \times \frac{5}{\cancel{8}_{\cancel{2}\,1}} = \frac{5}{26}$

11. P. 45. **11.** $4\frac{1}{8} \times \frac{18}{19} = \frac{33}{\cancel{8}_{4}} \times \frac{\cancel{18}^{9}}{19} = \frac{297}{76} = 3\frac{69}{76}$

12. P. 46. **12.** $\frac{4}{9} \div 4 = \frac{\cancel{4}^{1}}{9} \times \frac{1}{\cancel{4}_{1}} = \frac{1}{9}$

13. P. 46. **13.** A trip to Boston from New York will take you $4\frac{1}{2}$ hours. If you have traveled $\frac{1}{3}$ of the way, how much longer will the trip take?

$\frac{\cancel{2}^{1}}{\cancel{3}_{1}} \times \frac{\cancel{9}^{3}}{\cancel{2}_{1}} = 3$ hours

14. P. 46. **14.** Oak Ridge Corporation's new machine produces $20\frac{1}{4}$ widgets each hour. If the machine runs 18 hours, how many widgets will the machine produce?

$\frac{81}{\cancel{4}_{2}} \times \cancel{18}^{9} = \frac{729}{2} = 364\frac{1}{2}$ widgets

15. P. 45. **15.** A recent taste testing survey showed that $\frac{3}{5}$ of the people surveyed preferred the taste of chicken A over chicken B. If 17,500 people were in the survey, how many favored chicken A? How many chose chicken B?

A: $\frac{3}{5} \times 17{,}500 = 10{,}500$ people B: $\frac{2}{5} \times 17{,}500 = 7{,}000$ people

16. P. 41. **16.** Rene Foss, an employee of Budget Rent-A-Car, worked $9\frac{3}{4}$ hours on Monday, $2\frac{3}{4}$ hours on Tuesday, $7\frac{1}{2}$ hours on Wednesday, $7\frac{1}{4}$ hours on Thursday, and 9 hours on Friday. How many total hours did Rene work during the week?

$9\frac{3}{4} + 2\frac{3}{4} + 7\frac{2}{4} + 7\frac{1}{4} + 9 = 34\frac{9}{4} = 36\frac{1}{4}$ hours

17. P. 41. **17.** If the stock of Disney was $\$25\frac{1}{4}$ and rose $1\frac{5}{8}$ for the day, what is Disney's closing price?

$$\begin{array}{rcr} \$25\frac{1}{4} & = & \$25\frac{2}{8} \\ +\,1\frac{5}{8} & = & +\,1\frac{5}{8} \\ \hline & & \$26\frac{7}{8} \end{array}$$

Project A

AMR Chairman Sold Almost One-Fifth Of His Stake in Firm Early This Month

INSIDE TRACK

By GEORGETTE JASEN
Staff Reporter of THE WALL STREET JOURNAL

NEW YORK – Robert L. Crandall, chairman of American Airlines parent AMR Corp., sold nearly one-fifth of his holdings of the company's stock early this month.

Mr. Crandall sold 6,250 AMR shares at $65.25 each, or a total of $407,812, filings with the Securities and Exchange Commission show.

said he was prepared to launch a $7.54 lion bid for the quent was

"bu ter rat ca se in th

How many shares of stock did Crandall own before his selling?

$$6{,}250 \div \frac{1}{5} = 6{,}250 \times 5 = 31{,}250$$

Check $31{,}250 \times \frac{1}{5} = 6{,}250$

Project B

Heinz to Break Up Newly Acquired Unit; Dismissals Planned

By a WALL STREET JOURNAL *Staff Reporter*

PITTSBURGH—H.J. Heinz Co. said it would break up newly acquired JLFoods of Eugene, Ore., and assign that company's units to Heinz's North American affiliates.

As part of the move, about 200 of JLFoods' 2,400 workers will be dismissed in the next few months. Eighty of the 200 workers are located at JLFoods' Eugene headquarters.

The restructuring will bring a "greater focus on the North American food service industry," Chairman Anthony J.F. O'Reilly said. "Opportunities exist for Heinz to take advantage of the technology and production facilities of JLFoods and its operating units."

A Heinz spokeswoman said the company isn't ready yet to announce management changes that result from the restructuring.

The JLFoods units will be distributed as follows:

Chef Francisco, which makes frozen soups at plants in Eugene, Ore., and King of Prussia, Pa., will become part of Heinz U.S.A.

Delicious Foods and Oregon Farms will ...e operating ...

What fractional part of JLFoods workers will be retained?

$$\frac{200}{2{,}400} = \frac{1}{12}$$

$$\frac{12}{12} - \frac{1}{12} = \frac{11}{12} \text{ retained}$$

NOTES

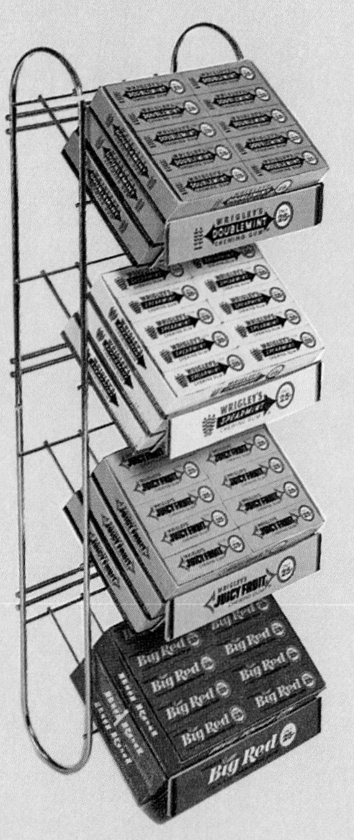

THAT WAS THEN . . .
. . . THIS IS NOW

In 1891, William Wrigley made soap and gave chewing gum away as advertising. This ad from 1918 shows the 3 gums William Wrigley made—Spearmint, Doublemint, and Juicy Fruit. The cost of a pack then was 5 cents or $.05. Today, the average cost is $.40

3

Decimals

LEARNING UNIT OBJECTIVES

LU 3-1: Rounding; Fraction and Decimal Conversions

1. Explain the relationship of place values. *p. 64*
2. Round decimals to indicated position. *p. 65*
3. Convert decimal fractions to decimal forms. *p. 66*
4. Convert proper fractions and mixed numbers to decimals. *p. 67*
5. Convert decimal forms and mixed decimals to decimal fractions. *p. 68*

LU 3-2: Decimal Addition, Subtraction, Multiplication, and Division; Shortcuts

1. Add, subtract, multiply, and divide with decimals and/or mixed decimals. *pp. 69–71*
2. Multiply and divide decimals by shortcut methods. *p. 71*
3. Dissect and solve a word problem. *p. 72*.

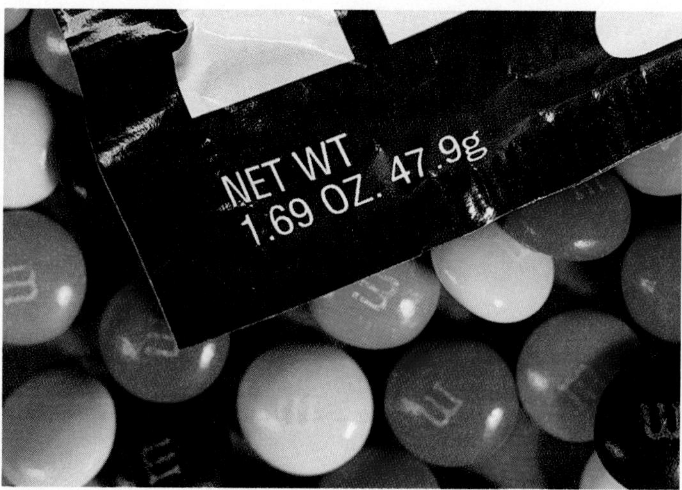

Sharon Hoogstraten

Chapter 2 introduced the 1.69-ounce bag of M&M's® Chocolate Candies shown above. In this chapter, we look again at this bag of 55 candies in six colors. In Table 3-1 we take the fractional breakdown of the six colors and express the values in decimal form.

This chapter is divided into two learning units. The first unit discusses rounding of decimals, converting fractions to decimals, and converting decimals to fractions. The second unit shows you how to add, subtract, multiply, and divide decimals, along with some shortcuts for multiplying and dividing decimals. You will find the procedural steps in these units easy to follow and remember.

LEARNING UNIT 3-1 ROUNDING; FRACTION AND DECIMAL CONVERSIONS

Remember to read the decimal point as and.

In Chapter 1, we stated that the **decimal point** is the center of the decimal system. So far we have studied whole numbers or fractional parts in divisional form that did not involve **decimals.** Now we will study the place values of the numbers to the right of the decimal point. See the diagram that follows. Note that the words to the right of the decimal point end in *ths*.

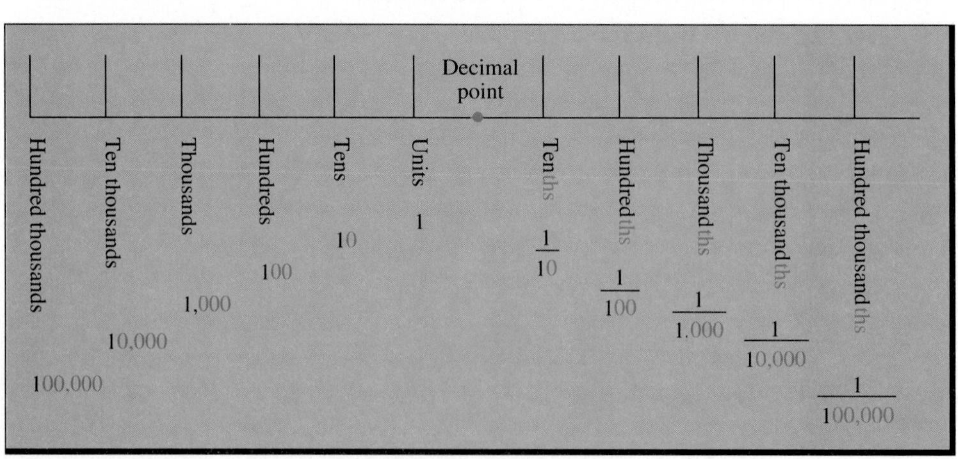

Reading decimals correctly helps you to write them correctly.

You should understand the relationship of the place values on either side of the decimal point. If you move a number to the left of the decimal point by place (units, tens, and so on), you *increase* its value 10 times for each point. If you move a number to the right of the decimal point by place (tenths, hundredths, and so on), you *decrease* its value 10 times for each place. This is why the decimal point is in the center of the decimal system.

TABLE 3–1
Analyzing a Bag of M&M's®

Note that decimals like .33, .11, and so on, have been rounded to nearest hundredths. Unit 3–1 explains how to round decimals.

Color	Fraction		Decimal
Yellow	$\frac{18}{55}$	or	.33
Red	$\frac{10}{55}$	or	.18
Tan	$\frac{9}{55}$	or	.16
Orange	$\frac{7}{55}$	or	.13
Brown	$\frac{6}{55}$	or	.11
Green	$\frac{5}{55}$	or	.09
	$\frac{55}{55} = 1$		1.00

Note: The color ratios currently given are a sample only, used for educational purposes, and do not represent the manufacturer's color ratios.

EXAMPLES

\$ .05 → The 5 is in the hundredths position. The .05 represents the cost of a bag of Wrigley's gum advertised in the 1918 chapter opener.

1.438 → The 4 is in the tenths place value.

1.9382 → The 2 is in the ten-thousandths place value.

.33 → The thirty-three hundred*ths* represents the yellow M&M's® in our M&M's® bag of 55 M&M's®.

1.69 oz. → The one ounce and sixty-nine hundred*ths* of another ounce is the weight of our bag of M&M's®.

Let's begin the unit by rounding decimals. Since you learned how to round whole numbers in Chapter 1, you should have no difficulty rounding decimals.

Rounding Decimals

From Table 3–1 describing the contents of a 1.69-ounce bag of M&M's®, you know that the bag contained $\frac{9}{55}$, or .16, tan M&M's®. The .16 was rounded to the nearest hundredth. **Rounding decimals** involves the following steps:

Steps for Rounding Decimals

Step 1. Identify digit you want to round.

Step 2. If digit to right of identified digit in Step 1 is 5 or more, increase identified digit by 1. If digit to right is less than 5, do not change identified digit.

Step 3. Drop all digits to right of identified digit.

Let's practice rounding by using the $\frac{9}{55}$ tan M&M's® that we rounded to .16 in Table 3–1. Before we rounded $\frac{9}{55}$ to .16, the number was .1636363.

EXAMPLE Round .1636363 to nearest hundredth.

Step 1. .1636363 — Identified digit is 6, which is in the hundredths position (two places to the right of decimal).

Step 2. Digit to right of 6 is less than 5 (3). Thus, 6, the identified digit in Step 1, is not changed.

.1636363

Step 3. .16 — Drop all other digits to right of identified digit 6.

We could also round the .1636363 M&M's® to the nearest tenth or thousandth like this:

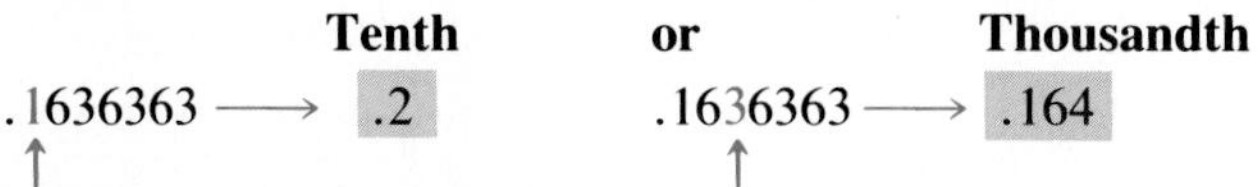

	Tenth	or	Thousandth
.1636363 ⟶	.2	.1636363 ⟶	.164

OTHER EXAMPLES

Round to nearest dollar	$155.38	⟶ $155
Round to nearest cent	$1,196.885	⟶ $1,196.89
Round to nearest hundredth	$38.563	⟶ $38.56
Round to nearest thousandth	$1,432.9981	⟶ $1,432.998

The rules for rounding can differ with the circumstances of the situation in which rounding is used. For example, have you ever bought one item from a supermarket produce department that was marked "3 for $1" and noticed what the cashier charged you? One item marked "3 for $1" would not cost you $33\frac{1}{3}$ cents rounded to 33 cents. You will pay 34 cents. Many retail stores round to the next cent even if the digit following the identified digit is less than $\frac{1}{2}$ of a penny. In this text, we round on the concept of 5 or more.

Fraction and Decimal Conversions

In business operations, we frequently need to convert fractions to decimal numbers and to convert decimal numbers to fractions. This section begins by discussing three types of fraction-to-decimal conversions.

Converting Decimal Fractions to Decimal Forms

A **decimal fraction** is a fraction with a denominator of 10, 100, 1,000, and so on. The fraction $\frac{7}{10}$ is a decimal fraction. To convert a decimal fraction to **decimal form,** take the following steps.

Steps for Converting Decimal Fractions to Decimal Forms

Step 1. Count number of zeros in denominator.

Step 2. Number of zeros tells how many digits to right of decimal your answer will be. Place numerator of decimal fraction in decimal form to right of decimal the same number of places as zeros in denominator. Be sure not to go over total number of denominator zeros.

Now let's change $\frac{7}{10}$ and its higher multiples of 10 to decimals.

EXAMPLES

	Verbal form	Decimal fraction	Decimal form	Number of decimal places to right of decimal
a.	Seven tenths	$\frac{7}{10}$	.7	1
b.	Seven hundredths	$\frac{7}{100}$	.07	2
c.	Seven thousandths	$\frac{7}{1,000}$	.007	3
d.	Seven ten thousandths	$\frac{7}{10,000}$	.0007	4

Note how the different values of the decimal fractions above are shown in the decimal forms. The zeros after the decimal and before the number 7 indicate these values. If you added zeros after the number 7, you would not change the value. Thus, the numbers .7, .70, and .700 have the same value. So seven tenths of a pizza, 70 hundredths of a pizza, or 700 thousandths of a pizza mean the same amount of pizza. The first pizza is sliced into 10 pieces. The next pizza is sliced into 100 slices. The third pizza is sliced into 1,000 slices. Also, we didn't need to place a zero to the left of the decimal point.

TABLE 3–2
Common Fraction to Decimal Conversions

Fraction	Decimal equivalent	Fraction	Decimal equivalent
$\frac{1}{2}$	.50	$\frac{1}{7}$	$.14\frac{2}{7}$ (.143)
$\frac{1}{3}$	$.33\frac{1}{3}$ ($.33\bar{3}$)	$\frac{1}{8}$	$.12\frac{1}{2}$ (.125)
$\frac{2}{3}$	$.66\frac{2}{3}$ ($.66\bar{6}$)	$\frac{3}{8}$	$.37\frac{1}{2}$ (.375)
$\frac{1}{4}$	.25	$\frac{5}{8}$	$.62\frac{1}{2}$ (.625)
$\frac{3}{4}$	.75	$\frac{7}{8}$	$.87\frac{1}{2}$ (.875)
$\frac{1}{5}$	.20	$\frac{1}{9}$	$.11\bar{1}$
$\frac{2}{5}$	.40	$\frac{1}{10}$	.10
$\frac{3}{5}$	.60	$\frac{1}{12}$	$.08\frac{1}{3}$ ($.08\bar{3}$)
$\frac{4}{5}$	.80	$\frac{1}{15}$	$.06\frac{2}{3}$ ($.06\bar{6}$)
$\frac{1}{6}$	$.16\frac{2}{3}$ ($.16\bar{6}$)	$\frac{1}{16}$	$.06\frac{1}{4}$ (.0625)
$\frac{5}{6}$	$.83\frac{1}{3}$ ($.83\bar{3}$)	$\frac{1}{20}$	.05
		$\frac{1}{25}$	.04

Converting Proper Fractions to Decimals

Recall from Chapter 2 that proper fractions are a form of division. This makes it possible for us to convert proper fractions to **decimal equivalents** by carrying out the division.

Steps for Converting Proper Fractions to Decimals

Step 1. Divide numerator or fraction by its denominator. (Additional zeros may have to be added to number in numerator.)

Step 2. Round as necessary.

EXAMPLES

$\frac{1}{4} = 4\overline{)1.00}$ = .25: 8, 20, 20

$\frac{5}{8} = 8\overline{)5.000}$ = .625: 4 8, 20, 16, 40, 40

$\frac{1}{3} = 3\overline{)1.000}$ = $.33\bar{3}$: 9, 10, 9, 10, 9, 1

Table 3–2 gives a quick reference for the decimal conversions of common fractions. Note in the example $\frac{1}{3}$ that the 3 in the quotient keeps repeating itself (never ends). We call this a **repeating decimal.** The short bar over the last 3 means that the number endlessly repeats.

Converting Mixed Numbers to Decimals

A mixed number, you recall, is a combination of a whole number and a proper fraction. We can convert mixed numbers to decimals by two simple steps.

Steps for Converting Mixed Numbers to Decimals

Step 1. Convert fractional part of mixed number to a decimal (as illustrated in the previous section).

Step 2. Add converted fractional part to a whole number.

EXAMPLE $8\frac{2}{5}$ = **(Step 1)** $5\overline{)2.0}$ = .4 (20) **(Step 2)** 8 + .4 = 8.4

Now that we have converted fractions to decimals, let's convert decimals to fractions.

Converting Decimal Forms and Mixed Decimals to Decimal Fractions

The term *decimal form* is familiar to you, let's define mixed decimals. A **mixed decimal** is a combination of a whole number and a decimal. Here is an example of a mixed decimal:

EXAMPLE 924.481 = Nine hundred twenty-four and four hundred eighty-one thousandths

Note the following conversion steps for converting decimal forms and mixed decimals to decimal fractions.

> **Steps for Converting Decimal Forms and Mixed Decimals to Decimal Fractions**
>
> **Step 1.** Place numbers to right of decimal point in numerator of fraction. Omit decimal point. (For a decimal fraction with a fractional part, see examples **c** and **d** below.)
>
> **Step 2.** Put a number 1 in denominator of fraction.
>
> **Step 3.** Count number of digits to right of decimal point. Add same number of zeros to denominator of fraction. For mixed decimals, add fraction to whole number.

If desired, you can reduce the fractions in Step 3.

EXAMPLES

	Step 1	Step 2	Places	Step 3
a. .4	$\frac{4}{}$	$\frac{4}{1}$	1	$\frac{4}{10}$
b. .48	$\frac{48}{}$	$\frac{48}{1}$	2	$\frac{48}{100}$
c. $.48\frac{1}{2}$	$\frac{485}{}$	$\frac{485}{1}$	3	$\frac{485}{1,000}$

Before completing Step 1 in example **c,** we must remove the fractional part, convert it to a decimal ($\frac{1}{2}$ = .5), and multiply it times .01 (.5 × .01 = .005). We use .01 because the 8 of .48 is in the hundredths place. Then we add the .005 + .48 = .485 (three places to right of the decimal). Now complete Steps 1, 2, and 3.

	Step 1	Step 2	Places	Step 3
d. $.06\frac{1}{4}$	$\frac{625}{}$	$\frac{625}{1}$	4	$\frac{625}{10,000}$

In example **d,** be sure to convert $\frac{1}{4}$ to .25 and multiply by .01. This gives .0025. Then add .0025 to .06 which is .0625 (four places). Now complete steps 1, 2, and 3.

	Step 1	Step 2	Places	Step 3
e. 17.45	$\frac{45}{}$	$\frac{45}{1}$	2	$\frac{45}{100} = 17\frac{45}{100}$

Example **e** is a mixed decimal. Since we substitute *and* for the decimal point, we read this mixed decimal as seventeen and forty-five hundredths. Note that after we converted the .45 of the mixed decimal to a fraction, we added it to the whole number 17.

Now try the following Practice Quiz.

LU 3-1 PRACTICE QUIZ

Write as a decimal number:

1. Three hundred one thousandths.

Name the place position of identified digit:

2. 3.4132 (↑ under 1) **3.** 4.8314 (↑ under 3)

Round each decimal to place indicated:

	Tenth	Thousandth
4. .41392	**a**	**b**
5. .68341	**a**	**b**

Convert to decimal form:

6. $\frac{8}{10{,}000}$ **7.** $\frac{12}{100{,}000}$

Convert to decimal fractions (do not reduce):

8. .819 **9.** 16.93 **10.** $.05\frac{1}{4}$

Convert the following fractions to decimals and round answer to nearest hundredth:

11. $\frac{1}{7}$ **12.** $\frac{3}{8}$ **13.** $12\frac{1}{8}$

SOLUTIONS TO LU 3-1 PRACTICE QUIZ

1. .301 (3 places to right of decimal)

2. hundredths **3.** thousandths

4. a. .4 (identified digit 4—digit to right less than 5) **b.** .414 (identified digit 3—digit to right greater than 5)

5. a. .7 (identified digit 6—digit to right greater than 5) **b.** .683 (identified digit 3—digit to right less than 5)

6. .0008 (4 places) **7.** .00012 (5 places)

8. $\frac{819}{1{,}000}\left(\frac{819}{1 + 3 \text{ zeros}}\right)$ **9.** $16\frac{93}{100}$

10. $\frac{525}{10{,}000}\left(\frac{525}{1 + 4 \text{ zeros}}\ \frac{1}{4} \times .01 = .0025 + .05 = .0525\right)$

11. .14285 = .14 **12.** .375 = .38 **13.** 12.125 = 12.13

LEARNING UNIT 3–2 DECIMAL ADDITION, SUBTRACTION, MULTIPLICATION, AND DIVISION; SHORTCUTS

Courtesy of the Chicago White Sox

Take Me Out to the Crowd

Average costs for a family of four to attend a major-league game

Tickets	$33.36
Parking	5.28
Beer (two)	5.74
Soft drinks (four)	5.04
Hot dogs (four)	6.68
Programs (two)	4.42
Baseball caps (two)	15.70
TOTAL COST	$76.22

Source: Team Marketing Report

of business with the Pittsburgh Pirates.

Making decisions about how to spend your entertainment dollars is a good example of using business math in your personal finances. Note how the above clipping from *The Wall Street Journal* uses decimals in totaling the average cost of a baseball game for a family of four.

The clipping says that for a family of four to attend a major-league game, the average total cost is $76.22. Rounding this all the way, the cost is $80 per game. If the family goes to a game four times a year, the total cost is $304.88. Rounding this all the way is $300. If you want to round $304.88 to the nearest dollar, you would have $305.

Remember that business math decisions are sometimes influenced by other decisions. For example, the family of four may not want to spend $305 to attend four games if their favorite team is not winning any games.

Now you are ready to make calculations involving decimals.

Addition and Subtraction of Decimals

Note how the decimals in the above "Take Me Out to the Crowd" clipping are aligned in the addition column. Remember that whole numbers such as $80, $300, and $305 above are assumed to have a decimal after the last digit.

Steps for Addition and Subtraction of Decimals

Step 1. Vertically write numbers and align decimal points. You can place additional zeros to right of a decimal point if needed without changing value.

Step 2. Add or subtract digits starting with right column moving to left.

Step 3. Align decimal point in answer with above decimals.

EXAMPLES Add 3 + 6.2 + 25.138 + .0008 + 7.33

```
Whole number to       →   3.0000    Extra zeros have been
right of last             6.2000 ←  added to make calculation
digit is assumed         25.1380    easier.
to have a decimal.         .0008
                          7.3300
                         -------
                         41.6688
```

Subtract 45.3 − 15.273   Subtract 7 − 6.9

```
    2 9 10            6 10
  45.300              7.0
− 15.273             −6.9
 -------             ----
  30.027               .1
```

Multiplication of Decimals

From the "Take Me Out to the Crowd" clipping at the beginning of this unit, you know that the average cost for a family of four to attend 1 game is $76.22. To find the cost of 4 games, you multiply this number by 4, which gives the total cost of $304.88. The steps that follow explain how to multiply decimals.

Steps for Multiplication of Decimals

Step 1. Multiply numbers as whole numbers ignoring decimals.

Step 2. Count and total number of decimal places in multiplier and multiplicand.

Step 3. Starting at right in product, count number of decimal places totaled in Step 2. Insert decimal at this point. If total number of places is greater than there are places in product, insert zeros in front of product.

EXAMPLES

```
          8.52 (2 decimal places)       2.36 (2 places)
        × 6.7  (1 decimal place)       ×.016 (3 places)
Step 1   5 964   ↖ Step 2              1416
        51 12                           236
        ------                        ------
        57.084                        .03776 Need to add zero
Step 3
```

Division of Decimals

If the divisor in your decimal division problem is a whole number, first place the decimal point in the quotient directly above the decimal in the dividend. Then divide as usual. If the divisor has a decimal, complete the steps that follow.

Steps for Division of Decimals

Step 1. Move decimal in divisor to right to make divisor a whole number.

Step 2. Move decimal in dividend to right the same number of positions that you moved decimal in divisor (Step 1).

Step 3. Put decimal in quotient above position of decimal in dividend. Divide as usual.

Since multiplication is the opposite of division, you can prove this example by multiplication.

EXAMPLE

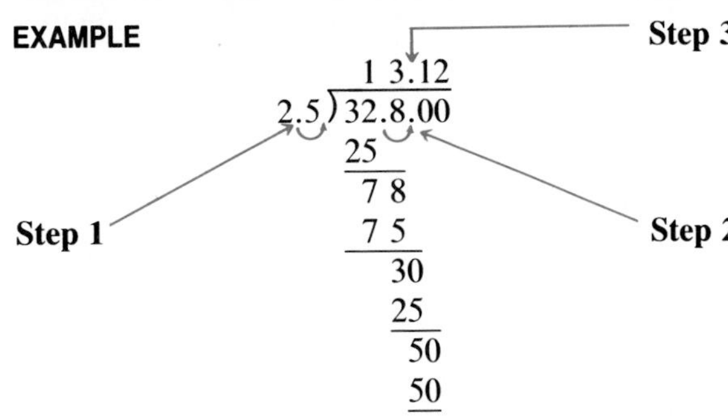

Stop a moment and study the above example. Note that the quotient does not change when we multiply the divisor and the dividend by the same number. This is why we can move the decimal point in division problems and always divide by a whole number.

The next section shows you some shortcuts you can use for multiplying and dividing decimal numbers.

Multiplication and Division Shortcuts for Decimal Numbers

In Unit 3–1, you saw how we worked with multiples of 10 when converting decimal fractions (fractions with denominators in multiples of 10) to decimal form. You can also take advantage of multiples of 10 when multiplying or dividing decimal numbers. Note the rules that follow.

Steps for Shortcuts for Multiples of 10

Multiplication

Step 1. Count zeros in multiplier.

Step 2. Move decimal in multiplicand same number of places to right as there are zeros in multiplier.

Division

Step 1. Count zeros in divisor.

Step 2. Move decimal in dividend same number of places to left as there are zeros in divisor.

In multiplication, the answers are *larger* than the original number.

EXAMPLES

$7.89 \times 10 = 78.9$ (1 place to right)

$7.89 \times 100 = 789$ (2 places to right)

$7.89 \times 1{,}000 = 7{,}890$ (3 places to right)

In division, the answers are *smaller* than the original number.

EXAMPLES

$7.89 \div 10 = .789$ (1 place to left)

$7.89 \div 100 = .0789$ (2 places to left)

$7.89 \div 1{,}000 = .00789$ (3 places to left)

$7.89 \div 10{,}000 = .000789$ (4 places to left)

Now let's dissect and solve a word problem.

How to Dissect and Solve a Word Problem

The Word Problem May O'Mally went to Sears, Roebuck to buy a wall-to-wall carpet. She needs 101.3 yards for downstairs, 16.3 yards for the upstairs bedrooms, and 6.2 yards for the halls. The carpet cost was $14.55 per yard. The padding cost $3.25 per yard. Sears quoted an installation charge of $6.25 per yard. What is May O'Mally's total cost?

By completing the following blueprint aid, we will slowly dissect this word problem. Note that before solving the problem, we gather the facts; identify what we are solving for; and list the steps that must be completed before solving the final answer, along with any key points we should remember. Let's go to it!

Blueprint Aid for Dissecting and Solving a Word Problem

A. Gather the facts	B. What am I solving for?	C. What must I know or calculate before solving problem?	D. Key points to remember
Carpet needed: 101.3 yards; 16.3 yards; 6.2 yards *Costs:* Carpet, $14.55 per yd.; padding, $3.25 per yd.; installation, $6.25 per yd.	Total cost of carpet.	Total yards × Total cost per yard = Total cost.	Align decimals. Round answer to nearest cent.

Steps to Solving Problem

1. Calculate total number of yards.

$$\begin{array}{r} 101.3 \\ 16.3 \\ \underline{6.2} \\ 123.8 \text{ yards} \end{array}$$

2. Calculate total cost per yard.

$$\begin{array}{r} \$14.55 \\ 3.25 \\ \underline{6.25} \\ \$24.05 \end{array}$$

3. Calculate total cost of carpet.

123.8 × $24.05 = **$2,977.39**

Now let's check your progress.

LU 3-2 PRACTICE QUIZ

1. Rearrange vertically and add:
   15, .189, 8.75, 14.18923
2. Rearrange and subtract:
   28.1549 − .885
3. Multiply and round answer to nearest tenth:
   28.53 × 17.4
4. Divide and round to nearest hundredth:
   2,182 ÷ 2.83

Complete by the shortcut method:

5. 11.28 × 100
6. 7,680 ÷ 1,000
7. 9,812 ÷ 10,000
8. Could you help Mel decide which product is the "better buy"?

Dog food A	**Dog food B**
$9.01 for 64 ounces	$7.95 for 50 ounces

   Round to nearest cent as needed.
9. At Avis Rent-A-Car, the cost per day to rent a medium-sized car is $39.99 plus 29 cents a mile. What is the charge to rent this car for 2 days if you drove 602.3 miles? You might want to complete a blueprint aid since the solution will show a completed one.

SOLUTIONS TO LU 3-2 PRACTICE QUIZ

1.
$$\begin{array}{r} 15.00000 \\ .18900 \\ 8.75000 \\ \underline{14.18923} \\ 38.12823 \end{array}$$

2.
$$\begin{array}{r} 28.1549 \\ \underline{-.8850} \\ 27.2699 \end{array}$$

3.

```
   28.53
 × 17.4
  11 412
 199 71
 285 3
 496.422 = 496.4
```

4.

```
          771.024 = 771.02
2.83)218200.000
     1981
      2010
      1981
        290
        283
          7 00
          5 66
          1 340
          1 132
```

5. 11.28 = 1,128   **6.** 7.680 = 7.680

7. .9812 = .9812

8. A: $9.01 ÷ 64 = $.14   Buy A.
B: $7.95 ÷ 50 = $.16

9. Avis Rent-A-Car total rental charge:

Blueprint Aid for Dissecting and Solving a Word Problem

A. Gather the facts	B. What am I solving for?	C. What must I know or calculate before solving problem?	D. Key points to remember
Cost per day, $39.99. 29 cents per mile. Drove 602.3 miles. 2-day rental	Total rental charge.	Total cost for 2 days' rental + Total cost of driving = Total rental charge.	In multiplication, count number of decimal places. Starting right to left in product, insert decimal to appropriate place. Round to nearest cent.

Steps to Solving Problem

1. Calculate total costs for 2 days' rental. $39.99 × 2 = $79.98
2. Calculate total cost of driving. $.29 × 602.3 = $174.667 = $174.67
3. Calculate total rental charge.

```
  $ 79.98
 + 174.67
  $254.65
```

CHAPTER ORGANIZER: A REFERENCE GUIDE

Page	Topic	Key point, procedure, formula	Example(s) to illustrate situation
64	Identify place value	$10, 1, \frac{1}{10}, \frac{1}{100}, \frac{1}{1,000}$, etc.	.439 in thousandths place value
65	Rounding	1. Identify digit you want to round. 2. If digit to right of identified digit in Step 1 is 5 or more, increase identified digit by 1. If digit to right is less than 5, do not change identified digit. 3. Drop all digits to right of identified digit.	.875 rounded to nearest tenth = .9 ↖ Identified digit
66	Converting decimal fractions to decimal forms	1. Decimal fraction has a denominator with multiples of 10. Count number of zeros in denominator. 2. Zeros show how many places are in decimal form.	$\frac{8}{1,000} = .008$ $\frac{6}{10,000} = .0006$

Page	Topic	Key point, procedure, formula	Example(s) to illustrate situation
67	Converting proper fractions to decimals	1. Divide numerator or fraction by its denominator. 2. Round as necessary.	$\frac{1}{3}$ (to nearest tenth) = .3
67	Converting mixed numbers to decimals	1. Convert fractional part of a mixed number to a decimal. 2. Add converted fractional part to whole number.	$6\frac{1}{4}$ $\frac{1}{4}$ = .25 + 6 = 6.25
68	Converting decimal forms and mixed decimals to decimal fractions	1. Place decimal number in numerator. 2. Put 1 in denominator. 3. Add zeros to denominator, depending on decimal places of original number. For mixed decimals add whole numbers to (3).	.984 (three places) 1. 984 2. $\frac{984}{1}$ 3. $\frac{984}{1{,}000}$
70	Addition and subtraction of decimals	1. Vertically write and align numbers and align decimal points. 2. Add or subtract digits starting with right column moving to left. 3. Align decimal point in answer with above decimals.	Add 1.3 + 2 + .4 1.3 2.0 .4 3.7 Subtract 5 − 3.9 $\overset{4}{\not 5}.\overset{10}{\not 0}$ − 3.9 1.1
70	Multiplication of decimals	1. Multiply numbers—ignore number of decimals. 2. Count and total number of decimal places in multiplier and multiplicand. 3. Starting at right in product, insert the number of decimal places counted in Step 2. If number of places is greater than space in answer, add zeros.	2.48 (2 places) × .018 (3 places) 1 984 2 48 .04464
71	Dividing a decimal by a whole number	1. Place decimal point in quotient directly above the decimal in the dividend. 2. Divide as usual.	1.1 42) 46.2 42 42 42
71	Dividing if the divisor is a decimal	1. Move decimal in divisor to right to make divisor a whole number. 2. Move decimal in dividend to right same number as Step 1. 3. Put decimal in quotient above the position of the decimal in dividend. Divide as usual.	1 4.2 2.9) 41.3 9 29 12 3 11 6 7 9 5 8 2 1
71	Shortcuts on multiplication and division of decimals	When multiplying by 10, 100, 1,000, and so on, move decimal in number being multiplied to right by number of zeros in the multiplier. For division, move decimal to the left.	4.85 × 100 = 485 4.85 ÷ 100 = .0485
	Key terms	Decimal form, *p. 66* Decimal equivalent, *p. 67* Decimal fractions, *p. 66* Decimal point, *p. 64*	Decimals, *p. 64* Mixed decimal, *p. 68* Repeating decimal, *p. 67* Rounding decimal, *p. 65*

Note: For information on dissecting and solving a word problem, see page 72 or page 73.

END-OF-CHAPTER PROBLEMS

Drill Problems

Additional homework assignments by learning unit are at the end of text in Appendix I (p. I–13). Solutions to odd problems are at the end of text in Appendix II.

Identify the place value:

3–1. 4.938 hundredths (arrow under 3)

3–2. 166.481 thousandths (arrow under 1)

Round as indicated:

		Tenth	Hundredth	Thousandth
3–3.	.4583	.5	.46	.458
3–4.	.4119	.4	.41	.412
3–5.	5.8931	5.9	5.89	5.893
3–6.	6.8415	6.8	6.84	6.842
3–7.	6.5555	6.6	6.56	6.556
3–8.	75.9913	76.0	75.99	75.991

Round to nearest cent:

3–9. \$1,822.583   \$1,822.58

3–10. \$6,000.045   \$6,000.05

Convert the following types of decimal fractions to decimal forms (round to nearest hundredth as needed):

3–11. $\frac{3}{100}$ .03

3–12. $\frac{4}{10}$ .40

3–13. $\frac{81}{1{,}000}$ .08

3–14. $\frac{810}{1{,}000}$ .81

3–15. $\frac{84}{100}$ .84

3–16. $\frac{979}{1{,}000}$ .98

3–17. $16\frac{82}{100}$ 16.82

Convert the following decimals to fractions (do not reduce to lowest terms):

3–18. .4 $\frac{4}{10}$

3–19. .33 $\frac{33}{100}$

3–20. .006 $\frac{6}{1{,}000}$

3–21. .0125 $\frac{125}{10{,}000}$

3–22. .609 $\frac{609}{1{,}000}$

3–23. .825 $\frac{825}{1{,}000}$

3–24. .9999 $\frac{9{,}999}{10{,}000}$

3–25. .7065 $\frac{7{,}065}{10{,}000}$

Convert to a mixed number (do not reduce to lowest terms):

3–26. 7.6 $7\frac{6}{10}$

3–27. 28.48 $28\frac{48}{100}$

3–28. 6.025 $6\frac{25}{1{,}000}$

Write the decimal equivalent:

3–29. Three thousandths
.003

3–30. Three hundred three and two hundredths
303.02

3–31. Sixty-five ten thousandths
.0065

3–32. Seven hundred seventy-five thousandths
.775

Rearrange the following and add:

3–33. .041,   9.8532,   2.6,   701.3821
713.8763

3–34. .005,   2,002.181,   795.41,   14.0,   .184
2,811.78

Rearrange and subtract:

3–35. 4.9 − 3.7 = 1.2

3–36. 7 − 2.0815 = 4.9185

3–37. 3.4 − 1.08 = 2.32

Estimate by rounding all the way and multiply the following (do not do rounding of final answer):

3–38. 7.54 × 2.8 = 21.112

Estimate 24 (8 × 3)

3–39. .413 × 3.07 = 1.26791

Estimate 1.2 (.4 × 3)

3–40. 675 × 1.92 = 1,296

Estimate 1,400 (700 × 2)

3–41. 4.9 × .825 = 4.0425

Estimate 4.0 (5 × .8)

Divide and round off to the nearest hundredth:

3–42. .5821 ÷ 5 = .12

3–43. 29.432 ÷ .0012 = 24,526.67

3–44. .0065 ÷ .07 = .09

3–45. 7,742.1 ÷ 48 = 161.29

3–46. 8.95 ÷ 1.18 = 7.58

3–47. 2,600 ÷ .381 = 6,824.15

Convert to decimals (round to nearest hundredth):

3–48. $\frac{1}{12}$ .08

3–49. $\frac{1}{25}$ .04

3–50. $\frac{5}{6}$ .83

3–51. $\frac{5}{8}$ .63

Complete these multiplications and divisions by the shortcut method (do not do any written calculations):

3–52. 75.8 ÷ 10 = 7.58

3–53. 258.5 ÷ 100 = 2.585

3–54. 8.51 × 1,000 = 8,510

3–55. .86 ÷ 100 = .0086

3–56. 9.015 × 100 = 901.5

3–57. 48.6 × 10 = 486

3–58. 750 × 10 = 7,500

3–59. 3,950 ÷ 1,000 = 3.950

3–60. 8.45 ÷ 10 = .845

3–61. 7.9132 × 1,000 = 7,913.2

Word Problems

3–62. At a demonstration for Apple Computer, 600 seats were set up. During the demonstration, 50 seats were vacant. In decimal form (to the nearest hundredth), show how many seats were filled.

$$\begin{array}{r} 600 \\ -\ 50 \\ \hline 550 \end{array} \qquad \frac{550}{600} = .92$$

3–63. Pete Williams got 4 hits out of 9 at bats. What was his average to the nearest thousandths place?

$\frac{4}{9} = .444$

3–64. A computer network using IBM computers charges $.35 per minute. If the bill for the first week of October is $24.95, how many minutes was the network used? (Round to nearest hundredth.)

```
         71.285 = 71.29
 .35)24.95.000
     24 5
        45
        35
        100
         70
        300
        280
         200
         175
```

3–65. Jackie Long purchased 12.48 yards of ribbon for the annual fair. Each yard cost 48 cents. What was the total cost of the ribbon?

12.48 × $.48 = $5.99

3–66. Douglas Noel went to Sommerville Lumber and bought 4 doors at $42.99 each and 6 bags of fertilizer at $8.99. What was the total cost to Douglas? If Douglas had $300 in his pocket, what does he have left to spend?

```
4 × $42.99 = $171.96        $300.00
6 ×   8.99 =    53.94       - 225.90
              $225.90       $  74.10
```

3-67. Alice did not feel well and went to her doctor. Alice's temperature was 102.83. If a normal temperature is 98.6, how much was Alice's temperature above normal?

$$\begin{array}{r} 102.83 \\ -\ 98.60 \\ \hline 4.23 \end{array}$$ degrees

3-68. The normal winter snowfall for Saye County is 109.48 inches. This winter, Saye County had the following snowfall:

	Inches
December	19.85
January	43.491
February	21.98
March	16.31
	101.631

$$\begin{array}{r} 109.480 \\ -\ 101.631 \\ \hline 7.849 \end{array} = 7.85 \text{ inches below normal}$$

What was this winter's total snowfall? How much was the snowfall below or above normal?

3-69. Howard is shopping for a top sirloin beef roast. At market A, a top sirloin roast is \$3.998 per pound. At market B, it is \$3.813 per pound. How much cheaper is market B?

$$\begin{array}{r} \$3.998 \\ -\ 3.813 \\ \hline \$\ .185 \end{array}$$ cheaper

3-70. Shannon is traveling to a carpet convention by car. Her company will reimburse her \$.33 per mile. If Shannon travels 750.8 miles, how much will Shannon receive from her company?

$\$.33 \times 750.8 = \$247.76$

3-71. Mark Ogara rented a truck for the weekend (2 days). The base rental price was \$29.95 per day plus $14\frac{1}{2}$ cents per mile. Mark drove 410.85 miles. How much does Mark owe?

$$\begin{array}{rr} 2 \times \$29.95 = & \$\ 59.90 \\ \$.145 \times 410.85 = & +59.57 \\ \hline & \$119.47 \end{array}$$

3-72. Timothy, Maurice, and Patty love to fly Piper airplanes. Timothy's plane uses 13.021 gallons of fuel per hour, Maurice's plane uses 16.15 gallons, and Patty's plane uses 18.153 gallons per hour. If Timothy, Maurice, and Patty fly for 4.82 hours, what is the total fuel consumed?

$$\begin{array}{r} 13.021 \\ 16.150 \\ 18.153 \\ \hline 47.324 \end{array} \times 4.82 = 228.10 \text{ gallons}$$

3-73. May Sweet bought a new sweater at Dayton's for \$169.48. She gave the salesperson two \$100 bills. What is May's change? Check your answer.

$$\begin{array}{r} \$200.00 \\ -\ 169.48 \\ \hline \$\ 30.52 \end{array} \text{ change} \qquad \begin{array}{r} \$\ 30.52 \\ +\ 169.48 \\ \hline \$200.00 \end{array}$$

3-74. The oil tank in Kent's basement read 310.51 gallons at the beginning of January. During the month, the oil company filled the tank with 110.88 gallons. Kent used 205.53 gallons in January. How many gallons of oil does Kent have to begin February?

$$\begin{array}{r} 310.51 \\ +\ 110.88 \\ \hline 421.39 \\ -\ 205.53 \\ \hline 215.86 \end{array}$$ gallons to begin February

3-75. Russell is preparing the daily bank deposit for his coffee shop. Before the deposit, the coffee shop had a checking account balance of \$3,185.66. The deposit contains the following checks:

No. 1	$ 99.50	No. 3	$8.75
No. 2	110.35	No. 4	6.83

Russell included $820.55 in currency with the deposit. What is the coffee shop's new balance assuming Russell writes no new checks?

$3,185.66
99.50
110.35
8.75
6.83
+ 820.55
$4,231.64

3–76. Meg Lions went to United Parcel to mail a 6.4-pound package for $5.32. On the next day she mailed a 4.5-pound package. What is her cost assuming the same postage rate for both days? (Round rate to nearest cent.)

$\frac{\$5.32}{6.4} = \$.83 \qquad \$.83 \times 4.5 = \$3.74$

3–77. Christine wants to install wall-to-wall carpeting in her home. She needs 110.8 yards for downstairs, 31.8 yards for halls, and 161.9 yards for the bedrooms upstairs. Christine chose a shag carpet that costs $14.99 per yard. She ordered foam padding at $3.10 per yard. The carpet installers quoted Christine a labor charge of $3.75 per yard. What will the total job cost Christine?

$14.99 + $3.10 + $3.75 = $ 21.84
110.8 yards + 31.8 yards + 161.9 yards = × 304.5
$6,650.28

3–78. Ralph Flanagan bought 4 new car tires for $79.99 per tire. The tire store charged $3.15 per tire for mounting, $2.75 per tire for valve stems, and $3.40 per tire for balancing. Assume Ralph paid no sales tax. What was Ralph's total cost for the 4 tires?

$79.99 + $3.15 + $2.75 + $3.40 = $ 89.29
$89.29 × 4 = $357.16

3–79. Shelly is shopping for laundry detergent, mustard, and canned tuna. She is trying to decide which of two products is the better buy. Using the following information, can you help Shelly?

Laundry detergent A ✓ $2.00 for 37 ounces $2.00 ÷ 37 = $.05	**Laundry detergent B** $2.37 for 38 ounces $2.37 ÷ 38 = .06
Mustard A $.88 for 6 ounces .88 ÷ 6 = $.15	**Mustard B** ✓ $1.61 for $12\frac{1}{2}$ ounces $1.61 ÷ 12.5 = $.13
Canned tuna A $1.09 for 6 ounces $1.09 ÷ 6 = $.18	**Canned tuna B** ✓ $1.29 for $8\frac{3}{4}$ ounces $1.29 ÷ 8.75 = $.15

3–80. Rick bought season tickets to professional basketball games. The cost was $695.10. The season package included 32 home games. What is the average price of the tickets per game? Round to the nearest cent. Marcelo, Rick's friend, offered to buy 4 of the tickets from Rick. What is the total amount Rick should receive?

$695.10 ÷ 32 = $21.72 × 4 = $86.88

3–81. Bee-Line Service owns a truck that can handle a maximum load of 1,700.00 pounds. Bee-Line loaded the following merchandise on the truck:

Wood, 450.813 pounds	Cement, 699.222 pounds
Nails, 229.118 pounds	Kitchen parts, 310.185 pounds

Bee-Line wants to add a refrigerator that weighs 340.324 pounds to the load. The company is afraid the truck cannot handle the additional weight. Can you help Bee-

Line decide whether or not to add the refrigerator to the load? How much is Bee-Line's truck over or under its maximum load capacity before adding the refrigerator?

```
  450.813         1,700.000
  229.118       − 1,689.338
  699.222            10.662 pounds under
  310.185                 = 10.66 (no room for refrigerator)
1,689.338
```

3-82. Printed pens cost $.147 each for an order of 20,600 pens. On Monday, Metrodome Company ordered 20,600 pens. What is Metrodome's total cost for the pens?
20,600 × $.147 = $3,028.20

Additional Set of Word Problems

When applicable, round answers to nearest hundredth.

3-83. The oil tank in Ron's Health Club read 287.85 gallons at the beginning of January. During the month, the oil company filled the tank with 102.35 gallons. The club used 104.95 gallons in January. How many gallons of oil are in the tank to begin February?
287.85 + 102.35 = 390.20 − 104.95 = 285.25 gallons

3-84. Tie Yang bought season tickets to the Boston Pops for $698.55. The season package included 38 performances. What is the average price of the tickets per performance? Round to nearest cent. Sam, Tie's friend, offered to buy 4 of the tickets from Tie. What is the total amount Tie should receive?
$698.55 ÷ 38 = $18.38 × 4 = $73.52

Hint: Use the fractional equivalent in your calculation.

3-85. Printed pencils cost $.33$\frac{1}{3}$ each for an order of 14,000 pencils. On Monday, Waldorf Company ordered 14,000 pencils. What is Waldorf's total cost for the pencils?
14,000 × $\frac{1}{3}$$ = $4,666.67

3-86. Morris Katz bought 4 new tires at Goodyear for $95.49 per tire. Goodyear also charged Morris $2.50 per tire for mounting, $2.40 per tire for valve stems, and $3.95 per tire for balancing. Assume no tax. What was Morris' total cost for the 4 tires?
$95.49 + $2.50 + $2.40 + $3.95 = $104.34
$104.34 × 4 = $417.36

3-87. Norma McMurry bought a new sweater at Marshall Field's for $89.45. She gave the salesperson a $100 bill. What is Norma's change?
$100.00 − $89.45 = $10.55

3-88. Steven is traveling to a computer convention by car. His company will reimburse him $.29 per mile. If Steven travels 890.5 miles, how much will he receive from his company?
890.5 × $.29 = $258.25

3-89. Irene went shopping for corn beef. At Marsha's Market, corn beef is $2.066 per pound. At Smith's Deli, corn beef is $2.05 per pound. How much cheaper is corn beef at Smith's? Round to nearest cent.

```
 $2.066
− 2.050
 $ .016 or 1 6/10 cents cheaper that rounds to 2 cents
```

3-90. Nancy wants to install wall-to-wall carpeting in her house. She needs 104.8 yards for downstairs, 17.4 yards for halls, and 165.8 yards for the upstairs bedrooms. Nancy chose a shag carpet that costs $13.95 per yard. She ordered foam padding at $2.75 per yard. The installers quoted Nancy a labor cost of $5.75 per yard in installation. What will the total job cost Nancy?
$13.95 + $2.75 + $5.75 = $22.45
104.8 yards + 17.4 yards + 165.8 yards = 288 yards
288 × $22.45 = $6,465.60

3-91. Elizabeth was not feeling well and visited her doctor. Her temperature was 102.87. If a normal temperature is 98.6, how much is Elizabeth's temperature over normal?
102.87 − 98.6 = 4.27

3–92. The normal winter snowfall at Ring Ski Hills is 114.85 inches. This winter, Ring Ski Hills had the following snowfall:

	Inches
December	28.13
January	44.358
February	18.95
March	17.15

Normal 114.850
Total − 108.588
Below 6.262 inches = 6.26 inches

What was this winter's total snowfall? How much was the snowfall below or above normal? Round to nearest hundredth.

Challenge Problem
Cost of Traveling

3–93. Susan and Alan decided to take a long weekend in Boston. Rome Hotel has a special getaway weekend for $79.95. This price is per person, per night, based on double occupancy. The hotel has a minimum two-night stay. For this price, Susan and Alan will receive $50 credit toward their dinners at Rome's Skylight Restaurant. Also included in the package is a $3.99 credit per person toward breakfast for two each morning.

Since Susan and Alan do not own a car, they plan to rent one. The car rental agency charges $19.95 a day with an additional charge of $.22 a mile and $1.19 per gallon of gas used.

From the following facts, calculate the total expenses of Susan and Alan (round all answers to nearest hundredth or cent as appropriate). Assume no taxes.

Dinner cost at Skylight	$182.12
Breakfast for two—morning No. 1	24.17
Breakfast for two—morning No. 2	26.88
Rental car (2-day rental):	
Beginning odometer reading	4,820
Ending odometer reading	4,940
Gas tank—beginning $\frac{3}{4}$ full	
Gas tank on return $\frac{1}{2}$ full	
Tank holds 24 gallons	

$79.95 × 2 = $159.90 × 2	= $319.80
$182.12 − 50.00 = $132.12	132.12
Breakfast No. 1: $24.17 − 7.98 = $16.19	16.19
Breakfast No. 2: $26.88 − 7.98 = $18.90	18.90
2 × $19.95	39.90
$.22 × 120 (4,940 − 4,820)	26.40
$\frac{1}{4}$ × 24 = 6 gallons × $1.19	7.14
	$560.45

Summary Practice Test

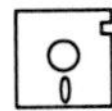

Solutions are at end of text in Appendix II.

Quick Reference

If you get any wrong answers, study the page numbers given for each problem.

1. Pp. 64, 70.
2. P. 66.
3. P. 66.
4. P. 66.
5. P. 68.
6. P. 68.
7. P. 68.
8. Pp. 67–68.
9. Pp. 67–68.
10. Pp. 67–68.
11. Pp. 67–68.

1. Add the following by translating the verbal form into the decimal equivalent:

Five hundred fifty-nine and nine hundred two thousandths	559.902	(Note:
Sixteen and fifty-eight hundredths	16.580	Zeros are
Five and three thousandths	5.003	added for
Seventy-two hundredths	.720	alignment.)
Two hundred three and five tenths	203.500	
	785.705	

Convert decimal fractions to decimal forms:

2. $\frac{9}{10}$ .9 **3.** $\frac{9}{100}$ .09 **4.** $\frac{9}{1,000}$ .009

Convert to proper fractions or mixed numbers (do not reduce to lowest terms):

5. .8 $\frac{8}{10}$ **6.** 2.66 $2\frac{66}{100}$ **7.** .951 $\frac{951}{1,000}$

Convert fractions to decimals (or mixed decimals) and round to nearest hundredth as needed:

8. $\frac{5}{7}$ .71 **9.** $\frac{3}{5}$ .60

10. $6\frac{7}{8}$ 6.88 **11.** $\frac{1}{2}$ .50

12. Pp. 69–70. **12.** Rearrange and add:

4.5, 9.81, 9.453, 151.0321, 99.1

```
  4.5000
  9.8100
  9.4530
151.0321
 99.1000
--------
273.8951
```

13. P. 70. **13.** Subtract and round to nearest tenth:

14.215 − 3.11 = 11.105 = 11.1

14. P. 70. **14.** Multiply (round solution to nearest hundredth):

8.532 × 11.834 = 100.96768 = 100.97

15. P. 71. **15.** Divide (round to nearest tenth):

295,115 ÷ 4.91 = 60,104.887 = 60,104.9

Complete by the shortcut method:

16. P. 71. **16.** 54.65 × 1,000 = 54,650

17. P. 71. **17.** 4,011,119.325 × 100 = 401,111,932.50

18. P. 70. **18.** The average pay of employees is $312.50 per week. John Sullivan earns $395.91 per week. How much is John's pay over the average?
$395.91 − $312.50 = $83.41

19. P. 70. **19.** The state reimburses Bill $.32 per mile. Bill submitted his travel log for a total of 670.8 miles. What will the state pay Bill? Round to nearest cent.
$.32 × 670.8 = $214.66

20. P. 70. **20.** Kevin Hoffman bought 2 new car tires from Big Wheel for $71.95 per tire. Big Wheel also charged Kevin $3.10 per tire for mounting, $2.80 per tire for valve stems, and $3.95 per tire for balancing. What is Kevin's final bill?

2 × $71.95 = $143.90
2 × $ 9.85 = 19.70
$163.60

21. P. 71. **21.** Could you help John decide which product is cheaper per ounce:

Canned fruit A ✓	**Canned fruit B**
$.77 for 5 ounces	$.86 for $5\frac{1}{2}$ ounces
$.77 ÷ 5 = $.154	$.86 ÷ 5.5 = $.156

Project A

Cartoon 'Cels' Animate a Sellers' Market

By JIM HERRON ZAMORA
Staff Reporter of THE WALL STREET JOURNAL

There's nothing Mickey Mouse about collecting celluloid frames of Walt Disney's famous rodent.

Animation art, once prized only by a small circle of cartoon memorabilia buffs and perhaps parents looking to spruce up the kids' room, is now big time. At the heart of the collection craze are 9-by-12-inch "cels"—individually hand-painted celluloid frames—tens of thousands of which go into each cartoon.

Experts caution that investing in cels requires sophistication. Despite the growing popularity of the often-colorful pieces that galleries, auction houses and well-heeled collectors now consider fine art, prices for some high-end cels have dropped recently, for example, as more large private collections have gone on the market. And then there are questions of whether both the art and its value might, quite literally, chip away with time.

'Piece of Childhood'

Mike Glad, though, continues to add to his 1,000-piece collection. "It's like buying a piece of art. A piece of history. A piece of childhood," says the 43-year-old Fremont, Calif., auto-store owner, who savors the "magical feeling when you freeze that same frame on your TV set and say, 'I've got it right here.' "

Though there are followings for the likes of Bugs Bunny, Woody Woodpecker, Fred Flintstone and the latter-day Teenage Mutant Ninja Turtles—their studio sells cels of Leonardo and friends for $60 to $80 each—Disney characters capture the greatest interest.

Esp[illegible]lly Mickey. New Y[illegible]k restaura-

'Cels,' hand-painted celluloid frames of cartoons, are becoming popular collectors' items, sending prices soaring. Disneyland for decades sold cels for $1.25 each, but in recent years, top auction prices have ranged from $20,000 to $286,000.

If Disney sold 40,000 cels at Disneyland years ago, what would be the total value? If the average cel costs approximately $1,000 today, what would be the total value?

Yesterday	Today
$1.25 × 40,000 = $50,000	$1,000 × 40,000 = $40,000,000

Project B

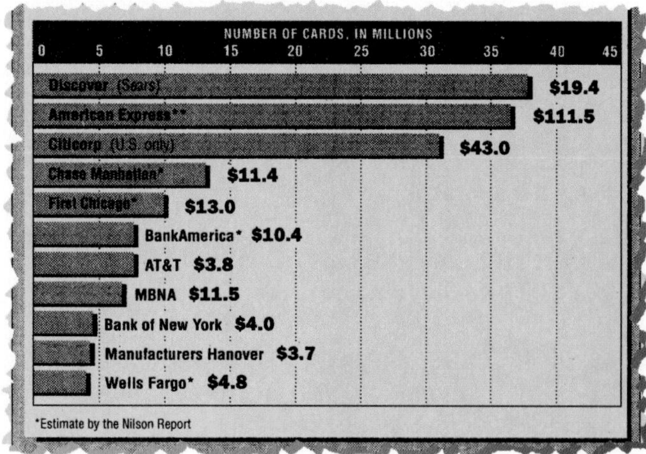

A. What is the total number of credit cards that have been issued?

19.4
111.5
43.0
11.4
13.0
10.4
3.8
11.5
4.0
3.7
4.8
236.5 million

B. How many more cards has American Express issued versus Citicorp?

111.5
− 43.0
68.5 million

CUMULATIVE REVIEW: A WORD PROBLEM APPROACH—CHAPTERS 1, 2, 3

Solutions are at end of text in Appendix II.

Quick Reference
If you get any wrong answers, study the page numbers given for each problem.

1. The top rate at the Waldorf Towers Hotel in New York is \$370. The top rate at the Ritz Carlton in Boston is \$335. If John spends 7 days at the hotel, how much can he save if he stays at the Ritz?

1. Pp. 10, 13.

$$\begin{array}{r} \$370 \\ -\ 335 \\ \hline \$\ 35 \end{array} \times 7 = \$245$$

2. Robert Half Placement Agency was rated best by 4 to 1 in an independent national survey. If 250,000 responded to the survey, how many rated Robert Half the best?

2. P. 45.

$\frac{4}{5} \times 250{,}000 = 200{,}000$

3. Of the 63.2 million people who watch professional football, only $\frac{1}{5}$ watch the commercials. How many viewers do not watch the commercials?

3. P. 45.

$\frac{4}{5} \times 63{,}200{,}000 = 50{,}560{,}000$

4. AT&T advertised a 10-minute call for \$2.27. MCI's rate was \$2.02. Assuming Bill Splat makes forty 10-minute calls, how much could he save by using MCI?

4. P. 70.

$$\begin{array}{r} \$2.27 \\ -\ 2.02 \\ \hline \$\ .25 \end{array} \times 40 = \$10.00$$

5. A square foot of rental space in New York, Boston, and Rhode Island is as follows: New York, \$6.25; Boston, \$5.75; and Rhode Island, \$3.75. If Compaq Computer wants to rent 112,500 square feet of space, what will Compaq save by renting in Rhode Island rather than Boston?

5. P. 70.

$$\begin{array}{r} \$5.75 \\ -\ 3.75 \\ \hline \$2.00 \end{array} \times 112{,}500 = \$225{,}000 \text{ savings from Boston}$$

6. American Airlines has a frequent-flier program. Coupon brokers who buy and sell these awards pay between 1 and $1\frac{1}{2}$ cents for each mile earned. Fred Dietrich earned a 50,000-mile award (worth two free tickets to any city). If Fred decides to sell his award to a coupon broker, approximately how much would he receive?

6. Pp. 64–70.

If 1 cent: $\$.01 \times 50{,}000 = \$500$

If $1\frac{1}{2}$ cents: $\$.015 \times 50{,}000 = \$750$

7. Lillie Wong bought 4 new Firestone tires at \$82.99 each. Firestone also charged Lillie \$2.80 per tire for mounting, \$1.95 per tire for valves, and \$3.15 per tire for balancing. Lillie turned her 4 old tires in to Firestone, which charged \$1.50 per tire to dispose of them. What was Lillie's final bill?

7. P. 70.

$$\begin{array}{rr} 4 \times \$82.99 = & \$331.96 \\ \$2.80 + \$1.95 + \$3.15 = \$7.90 \times 4 = & 31.60 \\ \hline & \$363.56 + \$6.00 = \$369.56 \end{array}$$

8. Tootsie Roll Industries bought Charms Company for \$65 million. Some analysts believe that in four years the purchase price could rise to 3 times as much. If the analysts are right, how much did Tootsie Roll save by purchasing Charms immediately?

8. Pp. 10, 13.

$$\begin{array}{rr} \$65{,}000{,}000 \times 3 = & \$195{,}000{,}000 \\ & -\ 65{,}000{,}000 \\ \hline & \$130{,}000{,}000 \end{array}$$

9. Today the average business traveler will spend almost \$50 a day on food. The breakdown is dinner, \$22.26; lunch, \$10.73; breakfast, \$6.53; tips, \$6.23; and tax, \$1.98. If Clarence Donato, an executive for Honeywell, spends only $.3\overline{3}$ of the average, what is Clarence's total cost for food for the day? If Clarence wanted to

9. Pp. 67–71.

spend one-third more than the average on the next day, what would be his total cost on the second day? Round to the nearest cent.

$22.26 + $10.73 + $6.53 + $6.23 + $1.98 = $47.73 actual

$\frac{1}{3} \times \$47.73 = \$15.91$

$1\frac{1}{3} \times \$47.73 = \frac{4}{3} \times \$47.73 = \$63.64$

Be sure you use the fractional equivalent in calculating $.3\overline{3}$.

10. Pp. 7, 10.

10. The projected cost to raise a child born in 1980 to age 22 is $214,957 (does not include college costs). Some costs included are food, $69,585; housing, $65,007; transportation, $29,255; and health, $14,973. Assume each cost given is rounded to nearest hundred. What will the total cost be? What is $214,957 rounded all the way?

$69,600 + $65,000 + $29,300 + $15,000 = $178,900
$214,957 = $200,000

What is the exact amount of the other costs not given?

$$\begin{array}{r} \$214{,}957 \\ -\ 178{,}820 \\ \hline \$\ 36{,}137 \end{array}$$

NOTES

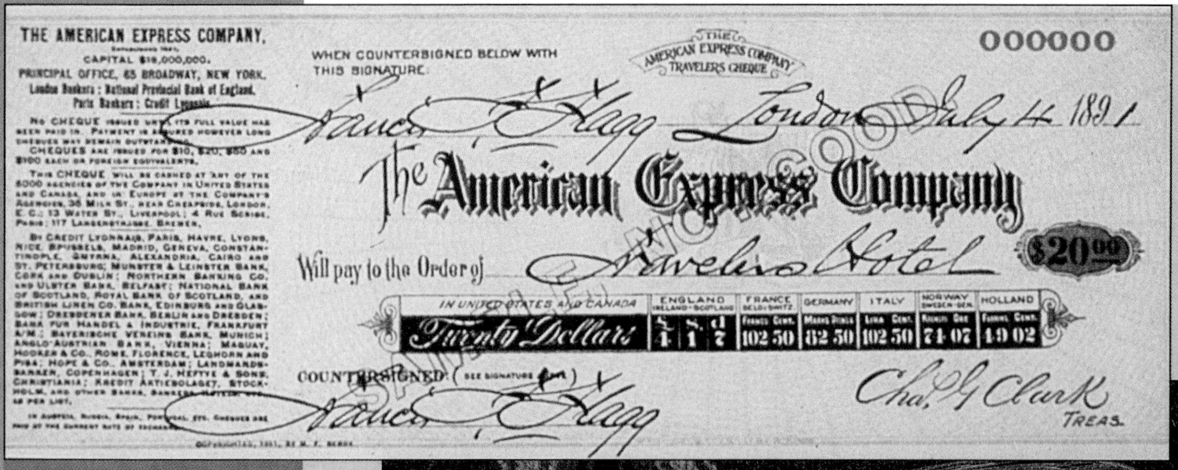

THAT WAS THEN . . .
. . . THIS IS NOW

The original traveler's check was created in 1891 in response to a challenge by the president of American Express to create a piece of paper accepted as money around the world. Today, American Express sells over $22 billion in checks.

4

Banking and Credit Card Transactions; with a Look into Future Trends

LEARNING UNIT OBJECTIVES

LU 4–1: The Checking Account; Credit Card Transactions

1. Define and state the purpose of signature cards, checks, deposit slips, check stubs, and check registers. *pp. 88–89*
2. Compare and contrast blank, full, and restrictive endorsements. *p. 90*
3. Explain how a merchant completes a credit card transaction for manual deposit or electronic deposit. *pp. 90–93*
4. Prepare deposit slips and write checks. *p. 89*
5. Complete a check register. *p. 89*
6. Complete a deposit for a credit card transaction using the merchant batch header slip. *p. 91*

LU 4–2: Bank Statement and Reconciliation Process; Insight into Current Trends

1. Define and state the purpose of the bank statement. *pp. 94–95*
2. List the steps to complete a bank reconciliation. *p. 95*
3. Explain and prepare a bank reconciliation. *pp. 95–97*
4. Dissect and solve a word problem. *pp. 97–98*
5. Explain new and future trends in the banking industry. *pp. 98–100*

Staff Reporter of THE WALL STREET JOURNAL

NEW YORK—Rafael Adorno paid $3.30 recently to cash a paycheck at the E.G.I. Check Cashing storefront in lower Manhattan. Mr. Adorno, a young New York blue-collar worker, explains that he willingly paid the hefty fee because he doesn't have a bank account.

Mr. Adorno isn't an oddity. An estimated 22% of adults don't have a bank account, according to the American Association of Retired Persons. Instead, they rely on costly check-cashing outlets and money orders to manage their finances.

Consumer advocates claim that many of these people would like to have a checking account but lack the minimum sum required to open an account or else can't maintain the necessary minimum balances.

Free checking for low-balance cus-

You may think that most adults have checking accounts. However, the above *Wall Street Journal* clipping states that an estimated 22 out of 100 adults do not have checking accounts. The reason given is that many of these adults do not have the minimum sum banks require to open an account. In New York, for example, many banks require a $3,000 minimum balance to have a checking account.

This chapter looks at the checking account and how merchants deposit credit card transactions at their bank. Then you will learn about the mechanics of verifying your checkbook balance. Be sure to read the section on future trends to see what the future may hold for you when you do your banking.

LEARNING UNIT 4–1 THE CHECKING ACCOUNT; CREDIT CARD TRANSACTIONS

Most small businesses depend on the checking account for efficient record keeping. In this chapter, you will follow the checking account procedures of a newly organized small business.

Elements of the Checking Account

Check Stub
It should be completed before the check is written.

No. 12 $ 75 35/100
December 15 19 94
To Avon Corporation
For Equipment

	DOLLARS	CENTS
BALANCE	7,100	00
AMT. DEPOSITED		
TOTAL	7,100	00
AMT. THIS CHECK	75	35
BALANCE FORWARD	7,024	65

Gayle Jensen, treasurer of Lantz Company, went to the Fleet Bank to open a business checking account. The bank manager gave Gayle a **signature card** to complete. The signature card contained space for the company's name and address, references, type of account, and the signature(s) of the person(s) authorized to sign **checks.** If necessary, the bank will use the signature card to verify that Gayle signed the checks. Some companies authorize more than one person to sign checks or require more than one signature on a check.

Gayle completed a deposit slip, which indicated the amount she was depositing in her company's business account. The bank gave Gayle a temporary checkbook to use until the company's printed checks arrived. Gayle also will receive *preprinted* checking account **deposit slips** like the one shown in Figure 4–1. Since deposit slips are in duplicate, Gayle can keep a record of her deposit.

Writing business checks is similar to writing personal checks. Before writing any checks, however, you must understand the structure of a check and know how to write a check. Carefully study Figure 4–2. Note that the verbal amount written in the check should match the figure amount. If these two amounts are different, by law the bank uses the verbal amount. Also note the bank imprint on the bottom right section of the check. When processing the check, the bank imprints the check's amount. This makes it easy to detect bank errors.

Once the check is written, the writer must keep a record of the check. Business checkbooks usually include attached **check stubs** to keep track of written checks. The sample check stub in the margin shows the information that the check writer will want to record. Some companies use a **check register** to keep their check records instead of check stubs. Figure 4–3 shows a check register.

FIGURE 4–1 Deposit Slip

Preprinted numbers in magnetic ink identify bank number, routing and sorting of the check, and Lantz account number.

Fleet Bank
Checking Deposit
TO THE ACCOUNT OF
DATE 2/20/94
NAME
(PLEASE PRINT)
PLEASE ENDORSE ALL CHECKS
PLEASE ENTER CLEARLY YOUR ACCOUNT NUMBER 150460

Lantz Company
80 Garfield Street
Boston, MA 01152

This deposit is subject to: proof and verification, the Uniform Commercial Code, the collection and availability policy of this bank.

DESCRIPTION	DOLLARS	CENTS
BILLS	410	XX
COIN		
1. 18-22	130	40
2. 19-61	150	66
3.		
4.		
5.		
6.		
SUB TOTAL ITEMS 1-6	691	06

ADDITIONAL CHECKS DESCRIPTION	DOLLARS	CENTS
7.		
8.		
9.		
10.		
11.		
12.		
13.		
14.		
SUB TOTAL ITEMS 7-14		
TOTAL	691	06

⑆011000138⑆ 15 046 0

The 18-22 is taken from the upper right corner of the check from the top part of the fraction. This number is known as the American Bankers Association transit number. The 18 identifies the city or state where the bank is located and the 22 identifies the bank.

FIGURE 4–2 The Structure of a Check

Date check written

Preprinted check number

To whom check is payable or **payee**

Verbal form of amount of check. Note spacing and use of "and" to represent the decimal.

Bank ordered to pay is **drawee**

Lantz Company
80 Garfield Street
Boston, MA 01152

No. 12

December 15 19 94

5-13/110

PAY TO THE ORDER OF Avon Corporation $ 75 35/100

Seventy-five and 35/100 DOLLARS

Fleet Bank
FLEET BANK OF MASSACHUSETTS, NATIONAL ASSOCIATION
BOSTON, MASSACHUSETTS

Gayle Jensen

⑆011000138⑆ 15 046 0 12 0000007535

Code number to identify bank

Amount of check

Signature–this is the same as on the signature card

One who writes check is called the **drawer**

Bank number printed with magnetic ink for computer processing matches printed number at upper right-hand corner of check above amount of check

Lantz Company's account number

Preprinted check number

When bank processes check, the 75.35 is imprinted here. Note that this should match what is written for amount of check.

FIGURE 4–3
Check Register

RECORD ALL CHARGES OR CREDITS THAT AFFECT YOUR ACCOUNT

NUMBER	DATE	DESCRIPTION OF TRANSACTION	PAYMENT/DEBT (–)		√ T	FEE (IF ANY) (–)	DEPOSIT/CREDIT (+)		BALANCE	
									$ 391	68
	1994		$			$	$			
190	4/12	Ranger Co.	55	91					335	77
191	4/17	Longin Co.	39	66					296	11
	4/18	Deposit					412	18	708	29
192	4/22	Flint Utilities	79	33					628	96

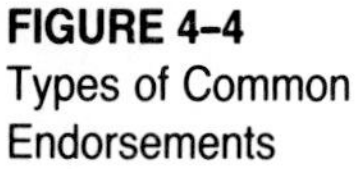

FIGURE 4–4
Types of Common Endorsements

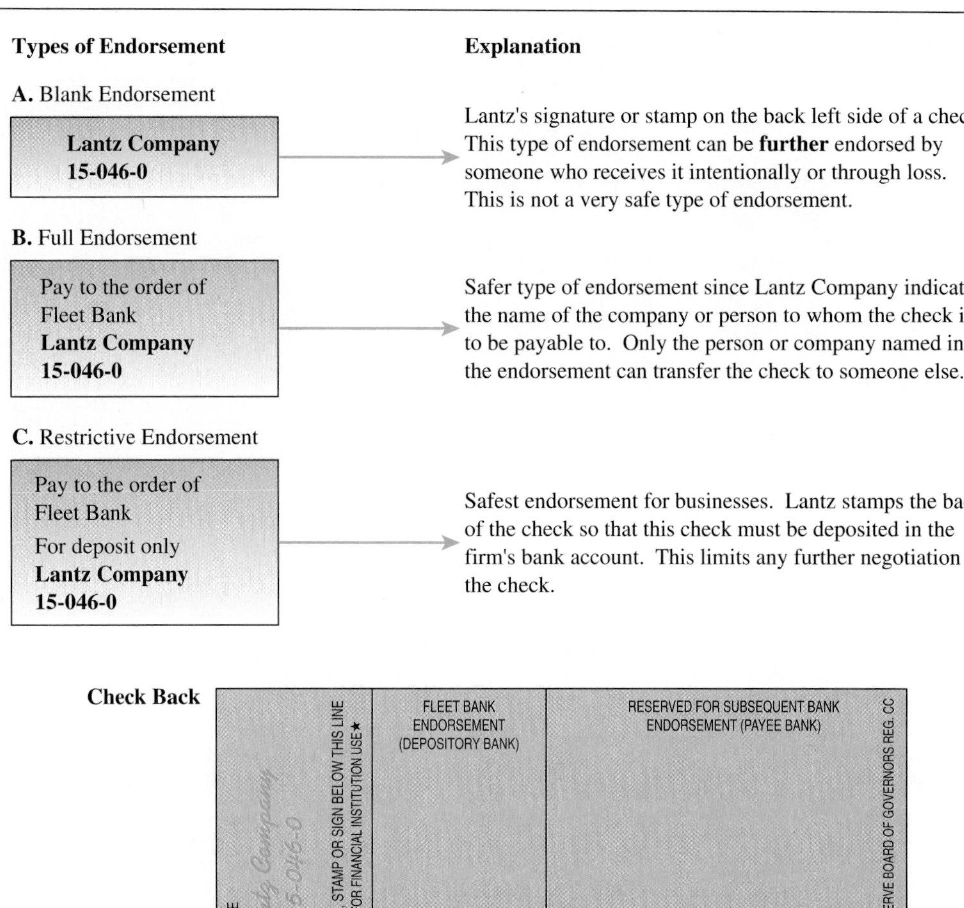

Lantz Company has had a busy week, and Gayle must deposit its checks in the company's checking account. However, before she can do this, Gayle must endorse the back left-hand side of the checks. Figure 4–4, above, explains the three types of check **endorsements: blank endorsement, full endorsement,** and **restrictive endorsement.** These endorsements transfer Lantz's ownership to the bank who collects the money from the person or company that issued the check. Federal Reserve regulation limits all endorsements to the top $1\frac{1}{2}$ inches of the trailing edge on the back side (Figure 4–4)

A credit to Lantz's account means the bank is increasing the account.

After the bank receives Gayle's deposit slip, shown in Figure 4–1, it increases (or credits) Lantz's account $691.06. Often Gayle leaves the deposit in a locked bag in a night depository. The bank credits (increases) Gayle's account when it processes the deposit on the next working day.

Gayle's company handles many credit card transactions. Let's see how Lantz records these transactions.

Depositing Credit Card Transactions

On November 1, 1994, Lantz Company will begin using MasterCard and Visa. This should increase its sales and will avoid the necessity of collecting past-due accounts.

Fleet Bank has given Lantz two options for depositing **credit card** transactions: Option 1, manual deposits; Option 2, electronic deposits. Let's study these options.

Option 1: Manual Deposits of Credit Card Transactions

When Lantz makes a charge sale with the **manual deposit** option, the salesperson fills out the MasterCard or Visa charge slip, Figure 4–5 which contains the specific details of the sale. Figure 4–5 shows a charge slip used by another company.

FIGURE 4–5
Charge Slip

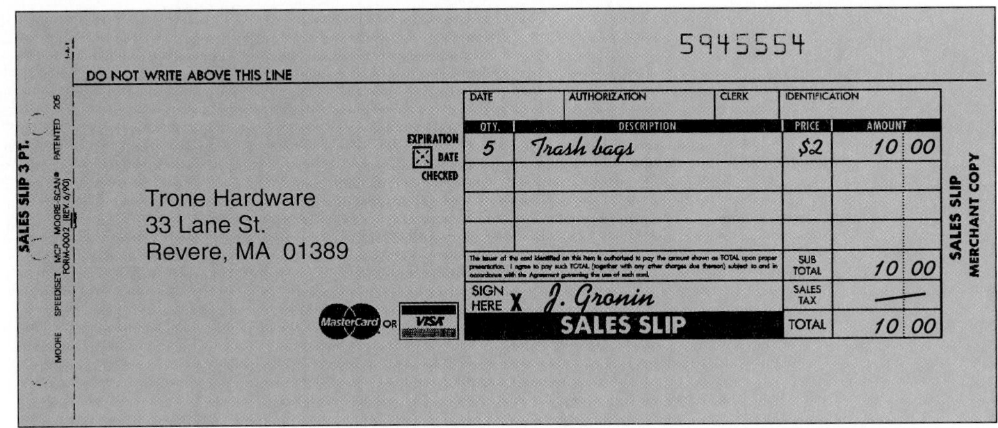

5945554

DO NOT WRITE ABOVE THIS LINE

DATE	AUTHORIZATION	CLERK	IDENTIFICATION

QTY.	DESCRIPTION	PRICE	AMOUNT
5	Trash bags	$2	10 00
		SUB TOTAL	10 00
SIGN HERE X J. Gronin		SALES TAX	—
SALES SLIP		TOTAL	10 00

EXPIRATION DATE CHECKED

Trone Hardware
33 Lane St.
Revere, MA 01389

MasterCard OR VISA

SALES SLIP
MERCHANT COPY

FIGURE 4–6
Merchant Batch Header Slip

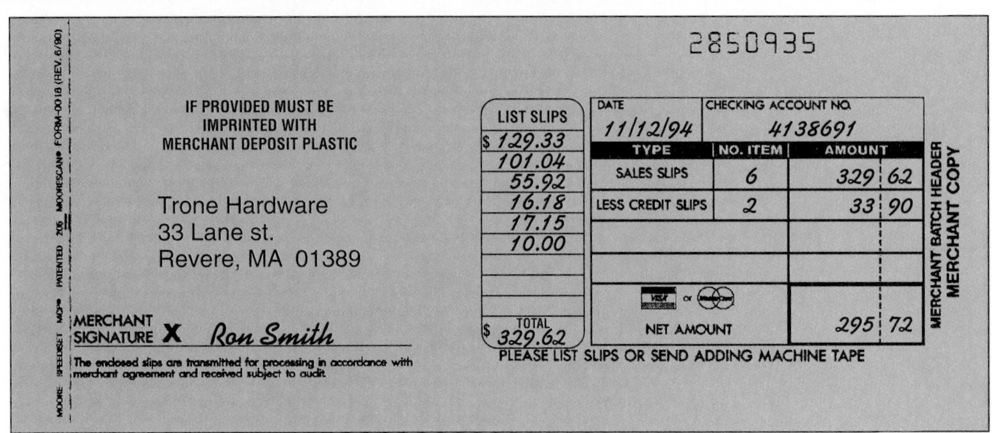

2850935

IF PROVIDED MUST BE IMPRINTED WITH MERCHANT DEPOSIT PLASTIC

Trone Hardware
33 Lane st.
Revere, MA 01389

MERCHANT SIGNATURE X Ron Smith

The enclosed slips are transmitted for processing in accordance with merchant agreement and received subject to audit.

LIST SLIPS
$ 129.33
101.04
55.92
16.18
17.15
10.00
TOTAL $ 329.62

DATE	CHECKING ACCOUNT NO.	
11/12/94	4138691	
TYPE	**NO. ITEM**	**AMOUNT**
SALES SLIPS	6	329 62
LESS CREDIT SLIPS	2	33 90
NET AMOUNT		295 72

PLEASE LIST SLIPS OR SEND ADDING MACHINE TAPE

MERCHANT BATCH HEADER
MERCHANT COPY

At the end of *each business day,* Lantz's bookkeeper completes a **merchant batch header slip** and attaches copies of the charge slips. Figure 4–6 shows a sample batch header slip used by another company. Note that the list of slips could be listed on the form, or an adding machine tape could be provided with the batch header slip. Also note that the total of all slips is shown less credit slips. The difference between the total sales less credit amount is called the **net deposit** (net amount). At the *end of statement period,* Fleet charges $3\frac{1}{4}\%$ (this means $3\frac{1}{4}$ cents per dollar) of the net deposit and subtracts this from Lantz's account.

Option 2: Electronic Deposits of Credit Card Transactions

Superstock, Inc.

Many retail stores use **electronic deposits.** Do you use a MasterCard or Visa credit card? If you do, have you watched the salesperson run your card through an authorizational terminal after you have made a purchase? The terminal not only approves (or disapproves) an amount but also immediately adds the amount to Lantz's balance. When a credit is given to the customer's charge card, this amount is subtracted from Lantz's balance.

Each day Fleet Bank sends Lantz a statement listing its MasterCard and Visa transactions. The bank charges Lantz $2\frac{1}{2}\%$ ($2\frac{1}{2}$ cents per dollar) since it wants to encourage the use of electronic deposits. The statement Lantz receives is similar to the following statement (on p. 92) for another company. When we work with percents in Chapter 6, you will see how to calculate the amount Lantz pays for using MasterCard and Visa. For now, focus on calculating net deposits.

DEPOSIT DETAILS:	CARDHOLDER	DATE	TRAN	AMOUNT	CST-TIME	CODE
	361060558	11/14/94	SALE	15.00	11:55:36	431011
	336808479		SALE	28.60	12:08:30	673011
	633615209		SALE	11.28	12:34:31	934440
	484383		SALE	7.77	14:03:38	482360
	611445		SALE	17.57	14:12:48	371224
	343103551		SALE	24.15	15:13:50	694492
	000115629		SALE	14.74	15:16:33	378823
	380057254		SALE	16.38	15:33:18	213011
	288121723		SALE	23.08	16:21:29	682011
	503999		SALE	9.96	16:27:41	714593
	309021229		SALE	38.82	16:32:29	891816
	005291394		SALE	19.93	16:42:43	731020
	387076		SALE	15.62	16:51:09	700644
	199011544		SALE	21.00	19:39:08	001640

	----- SALES -----		----- RETURNS -----		NET DEPOSIT
	14	263.90	0	.00	263.90
MASTERCARD	7	147.90	0	.00	147.90
VISA	7	116.00	0	.00	116.00

EXAMPLE From the following credit card sales and returns, calculate the net deposit for the day.

Credit card sales: $42.33, $16.88, $19.39, $47.66, $39.18.

Returns: $18.01, $13.04.

Solution:	Total credit card sales	$165.44
	Less returns	− 31.05
	Net deposit	$134.39

LU 4-1 PRACTICE QUIZ

1. Complete the following check and check stub for Jones Company. Note the $8,100.80 balance brought forward on check stub No. 113. You must make a $550.50 deposit on May 3. Sign the check for Roland Small.

Date	Check no.	Amount	Payable to	For
May 4, 1992	113	$94.75	Jill Corporation	Advertising

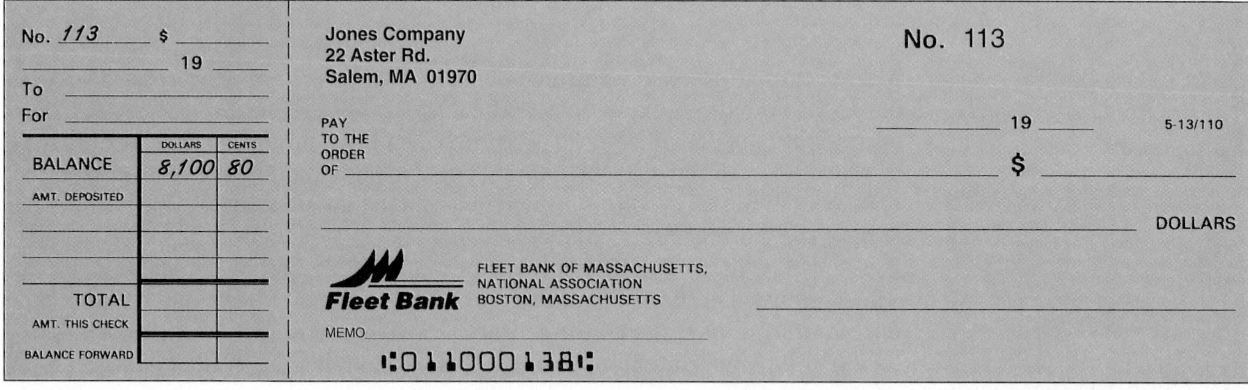

No. 113 $
19
To
For

	DOLLARS	CENTS
BALANCE	8,100	80
AMT. DEPOSITED		
TOTAL		
AMT. THIS CHECK		
BALANCE FORWARD		

Jones Company
22 Aster Rd.
Salem, MA 01970

No. 113

19 5-13/110

PAY TO THE ORDER OF $

DOLLARS

FLEET BANK OF MASSACHUSETTS, NATIONAL ASSOCIATION BOSTON, MASSACHUSETTS
Fleet Bank

MEMO

⑆011000138⑆

2. From the following information, complete Moore Company's merchant batch header slip for July 18, 1994. Sign the slip for John Moore, whose account number is 0139684.

Credit card sales	Credit card returns
$113.88	$13.01
22.55	12.15
66.10	
44.18	

MOORE SPEEDISET MC® PATENTED 705 MOORESCAN® FORM-0018 (REV. 6/90)

2850935

IF PROVIDED MUST BE IMPRINTED WITH MERCHANT DEPOSIT PLASTIC

Moore Co.
1817 Ridge Rd.
Homewood, IL 60430

MERCHANT SIGNATURE X

The enclosed slips are transmitted for processing in accordance with merchant agreement and received subject to audit.

LIST SLIPS
$
TOTAL $

DATE	CHECKING ACCOUNT NO.	
TYPE	NO. ITEM	AMOUNT
SALES SLIPS		
LESS CREDIT SLIPS		
VISA or MasterCard NET AMOUNT		

PLEASE LIST SLIPS OR SEND ADDING MACHINE TAPE

MERCHANT BATCH HEADER
MERCHANT COPY

SOLUTIONS TO LU 4–1 PRACTICE QUIZ

1.

No. 113 $ 94 75/100
May 4 19 92
To Jill Corp.
For Advertising

	DOLLARS	CENTS
BALANCE	8,100	80
AMT. DEPOSITED	550	50
TOTAL	8,651	30
AMT. THIS CHECK	94	75
BALANCE FORWARD	8,556	55

Jones Company
22 Aster Rd.
Salem, MA 01970

No. 113

May 4 19 92 5-13/110

PAY TO THE ORDER OF Jill Corporation $ 94 75/100

Ninety - four and 75/100 DOLLARS

Fleet Bank — FLEET BANK OF MASSACHUSETTS, NATIONAL ASSOCIATION BOSTON, MASSACHUSETTS

Roland Small

MEMO Advertising

⑆011000138⑆ 14 0380 113

2.

MOORE SPEEDISET MC® PATENTED 705 MOORESCAN® FORM-0018 (REV. 6/90)

2850935

IF PROVIDED MUST BE IMPRINTED WITH MERCHANT DEPOSIT PLASTIC

Moore Co.
1817 Ridge Rd.
Homewood, IL 60430

MERCHANT SIGNATURE X John Moore

The enclosed slips are transmitted for processing in accordance with merchant agreement and received subject to audit.

LIST SLIPS
$ 113.88
22.55
66.10
44.18
TOTAL $ 246.71

DATE 7/18/94	CHECKING ACCOUNT NO. 0139684	
TYPE	NO. ITEM	AMOUNT
SALES SLIPS	4	246 71
LESS CREDIT SLIPS	2	25 16
VISA or MasterCard NET AMOUNT		221 55

PLEASE LIST SLIPS OR SEND ADDING MACHINE TAPE

MERCHANT BATCH HEADER
MERCHANT COPY

LEARNING UNIT 4–2 BANK STATEMENT AND RECONCILIATION PROCESS; INSIGHT INTO CURRENT TRENDS

In a *Wall Street Journal* survey, only half of the adults surveyed said they balanced their checkbook every month. Almost one fourth said they never balanced their checkbook. This survey result is disappointing. Banks can make mistakes. By balancing your checkbook every month, you also catch your mistakes.

In this unit, Lantz Company reconciles its checkbook balance with the balance reported on its bank statement. You would use the same procedure in reconciling your personal checking account.

Bank Statement

As you will see, timing is an important cause of differences between bank and checkbook balances.

Each month Fleet Bank sends Lantz Company a **bank statement** (Figure 4–7). The statement gives different types of information. We are interested in the following:

1. The beginning bank balance.
2. The total of all the account increases. Each time the bank increases the account amount, it *credits* the account.

FIGURE 4–7
Bank Statement

Fleet Bank
Account
Number 150460

Lantz Company
80 Garfield St.
Boston, MA 01152

9/30/94 thru 10/29/94

DATE	Debits: CHECKS • WITHDRAWALS • PAYMENTS			Credits: DEPOSITS • INTEREST • ADVANCES	BALANCE
10/1	DM 10.00				16,250.00
10/2	DM 26.00				16,224.00
10/3	360.00				15,864.00
10/4	1,440.00	2,400.00			12,024.00
10/5				2,880.00	14,904.00
10/8	300.00	450.00			14,154.00
10/25				3,960.00	18,114.00
10/28	810.00			1,200.00	18,504.00
10/29	DM 204.00			CM 600.00	18,900.00
10/29				CM 15.18	18,915.18

Account Summary

	Beginning balance		$16,260.00
	Total credits/deposits		8,040.00
	Total debits/checks		5,760.00
Other debits	Bank charge	$ 10.00	
	NSF check	204.00	
	ATM withdrawal	26.00	240.00
Other credits	Interest credited	$ 15.18	
	Note collected	600.00	615.18
	Ending balance		$18,915.18

DM—Deductions
CM—Additions

3. The total of all the account decreases. Each time the bank decreases the account amount, it *debits* the account.
4. Final ending balance.

Due to differences in timing, the bank balance on the statement often doesn't match the customer's checkbook balance. To reconcile the difference between the amount on the bank statement and in the checkbook, the customer should complete a **bank reconciliation.** The following steps explain how this is done.

Steps for Reconciling a Bank Statement

Step 1. Identify outstanding checks (checks written but not yet processed by the bank).

Step 2. Identify deposits in transit (deposits made but not yet processed by the bank).

Step 3. Analyze bank statement for transactions not recorded in check stubs or check register.

Step 4. Check for recording errors, checks written, or deposits made.

Lantz keeps a record of its checks and deposits in a check register (Figure 4–8). By looking at Lantz's check register, you can see how to complete Steps 1 and 2. The explanation that follows for the four bank statement reconciliation steps will help you understand the procedure.

Step 1: Identify Outstanding Checks

Checks that Lantz has written but Fleet has not yet recorded for payment when it sends out the bank statement are called **outstanding checks.** Lantz's bookkeeper identifies checks No. 115 for $175 and No. 117 for $675 as outstanding by comparing the company's check register to the bank statement.

FIGURE 4–8
Lantz Company Check Register

RECORD ALL CHARGES OR CREDITS THAT AFFECT YOUR ACCOUNT

NUMBER	DATE	DESCRIPTION OF TRANSACTION	PAYMENT/DEBT (−)	√ T	FEE (IF ANY) (−)	DEPOSIT/CREDIT (+)	BALANCE
							$ 16,286 00
	1994		$		$	$	
114	9/30	French Co.	26 00				16,260 00
115	10/1	Lowe Co.	175 00				16,085 00
116	10/2	Able Co.	360 00				15,725 00
117	10/2	Ajax Co.	675 00				15,050 00
118	10/3	Blue Co.	1,440 00				13,610 00
119	10/4	Easter Co.	2,400 00				11,210 00
	10/4					2,880 00	14,090 00
120	10/7	Long Co.	300 00				13,790 00
121	10/7	Utah Co.	450 00				13,340 00
	10/24					3,960 00	17,300 00
	10/27					1,200 00	18,500 00
122	10/28	Last Co.	810 00				17,690 00
	10/29					1,000 00	18,690 00

REMEMBER TO RECORD AUTOMATIC PAYMENTS / DEPOSITS ON DATE AUTHORIZED

Step 2: Identify Deposits in Transit

A deposit that did not reach Fleet Bank by the time the bank prepared the bank statement is called a **deposit in transit.** The October 29 deposit of $1,000 did not reach Fleet Bank by the bank statement date. This can be seen by comparing the company's check register to the bank statement.

Step 3: Analyze Bank Statement for Transactions Not Recorded in Check Stubs or Check Register

The bank statement shown in Figure 4–7, page 94, gives "other debits" that Lantz was not aware of until the company reviewed the bank statement. When a bank debits Lantz's account, the account balance is reduced. Banks inform customers of a debit transaction by a **debit memo (DM).** The following items will result in debits to Lantz's account.

1. *Bank charge:* $10. — The bank charged $10 for printing the checks.

2. *NSF check:* $204. — One of Lantz's customers wrote Lantz a check for $204. Lantz deposited the check, but the check bounced for **nonsufficient funds (NSF).** Thus, Lantz has $204 less than it figured. (Today, banks charge $15 to $20 for NSF checks.)

3. *ATM withdrawal:* $26. — Lantz withdrew $26 from an automatic teller machine but forgot to update its checkbook for this withdrawal.

The bank statement contained two "other credits" that increased Lantz's account. These are the result of a **credit memo (CM).**

4. *Interest credited:* $15.18. — Since Lantz has a checking account that pays interest, the account has earned $15.18.

5. *Note collected:* $600.00. — As a service to Lantz, the bank acted as a collection agent and received $600 from one of Lantz's customers. Lantz did not know the bank collected this note until it received the bank statement.

Step 4: Check for Recording Errors, Checks Written, or Deposits Made

If Lantz's bookkeeper had recorded a check for the wrong amount, the checkbook balance would have to be adjusted. For example, if a $30 check was recorded for $10, the checkbook balance would have to be reduced $20. Also, the bookkeeper could have neglected to record a written check or a deposit. These errors would be caught in the reconciliation process.

Now we can complete the bank reconciliation on the back side of the bank statement as shown in Figure 4–9. This form usually is on the back of a bank statement. If necessary, however, the person reconciling the bank statement can construct this form as shown in Figure 4–10.

Next, let's try your skill at dissecting and solving a word problem.

How to Dissect and Solve a Word Problem

The Word Problem On December 31, Bill's Roast Beef had a $5,790.40 checkbook balance. Bill's bank statement showed a $5,981.50 balance. Outstanding checks were No. 101 for $290 and No. 104 for $160. A $221 deposit was in transit. The bank statement showed a NSF check of $40 along with a service charge of $10. For the month, the checking account earned interest of $12.10. Prepare a bank reconciliation.

FIGURE 4–9
Reconciliation Process

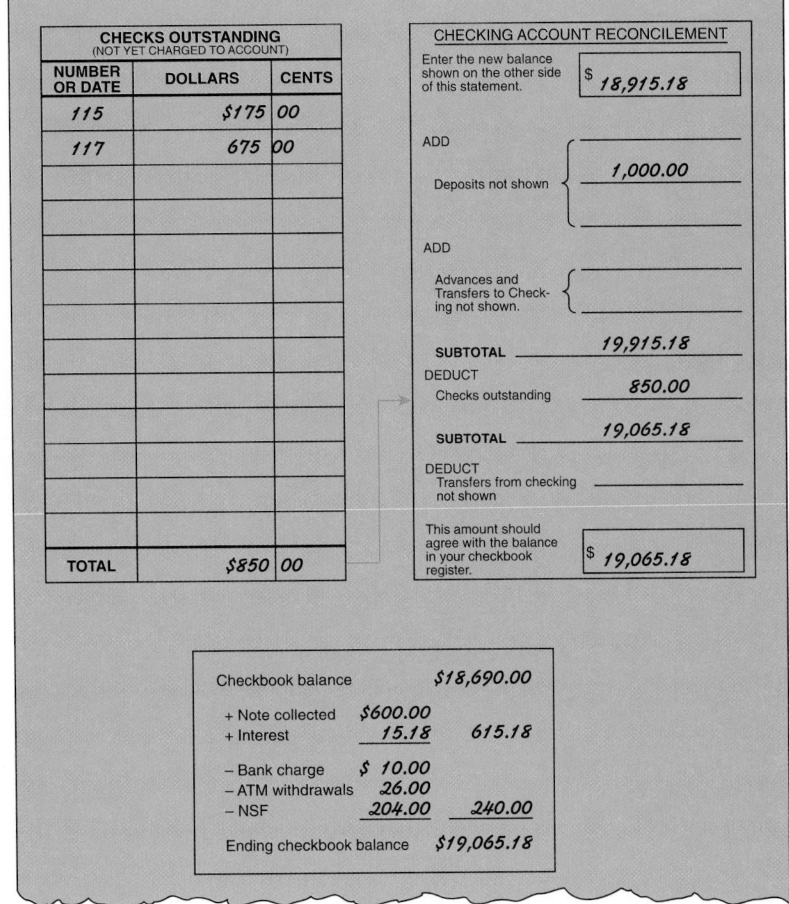

CHECKS OUTSTANDING (NOT YET CHARGED TO ACCOUNT)		
NUMBER OR DATE	DOLLARS	CENTS
115	$175	00
117	675	00
TOTAL	$850	00

CHECKING ACCOUNT RECONCILEMENT

Enter the new balance shown on the other side of this statement. $ 18,915.18

ADD
Deposits not shown 1,000.00

ADD
Advances and Transfers to Checking not shown.

SUBTOTAL 19,915.18

DEDUCT
Checks outstanding 850.00

SUBTOTAL 19,065.18

DEDUCT
Transfers from checking not shown

This amount should agree with the balance in your checkbook register. $ 19,065.18

Checkbook balance		$18,690.00
+ Note collected	$600.00	
+ Interest	15.18	615.18
– Bank charge	$ 10.00	
– ATM withdrawals	26.00	
– NSF	204.00	240.00
Ending checkbook balance		$19,065.18

FIGURE 4–10 Bank Reconciliation

LANTZ COMPANY
Bank Reconciliation as of October 31, 1994

Checkbook Balance			**Bank Balance**		
Lantz checkbook balance		$18,690.00	Bank balance		$18,915.18
Add:			Add:		
Collection of note	$600.00		Deposits in transit 10/29		1,000.00
Interest	15.18	615.18			$19,915.18
		$19,305.18			
Deduct:			Deduct:		
Check printing	$ 10.00		Outstanding checks:		
NSF check	204.00		No. 115	$175	
ATM withdrawals	26.00	240.00	No. 117	675	850.00
Reconciled balance		$19,065.18	Reconciled balance		$19,065.18

Blueprint Aid for Dissecting and Solving a Word Problem

A. Gather the facts	B. What am I solving for?	C. What must I know or calculate before solving problem?	D. Key points to remember
Checkbook balance: $5,790.40. *Bank balance:* $5,981.50. *Checks outstanding:* No. 101, $290.00; No. 104, $160.00. *Deposit in transit:* $221.00 *NSF:* $40.00. *Service charge:* $10.00 *Interest earned:* $12.10.	Reconciled balance.	Beginning bank balance + Total deposits in transit − Total checks outstanding = Ending bank balance. Beginning checkbook balance + Total CMs − Total DMs = Ending checkbook balance.	*Bank:* + Deposits in transit − Checks outstanding *Checkbook:* + Interest (CM) − NSF (DM) − SC (DM) DM—deducts from balance. CM—add to balance.

Steps to Solving Problem

1. Calculate ending bank balance.

    $5,981.50
    \+ 221.00 (deposit in transit)
    − 450.00 (total outstanding checks)
    = $5,752.50

2. Calculate ending checkbook balance.

    $5,790.40
    − 50.00 (NSF and service charge)
    \+ 12.10 (interest earned)
    = $5,752.50

Insight into Current Trends

Did you see in the chapter opener that now more than one person's name can be on an American Express Travelers' Cheque?

Software Makes Paying Your Bills Less of a Chore

WHAT if you could use your personal computer to pay bills electronically, doing away with stamps, checks and envelopes—without switching banks or paying through the nose?

For years, that's been one of the unrealized promises made by boosters of personal computers. Now, it's finally possible.

Anybody with a Macintosh or IBM-compatible computer and a modem can pay his or her bills electronically to just about any company or individual from nearly any bank—using relatively inexpensive and simple software. I've been doing it for about a year, and it has saved me immense time and hassle at little or no added cost.

There are two simple ways to do it. You can use a payment system run by Checkfree, Westerville, Ohio. Or you can join Prodigy, an on-line service that offers a national bill-paying system called BillPay USA. Of the two products, Checkfree has the edge, in my view, for someone

You have probably heard about the many tasks that the computers of the future will perform. The day has come for one of these tasks. The above *Wall Street Journal* clipping says that now you can pay your bills electronically. This means you do not have to look for a stamp, write a check, or save the envelope included with your bill.

You only have to turn on your computer and let your fingers go to work. Since more than 57 million checks are written daily, this new software will give people more hours to enjoy life.

Electronic Funds Transfer (EFT): Heart of ATM Technology

Citibank Japanese Unit Unveils New Cash Card

By a WALL STREET JOURNAL Staff Reporter

NEW YORK—Citibank Japan said it introduced Japan's first international cash card, which allows yen withdrawals from automatic teller machines in Japan and dollar withdrawals in the U.S.

The card is limited to Japanese residents who are holders of Citibank yen savings and checking accounts in Japan. The new arrangement is part of Citibank's effort to compete with credit cards or some bankcards that are part of an international ATM network.

A spokeswoman here for the Citicorp

Most people are familiar with the **ATM (automatic teller machine).** We see them in the supermarkets, the shopping malls, the airport, and almost everyplace where people will find ATMs convenient. Now, as stated in the above clipping from *The Wall Street Journal,* Japanese Citibank customers can withdraw U.S. dollars using ATMs.

The ATM allows customers the convenience of transferring, depositing, or withdrawing funds. New technology also allows ATMs to cash checks immediately. These machines allow you to cash a check instantly or deposit a portion of the check to your account.

ATMs were introduced in 1969. Today, we have more the 90,000 ATMs in the United States. Special telephone lines can immediately transmit data about your financial transaction to your financial institution, whether your bank is around the corner or across the country.

Now, let's return to the Lantz Company and see how it makes use of transferring funds electronically.

Lantz is planning to offer its employees the option of depositing their checks directly into each employee's checking account. This is accomplished through the **electronic funds transfer (EFT)**—a computerized operation that electronically transfers funds among parties without the use of paper checks. ATM technology is possible because of EFT, which is the heart of ATM.

Safekeeping

More than 57 million checks are written daily in the United States. The bank's cost to process and mail canceled checks to customers with their bank statements is substantial. Thus, many banks no longer return a customer's canceled checks. Instead, banks use a *safekeeping* procedure.

With the **safekeeping** procedure, the banks hold a customer's checks for a period of time (usually 90 days). Then the bank keeps microfilm copies of the checks for at least one year and sometimes as long as seven years. If a customer needs a check, the bank will return the check or a photocopy for a small fee. Some banks provide a picture of the canceled checks on one sheet of paper displayed in numerical order. The charge for this service is 25 cents monthly.

Point-of-Sale Terminals

Customers will be making more use of ATM cards at **point-of-sale** terminals. In the future, grocery stores, gas stations, fast-food restaurants, and so on, will accept ATM cards. Funds from the purchaser's account will be immediately deducted and transferred to the seller's account.

These ATM cards are **debit cards** that immediately deduct the amount spent from the customer's bank balance. They are different from the traditional credit card in which the customer pays the charges later. ATMs now issue rail passes in Portland, Oregon; gift certificates in Tacoma, Washington; postage stamps in Pittsburgh, Pennsylvania; and grocery coupons in the Midwest.

Now try the Practice Quiz to check your understanding of this unit.

LU 4–2 PRACTICE QUIZ

Moven Company's bank statement from Jass State Bank shows a bank balance of $10,880. Moven's check stubs showed an $8,420 ending checkbook balance. The bookkeeper of Moven noticed that checks No. 114 for $920 and No. 151 for $2,160 were not yet processed by the bank. Moven had made a deposit of $1,760 that had not reached the bank before the preparation of the bank statement. Bank service charges totaled $35. The statement showed that the bank collected a note for Moven for $1,200, charging a $20 collection fee. Moven's bookkeeper noticed that a check for $10 was recorded as $5. Prepare a bank reconciliation as of May 31, 1994.

SOLUTIONS TO LU 4–2 PRACTICE QUIZ

Blueprint Aid for Dissecting and Solving a Word Problem

A. Gather the facts	B. What am I solving for?	C. What must I know or calculate before solving problem?	D. Key points to remember
Bank balance: $10,880. *Checkbook balance:* $8,420. *Checks outstanding:* No. 114, $920; No. 151, $2,160. *Deposit in transit:* $1,760. *Service charge:* $35. *Note:* $1,200 less $20 collection fee. Check for $10 recorded as $5.	Reconciled balance.	Beginning bank balance + Total deposits in transit − Total checks outstanding = Ending bank balance. Beginning checkbook balance + Total CMs − Total DMs = Ending checkbook balance.	*Bank:* + Deposits in transit − Checks outstanding *Checkbook:* + Interest (CM) − NSF (DM) − SC (DM) DM—deducts from balance. CM—adds to balance.

Steps to Solving Problem

1. Calculate ending bank balance.

	$10,880	
+	1,760	(deposit in transit)
−	3,080	(total outstanding checks)
=	$ 9,560	

2. Calculate ending checkbook balance.

	$ 8,420	
+	1,180	(note less collection fee)
−	40	(service charge and error)
=	$ 9,560	

You should use the following setup for the bank reconciliation of end-of-chapter problems.

MOVEN COMPANY Bank Reconciliation as of May 31, 1994					
Checkbook Balance			**Bank Balance**		
Moven checkbook balance		$8,420	Bank balance		$10,880
Add:			Add:		
Collection of note (less fee)		1,180	Deposits in transit		1,760
		$9,600			$12,640
Deduct:			Deduct:		
Bank service charge	$35		Outstanding checks:		
Book error	5	40	No. 114	$ 920	
			No. 151	2,160	3,080
Reconciled balance		$9,560	Reconciled balance		$ 9,560

Since a $10 check was recorded as $5, we need to lower checkbook balance by another $5 to get back to original check of $10.

CHAPTER ORGANIZER: A REFERENCE GUIDE

Page	Topic	Key point, procedure, formula	Example(s) to illustrate situation
90	Types of endorsements	*Blank:* Not safe; can be further endorsed. *Full:* Only person or company named in endorsement can transfer check to someone else. *Restrictive:* Check must be deposited. Limits any further negotiation of the check.	Jones Co. 21-333-9 Pay to the order of Regan Bank Jones Co. 21-333-9 Pay to the order of Regan Bank. For deposit only. Jones Co. 21-333-9
91	Credit card transactions	*Manual deposit:* Need to calculate net deposit (credit card sales less returns). *Electronic deposit:* Eliminates deposit slips and summary batch header slip.	Calculate net deposit: Credit card sales $55.32 62.81 91.18 Credits − 10.16 − 8.15 $209.31 − 18.31 Net deposit = $191.00
95	Bank reconciliation	**Checkbook** Balance + Notes collected − Service charges − NSF ± Book errors* + Interest earned − ATM withdrawals − Overdrafts + EFT **Bank** Balance + Deposits in transit − Outstanding checks ± Bank errors CM—adds to balance DM—deducts from balance * If a $60 check is recorded as $50, we must decrease checkbook balance by $10.	**Checkbook** Balance $800 − NSF 40 $760 − Service charge 4 $756 **Bank** Balance $ 632 + Deposits in transit 416 $1,048 − Outstanding checks 292 $ 756

Page	Topic	Key point, procedure, formula	Example(s) to illustrate situation
	Key terms	ATM (automatic teller machine), *p. 99* Bank reconciliation, *p. 95* Bank statement, *p. 94* Blank endorsement, *p. 90* Check register, *p. 88* Check stub, *p. 88* Checks, *p. 88* Credit card, *p. 90* Credit memo (CM), *p. 96* Debit card, *p. 100* Debit memo (DM), *p. 96* Deposit in transit, *p. 96* Deposit slip, *p. 89* Drawee, *p. 89* Drawer, *p. 89*	Electronic deposit, *p. 91* Electronic funds transfer (EFT), *p. 99* Endorsements, *p. 90* Full endorsement, *p. 90* Manual deposit, *p. 90* Merchant batch header slip, *p. 91* Net deposit, *p. 91* Nonsufficient funds (NSF), *p. 96* Outstanding checks, *p. 95* Payee, *p. 89* Point of sale, *p. 100* Restrictive endorsement, *p. 90* Safekeeping, *p. 99* Signature card, *p. 88*

END-OF-CHAPTER PROBLEMS

Drill Problems

Additional homework assignments by learning unit are at the end of text in Appendix I (p. I–17). Solutions to odd problems are at the end of text in Appendix II.

4–1. Fill out the check register that follows with this information:

1995			
July 9	Check No. 430	Ryan's Clothing	$ 55.90
12	Check No. 431	Reel Tools	14.18
18	Deposit		410.11
19	Check No. 432	Loe Telephone	66.88
24	Check 433	Alice Decorating	31.84
29	Deposit		113.88

RECORD ALL CHARGES OR CREDITS THAT AFFECT YOUR ACCOUNT

NUMBER	DATE	DESCRIPTION OF TRANSACTION	PAYMENT/DEBT (−)	√ T	FEE (IF ANY) (−)	DEPOSIT/CREDIT (+)	BALANCE
							$ 510 99
	1995		$		$	$	
430	7/9	Ryan's Clothing	55 90				455 09
431	7/12	Reel Tools	14 18				440 91
	7/18	Deposit				410 11	851 02
432	7/19	Loe Telephone	66 88				784 14
433	7/24	Alice Decorating	31 84				752 30
	7/29	Deposit				113 88	866 18

4–2. On November 1, 1995, Moss Company has a $4,810.88 beginning checkbook balance. Record the following transaction(s) for Moss Company by completing the two checks and check stubs provided. Sign check Joe Moore, Treasurer.

a. November 5, 1995, deposited $148.99

b. November 5, check No. 187 payable to Ralph Corporation for supplies—$958.77

c. November 16, check No. 188 payable to Flynn Corporation for equipment—$66.10

No. 187 $ 958.77
November 5 19 95
To Ralph Corp.
For Supplies

	DOLLARS	CENTS
BALANCE	4,810	88
AMT. DEPOSITED	148	99
TOTAL	4,959	87
AMT. THIS CHECK	958	77
BALANCE FORWARD	4,001	10

MOSS COMPANY
2 ROUNDY ROAD
ST. PAUL, MN 55113

No. 187

November 5 19 95 5-13/110

PAY TO THE ORDER OF Ralph Corporation $ 958 77/100

Nine hundred fifty - eight and 77/100 DOLLARS

Fleet Bank — FLEET BANK OF MASSACHUSETTS, NATIONAL ASSOCIATION BOSTON, MASSACHUSETTS

Joe Moore
Treasurer

MEMO Supplies

⑆011000138⑆ 25 11103 187

No. 188 $ 66.10
November 16 19 95
To Flynn Corp.
For Equipment

	DOLLARS	CENTS
BALANCE	4,001	10
AMT. DEPOSITED		
TOTAL	4,001	10
AMT. THIS CHECK	66	10
BALANCE FORWARD	3,935	00

MOSS COMPANY
2 ROUNDY ROAD
ST. PAUL, MN 55113

No. 188

November 16 19 95 5-13/110

PAY TO THE ORDER OF Flynn Corporation $ 66 10/100

Sixty - six and 10/100 DOLLARS

Fleet Bank
FLEET BANK OF MASSACHUSETTS, NATIONAL ASSOCIATION BOSTON, MASSACHUSETTS

Joe Moore
Treasurer

MEMO Equipment

⑆011000138⑆ 25 11103 188

4–3. You are the bookkeeper of Reese Company and must complete a merchant batch header for July 8, 1995, from the following credit card transactions. The company lost the charge slips and doesn't include an adding machine tape. Reese's checking account number is 3158062. The merchant's signature can be left blank.

Credit card sales	Credit card returns
$191.85	$10.18
166.32	15.42
51.10	
66.18	

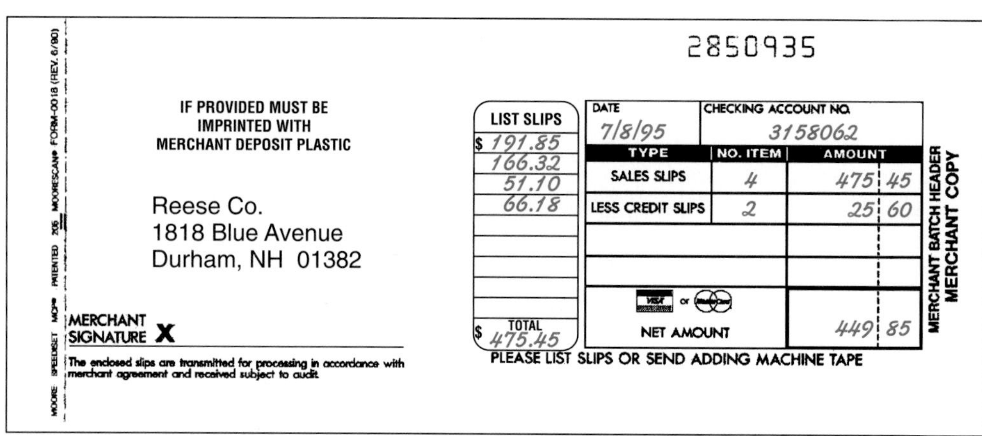
2850935

IF PROVIDED MUST BE IMPRINTED WITH MERCHANT DEPOSIT PLASTIC

Reese Co.
1818 Blue Avenue
Durham, NH 01382

MERCHANT SIGNATURE X

The enclosed slips are transmitted for processing in accordance with merchant agreement and received subject to audit.

MOORE SPEEDISET MOORESCAN FORM-0018 (REV. 6/90)

LIST SLIPS
$ 191.85
166.32
51.10
66.18
TOTAL $ 475.45

DATE	CHECKING ACCOUNT NO.	
7/8/95	3158062	
TYPE	NO. ITEM	AMOUNT
SALES SLIPS	4	475 45
LESS CREDIT SLIPS	2	25 60
VISA or MasterCard NET AMOUNT		449 85

PLEASE LIST SLIPS OR SEND ADDING MACHINE TAPE

MERCHANT BATCH HEADER
MERCHANT COPY

4–4. Using the check register in Problem 4–1 and the following bank statement, prepare a bank reconciliation for Chase Company.

Bank statement date	Checks	Deposits	Balance
7/1 balance			510.99
7/16	55.90		455.09
7/17		410.11	865.20
7/22	31.84		833.36
7/30	10.00 SC		823.36

Chase checkbook balance	$866.18	Bank balance			$823.36
Bank charge	10.00	+ Deposit in transit			113.88
		− Outstanding checks		$14.18	
				66.88	81.06
Ending book balance	$856.18	Ending bank balance			$856.18

Word Problems

4–5. On May 31, Safeway Swings Company showed an $8,000.10 bank statement balance. Safeway's bookkeeper noticed that the bank collected a $2,000 note. A $4,000.45 June 1 deposit was in transit. Outstanding checks for the month were $1,044.91. The bank charged a $44.80 service charge. Could you help Safeway's bookkeeper prepare a reconciliation assuming Safeway has a $9,000.44 checkbook balance?

Safeway checkbook balance	$ 9,000.44	Bank balance	$ 8,000.10
Add:		Add:	
Collection of note	2,000.00	Deposits in transit	4,000.45
Deduct:		Deduct:	
Service charge	44.80	Outstanding checks	1,044.91
Reconciled balance	$10,955.64	Reconciled balance	$10,955.64

4–6. First National Bank sent Joel Samaha his bank statement showing a $1,861.35 balance. Joel's checkbook showed a $1,763.31 balance. A $244.14 check was outstanding. The bank statement showed a $135.60 NSF check and a $10.50 service charge. Reconcile this bank statement for Joel.

Samaha checkbook balance	$1,763.31	Bank balance	$1,861.35
Deduct:		Deduct:	
Service charge	10.50	Outstanding checks	244.14
NSF check	135.60		
Reconciled balance	$1,617.21	Reconciled balance	$1,617.21

4–7. On July 19, 1995, Broom Company had the following MasterCard transactions (along with some returns):

Sales	Returns
$ 33.99	$10.15
142.31	16.41
139.88	

As the bookkeeper of Broom, you need to calculate the total net deposit.

Sales $33.99 + $142.31 + $139.88 = $316.18

− 26.56 ($10.15 + 16.41)

Net deposit = $289.62

4–8. Rent-A-Center Company's checkbook showed a $10,642.10 balance. The company's bank statement showed a $9,740.35 balance. Outstanding checks totaled $2,940.35. A $3,626.80 deposit was in transit. The bank statement showed a $229.00 NSF DM and $13.70 earned checking account interest. Prepare a bank reconciliation.

Rent-A-Center checkbook balance	$10,642.10	Bank balance	$ 9,740.35
Add:		Add:	
Interest	13.70	Deposits in transit	3,626.80
Deduct:		Deduct:	
NSF check	229.00	Outstanding checks	2,940.35
Reconciled balance	$10,426.80	Reconciled balance	$10,426.80

4–9. All Star Travel Company's bank statement showed a $10,256.67 balance. The company's checkbook showed an $11,176.65 balance. The bank did not return check No. 55 for $1,354.80 and check No. 59 for $685.68 with the bank statement. A $2,917.44 deposit was in transit. Monthly check charges were $26.82. The bank statement showed a $16.20 NSF check. Complete the company's bank reconciliation.

All Star checkbook balance	$11,176.65	Bank balance		$10,256.67
Deduct:		Add:		
Check charge	26.82	Deposits in transit		2,917.44
NSF check	16.20	Deduct:		
		Outstanding checks:		
		No. 55	$1,354.80	
		No. 59	685.68	2,040.48
Reconciled balance	$11,133.63	Reconciled balance		$11,133.63

4–10. Moore Company's checkbook showed a $4,170 balance. The bank statement showed a $5,353.50 balance. Check No. 59 for $675 and check No. 68 for $375 were outstanding. The bank statement did not list a $435 deposit. The bank collected a $600.00 note for Moore and charged a $31.50 service charge. Prepare a bank reconciliation.

Moore checkbook balance	$4,170.00	Bank balance		$5,353.50
Add:		Add:		
Collection of note:	600.00	Deposits in transit		435.00
Deduct:		Deduct:		
		Outstanding checks:		
Service charge	31.50	No. 59	$675.00	
		No. 68	375.00	1,050.00
Reconciled balance	$4,738.50	Reconciled balance		$4,738.50

4–11. Roe Company showed a $1,881.54 checkbook balance. The company's bank statement showed a $3,240.00 balance, $21.00 interest earned, and a $14.88 service charge. A $1,279.11 deposit was in transit. Outstanding checks total $1,881.45. In analyzing the bank statement, the bookkeeper noticed the bank collected a $2,100 note. During the month, Roe Company did not deduct a $1,350 check. Prepare a bank reconciliation.

Roe checkbook balance	$1,881.54	Bank balance	$3,240.00
Add:		Add:	
Interest	21.00	Deposits in transit	1,279.11
Collection of note	2,100.00	Deduct:	
Deduct:		Outstanding checks	1,881.45
Service charge	14.88		
Error	1,350.00		
Reconciled balance	$2,637.66	Reconciled balance	$2,637.66

4–12. Park State Bank sent a bank statement to Venice Company showing a $1,404.33 ending balance. The bank statement showed a $16.50 service charge. In the reconciliation process, Venice's bookkeeper noticed a $750.00 deposit in transit and

$520.50 in outstanding checks. Assume a beginning balance of $1,650.33 and complete the reconciliation.

Venice checkbook balance	$1,650.33	Bank balance	$1,404.33
Deduct:		Add:	
Service charge	16.50	Deposits in transit	750.00
		Deduct:	
		Outstanding checks	520.50
Reconciled balance	$1,633.83	Reconciled balance	$1,633.83

4–13. On December 31, Crocker Company had an $8,700.55 checkbook balance. The bank statement showed a $9,400.81 balance. Outstanding checks totaled $1,223.61. A $500 deposit was in transit. The bank statement showed a $22 check charge and $8.80 interest income earned by the company. The bookkeeper forgot to record a $10.15 check. Complete a reconciliation for Crocker.

Crocker checkbook balance	$8,700.55	Bank balance	$9,400.81
Add:		Add:	
Interest	8.80	Deposits in transit	500.00
Deduct:		Deduct:	
Check charges	22.00	Outstanding checks	1,223.61
Error	10.15		
Reconciled balance	$8,677.20	Reconciled balance	$8,677.20

4–14. Skol Company's checkbook had a $9,910.15 balance. The bank statement showed a $9,455.60 balance, $15.00 interest income, and $18.45 check charges. Skol recorded a $120 check as $100. Deposits in transit were $4,132.37. The bank did not return these checks: No. 85, $1,000.10; No. 88, $2,000.45; and No. 92, $700.72. Prepare a bank reconciliation for Skol.

Skol checkbook balance	$9,910.15	Bank balance		$9,455.60
Add:		Add:		
Interest	15.00	Deposits in transit		4,132.37
Deduct:		Deduct:		
		Outstanding checks:		
Check charges	18.45	No. 85	$1,000.10	
Error	20.00	No. 88	2,000.45	
		No. 92	700.72	3,701.27
Reconciled balance	$9,886.70	Reconciled balance		$9,886.70

4–15. On April 1, Jim Company received its bank statement showing a $1,422 balance. The company's checkbook balance showed $1,800. The bank statement showed a $9 service charge and a $90 NSF check. The following checks were outstanding: No. 150, $180; No. 156, $360; and No. 180, $117. A $936 deposit was in transit. Could you complete the bank reconciliation by using the form shown on page 109?

Bank Statement for Problem 4-15

Whenever you have a loan balance you may pay us more than the minimum due shown on the statement or pay us before the due date. If you do this your finance charge for the next month may be smaller.

U County Bank
8 Steel St.
Ron, Virginia

Jim Company
8894 Right Way
Ron, Virginia

AMOUNT ENCLOSED ....

DETACH THIS PART AND PRESENT, OR MAIL, WITH OVERDRAFT PROTECTION PLAN PAYMENT. Address Correction on Reverse Side ☐

CHECKING ACCOUNT

ON	YOUR BALANCE WAS	NO.	WE SUBTRACTED CHECKS TOTALING	LESS SERVICE CHARGE	NO.	WE ADDED DEPOSITS OF	MAKING YOUR PRESENT BALANCE
3/30/94	1,620.00	8	963.00	9.00	5	774.00	1,422.00

OVERDRAFT PROTECTION PLAN						FINANCE CHARGE	CURRENT PAYMENT DUE TO BE AUTOMATICALLY DEDUCTED 15 DAYS AFTER STATEMENT DATE	IF SHOWN "PAY THIS AMT." IT INCLUDES CURRENT AND PAST DUE AMTS.	
PREVIOUS BALANCE	AVERAGE DAILY BALANCE	NO.	PAYMENTS & CREDITS	NO.	LOANS & DEBITS				MAKING YOUR PRESENT LOAN BALANCE

DATE	CHECKS • WITHDRAWALS • PAYMENTS			DEPOSITS • INTEREST • ADVANCES	BALANCE
4/2					1,620.00
4/3	27.00	81.00			1,512.00
4/11	45.00			90.00	1,557.00
4/15	180.00			180.00	1,557.00
4/20	90.00 NSF			90.00	1,557.00
4/24	120.00	240.00		360.00	1,557.00
4/29	180.00	9.00 SC		54.00	1,422.00

Reconciliation Form for Problem 4-15

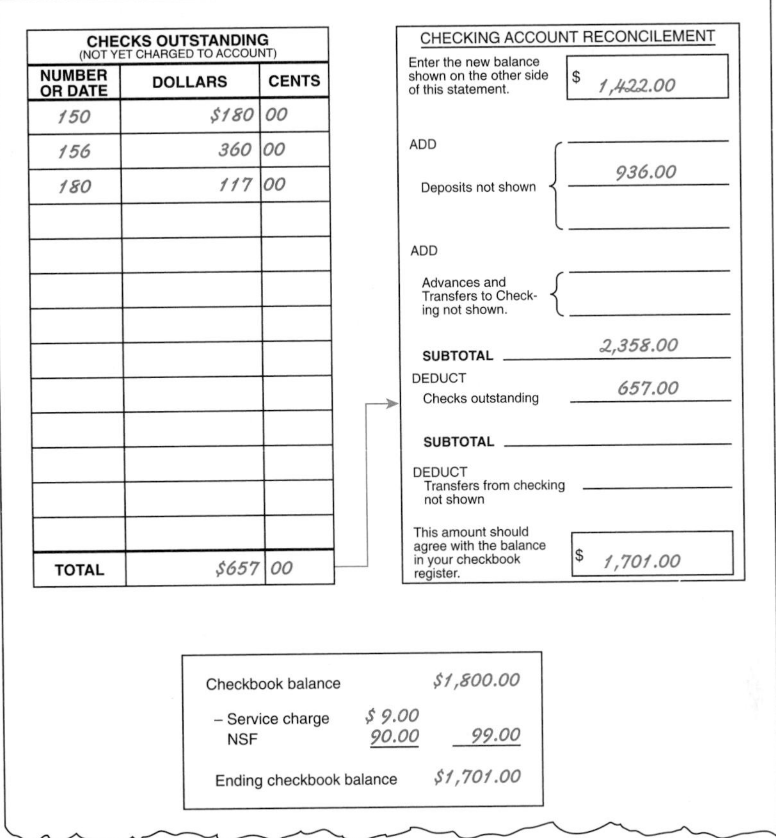

CHECKS OUTSTANDING (NOT YET CHARGED TO ACCOUNT)		
NUMBER OR DATE	DOLLARS	CENTS
150	$180	00
156	360	00
180	117	00
TOTAL	$657	00

CHECKING ACCOUNT RECONCILEMENT

Enter the new balance shown on the other side of this statement.	$ 1,422.00
ADD Deposits not shown	936.00
ADD Advances and Transfers to Checking not shown.	
SUBTOTAL	2,358.00
DEDUCT Checks outstanding	657.00
SUBTOTAL	
DEDUCT Transfers from checking not shown	
This amount should agree with the balance in your checkbook register.	$ 1,701.00

Checkbook balance		$1,800.00
− Service charge	$ 9.00	
NSF	90.00	99.00
Ending checkbook balance		$1,701.00

Challenge Problem
Bank Reconciliation

4–16. Melissa Jackson, bookkeeper for Kinko Company, cannot prepare a bank reconciliation. From the following facts, can you help her complete the June 30, 1995, reconciliation? The bank statement showed a $2,955.82 balance. Melissa's checkbook showed a $3,301.82 balance.

Melissa placed a $510.19 deposit in the bank's night depository on June 30. The deposit did not appear on the bank statement. The bank included two DMs and one CM with the returned checks: $690.65 DM for NSF check, $8.50 DM for service charges, and $400.00 CM (less $10 collection fee) for collecting a $400.00 non-interest-bearing note. Check No. 811 for $110.94 and check No. 912 for $82.50, both written and recorded on June 28, were not with the returned checks. The bookkeeper had correctly written check No. 884, $1,000, for a new cash register, but she recorded the check as $1,069. The May bank reconciliation showed check No. 748 for $210.90 and check No. 710 for $195.80 outstanding on April 30. The June bank statement included check No. 710 but not check No. 748.

KINKO COMPANY
Bank Reconciliation as of June 30, 1995

Checkbook Balance			**Bank Balance**		
Kinko checkbook balance		$3,301.82	Bank balance		$2,955.82
Add:			Add:		
Collection on notes receivable	$400.00		Deposit in transit		510.19
Less:					$3,466.01
Collection fee	10.00	390.00	Deduct:		
Error in recording check			Outstanding checks:		
No. 884		69.00	No. 748	$210.90	
		$3,760.82	No. 811	110.94	
			No. 912	82.50	404.34
Deduct:					
NSF check	$690.65				
Service charge	8.50	699.15			
Reconciled balance		$3,061.67	Reconciled balance		$3,061.67

Summary Practice Test

Solutions are at end of text in Appendix II.

Quick Reference
If you get any wrong answers, study the page numbers given for each problem.
1. P. 91.
2. P. 88.
3. P. 95.

1. Jane Company had the following MasterCard sales for the day: $43.18, $66.42, $39.50, $110.19. The company also issued two credits for returned merchandise: $31.50 and $16.19. What would be the amount of the net deposit for Jane Company on its merchant batch summary slip?

   $43.18 + $66.42 + $39.50 + $110.19 = $259.29
   − 47.69 ($31.50 + 16.19)
   Net deposit $211.60

2. Broadway Company has a $1,800.10 beginning checkbook balance. Record the following transactions in the check stubs provided.
   a. October 15, 19XX, check No. 188 payable to Abe Company, $612.55 for supplies.
   b. $700 deposit—October 16.
   c. October 28, 19XX, check No. 189 payable to R. G. Corporation, $719.84 for advertisement.

No. 188 $ 612.55
October 15 19 XX
To Abe Co.
For Supplies

	DOLLARS	CENTS
BALANCE	1,800	10
AMT. DEPOSITED		
TOTAL	1,800	10
AMT. THIS CHECK	612	55
BALANCE FORWARD	1,187	55

No. 189 $ 719.84
October 28 19 XX
To R.G. Corp.
For Advertisement

	DOLLARS	CENTS
BALANCE	1,187	55
AMT. DEPOSITED	700	00
TOTAL	1,887	55
AMT. THIS CHECK	719	84
BALANCE FORWARD	1,167	71

3. On November 1, Yang Company received a bank statement that showed a $3,150 balance. Yang showed a $3,080 checking account balance. The bank did not return check No. 108 for $75 and check No. 110 for $135. A $200 deposit made on October 28 was in transit. The bank charged Yang $6 for check printing and $24 for an NSF check. The bank also collected a $100 note for Yang. Yang forgot to record a $10 withdrawal at the ATM. Prepare a bank reconciliation.

YANG COMPANY
Bank Reconciliation as of October 31, 19XX

Checkbook Balance			Bank Balance		
Yang checkbook balance		$3,080	Bank balance		$3,150
Add:			Add:		
Collection of note		100	Deposits in transit 10/28		200
		$3,180			$3,350
Deduct:			Deduct:		
Check printing	$ 6		Outstanding checks:		
ATM	10		No. 108	$ 75	
NSF check	24	40	No. 110	135	210
Reconciled balance		$3,140	Reconciled balance		$3,140

4. P. 95. **4.** On December 31, Marcy Company's checkbook showed a $764.92 balance. Marcy's bank statement showed a $695.88 balance. Check No. 102 for $55.25 and check No. 104 for $66.28 are outstanding. A $185.40 deposit was in transit. The bank charged a $12 service charge. The statement showed a $6.83 earned interest income. Complete Marcy's bank reconciliation.

MARCY COMPANY
Bank Reconciliation as of December 31, 19XX

Book Balance		Bank Balance		
Marcy checkbook balance	$764.92	Bank balance		$695.88
Add:		Add:		
Interest income	6.83	Deposit in transit		185.40
	$771.75			$881.28
Deduct:		Deduct:		
Service charge	12.00	Outstanding checks:		
		No. 102	$55.25	
		No. 104	66.28	121.53
Reconciled balance	$759.75	Reconciled balance		$759.75

5. P. 95. **5.** On May 31, Snelling Company's bank statement showed a $10,189.02 bank balance. The bank statement also showed that it collected a $1,191 note for the company. A $1,095 June 1 deposit was in transit. Check No. 109 for $1,546.62 and check No. 111 for $2,000.58 were outstanding. Snelling's bank charges 20 cents per processed check. This month, Snelling wrote 75 checks. Snelling has a $6,560.42 checkbook balance. Prepare a reconciled statement.

SNELLING COMPANY
Bank Reconciliation as of May 31, 19XX

Book Balance		Bank Balance		
Snelling checkbook balance	$6,560.42	Bank balance		$10,189.02
Add:		Add:		
Collection of note	1,191.00	Deposit in transit		1,095.00
	$7,751.42			$11,284.02
Deduct:		Deduct:		
Check charges		Outstanding checks:		
(73* × $.20)	14.60	No. 109	$1,546.62	
		No. 111	2,000.58	3,547.20
Reconciled balance	$7,736.82	Reconciled balance		$ 7,736.82

* Due to two checks outstanding.

Project A

Complete this deposit account summary.

FLEET BANK

ACCOUNT NUMBER: 6125-1003

SNAPP III CHECKING STATEMENT
SNAPP SAVINGS
CASH RESERVE
STATEMENT PERIOD
SEP 04, 199X THRU OCT 02, 199X

JEFFREY SLATER
ROCHELLE SLATER
80 GARFIELD ST
MARBLEHEAD MA 01945

S4-001-E 21

DATE OF POSTING	TRANSACTION DESCRIPTION AND AMOUNT				BALANCES CHECKING	LOAN	SAVINGS
SEP 04	PREVIOUS BALANCES				3,690.65	.00	27,340.74
SEP 05	CHECKS PAID			187.36	3,503.29		
SEP 06	CHECKS PAID			187.20	3,316.09		
SEP 09	CHECKS PAID			5.00	3,311.09		
SEP 10	CHECKS PAID			31.00	3,280.09		
SEP 11	CHECKS PAID	14.00	13.00	10.00			
				919.90	2,323.19		
SEP 12	CHECKS PAID		230.00	90.00	2,003.19		
SEP 16	CHECKING DEPOSIT			291.00¤	2,294.19		
SEP 17	CHECKS PAID		35.58	32.02	2,226.59		
SEP 18	CHECKS PAID		177.00	16.93	2,032.66		
SEP 19	CHECKS PAID		50.00	34.00	1,948.66		
SEP 23	CHECKS PAID			25.00	1,923.66		
SEP 26	CHECKS PAID		329.10	56.82	1,537.74		
SEP 27	CHECKS PAID			121.45	1,416.29		
SEP 27	CHECKING DEPOSIT			1,600.00¤	3,016.29		
OCT 01	CHECKS PAID			83.23	2,933.06		
OCT 02	NOW INTEREST PAID			8.44¤	2,941.50		
OCT 02	SAVINGS INTEREST PAID			99.62¤			27,440.36
OCT 02	NEW BALANCES				2,941.50	.00	27,440.36

DATE OF POSTING	TRANSACTION DESCRIPTION AND AMOUNT	BALANCES CHECKING	LOAN	SAVINGS
	DEPOSIT ACCOUNT SUMMARY	**CHECKING**		**SAVINGS**
	BEGINNING BALANCE	3,690.65		27,340.74
	TOTAL CREDITS/DEPOSITS	1,891.00		.00
	TOTAL DEBITS/WITHDRAWALS	2,648.59		.00
	INTEREST CREDITED	8.44		99.62
	BANK CHARGES			
	NO BANK CHARGES THIS STATEMENT PERIOD			
	ENDING BALANCE	2,941.50		27,440.36
	MINIMUM BALANCE THIS PERIOD	1,537.74		27,340.74
	AVERAGE BALANCE THIS PERIOD	2,316.67		27,340.28
	COMBINED MINIMUM BALANCE THIS PERIOD 28,878.48			
	YEAR-TO-DATE INTEREST SUMMARY (199X):	EARNED	WITHHELD	PAID
	CHECKING INTEREST PAID	142.99	.00	142.99
	SAVINGS INTEREST PAID	1,259.43	.00	1,259.43

NOTES

THAT WAS THEN . . .
. . . THIS IS NOW

The globalization of Coca-Cola (as seen in the 1943 ad) began during World War II when it accompanied troops to the fighting fronts. The company faced many unknowns in its reach for global markets.

5

Solving for the Unknown: A How-to Approach for Solving Equations

LEARNING UNIT OBJECTIVES

LU 5–1: Solving Equations for the Unknown

1. Explain the mechanical steps needed to solve equations for the unknown. *pp. 116–120*
2. Check solution to unknown is correct. *pp. 116–120*

LU 5–2: Solving Word Problems for the Unknown

1. List the steps needed to solve a word problem. *p. 121*
2. Explain how the use of blueprint aids help to dissect and solve word problems. *pp. 122–123*
3. Solve and check word problems. *pp. 122–124*

This letter is based on a true story.

Smith's Decorating Service

Rose Smith
15 Locust Street
Lynn, MA 01915

Dear Professor Slater,

Thank you for helping me get through your Business Math class. When I first started, my math anxiety level was real high. I felt I had no head for numbers. When you told us we would be covering the chapter on solving equations, I'll never forget how I starting to shake. I started to panic. I felt I could never solve a word problem. I thought I was having an algebra attack.

Now that it's over (90 on the chapter on unknowns), I'd like to tell you what worked for me so you might pass this on to other students. It was your blueprint aids. Drawing boxes helped me think things out. They were a tool that helped me more clearly understand how to dissect each word problem. They didn't solve the problem for me, but gave me the direction I needed. Repetition was the key to my success. At first I got them all wrong but after the third time, things started to click. I felt more confident. Your gold sheets at the end of the chapter were great. Thanks for your patience – your repetition breeds success – now students are asking me to help them solve a word problem. Can you believe it!

Best,

Rose
Rose Smith

Where did you spend your last vacation? Assuming you have healthy finances, would you like to take a vacation in Japan? You say Japan has excellent golf courses and you would like to play golf in Japan? Wait a minute, do you know what it costs to play golf in Japan?

Japanese people are said to work longer and harder because housing and recreation are so expensive. If you played 18 holes of golf in a public course in Japan, your cost would average $150. In the United States, the average cost for 18 holes of golf is about $30.

Since this chapter is on solving for the unknown, let's assume you know the average cost of 18 holes of golf in Japan, but not in the United States. When talking to a friend, you mention that you plan to play golf in Japan. Your friend says, "Golf is 5 times more expensive in Japan." Now you have an unknown to solve: If golf is 5 times more expensive in Japan, what does it cost to play golf in the United States? This chapter teaches you how to use equations to solve problems with unknowns.

You may wonder why this is an important chapter. When you complete this chapter you will not have to memorize as many formulas to solve business and personal applications. Also, with an increasing use of computer software, a basic working knowledge of solving for the unknown has become necessary. Let's begin with Learning Unit 5–1 on solving equations for the unknown.

LEARNING UNIT 5–1 SOLVING EQUATIONS FOR THE UNKNOWN

Many of you are familiar with the terms *variables* and *constants*. If you are someone who is continuously on a diet, you know that your weight is a variable. Some days your weight is up; other days it is down. And probably you will never be able to say, "No matter what I eat, my weight is constant." Fortunately, in solving for unknowns, variables and constants are easier to control.

An Introduction to Solving for the Unknown

An **equation** is a math expression of equality. With equations, we can show that two numbers or two groups of numbers are equal. For example, $6 + 4 = 10$ shows an equation of equality.

Often equations use letters as symbols that represent one or more numbers. These letter symbols are called **variables.** For example, $A + 2 = 6$. A is a variable that represents the number, or *unknown* (4 in this case), for which we are solving. We distinguish variables from numbers, which have a fixed value. Numbers such as 3 or -7 are **constants,** while A and $3A$ (this means 3 times the variable A) are variables. In solving for the unknown, we place variable(s) on the left side of the equation and constants on the right. The following insight to understanding variables and constants is important.

Insight to Variables and Constants

1. If no number is in front of a letter, it is a 1: $B = 1B$; $C = 1C$.
2. If no sign is in front of a letter or number, it is a $+$; $C = +C$; $4 = +4$.

These variations result since X *may be confused with multiplication.* X *could also be a variable. We use letters like* A, B, *etc., to avoid confusion.*

You should be aware that in solving equations, the meaning of the $+$, $-$, $\times$, and $\div$ symbols has not changed. However, some variations occur. For example, we can write $A \times B$ (A times B) as (1) $A \cdot B$, (2) $A(B)$, or (3) AB. Also, A divided by B is the same as $\frac{A}{B}$. Now let's take a moment to look at how we can write variables from verbal phrases.

Assume Dick Hersh is 47 years old. Let's assign Dick Hersh's changing age to the symbol A. The symbol A is a variable.

Phrase	Variable A (age)
Dick's age 9 years ago	$A - 9$
Dick's age 9 years from today	$A + 9$
Three times Dick's age	$3A$
One fourth Dick's age	$\frac{A}{4}$

To visualize how equations work, think of the old-fashioned balancing scale shown in Figure 5–1. The pole of the scale is the equal sign. The two sides of the equation are the two pans of the scale. In the left pan or left side of the equation, we have $A + 9$. In the right pan or right side of the equation, we have 56. To solve for the unknown (Dick's present age), we isolate or place the unknown (variable) on the left side and the numbers on the right. We will do this soon. For now, remember that to keep an equation (or scale) in balance, we must perform mathematical operations (addition, subtraction, multiplication, and division) to *both* sides of the equation. This is our first rule in solving for **unknowns.**

Rule: Whatever you do to one side of an equation, you must do to the other.

FIGURE 5–1
Equality in Equations

Dick's age in 9 years will equal 56.

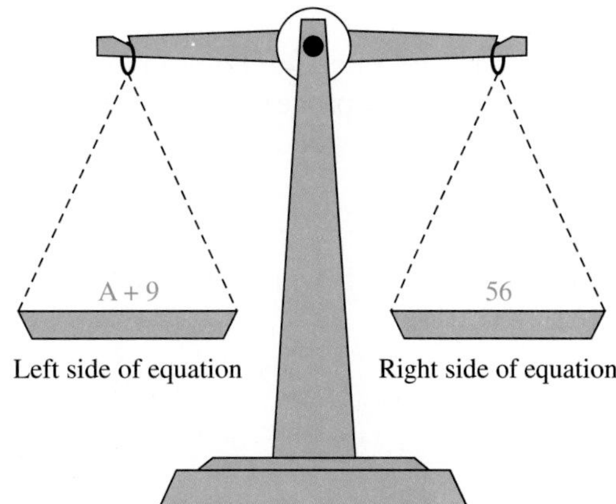

Before we look specifically at the mechanics of solving for an unknown in an equation, review the box below. This table gives some rules for using **positive** and **negative numbers.** It will aid you throughout the chapter. Do not memorize; use it as a reference.

Negative and Positive Numbers—Some Rules of the Game

1. Sum of two positive numbers is positive.
   $+4 + 3 = +7 \longrightarrow$ Positive plus positive equals positive
2. Sum of two negative numbers is negative.
   $-6 - 4 = -10 \longrightarrow$ Negative plus negative equals negative
3. Sum of a positive and a negative number can be:
   a. Zero.
   $+6 - 6 = 0 \longrightarrow$ Positive plus negative of equal value equals zero
   b. Positive.
   $+30 - 16 = 14 \longrightarrow$ Larger positive minus a positive equals positive
   $+30 - (-16) = 46 \longrightarrow$ Positive minus a negative (a minus and a minus are treated as a plus) means adding
   c. Negative.
   $-20 + 5 = -15$
   $-20 - (-5) = -15$
   $\longrightarrow$ Positive numbers are larger than all negatives even if negative looks larger; if negative number looks larger than the positive, then the sum will be negative
4. Product of two positive or two negative numbers is positive.
   $(+9)(+6) = 54 \longrightarrow$ Positive times positive equals positive
   $(-9)(-6) = 54 \longrightarrow$ Negative times negative equals positive
5. Product of a negative number and a positive number is negative.
   $(-9)(+6) = -54 \longrightarrow$ Negative times positive equals negative

If I loaned Elaine $20 and she paid me back $5, Elaine still owes me $15.

Solving Unknowns in Equations

Rule: If an equation indicates a process such as addition, subtraction, multiplication, or division, solve for the unknown or variable by using the opposite process. For example, if the equation process is addition, solve for the unknown by using subtraction.

Drill Situation 1: Subtracting Same Number from Both Sides of Equation

Problem	Mechanics	Explanation
$A + 9 = 56$ Dick's age A plus 9 equals 56	$A + 9 = 56$ $\quad -9 \quad -9$ $A = 47$	9 is subtracted from *both* sides of equation to isolate variable A on left. **Check** $47 + 9 = 56$ $56 = 56$

Note: Since the equation process used *addition,* we solve for variable A using the opposite process—*subtraction.* Remember that whatever you do to one side of the equation, you must do to the other side.

Drill Situation 2: Adding Same Number to Both Sides of Equation

Problem	Mechanics	Explanation
$B - 40 = 70$ Some number B less 40 equals 70	$B - 40 = 70$ $\quad +40 \quad +40$ $B = 110$	40 is added to *both* sides to isolate variable B on left. **Check** $110 - 40 = 70$ $70 = 70$

Note: Since the equation process used *subtraction,* we solve for variable B using the opposite process—*addition.*

Rule: You can add or subtract the same quantity or number from both sides of the equation without affecting the equality of the equation.

Drill Situation 3: Dividing Both Sides of Equation by Same Number

Problem	Mechanics	Explanation
$6G = 24$ Some number G times 6 equals 24	$6G = 24$ $\frac{6G}{6} = \frac{24}{6}$ $G = 4$	By dividing both sides by 6, G equals 4. **Check** $6(4) = 24$ $24 = 24$

Note: Since the equation process used *multiplication,* we solve for variable G using the opposite process—*division.*

Drill Situation 4: Multiplying Both Sides of Equation by Same Number

Problem	Mechanics	Explanation
$\frac{V}{5} = 70$ Some number V divided by 5 equals 70	$\frac{V}{5} = 70$ $5\left(\frac{V}{5}\right) = 70(5)$ $V = 350$	By multiplying both sides by 5, V is equal to 350. **Check** $\frac{350}{5} = 70$ $70 = 70$

Note: Since the equation process used *division,* we solve for variable V using the opposite process—*multiplication.*

Rule: You can divide or multiply both sides of the equation by the same quantity or number without affecting the equality of the equation. You do not multiply or divide an equation by zero.

Drill Situation 5: Equation That Uses Subtraction and Multiplication to Solve Unknown

Problem	Mechanics	Explanation
$\frac{H}{4} + 2 = 5$ When we divide unknown H by 4 and add the result to 2, the answer is 5	$\frac{H}{4} + 2 = 5$ $\frac{H}{4} + 2 = 5$ $-2 \quad -2$ $\frac{H}{4} = 3$ $4\left(\frac{H}{4}\right) = 4(3)$ $H = 12$	1. Move constant to right side by subtracting 2 from both sides. 2. To isolate H, which is divided by 4, we do the opposite process and multiply 4 times *both* sides of the equation. **Check** $\frac{12}{4} + 2 = 5$ $3 + 2 = 5$ $5 = 5$

Rule: When solving for unknown that involves more than one step, do addition and subtraction before multiplication and division.

Drill Situation 6: Using Parentheses in Solving for Unknown

Problem	Mechanics	Explanation
$5(P - 4) = 20$ The unknown P less 4 multiplied by 5 equals 20	$5(P-4) = 20$ $5P - 20 = 20$ $+20 = +20$ $\frac{\not{5}P}{\not{5}} = \frac{40}{5}$ $P = 8$	1. Parentheses tell us that everything inside parentheses is multiplied by 5. Multiply 5 times P and 5 times -4. 2. Add 20 to both sides to isolate $5P$ on left. 3. To remove 5 in front of P, divide both sides by 5 to result in P equals 8.

Check

$5(8 - 4) = 20$
$5(4) = 20$
$20 = 20$

Rule: When equations contain parentheses (which indicate grouping together), you solve for the unknown by first multiplying each item inside the parentheses by the number or letter just outside the parentheses. Then you continue solving for the unknown by using the opposite process used in the equation. Do additions and subtractions first, then multiplications and divisions.

Drill Situation 7: Combining Unknowns

Problem	Mechanics	Explanation
$4A + A = 20$	$4A + A = 20$ $\frac{\not{5}A}{\not{5}} = \frac{20}{5}$ $A = 4$	To solve this equation: $4A + 1A = 5A$. Thus, $5A = 20$. To solve for A, divide both sides by 5, leaving A equals 4.

Rule: To solve equations with like unknowns, you first combine unknowns and solve by using the opposite process used in the equation.

Before you go to Learning Unit 5–2, let's check your understanding of this unit.

LU 5-1 PRACTICE QUIZ

1. Write equations for the following (use the letter Q as the variable); do not solve for unknown:
   a. Seven less than one half a number is twelve.
   b. Nine times the sum of a number and thirty-one is forty.
   c. Twelve decreased by twice a number is four.
   d. Eight times a number less two equals twenty-one.
   e. The sum of four times a number and two is fifteen.
   f. If twice a number is decreased by eight, the difference is four.
2. Solve the following.
   a. $C + 19 = 48$ **b.** $D + 3D = 240$
   c. $12B = 144$ **d.** $\frac{B}{6} = 50$
   e. $\frac{B}{4} + 4 = 16$ **f.** $3(B - 8) = 18$

SOLUTIONS TO LU 5-1 PRACTICE QUIZ

1. **a.** $\frac{1}{2}Q - 7 = 12$ **b.** $9(Q + 31) = 40$
   c. $12 - 2Q = 4$ **d.** $8Q - 2 = 21$
   e. $4Q + 2 = 15$ **f.** $2Q - 8 = 4$

2. a.
$$\begin{aligned} C + 19 &= 48 \\ -19 &\quad -19 \\ \hline C &= \boxed{29} \end{aligned}$$

b.
$$\frac{\cancel{4}D}{\cancel{4}} = \frac{240}{4}$$
$$D = \boxed{60}$$

c.
$$\frac{\cancel{12}B}{\cancel{12}} = \frac{144}{12}$$
$$B = \boxed{12}$$

d.
$$\cancel{6}\left(\frac{B}{\cancel{6}}\right) = 50(6)$$
$$B = \boxed{300}$$

e.
$$\begin{aligned} \frac{B}{4} + 4 &= 16 \\ -4 &\quad -4 \\ \hline \frac{B}{4} &= 12 \\ \cancel{4}\left(\frac{B}{\cancel{4}}\right) &= 12(4) \\ B &= \boxed{48} \end{aligned}$$

f.
$$\begin{aligned} 3(B - 8) &= 18 \\ 3B - 24 &= 18 \\ +24 &\quad +24 \\ \hline \frac{\cancel{3}B}{\cancel{3}} &= \frac{42}{3} \\ B &= \boxed{14} \end{aligned}$$

LEARNING UNIT 5–2 SOLVING WORD PROBLEMS FOR THE UNKNOWN

Jeff Smith/The Image Bank

You are sitting in your business math class. Look around the class and count the students in class. If you were told that 5 more students are in this class than yesterday's class, do you know how many attended yesterday's class?

Whether you are in or out of class, you are continually solving word problems. For example, you plan to go to the theater. How much time must you allow to arrive at the theater before the movie begins? This probably depends on traffic, weather conditions, and other variables such as your car stalling at an intersection. Even the person selling popcorn at the movie works with variables. How much popcorn should be popped? The number of popcorn eaters could depend on the time of the movie, the day of the week, and the weather. So we can say that unknowns surround us.

In this unit, we give you a roadmap showing you how to solve word problems dealing with unknowns by using blueprint aids. Use these aids as a reference. The five steps below will help you dissect and solve these word problems. In Chapters 1 through 4, we also presented blueprint aids for dissecting and solving word problems. Now the blueprint aids focus on solving for the unknown.

This unit looks at six different situations. Be patient and *persistent*. The more problems you work, the easier the process becomes. Note how we dissect and solve each problem in the blueprint aids. Do not panic! Repetition is the key. Now let's study the five steps.

Steps for Solving Word Problems

Step 1. Carefully read the entire problem. You may have to read it several times.

Step 2. Ask yourself, "What is the problem looking for?"

Step 3. When you are sure what the problem is asking, let a variable represent the unknown. If the problem has more than one unknown, represent the second unknown in terms of the same variable. For example, if the problem has two unknowns, *Y* is one unknown. The second unknown is 4*Y*—four times the first unknown.

Step 4. Visualize the relationship between unknowns and variables. Then set up an equation to solve for unknown(s).

Step 5. Check your result to see if it is accurate.

Now let's look at some different word problem situations. Carefully note how we dissect each word problem in the blueprint aids.

Word Problem Situation 1: Number Problems

Problem

A pair of Nike sneakers were reduced $30. The sale price was $70. What was the original price?

Blueprint aid

Unknown(s)	Variable(s)	Relationship*
Original price	P	$P - \$30 =$ Sale price Sale price $= \$70$

* This column will help you visualize the equation before setting up the actual equation.

Mechanical steps

$$\begin{aligned} P - \$30 &= \$70 \\ +30 &\quad +30 \\ P &= \$100 \end{aligned}$$

Check

$$\$100 - \$30 = \$70$$
$$\$70 = \$70$$

Explanation

The original price less $30 equals $70. Note that we added $30 to both sides to isolate P on the left. Remember $1P = P$.

Word Problem Situation 2: Finding the Whole When Part Is Known

Problem

A local Burger King budgets $\frac{1}{8}$ of its monthly profits on salaries. Salaries for the month were $12,000. What were Burger King's monthly profits?

Blueprint aid

Unknown(s)	Variable(s)	Relationship
Monthly profits	P	$\frac{1}{8}P$ Salaries $= \$12,000$

Mechanical steps

$$\frac{1}{8}P = \$12,000$$
$$\not{8}\left(\frac{P}{\not{8}}\right) = \$12,000(8)$$
$$P = \$96,000$$

Check

$$\frac{1}{8}(\$96,000) = \$12,000$$
$$\$12,000 = \$12,000$$

Explanation

$\frac{1}{8}P$ represents Burger King's monthly salaries. Since the equation used division, we solve for S by multiplying both sides by 8.

Word Problem Situation 3: Difference Problems

Problem

ICM Company sold 4 times as many computers as Ring Company. The difference in their sales is 27. How many computers of each were sold?

Blueprint aid

Unknown(s)	Variable(s)	Relationship
ICM	$4C$	$4C$
Ring	C	$-C$
		27

Note: If problem has two unknowns, assign the variable to smaller item or one who sells the least. Then assign the other unknown using the same variable. *Use same letter.*

Mechanical steps

$$4C - C = 27$$
$$\frac{\not{3}C}{\not{3}} = \frac{27}{3}$$
$$C = 9$$

Ring = 9 computers
ICM = 4(9)
= 36 computers

Check

36 computers
−9 computers
27 computers

Explanation

The variables replace the names ICM and Ring. We assigned Ring the variable C since it sold the least amount of computers. We assigned ICM $4C$ since it sold 4 times as many computers.

Word Problem Situation 4: Calculating Unit Sales

Problem

Together, Barry Sullivan and Mitch Ryan sold 300 homes for Regis Realty. Barry sold 9 times as many homes as Mitch. How many did each sell?

Blueprint aid

Unknown(s)	Variable(s)	Relationship
Homes sold:		
B. Sullivan	$9H$	$9H$
M. Ryan	H*	$+H$
		300 homes

* Assign H to Ryan since he sold least.

Mechanical steps

$$9H + H = 300$$
$$\frac{\not{10}H}{\not{10}} = \frac{300}{10}$$
$$H = 30$$

Ryan: 30 homes
Sullivan: 9(30) =
270 homes

Check

$$30 + 270 = 300$$

Explanation

We assigned Mitch H since he sold fewer homes. We assigned Barry $9H$ since he sold 9 times as many homes. Together Barry and Mitch sold 300 homes.

Word Problem Situation 5: Calculating Unit and Dollar Sales (Cost per Unit) When Total Units Are Not Given

Problem

Andy sold watches ($9) and alarm clocks ($5) at a flea market. Total sales were $287. People bought 4 times as many watches as alarm clocks. How many of each did Andy sell? What was the total dollar sales of each?

Blueprint aid

Unknown(s)	Variable(s)	Price	Relationship
Unit sales:			
Watches	$4C$	$9	$36C$
Clocks	C	5	$+5C$
			$287 total sales

Mechanical steps

$$36C + 5C = 287$$
$$\frac{\not{41}C}{\not{41}} = \frac{287}{41}$$
$$C = 7$$

7 clocks
4(7) = 28 watches

Check

$$7(\$5) + 28(\$9) = \$287$$
$$\$35 + \$252 = \$287$$
$$\$287 = \$287$$

Explanation

Number of watches times $9 sales price plus number of alarm clocks times $5 equals $287 total sales.

Word Problem Situation 6: Calculating Unit and Dollar Sales (Cost per Unit) When Total Units Are Given

Problem

Andy sold watches ($9) and alarm clocks ($5) at a flea market. Total sales for 35 watches and alarm clocks were $287. How many of each did Andy sell? What was the total dollar sales of each?

Blueprint aid

Unknown(s)	Variable(s)	Price	Relationship
Unit sales:			
Watches	W*	$9	$9W$
Clocks	$35 - W$	5	$+5(35 - W)$
			$287 total sales

* The most expensive item is assigned to the variable first only for this situation to make the mechanical steps easier to complete.

Mechanical steps

$$9W + 5(35 - W) = 287$$
$$9W + 175 - 5W = 287$$
$$4W + 175 = 287$$
$$- 175 \quad - 175$$
$$\frac{4W}{4} = \frac{112}{4}$$
$$W = 28$$

Watches = 28

Clocks = 35 − 28 = 7

Check

28(9) + 7($5) = $287

$252 + $35 = $287

$287 = $287

Explanation

Number of watches (W) times price per watch plus number of alarm clocks times price per alarm clock equals $287. Total units given was 35.

Why did we use 35 − W? Assume we had 35 pizzas (some cheese, some meatball). If I said that I ate all the meatball pizzas (5), how many cheese pizzas are left? Thirty? Right, you subtract 5 from 35. Think of 35 − W as meaning one number.

Note in Word Problem Situations 5 and 6 that the situation is the same. In Word Problem Situation 5, we were not given total units sold (but we were told which sold better). In Word Problem Situation 6, we were given total units sold but we did not know which sold better.

Now try these six types of word problems in the Practice Quiz. Be sure to complete blueprint aids and the mechanical steps for solving the unknown(s).

LU 5-2 PRACTICE QUIZ

Situations

1. A Liz Claiborne sweater was reduced $40. The sale price was $85. What was the original price?
2. Kelly Doyle budgets $\frac{1}{8}$ of her yearly salary for entertainment. Kelly's total entertainment bill for the year is $6,500. What is Kelly's yearly salary?
3. Micro Knowledge sells 5 times as many computers as Morse Electronics. The difference in sales between the two stores is 20 computers. How many computers did each store sell?
4. Susie and Cara sell stoves at Elliott's Appliances. Together they sold 180 stoves in January. Susie sold 5 times as many stoves as Cara. How many stoves did each sell?
5. Pasquale's Pizza sells meatball pizzas ($6) and cheese pizzas ($5). In March, Pasquale's total sales were $1,600. People bought 2 times as many cheese pizzas as meatball pizzas. How many of each did Pasquale sell? What was the total dollar sales of each?
6. Pasquale's Pizza sells meatball pizzas ($6) and cheese pizzas ($5). In March, Pasquale's sold 300 pizzas for $1,600. How many of each did Pasquale's sell? What was the dollar sales price of each?

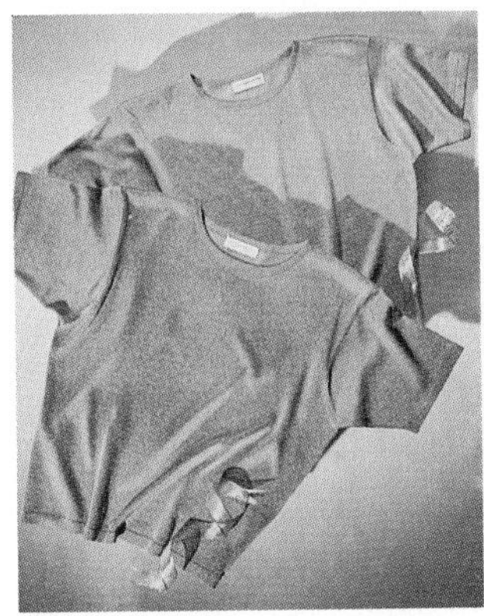

Courtesy of Liz Claiborne, Inc.

SOLUTIONS TO LU 5-2 PRACTICE QUIZ

1.

Unknown(s)	Variable(s)	Relationship
Original price	P*	P − $40 = Sale price Sale price = $85

* P = Original price.

Mechanical steps

$$P - \$40 = \$85$$
$$+ \ 40 \quad + 40$$
$$P = \$125$$

2.

Unknown(s)	Variable(s)	Relationship
Yearly salary	S*	$\frac{1}{8}S$ Entertainment = $6,500

* S = Salary.

Mechanical steps

$$\frac{1}{8}S = \$6,500$$
$$8\left(\frac{S}{8}\right) = \$6,500(8)$$
$$S = \$52,000$$

3.

Unknown(s)	Variable(s)	Relationship
Micro	$5C$*	$5C$
Morse	C	$-C$ 20 computers

*C = Computers.

Mechanical steps

$$5C - C = 20$$
$$\frac{4C}{4} = \frac{20}{4}$$
$$C = 5 \text{ (Morse)}$$
$$5C = 25 \text{ (Micro)}$$

4.

Unknown(s)	Variable(s)	Relationship
Stoves sold:		
Susie	$5S$*	$5S$
Cara	S	$+S$ 180 stoves

*S = Stoves.

Mechanical steps

$$5S + S = 180$$
$$\frac{6S}{6} = \frac{180}{6}$$
$$S = 30 \text{ (Cara)}$$
$$5S = 150 \text{ (Susie)}$$

5.

Unknown(s)	Variable(s)	Price	Relationship
Meatball	M	\$6	$6M$
Cheese	$2M$	5	$+10M$ \$1,600 total sales

Mechanical steps

$$6M + 10M = 1{,}600$$
$$\frac{16M}{16} = \frac{1{,}600}{16}$$
$$M = 100 \text{ (meatball)}$$
$$2M = 200 \text{ (cheese)}$$

Check

$$(100 \times \$6) + (200 \times \$5) = \$1{,}600$$
$$\$600 + \$1{,}000 = \$1{,}600$$
$$\$1{,}600 = \$1{,}600$$

6.

Unknown(s)	Variable(s)	Price	Relationship
Unit sales:			
Meatball	M*	\$6	$6M$
Cheese	$300 - M$	5	$+5(300 - M)$ \$1,600 total sales

*We assign the variable to the most expensive to make the mechanical steps easier to complete.

Mechanical steps

$$6M + 5(300 - M) = 1{,}600$$
$$6M + 1{,}500 - 5M = 1{,}600$$
$$M + 1{,}500 = 1{,}600$$
$$-1{,}500 \quad -1{,}500$$
$$M = 100$$

Meatball = 100

Cheese = 300 − 100 = 200

Check

100(\$6) + 200(\$5)

= \$600 + \$1,000

= \$1,600

CHAPTER ORGANIZER: A REFERENCE GUIDE

Page	Solving for unknowns from basic equations	Mechanical steps to solve unknowns	Key point(s)
118	Situation 1: Subtracting same number from both sides of equation	$D + 10 = 12$ $-10 \quad -10$ $D = 2$	Subtract 10 from both sides of equation to isolate variable D on the left. Since equation used addition, we solve by using opposite process—subtraction.

Page	Solving for unknowns from basic equations	Mechanical steps to solve unknowns	Key point(s)
118	Situation 2: Adding same number to both sides of equation	$L - 24 = 40$ $\underline{+24 \quad +24}$ $L = 64$	Add 24 to both sides to isolate unknown L on left. We solve by using opposite process of subtraction—addition.
119	Situation 3: Dividing both sides of equation by same number	$6B = 24$ $\frac{\cancel{6}B}{\cancel{6}} = \frac{24}{6}$ $B = 4$	To isolate B by itself on the left, divide both sides of the equation by 6. Thus, the 6 on the left cancels—leaving B equal to 4. Since equation used multiplication, we solve unknown by using opposite process—division.
119	Situation 4: Multiplying both sides of equation by same number	$\frac{R}{3} = 15$ $\cancel{3}\left(\frac{R}{\cancel{3}}\right) = 15(3)$ $R = 45$	To remove denominator, multiply both sides of the equation by 3—the 3 on the left side cancels, leaving R equal to 45. Since equation used division, we solve unknown by using opposite process—multiplication.
119	Situation 5: Equation that uses subtraction and multiplication to solve unknown	$\frac{B}{3} + 6 = 13$ $\underline{-6 \quad -6}$ $\frac{B}{3} = 7$ $\cancel{3}\left(\frac{B}{\cancel{3}}\right) = 7(3)$ $B = 21$	1. Move constant 6 to right side by subtracting 6 from both sides. 2. Isolate B by itself on left by multiplying both sides by 3.
120	Situation 6: Using parentheses in solving for unknown	$6(A - 5) = 12$ $6A - 30 = 12$ $\underline{+30 \quad +30}$ $\frac{\cancel{6}A}{\cancel{6}} = \frac{42}{6}$ $A = 7$	Parentheses indicate multiplication. Multiply 6 times A and 6 times -5. Result is $6A - 30$ on left side of the equation. Now add 30 to both sides to isolate $6A$ on left. To remove 6 in front of A, divide both sides by 6 to result in A equal to 7. Note that when deleting parentheses, we did not have to multiply the right side.
120	Situation 7: Combining unknowns	$6A + 2A = 64$ $\frac{\cancel{8}A}{\cancel{8}} = \frac{64}{8}$ $A = 8$	$6A + 2A$ combine to $8A$. To solve for A, we divide both sides by 8.

Page	Solving for unknowns from word problems	Blueprint aid	Mechanical steps to solve unknown with check
122	Situation 1: Number problems U.S. Air reduced its airfare to California by $60. The sale price was $95. What was the original price?	**Unknown(s):** Original price **Variable(s):** P **Relationship:** $P - \$60 =$ Sale price; Sale price $= \$95$	$P - \$60 = \$95$ $\underline{+60 \quad +60}$ $P = \$155$ **Check** $\$155 - \$60 = \$95$ $\$95 = \$95$
122	Situation 2: Finding the whole when part is known. K. McCarthy spends $\frac{1}{8}$ of her budget for school. What is the total budget if school costs $5,000?	**Unknown(s):** Total budget **Variable(s):** B **Relationship:** $\frac{1}{8}B$; School $= \$5{,}000$	$\frac{1}{8}B = \$5{,}000$ $\cancel{8}\left(\frac{B}{\cancel{8}}\right) = \$5{,}000(8)$ $B = \$40{,}000$ **Check** $\frac{1}{8}(\$40{,}000) = \$5{,}000$ $\$5{,}000 = \$5{,}000$

<table>
<tr><th>Page</th><th>Solving for unknowns from word problems</th><th>Blueprint aid</th><th>Mechanical steps to solve unknown with check</th></tr>
<tr><td>122</td><td>Situation 3: Difference problems.
Moe sold 8 times as many suitcases as Bill. The difference in their sales is 280 suitcases. How many suitcases did each sell?</td><td>
<table>
<tr><th>Unknown(s)</th><th>Variable(s)</th><th>Relationship</th></tr>
<tr><td>Suitcases sold:
Moe
Bill</td><td>
$8S$
S</td><td>
$8S$
$-S$
280 suitcases</td></tr>
</table>
</td><td>$8S - S = 280$ (Bill)
$\frac{7S}{7} = \frac{280}{7}$
$S = 40$ (Bill)
$8(40) = 320$ (Moe)

Check
$320 - 40 = 280$
$280 = 280$</td></tr>
<tr><td>122</td><td>Situation 4: Calculating unit sales.
Moe sold 8 times as many suitcases as Bill. Together they sold a total of 360. How many did each sell?</td><td>
<table>
<tr><th>Unknown(s)</th><th>Variable(s)</th><th>Relationship</th></tr>
<tr><td>Suitcases sold:
Moe
Bill</td><td>
$8S$
S</td><td>
$8S$
$+S$
360 suitcases</td></tr>
</table>
</td><td>$8S + S = 360$
$\frac{9S}{9} = \frac{360}{9}$
$S = 40$ (Bill)
$8S = 320$ (Moe)

Check
$320 + 40 = 360$
$360 = 360$</td></tr>
<tr><td>122</td><td>Situation 5: Calculating unit and dollar sales (cost per unit) when total units not given.
Blue Furniture Company ordered sleepers ($300) and nonsleepers ($200) that cost $8,000. Blue expects sleepers to outsell nonsleepers two to one. How many units of each were ordered? What were dollar costs of each?</td><td>
<table>
<tr><th>Unknown(s)</th><th>Variable(s)</th><th>Price</th><th>Relationship</th></tr>
<tr><td>Sleepers
Nonsleepers</td><td>$2N$
N</td><td>$300
200</td><td>$600N$
$+ 200N$
$8,000 total cost</td></tr>
</table>
</td><td>$600N + 200N = 8,000$
$\frac{800N}{800} = \frac{8,000}{800}$
$N = 10$ (nonsleepers)
$2N = 20$ (sleepers)

Check
10 × $200 = $2,000
20 × $300 = 6,000
$8,000</td></tr>
<tr><td>123</td><td>Situation 6: Calculating unit and dollar sales (cost per unit) when total units given.
Blue Furniture Company ordered 30 sofas that cost $8,000. The wholesale unit cost was $300 for the sleepers and $200 for the nonsleepers. How many units of each were ordered? What were dollar costs of each?</td><td>
<table>
<tr><th>Unknown(s)</th><th>Variable(s)</th><th>Price</th><th>Relationship</th></tr>
<tr><td>Unit cost:
Sleepers
Nonsleepers</td><td>
S
$30 - S$</td><td>
$300
200</td><td>
$300S$
$+ 200(30 - S)$
$8,000 total cost</td></tr>
</table>
When the total units are given, the highest priced item (sleepers) is assigned to the variable first. This makes the mechanical steps easier to complete.</td><td>$300S + 200(30 - S) = 8,000$
$300S + 6,000 - 200S = 8,000$
$100S + 6,000 = 8,000$
$-6,000 \quad -6,000$
$\frac{100S}{100} = \frac{2,000}{100}$
$S = 20$
Nonsleepers $= 30 - 20$
$= 10$

Check
20($300) + 10($200) = $8,000
$6,000 + $2,000 = $8,000
$8,000 = $8,000</td></tr>
<tr><td></td><td>Key terms</td><td>Constants, p. 117
Equation, p. 117
Negative number, p. 118</td><td>Positive number, p. 118
Unknown, p. 117
Variables, p. 117</td></tr>
</table>

END-OF-CHAPTER PROBLEMS

Drill Problems (First of Three Sets)

Additional homework assignments by learning unit are at the end of text in Appendix I (p. I-21). Solutions to odd problems are at the end of text in Appendix II.

Solve the unknown from the following equations:

5-1. $V + 16 = 42$
$$\begin{array}{rcr} V + 16 &=& 42 \\ -16 && -16 \\ \hline V &=& 26 \end{array}$$

5-2. $J + 19 = 68$
$$\begin{array}{rcr} J + 19 &=& 68 \\ -19 && -19 \\ \hline J &=& 49 \end{array}$$

5-3. $N + 60 = 180$
$$\begin{array}{rcr} N + 60 &=& 180 \\ -60 && -60 \\ \hline N &=& 120 \end{array}$$

5-4. $H - 88 = 66$
$$\begin{array}{rcr} H - 88 &=& 66 \\ +88 && +88 \\ \hline H &=& 154 \end{array}$$

5-5. $5Y = 75$
$$\frac{\not{5}Y}{\not{5}} = \frac{75}{5}$$
$$Y = 15$$

5-6. $\frac{P}{6} = 92$
$$\not{6}\left(\frac{P}{\not{6}}\right) = 92(6)$$
$$P = 552$$

5-7. $8Y = 96$
$$\frac{\not{8}Y}{\not{8}} = \frac{96}{8}$$
$$Y = 12$$

5-8. $\frac{N}{16} = 5$
$$\not{16}\left(\frac{N}{\not{16}}\right) = 5(16)$$
$$N = 80$$

5-9. $4(P - 9) = 64$
$$\begin{array}{rcr} 4P - 36 &=& 64 \\ +36 &=& +36 \\ \hline \frac{\not{4}P}{\not{4}} &=& \frac{100}{4} \\ P &=& 25 \end{array}$$

5-10. $3(P - 3) = 27$
$$\begin{array}{rcr} 3P - 9 &=& 27 \\ +9 && +9 \\ \hline \frac{\not{3}P}{\not{3}} &=& \frac{36}{3} \\ P &=& 12 \end{array}$$

Word Problems (First of Three Sets)

Complete the blueprint aid along with calculations.

Situation 1. P. 122.

5-11. American Airlines reduced its roundtrip ticket from Boston to Chicago by \$56. The sale price was \$299. What was the original price?

Unknown(s)	Variable(s)	Relationship
Original price	P	P − \$56 = Sale price Sale price = \$299

$$\begin{array}{rcr} P - \$56 &=& \$299 \\ +56 && +56 \\ \hline P &=& \$355 \end{array}$$

Situation 2. P. 122.

5-12. Molly's Diner receives cash for $\frac{1}{7}$ of its sales. During the first week in September, Molly's cash sales were \$490. What were Molly's total sales?

Unknown(s)	Variable(s)	Relationship
Total sales	S	$\frac{1}{7}S$ Cash sales = \$490

$$\frac{1}{7}S = \$490$$
$$7\left(\frac{S}{7}\right) = \$490(7)$$
$$S = \$3{,}430$$

Situation 4. P. 122.

5-13. Soo Lin and Hubert Krona sell cars for Northland Auto. Over the past year, they sold 150 cars. Soo sells 4 times as many cars as Hubert. How many cars did each sell?

Unknown(s)	Variable(s)	Relationship
Hubert Soo	C $4C$	C (30) + $4C$ (120) 150 cars

$$4C + C = 150$$
$$\frac{\not{5}C}{\not{5}} = \frac{150}{5}$$
$$C = 30 \text{ (Hubert)}$$
$$4C = 120 \text{ (Soo)}$$

Situation 4. P. 122.

5-14. Nanda Yueh and Lane Zuriff sell homes for Margate Realty. Over the past six months they sold 120 homes. Nanda sold 3 times as many homes as Lane. How many homes did each sell?

Unknown(s)	Variable(s)	Relationship
Nanda Lane	$3H$ H	$3H$ (90) $+\ H$ (30) 120 homes

$$3H + H = 120$$
$$\frac{\not{4}H}{\not{4}} = \frac{120}{4}$$
$$H = 30 \text{ (Lane)}$$
$$3H = 90 \text{ (Nanda)}$$

Situation 5. P. 122.

5-15. Runyon Company sells T-shirts ($2) and shorts ($4). In April, total sales were $600. People bought 4 times as many T-shirts as shorts. How many T-shirts and shorts did Runyon sell? Check your answer.

Unknown(s)	Variable(s)	Price	Relationship
T-shirts Shorts	$4S$ S	$2 4	$8S$ $+4S$ $600 total sales

$$8S + 4S = 600$$
$$\frac{\not{12}S}{\not{12}} = \frac{600}{12}$$
$$S = 50 \text{ shorts}$$
$$4S = 200 \text{ T-shirts}$$

Check

$$50(\$4) + 200(\$2) = \$600$$
$$\$200 + \$400 = \$600$$
$$\$600 = \$600$$

Hint: Let S = Shorts.
Situation 6. P. 123.

5-16. Runyon Company sells 250 T-shirts ($2) and shorts ($4). In April, total sales were $600. How many T-shirts and shorts did Runyon sell? Check your answer.

Unknown(s)	Variable(s)	Price	Relationship
T-shirts Shorts	$250 - S$ S	$2 4	$2(250 - S)$ $+\ 4S$ $600 total sales

$$2(250 - S) + 4S = 600$$
$$500 - 2S + 4S = 600$$
$$-500 \qquad -500$$
$$\frac{\not{2}S}{\not{2}} = \frac{100}{2}$$
$$S = 50 \text{ shorts}$$
$$250 - S = 200 \text{ T-shirts}$$

Check

$$200(\$2) + 50(\$4) = \$600$$
$$\$400 + \$200 = \$600$$
$$\$600 = \$600$$

Drill Problems (Second of Three Sets)

5-17.
$$18Y = 198$$
$$\frac{\not{18}Y}{\not{18}} = \frac{198}{18}$$
$$Y = 11$$

5-18.
$$9(B - 4) = 45$$
$$9B - 36 = 45$$
$$+36 \qquad +36$$
$$\frac{\not{9}B}{\not{9}} = \frac{81}{9}$$
$$B = 9$$

5-19.
$$\frac{N}{9} = 7$$
$$\not{9}\left(\frac{N}{\not{9}}\right) = 7(9)$$
$$N = 63$$

5-20.
$$18(C - 3) = 162$$
$$18C - 54 = 162$$
$$+54 \qquad +54$$
$$\frac{\not{18}C}{\not{18}} = \frac{216}{18}$$
$$C = 12$$

5-21.
$$9Y - 10 = 53$$
$$+10 \qquad +10$$
$$\frac{\not{9}Y}{\not{9}} = \frac{63}{9}$$
$$Y = 7$$

5-22.
$$7B + 5 = 26$$
$$-5 \qquad -5$$
$$\frac{\not{7}B}{\not{7}} = \frac{21}{7}$$
$$B = 3$$

Word Problems (Second of Three Sets)

5–23. Sears reduced its price on lawn mowers by \$45. The sale price was \$169. What was the original price?

Unknown(s)	Variable(s)	Relationship
Original price	P	$P - \$45 =$ Sale price Sale price $= \$169$

$$\begin{aligned} P - \$45 &= \$169 \\ +45 &\quad +45 \\ P &= \$214 \end{aligned}$$

5–24. Marge budgets $\frac{1}{4}$ of her yearly salary for clothing. Marge's total clothing bill for the year is \$15,000. What is her yearly salary?

Unknown(s)	Variable(s)	Relationship
Yearly salary	S	$\frac{1}{4}S$ Clothing $= \$15,000$

$$\begin{aligned} \frac{1}{4}S &= \$15,000 \\ 4\left(\frac{S}{4}\right) &= \$15,000(4) \\ S &= \$60,000 \end{aligned}$$

5–25. Bill's Roast Beef sells 5 times as many sandwiches as Pete's Deli. The difference between their sales is 360 sandwiches. How many sandwiches did each sell?

Unknown(s)	Variable(s)	Relationship
Bill's Pete's	$5S$ S	$5S$ (450) $-S$ (90) 360 sandwiches

$$\begin{aligned} 5S - S &= 360 \\ \frac{4S}{4} &= \frac{360}{4} \\ S &= 90 \\ 5S &= 450 \end{aligned}$$

5–26. In February, Shelly sold 4 times as many boats as Rusty. The difference between their sales is 21 boats. How many boats did each sell?

Unknown(s)	Variable(s)	Relationship
Shelly Rusty	$4B$ B	$4B$ (28) $-B$ (7) 21 boats

$$\begin{aligned} 4B - B &= 21 \\ \frac{3B}{3} &= \frac{21}{3} \\ B &= 7 \text{ (Rusty)} \\ 4B &= 28 \text{ (Shelly)} \end{aligned}$$

5–27. The Computer Store sells diskettes (\$3) and small boxes of computer paper (\$5). In August, total sales were \$960. Customers bought 5 times as many diskettes as boxes of computer paper. How many of each did the Computer Store sell? Check your answer.

Unknown(s)	Variable(s)	Price	Relationship
Diskettes Boxes of paper	$5P$ P	\$3 5	$15P$ $+5P$ \$960 total sales

$$\begin{aligned} 5P + 15P &= 960 \\ \frac{20P}{20} &= \frac{960}{20} \\ P &= 48 \text{ boxes of paper} \\ 5P &= 240 \text{ diskettes} \end{aligned}$$

Check

$$\begin{aligned} 48(\$5) + 240(\$3) &= \$960 \\ \$240 + \$720 &= \$960 \\ \$960 &= \$960 \end{aligned}$$

Hint: Let P = Pens.

5–28. St. Paul Stationery sells cartons of pens ($10) and rubber bands ($4). Leona ordered a total of 24 cartons for $210. How many cartons of each did Leona order? Check your answer.

Unknown(s)	Variable(s)	Price	Relationship
Pens	P	$10	$10P$
Rubber bands	$24 - P$	4	$+4(24 - P)$
			Total = $210

$$10P + 4(24 - P) = 210$$
$$10P + 96 - 4P = 210$$
$$6P + 96 = 210$$
$$-96 \quad -96$$
$$\frac{6P}{6} = \frac{114}{6}$$
$P = 19$ cartons of pens
$24 - P = 5$ cartons of rubber bands

Check
$19(\$10) + 5(\$4) = \$210$
$\$190 + \$20 = \$210$
$\$210 = \$210$

Drill Problems (Third of Three Sets)

Solve the unknown from the following equations.

5–29.
$$D + 95 - 13 = 129$$
$$D + 82 = 129$$
$$-82 \quad -82$$
$$D = 47$$

5–30.
$$5Y + 15(Y + 1) = 35$$
$$5Y + 15Y + 15 = 35$$
$$20Y + 15 = 35$$
$$-15 \quad -15$$
$$\frac{20Y}{20} = \frac{20}{20}$$
$$Y = 1$$

5–31.
$$3M + 20 = 2M + 80$$
$$-2M \quad -2M$$
$$M + 20 = +80$$
$$-20 \quad -20$$
$$M = 60$$

5–32.
$$20(C - 50) = 19,000$$
$$20C - 1,000 = 19,000$$
$$+1,000 \quad +1,000$$
$$\frac{20C}{20} = \frac{20,000}{20}$$
$$C = 1,000$$

Word Problems (Third of Three Sets)

5–33. Joan Madden decided to pay $\frac{1}{5}$ of the camp tuition for her grandson. Joan saved her daughter-in-law $250. What was the total cost of the tuition?

Unknown(s)	Variable(s)	Relationship
Total cost of camp	C	$\frac{1}{5}C$
		Savings = $250

$$\frac{1}{5}C = \$250$$
$$5\left(\frac{C}{5}\right) = \$250(5)$$
$$C = \$1,250$$

5–34. At Maplewood Marine, shift 1 produced 3 times as much as shift 2. Maplewood's total production for June was 6,400 row boats. What was the output for each shift?

Unknown(s)	Variable(s)	Relationship
Shift 1	$3S$	$3S$ (4,800)
Shift 2	S	$+ S$ (1,600)
		6,400

$$3S + S = 6,400$$
$$\frac{4S}{4} = \frac{6,400}{4}$$
$$S = 1,600$$

5–35. Ivy Corporation gave 84 people a bonus. If Ivy had given 2 more people bonuses, Ivy would have rewarded $\frac{2}{3}$ of the work force. What is Ivy's work force?

Unknown(s)	Variable(s)	Relationship
Total workers	W	$\frac{2}{3}W$ -2 workers 84

$$\frac{2}{3}W - 2 = 84$$
$$+2 \quad +2$$
$$\frac{2}{3}W = 86$$
$$3\left(\frac{2}{3}W\right) = 86(3)$$
$$\frac{2W}{2} = \frac{258}{2}$$
$$W = 129$$

5–36. Jim Murray and Phyllis Lowe received a total of $50,000 from a deceased relative's estate. They decided to put $10,000 in a trust for their nephew and divide the remainder. Phyllis received $\frac{3}{4}$ of the remainder; Jim received $\frac{1}{4}$. How much did Jim and Phyllis receive?

Unknown(s)	Variable(s)	Relationship
Jim	T	T ($10,000)
Phyllis	$3T$	$+\ 3T$ ($30,000) $40,000

$$T + 3T = \$40{,}000$$
$$\frac{4T}{4} = \frac{\$40{,}000}{4}$$
$$T = \$10{,}000$$

5–37. The first shift of the GME Corporation produced $1\frac{1}{2}$ times as many lanterns as the second shift. GME produced 5,600 lanterns in November. How many lanterns did GME produce on each shift?

Unknown(s)	Variable(s)	Relationship
Shift 1	$1.5L$	$1.5L$ (3,360)
Shift 2	L	$+\ L$ (2,240) 5,600

$$1.5L + L = 5{,}600$$
$$\frac{2.5L}{2.5} = \frac{5{,}600}{2.5}$$
$$L = 2{,}240$$
$$1.5L = 3{,}360$$

5–38. Jarvis Company sells thermometers ($2) and hot water bottles ($6). In December, Jarvis' total sales were $1,200. Customers bought 7 times as many thermometers as hot water bottles. How many of each did Jarvis sell? Check your answer.

Unknown(s)	Variable(s)	Price	Relationship
Thermometers	$7B$	$2	$14B$
Hot water bottles	B	6	$+\ 6B$ Total = $1,200

$$14B + 6B = 1{,}200$$
$$\frac{20B}{20} = \frac{1{,}200}{20}$$
$$B = 60 \text{ bottles}$$
$$7B = 420 \text{ thermometers}$$

Check

60($6) + 420($2) = $1,200
$360 + $840 = $1,200
$1,200 = $1,200

5–39. Ace Hardware sells cartons of wrenches ($100) and hammers ($300). Howard ordered 40 cartons of wrenches and hammers for $8,400. How many cartons of each are in the order? Check your answer.

Unknown(s)	Variable(s)	Price	Relationship
Wrenches	$40 - H$	\$100	$100(40 - H)$
Hammers	H	300	$+ 300H$
			Total = \$8,400

$$300H + 100(40 - H) = 8,400$$
$$300H + 4,000 - 100H = 8,400$$
$$200H + 4,000 = 8,400$$
$$- 4,000 \qquad -4,000$$
$$\frac{200H}{200} = \frac{4,400}{200}$$
$$H = 22 \text{ cartons of hammers}$$
$$40 - H = 18 \text{ cartons of wrenches}$$

Check

$$22(\$300) + 18(\$100) = \$8,400$$
$$\$6,600 + \$1,800 = \$8,400$$
$$\$8,400 = \$8,400$$

Challenge Problem
Distance Problem

Hint: Distance = Rate × Time.

a. 3 − .5 = 2.5 Sam starts ½ hour after Leona.
b. 15 miles.
c. 6 hours.

5–40. Myron Corporation is sponsoring a walking race at its company outing. Leona Jackson and Sam Peterson love to walk. Leona walks at the rate of 5 miles per hour. Sam walks at the rate of 6 miles per hour. Assume they start walking from the same place and walk in a straight line. Sam starts $\frac{1}{2}$ hour after Leona. Answer the questions that follow.

a. How long will it take Sam to meet Leona?
b. How many miles would each have walked?
c. Assume Leona and Sam meet in Lonetown Station where two buses leave along parallel routes in opposite directions. The bus traveling east has a 60 mph speed. The bus traveling west has a 40 mph speed. In how many hours will the buses be 600 miles apart?

	Distance =	Rate	× Time
Leona	Same	5	T
Sam	Same	6	$T - .5$

$$5T = 6(T - .5)$$
$$5T = 6T - 3$$
$$3 = T$$
$$5 \times 3 = 15 \text{ miles}$$
$$6 \times 2.5 = 15 \text{ miles}$$

	Rate	× Time	= Distance
East bus	60	T	600
West bus	40	T	600

$$60T + 40T = 600$$
$$100T = 600$$
$$T = 6 \text{ hours}$$

Summary Practice Test

Solutions are at end of text in Appendix II.
Quick Reference
If you get any wrong answers, study the page numbers given for each problem.
1. P. 122.
2. P. 122.

1. Amtrak reduced its round-trip ticket from Boston to Washington by \$49. The sale price was \$140. What was the original price?

Unknown(s)	Variable(s)	Relationship
Original price	P	P − \$49 = Sale price Sale price = \$140

$$P - \$49 = \$140$$
$$+ 49 \qquad +49$$
$$P = \$189$$

2. Glenn budgets $\frac{1}{6}$ of his weekly allowance for entertainment. Glenn's entertainment bill is \$29. What is his weekly allowance?

Unknown(s)	Variable(s)	Relationship
Weekly allowance	A	$\frac{1}{6}A$ Ent. = \$29

$$\frac{1}{6}A = \$29$$
$$\cancel{6}\left(\frac{A}{\cancel{6}}\right) = \$29(6)$$
$$A = \$174$$

3. P. 122.

3. TriCity Sales sells 4 times as many dishwashers as Solly Company. The difference between their sales is 96 dishwashers. How many dishwashers did each sell?

Unknown(s)	Variable(s)	Relationship
TriCity Solly	$4D$ D	$4D$ $-D$ 96 dishwashers

$$4D - D = 96$$
$$\frac{\not{3}D}{\not{3}} = \frac{96}{3}$$
$$D = 32$$
$$4D = 128$$

4. P. 122.

4. Alice Small and Rita Flynn sold a total of 400 cosmetic kits. Alice sold 3 times as many kits as Rita. How many did each sell?

Unknown(s)	Variable(s)	Relationship
Alice Rita	$3R$ R	$3R$ (300) $+R$ (100) 400

$$3R + R = 400$$
$$\frac{\not{4}R}{\not{4}} = \frac{400}{4}$$
$$R = 100$$
$$3R = 300$$

5. P. 122.

5. Sheffield Corporation sells sets of pots ($14) and dishes ($12) at a local charity. On Labor Day weekend, Sheffield's total sales were $1,080. People bought 3 times as many pots as dishes. How many of each did Sheffield sell? Check your answer.

Unknown(s)	Variable(s)	Price	Relationship
Pots Dishes	$3D$ D	$14 12	$42D$ $+12D$ Total = $1,080

$$42D + 12D = 1,080$$
$$\frac{\not{54}D}{\not{54}} = \frac{1,080}{54}$$
$$D = 20 \text{ dishes}$$
$$3D = 60 \text{ pots}$$

Check

20($12) + 60($14) = $1,080
$240 + $840 = $1,080
$1,080 = $1,080

6. P. 123.

6. Thorne's Diner sold a total of 500 small pizzas ($2) and hamburgers ($3) during the July 4 celebration. How many of each did the diner sell if total sales were $1,300. Check your answer.

Unknown(s)	Variable(s)	Price	Relationship
Hamburgers Pizzas	H $500 - H$	$3 2	$3H$ $+2(500 - H)$ Total = $1,300

$$3H + 2(500 - H) = 1,300$$
$$3H + 1,000 - 2H = 1,300$$
$$H + 1,000 = 1,300$$
$$-1,000 \quad -1,000$$
$$H = 300 \text{ hamburgers}$$
$$500 - H = 200 \text{ pizzas}$$

Check

300($3) + 200($2) = $1,300
$900 + $400 = $1,300
$1,300 = $1,300

Project A

ADVERTISING

Volvo Creates A Stir Again With TV Ads

By Jacqueline Mitchell
Staff Reporter of The Wall Street Journal

AB Volvo stirred up a hornet's nest a year ago when it admitted that commercials demonstrating the safety of its cars were rigged. Now the Swedish auto maker is back with new, hard-hitting commercials from a different ad agency. The initial result: more controversy.

Volvo's new commercials claim that its station wagons, which account for 30% of its U.S. sales, are twice as safe as minivans. And Volvo, which doesn't make a minivan, directly advises Americans to steer clear of the vehicles.

It's "deceptive and mislea[illegible]

Based on the article, if 30,000 deaths were reported and Volvo's claim is true, how many deaths would have occurred in minivans versus the Volvo wagon?

Volvo Minivan	D $2D$	D 10,000 $+2D$ 20,000 30,000

$$D + 2D = 30{,}000$$
$$\frac{3D}{3} = \frac{30{,}000}{3}$$
$$D = 10{,}000$$

Project B

THE WALL STREET JOURNAL

American Air Cuts Spending By $8 Billion

By Caleb Solomon
Staff Reporter of The Wall Street Journal

American Airlines said it slashed its capital spending plans by more than $8 billion through 1995 in a bid to keep its balance sheet unfettered amid an uncertain industry outlook.

The AMR Corp. unit said it told aircraft makers that it would "defer or pass" on options for 93 jets with a total value of $5.2 billion. American said it would reschedule deliveries of other aircraft and would cut other capital spending by about $3 billion, including expenditures on gates, facilities and other areas.

Until recently, American had an ambitious growth strategy to spend almost $22 billion through 1995 and was the industry pacesetter for expansion. American fueled massive expansion in the 1980s and explosive revenue growth by adding capacity.

But the Persian Gulf War and higher [illegible]

American Airlines reduced its budget by $8.2 billion. Assuming the new budget is $12.4 billion, what was the original budget?

Original budget	B	B – $8.2 billion = New budget New budget = $12.4 billion

$$B - \$8.2 = \$12.4$$
$$+\ 8.2 \quad +\ 8.2$$
$$B = \$20.6 \text{ billion}$$

NOTES

THAT WAS THEN . . .
. . . THIS IS NOW

In 1889, a test on Ivory Soap was run to see what impurities it had. The list was .11% uncombined alkali, .28% carbonates, and .17% mineral matter, equaling .56% foreign substances. Thus, 100% − .56% = $99\frac{44}{100}$% pure. The slogan was born and remains today.

6

Percents and Their Applications

LEARNING UNIT OBJECTIVES

LU 6–1: Conversions

1. Discuss the relationship of percents to numbers. *p. 138.*
2. Convert decimals to percents. *p. 138.*
3. Convert percents to decimals. *p. 139.*
4. Convert fractions to percents. *p. 139.*
5. Rounding percents to indicated digit. *p. 140.*
6. Convert percents to fractions. *p. 140.*

LU 6–2: Application of Percents—Portion Formula

1. List and define the key elements of the portion formula. *pp. 141–142.*
2. Dissect and solve a word problem. *p. 142.*
3. Solve for one unknown of the portion formula when the other two key elements are given. *pp. 142–145.*
4. Calculate rate of percent increases and decreases. *p. 145.*

Quaker Oats Reports Profit Increased 60%

By a WALL STREET JOURNAL *Staff Reporter*
CHICAGO—**Quaker Oats** Co. said earnings for its fourth quarter, ended June 30, rose 60% to $106.4 million, or $1.38 a share, from $66.3 million, or 86 cents a share.
The results include a charge of $10 million for the closing of a pasta-making plant. The year-earlier figures included a $34.4 million loss from discontinued operations.

Knott's Berry Farm

Theme Park Plans to Lower Children's Admission by 41%

Knott's Berry Farm, one of Southern California's largest theme parks, said it plans to lower its admission price for children by 41% on Dec. 21.
Knott's, based in Buena Park, is privately owned by the Knott family, said that the new price of $9.95 for children from three to 11 years old is permanent. Knott's current price for children is $17. Adults pay $21.95.

Companies frequently use percents to express various increases and decreases. For example, note the two *Wall Street Journal* clippings above. Quaker Oats reported their profits as an increase of 60%. Knott's Berry Farm decreased its admission price by 41%. Do you find it difficult to understand these percent increases and decreases? This chapter explains the conversions of percents and their application to personal and business events.

LEARNING UNIT 6–1 CONVERSIONS

Percents are the result of expressing numbers as a fraction of 100. Thus, 30% is 30 parts out of 100 parts. The percent symbol indicates hundredths (division by 100). Businesses use percents to see the relationship between two or more numbers. This relationship gives a more accurate picture of business events.

In the previous chapters on fractions and decimals, we saw how to express in fractional and decimal form the six colors in a bag of 55 M&M's®. Now look at Table 6–1 and see how each color is expressed in percent (rounded to nearest hundredth percent).

In Table 6–1, we illustrated the same value in terms of fractions, decimals, and percents. This unit shows you how to convert decimals to percents, percents to decimals, fractions to percents, and percents to fractions. We also explain how to round percents.

Converting Decimals to Percents

Let's begin by learning how decimals can be converted to percents.

Steps for Converting Decimals to Percents

Step 1. Move decimal point two places to the right. You are actually multiplying by 100.

Step 2. Place a percent symbol at end of number.

EXAMPLES

.65 = 65%　　.6 = 60%　　6 = 600%
.381 = 38.1%　　.007 = .7%　　2.51 = 251%

(.6 = 60% and .007 = .7%: Add one zero to make two places.)
(6 = 600% and 2.51 = 251%: Add two zeros to make two places.)

Caution: One percent means 1 out of every 100. Since .7% is less than 1%, it means $\frac{7}{10}$ of 1%—a very small amount. Less than 1% is less than .01. To show a number less than 1%, you must use more than two decimal places. Example: .7% = .007.

TABLE 6-1
Analyzing a Bag of M&M's®

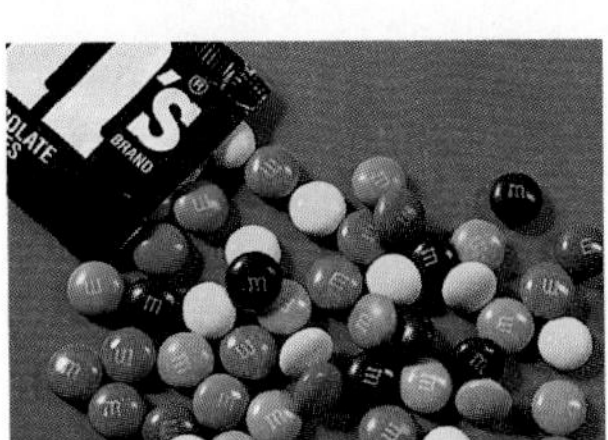

Sharon Hoogstraten

Color	Fraction	Decimal (hundredth)	Percent (hundredth)
Yellow	$\frac{18}{55}$	.33	32.73%
Red	$\frac{10}{55}$	.18	18.18
Tan	$\frac{9}{55}$	.16	16.36
Orange	$\frac{7}{55}$	.13	12.73
Brown	$\frac{6}{55}$	.11	10.91
Green	$\frac{5}{55}$	.09	9.09
	$\frac{55}{55} = 1$	1.00	100.00%

Note: The color ratios currently given are a sample only, used for educational purposes, and do not represent the manufacturer's color ratios.

Converting Percents to Decimals

Converting percents to decimals first involves learning two basic steps. Then you can learn the conversion steps for percents expressed in fractional form.

Steps for Converting Percents to Decimals

Step 1. Drop percent symbol.

Step 2. Move decimal point two places to the left. You are actually dividing by 100.

Steps for Conversion When Percent Is Expressed in Fractional Form

Step 1. Convert a fraction to a decimal by dividing numerator by denominator.

Step 2. Drop percent symbol.

Step 3. Move decimal point two places to the left.

Note that when a percent is less than 1%, the decimal conversion has at least two leading zeros before the whole number .009.

EXAMPLES

$.9\% = .009$
$9\% = .09$
$92\% = .92$
$92.4\% = .924$
$924.4\% = 9.244$

$8\frac{3}{4}\% = 8.75\% = .0875$
$5\frac{1}{2}\% = 5.5\% = .055$
$\frac{1}{5}\% = .20\% = .0020$
$\frac{1}{4}\% = .25\% = .0025$

Think of $8\frac{3}{4}\%$ as

$8\% = .08$
$+\frac{3}{4}\% = +.0075$
$8\frac{3}{4}\% = .0875$

Converting Fractions to Percents

To convert fractions to percents, use the following steps:

Steps for Converting Fractions to Percents

Step 1. Divide the numerator by the denominator.

Step 2. Move decimal point two places to the right.

Step 3. Add percent symbol.

EXAMPLES $\frac{1}{4} = .25. = 25\%$ $\quad \frac{1}{5} = .20. = 20\%$ $\quad \frac{1}{20} = .05. = 5\%$

Rounding Percents

Since you are familiar with rounding numbers, the following steps should be easy to remember.

Steps for Rounding Percents

Step 1. When converting from a fraction or decimal, be sure your answer is in percent form before rounding.

Step 2. Identify specific digit. If digit to the right of identified digit is 5 or greater, round up identified digit.

Step 3. Delete digits to the right of identified digit.

For example, Table 6–1 shows that the 18 yellow M&M's® rounded to the nearest hundredth percent is 32.73% of the bag of 55 M&M's®. Let's look at how we arrived at this figure.

Step 1.[1] $\frac{18}{55} = .3272727 = 32.72727\%$ ← Note number is in percent! Identify hundredth percent digit.

Step 2. 32.73727 Digit to the right of identified digit is greater than 5, so identified digit is increased by 1.

Step 3. **32.73%** Digits to the right of identified digit are deleted.

Converting Percents to Fractions

Converting percents to fractions first involves learning three basic steps. Then you can learn the conversion steps for mixed percents.

Steps for Converting a Whole Percent (or a Fractional Percent) to a Fraction

Step 1. Drop percent symbol.

Step 2. Multiply number by $\frac{1}{100}$.

Step 3. Reduce to lowest terms.

Do you recall that the chapter opener stated that Ivory soap is $99\frac{44}{100}$% pure? This is an example of a mixed percent.

Steps for Converting a Mixed Percent to a Fraction

Step 1. Drop percent symbol.

Step 2. Change mixed percent to an improper fraction.

Step 3. Multiply number by $\frac{1}{100}$.

Step 4. Reduce to lowest terms.

Note: If you have a decimal percent, change the decimal portion to fractional equivalent and continue with Steps 1 to 4.

EXAMPLES

$$76\% = 76 \times \frac{1}{100} = \frac{76}{100} = \frac{19}{25}$$

$$\frac{1}{9}\% = \frac{1}{9} \times \frac{1}{100} = \frac{1}{900}$$

$$156\% = 156 \times \frac{1}{100} = \frac{156}{100} = 1\frac{56}{100} = 1\frac{14}{25}$$

Remember, if a percent is a mixed number, convert it first to an improper fraction before multiplying by $\frac{1}{100}$.

$$12\frac{1}{2}\% = \frac{25}{2} \times \frac{1}{100} = \frac{25}{200} = \frac{1}{8}$$

$$12.5\% = 12\frac{1}{2}\% = \frac{25}{2} \times \frac{1}{100} = \frac{25}{200} = \frac{1}{8}$$

$$22.5\% = 22\frac{1}{2}\% = \frac{45}{2} \times \frac{1}{100} = \frac{45}{200} = \frac{9}{40}$$

It's time to check your progress with the following Practice Quiz.

[1] When using a calculator, press [18] [÷] [55] [%]. This allows you to go right to percent, avoiding the decimal step.

LU 6-1 PRACTICE QUIZ

Convert to percents (round to the nearest tenth percent as needed):

1. .4444 ______ 2. .567 ______
3. .009 ______ 4. 8.94444 ______

Convert to decimals (remember, decimals representing less than 1% will have at least two leading zeros before the number):

5. $\frac{1}{4}\%$ ______ 6. $6\frac{3}{4}\%$ ______
7. 87% ______ 8. 810.9% ______

Convert to percents (round to the nearest hundredth percent):

9. $\frac{1}{6}$ ______ 10. $\frac{2}{9}$ ______

Convert to fractions (remember, if it is a mixed number, first convert to an improper fraction):

11. 18% ______ 12. $71\frac{1}{2}\%$ ______ 13. 130% ______
14. $\frac{1}{2}\%$ ______ 15. 19.9% ______

SOLUTIONS TO LU 6-1 PRACTICE QUIZ

$6\frac{3}{4}\%$

$$\begin{aligned} 6\% &= .06 \\ +\tfrac{3}{4}\% &= +.0075 \\ \hline 6\tfrac{3}{4}\% &= .0675 \end{aligned}$$

1. 44.44% = 44.4%
2. 56.7%
3. .9%
4. 894.444% = 894.4%
5. $\frac{1}{4}\% \longrightarrow .25\% \longrightarrow .0025$
6. $6\frac{3}{4}\% \longrightarrow 6.75\% \longrightarrow .0675$
7. $87\% \longrightarrow .87$
8. $810.9\% \longrightarrow 8.109$
9. $\frac{1}{6} = .1666\bar{6} \longrightarrow 16.67\%$
10. $\frac{2}{9} = .2222\bar{2} \longrightarrow 22.22\%$
11. $18\% \longrightarrow 18 \times \frac{1}{100} = \frac{18}{100} = \frac{9}{50}$
12. $71\frac{1}{2}\% \longrightarrow \frac{143}{2} \times \frac{1}{100} = \frac{143}{200}$
13. $130\% \longrightarrow 130 \times \frac{1}{100} = \frac{130}{100} = 1\frac{3}{10}$
14. $\frac{1}{2}\% \longrightarrow \frac{1}{2} \times \frac{1}{100} = \frac{1}{200}$
15. $19\frac{9}{10}\% \longrightarrow \frac{199}{10} \times \frac{1}{100} = \frac{199}{1{,}000}$

LEARNING UNIT 6-2 APPLICATION OF PERCENTS—PORTION FORMULA

Sharon Hoogstraten

The bag of M&M's® we have been studying are M&M's® Plain Chocolate Candies. M&M/Mars also makes M&M's® Peanut Chocolate Candies and some other types of M&M's®. To study the application of percents to problems involving M&M's®, we make two key assumptions:

1. Total sales of M&M's® Plain, Peanut, and other M&M's® Chocolate Candies are $400,000.
2. Eighty percent of M&M's® sales are Plain Chocolate Candies. This leaves the Peanut and other M&M's® Chocolate Candies with 20% of the sales (100% − 80%).

Before we begin, you must understand the meaning of three terms—base, rate, and portion. These terms are the key elements in solving percent problems.

- □ **Base (*B*).** The **base** is the beginning whole quantity or value (100%) with which you will compare some other quantity or value. Often the problems give the base after the word *of*. For example, the whole (total) sales of M&M's®—Plain, Peanut, and other M&M's® Chocolate Candies—are $400,000.

T

- **Rate (*R*).** The **rate** is a percent, decimal, or fraction that indicates the part of the base that you must calculate. The percent symbol often helps you identify the rate. For example, M&M's® Plain Chocolate Candies currently account for 80% of sales. So the rate is 80%. Remember that 80% is also $\frac{4}{5}$ or .8.
- **Portion (*P*).** The **portion** is the amount or part that results from the base multiplied by the rate. For example, total sales of M&M's® are $400,000 (base); $400,000 times .80 (rate) equals $320,000 (portion), or the sales of M&M's® Plain Chocolate Candies. *A key point to remember is that portion is a number and not a percent. In fact, the portion can be larger than the base if the rate is greater than 100%.*

Solving Percents with the Portion Formula

Key Point
The rate and portion will refer to same part of base.

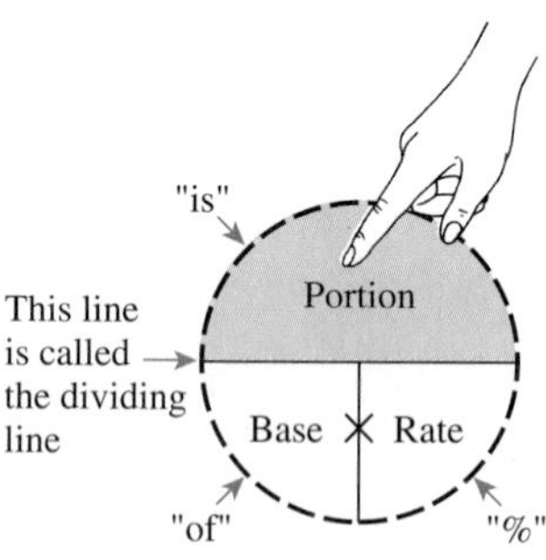

In problems involving portion, base, and rate, we give two of these elements. You must find the third element. The key formula to remember is:

$$\text{Portion } (P) = \text{Base } (B) \times \text{Rate } (R)$$

To help you solve the portion, base, and rate, this unit shows pie charts. The shaded area in each pie chart indicates the element that you must solve. For example, since we shaded *portion* in the pie chart at the left, you must solve for portion. To use the pie charts, put your finger on the shaded area (in this case portion). The formula that remains tells you what to do. So in the pie chart at the left, you solve the problem by multiplying base times rate. Note the circle around the pie chart is broken since we want to emphasize that portion can be larger than the base if the rate is greater than 100%. The horizontal line in the pie chart is called the dividing line, and we will use it when we solve for base or rate.

Now, let's begin with a closer look at the M&M's® example to see how we arrived at the $320,000 sales of M&M's® Plain Chocolate Candies, given earlier. We will be using blueprint aids to help dissect and solve each word problem.

Solving for Portion

The Word Problem Sales of M&M's® Plain Chocolate Candies are 80% of total M&M's® sales. Total M&M's® sales are $400,000. What are the sales of M&M's® Plain Chocolate Candies?

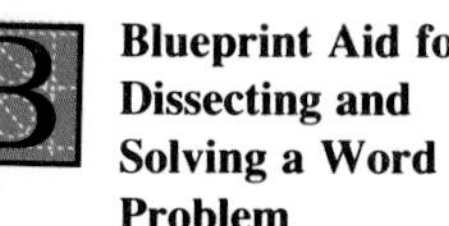

Blueprint Aid for Dissecting and Solving a Word Problem

A. Gather the facts	B. What am I solving for?	C. What must I know or calculate before solving problem?	D. Key points to remember
M&M's® Plain Chocolate Candies sales: 80%. *Total M&M's® sales:* $400,000.	Sales of M&M's® Plain Chocolate Candies.	Identify key elements. *Base:* $400,000. *Rate:* .80 *Portion:* ? Portion = Base × Rate.	Amount or part of beginning Portion (?) Base ($400,000) Rate (.80) Beginning whole quantity (often after "of") Percent symbol or word (here we put into decimal) Portion and rate must relate to same piece of base.

Steps to Solving Problem

1. Set up formula. Portion = Base × Rate
2. Calculate portion (sales of M&M's® Plain Chocolate Candies). $P = \$400{,}000 \times .80$
   $P = \$320{,}000$

Note how we gather the facts in Column A of the blueprint aid. In Column B, we state that we are looking for sales of M&M's® Plain Chocolate Candies. In Column C, we identify each key element along with the formula to solve the problem. Review the pie chart in Column D. Note that the portion and rate must relate to the same piece of the base. In this word problem, we can see from the solution below the blueprint aid that sales of M&M's® Plain Chocolate Candies are $320,000. The $320,000 does indeed represent 80% of the base. Note here that the portion ($320,000) is less than the base of $400,000 since the rate is less than 100%.

Now let's work an additional word problem that solves for the portion.

The Word Problem Sales of M&M's® Plain Chocolate Candies are 80% of total M&M's® sales. Total M&M's® sales are $400,000. What are the sales of Peanut and other M&M's® Chocolate Candies?

Blueprint Aid for Dissecting and Solving a Word Problem

A. Gather the facts	B. What am I solving for?	C. What must I know or calculate before solving problem?	D. Key points to remember
M&M's® *Plain* *Chocolate* *Candies* *sales:* 80%. *Total* *M&M's®* *sales:* $400,000.	Sales of Peanut and other M&M's® Chocolate Candies.	Identify key elements. *Base:* $400,000. *Rate:* .20 (100% − 80%) *Portion:* ? Portion = Base × Rate.	If 80% of sales are Plain, then 20% are Peanut and other M&M's® Chocolate Candies; Portion (?); Base ($400,000) × Rate (.20). Portion and rate must relate to same piece of base.

Steps to Solving Problem

1. Set up formula. — Portion = Base × Rate
2. Calculate portion (sale of Peanut and other M&M's® Chocolate Candies). — P = $400,000 × .20; P = $80,000

In the above blueprint aid, note that we must use a rate that agrees with the portion so the portion and rate refer to the same piece of the base. Thus, if 80% of sales are M&M's® Plain Chocolate Candies, 20% must be Peanut and other M&M's® Chocolate Candies (100% − 80% = 20%). So we use a rate of .20.

In Step 2, we multiplied $400,000 × .20 to get a portion of $80,000. This portion represents the part of the sales that were *not* M&M's® Plain Chocolate Candies. Note that the rate of .20 and the portion of $80,000 relate to the same piece of the base—$80,000 is 20% of $400,000. Also note that the portion ($80,000) is less than the base ($400,000) since the rate is less than 100%.

Take a moment to review the two blueprint aids in this section. Be sure you understand why the rate in the first blueprint aid was 80% and the rate in the second blueprint aid was 20%.

Solving for the Rate

The Word Problem Sales of M&M's® Plain Chocolate Candies are $320,000. Total M&M's® sales are $400,000. What is the percent of M&M's® Plain Chocolate Candies sales compared to total M&M's® sales?

Blueprint Aid for Dissecting and Solving a Word Problem

A. Gather the facts	B. What am I solving for?	C. What must I know or calculate before solving problem?	D. Key points to remember
M&M's® Plain Chocolate Candies sales: $320,000. *Total M&M's® sales:* $400,000.	Percent of M&M's® Plain Chocolate Candies sales to total M&M's® sales.	Identify key elements. *Base:* $400,000. *Rate:* ? *Portion:* $320,000. Rate = $\frac{\text{Portion}}{\text{Base}}$	Since portion is less than base, the rate must be less than 100% Portion ($320,000) Base ($400,000) × Rate (?) Portion and rate must relate to same piece of base.

Steps to Solving Problem

1. Set up formula. $\text{Rate} = \frac{\text{Portion}}{\text{Base}}$
2. Calculate rate (percent of M&M's® Plain Chocolate Candies sales). $R = \frac{\$320,000}{\$400,000}$

$R = 80\%$

Note that in this word problem, the rate of 80% and the portion of $320,000 refer to the same piece of the base. In the next word problem, we will look at an example where rate and portion refer to different pieces of the base.

The Word Problem Sales of M&M's® Plain Chocolate Candies are $320,000. Total sales of Plain, Peanut, and other M&M's® Chocolate Candies are $400,000. What percent of Peanut and other M&M's® Chocolate Candies are sold compared to total M&M's® sales?

Blueprint Aid for Dissecting and Solving a Word Problem

A. Gather the facts	B. What am I solving for?	C. What must I know or calculate before solving problem?	D. Key points to remember
M&M's® Plain Chocolate Candies sales: $320,000. *Total M&M's® sales:* $400,000.	Percent of Peanut and other M&M's® Chocolate Candies sales compared to total M&M's® sales.	Identify key elements. *Base:* $400,000. *Rate:* ? *Portion:* $80,000 ($400,000 − $320,000). Rate = $\frac{\text{Portion}}{\text{Base}}$	Represents sales of Peanut and other M&M's® Chocolate Candies Portion ($80,000) Base ($400,000) × Rate (?) When portion becomes $80,000, the portion and rate now relate to same piece of base.

Steps to Solving Problem

1. Set up formula. $\text{Rate} = \frac{\text{Portion}}{\text{Base}}$
2. Calculate rate. $R = \frac{\$80,000}{\$400,000}$ ($400,000 − $320,000)

$R = 20\%$

The above word problem asks for rate of candy sales that are *not* plain. Thus, $400,000 of total candy sales less sales of M&M's® Plain Chocolate Candies ($320,000) allows us to arrive at sales of Peanut and other M&M's® Chocolate Candies ($80,000).

The $80,000 portion represents 20% of total candy sales. The $80,000 portion and 20% rate refer to the same piece of the $400,000 base. Compare this blueprint aid with the blueprint aid for the previous word problem. Ask yourself why in the previous word problem the rate was 80% and in this word problem the rate is 20%. In both word problems, the portion was less than the base since the rate was less than 100%.

Now we go on to calculate the base. Remember to read the word problem carefully so that you match the rate and portion to the same piece of the base.

Solving for the Base

The Word Problem Sales of Peanut and other M&M's® Chocolate Candies are 20% of total M&M's® sales. Sales of M&M's® Plain Chocolate Candies are $320,000. What are the total sales of all M&M's®?

B **Blueprint Aid for Dissecting and Solving a Word Problem**

A. Gather the facts	B. What am I solving for?	C. What must I know or calculate before solving problem?	D. Key points to remember
Peanut and other M&M's® Chocolate Candies sales: 20% *M&M's® Plain Chocolate Candies sales:* $320,000.	Total M&M's® sales.	Identify key elements. *Base:* ? *Rate:* .80 (100% − 20%). *Portion:* $320,000. Base = $\frac{\text{Portion}}{\text{Rate}}$	Portion ($320,000) Base (?) × Rate (.80) (100% - 20%) Portion ($320,000) and rate (.80) do relate to same piece of base.

Steps to Solving Problem

1. Set up formula. Base $= \frac{\text{Portion}}{\text{Rate}}$

2. Calculate base. $B = \frac{\$320,000}{.80}$ ⟵ $320,000 is 80% of base.

   $B = \$400,000$

Note that we could not use 20% for the rate. The $320,000 of M&M's® Plain Chocolate Candies represents 80% (100% − 20%) of the total sales of M&M's®.We use 80% so that the portion and rate refer to same piece of the base. Remember that portion ($320,000) is less than the base ($400,000) since the rate is less than 100%.

Calculating Percent Increases and Decreases

Costs are continually increasing. In 1982, a ticket to watch the Boston Celtics play basketball cost $14. In 1992, a ticket cost $45. This is a 221% increase in cost. In this section, we will learn how to calculate **percent increases** and **percent decreases** using examples involving M&M's®.

Rate of Percent Increase

The Word Problem Sheila Leary went to her local supermarket and bought the bag of M&M's® shown on p. 145. The bag indicated a weight of 18.40 ounces of M&M's®, which was 15% more than a regular 1 pound bag of M&M's®. Sheila, who is a careful shopper, wanted to check and see if she was actually getting a 15% increase. Let's help Sheila dissect and solve this problem.

Blueprint Aid for Dissecting and Solving a Word Problem

A. Gather the facts	B. What am I solving for?	C. What must I know or calculate before solving problem?	D. Key points to remember
New bag of M&M's®: 18.40 oz. 15% increase in weight. *Original bag of M&M's®:* 16 oz. (1 lb.).	Checking percent increase of 15%.	Identify key elements. *Base:* 16 oz. *Rate:* ? *Portion:* 2.40 oz. (18.40 oz. − 16.00 = 2.40 oz.) $\text{Rate} = \frac{\text{Portion}}{\text{Base}}$	Difference between base and new weight Portion (2.40 oz.) Base × Rate (16 oz.) (?) Original amount sold

Steps to Solving Problem

1. Set up formula. $\text{Rate} = \frac{\text{Portion}}{\text{Base}}$

2. Calculate rate. $R = \frac{2.40 \text{ oz.}}{16.00 \text{ oz.}}$ ⟵ Difference between base and new weight. / ⟵ Old weight equals 100%.

$R = 15\%$ increase

The new weight of the bag of M&M's® is really 115% of the old weight:

16.00 oz.	=	100%
2.40	=	15
18.40 oz.	=	115%

We can check this by looking at the following pie chart.

Portion = Base × Rate

18.40 oz. = 16 oz. × 1.15

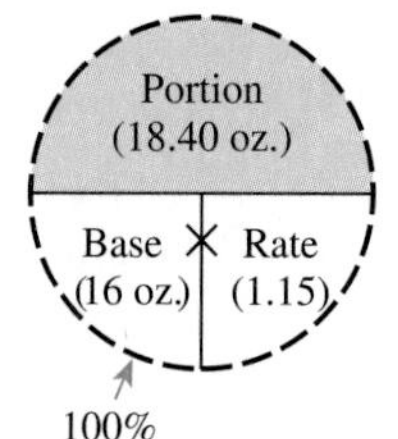

Why is the portion greater than the base? Remember that the portion can only be larger than the base if the rate is greater than 100%. Note how the portion and rate relate to the same piece of the base—18.40 oz. is 115% of the base (16 oz.).

Now let's see what could happen if M&M/Mars had a sugar shortage.

Rate of Percent Decrease

The Word Problem Because of a sugar shortage, M&M/Mars company decided to decrease the weight of each 1-pound bag of M&M's® to 12 ounces. What is the rate of percent decrease?

Blueprint Aid for Dissecting and Solving a Word Problem

A. Gather the facts	B. What am I solving for?	C. What must I know or calculate before solving problem?	D. Key points to remember
16 oz. bag of M&M's® reduced to 12 oz.	Rate of percent decrease.	Identify key elements. *Base:* 16 oz. *Rate:* ? *Portion:* 4 oz. (16 oz. − 12 oz.). $\text{Rate} = \frac{\text{Portion}}{\text{Base}}$	Amount of decrease Portion (4 oz.) Base × Rate (16 oz.) (?) Old base 100%

Steps to Solving Problem

1. Set up formula. $\text{Rate} = \dfrac{\text{Portion}}{\text{Base}}$

2. Calculate rate. $R = \dfrac{4 \text{ oz.}}{16.00 \text{ oz.}}$

$R = 25\%$ decrease

The new weight of the bag of M&M's® is really 75% of the old weight:

$$\begin{array}{rcl} 16 \text{ oz.} & = & 100\% \\ -4 & = & 25 \\ \hline 12 \text{ oz.} & = & 75\% \end{array}$$

We can check this by looking at the following pie chart:

$$\text{Portion} = \text{Base} \times \text{Rate}$$
$$12 \text{ oz.} = 16 \text{ oz.} \times .75$$

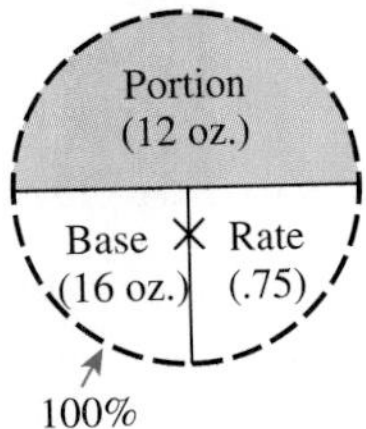

Note that the portion is smaller than the base because the rate is less than 100%. Also note how the portion and rate relate to the same piece of the base—12 ounces is 75% of the base (16 oz.).

LU 6–2 PRACTICE QUIZ

Solve for portion:

1. 41% of 700.
2. 40% of $6,000

Solve for rate (round to the nearest tenth percent as needed):

3. 540 is ______% of 6,000.
4. 150 is ______% of 900.

Solve for base (round to the nearest tenth as needed):

5. 55 is 40% of ______.
6. 900 is $4\frac{1}{2}\%$ of ______.

Solve the following (blueprint aids will be shown in solution; you might want to try some on scrap paper):

7. Five out of 25 students in Professor Ford's class received an "A" grade. What percent of the class *did not* receive the "A" grade?
8. Abby Biernet has yet to receive 60% of her lobster order. Abby received 80 lobsters to date. What was her original order?
9. In 1995, Dunkin Company had $300,000 in donut sales. In 1996, sales were up 40%. What are Dunkin sales for 1996?
10. The price of an Apple computer dropped from $1,600 to $1,200. What was the percent decrease?

SOLUTIONS TO LU 6–2 PRACTICE QUIZ

1. $287 = 700 \times .41$
   $(P) = (B) \times (R)$
2. $\$2{,}400 = \$6{,}000 \times .40$
   $(P) = (B) \times (R)$
3. $\dfrac{(P)\ 540}{(B)\ 6{,}000} = .09 = 9\%\ (R)$
4. $\dfrac{(P)\ 150}{(B)\ 900} = .1666 = 16.7\%\ (R)$
5. $\dfrac{(P)\ 55}{(R)\ .40} = 137.5\ (B)$
6. $\dfrac{(P)\ 900}{(R)\ .045} = 20{,}000\ (B)$

Blueprint Aid for Dissecting and Solving a Word Problem

7. Percent of Professor Ford's class that did not receive the "A" grade:

A. Gather the facts	B. What am I solving for?	C. What must I know or calculate before solving problem?	D. Key points to remember
5 "A"s. 25 in class.	Percent that did not receive "A".	Identify key elements. *Base:* 25 *Rate:* ? *Portion:* 20 (25 − 5) $\text{Rate} = \frac{\text{Portion}}{\text{Base}}$	Portion (20) Base (25) × Rate (?) The whole Portion and rate must relate to same piece of base.

Steps to Solving Problem

1. Set up formula. $\text{Rate} = \frac{\text{Portion}}{\text{Base}}$
2. Calculate rate. $R = \frac{20}{25}$

$R = 80\%$

Blueprint Aid for Dissecting and Solving a Word Problem

8. Abby Biernet's original order:

A. Gather the facts	B. What am I solving for?	C. What must I know or calculate before solving problem?	D. Key points to remember
60% of order not in. 80 lobsters received.	Total order of lobsters.	Identify key elements. *Base:* ? *Rate:* .40 (100% − 60%). *Portion:* 80 $\text{Base} = \frac{\text{Portion}}{\text{Rate}}$	Portion (80) Base (?) × Rate (.40) 80 lobsters represents 40% of the order Portion and rate must relate to same piece of base.

Steps to Solving Problem

1. Set up formula. $\text{Base} = \frac{\text{Portion}}{\text{Rate}}$
2. Calculate rate. $B = \frac{80}{.40}$ ← 80 lobsters is 40% of base.

$B = 200$ lobsters

9. Dunkin Company sales for 1996:

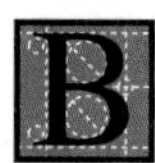

Blueprint Aid for Dissecting and Solving a Word Problem

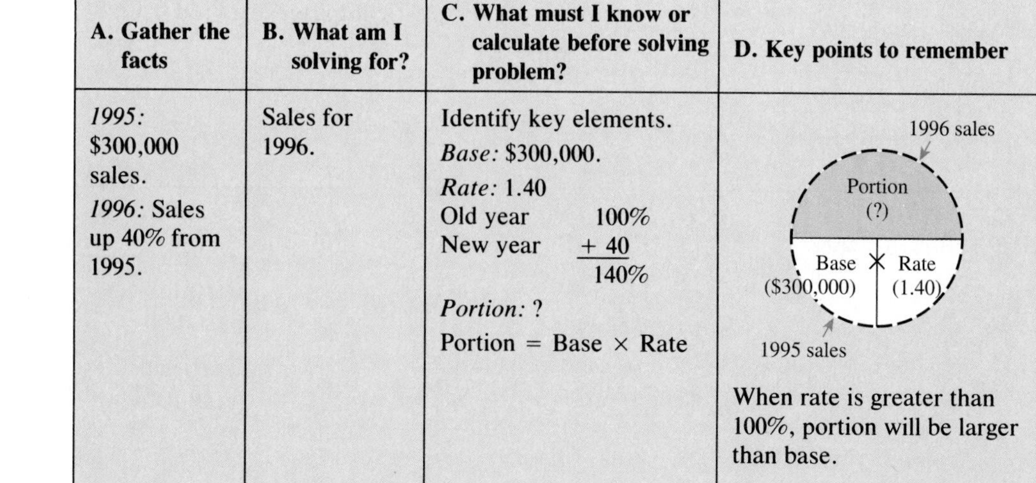

A. Gather the facts	B. What am I solving for?	C. What must I know or calculate before solving problem?	D. Key points to remember
1995: $300,000 sales. *1996:* Sales up 40% from 1995.	Sales for 1996.	Identify key elements. *Base:* $300,000. *Rate:* 1.40 Old year 100% New year + 40 140% *Portion:* ? Portion = Base × Rate	1996 sales Portion (?) Base ($300,000) × Rate (1.40) 1995 sales When rate is greater than 100%, portion will be larger than base.

Steps to Solving Problem

1. Set up formula. Portion = Base × Rate
$P = \$300{,}000 \times 1.40$
2. Calculate portion. $P = \$420{,}000$

10. Percent decrease in an Apple computer price:

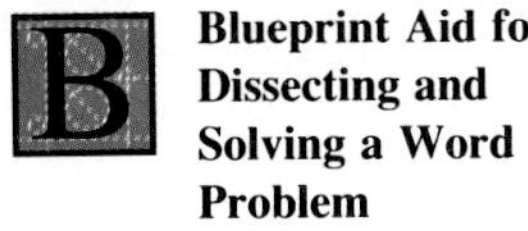

Blueprint Aid for Dissecting and Solving a Word Problem

A. Gather the facts	B. What am I solving for?	C. What must I know or calculate before solving problem?	D. Key points to remember
Apple computer was \$1,600; now, \$1,200.	Percent decrease in price.	Identify key elements. *Base:* \$1,600. *Rate:* ? *Portion:* \$400 (\$1,600 − \$1,200). $\text{Rate} = \frac{\text{Portion}}{\text{Base}}$	Difference in price Portion (\$400) Base (\$1,600) × Rate (?) Original price

Steps to Solving Problem

1. Set up formula. $\text{Rate} = \frac{\text{Portion}}{\text{Base}}$
2. Calculate rate. $R = \frac{\$400}{\$1{,}600}$
$R = 25\%$

CHAPTER ORGANIZER: A REFERENCE GUIDE

Page	Topic	Key point, procedure, formula	Example(s) to illustrate situation
138	Converting decimals to percents	1. Move decimal point two places to right. 2. Place a percent symbol at end of number.	.81 = 81% .008 = .8% 4.15 = 415%
139	Converting percents to decimals	1. Drop percent symbol. 2. Move decimal point two places to left. For fractional form: 1. Convert fraction to a decimal. 2. Drop percent symbol. 3. Move decimal two places to left.	.89% = .0089 $8\frac{3}{4}\%$ = 8.75% = .0875 95% = .95 $\frac{1}{4}\%$ = .25% = .0025 195% = 1.95 $\frac{1}{5}\%$ = .20% = .0020
139	Converting fractions to percents	1. Divide numerator by denominator. 2. Move decimal point two places to right. 3. Add percent symbol.	$\frac{4}{5}$ = 80%
139	Rounding percents	Be sure answer is in percent before rounding. Follow same rounding procedures as for decimals.	Round to nearest hundredth percent. $\frac{3}{7}$ = .4285714 = 42.85714% = 42.86%

Page	Topic	Key point, procedure, formula	Example(s) to illustrate situation
140	Converting percents to fractions	To convert whole percent (or a fractional percent) to fraction: 1. Drop percent symbol. 2. Multiply number by $\frac{1}{100}$. 3. Reduce to lowest terms. To convert a mixed percent to a fraction: 1. Drop percent symbol. 2. Change mixed percent to an improper fraction. 3. Multiply number by $\frac{1}{100}$. 4. Reduce to lowest terms. If you have a decimal percent, change decimal portion to fractional equivalent and continue with previous steps.	$64\% \rightarrow 64 \times \frac{1}{100} = \frac{64}{100} = \frac{16}{25}$ $\frac{1}{4}\% \rightarrow \frac{1}{4} \times \frac{1}{100} = \frac{1}{400}$ $119\% \rightarrow 119 \times \frac{1}{100} = \frac{119}{100} = 1\frac{19}{100}$ $16\frac{1}{4}\% \rightarrow \frac{65}{4} \times \frac{1}{100} = \frac{65}{400} = \frac{13}{80}$ $16.25\% \rightarrow 16\frac{1}{4}\% = \frac{65}{4} \times \frac{1}{100}$ $= \frac{65}{400} = \frac{13}{80}$
142	Solving for portion	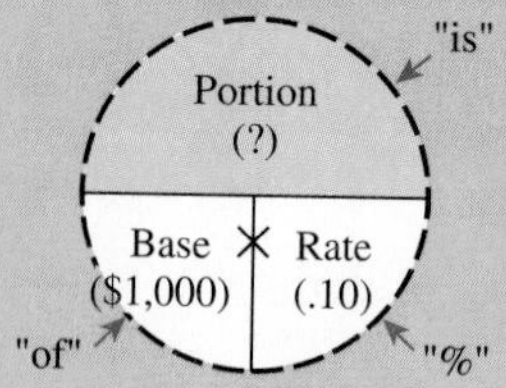 "is" Portion (?) "of" Base ($1,000) × Rate (.10) "%"	10% of Mel's paycheck of $1,000 goes for food. What portion is deducted for food? $100 = $1,000 × .10 Note: If question was what amount does not go for food, the portion would have been: $900 = $1,000 × .90 (100% − 10% = 90%)
144	Solving for rate	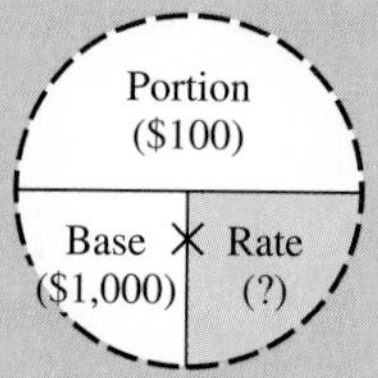 Portion ($100) Base ($1,000) × Rate (?)	Assume Mel spends $100 for food from his $1,000 paycheck. What percent of his paycheck is spent on food? $\frac{\$100}{\$1,000} = .10 = 10\%$ Note: Portion is less than base since rate is less than 100%.
145	Solving for base	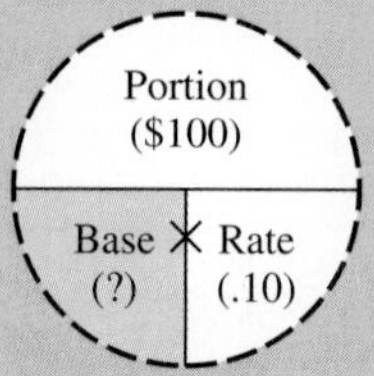 Portion ($100) Base (?) × Rate (.10)	Assume Mel spends $100 for food, which is 10% of his paycheck. What is Mel's total paycheck? $\frac{\$100}{.10} = \$1,000$
146	Calculate percent increases or decreases	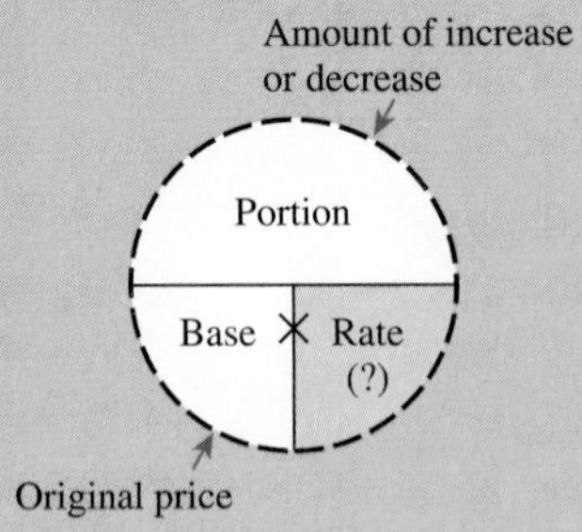 Amount of increase or decrease Portion Base × Rate (?) Original price	Stereo, $2,000 original price. Stereo, $2,500 new price. $\frac{\$500}{\$2,000} = .25 = 25\%$ increase **Check** $2,000 × 1.25 = $2,500 Note: Portion is greater than base since rate is greater than 100%. 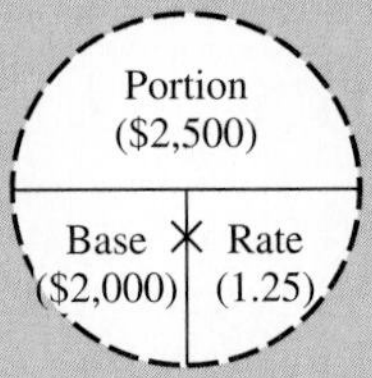 Portion ($2,500) Base ($2,000) × Rate (1.25)
	Key terms	Base, *p. 141* Percent, *p. 138* Percent decrease, *p. 145*	Percent increase, *p. 145* Portion, *p. 142* Rate, *p. 142*

Note: For how to dissect and solve a word problem, see page 142 or page 143.

END-OF-CHAPTER PROBLEMS

Drill Problems

Additional homework assignments by learning unit are at the end of text in Appendix I (p. I-25). Solutions to odd problems are at the end of text in Appendix II.

Convert the following decimals to percents:

6–1. .85 85%　　**6–2.** .713 71.3%　　**6–3.** .6 60%

6–4. 6.00 600%　　**6–5.** 2.145 214.5%　　**6–6.** 4.006 400.6%

Convert the following percents to decimals:

6–7. 4% .04　　**6–8.** 16% .16　　**6–9.** $45\frac{9}{10}\%$ .459

6–10. 86.8% .868　　**6–11.** 104% 1.04　　**6–12.** 99% .99

Convert the following fractions to percents (to the nearest tenth percent as needed):

6–13. $\frac{1}{15}$ $.0666 = 6.7\%$　　**6–14.** $\frac{1}{200}$ $.005 = .5\%$

6–15. $\frac{5}{8}$ $.625 = 62.5\%$　　**6–16.** $\frac{11}{8}$ $1.375 = 137.5\%$

Convert the following to fractions and reduce to lowest terms:

6–17. 5% $5 \times \frac{1}{100} = \frac{5}{100} = \frac{1}{20}$　　**6–18.** $18\frac{1}{2}\%$ $\frac{37}{2} \times \frac{1}{100} = \frac{37}{200}$

6–19. $31\frac{2}{3}\%$ $\frac{95}{3} \times \frac{1}{100} = \frac{95}{300} = \frac{19}{60}$　　**6–20.** $61\frac{1}{2}\%$ $\frac{123}{2} \times \frac{1}{100} = \frac{123}{200}$

6–21. 6.75% $6\frac{3}{4}\% = \frac{27}{4} \times \frac{1}{100} = \frac{27}{400}$　　**6–22.** 182% $182 \times \frac{1}{100} = \frac{182}{100} = 1\frac{82}{100} = 1\frac{41}{50}$

$P = R \times B$

Solve for the portion (round to nearest hundredth as needed):

6–23. 6% of 120
$.06 \times 120 = 7.2$

6–24. 125% of 4,320
$1.25 \times 4{,}320 = 5{,}400$

6–25. 25% of 410
$.25 \times 410 = 102.5$

6–26. 119% of 128.9
$1.19 \times 128.9 = 153.39$

6–27. 17.4% of 900
$.174 \times 900 = 156.6$

6–28. 11.2% of 85
$.112 \times 85 = 9.52$

6–29. $12\frac{1}{2}\%$ of 919
$.125 \times 919 = 114.88$

6–30. 45% of 300
$.45 \times 300 = 135$

6–31. 15% of 80
$.15 \times 80 = 12$

6–32. 30% of 2,000
$.30 \times 2{,}000 = 600$

$\frac{P}{R} = B$

Solve for the base (round to nearest hundredth as needed):

6–33. 115 is 150% of 76.67 $\left(\frac{115}{1.50}\right)$　　**6–34.** 36 is .75% of 4,800 $\left(\frac{36}{.0075}\right)$

6–35. 50 is .5% of 10,000 $\left(\frac{50}{.005}\right)$　　**6–36.** 10,800 is 90% of 12,000 $\left(\frac{10{,}800}{.90}\right)$

6–37. 800 is $4\frac{1}{2}\%$ of 17,777.78 $\left(\frac{800}{.045}\right)$

$\frac{P}{B} = R$

Solve for rate (round to nearest tenth percent as needed):

6–38. 50.6% of 180 is 91 $\left(\frac{91}{180}\right)$　　**6–39.** 108.2% of 85 is 92 $\left(\frac{92}{85}\right)$

6–40. 26% of 250 is 65 $\left(\frac{65}{250}\right)$　　**6–41.** 110 is 110% of 100 $\left(\frac{110}{100}\right)$

6–42. .09 is 4% of 2.25 $\left(\frac{.09}{2.25}\right)$　　**6–43.** 16 is 400% of 4 $\left(\frac{16}{4}\right)$

Solve the following—be sure to show your work (round to nearest hundredth or hundredth percent as needed):

6–44. What is 138% of 190? $1.38 \times 190 = 262.20$ $P = R \times B$

6–45. 66% of 90 is what? $.66 \times 90 = 59.40$ $P = R \times B$

6–46. 40% of what number is 20? $\frac{20}{.4} = 50$ $\frac{P}{R} = B$

6–47. 770 is 70% of what number? $\frac{770}{.7} = 1{,}100$ $\frac{P}{R} = B$

6–48. 4 is what percent of 90? $\frac{4}{90} = 4.44\%$ $\frac{P}{B} = R$

6–49. What percent of 150 is 60? $\frac{60}{150} = 40\%$ $\frac{P}{B} = R$

Complete the following table:

	Product	Sales in millions 1995	Sales in millions 1996	Amount of increase or decrease	Percent change (to nearest hundredth percent)
6–50.	Rugs	$810	$950	+ 140	+ 17.28% $\left(\frac{\$140}{\$810}\right)$
6–51.	Jewelry	$ 29	$ 15	− 14	− 48.28% $\left(\frac{-\$14}{\$29}\right)$

Word Problems (First of Four Sets)

6–52. At a local Dunkin Donuts shop, a survey showed that out of 5,000 customers coming in for breakfast, 4,500 ordered a cup of coffee with their meal. What percent of customers ordered coffee?

$\frac{4{,}500}{5{,}000} = 90\%$

Portion and rate must refer to same piece of the base.

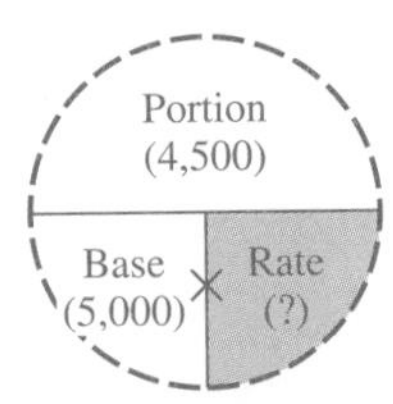

6–53. What percent of customers in Problem 6–52 did not order coffee?

$\frac{500}{5{,}000} = 10\%$

Portion and rate must refer to same piece of the base.

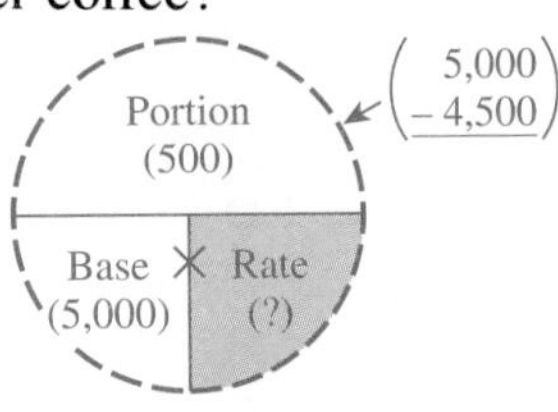

6–54. Ryan Ford is holding a fund-raiser for the Cancer Association. So far they have collected $9,500, which is 80% of their goal. What is Ryan Ford's goal and how much more money must they collect?

$\frac{\$9{,}500}{.80} = \$11{,}875$

$11,875
− 9,500
$ 2,375 to go

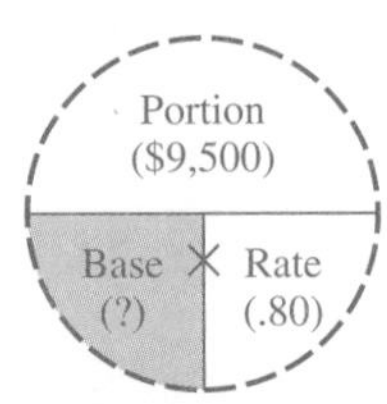

6–55. Pete Mill, the owner of a Texaco station, bought a new truck, paying $2,000 down. He still owes 80% of the selling price. What was the selling price of the truck?

$\frac{\$2{,}000}{.20} = \$10{,}000$

Rate and portion must relate to same piece of the base. $2,000 is 20% of the base.

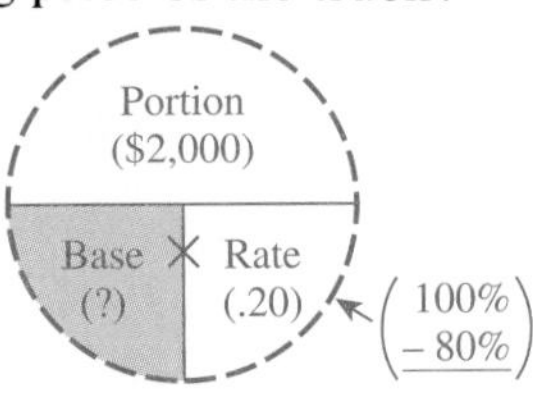

6–56. Matt Clark went to Sears and bought a Sony CD player. The purchase price was \$220. He made a down payment of 30%. How much was Matt's down payment?

$.30 \times \$220 = \$66$

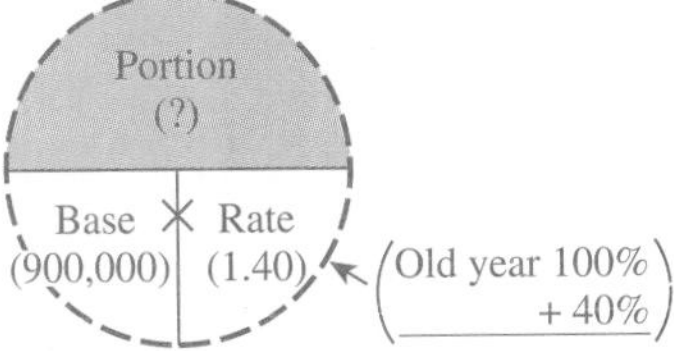

6–57. Assume that in 1995, 900,000 people attended the New Year's Eve celebration at Disney World. In 1996, attendance for the New Year's Eve celebration is expected to increase by 40%. What is the total number of people expected at Disney World for this event?

$900{,}000 \times 1.40 = 1{,}260{,}000$ people

Note: If rate is greater than 100%, the portion will be larger than the base.

6–58. Pete Smith found in his attic a Woody Woodpecker watch in its original box. It had a price tag on it for \$4.50. The watch was made in 1949. Pete brought the watch to an antique dealer and sold it for \$35. What was the percent of increase? Round to nearest hundredth percent.

$\frac{\$30.50}{\$4.50} = 677.78\%$

(The \$30.50 is $\begin{array}{r}\$35.00\\ -4.50\end{array}$)

Note: Portion is larger than base since rate is greater than 100%.

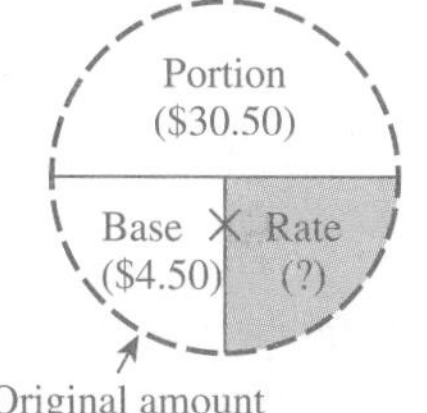

6–59. In 1996, the price of an IBM computer rose to \$1,200. This is 8% more than the 1995 price. What was the old selling price? Check your answer.

$\frac{\$1{,}200}{1.08} = \$1{,}111.11$

Portion and rate must refer to each piece of the base.

Check: $\underset{(B)}{\$1{,}111.11} \times \underset{(R)}{1.08} = \underset{(P)}{\$1{,}199.99}$ (not quite \$1,200 due to rounding)

Note: Portion is larger than base since rate is greater than 100%.

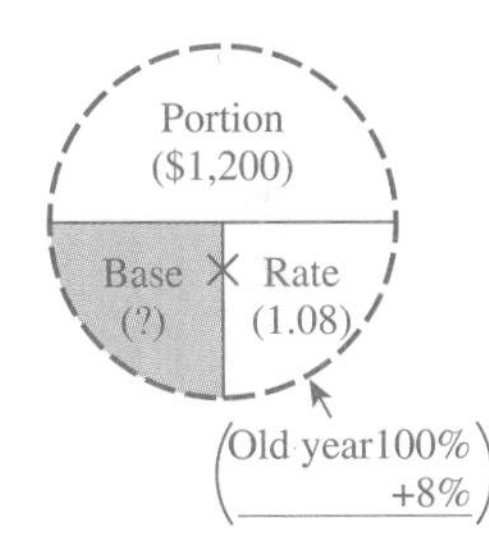

Word Problems (Second of Four Sets)

6–60. Out of 3,000 college students surveyed, 600 responded that they do not eat breakfast. What percent of the students do not eat breakfast?

$\frac{600}{3{,}000} = .20 = 20\%$

Note: Portion and rate refer to same part of base.

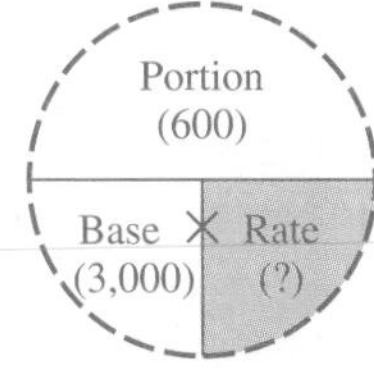

6–61. What percent of college students in Problem 6–60 eat breakfast?

$\frac{2{,}400}{3{,}000} = .80 = 80\%$

Note: Portion and rate refer to same part of base.

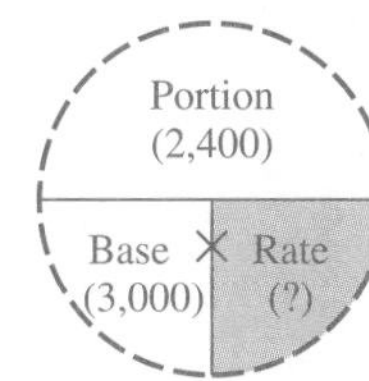

6–62. June Jackson made a $4,000 down payment on a new Jeep wagon. She still owes 90% of the selling price. What was the selling price of the wagon?

$\frac{\$4,000}{.10} = \$40,000$

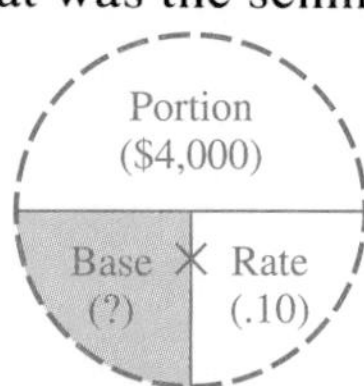

6–63. In Bob Grunzke's first week on the job as an insurance agent for Prudential Life, Bob earned $600 in commissions. Bob receives a 15% commission. What were Bob's total sales for the week? Round to the nearest dollar.

$\frac{\$600}{.15} = \$4,000$

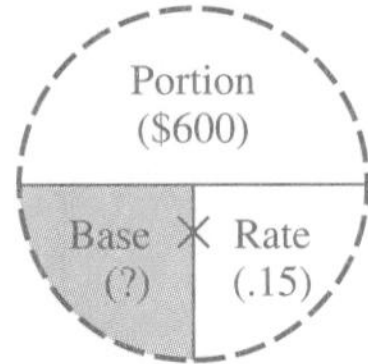

6–64. Charlie Wong bought an Apple personal computer for $1,200. He made a 30% down payment. What is the amount of Charlie's down payment?

$\$1,200 \times .30 = \$360$

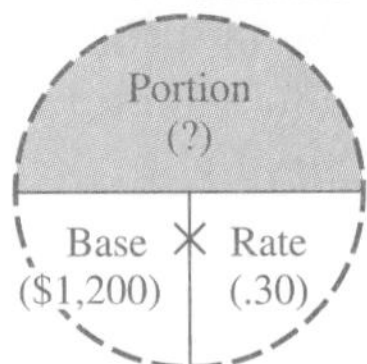

6–65. The price of a Timex watch dropped from $49.95 to $30.00. What was the percent decrease in price? Round to the nearest hundredth percent.

$\frac{\$19.95}{\$49.95} = 39.94\%$

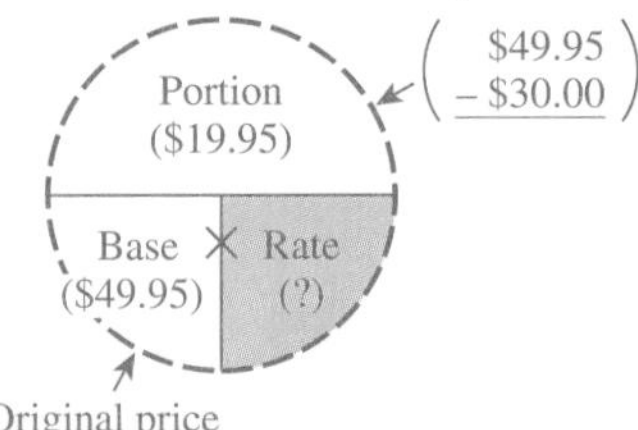

6–66. The Museum of Science estimated that 64% of all visitors came from within the state. On Saturday, 2,500 people attended the museum. How many attended the museum from out of state?

$2,500 \times .36 = 900$ people out of state

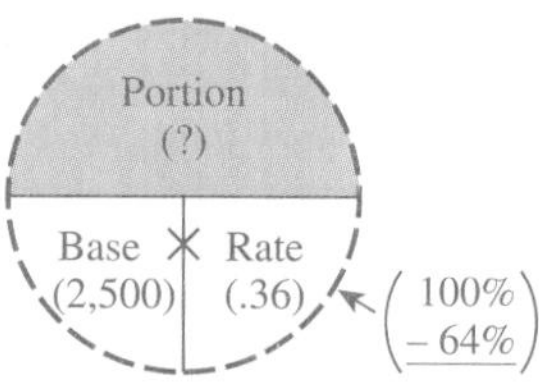

6–67. Cherokee Stationery pays George Nagovsky an annual salary of $36,000. Today, George's boss informs him that he will receive a $4,600 raise. What percent of George's old salary is the $4,600 raise? Round to the nearest tenth percent.

$\frac{\$4,600}{\$36,000} = 12.8\%$

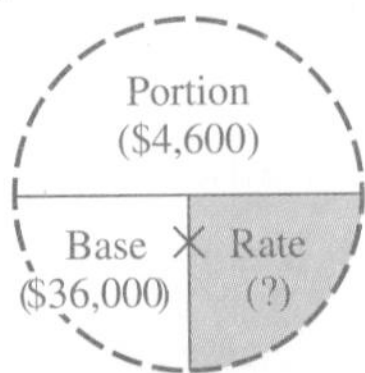

6–68. In 1995, Sweeney Brothers had $550,000 in sales. In 1996, Sweeney's sales were up 35%. What were Sweeney's sales in 1996?

$\$550,000 \times 1.35 = \$742,500$

100% old sales
+ 35% new sales

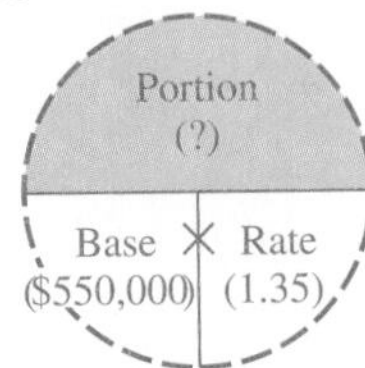

6–69. Blue Valley College has 600 female students. This is 60% of the total student body. How many students attend Blue Valley College?

$\frac{600}{.60} = 1{,}000$

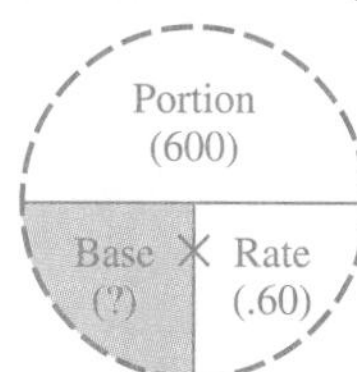

6–70. Dr. Grossman was reviewing his total accounts receivable. This month, credit customers paid $44,000, which represented 20% of all receivables (what customers owe) due. What was Dr. Grossman's total accounts receivable?

$\frac{\$44{,}000}{.20} = \$220{,}000$

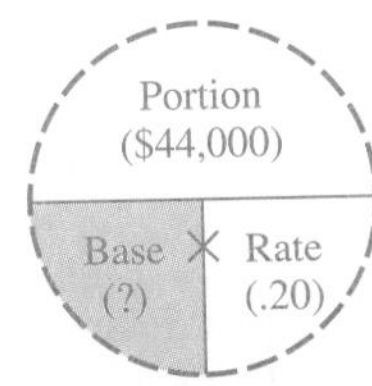

6–71. Massachusetts has a 5% sales tax. Timothy bought a Toro lawn mower and paid $20 sales tax. What was the cost of the lawn mower?

$\frac{\$20}{.05} = \$400$

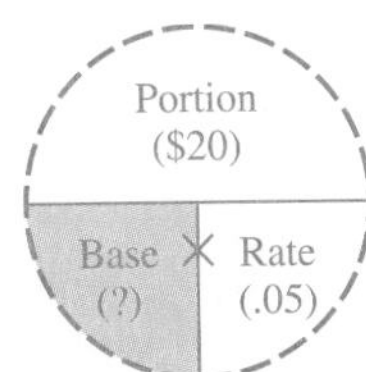

6–72. The price of a GE microwave oven increased from $600 to $800. What was the percent of increase? Round to the nearest tenth percent.

$\frac{\$200}{\$600} = 33.3\%$

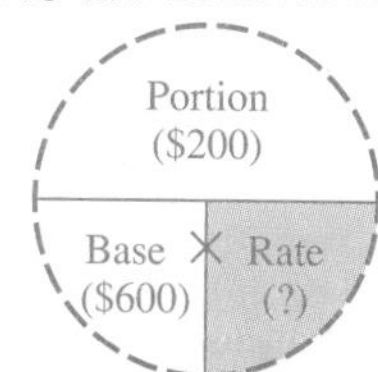

6–73. Leland's Bookseller ordered 60 marketing books but received 45 books. What percent of the order was missing?

$\frac{15}{60} = 25\%$

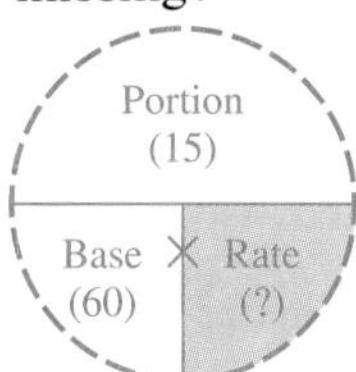

Word Problems (Third of Four Sets)

6–74. At a benefit auction, the auctioneer estimated that 38% of the audience was from within the state. Four thousand people attended the auction. How many out-of-state people attended?

$4{,}000 \times .62 = 2{,}480$ people from out of state

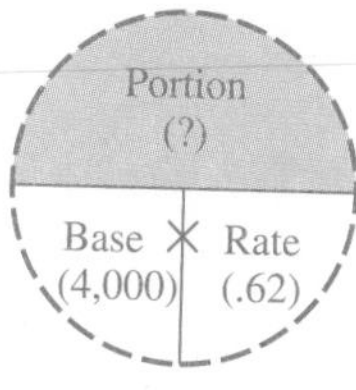

6–75. Red River Insurance pays its agents a 30% commission. Sharon Reed, an agent, earned $900 in commissions in one week. What were Sharon's total sales for the week?

$\frac{\$900}{.30} = \$3{,}000$

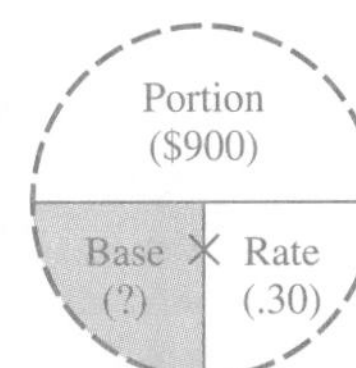

6–76. In 1996, Jim Goodman earned \$45,900, an increase of 17.5% over the previous year. What were Jim's earnings in 1995? Round to the nearest cent.

$B = \dfrac{\$45{,}900}{1.175} = \$39{,}063.83$

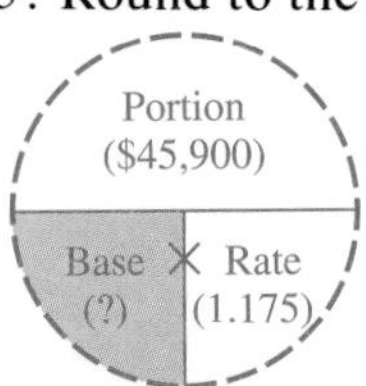

6–77. The price of Radio Shack's calculators dropped from \$29.95 to \$16.99. What was the percent decrease in price? Round to nearest hundredth percent.

$$\begin{array}{r} \$29.95 \\ -\ 16.99 \\ \hline \$12.96 \end{array} \qquad \frac{\$12.96}{\$29.95} = 43.27\%$$

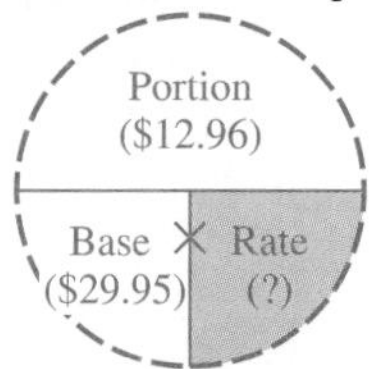

6–78. In 1995, the price of a business math text rose to \$34. This is 7% more than the 1994 price. What was the old selling price? Round to nearest cent.

$B = \dfrac{\$34}{1.07} = \$31.78$

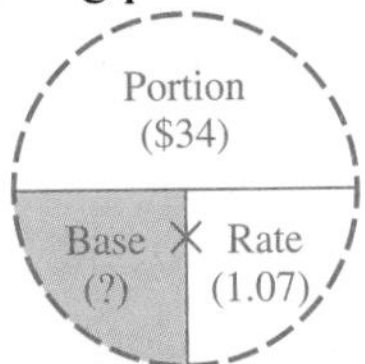

6–79. Pine Tree Company pays Alice Rose an annual salary of \$48,000. Today, Alice's boss informs her that she will receive a \$6,400 raise. What percent of Alice's old salary is the \$6,400 raise? Round to nearest tenth percent.

$\dfrac{\$6{,}400}{\$48{,}000} = 13.3\%$

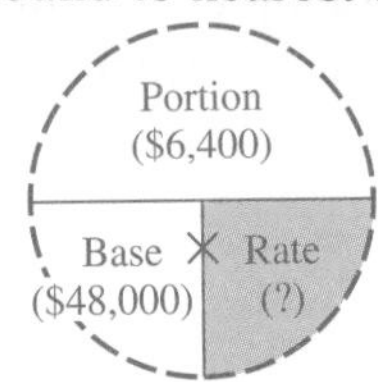

6–80. Forty percent of the students (900) at Northwest Technical College are female. How many students attend Northwest?

$\dfrac{900}{.40} = 2{,}250$ students

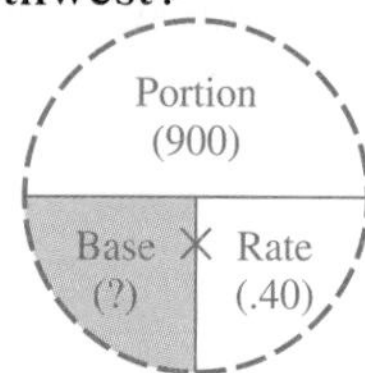

6–81. Rancho Bookstore ordered 100 calendars but received 60. What percent of the order was missing?

$\dfrac{40}{100} = 40\%$

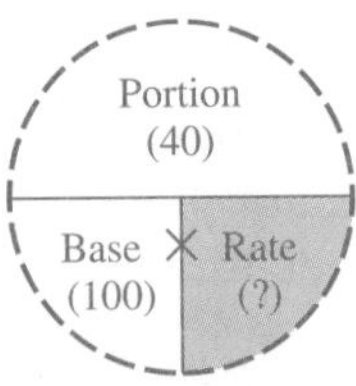

6–82. Peters Hardware uses MasterCard. MasterCard charges $2\frac{1}{2}\%$ on net deposits (credit slips less returns). Pete made a net deposit of \$4,100 for charge sales. How much did MasterCard charge Pete?

$\$4{,}100 \times .025 = \$102.50$

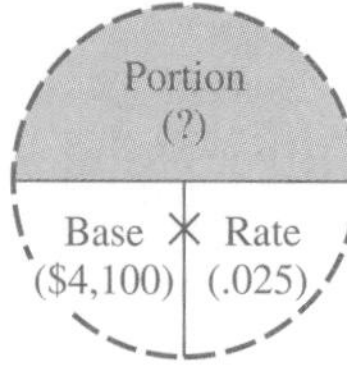

6–83. In 1995, Vetron computers had \$800,000 in sales. In 1996, Vetron's sales were up 45%. What are the sales for 1996?

$\$800{,}000 \times 1.45 = \$1{,}160{,}000$

Note: Portion is larger than base since rate is greater than 100%.

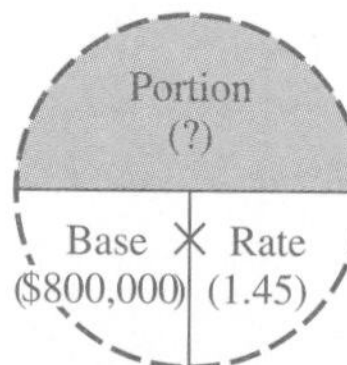

Word Problems (Fourth of Four Sets)

6–84. Toyota Motor raised the base price of its popular LS 400 by \$1,000 to \$36,000. What was the percent increase (round to nearest tenth percent).

$\frac{\$1,000}{\$35,000} = 2.9\%$

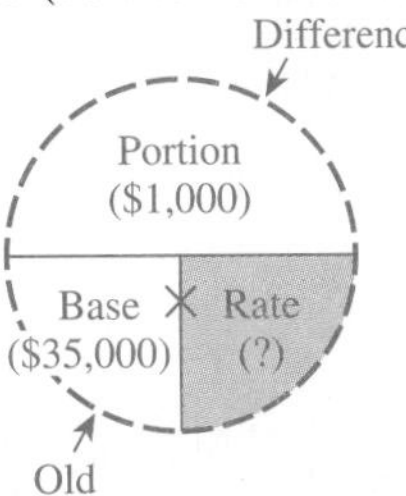

6–85. The sales tax rate is 8%. If Jim bought a new Saab and paid a sales tax of \$1,920, what was the cost of the Saab?

$\frac{\$1,920}{.08} = \$24,000$

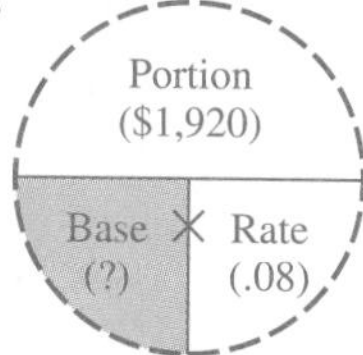

6–86. Alice Sey bought a new computer system on sale for \$2,400. It was advertised as 40% off the regular price. What was the original price of the computer?

$\frac{\$2,400}{.60} = \$4,000$

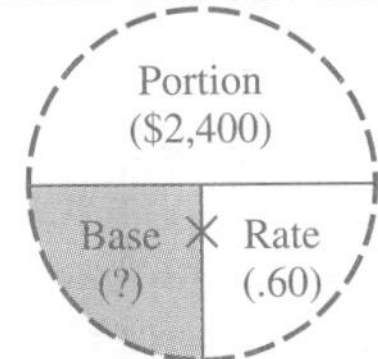

6–87. The cost of a telephone call from Chicago to Milwaukee is \$.50 using AT&T and \$.44 using MCI. Calculate the percent savings using MCI.

$\frac{\$.06}{\$.50} = 12\%$

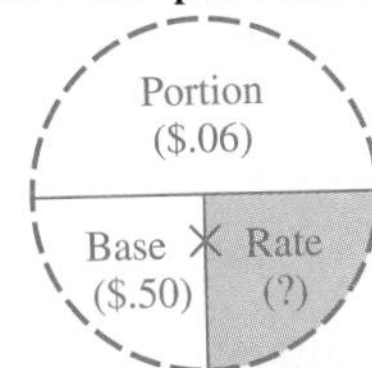

6–88. In 1996, Levin Furniture plans to ship furniture overseas for a sales volume of \$11.2 million, an increase of 40% from 1995. What was the sales volume in 1995?

$\frac{\$11.2}{1.40} = \$8 \text{ million}$

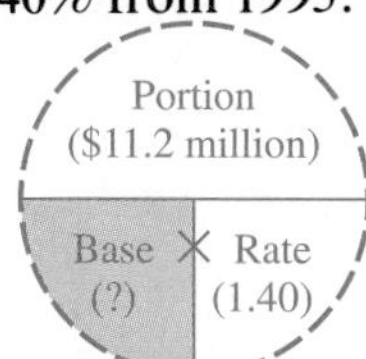

6–89. Peg Pouv sold her ski house for \$35,000. This sale represented a loss of 15% off the original price. What was the original price Peg paid for the ski house? Round answer to the nearest dollar.

$\frac{\$35,000}{.85} = \$41,176$

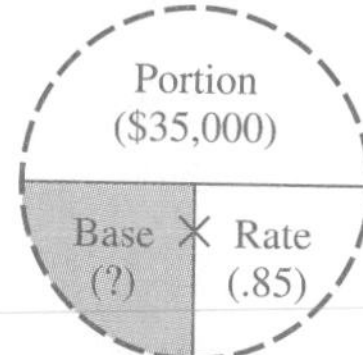

6–90. Out of 4,000 colleges surveyed, 60% reported that SAT scores were not used as a high consideration in viewing their applications. How many schools view the SAT as important in screening applicants?

$4,000 \times .40 = 1,600$

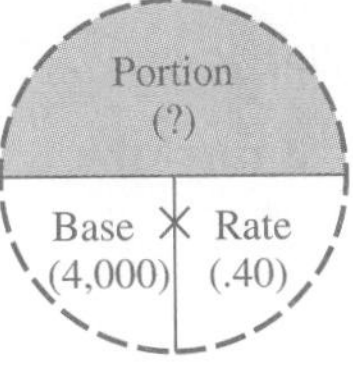

6–91. A road race raised \$6,000 to help the homeless. The committee had hoped to raise \$10,000. What percent of the goal was not achieved?

$\frac{\$4,000}{\$10,000} = 40\%$

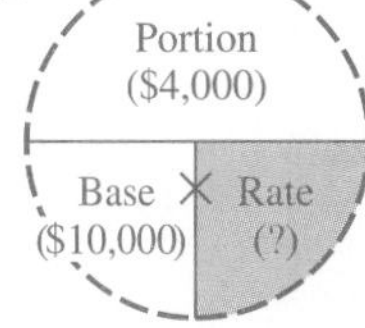

6–92. At a toy assembly line, 3% of all games were found to be defective. Assuming 360 games were pulled off the assembly line, how many total games were acceptable?

$\frac{360}{.03} = 12{,}000$ games

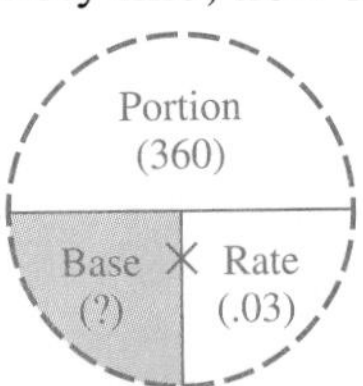

6–93. Assume 450,000 people line up on the streets to see the Orange Bowl Parade in 1995. If attendance is expected to increase 30%, what will be the number of people lined up on the streets to see the 1996 Orange Bowl Parade?

$450{,}000 \times 1.30 = 585{,}000$

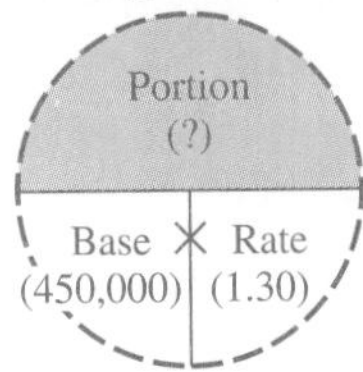

Challenge Problem

Airfare Special

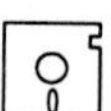

6–94. Each Tuesday, Ryan Airlines reduces its one-way ticket from Fort Wayne to Chicago from $125 to $40. To receive this special $40 price, the customer must buy a round-trip ticket. Ryan has a nonrefundable 25% penalty fare for cancellation; it estimates that about nine tenths of 1% will cancel their reservations. The airlines also estimates this special price will cause a passenger traffic increase from 400 to 900. Ryan expects revenue for the year to be 55.4% higher than the previous year. Last year, Ryan's sales were $482,000. To receive the special rate, Janice Miller bought two round-trip tickets. On other airlines, Janice has paid $100 round trip (with no cancellation penalty). Calculate the following:

a. Percent discount Ryan is offering.

$\$125 - 40 = \$85 \qquad \frac{\$85}{\$125} = 68\%$

b. Percent passenger travel will increase.

$\frac{500}{400} = 125\%$

c. Sales for new year. $1.554 \times \$482{,}000 = \$749{,}028$

d. Janice's loss if she cancels one round-trip flight. $\$80 \times .25 = \$20$

e. Approximately how many more cancellations can Ryan Airlines expect (after Janice's cancellation)?

$.009 \times 900 = 8.1$ people
$- 1.0$
7.1 people or 7

Summary Practice Test

Solutions are at end of text in Appendix II.

Quick Reference
If you get any wrong answers, study the page numbers given for each problem.

Convert the following decimals to percents:

1–4. P. 138.

1. .169 16.9%
2. .6 60%
3. 16.31 1,631%
4. 6 600%

Convert the following percents to decimals:

5–8. P. 139.

5. 19% .19
6. 4.14% .0414
7. 200% 2.0
8. $\frac{1}{5}\%$ .0020

Convert the following fractions to percents (round to nearest tenth percent):

9–10. P. 139.

9. $\frac{1}{8}$ 12.5%
10. $\frac{7}{9}$ 77.8%

Convert the following percents to fractions and reduce to lowest terms as needed:

11–12. P. 140.

11. $24\frac{2}{3}\%$ $\frac{74}{3} \times \frac{1}{100} = \frac{74}{300} = \frac{37}{150}$
12. 12.9% $12\frac{9}{10}\% = \frac{129}{10} \times \frac{1}{100} = \frac{129}{1{,}000}$

Solve for portion, base, or rate:

13. P. 142.

13. Magic Door Company has a net income before taxes of \$50,000. The company's treasurer estimates that 35% of the company's net income will go to federal and state taxes. How much will Magic Door have left?

$\$32,500 = \$50,000 \times .65$

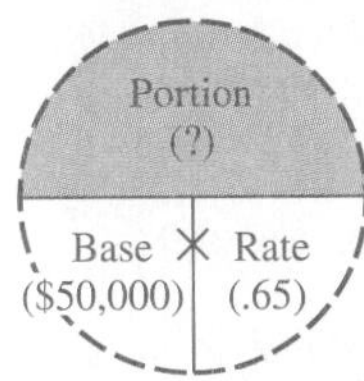

14. P. 145.

14. Safelite Corporation projects a year-end net income of \$90,000. The net income represents 12% of its projected annual sales. What are Safelite's projected annual sales?

$\frac{\$90,000}{.12} = \$750,000$

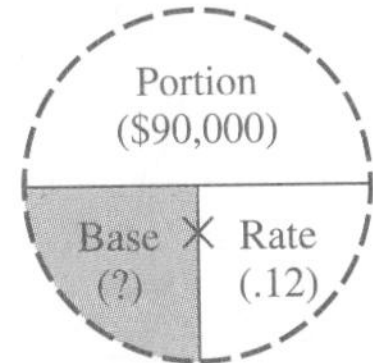

15. P. 144.

15. True Value Hardware ordered 100 rakes. When True Value received the order, 40 rakes were missing. What percent of the order did True Value receive?

$\frac{60}{100} = 60\%$

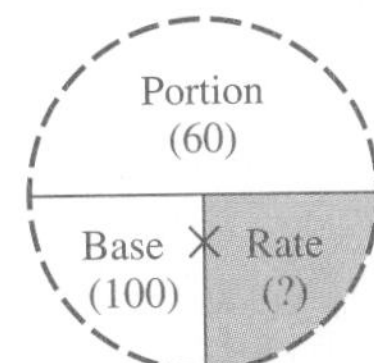

16. P. 144.

16. Joyce Workman receives an annual salary of \$70,000. Today, her boss informed her she would receive a \$5,000 raise. What percent of her old salary is the \$5,000 raise? Round to the nearest hundredth percent.

$\frac{\$5,000}{\$70,000} = 7.14\%$

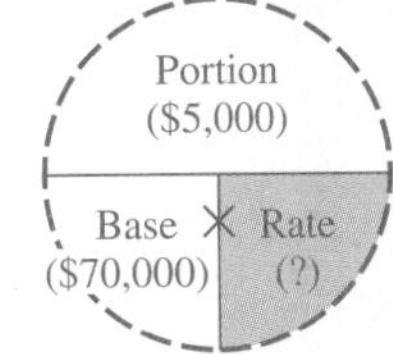

17. P. 146.

17. The price of an American airline ticket to Boston increased to \$600. This is a 15% increase. What was the old fare?

$\frac{\$600}{1.15} = \$521.74$

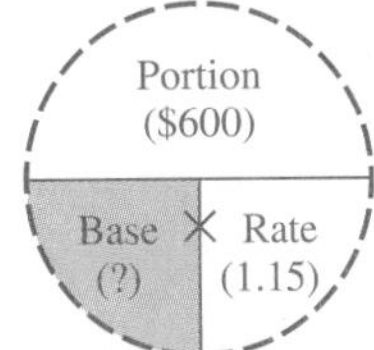

18. P. 142.

18. Joy Bell earns a gross pay of \$600 a week at JCPenney. Joy's payroll deductions are 35%. What is Joy's take-home pay?

$P = \$600 \times .65$

$P = \$390$

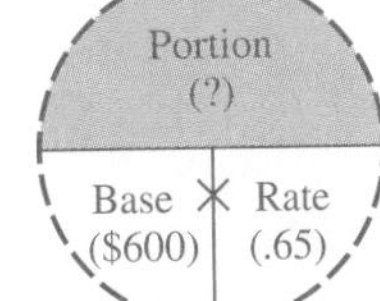

19. P. 145.

19. Lorenzo Flynn is reviewing the total accounts receivable of Dayton's Department Store. Credit customers paid \$60,000 this month. This represents 25% of all receivables due. What is Dayton's total accounts receivable?

$\frac{\$60,000}{.25} = \$240,000$

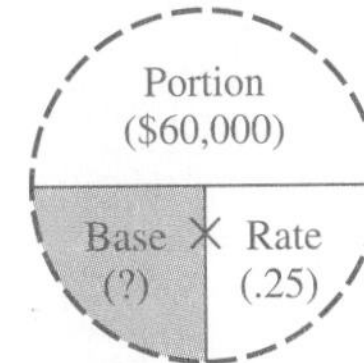

Project A

BRIEFS: The Charles Hotel in Cambridge, Mass., offers room service books—the concierge runs over to nearby Barillari Books (it's open until midnight), often fetching children's titles. . . . Send a math primer to Gloria Nilson Realtors in Shrewsbury, N.J., which advertises a Rumson, N.J., home that is "reduced 100%"—to $695,000 from $1.4 million.

—PAMELA SEBASTIAN

Show Gloria the correct answer. Round to the nearest tenth percent.

$$\begin{array}{r} \$1{,}400{,}000 \\ -\ 695{,}000 \\ \hline \$\ 705{,}000 \end{array} \qquad \frac{\$705{,}000}{\$1{,}400{,}000} = 50.4\%$$

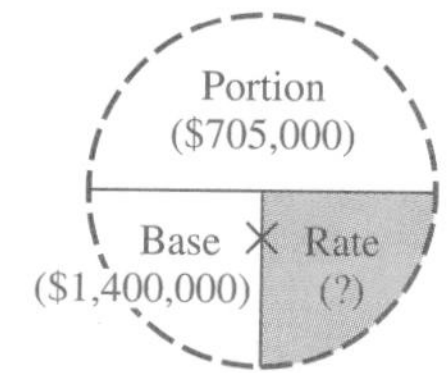

Project B

Impulse Item

Wrigley Is Thriving, Despite the Recession, In a Resilient Business

It Dominates the Gum Market By Stressing Old Values And Advertising Heavily

The Nickel Pack at 25 Cents

By BRETT PULLEY
Staff Reporter of THE WALL STREET JOURNAL

CHICAGO—Each year, Wm. Wrigley Jr. Co. makes more than 14,000 tons of a rubbery compound with ingredients found also in paint, underwear-elastic and petrochemicals. Machines roll out blobs of the stuff, slice it into thin sticks and sheathe it in foil wrap.

Chewing gum is a lucrative business, Wrigley's only business. Indeed, Wrigley dominates the world of chewing gum more thoroughly than Coca-Cola Co. looms over soft drinks. Wrigley has a 48% share of a $2.4 billion U.S retail market, nearly twice that of Warner-Lambert Co., its biggest competitor (Trident, Dentyne). And it soundly beats back the competitive threat from consumer-goods powerhouse RJR Nabisco Inc. (Beech-Nut, Care Free).

"We get a lot of letters about brands

What is the share of Wrigley's market?

$2.4 billion × .48 = $1.152 billion

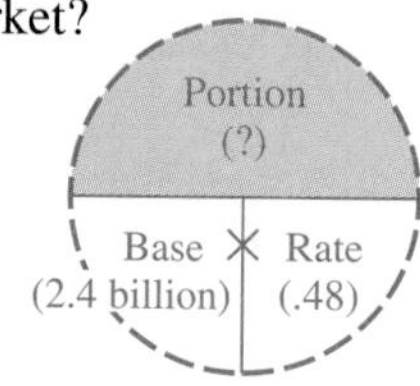

Project C

American Express Shortens Time for Levying Late Fee

By a WALL STREET JOURNAL *Staff Reporter*

NEW YORK—American Express Co., trying to get a better handle on charge card delinquencies, has cut the amount of time that cardholders have to pay their card bills before they are assessed a late charge.

In notices to cardholders, the company said the payment deadline is being reduced to 50 days from 60 days, effective Dec. 1. The amount of the late charge isn't changing, however.

Specifically, the notice, which has been sent recently to holders of green, gold and platinum cards, said that if any unpaid bill of $50 or more is 50 days late, it is considered delinquent, and will be charged the greater of $20, or 2.5% of the unpaid amount. The notice added that "by paying in full each month, this change will not affect you at all."

An American Express spokeswoman said the new payment requirement was instituted so that the company could "reclaim costs of administering overdue accounts."

If Pete Morse owes $5,200 on his American Express and the balance is 50 days late, what will be charged in late fees?

$5,200 × .025 = $130

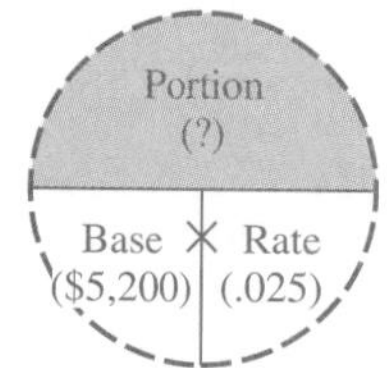

NOTES

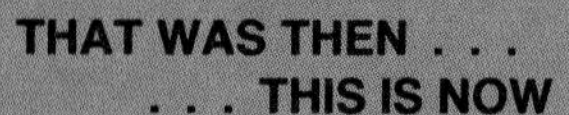

In this 1909 ad, terms of shipping are FOB Detroit. When you buy a car today are you paying the shipping charges? In both ads Ford stresses high quality.

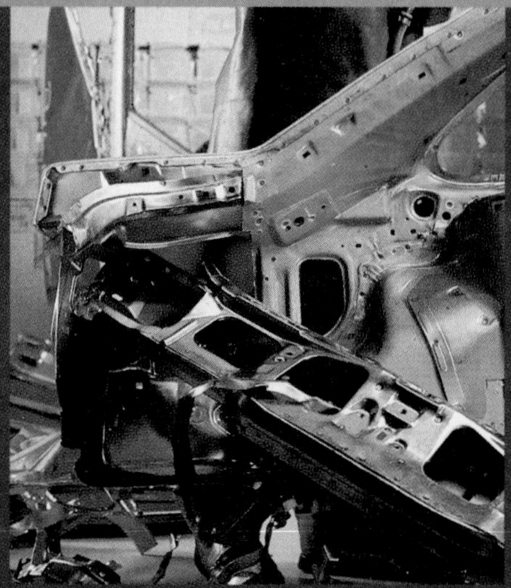

7

Discounts: Trade and Cash

LEARNING UNIT OBJECTIVES

LU 7–1: Trade Discounts—Single and Chain

1. Define and explain the reason for trade discounts. *p. 164.*
2. Calculate the amount of trade discount with a single discount. *p. 164.*
3. Dissect and solve a word problem. *p. 165.*
4. Solve for the list price, given net price and trade discount. *p. 166.*
5. Calculate net price and trade discount by net price equivalent rate and single equivalent discount rate. *p. 167.*

LU 7–2: Cash Discounts, Credit Terms, and Partial Payments

1. Compare and contrast cash discounts versus trade discounts. *p. 170.*
2. Explain the difference between FOB shipping point and FOB destination and their effect on cash discounts. *p. 171.*
3. List and explain typical discount periods and credit periods that a business may offer. *pp. 174–75.*
4. Dissect and solve a word problem. *p. 176.*
5. Calculate outstanding balance for partial payments. *p. 176.*

Lotus Fights To Regain Share With Discounts

By John R. Wilke
Staff Reporter of The Wall Street Journal

Moving to halt steep market share losses, **Lotus Development** Corp. for the first time will offer competitors' customers sharp discounts on its industry-leading Lotus 1-2-3 spreadsheet software.

Lotus yesterday said it will sell its latest 1-2-3 version to owners of **Microsoft** Corp.'s Excel or **Borland International**'s Quattro Pro for a suggested retail price of $150, or as low as $99 through distributors. The product now carries a list price of $595.

"Lotus is going to fight for every inch of

Sears to Delay Paying Vendors By 30 Days

Firm Says It Doesn't Have Cash-Flow Difficulties; Suppliers Assail Move

By Teri Agins
Staff Reporter of The Wall Street Journal

In a move reflecting the tough retail climate, **Sears, Roebuck** & Co. asked its vendors to wait at least an extra 30 days for payment.

In changing its payment terms "to a minimum of 60 days" from 30 days, Sears apparently broke ranks with most of its competitors. Sears says it is "absolutely not" experiencing cash-flow problems.

In the past two years only cash-short re-

Discount is a word that makes buyers stop and listen. For example, the sharp discounts in Lotus 1-2-3, announced in the above *Wall Street Journal* clipping, mean greater savings for buyers. This is an example of a trade discount.

We learn from the other clipping that Sears has asked its vendors for more time to pay its bills, which means that Sears could lose its cash discounts.

This chapter discusses two types of discounts—trade and cash. A **trade discount** is a reduction of an item's original selling price (list price). It is not related to early payment. A **cash discount** is the result of an early payment based on the terms of the sale.

LEARNING UNIT 7-1 TRADE DISCOUNTS—SINGLE AND CHAIN

Car manufacturers like Ford, in the chapter opener, can give trade discounts. For example, if you owned a delivery company and bought Ford trucks, you could get a trade discount for a fleet of trucks.

For many years, JCPenney, a *retail business,* has been selling merchandise directly to consumers. Retailers buy their merchandise from manufacturers and wholesalers. Manufacturers and wholesalers, which sell only to retailers and not to consumers, offer discounts so that retailers can resell the merchandise at a profit. These discounts are off the manufacturers' and wholesalers' **list price** (suggested retail price). The amount of discount that retailers receive off the list price is the **trade discount amount.**

To determine the trade discount amount, retailers are given a **trade discount rate.** This rate is a percent off the list price that retailers can deduct. Retailers use the following formula to determine the trade discount amount.

Formula for Calculating Trade Discount Amount
Trade discount amount = List price × Trade discount rate

The price that the retailer pays the manufacturer or wholesaler is the **net price.** To calculate the net price, use the following formula.

Formula for Calculating Net Price
Net price = List price − Trade discount amount

Courtesy of Apple Computer, Inc.

Frequently, manufacturers and wholesalers issue catalogs to retailers containing list prices of the seller's merchandise and the available trade discounts. To reduce printing costs when prices change, these sellers usually update the catalogs with new *discount sheets*. The discount sheet also gives the seller the flexibility of making different trade discounts to different classes of retailers. For example, some retailers buy in quantity and service the products. They may receive a larger discount than the retailer who wants the manufacturer to service the products. Sellers may also give discounts to meet a competitor's price, to attract new retailers, and to reward the retailers who buy product-line products. Sometimes the ability of the retailer to negotiate with the seller determines the trade discount amount.

Retailers cannot take trade discounts on freight, returned goods, sales tax, and so on. Trade discounts may be single discounts or a chain of discounts.

Single Trade Discount

Let's begin studying **single trade discounts** by dissecting and solving a word problem involving a single trade discount. Once again we will use a blueprint aid to help us dissect and solve the word problem.

The Word Problem The list price of a Macintosh computer is $900. The manufacturer offers dealers a 30% trade discount. What is the trade discount amount and the net price?

Blueprint Aid for Dissecting and Solving a Word Problem

A. Gather the facts	B. What am I solving for?	C. What must I know or calculate before solving problem?	D. Key points to remember
List price: $900. *Trade discount rate:* 30%.	Trade discount amount. Net price.	Trade discount amount = List price × Trade discount rate. Net price = List price − Trade discount amount.	Trade discount amount Portion (?) Base ($900) × Rate (.30) List price Trade discount rate

Steps to Solving Problem

1. Calculate trade discount amount. $900 × .30 = $270
2. Calculate net price. $900 − $270 = **$630**

Now let's learn how to check the dealers' net price of $630.

How to Calculate the $630 Net Price Using Complement of Trade Discount Rate

The following steps show you how to use the complement of a trade discount rate.

Steps for Calculating Net Price by Using Complement of Trade Discount Rate

Step 1. To find complement, subtract the single discount rate from 100%.

Step 2. Multiply the list price times the complement (from Step 1).

Think of a **complement** of any given percent (decimal) as the result of subtracting the percent from 100%.

Step 1. 100%
− 30 (trade discount rate)
70% or .70

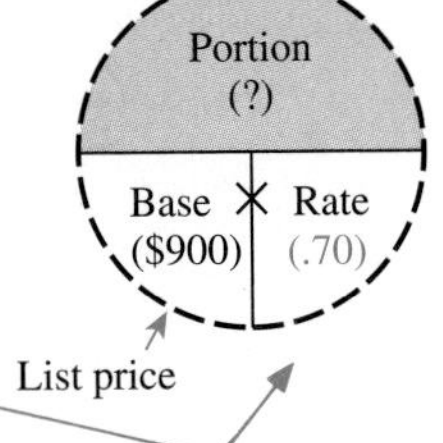

The complement means we are spending 70 cents per dollar because we save 30 cents per dollar. Since we planned to spend $900, we multiply the .70 times the $900 to get a net price of $630.

Step 2. $630 = $900 × .70

Note how the portion ($630) and rate (.70) relate to the same piece of the base ($900). The portion ($630) is smaller than the base since the rate is less than 100%.

Finding List Price When You Know Net Price and Trade Discount Rate

The formula that follows has many useful applications.

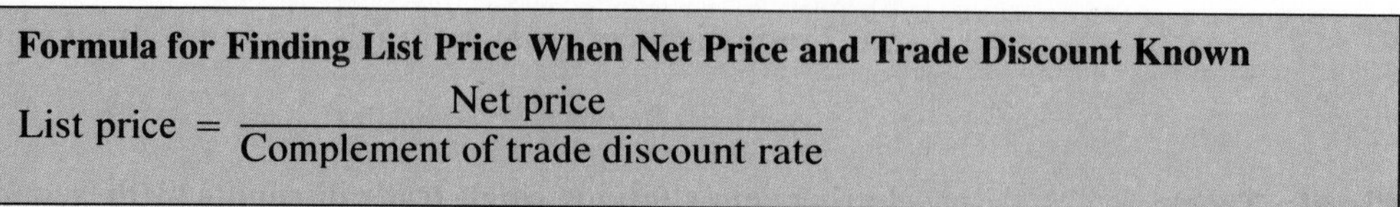

Formula for Finding List Price When Net Price and Trade Discount Known

$$\text{List price} = \frac{\text{Net price}}{\text{Complement of trade discount rate}}$$

Next, let's see how to dissect and solve a word problem involving list price.

The Word Problem A Macintosh computer has a $630 net price and a 30% trade discount. What would be its list price?

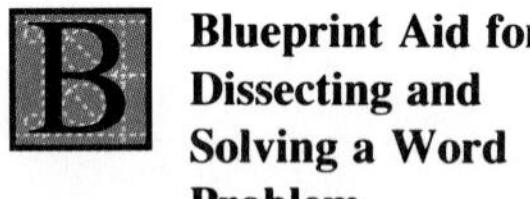

Blueprint Aid for Dissecting and Solving a Word Problem

A. Gather the facts	B. What am I solving for?	C. What must I know or calculate before solving problem?	D. Key points to remember
Net price: $630. *Trade discount rate:* 30%.	List price.	List price = $\frac{\text{Net price}}{\text{Complement of trade discount rate}}$	Portion ($630) / Base (?) × Rate (.70) Net price List price 100% − 30%

Steps to Solving Problem

1. Calculate complement of trade discount. 100% − 30 = 70% = .70
2. Calculate list price. $\frac{\$630}{.70} = \$900$

Note that the portion ($630) and rate (.70) relate to the same piece of the base. Now let's turn our attention to calculating chain discounts.

Chain Discounts

Frequently, manufacturers want more flexibility in setting trade discounts for different classes of customers, seasonal trends, promotional activities, and so on. To gain this flexibility, some sellers give **chain discounts**—trade discounts in a series of two or more successive discounts.

Sellers list chain discounts as a group, for example, 20/15/10. Let's look at how Mick Company arrives at the net price of office equipment with a 20/15/10 chain discount.

EXAMPLE The list price of the office equipment is $15,000. The chain discount is 20/15/10. The long way to calculate the net price is as follows:

Step 1	Step 2	Step 3	Step 4
$15,000	$15,000	$12,000	$10,200
× .20	− 3,000	− 1,800	− 1,020
$ 3,000	$12,000	$10,200	$ 9,180 (net price)
	× .15	× .10	
	$ 1,800	$ 1,020	

Never add the 20/15/10 together.

Note how we multiply the percent (in decimal) times the new balance after we subtract the previous trade discount amount. For example, in Step 3, we change the last discount 10%, to decimal form and multiply times $10,200. Remember that each percent is times a successively *smaller* base. You could write the 20/15/10 discount rate in any order and still arrive at the same net price. Thus, you would get the $9,180 net price if the discount was 10/15/20 or 15/20/10. However, sellers usually give the larger discounts first. *Never try to shorten this step process by adding the discounts.* Your net price will be incorrect because, when done properly, each percent is on a different base.

Net Price Equivalent Rate

In the example above, you could also find the $9,180 net price with the **net price equivalent rate**—a shortcut method. Let's see how to use this rate to calculate net price.

Steps for Calculating Net Price Using Net Price Equivalent Rate

Step 1. Subtract each chain discount rate from 100% (finding the complement) and convert each percent to a decimal.

Step 2. Multiply the decimals. Do not round off decimals since this number is the net price equivalent rate.

Step 3. Multiply the list price times the net price equivalent rate (Step 2).

The following word problem with its blueprint aid illustrates how to use the net price equivalent rate method.

The Word Problem The list price of office equipment is $15,000. The chain discount is 20/15/10. What is the net price?

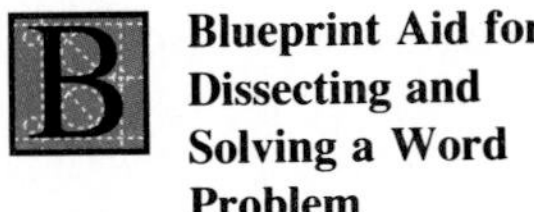

Blueprint Aid for Dissecting and Solving a Word Problem

A. Gather the facts	B. What am I solving for?	C. What must I know or calculate before solving problem?	D. Key points to remember
List price: $15,000. *Chain discount:* 20/15/10.	Net price.	Net price equivalent rate. Net price = List price × Net price equivalent rate.	Do not round net price equivalent rate.

Steps to Solving Problem

1. Calculate complement of each rate and convert each percent to a decimal.

$$\begin{array}{ccc} 100\% & 100\% & 100\% \\ -\ 20 & -\ 15 & -\ 10 \\ \hline 80\% & 85\% & 90\% \\ \downarrow & \downarrow & \downarrow \\ .8 & .85 & .90 \end{array}$$

2. Calculate net price equivalent rate (Do not round.)

$.8 \times .85 \times .9 = .612$ Net price equivalent rate. For each $1, you are spending about 61 cents.

3. Calculate net price (actual cost to buyer).

$\$15{,}000 \times .612 = \$9{,}180$

Next, we see how to calculate the trade discount amount with a simpler method.

Single Equivalent Discount Rate

In the previous word problem, we could calculate the trade discount amount as follows:

$15,000	List price
− 9,180	Net price
$ 5,820	Trade discount amount

You can use another method to find the trade discount by using the **single equivalent discount rate.**

Steps for Calculating Trade Discount Amount Using Single Equivalent Discount Rate

Step 1. Subtract net price equivalent rate from 1. This is the single equivalent discount rate.

Step 2. Multiply list price times single equivalent discount rate. This is the trade discount amount.

Let's now do the calculations.

Step 1.
```
  1.000 ← If you are using a calculator, just press 1.
 − .612
  .388 ← This is the single equivalent discount rate.
```

Step 2. $15,000 × .388 = **$5,820** → This is the trade discount amount.

Remember that when we used the net price equivalent rate, the buyer of the office equipment pays $.612 on each $1 of list price. With the single equivalent discount rate, we can say that the buyer saves $.388 on each $1 of list price. The .388 is the single equivalent discount rate for the 20/15/10 chain discount. Note how we use the .388 single equivalent discount rate as if it were the only discount.

Now let's check your progress.

LU 7-1 PRACTICE QUIZ[1]

1. The list price of a dining room set with a 30% trade discount is $10,000. What is the trade discount amount and net price (use complement method for net price)?
2. The net price of a video system with a 40% trade discount is $600. What is the list price?
3. Lamps Outlet bought a shipment of lamps from a wholesaler. The total list price was $12,000 with a 5/10/25 chain discount. Calculate the net price and trade discount amount. (Use the net price equivalent rate and single equivalent discount rates in your calculation.

SOLUTIONS TO LU 7-1 PRACTICE QUIZ

Blueprint Aid for Dissecting and Solving a Word Problem

1. Dining room set trade discount amount and net price:

A. Gather the facts	B. What am I solving for?	C. What must I know or calculate before solving problem?	D. Key points to remember
List price: $10,000. *Trade discount rate:* 30%	Trade discount amount. Net price.	Trade discount amount = List price × Trade discount rate. Net price = List price × Complement of trade discount rate.	Trade discount amount → Portion (?) ; Base ($10,000) × Rate (.30) ; List price, Trade discount rate

Steps to Solving Problem

1. Calculate trade discount amount. $10,000 × .30 = **$3,000** Trade discount amount
2. Calculate net price. $10,000 × .70 = **$7,000** (100% − 30% = 70%)

[1] For all three problems we will show blueprint aids. You might want to draw them on scrap paper.

Blueprint Aid for Dissecting and Solving a Word Problem

2. Video system list price:

A. Gather the facts	B. What am I solving for?	C. What must I know or calculate before solving problem?	D. Key points to remember
Net price: $600. *Trade discount rate:* 40%.	List price.	List price = $\frac{\text{Net price}}{\text{Complement of trade discount}}$	Portion ($600) = Base (?) × Rate (.60); Net price; List price; 100% − 40%

Steps to Solving Problem

1. Calculate complement of trade discount.

$$\begin{array}{r} 100\% \\ -\ 40 \\ \hline 60\% \end{array} = .60$$

2. Calculate list price.

$$\frac{\$600}{.60} = \$1{,}000$$

3. Lamps Outlet net price and trade discount amount:

Blueprint Aid for Dissecting and Solving a Word Problem

A. Gather the facts	B. What am I solving for?	C. What must I know or calculate before solving problem?	D. Key points to remember
List price: $12,000. *Chain discount:* 5/10/25.	Net price. Trade discount amount.	Net price = List price × Net price equivalent rate. Trade discount amount = List price × Single equivalent discount rate.	Do not round off net price equivalent rate or single equivalent discount rate.

Steps to Solving Problem

1. Calculate complement of each chain discount.

$$\begin{array}{r} 100\% \\ -\ 5 \\ \hline 95\% \end{array} \quad \begin{array}{r} 100\% \\ -\ 10 \\ \hline 90\% \end{array} \quad \begin{array}{r} 100\% \\ -\ 25 \\ \hline 75\% \end{array}$$

2. Calculate net price equivalent rate. $.95 \times .90 \times .75 = .64125$
3. Calculate net price. $\$12{,}000 \times .64125 = \$7{,}695$
4. Calculate single equivalent discount rate.

$$\begin{array}{r} 1.00000 \\ -\ .64125 \\ \hline .35875 \end{array}$$

5. Calculate trade discount amount $\$12{,}000 \times .35875 = \$4{,}305$

LEARNING UNIT 7–2 CASH DISCOUNTS, CREDIT TERMS, AND PARTIAL PAYMENTS

Liz Claiborne to Lift Standard Discount To Stores to 10% on Women's Apparel

By TERI AGINS
Staff Reporter of THE WALL STREET JOURNAL

NEW YORK—**Liz Claiborne** Inc. will raise its standard discount to stores on its shipments of women's apparel in a move calculated to earn the good will of department store retailers—and additional market share.

Liz Claiborne, already the dominant women's wear resource in most of the nation's department stores, said it will increase the discount to 10% from 8% to "help our retail partners overcome some of the increased costs of business . . . in a way that does not increase prices to consumers." The company said it will absorb the additional discount through cost cutting and the anticipated gains in market share.

The discount will apply to spring shipments that will arrive in stores later this year. It affects about 70% of Liz Claiborne's total business and excludes men's apparel, cosmetics and accessories.

As a rule, apparel makers give retailers an 8% discount on merchandise providing that bills are paid within the first 10 days of the month following delivery.

Deborah Bronston, an apparel analyst

Cash discounts for early payment of bills offer retail companies a way to save on the cost of resale merchandise. From the above *Wall Street Journal* clipping, you can see that Liz Claiborne will increase its cash discount to retailers from 8% to 10%. Apparel makers usually give an 8% discount if bills are paid within the first 10 days of the month following delivery.

This unit explains cash discounts and how they are determined. You will also learn about the common credit terms offered by sellers.

Cash Discounts

A cash discount is for prompt payment. A trade discount is not.

When a customer buys goods on credit, sellers issue an invoice or bill to the customer. The invoice states the **terms of the sale,** such as credit period, discount period, cash discount amount, and freight terms. For a better understanding of cash discounts, let's look at these terms now.

Buyers can often benefit from buying on credit. The time period that the seller gives buyers to pay their invoices is the **credit period.** Frequently, buyers can sell the goods they bought during this credit period. Then, at the end of the credit period, the buyer can pay the seller with the funds from the sales of the goods. When buyers can do this, they can use the consumer's money to pay the invoice instead of their own money.

Sellers can also offer a cash discount, or reduction from the invoice price, if buyers pay the invoice within a specified period of time. This time period is the **discount period,** which is part of the total credit period. Sellers offer this cash discount because they can use the dollars to better advantage sooner rather than later. Buyers who are not short of cash like cash discounts because the goods will cost less and provide opportunity for larger profits.

Trade discounts should be taken before the cash discounts.

Remember that buyers do not take cash discounts on freight, returned goods, sales tax, and so on. Buyers take cash discounts on the *net price* of the invoice (Figure 7–1). Before we can discuss how to calculate cash discounts, you should understand how companies determine freight charges.

Freight Terms

FOB Shipping Point
Buyer pays the freight cost.

The most common freight terms are **FOB shipping point** and **FOB destination.** These terms determine how the freight is to be paid. The key words in the terms are *shipping point* and *destination.* If you catalog shop, be careful! Many companies have raised the shipping fees due to increased postal and United Parcel Service rates. For example, JCPenney increased all merchandise shipping fees by as much as 27% to $4.64. L. L. Bean introduced charges for shipping for the *first time*—$3.50 an order. Spiegel, Sears, J. Crew, and others have all raised their shipping and handling fees.

FIGURE 7-1
Invoice

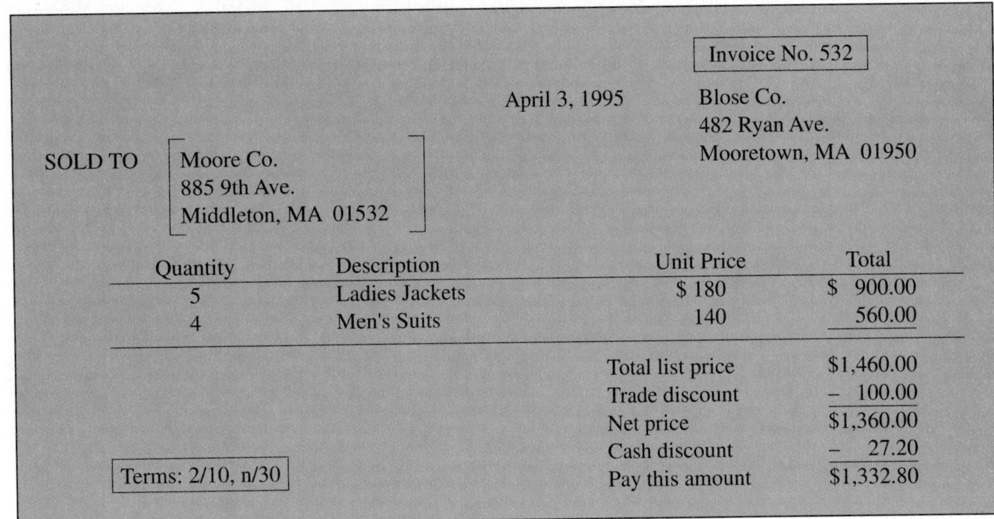

Invoice No. 532

April 3, 1995

Blose Co.
482 Ryan Ave.
Mooretown, MA 01950

SOLD TO Moore Co.
885 9th Ave.
Middleton, MA 01532

Quantity	Description	Unit Price	Total
5	Ladies Jackets	$ 180	$ 900.00
4	Men's Suits	140	560.00
		Total list price	$1,460.00
		Trade discount	– 100.00
		Net price	$1,360.00
		Cash discount	– 27.20
		Pay this amount	$1,332.80

Terms: 2/10, n/30

FOB Destination
Seller pays the freight cost.

FOB shipping point means free on board at shipping point; that is, the buyer pays the freight cost of getting the goods to the place of business. This freight term assumes that buyers take title to the goods once they reach the carrier (plane, boat, truck, etc.). For example, assume that IBM in San Diego bought goods from Avon suppliers in Boston. Avon ships the goods FOB Boston by plane. IBM takes title to the goods when the aircraft in Boston receives the goods, so IBM pays the freight from Boston to San Diego. Frequently the seller (Avon in this case) prepays the freight and adds the amount to the buyer's invoice (IBM). When paying the invoice, the buyer takes the cash discount off the net price and adds back the freight cost. FOB shipping point can be illustrated as follows:

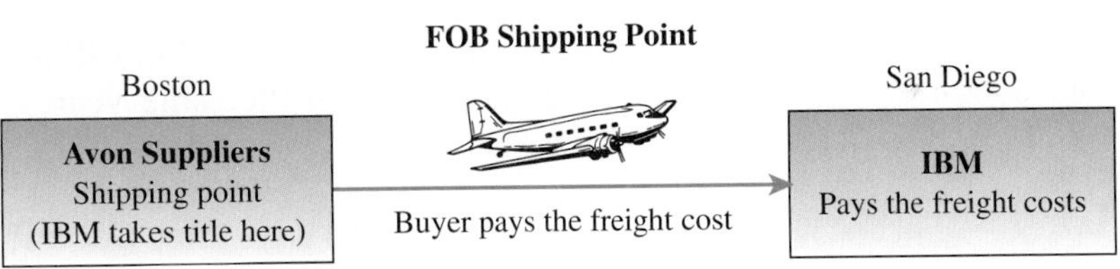

FOB destination means the seller pays the freight cost until it reaches the buyer's place of business. If Avon shipped its goods to IBM FOB destination or FOB San Diego, the title to the goods remains with Avon. Then it is Avon's responsibility to pay the freight from Boston to IBM's place of business in San Diego.

Before you learn how to calculate cash discounts, let's look at some aids that will help you calculate credit **due dates** and **end of credit periods.**

Aids in Calculating Credit Due Dates

Sellers usually give credit for 30, 60, or 90 days. All months of the year do not have 30 days. So you must count the credit days from the date of the invoice. The trick is to remember the number of days in each month. You can choose one of the following three options to help you do this.

Option 1: Days-in-a-Month Rule You may already know this rule. Remember that every four years is a leap year.

Years divisible by 4 are leap years. Leap years occur in 1996 and 2000.

Thirty days has September, April, June, and November; all the rest have 31 except February has 28, and 29 in leap years.

Option 2: Knuckle Months Some people like to use the knuckles on their hands to remember which months have 30 or 31 days. Note in the following diagram that each knuckle represents a month with 31 days. The short months are in between the knuckles.

31 days

Jan., March, May, July,
Aug., Oct., Dec.

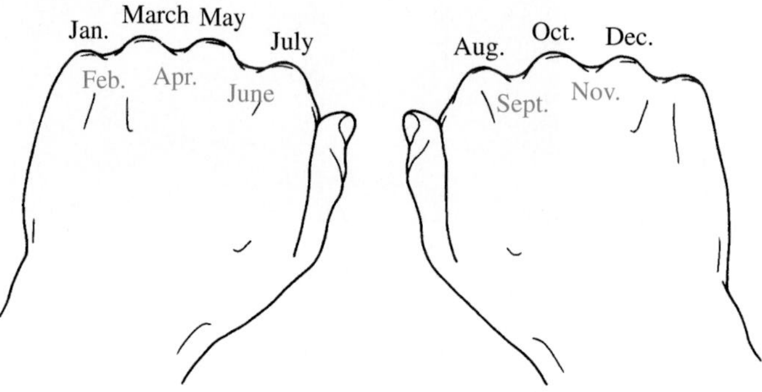

Option 3: Days-in-a-Year-Calendar The days-in-a-year calendar (excluding leap year) is another tool to help you calculate dates for discount and credit periods (Table 7–1). For example, let's use Table 7–1 to calculate 90 days from August 12.

EXAMPLE By Table 7–1: August 12 = 224 days
+ 90 days
314 days

Search for day 314 in Table 7–1. You will find that day 314 is November 10. In this example, we stayed within the same year. Now let's try an example in which we overlap from year to year.

EXAMPLE What date is 80 days after December 5?

Table 7–1 shows that December 5 is 339 days from the beginning of the year. Subtracting 339 from 365 (the end of the year) tells us that we have used up 26 days by the end of the year. This leaves 54 days in the new year. Go back in the table and start with the beginning of the year and search for 54 (80 − 26) days. The 54th day is February 23. So 80 days from December 5 is February 23 of the next year.

By table

365 days in the year
− 339 days until December 5
26 days used in the year

80 days from December 5
− 26 days used in the year
54 days in new year or
February 23

Without use of table

December 31
− December 5
26
+ 31 days in January
57
+ 23 due date (February 23)
80 total days

When you know how to calculate credit due dates, you can understand the common business terms sellers offer buyers involving discounts and credit periods. Remember that discount and credit terms vary from one seller to another.

TABLE 7-1 Exact Days-in-a-Year Calendar (Excluding Leap Year)

Day of month	31 Jan.	28 Feb.	31 Mar.	30 Apr.	31 May	30 June	31 July	31 Aug.	30 Sept.	31 Oct.	30 Nov.	31 Dec.
1	1	32	60	91	121	152	182	213	244	274	305	335
2	2	33	61	92	122	153	183	214	245	275	306	336
3	3	34	62	93	123	154	184	215	246	276	307	337
4	4	35	63	94	124	155	185	216	247	277	308	338
5	5	36	64	95	125	156	186	217	248	278	309	339
6	6	37	65	96	126	157	187	218	249	279	310	340
7	7	38	66	97	127	158	188	219	250	280	311	341
8	8	39	67	98	128	159	189	220	251	281	312	342
9	9	40	68	99	129	160	190	221	252	282	313	343
10	10	41	69	100	130	161	191	222	253	283	314	344
11	11	42	70	101	131	162	192	223	254	284	315	345
12	12	43	71	102	132	163	193	224	255	285	316	346
13	13	44	72	103	133	164	194	225	256	286	317	347
14	14	45	73	104	134	165	195	226	257	287	318	348
15	15	46	74	105	135	166	196	227	258	288	319	349
16	16	47	75	106	136	167	197	228	259	289	320	350
17	17	48	76	107	137	168	198	229	260	290	321	351
18	18	49	77	108	138	169	199	230	261	291	322	352
19	19	50	78	109	139	170	200	231	262	292	323	353
20	20	51	79	110	140	171	201	232	263	293	324	354
21	21	52	80	111	141	172	202	233	264	294	325	355
22	22	53	81	112	142	173	203	234	265	295	326	356
23	23	54	82	113	143	174	204	235	266	296	327	357
24	24	55	83	114	144	175	205	236	267	297	328	358
25	25	56	84	115	145	176	206	237	268	298	329	359
26	26	57	85	116	146	177	207	238	269	299	330	360
27	27	58	86	117	147	178	208	239	270	300	331	361
28	28	59	87	118	148	179	209	240	271	301	332	362
29	29	—	88	119	149	180	210	241	272	302	333	363
30	30	—	89	120	150	181	211	242	273	303	334	364
31	31	—	90	—	151	—	212	243	—	304	—	365

Common Credit Terms Offered by Sellers

Table 7–2, pp. 174–75, gives the common credit terms sellers offer buyers, along with explanations and examples. Terms such as **ordinary dating, receipt of goods (ROG), end of month (EOM),** and **proximo** are discussed. Take your time and go through each term step by step. To determine the due dates, we used the exact days-in-a-year calendar (Table 7–1). Remember that we do not take cash discounts on freight, goods returned, sales tax, or trade discount amounts.

Dissecting and Solving a Word Problem with Trade and Cash Discount

Now that we have studied trade and cash discounts, let's look at a combination that involves both a trade and cash discount.

The Word Problem Hardy Company sent Regan Corporation an invoice for office equipment with a $10,000 list price. Hardy dated the invoice July 29 with a 2/10 EOM (end of month) terms. Regan receives a 30% trade discount and paid the invoice on September 6. Since terms were FOB destination, Regan paid no freight charge. What was the cost of office equipment for Regan? (Solution is on p. 176.)

TABLE 7-2 Common Terms Offered by Sellers

Common credit terms of sale →	Explanation →	Worked-out example
1. Ordinary dating method **a. 2/10, n/30** 2% discount can be taken within 10 days of invoice date. Full amount of price or net with no discount. Credit period is 30 days from date of invoice.	Today, businesses frequently use the ordinary dating method. Buyers can take a 2% cash discount off the gross amount* of the invoice if they pay the bill within 10 days from the invoice date. If buyers miss the discount period, the net amount—without a discount—is due between day 11 and day 30. *Remember that freight, trade discounts, etc., are subtracted from the gross before calculating cash discount. Note a 2% cash discount means we save 2¢ on the dollar and pay 98¢ on the dollar. Thus, $.98 × $400 = $392.	$400 invoice dated July 5; terms 2/10, n/30; no freight; paid on July 11. **Step 1. Calculate end of 2% discount period:** July 5 date of invoice + 10 days July 15 end of 2% discount period **Step 2. Calculate end of credit period:** July 5 by Table 7-1 → 186 days + 30 days 216 days Search in Table 7-1 for 216 August 4 → end of credit period **Step 3. Calculate payment on July 11:** .02 × $400 = $8 cash discount $400 − $8 = $392 paid
b. 2/10, 1/15 n/30 2% discount can be taken within 10 days of date of invoice. If 2% discount missed, a 1% discount can be taken from day 11 to day 15. Full amount. End of credit period.	The seller will give buyers a 2% (2 cents on the dollar) cash discount if they pay within 10 days of invoice date. If buyers pay between day 11 to day 15 from date of invoice, they can save 1 cent on the dollar. If buyers do not pay on day 15, the net or full amount is due 30 days from the invoice date. A 1% discount means we pay $.99 on the dollar or $500 × $.99 = $495 + $100 freight = $595. Note: Freight is added back since no cash discount is taken on freight.	$600 invoice dated May 8; $100 of freight included in invoice price; paid on May 22. **Step 1. Calculate end of 2% discount period:** May 8 date of invoice + 10 days May 18 end of 2% discount period **Step 2. Calculate end of 1% discount period:** May 18 end of 2% discount period + 5 days May 23 end of 1% discount period **Step 3. Calculate end of credit period:** May 8 by Table 7-1 → 128 days + 30 days 158 days Search in Table 7-1 for 158 June 7 → end of credit period **Step 4. Calculate payment on May 22 (14 days after date of invoice):** $600 invoice − 100 freight $500 × .01 $5.00 $500 − $5.00 + $100 freight = $595

TABLE 7-2 (*Concluded*)

Common credit terms of sale →	Explanation →	Worked-out example
2. Receipt of goods (ROG) 3/10, n/30 ROG A 3% discount can be taken within 10 days *after* receipt of goods. Full amount due between day 11 to day 30 if cash discount period missed. Receipt of goods.	Cash discount period begins when buyer receives goods and *not* the invoice date. Industry often uses the ROG terms when buyers cannot expect delivery until a long time after they place the order.	$900 invoice dated May 9; no freight or returned goods; the goods were received on July 8; terms 3/10, n/30 ROG; payment made on July 20. **Step 1. Calculate end of 3% discount period:** July 8 date goods arrive + 10 days July 18 end of 3% discount period **Step 2. Calculate end of credit period:** July 8 by Table 7-1 189 days + 30 days 219 days Search in Table 7-1 for 219 August 7 → end of credit period **Step 3. Calculate paid on July 20:** Missed discount period and paid net or full amount of $900.
3. End of month (EOM)* For EOM: (1) We assume a 30-day month. (2) Buyer is guaranteed at least 15 days' credit.		
a. Invoice dated 25th or earlier in month 1/10 EOM* A 1% cash discount can be taken if invoice is paid by the 10th day of the month that *follows* the sale. If discount not taken, full amount due within 20 days after end of discount period.	If seller dates invoice on the 25th or earlier in the month, buyer can take the cash discount if buyer pays the invoice within first 10 days of month following sale (next month). If buyers miss the discount period, the full amount is due within 20 days after end of discount period. Note that discount period begins with next month after seller prepares invoice.	$600 invoice dated July 6; no freight or returns; terms 1/10 EOM; paid on August 8. **Step 1. Calculate end of 1% discount period:** August 10 Note by end of discount period buyer has received the guaranteed 15 days' credit **Step 2. Calculate end of credit period:** August 10 + 20 days August 30 **Step 3. Calculate paid on August 8:** .99 × $600 = $594
Note: Discount, as well as credit period, starts from end of month sale made.		
b. Invoice dated after 25th of month 2/10 EOM A 2% cash discount can be taken if invoice paid by 10th day of *second* month following the sale. Full amount due within 20 days after end of discount period.	When seller sells goods after 25th of month, buyers gain an additional month. The cash discount ends on the 10th day of the second month that follows the sale. Why? This occurs because the seller guarantees the 15 days' credit of the buyer. If a buyer bought goods on August 29, September 10 would be only 12 days. So buyer gets the extra month.	$800 invoice dated April 29; no freight or returns; terms 2/10 EOM; payment made on June 18. **Step 2. Calculate end of 2% discount period:** June 10 If the discount period was May 10, buyer would have only 11 days' credit. Must have at least 15 for EOM. **Step 2. Calculate end of credit period:** June 10 + 20 June 30 **Step 3. Calculate paid on June 18:** No discount; $800 paid.

*Sometimes Latin term *proximo* is used. Other variations of EOM exist, but the key point is that the seller guaranteed the buyer 15 days' credit.

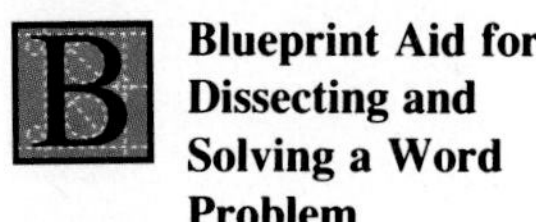

Blueprint Aid for Dissecting and Solving a Word Problem

A. Gather the facts	B. What am I solving for?	C. What must I know or calculate before solving problem?	D. Key points to remember
List price: $10,000. *Trade discount rate:* 30%. *Terms:* 2/10 EOM. *Invoice date:* 7/29. *Date paid:* 9/6.	Cost of office equipment.	Net price = List price × Complement of trade discount rate. After 25th of month for EOM. Discount period is 1st 10 days of second month that follows sale.	Trade discounts are deducted before taking cash discounts. Cash discounts are not taken on freight or returns.

Steps to Solving Problem

1. Calculate net price. $10,000 × .70 = $7,000 ← 100% − 30 (trade discount)
2. Calculate discount period. Sale: 7/29 Month 1: Aug. Month 2: Sept 10 ← Paid on Sept. 6—is entitled to 2% off.
3. Calculate cost of office equipment. $7,000 × .98 = **$6,860** (↑ 100% − 2%) If you save 2 cents on a dollar, you are spending 98 cents.

Partial Payments

Often the buyer cannot pay the entire invoice before the end of the discount period.

Steps for Calculating Partial Payments and Amount of Outstanding Balance

Step 1. Calculate complement of discount rate.

Step 2. Divide partial payments by complement of discount rate (Step 1). This gives the amount credited.

Step 3. Subtract Step 2 amount from the total owed. This is the outstanding balance.

EXAMPLE Molly McGrady owed $400. Molly's terms were 2/10, n/30. Within 10 days, Molly sent a check for $80. The actual credit the buyer gave Molly is:

Partial payment

$$\frac{\$80}{1 - .02}$$

↗ *Discount rate*

Step 1. 100% − 2% = 98% → .98

Step 2. $\frac{\$80}{.98} = \$81.63$

Step 3. $400.00
− 81.63 (partial payment—although sent in $80)
$318.37 (outstanding balance)

Note: We do not multiply the .02 × $80 because the seller did not base the original discount on the $80. When Molly makes a payment within the 10-day discount period, 98 cents pays each $1 she owes. Before buyers take discounts on partial payments, they must have permission from the seller. Not all states allow partial payments.

It's time to try the Practice Quiz and test what you have learned.

LU 7-2 PRACTICE QUIZ

Complete the following table:

	Date of invoice	Date goods received	Terms	Last day* of discount period	End of credit period
1.	November 6		2/10, n/30		
2.	February 19	June 9	3/10, n/30 ROG		
3.	May 9		4/10, 1/30, n/60		
4.	May 12		2/10 EOM		
5.	May 29		2/10 EOM		

*If more than one discount, assume date of last discount.

6. Metro Corporation sent Vasko Corporation an invoice for equipment with an $8,000 list price. Metro dated the invoice May 26. Terms were 2/10 EOM. Vasco receives a 20% trade discount and paid the invoice on July 3. What was the cost of equipment for Vasko? (A blueprint aid will be in the solution to help dissect this problem.)
7. Complete amount to be credited and balance outstanding:
   Amount of invoice: $600
   Terms: 2/10, 1/15, n/30
   Date of invoice: September 30
   Paid October 3: $400

SOLUTIONS TO LU 7-2 PRACTICE QUIZ

1. End of discount period: November 6 + 10 days = November 16
   End of credit period: By Table 7-1, November 6 = 310 days
   + 30 days
   340 → search → Dec. 6
2. End of discount period: June 9 + 10 days = June 19
   End of credit period: By Table 7-1, June 9 = 160 days
   + 30 days
   190 → search → July 9
3. End of discount period: By Table 7-1, May 9 = 129 days
   + 30 days
   159 → search → June 8
   End of credit period: By Table 7-1, May 9 = 129 days
   + 60 days
   189 → search → July 8
4. End of discount period: June 10
   End of credit period: June 10 + 20 = June 30
5. End of discount period: July 10
   End of credit period: July 10 + 20 = July 30
6. Vasko Corporation's cost of equipment:

Blueprint Aid for Dissecting and Solving a Word Problem

A. Gather the facts	B. What am I solving for?	C. What must I know or calculate before solving problem?	D. Key points to remember
List price: $8,000. *Trade discount rate:* 20%. *Terms:* 2/10 EOM. *Invoice date:* 5/26. *Date paid:* 7/3	Cost of equipment.	Net price = List price × Complement of trade discount rate. *EOM before 25th:* Discount period is 1st 10 days of month that follows sale. If goods are sold after the 25th, buyer gains an additional month.	Trade discounts are deducted before taking cash discounts. Cash discounts are not taken on freight or returns.

Steps to Solving Problem

1. Calculate net price. $8,000 × .80 = $6,400 (100% − 20)
2. Calculate discount period. Until July 10
3. Calculate cost of equipment. $6,400 × .98 = $6,272 (100% − 2)

7. $\frac{\$400}{.98}$ = $408.16, amount credited.

$600 − $408.16 = $191.84, balance outstanding.

CHAPTER ORGANIZER: A REFERENCE GUIDE

Page	Topic	Key point, procedure, formula	Example(s) to illustrate situation
164	Trade discount amount	Trade discount amount = List price × Trade discount rate	$600 list price 30% trade discount rate Trade discount amount = $600 × .30 = $180
164	Calculating net price	Net price = List price × Complement of trade discount rate or List price − Trade discount amount	$600 list price 30% trade discount rate Net price = $600 × .70 = $420 1.00 − .30 .70
166	Calculating list price when net price and trade discount rate are known	List price = $\frac{\text{Net price}}{\text{Complement of trade discount rate}}$	40% trade discount rate Net price, $120 $\frac{\$120}{.60}$ = $200 list price (1.00 − .40)
167	Chain discounts	Can never be added together because rate is based on a successively lower base.	5/10 on a $100 list item $100 × .05 = $5.00; $ 95 × .10 = $9.50 (running balance) $95.00 − 9.50 = $85.50 net price
167	Net price equivalent rate	Actual cost to buyer = List price × Net price equivalent rate Take complement of each chain discount and multiply—do not round. Trade discount amount = List price − Actual cost to buyer	Given: 5/10 on $1,000 list price Take complement: .95 × .90 = .855 (net price equivalent) $1,000 × .855 = $855 (actual cost or net price) $1,000 − 855 $ 145 trade discount amount
168	Single equivalent discount rate	Trade discount amount = List price × 1 − Net price equivalent rate	See example above for facts: 1 − .855 = .145 .145 × $1,000 = $145

Page	Topic	Key point, procedure, formula	Example(s) to illustrate situation
170	Cash discount	Cash discounts, due to prompt payment, are not taken on freight, returns, etc.	Gross $1,000 (includes freight) Freight $25 Terms, 2/10, n/30 Returns $25 Purchased: Sept. 9; paid Sept. 15 Cash discount = $950 × .02 = $19
171	Freight	FOB destination—seller pays freight FOB shipping point—buyer pays freight	Moose Company of New York sells equipment to Agee Company of Oregon. Terms of shipping are FOB New York. Agee pays cost of freight since terms are FOB shipping point.
171	Calculating due dates	*Option 1:* Thirty days has September, April, June, and November, all the rest have 31 except February has 28, and 29 in leap years. *Option 2:* Knuckles—31-day month; in between knuckles are short months. *Option 3:* Days-in-a-year table.	Invoice $500 on March 5; terms 2/10, n/30. March 5 *End of discount* + 10 *period:* → March 15 *End of credit* March 5 = 64 days *period by* + 30 days *Table 7–1:* → 94 days Search in Table 7–1 → April 4
174	Common terms of sale **a.** Ordinary method	Discount period begins from date of invoice. Credit period ends 20 days from the end of the discount period unless otherwise stipulated; example, 2/10, n/60—the credit period ends 50 days from end of discount period.	Invoice $600 (freight of $100 included in price) dated March 8; payment on March 16; 3/10, n/30. March 8 *End of discount* + 10 *period:* → March 18 *End of credit* March 8 = 67 days *period by* + 30 days *Table 7–1:* → 97 days Search in Table 7–1 → April 7 *If paid on March 16:* .97 × $500 = $485 + 100 freight $585
174	**b.** Receipt of goods (ROG)	Discount period begins when goods are received. Credit period ends 20 days from end of discount period.	4/10, n/30, ROG. $600 invoice; no freight; dated August 5; goods received October 2; payment made October 20. October 2 *End of discount* + 10 *period:* → October 12 *End of credit* October 2 = 275 *period by* + 30 *Table 7–1:* → 305 ↓ Search in Table 7–1 November 1 *Payment on October 20:* No discount; pay $600
175	End of month (EOM)	Assume: (1) A 30-day month. (2) Buyer is guaranteed at least 15 days' credit. After 25th an additional extra month is gained.	$1,000 invoice dated May 12; no freight or returns; terms 2/10 EOM. *End of discount period* → June 10 *End of credit period* → June 30
176	Partial payments	$\text{Amount credited} = \frac{\text{Partial payment}}{1 - \text{Discount rate}}$	$200 invoice, terms 2/10, n/30, dated March 2; paid $100 on March 5. $\frac{\$100}{1 - .02} = \frac{\$100}{.98} = \$102.04$

Page	Topic	Key point, procedure, formula	Example(s) to illustrate situation
	Key terms	Cash discount, *p. 170* Chain discounts, *p. 166* Complement, *p. 165* Credit period, *p. 170* Discount period, *p. 170* Due dates, *p. 171* End of credit period, *p. 171* End of month (EOM), *p. 175* FOB destination, *p. 170* FOB shipping point, *p. 170* List price, *p. 164*	Net price, *p. 164* Net price equivalent rate, *p. 167* Ordinary dating, *p. 174* Proximo, *p. 175* Receipt of goods (ROG), *p. 175* Single equivalent discount rate, *p. 167* Single trade discounts, *p. 165* Terms of the sale, *p. 170* Trade discount, *p. 164* Trade discount amount, *p. 164* Trade discount rate, *p. 164*

END-OF-CHAPTER PROBLEMS

Drill Problems

Additional homework assignments by learning unit are at the end of text in Appendix I (p. I–29). Solutions to odd problems are at the end of text in Appendix II.

For all problems, round final answer to nearest cent. Do not round net price equivalent rates or single equivalent discount rates.

Complete the following:

	Item	List price	Chain discount	Net price equivalent rate (in decimals)	Single equivalent discount rate (in decimals)	Trade discount	Net price
7–1.	CD player	$650	10/5	.855	.145	$94.25	$555.75

1.00 − .10 = .90 × (1.00 − .05 =) .95 = .855 × $650 = $555.75

1.000 − .855 = .145 × $650 = $94.25

	Item	List price	Chain discount	Net price equivalent rate (in decimals)	Single equivalent discount rate (in decimals)	Trade discount	Net price
7–2.	Video camcorder	$349	20/10/10	.648	.352	122.85	226.15

1.00 − .20 = .80 × (1.00 − .10 =) .90 × (1.00 − .10 =) .90 = .648 × $349 = $226.15

1.000 − .648 = .352 × $349 = $122.85

	Item	List price	Chain discount	Net price equivalent rate (in decimals)	Single equivalent discount rate (in decimals)	Trade discount	Net price
7–3.	Cassette recorder	$150	14/3/2	.817516	.182484	27.37	122.63

1.00 − .14 = .86 × (1.00 − .03 =) .97 × (1.00 − .02 =) .98 = .817516 × $150 = $122.63

1.000000 − .817516 = .182484 × $150 = $27.37

Complete the following:

	Item	List price	Chain discount	Net price	Trade discount
7–4.	Sony Portable T.V.	$150	15/10	$114.75	$35.25

$150 × .765 = $114.75 (.765 = .85 × .9)
$150 × .235 = $35.25 (1 − .765 = .235)

	Item	List price	Chain discount	Net price	Trade discount
7–5.	Maytag diswasher	$450	8/5/6	$369.70	$80.30

$450 × .82156 = $369.70 (.82156 = .92 × .95 × .94)
$450 × .17844 = $80.30 (1 − .82156 = .17844)

	Item	List price	Chain discount	Net price	Trade discount
7–6.	Word processor	$320	3/5/9	$268.34	$51.66

$320 × .838565 = $268.34 (.838565 = .97 × .95 × .91)
$320 × .161435 = $51.66 (1 − .838565 = .161435)

	Item	List price	Chain discount	Net price	Trade discount
7–7.	Nautilus Equip.	$1,850	12/9/6	$1,392.59	$457.41

$1,850 × .752752 = $1,392.59 (.752752 = .88 × .91 × .94)
$1,850 × .247248 = $457.41 (1 − .752752 = .247248)

7-8. Which of the following companies, A or B, gives a higher discount? Use the single equivalent discount rate to make your choice (convert your equivalent rate to the nearest hundredth percent).

Company A	**Company B**
8/10/15/3	10/6/16/5

A: .92 × .90 × .85 × .97 = 1.000000 − .682686 = .317314 = 31.73%

B: .90 × .94 × .84 × .95 = 1.000000 − .675108 = .324892 = 32.49% Better

Complete the following:

	Invoice	Dates when goods received	Terms	Last day* of discount period	Final day bill is due (end of credit period)
7-9.	June 14		1/10, n/30	June 24	July 14
	By Table 7-1, June 14 = 165 + 30 = 195 → search in Table 7-1				
7-10.	Nov. 27		2/10 EOM	Jan. 10	Jan. 30 Extra month since after the 25th. Credit period ends 20 days from end of discount period.
7-11.	May 15	June 5	3/10, ROG	June 15	July 5
7-12.	Apr. 10		2/10, 1/30, n/60	May 10	June 9
	By Table 7-1, April 10 = 100 + 60 = 160 → search in Table 7-1.				
7-13.	June 12		3/10 EOM	July 10	July 30 Discount and credit period begin at end of month of sale.
7-14.	Jan. 10	Feb. 3 (no leap year)	4/10, n/30, ROG	Feb. 13	March 5
	By Table 7-1, February 3 = 34 + 30 = 64 → search in Table 7-1.				

* If more than one discount, assume date of last discount.

Complete the following by calculating the cash discount and net amount paid:

	Gross amount of invoice (freight charge already included)	Freight charge	Date of invoice	Terms of invoice	Date of payment	Cash discount	Net amount paid
7-15.	$6,000	$100	9/6	2/10, n/60	9/15	$118 (.02 × $5,900)	$5,882 ($5,900 × .98 = $5,782 + $100 freight)
7-16.	$ 600	None	8/1	3/10, 2/15, n/30	8/13	$12 (.02 × $600)	$588 (.98 × $600)
7-17.	$ 200	None	11/13	1/10 EOM	12/3	$2 (.01 × $200)	$198 (.99 × $200)
7-18.	$ 500	$100	11/29	1/10 EOM	1/4	$4 (.01 × $400)	$496 (.99 × $400 = $396 + $100 = $496)

Complete the following:

	Amount of invoice	Terms	Invoice date	Actual partial payment made	Date of partial payment	Amount of payment to be credited	Balance outstanding
7–19.	$450	2/10, n/60	6/6	$110	6/15	$112.24	$337.76
7–20.	$600	4/10, n/60	7/5	$400	7/14	$416.67	$183.33

7–19: $\frac{\$110}{.98} = \$450.00 - 112.24 = \$337.76$

7–20: $\frac{\$400}{.96} = \$600.00 - 416.67 = \$183.33$

Word Problems

7–21. The list price of a Timex watch is $39.95. Marvin Jewelers receives a trade discount of 15%. Find the trade discount amount and the net price.
$39.95 × .15 = $5.99 trade discount
$39.95 × .85 = $33.96 net price

7–22. A Minolta camera lists for $1,999 with a trade discount of 10%. What is the net price of the camera?
$1,999 × .90 = $1,799.10

7–23. Fireside Corporation buys its wood stoves from a wholesaler. The stove has a $400 list price with a 40% trade discount. What is the trade discount? What is the net price of the stove? Freight is FOB destination.
$400 × .40 = $160 trade discount
$400 × .60 = $240 net price

7–24. Pacesetter Furniture buys a living room set with a $4,000 list price and a 55% trade discount. Freight (FOB shipping point) of $50 is not part of the list price. What is the delivered price (including freight) of the living room set assuming a cash discount of 2/10, n/30, ROG? The invoice had an April 8 date. Pacesetter received the goods on April 19 and paid the invoice on April 25.
$4,000 × .55 = $2,200 Amount of trade discount
$4,000 − 2,200 = $1,800 × .98 = $1,764 + $50 = $1,814
or
($4,000 × .45 = $1,800)

7–25. A roller blades manufacturer offered a 5/2/1 chain discount to many customers. Bob's Sporting Goods ordered 20 pairs of roller blades for a total $625 list price. What was the net price of the roller blades? What was the trade discount amount?
NP: .95 × .98 × .99 = .92169 × $625 = $576.05625 = $576.06
TD: .07831 × $625 = $48.94

7–26. Radio Shack wants to buy a new line of shortwave radios. Manufacturer A offers a 21/13 chain discount. Manufacturer B offers a 26/8 chain discount. Both manufacturers have the same list price. Which manufacturer should Radio Shack buy from?
A: .79 × .87 = 1.0000 − .6873 = .3127
B: .74 × .92 = 1.0000 − .6808 = .3192 ✓

7–27. Maplewood Supply received a \$5,250 invoice dated 4/15/95. The \$5,250 included \$250 freight. Terms were 4/10, 3/30, n/60. If Maplewood pays the invoice on April 27, what will it pay? If Maplewood pays the invoice on May 21, what will it pay?

\$5,250 − \$250 = \$5,000 × .97 = \$4,850
+ 250 freight
\$5,100

May 21
\$5,250

7–28. Ethan Furniture Barn paid \$90 for a lamp after discounts of 30% and 20% from the list price. What was the list price to the nearest cent?

1.00 − .30 = .70 × (1.00 − .20 = .80) = .56

$B = \frac{P}{R}$ $\frac{\$90}{.56} = \$160.71$

7–29. Suburban Tool Manufacturing sold Hamline Hardware a set of jigsaws for a \$1,050 list price. Suburban offered a 4/3/1 chain discount. What was the net price of the jigsaws? What was the trade discount amount? (Round final answers to nearest cent.)

.96 × .97 × .99 = .921888

\$1,050 × .921888 = \$967.9824 NP

.078112 × \$1,050 = \$82.0176 TD

\$967.98 NP + 82.02 TD = \$1,050.00

7–30. Macy of New York sold Marriott of Chicago office equipment with a \$6,000 list price. Sale terms were 3/10, n/30 FOB New York. Macy agreed to prepay the \$30 freight. Marriott pays the invoice within the discount period. What does Marriott pay Macy?

.97 × \$6,000 = \$5,820 + \$30 freight = \$5,850

7–31. Quality Furniture bought a sofa for \$900. The sofa had a \$1,200 list price. What was the trade discount rate Quality received?

$\frac{(P)\$300}{(B)\$1,200} = \frac{1}{4} = 25\%(R)$

7–32. Dalton Bookseller paid a \$4,500 net price for textbooks. The publisher offered a 25% trade discount. What was the publisher's list price?

$\frac{(P)\$4,500}{(R).75} = \$6,000\ (B)$

7–33. Heartland Manufacturing sent Sully Corporation an invoice for machinery with a \$9,000 list price. Heartland dated the invoice July 23 with 2/10 EOM terms. Sully receives a 30% trade discount. Sully pays the invoice on August 5. What does Sully pay Heartland?

\$9,000 × .70 = \$6,300   \$6,300 × .98 = \$6,174

7–34. On August 1, Sully Corporation (Problem 7–33) returns \$100 of the machinery due to defects. What does Sully pay Heartland on August 5?

\$9,000
− 100 returns
\$8,900 × .70 = \$6,230   \$6,230 × .98 = \$6,105.40

7–35. Stacy's Dress Shop received a \$1,050 invoice dated July 8 with 2/10, 1/15, n/60 terms. On July 22, Stacy's sent a \$242 partial payment. What credit should Stacy receive? What is Stacy's outstanding balance?

$\frac{\$242}{.99} = \$244.44$ \$1,050 − \$244.44 = \$805.56

7–36. On March 11, Jangles Corporation received a \$20,000 invoice dated March 8. Cash discount terms were 4/10, n/30. On March 15, Jangles sent an \$8,000 partial payment. What credit should Jangles receive? What is Jangles' outstanding balance?

$\frac{\$8,000}{.96} = \$8,333.33$

\$20,000.00
− 8,333.33
\$11,666.67 balance outstanding

Additional Set of Word Problems

7–37. Medco Healthcare wants to buy a new line of wheelchairs. Manufacturer A offers a 20/15 chain discount. Manufacturer B offers a 19/16 chain discount. Both manufacturers have the same list price. Which manufacturer should Medco buy from?

A: .80 × .85 = .68; 1.00 − .68 = .32
Better discount

B: .81 × .84 = .6804; 1.0000 − .6804 = .3196

7–38. The Sandstorm Bookstore paid a $6,600 net price for novels. The publisher offered a 20% trade discount. What was the publisher's list price?

$\frac{\$6,600}{.80} = \$8,250$

7–39. Lechmere Corporation buys word processors from a wholesaler. The word processors have a $425 list price with a 40% trade discount. What is the trade discount amount? What is the net price of the word processor? Freight charges are FOB destination.

$425 × .40 = $170 trade discount $425 × .60 = $255 net price

7–40. The Vail Ski Shop received a $1,201 invoice dated July 8 with 2/10, 1/15, n/60 terms. On July 22, Vail sent a $485 partial payment. What credit should Vail receive? What is Vail's outstanding balance?

$\frac{\$485}{.99} = \$489.90$

$1,201.00
− 489.90
$711.10 balance outstanding

7–41. Hiawatha Supply received an invoice dated 4/15/96. The invoice had a $5,500 balance that included $300 freight. Terms were 4/10, 3/30, n/60. Hiawatha pays the invoice on April 29. What amount does Hiawatha pay?

$5,500 − $300 = $5,200 × .97 = $5,044
+ 300
$5,344

7–42. Jebco Manufacturing sold Faraday Hardware a set of lawn furniture with a $1,350 list price. Jebco offered a 5/4/2 chain discount. What was the net price of the lawn furniture? What was the trade discount amount? Round to nearest cent.

.95 × .96 × .98 = .89376

$1,350
× .89376
$1,206.58 NP

$1,350
× .10624
$143.42 TD

7–43. On May 14, Bryant of Boston sold Forrest of Los Angeles $6,000 of office equipment. Terms were 2/10 EOM FOB Boston. Bryant agreed to prepay the $90 freight. If Forrest pays the invoice on June 8, what will Forrest pay? If Forrest pays on June 20, what will Forrest pay?

.98 × $6,000 = $5,880 + $90 freight = $5,970
June 20: $6,090 ($6,000 + $90)

7–44. Steele Roller Skates offers 4/3/1 chain discounts to many of its customers. Bob's Sporting Goods ordered 20 pairs of roller skates with a total list price of $900. What is the net price of the roller skates? What was the trade discount amount? Round to nearest cent.

.96 × .97 × .99 = .921888

$900
× .921888
$829.70 NP

$900
× .078112
$70.30 TD

7–45. Majestic Manufacturing sold McCormack Furniture a living room set for $8,500 list price with 35% trade discount. The $100 freight (FOB shipping point) was not part of the list price. Terms were 3/10, n/30 ROG. The invoice date was May 30. McCormack received the goods on July 18 and paid the invoice on July 20. What was the net price (include cost of freight) of the living room set?

$8,500 × .35 = $2,975 TD
$8,500 − $2,975 = $5,525 × .97 = $5,359.25 + $100 = $5,459.25
(or .65 × $8,500) ↑

7–46. Boeing Truck Company received an invoice showing 8 tires at $110 each, 12 tires at $160 each, and 15 tires at $180 each. Shipping terms are FOB shipping point. Freight is $400, trade discount is 10/5, and a cash discount of 2/10, n/30 is offered. Assuming Boeing pays within the discount period, what did Boeing pay?

8 × $110 = $ 880
12 × $160 = $1,920
15 × $180 = $2,700
$5,500 list

1.00 − .10 = .90 × (1.00 − .05 = .95) = .855

.855
× $5,500
$4,702.50 × .98 = $4,608.45
+ 400.00
$5,008.45

Challenge Problem
Buying Televisions —the Bottom Line

7–47. On March 30, Century Television received an invoice dated March 28 from ACME Manufacturing for 50 televisions at a cost of $125 each. Century received a 10/4/2 chain discount. Shipping terms were FOB shipping point. ACME prepaid the $70 freight. Terms were 2/10 EOM. When Century received the goods, 3 sets were defective. Century returned these sets to ACME. On April 8, Century sent a $150 partial payment. Century will pay the balance on May 6. What is Century's final payment on May 6? Assume no taxes.

List price (50 − 3) × $125 = $5,875
Less trade discount .90 × .96 × .98 × $5,875 = $4,974.48 + Freight
April 8 pays $150 $\frac{\$150}{.98}$ = $153.06

$4,974.48 − $153.06 = $4,821.42 due + $70

May 6 $4,821.42 − (.02 × $4,821.42) = $96.43
$4,821.42 − $96.43 = $4,724.99
+ 70.00
$4,794.99

Summary Practice Test

Solutions are at end of text in Appendix II.
Quick Reference
If you get any wrong answers, study the page numbers given for each problem.
1. P. 164.
2. P. 166.
3. P. 164.
4. Pp. 174–75.
5. P. 164.

Complete the following.

	Item	List price	Single trade discount	Net price
1.	GoodYear tires	$600	40%	? $360 = $600 × .60 $P = B \times R$
2.	Sony stereo $\left(\frac{\$600\ P}{.75\ R}\right)$	? $800 ($B$)	25%	$600

Calculate the net price and trade discount (use net price equivalent rate and single equivalent discount rate):

	Item	List price	Chain discount	Net price	Trade discount
3.	Amana oven	$400	8/10	? $331.20 (.92 × .90 = .828 × $400)	$68.80 (.172 × $400)

4. From the following, what is the last date for each discount period and credit period?

	Date of invoice	Terms	End of discount period	End of credit period
a.	July 15	2/10, n/30	July 25 (July 15 + 10)	Aug. 14 (July 15 → 196 days + 30 = 226)
b.	Aug. 10 (1994)	4/10, n/30 ROG (Goods received June 3, 1995)	June 13, 1995	July 3, 1995 (June 3 → 154 days + 30 = 184)
c.	Apr. 5	2/10 EOM	May 10	May 30
d.	May 29	2/10 EOM	July 10	July 30

5. Stanley Television buys a television from a wholesaler with an $800 list price and a 34% trade discount. What is the trade discount amount? What is the net price of the television?

$800 × .34 = $272
$800 × .66 = $528

6. *P. 171.*

6. French of Los Angeles sold Moore of Omaha office equipment with a $7,000 list price. Sale terms were 2/10, n/30 FOB Los Angeles. French agreed to prepay the $40 freight. Moore pays the invoice within the discount period. What does Moore pay French?

.98 × $7,000 = $6,860 + $40 = $6,900

7. *Pp. 166–68.*

7. Joyce Rich wants to buy a new line of stereos for her shop. Manufacturer A offers a 19/14 chain discount. Manufacturer B offers a 24/8 chain discount. Both manufacturers have the same list price. Which manufacturer should Joyce buy from?

Manufacturer A ✓

1.00 − .19 = .81; 1.00 − .14 = .86

.81 × .86 = .6966

1.0000 − .6966 = .3034 discount ✓

Manufacturer B

1.00 − .24 = .76; 1.00 − .08 = .92

.76 × .92 = .6992

1.0000 − .6992 = .3008 discount

8. *P. 176.*

8. Ed's Print Shop received a $4,000 invoice dated May 12. Terms were 3/10, 1/15, n/60. On May 24, Ed's Print Shop sent a $1,900 partial payment. What credit should Ed's Print Shop receive? What is Ed's Print Shop's outstanding balance? Round to nearest cent.

$\frac{\$1,900}{.99} = \$1,919.19$

$4,000.00 − 1,919.19 = $2,080.81

9. *P. 175.*

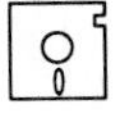

9. Lenore Company received from Murphy Company an invoice dated August 27. Terms were 2/10 EOM. List price on the invoice was $2,500 (freight not included). Lenore receives a 10/8 chain discount. Freight charges are Lenore's responsibility, but Murphy agreed to prepay the $200 freight. Lenore pays the invoice on October 8. What does Lenore Company pay Murphy?

.90 × .92 = .828 × $2,500 = $2,070 amount after trade discount

$2,070 × .98 = $2,028.60

$2,028.60 + 200.00 freight = $2,228.60

Project A

Digital Equipment Offer Aims to Aid Massachusetts

By a WALL STREET JOURNAL *Staff Reporter*

MAYNARD, Mass. – Responding to the beleaguered Massachusetts economy, **Digital Equipment** Corp. said it will give new companies incorporated in the state 40% to 50% discounts on computers.

Kenneth Olsen, president, who founded the company with a $70,000 investment in 1957, said the offer will help "by freeing the entrepreneurs to focus on their uniqueness," rather than on affording computers. "Computers can make startups successful faster," he said.

Mr. Olsen, subject of a biography called "The Ultimate Entrepreneur," has led Digital to No. 30 rank in the Fortune 500.

The offer will let start-up companies buy computers from Digital more cheaply than even Digital's biggest customers can. But it is tightly circumscribed. Only companies incorporated between May 1, 1990, and June 30, 1992, are eligible. And they can only order products at the reduced rate once.

If Digital sells Moore Company a $1,500,000 computer, what will Moore pay assuming a 40% discount?

$\$1{,}500{,}000 \times .60 = \$900{,}000$

Project B

MCI Unveils Service With 20% Discount On Some Phone Calls

NEW YORK – **MCI Communications** Corp., the nation's No. 2 long-distance company, introduced a service called Friends and Family, which offers a 20% discount to any customer who sends MCI a list of the numbers he calls the most. Those numbers also receive a 20% discount when they call the customer. The catch: Everybody must be an MCI customer to qualify for the discount.

"The idea is instead of [MCI] creating geographic areas for discounts, you tell us if you want the discount," said Timothy Price, senior vice president of sales and marketing.

Some analysts expressed doubts about the move. "The bigger the turnout among MCI's existing customer base, the worse it is financially," said Jack B. Grubman, an analyst at PaineWebber Inc. "The only way MCI gains is if they are able to attract

Assume Abby and Lorrette are MCI customers. What would a $6.24 call cost if they have Friends and Family?

$\$6.24 \times .80 = \$4.99$

Project C

ASEW INCORPORATED
6 Marsh-Creek Road
Waterville, Indiana 06766

INVOICE
No. 1418

Sold To: RYAN TOY SUPPLY
12 RUNNING-BROOK LANE
WOBURN, MA 01888

Shipped To:

DATE	OUR ORDER #	YOUR ORDER #	SHIPPING #	SHIPPED VIA	TERMS
10-27-xx		WM 11662		UPS	2/10, EOM

Quantity	DESCRIPTION	Price	Per	Amount
15	Toy wagons	32.95	Ea.	$ 494.25
5	Dolls	32.95	Ea.	164.75
3	Badminton sets	26.95	Ea.	80.85
5	Robots	41.95	Ea.	209.75
5	Footballs	28.55	Ea.	142.75
4	Doll carriages	41.55	Ea.	166.20
				$1,258.55
			SHIPPING......	43.40
				$1,301.95

Assume Asew gives a trade chain discount of 9/8/3 to Ryan (note that Asew prepaid the freight of $43.40) and Ryan pays the bill on December 7. What amount does Asew receive?

$.91 \times .92 \times .97 = .812084 \times \$1{,}258.55 = \$1{,}022.05$

$\times\ .98$

$\$1{,}001.61$

$+\ 43.40$

$\$1{,}045.01$

NOTES

THAT WAS THEN . . .
. . . THIS IS NOW

In this 1913 ad, the Arrow Shirt Man was illustrated by J. C. Leyendecker. That year shirts sold at retail for $1.50 and up, and collars were 2 for 25 cents. Today, 70% of all shirts sold are sports models.

ARROW
COLLARS
& SHIRTS
FOR DRESS

8

Markups and Markdowns; Insight into Perishables

LEARNING UNIT OBJECTIVES

LU 8–1: Markups[1] Based on Cost (100%)

1. Calculate markup amount and percent markup on cost. *p. 193.*
2. Calculate cost when markup amount and percent markup on cost are known. *p. 193.*
3. Calculate selling price when you know cost and percent markup on cost. *p. 194.*
4. Calculate cost when you know selling price and percent markup on cost. *p. 194.*

LU 8–2: Markups Based on Selling Price (100%)

1. Calculate markup amount and percent markup on selling price. *pp. 196–97.*
2. Calculate selling price when markup amount and percent markup on selling price are known. *p. 197.*
3. Calculate selling price when you know cost and percent markup on selling price. *p. 197.*
4. Calculate cost when you know selling price and percent markup on selling price. *p. 197.*
5. Convert markup percent on selling price to percent markup on cost. *p. 198.*
6. Convert percent markup on cost to percent markup on selling price. *p. 198.*

LU 8–3: Markdowns and Perishables

1. Calculate markdowns. *p. 201.*
2. Compare and contrast markdowns and markups. *p. 201.*
3. Price perishable items to cover spoilage loss. *p. 201.*

[1] Some texts use the term *markon* (selling price minus cost).

Courtesy of AT&T Archives

Did you ever wonder what it would be like to answer the telephone and not only hear the caller's voice but also see the caller? AT&T now has a video phone that sells for approximately $1,000. Do you think the convenience of hearing and seeing the person on the other end of the telephone will become popular? Will everyone be using a video phone in the 21st century?

If AT&T sells video phones for approximately $1,000, what is the cost to manufacture a video phone? What percent of profit will AT&T need to receive to make the phones profitable?

In this chapter, we discuss markup on cost and selling price. We begin by looking at the operation of a True Value Hardware store owned for 20 years by Nancy Ford.

When Nancy calculates the selling price of her goods, she considers these elements.

1. **Cost:** The price Nancy pays suppliers to bring goods into the store.
2. **Gross profit:** Net sales (sales less returns, discounts, and allowances) minus cost.
3. **Operating expenses:** The regular expenses of doing business such as rent, salaries, taxes, insurance, advertising, and so on.
4. **Net income (net profit):** Profit remaining after subtracting costs and operating expenses from net sales.

Nancy arrives at her selling price by adding a **markup** (or gross profit) to the cost of her goods. This markup represents the amount Nancy needs to cover her operating expenses and make a profit (net income). For this chapter, think of markup as selling price (S) less cost (C). To help you understand the basic formula that follows, let's use the example of a lawn mower that Nancy bought from a supplier and plans to sell for $300.

Selling price (S)	=	Cost (C)	+	Markup (M)
↑		↑		↑
$300 (mower)	=	$210 (price paid to bring mower into store)	+	$90 (amount to cover operating expenses and make a profit)

Retailers can use two methods to mark up goods: markups based on cost and markups based on selling price. Let's begin by studying markups based on cost.

LEARNING UNIT 8–1 MARKUPS BASED ON COST (100%)

In Chapter 6, you were introduced to the portion formula, which we used to solve percent problems. We also used the portion formula in Chapter 7 to solve problems involving trade and cash discounts. In this unit, you will see how we use the portion formula to solve three markup situations. We will be using blueprint aids to show how to dissect and solve all word problems in this chapter.

Many manufacturers mark up goods on cost since manufacturers can get cost information easier than sales information. Businesses that mark up their goods on cost recognize that cost is 100%. This 100% represents the base of the portion formula. All situations in this unit use cost as 100%.

To illustrate calculating **markup amount** and **percent markup on cost,** let's use Nancy Ford's lawn mower purchase at the beginning of the chapter and the basic formula for selling price.

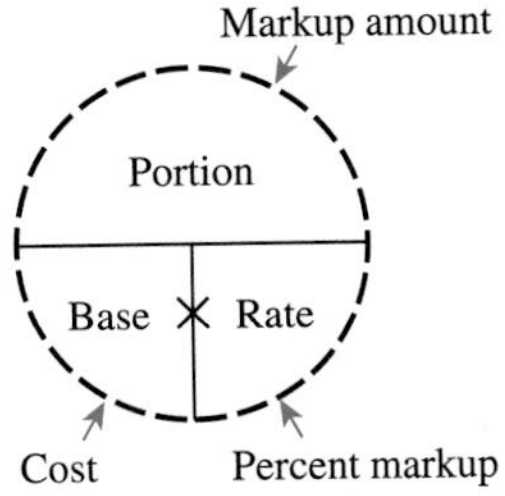

Cost	100% →	Cost is 100%—the base. Markup amount is the portion, and percent markup on cost is the rate.
+ Markup	42.86%	
= Selling price	142.86%	

In Situation 1 (below), we show why Nancy has a 42.86% markup based on cost by presenting Nancy's lawn mower purchase in the form of a word problem. To solve the word problem, we use the same type of blueprint aid we have used in the first seven chapters. In Column B, however, you will see subscripts after two numbers. These refer to the steps we use below the blueprint aid to solve the problem. Remember that cost is the base for this unit.

Situation 1: Calculating Markup Amount and Percent Markup on Cost

The Word Problem Nancy Ford bought a lawn mower for her True Value Hardware store that cost $210. She plans to sell the mower for $300. What is Nancy's markup amount and percent markup on cost (round to nearest hundredth percent)?

Blueprint Aid for Dissecting and Solving a Word Problem

A. Gather the facts	B. What am I solving for?	C. What must I know or calculate before solving problem?	D. Key points to remember
Mower cost: $210. *Mower selling price:* $300.	% / $ *C* 100.00% $210 + *M* 42.86[2] 90[1] = *S* 142.86% $300 [1] Markup amount. [2] Percent markup on cost.	Markup amount = Selling price − Cost Percent markup on cost = $\frac{\text{Markup amount}}{\text{Cost}}$	Markup amount Portion ($90) Base ($210) × Rate (?) Cost

Steps to Solving Problem

1. Calculate markup amount.

$$\text{Markup amount} = \text{Selling price} - \text{Cost}$$
$$\$90 = \$300 - \$210$$

2. Calculate percent markup on cost.

$$\text{Percent markup on cost} = \frac{\text{Markup amount}}{\text{Cost}}$$
$$= \frac{\$90}{\$210} = 42.86\%$$

Check

Selling price = Cost + Markup

$$\$300 = \$210 + .4286(\$210)$$
$$\$300 = \$210 + \$90^*$$
$$\$300 = \$300$$

Parentheses mean multiplication

or

$$\text{Cost} = \frac{\text{Markup amount}}{\text{Percent markup on cost}}$$
$$= \frac{\$90}{.4286} = \$209.99^*$$

* Off 1 cent due to rounding of percent.

In the check, note how we can calculate the cost when we know the markup amount and the percent markup on cost.

Situation 2: Calculating Selling Price When You Know Cost and Percent Markup on Cost

Blueprint Aid for Dissecting and Solving a Word Problem

The Word Problem Mel's Furniture bought a lamp for his store that cost $100. To make his desired profit, Mel needs a 65% markup on cost. What are Mel's markup amount and selling price?

A. Gather the facts	B. What am I solving for?	C. What must I know or calculate before solving problem?	D. Key points to remember
Lamp cost: $100. *Markup on cost:* 65%	% | $ C 100% $100 $+M$ 65 65[1] $= S$ 165% $165[2] [1] Markup amount. [2] Selling price.	Markup amount. $S = C + M$ or $S = \left(1 + \begin{array}{c}\text{Percent markup}\\\text{on cost}\end{array}\right) \times \text{Cost}$	Selling price Portion (?) Base ($100) × Rate (1.65) Cost 100% + 65%

Steps to Solving Problem

1. Calculate markup amount.
   $S = C + M$
   $S = \$100 + .65(\$100)$ ←Parentheses mean multiplication
   $S = \$100 + \$65$ ←Markup amount
2. Calculate selling price.
   $S = \$165$

Check Selling price = (1 + Percent markup on cost) × Cost

$165 = 1.65 × $100

Situation 3: Calculating Cost When You Know Selling Price and Percent Markup on Cost

Blueprint Aid for Dissecting and Solving a Word Problem

The Word Problem Jill Sport, owner of Sports, Inc., sells tennis rackets for $50. To make her desired profit, Jill needs a 40% markup on cost. What do the tennis rackets cost Jill? What is dollar markup?

A. Gather the facts	B. What am I solving for?	C. What must I know or calculate before solving problem?	D. Key points to remember
Selling price: $50. *Markup on cost:* 40%.	% | $ C 100% $35.71[1] $+M$ 40 14.29[2] $= S$ 140% $50.00 [1] Cost. [2] Dollar markup.	$S = C + M$ or $\text{Cost} = \dfrac{\text{Selling price}}{1 + \text{Percent markup on cost}}$ $M = S - C$	Selling price Portion ($50) Base (?) × Rate (1.40) Cost 100% + 40%

Steps to Solving Problem

1. Calculate cost.
   $S = C + M$
   $\$50.00 = C + .40C$
   $\dfrac{\$50.00}{1.40} = \dfrac{1.40C}{1.40}$
   $\$35.71 = C$
2. Calculate dollar markup.
   $M = S - C$
   $M = \$50.00 - \$35.71$
   $M = \$14.29$

Check $\text{Cost} = \dfrac{\text{Selling price}}{1 + \text{Percent markup on cost}} = \dfrac{\$50.00}{1.40} = \$35.71$

Now try the following Practice Quiz to check your understanding of this unit.

LU 8–1 PRACTICE QUIZ

Solve the following situations (markups based on cost):

1. Irene Westing bought a desk for $400 from an office supply house. She plans to sell the desk for $600. What is Irene's markup amount and her percent markup on cost? Check your answer.
2. Suki Komar bought dolls for her toy store that cost $12 each. To make her desired profit, Suki must mark up each doll 35% on cost. What is the amount of markup? What is the selling price of each doll? Check your answer.
3. Jay Lyman sells calculators. His competitor sells a new calculator line for $14 each. Jay needs a 40% markup on cost to make his desired profit, and he must meet price competition. What cost can Jay afford to bring these calculators into the store? What is the dollar markup? Check your answer.

SOLUTIONS TO LU 8–1 PRACTICE QUIZ

Blueprint Aid for Dissecting and Solving a Word Problem

1. Irene's markup amount and percent markup on cost:

A. Gather the facts	B. What am I solving for?	C. What must I know or calculate before solving problem?	D. Key points to remember
Desk cost: $400. *Desk selling price:* $600.	% $ C 100% $400 $+ M$ 50[2] 200[1] $= S$ 150% $600 [1] Markup amount. [2] Percent markup on cost.	Markup amount = Selling price − Cost $\text{Percent markup on cost} = \frac{\text{Markup amount}}{\text{Cost}}$	Markup amount: Portion ($200) Cost: Base ($400) × Rate (?)

Steps to Solving Problem

1. Calculate markup amount. Markup amount = Selling price − Cost
   $200 = $600 − $400
2. Calculate percent markup on cost. $\text{Percent markup on cost} = \frac{\text{Markup amount}}{\text{Cost}}$
   $= \frac{\$200}{\$400} = 50\%$

Check

Selling price = Cost + Markup
$600 = $400 + .50($400)
$600 = $400 + $200
$600 = $600

or

$\text{Cost} = \frac{\text{Markup amount}}{\text{Percent markup on cost}}$

$= \frac{\$200}{.50} = \$400$

2. Amount of markup and selling price of doll:

Blueprint Aid for Dissecting and Solving a Word Problem

A. Gather the facts	B. What am I solving for?	C. What must I know or calculate before solving problem?	D. Key points to remember
Doll cost: $12 each. *Markup on cost:* 35%.	% $ C 100% $12.00 $+ M$ 35 4.20[1] $= S$ 135% $16.20[2] [1] Markup amount. [2] Selling price.	Markup amount. $S = C + M$ or $S = \left(1 + \text{Percent markup on cost}\right) \times \text{Cost}$	Selling price: Portion (?) Cost: Base ($12) × Rate (1.35) 100% + 35%

Steps to Solving Problem

1. Calculate markup amount.
   $S = C + M$
   $S = \$12.00 + .35(\$12.00)$
   $S = \$12.00 + \$4.20$ ← Markup amount
2. Calculate selling price. $S = \$16.20$

Check Selling price = (1 + Percent markup on cost) × Cost = 1.35 × $12.00 = $16.20

3. Cost and dollar markup:

Blueprint Aid for Dissecting and Solving a Word Problem

A. Gather the facts	B. What am I solving for?	C. What must I know or calculate before solving problem?	D. Key points to remember
Selling price: $14. *Markup on cost:* 40%	% $ C 100% $10[1] $+ M$ 40 4[2] $= S$ 140% $14[2] [1] Cost. [2] Dollar markup.	$S = C + M$ or $\text{Cost} = \dfrac{\text{Selling price}}{\text{Percent } 1 + \text{markup on cost}}$ $M = S - C$	Selling price Portion ($14) Base (?) × Rate (1.40) Cost 100% + 40%

Steps to Solving Problem

1. Calculate cost.

$$S = C + M$$
$$\$14 = C + .40C$$
$$\frac{\$14}{1.40} = \frac{1.40C}{1.40}$$
$$\$10 = C$$

2. Calculate dollar markup.

$$M = S - C$$
$$M = \$14 - \$10$$
$$M = \$4$$

Check $\text{Cost} = \dfrac{\text{Selling price}}{1 + \text{Percent markup on cost}} = \dfrac{\$14}{1.40} = \$10$

LEARNING UNIT 8–2 MARKUPS BASED ON SELLING PRICE (100%)

Many retailers, like Neiman Marcus, Sears, and so on, mark their goods up on selling price since sales information is easier to get than cost information. These retailers use retail prices in their inventory and report their expenses as a percent of sales.

Businesses that mark up their goods on **selling price** recognize that selling price is 100%. We illustrate this by using the **percent markup on selling price,** Situation 1 below.

Cost	70%
+ Markup	30%
= Selling price	100%

Selling price is 100%—the base. Markup amount is the portion, and percent markup on selling price is the rate.

Now, we will show why Nancy Ford in Situation 1 has a 30% markup based on selling price as 100%. In the last unit, markups were on cost. In this unit, markups are on *selling price*.

Situation 1: Calculating Markup Amount and Percent Markup on Selling Price

The Word Problem Nancy Ford bought a lawn mower for her True Value Hardware store that cost $210. She plans to sell the mower for $300. What is Nancy's markup amount and percent markup on selling price?

Blueprint Aid for Dissecting and Solving a Word Problem

A. Gather the facts	B. What am I solving for?	C. What must I know or calculate before solving problem?	D. Key points to remember
Mower cost: $210. *Mower selling price:* $300.	% $ C 70% $210 $+ M$ 30[2] 90[1] $= S$ 100% $300 [1] Markup amount. [2] Percent markup on selling price.	$\text{Markup amount} = \text{Selling price} - \text{Cost}$ $\text{Percent markup on selling price} = \dfrac{\text{Markup amount}}{\text{Selling price}}$	Markup amount Portion ($90) Base ($300) × Rate (?) Selling price

Steps to Solving Problem

1. Calculate markup amount.

$$\text{Markup amount} = \text{Selling price} - \text{Cost}$$
$$\$90 = \$300 - \$210$$

2. Calculate percent markup on selling price.

$$\text{Percent markup on selling price} = \frac{\text{Markup amount}}{\text{Selling price}} = \frac{\$90}{\$300} = 30\%$$

Check

Selling price = Cost + Markup **or** Selling price = $\dfrac{\text{Markup amount}}{\text{Percent markup on selling price}}$

$$\$300 = \$210 + .30(\$300)$$
$$\$300 = \$210 + \$90$$
$$\$300 = \$300$$

$$= \frac{\$90}{.30} = \$300$$

Note in the check how selling price can be calculated when markup amount and percent markup on selling price are known.

Situation 2: Calculating Selling Price When You Know Cost and Percent Markup on Selling Price

Blueprint Aid for Dissecting and Solving a Word Problem

The Word Problem Mel's Furniture bought a lamp for his store that cost $100. To make his desired profit, Mel needs a 65% markup on selling price. What is Mel's selling price and dollar markup?

A. Gather the facts	B. What am I solving for?	C. What must I know or calculate before solving problem?	D. Key points to remember
Lamp cost: $100. *Markup on selling price:* 65%.	% / $ C 35% $100.00 $+ M$ 65 185.71[2] $= S$ 100% $285.71[1] [1] Selling price. [2] Dollar markup.	S = C + M or $S = \dfrac{\text{Cost}}{1 - \text{Percent markup on selling price}}$	Cost; Portion ($100); Base (?) × Rate (.35); Selling price; 100% − 65%

Steps to Solving Problem

1. Calculate selling price.

$$S = C + M$$
$$S = \$100.00 + .65S$$
$$-.65S \qquad -.65S$$
$$\frac{.35S}{.35} = \frac{\$100.00}{.35}$$
$$S = \$285.71$$

$1.00S - .65S = .35S$

Do not multiply the .65 times $100.00. The 65% is based on selling price not cost.

2. Calculate dollar markup.

$$M = S - C$$
$$\$185.71 = \$285.71 - \$100.00$$

Check $\text{Selling price} = \dfrac{\text{Cost}}{1 - \text{Percent markup on selling price}} = \dfrac{\$100.00}{1 - .65} = \dfrac{\$100.00}{.35} = \$285.71$

Situation 3: Calculating Cost When You Know Selling Price and Percent Markup on Selling Price

Blueprint Aid for Dissecting and Solving a Word Problem

The Word Problem Jill Sport, owner of Sports, Inc., sells tennis rackets for $50. To make her desired profit, Jill needs a 40% markup on the selling price. What is the dollar markup? What do the tennis rackets cost Jill?

A. Gather the facts	B. What am I solving for?	C. What must I know or calculate before solving problem?	D. Key points to remember
Selling price: $50. *Markup on selling price:* 40%.	% / $ C 60% $30[2] $+ M$ 40 20[1] $= S$ 100% $50 [1] Dollar markup. [2] Cost.	$S = C + M$ or $\text{Cost} = \text{Selling price} \times \left(1 - \text{Percent markup on selling price}\right)$	Cost; Portion (?); Base ($50) × Rate (.60); Selling price; 100% − 40%

TABLE 8-1
Comparison of Markup on Cost versus Markup on Retail

	Learning Unit 8-1: Cost is 100%		Learning Unit 8-2: Selling price is 100%	
	Markup amount	**Percent markup on cost**	**Markup amount**	**Percent markup on selling price**
Situation 1: Mower cost, $210 Mower selling price, $300	$90 (p. 193)	42.86%	$90 (p. 196)	30%
Situation 2: Lamp cost, $100	Selling price, $165 (p. 194)	65%	Selling price, $285.71 (p. 197)	65%
Situation 3: Tennis racket selling price, $50	Cost, $35.71 (p. 194)	40%	Cost, $30 (p. 198)	40%

Steps to Solving Problem

1. Calculate dollar markup. $S = C + M$
   $\$50 = C + .40(\$50)$
2. Calculate cost. $\$50 = C + \$20$ ← Dollar markup
   $-20 \qquad -20$
   $\$30 = C$

Check Cost = Selling price × (1 − Percent markup on selling price)
$\$30 = \$50 \times .60$ (1.00 − .40)

In Table 8-1, we compare percent markup on cost with percent markup on retail (selling price). This table is a summary of the answers we calculated from the word problems in Learning Units 8-1 and 8-2. The word problems in the units were the same except that in Learning Unit 8-1, we assumed markups were on cost, while in Learning Unit 8-2, markups were on selling price. Note that in Situation 1, the dollar markup is the same $90, although the percent markup is different.

Let's now look at how to convert from percent markup on cost to percent markup on selling price and vice versa. We will use Situation 1 from Table 8-1.

Formula for Converting Percent Markup on Selling Price to Percent Markup on Cost

To convert percent markup on selling price to percent markup on cost

$$\frac{\text{Percent markup on selling price}}{1 - \text{Percent markup on selling price}}$$

$$\frac{.30}{1 - .30} = \frac{.30}{.70} = 42.86\%$$

Formula for Converting Percent Markup on Cost to Percent Markup on Selling Price

To convert percent markup on cost to percent markup on selling price

$$\frac{\text{Percent markup on cost}}{1 - \text{Percent markup on cost}}$$

$$\frac{.4286}{1 + .4286} = 30\%$$

Key point: A 30% markup on selling price or a 42.86% markup on cost results in same dollar markup of $90.

Table 8-2 summarizes the calculations of these two formulas. As stated in the table, the rate of markup on selling price is always *lower* than the rate of markup on cost. Before going on to the topic of markdowns and perishables, check your progress with the following Practice Quiz.

TABLE 8-2
Equivalent Markup

Percent markup on selling price	Percent markup on cost (round to nearest tenth percent)
20	25.0
25	33.3
30	42.9
33	49.3
35	53.8
40	66.7
50	100.0

Note: Rate of markup on selling price is always lower than on cost because the cost base is always lower than the selling price base.

LU 8-2 PRACTICE QUIZ

Solve the following situations (markups based on selling price):

1. Irene Westing bought a desk for $400 from an office supply house. She plans to sell the desk for $600. What are Irene's markup amount and her percent markup on selling price (round to nearest tenth percent)? Check your answer. Selling price will be slightly off due to rounding.
2. Suki Komar bought dolls for her toy store that cost $12 each. To make her desired profit, Suki must mark up each doll 35% on selling price. What is the selling price of each doll? What is the amount of markup? Check your answer.
3. Jay Lyman sells calculators. His competitor sells a new calculator line for $14 each. Jay needs a 40% markup on selling price to make his desired profit, and he must meet price competition. What cost can Jay afford to bring these calculators into the store? What is the dollar markup? Check your answer.
4. Dan Flow sells wrenches for $10 that cost $6. What is Dan's percent markup at cost? Round to nearest tenth percent. What is Dan's percent markup on selling price? Check your answer.

SOLUTIONS TO LU 8-2 PRACTICE QUIZ

Blueprint Aid for Dissecting and Solving a Word Problem

1. Irene's markup and percent markup on selling price:

A. Gather the facts	B. What am I solving for?	C. What must I know or calculate before solving problem?	D. Key points to remember
Desk cost: $400. *Desk selling price:* $600.	% $ *C* 66.7% $400 + *M* 33.3[2] 200[1] = *S* 100% $600 [1] Markup amount. [2] Percent markup on selling price.	Markup amount = Selling price − Cost Percent markup on selling price = Markup amount / Selling price	Markup Portion ($200) Base ($600) × Rate (?) Selling price

Steps to Solving Problem

1. Calculate markup amount.

$$\text{Markup amount} = \text{Selling price} - \text{Cost}$$
$$\$200 = \$600 - \$400$$

2. Calculate percent markup on selling price.

$$\text{Percent markup on selling price} = \frac{\text{Markup amount}}{\text{Selling price}}$$
$$= \frac{\$200}{\$600} = 33.3\%$$

Check

Selling price = Cost + Markup
$600 = $400 + .333($600)
$600 = $400 + $199.80
$600 = $599.80*

* Off due to rounding.

or

$$\text{Selling price} = \frac{\text{Markup amount}}{\text{Percent markup on selling price}}$$
$$= \frac{\$200}{.333} = \$600.60$$

(not exactly $600 due to rounding)

2. Selling price of doll and markup amount:

Blueprint Aid for Dissecting and Solving a Word Problem

A. Gather the facts	B. What am I solving for?	C. What must I know or calculate before solving problem?	D. Key points to remember
Doll cost: $12 each. *Markup on selling price:* 35%.	% $ C 65% $12.00 $+M$ 35 6.46[2] $=S$ 100% $18.46[1] [1] Selling price. [2] Markup amount.	$S = C + M$ or $S = \dfrac{\text{Cost}}{1 - \text{Percent markup on selling price}}$	Cost Portion ($12) Base (?) × Rate (.65) Selling price 100% − 35%

Steps to Solving Problem

1. Calculate selling price.

$$S = C + M$$
$$S = \$12.00 + .35S$$
$$-.35S \qquad -.35S$$
$$\frac{.65S}{.65} = \frac{\$12.00}{.65}$$
$$S = \$18.46$$

2. Calculate markup amount.

$$M = S - C$$
$$\$6.46 = \$18.46 - \$12.00$$

Check Selling price $= \dfrac{\text{Cost}}{1 - \text{Percent markup on selling price}} = \dfrac{\$12.00}{.65} = \$18.46$

3. Cost and dollar markup:

Blueprint Aid for Dissecting and Solving a Word Problem

A. Gather the facts	B. What am I solving for?	C. What must I know or calculate before solving problem?	D. Key points to remember
Selling price: $14. *Markup on selling price:* 40%.	% $ C 60% $ 8.40[1] $+M$ 40 5.60[2] $=S$ 100% $14.00 [1] Cost. [2] Dollar markup.	$S = C + M$ or $\text{Cost} = \text{Selling price} \times \left(1 - \text{Percent markup on selling price}\right)$	Cost Portion (?) Base ($14) × Rate (.60) Selling price 100% − 40%

Steps to Solving Problem

1. Calculate cost.

$$S = C + M$$
$$\$14.00 = C + .40(\$14.00)$$
$$\$14.00 = C + \$5.60$$
$$-5.60 \qquad -5.60$$
$$\$8.40 = C$$

2. Calculate dollar markup.

$$M = S - C$$
$$M = \$14.00 - \$8.40$$
$$M = \$5.60$$

Check Cost $= \text{Selling price} \times \left(1 - \text{Percent markup on selling price}\right) = \$14.00 \times (1 - .40) = \$8.40$

4. Cost $= \dfrac{\$4}{\$6} = 66.7\%$ $\qquad \dfrac{.40}{1 - .40} = \dfrac{.40}{.60} = \dfrac{2}{3} = 66.7\%$

Selling price $= \dfrac{\$4}{\$10} = 40\%$ $\qquad \dfrac{.667}{1 + .67} = \dfrac{.667}{1.67} = 39.9\%$
(due to rounding)

LEARNING UNIT 8–3 MARKDOWNS AND PERISHABLES

In a few moments, we'll look at how businesses price perishable items that may spoil before customers buy them. First, let's focus our attention on how to calculate markdowns.

Markdowns

Markdowns are reductions from the original selling price caused by seasonal changes, special promotions, style changes, and so on. We calculate the markdown percent as follows:

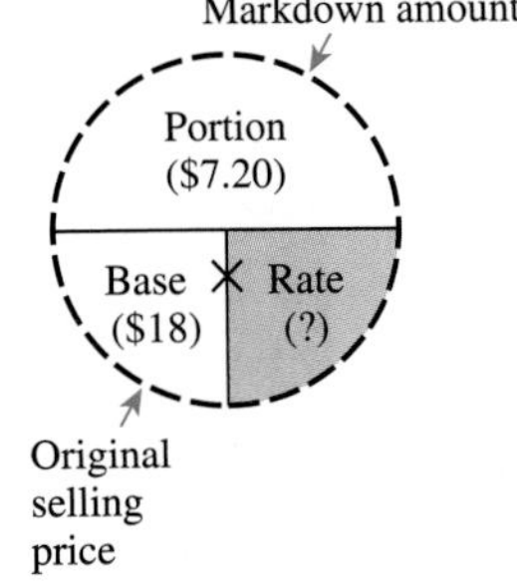

$$\text{Markdown percent} = \frac{\text{Markdown amount}}{\text{Selling price (original)}}$$

EXAMPLE A store marked down an $18 calculator to $10.80. What is the **markdown amount** and the markdown percent?

$18.00	Original selling price
− 10.80	Sale price
$ 7.20	Markdown

$$\frac{\text{Markdown amount, \$7.20}}{\text{Selling price (original), \$18.00}} = 40\%$$

Calculating a Series of Markdowns and Markups

Often the final selling price is the result of a series of markdowns (and possibly a markup in between markdowns). We calculate additional markdowns on the previous selling price. Note in the following example how we calculate markdown on selling price after we add a markup.

EXAMPLE Jones Department Store paid its supplier $400 for a TV. On January 10, Jones marked the TV up 60% on selling price. As a special promotion, Jones marked the TV down 30% on February 8 and another 20% on February 28. No one purchased the TV, so Jones marked it up 10% on March 11. What was the selling price of the TV on March 11?

January 10: Selling price = Cost + Markup

$$S = \$400 + .60S$$
$$-.60S \qquad -.60S$$
$$\frac{.40S}{.40} = \frac{\$400}{.40}$$
$$S = \$1{,}000$$

Check

$$S = \frac{\text{Cost}}{1 - \text{Percent markup on selling price}}$$

$$S = \frac{\$400}{1 - .60} = \frac{\$400}{.40} = \$1{,}000$$

February 8 markdown: 100% − 30% = 70% → .70 × $1,000 = $700 selling price

February 28 additional markdown: 100% − 20% = 80% → .80 × $700 = $560

March 11 additional markup: 100% + 10% = 110% → 1.10 × $560 = $616

Pricing Perishable Items

Let's see how companies determine the price of goods that have a short shelf life such as fruit, flowers, and pastry. (We limit this discussion to obvious **perishable** items.)

The Word Problem Audrey's Bake Shop baked 20 dozen bagels. Audrey expects 10% of the bagels to become stale and not salable. The bagels cost Audrey \$1.20 per dozen. Audrey wants a 60% markup on cost. What should Audrey charge for each dozen bagels so she will make her profit? Round to nearest cent.

Blueprint Aid for Dissecting and Solving a Word Problem

A. Gather the facts	B. What am I solving for?	C. What must I know or calculate before solving problem?	D. Key points to remember
Bagels cost: \$1.20 per dozen. *Not salable:* 10% *Baked:* 20 dozen. *Markup on cost:* 60%.	Price of a dozen bagels.	Total cost. Total markup. Total selling price. Bagel loss. $TS = TC + TM$.	Markup is based on cost.

Steps to Solving Problem

1. Calculate total cost. $TC = 20 \text{ dozen} \times \$1.20 = \$24.00$
2. Calculate total markup. $TS = TC + TM$

   $TS = \$24.00 + .60(\$24.00)$

   $TS = \$24.00 + \$14.40$ ← Total markup
3. Calculate total selling price. $TS = \$38.40$ ← Total selling price
4. Calculate bagel loss. $20 \text{ dozen} \times .10 = 2 \text{ dozen}$
5. Calculate selling price for dozen bagels. $\dfrac{\$38.40}{18} = \$2.13$ per dozen $\left[\begin{array}{r} 20 \\ -2 \\ \hline \end{array}\right.$

LU 8-3 PRACTICE QUIZ

1. Sunshine Music Shop bought a stereo for \$600 and marked it up 40% on selling price. To promote customer interest, Sunshine marked the stereo down 10% for one week. Since business was slow, Sunshine marked the stereo down an additional 5%. After a week, Sunshine marked the stereo up 2%. What is the new selling price of the stereo to the nearest cent? What is the markdown percent based on the original selling price to the nearest hundredth percent?
2. Alvin Rose owns a fruit and vegetable stand. He knows that he cannot sell all his produce at the full price. Some of his produce will be markdowns, and he will throw out some produce. Alvin must put a high enough price on the produce to cover markdowns and rotted produce and still make his desired profit. Alvin bought 300 pounds of tomatoes at 14 cents per pound. He expects a 5% spoilage and marks up tomatoes 60% on cost. What price per pound should Alvin charge for the tomatoes?

SOLUTIONS TO LU 8-3 PRACTICE QUIZ

1.
$$S = C + M$$
$$S = \$600 + .40S$$
$$-.40S \qquad -.40S$$
$$\frac{\cancel{.60}S}{\cancel{.60}} = \frac{\$600}{.60}$$
$$S = \$1,000$$

Check

$$S = \frac{\text{Cost}}{1 - \text{Percent markup on selling price}}$$
$$S = \frac{\$600}{1 - .40} = \frac{\$600}{.60} = \$1,000$$

First markdown: $.90 \times \$1,000 = \$900$ selling price
Second markdown: $.95 \times \$900 = \$855$ selling price
Markup: $1.02 \times \$855 = \$872.10$ final selling price

$$\$1,000 - \$872.10 = \frac{\$127.90}{\$1,000} = 12.79\%$$

2. Price of tomatoes per pound:

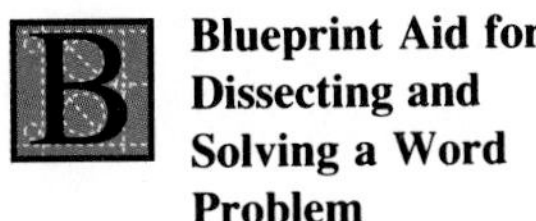

Blueprint Aid for Dissecting and Solving a Word Problem

A. Gather the facts	B. What am I solving for?	C. What must I know or calculate before solving problem?	D. Key points to remember
300 lbs. tomatoes at \$.14 per pound. *Spoilage: 5%.* *Markup on cost: 60%.*	Price of tomatoes per pound.	Total cost. Total markup. Total selling price. Spoilage amount. $TS = TC + TM$.	Markup is based on cost.

Steps to Solving Problem

1. Calculate total cost. — $TC = 300 \text{ lbs.} \times \$.14 = \$42.00$
2. Calculate total markup. — $TS = TC + TM$
   $TS = \$42.00 + .60(\$42.00)$
   $TS = \$42.00 + \$25.20$ ← Total markup
3. Calculate total selling price. — $TS = \$67.20$ ← Total selling price
4. Calculate tomato loss. — 300 pounds × .05 = 15 pounds spoilage
5. Calculate selling price per pound of tomatoes. — $\frac{\$67.20}{285} = \$.24$ per pound (rounded to nearest hundredth)

CHAPTER ORGANIZER: A REFERENCE GUIDE

Page	Topic	Key point, procedure, formula	Example(s) to illustrate situation
192	**Markups based on cost: cost is 100% (base)**	Selling price (S) = Cost (C) + Markup (M)	\$400 = \$300 + \$100 $S = C + M$
193	Percent markup on cost Cost	$\frac{\text{Markup amount (portion)}}{\text{Cost (base)}} = \frac{\text{Percent markup}}{\text{on cost (rate)}}$ $C = \frac{\text{Markup amount}}{\text{Percent markup on cost}}$	$\frac{\$100}{\$300} = \frac{1}{3} = 33\frac{1}{3}\%$ $\frac{\$100}{.33} = \$303$ Off slightly due to rounding
194	Calculating selling price	$S = C + M$ **Check** $S = (1 + \text{Percent markup on cost}) \times \text{Cost}$	Cost, \$6; percent markup on cost, 20% $S = \$6 + .20(\$6)$ $S = \$6 + \$1.20$ $S = \$7.20$ **Check** ↓ 1.20 × \$6 = \$7.20
194	Calculating cost	$S = C + M$ **Check** $\text{Cost} = \frac{\text{Selling price}}{1 + \text{Percent markup on cost}}$	$S = \$100$; M = 70% of cost $S = C + M$ $\$100 = C + .70C$ $\$100 = 1.7C$ *(Remember $C = 1.00C$)* $\frac{\$100}{1.7} = C$ $\$58.82 = C$ **Check** ↓ $\frac{\$100}{1 + .70} = \$58.82$

Page	Topic	Key point, procedure, formula	Example(s) to illustrate situation
196	**Markups based on selling price; selling price is 100% (base):**	Markup amount = Selling price − Cost	$M = S - C$ $600 = $1,000 − $400
196	Percent markup on selling price	$\frac{\text{Markup amount (portion)}}{\text{Selling price (base)}} = \text{Percent markup on selling price (rate)}$	$\frac{\$600}{\$1,000} = 60\%$
197	Selling price	$S = \frac{\text{Markup amount}}{\text{Percent markup on selling price}}$	$\frac{\$600}{.60} = \$1,000$
197	Calculating selling price	$S = C + M$ **Check** $\text{Selling price} = \frac{\text{Cost}}{1 - \text{Percent markup on selling price}}$	Cost, $400; percent markup on *S*, 60% $S = C + M$ $S = \$400 + .60S$ $S - .60S = \$400 + .60S - .60S$ $\frac{\not{.40}S}{\not{.40}} = \frac{\$400}{.40}$ $S = \$1,000$ **Check** → $\frac{\$400}{1 - .60} = \frac{\$400}{.40} = \$1,000$
197	Calculating cost	$S = C + M$ **Check** $\text{Cost} = \text{Selling price} \times \left(1 - \text{Percent markup on selling price}\right)$	$1,000 = *C* + 60%($1,000) $1,000 = *C* + $600 $400 = *C* **Check** → $1,000 × (1 − .60) $1,000 × .40 = $400
198	Conversion of markup percent	Percent markup on selling price to Percent markup on cost $\frac{\text{Percent markup on selling price}}{1 - \text{Percent markup on selling price}}$ Percent markup on cost to Percent markup on selling price $\frac{\text{Percent markup on cost}}{1 + \text{Percent markup on cost}}$	*Round to nearest percent:* 35% markup on selling price → 54% markup on cost $\frac{.35}{1 - .35} = \frac{.35}{.65} = 54\%$ 54% markup on cost → 35% markup on selling price $\frac{.54}{1 + .54} = \frac{.54}{1.54} = 35\%$
201	Markdowns	$\text{Markdown percent} = \frac{\text{Markdown amount}}{\text{Selling price (original)}}$	$40 selling price 10% markdown $40 × .10 = $4.00 markdown $\frac{\$4}{\$40} = 10\%$
202	Pricing perishables	1. Calculate total cost and total selling price. 2. Calculate selling price per unit by dividing total sales in Step 1 by units expected to be sold after taking perishables into account.	50 pastries cost 20 cents each; 10 will spoil before being sold. Markup is 60% on cost. 1. $TC = 50 \times \$.20 = \$10$ $TS = TC + TM$ $TS = \$10 + .60(\$10)$ $TS = \$10 + \$6$ $TS = \$16$ 2. $\frac{\$16}{40 \text{ pastries}} = \$.40$ per pastry
	Key terms	Cost, *p. 192* Gross profit, *p. 192* Markdown amount, *p. 201* Markdowns, *p. 201* Markup, *p. 192* Markup amount, *p. 193*	Net income (net profit), *p. 192* Operating expenses, *p. 192* Percent markup on cost, *p. 192* Percent markup on selling price, *p. 196* Perishables, *p. 201* Selling price, *p. 196*

END-OF-CHAPTER PROBLEMS

Drill Problems

Additional homework assignments by learning unit are at the end of text in Appendix I (p. I-33). Solutions to odd problems are at the end of text in Appendix II.

Markups in Problems 8-1 to 8-6 are based on cost.

Find the markup amount and selling price (round answers to nearest cent):

	Item	Cost	Markup percent	Markup amount	Selling price
8-1.	Sony CD player	$150	60%	$90	$240

$S = C + M$
$S = \$150 + .60(\$150)$
$S = \$150 + \$90$
$S = \$240$

Check: $S = \left(1 + \frac{\text{Markup}}{\text{on cost}}\right) \times \text{Cost}$
$\$240 = 1.60 \times \$150$

	Item	Cost	Markup percent	Markup amount	Selling price
8-2.	Dining room table	$400	50%	$200	$600

$S = \$400 + .50(\$400)$
$S = \$400 + \$200$
$S = \$600$

Check: $\$600 = 1.50 \times \$400$

8-3. Selling price of RCA entertainment center, $6,000
Percent markup on cost, 40%
Actual cost, ?

$\$6,000 = C + .40C$
$\frac{\$6,000}{1.40} = \frac{1.40C}{1.40}$
$\$4,285.71 = C$

Check
$\frac{\$6,000}{1.40} = \$4,285.71$

Solve for cost (round to nearest cent):

8-4. Selling price of sofa, $4,000
Percent markup on cost, 30%
Actual cost, ?

$\$4,000 = C + .30C$
$\frac{\$4,000}{1.30} = \frac{1.30C}{1.30}$
$\$3,076.92 = C$

Check
$\frac{\$4,000}{1.30} = \$3,076.92$

$C = \frac{\text{Selling price}}{1 + \text{Percent markup on cost}}$

Complete the following:

	Cost	Selling price	Markup amount	Percent markup on cost*
8-5.	$15.10	$22.00	$6.90	45.70% $\left(\frac{\$6.90}{\$15.10}\right)$
8-6.	$ 4.60	$ 9.30	$4.70	102.17%

$C = \frac{\$4.70}{1.0217}$

* Round to nearest hundredth percent.

Assume markups in Problems 8-7 to 8-12 are based on selling price.

Find the markup amount and cost (round answers to nearest cent):

	Item	Selling price	Markup percent	Markup amount	Cost
8-7.	Maytag washer	$325	40%	$130	$195

$\$325 = C + .40(\$325)$
$\$325 = C + \$130$
$-130 \quad\quad -130$
$\$195 = C$

Check
$\$195 = \$325 \times .60$

	Item	Selling price	Markup percent	Markup amount	Cost
8-8.	Timex watch	$ 80	30%	$ 24	$ 56

Note: Markup is on selling price not cost.

$\$80 = C + .30(\$80)$
$\$80 = C + \$24$
$-24 \quad\quad -24$
$\$56 = C$

Check
$\$56 = \$80 \times .70$

$C = \text{Selling price} \times \left(1 - \frac{\text{Percent markup}}{\text{on selling price}}\right)$

8–9. Selling price of dishes,?
40% markup on selling price
Cost, actual, $66.50

Check

$$\frac{\$66.50}{.60} = \$110.83$$

$$S = \$66.50 + .40S$$
$$\frac{-.40S \qquad -.40S}{\frac{.60S}{.60} = \frac{\$66.50}{.60}}$$
$$S = \$110.83$$
$$S = \frac{\text{Cost}}{1 - \text{Percent markup on selling price}}$$

Solve for selling price (round to nearest cent):

8–10. Selling price of an antique, ?
65% markup on selling price
Cost, actual, $1,200

Check

$$\frac{\$1,200}{.35} = \$3,428.57$$

$$S = \$1,200 + .65S$$
$$\frac{-.65S \qquad -.65S}{\frac{.35S}{.35} = \frac{\$1,200}{.35}}$$
$$S = \$3,428.57$$

Complete the following:

	Cost	Selling price	Markup amount	Percent markup on selling price (round to nearest tenth percent)
8–11.	$14.80	$49.00	$34.20	69.8% $\left(\frac{\$34.20}{\$49.00}\right)$
8–12.	$16	$20	$4	20% $\quad S = \frac{\$4}{.20}$

By conversion of markup formula, solve the following (round to nearest whole percent as needed):

	Percent markup on cost	Percent markup on selling price
8–13.	12.4%	? 11% $\frac{.124}{1 + .124}$
8–14.	? 15% $\frac{.13}{1 - .13}$	13%

Complete the following:

8–15. Calculate the final selling price to nearest cent and markdown percent to nearest hundredth percent:

Original selling price	First markdown	Second markdown	Markup	Final markdown
$5,000	20%	10%	12%	5%

$\$5,000 \times .80 = \$4,000.00$
$\$4,000 \times .90 = \$3,600.00$
$\$3,600 \times 1.12 = \$4,032.00$
$\$4,032 \times .95 = \$3,830.40$

$$\$5,000.00 - 3,830.40 = \$1,169.60 \qquad \frac{\$1,169.60}{\$5,000.00} = 23.39\%$$

	Item	Total quantity bought	Unit cost	Total cost	Percent markup on cost	Total selling price	Percent that will spoil	Selling price per eclair
8–16.	Eclairs	20	$.79	$15.80	60%	$25.28	10%	$1.40

$$\text{Total cost} = 20 \times \$.79 = \$15.80$$
$$\text{Total selling price} = TC + TM$$
$$TS = \$15.80 + .60(\$15.80)$$
$$TS = \$15.80 + \$9.48$$
$$TS = \$25.28$$

$$\frac{\$25.28}{18} = \$1.40 \text{ per eclair}$$

Word Problems

8–17. Joan Trembly Jewelers bought a Mickey Mouse watch for $40 and plans to sell it for $75. What is the markup amount and the percent markup on cost (to the nearest tenth percent)? Check the cost figure.

Markup amount = $S - C$
$35 = $75 − $40

Percent markup on cost $= \frac{\$35}{\$40} = 87.5\%$

$$C = \frac{\text{Markup amount}}{\text{Percent markup on cost}} = \frac{\$35}{.875} = \$40$$

8–18. Harvey Drew, store manager for Drake Appliance, does not know how to price a refrigerator that cost $800. Harvey knows his boss wants a 38% markup on cost. Can you help Harvey price the refrigerator?

Note: The markup of 38% is based on cost, not selling price.

$S = \$800 + .38(\$800)$
$S = \$800 + \$304$
$S = \$1{,}104$

Check

$S = (1 + \text{Percent markup on cost}) \times \text{Cost}$
$\$1{,}104 = 1.38 \times \$800$

8–19. Cecil Green sells ski hats. He knows that most people will not pay more than $20 for a ski hat. Cecil needs a 40% markup on cost. What should Cecil pay for his ski hats? Round to nearest cent.

Note: The markup of 40% is based on cost not selling price.

$\$20 = C + .40C$
$\frac{\$20}{1.40} = \frac{1.40C}{1.40}$
$\$14.29 = C$

Check

$\text{Cost} = \frac{\text{Selling price}}{1 + \text{Percent markup on cost}}$
$\$14.29 = \frac{\$20}{1.40}$

8–20. Thrifty Computers sells an IBM computer for $699. Thrifty marked the computer up 35% on selling price. What is the cost of the computer?

Note: The markup of 35% is based on the selling price not cost.

$\$699.00 = C + .35(\$699)$
$\$699.00 = C + \$244.65$
$-244.65 \qquad -244.65$
$\$454.35 = C$

Check

$C = \text{Selling price} \times \left(1 - \text{Percent markup on selling price}\right)$
$= \$699 \times (1 - .35)$
$\$454.35 = \$699 \times .65$

8–21. Copperfield Jewelers bought a sterling silver flatware set for $1,200. Copperfield has a 40% markup on selling price. What is the selling price of the sterling set?

Note: The markup is on the selling price, not the cost.

$S = \$1{,}200 + .40S$
$-.40S \qquad -.40S$
$\frac{.60S}{.60} = \frac{\$1{,}200}{.60}$
$S = \$2{,}000$

Check

$S = \frac{\text{Cost}}{1 - \text{Percent markup on selling price}}$
$\$2{,}000 = \frac{\$1{,}200}{.60}$

8–22. Katie Herscher sells a light fixture for $98.50 that cost $62.50. What is Katie's percent markup on selling price? Round to nearest hundredth percent. Check the selling price.

Markup = Selling price − Cost
$36.00 = $98.50 − $62.50

$\frac{\$36.00}{\$98.50} = 36.55\%$

$\frac{\text{Markup amount}}{\text{Percent markup on selling price}}$ $\frac{\$36}{.3655} = \$98.50$

8–23. Misu Sheet, owner of the Bedspread Shop, knows his customers will pay no more than $120 for a comforter. Misu wants a 30% markup on selling price. What is the most that Misu can pay for a comforter?

Note: The markup is on the selling price, not the cost.

$\$120 = C + .30(\$120)$
$\$120 = C + \$36$
$-36 \qquad -36$
$\$84 = C$

Check

$C = \text{Selling price} \times \left(1 - \text{Percent markup on selling price}\right)$
$\$84 = \$120 \times .70$

8–24. Assume Misu Sheet (Problem 8–23) wants a 30% markup on cost instead of on selling price. What is Misu's cost? Round to nearest cent.

Note: The markup is on the cost, not the selling price.

$\$120 = C + .30C$
$\frac{\$120}{1.3} = \frac{1.3C}{1.3}$
$\$92.31 = C$

Check

$C = \frac{\text{Selling price}}{1 + \text{Percent markup on cost}}$
$\$92.31 = \frac{\$120}{1.30}$

8–25. Misu Sheet (Problem 8–23) wants to advertise the comforter as "percent markup on cost." What is the equivalent rate of percent markup on cost compared to the

30% markup on selling price? Check your answer. Is this a wise marketing decision? Round to nearest hundredth percent.

$\frac{.30}{1 - .30} = \frac{.30}{.70} = 42.86\%$

Check

$\frac{.4286}{1 + .4286} = \frac{.4286}{1.4286} = 30\%$

No, customers will see 42.86% instead of 30%. They will think markup is higher, although dollar amount of $36 is the same.

8-26. DeWitt Company sells a kitchen set for $475. To promote July 4, DeWitt ran the following advertisement:

> Beginning each hour up to 4 hours we will mark down the kitchen set 10%. At the end of each hour, we will mark up the set 1%.

Assume Ingrid Swenson buys the set 1 hour and 50 minutes into the sale. What will Ingrid pay? Round each calculation to nearest cent. What is the markdown percent? Round to nearest hundredth percent.

$475.00 × .90 = $427.50 beginning of hour 1
$427.50 × 1.01 = $431.78 end of hour 1
$431.78 × .90 = $388.60 beginning of hour 2

$475.00
− 388.60
$86.40

$\frac{\$86.40}{\$475.00} = 18.19\%$

8-27. Angie Bake Shop makes birthday chocolate chip cookies that cost $2 each. Angie expects that 10% of the cookies will crack and be discarded. Angie wants a 60% markup on cost and produces 100 cookies. What should Angie price each cookie? Round to nearest cent.

$$\text{Total cost} = 100 \times \$2.00 = \$200$$
$$\text{Total selling price} = TC + TM$$
$$TS = \$200 + .60(\$200)$$
$$TS = \$200 + \$120$$
$$TS = \$320$$
$$\text{Selling price per cookie} = \frac{\$320}{90 \text{ cookies}} = \$3.56$$

8-28. Assume that Angie (Problem 8-27) can sell the cracked cookies for $1.10 each. What should Angie price each cookie?

$$\frac{\$320 - (10 \text{ cookies} \times \$1.10)}{90 \text{ cookies}} = \frac{\$320 - \$11}{90} = \frac{\$309}{90} = \$3.43$$

The 90 cookies are sold for the $320 less what is received from cracked cookies.

Additional Set of Word Problems

8-29. Facets Jewelry bought a sterling silver tea set for $499. Facets has a 55% markup on selling price. What is the selling price of the sterling set? Round to nearest cent?

Note: Markup is on selling price, not cost.

$$S = \$499 + .55S$$
$$-.55S \qquad -.55S$$
$$\frac{.45S}{.45} = \frac{\$499}{.45}$$
$$S = \$1,108.89$$

Check

$$S = \frac{\text{Cost}}{1 - \text{Percent markup on selling price}}$$
$$\$1,108.89 = \frac{\$499}{.45}$$

8-30. Sachi Wong, store manager for Hawk Appliance, does not know how to price a refrigerator that cost $399. Sachi knows her boss wants a 40% markup on cost. Can you help Sachi price the refrigerator?

Note: Markup is on cost, not selling price.

$$S = \$399 + .40(\$399)$$
$$S = \$399 + \$159.60$$
$$S = \$558.60$$

Check

$$S = (1 + \text{Percent markup on cost}) \times \text{Cost}$$
$$\$558.60 = 1.40 \times \$399$$

8-31. Morse Bookstore bought a cookbook for $39.95. Morse plans to sell the cookbook for $69.95. What is the markup amount and the percent markup on cost? Round to nearest hundredth percent. Check the cost figure.

$69.95
− 39.95
$30.00

$\frac{\$30.00}{\$39.95} = 75.09\%$

$$C = \frac{\text{Markup amount}}{\text{Percent markup on cost}} = \frac{\$30}{.7509} = \$39.95$$

8–32. Heather Jenkins, owner of Jenkins Bed Shop, knows her customers will pay no more than $250 for a bedspread. Heather wants a 40% markup on selling price. What is the most that Heather can pay for a bedspread?

Note: Markup is on selling price, not cost.

$$\begin{aligned} \$250 &= C + .40(\$250) \\ \$250 &= C + \$100 \\ -100 &\quad\ \ -100 \\ \$150 &= C \end{aligned}$$

Check

$$C = \text{Selling price} \times \left(1 - \frac{\text{Percent markup}}{\text{on selling price}}\right)$$

$$\$150 = \$250 \times .60$$

8–33. Salvador Spring sells mittens. He knows the most that people will pay for a pair of mittens is $29.95. Salvador needs a 35% markup on cost. What is the most that Salvador can pay for a pair of mittens? Round to nearest cent.

Note: Markup is on cost, not selling price.

$$\$29.95 = C + .35C$$

$$\frac{\$29.95}{1.35} = \frac{1.35C}{1.35}$$

$$\$22.19 = C$$

Check

$$C = \frac{\text{Selling price}}{1 + \text{Percent markup on cost}} \qquad \$22.19 = \frac{\$29.95}{1.35}$$

8–34. Radio Shack sells a radio for $90.50 that cost $51.45. What is the percent markup on selling price? Round to nearest percent.

$$\begin{aligned} &\$90.50 \\ -&\ 51.45 \\ &\$39.05 \end{aligned} \qquad \frac{\$39.05}{\$90.50} = 43\%$$

8–35. Hilda's Camera Shop sells a camcorder for $799. Hilda marked up the camcorder 45% on the selling price. What is the cost of the camcorder?

Note: Markup is on selling price, not cost.

$$\begin{aligned} \$799.00 &= C + .45(\$799) \\ \$799.00 &= C + \$359.55 \\ -359.55 &\quad\ \ -359.55 \\ \$439.45 &= C \end{aligned}$$

Check

$$C = \text{Selling price} \times \left(1 - \frac{\text{Percent markup}}{\text{on selling price}}\right)$$

$$\$439.45 = \$799 \times .55$$

8–36. Arley's Bakery makes oat bran cookies that cost $1.50 each. Arley expects 15% of the cookies to fall apart and be discarded. Arley wants a 45% markup on cost and produces 200 cookies. What should Arley price each cookie? Round to nearest cent.

$$\begin{aligned} \text{Total cost} &= 200 \times \$1.50 = \$300 \\ TS &= \$300 + .45(\$300) \\ TS &= \$300 + \$135 \\ TS &= \$435 \end{aligned} \qquad \frac{\$435}{170 \text{ cookies}} = \$2.56$$

8–37. Assume that Arley (Problem 8–36) can sell the broken cookies for $1.40 each. What should Arley price each cookie?

$$\frac{\$435 - (30 \text{ cookies} \times \$1.40)}{170 \text{ cookies}} = \frac{\$435 - \$42}{170} = \$2.31$$

Challenge Problem

How to Be Competitive in the Marketplace

8–38. On July 8, 1995, Leon's Kitchen Hut bought a set of pots with a $120 list price from Lambert Manufacturing. Leon's receives a 25% trade discount. Terms of the sale were 2/10, n/30. On July 14, Leon's sent a check to Lambert for the pots. Leon's expenses are 20% of the selling price. Leon's must also make a profit of 15% of the selling price. A competitor marked down the same set of pots 30%. Assume Leon's reduces its selling price by 30%.

a. What is the sale price at the Kitchen Hut?

b. What was the operating profit or loss?

a. $\$120 \times .75 = \$90 \times .98 = \$88.20$

$$\begin{aligned} S &= \$88.20 + .20S + .15S \\ S &= \$88.20 + .35S \\ .65S &= \$88.20 \\ S &= \$135.69 \end{aligned}$$

Sale price: $94.98, or (.70 × $135.69)

b.

$$\begin{aligned} \text{Total cost} &= \$88.20 + .20(\$135.69) \\ &= \$88.20 + \$27.14 \\ &= \$115.34 \end{aligned} \qquad \begin{aligned} P &= SP - TC \\ &\$94.98 - \$115.34 \\ \text{Loss} &= \$20.36 \end{aligned}$$

Summary Practice Test

Solutions are at end of text in Appendix II.

Quick Reference
If you get any wrong answers, study the page numbers given for each problem.

1. P. 194.

1. Jonathan Katz marks up his goods 42% on cost. A TV cost Jonathan \$240. What is Jonathan's selling price? Round to nearest cent.

$S = \$240 + .42(\$240)$
$S = \$240 + \$100.80$
$S = \$340.80$

Check

$S = (1 + \text{Percent markup on cost}) \times \text{Cost}$
$\$340.80 = 1.42 \times \$240$

2. P. 193.

2. Moore, Inc., sells jeans for \$39.99 that cost \$16.99. What is the percent markup on cost? Round to nearest hundredth percent. Check the cost.

$\$39.99 = \$16.99 + M$
$-16.99 \quad -16.99$
$\$23.00 = M$

$\frac{\$23.00}{\$16.99} = 135.37\% \quad C = \frac{\$23}{1.3537} = \$16.99$

3. P. 194.

3. Jason's Appliance sells an oven for \$650. Jason's marks up the oven 100% on cost. What is the cost and markup of the oven?

$\$650 = C + 1.00C$
$\frac{\$650}{2} = \frac{\not{2}C}{\not{2}}$
$\$325 = C$

Check

$\text{Cost} = \frac{\text{Selling price}}{1 + \text{Percent markup on cost}}$
$\$325 = \frac{\$650}{2}$

Markup $= \$650 - \$325 = \$325$

4. Pp. 193–194.

4. A lumberyard marks up a bench \$25 and sells it for \$65. Markup is on cost. What is the cost and percent markup to nearest tenth percent?

$\$65$
-25
$\$40$ cost

$\frac{\$25}{\$40} = 62.5\%$

5. P. 197.

5. Bill's Hatshop bought a hat for \$88. Bill marks up his hats 55% on the selling price. What is the selling price of the hat? Round to nearest cent.

$S = \$88 + .55S$
$-.55S \quad -.55S$
$\frac{\not{.45}S}{\not{.45}} = \frac{\$88}{.45}$
$S = \$195.56$

Check

$S = \frac{\text{Cost}}{1 - \text{Percent markup on selling price}}$
$\$195.56 = \frac{\$88}{.45}$

6. P. 197.

6. Worldwide Computers sells a computer monitor for \$499.95. Worldwide marks up the monitor 25% on the selling price. What did the computer monitor cost Worldwide? Round to nearest cent.

$\$499.95 = C + .25(\$499.95)$
$\$499.95 = C + \$124.99$
$-124.99 \quad -124.99$
$\$374.96 = C$

Check

$C = \text{Selling price} \times \left(1 - \text{Percent markup on selling price}\right)$
$\$374.96 = \$499.95 \times .75$

7. P. 197.

7. Camille Royce sells lamps for \$88.50 that cost \$59. What is Camille's percent markup on selling price? Round to nearest hundredth percent. Check the selling price.

$\$88.50$
-59.00
$\$29.50$

$\frac{\$29.50}{\$88.50} = 33.33\%$

Check

$S = \frac{\$29.50}{.3333} = \$88.51$ ← Off 1¢ due to rounding

8. P. 197.

8. Abby Ring, a customer of Rudolf Roy, will pay \$160 for a tea set. Roy has a 40% markup on selling price. What is the most that Rudolf can pay for this tea set?

$\$160 = C + .40(\$160)$
$\$160 = C + \$64$
$-64 \quad -64$
$\$96 = C$

Check

$C = \text{Selling price} \times \left(1 - \text{Percent markup on selling price}\right)$
$\$96 = \$160 \times .60$

9. P. 198.

9. Whitney Company marks up its goods 50% on cost. What is Whitney's equivalent markup on selling price? Round to nearest tenth percent.

$\frac{.50}{1 + .50} = 33.3\%$

10. P. 202.

10. Sam's Bakeshop makes triple chocolate brownies that cost $1.25 each. Sam knows that 30% of the brownies will spoil. Assume Sam wants 45% markup on cost and produces 400 brownies. What should Sam price each brownie? Round to nearest cent.

$TC = \$1.25 \times 400 = \$500$

$TS = \$500 + .45(\$500)$

$TS = \$500 + \$225$

$TS = \$725$

$$\frac{\$725}{280} = \$2.59 \text{ per brownie}$$

Project A

MARKETING

Izod Lacoste Gets Restyled and Repriced

By Teri Agins
Staff Reporter of The Wall Street Journal

The Izod Lacoste polo shirt, whose alligator logo was once the favorite mascot of the Chardonnay set, is struggling to save its hide.

This fall, the shirt's maker, **Crystal Brands** Inc. of Southport, Conn., will introduce an embroidered crest—with nary an alligator in sight—on the chest of its classic cotton knit shirt. The new version will be priced at $30 to $35, some 20% lower than the venerable $42.50 version with the alligator. The company is betting that within the next few years the crest shirt will largely supplant the alligator.

(The alligator logo is actually a crocodile, stemming from the nickname—Le Crocodile—of 1920s French tennis champ Rene Lacoste; but the product has long been known as the alligator shirt.)

The price-cutting move is the latest attempt by Crystal Brands to stage a comeback for its troubled Izod Lacoste line. This spring, Crystal Brands introduced a restyled alligator shirt with the looser fit that men prefer nowadays—a full two years after its competitors. At about the same time, Izod Lacoste aired its first television commercial since 1983.

If the new version costs $20 and is sold for $35, what is the percent markup on cost? Check the cost.

$$\begin{array}{r} \$35 \\ -20 \\ \hline \$15 \end{array} \qquad \frac{\$15}{\$20} = 75\% \qquad \textbf{Check} \quad \frac{\$15}{.75} = \$20$$

Project B

Assume the sweater is marked up 40% on selling price. What is the actual cost before the markdown?

$\$32.50 = C + .40\ (\$32.50)$
$\$32.50 = C + \$13$
$\underline{-13} \qquad \underline{-13}$
$\$19.50 = C$

What is the percent markdown (to the nearest hundredth percent)?

$$\begin{array}{r} \$32.50 \\ -26.50 \\ \hline \$\ 6.00 \end{array} \qquad \frac{\$\ 6.00}{\$32.50} = 18.46\%$$

Check

Selling price × (1 – Percent markup on selling price) = Cost
$32.50 × .60 = $19.50

Huntington

world...the very best in premium country called California.

Crew Neck Special Pricing!
Now $26.50
Stock Up!

Our traditional nine-gauge crew and v-neck sweaters have always been favorites with our customers, so we offer them in a full range of attractive colors. Our new fifteen-gauge, bold stripe pullover includes a continuous rugby-styled placket front, with contrasting tape and de rigueur, rugby rubber buttons.

Our lycra-reinforced rib cuffs and waistbands, and our stitched neckbands (on crew and v-necks) will retain their great shape year after year. Full fashioned shoulder, armhole and side seams on crew necks and v-necks. Our placket front has set-in sleeves. USA.

Available in sizes: M, L, XL.
No. 4137 Cotton v-neck sweater available in navy, yellow, or red...$32.50
No. 4130 Cotton crew neck sweater available in shell pink, navy, white, red, or yellow...~~$32.50~~ *Now $26.50*
No. 4188 Cotton rugby stripe sweater available in navy/white stripes, or green/white stripes...$39.50

Courtesy Huntington Clothiers, Inc.

CUMULATIVE REVIEW: A WORD PROBLEM APPROACH—CHAPTERS 6, 7, 8

Solutions are at end of text in Appendix II.

Quick Reference
If you get any wrong answers, study the page numbers given for each problem.
1. P. 146.
2. P. 173.
3. P. 167.
4. P. 193.
5. P. 143.
6. P. 173.
7. P. 197.

1. Assume Kellogg's produced 675,000 boxes of Rice Krispies this year. This was 120% of the annual production last year. What was last year's annual production?

$\frac{675{,}000}{1.20} = 562{,}500$

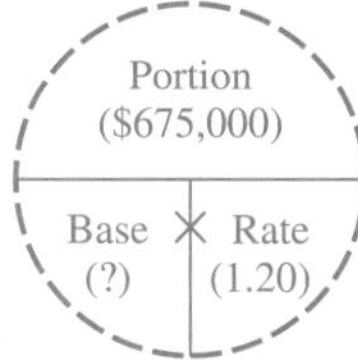

2. A new Sony TV has a list price of $420. The trade discount is 10/20 with terms of 2/10, n/30. Assuming that a retailer pays the invoice within the discount period, what is the amount the retailer must pay?

$.9 \times .8 = .72$

$\$420 \times .72 = \$302.40$ (net price)
$\times\ .98$
$\$296.35$

3. Florsheim shoes is selling loafers with a markup of $40. If the markup is 30% on cost, what was Florsheim's cost? Round to nearest dollar.

$\frac{\$40}{.30} = \$133$

4. In 1995, the national sales manager of Challenger Corporation reported the following sales by region:

Northeast	$185,915
Southeast	515,812
Central	621,510

After analyzing the numbers, Challenger's accountant issued the following statements: "Of the total sales, Northeast accounted for 38.9% of the company's sales." Is the accountant correct? If not, could you rewrite his statement to the nearest tenth percent?

No.

$\$185{,}915 + \$515{,}812 + \$621{,}510 = \$1{,}323{,}237$

$\frac{\$185{,}915}{\$1{,}323{,}237} = 14.05\% = 14.1\%$

"Of the total sales, Northeast accounted for 14.1% of the company's sales."

5. If the sales in Problem 4 increased 6% in 1995, what were the total 1995 sales?

$\$1{,}323{,}237 \times 1.06 = \$1{,}402{,}631.20$

Why is the portion going to be greater than the base?

The rate is greater than 100% → 106%

6. Aster Computers received from Ring Manufacturers an invoice dated August 28 with terms 2/10 EOM. The list price of the invoice is $3,000 (freight not included). Ring offers Aster a 9/8/2 trade chain discount. Terms of freight are FOB shipping point, but Ring prepays the $150 freight. Assume Aster pays the invoice on October 9. How much will Ring receive?

$.91 \times .92 \times .98 = .820456 \times \$3{,}000 = \$2{,}461.37$
$\times\ .98$
$\$2{,}412.14$
$+\ 150.00$
$\$2{,}562.14$

7. Runners World marks up its Nike jogging shoes 25% on selling price. The Nike sells for $65. How much did the store pay for them?

$S = C + M$
$\$65.00 = C + .25(\$65)$
$\$65.00 = C + \$16.25$
$-\ 16.25 \qquad -\ 16.25$
$\$48.75 = C$

$C = \text{Selling price} \times \left(1 - \frac{\text{Percent markup}}{\text{on selling price}}\right)$
$C = \$65 \times .75$
$C = \$48.75$

8. P. 194.

8. Ivan Rone sells antique sleds. He knows that the most he can get for a sled is $350. Ivan needs a 35% markup on cost. Since Ivan is going to an antique show, he wants to know what is the most he can offer a dealer for an antique sled.

$$S = C + M$$
$$\$350 = C + .35C$$
$$\frac{\$350}{1.35} = \frac{\cancel{1.35}C}{\cancel{1.35}}$$
$$\$259.26 = C$$

$$\text{Cost} = \frac{\text{Selling price}}{1 + \text{Percent markup on cost}} = \frac{\$350}{1.35} = \$259.26$$

9. P. 202.

9. Bonnie's Bakery bakes 60 loaves of bread for $1.10 each. Bonnie's estimates that 10% of the bread will spoil. Assume a 60% markup on cost. What is the selling price of each loaf? If Bonnie's can sell the old bread for half price, what is the selling price of each loaf?

$$TC = 60 \times \$1.10 = \$66$$
$$TS = TC + TM$$
$$TS = \$66 + .60(\$66)$$
$$TS = \$66 + \$39.60$$
$$TS = \$105.60$$

$$\frac{\$105.60}{54} = \$1.96 \quad (54 = 60 \times .90)$$

$$\frac{\$105.60 - (6 \times \$.55)}{54} = \frac{\$105.60 - \$3.30}{54} = \$1.89$$

NOTES

THAT WAS THEN . . .
. . . THIS IS NOW

From 1920 to the 1940s, accounting machines were common for doing payroll records. Today, computers and special software packages quickly handle payroll requirements.

9

Payroll

LEARNING UNIT OBJECTIVES

LU 9–1: Calculating Various Types of Employees' Gross Pay

1. Define, compare, and contrast weekly, biweekly, semimonthly, and monthly pay periods. *p. 218*
2. Calculate gross pay with overtime on the basis of time. *p. 219*
3. Calculate gross pay for piecework, differential pay scales, straight commission, and salary plus commission. *pp. 220–21*

LU 9–2: Computing Payroll Deductions for Employees' Pay; Insight into Employers' Responsibilities

1. Prepare and explain the parts of a payroll register. *p. 222*
2. Explain and calculate federal and state unemployment. *pp. 227–28*

Burger King Faces Charges of Violating Child-Labor Laws

MIAMI (AP)—The U.S. is suing Burger King Corp. for alleged violations of federal child-labor laws, in the first major suit since Labor Secretary Elizabeth Dole announced a campaign for tougher enforcement of regulations protecting young workers.

The suit, filed Wednesday in U.S. district court, charges the nation's second-largest fast-food chain with assigning workers under 16 to more hours per week than permitted under federal laws and allowing the young employees to work at times of the day not allowed under the Fair Labor Standards Act.

The suit also claims Miami-based Burger King, which is second in size to McDonald's Corp., had workers under 16 handling prohibited duties, such as most cooking and baking activities.

Violations [illegible] back to at [illegible]

In Situation 1, Learning Unit 9–1, you will learn about the Fair Labor Standards Act that protects workers. You have probably heard about how the child-labor laws of this act protect young children working in the TV and movie industry. As you can see from the above *Wall Street Journal* clipping, these laws also protect workers under 16 who work in the fast-food chains. The child-labor laws are enforced by the Secretary of Labor.

This chapter discusses (1) the type of pay people work for, (2) how employers calculate paychecks and deductions, and (3) what employers must report and pay in taxes.

LEARNING UNIT 9–1 CALCULATING VARIOUS TYPES OF EMPLOYEES' GROSS PAY

Angel Company manufactures dolls of all shapes and sizes. These dolls are sold worldwide. We study Angel Company in this unit because of the variety of methods Angel uses to pay its employees.

Companies usually pay employees **weekly, biweekly, semimonthly,** or **monthly.** How often employers pay employees can affect how employees manage their money. Some employees prefer a weekly paycheck that spreads the inflow of their money. Employees who have monthly bills may find the twice a month or monthly paycheck more convenient. All employees would like more money to manage.

Let's assume you earn $40,000 a year. The following table shows what you would earn each pay period:

Salary paid	Period (based on a year)	Earnings for period (dollars)	
Weekly	52 times (once a week)	$ 769.23	($40,000 ÷ 52)
Biweekly	26 times (every two weeks)	$1,538.46	($40,000 ÷ 26)
Semimonthly	24 times (twice a month)	$1,666.67	($40,000 ÷ 24)
Monthly	12 times (once a month)	$3,333.33	($40,000 ÷ 12)

Now let's look at some pay schedule situations and examples showing how Angel Company calculates its payroll for employees of different pay status.

Situation 1: Hourly Rate of Pay; Calculation of Overtime

Murray Alcosser/The Image Bank

The **Fair Labor Standards Act** sets minimum wage standards and overtime regulations for employees of companies covered by this federal law. The law provides that employees working for an hourly rate receive time-and-a-half pay for hours over their regular 40-hour week. Effective April 1991, the minimum wage was $4.25. Many managerial people, however, are exempt from the time-and-a-half pay for hours over a 40-hour week.

Angel Company is calculating the weekly pay of Julian Valdez who works in its manufacturing division. For the first 40 hours Julian works, Angel calculates his **gross pay** (earnings before **deductions**) as follows:

$$\text{Gross pay} = \text{Hours employee worked} \times \text{Rate per hour}$$

Julian works more than 40 hours in a week, so he will receive **overtime** pay at time and a half. Angel Company must include Julian's overtime pay with his regular pay. To determine Julian's gross pay, Angel uses the following formula:

$$\text{Gross pay} = \begin{array}{c}\text{Earnings for}\\ \text{40 hours}\end{array} + \begin{array}{c}\text{Earnings at}\\ \text{time-and-a-half}\\ \text{rate (1.5)}\end{array}$$

Now let's calculate Julian's gross pay from the following data:

EXAMPLE

Employee	M	T	W	Th	F	S	Total hours	Rate per hour
Julian Valdez	11	$8\frac{1}{2}$	10	8	$11\frac{1}{4}$	$10\frac{3}{4}$	$59\frac{1}{2}$	$8

$59\frac{1}{2}$ total hours
$-\ 40$ regular hours
$19\frac{1}{2}$ hours overtime[1] Time-and-a-half: $8 × 1.5 = $12

$$\begin{aligned}\text{Gross pay} &= (40 \text{ hours} \times \$8) + \left(19\tfrac{1}{2} \text{ hours} \times \$12\right)\\ &= \$320 + \$234\\ &= \boxed{\$554}\end{aligned}$$

Note that the $12 overtime rate came out even. However, throughout the text, *if an overtime rate is greater than two decimal places, do not round it. Round only the final answer. This gives more accuracy.*

Situation 2: Straight Piece Rate Pay

Some companies, especially manufacturers, pay workers according to how much they produce. Angel Company pays Ryan Foss for the number of dolls he produces in a week. This gives Ryan an incentive to make more money by producing more dolls. Ryan receives $.84 per doll, less any defective units. The following formula determines Ryan's gross pay:

$$\text{Gross pay} = \text{Number of units produced} \times \text{Rate per unit}$$

Companies may also pay a guaranteed hourly wage and use piece rate as a bonus. However, Angel uses straight piece rate as wages for some of its employees.

[1] Some companies pay overtime for time over 8 hours in one day; Angel Company pays overtime for time over 40 hours per week.

EXAMPLE During the last week of April, Ryan Foss produced 750 dolls. Using the above formula, Angel Company paid Ryan $630.

Gross pay = 750 dolls × $.84
= $630

Situation 3: Differential Pay Schedule

Some of Angel's employees can earn more than the $.84 straight piece rate for every doll they produce. Angel Company has set up a **differential pay schedule** for these employees. The company determines the rate these employees make by the amount of units the employee produces at different levels of production.

EXAMPLE Angel Company pays Abby Rogers on the basis of the following schedule:

Units produced	Amount per unit
1–50	$.45
51–150	.49
151–200	.54
Over 200	.95

Last week Abby produced 300 dolls. What is Abby's gross pay?

Angel calculated Abby's gross pay as follows:

(50 × $.45) + (100 × $.49) + (50 × $.54) + (100 × $.95)
$22.50 + $49 + $27 + $95 = $193.50

Before we see how Angel pays some of its sales force, read the following *Wall Street Journal* clipping and note that it isn't always easy for retailers to switch to an incentive-pay plan. Although retailers believe that these plans are necessary to compete in today's markets, employees often feel intimidated by unrealistic high sales goals and threats of dismissal.

RETAILING

Chain Finds Incentives A Hard Sell

By FRANCINE SCHWADEL
Staff Reporter of THE WALL STREET JOURNAL

Retailers claim better service depends on linking clerks' pay to performance. But Dayton Hudson Corp. is discovering it isn't easy to switch to an incentive-pay plan.

Unhappy workers at half a dozen Hudson's department stores in Michigan are attempting to unionize. In the first election in May, salespeople at the Westland store voted 274 to 179 in favor of joining the United Auto Workers union. The company has challenged the results. But one fact is undisputed: Complaints about the company's Performance Plus pay plan fueled the union drive.

The experience of the Minneapolis-based department store chain illustrates the pitfalls retailers are likely to encounter as more of them attempt to link pay to performance. Store managers say incentive plans are necessary in today's competitive environment. But store clerks often say they feel intimidated by unrealistically high sales goals and threats of dismissal.

Stores from Bloomingdale's Inc. to R.H. Macy & Co. have switched to incentive-pay plans in recent years to better compete with the likes of Nordstrom Inc. The Seattle-based retailer built a reputation for stellar service by paying clerks commis-[illegible]

Now let's go back to Angel Company and look at some of its other types of employee payment plans.

Situation 4: Straight Commission with Draw

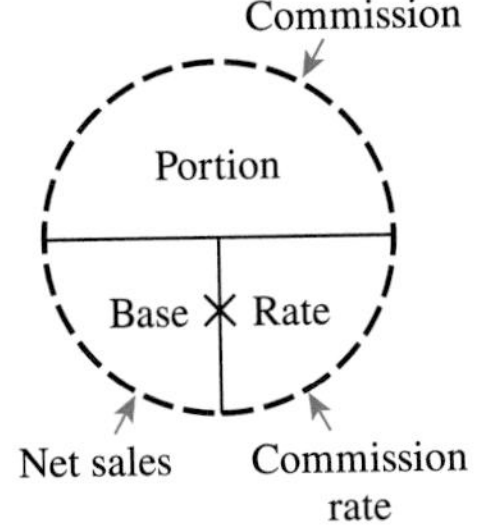

Companies frequently use **straight commission** to determine the pay of salespersons. This commission is usually a certain percentage of the amount the salesperson sells. Angel Company allows some of its salespersons to draw against this commission at the beginning of each month.

A **draw** is an advance on the salesperson's commission. Angel subtracts this advance later from the employee's commission earned based on sales. When the commission does not equal the draw, the salesperson owes Angel the difference between the draw and the commission.

EXAMPLE Angel Company pays Jackie Okamoto a straight commission of 15% on her net sales (net sales are total sales less sales returns). In May, Jackie had net sales of \$56,000. Angel gave Jackie a \$600 draw in May. What is Jackie's gross pay?

Angel calculated Jackie's commission minus her draw as follows:

$$\begin{aligned} \$56{,}000 \times .15 &= \$8{,}400 \\ &\quad - 600 \\ &\quad \$7{,}800 \end{aligned}$$

Angel Company pays some people in the sales department on a variable commission scale. Let's look at this assuming the employee had no draw.

Situation 5: Variable Commission Scale

A company with a **variable commission scale** uses different commission rates for different levels of net sales.

EXAMPLE Last month, Jane Ring's net sales were \$160,000. What is Jane's gross pay based on the following schedule?

Up to \$35,000	4%
Excess of \$35,000 to \$45,000	6%
Over \$45,000	8%

$$\begin{aligned} \text{Gross pay} &= (\$35{,}000 \times .04) + (\$10{,}000 \times .06) + (\$115{,}000 \times .08) \\ &= \$1{,}400 + \$600 + \$9{,}200 \\ &= \$11{,}200 \end{aligned}$$

Situation 6: Salary Plus Commission

Angel Company pays Joe Roy a \$3,000 monthly salary plus a 4% commission for sales over \$20,000. Last month Joe's net sales were \$50,000. Angel calculated Joe's gross monthly pay as follows:

$$\begin{aligned} \text{Gross pay} &= \text{Salary} + (\text{Commission} \times \text{Sales over } \$20{,}000) \\ &= \$3{,}000 + (\$.04 \times \$30{,}000) \\ &= \$3{,}000 + \$1{,}200 \\ &= \$4{,}200 \end{aligned}$$

Before you take the Practice Quiz, you should know that many managers today receive **overrides.** These managers receive a commission based on the net sales of the people they supervise.

LU 9-1 PRACTICE QUIZ

1. Lynn Sullivan worked $49\frac{1}{2}$ hours in one week for American Airways. Lynn earns \$6 per hour. What is Lynn's gross pay assuming overtime is time and a half?
2. Matt Long had \$180,000 in sales for the month. Matt's commission rate is 9%, and he had a \$3,500 draw. What was Matt's end-of-month commission?
3. Bob Meyers receives a \$1,000 monthly salary. He also receives a variable commission on net sales based on the following schedule (commission doesn't begin until Bob earns \$8,000 in net sales):

\$8,000–\$12,000	1%	Excess of \$20,000 to \$40,000	5%
Excess of \$12,000 to \$20,000	3%	Over \$40,000	8%

Assume Bob earns \$40,000 net sales for the month. What is his gross pay?

SOLUTIONS TO LU 9-1 PRACTICE QUIZ

1. 40 hours × \$6.00 = \$240.00

$9\frac{1}{2}$ hours × \$9.00 = 85.50 (\$6.00 × 1.5 = \$9.00)

\$325.50

2. \$180,000 × .09 = \$16,200

− 3,500

\$12,700

3. Gross pay = \$1,000 + (\$4,000 × .01) + (\$8,000 × .03) + (\$20,000 × .05)

= \$1,000 + \$40 + \$240 + \$1,000

= \$2,280

LEARNING UNIT 9-2 COMPUTING PAYROLL DEDUCTIONS FOR EMPLOYEES' PAY; INSIGHT INTO EMPLOYERS' RESPONSIBILITIES

When you get your weekly paycheck, do you take the time to check all the numbers? Do you understand the difference between Social Security and Medicare? This unit begins by dissecting a paycheck. Then we give you an insight into the tax responsibilities of employers.

Computing Payroll Deductions for Employees

Companies often record employee payroll information in a multicolumn form called a **payroll register.** The increased use of computers in business has made computerized registers a time saver for many companies.

Moore Company uses a multicolumn payroll register. Below is Moore's partial register showing the payroll information for Gail Koro during week #45. Let's check each column to see if Gail's take-home pay of \$910.01 is correct. Note how the circled letters in the register correspond to the explanations given below the register.

MOORE COMPANY
Payroll Register
November 11, 19XX Week #45

				Earnings				FICA taxable earnings		Deductions						
										FICA						
Employee name	**Allow. & marital status**	**Cum. earn.**	**Sal. per week**	**Reg.**	**Ovt.**	**Gross**	**Cum. earn.**	**SS.**	**Med.**	**Soc. Sec.**	**Med.**	**FIT**	**SIT**	**Health ins.**	**Net pay**
Koro, Gail	M-2	55,440	1,260	1,260	—	1,260	56,700	60	1,260	3.72	18.27	220	63	45	910.01
	(A)	(B)	(C)		(D)		(E)	(F)	(G)	(H)	(I)	(J)	(K)	(L)	(M)

Payroll Register Explanations

A—Allowance and marital status

When Gail was hired, she completed the **W-4 (Employee's Withholding Allowance Certificate)** form shown in Figure 9-1 stating that she is married and claims an allowance (exemption) of 2. Moore Company will need this information to calculate federal income tax (Column J).

B, C, D—Cumulative earnings before payroll, salaries, earnings

Before this pay period, Gail has earned \$55,440 (44 weeks × \$1,260 salary per week). Since Gail receives no overtime, her \$1,260 salary per week represents her gross pay (pay before any deductions).

E—Cumulative earnings after payroll

After this pay period, Gail has earned \$56,700 (\$55,440 + \$1,260).

F, G—Taxable earnings for Social Security and Medicare

The **Federal Insurance Contribution Act (FICA)** funds the **Social Security** program. The program includes Old Age and Disability, Medicare, Survivor Benefits, and so on. Beginning in 1991, the FICA tax required separate reporting for Social Security and **Medicare.** We will use the following rates for Moore Company:

FIGURE 9–1
Employee's W-4 Form

Form **W-4** Department of the Treasury Internal Revenue Service | **Employee's Withholding Allowance Certificate** ▶ For Privacy Act and Paperwork Reduction Act Notice, see reverse. | OMB No. 1545-0010 **19XX**

1 Type or print your first name and middle initial: Gail | Last name: Koro | 2 Your social security number: 021369494

Home address (number and street or rural route): 2 Roundy Road | 3 ☐ Single ☒ Married ☐ Married, but withhold at higher Single rate. Note: If married, but legally separated, or spouse is a nonresident alien, check the Single box.

City or town, state, and ZIP code: Marblehead, MA 01945 | 4 If your last name differs from that on your social security card, check here and call 1-800-772-1213 for more information . . . . ▶ ☐

5 Total number of allowances you are claiming (from line G above or from the worksheets on page 2 if they apply) . | 5 | 2
6 Additional amount, if any, you want withheld from each paycheck . . . . | 6 | $
7 I claim exemption from withholding for 1993 and I certify that I meet **ALL** of the following conditions for exemption:
- Last year I had a right to a refund of **ALL** Federal income tax withheld because I had **NO** tax liability; **AND**
- This year I expect a refund of **ALL** Federal income tax withheld because I expect to have **NO** tax liability; **AND**
- This year if my income exceeds $600 and includes nonwage income, another person cannot claim me as a dependent.

If you meet all of the above conditions, enter "EXEMPT" here . . . . ▶ | 7 |

Under penalties of perjury, I certify that I am entitled to the number of withholding allowances claimed on this certificate or entitled to claim exempt status.

Employee's signature ▶ Gail Koro Date ▶ 1/1 , 19 XX

8 Employer's name and address (Employer: Complete 8 and 10 only if sending to the IRS) | 9 Office code (optional) | 10 Employer identification number

	Rate	Base
Social Security*	6.20%	$ 55,500
Medicare†	1.45	130,200

* The 1993 rate of Social Security is 6.2% on $57,600.
† The 1993 rate for Medicare is 1.45% on $135,000.

These rates mean that Gail Koro will pay Social Security taxes on the first $55,500 she earns this year. After earning $55,500, Gail's wages will be exempt from Social Security. Note that Gail will be paying Medicare taxes until she earns $130,200 (which she will never reach).

To help keep Moore's record straight, the *taxable earnings column only shows what wages will be taxed. This amount is not the tax.* For example, in week #45, only $60 of Gail's salary will be taxable for Social Security.

$55,500	Social Security base
− 55,440	(B)
$ 60	

Gail's entire salary of $1,260 will be taxed for Medicare since she is not over $130,200.

H—Social Security

To calculate Gail's Social Security tax, we multiply $60 (F) times 6.2%

$60 × .062 = $3.72

I—Medicare

Since Gail's total salary is taxed for Medicare, we multiply $1,260 (G) times 1.45%.

$1,260 × .0145 = $18.27

J—FIT

Using the W-4 form Gail completed, Moore deducts **federal income tax withholding (FIT).** The more allowances an employee claims, the less money Moore deducts from the employee's paycheck. Two methods are used to determine FIT: wage bracket method and percentage method. Moore uses the wage bracket method. We will also show the percentage method.

1. Wage Bracket Method The **wage bracket method** uses the tables in Circular E of the federal government's Employer's Guide. Circular E contains many tables for pay paid weekly, biweekly, semimonthly, monthly, and so on. Table 9–1 (p. 224) shows a table for married persons paid weekly. Table 9–2 (p. 225) shows a table for a single person paid monthly. (Be sure to check each year with the Internal Revenue for the latest tables.) Since Gail is married and her weekly pay is $1,260, we go down the left of Table 9–1 until we see at least $1,260. Then we go across to 2 withholding allowances. At the intersection, we see $220. This is Gail's federal income tax. Note that if Gail's pay were $1,270, we would have used the next row down.

TABLE 9-1 Weekly Payroll Table for Married Persons

MARRIED Persons—WEEKLY Payroll Period

And the wages are–		And the number of withholding allowances claimed is—										
At least	But less than	0	1	2	3	4	5	6	7	8	9	10
		The amount of income tax to be withheld shall be—										
$640	$650	$86	$79	$73	$66	$60	$53	$46	$40	$33	$26	$20
650	660	88	81	74	68	61	54	48	41	35	28	21
660	670	89	82	76	69	63	56	49	43	36	29	23
670	680	91	84	77	71	64	57	51	44	38	31	24
680	690	92	85	79	72	66	59	52	46	39	32	26
690	700	94	87	80	74	67	60	54	47	41	34	27
700	710	95	88	82	75	69	62	55	49	42	35	29
710	720	97	90	83	77	70	63	57	50	44	37	30
720	730	98	91	85	78	72	65	58	52	45	38	32
730	740	100	93	86	80	73	66	60	53	47	40	33
740	750	101	94	88	81	75	68	61	55	48	41	35
750	760	103	96	89	83	76	69	63	56	50	43	36
760	770	105	97	91	84	78	71	64	58	51	44	38
770	780	108	99	92	86	79	72	66	59	53	46	39
780	790	110	100	94	87	81	74	67	61	54	47	41
790	800	113	102	95	89	82	75	69	62	56	49	42
800	810	116	104	97	90	84	77	70	64	57	50	44
810	820	119	106	98	92	85	78	72	65	59	52	45
820	830	122	109	100	93	87	80	73	67	60	53	47
830	840	124	112	101	95	88	81	75	68	62	55	48
840	850	127	115	103	96	90	83	76	70	63	56	50
850	860	130	118	105	98	91	84	78	71	65	58	51
860	870	133	120	108	99	93	86	79	73	66	59	53
870	880	136	123	111	101	94	87	81	74	68	61	54
880	890	138	126	114	102	96	89	82	76	69	62	56
890	900	141	129	116	104	97	90	84	77	71	64	57
900	910	144	132	119	107	99	92	85	79	72	65	59
910	920	147	134	122	110	100	93	87	80	74	67	60
920	930	150	137	125	112	102	95	88	82	75	68	62
930	940	152	140	128	115	103	96	90	83	77	70	63
940	950	155	143	130	118	106	98	91	85	78	71	65
950	960	158	146	133	121	108	99	93	86	80	73	66
960	970	161	148	136	124	111	101	94	88	81	74	68
970	980	164	151	139	126	114	102	96	89	83	76	69
980	990	166	154	142	129	117	104	97	91	84	77	71
990	1,000	169	157	144	132	120	107	99	92	86	79	72
1,000	1,010	172	160	147	135	122	110	100	94	87	80	74
1,010	1,020	175	162	150	138	125	113	102	95	89	82	75
1,020	1,030	178	165	153	140	128	116	103	97	90	83	77
1,030	1,040	180	168	156	143	131	118	106	98	92	85	78
1,040	1,050	183	171	158	146	134	121	109	100	93	86	80
1,050	1,060	186	174	161	149	136	124	112	101	95	88	81
1,060	1,070	189	176	164	152	139	127	114	103	96	89	83
1,070	1,080	192	179	167	154	142	130	117	105	98	91	84
1,080	1,090	194	182	170	157	145	132	120	108	99	92	86
1,090	1,100	197	185	172	160	148	135	123	110	101	94	87
1,100	1,110	200	188	175	163	150	138	126	113	102	95	89
1,110	1,120	203	190	178	166	153	141	128	116	104	97	90
1,120	1,130	206	193	181	168	156	144	131	119	107	98	92
1,130	1,140	208	196	184	171	159	146	134	122	109	100	93
1,140	1,150	211	199	186	174	162	149	137	124	112	101	95
1,150	1,160	214	202	189	177	164	152	140	127	115	103	96
1,160	1,170	217	204	192	180	167	155	142	130	118	105	98
1,170	1,180	220	207	195	182	170	158	145	133	121	108	99
1,180	1,190	222	210	198	185	173	160	148	136	123	111	101
1,190	1,200	225	213	200	188	176	163	151	138	126	114	102
1,200	1,210	228	216	203	191	178	166	154	141	129	117	104
1,210	1,220	231	218	206	194	181	169	156	144	132	119	107
1,220	1,230	234	221	209	196	184	172	159	147	135	122	110
1,230	1,240	236	224	212	199	187	174	162	150	137	125	113
1,240	1,250	239	227	214	202	190	177	165	152	140	128	115
1,250	1,260	242	230	217	205	192	180	168	155	143	131	118
1,260	1,270	245	232	220	208	195	183	170	158	146	133	121
1,270	1,280	248	235	223	210	198	186	173	161	149	136	124
1,280	1,290	250	238	226	213	201	188	176	164	151	139	127

TABLE 9–2 Monthly Payroll Table for Single Persons

SINGLE Persons—MONTHLY Payroll Period

And the wages are–		And the number of withholding allowances claimed is—										
At least	But less than	0	1	2	3	4	5	6	7	8	9	10
		The amount of income tax to be withheld shall be—										
$1,800	$1,840	$257	$228	$199	$171	$142	$113	$84	$56	$27	$0	$0
1,840	1,880	263	234	205	177	148	119	90	62	33	4	0
1,880	1,920	269	240	211	183	154	125	96	68	39	10	0
1,920	1,960	280	246	217	189	160	131	102	74	45	16	0
1,960	2,000	292	252	223	195	166	137	108	80	51	22	0
2,000	2,040	303	258	229	201	172	143	114	86	57	28	0
2,040	2,080	314	264	235	207	178	149	120	92	63	34	5
2,080	2,120	325	272	241	213	184	155	126	98	69	40	11
2,120	2,160	336	283	247	219	190	161	132	104	75	46	17
2,160	2,200	348	294	253	225	196	167	138	110	81	52	23
2,200	2,240	359	305	259	231	202	173	144	116	87	58	29
2,240	2,280	370	316	265	237	208	179	150	122	93	64	35
2,280	2,320	381	328	274	243	214	185	156	128	99	70	41
2,320	2,360	392	339	285	249	220	191	162	134	105	76	47
2,360	2,400	404	350	296	255	226	197	168	140	111	82	53
2,400	2,440	415	361	308	261	232	203	174	146	117	88	59
2,440	2,480	426	372	319	267	238	209	180	152	123	94	65
2,480	2,520	437	384	330	276	244	215	186	158	129	100	71
2,520	2,560	448	395	341	287	250	221	192	164	135	106	77
2,560	2,600	460	406	352	299	256	227	198	170	141	112	83
2,600	2,640	471	417	364	310	262	233	204	176	147	118	89
2,640	2,680	482	428	375	321	268	239	210	182	153	124	95
2,680	2,720	493	440	386	332	279	245	216	188	159	130	101
2,720	2,760	504	451	397	343	290	251	222	194	165	136	107
2,760	2,800	516	462	408	355	301	257	228	200	171	142	113
2,800	2,840	527	473	420	366	312	263	234	206	177	148	119
2,840	2,880	538	484	431	377	323	270	240	212	183	154	125
2,880	2,920	549	496	442	388	335	281	246	218	189	160	131
2,920	2,960	560	507	453	399	346	292	252	224	195	166	137
2,960	3,000	572	518	464	411	357	303	258	230	201	172	143
3,000	3,040	583	529	476	422	368	315	264	236	207	178	149
3,040	3,080	594	540	487	433	379	326	272	242	213	184	155
3,080	3,120	605	552	498	444	391	337	283	248	219	190	161
3,120	3,160	616	563	509	455	402	348	294	254	225	196	167
3,160	3,200	628	574	520	467	413	359	306	260	231	202	173
3,200	3,240	639	585	532	478	424	371	317	266	237	208	179
3,240	3,280	650	596	543	489	435	382	328	274	243	214	185
3,280	3,320	661	608	554	500	447	393	339	286	249	220	191
3,320	3,360	672	619	565	511	458	404	350	297	255	226	197
3,360	3,400	684	630	576	523	469	415	362	308	261	232	203
3,400	3,440	695	641	588	534	480	427	373	319	267	238	209
3,440	3,480	706	652	599	545	491	438	384	330	277	244	215
3,480	3,520	717	664	610	556	503	449	395	342	288	250	221
3,520	3,560	728	675	621	567	514	460	406	353	299	256	227
3,560	3,600	740	686	632	579	525	471	418	364	310	262	233
3,600	3,640	751	697	644	590	536	483	429	375	322	268	239
3,640	3,680	762	708	655	601	547	494	440	386	333	279	245
3,680	3,720	773	720	666	612	559	505	451	398	344	290	251
3,720	3,760	784	731	677	623	570	516	462	409	355	301	257
3,760	3,800	796	742	688	635	581	527	474	420	366	313	263
3,800	3,840	807	753	700	646	592	539	485	431	378	324	270
3,840	3,880	818	764	711	657	603	550	496	442	389	335	281
3,880	3,920	829	776	722	668	615	561	507	454	400	346	293
3,920	3,960	840	787	733	679	626	572	518	465	411	357	304
3,960	4,000	852	798	744	691	637	583	530	476	422	369	315
4,000	4,040	863	809	756	702	648	595	541	487	434	380	326
4,040	4,080	874	820	767	713	659	606	552	498	445	391	337
4,080	4,120	885	832	778	724	671	617	563	510	456	402	349
4,120	4,160	896	843	789	735	682	628	574	521	467	413	360
4,160	4,200	908	854	800	747	693	639	586	532	478	425	371
4,200	4,240	919	865	812	758	704	651	597	543	490	436	382
4,240	4,280	930	876	823	769	715	662	608	554	501	447	393
4,280	4,320	941	888	834	780	727	673	619	566	512	458	405
4,320	4,360	952	899	845	791	738	684	630	577	523	469	416

TABLE 9-3
Percentage Method Income Tax Withholding Table

Payroll Period	One withholding allowance
Weekly	$44.23
Biweekly.	88.46
Semimonthly	95.83
Monthly	191.67
Quarterly.	575.00
Semiannually	1,150.00
Annually	2,300.00
Daily or miscellaneous (each day of the payroll period)	8.85

$44.23 × 2 = $88.46

2. Percentage Method Today, many companies do not want to store the wage bracket tables, and they use computers for their payroll. These companies use the **percentage method.** For this method we use Table 9-3 above and Table 9-4 from Circular E to calculate Gail's FIT.

Step 1. In Table 9-3, locate the weekly withholding for one allowance. Multiply this number by 2.

Step 2. Subtract $88.46 in Step 1 from the Gail's total pay.

$1,260.00
− 88.46
$1,171.54

Step 3. In Table 9-4 locate the married person's weekly pay table. The $1,171.54 falls between $760 and $1,735. The tax is $103.35 plus 28% of the excess over $760.

$1,171.54
− 760.00
$ 411.54

Tax: $103.35 + .28 ($411.54)
$103.35 + $115.23 = $218.58

Note that the percentage method results in a slightly different tax than the wage bracket method due to the range in table bracket intervals. If we use the middle of each range, our answer is close.

K—SIT

We assume a 5% **state income tax (SIT).**

$1,260 × .05 = $63

L—Health insurance

Gail contributes $45 per week for health insurance.

M—Net pay

Gail's **net pay** is her gross pay less all deductions.

	$1,260.00	gross
−	3.72	Social Security
−	18.27	Medicare
−	220.00	FIT
−	63.00	SIT
−	45.00	health insurance
=	$ 910.01	net pay

Insight into Employers' Responsibilities[2]

T

In the first section of this unit, we saw that Gail Koro contributed to Social Security and Medicare. Moore Company has the legal responsibility to match her contributions. Besides matching Social Security and Medicare, Moore must pay two important taxes that employees do not have to pay—federal and state unemployment taxes.

[2] Effective January 1, 1993, the IRS issued new rules regulating how companies must deposit payroll taxes (federal income tax, Social Security, and Medicare). If a business reported $50,000 or less for payroll tax liability in the prior

TABLE 9-4 Percentage Method Income Tax Withholding Tables

Tables for Percentage Method of Withholding
(For Wages Paid After December 1991)

TABLE 1—If the Payroll Period With Respect to an Employee is Weekly

(a) SINGLE person—including head of household:

If the amount of wages (after subtracting withholding allowances) is: Not over $25 . . . . . The amount of income tax to be withheld shall be: 0

Over—	But not over—		of excess over—
$25	—$438 . . .	15%	—$25
$438	—$1,023 . .	$61.95 plus 28%	—$438
$1,023		$225.75 plus 31%	—$1,023

(b) MARRIED person

If the amount of wages (after subtracting withholding allowances) is: Not over $71 . . . . . The amount of income tax to be withheld shall be: 0

Over—	But not over—		of excess over—
$71	—$760 . . .	15%	—$71
$760	—$1,735 . . .	$103.35 plus 28%	—$760
$1,735		$376.35 plus 31%	—$1,735

TABLE 2—If the Payroll Period With Respect to an Employee is Biweekly

(a) SINGLE person—including head of household:

If the amount of wages (after subtracting withholding allowances) is: Not over $50. . . . . The amount of income tax to be withheld shall be: 0

Over—	But not over—		of excess over—
$50	—$875 . . .	15%	—$50
$875	—$2,046 . .	$123.75 plus 28%	—$875
$2,046		$451.63 plus 31%	—$2,046

(b) MARRIED person

If the amount of wages (after subtracting withholding allowances) is: Not over $142 . . . . The amount of income tax to be withheld shall be: 0

Over—	But not over—		of excess over—
$142	—$1,519 . . .	15%	—$142
$1,519	—$3,469 . . .	$206.55 plus 28%	—$1,519
$3,469		$752.55 plus 31%	—$3,469

TABLE 3—If the Payroll Period With Respect to an Employee is Semimonthly

(a) SINGLE person—including head of household:

If the amount of wages (after subtracting withholding allowances) is: Not over $54. . . . . The amount of income tax to be withheld shall be: 0

Over—	But not over—		of excess over—
$54	—$948 . . .	15%	—$54
$948	—$2,217 . .	$134.10 plus 28%	—$948
$2,217		$489.42 plus 31%	—$2,217

(b) MARRIED person—

If the amount of wages (after subtracting withholding allowances) is: Not over $154 . . . . The amount of income tax to be withheld shall be: 0

Over—	But not over—		of excess over—
$154	—$1,646 . . .	15%	—$154
$1,646	—$3,758 . . .	$223.80 plus 28%	—$1,646
$3,758		$815.16 plus 31%	—$3,758

TABLE 4—If the Payroll Period With Respect to an Employee is Monthly

(a) SINGLE person—including head of household:

If the amount of wages (after subtracting withholding allowances) is: Not over $108 . . . . The amount of income tax to be withheld shall be: 0

Over—	But not over—		of excess over—
$108	—$1,896 . .	15%	—$108
$1,896	—$4,433 . .	$268.20 plus 28%	—$1,896
$4,433		$978.56 plus 31%	—$4,433

(b) MARRIED person—

If the amount of wages (after subtracting withholding allowances) is: Not over $308 . . . . The amount of income tax to be withheld shall be: 0

Over—	But not over—		of excess over—
$308	—$3,292 . . .	15%	—$308
$3,292	—$7,517 . . .	$447.60 plus 28%	—$3,292
$7,517		$1,630.60 plus 31%	—$7,517

Federal Unemployment Tax Act (FUTA)

In all our calculations, FUTA is .008.

The federal government participates in a joint federal-state unemployment program to help unemployed workers. At this writing, employers pay the government a 6.2% **FUTA** tax on the first $7,000 paid to employees as wages during the calendar year. Any wages over $7,000 per worker are exempt wages and not taxed for FUTA. If the total cumulative amount the employer owes the government is less than $100, the employer can pay the liability yearly (end of January in the following calendar year). If the tax is greater than $100, the employer must pay it quarterly.

year, deposits will be due monthly. If more than $50,000 was reported by a company in a prior year, deposits would be made up to two times weekly. Check with the IRS for the latest details.

Companies involved in a state unemployment tax fund can usually take a credit against their FUTA tax. *In reality, then, companies are paying .8% (.008) to the federal unemployment program.*

EXAMPLE Assume a company had total wages of $19,000 in a calendar year. No employee earned more than $7,000 during the calendar year. The FUTA tax is .8% (6.2% minus the company's 5.4% credit for state unemployment tax). How much does the company pay in FUTA tax?

The company calculates its FUTA tax as follows:

6.2% FUTA tax
− 5.4% credit for SUTA tax
= .8% tax for FUTA

.008 × $19,000 = **$152** FUTA tax due the federal government.

State Unemployment Tax (SUTA)

The current **SUTA** tax in most states is 5.4% on the first $7,000 the employer pays an employee. Some states offer a merit rating system that results in a lower SUTA rate for companies with a stable employment period. The federal government still allows 5.4% credit on FUTA tax to companies entitled to the lower SUTA rate. States also charge companies with a poor employment record a higher SUTA rate. However, these companies cannot take any more than the 5.4% credit against the 6.2% federal unemployment rate.

EXAMPLE Assume a company has total wages of $20,000 and $4,000 of the wages are exempt from SUTA. What are the company's SUTA and FUTA taxes if the company's SUTA rate is 5.8% due to a poor employment record?

The exempt wages (over $7,000 earnings per worker) are not taxed for SUTA or FUTA. So the company owes the following SUTA and FUTA taxes:

$20,000
− 4,000 (exempt wages)
$16,000 × .058 = **$928** SUTA

Federal FUTA tax would then be:
$16,000 × .008 = **$128**

LU 9-2 PRACTICE QUIZ

1. Calculate Social Security, Medicare, and FIT taxes for Allison Reese. Allison's company pays her a monthly salary of $4,080. She is single and claims one deduction. Before this payroll, Allison's cumulative earnings were $53,000. (Social Security maximum is 6.2% on $55,500, and Medicare is 1.45% on $130,200.) Calculate FIT with the wage bracket method and the percentage method.
2. Jim Brewer, owner of Arrow Company, has three employees who earn $300, $700, and $900 a week. Assume a state SUTA rate of 5.1%. What will Jim pay for state and federal unemployment for the first quarter?

SOLUTIONS TO LU 9-2 PRACTICE QUIZ

1. *Social Security:*

$55,500
− 53,000
$ 2,500 × .062 = $155

Medicare:

$4,080 × .0145 = $59.16

FIT: **a.** (Wage bracket method) (Table 9-2) — $4,080 − $4,120, 1 withholding ⟶ $832 tax

b. (Percentage method)
$191.67 × 1 = (Table 9-3)

$4,080.00
− 191.67
$3,888.33

(Table 9-4)
$1,896 − $4,433 ⟶ $268.20 plus 28%

$3,888.33
− 1,896.00
$1,992.33 × .28 = $557.85
+ 268.20
$826.05

2. 13 weeks × \$300 = \$ 3,900 → -0-
13 weeks × \$700 = 9,100 (\$9,100 − \$7,000) → \$2,100
13 weeks × \$900 = 11,700 (\$11,700 − \$7,000) → 4,700
\$24,700 — \$6,800

Exempt wages (not taxed for FUTA or SUTA)

\$24,700 − \$6,800 = \$17,900 taxable wages
SUTA = .051 × \$17,900 = \$912.90
FUTA = .008 × \$17,900 = \$143.20

Note: FUTA remains at .008 whether SUTA rate is higher or lower than standard.

CHAPTER ORGANIZER: A REFERENCE GUIDE

Page	Topic	Key point, procedure, formula	Example(s) to illustrate situation
219	Gross pay	Hours employee worked × Rate per hour	\$6.50 per hour at 36 hours Gross pay = 36 × \$6.50 = \$234
219	Overtime	Gross earnings (pay) = Regular pay + Earnings at overtime rate ($1\frac{1}{2}$)	\$6 per hour; 42 hours Gross pay = (40 × \$6) + (2 × \$9) = \$240 + \$18 = \$258
219	Straight piece rate	Gross pay = Number of units produced × Rate per unit	1,185 units; rate per unit, \$.89 Gross pay = 1,185 × \$.89 = \$1,054.65
220	Differential pay schedule	Rate on each item is related to the number of items produced.	1–500 at \$.84; 501–1,000 at \$.96; 900 units produced Gross pay = (500 × \$.84) + (400 × \$.96) = \$420 + \$384 = \$804
221	Straight commission	Total sales × Commission rate Any draw would be subtracted from earnings.	\$155,000 sales; 6% commission \$155,000 × .06 = \$9,300
221	Variable commission scale	Sales at different levels pay different rates of commission.	Up to \$5,000, 5%; \$5,001 to \$10,000, 8%; over \$10,000, 10% Sold: \$6,500 Solution: (\$5,000 × .05) + (\$1,500 × .08) = \$250 + \$120 = \$370
221	Salary plus commission	Regular wages (fixed) + Commissions earned	Base \$400 per week + 2% on sales over \$14,000 Actual sales: \$16,000 \$400(base) + (.02 × \$2,000) = \$440
222	Payroll register	Multicolumn form to record payroll. Married and paid weekly. Claims 0 allowances. FICA rates from chapter.	Earnings: Gross 1,100; Deductions: FICA Soc. Sec. 68.20, FICA Med. 15.95, FIT 200; Net pay 815.85
223	FICA Social Security Medicare	6.2% on \$55,500 1.45% on \$130,200 (Check IRS for latest rates.)	If John earns \$60,000, what did he contribute to Social Security and Medicare? S.S. \$55,500 × .062 = \$3,441 Med. \$60,000 × .0145 = \$ 870

Payroll register example (page 222):

Earnings	Deductions			Net pay
Gross	FICA			
	Soc. Sec.	Med.	FIT	
1,100	68.20	15.95	200	815.85

Page	Topic	Key point, procedure, formula	Example(s) to illustrate situation
223	FIT calculation (wage bracket method)	FIT has no maximum, unlike Social Security and Medicare.	Al Doy—married and 2 allowances. Paid weekly, $1,200. Table 9–1 → $203 $1,200 — $1,210
226	FIT (percentage method)	The percentage method will produce approximately the same answer as wage bracket method. Companies with computers would utilize the percentage method.	Use same example as above. $1,200.00 − 88.46 ($44.23 × 2) Table 9–3 $1,111.54 By Table 9–4 $1,111.54 − 760.00 $ 351.54 $103.35 + .28 ($351.54) $103.35 + $98.43 $201.78
228	State and federal unemployment	Employer pays these taxes. Rates are 6.2% on $7,000 for federal and 5.4% for state on $7,000. 6.2% − 5.4% = .8% federal rate after credit. If state unemployment rate is higher than 5.4%, no additional credit is taken. If state unemployment rate is less than 5.4%, the full 5.4% credit can be taken for federal unemployment.	Cumulative pay before payroll, $6,400; this week's pay, $800. What is state and federal unemployment for employer assuming a 5.2% state unemployment rate? State → .052 × $600 = $31.20 Federal → .008 × $600 = $4.80 ($6,400 + $600 = $7,000 maximum)
	Key terms	Biweekly, *p. 218* Deductions, *p. 219* Differential pay schedule, *p. 220* Draw, *p. 221* Employee's Withholding Allowance Certificate (W-4), *p. 223* Fair Labor Standards Act, *p. 219* Federal income tax withholding (FIT), *p. 223* Federal Insurance Contribution Act (FICA), *p. 222* Federal Unemployment Tax Act (FUTA), *p. 227* Gross pay, *p. 219* Medicare, *p. 223* Monthly, *p. 218*	Net pay, *p. 226* Overrides, *p. 221* Overtime, *p. 219* Payroll register, *p. 222* Percentage method, *p. 226* Semimonthly, *p. 218* Social Security, *p. 222* State income tax (SIT), *p. 226* State Unemployment Tax (SUTA), *p. 228* Straight commission, *p. 221* Variable commission scale, *p. 221* W-4, *p. 223* Wage bracket method, *p. 223* Weekly, *p. 218*

END-OF-CHAPTER PROBLEMS

Drill Problems

Additional homework assignments by learning unit are at the end of text in Appendix I (p. I–39). Solutions to odd problems are at the end of text in Appendix II.

Complete the following table:

	Employee	M	T	W	Th	F	Hours	Rate per hour	Gross pay
9–1.	Jim Gota	8	5	8	7	7	35	$4.95	$173.25
9–2.	Pete Joll	7	9	8	8	8	40	$7.00	$280.00

Complete the following table (assume the overtime for each employee is a time-and-a-half rate after 40 hours):

	Employee							Total regular hours	Total overtime hours	Regular rate	Overtime rate	Gross earnings
9–3.	Fast	10	9	9	9	9	3	40	9	$6.20	$ 9.30	$331.70
9–4.	Tagney	14	8	9	9	5	1	40	6	$7.60	$11.40	$372.40

9–3 work:
40 × $6.20 = $248.00
9 × $9.30 = 83.70
$331.70

9–4 work:
40 × $7.60 = $304.00
6 × $11.40 = 68.40
$372.40

Calculate gross earnings:

	Worker	Number of units produced	Rate per unit	Gross earnings
9–5.	Lang	315	$2.10	$661.50 (315 × $2.10)
9–6.	Swan	846	$ .58	$490.68($.58 × 846)

Calculate the gross earnings for each apple picker based on the following differential pay scale:

1–1,000	$.03 each
1,001–1,600	.05 each
Over 1,600	.07 each

	Apple picker	Number of apples picked	Gross earnings
9–7.	Ryan	1,600	$60 = (1,000 × $.03) + (600 × $.05)
9–8.	Rice	1,925	$82.75 = (1,000 × $.03) + (600 × $.05) + (325 × $.07)

	Employee	Total sales	Commission rate	Draw	End of month commission received
9–9.	Reese	$300,000	7%	$8,000	$13,000

(.07 × $300,000 = $21,000
− 8,000
$13,000)

Ron Company has the following commission schedule:

Commission rate	Sales
2%	Up to $80,000
3.5%	Excess of $80,000 to $100,000
4%	More than $100,000

Calculate the gross earnings of Ron Company's two employees:

	Employee	Total sales	Gross earnings
9-10.	Bill Moore	$ 70,000	$1,400 ($70,000 × .02)
9-11.	Ron Ear	$155,000	$4,500 ($80,000 × .02 = $1,600; $20,000 × .035 = 700; $55,000 × .04 = 2,200; $4,500)

Complete the following table, given that A Publishing Company pays its salespeople a weekly salary plus a 2% commission on all net sales over $5,000 (no commission on returned goods):

	Employee	Gross sales	Return	Net sales	Given quota	Commission sales	Commission rates	Total commission	Regular wage	Total wage
9-12.	Ring	$ 8,000	$ 25	$ 7,975	$5,000	$2,975	2%	$ 59.50	$250	$309.50
9-13.	Porter	$12,000	$100	$11,900	$5,000	$6,900	2%	$138.00	$250	$388.00

Calculate the Social Security and Medicare deduction for the following employees (assume a tax rate of 6.2% on $55,500 for Social Security and 1.45% on $130,200 for Medicare).

	Employee	Cumulative earnings before this pay period	Pay amount this period	Social Security	Medicare
9-14.	Wilson	$40,000	$1,200	$74.40	$17.40
		$1,200 × .062 = $74.40	$1,200 × .0145 = $17.40		
9-15.	Rosen	$55,400	$1,600	$ 6.20	$23.20
		$100 × .062 = $6.20	$1,600 × .0145 = $23.20		
9-16.	Brown	$70,000	$800	-0-	$11.60
			$800 × .0145 = $11.60		

Complete the following payroll register; calculate FIT by the wage bracket method for this weekly period; Social Security and Medicare are the same rates as in the previous problems. No one will reach the maximum for FICA.

	Employee	Marital status	Allowances claimed	Gross pay	FIT	FICA S.S.	FICA Med.	Net Pay
9-17.	Al Holland	M	2	$850	$105	$52.70	$12.33	$679.97
		S.S.: $850 × .062 = $52.70		Med.: $850 × .0145 = $12.33				
9-18.	Jill West	M	3	$1,250	$205	$77.50	$18.13	$949.37
		S.S.: $1,250 × .062 = $77.50		Med.: $1,250 × .0145 = $18.13				

Complete the following weekly payroll register; calculate FIT by percentage method; assume FICA maximum will not be reached by an employee; Social Security and Medicare are the same rates as in previous problems.

	Employee	Marital status	Exemptions claimed	Gross pay	FIT	FICA S.S.	FICA Med.	Net Pay
9-19.	Long	M	4	$1,700	$317.01	$105.40	$24.65	$1,252.94

$1,700.00
− 176.92 (4 × $44.23)
$1,523.08 = $103.35 + .28($763.08)
− 760.00 $103.35 + $213.66
$ 763.08 $317.01

S.S. = $1,700 × .062 = $105.40
Med. = $1,700 × .0145 = $24.65

9-20. Given the following, calculate amount of state (assume 5.3%) and federal unemployment tax the employer must pay for each of the first two quarters. Federal is .8% on first $7,000.

	Payroll summary	
	Quarter 1	Quarter 2
Bill Adams	$4,000	$ 8,000
Rich Haines	8,000	14,000
Alice Smooth	3,200	3,800

Quarter 1
Adams $ 4,000
Haines 7,000 *
Smooth 3,200
$14,200
× .053
SUTA = $752.60

Quarter 2
Adams $ 3,000 †
Haines -0-
Smooth 3,800
$ 6,800
× .053
SUTA = $360.40
FUTA = $ 54.40
($6,800 × .008)

.008 × $14,200 = $113.60 FUTA

* Note only first $7,000 is taxed.
† Only first $3,000 is taxed since that puts Adams over $7,000 for the year.

9–21. Jill Owens is married and is paid weekly. Her gross pay is $1,500. Calculate FIT by the percentage method. Jill claims three allowances.
$1,500.00
− 132.69 (3 × $44.23)
$1,367.31 = $103.35 + .28($607.31)
− 760.00 $103.35 + $170.05
$ 607.31 $273.40

Word Problems

9–22. Lion Corporation pays Red Roff $9.50 per hour. Last week Red worked 40 hours. This week Red worked 70 hours. Calculate Red's pay for each week. Red received time and a half for overtime.
Last week: 40 hours × $9.50 = $380.00 week 1
This week: 40 hours × $9.50 = $380.00
30 hours × $14.25 = 427.50
$807.50 week 2
($9.50 × 1.5)

9–23. Continental Corporation pays its employees on a 40-hour workweek. The company pays $1\frac{1}{2}$ times the regular hourly rate for time over 40 hours. Workers working on Sunday receive double time. Alice Soze worked the following hours:

M	T	W	Th	F	Sat	Sun
8	$7\frac{1}{2}$	$7\frac{1}{2}$	8	8	$7\frac{1}{2}$	$6\frac{1}{2}$

40 hours × $6 = $240.00
6.5 hours × $9 = 58.50
6.5 hours × $12 = 78.00 (Sunday)
$376.50

Assume a rate of $6 per hour. What is Alice's gross pay?

9–24. Dennis Toby is a salesclerk at Northwest Department Store. Dennis receives $8 per hour plus a commission of 3% on all sales. Assume Dennis works 30 hours and has sales of $1,900. What is his gross pay?
(30 hours × $8) + ($1,900 × .03) = $240 + $57 = $297

9–25. Blinn Corporation pays its employees on a graduated commission scale: 3% on first $40,000 sales; 4% on sales above $40,000 to $85,000; and 6% on sales greater than $85,000. Bill Burns had $87,000 sales. What commission did Bill earn?
$40,000 × .03 = $1,200
45,000 × .04 = 1,800
2,000 × .06 = 120
$3,120

9–26. Robin Hartman earns $600 per week plus 3% of sales over $6,500. Robin's sales are $14,000. How much does Robin earn?
$600 + (.03 × $7,500) = $600 + $225 = $825

9–27. Tom Mitchell is a salesperson who receives a $200 draw per week. He receives a 4% commission on all sales. Sales for Tony were $155,000 for the month. Assume a 5-week month. What did Tony receive after his draw?
.04 × $155,000 = $6,200
− 1,000
$5,200

9–28. Jewel Ross sells automobiles. She receives a $200 salary per week plus a 3% commission on all sales. During a 4-week period, Jewel's sales were $34,800. What were Jewel's average weekly earnings?
$\$800 + (.03 \times \$34{,}800) = \frac{\$800 + \$1{,}044}{4} = \$461$ per week

9–29. Warren Shanesy earns a gross salary of $1,200 each week. What is Warren's first week's deduction for Social Security and Medicare? Will any of Warren's wages be exempt from Social Security and Medicare for the calendar year? Assume a rate of 6.2% on $55,500 for Social Security and 1.45% on $130,200 for Medicare.

Social Security $1,200 × .062 = $74.40 Medicare $1,200 × .0145 = $17.40

Yes for Social Security 52 weeks × $1,200 = $62,400
− 55,500
$ 6,900 exempt

9–30. Richard Gaziano is a manager for Health Care, Inc. Health Care deducts Social Security, Medicare, and FIT from his earnings. Assume the same Social Security and Medicare rates as Problem 9–29. Before this payroll, Richard is $500 below the maximum level for Social Security earnings. Richard is married, paid weekly, and claims two exemptions. Use wage bracket Table 9–1 for FIT. What is Richard's net pay for the week if he earns $1,200?

Social Security $1,200
− 700
$ 500 × .062 = $31.00; FIT $203

Medicare $1,200 × .0145 = $17.40

$1,200 − $31 − $17.40 − $203 = $948.60

9–31. Joe Palino earned $1,750 for the last two weeks. He is married, paid biweekly, and claims three exemptions. What is Joe's income tax? Use the percentage method.

$1,750.00
− 265.38 ($88.46 × 3) Table 9–3
$1,484.62
− 142.00
$1,342.62 × .15 = $201.39

9–32. Westway Company pays Suzie Chan $1,500 per week. By the end of week 49, how much did Westway deduct for Suzie's Social Security and Medicare for the year? Assume Social Security is 6.2% on $55,500 and 1.45% for Medicare on $130,200. What state and federal unemployment tax does Westway pay on Suzie's yearly salary? The state unemployment rate is 5.1%. FUTA is .8%.

49 weeks × $1,500 = $73,500
Social Security $55,500 × .062 = $3,441
Medicare $73,500 × .0145 = $1,065.75

SUTA .051 × $7,000 = $357
FUTA .008 × $7,000 = $56

9–33. Morris Leste, owner of Carlson Company, has three employees who earn $400, $500, and $700 per week. What is the total state and federal unemployment taxes that Morris owes for the first 11 weeks of the year and for week 30? Assume a state rate of 5.6% and federal rate of .8%.

11 × $400 = $ 4,400
11 × $500 = 5,500
11 × $700 = 7,700
$17,600
− 700
$16,900

State: $16,900 × .056 = $946.40
Federal: $16,900 × .008 = $135.20
$0 for week 30

9–34. Barry Katz earned $150,000 this year. What did he pay in for Social Security and Medicare? Assume 6.2% on $55,500 for Social Security and 1.45% on $130,200 for Medicare.

Social Security $55,500 × .062 = $3,441
Medicare $130,200 × .0145 = $1,887.90

Challenge Problem
Checking Your Paycheck

9–35. Bill Rose is a salesperson for Boxes, Inc. He believes his $1,460.47 monthly paycheck is in error. Bill earns a $1,400 salary per month plus a 9.5% commission on sales over $1,500. Last month, Bill had $8,250 in sales. Bill believes his traveling expenses are 16% of his weekly gross earnings before commissions. Monthly deductions include Social Security, $120; Medicare, $33.30; FIT, $382.50; union dues, $25; and health insurance, $16.99. Calculate the following: **(a)** Bill's monthly take-home pay and indicate the amount his check was under- or overstated, and **(b)** Bill's weekly traveling expenses. Round final answer to nearest dollar.

a. $8,250
− 1,500
$6,750 × .095 = $641.25

$1,400.00 monthly salary
+ 641.25 commission
$2,041.25
− 120.00
− 33.30
− 382.50
− 25.00
− 16.99
$1,463.46 net pay Difference $2.99 too low.

b. $\frac{\$1{,}400 \times 12}{52} \times .16 = \$51.69 = \$52$

Summary Practice Test

Solutions are at end of text in Appendix II.

Quick Reference

If you get any wrong answers, study the page numbers given for each problem.

1. Calculate Bill's Gross pay (he is entitled to time and a half).

1. P. 219.

M	T	W	Th	F	Total hours	Rate per hour	Gross pay
$8\frac{1}{2}$	$9\frac{1}{2}$	$10\frac{1}{4}$	$9\frac{1}{2}$	$8\frac{3}{4}$	46.5	$6.50	$323.38

40 hours × $6.50 = $260.00
6.5 hours × $9.75 = $ 63.38
$323.38

2. Eartha Jackson sells shoes for Hall Shoes. Hall pays Eartha $6.25 per hour plus a 4% commission on all sales. Assume Eartha works 28 hours for the week and has $3,700 sales. What is Eartha's gross pay?

2. P. 221.

28 hours × $6.25 = $175
$3,700 × .04 = 148
$323

3. Riveria Company pays its employees on a graduated commission scale: 2% on the first $25,000 sales; 4% on sales from $25,000 to $95,000; and 6% on sales more than $95,000. Lisa Rooney, an employee of Riveria, has $120,000 in sales. What commission did Lisa earn?

3. P. 221.

.02 × $25,000 = $ 500
.04 × $70,000 = 2,800
.06 × $25,000 = 1,500
$4,800

4. Janice Tax, an accountant for Shakopee Corporation, earned $50,000 from January to June. In July, Janice earned $16,000. Assume a tax rate of 6.2% for Social Security on $55,500 and 1.45% on $130,200 for Medicare. How much is the July tax for Social Security and Medicare?

4. P. 223.

Social Security $55,500
− 50,000
$ 5,500 × .062 = $341

Medicare $16,000 × .0145 = $232

5. Barry Katz earns $1,275 per week. He is married and claims two exemptions. What is Barry's income tax? Use the percentage method.

5. P. 226.

$1,275.00
− 88.46 (2 × $44.23)
$1,186.54
− 760.00 $103.35 + .28($426.54) = $222.78
$ 426.54

6. Dave Newhall pays his two employees $390 and $625 per week. Assume a state unemployment rate of 5.8% and a federal unemployment rate of .8%. What state and federal unemployment tax will Dave pay at end of quarter 1 and quarter 2?

6. P. 228.

Quarter 1 13 weeks × $390 = $5,070
13 weeks × $625 = $8,125

Taxable $5,070 + $7,000 = $12,070 × .058 = $700.06 SUTA
FUTA = $12,070 × .008 = $96.56

Quarter 2 $7,000 − $5,070 = $1,930 × .058 = $111.94 SUTA
$1,930 × .008 = $15.44 FUTA

Project A

Airlines Boost Travel Agent Payments for Some Flights

By JONATHAN DAHL
Staff Reporter of THE WALL STREET JOURNAL

TRAVEL

Travel agent commissions have just jumped on some key East Coast flights, and some industry followers say the increases could spread elsewhere.

Continental Airlines and USAir this month started offering major travel agencies a $50 bonus—on top of their usual 10% to 15% commission—for round trip flights on 10 major routes out of New York City Travel experts call the commission an alarmingly large reward that could easily sway agencies to recommend those carriers even if the fares or flights aren't in the traveler's best interest.

"The airlines wouldn't be offering this if they didn't think it would affect a travel agent's behavior," says Doug Birdsall, president of Travelmation Inc., a Stamford, Conn.-based travel management company. Adds John Holland, publisher of the Business Flyer: "To me, this is like bribery."

Continental concedes the size of the offer is unusual; other industry followers called it unprecedented. The carrier also says the offer will expire at the end of June and insists it won't spread to other markets. The unit of **Continental Holdings Inc.** said it only raised the commission ante to promote some new flights out of New York.

But industry followers note that the offer already has spread from four routes out of New York to 10 in less than a week. And Northwest Airlines, another major New York carrier, says it is studying the move. "I think you'll start to see this in some other major cities," says Mr. Holland. "The airlines are fighting ways to get more market share without having to lower fares and go bankrupt."

Travel agents insist they wouldn't go against a customer's best interest because that could risk losing their business. "Nobody's going to push a flight that's a lot more expensive," says Philip Davidoff, president of the American Society of Travel Agents. But industry followers say that because air fares change so fast, travelers have no way of knowing if their agent is getting the best deal. And agents are unlikely to tell travelers about any special commissions.

Many agents are also under pressure to boost revenue because the travel business is coming off one of its worst slumps in years. Airline traffic—and thus travel agent commissions—began slowing last year and dropped sharply during the Mideast war. Some agencies are also hurting because corporate clients are starting to demand part of an agent's commission. Agencies that don't agree to this arrangement can risk losing the client.

Although travelers can contact airlines directly, more than 80% of them book their flights with travel agencies. Agents usually get 10% commission on tickets, plus an additional 1% to 5% that is often based on the number of flights they ticket on a certain carrier. Under the new offer, an agent could almost double his or her take on certain tickets. The extra money, at a minimum, would mean that an agent wouldn't lose money on very low-priced tickets; the cost of booking a ticket sometimes exceeds the actual commission on fares of less than $200.

USAir, a unit of **USAir Group Inc.**, wouldn't provide many details on its offer. A spokesman for Continental said the bonus was offered mainly to the major agencies that book flights for corporate customers, although vacation travelers sometimes book flights with these agents, too. The bonus of $25 on one-way tickets and $50 on round trip flights applies to unrestricted fares—those used mainly by business fliers.

Continental said it originally offered the bonus on flights out of New York to Detroit, Atlanta, Buffalo, N.Y., and Columbus, Ohio. The carrier said it started the offer because it recently added some new service out of LaGuardia airport.

Visit a travel agency and see their reaction to this article. What are the current commission rates?

NOTES

THAT WAS THEN . . .
. . . THIS IS NOW

In the 1930s, all bank dealings needed to be done in the bank itself. Today, computerized operations using ATMs allow transactions to occur without having to wait for the bank to open and funds to be transferred electronically.

10

Simple Interest

LEARNING UNIT OBJECTIVES

LU 10–1: Calculation of Simple Interest

1. Define interest, principal, rate, and time. *p. 240.*
2. Calculate simple interest for months and years. *p. 241.*
3. Calculate interest by:
   a. Exact time, exact interest. *p. 241*
   b. Exact time, ordinary interest. *p. 242.*
4. Explain the advantage of borrowing to get a cash discount. *pp. 242–43.*

LU 10–2: Finding Unknown in Simple Interest Formula

1. Using the interest formula, calculate the unknown when the other two are given (principal, rate, or time). *pp. 244–45.*

LU 10–3: U.S. Rule versus Merchant's Rule in Making Partial Note Payments before Due Date

1. List the steps to complete the U.S. Rule and Merchant's Rule. *pp. 246–47.*
2. Complete the proper interest credits under the U.S. Rule and Merchant's Rule. *pp. 246–47.*

We live in a credit society. Many people—and businesses—"buy now and pay later." We may be short of cash and still buy a luxury item, especially if we can buy it at a discount. However, everything has a price. The price we pay for "buy now and pay later" is **interest.** Think of interest as a rental charge for money.

When we borrow money from banks or mortgage companies, the rate of interest greatly affects our payments. This is why homeowners often refinance their mortgage when interest rates are low. As you can see from the following *Wall Street Journal* clipping, large corporations also try to cut their interest expense.

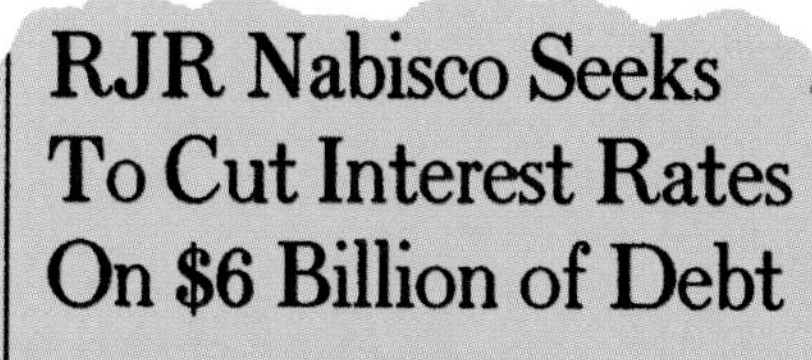
RJR Nabisco Seeks To Cut Interest Rates On $6 Billion of Debt

By a WALL STREET JOURNAL *Staff Reporter*

NEW YORK—**RJR Nabisco** Inc. is seeking to reduce the interest rates it is paying on some of its $6 billion in bank debt.

According to individuals with knowledge of the negotiations, RJR approached its banks in recent weeks to try to renegotiate at least a portion of its debt.

An RJR spokesman said the company

If you have money in a savings institution, the institution pays *you* interest. Often it is difficult to determine the actual rate of interest you are receiving. The new Truth in Savings law enacted in March 1993 forces savings institutions to reveal their real rate of interest, or **annual percentage yield** (APY). Under this law, depositors must be told the actual return they will receive on a $100 deposit for a year (365 days). No longer will depositors receive interest determined by their lowest balance during the month. Obviously, all depositors welcome this long-awaited law.

The principles in this chapter apply whether we are paying interest or receiving interest. Let's begin by learning how to calculate simple interest.

LEARNING UNIT 10–1 CALCULATION OF SIMPLE INTEREST

Garry Gray/The Image Bank

Jim Edward, a young attorney, rented an office in a professional building. Since Jim recently graduated from law school, he was short of cash. To purchase office furniture for his new office, Jim went to his bank and borrowed $30,000 for 6 months at an 8% annual interest rate.

The original amount Jim borrowed ($30,000) is the **principal** (face value) of the loan. Jim's price for using the $30,000 is the interest rate (8%) the bank charges on a yearly basis. Since Jim is borrowing the $30,000 for six months, this is the **time** or period that Jim has to repay the loan. *Loan time periods can be days, months, or years.*

At the end of six months, Jim's loan will have a **maturity value** of $31,200—the principal plus the interest on the loan. Thus, Jim's price for using the furniture before he can pay for it is $1,200. To make this calculation, we use the following formula:

$$\text{Maturity value } (MV) = \text{Principal } (P) + \text{Interest } (I)$$

$$\downarrow \qquad \downarrow \qquad \downarrow$$

$$\$31,200 = \$30,000 + \$1,200$$

Jim's furniture purchase introduces **simple interest**—the cost of a loan, usually for one year or less. Simple interest is only on the original principal or amount borrowed. Let's begin this unit by examining how the bank calculated Jim's $1,200 interest.

Simple Interest Formula

The **simple interest formula** is:

$$\text{Interest } (I) = \text{Principal } (P) \times \text{Rate } (R) \times \text{Time } (T)$$

We can use this formula to determine the cost of borrowing money for months and years.

In your calculator, multiply $30,000 times .08 times 6. Divide your answer by 12.

EXAMPLE Jim Edwards borrowed $30,000 for office furniture. The loan was for six months at an annual interest rate of 8%. What is Jim's interest and maturity value?

Using the simple interest formula, the bank determined Jim's interest as follows:

Step 1: Calculate interest.

$$I = \underset{(P)}{\$30{,}000} \times \underset{(R)}{.08} \times \underset{(T)}{\frac{6}{12}} = \$1{,}200$$

Step 2: Calculate maturity value.

$$MV = \underset{(P)}{\$30{,}000} + \underset{(I)}{\$1{,}200} = \boxed{\$31{,}200}$$

Now let's use the same example and assume Jim borrowed the $30,000 for 1 year. The bank would calculate Jim's interest and maturity value as follows:

Step 1: Calculate interest.

$$I = \underset{(P)}{\$30{,}000} \times \underset{(R)}{.08} \times \underset{(T)}{1 \text{ year}} = \$2{,}400$$

Step 2. Calculate maturity value.

$$MV = \$30{,}000 + \$2{,}400 = \boxed{\$32{,}400}$$

Let's use the same example again and assume Jim borrowed the $30,000 for 18 months. Then the interest would be:

Step 1: Calculate interest.

$$I = \underset{(P)}{\$30{,}000} \times \underset{(R)}{.08} \times \underset{(T)}{\frac{18}{12}}\text{[1]} = \$3{,}600$$

Step 2: Calculate maturity value.

$$MV = \underset{(P)}{\$30{,}000} + \underset{(I)}{\$3{,}600} = \boxed{\$33{,}600}$$

Now we'll turn our attention to two common methods we can use to calculate simple interest.

Two Methods for Calculating Simple Interest

From the Business Math Handbook

July 6 187th day
March 4 − 63rd day
124 days (exact time of loan)

Note: If Handbook is not used, first day of note is not counted but last day is.

March	*31*
	− 4
	27
April	*30*
May	*31*
June	*30*
July	*+ 6*
	124 days

Method 1: Exact Time, Exact Interest (365 days) The Federal Reserve Banks and the federal government use the **exact time, exact interest** method. This method calculates interest by using the following fraction to represent the time in the formula $I = P \times R \times T$:

$$\text{Time} = \frac{\text{Exact number of days}}{365}$$

Exact number of days ← Exact time; 365 ← Exact interest

For this calculation, we will use the exact day-in-a-year calendar from the Business Math Handbook. In Chapter 7, page 173, we covered how to use the calendar.

EXAMPLE On March 4, Peg Carry borrowed $40,000 at 8% interest. Interest and principal are due on July 6. What is the interest cost and the maturity value?

Step 1: Calculate interest.

$$I = P \times R \times T$$
$$= \$40{,}000 \times .08 \times \frac{124}{365}$$
$$= \$1{,}087.12 \text{ (rounded to nearest cent)}$$

[1] This is the same as 1.5 years.

Step 2. Calculate maturity value.

$$MV = P + I$$
$$= \$40{,}000 + \$1{,}087.12$$
$$= \$41{,}087.12$$

Method 2: Exact Time, Ordinary Interest (360 Days) In the **exact time, ordinary interest** method, time in the formula $I = P \times R \times T$ is equal to:

$$\text{Time} = \frac{\text{Exact number of days}}{360}$$

Exact time (just like Method 1)

Ordinary interest

Courtesy of Board of Governors of the Federal Reserve System

Since banks commonly use the exact time, ordinary interest method, it is known as the **Banker's Rule.** Banks charge a slightly higher rate of interest because they use 360 days instead of 365 in the denominator. By using 360 instead of 365, the calculation is supposedly simplified. Consumer groups, however, are questioning why banks can use 360 days since this benefits the bank and not the customer. The use of computers and calculators no longer makes the simplified calculation necessary. For example, after a court case in Oregon, banks began calculating interest on 365 days except in mortgages.

Now let's replay the Peg Carry example we used to illustrate Method 1 to see the difference in bank interest when we use Method 2.

EXAMPLE On March 4, Peg Carry borrowed $40,000 at 8% interest. Interest and principal are due on July 6. What is the interest cost and the maturity value?

The exact time, ordinary interest method results in higher interest because the bank bases the loan on 360 days instead of 365.

Step 1: Calculate interest.

$$I = \$40{,}000 \times .08 \times \frac{124}{360}$$
$$= \$1{,}102.22$$

Step 2. Calculate maturity value.

$$MV = P + I$$
$$= \$40{,}000 + \$1{,}102.22$$
$$= \$41{,}102.22$$

Note: By using Method 2, the bank increases its interest by $15.10.

$1,102.22	(Method 2)
− 1,087.12	(Method 1)
$ 15.10	

Cash Discounts versus Borrowing

You can use the following steps to decide whether you should borrow money to take advantage of a cash discount.

Steps for Computing Cash Discounts versus Borrowing

Step 1. Calculate cash discount.

Step 2. Calculate interest.

$$I = P \times R \times \frac{T}{360}$$

P ↑ Price after discount

T: Difference between the credit and discount period

Step 3. Calculate savings.
Cash discount − Cost of borrowing

EXAMPLE Tina Meese bought a $600 computer desk with 2/10, n/60 terms. She does not have the cash to pay for the desk in 10 days. Is it worthwhile for Tina to borrow the money (using ordinary interest) at 11% and take advantage of the cash discount?

The following calculations answer this question for Tina:

Step 1. Cash discount = $600 × .02 = $12.00

Step 2. Interest = Purchase price after cash discount × Rate × Time

$I = \$588 \times .11 \times \frac{50}{360}$

↑

(\$600 − \$12)

$I = \$8.98$

Since the cash discount is for the first 10 days, we need not borrow the money till the 10th day, leaving 50 $\left(\begin{array}{r}60\\-10\end{array}\right)$ days for loan. Note we only borrow \$588.

Step 3. Savings from borrowing:

\$12.00	cash discount
− 8.98	interest on loan
\$3.02	savings

Many banks will have a minimum charge for loans.

Now let's check your progress with the Practice Quiz.

LU 10–1 PRACTICE QUIZ

Calculate simple interest (round to nearest cent):

1. \$13,000 at 5% for 7 months.
2. \$25,000 at 7% for 5 years.
3. \$40,000 at $10\frac{1}{2}\%$ for 19 months.
4. On May 4, Dawn Kristal borrowed \$15,000 at 8%. Dawn must pay the principal and interest on August 10. What are Dawn's simple interest and maturity value if you use the exact time, exact interest method?
5. What are Dawn Kristal's (Problem 4) simple interest and maturity value if you use exact time, ordinary interest?
6. Glenn Eshun bought a \$10,000 computer with 2/10, n/30 terms. Assume Glenn pays for the computer with 12% borrowed funds to take advantage of the cash discount. What would be Glenn's net savings? Use the exact time, ordinary interest method.

SOLUTIONS TO LU 10–1 PRACTICE QUIZ

1. $\$13{,}000 \times .05 \times \frac{7}{12} = \$379.17$
2. $\$25{,}000 \times .07 \times 5 = \$8{,}750$
3. $\$40{,}000 \times .105 \times \frac{19}{12} = \$6{,}650$
4. August 10 → 222
   May 4 → − 124
   98

   $\$15{,}000 \times .08 \times \frac{98}{365} = \$322.19$

   $MV = \$15{,}000 + \$322.19 = \$15{,}322.19$
5. $\$15{,}000 \times .08 \times \frac{98}{360} = \$326.67$ $\quad MV = \$15{,}000 + \$326.67 = \$15{,}326.67$
6. $\$10{,}000 \times .02 = \$200$ cash discount

   $I = \$9{,}800 \times .12 \times \frac{20}{360} = \$65.33$

   Savings: $\$200 - \$65.33 = \$134.67$

LEARNING UNIT 10–2 FINDING UNKNOWN IN SIMPLE INTEREST FORMULA

Up to this point, we solved for interest in the formula:

$$\text{Interest } (I) = \text{Principal } (P) \times \text{Rate } (R) \times \text{Time } (T)$$

Now we will show how to solve for principal, rate, and time. In all our calculations, we use 360 days and round only final answers.

Finding the Principal

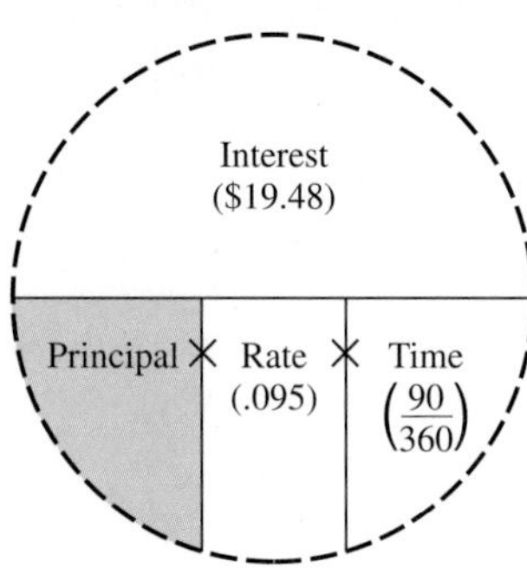

EXAMPLE Tim Jarvis paid the bank $19.48 interest at 9.5% for 90 days. How much did Tim borrow?

The formula for calculating the principal of a loan is:

$$\text{Principal} = \frac{\text{Interest}}{\text{Rate} \times \text{Time}}$$

Note how we illustrated this in the margin. The shaded area is what we are solving for. When solving for principal, rate, or time, you are dividing. Interest will be in the numerator, and the denominator will be the other two elements multiplied times each other.

Step 1. Set up formula. $P = \dfrac{\$19.48}{.095 \times \dfrac{90}{360}}$

Step 2. Multiply denominator. .095 times 90 divided by 360 (do not round)

$P = \dfrac{\$19.48}{.02375}$

When using a calculator, press:

[.095] [×] [90] [÷] [360] [M+]

Step 3. Divide numerator by the result of Step 2. $P = \$820.21$

When using a calculator, press:

[19.48] [÷] [MR] [=]

Step 4. Check your answer. $\$19.48 = \$820.21 \times .095 \times \dfrac{90}{360}$

(*I*) (*P*) (*R*) (*T*)

Finding the Rate

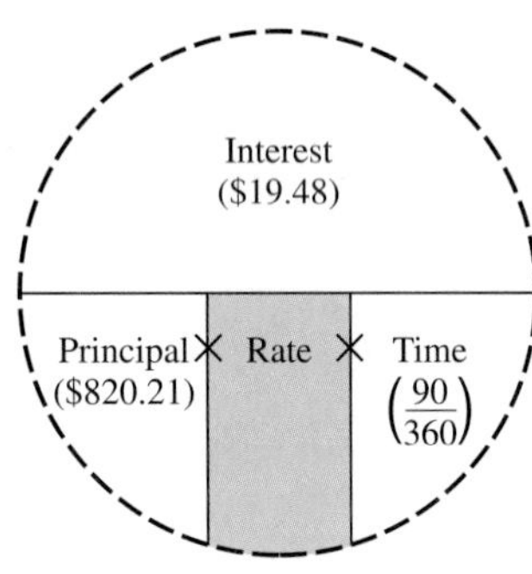

EXAMPLE Tim Jarvis borrowed $820.21 from a bank. Tim's interest is $19.48 for 90 days. What rate of interest did Tim pay?

The formula to calculate the rate of interest is:

$$\text{Rate} = \frac{\text{Interest}}{\text{Principal} \times \text{Time}}$$

Step 1. Set up formula. $R = \dfrac{\$19.48}{\$820.21 \times \dfrac{90}{360}}$

Step 2. Multiply denominator. $R = \dfrac{\$19.48}{\$205.0525}$

Do not round answer. $820.21 times 90 divided by 360

When using a calculator, press:

[820.21] [×] [90] [÷] [360] [M+]

Step 3. Divide numerator by the result of Step 2. $R = 9.5\%$

When using a calculator, press:

[19.48] [÷] [MR] [%]

Step 4. Check your answer. $\$19.48 = \$820.21 \times .095 \times \dfrac{90}{360}$

(*I*) (*P*) (*R*) (*T*)

Finding the Time

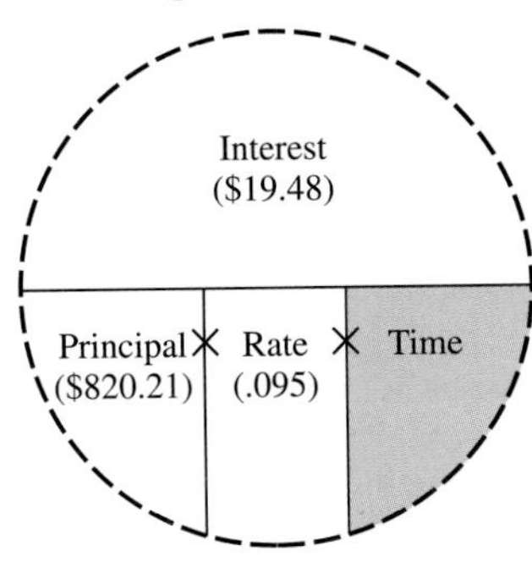

EXAMPLE Tim Jarvis borrowed $820.21 from a bank. Tim's interest is $19.48 at 9.5%. How much time does Jim have to repay the loan?

The formula to calculate time is:

$$\text{Time (in years)} = \frac{\text{Interest}}{\text{Principal} \times \text{Rate}}$$

Step 1. Set up formula. $T = \dfrac{\$19.48}{\$820.21 \times .095}$

Step 2. Multiply denominator. $T = \dfrac{\$19.48}{\$77.91995}$

Do not round the answer.
When using a calculator, press:

820.21 × .095 M+

Step 3. Divide numerator by the result of Step 3. $T = .25$ years
When using a calculator, press:

19.48 ÷ MR =

Step 4. Convert years to days (assume 360 days). $.25 \times 360 =$ **90 days**

Step 5. Check your answer. $\$19.48 = \$820.21 \times .095 \times \dfrac{90}{360}$

$(I) \quad (P) \quad (R) \quad (T)$

LU 10-2 PRACTICE QUIZ

Complete (assume 360 days):

	Principal	Interest rate	Time (days)	Simple interest
1.	?	9%	60 days	$15,000
2.	$7,000	?	220 days	350
3.	$1,000	8%	?	300

SOLUTIONS TO LU 10-2 PRACTICE QUIZ

1. $\dfrac{\$15{,}000}{.09 \times \dfrac{60}{360}} = \dfrac{\$15{,}000}{.015} = \$1{,}000{,}000 \qquad P = \dfrac{I}{R \times T}$

2. $\dfrac{\$350}{\$7{,}000 \times \dfrac{220}{360}} = \dfrac{\$350}{\$4{,}277.7777} = 8.18\% \qquad R = \dfrac{I}{P \times T}$
(do not round)

3. $\dfrac{\$300}{\$1{,}000 \times .08} = \dfrac{\$300}{\$80} = 3.75 \times 360 = 1{,}350 \text{ days} \qquad T = \dfrac{I}{P \times R}$

LEARNING UNIT 10-3 U.S. RULE VERSUS MERCHANT'S RULE IN MAKING PARTIAL NOTE PAYMENTS BEFORE DUE DATE

Often a person may want to pay off a debt in more than one payment before the maturity date. The U.S. Rule and Merchant's Rule allow the borrower to receive proper interest credits. Let's first look at the U.S. Rule.

U.S. Rule

The Supreme Court originated the U.S. Rule in the case of Story v. Livingston.

The **U.S. Rule** states that any partial loan payment first covers any interest that has built up. The remainder of the partial payment reduces the loan principal. Courts or legal proceedings generally use the U.S. Rule.

EXAMPLE Joe Mill owes $5,000 on an 11%, 90-day note. On day 50, Joe pays $600 on the note. On day 80, Joe makes an $800 additional payment. Assume a 360-day year. What is Joe's adjusted balance after day 50 and day 80? What is the ending balance due?

U.S. Rule	**U.S. Rule calculations**
To calculate $600 payment on day 50:	
Step 1. Calculate interest on principal from date of loan to date of first principal payment. Round to nearest cent.	$I = P \times R \times T$ $I = \$5{,}000 \times .11 \times \frac{50}{360}$ $I = \$76.39$
Step 2. Apply partial payment to interest due. Subtract remainder of payment from principal. This is the **adjusted balance** (principal).	$600.00 payment − 76.39 interest $523.61 → $5,000.00 principal − 523.61 $4,476.39 adjusted balance—(principal)
To calculate $800 payment on day 80:	
Step 3. Calculate interest on adjusted balance that starts from previous payment date and goes to new payment date. Then apply Step 2 above.	Compute interest on $4,476.39 for 30 days (80 − 50) $I = \$4{,}476.39 \times .11 \times \frac{30}{360}$ $I = \$41.03$ $800.00 payment − 41.03 interest $758.97 → $4,476.39 − 758.97 $3,717.42 adjusted balance
Step 4. At maturity, calculate interest from last partial payment. *Add* this interest to adjusted balance.	Ten days are left on note since last payment. $I = \$3{,}717.42 \times .11 \times \frac{10}{360}$ $I = \$11.36$ Balance owed = $3,728.78 ($3,717.42 + $11.36)

Note that when Joe makes two partial payments, Joe's total interest is $128.78 ($76.39 + $41.03 + $11.36). If Joe repaid the entire loan after 90 days, his interest payment would have been $137.50—a total savings of $8.72.

Now let's see how Joe would come out under the Merchant's Rule.

Merchant's Rule

Some customers prefer the **Merchant's Rule** since it results in less interest costs. When the loan does not involve court action, the merchant's rule is sometimes used. Let's replay our example.

EXAMPLE Joe Mill owes \$5,000 on a 11%, 90-day note. On day 50, Joe pays \$600 on the note. On day 80, Joe makes an \$800 additional payment. Assume a 360-day year. What is Joe's adjusted balance after day 50 and day 80? What is the ending balance due?

Merchant's Rule	**Merchant's Rule calculations**
Step 1. Calculate maturity value.	$I = P \times R \times T$ $I = \$5{,}000 \times .11 \times \frac{90}{360}$ total length of loan $I = \$137.50$ $MV = P + I$ $= \$5{,}000 + \$137.50$ $= \$5{,}137.50$
To calculate \$600 payment on day 50:	
Step 2. Calculate days remaining on loan from date of partial payment. Then calculate interest for this period on the *partial payment*. Why? To save on interest costs from date of payment until end of period on amount paid.	$90 - 50 = 40$ days left — Numerator is number of days left to go. $I = \$600 \times .11 \times \frac{40}{360} = \$7.33$
Step 3. Add partial payment *plus* interest and subtract it from total amount of loan to arrive at new balance.	\$5,137.50 (Step 1) − 607.33 (\$600.00 + \$7.33) \$4,530.17
To calculate \$800 payment on day 80:	
Step 4. Continue Steps 2 and 3 for each partial payment. This results in lowering adjusted balance until you reach ending balance.	10 days left $I = \$800 \times .11 \times \frac{10}{360} = \$\ 2.44$ + 800.00 (partial payment) \$802.44 \$4,530.17 − 802.44 **\$3,727.73** ending balance due

We can prove the ending balance by taking the total amount of the loan less each partial payment plus the interest that we saved. Joe's total interest under the Merchant's Rule is \$127.73 (\$137.50 − \$7.33 − \$2.44) compared to \$128.78 (p. 246) under the U.S. Rule. The Merchant's Rule also has a lower ending balance due (\$3,727.73 versus \$3,728.78).

Once again, it's time to test what you have learned by taking the following Practice Quiz.

LU 10-3 PRACTICE QUIZ

Polly Flin borrowed \$5,000 for 60 days at 8%. On day 10, Polly made a \$600 partial payment. On day 40, Polly made a \$1,900 partial payment. What is Polly's ending balance due under the U.S. Rule and the Merchant's Rule (assume a 360-day year)?

SOLUTIONS TO LU 10–3 PRACTICE QUIZ

U.S. Rule

$\$5{,}000 \times .08 \times \frac{10}{360} = \$11.11$

\$600.00	\$5,000.00
− 11.11	− 588.89
\$588.89	\$4,411.11

$\$4{,}411.11 \times .08 \times \frac{30}{360} = \$29.41$

\$1,900.00	\$4,411.11
− 29.41	− 1,870.59
\$1,870.59	\$2,540.52

$\$2{,}540.52 \times .08 \times \frac{20}{360} = \$11.29$

\$ 11.29
+ 2,540.52
\$2,551.81

Merchant's Rule

$\$5{,}000 \times .08 \times \frac{60}{360} = $ \$ 66.67
+ 5,000.00
\$5,066.67 *MV*

$\$600 \times .08 \times \frac{50}{360} = $ \$ 6.67
+ 600.00
\$606.67

\$5,066.67
− 606.67
\$4,460.00

$\$1{,}900 \times .08 \times \frac{20}{360} = $ \$ 8.44
+ 1,900.00
\$1,908.44

\$4,460.00
− \$1,908.44
\$2,551.56

CHAPTER ORGANIZER: A REFERENCE GUIDE

Page	Topic	Key point, procedure, formula	Example(s) to illustrate situation
240	Simple interest for months	Interest = Principal × Rate × Time (*I*) (*P*) (*R*) (*T*)	\$2,000 at 9% for 17 months $I = \$2{,}000 \times .09 \times \frac{17}{12}$ $I = \$255$
241	Exact time, exact interest	$T = \frac{\text{Exact number of days}}{365}$ $I = P \times R \times T$	\$1,000 at 10% from January 5 to February 20 $I = \$1{,}000 \times .10 \times \frac{46}{365}$ Feb. 20: 51 days Jan. 5: − 5 days 46 days $I = \$12.60$
242	Exact time, ordinary interest (Banker's Rule)	$T = \frac{\text{Exact number of days}}{360}$ $I = P \times R \times T$ Higher interest costs	$I = \$1{,}000 \times .10 \times \frac{46}{360}$ (51 − 5) $I = \$12.78$
242	Cash discounts versus borrowing	Borrowing could make cash discounts attractive. Interest is calculated by: (Purchase price after cash discount) × Rate × $\frac{\text{Days money borrowed}}{360}$ Days money borrowed = Credit period − Discount period	Use the example above for Banker's Rule if terms were 2/10, n/30 to borrow the \$1,000 to buy a chair: $\$980 \times .10 \times \frac{20 \text{ days}}{360} = \$5.44$ \$20.00 (cash discount) − \$5.44 (cost of borrowing) = \$14.56 (savings)
244	Finding unknown in simple interest formula (use 360 days)	$I = P \times R \times T$	Use this example for illustrations of simple interest formula parts: \$1,000 loan at 9%, 60 days $I = \$1{,}000 \times .09 \times \frac{60}{360} = \$15$

Page	Topic	Key point, procedure, formula	Example(s) to illustrate situation
244	Finding the principal	$P = \frac{I}{R \times T}$	$P = \frac{\$15}{.09 \times \frac{60}{360}} = \frac{\$15}{.015} = \$1{,}000$
244	Finding the rate	$R = \frac{I}{P \times T}$	$R = \frac{\$15}{\$1{,}000 \times \frac{60}{360}} = \frac{\$15}{166.66666} = .09$ $= 9\%$ Note: We did not round the denominator.
245	Finding the time	$T = \frac{I}{P \times R}$ (in years) Multiply answer times 360 days to convert answer to days for ordinary interest.	$T = \frac{\$15}{\$1{,}000 \times .09} = \frac{\$15}{\$90} = .1666666$ $.1666666 \times 360 = 59.99 = 60$ days
246	U.S. Rule (use 360 days)	Calculate interest on principal from date of loan to date of first partial payment. Calculate adjusted balance by subtracting from principal the partial payment less interest cost. The process continues for future partial payments with the adjusted balance used to calculate cost of interest from last payment to present payment. Balance owed equals last adjusted balance plus interest cost from last partial payment to final due date.	12%, 120 days, \$2,000 *Partial payments:* On day 40; \$250 On day 60; \$200 *First payment:* $I = \$2{,}000 \times .12 \times \frac{40}{360}$ $I = \$26.67$ \$250.00 payment − 26.67 interest \$223.33 \$2,000.00 principal − 223.33 \$1,776.67 adjusted balance *Second payment:* $I = \$1{,}776.67 \times .12 \times \frac{20}{360}$ $I = \$11.84$ \$200.00 payment − 11.84 interest \$188.16 \$1,776.67 − 188.16 \$1,588.51 adjusted balance *60 days left:* $\$1{,}588.51 \times .12 \times \frac{60}{360} = \$31.77$ \$1,588.51 + \$31.77 = \$1,620.28 balance due Total interest = \$26.67 11.84 + 31.77 \$70.28

Page	Topic	Key point, procedure, formula	Example(s) to illustrate situation
247	Merchant's Rule	Calculate maturity value. Calculate number of days left on loan from date of partial payment. Interest is calculated on partial payment for this period of time. Add partial payment plus interest and subtract it from total amount of loan to arrive at new balance. This continues for each partial payment. Final balance due Total interest cost	Same situation as U.S. Rule: $I = \$2,000 \times .12 \times \frac{120}{360} = \$80$ $80.00 + $2,000 = $2,080.00 *MV* *First payment:* 120 days − 40 = 80 days left to go $\$250 \times .12 \times \frac{80}{360} = \$6.67 + \$250$ $2,080.00 total amount of loan − 256.67 partial payment plus interest $1,823.33 adjusted balance *Second payment:* $\$200 \times .12 \times \frac{60}{360} = \$4.00 + \$200$ $1,823.33 − 204.00 $1,619.33 ending balance $69.33 interest cost ($80.00 − $6.67 − $4.00)
	Key terms	Adjusted balance, *p. 246* Annual percentage yield, *p. 240* Banker's Rule, *p. 242* Exact time, exact interest, *p. 241* Exact time, ordinary interest, *p. 242* Interest, *p. 240* Maturity value, *p. 240*	Merchant's Rule, *p. 247* Principal, *p. 240* Simple interest, *p. 240* Simple interest formula, *p. 243* Time, *p. 241* U.S. Rule, *p. 246*

END-OF-CHAPTER PROBLEMS

Drill Problems

Additional homework assignments by learning unit are at the end of text in Appendix I (p. I–43). Solutions to odd problems are at the end of text in Appendix II.

Calculate the simple interest and maturity value (round to nearest cent as needed):

	Principal	Interest rate	Time	Simple interest	Maturity value
10–1.	$3,000	$5\frac{1}{2}\%$	18 mos.	$247.50	$3,247.50
			$\$3{,}000 \times .055 \times \frac{18}{12} = \$247.50$		
10–2.	$4,000	6%	$1\frac{1}{4}$ yrs.	$300.00	$4,300.00
			$\$4{,}000 \times .06 \times \frac{15}{12} = \$300$		
10–3.	$600	$9\frac{1}{4}\%$	7 mos.	$32.38	$632.38
			$\$600 \times .0925 \times \frac{7}{12} = \$32.38$		

Complete the following using exact time, ordinary interest: $T = \frac{\text{Exact no. of days}}{360}$

	Principal	Interest rate	Date borrowed	Date repaid	Exact time	Interest	Maturity value
10–4.	$1,000	8%	Mar. 8	June 9	93	$20.67	$1,020.67
			67	160			
			$\$1{,}000 \times .08 \times \frac{93}{360} = \$20.67$				
10–5.	$585	9%	June 5	Dec. 15	193	$28.23	$ 613.23
			156	349			
			$\$585 \times .09 \times \frac{193}{360} = \$28.23$				
10–6.	$1,200	12%	July 7	Jan. 10	187	$74.80	$1,274.80
			188	10			
			(365 − 188 = 177 + 10) $\$1{,}200 \times .12 \times \frac{187}{360} = \$74.80$				

Complete the following using exact time, exact interest: $T = \frac{\text{Exact no. of days}}{365}$

	Principal	Interest rate	Date borrowed	Date repaid	Exact time	Interest	Maturity value
10–7.	$1,000	8%	Mar. 8	June 9	93	$20.38	$1,020.38
			67	160			
			$\$1{,}000 \times .08 \times \frac{93}{365} = \$20.38$				
10–8.	$585	9%	June 5	Dec. 15	193	$27.84	$ 612.84
			156	349			
			$\$585 \times .09 \times \frac{193}{365} = \$27.84$				
10–9.	$1,200	12%	July 7	Jan. 10	187	$73.78	$1,273.78
			188	10			
			(365 − 188 = 177 + 10) $\$1{,}200 \times .12 \times \frac{187}{365} = \$73.78$				

Is it worth borrowing to take advantage of a cash discount? If so, by how much?

10–10. **Given** $7,000 dining set, terms 3/10, n/30. Cost of borrowing is $11\frac{1}{2}\%$.

$I = \$6{,}790 \times .115 \times \frac{20}{360}$
↑
($7,000 × .97)
= $43.38

Savings = $210 − $43.38 = $166.62
↑
(.03 × $7,000)

Solving the missing item:

	Principal	Interest rate	Time (months years)	Simple interest	
10–11.	$500	10%	? 2 years	$100	$T = \frac{\$100}{\$500 \times .10} = \frac{\$100}{\$50} = 2$
10–12.	? $1,904.76	7%	$1\frac{1}{2}$ years	$200	$P = \frac{\$200}{.07 \times \frac{18}{12}} = \$1{,}904.76$
10–13.	$5,000	? 12%	6 months	$300	$R = \frac{\$300}{\$5{,}000 \times \frac{6}{12}} = .12$

10–14. Solve by the U.S. Rule and the Merchant's Rule for total interest costs, balances, and final payments (use ordinary interest).

Given Principal: $10,000, 8%, 240 days
Partial payments: On 100th day, $4,000
On 180th day, $2,000

U.S. Rule

8%, 100 days, $10,000

$I = \$10{,}000 \times .08 \times \frac{100}{360} = \$222.22$

$4,000.00 − 222.22 = $3,777.78
$10,000.00 − 3,777.78 = $ 6,222.22 adjusted balance

$\$6{,}222.22 \times .08 \times \frac{80}{360} = \$110.62$

$2,000.00 − 110.62 = $1,889.38
$6,222.22 − 1,889.38 = $4,332.84 adjusted balance

$\$4{,}332.84 \times .08 \times \frac{60}{360} = \$57.77$

$4,332.84 + 57.77 = $4,390.61 balance due

Interest paid:
$222.22
110.62
+ 57.77
$390.61

Merchant's Rule

$I = \$10{,}000 \times .08 \times \frac{240}{360} = \$533.33$

$533.33 + $10,000 = $10,533.33 total amount of loan

240 days
− 100
140 days left

$I = \$4{,}000 \times .08 \times \frac{140}{360} = \$124.44$

$4,000.00 + 124.44 = $4,124.44
$10,533.33 − 4,124.44 = $ 6,408.89 adjusted balance

$I = \$2{,}000 \times .08 \times \frac{60}{360} = \$26.67$

$2,000.00 + 26.67 = $2,026.67
$6,408.89 − 2,026.67 = $4,382.22 balance due

Interest paid: $533.33 (if no partial payments)
− 124.44
− 26.67
$382.22

Difference in interest of $8.39. Cheaper by Merchant's Rule.

Word Problems

10–15. Heather Grant borrowed $12,000 to pay for her child's education. Heather must repay the loan at the end of 7 months in one payment with $7\frac{1}{2}$% interest. How much interest must Heather pay? What is the maturity value?

$\$12{,}000 \times .075 \times \frac{7}{12} = \$525$ interest

$MV = P + I$

$12,525 = $12,000 + $525

Sept. 12 $\begin{array}{r} 365 \\ -255 \\ \hline 110 \\ +27 \\ \hline 137 \end{array}$

10–16. On September 12, Jody Jansen went to Sunshine Bank to borrow $2,300 at 9% interest. Jody plans to repay the loan on January 27. Assume the loan is on exact time, ordinary interest. What interest will Jody owe on January 27? What is the total amount Jody must repay at maturity?

$\$2{,}300 \times .09 \times \frac{137}{360} = \$78.78$ interest

$\$78.78 + \$2{,}300 = \$2{,}378.78$

10–17. Kelly O'Brien met Jody Jansen (Problem 10–16) at Sunshine Bank and suggested she consider the loan on exact time, exact interest. Recalculate the loan for Jody under this assumption.

$\$2{,}300 \times .09 \times \frac{137}{365} = \$77.70 + \$2{,}300 = \$2{,}377.70$

Save $1.08

10–18. Victor Ohno bought a $250 typewriter with 2/10, n/60 terms. Victor does not have the cash to pay for the typewriter in 10 days. His aunt told him to borrow the money from Bloss Bank at 11% and pay cash for the typewriter taking advantage of the cash discount. Victor does not think the cash discount warrants taking out a loan. Calculate the savings from borrowing. Use 360 days in a year.

$I = \$245 \times .11 \times \frac{50}{360}$ ← ($250 × .98)

$= \$3.74$

Savings from borrowing:

$\begin{array}{r} \$5.00 \\ -\ 3.74 \\ \hline \$1.26 \end{array}$ saved

10–19. Gordon Rosel went to his bank to find out how long it will take for $1,200 to amount to $1,650 at 8% simple interest. Please solve Gordon's problem. Round time in years to nearest tenth.

$\frac{\$450}{\$1{,}200 \times .08} = \frac{\$450}{\$96} = 4.7$ years

I ($450)
P × R × T
($1,200) (.08)

10–20. Bill Moore is buying a van. His April monthly interest at 12% was $125. What was Bill's principal balance at the beginning of April? Use 360 days.

$\frac{\$125}{.12 \times \frac{30}{360}} = \frac{\$125}{.01} = \$12{,}500$

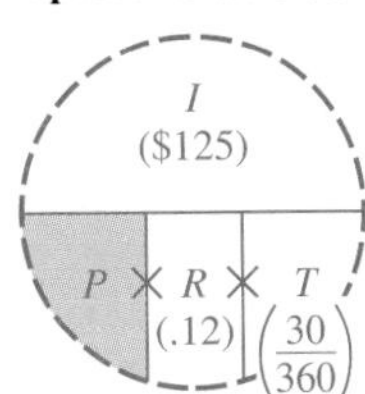

$\begin{array}{r} 365 \\ -\ 67 \\ \hline 298 \end{array} + 8 = 306$

10–21. On March 8, 1994, Jane King took out an $8\frac{3}{4}\%$ loan for $12,000. The loan is due January 8, 1995. Use exact time, ordinary interest to calculate the interest. What total amount will Jane pay on January 8, 1995?

$\$12{,}000 \times .0875 \times \frac{306}{360} = \$892.50 + \$12{,}000 = \$12{,}892.50$

10–22. Alice Hall took out the same loan as Jane (Problem 10–21). Alice's terms, however, are exact time, exact interest. What is Alice's difference in interest? What will she pay on January 8, 1995?

$\$12{,}000 \times .0875 \times \frac{306}{365} = \$880.27$ ⟶ $\begin{array}{r} \$880.27 \\ +\ \$12{,}000.00 \\ \hline \$12{,}880.27 \end{array}$

Difference in interest ⟶ $\begin{array}{r} \$892.50 \\ -\ 880.27 \\ \hline \$\ 12.23 \end{array}$

10–23. Max Wholesaler borrowed $2,000 on a 10%, 120-day note. After 45 days, Max paid $700 on the note. Thirty days later, Max paid an additional $630. What is the final balance due? Determine the total interest and ending balance due for the U.S. Rule and the Merchant's Rule. Use ordinary interest.

U.S. Rule

45 days

$\$2{,}000 \times .10 \times \frac{45}{360} = \$25.00$ interest

$2,000
− 675 ($700 − $25)
$1,325 adjusted balance

75th day

$\$1{,}325 \times .10 \times \frac{30}{360} = \$11.04$ interest

$1,325.00
− 618.96 ($630.00 − $11.04)
$ 706.04 adjusted balance

120th day

$\$706.04 \times .10 \times \frac{45}{360} = \$8.83$

$706.04
+ 8.83
$714.87 ending balance due

Total interest, $44.87
($25 + $11.04 + $8.83)

Merchant's Rule

$\$2{,}000 \times .10 \times \frac{120}{360} = \$\ 66.67$
+ 2,000.00
$2,066.67 (total amount of loan)

First payment:

120 − 45 = 75 days left

$I = \$700 \times .10 \times \frac{75}{360} = \$14.58$

$2,066.67
− 714.58 ($700 + $14.58)
$1,352.09 adjusted balance

Second payment:

$I = \$630 \times .10 \times \frac{45}{360} = \$7.88$

$1,352.09
− 637.88 ($630 + $7.88)
$ 714.21 ending balance due

Total interest cost = $44.21
($66.67 − $14.58 − $7.88)

Additional Set of Word Problems

10–24. Bill Blanc bought a $300 computer printer with 2/10, n/60 terms. Bill does not have the cash to pay for the computer in 10 days. His aunt told him to borrow the money from Roosevelt Bank at 12% and pay cash for the computer printer taking advantage of the discount. Bill does not think the cash discount warrants taking out a loan. What would you advise Bill? Use 360 days in a year.

$I = \$294 \times .12 \times \frac{50}{360} = \$4.90$

$\$300 \times .02 = \$6.00$ Save $1.10 by taking out loan.

Sept. 14 365 − 257 = 108; + 27 = 135

10–25. On September 14, Jennifer Rick went to Park Bank to borrow $2,500 at $11\frac{3}{4}\%$ interest. Jennifer plans to repay the loan on January 27. Assume the loan is on exact time, ordinary interest. What interest will Jennifer owe on January 27? What is the total amount Jennifer must repay at maturity?

$\$2{,}500 \times .1175 \times \frac{135}{360} = \$110.16 + \$2{,}500 = \$2{,}610.16$

10–26. Steven Linden met Jennifer Rick (Problem 10–25) at Park Bank and suggested she consider the loan on exact time, exact interest. Recalculate the loan for Jennifer under this assumption.

$\$2{,}500 \times .1175 \times \frac{135}{365} = \$108.65 + \$2{,}500 = \$2{,}608.65$

10–27. Lance Lopes went to his bank to find out how long it will take for $1,000 to amount to $1,700 at 12% simple interest. Can you solve Lance's problem? Round time in years to nearest tenth.

$\frac{\$700}{\$1{,}000 \times .12} = \frac{\$700}{\$120} = 5.8 \text{ years}$

10–28. Margie Pagano is buying a car. Her June monthly interest at $12\frac{1}{2}\%$ was $195. What was Margie's principal balance at the beginning of June? Use 360 days. Do not round denominator before dividing.

$\frac{\$195}{.125 \times \frac{30}{360}} = \frac{\$195}{.0104166} = \$18{,}720.12$

10–29. Shawn Bixby borrowed \$17,000 on a 120-day, 12% note. After 65 days, Shawn paid \$2,000 on the note. On day 89, Shawn paid an additional \$4,000. What is the final balance due? Determine total interest and ending balance due by the U.S. Rule. Use ordinary interest.

\$368.33
+ 122.95
+ 118.74
\$610.02 total interest

$\$17{,}000 \times .12 \times \frac{65}{360} = \$368.33$ interest

\$2,000 − \$368.33 = \$1,631.67 payment

\$17,000 − \$1,631.67 = \$15,368.33 adjusted balance

$\$15{,}368.33 \times .12 \times \frac{24}{360} = \$122.95$ interest

\$4,000 − \$122.95 = \$3,877.05 payment

\$15,368.33 − \$3,877.05 = \$11,491.28 adjusted balance

$\$11{,}491.28 \times .12 \times \frac{31}{360} = \$118.74$ interest

\$11,491.28 + \$118.74 = \$11,610.02 ending balance due

10–30. Shawn (Problem 10–29) asked you to recalculate the final balance due and total interest by the Merchant's Rule. Use ordinary interest.

\$680.00
− 36.67
− 41.33
\$602.00 total interest

$\$17{,}000 \times .12 \times \frac{120}{360} = \$680$

\$17,000 + \$680 = \$17,680 total amount of loan

$\$2{,}000 \times .12 \times \frac{55}{360} = \$36.67$ interest

\$2,000 + \$36.67 = \$2,036.67 payment

\$17,680 − \$2,036.67 = \$15,643.33 adjusted balance

$\$4{,}000 \times .12 \times \frac{31}{360} = \$41.33$ interest

\$4,000 + \$41.33 = \$4,041.33 payment

\$15,643.33 − \$4,041.33 = \$11,602.00 ending balance due

Challenge Problem
Equal Payments?

10–31. Janet Foster bought a computer and printer at Computerland. The printer had a \$600 list price with a \$100 trade discount and 2/10, n/30 terms. The computer had a \$1,600 list price with a 25% trade discount but no cash discount. On the computer, Computerland offered Janet the choice of (1) paying \$50 per month for 17 months with the 18th payment paying the remainder of the balance or (2) paying 8% interest for 18 months in equal payments.

a. Assume Janet could borrow the money for the printer at 8% to take advantage of the cash discount. How much would Janet save?

b. On the computer, what is the difference in the final payment between choices 1 and 2?

a. $\$490 \times .08 \times \frac{20}{360} = \$2.18$

(\$600 − \$100) × .98

\$10.00
− 2.18
\$ 7.82 (savings—worth borrowing)

b. (1) \$50 × 17 = \$850 Last payment \$1,200 − \$850 = \$350

(2) \$1,200 × .08 × 1.5 = \$144

$\$1{,}200 + \$144 = \frac{\$1{,}344}{18} = \$74.67$

\$350.00
− 74.67
\$275.33

Summary Practice Test

Solutions are at end of text in Appendix II.

Quick Reference
If you get any wrong answers, study the page numbers given for each problem.

1. P. 242.
2. P. 240.

1. Pete Regan's real estate tax of $795.18 was due on November 1, 1995. Due to loss of job, Pete was unable to pay his tax bill until January 18, 1996. The penalty for late payment is $9\frac{3}{4}$% ordinary interest.

a. What is the penalty Pete will have to pay?
b. What will Pete totally pay on January 18?

Dec. 31	365
− Nov. 1	305
	60
+ Jan. 18	+ 18
	78

a. $I = P \times R \times T$

$I = \$795.18 \times .0975 \times \frac{78}{360} = \$16.80$

b. $MV = \$795.18 + \$16.80$
$= \$811.98$

2. Meg O'Brien borrowed $75,000 to pay for her child's education. She must repay the loan at the end of 8 years in one payment with $8\frac{3}{4}$% interest. What is the maturity value Meg must repay?

$\$75,000 \times .0875 \times 8 = \$52,500 + \$75,000 = \$127,500$

3. P. 242.

	365
Sept. 14	*− 257*
	108
Feb. 8	*+ 39*
	147

3. On September 14, Don Hiroshi borrowed $5,000 from the Burlington Bank at $11\frac{3}{4}$% interest. Don plans to repay the loan on February 8. Assume the loan is on exact time, ordinary interest. How much will Don repay on February 8?

$\$5,000 \times .1175 \times \frac{147}{360} = \$239.90 + \$5,000 = \$5,239.90$

4. P. 241.

4. Jane Perks met Don Hiroshi (Problem 3) at the Burlington Bank. After talking with Don, Jane decided she would like to consider the same loan on exact time, exact interest. Can you recalculate the loan for Jane under this assumption?

$\$5,000 \times .1175 \times \frac{147}{365} = \$236.61 + \$5,000 = \$5,236.61$

5. P. 244.

5. Suki Wong is buying her car. Her June monthly interest was $180 at $11\frac{1}{2}$% interest. What is Suki's principal balance at the beginning of June? Use 360 days. Do not round the denominator in your calculation.

$$\frac{\$180}{.115 \times \frac{30}{360}} = \frac{\$180}{.0095833} = \$18,782.67$$

6. P. 246.

6. David Ring borrowed $6,000 on a 13%, 60-day note. After 10 days, David paid $500 on the note. On day 40, David paid $900 on the note. What is the total interest and ending balance due by the U.S. Rule? Use ordinary interest.

U.S. Rule

$\$6,000 \times .13 \times \frac{10}{360} = \$21.67$

$500.00	$6,000.00	principal
− 21.67	− 478.33	
$478.33	$5,521.67	adjusted balance (principal)

$\$5,521.67 \times .13 \times \frac{30}{360} = \$59.82$

$900.00	$5,521.67
− 59.82	− 840.18
$840.18	$4,681.49

$\$4,681.49 \times .13 \times \frac{20}{360} = \$33.81$

$4,681.49		$ 21.67	
+ 33.81		59.82	
$4,715.30	ending balance due	+ 33.81	
		$115.30	total interest

7. P. 247.

7. David (Problem 6) asked you to recalculate the total interest and ending balance due by the Merchant's Rule. Use ordinary interest.

Merchant's Rule

$$\$6{,}000 \times .13 \times \frac{60}{360} = \$\ 130$$

$$\begin{array}{r} \$\ 130 \\ +\ 6{,}000 \\ \hline \$6{,}130 \end{array} \quad \text{total amount of loan}$$

First payment:

60 − 10 = 50 days left

$$I = \$500 \times .13 \times \frac{50}{360} = \$9.03$$

$$\begin{array}{rl} \$6{,}130.00 & \\ -\ 509.03 & (\$500 + \$9.03) \\ \hline \$5{,}620.97 & \text{adjusted balance} \end{array}$$

Second payment:

$$I = \$900 \times .13 \times \frac{20}{360} = \$6.50$$

$$\begin{array}{rl} \$5{,}620.97 & \\ -\ 906.50 & (\$900 + \$6.50) \\ \hline \$4{,}714.47 & \text{ending balance due} \end{array}$$

Total interest, $114.47
($130 − $9.03 − $6.50)

Project A

IF YOUR BANK DOESN'T OFFER YOU INTEREST LIKE THIS:

	30 DAYS
$5000	10%
$100,000	12%

Annual Rates

Offer may be modified or withdrawn at any time. Interest is based on simple interest, 365-day year, and is payable at maturity. Certificates may not be redeemed before maturity dates. This offer may be modified or withdrawn at any time, without notice.

1. Find the interest on the $5,000.
2. Check the $5,000 amount by formula.
3. Check the 10% by formula.
4. Check the time by formula.

1. $I = P \times R \times T$

$$\$5{,}000 \times .10 \times \frac{30}{365} = \$41.10$$

2. $$P = \frac{I}{R \times T} = \frac{\$41.10}{.10 \times \frac{30}{365}} = \frac{\$41.10}{.0082191} = \$5{,}000.55$$

3. $$R = \frac{I}{P \times T} = \frac{\$41.10}{\$5{,}000 \times \frac{30}{365}} = \frac{\$41.10}{\$410.9589} = 10.001\%$$

4. $$T = \frac{I}{P \times R} = \frac{\$41.10}{\$5{,}000 \times .10} = \frac{\$41.10}{\$500} = .0822 \times 365 = 30.003 \text{ days}$$

NOTES

THAT WAS THEN . . .
. . . THIS IS NOW

This 1869 ad for a washing machine would require the buyer to make a downpayment and sign a promissory note for the balance. Today, if you make a major purchase and don't pay cash or use a credit card you could be asked to sign a note.

11

Structure of Promissory Notes, Simple Discount Notes, and the Discounting Process

LEARNING UNIT OBJECTIVES

LU 11–1: Structure of Promissory Notes; the Simple Discount Note

1. Define a promissory note and identify its parts. *p. 262.*
2. Differentiate between interest-bearing and noninterest-bearing notes. *p. 262.*
3. Calculate bank discount and proceeds for simple discount notes. *p. 263.*
4. Compare and contrast the simple discount note with the simple interest note. *p. 264.*
5. Calculate the true rate of interest for a simple discount note. *p. 263.*
6. Explain and calculate the effective rate for a Treasury bill. *pp. 264–65.*

LU 11–2: Discounting an Interest-Bearing Note before Maturity

1. Define and calculate the maturity value, bank discount, and proceeds. *pp. 266–67.*
2. Identify and complete the four steps of the discounting process. *pp. 266–67.*

Have you ever received a loan from a financial institution? If you have, you probably had to sign a note stating when you promised to repay the loan. What would happen if you did not repay your loan? Like the Japanese company in the following *Wall Street Journal* clipping, you could experience a financial crisis.

Bankruptcy Toll On Japan Firms May Increase

Special to THE WALL STREET JOURNAL

TOKYO—Nippon Saiken Toshi K.K., a securities investment company known for speculative activities, was unable for the second time to repay promissory notes owed to financial institutions, a private corporate debt research company said.

The failure to repay is likely to spell

LEARNING UNIT 11–1 STRUCTURE OF PROMISSORY NOTES; THE SIMPLE DISCOUNT NOTE

Although businesses frequently sign promissory notes, customers also sign promissory notes. For example, some student loans may require the signing of promissory notes. Appliance stores often ask customers to sign a promissory note when they buy large appliances on credit. As you will see in this unit, promissory notes usually involve the payment of interest.

Structure of Promissory Notes

To borrow money, you must find a lender (a bank or a company selling goods on credit). You must also be willing to pay for the use of the money. In Chapter 10, you learned that interest is the cost of borrowing money for periods of time.

Money lenders usually require that borrowers sign a **promissory note.** This note states that the borrower will repay a certain sum at a fixed time in the future. The note often includes the charge for the use of the money, or the rate of interest. Figure 11–1 shows a sample promissory note with its terms identified and defined. Take a moment to look at each term.

In this section, you will learn the difference between interest-bearing notes and noninterest-bearing notes.

Interest-Bearing versus Noninterest-Bearing Notes

A promissory note can be interest bearing or noninterest bearing. To be **interest bearing,** the note must state the rate of interest. Since the promissory note in Figure 11–1 states that its interest is 9%, it is an interest-bearing note. When the note matures, Bob Corporation will pay back the original amount (**face value**) borrowed plus interest. We use the following formulas to calculate interest and maturity value:

$$\text{Interest} = \text{Face value (principal)} \times \text{Rate} \times \text{Time}$$

$$\text{Maturity value} = \text{Face value (principal)} + \text{Interest}$$

The maturity value of a noninterest-bearing note is the same as its face value.

If you sign a **noninterest-bearing** promissory note for $10,000, you pay back $10,000 at maturity. The maturity value of a noninterest-bearing note is the same as its face value. Usually noninterest-bearing notes occur for short time periods under special conditions. For example, money borrowed from a relative could be secured by a noninterest-bearing promissory note.

FIGURE 11-1
Interest-Bearing Promissory Note

$10,000 a.	LAWTON, OKLAHOMA October 2, 1996 c.
Sixty days b. AFTER DATE we PROMISE TO PAY TO	
THE ORDER OF G. J. Equipment Company d.	
Ten thousand and 00/100---------------- DOLLARS.	
PAYABLE AT Able National Bank	
VALUE RECEIVED WITH INTEREST AT 9% e.	BOB CORPORATION f.
NO. 114 DUE December 1, 1996 g.	J.M. Moore TREASURER

a. **Face value:** Amount of money borrowed—$10,000. The face value is also the principal of the note.
b. **Time:** Length of time that the money is borrowed—60 days.
c. **Date:** The date that the note is issued—October 2, 1996.
d. **Payee:** The company extending the credit—G. J. Equipment Company.
e. **Rate:** The annual rate for the cost of borrowing the money—9%.
f. **Maker:** The company issuing the note and borrowing the money—Bob Corporation.
g. **Maturity date:** The date the principal and interest are due—December 1, 1996.

Simple Discount Note

The total amount due at the end of the loan, or the **maturity value (MV),** is the sum of the face value (principal) and interest. Some banks deduct the loan interest in advance. When banks do this, the note is a **simple discount note.**

The interest banks deduct in advance is the **bank discount.** The amount the borrower receives after the bank deducts its discount from the loan's maturity value is the note's **proceeds.** Sometimes we refer to simple discount notes as noninterest-bearing notes. Remember, however, that borrowers *do* pay interest on these notes.

In the example that follows, Pete Runnels has the choice of a note with a simple interest rate (Chapter 10) or a note with a simple discount rate (Chapter 11). Table 11-1 provides a summary of the calculations made in the example and gives the key points that you should remember. Now let's study the example, and then you can review Table 11-1.

EXAMPLE (These final calculations are also shown in Table 11-1.) Pete Runnels has a choice of two different notes that both have a face value (principal) of $14,000 for 60 days. One note has a simple interest rate of 8%, while the other note has a simple discount rate of 8%. For each type of note, calculate (a) interest owed, (b) maturity value, (c) proceeds, and (d) effective rate.

Simple interest note—Chapter 10	Simple discount note—Chapter 11
Interest **a.** I = Face value (principal) $\times R \times T$ $I = \$14{,}000 \times .08 \times \frac{60}{360}$ $I = \$186.67$	**Interest** **a.** I = Face value (principal) $\times R \times T$ $I = \$14{,}000 \times .08 \times \frac{60}{360}$ $I = \$186.67$
Maturity value **b.** MV = Face value + Interest $MV = \$14{,}000 + \$186.67$ $MV = \$14{,}186.67$	**Maturity value** **b.** MV = Face value $MV = \$14{,}000$
Proceeds **c.** Proceeds = Face value = $14,000	**Proceeds** **c.** Proceeds = MV − Bank discount = $14,000 − $186.67 = $13,813.33
Effective rate **d.** $\text{Rate} = \frac{\text{Interest}}{\text{Proceeds} \times \text{Time}}$ $= \frac{\$186.67}{\$14{,}000 \times \frac{60}{360}}$ = 8%	**Effective rate** **d.** $\text{Rate} = \frac{\text{Interest}}{\text{Proceeds} \times \text{Time}}$ $= \frac{\$186.67}{\$13{,}813.33 \times \frac{60}{360}}$ = 8.11%

TABLE 11–1
Comparison of Simple Interest Note and Simple Discount Note (Calculations from the Pete Runnels Example, p. (263)

Simple interest note (Chapter 10)	Simple discount note (Chapter 11)
1. A promissory note for a loan with a term of usually less than one year. Example: 60 days.	1. A promissory note for a loan with a term of usually less than one year. Example: 60 days.
2. Paid back by one payment at maturity. Face value equals actual amount (or principal) of loan (this is not maturity value).	2. Paid back by one payment at maturity. Face value equals maturity value (what will be repaid).
3. Interest computed on face value or what is actually borrowed. Example: $186.67.	3. Interest computed on maturity value or what will be repaid and not on actual amount borrowed. Example: $186.67.
4. Maturity value = Face value + Interest. Example: $14,186.67.	4. Maturity value = Face value. Example: $14,000.
5. Borrower receives the face value. Example: $14,000.	5. Borrower receives proceeds = Face value − Bank discount. Example: $13,813.33.
6. Effective rate (true rate is same as rate stated on note). Example: 8%.	6. Effective rate is higher since interest was deducted in advance. Example: 8.11%.
7. Used frequently instead of the simple discount note. Example: 8%.	7. Not used as much now because in 1969 congressional legislation required that the true rate of interest be revealed. Still used where legislation does not apply, such as personal loans.

Note that the interest of $186.67 is the same for the simple interest note and the simple discount note. The maturity value of the simple discount note is the same as the face value. In the simple discount note, interest is deducted in advance, so the proceeds are less than the face value. Note that the effective rate for a simple discount note is higher than the stated rate since the bank calculated the rate on the face of the note and not on what Pete received.

Courtesy of Department of the Treasury, Bureau of the Public Debt

Application of Discounting—Treasury Bills

A **Treasury bill** is a loan to the federal government for 91 days (13 weeks), 182 days (26 weeks), or one year. When the government needs money, it sells Treasury bills. For example, the following *Wall Street Journal* clipping states that the Treasury plans to reduce $275 million of the public debt by selling short-term bills.

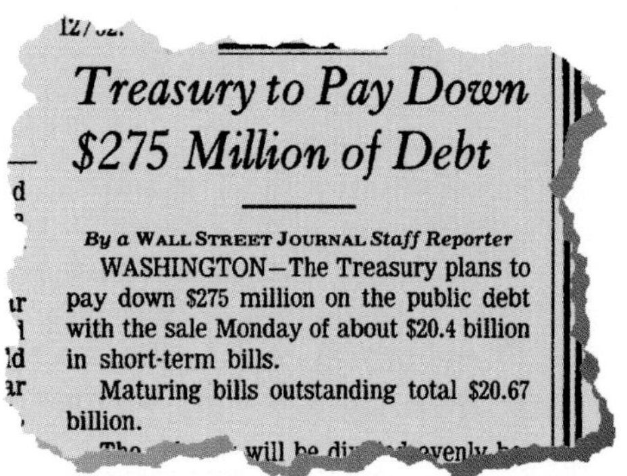
Treasury to Pay Down $275 Million of Debt

By a WALL STREET JOURNAL Staff Reporter
WASHINGTON–The Treasury plans to pay down $275 million on the public debt with the sale Monday of about $20.4 billion in short-term bills.
Maturing bills outstanding total $20.67 billion.

The government sells Treasury bills in minimum units of $10,000. The purchase price (or proceeds) of a Treasury bill is the value of the Treasury bill less the discount. Say you buy a $10,000 one-year Treasury bill at 8%. Since you have not yet earned your interest, you pay $9,200. At maturity—one year—the government pays you $10,000. You would calculate your effective yield (8.7% rounded to nearest tenth percent) as follows:

$$\frac{\$800}{\$9{,}200 \times 1 \text{ year}} = 8.7\% \text{ effective rate}$$

Now it's time to try the Practice Quiz and check your progress.

LU 11-1 PRACTICE QUIZ

1. Warren Ford borrowed $12,000 on a noninterest-bearing, simple discount note, $9\frac{1}{2}\%$, 60-day note. Assume exact time, ordinary interest. What is **(a)** the maturity value, **(b)** the bank's discount, **(c)** Warren's proceeds, and **(d)** the effective rate to nearest hundredth percent?
2. Jane Long buys a $10,000 one-year treasury bill at $6\frac{1}{2}\%$. What is her effective rate? Round to nearest hundredth percent.

SOLUTIONS TO 11-1 PRACTICE QUIZ

1. **a.** Maturity value = Face value = $12,000

   b. $\text{Bank discount} = MV \times \text{Bank discount rate} \times \text{Time}$
   $$= \$12{,}000 \times .095 \times \frac{60}{360}$$
   $$= \$190$$

   c. $\text{Proceeds} = MV - \text{Bank discount}$
   $$= \$12{,}000 - \$190$$
   $$= \$11{,}810$$

   d. $$\text{Effective rate} = \frac{\text{Interest}}{\text{Proceeds} \times \text{Time}} = \frac{\$190}{\$11{,}810 \times \frac{60}{360}} = 9.65\%$$

2. $$\frac{\text{Interest}}{\text{Proceeds} \times 1} = \frac{\$650}{\$9{,}350 \times 1} = 6.95\%$$

LEARNING UNIT 11-2 DISCOUNTING AN INTEREST-BEARING NOTE BEFORE MATURITY

Manufacturers frequently deliver merchandise to retail companies and do not request payment for several months. For example, Roger Company manufactures outdoor furniture that it delivers to its retailers in March. Payment for the furniture is not due until September. Roger will have its money tied up in this furniture until September. So Roger requests that its retailers sign promissory notes.

If Roger Company needs cash sooner than September, what can it do? Roger Company can take one of its promissory notes to the bank, assuming the company that signed the note is reliable. The bank will buy the note from Roger. Now Roger has discounted the note and has cash instead of waiting until September when the retailer would have paid Roger.

Think of **discounting a note** as a three-party arrangement. Roger Company realizes that the bank will charge for this service. The bank's charge is a *bank discount*. The actual amount Roger receives is the *proceeds* of the note. The steps and example that follow will help you understand this discounting process.

Steps for Discounting a Note

Step 1. Calculate maturity value.

Step 2. Calculate discount period.

Step 3. Calculate bank discount.

Step 4. Calculate proceeds.

EXAMPLE Roger Company sold the following promissory note to the bank:

Date of note	Face value of note	Length of note	Interest rate	Bank discount rate	Date of discount
Mar. 8	$2,000	185 days	10%	9%	Aug. 9

What is Roger's (1) interest and maturity value (MV)? (2) What is the discount period, (3) bank discount, and (4) proceeds?

1. *Calculate Roger's interest and maturity value (MV):*

$$MV = \text{Face value (principal)} + \text{Interest}$$

$$\text{Interest} = \$2{,}000 \times .10 \times \frac{185}{360} \quad \leftarrow \text{Exact number of days over 360}$$

$$= \$102.78$$

$$MV = \$2{,}000 + \$102.78$$

$$= \$2{,}102.78$$

2. *Calculate discount period:* Determine the number of days that the bank will have to wait for the note to come due (discount period).

August 9	221 days	
March 8	− 67 days	
	154 days passed before note is discounted	
	185 days	
	− 154 days	
	31 days bank waits for note to come due	

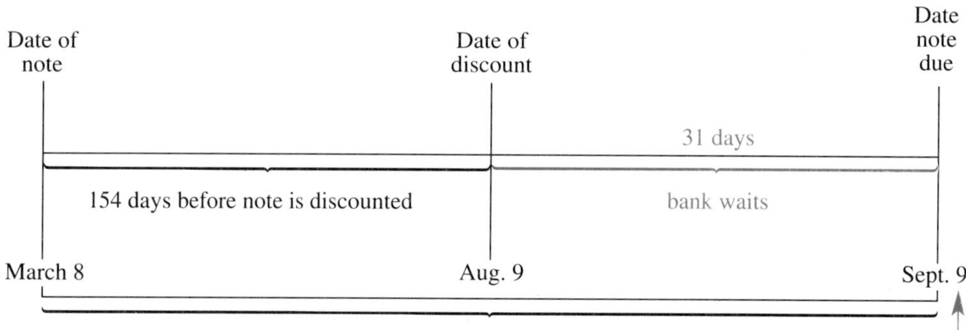

By table:
March 8 = 67 days
+ 185
252 search in table

3. *Calculate bank discount (bank charge):*

$\$2{,}102.78 \times .09 \times \frac{31}{360} = \$16.30$

$$\text{Bank discount} = MV \times \text{Bank discount rate} \times \frac{\text{Number of days bank waits for note to come due}}{360}$$

4. *Calculate proceeds:*

   $2,102.78
   − 16.30
   $2,086.48

   If Roger had waited until September 9, it would have received $2,102.78. Now, on August 9, Roger received $2,000 plus $86.48 interest.

$$\text{Proceeds} = MV - \text{Bank discount (charge)}$$

(MV: Step 1; Bank discount: Step 3)

Now let's assume Roger Company received a noninterest-bearing note. Then we would follow the above steps except the maturity value would be the amount of the loan. No interest accumulates on a noninterest-bearing note. Today, many banks use simple interest instead of discounting. Also, instead of discounting notes, many companies set up *lines of credit* so that additional financing is immediately available. In the following clipping, *The Wall Street Journal* reports that 10 NFL teams will use a $300 million line of credit to ease high interest payments.

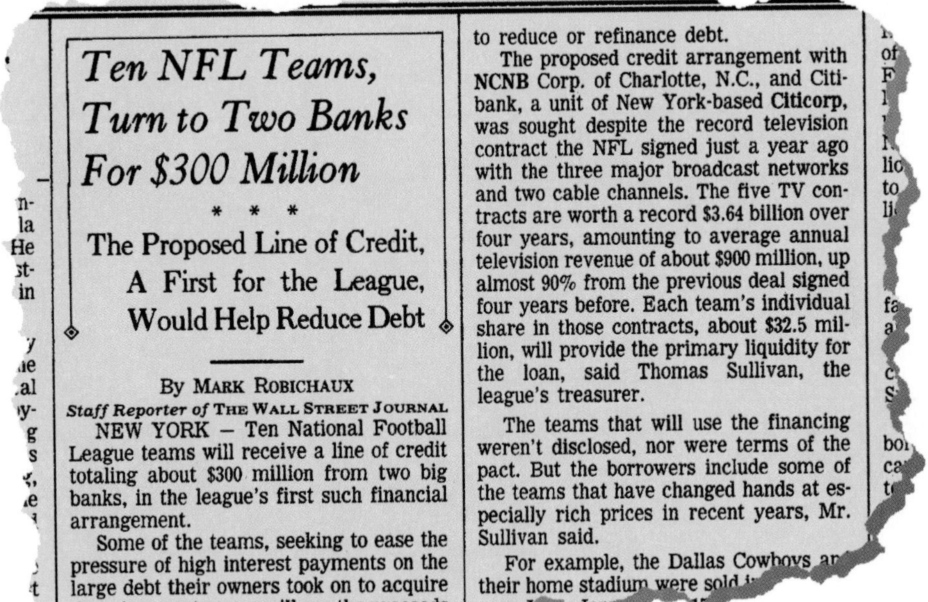

Ten NFL Teams, Turn to Two Banks For $300 Million

* * *

The Proposed Line of Credit, A First for the League, Would Help Reduce Debt

By MARK ROBICHAUX
Staff Reporter of THE WALL STREET JOURNAL

NEW YORK – Ten National Football League teams will receive a line of credit totaling about $300 million from two big banks, in the league's first such financial arrangement.

Some of the teams, seeking to ease the pressure of high interest payments on the large debt their owners took on to acquire them in recent years, will use the proceeds to reduce or refinance debt.

The proposed credit arrangement with NCNB Corp. of Charlotte, N.C., and Citibank, a unit of New York-based Citicorp, was sought despite the record television contract the NFL signed just a year ago with the three major broadcast networks and two cable channels. The five TV contracts are worth a record $3.64 billion over four years, amounting to average annual television revenue of about $900 million, up almost 90% from the previous deal signed four years before. Each team's individual share in those contracts, about $32.5 million, will provide the primary liquidity for the loan, said Thomas Sullivan, the league's treasurer.

The teams that will use the financing weren't disclosed, nor were terms of the pact. But the borrowers include some of the teams that have changed hands at especially rich prices in recent years, Mr. Sullivan said.

For example, the Dallas Cowboys ar[illegible] their home stadium were sold [illegible]

Now test your understanding of this unit with the following Practice Quiz.

LU 11-2 PRACTICE QUIZ

Date of note	Face value (principal) of note	Length of note	Interest rate	Bank discount rate	Date of discount
April 8	$35,000	160 days	11%	9%	June 8

From the above, calculate (**a**) interest and maturity value, (**b**) discount period, (**c**) bank discount, and (**d**) proceeds. Assume ordinary interest.

SOLUTIONS TO LU 11-2 PRACTICE QUIZ

a. $I = \$35{,}000 \times .11 \times \frac{160}{360} = \$1{,}711.11$

$MV = \$35{,}000 + \$1{,}711.11 = \$36{,}711.11$

b. Discount period = 160 − 61 = 99 days.

April	30	
	− 8	
	22	
May	+ 31	
	53	
June	+ 8	
	61	

Or by table:

June 8	159
April 8	− 98
	61

c. Bank discount $= \$36{,}711.11 \times .09 \times \frac{99}{360} = \$908.60$

d. Proceeds = $36,711.11 − $908.60 = $35,802.51

CHAPTER ORGANIZER: A REFERENCE GUIDE

Page	Topic	Key point, procedure, formula	Example(s) to illustrate situation
263	Simple discount note	Bank discount (interest) = MV × Bank discount rate × Time Interest based on amount paid back and not what received.	$\$6{,}000 \times .09 \times \frac{60}{360} = \$90$ Borrower receives $5,910 (the proceeds) and pays back $6,000 at maturity after 60 days. A Treasury bill is a good example of a simple discount note.
263	Effective rate	$\frac{\text{Interest}}{\text{Proceeds} \times \text{Time}}$ ↑ What borrower receives (Face value − Discount)	*Example.* $10,000 note, discount rate 12% for 60 days. $I = \$10{,}000 \times .12 \times \frac{60}{360} = \$200$ Effective rate: $\frac{\$200}{\$9{,}800 \times \frac{60}{360}} = \frac{\$200}{\$1{,}633.3333} = 12.24\%$ ↑ Amount borrower received
266	Discounting an interest-bearing note	1. Calculate interest and maturity value. I = Face value × Rate × Time MV = Face value + Interest 2. Calculate number of days bank will wait for note to come due (discount period). 3. Calculate bank discount (bank charge). MV × Bank discount rate × $\frac{\text{Number of days bank waits}}{360}$ 4. Calculate proceeds. MV − Bank discount (charge)	*Example.* $1,000 note, 6%, 60-day, dated November 1 and discounted on December 1 at 8%. 1. $I = \$1{,}000 \times .06 \times \frac{60}{360} = \$10$ $MV = \$1{,}000 + \$10 = \$1{,}010$ 2. 30 days 3. $\$1{,}010 \times .08 \times \frac{30}{360} = \$6.73$ 4. $1,010 − $6.73 = $1,003.27
	Key terms	Bank discount, *p. 263* Discounting a note, *p. 266* Discount period, *p. 266* Effective rate, *p. 263* Face value, *p. 262* Interest-bearing note, *p. 262* Maker, *p. 263* Maturity date, *p. 266*	Maturity value (MV), *p. 263* Noninterest-bearing note, *p. 262* Payee, *p. 263* Proceeds, *p. 263* Promissory note, *p. 263* Simple discount note, *p. 262* Treasury bill, *p. 264*

END-OF-CHAPTER PROBLEMS

Drill Problems

Additional homework assignments by learning unit are at the end of text in Appendix I (p. I–49). Solutions to odd problems are at the end of text in Appendix II. Use ordinary interest as needed.

Complete the following table for these simple discount notes; use the exact time, ordinary interest method.

	Amount due at maturity	Discount rate	Time	Bank discount	Proceeds
11–1.	$7,000	$6\frac{1}{2}\%$	85 days	$107.43	$6,892.57
11–2.	$6,000	$7\frac{1}{4}\%$	110 days	$132.92	$5,867.08

11–1. $\$7{,}000 \times .065 \times \frac{85}{360} = \$107.43$ $\$7{,}000 - \$107.43 = \$6{,}892.57$

11–2. $\$6{,}000 \times .0725 \times \frac{110}{360} = \$132.92$ $\$6{,}000 - \$132.92 = \$5{,}867.08$

Calculate the discount period for the bank to wait to receive its money:

	Date of note	Length of note	Date note discounted	Discount period
11–3.	Nov. 5	38 days	Dec. 10	38 − 35 = 3
11–4.	Mar. 7	120 days	June 8	120 − 93 = 27

11–3. Dec. 10 344 days; Nov. 5 − 309 days; 35 days

11–4. June 8 159 days; Mar. 7 − 66 days; 93 days

Solve for maturity value, discount period, bank discount, and proceeds (assume for Problems 11–5 and 11–6 a bank discount rate of 9%).

	Face value (principal)	Rate of interest	Length of note	Maturity value	Date of note	Date note discounted	Discount period	Bank discount	Proceeds
11–5.	$40,000	8%	180 days	$41,600	July 8	Nov. 6	59	$613.60	$40,986.40
11–6.	$25,000	9%	60 days	$25,375	June 8	July 10	28	$177.63	$25,197.37

11–5. Nov. 6 310 days; July 8 − 189 days; 121 days

$\$40{,}000 \times .08 \times \frac{180}{360} = \$1{,}600 + \$40{,}000 = \$41{,}600\ MV$

Discount period = 180 − 121 = 59

Bank discount = $\$41{,}600 \times .09 \times \frac{59}{360} = \$613.60$

Proceeds = $41,600 − $613.60 = $40,986.40

11–6. July 10 191 days; June 8 − 159 days; 32 days

$\$25{,}000 \times .09 \times \frac{60}{360} = \$375 + \$25{,}000 = \$25{,}375\ MV$

Discount period = 60 − 32 = 28

Bank discount = $\$25{,}375 \times .09 \times \frac{28}{360} = \$177.63$

Proceeds = $25,375 − $177.63 = $25,197.37

Word Problems

(Use ordinary interest as needed)

11–7. Alana Olsen borrowed $5,000 for 90 days from First Bank. The bank discounted the note at 10%. What proceeds does Olsen receive? Calculate the effective rate to the nearest hundredth percent.

$\$5{,}000 \times .10 \times \frac{90}{360} = \$125$

$\$5{,}000 - \$125 = \$4{,}875$

$\frac{\$125}{\$4{,}875 \times \frac{90}{360}} = \frac{\$125}{\$1{,}218.75} = 10.26\%$

11–8. Wally Hersey signed an $8,000 note at French Bank. French charges an $8\frac{3}{4}\%$ discount rate. If the loan is for 180 days, find **(a)** the proceeds and **(b)** the effective rate charged by the bank (to the nearest tenth percent).

a. $\$8{,}000 \times .0875 \times \frac{180}{360} = \$350$

$\$8{,}000 - \$350 = \$7{,}650$

b. $\frac{\$350}{\$7{,}650 \times \frac{180}{360}} = \frac{\$350}{\$3{,}825} = 9.2\%$

$4,000 × .09 × $\frac{60}{360}$ =
$60 interest

11–9. The face value of a simple interest note and simple discount note is $4,000. Assume both notes have 9% interest rates for 60 days. Calculate the following:

a. Amount of interest charged for each note. $60

b. Maturity value.
Simple interest note: $4,060
Simple discount note: $4,000

c. Amount each borrower receives. $4,000 simple interest
$3,940 simple discount

Sept. 5 248 days
June 5 − 156 days
92 days passed
120 − 92 = 28 days (discount period)

11–10. On September 5, Sheffield Company discounted at the Sunshine Bank a $9,000, 120-day note dated June 5. Sunshine's discount rate was 9%. What proceeds did Sheffield Company receive?

$\$9{,}000 \times .09 \times \frac{28}{360} = \$63$ $\$9{,}000 - \$63 = \$8{,}937$

11–11. On July 18, Eastgate Corporation accepted a $9,000, 8%, 90-day note. On September 3, Eastgate discounted the note at Shaw State Bank at 9%. What proceeds did Eastgate receive?

Sept. 3 246 days
July 18 − 199 days
47 days passed
90 − 47 = 43 days (discount period)

$\$9{,}000 \times .08 \times \frac{90}{360} = \$180$

$\$9{,}000 + \$180 = \$9{,}180$ *MV*

Bank discount

$\$9{,}180.00 \times .09 \times \frac{43}{360} = \$98.69$

$9,180.00
− 98.69
$9,081.31 proceeds

11–12. Ron Prentice bought goods from Shelly Katz. On May 8, Shelly gave Ron a time extension on his bill by accepting a $3,000, 8%, 180-day note. On August 16, Shelly discounted the note at Roseville Bank at 9%. What proceeds does Shelly Katz receive?

Aug. 16 228 days
May 8 − 128 days
100 days passed
180 − 100 = 80 days (discount period)

$\$3{,}000 \times .08 \times \frac{180}{360} = \$120$

$\$3{,}000 + \$120 = \$3{,}120$ *MV*

Bank discount

$\$3{,}120 \times .09 \times \frac{80}{360} = \$62.40$

$3,120.00
− 62.40
$3,057.60 proceeds

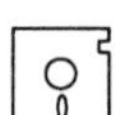

11–13. Rex Corporation accepted a $5,000, 8%, 120-day note dated August 8 from Regis Company in settlement of a past bill. On October 11, Rex discounted the note at Park Bank at 9%. What is the note's maturity value, discount period, and bank discount? What proceeds does Rex receive?

Oct. 11 284 days
Aug. 8 − 220 days
64 days passed
120 − 64 = 56 days (discount period)

$\$5{,}000 \times .08 \times \frac{120}{360} = \$133.33$

$\$5{,}000 + \$133.33 = \$5{,}133.33$ *MV*

Bank discount

$\$5{,}133.33 \times .09 \times \frac{56}{360} = \$71.87$

$5,133.33
− 71.87
$5,061.46 proceeds

11–14. On May 12, Scott Rinse accepted an $8,000, 12%, 90-day note for a time extension of a bill for goods bought by Ron Prentice. On June 12, Scott discounted the note at Able Bank at 10%. What proceeds does Scott receive?

June 12 163 days
May 12 − 132 days
31 days passed
90 − 31 = 59 days (discount period)

Maturity value $= \$8{,}000 \times .12 \times \frac{90}{360} = \$240 + \$8{,}000 = \$8{,}240$

Discount period = 90 − 31 = 59

Bank discount $= \$8{,}240 \times .10 \times \frac{59}{360} = \$135.04$

Proceeds = $8,240 − $135.04 = $8,104.96

11–15. Jensen Furniture wants to buy a $6,000 computer with a 5% cash discount. Jensen needs more cash to pay for the computer. On June 5, it is considering discounting a 90-day note dated May 12 with a $5,000 maturity value at Hunt Bank that has a 14% discount rate. Should Jensen discount the note?

June 5 156 days
May 12 − 132 days
24 days passed
90 − 24 = 66 days (discount period)

Bank discount $= \$5{,}000 \times .14 \times \frac{66}{360} = \$128.33$

$300 cash discount justifies the discounting cost of $128.33
Save $171.67 ($300 − $128.33)

Challenge Problem
Requesting a Loan

11–16. Tina Mier must pay a $2,000 furniture bill. A finance company will loan Tina $2,000 for 8 months at a 9% discount rate. The finance company told Tina that if she wants to receive exactly $2,000, she must borrow more than $2,000. The finance company gave Tina the following formula:

$$\text{What to ask for} = \frac{\text{Amount in cash to be received}}{1 - (\text{Discount rate} \times \text{Time of loan})}$$

Calculate Tina's loan request and the effective rate of interest.

$$\frac{\$2{,}000}{1 - \left(.09 \times \frac{8}{12}\right)} = \frac{\$2{,}000}{1 - .06} = \frac{\$2{,}000}{.94} = \$2{,}127.66$$

Check $\$2{,}127.66 \times .09 \times \frac{8}{12} = \$127.66$ $\qquad \frac{\$127.66}{\$2{,}000 \times \frac{8}{12}} = 9.57\%$

Summary Practice Test

Solutions are at end of text in Appendix II.
Quick Reference
If you get any wrong answers, study the page numbers given for each problem.
Use ordinary interest as needed.

1. P. 263.
2. P. 263.
3. P. 266.

1. On September 9, MCI Corporation accepted a $200,000, 80-day, noninterest-bearing note from Universal Corporation. What is the maturity value of the note?
$200,000

2. The face value of a simple discount note is $6,000. The discount is 11% for 80 days. Calculate the following:

a. Amount of interest charged for each note. $146.67
b. Amount borrower would receive. $5,853.33
c. Amount payee would receive at maturity. $6,000
d. Effective rate (to nearest tenth percent). 11.3%

$\$6{,}000 \times .11 \times \frac{80}{360} = \$146.67$ $\qquad \frac{\$146.67}{\$5{,}853.33 \times \frac{80}{360}} = \frac{\$146.67}{\$1{,}300.74} = 11.3\%$

↑ ($6,000 − $146.67)

3. On June 2, Ron Smith accepted an $8,000, 9%, 160-day note from Dick Shea. On September 6, Ron discounted the note at Tover Bank at 10%. What proceeds did Ron receive?

(1). $MV = \$8{,}000 \times .09 \times \frac{160}{360} = \$320 + \$8{,}000 = \$8{,}320$

(2). Sept. 6 249 days
June 2 − 153 days
96 days elapsed $\qquad 160 - 96 = 64$ days

(3) Bank discount $= \$8{,}320 \times .10 \times \frac{64}{360} = \$147.91$

(4) Proceeds $= \$8{,}320 - \$147.91 = \$8{,}172.09$

4. P. 266.

4. Mainline Corporation accepted an $18,000, 12%, 90-day note on July 2. Mainline discounts the note on August 10 at the Victor Bank at 11%. What proceeds did Mainline receive?

(1). $MV = \$18{,}000 \times .12 \times \frac{90}{360} = \$540 + \$18{,}000 = \$18{,}540$

(2). Aug. 10 222 days
July 2 − 183 days
39 days elapsed $\qquad 90 - 39 = 51$ days

(3). Bank discount $= \$18{,}540 \times .11 \times \frac{51}{360} = \$288.92$

(4). Proceeds $= \$18{,}540 - \$288.92 = \$18{,}251.08$

5. P. 263.

5. Walter Lantz signed a $7,500 note at Bloss Bank. Bloss charges a $6\frac{1}{2}\%$ discount rate. If the loan is for 95 days, find **(a)** the proceeds and **(b)** the effective rate charged by the bank (to nearest tenth percent).

a. $\$7{,}500 \times .065 \times \frac{95}{360} = \$128.65$
$\$7{,}500 - \$128.65 = \$7{,}371.35$

b. $\frac{\$128.65}{\$7{,}371.35 \times \frac{95}{360}} = \frac{\$128.65}{\$1{,}945.2173} = 6.6\%$

Project A

LYNN, MASSACHUSETTS March 5 19 95

$ 20,000

ON DEMAND the undersigned (jointly and severally, if more than one) promise to pay to the order of

SECURITY NATIONAL BANK, LYNN, MASSACHUSETTS

at said Bank Twenty Thousand and xx/100 DOLLARS with interest at the rate fixed by the Bank from time to time, having deposited with the Bank as collateral security for the payment of this and any and all other liabilities of the undersigned or any of them to the holder, direct or indirect, absolute or contingent, due or to become due or that may hereafter be contracted, the following property:

1995 Volvo Wagon

The undersigned do hereby fully authorize and empower the holder, on the non-performance of any promise made herein, or the non-payment of any of the liabilities above mentioned, or at any time or times thereafter, to sell, assign and deliver, all of the security herefor or any part thereof or any substitutes therefor, or any additions thereto, at any Broker's Board, or at public or private sale, at the option of the holder, or any officer or anyone acting in behalf of the holder, without advertisement or any notice to the undersigned or any other person, and the holder, its officers or assigns may bid and become purchasers at any such sale, if public, or at any Broker's Board. Right is expressly granted to the holder at its option to transfer at any time to itself or to its nominee any securities pledged hereunder and to receive the income thereon and hold the same as security herefor, or apply it on the principal or interest due hereon or due on any liability secured hereby.

Any and all deposits or other sums at any time or times credited by or due from the holder to, and all securities or other property in possession of the holder for safekeeping or otherwise and belonging to, any maker, endorser, or guarantor of this note are and shall be subject to a security interest in favor of the holder to secure payment of this note and the payment and performance of any and all other liabilities and obligations, direct or indirect, absolute or contingent, due or to become due or that may hereafter be contracted, of said respective maker, endorser, or guarantor to the holder. Upon any of the events specified above or upon non-payment of this note, or of any such liability whenever due, and at any time or times thereafter, without any demand or notice, except to such extent as notice may be required by applicable law, the holder may sell or dispose of any or all of such securities or other property and may exercise any and all of the rights accorded the holder by the Massachusetts Uniform Commercial Code. The holder may apply or set off such deposits or other sums at any time in the case of deposits of, or other sums due to, makers of this note, but only with respect to matured liabilities in the case of endorsers or guarantors of this note. The provisions of this paragraph are cumulative to, and not exclusive of, any other rights that the holder has with respect to such deposits, sums, securities, or other property under other agreements or applicable principles of law.

The undersigned will pay all expenses of every kind of the enforcement of this note or of any of the rights hereunder, and hereby agree to pay to the holder on demand the amount of any and all such expenses incurred by it including a reasonable attorney's fee of at least fifteen (15) percentum per annum of the unpaid principal balance. After deducting all legal or other expenses and costs of collection of this note and all legal or other expenses and costs of collection, storage, custody, sale, and delivery of collateral held hereunder, the residue of any proceeds of collection or sale shall be applied to the payment of principal or interest on this note or on any or all the other liabilities aforesaid, due or to become due, in such order of preference as the holder shall determine, proper allowance for interest on liabilities not then due being made, and any overplus shall be returned to the undersigned.

Under the provisions of Regulation U issued by the Board of Governors of the Federal Reserve System pursuant to the authority of the Securities Exchange Act, I/We certify that this loan is not made for the purpose of purchasing or carrying any stock registered on a National Securities Exchange.

I/We acknowledge that I/we have read all of the above terms and have received a conformed copy of this note.

This note shall have the effect of a sealed instrument.

NO. 8450 9/1/96 DUE

Signature Morris Katz
87 Garfield Ave.
Revere, Mass.

THIS NOTE IS SUBJECT TO THE ADDITIONAL PROVISIONS SET FORTH ON THE REVERSE SIDE HEREOF, THE SAME BEING INCORPRATED HEREIN BY REFERENCE.

AMOUNT FINANCED	$18,700.00
FINANCE CHARGE	$1,300.00
TOTAL PAYMENT DUE	$20,000
ANNUAL PERCENTAGE RATE	13.9%

(Effective Rate)
(May be changed at option of holder)

For purposes of disclosure, a demand note is treated as having a half-year maturity for the purposes of computing the FINANCE CHARGE with interest payable quarterly, monthly. Unearned Finance Charges (if any) will be refuned in accordance with actuarial method.

Acceptance of the above Regulation U statement as given in good faith.

SECURITY NATIONAL BANK

By. John Doe

Reprinted by permission of Security National Bank

Morris signed this simple collateral note (loan is secured by the auto). Could you show Morris how the the bank arrived at a finance charge (bank discount) of $1,300 given a bank discount rate of 13%? Use the bankers' method. How is the effective rate of 13.9% arrived at?

$$\$20{,}000 \times .13 \times \frac{180}{360} = \$1{,}300$$

Sept. 1 =	244 days
March 5 =	− 64 days
	180 days

$$\text{Effective rate} = \frac{\$1{,}300}{\$18{,}700 \times \frac{180}{360}} = \frac{\$1{,}300}{\$9{,}350} = 13.9\%$$

NOTES

THAT WAS THEN . . .
. . . THIS IS NOW

Did you know that Zenith is the only American television set maker? If this boy in the 1951 photo put $100 in a bank at 6% interest, would he have enough to buy the big screen television shown that might cost $1,100 in 1995?

12

Compound Interest and Present Value

LEARNING UNIT OBJECTIVES

LU 12–1: Compound Interest (Future Value)—The Big Picture and Specific Calculations

1. Compare and contrast compound interest and simple interest. *pp. 276–77.*
2. Calculate compound interest manually and by table lookup. *pp. 277–79.*
3. Explain and compute effective rate. *p. 280.*

LU 12–2: Present Value—The Big Picture and Specific Calculations

1. Compare and contrast present value (PV) and compound interest (FV). *p. 282.*
2. Compute the present value by table lookup. *pp. 282–84.*
3. Check the present value answer by compounding. *p. 285.*

If you have a savings account, you know that in recent years your interest has been declining. The following *Wall Street Journal* clipping states that Citicorp's Chicago bank is lowering its savings account interest rate from 4.34% to 3.15%. Interest rates have not been this low since 1966.

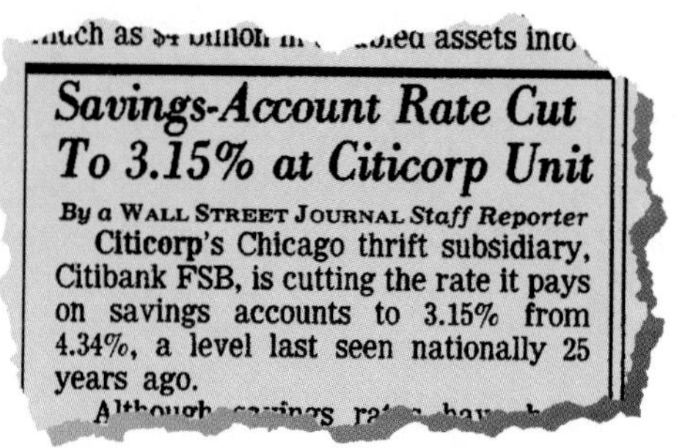
Savings-Account Rate Cut To 3.15% at Citicorp Unit

By a WALL STREET JOURNAL *Staff Reporter*

Citicorp's Chicago thrift subsidiary, Citibank FSB, is cutting the rate it pays on savings accounts to 3.15% from 4.34%, a level last seen nationally 25 years ago.

Courtesy of First National Bank of Chicago

Do you leave the interest in your savings account? Then you are paid interest on your earned interest. In this chapter, you will see the power of this compounding.

If you want to determine how long it will take to double a sum of money at different interest rates with annual compounding, divide 72 by the interest rate. For example, if you have a $10,000 investment that pays 8%, divide 72 by 8. Your answer is 9. This means that in 9 years your money will double.

Let's begin by studying Learning Unit 12–1, which shows you how to calculate compound interest.

LEARNING UNIT 12–1 COMPOUND INTEREST (FUTURE VALUE)—THE BIG PICTURE AND SPECIFIC CALCULATIONS

So far we have discussed only simple interest, which is interest on the principal alone. Simple interest is either paid at the end of the loan period or deducted in advance. From the above introduction, you know that interest can also be compounded.

In **compounding,** we calculate the interest periodically over the life of the loan and add it to the principal. Then for each next period we base the interest calculation on the adjusted principal (old principal plus interest). **Compound interest** is the interest on the sum of principal plus the interest of prior periods. In the beginning of this unit, do not be concerned with how we calculate compounding but try to understand the meaning of compounding.

Figure 12–1 shows you how $1 will grow if it is compounded for 4 years at 8% annually. This means the interest is calculated on the balance once a year. In Figure 12–1, we start with $1. This is the **present value.** After year 1, the dollar with interest is worth $1.08. At the end of year 2, the dollar is worth $1.17. By the end of year 4, the dollar is worth $1.36. Note how we start with the present and look to see what the dollar will be worth in the future. *Compounding goes from present value to future value.*

Before we show you how to calculate compound interest and compare it to simple interest, you must understand the terms that follow. We will also be using these terms in Chapter 13.

- **Compounded annually:** Interest calculated on balance once a year.
- **Compounded semiannually:** Interest calculated on balance every 6 months or every $\frac{1}{2}$ year.
- **Compounded quarterly:** Interest calculated on balance every 3 months or every $\frac{1}{4}$ year.
- **Compounded monthly:** Interest calculated on balance monthly.
- **Compounded daily:** Interest calculated on balance each day.

FIGURE 12-1
Future Value of $1 at 8% for Four Periods

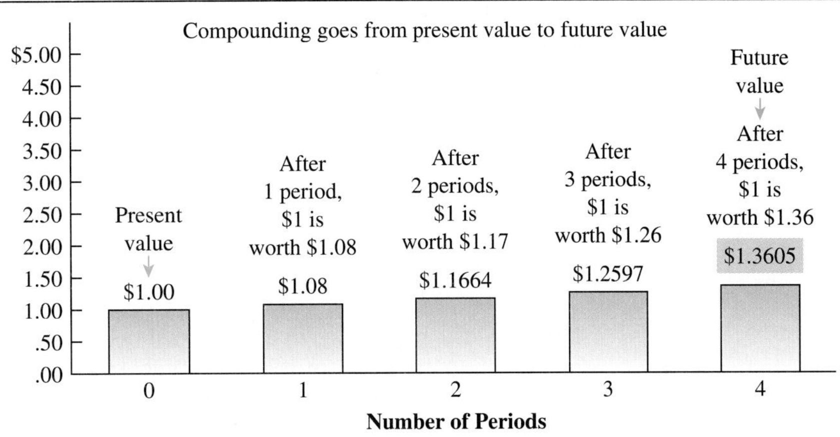

- □ **Rate for each period:** Annual rate divided by number of times compounded per year. For example:

$$\frac{8\%}{4\text{ (quarterly)}} = 2\%$$

- □ **Periods:** Number of years times number of times compounded per year. For example, $12,000 at 8% compounded quarterly for 8 years is:

Compounded 4 times per year
8 years × 4 = 32 periods

Note: The rate would be 2% or $\frac{8\%}{4}$.

Now you are ready to learn the difference between simple interest and compound interest.

Simple versus Compound Interest

The following three situations of Bill Smith will clarify the difference between simple interest and compound interest.

Situation 1: Calculating Simple Interest

EXAMPLE Bill Smith deposited $80 in a savings account at an annual interest rate of 8% for 4 years. What is Bill's simple interest?

We calculate simple interest as follows:

$$\text{Interest } (I) = \text{Principal } (P) \times \text{Rate } (R) \times \text{Time } (T)$$

$$\$25.60 = \$80 \times .08 \times 4$$

In 4 years, Bill receives a total of $105.60 ($80.00 + $25.60)—principal plus simple interest.

Now let's look at the interest Bill would earn if the bank compounded Bill's interest on his savings.

Situation 2: Calculating Compound Interest without Tables[1]

You can use the following steps to calculate compound amount and interest manually.

Steps for Calculating Compound Amount and Interest

Step 1. Calculate interest and add it to principal. Use this total to figure next year's interest.

Step 2. Repeat for total number of periods.

Step 3. Compound amount − Principal = Compound interest.

[1] For simplicity of presentation, round each calculation to nearest cent before continuing the compounding process.

EXAMPLE Bill Smith deposited $80 in a savings account at an annual compounded rate of 8% for 4 years. What is Bill's compound interest?

The following shows how the compounded rate affects Bill's interest:

	Year 1	Year 2	Year 3	Year 4
	$80.00	$86.40	$ 93.31	$100.77
	× .08	× .08	× .08	× .08
Interest	$ 6.40	$ 6.91	$ 7.46	$ 8.06
Beginning balance	+ 80.00	+ 86.40	+ 93.31	+ 100.77
Amount at year-end	$86.40	$93.31	$100.77	$108.83

Note that the beginning year 2 interest is the result of the interest of year 1 added to the principal. At the end of each interest period, we add on the period's interest. This interest becomes part of the principal we use for the calculation of the next period's interest. We can determine Bill's compound interest as follows:

Compound amount	$108.83
Principal	− 80.00
Compound interest	$ 28.83

Note in Situation 1 that interest was $25.60.

We could have used the following simplified process to calculate the compound interest:

Year 1	Year 2	Year 3	Year 4	
$80.00	$86.40	$93.31	$100.77	
× 1.08	× 1.08	× 1.08	× 1.08	
$86.40	$93.31	$100.77	$108.83	← Future value

When using this simplification, you do not have to add the new interest to the previous balance. Remember that compounding results in higher interest than simple interest. Compounding is the *sum* of principal and interest multiplied by the interest rate we use to calculate interest for the next period. So, 1.08 above is 108%, with 100% as the base and 8% as the interest.

Situation 3: Calculating Compound Interest by Tables[2]

To calculate compound interest with a table, use the following steps:

Steps for Calculating Compound Amount by Table

Step 1. Find periods: Years multiplied by number of times compounded in one year.

Step 2. Find rate: Annual rate divided by number of times compounded in one year.

Step 3: Go down Period column of table to number of periods desired; look across the row to find rate. At intersection of two columns is table factor for compound amount of $1.

Step 4. Multiply table factor times amount of loan. This gives the compound amount.

8% Rate

8% rate = 8% → Annual rate / 1 → No. of times compounded in 1 year

Four Periods

No. of times compounded in 1 year × No. of years

1 × 4

In Situation 2, Bill deposited $80 into a savings account for 4 years at an interest rate of 8% compounded annually. Bill heard that he could calculate compound interest by using tables. In Situation 3, Bill learns how to do this. Again, Bill wants to know the value of $80 in 4 years at 8%. He begins by using Table 12–1.

Looking at Table 12–1 (p. 279), Bill goes down the Period column to Period 4, then across the row to the 8% column. At intersection, Bill sees the number 1.3605. The marginal note shows how Bill arrived at the rate and periods. The 1.3605 table number means that $1 compounded at this rate will increase in value in 4 years to about $1.36.

[2] The formula for compounding is $A = P(1 + i)^N$, where A equals compound amount, i equals interest per period, and N equals number of periods.

TABLE 12–1 Future Value of $1 at Compound Interest

Period	1	$1\frac{1}{2}$%	2%	3%	4%	5%	6%	7%	8%	9%	10%
1	1.0100	1.0150	1.0200	1.0300	1.0400	1.0500	1.0600	1.0700	1.0800	1.0900	1.1000
2	1.0201	1.0302	1.0404	1.0609	1.0816	1.1025	1.1236	1.1449	1.1664	1.1881	1.2100
3	1.0303	1.0457	1.0612	1.0927	1.1249	1.1576	1.1910	1.2250	1.2597	1.2950	1.3310
4	1.0406	1.0614	1.0824	1.1255	1.1699	1.2155	1.2625	1.3108	1.3605	1.4116	1.4641
5	1.0510	1.0773	1.1041	1.1593	1.2167	1.2763	1.3382	1.4026	1.4693	1.5386	1.6105
6	1.0615	1.0934	1.1262	1.1941	1.2653	1.3401	1.4185	1.5007	1.5869	1.6771	1.7716
7	1.0721	1.1098	1.1487	1.2299	1.3159	1.4071	1.5036	1.6058	1.7138	1.8280	1.9487
8	1.0829	1.1265	1.1717	1.2668	1.3686	1.4775	1.5938	1.7182	1.8509	1.9926	2.1436
9	1.0937	1.1434	1.1951	1.3048	1.4233	1.5513	1.6895	1.8385	1.9990	2.1719	2.3579
10	1.1046	1.1605	1.2190	1.3439	1.4802	1.6289	1.7908	1.9672	2.1589	2.3674	2.5937
11	1.1157	1.1780	1.2434	1.3842	1.5395	1.7103	1.8983	2.1049	2.3316	2.5804	2.8531
12	1.1268	1.1960	1.2682	1.4258	1.6010	1.7959	2.0122	2.2522	2.5182	2.8127	3.1384
13	1.1381	1.2135	1.2936	1.4685	1.6651	1.8856	2.1329	2.4098	2.7196	3.0658	3.4523
14	1.1495	1.2318	1.3195	1.5126	1.7317	1.9799	2.2609	2.5785	2.9372	3.3417	3.7975
15	1.1610	1.2502	1.3459	1.5580	1.8009	2.0789	2.3966	2.7590	3.1722	3.6425	4.1772
16	1.1726	1.2690	1.3728	1.6047	1.8730	2.1829	2.5404	2.9522	3.4259	3.9703	4.5950
17	1.1843	1.2880	1.4002	1.6528	1.9479	2.2920	2.6928	3.1588	3.7000	4.3276	5.0545
18	1.1961	1.3073	1.4282	1.7024	2.0258	2.4066	2.8543	3.3799	3.9960	4.7171	5.5599
19	1.2081	1.3270	1.4568	1.7535	2.1068	2.5270	3.0256	3.6165	4.3157	5.1417	6.1159
20	1.2202	1.3469	1.4859	1.8061	2.1911	2.6533	3.2071	3.8697	4.6610	5.6044	6.7275
21	1.2324	1.3671	1.5157	1.8603	2.2788	2.7860	3.3996	4.1406	5.0338	6.1088	7.4002
22	1.2447	1.3876	1.5460	1.9161	2.3699	2.9253	3.6035	4.4304	5.4365	6.6586	8.1403
23	1.2572	1.4084	1.5769	1.9736	2.4647	3.0715	3.8197	4.7405	5.8715	7.2579	8.9543
24	1.2697	1.4295	1.6084	2.0328	2.5633	3.2251	4.0489	5.0724	6.3412	7.9111	9.8497
25	1.2824	1.4510	1.6406	2.0938	2.6658	3.3864	4.2919	5.4274	6.8485	8.6231	10.8347
26	1.2953	1.4727	1.6734	2.1566	2.7725	3.5557	4.5494	5.8074	7.3964	9.3992	11.9182
27	1.3082	1.4948	1.7069	2.2213	2.8834	3.7335	4.8223	6.2139	7.9881	10.2451	13.1100
28	1.3213	1.5172	1.7410	2.2879	2.9987	3.9201	5.1117	6.6488	8.6271	11.1672	14.4210
29	1.3345	1.5400	1.7758	2.3566	3.1187	4.1161	5.4184	7.1143	9.3173	12.1722	15.8631
30	1.3478	1.5631	1.8114	2.4273	3.2434	4.3219	5.7435	7.6123	10.0627	13.2677	17.4494

Note: For more detailed tables, see your reference booklet, the Business Math Handbook.

Sound familiar? Figure 12–1 showed how the dollar grew to $1.36. Since Bill wants to know the value of $80, he multiplies as follows:

$80.00 × 1.3605 = $108.84[3]
Dollar amount × Table factor = Compound amount (future value)

Figure 12–2 illustrates this compounding procedure. We could say future value (FV) stands for compounding since we are looking into the future. Thus:

$108.84 − $80.00 = $28.84 interest for 4 years at 8% compounded annually on $80.00

Let's look at examples that show compounding more than once a year.

EXAMPLE Find the interest on $6,000 at 10% compounded semiannually for 5 years.

We calculate the interest as follows:

Rate = 10% ÷ 2 = 5%
Periods = 2 × 5 years = 10
5%, 10 periods in Table 12–1 = 1.6289 (table factor)

$6,000 × 1.6289 = $9,773.40
− 6,000.00
$3,773.40 interest

[3] Off 1 cent due to rounding of table factor.

FIGURE 12-2
Compounding (FV)

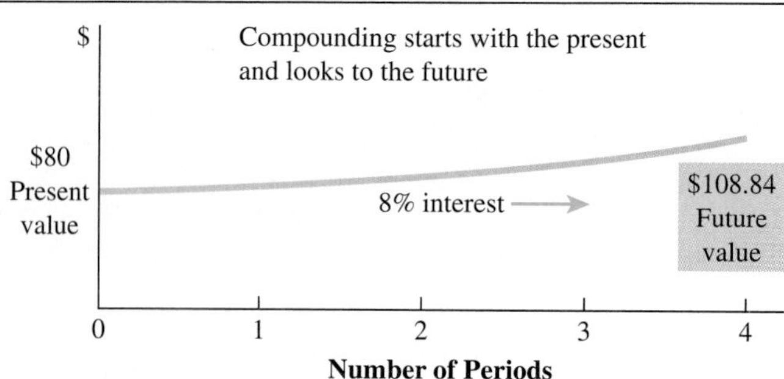

EXAMPLE Pam Donahue deposits $8,000 in her savings account that pays 6% interest compounded quarterly. What will be the balance of her account at the end of 5 years?

Rate = 6% ÷ 4 = $1\frac{1}{2}$%
Periods = 4 × 5 years = 20
$1\frac{1}{2}$%, 20 periods in Table 12-1 = 1.3469 (table factor)
$8,000 × 1.3469 = **$10,775.20**

Next, let's look at bank rates and how they affect interest.

Bank Rates—Nominal versus Effective Rates

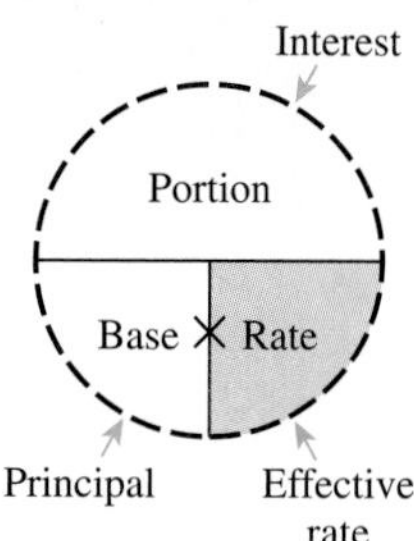

Today, banks often advertise their annual rates (nominal) and not their true (effective) rates. Let's study the rates of two banks to see which bank has the best return for the investor.

Blue Bank pays 8% interest compounded quarterly on $8,000. Sun Bank offers 8% interest compounded semiannually on the $8,000. The 8% rate is the **nominal rate,** or stated rate, on which the bank calculates the interest. However, we can calculate the true rate or **effective rate** as follows:

$$\text{Effective rate}^{4} \text{ (true)} = \frac{\text{Interest for 1 year}}{\text{Principal}}$$

Now let's calculate the effective rate for Blue Bank and Sun Bank.

Note the effective rates can be seen from Table 12-1 for $1:
1.0824 ← 2%, 4 periods
1.0816 ← 4%, 2 periods

Blue, 8% compounded quarterly	**Sun, 8% compounded semiannually**
Percent = $\frac{8\%}{4}$ = 2%	Percent = $\frac{8\%}{2}$ = 4%
Periods = 4 (4 × 1)	Periods = 2 (2 × 1)
Principal = $8,000	Principal = $8,000
Table 12-1 look-up: 2%, 4 periods	Table 12-1 look-up: 4%, 2 periods
1.0824	1.0816
× $8,000	× $8,000
Less $8,659.20	$8,652.80
principal − 8,000.00	− 8,000.00
$ 659.20	$ 652.80
Effective rate = $\frac{\$659.20}{\$8{,}000}$ = .0824 = **8.24%**	$\frac{\$652.80}{\$8{,}000}$ = .0816 = **8.16%**

Figure 12-3 illustrates a comparison of nominal and effective rates of interest. This comparison should make you question any advertisement of interest rates before depositing your money.

Before concluding this unit, let's briefly discuss compounding interest daily.

[4] Round to nearest hundredth percent as needed. In practice, the rate is often rounded to nearest thousandth.

FIGURE 12-3
Nominal and Effective Rates of Interest Compared

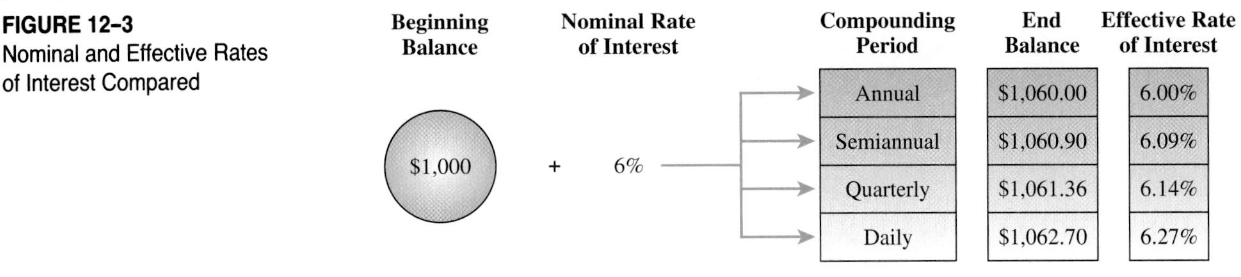

TABLE 12-2 Interest on a $1 Deposit Compounded Daily—360-Day Basis

Number of years	6.00%	6.50%	7.00%	7.50%	8.00%	8.50%	9.00%	9.50%	10.00%
1	1.0618	1.0672	1.0725	1.0779	1.0833	1.0887	1.0942	1.0996	1.1052
2	1.1275	1.1388	1.1503	1.1618	1.1735	1.1853	1.1972	1.2092	1.2214
3	1.1972	1.2153	1.2337	1.2523	1.2712	1.2904	1.3099	1.3297	1.3498
4	1.2712	1.2969	1.3231	1.3498	1.3771	1.4049	1.4333	1.4622	1.4917
5	1.3498	1.3840	1.4190	1.4549	1.4917	1.5295	1.5682	1.6079	1.6486
6	1.4333	1.4769	1.5219	1.5682	1.6160	1.6652	1.7159	1.7681	1.8220
7	1.5219	1.5761	1.6322	1.6904	1.7506	1.8129	1.8775	1.9443	2.0136
8	1.6160	1.6819	1.7506	1.8220	1.8963	1.9737	2.0543	2.1381	2.2253
9	1.7159	1.7949	1.8775	1.9639	2.0543	2.1488	2.2477	2.3511	2.4593
10	1.8220	1.9154	2.0136	2.1168	2.2253	2.3394	2.4593	2.5854	2.7179
15	2.4594	2.6509	2.8574	3.0799	3.3197	3.5782	3.8568	4.1571	4.4808
20	3.3198	3.6689	4.0546	4.4810	4.9522	5.4728	6.0482	6.6842	7.3870
25	4.4811	5.0777	5.7536	6.5195	7.3874	8.3708	9.4851	10.7477	12.1782
30	6.0487	7.0275	8.1645	9.4855	11.0202	12.8032	14.8747	17.2813	20.0772

Compounding Interest Daily

Often banks pay interest that is **compounded daily.** Some banks also use *continuous compounding*. Remember that continuous compounding sounds great, but in fact, it yields only a fraction of a percent more interest over a year than daily compounding. Today, we use computers to perform these calculations.

Table 12-2 is a partial table showing what a dollar will grow to in the future by daily compounded interest, 360-day basis. For example, we can calculate interest compounded daily on $900 at 6% per year for 25 years as follows:

$900 × 4.4811 = $4,032.99 daily compounding

Now it's time to check your progress with the following Practice Quiz.

LU 12-1 PRACTICE QUIZ

1. Complete without a table (round to nearest cent each calculation as needed):

Principal	Time	Rate of compound interest	Compounded	Number of periods to be compounded	Total amount	Total interest
$200	1 year	8%	Quarterly	**a.**	**b.**	**c.**

2. Solve No. 1 by using compound value (FV) Table 12-1.
3. Lionel Rodgers deposits $6,000 in Victory Bank, which pays 3% interest compounded semiannually. How much will Lionel have in his account at the end of 8 years?
4. Find the effective rate for the year:
principal, $7,000; interest rate, 12%; and compounded quarterly.
5. Calculate by Table 12-2 what $1,500 compounded daily for 5 years will grow to at 7%.

SOLUTIONS TO LU 12-1 PRACTICE QUIZ

1. a. 4 b. $216.48 c. $16.48
 $200 × 1.02 = $204 × 1.02 = $208.08 × 1.02 = $212.24 × 1.02 = $216.48
2. $200 × 1.0824 = $216.48 (2%, 4 periods)
3. $1\frac{1}{2}\%$ 16 periods $6,000 × 1.2690 = $7,614
4. 3% 4 periods

 $7,000 × 1.1255 = $7,878.50 − 7,000.00 = $ 878.50 $\frac{\$878.50}{\$7{,}000.00} = 12.55\%$
5. $1,500 × 1.4190 = $2,128.50

LEARNING UNIT 12-2 PRESENT VALUE—THE BIG PICTURE AND SPECIFIC CALCULATIONS

In Learning Unit 12-1 (p. 277), we saw how $1 in the present grew in the future to $1.36 by compounding. Now before we look at specific calculations involving present value, let's discuss the concept of present value.

Figure 12-4 shows that if we invested 74 cents today, it would grow to $1 in the future. This is the result of compounding. For example, let's assume you ask this question: "If I need $1 in 4 years in the future, how much must I put in the bank *today* (assume an 8% annual interest)?" To answer the question, you must know the present value of that $1 today. From Figure 12-4, you can see that the present value of $1 is .7350. Remember that $1 is only worth 74 cents if you have to wait 4 periods to receive it. This is one reason why so many athletes get such big contracts—much of the money is paid in later years when it is not worth as much.

Relationship of Compounding (FV) to Present Value (PV)—The Bill Smith Example Continued

In Learning Unit 12-1, our consideration of compounding started in the *present* ($80) and looked to find the *future* amount of $108.83. Present value (PV) starts with the *future* and tries to calculate its worth in the *present* ($80). For example, in Figure 12-5, we assume Bill Smith knew that in 4 years he wanted to buy a bike that cost $108.83 (future). Bill's bank pays 8% interest compounded annually. How much money must Bill put in the bank *today* (present) to have $108.83 in 4 years? To work from the future to the present, we can use a present value (PV) table. In the next section, you will learn how to use this table.

How to Use Present Value (PV) Table[5]

You can use the following steps to calculate the present value amount by table.

Steps for Calculating Present Value Amount by Table

Step 1. Find periods: Years multiplied by number of times compounded in one year.

Step 2. Find rate: Annual rate divided by number of times compounded in one year.

Step 3. Go down Period column of table to number of periods desired; look across the row to find rate. At intersection of the two columns is table factor for present value of $1.

Step 4. Multiply table factor times future value. This gives the present value amount.

[5] The formula for present value is $PV = \frac{A}{(1 + i)^N}$, where *A* equals future amount (compound amount), *N* equals number of compounding periods, and *i* equals interest rate per compounding period.

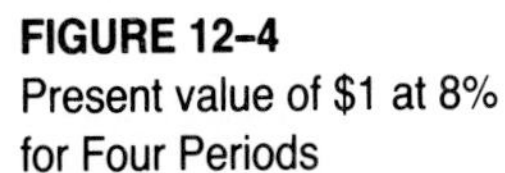

FIGURE 12-4
Present value of $1 at 8% for Four Periods

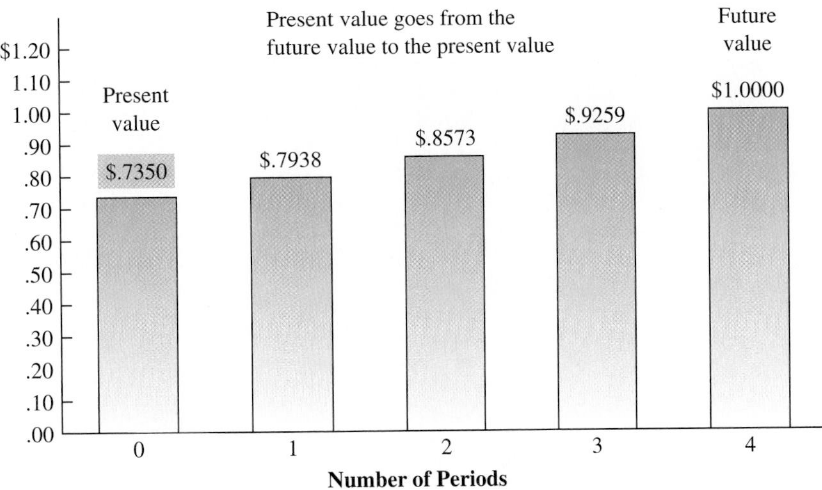

FIGURE 12-5
Present Value

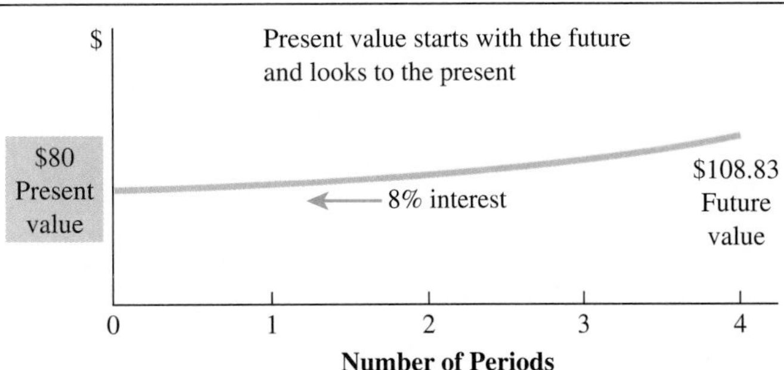

Periods
4 × 1 = 4
Quarterly — *No. of times compounded in 1 year*

Table 12–3 (p. 284) is a present value (PV) table that tells you what $1 is worth today at different interest rates. To continue our Bill Smith example, go down the Period column in Table 12–3 to 4. Then go across to the 8% column. At 8% for 4 periods, we see a table factor of .7350. This means that $1 in the future is worth approximately 74 cents today. If Bill invested 74 cents today at 8% for 4 periods, Bill would have $1.

Since Bill knows the bike will cost $108.83 in the future, he completes the following calculation:

$108.83 × .7350 = $79.99[6]

This means the $108.83 in today's dollar is worth $80.00. Now let's check this.

Comparing Compound Interest (FV) Table 12–1 with Present Value (PV) Table 12–3

We know from our calculations that Bill needs to invest $80 for 4 years at 8% compound interest annually to buy his bike. We can check this by going back to Table 12–1 and comparing it with Table 12–3. Let's do this now.

Compound value Table 12–1				**Present value Table 12–3**			
Table 12–1	**Present value**		**Future value**	**Table 12–3**	**Future value**		**Present value**
1.3605	× $80.00	=	$108.84*	.7350	× $108.83	=	$79.99*
(8%, 4 per.)	↗			(8%, 4 per.)	↗		
We know the present dollar amount and find what the dollar amount is worth in the future.				We know the future dollar amount and find what the dollar amount is worth in the present.			

* Off 1 cent due to rounding of table factors.

[6] Off 1 cent due to rounding of table factors.

TABLE 12–3 Present Value of $1 at End of Period

Period	1%	$1\frac{1}{2}$%	2%	3%	4%	5%	6%	7%	8%	9%	10%
1	.9901	.9852	.9804	.9709	.9615	.9524	.9434	.9346	.9259	.9174	.9091
2	.9803	.9707	.9612	.9426	.9246	.9070	.8900	.8734	.8573	.8417	.8264
3	.9706	.9563	.9423	.9151	.8890	.8638	.8396	.8163	.7938	.7722	.7513
4	.9610	.9422	.9238	.8885	.8548	.8227	.7921	.7629	.7350	.7084	.6830
5	.9515	.9283	.9057	.8626	.8219	.7835	.7473	.7130	.6806	.6499	.6209
6	.9420	.9145	.8880	.8375	.7903	.7462	.7050	.6663	.6302	.5963	.5645
7	.9327	.9010	.8706	.8131	.7599	.7107	.6651	.6227	.5835	.5470	.5132
8	.9235	.8877	.8535	.7894	.7307	.6768	.6274	.5820	.5403	.5019	.4665
9	.9143	.8746	.8368	.7664	.7026	.6446	.5919	.5439	.5002	.4604	.4241
10	.9053	.8617	.8203	.7441	.6756	.6139	.5584	.5083	.4632	.4224	.3855
11	.8963	.8489	.8043	.7224	.6496	.5847	.5268	.4751	.4289	.3875	.3505
12	.8874	.8364	.7885	.7014	.6246	.5568	.4970	.4440	.3971	.3555	.3186
13	.8787	.8240	.7730	.6810	.6006	.5303	.4688	.4150	.3677	.3262	.2897
14	.8700	.8119	.7579	.6611	.5775	.5051	.4423	.3878	.3405	.2992	.2633
15	.8613	.7999	.7430	.6419	.5553	.4810	.4173	.3624	.3152	.2745	.2394
16	.8528	.7880	.7284	.6232	.5339	.4581	.3936	.3387	.2919	.2519	.2176
17	.8444	.7764	.7142	.6050	.5134	.4363	.3714	.3166	.2703	.2311	.1978
18	.8360	.7649	.7002	.5874	.4936	.4155	.3503	.2959	.2502	.2120	.1799
19	.8277	.7536	.6864	.5703	.4746	.3957	.3305	.2765	.2317	.1945	.1635
20	.8195	.7425	.6730	.5537	.4564	.3769	.3118	.2584	.2145	.1784	.1486
21	.8114	.7315	.6598	.5375	.4388	.3589	.2942	.2415	.1987	.1637	.1351
22	.8034	.7207	.6468	.5219	.4220	.3418	.2775	.2257	.1839	.1502	.1228
23	.7954	.7100	.6342	.5067	.4057	.3256	.2618	.2109	.1703	.1378	.1117
24	.7876	.6995	.6217	.4919	.3901	.3101	.2470	.1971	.1577	.1264	.1015
25	.7798	.6892	.6095	.4776	.3751	.2953	.2330	.1842	.1460	.1160	.0923
26	.7720	.6790	.5976	.4637	.3607	.2812	.2198	.1722	.1352	.1064	.0839
27	.7644	.6690	.5859	.4502	.3468	.2678	.2074	.1609	.1252	.0976	.0763
28	.7568	.6591	.5744	.4371	.3335	.2551	.1956	.1504	.1159	.0895	.0693
29	.7493	.6494	.5631	.4243	.3207	.2429	.1846	.1406	.1073	.0822	.0630
30	.7419	.6398	.5521	.4120	.3083	.2314	.1741	.1314	.0994	.0754	.0573
35	.7059	.5939	.5000	.3554	.2534	.1813	.1301	.0937	.0676	.0490	.0356
40	.6717	.5513	.4529	.3066	.2083	.1420	.0972	.0668	.0460	.0318	.0221

Note: For more detailed tables, see your booklet, the Business Math Handbook.

Note that the table factor for compounding is over 1 (1.3605) and the table factor for present value is less than 1 (.7350). The compound value table starts with the present and goes to the future. The present value table starts with the future and goes to the present.

Let's look at another example before trying the Practice Quiz.

EXAMPLE Rene Weaver needs $20,000 for college in 4 years. She can earn 8% compounded quarterly at her bank. How much must Rene deposit at the beginning of the year to have $20,000 in 4 years?

Remember that in this example the bank compounds the interest *quarterly*. Let's first determine the rate and period on a quarterly basis:

$$\text{Rate} = \frac{8\%}{4} = 2\% \qquad \text{Periods} = 4 \times 4 \text{ years} = 16 \text{ periods}$$

Now we go to Table 12–3 and find 16 under the Period column. We then move across to the 2% column and find the .7284 table factor.

$20,000	× .7284 =	$14,568
(future value)		(present value)

We illustrate this in Figure 12–6.

FIGURE 12–6
Present Value

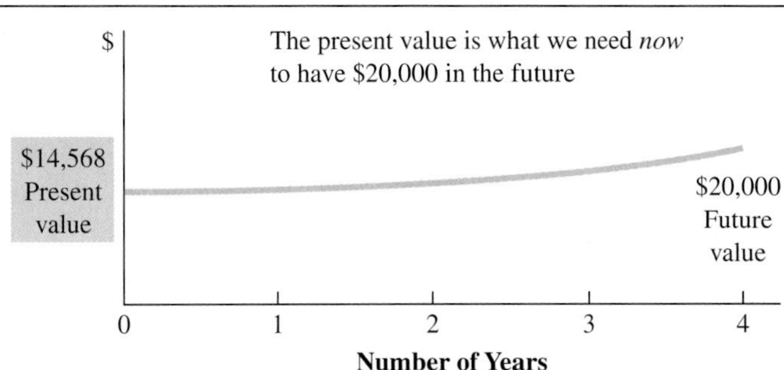

We can check the $14,568 present value by using the compound value Table 12–1:

2% column, 16 periods = 1.3728 × $14,568 = $19,998.95[7]

Let's test your understanding of this unit with the Practice Quiz.

LU 12–2 PRACTICE QUIZ

Courtesy of Ford Motor Company

Use the present value Table 12–3 to complete:

	Future amount desired	Length of time	Rate compounded	Table period	Rate used	PV factor	PV amount
1.	$ 7,000	6 years	6% semiannually	______	______	______	______
2.	$15,000	20 years	10% annually	______	______	______	______

3. Bill Blum needs $20,000 6 years from today to attend V.P.R. Tech. How much must Bill put in the bank today (12% quarterly) to reach his goal?
4. Bob Fry wants to buy his grandson a Ford Taurus in 4 years. The cost of a car should be $24,000. Assuming a bank rate of 8% compounded quarterly, how much must Bob put in the bank today?

SOLUTIONS TO LU 12–2 PRACTICE QUIZ

1. 12 periods 3% .7014 $4,909.80 ($7,000 × .7014)
2. 20 periods 10% .1486 $2,229.00 ($15,000 × .1486)
3. $\frac{12\%}{4} = 3\%$ 6 years × 4 = 24 periods
   .4919 × $20,000 = $9,838
4. $\frac{8\%}{4} = 2\%$ 4 × 4 years = 16 periods
   .7284 × $24,000 = $17,481.60

CHAPTER ORGANIZER: A REFERENCE GUIDE

Page	Topic	Key point, procedure, formula	Example(s) to illustrate situation
277	Calculating compound interest without tables (future value)*	Determine new interest by multiplying rate times new balance (that includes interest added on). Start in present and look to future. Compound interest = Compound amount − Principal PV ← Compounding → FV	$100 in savings account, compounded annually for 2 years at 8%: $100 × 1.08 = $108 $108 × 1.08 = $116.64 (future value)

* $A = P(1 + i)^N$.

[7] Not quite $20,000 due to rounding of table factors.

Page	Topic	Key point, procedure, formula	Example(s) to illustrate situation
278	Calculating compound interest (future value) by tables	$\text{Rate} = \frac{\text{Annual rate}}{\text{Number of times compounded per year}}$ $\text{Periods} = \begin{matrix}\text{Number of times}\\\text{compounded}\\\text{per year}\end{matrix} \times \begin{matrix}\text{Years of}\\\text{loan}\end{matrix}$ Multiply table factor (intersection of rate and period) times amount of loan.	*Example:* \$2,000 @ 12% 5 years compounded quarterly: $\text{Rate} = \frac{12\%}{4} = 3\%$ Periods = 4 × 5 years = 20 3%, 20 periods = 1.8061 (table factor) \$2,000 × 1.8061 = \$3,612.20 (future value)
280	Effective rate	$\frac{\text{Interest for 1 year}}{\text{Principal}}$ or Rate can be seen in Table 12-1 factor.	\$1,000 at 10% compounded semiannually for one year. By Table 12-1: 5%, 2 periods 1.1025 means at end of year investor has earned 110.25% of original principal. Thus the interest is 10.25%. \$1,000 × 1.1025 = \$1,102.50 − 1,000.00 \$ 102.50 $\frac{\$102.50}{\$1,000} = 10.25\%$ effective rate
282	Calculating present value (PV) with tables†	Start with future and calculate worth in the present. Rate and periods computed like in compound interest. PV ← Present value — FV Find rate and periods. Multiply table factor (intersection of rate and period) times amount of loan	*Example:* Want \$3,612.20 after 5 years with rate of 12% compounded quarterly: % = 3%; periods = 4 × 5 = 20 By Table 12-3: 3%, 20 periods = .5537 \$3,612.20 × .5537 = \$2,000.08 Invested today will yield desired amount in future
	Key terms	Compounded annually, *p. 276* Compounded daily, *p. 281* Compounded monthly, *p. 276* Compounded quarterly, *p. 276* Compounded semiannually, *p. 276* Compounding (FV), *p. 277*	Compound interest, *p. 277* Effective rate, *p. 280* Nominal rate, *p. 280* Periods, *p. 277* Present value (PV), *p. 282* Rate for each period, *p. 277*

† $\frac{A}{(1+i)^N}$ if table not used.

END-OF-CHAPTER PROBLEMS

Drill Problems

Additional homework assignments by learning unit are at the end of text in Appendix I (p. I–53). Solutions to odd problems are at the end of text in Appendix II.

Complete without using Table 12–1 (round to nearest cent for each calculation) and then check by Table 12–1 (check will be several cents off due to rounding):

	Principal	Time (years)	Rate of compound interest	Compounded	Periods	Rate	Total amount	Total interest
12–1.	$800	4	8%	Semiannually	8	4%	$1,094.86	$294.86

$\frac{8\%}{2} = 4\%$

4 years × 2 = 8 periods

$800.00	$ 935.89
× 1.04	× 1.04
$832.00	$ 973.33
× 1.04	× 1.04
$865.28	$1,012.26
× 1.04	× 1.04
$899.89	$1,052.75
× 1.04	× 1.04
$935.89	$1,094.86
	− 800.00
	$ 294.86

Check

$800 × 1.3686 = $1,094.88 (8 periods, 4%)

Complete the following using compound future value Table 12–1:

	Time	Principal	Rate	Compounded	Amount	Interest
12–2.	4 yrs.	$ 6,000	6%	Semiannually	$7,600.80	$1,600.80

$\frac{6\%}{2} = 3\%$

4 years × 2 = 8 periods

$6,000 × 1.2668 = $7,600.80
− 6,000.00
$1,600.80

	Time	Principal	Rate	Compounded	Amount	Interest
12–3.	6 mos.	$10,000	8%	Quarterly	$10,404.00	$ 404.00

$\frac{8\%}{4} = 2\%$

$\frac{6}{12} \times 4 = 2$ periods $10,000 × 1.0404 = $10,404
− 10,000
$ 404

	Time	Principal	Rate	Compounded	Amount	Interest
12–4.	3 yrs.	$2,000	12%	Semiannually	$ 2,837.00	$ 837.00

$\frac{12\%}{2} = 6\%$

3 years × 2 = 6 periods $2,000 × 1.4185 = $2,837
− 2,000
$ 837

Calculate the effective rate of interest for one year:

12–5. Principal: $15,500
Interest rate: 12%
Compounded quarterly
Effective rate: 12.55%

$\frac{12\%}{4} = 3\%$ 4 periods

$15,500 × 1.1255 = $17,445.25
− 15,500.00
$ 1,945.25

$\frac{\$1,945.25}{\$15,500} = .1255 = 12.55\%$

12–6. Using Table 12–2, calculate what $700 would grow to at $6\frac{1}{2}\%$ per year compounded daily for 7 years.

$700 × 1.5761 = $1,103.27

Complete the following using present value Table 12-3:

	Amount desired at end of period	Length of time	Rate	Compounded	On PV Table 12-3 Period used	Rate used	PV factor used	PV of amount desired at end of period
12-7.	$ 900	4 years	4%	Semiannually	8	2%	.8535	$ 768.15
				$900 × .8535 = $768.15				
12-8.	$ 7,650	2 years	12%	Monthly	24	1%	.7876	$6,025.14
				$7,650 × .7876 = $6,025.14				
12-9.	$17,600	7 years	12%	Quarterly	28	3%	.4371	$7,692.96
				$17,600 × .4371 = $7,692.96				
12-10.	$20,000	20 years	8%	Annually	20	8%	.2145	$4,290
				$20,000 × .2145 = $4,290				

12-11. Check your answer in Problem 12-9 by the compound value Table 12-1. (Answer will be off due to rounding.)
2.2879 × $7,692.96 = $17,600.72
(3%, 28 periods)

Word Problems

$\frac{10\%}{2} = 5\%$
3 years × 2 = 6 periods

12-12. Katie Kosiak deposited $25,100 in Ranch Bank. Ranch pays 10% interest compounded semiannually. How much will Katie have in her account at the end of 3 years?
$25,100 × 1.3401 = $33,636.51

$\frac{8\%}{2} = 4\%$
5 years × 2 = 10 periods

12-13. Alice Horn, owner of Horn's Ceramics Shop, loaned $12,000 to Pete Hall to help him open a deli. Pete plans to repay Alice at the end of 5 years with 8% interest compounded semiannually. How much will Alice receive at the end of 5 years?
$12,000 × 1.4802 = $17,762.40

$\frac{6\%}{4} = 1.5\%$
1 year × 4 = 4 periods

12-14. Molly Slate deposited $35,000 at Quazi Bank at 6% interest compounded quarterly. What is the effective rate to nearest hundredth percent?
$35,000 × 1.0614 = $37,149 − $35,000 = $\frac{\$2,149}{\$35,000}$ = 6.14%

12-15. Melvin Indecision has difficulty deciding whether to put his savings in Mystic Bank or in Four Rivers Bank. Mystic offers 10% interest compounded semiannually. Four Rivers offers 8% interest compounded quarterly. Melvin has $10,000 to invest. He expects to withdraw the money at the end of 4 years. Which bank gives Melvin the best deal? Check your answer.

Mystic ✔

$\frac{10\%}{2} = 5\%$
4 years × 2 = 8 periods
$10,000 × 1.4775 = $14,775
− 10,000
$ 4,775

Four Rivers

$\frac{8\%}{4} = 2\%$
4 years × 4 = 16 periods
$10,000 × 1.3728 = $13,728
− 10,000
$ 3,728

$\frac{12\%}{2} = 6\%$
3 years × 2 = 6 periods

12-16. Brian Costa deposited $20,000 in a new savings account at 12% interest compounded semiannually. At the beginning of year 4, Brian deposits an additional $30,000 at 12% interst compounded semiannually. At the end of 6 years, what is the balance in Brian's account?
$20,000 × 1.4185 = $28,370
+ 30,000
$58,370
$58,370 × 1.4185 = $82,797.85

$\frac{12\%}{4} = 3\%$
5 years × 4 = 20 periods

12-17. Carol Mores loaned Jeff Sales $12,000 to open up a coffee shop. After 5 years, Jeff will repay Carol with 12% interest compounded quarterly. How much will Carol receive at the end of 5 years?
$12,000 × 1.8061 = $21,673.20

12–18. John Bienet signed a 5-year note with a face value of $20,000 and interest of 8% compounded quarterly. What is the present value of the note to the *holder* if he can invest his money at 8% compounded semiannually?

Future value: $\frac{8\%}{4} = 2\%$ 1.4859 × $20,000 = $29,718

4 × 5 years = 20 periods

Present value: $\frac{8\%}{2} = 4\%$ .6756 × $29,718 = $20,077.48

2 × 5 years = 10 periods

12–19. Jeff Jones loans $9,500 to his brother-in-law. He will be repaid at the end of 8 years with interest at 6% compounded semiannually. Find out how much will be repaid.

3% 16 periods 6% ÷ 2 = 3% 8 years × 2 = 16 periods

1.6047 × $9,500 = $15,244.65

12–20. Jim Jones, an owner of a Burger King restaurant, assumes that his restaurant will need a new roof in seven years. He estimates the roof will cost him $9,000 at that time. What amount should Jim invest today at 6% compounded quarterly to be able to pay off the roof? Check your answer.

1.5% 28 periods 6% ÷ 4 = 1.5% 7 years × 4 = 28 periods

.6591 × $9,000 = $5,931.90

Check $5,931.90 × 1.5172 = $8,999.88 (due to rounding)

$\frac{12\%}{2} = 6\%$

4 years × 2 = 8 periods

12–21. Tony Ring wants to attend Northeast College. He will need $60,000 4 years from today. Assume Tony's bank pays 12% interest compounded semiannually. What must Tony deposit today so he will have $60,000 in 4 years?

$60,000 × .6274 = $37,644

6%, 8 periods

12–22. Could you check your answer (to nearest dollar) in Problem 12–21 by using the compound value Table 12–1? The answer will be off slightly due to rounding.

$37,644 × 1.5938 = $59,997

$\frac{12\%}{2} = 6\%$

5 years × 2 = 10 periods

12–23. Pete Air wants to buy a new Jeep in 5 years. He estimates the Jeep will cost $15,000. Assume Pete invests $10,000 now at 12% interest compounded semiannually. Will Pete have enough money to buy his Jeep at the end of 5 years?

$10,000 × 1.7908 = $17,908 Yes.

12–24. Lance Jackson deposited $5,000 at Basil Bank at 9% interest compounded daily. What is Lance's investment at the end of 4 years?

$5,000 × 1.4333 = $7,166.50

$\frac{6\%}{2} = 3\%$

8 years × 2 = 16 periods

12–25. Paul Havlik promised his grandson Jamie that he would give him $6,000 8 years from today for graduating from high school. Assume money is worth 6% interest compounded semiannually. What is the present value of this $6,000?

$6,000 × .6232 = $3,739.20

$\frac{6\%}{2} = 3\%$

15 years × 2 = 30 periods

12–26. Earl Ezekiel wants to retire in San Diego when he is 65 years old. Earl is now 50. He believes he will need $300,000 to retire comfortably. To date, Earl has set aside no retirement money. Assume Earl gets 6% interest compounded semiannually. How much must Earl invest today to meet his $300,000 goal?

$300,000 × .4120 = $123,600

$\frac{8\%}{2} = 4\%$

4 years × 2 = 8 periods

12–27. Lorna Evenson would like to buy a $19,000 car in 4 years. Lorna wants to put the money aside now. Lorna's bank offers 8% interest compounded semiannually. How much must Lorna invest today?

$19,000 × .7307 = $13,883.30

Challenge Problem

Certificate of Deposit

12–28. John Tobas hit the numbers game in the Tri-State Lottery. He received a $40,000 check. John decided he would buy a 30-month Certificate of Deposit. In a local advertisement, National Bank offered 30-month certificates with 6% interest compounded quarterly. John bought this $40,000 certificate on January 1. Later in the day, John became upset when he saw another advertisement for a 30-month certificate with 8% interest compounded quarterly. What is the difference in interest between these two certificates of deposit? Calculate the effective yield for each to nearest hundredth percent.

$\frac{6\%}{4} = 1.5\%$ $\frac{8\%}{4} = 2\%$

2.5 yr. × 4 = 10 periods 2.5 yr. × 4 = 10 periods

$40,000 × 1.1605 = $46,420 $40,000 × 1.2190 = $48,760

$48,760
− 46,420
$ 2,340

6.14% 4 periods = 1.0614 8.24% 4 periods = 1.0824

Summary Practice Test

Solutions are at end of text in Appendix II.

Quick Reference
If you get any wrong answers, study the page numbers given for each problem.

1. Jane Joy, owner of The Clock Shop, loaned $12,000 to Carol Miller to help her open an art shop. Carol plans to repay Jane at the end of 7 years with 6% interest compounded quarterly. How much will Jane receive at the end of 7 years?
   $\frac{6\%}{4} = 1.5\%$ 7 years × 4 = 28 periods $12,000 × 1.5172 = $18,206.40

   1. Pp. 278–79.

2. Abby Ellen wants to attend Ithaca College. She will need $75,000 6 years from today. Assume Abby's bank pays 6% interest compounded semiannually. What must Abby deposit today to have $75,000 in 6 years?
   $\frac{6\%}{2} = 3\%$ 6 years × 2 = 12 periods $75,000 × .7014 = $52,605

   2. Pp. 282–83.

3. Jacob Fonda deposited $25,000 in a savings account at 10% interest compounded semiannually. At the beginning of year 4, Jacob deposits an additional $40,000 at 10% interest compounded semiannually. At the end of 6 years, what is the balance in Jacob's account?
   $\frac{10\%}{2} = 5\%$ 3 years × 2 = 6 periods $25,000 × 1.3401 = $33,502.50
   $73,502.50 × 1.3401 = $98,500.70

   3. Pp. 278–79.

4. Margaret Foster wants to buy a new camper in 6 years. She estimates the camper will cost $6,400. Assume Margaret invests $3,800 now at 8% interest compounded semiannually. Will Margaret have enough money to buy her camper at the end of the 6 years?
   $\frac{8\%}{2} = 4\%$ 6 years × 2 = 12 periods
   $3,800 × 1.6010 = $6,083.80 No; $6,400 − $6,083.80 = $316.20 shortage

   4. Pp. 278–79.

5. Ed Sullivan deposited $14,000 at Roll Bank at 8% interest compounded semiannually. What was the effective rate? Round to nearest hundredth percent.
   $\frac{8\%}{2} = 4\%$, 2 periods $\frac{\$1,142.40}{\$14,000} = 8.16\%$
   $14,000 × 1.0816 = $15,142.40
   − 14,000.00
   $ 1,142.40

   5. P. 280.

6. Alvin Miller, owner of Miller Garage, estimates that he will need $18,000 for new equipment in 20 years. Alvin decided to put aside the money today so it will be available in 20 years. Sound Bank offers Alvin 12% interest compounded semiannually. How much must Alvin invest today to have $18,000 in 20 years?
   $\frac{12\%}{2} = 6\%$ 20 × 2 = 40 periods
   $18,000 × .0972 = $1,749.60

   6. Pp. 282–83.

7. Pp. 282–83.

7. Ray Long wants to retire in Arizona when he is 70 years of age. Ray is now 50. He believes he will need \$130,000 to retire comfortably. To date, Ray has set aside no retirement money. Assume Ray gets 14% interest compounded semiannually. How much must Ray invest today to meet his \$130,000 goal?

$\frac{14\%}{2} = 7\%$ 20 years $\times$ 2 = 40 periods

\$130,000 $\times$ .0668 = \$8,684

8. P. 281.

8. Rose Ray deposited \$24,000 in a savings account at $6\frac{1}{2}\%$ interest compounded daily. At the end of 7 years, what is the balance in Rose Ray's account?

\$24,000 $\times$ 1.5761 = \$37,826.40

Project A

	When you deposit	30-month C.D. interest rate	30-month interest at maturity	If 12% interest at maturity	Interest difference
A.	$100,000	12.28% EFFECTIVE ANNUAL YIELD ON 11.75% INTEREST RATE	$33,578	$34,390	$812
B.	$80,001	12.28% EFFECTIVE ANNUAL YIELD ON 11.75% INTEREST RATE	$26,863	$27,512.34	$649.34
C.	$60,001	12.28% EFFECTIVE ANNUAL YIELD ON 11.75% INTEREST RATE	$20,147	$20,634.34	$487.34
D.	$40,001	12.28% EFFECTIVE ANNUAL YIELD ON 11.75% INTEREST RATE	$13,431	$13,756.34	$325.34
E.	$20,001	12.28% EFFECTIVE ANNUAL YIELD ON 11.75% INTEREST RATE	$6,716	$6,878.34	$162.34
F.	$15,001	12.28% EFFECTIVE ANNUAL YIELD ON 11.75% INTEREST RATE	$5,037	$5,158.84	$121.84
G.	$10,001	12.28% EFFECTIVE ANNUAL YIELD ON 11.75% INTEREST RATE	$3,358	$3,439.34	$81.34

This yield assumes that principal and interest remain on deposit for a full year. Interest compounded quarterly

Bill Smith saw this bank advertisement. He feels the interest rate may rise to 12% next month. Using the compound interest Table 12-1 in the text, what would the interest be at maturity for each amount below? By waiting until next month, how much interest could Bill gain over depositing now? Assume that Bill wants to work out the interest rate for each deposit shown. What would be the annual effective yield with an interest rate of 12%.

$\frac{12\%}{4} = 3\%$ 2.5 years × 4 = 10 periods

A. $100,000 × 1.3439 = $134,390 − 100,000 = $ 34,390; $34,390 − 33,578 = $ 812

B. $80,001 × 1.3439 = $107,513.34 − 80,001.00 = $ 27,512.34; $27,512.34 − 26,863.00 = $ 649.34

C. $60,001 × 1.3439 = $80,635.34 − 60,001.00 = $20,634.34; $20,634.34 − 20,147.00 = $ 487.34

D. $40,001 × 1.3439 = $53,757.34 − 40,001.00 = $13,756.34; $13,756.34 − 13,431.00 = $ 325.34

E. $20,001 × 1.3439 = $26,879.34 − 20,001.00 = $ 6,878.34; $ 6,878.34 − 6,716.00 = $ 162.34

F. $15,001 × 1.3439 = $20,159.84 − 15,001.00 = $ 5,158.84; $5,158.84 − 5,037.00 = $ 121.84

G. $10,001 × 1.3439 = $13,440.34 − 10,001.00 = $ 3,439.34; $3,439.34 − 3,358.00 = $ 81.34

Effective rate, 12.55%

Note: Have students visit a bank to see the current rate of CDs.

NOTES

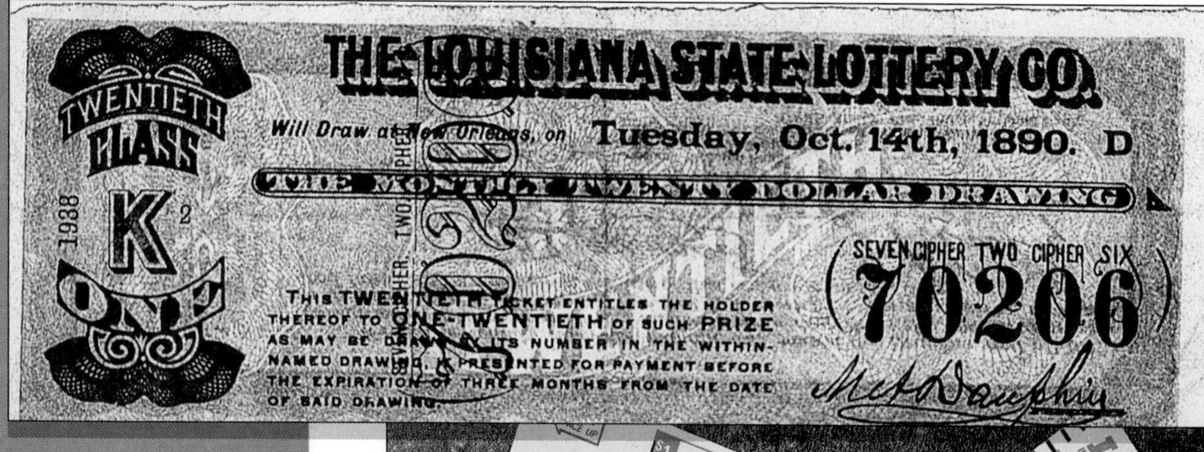

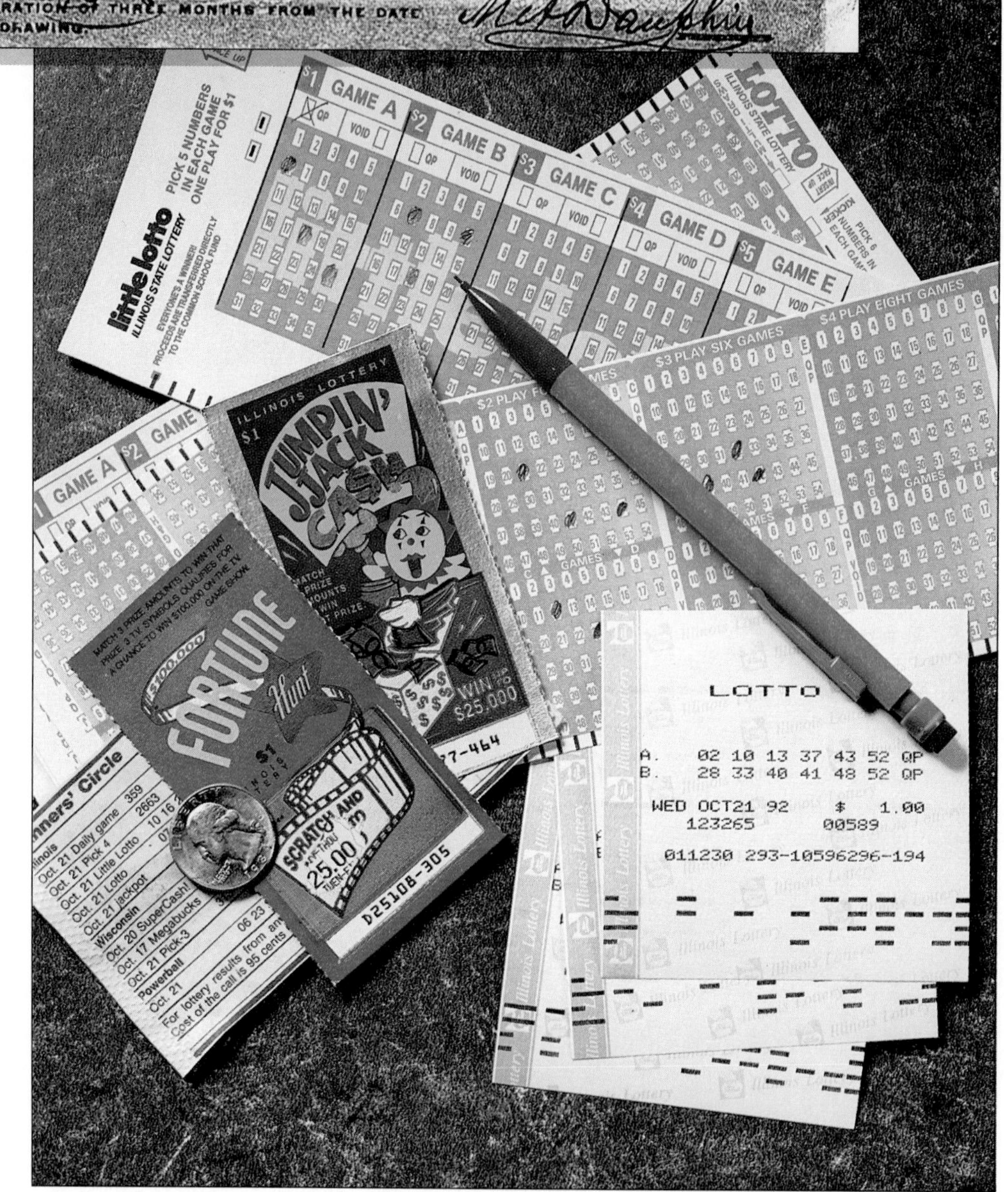

THAT WAS THEN . . .
. . . THIS IS NOW

Lotteries have been around for many years, as seen by this 1890 Louisiana State Lottery ticket. If you win $1,000,000 is it really worth one million in today's dollars? If paid $50,000 for 20 years you would be receiving an annuity.

13

Annuities and Sinking Funds

LEARNING UNIT OBJECTIVES

LU 13-1: Annuities: Ordinary Annuity and Annuity Due

1. Differentiate between contingent annuities and annuities certain. *p. 297.*
2. Calculate manually the value of an ordinary annuity and annuity due. *pp. 298–300.*
3. Calculate the value of an annuity by tables for ordinary and annuity due. *pp. 298–300.*

LU 13-2: Present Value of an Ordinary Annuity (Finds Present Worth)

1. Differentiate between the present value of one lump sum versus the present value of an ordinary annuity. *p. 301.*
2. Calculate the present value of an ordinary annuity by table lookup and manually check the calculation. *p. 302.*

LU 13-3: Sinking Funds (Finds Payment Amount)

1. Calculate payment made at end of each period by table lookup. *pp. 304–5.*
2. Check table lookup by using ordinary annuity table. *p. 305.*

In Chapter 12, we explained how to calculate compound interest on a lump-sum payment deposited at the beginning of a particular time. In this chapter, we study interest compounding that results from a *stream* of payments, or an annuity. The following article from *The Wall Street Journal* gives an example of a common form of annuity—the IRA.

A Strategy for Young Savers

If you've got a teen-ager and are wondering if he will ever save a penny, you may want to take a second look at individual retirement accounts—not for yourself, but as a way of helping your kid retire a millionaire.

Say your son or daughter starts working at the age of 18, earning money from a summer job. Put $2,000 of those earnings into an IRA, and reimburse your child with spending money. In return, there's a small tax deduction on your child's tax return.

Do this for seven years, until the child is 24. Then, just sit back, says Albert Margeson, a vice president at TNE Funds Group in Boston. If the IRA averages a 10% annual return for the next 40 years, the account would grow to over $1 million when your child turns 65. But if you wait until your child turns 24 to start the IRA, it would require 41 $2,000 deposits to get the same outcome, Mr. Margeson says.

The principle remains the same if your children don't earn $2,000 a year, although the numbers are lower. P. Kemp Fain Jr., a Knoxville, Tenn., financial planner who helped his children get started with IRAs, says he simply invested an amount equal to whatever the kids earned. "Let's say they earned $500, I would put that in," he says.

The downside? Penalties on withdrawals before age 59 1/2 mean that "a 16-year-old will not be able to use that money for their college education or their house down payment," says William J. Goldberg, national director of personal financial planning services at KPMG Peat Marwick. He says these needs should probably be addressed before considering an IRA for your teen. "But if you put it in there and left it in there for 10 years—even with the penalties—you could be ahead of the game," he says.

—Lynn Asinof

Knowing how to calculate interest compounding on a lump sum will make the calculation of interest compounding on annuities easier to understand. The first unit of this chapter explains the difference between an ordinary annuity and an annuity due.

LEARNING UNIT 13–1 ANNUITIES: ORDINARY ANNUITY AND ANNUITY DUE

Let's begin by studying the concept of the future value of annuities.

Concept of an Annuity—The Big Picture

You would all probably like to win $1 million in a state lottery. As soon as you know you have won, you would take the winning ticket to the lottery headquarters. You may think that when you turn in the winning ticket, you will immediately receive in return a check for $1 million. This is not how lottery payoffs occur.

Lottery winners receive a series of payments over a period of time—usually years. This *stream* of payments is an **annuity.** By paying the winners an annuity, lotteries do not actually spend $1 million. The lottery deposits a sum of money in a financial institution. The continual growth of this sum through compound interest provides the lottery winner with a series of payments.

FIGURE 13–1
Future Value of an Annuity of $1 at 8%

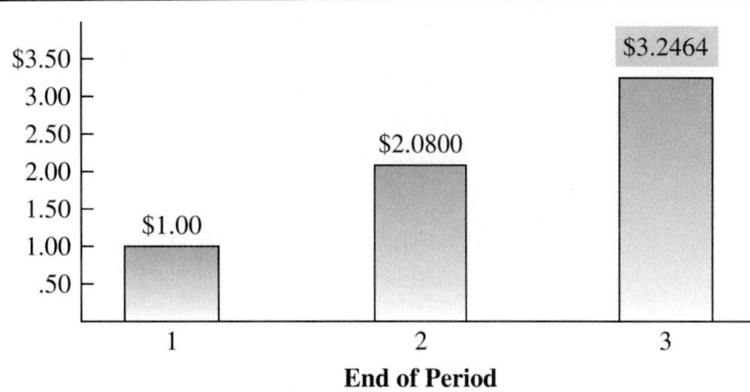

Courtesy of Illinois Lottery

When we calculated the maturity value of a lump-sum payment in Chapter 12, the maturity value was the principal and its interest. Now we are not looking at lump-sum payments but a series of payments (usually of equal amount over regular periods) plus the interest that accumulates. So the **value of an annuity** is the value of a series of payments plus interest.

The concept of the future value of an annuity is illustrated in Figure 13–1. Do not be concerned about the calculations (we will do them soon). Let's first focus on the big picture of annuities. In Figure 13–1, we see the following:

At end of period 1:	The $1 is still worth $1 because it was invested at the *end* of the period.
At end of period 2:	An additional $1 is invested. The $2 are now worth $2.08. Note the $1 from period 1 earns interest but not the $1 invested at the end of period 2.
At end of period 3:	An additional $1 is invested. The $3 are now worth $3.25. Remember that the last dollar invested earns no interest.

Before learning how to calculate annuities, you should understand the types of annuities.

Classifications of Annuities

Annuities have many uses in addition to lottery payoffs. Some of the uses are insurance companies' pension installments, social security payments, home mortgages, businesses paying off notes, bond interest, and saving for a vacation trip or college education.

The two basic classes of annuities are contingent annuities and annuities certain. **Contingent annuities** have no fixed amount of payments (like paying so much per month, until retirement, or until death). **Annuities certain** have a specific stated number of payments. Based on the time of payment, we can break down these two types of annuities into:

1. **Ordinary annuity**—regular deposits (payments) made at the *end* of the period. Periods could be months, quarters, years, and so on. An ordinary annuity could be salaries, stock dividends, and so on.
2. **Annuity due**—regular deposits (payments) made at the *beginning* of the period, such as rent or life insurance premiums.

The remainder of this unit shows you how to calculate and check ordinary annuities and annuities due.

Ordinary Annuities (Finds Future Value)

Before we explain how to use tables that simplify calculating ordinary annuities, let's first determine how to calculate an ordinary annuity manually.

Calculating Ordinary Annuities Manually

Remember that an ordinary annuity invests money at the *end* of each year (period). After we calculate ordinary annuities manually, you will see that the total value of the investment comes from the *stream* of yearly investments and the buildup of interest on the current balance.

Steps for Calculating Value of an Ordinary Annuity Manually

Step 1. For period 1, no interest calculation is necessary since money is invested at end of period.

Step 2. For period 2, calculate interest on balance and add to previous balance.

Step 3. Add additional investment at end of period 2 to new balance.

Step 4. Repeat Steps 2 and 3 until end of desired period is reached.

EXAMPLE Find the value of an investment after three years for a $3,000 ordinary annuity at 8%.

We calculate this manually as follows:

Money invested at the end of each year is an ordinary annuity.

Step 1.	→ End of year 1:	$3,000.00	→ No interest, since this is put in at end of year 1. (Remember, payment is made at end of period.)
	Year 2:	$3,000.00	→ Value of investment before investment at end of year 2.
Step 2.	→	+ 240.00	→ Interest (.08 × $3,000) for year 2.
		$3,240.00	→ Value of investment at end of year 2 before second investment.
Step 3.	→ End of year 2:	+ 3,000.00	→ Second investment at end of year 2.
	Year 3:	$6,240.00	→ Investment balance going into year 3.
		+ 499.20	→ Interest for year 3 (.08 × $6,240).
Step 4.	→	$6,739.20	→ Value before investment at end of year 3.
	→	+ 3,000.00	→ Investment at end of year 3.
	End of year 3:	$9,739.20	→ Total value of investment after investment at end of year 3.

Years

1 2 3

$3,000 ⟶

$3,000 ⟶

$3,000 ⟶

Note: We totally invested $9,000 over three different periods. It is now worth $9,739.20.

The value of the annuity is called the maturity value in compounding. Today, you can make these calculations quicker with a computer.

When you deposit $3,000 at the end of each year at an annual rate of 8%, the total value of the annuity is $9,739.20. What we called *maturity value* in compounding is now called the *value of annuity*. We can make this calculation easier by using Table 13–1 (p. 299).

Calculating Value of Ordinary Annuity by Table Lookup

Use the following steps to calculate the value of an ordinary annuity by table.

Steps for Calculating Value of an Ordinary Annuity by Table

Step 1. Calculate rate per period and number of periods.

Step 2. Look up in ordinary annuity table the rate and periods. Intersection gives table factor for future value of $1.

Step 3. Multiply payment each period times table factor. This gives value of annuity.

EXAMPLE Find the value of an investment after 3 years for a $3,000 ordinary annuity at 8%.

Step 1. Rate $= \frac{8\%}{\text{Annually}} = 8\%$ Periods = 3 years × 1 = 3

TABLE 13–1 Ordinary Annuity Table: Compound Sum of an Annuity of $1

Period	2%	3%	4%	5%	6%	7%	8%	9%	10%	11%	12%	13%
1	1.0000	1.0000	1.0000	1.0000	1.0000	1.0000	1.0000	1.0000	1.0000	1.0000	1.0000	1.0000
2	2.0200	2.0300	2.0400	2.0500	2.0600	2.0700	2.0800	2.0900	2.1000	2.1100	2.1200	2.1300
3	3.0604	3.0909	3.1216	3.1525	3.1836	3.2149	3.2464	3.2781	3.3100	3.3421	3.3744	3.4069
4	4.1216	4.1836	4.2465	4.3101	4.3746	4.4399	4.5061	4.5731	4.6410	4.7097	4.7793	4.8498
5	5.2040	5.3091	5.4163	5.5256	5.6371	5.7507	5.8666	5.9847	6.1051	6.2278	6.3528	6.4803
6	6.3081	6.4684	6.6330	6.8019	6.9753	7.1533	7.3359	7.5233	7.7156	7.9129	8.1152	8.3227
7	7.4343	7.6625	7.8983	8.1420	8.3938	8.6540	8.9228	9.2004	9.4872	9.7833	10.0890	10.4047
8	8.5829	8.8923	9.2142	9.5491	9.8975	10.2598	10.6366	11.0285	11.4359	11.8594	12.2997	12.7573
9	9.7546	10.1591	10.5828	11.0265	11.4913	11.9780	12.4876	13.0210	13.5795	14.1640	14.7757	15.4157
10	10.9497	11.4639	12.0061	12.5779	13.1808	13.8164	14.4866	15.1929	15.9374	16.7220	17.5487	18.4197
11	12.1687	12.8078	13.4863	14.2068	14.9716	15.7836	16.6455	17.5603	18.5312	19.5614	20.6546	21.8143
12	13.4120	14.1920	15.0258	15.9171	16.8699	17.8884	18.9771	20.1407	21.3843	22.7132	24.1331	25.6502
13	14.6803	15.6178	16.6268	17.7129	18.8821	20.1406	21.4953	22.9534	24.5227	26.2116	28.0291	29.9847
14	15.9739	17.0863	18.2919	19.5986	21.0150	22.5505	24.2149	26.0192	27.9750	30.0949	32.3926	34.8827
15	17.2934	18.5989	20.0236	21.5785	23.2759	25.1290	27.1521	29.3609	31.7725	34.4054	37.2797	40.4174
16	18.6392	20.1569	21.8245	23.6574	25.6725	27.8880	30.3243	33.0034	35.9497	39.1899	42.7533	46.6717
17	20.0120	21.7616	23.6975	25.8403	28.2128	30.8402	33.7503	36.9737	40.5447	44.5008	48.8837	53.7390
18	21.4122	23.4144	25.6454	28.1323	30.9056	33.9990	37.4503	41.3014	45.5992	50.3959	55.7497	61.7251
19	22.8405	25.1169	27.6712	30.5389	33.7599	37.3789	41.4463	46.0185	51.1591	56.9395	63.4397	70.7494
20	24.2973	26.8704	29.7781	33.0659	36.7855	40.9954	45.7620	51.1602	57.2750	64.2028	72.0524	80.9468
25	32.0302	36.4593	41.6459	47.7270	54.8644	63.2489	73.1060	84.7010	98.3471	114.4133	133.3338	155.6194
30	40.5679	47.5754	56.0849	66.4386	79.0580	94.4606	113.2833	136.3077	164.4941	199.0209	241.3327	293.1989
40	60.4017	75.4012	95.0254	120.7993	154.7616	199.6346	259.0569	337.8831	442.5928	581.8260	767.0913	1013.7030
50	84.5790	112.7968	152.6669	209.3470	290.3351	406.5277	573.7711	815.0853	1163.9090	1668.7710	2400.0180	3459.5010

Note: This is only a sampling of tables available. The Business Math Handbook shows tables from ½% to 15%.

Step 2. Go to Table 13–1, ordinary annuity table. Look for 3 under Period column. Go across to 8%. At intersection is the table factor, 3.2464. (This was the example we showed in Figure 13–1.)

Step 3. Multiply $3,000 × 3.2464 = $9,739.20 (the same figure we calculated manually).

Now let's look at what the difference in the total investment would be for an annuity due.

Annuity Due: Money Invested at Beginning of Year (Finds Future Value)

As in the previous section, we will first make the calculation manually and then use the table lookup.

Calculating Annuity Due Manually

Use the steps that follow to manually calculate an annuity due.

Steps for Calculating Value of an Annuity Due Manually

Step 1. Calculate interest on balance for period and add to previous balance.

Step 2. Add additional investment at *beginning* of period to new balance.

Step 3. Repeat Steps 1 and 2 until end of desired period is reached.

Common sense should tell us that the *annuity due* will give a higher final value. Remember that in an annuity due, we put the money in at the *beginning* of the year and gain more interest. We will use the same example that we used before.

EXAMPLE Find the value of an investment after 3 years for $3,000 annuity due at 8%.

We calculate this manually as follows:

Beginning year 1:	$3,000.00	→	First investment (will earn interest for 3 years).
Step 1. →	+ 240.00	→	Interest (.08 × $3,000).
	$3,240.00	→	Value of investment at end of year 1.
Step 2. → Year 2:	+ 3,000.00	→	Second investment (will earn interest for 2 years).
	$6,240.00		
Step 3. →	+ 499.20	→	Interest for year 2 (.08 × $6,240).
	$6,739.20	→	Value of investment at end of year 2.
Year 3:	+ 3,000.00		
	$9,739.20	→	Third investment (will earn interest for one year).
	+ 779.14	→	Interest (.08 × $9,739.20)
End of year 3:	**$10,518.34**	→	At end of year 3, final value.

Years

1 2 3

$3,000 →
$3,000 →
$3,000 →

Note: Our total investment of $9,000 is worth $10,518.34. For an ordinary annuity it was only worth $9,739.20.

Calculating Value of Annuity Due by Table Lookup

To calculate the value of an annuity due with a table, use the steps that follow.

Steps for Calculating Value of an Annuity Due by Table

Step 1. Calculate rate per period and number of periods. Add one extra period.

Step 2. Look up in ordinary annuity table the rate and periods. Intersection gives table *factor* for future value of $1.

Step 3. Multiply payment each period times table factor.

Step 4. Subtract 1 payment from Step 3.

Let's check the $10,518.34 by table lookup.

Step 1. Rate $= \frac{8\%}{\text{Annually}} = 8\%$ Periods = 3 years × 1 = 3
+1 extra
4

Step 2. Table factor, 4.5061

Step 3. $3,000 × 4.5061 = $13,518.30

Step 4. − 3,000.00

= $10,518.30 (off 4 cents due to rounding)

Note that the annuity due shows an ending value of $10,518.30, while the ending value of ordinary annuity was $9,739.20. We had a higher ending value with the annuity due because the investment took place at the beginning of each period.

Annuity payments do not have to be yearly. They could be semiannually, monthly, quarterly, and so on. Let's look at one more example with a different rate and number of periods.

Different Rates and Number of Periods

By using different rates and periods, we will contrast an ordinary annuity with an annuity due in the following example:

EXAMPLE Using Table 13–1, find the value of a $3,000 investment after 3 years made quarterly at 8%.

In the annuity due calculation, be sure to add one period and subtract one payment from the total value.

	Ordinary annuity		**Annuity due**		
Step 1.	Rate = 8% ÷ 4 = 2%		Rate = 8% ÷ 4 = 2%		**Step 1.**
	Periods = 3 years × 4 = 12		Periods = 3 years × 4 = 12		
	Table 13–1:		Table 13–1:		
Step 2.	2%, 12 periods =	13.4120	2%, 13 periods =	14.6803	**Step 2.**
Step 3.	$3,000 × 13.4120 =	$40,236	$3,000 × 14.6803 =	$44,040.90	**Step 3.**
				− $3,000.00	**Step 4.**
			=	$41,040.90	

Again, note that with annuity due, total value is greater since you invest the money at the beginning of each period.

Now check your progress with the Practice Quiz.

LU 13-1 PRACTICE QUIZ

1. Using Table 13–1, (**a**) find the value of an investment after 4 years on an ordinary annuity of $4,000 made semiannually at 10% and (**b**) recalculate assuming an annuity due.
2. Wally Beaver won a lottery and will receive a check for $4,000 at the beginning of each 6 months for the next 5 years. If Wally deposits each check into an account that pays 6%, how much will he have at the end of the 5 years?

SOLUTIONS TO LU 13-1 PRACTICE QUIZ

1. a. Step 1. 10% ÷ 2 = 5%
Periods = 4 years × 2 = 8
Step 2. Factor = 9.5491
Step 3. $4,000 × 9.5491 = $38,196.40

b. 10% ÷ 2 = 5% **Step 1.**
Periods = 4 years × 2 = 8 + 1 = 9
Factor = 11.0265 **Step 2.**
$4,000 × 11.0265 = $44,106 **Step 3.**
− 1 payment − 4,000 **Step 4.**
$40,106

2. Step 1. $\frac{6\%}{2}$ = 3% 5 years × 2 = 10
+ 1
11 periods

Step 2. Table factor, 12.8078
Step 3. $4,000 × 12.8078 = $51,231.20
Step 4. − 4,000.00
$47,231.20

LEARNING UNIT 13–2 PRESENT VALUE OF AN ORDINARY ANNUITY (FINDS PRESENT WORTH)

This unit begins by presenting the concept of present value of an ordinary annuity. Then you will learn how to use a table to calculate the present value of an ordinary annuity.

Concept of Present Value of an Annuity—The Big Picture

Let's assume that we want to know how much money we need to invest *today* to receive a stream of payments for a given number of years in the future. This is called the **present value of an ordinary annuity.**

In Figure 13–2, p. 302, you can see that if you wanted to withdraw $1 at the end of one period, you would have to invest 93 cents *today*. If at the end of each period for three periods, you wanted to withdraw $1, you would have to put $2.58 in the bank *today* at 8% interest. (Note that we go from the future back to the present.)

Now let's look at how we could use tables to calculate the present value of annuities and then check our answer.

FIGURE 13-2
Present Value of an Annuity of $1 at 8%

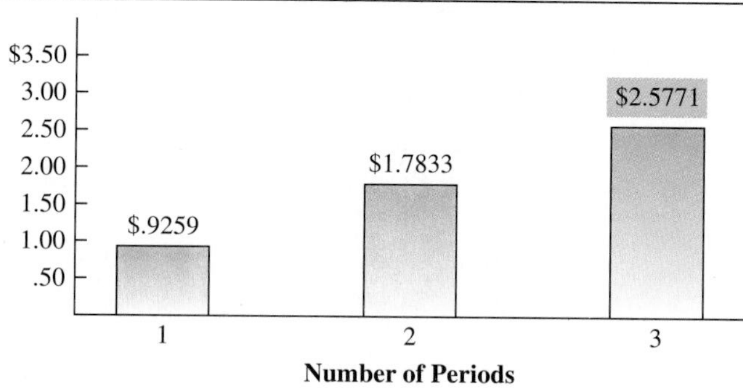

Calculating Present Value of Ordinary Annuity by Table

Use the following steps to calculate by table the present value of an ordinary annuity.

Steps for Calculating Present Value of Ordinary Annuity by Table

Step 1. Calculate rate per period and number of periods.

Step 2. Look up rate and periods in the present value of an annuity table. Intersection gives table factor for present value of $1.

Step 3. Multiply withdrawal for each period times table factor. This gives present value of ordinary annuity.

Remember that interest could be earned semiannually, quarterly, and so on, as shown in previous unit.

EXAMPLE John Fitch wants to receive an $8,000 annuity in 3 years. Interest on the annuity is 8% annually. John will make withdrawals at the end of each year. How much must John invest today to receive a stream of payments for 3 years? Use Table 13-2.

Step 1. $\frac{8\%}{\text{Annually}} = 8\%$ 3 years × 1 = 3 periods

Step 2. Table factor, 2.5771 (we saw this in Figure 13-2)

Step 3. $8,000 × 2.5771 = $20,616.80

If John wants to withdraw $8,000 at the end of each period for 3 years, he will have to deposit $20,616.80 in the bank *today*.

$20,616.80	
+ 1,649.34	→ Interest at end of year 1 (.08 × $20,616.80)
$22,266.14	
− 8,000.00	→ First payment to John
$14,266.14	
+ 1,141.29	→ Interest at end of year 2 (.08 × $14,266.14)
$15,407.43	
− 8,000.00	→ Second payment to John
$ 7,407.43	
+ 592.59	→ Interest at end of year 3 (.08 × $7,407.43)
$8,000.02	
−8,000.00	→ After end of year 3 John receives his last $8,000
.02[1]	

Before leaving this unit, let's work out two examples that show the relationship of Chapter 13 to Chapter 12. Use your Business Math Handbook.

Chapter 12 versus Chapter 13—Lump Sums versus Annuities

EXAMPLE John Sands made deposits of $200 semiannually to Floor Bank, which pays 8% interest compounded semiannually. After 5 years, John makes no more deposits. What will be the balance in the account 6 years after the last deposit?

[1] Off due to rounding.

TABLE 13–2 Present Value of an Annuity of $1

Period	2%	3%	4%	5%	6%	7%	8%	9%	10%	11%	12%	13%
1	0.9804	0.9709	0.9615	0.9524	0.9434	0.9346	0.9259	0.9174	0.9091	0.9009	0.8929	0.8850
2	1.9416	1.9135	1.8861	1.8594	1.8334	1.8080	1.7833	1.7591	1.7355	1.7125	1.6901	1.6681
3	2.8839	2.8286	2.7751	2.7232	2.6730	2.6243	2.5771	2.5313	2.4869	2.4437	2.4018	2.3612
4	3.8077	3.7171	3.6299	3.5459	3.4651	3.3872	3.3121	3.2397	3.1699	3.1024	3.0373	2.9745
5	4.7134	4.5797	4.4518	4.3295	4.2124	4.1002	3.9927	3.8897	3.7908	3.6959	3.6048	3.5172
6	5.6014	5.4172	5.2421	5.0757	4.9173	4.7665	4.6229	4.4859	4.3553	4.2305	4.1114	3.9975
7	6.4720	6.2303	6.0021	5.7864	5.5824	5.3893	5.2064	5.0330	4.8684	4.7122	4.5638	4.4226
8	7.3255	7.0197	6.7327	6.4632	6.2098	5.9713	5.7466	5.5348	5.3349	5.1461	4.9676	4.7988
9	8.1622	7.7861	7.4353	7.1078	6.8017	6.5152	6.2469	5.9952	5.7590	5.5370	5.3282	5.1317
10	8.9826	8.5302	8.1109	7.7217	7.3601	7.0236	6.7101	6.4177	6.1446	5.8892	5.6502	5.4262
11	9.7868	9.2526	8.7605	8.3064	7.8869	7.4987	7.1390	6.8052	6.4951	6.2065	5.9377	5.6869
12	10.5753	9.9540	9.3851	8.8632	8.3838	7.9427	7.5361	7.1607	6.8137	6.4924	6.1944	5.9176
13	11.3483	10.6350	9.9856	9.3936	8.8527	8.3576	7.9038	7.4869	7.1034	6.7499	6.4235	6.1218
14	12.1062	11.2961	10.5631	9.8986	9.2950	8.7455	8.2442	7.7862	7.3667	6.9819	6.6282	6.3025
15	12.8492	11.9379	11.1184	10.3796	9.7122	9.1079	8.5595	8.0607	7.6061	7.1909	6.8109	6.4624
16	13.5777	12.5611	11.6523	10.8378	10.1059	9.4466	8.8514	8.3126	7.8237	7.3792	6.9740	6.6039
17	14.2918	13.1661	12.1657	11.2741	10.4773	9.7632	9.1216	8.5436	8.0216	7.5488	7.1196	6.7291
18	14.9920	13.7535	12.6593	11.6896	10.8276	10.0591	9.3719	8.7556	8.2014	7.7016	7.2497	6.8399
19	15.6784	14.3238	13.1339	12.0853	11.1581	10.3356	9.6036	8.9501	8.3649	7.8393	7.3658	6.9380
20	16.3514	14.8775	13.5903	12.4622	11.4699	10.5940	9.8181	9.1285	8.5136	7.9633	7.4694	7.0248
25	19.5234	17.4131	15.6221	14.0939	12.7834	11.6536	10.6748	9.8226	9.0770	8.4217	7.8431	7.3300
30	22.3964	19.6004	17.2920	15.3724	13.7648	12.4090	11.2578	10.2737	9.4269	8.6938	8.0552	7.4957
40	27.3554	23.1148	19.7928	17.1591	15.0463	13.3317	11.9246	10.7574	9.7790	8.9511	8.2438	7.6344
50	31.4236	25.7298	21.4822	18.2559	15.7619	13.8007	12.2335	10.9617	9.9148	9.0417	8.3045	7.6752

Step 1. Calculate amount of annuity: ← Table 13–1
4%, 10 periods $200 × 12.0061 = $2,401.22

Step 2. Calculate how much final value of annuity will grow by the compound interest table. ← Table 12–1
4%, 12 periods $2,401.22 × 1.6010 = **$3,844.35**

For John, the stream of payments grows to $2,401.22. Then this *lump sum* grows for 6 years to $3,844.35. Now let's look at a present value example.

EXAMPLE Mel Rich decided to retire in 8 years to Florida. What amount should Mel invest today so he will be able to withdraw $40,000 at the end of each year for 25 years *after* he retires? Assume Mel can invest money at 5% interest (compounded annually).

Step 1. Calculate present value of annuity: ← Table 13–2
5%, 25 periods $40,000 × 14.0939 = $563,756

Step 2. Find the present value of $563,756 since Mel will not retire for 8 years: Table 12–3 →
5%, 8 periods (PV table) $563,756 × .6768 = **$381,550.06**

If Mel deposits $381,550 in year 1, it will grow to $563,756 after 8 years.

It's time to try the Practice Quiz and check your understanding of this unit.

LU 13–2 PRACTICE QUIZ

1. What must you invest today to receive an $18,000 annuity for 5 years semiannually at a 10% annual rate? All withdrawals will be made at the end of each year.
2. Rase High School wants to set up a scholarship fund to provide 5 $2,000 scholarships for the next 10 years. If money can be invested at an annual rate of 9%, how much should the scholarship committee invest today?

SOLUTIONS TO LU 13-2 PRACTICE QUIZ

1. **Step 1.** Rate = 10% ÷ 2 = 5%; Periods = 5 years × 2 = 10
   Step 2. Factor, 7.7217
   Step 3. $18,000 × 7.7217 = $138,990.60
2. **Step 1.** Rate = 9% Periods = 10
   Step 2. Factor, 6.4177
   Step 3. $10,000 × 6.4177 = $64,177

LEARNING UNIT 13-3 SINKING FUNDS (FINDS PAYMENT AMOUNT)

A sinking fund sets up an annuity to meet a future obligation.

A **sinking fund** is a financial arrangement that sets aside regular periodic payments of a particular amount of money. Compound interest accumulates on these payments to a specific sum at a predetermined future date. Corporations use sinking funds to discharge bonded indebtedness, to replace worn-out equipment, to purchase plant expansion, and so on.

A sinking fund is different from an annuity. In a sinking fund, you determine the amount of periodic payments you need to achieve a given financial goal. In the annuity, you know the amount of each payment and must determine its future value. Let's work with the following example.

Sinking fund payment = Future value × Sinking fund table factor

EXAMPLE To retire a bond issue, Moore Company needs $60,000 18 years from today. The interest rate is 10% compounded annually. What payment must Moore make at the end of each year? Use Table 13-3.

TABLE 13-3 Sinking Fund Table Based on $1

Period	2%	3%	4%	5%	6%	8%	10%
1	1.0000	1.0000	1.0000	1.0000	1.0000	1.0000	1.0000
2	0.4951	0.4926	0.4902	0.4878	0.4854	0.4808	0.4762
3	0.3268	0.3235	0.3203	0.3172	0.3141	0.3080	0.3021
4	0.2426	0.2390	0.2355	0.2320	0.2286	0.2219	0.2155
5	0.1922	0.1884	0.1846	0.1810	0.1774	0.1705	0.1638
6	0.1585	0.1546	0.1508	0.1470	0.1434	0.1363	0.1296
7	0.1345	0.1305	0.1266	0.1228	0.1191	0.1121	0.1054
8	0.1165	0.1125	0.1085	0.1047	0.1010	0.0940	0.0874
9	0.1025	0.0984	0.0945	0.0907	0.0870	0.0801	0.0736
10	0.0913	0.0872	0.0833	0.0795	0.0759	0.0690	0.0627
11	0.0822	0.0781	0.0741	0.0704	0.0668	0.0601	0.0540
12	0.0746	0.0705	0.0666	0.0628	0.0593	0.0527	0.0468
13	0.0681	0.0640	0.0601	0.0565	0.0530	0.0465	0.0408
14	0.0626	0.0585	0.0547	0.0510	0.0476	0.0413	0.0357
15	0.0578	0.0538	0.0499	0.0463	0.0430	0.0368	0.0315
16	0.0537	0.0496	0.0458	0.0423	0.0390	0.0330	0.0278
17	0.0500	0.0460	0.0422	0.0387	0.0354	0.0296	0.0247
18	0.0467	0.0427	0.0390	0.0355	0.0324	0.0267	0.0219
19	0.0438	0.0398	0.0361	0.0327	0.0296	0.0241	0.0195
20	0.0412	0.0372	0.0336	0.0302	0.0272	0.0219	0.0175
24	0.0329	0.0290	0.0256	0.0225	0.0197	0.0150	0.0113
28	0.0270	0.0233	0.0200	0.0171	0.0146	0.0105	0.0075
32	0.0226	0.0190	0.0159	0.0133	0.0110	0.0075	0.0050
36	0.0192	0.0158	0.0129	0.0104	0.0084	0.0053	0.0033
40	0.0166	0.0133	0.0105	0.0083	0.0065	0.0039	0.0023

We begin by looking down the Period column in Table 13–3 until we come to 18. Then we go across until we reach the 10% column. The table factor is .0219.

Now we multiply $60,000 times the factor as follows:

$60,000 × .0219 = **$1,314**

This states that if Moore Company pays $1,314 at the end of each period for 18 years, $60,000 will be available to pay off the bond issue at maturity.

We can check this by using Table 13–1 (the ordinary annuity table):

$1,314 × 45.5992 = $59,917.35[2]

It's time to try the following Practice Quiz.

LU 13–3 PRACTICE QUIZ

Today, Arrow Company issued bonds that will mature to a value of $90,000 in 10 years. Arrow's controller is planning to set up a sinking fund. Interest rates are 12% compounded semiannually. What will Arrow Company have to set aside to meet its obligation in 10 years? Check your answer. Your answer will be off due to the rounding of Table 13–3.

SOLUTION TO LU 13–3 PRACTICE QUIZ

$\frac{12\%}{2} = 6\%$ 10 years × 2 = 20 periods $90,000 × .0272 = $2,448

Check $2,448 × 36.7855 = $90,050.90

CHAPTER ORGANIZER: A REFERENCE GUIDE

Page	Topic	Key point, procedure, formula	Example(s) to illustrate situation
297	Ordinary annuities (finds future value)	Invest money at end of each period. Find future value at maturity. Answers question how much does money accumulate.	Use Table 13–1: 2 years, $4,000 ordinary annuity at 8% annually. Value = $4,000 × 2.0800 = $8,320 (8%, 2 periods)
299	Annuity due (finds future value)	Invest money at beginning of each period. Find future value at maturity. Should be higher than ordinary annuity since invested at beginning of each period. Use Table 13–1 but add one period and subtract one payment from answer.	*Example:* Same example as above but invest money at beginning of period. $4,000 × 3.2464 = $12,985.60 − 4,000.00 $8,985.60 (8%, 3 periods)
301	Present value of an ordinary annuity (finds present worth)	How much must you invest today to be able to withdraw an amount each period?	*Example:* Receive $10,000 for 5 years. Interest is 10% annually. Table 13–2: 10%, 5 periods (10%, 5 periods) 3.7908 × $10,000 What you put in today = $37,908

[2] Off due to rounding.

Page	Topic	Key point, procedure, formula	Example(s) to illustrate situation
304	Sinking fund (finds amount of payment)	Paying a particular amount of money for a set number of periodic payments to accumulate a specific sum. We know the future and must calculate the periodic payments needed. Answer can be proved by ordinary annuity table.	*Example:* \$200,000 bond to retire 15 years from now. Interest is 6% compounded annually. By Table 13-3: \$200,000 × .0430 = \$8,600 Check by Table 13-1: \$8,600 × 23.2759 = \$200,172.74
	Key terms	Annuities certain, *p. 297* Annuity, *p. 296* Annuity due, *p. 299* Contingent annuities, *p. 297*	Ordinary annuities, *p. 297* Present value of annuity, *p. 301* Sinking fund, *p. 304* Value of an annuity, *p. 297*

END-OF-CHAPTER PROBLEMS

Drill Problems

Additional homework assignments by learning unit are at the end of text in Appendix I (p. I–57).

Solutions to odd problems are at the end of text in Appendix II.

Complete the ordinary annuities using Table 13–1:

	Amount of payment	Payment payable	Years	Interest rate	Value of annuity
13–1.	$1,200	Quarterly (16)	4 20.1569	12% (3%)	$24,188.28 ($1,200 × 20.1569)
13–2.	3,000	Semiannually (20)	10 (33.0659)	10% (5%)	$99,197.70 ($3,000 × 33.0659)

Redo Problem 13–1 as an annuity due:

13–3. $1,200, 3%, 17 periods = 21.7616 × $1,200 = $26,113.92
− 1,200.00
$24,913.92

Calculate the value of the following annuity due without a table, check your results by Table 13–1 (it will be slightly off due to rounding):

	Amount of payment	Payment payable	Years	Interest rate
13–4.	$2,000	Annually	3	6%

$2,000.00
+ 120.00
$2,120.00
+ 2,000.00
$4,120.00
+ 247.20
$4,367.20
+ 2,000.00
$6,367.20
+ 382.03
$6,749.23

Check 6%, 4 periods
$2,000 × 4.3746 = $8,749.20
− 2,000.00
$6,749.20

Complete the following using Table 13–2, present value of an ordinary annuity:

	Amount of annuity expected	Payment	Time	Interest rate earned	Present value (amount needed now to invest to receive annuity)
13–5.	$ 600	Annually	3 years	8%	$1,546.26 ($600 × 2.5771) (8%, 3 periods)
13–6.	$9,000	Semiannually	2 years	10%	$31,913.10 ($9,000 × 3.5459) (5%, 4 periods)

13–7. Check Problem 13–5 without the use of Table 13–2.

	$1,546.26	$1,069.96	$555.56
($1,546.26 × .08)	+ 123.70	+ 85.60	+ 44.44
	$1,669.96	$1,155.56	$600.00
	− 600.00	− 600.00	− 600.00
	$1,069.96	$ 555.56	$ .00

Using sinking fund Table 13-3, complete the following:

	Required amount	Frequency of payment	Length of time	Interest rate	Payment amount end of each period
13-8.	$25,000	Quarterly	6 years	8%	$822.50 (2%, 24 periods = .0329) $25,000 × .0329 = $822.50
13-9.	$15,000	Annually	8 years	8%	$1,410 (8%, 8 periods = .0940) $15,000 × .0940 = $1,410

13-10. Check answer in Problem 13-9 by Table 13-1.

$1,410 × 10.6366 = $14,997.61 (due to rounding of table factors)

Word Problems

13-11. Lani Koko made deposits of $700 at the end of each year for 4 years. Interest is 10% compounded annually. What is the value of Lani's annuity at the end of 4 years?

10%, 4 periods (Table 13-1)

$700 × 4.6410 = $3,248.70

13-12. James Will promised to pay his son $200 semiannually for 8 years. Assume James can invest his money at 10% in an ordinary annuity. How much must James invest today to pay his son $200 semiannually for 8 years?

16 periods, 5% (Table 13-2)

$200 × 10.8378 = $2,167.56

13-13. Josef Company borrowed money that must be repaid in 20 years. The company wants to make sure the loan will be repaid at the end of year 20. So it invests $12,500 at the end of each year at 12% interest compounded annually. What was the amount of the original loan?

12%, 20 periods (Table 13-1)

$12,500 × 72.0524 = $900,655

13-14. Jane Frost wants to receive yearly payments of $15,000 for 10 years. How much must she deposit at her bank today at 11% interest compounded annually?

11%, 10 periods (Table 13-2)

$15,000 × 5.8892 = $88,338

13-15. Toby Martin invests $2,000 at the end of each year for 10 years in an ordinary annuity at 11% interest compounded annually. What is the final value of Toby's investment at the end of year 10?

10 periods, 11%, 16.7220 (Table 13-1)

$2,000 × 16.7220 = $33,444

13-16. Alice Longtree has decided to invest $400 quarterly for 4 years in an ordinary annuity at 8%. As her financial advisor, calculate for Alice the total cash value of the annuity at the end of year 4?

16 periods, 2% (Table 13-1)

$400 × 18.6392 = $7,455.68

13-17. At the beginning of each year for 8 years, Segel Flynn invests $300 semiannually at 8%. What is the cash value of this annuity due at the end of year 8?

16 + 1, 4% (Table 13-1)

$300 × 23.6975 = $7,109.25
− 300.00
$6,809.25

13-18. Jeff Associates borrowed $30,000. The company plans to set up a sinking fund that will repay the loan at the end of 8 years. Assume a 12% interest rate compounded semiannually. What must Jeff pay into the fund each period of time? Check your answer by Table 13-1.

6%, 16 periods = .0390 (Table 13-3)

$30,000 × .0390 = $1,170

Check $1,170 × 25.6725 = $30,036.83 (due to table rounding) (by Table 13-1)

13–19. Joe Martin's uncle promised him upon graduation a gift of $12,000 in cash or $900 every quarter for the next 4 years. If money could be invested at 8% compounded quarterly, which offer is best for Joe?

$\frac{8\%}{4}$ = 2%, 16 periods (Table 13–2)

$900 × 13.5777 = $12,219.93

Choose the annuity.

13–20. Pete Moore is considering loaning Jim Fox, owner of a deli, $7,000. Jim told Pete he will repay $850 every 6 months for the 4 years. If money can be invested at 6% compounded semiannually, calculate the cash value of the offer today. Should Pete go through with the loan?

$\frac{6\%}{2}$ = 3%, 8 periods (Table 13–2)

$850 × 7.0197 = $5,966.75 Pete should not take the deal.

13–21. GU Corporation must buy a new piece of equipment in 5 years that will cost $88,000. The company is setting up a sinking fund to finance the purchase. What will their quarterly deposit be if the fund earns 8% interest?

2%, 20 periods (Table 13–3)

.0412 × $88,000 = $3,625.60 (quarterly payment)

13–22. Mike Macaro is selling a piece of land. Two offers are on the table. Morton Company offered a $40,000 down payment and $35,000 a year for the next 5 years. Flynn Company offered $25,000 down and $38,000 a year for the next 5 years. If money can be invested at 8% compounded annually, which offer is best for Mike?

Morton: 8%, 5 periods (Table 13–2)

3.9927 × $35,000 = $139,744.50 + $40,000 = $179,744.50

Flynn: 8%, 5 periods (Table 13–2)

3.9927 × $38,000 = $151,722.60 + $25,000 = $176,722.60

Morton offer is the better deal.

Note: Problems 13–23 and 13–24 integrate Chapters 12 and 13 together. Use your Business Math Handbook.

13–23. Al Vincent has decided to retire to Arizona in 10 years. What amount should Al invest today so that he will be able to withdraw $28,000 at the end of each year for 15 years *after* he retires? Assume he can invest the money at 8% interest compounded annually. (Use your Business Math Handbook for this problem.)

PV annuity table: 8%, 15 periods (Table 13–2) 8.5595 × $28,000 = $239,666

PV table: 8%, 10 years (Table 12–3) .4632 × $239,666 = $111,013.29

13–24. Victor French made deposits of $5,000 at the end of each quarter to Book Bank, which pays 8% interest compounded quarterly. After 3 years, Victor made no more deposits. What would be the balance in the account 2 years later from the last deposit?

Amount of annuity table: $\frac{8\%}{4}$ = 2% 3 years × 4 = 12 periods (Table 13–1)

13.4120 × $5,000 = $67,060

Compound table: 2%, 2 years × 4 = 8 periods (Table 12–1)

1.1717 × $67,060 = $78,574.20

Challenge Problem
Calculating a Monthly Payment

13–25. Assume that you can buy a $6,000 computer system in monthly installments for 3 years. The seller charges you 12% interest compounded monthly. What is your monthly payment? Assume your first payment is due at the end of the month. Use tables in the Business Math Handbook.

$$\text{Monthly payment} = \frac{\text{Amount owed}}{\text{Table factor for PV of annuity}}$$

$\frac{12\%}{12}$ = 1% 36 periods 30.1075 factor $\frac{\$6{,}000}{30.1075}$ = $199.29

Summary Practice Test

Solutions are at end of text in Appendix II.

Quick Reference
If you get any wrong answers, study the page numbers given for each problem.
1. Pp. 298–99.
2. P. 303.
3. P. 303.
4. P. 304.
5. Pp. 304–5.
6. P. 303.
7. Pp. 299–300.
8. Pp. 298–99.
9. P. 303.

1. Todd Rane plans to deposit $600 at the end of every 6 months for the next 10 years at 12% interest compounded semiannually. What is the value of Todd's annuity at the end of 10 years?
6%, 20 periods (Table 13–1) $600 × 36.7855 = $22,071.30

2. Janet Fog's uncle, Pete Moore, promised her a gift of $14,000 upon her graduation from law school or $1,200 every quarter for the next 4 years. If money could be invested at 12% compounded quarterly, which offer should Janet choose?
$\frac{12\%}{4} = 3\%$, 16 periods (Table 13–2) $1,200 × 12.5611 = $15,073.32
Choose the annuity.

3. Jim Green wants to receive $3,500 each year for 12 years. How much must Jim invest today at 12% interest compounded annually?
12%, 12 periods (Table 13–2) $3,500 × 6.1944 = $21,680.40

4. In $3\frac{1}{2}$ years Regan Company will have to repay a $30,000 loan. Assume an 8% interest rate compounded quarterly. How much must Regan pay each period to have the $30,000 at the end of $3\frac{1}{2}$ years?
Periods $= 3\frac{1}{2} \times 4 = 14$ $\frac{8\%}{4} = 2\%$ $30,000 × .0626 = $1,878
(Table 13–3)

5. Jeff Associates borrowed $50,000. The company plans to set up a sinking fund that will repay the loan at the end of 10 years. Assume a 10% interest rate compounded semiannually. What amount must Jeff Associates pay into the fund each period. Check your answer by Table 13–1.
5%, 20 periods
$50,000 × .0302 = $1,510
$1,510 × 33.0659 = $49,929.51 (due to rounding)

6. Jim Green wants to receive $5,000 each year for the next 14 years. Assume a 13% interest rate compounded annually. How much must Jim invest today?
13%, 14 periods (Table 13–2) $5,000 × 6.3025 = $31,512.50

7. Twice a year for 6 years, Wendy Cortez invested $800 compounded semiannually at 12% interest. What is the value of this annuity due?
6%, 13 periods (Table 13–1) $800 × 18.8821 = $15,105.68
− 800.00
$14,305.68

8. Darlene Grimes invested $600 semiannually for 9 years at 10% interest compounded semiannually. What is the value of this annuity due?
5%, 19 periods (Table 13–1) $600 × 30.5389 = $18,323.34
− 600.00
$17,723.34

9. Garth Scholten decided to retire to San Diego in 5 years. What amount should Garth deposit so that he will be able to withdraw $40,000 at the end of each year for 20 years after he retires? Assume Garth can invest money at 6% interest compounded annually (use the Business Math Handbook).
Present value annuity table: 6%, 20 periods
$40,000 × 11.4699 = $458,796
Present value table: 6%, 5 periods
$458,796 × .7473 = $342,858.25

Project A

Oh, the Trials of Instant Wealth! (Or, Problems We'd Like to Have)

YOUR MONEY MATTERS

By Earl C. Gottschalk Jr.
Staff Reporter of The Wall Street Journal

So you think you'd really have it made if you could score just one big hit?

Do you dream of finding that tiny start-up stock that actually does turn out to be the next IBM? Or selling your nice little family business to Japan Inc.? Or, maybe, just winning the lottery?

Forget it.

"Wealth in and of itself isn't necessarily a blessing," says Dirk L. Edwards, a partner in Edwards & Meyers, a Portland, Ore., accounting firm that specializes in advising people who suddenly strike it rich. "We have clients whose assets have destroyed them. They would have been better off without the windfall."

Okay, okay. You know you could handle the psychological strain—or you're more than willing to take the chance. What about the maze of legal and tax complexities?

R. Milton Laird, a Sherman Oaks, Calif., accountant who specializes in money management, knows how much is involved. He won $27.5 million in the California Lottery last June. Mr. Laird, who is 59, will get $1.1 million a year for 20 years. That's after the state withholds 20% of the yearly payment for federal income taxes.

So what's the problem? Estate taxes.

After Mr. Laird and his 60-year-old wife, Carlene, are dead, their estate will pass to their three grown children. Federal estate tax of 55% of the present value of the lottery winnings will be due within nine months.

The Internal Revenue Service wants the money right away—not over the remaining years that California will actually be paying the money out. That means the children would have to come up with $5 million to $6 million to pay the federal estate tax, Mr. Laird says.

Do you have that kind of money lying around? "Estate taxes can be very oppressive at these levels," says Mr. Laird, who has retained a knack for understatement despite his good fortune.

One alternative would be for the children to apply to the IRS for an extension on the estate tax and pay it out year by year up to a possible maximum of 10 years—all the while paying the IRS interest of 1 percentage point over the prime rate on the remainder of the outstanding tax bill.

There's no guarantee that they would be granted this extension, however. And they might have to post a bond to guarantee they'd pay in full.

What to do? Mr. Laird bought a $6 million life insurance policy and placed it in an irrevocable trust outside his estate with his three children as beneficiaries. The premium: $75,000 a year.

That's a lot of money, even if you are getting over $1 million a year. In the long run, leaving it up to the kids to work things out with Uncle Sam might actually be cheaper, depending on how long Mr. and Mrs. Laird live and what happens to interest rates over the next two decades. There isn't a clear-cut answer, says Houston estate planner Ross Nager, world-wide director of family wealth planning for Arthur Anderson & Co.

Whatever the case, Mr. Laird says the insurance is worth the cost, because he doesn't want to "tie up my children with a long-term commitment to the income tax people."

Being an accountant like Mr. Laird helps a lot when you have to deal... questions. Just imagine... most of your working... money matters.

Glee... school... lif., s... nia... then... a fl... som... abo... bucks... Su... the... h...

Assuming Mr. Laird pays $75,000 at the end of each year for 20 years for life insurance, what is the amount he would have to invest today to ensure this payment? Assume he can invest his money at 8% compounded annually.

8%, 20 periods
(Table 13-2)

9.8181
× $ 75,000.00
$736,357.50

CUMULATIVE REVIEW: A WORD PROBLEM APPROACH—CHAPTERS 10, 11, 12, 13

Solutions are at end of text in Appendix II.
Quick Reference
If you get any wrong answers, study the page numbers given for each problem.

1. P. 303.

1. Amy O'Mally graduated from high school. Her uncle promised her as a gift a check for \$2,000 or \$275 every quarter for 2 years. If money could be invested at 6% compounded quarterly, which offer is best for Amy? (Use the tables in the Business Math Handbook.)

$\frac{6\%}{4} = 1\frac{1}{2}\%$ 2 years × 4 = 8 periods

\$275 × 7.4859 = \$2,058.62

Take the annuity.

2. P. 303.

2. Alan Angel made deposits of \$400 semiannually to Sag Bank, which pays 10% interest compounded semiannually. After 4 years, Alan made no more deposits. What would be the balance in the account 3 years after the last deposit? (Use tables in the Business Math Handbook.)

$\frac{10\%}{2} = 5\%$ (Table 13–1   4 years × 2 = 8 periods

9.5491 × \$400 = \$3,819.64

5%   (Table 12–1)   3 years × 2 = 6 periods

1.3401 × \$3,819.64 = \$5,118.70

3. P. 303.

3. Roger Disney decided to retire to Florida in 12 years. What amount should Roger invest today so that he will be able to withdraw \$30,000 at the end of each year for 20 years *after* he retires? Assume he can invest money at 8% interest compounded annually. (Use tables in the Business Math Handbook.)

8%, 20 periods   (Table 13–2)   9.8181 × \$30,000 = \$294,543

8%, 12 periods   (Table 12–2)   .3971 × \$294,543 = \$116,963.02

4. P. 241.

4. On September 15, Arthur Westering borrowed \$3,000 from Vermont Bank at $10\frac{1}{2}\%$ interest. Arthur plans to repay the loan on January 25. Assume the loan is based on exact time, exact interest. How much will Arthur totally repay?

	365	$I = P \times R \times T$
Sept. 15	− 258	$I = \$3{,}000 \times .105 \times \frac{132}{365}$
	107	
	+ 25	= \$113.92
	132	\$113.92 + \$3,000 = \$3,113.92

5. P. 246.

5. Sue Cooper borrowed \$6,000 on an $11\frac{3}{4}\%$, 120-day note. Sue paid \$300 towards the note on day 50. On day 90, Sue paid an additional \$200. Using the U.S. Rule, Sue's adjusted balance after her first payment is:

$\$6{,}000 \times .1175 \times \frac{50}{360} = \$97.92$ \$300.00 − 97.92 = \$202.08   \$6,000 − \$202.08 = \$5,797.92

6. P. 266.

6. On November 18, Northwest Company discounted an \$18,000, 12%, 120-day note dated September 8. Assume a 10% discount rate. What would be the proceeds? Use ordinary interest.

$MV = \$18{,}000 \times .12 \times \frac{120}{360} = \$720 + \$18{,}000 = \$18{,}720$

Nov. 18	322	120	
Sept. 8	− 251	− 71	$\$18{,}720 \times .10 \times \frac{49}{360} = \$254.80$
	71	49	

Proceeds = \$18,720 − \$254.80 = \$18,465.20

7. P. 279.

7. Alice Reed deposits \$16,500 into Rye Bank, which pays 10% interest compounded semiannually. Using the appropriate table, what will Alice have in her account at the end of 6 years?

$\frac{10\%}{2} = 5\%$ 6 years × 2 = 12 periods   Table 12–1

5%, 12 periods = 1.7959   \$16,500 × 1.7959 = \$29,632.35

8. P. 284.

8. Peter Regan needs \$90,000 5 years from today to retire in Arizona. Peter's bank pays 10% interest compounded semiannually. What will Peter have to put in the bank today to have \$90,000 in 5 years?

$\frac{10\%}{2} = 5\%$ 5 years × 2 = 10 periods   \$90,000 × .6139 = \$55,251
Table 12–3

NOTES

THAT WAS THEN . . .
. . . THIS IS NOW

Although no longer in the catalog business, Sears Roebuck and Company has had a long history in retailing. This 1896 catalog had a circulation of over 300,000.

14

Installment Buying, Rule of 78, and Revolving Charge and Credit Card Accounts

LEARNING UNIT OBJECTIVES

LU 14–1: Cost of Installment Buying: The Cost of Buying a Pickup Truck

1. Calculate amount financed, finance charge, and deferred payment. *p. 317.*
2. Compute estimated APR by formula and by table. *pp. 317–19.*
3. Compute monthly payments for formula and table lookup. *p. 320.*

LU 14–2: Paying Off Installment Loan before Due Date

1. Calculate rebate by Rule of 78 and final payoff amount. *pp. 321–23.*

LU 14–3: Revolving Charge and Credit Cards

1. Calculate by various methods finance charges on revolving charge and credit card accounts. *pp. 324–25.*

You probably know that when customers use credit cards such as MasterCard, Visa, and American Express, retailers pay a fee to the credit company. As a retailer of women's apparel and home furnishings, Laura Ashley's yearly sales are approximately $500 million. About $35 million or 17% of the total U.S. sales were charged on American Express. The following *Wall Street Journal* clipping states that American Express will drop the Laura Ashley account, which could hurt potential sales. The dispute between Ashley and American Express came about because MasterCard and Visa charge 1% to 1.5% on each customer purchase and American Express charges between 2.5% and 4.5%.

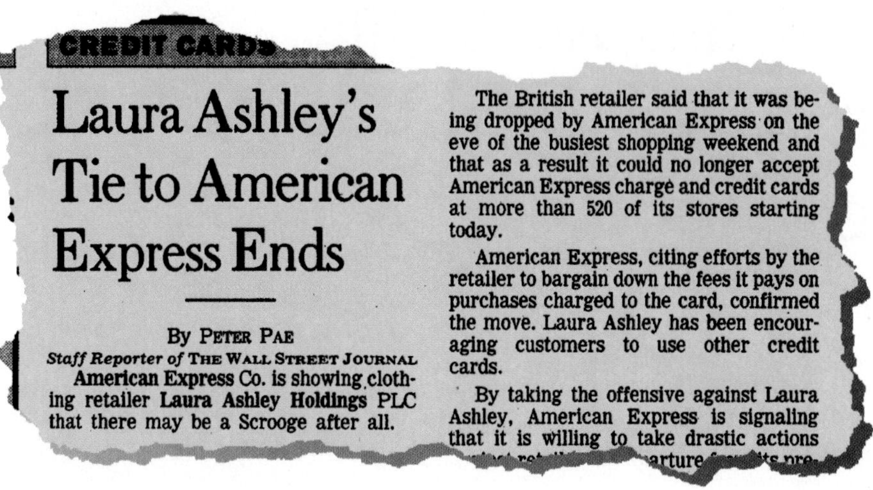

CREDIT CARDS

Laura Ashley's Tie to American Express Ends

By PETER PAE
Staff Reporter of THE WALL STREET JOURNAL

American Express Co. is showing clothing retailer Laura Ashley Holdings PLC that there may be a Scrooge after all.

The British retailer said that it was being dropped by American Express on the eve of the busiest shopping weekend and that as a result it could no longer accept American Express charge and credit cards at more than 520 of its stores starting today.

American Express, citing efforts by the retailer to bargain down the fees it pays on purchases charged to the card, confirmed the move. Laura Ashley has been encouraging customers to use other credit cards.

By taking the offensive against Laura Ashley, American Express is signaling that it is willing to take drastic actions

This chapter discusses the various types of installment buying and revolving charge credit cards. We begin by learning how to buy a vehicle on installment.

LEARNING UNIT 14–1 COST OF INSTALLMENT BUYING: THE COST OF BUYING A PICKUP TRUCK

In this unit, we follow the procedure of buying a pickup truck, including the amount financed, finance charge, and deferred payment. Then we study the effect of the Truth in Lending Act.

Amount Financed, Finance Charge, and Deferred Payment

The following advertisement for the sale of a pickup truck appeared in a local paper:

As you can see from the advertisement, after customers make a **down payment,** they can buy the truck with an installment loan. This loan is paid off with a series of equal periodic payments. These payments include both interest and principal. The payment process is called **amortization.** In the promissory notes of earlier chapters, the loan was paid off in one ending payment. Now let's look at the calculations involved in buying a pickup truck.

Checking Calculations in Pickup Advertisement

Calculating Amount Financed The **amount financed** is what you actually borrow. To calculate this amount, use the following formula:

Amount financed	=	Cash price	−	Down payment
↑		↑		↑
$9,045	=	$9,345	−	$300

Calculating Finance Charge The words **finance charge** in the advertisement represents the **interest** charge. The interest charge resulting in the finance charge includes the cost of credit reports, mandatory bank fees, and so on. You can use the following formula to calculate the total interest on the loan:

Total finance charge (interest charge)	=	Total of all monthly payments	−	Amount financed
↑		↑		↑
$2,617.80	=	$11,662.80 ($194.38 × 60 months)	−	$9,045

Calculating Deferred Payment Price The **deferred payment price** represents the total of all monthly payments plus the down payment. The following formula is used to calculate deferred payment price:

Deferred payment price	=	Total of all monthly payments	+	Down payment
↑		↑		↑
$11,962.80	=	$11,662.80 ($194.38 × 60)	+	$300

Truth in Lending: APR Defined and Calculated

In 1969, the Federal Reserve Board established the **Truth in Lending Act** (Regulation Z). The law doesn't regulate interest charges; its purpose is to make the consumer aware of the true cost of credit.

The Truth in Lending Act requires that creditors provide certain basic information about the actual cost of buying on credit. Before signing a credit agreement, the creditor must inform you in writing the amount of the finance charge and the **APR (annual percentage rate).** The APR represents the true effective annual interest sellers charge. This is helpful to buyers who repay loans over different periods of time (1 month, 48 months, and so on).

To illustrate how the APR affects your interest rate, assume you borrow $100 for a year and pay a finance charge of $9. Your interest rate would be 9%. The APR would also be 9% if you waited until the end of the year to pay back the loan. Now let's say you pay off the loan and finance charge in 12 monthly payments. Each month that you make a payment, you are losing the value or use of the some of that money. So the effective or true annual interest rate (APR) is actually over 9%.

The APR can be calculated by formula or by the use of tables. The table method is more exact. The formula only gives an estimate of the APR.[1]

Calculating APR Rate by Formula

Remember

Amount financed equals cash price less down payment. Finance charge equals total of all monthly payments less amount financed

With the following formula, we can calculate the estimated APR for the pickup truck to the nearest hundredth percent.

$$\text{APR} = \frac{2 \times \text{Number of payment periods in 1 year}^{2} \times \text{Finance charge}}{\text{Amount financed} \times (\text{Total number of payments} + 1)}$$

$$= \frac{2 \times 12 \times \$2{,}617.80}{\$9{,}045.00 \times (60 + 1)} = \frac{\$62{,}827.20}{\$551{,}745} = 11.39\%$$

[1] More complex formulas are available that provide additional accuracy.

[2] Does not refer to length of loan: if payments made weekly, 52; if made monthly, 12.

TABLE 14–1 Annual Percentage Rate Table per $100

NUMBER OF PAYMENTS	ANNUAL PERCENTAGE RATE															
	10.00%	10.25%	10.50%	10.75%	11.00%	11.25%	11.50%	11.75%	12.00%	12.25%	12.50%	12.75%	13.00%	13.25%	13.50%	13.75%
	(FINANCE CHARGE PER $100 OF AMOUNT FINANCED)															
1	0.83	0.85	0.87	0.90	0.92	0.94	0.96	0.98	1.00	1.02	1.04	1.06	1.08	1.10	1.12	1.15
2	1.25	1.28	1.31	1.35	1.38	1.41	1.44	1.47	1.50	1.53	1.57	1.60	1.63	1.66	1.69	1.72
3	1.67	1.71	1.76	1.80	1.84	1.88	1.92	1.96	2.01	2.05	2.09	2.13	2.17	2.22	2.26	2.30
4	2.09	2.14	2.20	2.25	2.30	2.35	2.41	2.46	2.51	2.57	2.62	2.67	2.72	2.78	2.83	2.88
5	2.51	2.58	2.64	2.70	2.77	2.83	2.89	2.96	3.02	3.08	3.15	3.21	3.27	3.34	3.40	3.46
6	2.94	3.01	3.08	3.16	3.23	3.31	3.38	3.45	3.53	3.60	3.68	3.75	3.83	3.90	3.97	4.05
7	3.36	3.45	3.53	3.62	3.70	3.78	3.87	3.95	4.04	4.12	4.21	4.29	4.38	4.47	4.55	4.64
8	3.79	3.88	3.98	4.07	4.17	4.26	4.36	4.46	4.55	4.65	4.74	4.84	4.94	5.03	5.13	5.22
9	4.21	4.32	4.43	4.53	4.64	4.75	4.85	4.96	5.07	5.17	5.28	5.39	5.49	5.60	5.71	5.82
10	4.64	4.76	4.88	4.99	5.11	5.23	5.35	5.46	5.58	5.70	5.82	5.94	6.05	6.17	6.29	6.41
11	5.07	5.20	5.33	5.45	5.58	5.71	5.84	5.97	6.10	6.23	6.36	6.49	6.62	6.75	6.88	7.01
12	5.50	5.64	5.78	5.92	6.06	6.20	6.34	6.48	6.62	6.76	6.90	7.04	7.18	7.32	7.46	7.60
13	5.93	6.08	6.23	6.38	6.53	6.68	6.84	6.99	7.14	7.29	7.44	7.59	7.75	7.90	8.05	8.20
14	6.36	6.52	6.69	6.85	7.01	7.17	7.34	7.50	7.66	7.82	7.99	8.15	8.31	8.48	8.64	8.81
15	6.80	6.97	7.14	7.32	7.49	7.66	7.84	8.01	8.19	8.36	8.53	8.71	8.88	9.06	9.23	9.41
16	7.23	7.41	7.60	7.78	7.97	8.15	8.34	8.53	8.71	8.90	9.08	9.27	9.46	9.64	9.83	10.02
17	7.67	7.86	8.06	8.25	8.45	8.65	8.84	9.04	9.24	9.44	9.63	9.83	10.03	10.23	10.43	10.63
18	8.10	8.31	8.52	8.73	8.93	9.14	9.35	9.56	9.77	9.98	10.19	10.40	10.61	10.82	11.03	11.24
19	8.54	8.76	8.98	9.20	9.42	9.64	9.86	10.08	10.30	10.52	10.74	10.96	11.18	11.41	11.63	11.85
20	8.98	9.21	9.44	9.67	9.90	10.13	10.37	10.60	10.83	11.06	11.30	11.53	11.76	12.00	12.23	12.46
21	9.42	9.66	9.90	10.15	10.39	10.63	10.88	11.12	11.36	11.61	11.85	12.10	12.34	12.59	12.84	13.08
22	9.86	10.12	10.37	10.62	10.88	11.13	11.39	11.64	11.90	12.16	12.41	12.67	12.93	13.19	13.44	13.70
23	10.30	10.57	10.84	11.10	11.37	11.63	11.90	12.17	12.44	12.71	12.97	13.24	13.51	13.78	14.05	14.32
24	10.75	11.02	11.30	11.58	11.86	12.14	12.42	12.70	12.98	13.26	13.54	13.82	14.10	14.38	14.66	14.95
25	11.19	11.48	11.77	12.06	12.35	12.64	12.93	13.22	13.52	13.81	14.10	14.40	14.69	14.98	15.28	15.57
26	11.64	11.94	12.24	12.54	12.85	13.15	13.45	13.75	14.06	14.36	14.67	14.97	15.28	15.59	15.89	16.20
27	12.09	12.40	12.71	13.03	13.34	13.66	13.97	14.29	14.60	14.92	15.24	15.56	15.87	16.19	16.51	16.83
28	12.53	12.86	13.18	13.51	13.84	14.16	14.49	14.82	15.15	15.48	15.81	16.14	16.47	16.80	17.13	17.46
29	12.98	13.32	13.66	14.00	14.33	14.67	15.01	15.35	15.70	16.04	16.38	16.72	17.07	17.41	17.75	18.10
30	13.43	13.78	14.13	14.48	14.83	15.19	15.54	15.89	16.24	16.60	16.95	17.31	17.66	18.02	18.38	18.74
31	13.89	14.25	14.61	14.97	15.33	15.70	16.06	16.43	16.79	17.16	17.53	17.90	18.27	18.63	19.00	19.38
32	14.34	14.71	15.09	15.46	15.84	16.21	16.59	16.97	17.35	17.73	18.11	18.49	18.87	19.25	19.63	20.02
33	14.79	15.18	15.57	15.95	16.34	16.73	17.12	17.51	17.90	18.29	18.69	19.08	19.47	19.87	20.26	20.66
34	15.25	15.65	16.05	16.44	16.85	17.25	17.65	18.05	18.46	18.86	19.27	19.67	20.08	20.49	20.90	21.31
35	15.70	16.11	16.53	16.94	17.35	17.77	18.18	18.60	19.01	19.43	19.85	20.27	20.69	21.11	21.53	21.95
36	16.16	16.58	17.01	17.43	17.86	18.29	18.71	19.14	19.57	20.00	20.43	20.87	21.30	21.73	22.17	22.60
37	16.62	17.06	17.49	17.93	18.37	18.81	19.25	19.69	20.13	20.58	21.02	21.46	21.91	22.36	22.81	23.25
38	17.08	17.53	17.98	18.43	18.88	19.33	19.78	20.24	20.69	21.15	21.61	22.07	22.52	22.99	23.45	23.91
39	17.54	18.00	18.46	18.93	19.39	19.86	20.32	20.79	21.26	21.73	22.20	22.67	23.14	23.61	24.09	24.56
40	18.00	18.48	18.95	19.43	19.90	20.38	20.86	21.34	21.82	22.30	22.79	23.27	23.76	24.25	24.73	25.22
41	18.47	18.95	19.44	19.93	20.42	20.91	21.40	21.89	22.39	22.88	23.38	23.88	24.38	24.88	25.38	25.88
42	18.93	19.43	19.93	20.43	20.93	21.44	21.94	22.45	22.96	23.47	23.98	24.49	25.00	25.51	26.03	26.55
43	19.40	19.91	20.42	20.94	21.45	21.97	22.49	23.01	23.53	24.05	24.57	25.10	25.62	26.15	26.68	27.21
44	19.86	20.39	20.91	21.44	21.97	22.50	23.03	23.57	24.10	24.64	25.17	25.71	26.25	26.79	27.33	27.88
45	20.33	20.87	21.41	21.95	22.49	23.03	23.58	24.12	24.67	25.22	25.77	26.32	26.88	27.43	27.99	28.55
46	20.80	21.35	21.90	22.46	23.01	23.57	24.13	24.69	25.25	25.81	26.37	26.94	27.51	28.08	28.65	29.22
47	21.27	21.83	22.40	22.97	23.53	24.10	24.68	25.25	25.82	26.40	26.98	27.56	28.14	28.72	29.31	29.89
48	21.74	22.32	22.90	23.48	24.06	24.64	25.23	25.81	26.40	26.99	27.58	28.18	28.77	29.37	29.97	30.57
49	22.21	22.80	23.39	23.99	24.58	25.18	25.78	26.38	26.98	27.59	28.19	28.80	29.41	30.02	30.63	31.24
50	22.69	23.29	23.89	24.50	25.11	25.72	26.33	26.95	27.56	28.18	28.80	29.42	30.04	30.67	31.29	31.92
51	23.16	23.78	24.40	25.02	25.64	26.26	26.89	27.52	28.15	28.78	29.41	30.05	30.68	31.32	31.96	32.60
52	23.64	24.27	24.90	25.53	26.17	26.81	27.45	28.09	28.73	29.38	30.02	30.67	31.32	31.98	32.63	33.29
53	24.11	24.76	25.40	26.05	26.70	27.35	28.00	28.66	29.32	29.98	30.64	31.30	31.97	32.63	33.30	33.97
54	24.59	25.25	25.91	26.57	27.23	27.90	28.56	29.23	29.91	30.58	31.25	31.93	32.61	33.29	33.98	34.66
55	25.07	25.74	26.41	27.09	27.77	28.44	29.13	29.81	30.50	31.18	31.87	32.56	33.26	33.95	34.65	35.35
56	25.55	26.23	26.92	27.61	28.30	28.99	29.69	30.39	31.09	31.79	32.49	33.20	33.91	34.62	35.33	36.04
57	26.03	26.73	27.43	28.13	28.84	29.54	30.25	30.97	31.68	32.39	33.11	33.83	34.56	35.28	36.01	36.74
58	26.51	27.23	27.94	28.66	29.37	30.10	30.82	31.55	32.27	33.00	33.74	34.47	35.21	35.95	36.69	37.43
59	27.00	27.72	28.45	29.18	29.91	30.65	31.39	32.13	32.87	33.61	34.36	35.11	35.86	36.62	37.37	38.13
60	27.48	28.22	28.96	29.71	30.45	31.20	31.96	32.71	33.47	34.23	34.99	35.75	36.52	37.29	38.06	38.83

Note: For a more detailed set of tables from 2% to 21.75%, see the reference tables in the Business Math Handbook.

Remember that the 11.39% is only an approximation. The advertisement gives the actual APR rate as 10.5%. Now let's use Table 14–1 to calculate the APR with more accuracy.

Calculating APR Rate by Table 14–1

To calculate the APR using Table 14–1, we first divide the finance charge by the amount financed and multiply by $100:

TABLE 14-1 (concluded)

NUMBER OF PAYMENTS	ANNUAL PERCENTAGE RATE															
	14.00%	14.25%	14.50%	14.75%	15.00%	15.25%	15.50%	15.75%	16.00%	16.25%	16.50%	16.75%	17.00%	17.25%	17.50%	17.75%
	(FINANCE CHARGE PER $100 OF AMOUNT FINANCED)															
1	1.17	1.19	1.21	1.23	1.25	1.27	1.29	1.31	1.33	1.35	1.37	1.40	1.42	1.44	1.46	1.48
2	1.75	1.78	1.82	1.85	1.88	1.91	1.94	1.97	2.00	2.04	2.07	2.10	2.13	2.16	2.19	2.22
3	2.34	2.38	2.43	2.47	2.51	2.55	2.59	2.64	2.68	2.72	2.76	2.80	2.85	2.89	2.93	2.97
4	2.93	2.99	3.04	3.09	3.14	3.20	3.25	3.30	3.36	3.41	3.46	3.51	3.57	3.62	3.67	3.73
5	3.53	3.59	3.65	3.72	3.78	3.84	3.91	3.97	4.04	4.10	4.16	4.23	4.29	4.35	4.42	4.48
6	4.12	4.20	4.27	4.35	4.42	4.49	4.57	4.64	4.72	4.79	4.87	4.94	5.02	5.09	5.17	5.24
7	4.72	4.81	4.89	4.98	5.06	5.15	5.23	5.32	5.40	5.49	5.58	5.66	5.75	5.83	5.92	6.00
8	5.32	5.42	5.51	5.61	5.71	5.80	5.90	6.00	6.09	6.19	6.29	6.38	6.48	6.58	6.67	6.77
9	5.92	6.03	6.14	6.25	6.35	6.46	6.57	6.68	6.78	6.89	7.00	7.11	7.22	7.32	7.43	7.54
10	6.53	6.65	6.77	6.88	7.00	7.12	7.24	7.36	7.48	7.60	7.72	7.84	7.96	8.08	8.19	8.31
11	7.14	7.27	7.40	7.53	7.66	7.79	7.92	8.05	8.18	8.31	8.44	8.57	8.70	8.83	8.96	9.09
12	7.74	7.89	8.03	8.17	8.31	8.45	8.59	8.74	8.88	9.02	9.16	9.30	9.45	9.59	9.73	9.87
13	8.36	8.51	8.66	8.81	8.97	9.12	9.27	9.43	9.58	9.73	9.89	10.04	10.20	10.35	10.50	10.66
14	8.97	9.13	9.30	9.46	9.63	9.79	9.96	10.12	10.29	10.45	10.62	10.78	10.95	11.11	11.28	11.45
15	9.59	9.76	9.94	10.11	10.29	10.47	10.64	10.82	11.00	11.17	11.35	11.53	11.71	11.88	12.06	12.24
16	10.20	10.39	10.58	10.77	10.95	11.14	11.33	11.52	11.71	11.90	12.09	12.28	12.46	12.65	12.84	13.03
17	10.82	11.02	11.22	11.42	11.62	11.82	12.02	12.22	12.42	12.62	12.83	13.03	13.23	13.43	13.63	13.83
18	11.45	11.66	11.87	12.08	12.29	12.50	12.72	12.93	13.14	13.35	13.57	13.78	13.99	14.21	14.42	14.64
19	12.07	12.30	12.52	12.74	12.97	13.19	13.41	13.64	13.86	14.09	14.31	14.54	14.76	14.99	15.22	15.44
20	12.70	12.93	13.17	13.41	13.64	13.88	14.11	14.35	14.59	14.82	15.06	15.30	15.54	15.77	16.01	16.25
21	13.33	13.58	13.82	14.07	14.32	14.57	14.82	15.06	15.31	15.56	15.81	16.06	16.31	16.56	16.81	17.07
22	13.96	14.22	14.48	14.74	15.00	15.26	15.52	15.78	16.04	16.30	16.57	16.83	17.09	17.36	17.62	17.88
23	14.59	14.87	15.14	15.41	15.68	15.96	16.23	16.50	16.78	17.05	17.32	17.60	17.88	18.15	18.43	18.70
24	15.23	15.51	15.80	16.08	16.37	16.65	16.94	17.22	17.51	17.80	18.09	18.37	18.66	18.95	19.24	19.53
25	15.87	16.17	16.46	16.76	17.06	17.35	17.65	17.95	18.25	18.55	18.85	19.15	19.45	19.75	20.05	20.36
26	16.51	16.82	17.13	17.44	17.75	18.06	18.37	18.68	18.99	19.30	19.62	19.93	20.24	20.56	20.87	21.19
27	17.15	17.47	17.80	18.12	18.44	18.76	19.09	19.41	19.74	20.06	20.39	20.71	21.04	21.37	21.69	22.02
28	17.80	18.13	18.47	18.80	19.14	19.47	19.81	20.15	20.48	20.82	21.16	21.50	21.84	22.18	22.52	22.86
29	18.45	18.79	19.14	19.49	19.83	20.18	20.53	20.88	21.23	21.58	21.94	22.29	22.64	22.99	23.35	23.70
30	19.10	19.45	19.81	20.17	20.54	20.90	21.26	21.62	21.99	22.35	22.72	23.08	23.45	23.81	24.18	24.55
31	19.75	20.12	20.49	20.87	21.24	21.61	21.99	22.37	22.74	23.12	23.50	23.88	24.26	24.64	25.02	25.40
32	20.40	20.79	21.17	21.56	21.95	22.33	22.72	23.11	23.50	23.89	24.28	24.68	25.07	25.46	25.86	26.25
33	21.06	21.46	21.85	22.25	22.65	23.06	23.46	23.86	24.26	24.67	25.07	25.48	25.88	26.29	26.70	27.11
34	21.72	22.13	22.54	22.95	23.37	23.78	24.19	24.61	25.03	25.44	25.86	26.28	26.70	27.12	27.54	27.97
35	22.38	22.80	23.23	23.65	24.08	24.51	24.94	25.36	25.79	26.23	26.66	27.09	27.52	27.96	28.39	28.83
36	23.04	23.48	23.92	24.35	24.80	25.24	25.68	26.12	26.57	27.01	27.46	27.90	28.35	28.80	29.25	29.70
37	23.70	24.16	24.61	25.06	25.51	25.97	26.42	26.88	27.34	27.80	28.26	28.72	29.18	29.64	30.10	30.57
38	24.37	24.84	25.30	25.77	26.24	26.70	27.17	27.64	28.11	28.59	29.06	29.53	30.01	30.49	30.96	31.44
39	25.04	25.52	26.00	26.48	26.96	27.44	27.92	28.41	28.89	29.38	29.87	30.36	30.85	31.34	31.83	32.32
40	25.71	26.20	26.70	27.19	27.69	28.18	28.68	29.18	29.68	30.18	30.68	31.18	31.68	32.19	32.69	33.20
41	26.39	26.89	27.40	27.91	28.41	28.92	29.44	29.95	30.46	30.97	31.49	32.01	32.52	33.04	33.56	34.08
42	27.06	27.58	28.10	28.62	29.15	29.67	30.19	30.72	31.25	31.78	32.31	32.84	33.37	33.90	34.44	34.97
43	27.74	28.27	28.81	29.34	29.88	30.42	30.96	31.50	32.04	32.58	33.13	33.67	34.22	34.76	35.31	35.86
44	28.42	28.97	29.52	30.07	30.62	31.17	31.72	32.28	32.83	33.39	33.95	34.51	35.07	35.63	36.19	36.76
45	29.11	29.67	30.23	30.79	31.36	31.92	32.49	33.06	33.63	34.20	34.77	35.35	35.92	36.50	37.08	37.66
46	29.79	30.36	30.94	31.52	32.10	32.68	33.26	33.84	34.43	35.01	35.60	36.19	36.78	37.37	37.96	38.56
47	30.48	31.07	31.66	32.25	32.84	33.44	34.03	34.63	35.23	35.83	36.43	37.04	37.64	38.25	38.86	39.46
48	31.17	31.77	32.37	32.98	33.59	34.20	34.81	35.42	36.03	36.65	37.27	37.88	38.50	39.13	39.75	40.37
49	31.86	32.48	33.09	33.71	34.34	34.96	35.59	36.21	36.84	37.47	38.10	38.74	39.37	40.01	40.65	41.29
50	32.55	33.18	33.82	34.45	35.09	35.73	36.37	37.01	37.65	38.30	38.94	39.59	40.24	40.89	41.55	42.20
51	33.25	33.89	34.54	35.19	35.84	36.49	37.15	37.81	38.46	39.12	39.79	40.45	41.11	41.78	42.45	43.12
52	33.95	34.61	35.27	35.93	36.60	37.27	37.94	38.61	39.28	39.96	40.63	41.31	41.99	42.67	43.36	44.04
53	34.65	35.32	36.00	36.68	37.36	38.04	38.72	39.41	40.10	40.79	41.48	42.17	42.87	43.57	44.27	44.97
54	35.35	36.04	36.73	37.42	38.12	38.82	39.52	40.22	40.92	41.63	42.33	43.04	43.75	44.47	45.18	45.90
55	36.05	36.76	37.46	38.17	38.88	39.60	40.31	41.03	41.74	42.47	43.19	43.91	44.64	45.37	46.10	46.83
56	36.76	37.48	38.20	38.92	39.65	40.38	41.11	41.84	42.57	43.31	44.05	44.79	45.53	46.27	47.02	47.77
57	37.47	38.20	38.94	39.68	40.42	41.16	41.91	42.65	43.40	44.15	44.91	45.66	46.42	47.18	47.94	48.71
58	38.18	38.93	39.68	40.43	41.19	41.95	42.71	43.47	44.23	45.00	45.77	46.54	47.32	48.09	48.87	49.65
59	38.89	39.66	40.42	41.19	41.96	42.74	43.51	44.29	45.07	45.85	46.64	47.42	48.21	49.01	49.80	50.60
60	39.61	40.39	41.17	41.95	42.74	43.53	44.32	45.11	45.91	46.71	47.51	48.31	49.12	49.92	50.73	51.55

$$\frac{\text{Finance charge}}{\text{Amount financed}} \times \$100 = \text{Table 14-1 lookup number}$$

$$\uparrow \qquad\qquad \uparrow \qquad\qquad \uparrow$$

$$\frac{\$2{,}617.80}{\$9{,}045.00} \times \$100 = \$28.94$$

We multiply by $100 since the table is based on $100 of financing.

Now we use the $28.94 for Table 14-1. We go down the left side of the table until we come to 60 payments (the advertisement states 60 months). Then, moving to the right,

TABLE 14–2 Loan Amortization Table (Monthly Payment per $1,000 to Pay Principal and Interest on Installment Loan)

Terms in months	10.00%	10.50%	11.00%	11.50%	12.00%	12.50%	13.00%	13.50%	14.00%	14.50%	15.00%	15.50%	16.00%
6	$171.56	$171.81	$172.05	$172.30	$172.55	$172.80	$173.04	$173.29	$173.54	$173.79	$174.03	$174.28	$174.53
12	87.92	88.15	88.38	88.62	88.85	89.08	89.32	89.55	89.79	90.02	90.26	90.49	90.73
18	60.06	60.29	60.52	60.75	60.98	61.21	61.45	61.68	61.92	62.15	62.38	62.62	62.86
24	46.14	46.38	46.61	46.84	47.07	47.31	47.54	47.78	48.01	48.25	48.49	48.72	48.96
30	37.81	38.04	38.28	38.51	38.75	38.98	39.22	39.46	39.70	39.94	40.18	40.42	40.66
36	32.27	32.50	32.74	32.98	33.21	33.45	33.69	33.94	34.18	34.42	34.67	34.91	35.16
42	28.32	28.55	28.79	29.03	29.28	29.52	29.76	30.01	30.25	30.50	30.75	31.00	31.25
48	25.36	25.60	25.85	26.09	26.33	26.58	26.83	27.08	27.33	27.58	27.83	28.08	28.34
54	23.07	23.32	23.56	23.81	24.06	24.31	24.56	24.81	25.06	25.32	25.58	25.84	26.10
60	21.25	21.49	21.74	21.99	22.24	22.50	22.75	23.01	23.27	23.53	23.79	24.05	24.32

we look for $28.94 or the two numbers closest to it. The number $28.94 is between $28.22 and $28.96. So we look up to the top heading and see a rate of between 10.25% and 10.5%. The Truth in Lending Act requires that when creditors state the APR, it must be accurate to nearest $\frac{1}{4}$ of 1%.[3]

Calculating the Monthly Payment by Formula and Table 14–2

The advertisement showed a $194.38 monthly payment. We can check this by formula and by table lookup.

By Formula

$$\frac{\text{Finance charge} + \text{Amount financed}}{\text{Number of payments of loan}} = \frac{\$2{,}617.80 + \$9{,}045}{60} = \$194.38$$

By Table 14–2 The **loan amortization table** in Table 14–2 can be used to calculate the pickup monthly payment (many variations of this table are available). To calculate a monthly payment with a table, use the following steps:

Steps for Calculating Monthly Payment by Table

Step 1. Divide loan amount by $1,000 (since Table 14–2 is per $1,000):

$$\frac{\$9{,}045}{\$1{,}000} = 9.045$$

Step 2. Look up rate (10.5%) and months (60). At the intersection is the table factor showing the monthly payment per $1,000.

Step 3. Multiply quotient in Step 1 times the table factor in Step 2:

$9.045 \times \$21.49 = \$194.38$

Remember that this $194.38 fixed payment both covers interest and reduces the balance of the loan. As the number of payments increase, interest payments get smaller, and the reduction of the principal gets larger.[4]

Now let's check your progress with the Practice Quiz.

[3] If we wanted an exact reading of APR when the number is not exactly in the table, we would use a process of interpolating. We do not cover this in this course.

[4] In Chapter 15, we give an amortization schedule for home mortgages (p. 345) that shows how much of each fixed payment goes to interest and how much reduces the principal. This repayment schedule also gives a running balance of the loan.

LU 14-1 PRACTICE QUIZ

From the partial advertisement at the right calculate:

1. **a.** Amount financed.
   b. Finance charge.
   c. Deferred payment price.
   d. APR by Table 14-1.
   e. Calculate monthly payment by formula.
   f. Also estimate APR to nearest hundredth percent by formula.
2. Jay Miller bought a new Brunswick boat for $7,500. Jay put down $1,000 and financed the balance at 10% for 60 months. What is his monthly payment? Use Table 14-2.

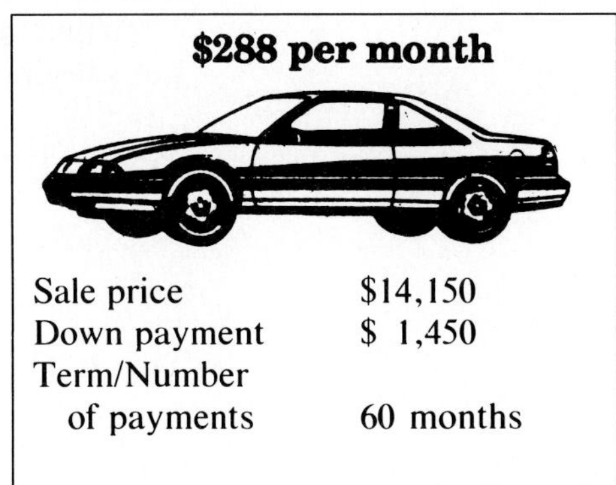

SOLUTIONS TO LU 14-1 PRACTICE QUIZ

Courtesy of Brunswick Corporation

1. **a.** $\$14{,}150 - \$1{,}450 = \$12{,}700$
   b. $\$17{,}280\ (\$288 \times 60) - \$12{,}700 = \$4{,}580$
   c. $\$17{,}280\ (\$288 \times 60) + \$1{,}450 = \$18{,}730$
   d. $\dfrac{\$4{,}580}{\$12{,}700} \times \$100 = \$36.06$; between 12.75% and 13%
   e. $\dfrac{\$4{,}580 + \$12{,}700}{60} = \$288$
   f. $\dfrac{2 \times 12 \times \$4{,}580}{\$12{,}700 \times (60 + 1)} = \dfrac{\$109{,}920}{\$774{,}700} = 14.19\%$
2. $\dfrac{\$6{,}500}{\$1{,}000} = 6.5 \times \$21.25 = \$138.13$
   (10%, 60 months)

LEARNING UNIT 14-2 PAYING OFF INSTALLMENT LOAN BEFORE DUE DATE

In Learning Unit 10-3, Chapter 10 (p. 246), you learned about the U.S. Rule. This rule applies partial payments to the interest *first* and then the remainder of the payment reduces the principal. Many states and the federal government use this rule.

Some states use another method for prepaying a loan, called **the Rule of 78.** It is a variation of the U.S. Rule. The Rule of 78 got its name because it bases the finance charge rebate and the payoff on a 12-month loan. (Any number of months can be used.)

With the Rule of 78, the finance charge earned the first month is $\frac{12}{78}$. The 78 comes from summing the 12 months. The second month the finance charge would be $\frac{11}{78}$. We will use tables to simplify this process. Remember that the Rule of 78 charges a larger portion of the finance charges to the earlier payments.

To calculate the **rebate** amount of the finance charge and the payoff for the Rule of 78, use the steps that follow.

Steps for Calculating Rebate and Payoff for Rule of 78

Step 1. Find balance of loan outstanding.
Step 2. Calculate total finance charge.
Step 3. Find number of payments remaining.
Step 4. Set up rebate fraction from Table 14-3.
Step 5. Calculate rebate amount of finance charge.
Step 6. Calculate payoff.

Let's see what the rebate of finance charge and payoff would be if the pickup truck loan was paid off after 27 months (instead of 60).

To find the finance charge rebate and the final payoff, we follow six specific steps. Let's begin.

Step 1. Find balance of loan outstanding:

Total of monthly payments (60 × $194.38)	$11,662.80
Payments to date: 27 × $194.38	− 5,248.26
Balance of loan outstanding	$ 6,414.54

Step 2. Calculate total finance charge:

$11,662.80	Total of all payments (60 × $194.38)
− 9,045.00	Amount financed ($9,345 − $300)
$ 2,617.80	Total finance charge

Step 3. Find number of payments remaining:

60 − 27 = 33

TABLE 14-3
Rebate Fraction Table Based on Rule of 78

Months to go	Sum of digits	Months to go	Sum of digits	
1	1	31	496	
2	3	32	528	
3	6	33	561	→ 33 months to go
4	10	34	595	
5	15	35	630	
6	21	36	666	
7	28	37	703	
8	36	38	741	
9	45	39	780	
10	55	40	820	
11	66	41	861	
12	78	42	903	
13	91	43	946	
14	105	44	990	
15	120	45	1,035	
16	136	46	1,081	
17	153	47	1,128	
18	171	48	1,176	
19	190	49	1,225	
20	210	50	1,275	
21	231	51	1,326	
22	253	52	1,378	
23	276	53	1,431	
24	300	54	1,485	
25	325	55	1,540	
26	351	56	1,596	
27	378	57	1,653	
28	406	58	1,711	
29	435	59	1,770	
30	465	60	1,830	→ 60 months = 1,830

Step 4. Set up **rebate fraction** based on Table 14–3[5] (p. 322).

$$\frac{\text{Sum of digits based on number of months to go}}{\text{Sum of digits based on total number of months of loan}} = \frac{561 \leftarrow 33 \text{ months to go}}{1{,}830 \leftarrow 60 \text{ months in loan}}$$

Note: If this loan were for 12 months, the denominator would have been 78.

Step 5. Calculate rebate amount of finance charge:

Rebate fraction	×	Total finance charge	=	Rebate amount
$\frac{561}{1{,}830}$ **(Step 4)**	×	$2,617.80 **(Step 2)**	=	$802.51

Step 6. Calculate payoff:

Balance of loan outstanding	−	Rebate	=	Payoff
$6,414.54 **(Step 1)**	−	$802.51 **(Step 5)**	=	$5,612.03

It's time to test your skill with the Practice Quiz.

LU 14–2 PRACTICE QUIZ

Calculate the finance charge rebate and payoff (calculate all six steps):

Loan	Months of loan	End of month loan is repaid	Monthly payment	Finance charge rebate	Final payoff
$5,500	12	7	$510		

SOLUTIONS TO LU 14–2 PRACTICE QUIZ

Step 1. 12 × $510 = $6,120
7 × $510 = − 3,570
$2,550 (balance outstanding)

Step 2. 12 × $510 = $6,120
− 5,500
$ 620 (total finance charge)

Step 3. 12 − 7 = 5

Step 4. $\frac{15}{78}$ (by Table 14–3)

Step 5. $\frac{15}{78}$ × $620 = $119.23 rebate
(Step 4) (Step 2)

Step 6. **Step 1** − **Step 5**
$2,550 − $119.23
= $2,430.77 payoff

---

[5] If no table is available, the following formula is available:

$$\frac{\frac{N(N+1)}{2}}{\frac{T(T+1)}{2}} = \frac{\frac{33(33+1)}{2}}{\frac{60(60+1)}{2}} = \frac{561}{1{,}830}$$

In the numerator, N stands for number of months to go and in the denominator, T is total months of loan.

LEARNING UNIT 14–3 REVOLVING CHARGE AND CREDIT CARDS

Revolving charge and credit cards are widely used today. Businesses find that consumers tend to buy more when they can use a credit card for their purchases. Consumers find credit cards convenient to use and valuable in establishing credit.

In the following *Wall Street Journal* clipping, you can see that over 75 million credit card holders vow to pay off credit card debt but they still only make the minimum payment.

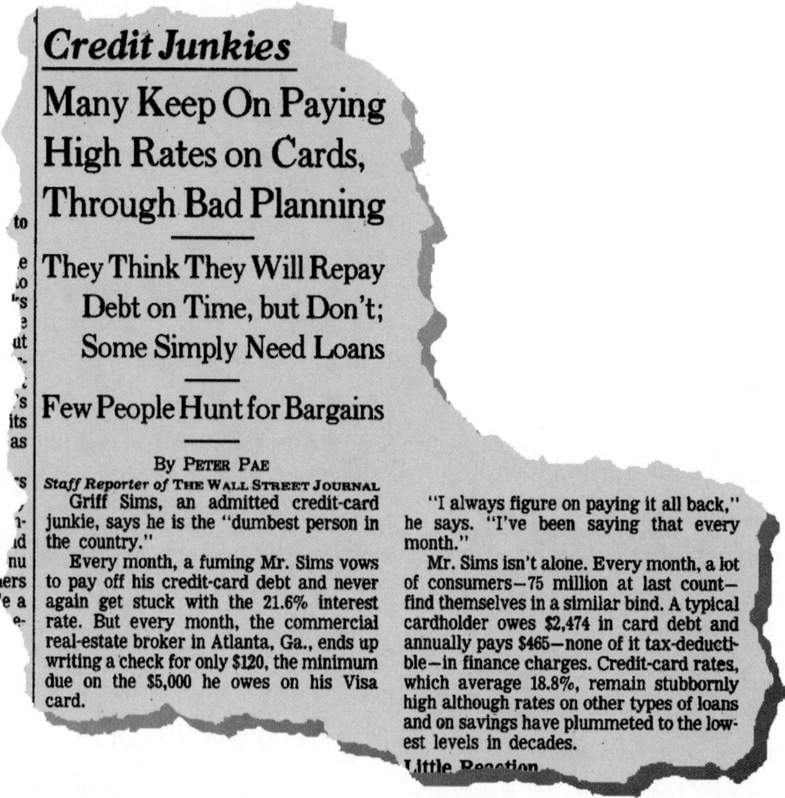

Credit Junkies

Many Keep On Paying High Rates on Cards, Through Bad Planning

They Think They Will Repay Debt on Time, but Don't; Some Simply Need Loans

Few People Hunt for Bargains

By PETER PAE
Staff Reporter of THE WALL STREET JOURNAL

Griff Sims, an admitted credit-card junkie, says he is the "dumbest person in the country."

Every month, a fuming Mr. Sims vows to pay off his credit-card debt and never again get stuck with the 21.6% interest rate. But every month, the commercial real-estate broker in Atlanta, Ga., ends up writing a check for only $120, the minimum due on the $5,000 he owes on his Visa card.

"I always figure on paying it all back," he says. "I've been saying that every month."

Mr. Sims isn't alone. Every month, a lot of consumers—75 million at last count—find themselves in a similar bind. A typical cardholder owes $2,474 in card debt and annually pays $465—none of it tax-deductible—in finance charges. Credit-card rates, which average 18.8%, remain stubbornly high although rates on other types of loans and on savings have plummeted to the lowest levels in decades.

Little Reaction

To protect consumers, Congress in 1988 passed the **Fair Credit and Charge Card Disclosure Act of 1988.** This act requires that for direct mail application or solicitation, credit card companies must provide specific details involving all fees, grace period, calculation of finance charges, and so on.

We begin the unit by seeing how Moe's Furniture Store calculates the finance charge on Abby Jordan's previous month's credit card balance. Then we learn how to calculate the average daily balance on the partial bill of Joan Ring.

Calculating Finance Charge on Previous Month's Balance

Abby Jordan bought a dining room set for $8,000 on credit. She has a **revolving charge account** at Moe's Furniture Store. Since Abby has a good credit record, she has a $10,000 credit limit. So Abby can make purchases on her revolving charge account up to $10,000.

Often customers do not completely pay their revolving charge accounts at the end of a billing period. When this occurs, stores add interest charges to the customer's bill. Moe's Furniture Store charges $1\frac{1}{2}\%$ interest on the previous month's balance, or 18% per year. Moe's has no minimum monthly payment (many stores require $10 or $15 or a percent of outstanding balance).

Abby has no other charges on her revolving charge account. She plans to pay $500 per month until she completely pays off her dining room set. Abby's revolving charge

TABLE 14–4 Schedule of Payments

Monthly payment number	Outstanding balance due	$1\frac{1}{2}\%$ interest payment	Amount of monthly payment	Reduction in balance due	Outstanding balance due
1	$8,000.00	$120.00 (.015 × $8,000.00)	$500	$380.00 ($500 − $120.00)	$7,620.00 ($8,000 − $380)
2	$7,620.00	$114.30 (.015 × $7,620.00)	$500	$385.70 ($500 − $114.30)	$7,234.30 ($7,620 − $385.70)
3	$7,234.30	$108.51 (.015 × $7,234.30)	$500	$391.49 ($500 − $108.51)	$6,842.81 ($7,234.30 − $391.49)

has **open-end credit,** so Abby can make as many purchases on credit as she wants until she reaches her maximum $10,000 credit limit. Abby realizes that when she makes a payment, Moe's Furniture Store first applies the money toward the interest and then to reduce the **outstanding balance** due. (This is the U.S. Rule we discussed in Chapter 10.) For her own information, Abby worked out the schedule of payments shown in Table 14–4 for the first three months. Note how interest payment is the rate times the outstanding balance.

Today, most companies with credit card accounts calculate the finance charge as a percentage of the average daily balance.

Calculating Average Daily Balance

Let's look at the following steps for calculating the **average daily balance**. Keep in mind a **cash advance** is a cash loan from a credit card company.

Steps for Calculating Average Daily Balance

Step 1. Calculate daily balance:

$$\text{Daily balance} = \text{Previous balance} + \text{Cash advances} + \text{Purchases} - \text{Payments}$$

Step 2. Multiply daily balance times number of days of current balance. This gives an extension, or cumulative daily balance.

Step 3. Add sum of cumulative daily balances.

Step 4. Divide sum of cumulative daily balances by number of days in billing cycle.

Following is the partial bill of Joan Ring and an explanation of how Joan's average daily balance was calculated. Note how we calculated each **daily balance** and then multiplied each number times the number of days of the current balance. Take a moment to study how we arrived at the 8 days. The total of the cumulative daily balances was $16,390. To get the average daily balance, we divided by the number of days in the billing cycle—30.

30-day billing cycle

6/20	Billing date	Previous balance		$450
6/27	Payment		$ 50	
6/30	Charge		200	
7/9	Payment		40	
7/12	Cash advance		60	

7 days had a balance of $450.

	No. of days of current balance	Current daily balance	Extension	
Step 1 →	7	$450	$ 3,150	← Step 2
	3	400	1,200	
	9	600	5,400	
	3	560	1,680	
	8	620	4,960	
	30		$16,390	← Step 3

30-day cycle − 22 (7 + 3 + 9 + 3) equals 8 days left with a balance of $620.

$$\text{Average daily balance} = \frac{\$16,390}{30} = \$546.33 \leftarrow \textbf{Step 4}$$

Now try the following quiz to check your understanding of this unit.

LU 14-3 PRACTICE QUIZ

1. Calculate balance outstanding at end of month 2 (use U.S. Rule) given the following: purchased $600 desk; pay back $40 per month; and charge of $2\frac{1}{2}\%$ interest on unpaid balance.
2. Calculate the average daily balance from the following information:

31-day billing cycle

8/20	Billing date	Previous balance		$210
8/27	Payment		$50 cr.	
8/31	Charge		30	
9/5	Payment		10 cr.	
9/10	Cash advance		60	

SOLUTIONS TO LU 14-3 PRACTICE QUIZ

1.

Month	Balance due	Interest	Monthly payment	Reduction in balance	Balance outstanding
1	$600	$15.00 (.025 × $600)	$40	$25.00 ($40 − $15)	$575.00
2	575	14.38 (.025 × $575)	40	25.62	549.38

2. Average daily balance calculated as follows:

No. of days of current balance	Current balance	Extension
7	$210	$1,470
4	160 ($210 − $50)	640
5	190 ($160 + $30)	950
5	180 ($190 − $10)	900
10	240 ($180 + $60)	2,400
31		$6,360

31 − 21 (7 + 4 + 5 + 5) → 10

$$\text{Average daily balance} = \frac{\$6,360}{31} = \$205.16$$

CHAPTER ORGANIZER: A REFERENCE GUIDE

Page	Topic	Key point, procedure, formula	Example(s) to illustrate situation
317	Amount financed	Amount financed = Cash price − Down payment	60 payments at $125.67 per month; cash price $5,295 with a $95 down payment Cash price $5,295 − Down payment − 95 = Amount financed $5,200

Page	Topic	Key point, procedure, formula	Example(s) to illustrate situation
317	Total finance charge (interest)	Total finance charge = Total of all monthly payments − Amount financed	*(continued from above)* $125.67 per month × 60 months = $7,540.20 − Amount financed − $5,200.00 = Finance charge $2,340.20
317	Deferred payment price	Total of all monthly payments + Down payment	*(continued from above)* $7,540.20 + $95 = $7,635.20
317	Calculating APR by formula	$\text{APR} = \dfrac{2 \times \text{Number of payment periods in 1 year} \times \text{Finance charge}}{\text{Amount financed} \times (\text{Total number of payments} + 1)}$ Amount financed ↑ (Cash price − Down payment)	*(continued from above)* $\text{APR} = \dfrac{2 \times 12 \times \$2{,}340.20}{\$5{,}200 \times (60 + 1)}$ $= .1771 = 17.71\%$
318	Calculating APR by Table 14-1	$\dfrac{\text{Finance charge}}{\text{Amount financed}} \times \$100 =$ Table 14-1 lookup number	*(continued from above)* $\dfrac{\$2{,}340.20}{\$5{,}200.00} \times \$100 = \$45.004$ Search in Table 14-1 between 15.50% and 15.75% for 60 payments.
320	Monthly payment	*By formula:* $\dfrac{\text{Finance charge} + \text{Amount financed}}{\text{Number of payments of loan}}$ *By table:* $\dfrac{\text{Loan}}{\$1{,}000} \times$ Table factor (rate, months)	*(continued from above)* $\dfrac{\$2{,}340.20 + \$5{,}200.00}{60} = \$125.67$ Given: 15.5% 60 months $5,200 loan $\dfrac{\$5{,}200}{\$1{,}000} = 5.2 \times \$24.05 = \$125.06$* *Off due to rounding of rate.
321	Paying off installment loan before due date	1. Find balance of loan outstanding (Total of monthly payments − Payments to date). 2. Calculate total finance charge. 3. Find number of payments remaining. 4. Set up rebate fraction from Table 14-3. 5. Calculate rebate amount of finance charge. 6. Calculate payoff.	*Example:* Loan, $8,000; 20 monthly payments of $420; end of month repaid 7. 1. $8,400 (20 × $420) − 2,940 (7 × $420) $5,460 (balance of loan outstanding) 2. $8,400 (total payments) − 8,000 (amount financed) $ 400 (total finance charge) 3. 20 − 7 = 13 4 and 5. $\dfrac{91}{210} \times \$400 = \$173.33$ 6. $5,460.00 (Step 1) − 173.33 rebate (Step 4) $5,286.67 payoff
325	Open-end credit	Monthly payment applied to interest first before reducing balance outstanding.	$4,000 purchase $250 a month payment $2\frac{1}{2}\%$ interest on unpaid balance $4,000 × .025 = $100 interest $250 − $100 = $150 to lower balance $4,000 − $150 = $3,850 Balance outstanding after month 1.

Page	Topic	Key point, procedure, formula	Example(s) to illustrate situation
326	Average daily balance	$\text{Average daily balance} = \dfrac{\text{Sum of cumulative daily balances}}{\text{Number of days in billing cycle}}$ 30-day cycle less the 8 and 14. ← $\text{Daily balance} = \text{Previous balance} + \text{Cash advances} + \text{Purchases} - \text{Payments}$	*30-day billing cycle:* *Example:* 8/21 Balance $100 8/29 Payment $10 9/12 Charge 50 *Average daily balance equals:* 8 days × $100 = $ 800 14 days × 90 = 1,260 8 days × 140 = 1,120 $3,180 ÷ 30 Average daily balance = $106
	Key terms	Amortization, *p. 316* Amount financed, *p. 317* APR (annual percentage rate), *p. 317* Average daily balance, *p. 325* Cash advance, *p. 325* Daily balance, *p. 325* Deferred payment price, *p. 317* Down payment, *p. 317* Fair Credit and Charge Card Disclosure Act of 1988, *p. 324*	Finance charge, *p. 317* Interest, *p. 317* Loan amortization table, *p. 320* Open-end credit, *p. 325* Outstanding balance, *p. 325* Rebate, *p. 321* Rebate fraction, *p. 323* Revolving charge account, *p. 324* Rule of 78, *p. 321* Truth in Lending Act, *p. 317*

END-OF-CHAPTER PROBLEMS

Drill Problems

Additional homework assignments by learning unit are at the end of text in Appendix I (p. I–61). Solutions to odd problems are at the end of text in Appendix II.

Complete the following table:

	Purchase price of product		Down payment		Amount financed	Number of monthly payments		Amount of monthly payments		Total of monthly payments	Total finance charge
14–1.	Jeep $18,000	−	$1,000	=	$17,000	60	×	$299	=	$17,940	$940 ($17,940 − $17,000)
14–2.	Washer-dryer $1,100	−	$100	=	$ 1,000	12	×	$109.99	=	$1,319.88	$319.88 ($1,319.88 − $1,000)

Calculate **(a)** amount financed, **(b)** total finance charge, and **(c)** estimated annual percentage rate to nearest hundredth percent by formula:

	Purchase price of a used car	Down payment	Number of monthly payments	Amount financed	Total of monthly payments	Total finance charge	APR
14–3.	$5,673	$1,223	48	$4,450	$5,729.76	$1,279.76	14.09%
14–4.	$4,195	$95	60	$4,100	$5,944.00	$1,844.00	17.70%

$5,673 − 1,223 = $4,450 *$5,729.76 − 4,450.00 = $1,279.76*

$$\frac{2 \times 12 \times \$1{,}279.76}{\$4{,}450 \times (48 + 1)} = 14.09\%$$

$4,195 − 95 = $4,100 *$5,944 − 4,100 = $1,844*

$$\frac{2 \times 12 \times \$1{,}844}{\$4{,}100 \times (60 + 1)} = 17.70\%$$

Recalculate Problems 14–3 and 14–4 to solve for annual percentage rate by Table 14–1:

14–5. **(14–3)** $\frac{\$1{,}279.76}{\$4{,}450.00} \times \$100 = \$28.76$ is between 12.75% to 13% at 48 months

14–6. **(14–4)** $\frac{\$1{,}844}{\$4{,}100} \times \$100 = \$44.98$ at 60 months is between 15.50% to 15.75%

Calculate the monthly payment for Problems 14–3 and 14–4 by table and formula. (Answer will not be exact due to rounding off of percents in table lookup.)

14–7. **(14–3)** (Use 13% for table.)

Table: $5,673 − 1,223 = $4,450 ÷ $1,000 = 4.45 × 26.83 (13%, 48 months) = $119.39

Formula: $\frac{\$1{,}279.76 + \$4{,}450}{48} = \$119.37$

14–8. **(14–4)** (Use 15.5% for table.)

Table: $4,195 − 95 = $4,100 ÷ $1,000 = 4.1 × 24.05 = $98.61 (15.5%, 60 months)

Formula: $\frac{\$1{,}844 + \$4{,}100}{60} = \$99.07$

Complete the following table:

	Number of months of loan	Number of months of loan remaining when note paid in full	Fractional rate		Finance charge		Rebate of finance charge (round to nearest cent)
14–9.	10	3	$\frac{6}{55}$	×	$400	=	$ 43.64
14–10.	24	12	$\frac{78}{300}$	×	$900	=	$234.00

Calculate the finance charge rebate and payoff:

	Loan	Months of loan	End of month loan is repaid	Monthly payment	Finance charge rebate	Final payoff
14–11.	$5,500	12	7	$510	$119.23	$2,430.77

Step 1.

12 × $510 =	$6,120
7 × $510 =	− 3,570
Balance outstanding	$2,550

Step 2.

12 × $510 =	$6,120
− Amount financed	− 5,500
Total finance charge	$ 620

Step 3.

12 − 7 = 5

Step 4.

$\frac{15}{78}$ (by Table 14–3)

Step 5.

$\frac{15}{78}$ × $620 = $119.23 rebate
(Step 4) (Step 2)

Step 6.

$2,550 − $119.23 = $2,430.77
(Step 1) (Step 5) (payoff)

	Loan	Months of loan	End of month loan is repaid	Monthly payment	Finance charge rebate	Final payoff
14–12.	$9,000	24	9	$440	$624.00	$5,976.00

Step 1.

Total payments	
$440 × 24	$10,560
$440 × 9	− 3,960
Balance outstanding	$ 6,600

Step 2.

Total of all payments	$10,560
− Amount financed	− 9,000
Total finance charge	$ 1,560

Step 3.

24 − 9 = 15

Step 4.

By Table 14–3, $\frac{120 \rightarrow 15 \text{ months to go}}{300 \rightarrow 24 \text{ months total loan}}$

Step 5.

$\frac{120}{300}$ × $1,560 = $624 finance charge rebate
(Step 4) (Step 2)

Step 6.

$6,600 − $624 = $5,976
(Step 1) (Step 5) (payoff)

14–13. Calculate the average daily balance:

30-day billing cyle

9/16	Billing date	Previous balance		$2,000
9/19	Payment		$ 60	
9/30	Charge		1,500	
10/3	Payment		60	
10/7	Cash advance		70	

No. of days of current balance	Current balance	Extension
3	$2,000	$ 6,000
11	1,940	21,340
3	3,440	10,320
4	3,380	13,520
9	3,450	31,050

$\frac{\$82,230}{30}$ = $2,741 average daily balance

Word Problems

14–14. Tom Connolly saw the following advertisement and decided to work out the numbers to be sure there were no errors in the ad. Please help Tom by calculating **(a)** amount financed, **(b)** finance charge, **(c)** deferred payment, **(d)** APR by table, (**e**) monthly payment by formula, (**f**) monthly payment by table (will be off slightly), and (**g**) APR by formula (to nearest hundredth percent).

a. Amount financed: $8,984 (Selling price) − $500 (Down payment) = $8,484 (Amount financed)

b. Finance charge: ($186.77 × 60) − $8,484 = $2,722.20

c. Deferred payment: ($186.77 × 60) (Monthly payment) + $500 (Down payment) = $11,706.20 (Deferred price)

d. APR by table: $\frac{\$2,722.20}{\$8,484} \times 100 = 32.09$ 11.50% − 11.75%

e. Monthly payment by formula: $\frac{\$2,722.20 + \$8,484}{60} = \$186.77$

f. Monthly payment by table: $\frac{\$8,484}{1,000} = 8.484 \times \$21.99 = \$186.56$ (11.5%, 60 months)

g. APR by formula: $\frac{2 \times 12 \times \$2,722.20}{\$8,484 \times (60 + 1)} = 12.62\%$

14–15. From this partial advertisement calculate:

a. Amount financed.
b. Finance charge.
c. Deferred payment price.
d. APR by Table 14–1.
e. Check monthly payment (by formula).
f. APR by formula.

$89.11 per month
#969531 Used car. Cash price $3,984. Down payment $95 for 60 months.

Michael Hruby/Courtesy Shaver Chevrolet

a. Amount financed = $3,984 − $95 = $3,889

b. Finance charge = $5,346.60 ($89.11 × 60) − $3,889 = $1,457.60

c. Deferred payment price = $5,346.60 ($89.11 × 60) + $95 = $5,441.60

d. $\frac{\$1,457.60}{\$3,889.00} \times \$100 = \$37.48$ (in Table 14–1, between 13.25% to 13.50%)

e. $\frac{\$1,457.60 + \$3,889.00}{60} = \$89.11$

f. $\frac{2 \times 12 \times \$1,457.60}{\$3,889.00 \times (60 + 1)} = \frac{\$34,982.40}{\$237,229.00} = .14746 = 14.75\%$

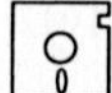

14–16. Paula Westing borrowed $6,200 to travel to Sweden to see her son Arthur. Her loan was to be paid in 48 monthly installments of $170. At the end of 9 months, Paula's daughter Irene convinced her that she should pay off the loan early. What is Paula's rebate and her payoff amount?

Step 1. Total payments $8,160 (48 × $170)
Payments to date − 1,530 (9 × $170)
$6,630

Step 2. $8,160 (total payments)
− 6,200 (amount financed)
$1,960 (total finance charge)

Step 3. 48 − 9 = 39

Step 4. $\frac{780}{1,176}$

Step 5. $\frac{780}{1,176} \times \$1,960 = \$1,300$ rebate

Step 6. $6,630 − $1,300 = $5,330 payoff

14–17. Al Rolf bought an air conditioner with $100 down and 40 equal monthly installments of $30. The total purchase price (cash price) of the air conditioner was $900. Al decided to pay off the bill after the 29th payment. What is Al entitled to as a rebate on the finance charge? What will Al's payoff be?

Step 1. 40 × $30 = $1,200
29 × $30 = 870
$ 330 balance outstanding

Step 2. $1,200 (40 × $30)
− 800 ($900 − $100)
$ 400 total finance charge

Step 3. 40 − 29 = 11

Step 4. $\frac{66}{820}$

Step 5. $\frac{66}{820} \times \$400 = \$32.20$ rebate

Step 6. $330.00
− 32.20
$297.80 payoff

14–18. Joanne Flynn bought a new boat for $14,500. She put a $2,500 down payment on it. The bank's loan was for 48 months. Finance charges totaled $4,400.16. Assume Joanne decides to pay off the loan at the end of the 28th month. What rebate would she be entitled to and what is the actual payoff amount?

$$\text{Monthly payment} = \frac{\$4,400.16 + \$12,000}{48} = \$341.67$$

Step 1. 48 × $341.67 = $16,400.16
28 × $341.67 = − 9,566.76
$ 6,833.40 balance outstanding

Step 2. $16,400.16
− 12,000.00
$ 4,400.16

Step 3. 48 − 28 = 20

Step 4. $\frac{210}{1,176}$

Step 5. $\frac{210}{1,176} \times \$4,400.16 = \$785.74$ rebate

Step 6. $6,833.40
− 785.74
$6,047.66 payoff

14–19. Check APR by Table 14–1 for the following advertisement: $99.28 per month; cash price, $2,999; down payment, $99, cash or trade; annual percentage rate, 14.22 for 36 months with bank approved credit; amount financed, $2,900; finance charge $674.08; deferred payment price, $3,673.08; and total payments, $3,574.08.

$\frac{\$674.08}{\$2,900} \times \$100 = \$23.24$ Between 14% and 14.25%

14–20. From the following facts, Molly Roe has requested you to calculate the average daily balance. The customer believes the average daily balance should be $877.67. Respond to the customer's concern.

28-day billing cycle

3/18	Billing date	Previous balance		$800
3/24	Payment		$ 60	
3/29	Charge		250	
4/5	Payment		20	
4/9	Charge		200	

No. of days of current balance	Current balance	Extension	
6	$ 800	$ 4,800	
5	740	3,700	
7	990	6,930	
4	970	3,880	
6	1,170	7,020	
		$26,330	÷ 28 = $940.36

Customer divided by 30 days instead of 28 days; should be $940.36

14–21. Jill bought a $500 rocking chair. Terms of her revolving charge are $1\frac{1}{2}\%$ on the unpaid balance from previous month. If she pays $100 per month, complete a schedule for the first 3 months like Table 14–4. Be sure to use the U.S. Rule.

Monthly payment number	Outstanding balance due	$1\frac{1}{2}\%$ interest payment	Amount of monthly payment	Reduction in balance due	Outstanding balance due
1	$500.00	$7.50 ($500.00 × .015)	$100.00	$92.50 ($100.00 − $7.50)	$407.50 ($500.00 − $92.50)
2	$407.50	$6.11 ($407.50 × .015)	$100.00	$93.89 ($100.00 − $6.11)	$313.61 ($407.50 − $93.89)
3	$313.61	$4.70 ($313.61 × .015)	$100.00	$95.30 ($100.00 − $4.70)	$218.31 ($313.61 − $95.30)

Challenge Problem
Is Life Insurance's Finance Charge Correct?

14–22. Peg Gasperoni bought a $50,000 life insurance policy for $100 per year. Ryan Life Insurance Company sent her the following billing instructions along with a premium plan example:

"Your insurance premium notice will be mailed to you in a few days. You may pay the entire premium in full without a finance charge or you may pay the premium in installments after a down payment and the balance in monthly installments of $30. The finance charge will be added to the unpaid balance. The finance charge is based on an annual percentage rate of 15%."

If the total policy premium is:	And you put down:	The balance subject to finance charge will be:	The total number of monthly installments ($30 minimum) will be:	The monthly installment before adding the finance charge will be:	The total finance charge for all installments will be:	And the total deferred payment price will be:
$100	$30.00	$ 70.00	3	$30.00	$ 1.75	$101.75
200	50.00	150.00	5	30.00	5.67	205.67
300	75.00	225.00	8	30.00	12.84	312.84

Peg feels that the finance charge of $1.75 is in error. Who is correct? Check your answer.

$100
− 30
$70 × .0125 = $.875 $30 − $.875 = $29.125
$70.00
− 29.125
$ 40.875 × .0125 = $.51 $30 − $.51 = $29.49
− 29.49
$ 11.385 × .0125 = $.142
+ .142
$11.527 $1.53 not $1.75

$.875
+ .51
+ .142

Summary Practice Test

Solutions are at end of text in Appendix II.

Quick Reference

If you get any wrong answers, study the page numbers given for each problem.

1. Al Ranch bought a Chevy truck for $16,000. Al made a down payment of $3,000 and paid $250 monthly for 60 months. What is the total amount financed and the total finance charge that Al paid at the end of the 60 months? *(1. P. 317.)*

   $16,000 − $3,000 = $13,000 amount financed
   Total finance charge = ($250 × 60) − $13,000
   = $15,000 − $13,000
   = $2,000

2. Joy Abbot bought a computer for $3,500. Joy put down $500 and financed the balance at 11% for 48 months. What is her monthly payment (use loan amortization table)? *(2. P. 320.)*

   $\$3{,}500 - \$500 = \dfrac{\$3{,}000}{\$1{,}000} = 3 \times \$25.85 = \$77.55$

3. Joan Porl read the following partial advertisement: Price, $16,988; down payment, $488, cash or trade; and $385.19 per month for 60 months. Calculate **(a)** the total finance charge and **(b)** the APR by formula and by Table 14–1 to the nearest hundredth percent. *(3. Pp. 317–19.)*

   a. $16,988 $385.19 × 60 = $23,111.40
   − 488   − 16,500.00
   $16,500 $ 6,611.40 total finance charge

   b. Formula $\dfrac{2 \times 12 \times \$6{,}611.40}{\$16{,}500(60 + 1)} = \dfrac{\$158{,}673.60}{\$1{,}006{,}500} = 15.76\%$

   Table 14–1 $\dfrac{\$6{,}611.40}{\$16{,}500} \times \$100 = \$40.07$ between 14% and 14.25%

4. Barry Crate bought a $9,000 desk. Based on his income, Barry could only afford to pay back $800 per month. The charge on the unpaid balance is $1\frac{1}{2}\%$. The U.S. Rule is used in the calculation. Could you calculate at the end of month 2 the balance outstanding? *(4. P. 325.)*

Month	Balance due	Interest	Monthly payment	Reduction in balance	Balance outstanding
1	$9,000	$135.00 (.015 × $9,000)	$800	$665.00 ($800 − $135)	$8,335.00
2	$8,335	$125.03 (.015 × $8,335)	$800	$674.97 ($800 − $125.03)	$7,660.03

5. Jim Jean borrowed $8,000 to travel to Europe to see his son Bill. His loan was to be paid in 48 monthly installments of $195. At the end of 12 months, his daughter Joan convinced him that he should pay off the loan early. What is Jim's rebate and payoff amount? *(5. Pp. 321–22.)*

   Step 1. Total payments $9,360 ($195 × 48)
   Payments to date − 2,340 ($195 × 12)
   Balance of loan outstanding $7,020

   Step 2. Total payments $9,360
   − Amount financed − 8,000
   Total finance charge $1,360

Step 3. 48 − 12 = 36

Step 4. $\frac{666}{1,176}$

Step 5. $\frac{666}{1,176}$ × \$1,360 = \$770.20 rebate

Step 6. \$7,020 − \$770.20 = \$6,249.80

6. P. 326.

6. Calculate average daily balance.

29-day billing cycle

9/4	Balance	\$500
9/13	Payment	20
9/19	Charge	100

9 days × \$500 = \$ 4,500
6 days × 480 = 2,880
14 days × 580 = 8,120
\$15,500 ÷ 29 = \$534.48

Project A

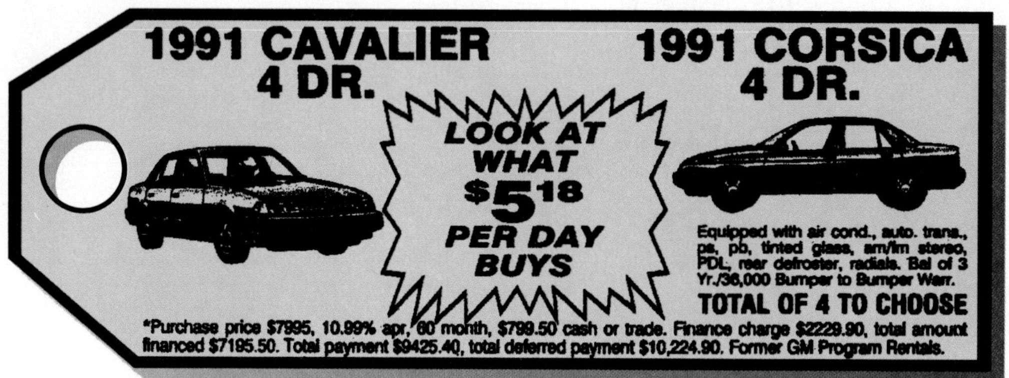

Is the $5.18 figure correct?

60 months = 5 years × 365 days = 1,825 days

Total payments $\frac{\$9,425.40}{1,825 \text{ days}} = \$5.16$

Doesn't quite match ad.

15

The Cost of Home Ownership

LEARNING UNIT OBJECTIVES

LU 15-1: Types of Mortgages and the Monthly Mortgage Payment

1. List types of mortgages available. *p. 341.*
2. Utilize an amortization chart to compute monthly payment. *p. 341.*
3. Calculate total cost of interest over life of mortgage. *p. 342.*

LU 15-2: Amortization Schedule—Breaking Down the Monthly Payment

1. Calculate and identify the interest and principal portion of each monthly payment. *p. 343.*
2. Prepare an amortization schedule. *p. 345.*

Chapter 15 could save you thousands of dollars! Read the following true story.

Last year, your author bought a new home. This is how I was able to save $70,121.40. Over the life of the mortgage, a 30-year **fixed rate mortgage** (Figure 15–1) of $100,000 would have cost me $207,235 in interest. My monthly payment would have been $849.99. This does not include taxes, insurance, repairs, and so on.

I chose a **biweekly mortgage** (Figure 15–1). This meant that every two weeks I would pay the bank $425. This would be paid 26 times a year. By paying every two weeks instead of once a month, my mortgage would be paid off in 23 years (instead of 30), and my *savings* on interest would be $70,121.40! Why? When a payment is made every two weeks, the principal is reduced quicker, which substantially reduces the interest cost.

This chapter gives valuable insights into home buying. Let's first look at different types of mortgages and the monthly mortgage payment.

LEARNING UNIT 15–1 TYPES OF MORTGAGES AND THE MONTHLY MORTGAGE PAYMENT

Did you know that the elderly can use their home to get cash or monthly income? The following clipping from *The Wall Street Journal* explains how **reverse mortgages** for elderly will be expanded.

Reverse Mortgages For Elderly Slated To Be Expanded

By MITCHELL PACELLE
Staff Reporter of THE WALL STREET JOURNAL

Elderly homeowners who are house-rich and cash-poor may no longer have to sell their homes to meet living expenses under a new federal loan program.

The Federal Housing Administration announced it is expanding a pilot program that allows homeowners at least 62 years old to convert equity in their homes into cash or monthly incomes. Many older homeowners don't have sufficient income to qualify for traditional home equity loans.

Under the new "reverse mortgages," homeowners can choose from five different payment plans, ranging from a line of credit to monthly payments for as long as they occupy their homes, even if it means receiving more than the value of the home.

The program includes condominiums but not cooperatives, which are shareholder-owned.

The loans don't have to be repaid during the lifetime of the homeowner, unless the property is no longer occupied as a primary residence. When the homeowner moves or dies, the principal and interest come due. The heirs can either repay the loan and keep the home or sell the home to pay off the loan.

If the loan amount exceeds the sale price, the FHA will absorb the loss. The FHA will also cover the cost of lifelong monthly payments to homeowners who outlive the values of their homes.

Many types of **mortgages** are available for all age levels. Figure 15–1 lists the types of mortgages available. In the past few years, interest rates and house prices have decreased. Depending on how interest rates are moving when you purchase a home, you may find one type of mortgage to be more advantageous for you.

Now let's learn how to calculate a monthly mortgage payment and the total cost of loan interest over the life of a mortgage. We will use the following example in our discussion.

EXAMPLE Gary bought a home for $200,000. He made a 20% down payment. The 9% mortgage is for 30 years (30 × 12 = 360 payments). What is Gary's monthly payment and total cost of interest?

FIGURE 15–1 Types of Mortgages Available

Loan type	Advantages	Disadvantages
30-year fixed rate mortgage	A predictable monthly payment.	If interest rates fall, you are locked in to higher rate unless you refinance. (Application and appraisal fees along with other closing costs will result.)
15-year fixed rate mortgage	Interest rate lower than 30-year fixed (usually $\frac{1}{4}$ to $\frac{1}{2}$ of a percent). Your equity builds up faster while cutting interest costs by more than half.	A larger down payment needed. Monthly payment will be higher.
Graduated-payment mortgage (GPM)	Easier to qualify for loan than 30- or 15-year fixed rate. Monthly payments start low and increase over time.	May have higher APR than fixed or variable rates.
Biweekly mortgage	Shortens term loan; saves substantial amount of interest. 26 biweekly payments a year. Builds equity twice as fast.	Those not seeking an early loan payoff.
Adjustable rate mortgage (ARM)	Lower rate than fixed. If rates fall, could be adjusted down without refinancing. Caps available that limit how high rate could go for each adjustment period over term of loan.	Monthly payment could rise if interest rates rise. Riskier than fixed rate mortgage where monthly payment is stable.
Home equity loan	Cheap and reliable accessible lines of credit backed by equity in your home. Tax deductible. Rates can be locked in. Reverse mortgages may be available to those 62 or older. See clipping on p. 340.	Could lose home if not paid. No annual or interest caps.

TABLE 15–1 Amortization Chart (Mortgage Principal and Interest per Thousand Dollars)

Term in years	Interest																
	8%	9%	10%	$10\frac{1}{2}$%	11%	$11\frac{1}{2}$%	$11\frac{3}{4}$%	12%	$12\frac{1}{2}$%	$12\frac{3}{4}$%	13%	$13\frac{1}{2}$%	$13\frac{3}{4}$%	14%	$14\frac{1}{2}$%	$14\frac{3}{4}$%	15%
10	12.14	12.67	13.22	13.50	13.78	14.06	14.21	14.35	14.64	14.79	14.94	15.23	15.38	15.53	15.83	15.99	16.14
12	10.83	11.39	11.96	12.25	12.54	12.84	12.99	13.14	13.44	13.60	13.75	14.06	14.22	14.38	14.69	14.85	15.01
15	9.56	10.15	10.75	11.06	11.37	11.69	11.85	12.01	12.33	12.49	12.66	12.99	13.15	13.32	13.66	13.83	14.00
17	8.99	9.59	10.22	10.54	10.86	11.19	11.35	11.52	11.85	12.02	12.19	12.53	12.71	12.88	13.23	13.41	13.58
20	8.37	9.00	9.66	9.99	10.33	10.67	10.84	11.02	11.37	11.54	11.72	12.08	12.26	12.44	12.80	12.99	13.17
22	8.07	8.72	9.39	9.73	10.08	10.43	10.61	10.78	11.14	11.33	11.51	11.87	12.06	12.24	12.62	12.81	12.99
25	7.72	8.40	9.09	9.45	9.81	10.17	10.35	10.54	10.91	11.10	11.28	11.66	11.85	12.04	12.43	12.62	12.81
30	7.34	8.05	8.78	9.15	9.53	9.91	10.10	10.29	10.68	10.87	11.07	11.46	11.66	11.85	12.25	12.45	12.65
35	7.11	7.84	8.60	8.99	9.37	9.77	9.96	10.16	10.56	10.76	10.96	11.36	11.56	11.76	12.17	12.37	12.57

Computing the Monthly Payment for Principal and Interest

With Table 15–1, we use the following steps to calculate the principal and interest of Gary's **monthly payment.** (Remember this is the same type of amortization table we used in Chapter 14 for installment loans.)

Steps for Computing Monthly Payment from Amortization Chart

Step 1. Divide amount of mortgage by $1,000.

Step 2. Look up rate and term. At intersection is the table factor.

Step 3. Multiply Step 1 times Step 2.

TABLE 15-2 Effect of Interest Rates on Monthly Payments

	9%	11%	Difference
Monthly payment	\$1,288 (160 × \$8.05)	\$1,524.80 (160 × \$9.53)	\$236.80 per month
Total cost of interest	\$303,680 (\$1,288 × 360) − \$160,000	\$388,928 (\$1,524.80 × 360) − \$160,000	\$85,248 (\$236.80 × \$360)

For Gary, we calculate the following:

$$\frac{\$160{,}000 \text{ (amount of mortgage)}}{\$1{,}000} = 160 \times \$8.05 \text{ (table rate)} = \$1{,}288$$

\$160,000 is the amount of the mortgage (\$200,000 less 20%). The \$8.05 is the table factor of 9% for 30 years per \$1,000. Since Gary is mortgaging 160 units of \$1,000, the factor of \$8.05 is multiplied by 160. Remember that the \$1,288 payment does not include taxes, insurance, and so on.

What Is the Total Cost of Interest over the Life of the Loan?

We can use the following formula to calculate Gary's total interest cost over the life of the mortgage:

$$\text{Total cost of interest} = \text{Total of all monthly payments} - \text{Amount of mortgage}$$

$$\$303{,}680 = \$463{,}680 \ (\$1{,}288 \times 360) - \$160{,}000$$

Effects of Interest Rates on Monthly Payment and Total Cost of Interest

To show the effect that interest rates have on Gary's monthly payment and to determine his total cost of interest, let's look at Table 15-2. This table shows that if interest rates rise to 11%, the 2% increase will result in Gary paying an additional \$85,248 in total interest.

For most people, purchasing a home is a major lifetime decision. Many factors must be considered before making this decision. One of these factors is how to pay for the home. The purpose of this unit is to tell you that being informed on the types of available mortgages can save you thousands of dollars. You should remember that the interest on a mortgage is tax deductible.

Courtesy of Baird & Warner

When buying a home, here are some *additional* costs you may face besides the monthly payment for principal and interest.

Closing costs—When property passes from seller to buyer, **closing costs** may include credit reports, recording costs, lawyer's fees, points, title search, and so on. A **point** is a one-time charge that is a percent of the mortgage. Two points means 2% of the mortgage.

Escrow account—Usually the lending institution, for its protection, requires that each month $\frac{1}{12}$ of the cost of the insurance and $\frac{1}{12}$ of the cost of real estate taxes be kept in a special account called the **escrow account.** Your monthly balance in this account will change depending on the cost of insurance and taxes. Interest is paid on escrow accounts.

Repairs and maintenance—This includes paint, paper, landscaping, plumbing, and electrical expenses.

As you can see, the cost of running a home can be expensive. But remember that all interest costs of your monthly payment are tax deductible, and that owning a home has many advantages over renting.

Now let's check your understanding of this unit with a Practice Quiz.

LU 15-1 PRACTICE QUIZ

Given Price of home, $225,000; 20% down payment; 9% interest rate; 25-year mortgage.

Solve for

1. Monthly payment and total cost of interest over 25 years.
2. If rate fell to 8%, what would be total decrease in interest cost over life of mortgage?

SOLUTIONS TO LU 15-1 PRACTICE QUIZ

1. $225,000 − $45,000 = $180,000

   $\frac{\$180{,}000}{\$1{,}000} = 180 \times \$8.40 = \$1{,}512$

   $273,600 = $453,600 ($1,512 × 300) − $180,000 (300 = 25 years × 12 payments per year)

2. 8% = $1,389.60 (180 × $7.72) monthly payment

   Total interest cost $236,880 = ($1,389.60 × 300) − $180,000

   Savings $36,720 = ($273,600 − $236,880)

LEARNING UNIT 15-2 AMORTIZATION SCHEDULE—BREAKING DOWN THE MONTHLY PAYMENT

In Learning Unit 15-1, we saw that over the life of Gary's $160,000 loan, he would pay $303,680 in interest. Now let's see what portion of Gary's first monthly payment reduces the principal and what portion is interest. We will complete the following steps:

Steps for Calculating Interest, Principal, and New Balance of Monthly Payment

Step 1. Calculate interest for a month (use current principal):
Interest = Principal × Rate × Time.

Step 2. Calculate amount used to reduce principal:
Principal reduction = Monthly payment − Interest (Step 1).

Step 3. Calculate new principal: Current principal − Reduction of principal (Step 2) = New principal.

Step 1. Interest (I) = Principal (P) × Rate (R) × Time (T)

$$\$1{,}200 = \$160{,}000 \times .09 \times \frac{1}{12}$$

Step 2. The reduction of the $160,000 principal each month is equal to the payment less interest. So we can calculate Gary's new principal balance at the end of month 1 as follows:

Monthly payment at 9% (from Table 15-1)	$1,288 (160 × $8.05)
− Interest for first month	− 1,200
= Principal reduction	$ 88

Step 3. As the years go along, the interest portion of the payment decreases and the principal portion increases.

Principal balance	$160,000
Principal reduction	− 88
Balance of principal	$159,912

Let's do month 2:

Step 1. Interest = Principal × Rate × Time

$$= \$159{,}912 \times .09 \times \frac{1}{12}$$

$$= \$1{,}199.34$$

Step 2.

$1,288.00	monthly payment
− 1,199.34	interest for month 2
$ 88.66	principal reduction

Step 3.

$159,912.00	principal balance
− 88.66	principal reduction
$159,823.34	balance of principal

Note that in month 2, interest costs drop 66 cents ($1,200 − $1,199.34). So in two months, Gary has reduced his mortgage balance by $176.66 ($88 + $88.66). After two months, Gary has paid a total interest of $2,399.34 ($1,200 + $1,199.34).

Example of an Amortization Schedule

The partial **amortization schedule** given in Table 15–3 shows the breakdown of Gary's monthly payment. Note the amount that goes toward reducing the principal and toward payment of actual interest. Also note how the outstanding balance of the loan is reduced. After seven months, Gary still owes $159,369.97. Often when you take out a mortgage loan, you will receive an amortization schedule from the company that holds your mortgage.

As a final note, you should be aware that with changing interest rates, it may pay you to refinance a mortgage. The information in the following table is valuable if you already have a mortgage or if you buy a home in the future at a time when interest rates are high.

Mortgage Refinancing Calculator

When does it pay to refinance? Find the amount on the left that's closest to what it would cost to refinance your mortgage. Follow that row to the right, until the column is over the amount that's closest to what you would save each month by refinancing. Where the cost row and the savings column intersect shows the approximate number of months it will take for refinancing to begin paying off. Actual payback periods will be affected by tax considerations.

Costs of refinancing									
$7,000	140	94	70	56	47	40	35	32	28
6,000	120	80	60	48	40	35	30	27	24
5,000	100	67	50	40	34	29	25	23	20
4,000	80	54	40	32	27	23	20	18	16
3,000	60	40	30	24	20	18	15	14	12
2,000	40	27	20	16	14	12	10	9	8
1,000	20	14	10	8	7	6	5	5	4
Monthly savings ($)	**50**	**75**	**100**	**125**	**150**	**175**	**200**	**225**	**250**

Now let's take another Practice Quiz.

TABLE 15-3 Partial Amortization Schedule

Payment number	Principal (current)	Interest	Principal reduction	Balance of principal
		Monthly payment, $1,288		
1	$160,000	$1,200.00 $\left(\$160{,}000 \times .09 \times \frac{1}{12}\right)$	$88.00 ($1,288 − $1,200)	$159,912 ($160,000 − $88)
2	$159,912	$1,199.34 $\left(\$159{,}912 \times .09 \times \frac{1}{12}\right)$	$88.66 ($1,288 − $1,199.34)	$159,823.34 ($159,912 − $88.66)
3	$159,823.34	$1,198.68	$89.32	$159,734.02
4	$159,734.02	$1,198.01	$89.99	$159,644.03
5	$159,644.03	$1,197.33	$90.67	$159,553.36
6	$159,553.36	$1,196.65	$91.35	$159,462.01
7	$159,462.01	$1,195.97	$92.04	$159,369.97

LU 15-2 PRACTICE QUIZ

Prepare an amortization schedule for first three periods for the following: mortgage, $100,000; 11%; 30 years.

SOLUTIONS TO LU 15-2 PRACTICE QUIZ

$100,000 mortgage; monthly payment, $953 (100 × $9.53)

Payment number	Principal (current)	Interest	Principal reduction	Balance of principal
		Portion to—		
1	$100,000	$916.67 $\left((\$100{,}000 \times .11 \times \frac{1}{12}\right)$	$36.33 ($953 − $916.67)	$99,963.67 ($100,000 − $36.33)
2	$99,963.67	$916.33 $\left(\$99{,}963.67 \times .11 \times \frac{1}{12}\right)$	$36.67 ($953 − $916.33)	$99,927.00 ($99,963.67 − $36.67)
3	$99,927	$916.00 $\left(\$99{,}927 \times .11 \times \frac{1}{12}\right)$	$37.00 ($953 − $916)	$99,890.00 ($99,927 − $37)

CHAPTER ORGANIZER: A REFERENCE GUIDE

Page	Topic	Key point, procedure, formula	Example(s) to illustrate situation
342	Computing monthly mortgage payment	Based on per $1,000 Table 15-1: $\frac{\text{Amount of mortgage}}{\$1{,}000} \times \text{Table rate}$	Use Table 15-1: 12% on $60,000 mortgage for 30 years. $\frac{\$60{,}000}{\$1{,}000} = 60 \times \$10.29$ $= \$617.40$

Page	Topic	Key point, procedure, formula	Example(s) to illustrate situation
342	Calculating total interest cost	Total of all monthly payments − Amount of mortgage	Using example above: 30 years = 360 (payments) × \$617.40 \$222,264 − 60,000 \$162,264 (mortgage interest over life of mortgage)
344	Amortization schedule	$I = P \times R \times T$ $\left(I \text{ for month} = P \times R \times \frac{1}{12}\right)$ Principal reduction = Monthly payment − Interest New principal = Current principal − Reduction of principal	Using same example: **Portion to—** **Payment number** / **Interest** / **Principal reduction** / **Balance of principal** 1 / \$600 / \$17.40 / \$59,982.60 $\left(\$60{,}000 \times .12 \times \frac{1}{12}\right)$ $\left(\begin{array}{r}\$617.40\\ -\ \$600.00\end{array}\right)$ $\left(\begin{array}{r}\$60{,}000.00\\ -\ \$17.40\end{array}\right)$ 2 / \$599.83 / \$17.57 / \$59,965.03 $\left(\$59{,}982.60 \times .12 \times \frac{1}{12}\right)$ $\left(\begin{array}{r}\$617.40\\ -\ \$599.83\end{array}\right)$ $\left(\begin{array}{r}\$59{,}982.60\\ -\ \$17.57\end{array}\right)$
	Key terms	Adjustable rate mortgage, (ARM), *p. 341* Amortization schedule, *p. 345* Biweekly mortgage, *p. 341* Closing costs, *p. 342* Escrow account, *p. 342* Fixed rate mortgage, *p. 341*	Graduated-payment mortgages (GPM), *p. 341* Home equity, *p. 341* Monthly payment, *p. 341* Mortgages, *p. 340* Points, *p. 342* Reverse mortgages, *p. 340*

NOTES

THAT WAS THEN . . .
. . . THIS IS NOW

Disney has provided great memories through movies and theme parks, from the original Disneyland in 1955 to the new Euro Disneyland. But Disney is also a corporation responsible for preparing annual reports to its stockholders.

16

How to Read, Analyze, and Interpret Financial Reports

LEARNING UNIT OBJECTIVES

LU 16–1: Balance Sheet: Report as of a Particular Date

1. Explain the purpose and the key items on the balance sheet. *p. 356.*
2. Explain and complete vertical and horizontal analysis. *pp. 357–58.*

LU 16–2: Income Statement: Report for a Specific Period of Time

1. Explain the purpose and the key items on the income statement. *pp. 360–61.*
2. Explain and complete vertical and horizontal analysis. *p. 363.*

LU 16–3: Trend and Ratio Analysis

1. Explain and complete a trend analysis. *p. 364.*
2. List, explain, and calculate key financial ratios. *p. 365.*

Many companies today find it necessary to cut expenses. The following *Wall Street Journal* clipping states that USF&G is trying to avoid financial difficulties by reducing expenses and shoring up its balance sheet.

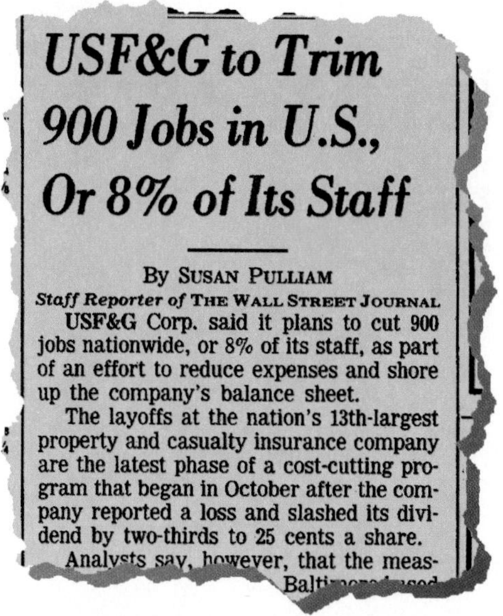
USF&G to Trim 900 Jobs in U.S., Or 8% of Its Staff

By SUSAN PULLIAM
Staff Reporter of THE WALL STREET JOURNAL

USF&G Corp. said it plans to cut 900 jobs nationwide, or 8% of its staff, as part of an effort to reduce expenses and shore up the company's balance sheet.

The layoffs at the nation's 13th-largest property and casualty insurance company are the latest phase of a cost-cutting program that began in October after the company reported a loss and slashed its dividend by two-thirds to 25 cents a share.

Analysts say, however, that the meas-

In this chapter, we focus our attention on analyzing financial reports. Business owners must understand their own financial statements to avoid financial difficulties. This includes knowing how to read, analyze, and interpret financial reports.

The two key financial reports that we discuss in this chapter are the *balance sheet* (shows a company's financial condition at a particular date) and the *income statement* (shows a company's profitability over a time period).[1] Let's first turn our attention to the balance sheet.

LEARNING UNIT 16–1 BALANCE SHEET: REPORT AS OF A PARTICULAR DATE

The **balance sheet** gives a financial picture of what a business is worth as of a particular date. This report lists (1) how much the business owns (assets), (2) how much the business owes (liabilities), and (3) how much the owner (owner's equity) is worth. So we have the following formula:

Assets − Liabilities = Owner's equity

Like this formula, the items on both sides of the equal sign must balance.

By reversing this formula, we have the common balance sheet layout:

Assets = Liabilities + Owner's equity

[1] The third key financial report is the statement of cash flows. We do not discuss this statement. For more information on the statement of cash flows, check your accounting text.

Sharon Hoogstraten

To introduce you to the balance sheet, let's assume that you collect baseball cards and decide to open a baseball card shop. As the owner of The Card Shop, your investment, or owner's equity, is called **capital**. Since your business is small, your balance sheet is short. After the first year of operation, The Card Shop balance sheet looks like this:

You will learn the meaning of these balance sheet terms later in the chapter.

Capital does not mean cash. It is the owner's investment into the company.

THE CARD SHOP
Balance Sheet
December 31, 1995

Assets		**Liabilities**	
Cash	$ 3,000	Accounts payable	$ 2,500
Merchandise inventory		**Owner's Equity**	
(baseball cards)	4,000		
Equipment	3,000	E. Slott, capital	7,500
Total assets	$10,000	Total liabilities and owner's equity	$10,000

The heading gives the name of the company, title of the report, and date or period of the report. Note how the totals of both sides of the balance sheet are the same. This is true of all balance sheets.

We can take figures from the The Card Shop balance sheet and use our first formula to determine how much your business is worth:

Assets	−	Liabilities	=	Owner's equity (capital)
$10,000	−	$2,500	=	$7,500

Now you are ready to study the balance sheet elements of a corporation. As the single owner of The Card Shop, you are a **sole proprietorship.** If a company has two or more owners, it is called a **partnership. A corporation** has many owners or stockholders. So the owner's equity of a corporation is called **stockholders' equity.**

Elements of the Balance Sheet of a Corporation

The format and contents of all company balance sheets are similar. Figure 16–1 shows the balance sheet of Mool Company. As you can see, the formula Assets = Liabilities + Stockholders' equity (remember now we have a corporation) is also the framework of this balance sheet.

FIGURE 16–1 Balance Sheet

Break assets into current assets and plant and equipment

MOOL COMPANY
Balance Sheet
December 31, 1995

Put in heading who, what, when

Liabilities broken down by current and long-term

		Assets		
1.	a.	Current assets:		
	b.	Cash	$ 7,000	
	c.	Accounts receivable	9,000	
	d.	Merchandise inventory	30,000	
	e.	Prepaid expenses	15,000	
	f.	Total current assets		$ 61,000
	g.	Plant and equipment:		
	h.	Building (net)	$60,000	
	i.	Land	84,000	
	j.	Total plant and equipment		144,000
	k.	Total assets		$205,000

		Liabilities		
2.	a.	Current liabilities:		
	b.	Accounts payable	$80,000	
	c.	Salaries payable	12,000	
	d.	Total current liabilities		$ 92,000
	e.	Long-term liabilities:		
	f.	Mortgage note payable		58,000
	g.	Total liabilities		$150,000
		Stockholders' Equity		
3.	a.	Common stock	$20,000	
	b.	Retained earnings	35,000	
	c.	Total stockholders' equity		55,000
	d.	Total liabilities and stockholders' equity		$205,000

Total of current assets and plant and equipment

Total is double ruled

Total of all liabilities and stockholders' equity

To help you understand the three main balance sheet groups (assets, liabilities, and stockholders' equity) and their elements, we have labeled them in Figure 16–1. An explanation of these elements follows. Do not try to memorize the elements. Just try to understand their meaning. Think of Figure 16–1 as a reference aid. You will find that the more you work with balance sheets, the easier it is for you to understand them.

1. **Assets:** Things of value *owned* by an individual or enterprise (economic resources of the business) that can be measured and expressed in monetary terms.
   a. **Current assets:** Assets that companies consume or convert into cash *within one year* or a normal operating cycle.
   b. **Cash:** Cash includes checking accounts, currency, and the like.
   c. **Accounts receivable:** Amount *owed* by customers to a business from sales on account (buy now, pay later).
   d. **Merchandise inventory:** Cost of goods in stock for resale to customers.
   e. **Prepaid expenses:** When a company buys items, they are assets. As these items expire and are consumed, they become expenses. Example: insurance and rent.
   f. **Total current assets:** Sum of all assets that the company will consume or convert into cash within one year.
   g. **Plant and equipment:** Assets that will last longer than one year. Companies use these assets in their business operation rather than for resale.
   h. **Building (net):** This item is the cost of the building minus the depreciation amount that has accumulated. Usually, the balance sheet shows this item as "Building less accumulated depreciation." In Chapter 17, we will talk more about accumulated depreciation.
   i. **Land:** An asset that does not depreciate.
   j. **Total plant and equipment:** Total of building, machinery, equipment, and land.
   k. **Total assets:** Sum of current assets and plant and equipment.

2. **Liabilities:** Debts or obligations of the company.
   a. **Current liabilities:** Debts or obligations of a company that are *due within one year.*
   b. **Accounts payable:** A current liability that shows the amount a company owes to creditors for services or item purchased.
   c. **Salaries payable:** Obligations that the company must pay within a year for salaries earned but unpaid.
   d. **Total current liabilities:** The sum of obligations that the company must pay within one year.
   e. **Long-term liabilities:** The debts or obligations that the company does not have to pay within one year.
   f. **Mortgage note payable:** The debt owed on a building that is a long-term liability; often the building is collateral.
   g. **Total liabilities:** The total of current and long-term liabilities.
3. **Stockholders' equity (owner's equity):** The rights or interest of the stockholders to assets of a corporation. If the company is not a corporation, the term *owner's equity* is used. The word *capital* follows the owner's name under the title *Owner's Equity.*
   a. **Common stock:** The amount of inital and additional investment of corporation owners by the purchase of stock.
   b. **Retained earnings:** The amount of corporation earnings that the company retains in the business, not necessarily in cash form.
   c. **Total stockholders' equity:** Total of stock plus retained earnings.
   d. **Total liabilities and stockholders' equity:** Sum of current liabilities, long-term liabilities, stock, and retained earnings. This sum represents the total claims on assets: prior and present claims of creditors, owners' residual claims, and any other claims.

Now that you are familiar with the common balance sheet items, you are ready to analyze a balance sheet.

Vertical Analysis and the Balance Sheet

Often financial statement readers want to analyze reports that contain data for two or more successive accounting periods. To make this possible, companies present a statement showing the data from these periods side by side. As you might expect, this statement is called a **comparative statement.**

Comparative reports help illustrate changes in data. Statement readers should compare the percents in the reports to industry percents and the percents of competitors.

Figure 16–2 shows the comparative balance sheet of Roger Company. Note that the statement analyzes each asset as a percent of total assets for a single time period. The statement then analyzes each liability and equity as a percent of total liabilities and stockholders' equity. We call this type of analysis **vertical analysis.**

The following steps are used to prepare a vertical analysis of a balance sheet.

Steps for Preparing Vertical Analysis of a Balance Sheet

Step 1. Divide each asset (the portion) as a percent of total assets (the base). Round as indicated.

Step 2. Divide each liability and stockholders' equity (the portions) as a percent of total liabilities and stockholders' equity (the base). Round as indicated.

FIGURE 16–2
Comparative Balance Sheet: Vertical Analysis

We divide each item by the total of assets.

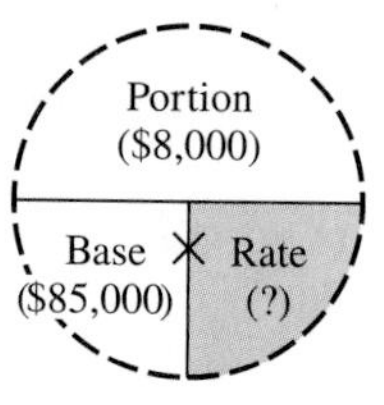

We divide each element by total of liabilities and stockholders' equity.

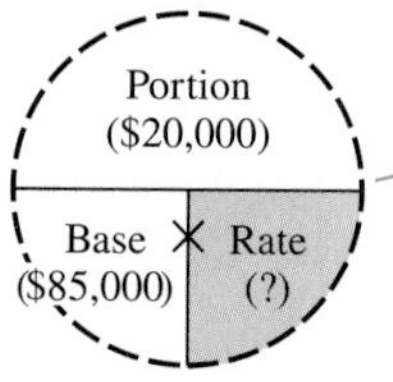

ROGER COMPANY
Comparative Balance Sheet
December 31, 1994, and 1995

	1995		1994	
	Amount	**Percent**	**Amount**	**Percent**
Assets				
Current assets:				
Cash	$22,000	25.88	$18,000	22.22
Accounts receivable	8,000	9.41	9,000	11.11
Merchandise inventory	9,000	10.59	7,000	8.64
Prepaid rent	4,000	4.71	5,000	6.17
Total current assets	$43,000	50.59	$39,000	48.15 *
Plant and equipment:				
Building (net)	$18,000	21.18	$18,000	22.22
Land	24,000	28.24	24,000	29.63
Total plant and equipment	$42,000	49.41 *	$42,000	51.85
Total assets	$85,000	100.00	$81,000	100.00
Liabilities				
Current liabilities:				
Accounts payable	$14,000	16.47	$ 8,000	9.88
Salaries payable	18,000	21.18	17,000	20.99
Total current liabilities	$32,000	37.65	$25,000	30.86 *
Long-term liabilities				
Mortgage note payable	12,000	14.12	20,000	24.69
Total liabilities	$44,000	51.76 *	$45,000	55.56 *
Stockholders' Equity				
Common stock	$20,000	23.53	$20,000	24.69
Retained earnings	21,000	24.71	16,000	19.75
Total stockholders' equity	$41,000	48.24	$36,000	44.44
Total liabilities and stockholders' equity	$85,000	100.00	$81,000	100.00

Note: All percents are rounded to nearest hundredth percent.
* Due to rounding.

Horizontal Analysis and the Balance Sheet

We can also analyze balance sheets for two or more periods by using **horizontal analysis.** Horizontal analysis compares each item in one year, by amount, percent, or both, with the same item of the previous year. Note the Abby Ellen Company horizontal analysis shown in Figure 16–3. To make a horizontal analysis, we use the steps that follow.

Steps for Preparing a Horizontal Analysis of a Comparative Balance Sheet

Step 1. Calculate the increase or decrease in each item from the base year.

Step 2. Divide the increase or decrease in Step 1 by the old, or base, year.

Step 3. Round as indicated.

You can see the difference between vertical analysis and horizontal analysis by looking at the example of vertical analysis in Figure 16–2. The percent calculations in Figure 16–2 are for each item of a particular year as a percent of that year's total assets or total liabilities and stockholders' equity.

Horizontal analysis needs comparative columns because we take the difference *between* periods of time. In Figure 16–3, for example, the accounts receivable decreased $1,000 from 1994 to 1995. Thus, by dividing $1,000 (amount of change) by $6,000 (base year), we see that Abby's receivables decreased 16.67%.

FIGURE 16–3
Comparative Balance Sheet: Horizontal Analysis

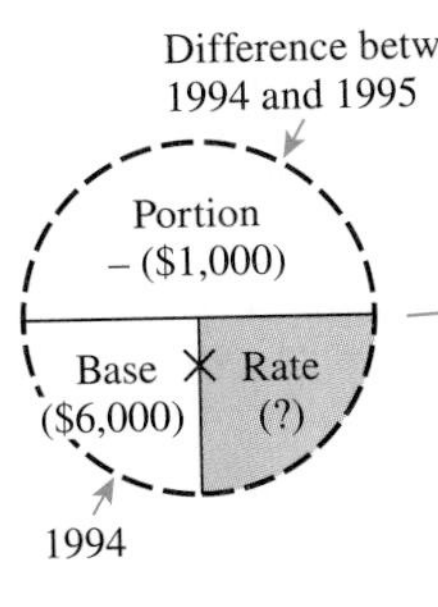

ABBY ELLEN COMPANY
Comparative Balance Sheet
December 31, 1994, and 1995

	1995	1994	Increase (decrease) Amount	Percent
Assets				
Current assets:				
Cash	$ 6,000	$ 4,000	$ 2,000	50.00*
Accounts receivable	5,000	6,000	(1,000)	– 16.67
Merchandise inventory	9,000	4,000	5,000	125.00
Prepaid rent	5,000	7,000	(2,000)	– 28.57
Total current assets	$25,000	$21,000	$ 4,000	19.05
Plant and equipment:				
Building (net)	$12,000	$12,000	-0-	-0-
Land	18,000	18,000	-0-	-0-
Total plant and equipment	$30,000	$30,000	-0-	-0-
Total assets	$55,000	$51,000	$ 4,000	7.84
Liabilities				
Current liabilities:				
Accounts payable	$ 3,200	$ 1,800	$ 1,400	77.78
Salaries payable	2,900	3,200	(300)	– 9.38
Total current liabilities	$ 6,100	$ 5,000	$ 1,100	22.00
Long-term liabilities:				
Mortgage note payable	17,000	15,000	2,000	13.33
Total liabilities	$23,100	$20,000	$ 3,100	15.50
Owner's equity				
Abby Ellen, capital	$31,900	$31,000	$ 900	2.90
Total liabilities and owner's equity	$55,000	$51,000	$ 4,000	7.84

* The percents are not summed vertically in horizontal analysis.

Let's now try the following Practice Quiz.

LU 16–1 PRACTICE QUIZ

1. Complete this partial comparative balance sheet by vertical analysis. Round percents to nearest hundredth.

	1995 Amount	1995 Percent	1994 Amount	1994 Percent
Assets				
Current assets:				
a. Cash	$ 42,000		$ 40,000	
b. Accounts receivable	18,000		17,000	
c. Merchandise inventory	15,000		12,000	
d. Prepaid expenses	17,000		14,000	
.	.		.	
.	.		.	
.	.		.	
Total current assets	$160,000		$150,000	

2. What is the amount of change in merchandise inventory and the percent increase?

SOLUTIONS TO LU 16-1 PRACTICE QUIZ

	1995	1994
1. a. Cash	$\frac{\$42,000}{\$160,000} = 26.25\%$	$\frac{\$40,000}{\$150,000} = 26.67\%$
b. Accounts receivable	$\frac{\$18,000}{\$160,000} = 11.25\%$	$\frac{\$17,000}{\$150,000} = 11.33\%$
c. Merchandise inventory	$\frac{\$15,000}{\$160,000} = 9.38\%$	$\frac{\$12,000}{\$150,000} = 8\%$
d. Prepaid expenses	$\frac{\$17,000}{\$160,000} = 10.63\%$	$\frac{\$14,000}{\$150,000} = 9.33\%$

2. $15,000
 − 12,000
Amount = $ 3,000

Percent $= \frac{\$3,000}{\$12,000} = 25\%$

LEARNING UNIT 16-2 INCOME STATEMENT: REPORT FOR A SPECIFIC PERIOD OF TIME

The **income statement** is a financial report that tells how well a company is performing (its profitability) during a specific period of time (month, year, and so on). In general, the income statement reveals the inward flow of revenues (sales) against the outward or potential outward flow of costs and expenses.

The form of income statements varies depending on the company's type of business. However, the basic formula of the income statement is the same:

Revenues − Operating expenses = Net income

In a merchandising business like The Card Shop, we can enlarge on this formula:

Revenues (sales) ← After any returns or discounts
− Cost of merchandise or goods ← Baseball cards
= Gross profit from sales
− Operating expenses
= Net income (profit)

Sharon Hoogstraten

Now let's look at The card Shop's income statement to see how much profit The Card Shop made during its first year of operation. For simplicity, we assume The Card Shop sold all the cards it bought during the year.

THE CARD SHOP
Income Statement
For Month Ended December 31, 1995

Revenues (sales)	$8,000
Cost of merchandise sold	3,000
Gross profit from sales	$5,000
Operating expenses	750
Net income	$4,250

For its first year of business, The Card Shop made a profit of $4,250.

We can now go more deeply into these elements as we study the income statement of a corporation. Remember to use the vocabulary list in Learning Unit 16-1 as a reference tool. The more you use the terms, the more familiar they will become.

FIGURE 16–4 Income Statement

MOOL COMPANY
Income Statement
For Month Ended December 31, 1995

← Put in heading who, what, when

		Revenues:					
1.	a.	Gross sales			$22,080		
	b.	Less: Sales returns and allowances		$ 1,082			Actual sales after discounts and returns
	c.	Sales discounts		432	1,514		
	d.	Net sales				$20,566	
		Cost of merchandise (goods) sold:					
2.	a.	Merchandise inventory December 1, 1995			$ 1,248		
	b.	Purchases		$10,512			
	c.	Less: Purchase returns and allowances	$336				
	d.	Less: Purchase discounts	204	540			
	e.	Cost of net purchases			9,972		
	f.	Cost of merchandise (goods available for sale)			$11,220		
	g.	Less: Merchandise inventory, December 31, 1995			1,600		Inventory not yet sold
	h.	Cost of merchandise (goods) sold				9,620	
3.		Gross profit from sales				$10,946	Net sales − Cost of goods sold
		Operating expenses:					
4.	a.	Salary		$ 2,200			
	b.	Insurance		1,300			
	c.	Utilities		400			
	d.	Plumbing		120			
	e.	Rent		410			
	f.	Depreciation		200			
	g.	Total operating expenses				4,630	
5.		Net income				$ 6,316	Gross profit − Operating expenses

Note: Numbers are subtotaled from left to right.

Elements of the Income Statement of a Corporation

Figure 16–4 gives the format and content of the Mool company income statement—a corporation. The five main items of an income statement are revenues, cost of merchandise (goods) sold, gross profit on sales, operating expenses, and net income. We will follow the same pattern we used in explaining the balance sheet and define the main items and the letter coded subitems.

1. **Revenues:** Total earned sales (cash or credit) less any sales discounts, returns, or allowances.
   a. **Gross sales:** Total earned sales before sales returns and allowances or sales discounts.
   b. **Sales returns and allowances:** Reductions in price or reductions in revenue due to goods returned because of product defects, errors, and so on. When the buyer keeps damaged goods, an allowance results.
   c. **Sales (not trade) discounts:** Reductions in the selling price of goods due to early customer payment. For example, a store may give 2% discount to a customer who pays a bill within 10 days.
   d. **Net sales:** Gross sales less sales returns and allowances less sales discounts.
2. **Cost of merchandise (goods) sold:** All the company's costs of getting the merchandise that the company sold. The cost of all unsold merchandise (goods) will be subtracted from this item (ending inventory).
   a. **Merchandise inventory, December 1, 1995:** Cost of inventory in the store that was for sale to customers at the beginning of the month.
   b. **Purchases:** Cost of additional merchandise brought into the store for resale to customers.

c. **Purchase returns and allowances:** Cost of merchandise returned to the store due to damage, defects, errors, and so on. Damaged goods kept by the buyer result in a cost reduction called an *allowance*.

d. **Purchase discounts:** Savings received by the buyer for paying for merchandise before a certain date. These discounts can result in a substantial savings to a company.

e. **Cost of net purchases:** Cost of purchases less purchase returns and allowances less purchase discounts.

f. **Cost of merchandise (goods available for sale):** Sum of beginning inventory plus cost of net purchases.

g. **Merchandise inventory, December 31, 1995:** Cost of inventory remaining in the store to be sold.

h. **Cost of merchandise (goods) sold:** Beginning inventory plus net purchases less ending inventory.

3. **Gross profit from sales:** Net sales less cost of merchandise (goods) sold.
4. **Operating expenses:** Additional costs of operating the business beyond the actual cost of inventory sold.

   a.–f. **Expenses:** Individual expenses broken down.

   g. **Total operating expenses:** Total of all the individual expenses.
5. **Net income:** Gross profit less operating expenses.

In the next section, you will learn some formulas that companies use to calculate various items on the income statement.

Calculating Net Sales, Cost of Merchandise (Goods) Sold, Gross Profit from Sales, and Net Income of an Income Statement

It is time to look closely at Figure 16–4 and see how each section is built. Use the above vocabulary as a reference. We will study Figure 16–4 step by step.

Step 1. Calculate net sales. What Mool earned:

Net sales	=	Gross sales	−	Sales returns and allowances	−	Sales discount
↑		↑		↑		↑
$20,566	=	$22,080	−	$1,082	−	$432

Step 2. Calculate cost of merchandise (goods) sold. What it cost to sell baseball cards before operating expenses:

Cost of merchandise (goods) sold	=	Beginning inventory	+	Net purchases (purchases less returns and discounts)	−	Ending inventory
↑		↑		↑		↑
$9,620	=	$1,248	+	$9,972	−	$1,600

Step 3. Calculate gross profit from sales. Profit before operating expenses:

Gross profit from sales	=	Net sales	−	Cost of merchandise (goods) sold
↑		↑		↑
$10,946	=	$20,566	−	$9,620

Step 4. Calculate net income. Profit after operating expenses:

Net income	=	Gross profit	−	Operating expenses
↑		↑		↑
$6,316	=	$10,946	−	$4,630

FIGURE 16–5
Vertical Analysis

Individual amount
Portion ($12,000)
Base × Rate
($29,000) (?)
Net sales

ROYAL COMPANY
Comparative Income Statement
For Years Ended December 31, 1994, and 1995

	1995	Percent of net	1994	Percent of net
Net sales	$45,000	100.00	$29,000	100.00 *
Cost of merchandise sold	19,000	42.22	12,000	41.38
Gross profit from sales	$26,000	57.78	$17,000	58.62
Operating expenses:				
Depreciation	$ 1,000	2.22	$ 500	1.72
Selling and advertising	4,200	9.33	1,600	5.52
Research	2,900	6.44	2,000	6.90
Miscellaneous	500	1.11	200	.69
Total operating expenses	$ 8,600	19.11 †	$ 4,300	14.83
Income before interest and taxes	$17,400	38.67	$12,700	43.79
Interest expense	6,000	13.33	3,000	10.34
Income before taxes	$11,400	25.33 †	$ 9,700	33.45
Provision for taxes	5,500	12.22	3,000	10.34
Net income	$ 5,900	13.11	$ 6,700	23.10 †

* Net sales = 100%.
† Off due to rounding.

FIGURE 16–6
Horizontal Analysis

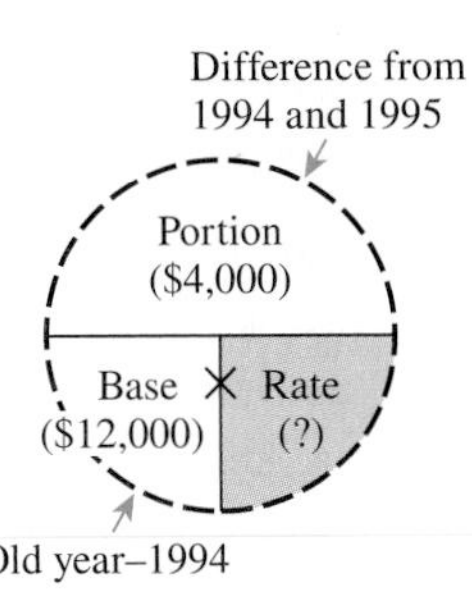

FLINT COMPANY
Comparative Income Statement
For Years Ended December 31, 1994, and 1995

	1995	1994	Increase (decrease) Amount	Percent
Sales	$90,000	$80,000	$10,000	
Sales returns and allowances	2,000	2,000	-0-	
Net sales	$88,000	$78,000	$10,000	+ 12.82
Cost of merchandise (goods) sold	45,000	40,000	5,000	+ 12.50
Gross profit from sales	$43,000	$38,000	$ 5,000	+ 13.16
Operating expenses:				
Depreciation	$ 6,000	$ 5,000	$ 1,000	+ 20.00
Selling and administrative	16,000	12,000	4,000	+ 33.33
Research	600	1,000	(400)	− 40.00
Miscellaneous	1,200	500	700	+ 140.00
Total operating expenses	$23,800	$18,500	$ 5,300	+ 28.65
Income before interest and taxes	$19,200	$19,500	$ (300)	− 1.54
Interest expense	4,000	4,000	-0-	
Income before taxes	$15,200	$15,500	$ (300)	− 1.94
Provision for taxes	3,800	4,000	(200)	− 5.00
Net income	$11,400	$11,500	$ (100)	− .87

Analyzing Comparative Income Statements

We can apply the same procedures of vertical and horizontal analysis to the income statement that we used in analyzing the balance sheet. Let's first look at the vertical analysis for Royal Company, Figure 16–5. Then we will look at the horizontal analysis of Flint Company's 1994 and 1995 income statements shown in Figure 16–6. Note in the margin of these figures how numbers are calculated.

It's time once again to try a Practice Quiz on this unit.

LU 16-2 PRACTICE QUIZ

From the following information, calculate:

a. Net sales. **b.** Cost of merchandise (goods) sold.
c. Gross profit from sales. **d.** Net income.

Given Gross sales, $35,000; sales returns and allowances, $3,000; beginning inventory, $6,000; net purchases, $7,000; ending inventory, $5,500; operating expenses, $7,900.

SOLUTIONS TO LU 16-2 PRACTICE QUIZ

a. $35,000 − $3,000 = $32,000 (Gross sales − Sales returns and allowances)

b. $6,000 + $7,000 − $5,500 = $7,500 (Beginning inventory + Net purchases − Ending inventory)

c. $32,000 − $7,500 = $24,500 (Net sales − Cost of merchandise sold)

d. $24,500 − $7,900 = $16,600 (Gross profit from sales − Operating expenses)

LEARNING UNIT 16-3 TREND AND RATIO ANALYSIS

Tootsie Roll Industries has reported record sales and earnings. The company looks to expand its market share in the future by entering the large teen and adult chocolate segment of the market. New state-of-the-art plant and equipment is planned. These decisions come after careful corporate planning and analyzing financial reports for over 14 years.

Analyzing financial reports can indicate various trends. The study of these trends is valuable to businesses, financial institutions, and consumers. We begin this unit with a discussion of trend analysis.

Trend Analysis

Many tools are available to analyze financial reports. When data covers several years, we can analyze changes that occur by expressing each number as a percent of the base year. The base year is a past period of time that we use to compare sales, profits, and so on, with other years. We call this **trend analysis.**

Using the following example of Rose Company, let's complete a trend analysis with the following steps:

Steps for Completing a Trend Analysis

Step 1. Select the base year (100%).

Step 2. Express each amount as a percent of the base year amount (rounded to nearest whole percent).

Given (base year 1994)

	1997	1996	1995	1994
Sales	$621,000	$460,000	$340,000	$420,000
Gross profit	182,000	141,000	112,000	124,000
Net income	48,000	41,000	22,000	38,000

Trend analysis

	1997	1996	1995	1994
Sales	148%	110%	81%	100%
Gross profit	147	114	90	100
Net income	126	108	58	100

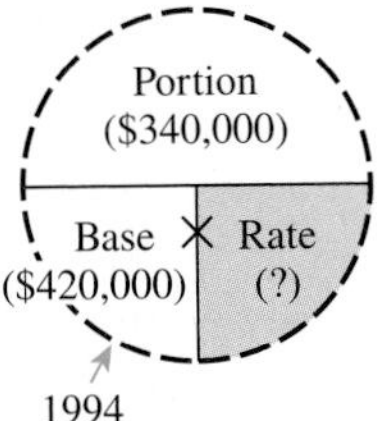

How to calculate trend analysis

$$\frac{\text{Each item}}{\text{Base amount}} = \frac{\$340{,}000}{\$420{,}000} = 80.95\% = 81\%$$

Sales for 1995 (numerator); Sales for 1994 (denominator)

What trend analysis means

Sales of 1995 were 81% of the sales of 1994. Note that you would follow the same process no matter which of the three areas you are analyzing. All categories are compared to the base year—sales, gross profit, or net income.

TABLE 16–1 Summary of Key Ratios: A Reference Guide* (see explanation on page 366)

Ratio	Formula	Actual calculations	What it says	Questions that could be raised
1. Current ratio	$\frac{\text{Current assets}}{\text{Current liabilities}}$ (Current assets include cash, accounts receivable, and marketable securities.)	$\frac{\$61{,}000}{\$92{,}000} = .66:1$ Industry average, 2 to 1	Business has 66¢ of current assets to meet each $1 of current debt.	Not enough current assets to pay off current liabilities. Industry standard is $2 for each $1 of current debt.
2. Acid test (quick ratio) Top of fraction often referred to as quick assets	$\frac{\text{Current assets} - \text{Inventory} - \text{Prepaid expenses}}{\text{Current liabilities}}$ (Inventory and prepaid expenses are excluded because it may not be easy to convert these to cash.)	$\frac{\$61{,}000 - \$30{,}000 - \$15{,}000}{\$92{,}000} = .17:1$ Industry average, 1 to 1	Business has only 17¢ to cover each $1 of current debt. This calculation excludes inventory and prepaid expenses.	Same as above but more severe.
3. Average day's collection	$\frac{\text{Accounts receivable}}{\frac{\text{Net sales}}{360}}$	$\frac{\$9{,}000}{\frac{\$20{,}566}{360}} = 158 \text{ days}$ Industry average, 90–120 days	On the average, it takes 158 days to collect accounts receivable.	Could we speed up collection since industry average is 90–120 days?
4. Total debt to total assets	$\frac{\text{Total liabilities}}{\text{Total assets}}$	$\frac{\$150{,}000}{\$205{,}000} = 73.17\%$ Industry average, 50%–70%	For each $1 of assets, the company owes 73¢ in current and long-term debt.	73% is slightly higher than industry average.
5. Return on equity	$\frac{\text{Net income}}{\text{Stockholders' equity}}$	$\frac{\$6{,}316}{\$55{,}000} = 11.48\%$ Industry average, 15%–20%	For each $1 invested by the owner, a return of 11¢ results.	Could we get a higher return on money somewhere else?
6. Asset turnover	$\frac{\text{Net sales}}{\text{Total assets}}$	$\frac{\$20{,}566}{\$205{,}000} = 10¢$ Industry average, 3¢ to 8¢	For each $1 invested in assets, it returns 10¢ in sales.	Are assets being utilized efficiently?
7. Profit margin on net sales	$\frac{\text{Net income}}{\text{Net sales}}$	$\frac{\$6{,}316}{\$20{,}566} = 30.71\%$ Industry average, 25%–40%	For each $1 of sales, company produces 31¢ in profit	Compared to competitors, are we showing enough profits versus our increased sales?

* Inventory turnover is discussed in Chapter 18.

We now will examine **ratio analysis**—another tool companies use to analyze performance.

Ratio Analysis

A *ratio* is the relationship of one number to another. Many companies compare their ratios with those of previous years and with ratios of other companies in their industry. Companies can get ratios of the performance of other companies from their banker, accountant, local small business center, libraries, and newspaper articles.

Tootsie Roll reported in its annual report "our current ratio increased from 2.6:1 to 3.5:1. Quick ratio increased from 1.5:1 to 2.3:1. Current debt to net worth declined from 18.9% to 17.4%." Let's see what these ratios mean. (In the Business Math Scrapbook, we will calculate the current ratio and quick ratio for Tootsie Roll from their actual financial report.)

Companies use percentage ratios to determine:

1. How well they manage their assets—*asset management ratios*.
2. The debt situation—*debt management ratios*.
3. The profitability picture of the firm—*profitability ratios*.

Each company must decide the true meaning of what the ratios are saying. Table 16–1 (p. 365) gives a summary of key ratios, their calculations (rounded to nearest hundredth), and what they mean. All calculations are from Figures 16–1 and 16–4.

Now you can check your knowledge with the Practice Quiz that follows

---

LU 16–3 PRACTICE QUIZ

1. Prepare a trend analysis from the following sales assuming a base year of 1994. Round to nearest whole percent.

	1997	1996	1995	1994
Sales	$29,000	$44,000	$48,000	$60,000

2. **Given** Total current assets (CA), $15,000; accounts receivable (AR), $6,000; total current liabilities (CL), $10,000; inventory (Inv.), $4,000; net sales, $36,000; total assets, $30,000; net income (NI), $7,500.

Calculate

a. Current ratio.
b. Acid test.
c. Average day's collection.
d. Profit margin on sales (round to nearest hundredth percent).

SOLUTIONS TO LU 16–3 PRACTICE QUIZ

1.

	1997	1996	1995	1994
Sales	48% $\left(\frac{\$29,000}{\$60,000}\right)$	73% $\left(\frac{\$44,000}{\$60,000}\right)$	80% $\left(\frac{\$48,000}{\$60,000}\right)$	100%

2. a. $\frac{\text{CA}}{\text{CL}} = \frac{\$15,000}{\$10,000} = 1.5$

b. $\frac{\text{CA} - \text{Inv}}{\text{CL}} = \frac{\$15,000 - \$4,000}{\$10,000} = 1.1$

c. $\frac{\text{AR}}{\frac{\text{Net sales}}{360}} = \frac{\$6,000}{\frac{\$36,000}{360}} = 60 \text{ days}$

d. $\frac{\text{NI}}{\text{Net sales}} = \frac{\$7,500}{\$36,000} = 20.83\%$

CHAPTER ORGANIZER: A REFERENCE GUIDE

Page	Topic	Key point, procedure, formula	Example(s) to illustrate situation
356	**Balance sheet**		
357	Vertical analysis	Process of relating each figure on a financial report (down the column) to a total figure.	Current assets $ 520 52% Plant and equipment 480 48% Total assets $1,000 100%
358	Horizontal analysis	Analyzing comparative financial reports shows rate and amount of change across columns item by item.	1995 | 1994 | Change | % Cash, $5,000 | $4,000 | $1,000 \| 25% ← ($\frac{\$1,000}{\$4,000}$)
360	**Income statement formulas**	(Horizontal and vertical analysis can also be done for income statements.)	
362	Net sales	Gross sales − Sales returns and allowances − Sales discounts	$200 gross sales − 10 sales returns and allowances − 2 sales discounts $188 net sales
362	Cost of merchandise (goods) sold	Beginning inventory + Net purchases − Ending inventory	$50 + $100 − $20 = $130 Beginning inventory + Net purchases − Ending inventory = Cost of merchandise (goods) sold
362	Gross profit from sales	Net sales − Cost of merchandise (goods) sold	$188 − $130 = $58 gross profit from sales Net sales − Cost of merchandise (goods) sold = Gross profit from sales
362	Net income	Gross profit − Operating expenses	$58 − $28 = $30 Gross profit from sales − Operating expenses = Net income
364	Trend analysis	Each number expressed as a percent of the base year. $\frac{\text{Each item}}{\text{Base amount}}$	1996 1995 1994 Sales $200 $300 $400 ← Base year 50% 75% 100% ($\frac{\$200}{\$400}$) ($\frac{\$300}{\$400}$)
365	**Ratios**	Tools to interpret items on financial reports.	Use this example for calculating the following ratios: current assets, $30,000; accounts receivable, $12,000; total current liabilities, $20,000; inventory, $6,000; prepaid expenses, $2,000; net sales, $72,000; total assets, $60,000; net income, $15,000; total liabilities, $30,000.
365	Current ratio	$\frac{\text{Current assets}}{\text{Current liabilities}}$	$\frac{\$30,000}{\$20,000} = 1.5$
365	Acid test (quick ratio)	$\frac{\text{Current assets} - \text{Inventory} - \text{Prepaid expenses}}{\text{Current liabilities}}$ ← Called quick assets	$\frac{\$30,000 - \$6,000 - \$2,000}{\$20,000} = 1.1$
365	Average day's collection	$\frac{\text{Accounts receivable}}{\frac{\text{Net sales}}{360}}$	$\frac{\$12,000}{\frac{\$72,000}{360}} = 60$ days
365	Total debt to total assets	$\frac{\text{Total liabilities}}{\text{Total assets}}$	$\frac{\$30,000}{\$60,000} = 50\%$

Page	Topic	Key point, procedure, formula	Example(s) to illustrate situation
365	Return on equity	$\frac{\text{Net income}}{\text{Stockholders' equity (A - L)}}$	$\frac{\$15{,}000}{\$30{,}000} = 50\%$
365	Asset turnover	$\frac{\text{Net sales}}{\text{Total assets}}$	$\frac{\$72{,}000}{\$60{,}000} = 1.2$
365	Profit margin on net sales	$\frac{\text{Net income}}{\text{Net sales}}$	$\frac{\$15{,}000}{\$72{,}000} = .2083 = 20.83\%$
	Key terms	Accounts payable, *p. 357* Accounts receivable, *p. 356* Acid test, *p. 365* Assets, *p. 356* Asset turnover, *p. 365* Balance sheet, *p. 354* Capital, *p. 355* Comparative statement, *p. 357* Corporation, *p. 350* Cost of merchandise (goods) sold, *p. 362* Current assets, *p. 356* Current liabilities, *p. 357* Current ratio, *p. 365* Gross profit from sales, *p. 362* Horizontal analysis, *p. 358* Income statement, *p. 361* Liabilities, *p. 357* Long-term liabilities, *p. 357*	Merchandise inventory, *p. 356* Net income, *p. 362* Net purchases, *p. 362* Net sales, *p. 362* Owner's equity, *p. 355* Partnership, *p. 355* Plant and equipment, *p. 356* Prepaid expenses, *p. 356* Quick assets, *p. 365* Quick ratio, *p. 365* Ratio analysis, *p. 366* Retained earnings, *p. 357* Return on equity, *p. 365* Revenues, *p. 360* Sole proprietorship, *p. 355* Stockholders' equity, *p. 355* Trend analysis, *p. 364* Vertical analysis, *p. 357*

END-OF-CHAPTER PROBLEMS

Drill Problems

Additional homework assignments by learning unit are at the end of text in Appendix I (p. I–68). Solutions to odd problems are at the end of text in Appendix II.

16–1. From the following, prepare a balance sheet like The Card Shop (LU 16–1) for Jane's Grocery Shop on December 31, 1995: cash, $5,000; accounts payable, $8,000; merchandise inventory, $6,000; J. Reel, capital, $10,000; and equipment, $7,000.

JANE'S GROCERY SHOP
Balance Sheet
December 31, 1995

Assets		**Liabilities**	
Cash	$ 5,000	Accounts payable	$ 8,000
Merchandise inventory	6,000	**Owner's Equity**	
Equipment	7,000	J. Reel, capital	10,000
		Total liabilities and	
Total assets	$18,000	owner's equity	$18,000

16–2. From the following, prepare a classified balance sheet for Rug Company as of December 31, 1995. Ending merchandise inventory was $3,000 for the year.

Cash	$1,000	Accounts payable	$1,200
Prepaid rent	1,200	Salaries payable	1,500
Prepaid insurance	2,000	Note payable (long term)	1,000
Office equipment (net)	3,000	B. Rug, capital*	6,500

* What owner supplies to the business. Replaces common stock and retained earnings section.

RUG COMPANY
Balance Sheet
December 31, 1995

Assets			**Liabilities**		
Current assets:			Current liabilities:		
Cash	$1,000		Accounts payable	$1,200	
Merchandise inventory	3,000		Salaries payable	1,500	
Prepaid insurance	2,000		Total liabilities		$ 2,700
Prepaid rent	1,200		Long-term liabilities:		
Total current assets		$7,200	Notes payable		1,000
Plant and equipment:			Total liabilities		$ 3,700
Office equipment (net)		3,000	**Owner's Equity**		
			B. Rug, capital		6,500
Total assets		$10,200	Total liabilities and owner's equity		$10,200

$\frac{\$5,250}{\$10,500} = 50\%$

16–3. Complete a horizontal analysis for the Ray Lowe Company (round percents to nearest hundredth):

RAY LOWE COMPANY
Comparative Balance Sheet
December 31, 1994, and 1995

	1995	1994	Increase (decrease) Amount	Percent
Assets				
Current assets:				
Cash	$ 15,750	$ 10,500	$ 5,250	+50.00
Accounts receivable	18,000	13,500	4,500	+33.33
Merchandise inventory	18,750	22,500	(3,750)	−16.67
Prepaid advertising	54,000	45,000	9,000	+20.00
Total current assets	$106,500	$ 91,500	$15,000	+16.39
Plant and equipment:				
Building (net)	$120,000	$126,000	$ (6,000)	−4.76
Land	90,000	90,000	-0-	-0-
Total plant and equipment	$210,000	$216,000	(6,000)	−2.78
Total assets	$316,500	$307,500	$ 9,000	+2.93
Liabilities				
Current liabilities:				
Accounts payable	$132,000	$120,000	$12,000	+10.00
Salaries payable	22,500	18,000	4,500	+25.00
Total current liabilities	$154,500	$138,000	$16,500	+11.96
Long-term liabilities:				
Mortgage note payable	99,000	87,000	12,000	+13.79
Total liabilities	$253,500	$225,000	$28,500	+12.67
Owner's Equity				
Ray Lowe, capital	63,000	82,500	(19,500)	−23.64
Total liabilities and owner's equity	$316,500	$307,500	$ 9,000	+2.93

16–4. Prepare an income statement for Munroe Sauce for the year ended December 31, 1995. Beginning inventory was $1,248. Ending inventory was $1,600.

Net sales = $34,900
− 1,092
− 1,152

Beginning inventory	*$1,248*
+ Net purchases	*9,972*
− Ending inventory	*1,600*
= COGS	*9,620*

Sales	$34,900
Sales returns and allowances	1,092
Sales discount	1,152
Purchases	10,512
Purchase discounts	540
Salary expense	5,200
Insurance expense	2,600
Utilities expense	210
Plumbing expense	250
Rent expense	180
Depreciation expense	115

MUNROE SAUCE
Income Statement
For Year Ended December 31, 1995

Net sales		$32,656
Cost of merchandise (goods) sold		9,620
Gross profit from sales		$23,036
Operating expenses:		
Depreciation	$ 115	
Salary	5,200	
Insurance	2,600	
Utilities	210	
Plumbing	250	
Rent	180	
Total operating expenses		8,555
Net income		$14,481

16–5. Complete the following (round percents to nearest hundredth):

$\frac{\$22,000}{\$68,000} = 32.35\%$

BOMB COMPANY
Comparative Income Statement
For Years Ended December 31, 1994, and 1995

	1995	Percent of net	1994	Percent of net
Net sales	$110,000	100.00	$68,000	100.00
Cost of merchandise sold	75,000	68.18	22,000	32.35
Gross profit from sales	$ 35,000	31.82	$46,000	67.65
Operating expenses:				
Depreciation	$ 850	.77	$ 450	.66
Selling and administrative	1,900	1.73	1,250	1.84
Research	2,900	2.64	1,600	2.35
Miscellaneous	3,500	3.18	150	.22
Total operating expenses	$ 9,150	8.32	$ 3,450	5.07
Income before interest and taxes	$ 25,850	23.50	$42,550	62.57
Interest expense	8,000	7.27	$ 8,500	12.50
Income before taxes	$ 17,850	16.23	$34,050	50.07
Provision for taxes	7,000	6.36	14,000	20.59
Net income	$ 10,850	9.86	$20,050	29.49

16–6. Complete a vertical analysis for Lang Company (round percents to nearest hundredth):

$\frac{\$9,000}{\$65,500}$

LANG COMPANY
Comparative Balance Sheet
December 31, 1994, and 1995

	1995		1994	
	Amount	Percent	Amount	Percent
Assets				
Current assets:				
Cash	$12,000	13.48	$ 9,000	13.74
Accounts receivable	16,500	18.54	12,500	19.08
Merchandise inventory	8,500	9.55	14,000	21.37
Prepaid expenses	24,000	26.97	10,000	15.27
Total current assets	$61,000	68.54	$45,500	69.47 *
Plant and equipment:				
Building (net)	$14,500	16.29	$11,000	16.79
Land	13,500	15.17	9,000	13.74
Total plant and equipment	$28,000	31.46	$20,000	30.53
Total assets	$89,000	100.00	$65,500	100.00
Liabilities				
Current liabilities:				
Accounts payable	$13,000	14.61	$ 7,000	10.69
Salaries payable	7,000	7.87	5,000	7.63
Total current liabilities	$20,000	22.47 *	$12,000	18.32
Long-term liabilities:				
Mortgage note payable	22,000	24.72	20,500	31.30
Total liabilities	$42,000	47.19	$32,500	49.62
Stockholders' Equity				
Common stock	$21,000	23.60	$21,000	32.06
Retained earnings	26,000	29.21	12,000	18.32
Total stockholders' equity	$47,000	52.81	$33,000	50.38
Total liabilities and stockholders' equity	$89,000	100.00	$65,500	100.00

* Due to rounding.

16–7. Complete the following (round percents to nearest hundredth):

LANG COMPANY
Comparative Income Statement
For Years Ended December 31, 1994, and 1995

$\frac{\$3,100}{\$14,900}$

	1995	1994	Increase Amount	(decrease) Percent
Gross sales	$19,000	$15,000	$4,000	26.67
Sales returns and allowances	1,000	100	900	900.00
Net sales	$18,000	$14,900	$3,100	+ 20.81
Cost of merchandise (goods) sold	12,000	9,000	3,000	+ 33.33
Gross profit	$ 6,000	$ 5,900	$ 100	+ 1.69
Operating expenses:				
Depreciation	$ 700	$ 600	$ 100	+ 16.67
Selling and administrative	2,200	2,000	200	+ 10.00
Research	550	500	50	+ 10.00
Miscellaneous	360	300	60	+ 20.00
Total operating expenses	$ 3,810	$ 3,400	$ 410	+ 12.06
Income before interest and taxes	$ 2,190	$ 2,500	$ (310)	− 12.40
Interest expense	560	500	60	+ 12.00
Income before taxes	$ 1,630	$ 2,000	$ (370)	− 18.50
Provision for taxes	640	800	(160)	− 20.00
Net income	$ 990	$ 1,200	$ (210)	− 17.50

From Problems 16–6 and 16–7, your supervisor has requested you calculate the following ratios (round to nearest hundredth):

		1995	1994
16–8.	Current ratio.	3.05	3.79
16–9.	Acid test.	1.43	1.79
16–10.	Average day's collection.	330.00	302.01
16–11.	Asset turnover.	.20	.23
16–12.	Total debt to total assets.	.47	.50
16–13.	Net income (after tax) to the net sales.	.06	.08
16–14.	Return on equity (after tax).	.02	.04

		1995	1994
16–8.	$\frac{CA}{CL}$	$\frac{\$61,000}{\$20,000} = 3.05$	$\frac{\$45,500}{\$12,000} = 3.79$
16–9.	$\frac{CA - Inv. - Prep.\ Exp.}{CL}$	$\frac{\$61,000 - \$8,500 - \$24,000}{\$20,000} = 1.43$	$\frac{\$45,500 - \$14,000 - \$10,000}{\$12,000} = 1.79$
16–10.	$\frac{AR}{\frac{Net\ sales}{360}}$	$\frac{\$16,500}{\frac{\$18,000}{360}} = 330$	$\frac{\$12,500}{\frac{\$14,900}{360}} = 302.01$
16–11.	$\frac{Net\ sales}{TA}$	$\frac{\$18,000}{\$89,000} = .202 = .20$	$\frac{\$14,900}{\$65,500} = .227 = .23$
16–12.	$\frac{T.\ Liab.}{TA}$	$\frac{\$42,000}{\$89,000} = .471 = .47$	$\frac{\$32,500}{\$65,500} = .496 = .50$
16–13.	$\frac{NI}{Net\ sales}$	$\frac{\$990}{\$18,000} = .055 = .06$	$\frac{\$1,200}{\$14,900} = .0805 = .08$
16–14.	$\frac{NI}{Equity}$	$\frac{\$990}{\$47,000} = .021 = .02$	$\frac{\$1,200}{\$33,000} = .036 = .04$

Word Problems

16–15. The total debt to total assets of the Jones Company was .85. Jones's total assets were $300,000. What is the amount of total debt to Jones Company?
$300,000 × .85 = $255,000

16–16. Beaver Company has a current ratio of 1.95. The acid-test ratio is 1.72. The current liabilities of Beaver are $34,000. Could you calculate the dollar amount of merchandise inventory? Assume no prepaid expenses.
$34,000 × 1.95 = $66,300 CA
$34,000 × 1.72 = − 58,480
$ 7,820

16–17. The asset turnover of River Company is 4.2. The total assets of River are $71,000. What are River's net sales?
$71,000 × 4.2 = $298,200

16–18. Jangles Corporation has earned $92,000 after tax. The accountant calculated the return on equity as 16%. What was Jangles Corporation's stockholders' equity?
$\frac{\$92,000}{.16} = \$575,000$

16–19. In analyzing the income statement of Ryan Company, cost of goods sold has decreased from 1994 to 1995 by 6.2%. The cost of goods sold was $15,000 in 1995. What was the cost of goods sold in 1994?
$\frac{\$15,000}{.938} = \$15,991.47$
.938 ← (100% − 6.2%)

16–20. Don Williams received a memo requesting that he complete a trend analysis of the following using 1993 as the base year and rounding each percent to nearest whole percent. Could you help Don with the request?

	1996	1995	1994	1993
Sales	$340,000	$400,000	$420,000	$500,000
Gross profit	180,000	240,000	340,000	400,000
Net income	$ 70,000	$ 90,000	$ 40,000	$ 50,000

$\frac{\$340,000}{\$500,000}$ (→ 1996 Sales)

	1996	1995	1994	1993
Sales	68%	80%	84%	100%
Gross profit	45	60	85	100
Net income	140	180	80	100

16–21. Al Downey has requested that you calculate the asset turnover from the following (round answer to nearest tenth):

Gross sales	$60,000
Sales discount	1,000
Sales returns and allowances	7,000
Total assets	36,000

$\frac{\$52,000}{\$36,000} = 1.44 = 1.4$

Challenge Problem: *Return on Investment*

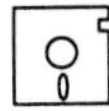

16–22. On January 1, Pete Rowe bought a ski chalet for $51,000. Pete is renting the chalet for $55 per night. He estimates he can rent the chalet for 190 nights. Pete's mortgage for principal and interest is $448 per month. Real estate tax on the chalet is $500 per year.

Pete estimates that his heating bill will run $60 per month. He expects his monthly electrical bill to be $20 per month. He pays $12 per month for cable television.

What is Pete's return on the initial investment for this year? Assume rentals drop by 30% and monthly bills for heat and light drop by 10% each month. What would be Pete's return on initial investment? Round to nearest tenth percent as needed.

190 days at $55 each ↘

	Rental income		$10,450	
	Less expenses:			$\frac{\$3,470}{\$51,000} = 6.8\%$
($448 × 12)	Principal and interest	$5,376		
	Tax	500		
($60 × 12)	Heat	720		
($20 × 12)	Electricity	240		
($12 × 12)	Cable	144	6,980	
	Net income		$ 3,470	

133 days (190 × .70) ↘

Rental income		$ 7,315	
Less expenses:			$\frac{\$431}{\$51,000} = .8\%$
Principal and interest	$5,376		
Tax	500		
Heat	648		
Electricity	216		
Cable	144	6,884	
Net income		$ 431	

Summary Practice Test

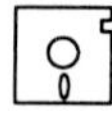

Solutions are at end of text in Appendix II.

Quick Reference

If you get any wrong answers, study the page numbers given for each problem.

1. P. 362.

1. Given Gross sales, $50,000; sales returns and allowances, $6,000; beginning inventory, $4,000; net purchases, $8,000; ending inventory, $2,000; operating expenses, $4,500. Calculate **(a)** net sales, **(b)** cost of merchandise (goods) sold, **(c)** gross profit from sales, and **(d)** net income.

a.

Gross sales	$50,000
− Sales discount	-0-
− SRA	6,000
Net sales	$44,000

b. Cost of merchandise (goods) sold:

Beginning inventory	$ 4,000
+ Net purchases	8,000
− Ending inventory	2,000
Cost of merchandise (goods) sold	$10,000

c. Gross profit from sales:

Net sales	$44,000
− COGS	10,000
Gross profit from sales	$34,000

d.

Gross profit from sales	$34,000
− Operating expenses	4,500
= Net income	$29,500

2. P. 359.

2. Complete this partial comparative balance sheet by filling in total current assets and the percent column; assume no plant and equipment (round to nearest hundredth percent):

	Amount	Percent	Amount	Percent
Assets				
Current assets:				
Cash	$ 3,000	15.79	$ 6,000	26.09
Accounts receivable	4,000	21.05	3,500	15.22
Merchandise inventory	2,000	10.53	2,500	10.87
Prepaid expenses	10,000	52.63	11,000	47.83
Total current assets	$19,000	100.00	$23,000	100.00 (due to rounding)

3. P. 359.

3. Calculate the amount of increase or decrease and the percent change of each title (round to nearest hundredth percent):

	1995	1994	Amount	Percent
Cash	$13,000	$ 8,000	$5,000	+ 62.50
Land	36,000	28,000	8,000	+ 28.57
Accounts payable	18,000	12,000	6,000	+ 50.00

4. P. 364.

4. Complete a trend analysis for sales (round to nearest whole percent and use 1993 as the base year):

	1996	1995	1994	1993
Sales	$200,000	$300,000	$350,000	$400,000
	50%	75%	88%	100%
	$\left(\frac{\$200,000}{\$400,000}\right)$	$\left(\frac{\$300,000}{\$400,000}\right)$	$\left(\frac{\$350,000}{\$400,000}\right)$	

5. P. 356.

5. From the following prepare a balance sheet for Moll Company as of December 31, 1995:

Building	$70,000	Mortgage note payable	$44,000
Merchandise inventory	15,000	Common stock	26,000
Cash	4,000	Retained earnings	31,000
Land	20,000	Accounts receivable	8,000
Accounts payable	18,000	Salaries payable	8,000
Prepaid rent	10,000		

MOLL COMPANY
Balance Sheet
December 31, 1995

Assets		
Current assets:		
Cash	$ 4,000	
Accounts receivable	8,000	
Merchandise inventory	15,000	
Prepaid rent	10,000	
Total current assets		$ 37,000
Plant and equipment:		
Land	$20,000	
Building	70,000	
Total plant and equipment		$ 90,000
Total assets		$127,000

Liabilities			
Current liabilities:			
Accounts payable	$18,000		
Salaries payable	8,000		
Total current liabilities		$26,000	
Long-term liabilities:			
Mortgage note payable		44,000	
Total liabilities			$ 70,000
Stockholders' Equity			
Common stock		$26,000	
Retained earnings		31,000	
Total stockholders' equity			57,000
Total liabilities and stockholders' equity			$127,000

6. P. 365.

6. Solve from the following facts (round to nearest hundredth):

Current assets	$20,000	Net sales	40,000
Accounts receivable	4,000	Total assets	30,000
Current liabilities	15,000	Net income	5,000
Inventory	3,000		

a. Current ratio. 1.33
b. Acid test. 1.13
c. Average day's collection. 36 days
d. Asset turnover. 1.33
e. Profit margin on sales. .13

a. $\frac{\$20,000}{\$15,000}$ b. $\frac{\$20,000 - \$3,000}{\$15,000}$

c. $\frac{\$4,000}{\$111.11}$ d. $\frac{\$40,000}{\$30,000}$ e. $\frac{\$5,000}{\$40,000}$

Project A

From this partial balance sheet of Tootsie Roll, calculate the current and quick ratio for 19X2 (to the nearest tenth). By what percent (to nearest tenth) has the cash balance increased in 19X2?

CONSOLIDATED STATEMENTS OF
Financial Position

TOOTSIE ROLL INDUSTRIES, INC. AND SUBSIDIARIES

Assets

	December 31, 19X2	19X1
CURRENT ASSETS:		
Cash and cash equivalents (Note 1)	$ 4,224,190	$ 1,835,228
Investments (Note 1)	32,533,769	16,656,472
Accounts receivable, less allowances of $748,000 and $744,000	16,206,648	12,060,954
Inventories (Note 1):		
Finished goods and work in progress	12,650,955	14,456,528
Raw materials and supplies	10,275,858	7,839,863
Prepaid expenses	2,037,710	1,358,694
Total current assets	77,929,130	54,207,739
PROPERTY, PLANT AND EQUIPMENT, at cost (Note 1):		
Land	230,667	230,667
Buildings	4,087,964	4,087,964
Machinery and equipment	58,815,077	53,986,981
Leasehold improvements	4,840,902	4,840,902
	67,974,610	63,146,514
Less—Accumulated depreciation and amortization	35,875,750	32,239,636
	32,098,860	30,906,878
OTHER ASSETS:		
Excess of cost over acquired net assets (Note 1)	47,724,214	49,254,837
Other assets	1,949,408	1,972,546
	49,673,622	51,227,383
	$159,701,612	$136,342,000
CURRENT LIABILITIES:		
Notes payable to banks	$ 672,221	$ 1,473,449
Accounts payable	7,004,075	5,533,028
Dividends payable	576,607	559,858
Accrued liabilities (Note 5)	9,826,534	9,496,354
Income taxes payable	4,471,429	3,658,909
Total current liabilities	22,550,866	20,721,598

$$\text{Current ratio} = \frac{\text{CA}}{\text{CL}} \quad \frac{\$77{,}929{,}130}{\$22{,}550{,}866} = 3.45 = 3.5$$

$$\text{Quick ratio} = \frac{\text{CA} - \text{Prep. exp.} - \text{Inv.}}{\text{CL}} = \frac{\$77{,}929{,}130 - \$12{,}650{,}955 - \$10{,}275{,}858 - \$2{,}037{,}710}{\$22{,}550{,}860}$$

$$= \frac{\$52{,}964{,}607}{\$22{,}550{,}866}$$

$$= 2.3$$

$4,224,190
−1,835,228
$2,388,962 ÷ 1,835,228 = 130.2%

NOTES

THAT WAS THEN . . .
. . . THIS IS NOW

Before video stores, movies were seen in movie palaces like the restored Fox Theater in Detroit. The cost of those theaters was depreciated over a period of years. Note that depreciation is an estimate and not an exact science.

17

Depreciation

LEARNING UNIT OBJECTIVES

LU 17–1: Concepts of Depreciation and the Straight-Line Method

1. Explain the concept of depreciation. *p. 380.*
2. Define residual value, accumulated depreciation, and book value. *p. 380.*
3. Prepare a depreciation schedule. *p. 382.*
4. Calculate depreciation for partial years. *p. 382.*

LU 17–2: Units-of-Production Method

1. Explain how use and not time affects the units-of-production method. *pp. 383–84.*
2. Prepare a depreciation schedule. *p. 383.*

LU 17–3: Sum-of-the-Years'-Digits Method

1. Explain how to use the fraction in the sum-of-the-years'-digits method. *p. 384.*
2. Prepare a depreciation schedule. *p. 384.*

LU 17–4: Declining-Balance Method

1. Explain the importance of residual value and book value in the depreciation schedule. *p. 385.*
2. Prepare a depreciation schedule. *p. 386.*

LU 17–5: Modified Accelerated Cost Recovery System (MACRS)

1. Explain the goals of MACRS and their limitations. *pp. 387–88.*
2. Calculate depreciation using the MACRS guidelines. *pp. 387–88.*

This chapter concentrates on the operating expense called *depreciation*. You will learn that a company like Morse (Figure 17–1) may compute depreciation twice—for financial reporting and for tax purposes. In Learning Units 17–1 to 17–4, we discuss methods of calculating depreciation for financial reporting. In Learning Unit 17–5, we look at how, by tax law, a company reports depreciation for tax purposes. Both methods are legal.

LEARNING UNIT 17–1 CONCEPTS OF DEPRECIATION AND THE STRAIGHT-LINE METHOD

The Internal Revenue has guidelines available for estimating the useful life of assets and for calculating depreciation.

Photo courtesy of Hewlett-Packard Company

Frequently, a company buys assets, such as equipment or a building, that will last longer than one year. These assets depreciate, or lose some of their market value, as time passes. The total cost of the purchase price of these assets cannot be shown in *one year* as an expense of running the business. Companies must estimate in a systematic and logical way the asset cost they show as an expense of a particular period of time. We call this process **depreciation.**

The depreciation process results in **depreciation expense,** which involves three key factors: (1) **asset cost**—amount the company paid for the asset; (2) **estimated useful life**—number of years or time periods that the company can use the asset; and (3) **residual value (salvage or trade-in value)**—expected cash value at the end of the asset's useful life.

Depreciation expense is listed on the income statement. The **accumulated depreciation** title on the balance sheet stores the history of the asset's amount of depreciation taken to date. Asset cost less accumulated depreciation is the asset's **book value.** The book value shows the unused amount of the asset cost that the company may depreciate in future periods. At the end of the asset's life, the asset's book value is the same as its residual value—book value cannot be less than residual value.

Depending on the amount and timetable of the asset's depreciation, a company can increase or decrease its profit. If a company shows more depreciation in earlier years, the company will have a lower reported profit and pay less in taxes. Thus, depreciation can be an indirect tax savings for the company.

Note in the following *Wall Street Journal* clipping that a change in the method of calculating depreciation will result in a bottom line profit increase for two real estate investment trusts.

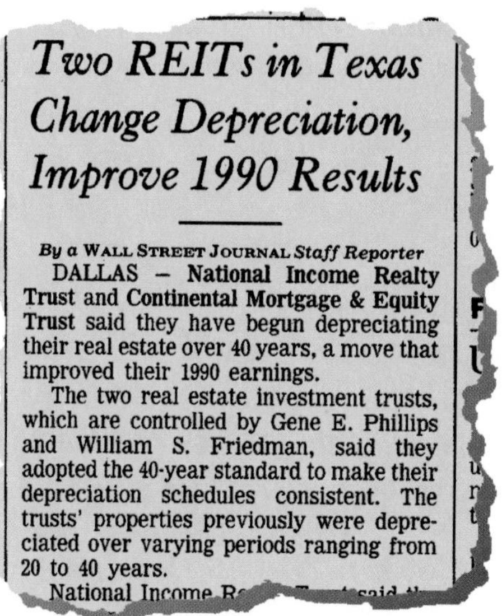

Two REITs in Texas Change Depreciation, Improve 1990 Results

By a WALL STREET JOURNAL *Staff Reporter*

DALLAS – **National Income Realty Trust** and **Continental Mortgage & Equity Trust** said they have begun depreciating their real estate over 40 years, a move that improved their 1990 earnings.

The two real estate investment trusts, which are controlled by Gene E. Phillips and William S. Friedman, said they adopted the 40-year standard to make their depreciation schedules consistent. The trusts' properties previously were depreciated over varying periods ranging from 20 to 40 years.

National Income R...

FIGURE 17–1
Income Statement

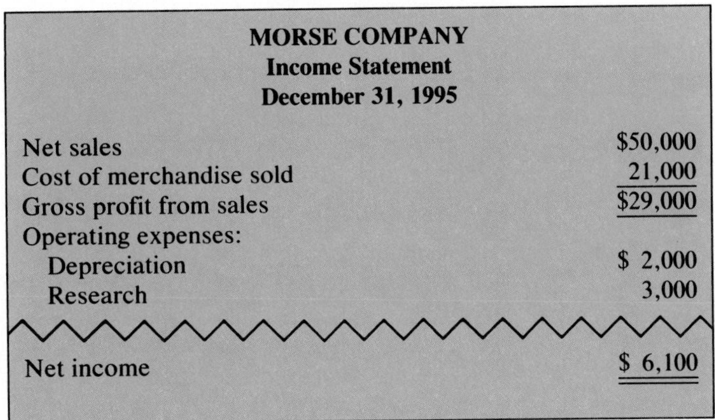

MORSE COMPANY
Income Statement
December 31, 1995

Net sales	$50,000
Cost of merchandise sold	21,000
Gross profit from sales	$29,000
Operating expenses:	
Depreciation	$ 2,000
Research	3,000
Net income	$ 6,100

Can factory workers be depreciated? See the case of Ithaca Industries in the Business Math Scrapbook.

Later in the chapter we will discuss the different methods of computing depreciation that spread the cost of an asset over specified periods of time. However, first let's look at some of the major causes of depreciation.

Causes of Depreciation

As assets, all machines have an estimated amount of usefulness simply because as companies use the assets they gradually wear out. The cause of this depreciation is *physical deterioration.*

The growth of a company can also cause depreciation. Many companies begin on a small scale. As the companies grow, they often find their equipment and buildings inadequate. The use of depreciation enables these businesses to "write off" their old, inadequate equipment and buildings. Companies cannot depreciate land. For example, a garbage dump can be depreciated but not the land.

Another cause of depreciation is the result of advances in technology. The computers that companies bought a few years ago may be in perfect working condition but outdated. Companies may find it necessary to replace these old computers with more sophisticated, faster, and possibly more economical machines. Thus, *product obsolescence* is a key factor contributing to depreciation.

Now we are ready to begin our study of depreciation methods that could be used for financial reporting. The first method we will study is straight-line depreciation. It is also the most common of the four depreciation methods.

Straight-Line Method

The **straight-line method** of depreciation tries to distribute the same amount of depreciation expense to each period of time. For example, assume Ajax Company bought equipment for $2,500. The company estimates that the equipment's period of "usefulness"—*or useful life*—will be 5 years. After 5 years, the equipment will have a residual value (salvage value) of $500. The company decides to calculate its depreciation with the straight-line method and uses the following formula:

$$\text{Depreciation expense each year} = \frac{\text{Cost} - \text{Residual value}}{\text{Estimated useful life in years}}$$

$$\frac{\$2{,}500 - \$500}{5 \text{ years}} = \$400 \quad \text{depreciation expense taken each year}$$

Table 17–1 gives a summary of the equipment depreciation that Ajax Company will take over the next 5 years. Companies call this summary a **depreciation schedule.**

TABLE 17–1
Depreciation Schedule for Straight-Line Method

$$\frac{100\%}{\text{Number of years}} = \frac{100\%}{5} = 20\%$$

Thus, the company is depreciating the equipment at a 20% rate each year.

End of year	Cost of equipment	Depreciation expense for year	Accumulated depreciation end of year	Book value end of year (Cost − Accumulated depreciation)
1	$2,500	$400	$ 400	$2,100 ($2,500 − $400)
2	2,500	400	800	1,700
3	2,500	400	1,200	1,300
4	2,500	400	1,600	900
5	2,500	400	2,000	500
	↑ Cost stays the same.	↑ Depreciation expense is same each year.	↑ Accumulated depreciation increases by $400 each year.	↑ Book value is lowered by $400 until the residual value of $500 is reached.

Depreciation for Partial Years

If a company buys an asset before the 15th of the month, the company calculates the asset's depreciation for a full month. Companies do not take the full month's depreciation for assets bought after the 15th of the month. For example, assume Ajax Company (Table 17–1) bought the equipment on May 6. The company would calculate the depreciation for the first year as follows:

$$\frac{\$2,500 - \$500}{5 \text{ years}} = \$400 \times \frac{8}{12} = \$266.67$$

Now let's check your progress with the Practice Quiz before looking at the next depreciation method.

LU 17–1 PRACTICE QUIZ

1. Prepare a depreciation schedule using straight-line depreciation for the following:

Cost of truck	$16,000
Residual value	1,000
Life	5 years

2. If the truck was bought on February 3, what would the depreciation expense be in the first year?

SOLUTIONS TO LU 17–1 PRACTICE QUIZ

1.

End of year	Cost of truck	Depreciation expense for year	Accumulated depreciation end of year	Book value end of year (Cost − Accumulated depreciation)
1	$16,000	$3,000	$ 3,000	$13,000 ($16,000 − $3,000)
2	16,000	3,000	6,000	10,000
3	16,000	3,000	9,000	7,000
4	16,000	3,000	12,000	4,000
5	16,000	3,000	15,000	1,000 ← Note that we are down to residual value

2. $\frac{\$16,000 - \$1,000}{5} = \$3,000 \times \frac{11}{12} = \$2,750$

LEARNING UNIT 17–2 UNITS-OF-PRODUCTION METHOD

Unlike the straight-line depreciation method, the **units-of-production method** does not use the passage of time to determine an asset's depreciation amount. Instead, the company determines the asset's depreciation according to how much the company uses the asset. This use could be miles driven, tons hauled, or units that a machine produces. For example, when a company such as Ajax Company, in Learning Unit 17–1, buys equipment, the company estimates how many units the equipment can produce. Let's assume the equipment has a useful life of 4,000 units. The following formula is used to calculate the equipment's depreciation for the units-of-production method.

$$\text{Depreciation per unit} = \frac{\text{Cost} - \text{Residual value}}{\text{Estimated units of useful life production}} = \frac{\$2{,}500 - \$500}{4{,}000 \text{ units}} = \$.50 \text{ per unit}$$

$$\text{Depreciation amount} = \text{Unit depreciation} \times \text{Units produced} = .50 \text{ times actual number of units}$$

Now we can complete Table 17–2. Note that the table gives the units produced each year.

Let's check your understanding of this unit with the Practice Quiz.

TABLE 17–2 Depreciation Schedule for Units-of-Production Method

End of year	Cost of equipment	Units produced	Depreciation expense for year	Accumulated depreciation end of year	Book value end of year (Cost − Accumulated depreciation)
1	$2,500	300	$ 150 (300 × $.50)	$ 150	$2,350 ($2,500 − $150)
2	2,500	400	200	350	2,150
3	2,500	600	300	650	1,850
4	2,500	2,000	1,000	1,650	850
5	2,500	700	350	2,000	500
		↑ At the end of 5 years, the equipment produced 4,000 units. If in year 5 the equipment produced 1,500 units, only 700 could be used in the calculation, or it will go below the equipment's residual value.	↑ Units produced per year times $.50 equals depreciation expense.		↑ Residual value of $500 is reached. (Be sure depreciation is not taken below the residual value.)

LU 17–2 PRACTICE QUIZ

From the following facts prepare a depreciation schedule:

Machine cost $20,000
Residual value 4,000
Expected to produce 16,000 units over its expected life

	19X1	19X2	19X3	19X4	19X5
Units produced:	2,000	8,000	3,000	1,800	1,600

SOLUTIONS TO LU 17-2 PRACTICE QUIZ

$$\frac{\$20{,}000 - \$4{,}000}{16{,}000} = \$1$$

End of year	Cost of machine	Units produced	Depreciation expense for year	Accumulated depreciation end of year	Book value end of year (Cost − Accumulated depreciation)
1	$20,000	2,000	$2,000 (2,000 × $1)	$ 2,000	$18,000
2	20,000	8,000	8,000	10,000	10,000
3	20,000	3,000	3,000	13,000	7,000
4	20,000	1,800	1,800	14,800	5,200
5	20,000	1,600	1,200*	16,000	4,000

*Note that we only can depreciate 1,200 units since we cannot go below the residual value of $4,000.

LEARNING UNIT 17–3 SUM-OF-THE-YEARS'-DIGITS METHOD

Now we look at the **sum-of-the-years'-digits method.** This is an **accelerated method** that computes more depreciation expense in the early years of the asset's life than in the later years. The basic formula to calculate depreciation expense for the sum-of-the-years'-digits method is:

$$\text{Depreciation expense} = (\text{Cost} - \text{Residual value}) \times \frac{\text{Remaining life}}{\text{Sum-of-the-years'-digits}}$$

The fraction in the formula is the key to understanding the sum-of-the-years'-digits method. We can explain this fraction by assuming an asset has 5 years of remaining life.

$\left(\frac{5}{15}\right)$ ← Numerator of fraction is years remaining

↖ Denominator of fraction is the sum of the asset's service life (5 + 4 + 3 + 2 + 1)

TABLE 17–3 Depreciation Schedule for Sum-of-the-Years'-Digits Method

End of year	Cost − Residual value	×	Fraction for year	=	Yearly depreciation expense	Accumulated depreciation end of year	Book value end of year (Cost − Accumulated depreciation)
1	$2,000 ($2,500 − $500)	×	$\frac{5}{15}$	=	$666.67	$ 666.67	$1,833.33 ($2,500 − $666.67)
2	$2,000	×	$\frac{4}{15}$	=	533.33	1,200.00	$1,300.00 ($2,500 − $1,200)
3	2,000	×	$\frac{3}{15}$	=	400.00	1,600.00	$ 900.00
4	2,000	×	$\frac{2}{15}$	=	266.67	1,866.67	633.33
5	2,000	×	$\frac{1}{15}$	=	133.33	2,000.00	500.00
	↑ Cost less residual value is multiplied times fraction for year.		↑ Large numerator occurs in early years.		↑ Note: Depreciation of $666.67 in year 1 is highest.	↑ Accumulated depreciation increases slower in later years.	↑ Note: We used cost of $2,500 − $2,000 accumulated depreciation to equal book value of $500.

We can calculate the denominator of the fraction by this formula:

$$\frac{N(N+1)}{2} = \frac{5(5+1)}{2} = \frac{30}{2} = 15$$

where N is the estimated life of the asset. Remember that the numerator of the fraction—remaining years left—changes each year as the asset gets older. The denominator of the fraction—sum-of-the-years' digits—remains the same for the life of the asset.

Now let's use the sum-of-the-years'-digits method and prepare the depreciation schedule shown in Table 17–3 for the Ajax Company in Learning Unit 17–2. Keep in mind that partial years for depreciation could result, as we showed in the straight-line method.

It's time for another Practice Quiz.

LU 17–3 PRACTICE QUIZ

Prepare a depreciation schedule for the sum-of-the-years'-digits method from the following:

Cost of machine, 5-year life	$16,000
Residual value	1,000

SOLUTIONS TO LU 17–3 PRACTICE QUIZ

End of year	Cost − Residual value	×	Fraction for year	=	Yearly depreciation expense	Accumulated depreciation end of year	Book value end of year (Cost − Accumulated depreciation)
1	$15,000	×	$\frac{5}{15}$	=	$5,000	$ 5,000	$11,000 ($16,000 − $5,000)
2	15,000	×	$\frac{4}{15}$	=	4,000	9,000	7,000
3	15,000	×	$\frac{3}{15}$	=	3,000	12,000	4,000
4	15,000	×	$\frac{2}{15}$	=	2,000	14,000	2,000
5	15,000	×	$\frac{1}{15}$	=	1,000	15,000	1,000

LEARNING UNIT 17–4 DECLINING-BALANCE METHOD

In the declining-balance method, we cannot depreciate below the residual value.

The **declining-balance method** is another type of accelerated depreciation that takes larger amounts of depreciation expense in the earlier years of the asset. The straight-line method, you recall, estimates the life of the asset and distributes the same amount of depreciation expense to each period of time. To take larger amounts of depreciation expense in the asset's earlier years, the declining-balance method uses up to twice the **straight-line rate** in the first year of depreciation. A key point to remember is that the declining-balance method does *not* deduct the residual value in calculating depreciation expense.

For all problems, we will use double the straight-line rate unless we indicate otherwise. Today, the rate is often 1.5 or 1.25 times the straight-line rate. Again, we use our $2,500 equipment with its estimated useful life of 5 years. As we build the depreciation schedule in Table 17–4, (p. 386), note the following steps:

Step 1. Rate is equal to $\frac{100\%}{5 \text{ years}} \times 2 = 40\%$

Or another way to look at it is that the straight-line rate is $\frac{1}{5} \times 2 = \frac{2}{5} = 40\%$.

Step 2. $\text{Depreciation expense each year} = \text{Book value of equipment at beginning of year} \times \text{Depreciation rate}$

TABLE 17-4 Depreciation Schedule for Declining-Balance Method

End of year	Cost of equipment	Accumulated depreciation beginning of year	Book value beginning of year (Cost − Accumulated depreciation)	Depreciation (Book value beginning of year × Rate)	Accumulated depreciation end of year	Book value end of year (Cost − Accumulated depreciation)
1	$2,500	—	$2,500	$1,000 ($2,500 × .40)	$1,000	$1,500 ($2,500 − $1,000)
2	2,500	$1,000	1,500	$ 600 ($1,500 × .40)	1,600	900
3	2,500	1,600	900	$ 360 ($900 × .40)	1,960	540
4	2,500	1,960	540	$ 40	2,000	500
5	2,500	2,000	500		2,000	500
	↑ Original cost of $2,500 does not change. Residual value was not subtracted.	↑ Ending accumulated depreciation of one year becomes next year's beginning.	↑ Cost less accumulated depreciation.	↑ Note: In year 4 only, $40 is taken since we cannot depreciate below residual value of $500. In year 5, no depreciation is taken.	↑ Accumulated depreciation balance plus depreciation expense this year.	↑ Book value now equals residual value.

Step 3. We cannot depreciate the equipment below its residual value ($500). The straight-line method and the sum-of-the-years'-digits method automatically reduced the asset's book value to the residual value. This is not true with the declining-balance method. So you must be careful when you prepare the depreciation schedule.

Now let's check your progress again with another Practice Quiz.

LU 17-4 PRACTICE QUIZ

Prepare a depreciation schedule from the following:

Cost of machine: $16,000
Rate: 40% (this is twice the straight-line rate)
Estimated life: 5 years
Residual value: $1,000

SOLUTIONS TO LU 17-4 PRACTICE QUIZ

Note in this case we never reach residual value.

End of year	Cost of machine	Accumulated depreciation beginning of year	Book value beginning of year (Cost − Accumulated depreciation)	Depreciation (Book value beginning of year × Rate)	Accumulated depreciation end of year	Book value end of year (Cost − Accumulated depreciation)
1	$16,000	$ -0-	$16,000.00	$6,400.00	$ 6,400.00	$9,600.00
2	16,000	6,400.00	9,600.00	3,840.00	10,240.00	5,760.00
3	16,000	10,240.00	5,760.00	2,304.00	12,544.00	3,456.00
4	16,000	12,544.00	3,456.00	1,382.40	13,926.40	2,073.60
5	16,000	13,926.40	2,073.60	829.44*	14,755.84	1,244.16

*Since we do not reach the residual value of $1,000, another $244.16 could have been taken as depreciation expense to bring it to the estimated residual value of $1,000.

LEARNING UNIT 17–5 MODIFIED ACCELERATED COST RECOVERY SYSTEM (MACRS)

In Learning Units 17–1 and 17–4, we discussed the depreciation methods used for financial reporting. Since 1981, federal tax laws have been passed that state how depreciation must be taken for income tax purposes. We will look at the **Modified Accelerated Cost Recovery System (MACRS)** that was made law for all property placed into service after December 31, 1986. We will also look at a 1989 update.

Depreciation for Tax Purposes Based on the Tax Reform Act of 1986 (MACRS)

Tables 17–5 and 17–6 give the classes of recovery and annual depreciation percentages that the MACRS established in 1986.

The key points of MACRS are:

1. Calculates depreciation for tax purposes.
2. Ignores residual value.
3. Depreciation in the first year (for personal property) is based on the assumption that the asset was purchased half way through the year.[1]
4. Classes 3, 5, 7, and 10 use a 200% declining-balance method for a period of years before switching to straight-line. You do not have to determine the year in which to switch since Table 17–6 builds this into the calculation.
5. Classes 15 and 20 use a 150% declining-balance method before switching to straight-line.
6. Classes 27.5 and 31.5 use straight-line.

EXAMPLE Using the same equipment of $2,500 for Ajax, prepare a depreciation schedule under MACRS assuming the equipment is a 5-year class and not part of the tax bill of 1989.

End of year	Cost	Depreciation expense	Accumulated depreciation	Book value end of year
1	$2,500	$500 (.20 × $2,500)	$ 500	$2,000
2	2,500	$800 (.32 × $2,500)	1,300	1,200
3	2,500	$480 (.1920 × $2,500)	1,780	720
4	2,500	$288 (.1152 × $2,500)	2,068	432
5	2,500	$288 (.1152 × $2,500)	2,356	144
6	2,500	$144 (.0576 × $2,500)	2,500	-0-

Update on MACRS: The 1989 Tax Bill

Before the 1989 tax bill **(Omnibus Budget Reconciliation Act of 1989),** cellular phones and similar equipment were depreciated under the MACRS system. Since cellular phones are subject to personal use, the 1989 act now treats them as "listed" property. This means that unless business use is greater than 50%, the straight-line method of depreciation is required.

Let's try another Practice Quiz.

[1] New law adds a midquarter convention for all personal property if more than 40% is placed in service during the last three months of the taxable year.

TABLE 17–5
Modified Accelerated Cost Recovery System for Assets Placed in Service after December 31, 1986 (MACRS)

The tax bill of 1989 updates how cellular phones and similar equipment are to be depreciated.

Class recovery period (life)	Asset types
3-year*	Race horses more than 2 years old or any horse other than a race horse that is more than 12 years old at the time placed into service; special tools of certain industries.
5-year*	Automobiles (not luxury); taxis; light general-purpose trucks; semiconductor manufacturing equipment; computer-based telephone central-office switching equipment; qualified technological equipment; property used in connection with research and experimentation.
7-year*	Railroad track; single-purpose agricultural (pigpens) or horticultural structures; fixtures; equipment; furniture.
10-year*	New law doesn't add any specific property under this class.
15-year†	Municipal wastewater treatment plants; telephone distribution plants and comparable equipment used for two-way exchange of voice and data communications.
20-year†	Municipal sewers.
27.5-year‡	Only residential rental property.
31.5-year‡	Only nonresidential real property.

*These classes use a 200% declining-balance method switching to the straight-line method.
†These classes use a 150% declining-balance method switching to straight-line.
‡These classes use a straight-line method.

TABLE 17–6 Annual Recovery for MACRS

Recovery year	3-year class (200% D.B.)	5-year class (200% D.B.)	7-year class (200% D.B.)	10-year class (200% D.B.)	15-year class (150% D.B.)	20-year class (150% D.B.)
1	33.00	20.00	14.28	10.00	5.00	3.75
2	45.00	32.00	24.49	18.00	9.50	7.22
3	15.00*	19.20	17.49	14.40	8.55	6.68
4	7.00	11.52*	12.49	11.52	7.69	6.18
5		11.52	8.93*	9.22	6.93	5.71
6		5.76	8.93	7.37	6.23	5.28
7			8.93	6.55*	5.90*	4.89
8			4.46	6.55	5.90	4.52
9				6.55	5.90	4.46*
10				6.55	5.90	4.46
11				3.29	5.90	4.46
12					5.90	4.46
13					5.90	4.46
14					5.90	4.46
15					5.90	4.46
16					3.00	4.46

*Identifies when switch is made to straight-line.

LU 17–5 PRACTICE QUIZ

1. In 1991, Rancho Corporation bought semiconductor equipment for $80,000. Using MACRS, what is depreciation expense in year 3?
2. What would depreciation be the first year for a waste water sewer plant that cost $800,000.

SOLUTIONS TO LU 17-5 PRACTICE QUIZ

1. $80,000 × .1920 = $15,360
2. $800,000 × .05 = $40,000

CHAPTER ORGANIZER: A REFERENCE GUIDE

Page	Topic	Key point, procedure, formula	Example(s) to illustrate situation
381	Straight-line depreciation method	$\text{Depreciation} = \dfrac{\text{Cost} - \text{Residual value}}{\text{Estimated useful life in years}}$ For partial years if purchased before 15th of month depreciation is taken.	Truck, $25,000; $5,000 residual value, 4-year life. $\text{Depreciation expense} = \dfrac{\$25{,}000 - \$5{,}000}{4}$ $= \$5{,}000$ per year
383	Units-of-production method	$\text{Depreciation expense} = \dfrac{\text{Cost} - \text{Residual value}}{\text{Estimated units of useful life production}}$ Do not depreciate below residual value even if actual units are greater than estimate.	Machine, $5,000; estimated life in units, 900; residual value, $500. Assume first year produced 175 units. $\text{Depreciation expense} = \dfrac{\$5{,}000 - \$500}{900}$ $= \dfrac{\$4{,}500}{900}$ = $5 depreciation per unit 175 units × $5 = $875 depreciation expense
384	Sum-of-the-years'-digits method	$\text{Depreciation expense} = (\text{Cost} - \text{Residual value}) \times \dfrac{\text{Remaining life}}{\text{Sum-of-the-years' digits}}$ Sum-of-the-years' digits ↑ $\dfrac{N(N+1)}{2}$	Truck, $32,000; estimated life, 5 years; residual value, $2,000. **Year** | **Cost (less residual value)** × **Rate** = **Depreciation expense** 1 | $30,000 × $\frac{5}{15}$ = $10,000 2 | 30,000 × $\frac{4}{15}$ = 8,000
385	Declining-balance method	An accelerated method. Residual value not subtracted from cost in depreciation schedule. Do not depreciate below residual value. $\text{Depreciation expense} = \text{Book value} \times \text{Depreciation rate}$	Truck, $50,000; estimated life, 5 years; residual value, $10,000. $\frac{1}{5}$ = 20% × 2 = 40% (assume double the straight-line rate) **Year** | **Cost** | **Depreciation expense** | **Book value end of year** 1 | $50,000 | $20,000 ($50,000 × .40) | $30,000 ($50,000 − $20,000) 2 | 50,000 | $12,000 ($30,000 × .40) | $18,000 ($50,000 − $32,000)
387	MACRS/tax bill of 1989	After December 31, 1986, depreciation calculation is modified. Tax Act of 1989 modifies way to depreciate cellular phones and similar equipment.	Auto: 5 years. First year, .20 × $8,000 = $1,600 depreciation expense

Page	Topic	Key point, procedure, formula	Example(s) to illustrate situation
	Key terms	Accelerated method, *p. 385* Accumulated depreciation, *p. 380* Asset cost, *p. 380* Book value, *p. 380* Declining-balance method, *p. 385* Depreciation, *p. 380* Depreciation expense, *p. 380* Depreciation schedule, *p. 381* Estimated useful life, *p. 381* Modified Accelerated Cost Recovery System (MACRS), *p. 387*	Omnibus Budget Reconciliation Act of 1989, *p. 387* Residual value, *p. 380* Salvage value, *p. 380* Straight-line method, *p. 381* Straight-line rate, *p. 382* Sum-of-the-years'-digits method, *p. 384* Trade-in value, *p. 380* Units-of-production method, *p. 383*

END-OF-CHAPTER PROBLEMS

Drill Problems

Additional homework assignments by learning unit are at the end of text in Appendix I (p. I–74).

Solutions to odd problems are at the end of text in Appendix II.

From the following facts, complete a depreciation schedule using the straight-line method:

Given Cost of car $8,000
Residual value $800
Estimated life 5 years

	End of year	Cost of car	Depreciation expense for year	Accumulated depreciation end of year	Book value end of year
17–1.	1	$8,000	$1,440	$1,440	$6,560 ($8,000 − $1,440)
17–2.	2	8,000	1,440	2,880	5,120
17–3.	3	8,000	1,440	4,320	3,680
17–4.	4	8,000	1,440	5,760	2,240
17–5.	5	8,000	1,440	7,200	800

$$\frac{\$8{,}000 - \$800}{5 \text{ years}} = \$1{,}440$$

Prepare a depreciation schedule using the sum-of-the-years' digits method:

Given Truck cost $11,000
Residual value 1,000
Estimated life 4 years

	End of year	Cost − Residual value	×	Fraction for year	Depreciation expense for year	Accumulated depreciation end of year	Book value end of year
17–6.	1	$10,000	×	$\frac{4}{10}$	$4,000	$ 4,000	$7,000 ($11,000 − $4,000)
17–7.	2	10,000	×	$\frac{3}{10}$	3,000	7,000	$4,000
17–8.	3	10,000	×	$\frac{2}{10}$	2,000	9,000	2,000
17–9.	4	10,000	×	$\frac{1}{10}$	1,000	10,000	1,000

$$\frac{N(N+1)}{2} = \frac{4(4+1)}{2} = \frac{20}{2} = 10$$

Prepare a depreciation schedule using the declining-balance method (twice the straight-line rate):

Given Cost of truck $25,000
Residual value 5,000
Estimated life 5 years

	End of year	Cost of truck	Accumulated depreciation beginning of year	Book value beginning of year	Depreciation expense	Accumulated depreciation end of year	Book value end of year
17–10.	1	$25,000	–0–	$25,000	$10,000 ($25,000 × .40)	$10,000	$15,000 ($25,000 − $10,000)
17–11.	2	25,000	$10,000	15,000	$ 6,000 ($15,000 × .40)	16,000	$ 9,000 ($25,000 − $16,000)
17–12.	3	25,000	16,000	9,000	$ 3,600 ($9,000 × .40)	19,600	$ 5,400 ($25,000 − $19,600)
17–13.	4	25,000	19,600	5,400	$ 400* ($5,400 − $5,000)	20,000	$ 5,000

*Cannot be depreciated below book value.

For the first two years, calculate the depreciation expense for a $7,000 car under MACRS. This is a nonluxury car.

		MACRS			MACRS
17–14.	Year 1	$1,400 ($7,000 × .20)	**17–15.**	Year 2	$2,240 ($7,000 × .32)

Complete the following table given this information:

Cost of machine	$94,000	Estimated units machine will produce		100,000
Residual value	4,000			
Useful life	5 years	Actual production:	**Year 1**	**Year 2**
			60,000	15,000

		Depreciation expense	
	Method	**Year 1**	**Year 2**
17–16.	Straight-line	$18,000	$18,000
17–17.	Units-of-production	54,000	13,500
17–18.	Sum-of-the-years'-digits	30,000	24,000
17–19.	Declining-balance	37,600	22,560
17–20.	MACRS (5-year class)	18,800	30,080

17–16. $\frac{\$94{,}000 - \$4{,}000}{5} = \$18{,}000$

17–17. $\frac{\$94{,}000 - \$4{,}000}{100{,}000} = \$.90$ depreciation per unit

Year 1: 60,000 × $.90 = $54,000
Year 2: 15,000 × $.90 = $13,500

17–18. $\frac{5}{15} \times \$90{,}000 = \$30{,}000$

$\frac{4}{15} \times \$90{,}000 = \$24{,}000$

17–19. $\frac{1}{5} = .20 \times 2 = .40$

$94,000 × .40 = $37,600
$94,000 − $37,600 = $56,400
× .40
$22,560

17–20. $94,000 × .20 = $18,800
$94,000 × .32 = $30,080

Word Problems

17–21. Alvin Ross bought a truck for $18,000 with an estimated life of 3 years. The residual value of the truck is $3,000. Assume a straight-line method of depreciation. What will be the book value of the truck at the end of year 2? If truck was bought the first year on April 12, how much depreciation would be taken the first year?

$\frac{\$18{,}000 - \$3{,}000}{3 \text{ years}} = \$5{,}000$ depreciation expense

$18,000 − $10,000 = $8,000 book value
Cost − Accumulated depreciation

$\$5{,}000 \times \frac{9}{12} = \$3{,}750$

17–22. Jim Company bought a machine for $36,000 with an estimated life of 5 years. The residual value of the machine is $6,000. Calculate (**1**) the annual depreciation and (**2**) the book value at end of year 3. Assume straight-line depreciation.

1. $\frac{\$36{,}000 - \$6{,}000}{5 \text{ years}} = \frac{\$30{,}000}{5 \text{ years}} = \$6{,}000$ depreciation expense
2. $36,000 − $18,000 = $18,000
Cost − Accumulated depreciation

17–23. Using Problem 17–22, calculate the first two years' depreciation assuming units-of-production method. This machine is expected to produce 120,000 units. In year 1, it produced 19,000 units; and in year 2, 38,000 units.

$\frac{\$36{,}000 - \$6{,}000}{120{,}000 \text{ units}} = \frac{\$30{,}000}{120{,}000} = \$.25$ Year 1: 19,000 × \$.25 = \$4,750
Year 2: 38,000 × \$.25 = \$9,500

17–24. Assume Jim Company (Problem 17–22) used the sum-of-the-years'-digits method. How much more or less depreciation expense over the first 2 years would have been taken compared to straight-line depreciation?

$\$30{,}000 \times \frac{5}{15} =$ \$10,000

$\$30{,}000 \times \frac{4}{15} =$ \$ 8,000
\$18,000
− 12,000
\$ 6,000 more using sum-of-the-years'-digits

17–25. Using Problem 17–22, calculate the first two years' depreciation, assuming Jim Company used the declining-balance method at twice the straight-line rate.

Year 1: \$36,000 × .40 = \$14,400
Year 2: \$36,000 − \$14,400 = \$21,600 × .40 = \$8,640
Total: \$14,400 + \$8,640 = \$23,040

17–26. For tax purposes, Jim in Problem 17–22 has requested his accountant to calculate what his depreciation expense per year will be for his 5-year class piece of machinery over the first 3 years using MACRS.

\$ 7,200 (\$36,000 × .20)
11,520 (\$36,000 × .32)
6,912 (\$36,000 × .1920)

17–27. Mr. Fix Company bought a new delivery truck for \$26,000 with an estimated life of 5 years. The residual value of the truck is \$1,000. As Mr. Fix's accountant, prepare depreciation schedules for straight-line, sum-of-the-years'-digits, and declining balance ($1\frac{1}{2}$ times the straight-line rate) methods.

Straight-line method: $\frac{\$26{,}000 - \$1{,}000}{5} = \$5{,}000$ per year

End of year	Cost of truck	Depreciation expense	Accumulated depreciation
1	\$26,000	\$5,000	\$ 5,000
2	26,000	5,000	10,000
3	26,000	5,000	15,000
4	26,000	5,000	20,000
5	26,000	5,000	25,000

Sum-of-the-years' digits method:

End of year	Cost of truck − Residual		Depreciation expense	Accumulated depreciation
1	\$25,000 ×	$\frac{5}{15}$	= \$8,333.33	\$ 8,333.33
2	25,000 ×	$\frac{4}{15}$	= 6,666.67	15,000.00
3	25,000 ×	$\frac{3}{15}$	= 5,000.00	20,000.00
4	25,000 ×	$\frac{2}{15}$	= 3,333.33	23,333.33
5	25,000 ×	$\frac{1}{15}$	= 1,666.67	25,000.00

Declining-balance method: 1.5 × .20 = .30 = 30%

End of year	Cost of truck	Accumulated depreciation beginning of year	Book value beginning of year	Depreciation expense	Accumulated depreciation end of year	Book value end of year
1	$26,000	-0-	$26,000.00	$7,800.00 ($26,000 × .30)	$ 7,800.00	$18,200.00 ($26,000 − $7,800)
2	26,000	$ 7,800.00	18,200.00	$5,460.00 ($18,200 × .30)	13,260.00	$12,740.00
3	26,000	13,260.00	12,740.00	$3,822.00	17,082.00	8,918.00
4	26,000	17,082.00	8,918.00	2,675.40	19,757.40	6,242.60
5	26,000	19,757.40	6,242.60	1,872.78*	21,630.18	4,369.82

* Since we have not reached the $1,000 residual value, another $3,369.82 ($4,369.82 − $1,000) could have been taken as depreciation expense in year 5.

Challenge Problem

Depreciation for Partial Years

17–28. On October 1, 1994, Ranger Corporation purchased a new printing press for $240,000. The fiscal year for Ranger Company ends on December 31, 1994. The printing press has a life expectancy of 5 years with a residual value of $30,000. Could you calculate the depreciation expense for the partial year 1994 and the depreciation expense for years 1995 and 1996 using the sum-of-the-years'-digits method?

Year		Depreciation expense
1994	$\left(\frac{5}{15} \times \$210{,}000\right) \times \frac{3}{12} =$	$17,500
1995	$\left(\frac{5}{15} \times \$210{,}000\right) \times \frac{9}{12} = \$52{,}500$	
	$\left(\frac{4}{15} \times \$210{,}000\right) \times \frac{3}{12} = \underline{14{,}000}$	$66,500
1996	$\left(\frac{4}{15} \times \$210{,}000\right) \times \frac{9}{12} = \$42{,}000$	
	$\left(\frac{3}{15} \times \$210{,}000\right) \times \frac{3}{12} = \underline{10{,}500}$	$52,500

Summary Practice Test

Solutions are at end of text in Appendix II.

Quick Reference
If you get any wrong answers, study the page numbers given for each problem.

1. P. 385.

1. Marika Katz, owner of Katz Ice Cream, is discussing with her accountant which method of depreciation would be best for her ice cream truck. The cost of the truck was $17,000 with an estimated life of 4 years. The residual value of the truck is $2,000. Marika wants you to prepare a depreciation schedule using the declining-balance method at twice the straight-line rate.

End of year	Cost of truck	Accumulated depreciation beginning of year	Book value beginning of year	Depreciation expense	Accumulated depreciation end of year	Book value end of year
1	$17,000	-0-	$17,000	$8,500 (.50 × $17,000)	$ 8,500	$8,500
2	17,000	$ 8,500	8,500	$4,250 (.50 × $8,500)	12,750	4,250
3	17,000	12,750	4,250	$2,125 (.50 × $4,250)	14,875	2,125

In year 4, $125 of depreciation is taken since it cannot go below the residual value.

2. P. 387.

2. Using MACRS, what is depreciation for the first year on furniture costing $8,000?
$1,142.40 ($8,000 × .1428) (7-year class)

3. P. 384.

3. Jerry Jeves bought a new delivery truck for $16,000 with an estimated life of 3 years. The residual value of the truck is $4,000. Prepare a depeciation schedule for the sum-of-the-years'-digits method.

Year	Cost	Depreciation expense	Accumulated depreciation
1	$\$12{,}000 \times \frac{3}{6} =$	$6,000	$ 6,000
2	$12{,}000 \times \frac{2}{6} =$	4,000	10,000
3	$12{,}000 \times \frac{1}{6} =$	2,000	12,000

4. P. 381.

4. Able Corporation bought a car for $19,000 with an estimated life of 4 years. The residual value of the car is $3,000. After 2 years, the car was sold for $6,000. What was the difference between the book value and the amount received from selling the car if Able used the straight-line method of depreciation?

$$\frac{\$19{,}000 - \$3{,}000}{4 \text{ years}} = \frac{\$16{,}000}{4 \text{ years}} = \$4{,}000 \times 2 = \$8{,}000$$

$19,000
− 8,000
$11,000 book value
− 6,000
$ 5,000 difference

5. P. 384.

5. If Able Corporation (Problem 4) used the sum-of-the-years'-digits method, what would have been the difference between the book value and the price at which the car was sold?

$$\$16{,}000 \times \frac{4}{10} = \$\ 6{,}400$$

$$\$16{,}000 \times \frac{3}{10} = \$\ 4{,}800$$

$11,200

$19,000
− 11,200
$ 7,800
− 6,000
$ 1,800 difference

Project A

Check with the IRS to see if any new tax laws have been enacted as a result of the Ithaca Industries case. Report back to your professor.

IRS Victory on 'Intangible' Depreciation May Mean Back Taxes in Old Buy-Outs

By CRAIG S. SMITH
Special to THE WALL STREET JOURNAL

NEW YORK—Companies taken private in some leveraged buy-outs may face millions of dollars in back taxes, following a recent tax case won by the Internal Revenue Service.

Earlier this month, the IRS won a case in U.S. Tax Court challenging underwear-maker **Ithaca Industries**' classification of its "assembled work force," made up mostly of factory workers, as a depreciable asset.

Ithaca wrote off the value of the work force that it acquired in a leveraged buy-out in 1983, arguing that the work force had a "life" of just under seven years from the day it was acquired, much like the knitting mills and other assets it purchased. The Tax Court disagreed.

Taking tax deductions for the depreciation of something you can't touch has been a game that has fattened leverage buy-out investors and rankled tax collectors for years.

The IRS has long tilted its lance at "intangibles" that taxpayers claim are assets declining in value and deserving to be written down over time. But it wasn't until recently that the government has made any headway in its efforts to pin down such deductions.

Ithaca hasn't yet decided whether to appeal the case or cough up the few million owed in back taxes and interest if the Tax Court's decision stands. But word of the decision spread quickly through the network of tax attorneys, asset appraisers and leveraged buy-out advisers that blanket the country.

"You can be sure that just about anybody who did an LBO has got to be looking at this case, and just about everyone I know used an assembled work force" as a depreciable asset, says Lehman Brothers tax expert Robert Willens.

He estimates that some companies may owe as much as $60 million or $70 million to the IRS if their write-offs are reversed.

Appraisers, responsible for putting a dollar value and a depreciable life on any asset set before them, say assembled work forces have been commonly treated as amortizable assets for tax purposes—particularly in leveraged buy-outs done before the tax code changed in 1986.

The problem arises in some transactions when a buyer pays more for a company than the appraised value of the underlying hard assets, such as property and equipment. The excess amount is considered good will, which can't be written off under current tax law.

To maximize tax benefits, some buyers assigned value to all sorts of "intangibles," which then could be written off. In some cases, these "intangibles" included employees, as well as customer lists, relationships with suppliers, patents, and contract rights. These were all treated as amortizable assets to stave off the day that the company would have to pay tax.

Lehman's Mr. Willens says the Ithaca case opens the door for the IRS to attack the write-off of other intangible assets.

An Arthur Andersen & Co. partner, Karl Eschelbach, says acquirers often came up with intangible assets "with a wink and a nod, on the expectation that if they were challenged they would negotiate their way out of it" later on.

Some experts believe the IRS victory will make the taxmen more aggressive in tracking down other such deductions. "I think the government will be encouraged by this victory to go after these types of intangibles that have not yet been litigated," says Burton Mirsky, partner at KPMG Peat Marwick.

Others argue that only a fraction of the leveraged buy-outs completed in the last 20 years are likely to have questionable intangibles listed in their tax returns. And most of those aren't paying taxes anyway, because interest expenses eat up any taxable profits they might otherwise have.

The question might become moot if Dan Rostenkowski has his way. The Democratic representative from Illinois, who is also the chairman of the powerful House Ways and Means Committee, has introduced a bill that would set a standard 14-year amortization period for all intangible assets—including good will.

That would end the tricky job of allocating the dollars paid for a business to various assets, imagined or real. It would also ease the IRS's burden of scrutinizing mountains of deductions for intangibles and challenging those that it considers too ethereal.

"The government ... police these

NOTES

THAT WAS THEN . . .
. . . THIS IS NOW

Compare the first Hertz station in 1926 to those of today. Hertz has more than 300,000 autos in 5,400 locations worldwide. How a company controls its inventory affects its profits.

18

Inventory and Overhead

LEARNING UNIT OBJECTIVES

LU 18–1: Assigning Costs to Ending Inventory: Specific Identification; Weighted Average; FIFO; LIFO

1. List the key assumptions of each inventory method. *pp. 400–404.*
2. Calculate the cost of ending inventory and cost of goods sold for each inventory method. *pp. 400–404.*

LU 18–2: Retail Method; Gross Profit Method; Inventory Turnover; Distribution of Overhead

1. Calculate the cost ratio and ending inventory at cost for the retail method. *p. 405.*
2. Calculate the estimated inventory using the gross profit method. *p. 406.*
3. Explain and calculate inventory turnover. *p. 406.*
4. Explain overhead expenses. *p. 407.*
5. Allocate overhead according to (1) floor space and (2) sales. *pp. 407–8.*

Whether you shop at Sears, Toys "R" Us, or Wal-Mart, cashiers no longer punch into cash registers the codes and prices of merchandise from the merchandise ticket. Today, cashiers run scanners across the product code of each item sold. These scanners read pertinent information into a computer terminal, such as the item's number, department, price, and so on. This information has several important uses for business managers and owners.

Every customer knows the frustration of shopping for items that are "temporarily out of stock." To the store, this means not only the loss of a sale but a dissatisfied customer. Computers provide immediate access to the store's inventory.

When store managers use computers to update the merchandise in stock, they are using the **perpetual inventory system.** However, as you probably know, stores cannot rely completely on their computer for an accurate count of merchandise in stock. Some merchandise escapes the computer—stolen or lost merchandise, for example. Periodically, the store must take a physical count of its merchandise to verify the computer count.

Smaller stores that sell high-ticket merchandise such as appliances often keep a manual system of perpetual inventory. The store records the individual items and their serial numbers on inventory cards. Bookkeepers manually enter new merchandise into the cards and remove sold merchandise.

Many stores, such as your local corner variety store, find the perpetual system too costly. These stores use the **periodic inventory system.** This system usually does not keep a running account of its inventory but relies only on a physical inventory count taken at least once a year. The store then uses various accounting methods to value the cost of its merchandise. In this chapter, we discuss the periodic method of inventory.

Photo courtesy of Hewlett-Packard Company

You may wonder why a company should know the status of its inventory. In Chapter 16, we introduced you to the balance sheet and the income statement. Companies cannot accurately prepare these statements unless they have placed the correct value on their inventory. To do this, a company must know (1) the cost of its ending inventory (found on the balance sheet) and (2) the cost of the goods (merchandise) sold (found on the income statement).

Frequently, the same type of merchandise flows into a business at different costs. Depending on the value assumptions that a business makes about the goods it sells first, the company will assign different flows of costs to its ending inventory. Remember that different costs result in different levels of profit on a firm's financial reports. This chapter discusses four common methods that businesses use to calculate costs of ending inventory and cost of goods sold. In these methods, the flow of costs does not always match the flow of goods. Let's begin by following a case study of the Blue Company.

LEARNING UNIT 18-1 ASSIGNING COSTS TO ENDING INVENTORY: SPECIFIC IDENTIFICATION; WEIGHTED AVERAGE; FIFO; LIFO

Blue Company is a small artist supply store. Its beginning inventory is 40 tubes of art paint that cost $320 (at $8 a tube) to bring into the store. As shown in Figure 18-1, Blue made additional purchases in April, May, October, and December. Note that because of inflation and other competitive factors, the cost of the paint rose from $8 to $13 per tube. At the end of December, Blue had 48 unsold paint tubes. During the year, Blue had 120 paint tubes to sell. Blue wants to calculate (1) a cost of ending inventory (not sold) and (2) the cost of goods sold.

Specific Identification Method

Companies use the **specific identification method** when they can identify the original purchase cost of an item with the item. For example, Blue Company color codes its paint tubes as they come into the store. Blue can then attach a specific invoice price to

FIGURE 18–1
Blue Company—A Case Study

	Number of units purchased	Cost per unit	Total cost	
Beginning inventory	40	$ 8	$ 320	
First purchase (April 1)	20	9	180	
Second purchase (May 1)	20	10	200	
Third purchase (October 1)	20	12	240	
Fourth purchase (December 1)	20	13	260	
Goods (merchandise) available for sale	120		$1,200	← **Step 1**
Units sold	72			
Units in ending inventory	48			

Companies that sell high-cost items such as autos, jewelry, antiques, and so on, usually use the specific identification method.

each paint tube. This makes the flow of goods and flow of costs the same. Then, when Blue computes its ending inventory and cost of goods sold, it can associate the actual invoice cost with each item sold and in inventory.

To help Blue calculate its inventory with the specific identification method, use the steps that follow.

Steps for Calculating the Specific Identification Method

Step 1. Calculate cost of goods (merchandise available for sale).

Step 2. Calculate cost of ending inventory.

Step 3. Calculate cost of goods sold (Step 1 − Step 2).

First, Blue must actually count the tubes of paint on hand. Since Blue coded these paint tubes, it can identify the tubes with their purchase cost and multiply them by this cost to arrive at a total cost of ending inventory. Let's do this now:

Blue could have identified each tube by serial number, physical description, or location.

	Cost per unit	Total cost	
20 units from April 1	$ 9	$180	
20 units from October 1	12	240	
8 units from December 1	13	104	
Cost of ending inventory		$524	←**Step 2**

Blue uses the following cost of goods sold formula to determine its cost of goods sold:

Cost of goods available for sale	−	Cost of ending inventory	=	Cost of goods sold	←**Step 3**
↑		↑		↑	
$1,200 (Figure 18–1)	−	$524	=	$676	

Note that the $1,200 for cost of goods available for sale comes from Figure 18–1. Remember, we are focusing our attention on Blue's *purchase costs*. Blue's actual *selling price* does not concern us.

Now let's look at how Blue would use the weighted-average method.

Weighted-Average Method

Often grains that are stored in silos will use the weighted-average method.

The **weighted-average method** prices the ending inventory by using an average unit cost. Let's replay Blue Company and use the weighted-average method to find the average unit cost of its ending inventory and its cost of goods sold. Blue would use the steps that follow.

Steps for Calculating the Weighted-Average Method

Step 1. Calculate average unit cost.

Step 2. Calculate cost of ending inventory.

Step 3. Calculate cost of goods sold.

In the table that follows, Blue makes the calculation.

	Number of units purchased	Cost per unit	Total cost
Beginning inventory	40	$ 8	$ 320
First purchase (April 1)	20	9	180
Second purchase (May 1)	20	10	200
Third purchase (October 1)	20	12	240
Fourth purchase (December 1)	20	13	260
Goods (merchandise) available for sale	120		$1,200
Units sold	72		
Units in ending inventory	48		

$$\text{Weighted-average unit cost} = \frac{\text{Total cost of goods available for sale}}{\text{Total number of units available for sale}} = \frac{\$1{,}200}{120 \text{ units}} = \$10 \text{ average unit cost} \leftarrow \textbf{Step 1}$$

Average cost of ending inventory: 48 units at $10 = $480 ← **Step 2**

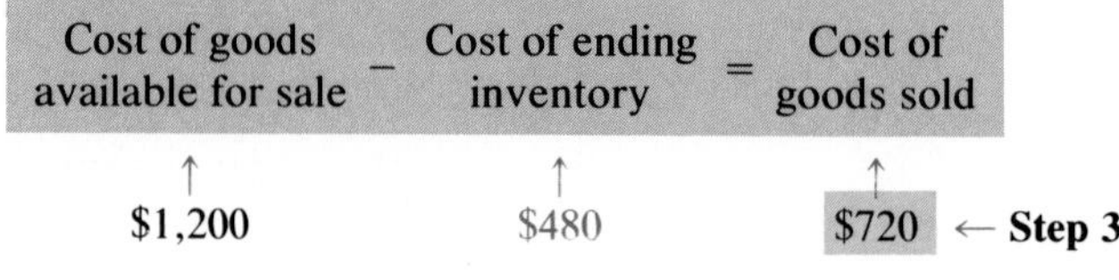

← **Step 3**

Remember that some of the costs we used to determine the average unit cost were higher and some lower. The weighted-average method, then, calculates an *average unit price* for goods. Companies with similar units of goods, such as rolls of wallpaper, often use the weighted-average method. Also, companies with homogenous products like fuels and grains may use the weighted-average method.

Now let's see how Blue Company would value its inventory with the FIFO method.

FIFO—First-In, First-Out Method

The **first-in, first-out (FIFO)** inventory valuation method assumes that the first goods (paint tubes for Blue) brought into the store are the first goods sold. Thus, FIFO assumes that each sale is from the oldest goods in inventory. FIFO also assumes that the inventory remaining in the store at the end of the period of time is the most recently acquired goods. This cost flow assumption may or may not exist in the actual physical flow of the goods.

Use the following steps to calculate inventory with the FIFO method.

Steps for Calculating the FIFO Inventory
Step 1. List units and their costs to be included in ending inventory.
Step 2. Calculate cost of ending inventory.
Step 3. Calculate cost of goods sold.

In the table that follows, we show how to calculate FIFO for Blue using these steps.

FIFO (bottom up)	Number of units purchased	Cost per unit	Total cost
Beginning inventory	40	$ 8	$ 320
First purchase (April 1)	20	9	180
Second purchase (May 1)	20	10	200
Third purchase (October 1)	20	12	240
Fourth purchase (December 1)	20	13	260
Goods (merchandise) available for sale	120		$1,200
Units sold	72		
Units in ending inventory	48		

20 units from December 1 purchased at $13	← Step 1 →	$260	
20 units from October 1 purchased at $12		240	
8 units from May 1 purchased at $10		80	Step 2
48 units result in an ending inventory cost of		$580	

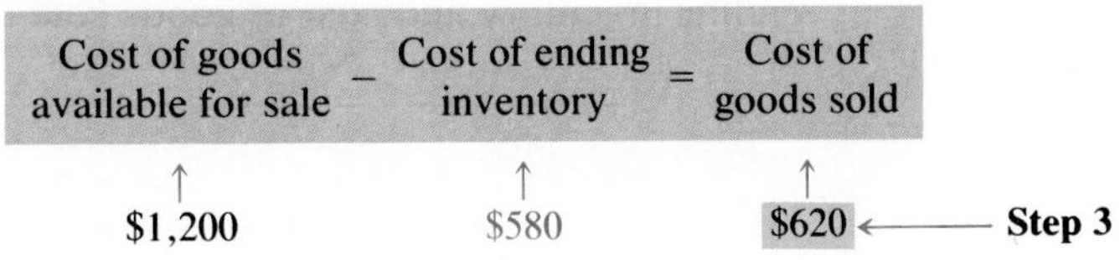

In FIFO, the cost flow of goods tends to follow the physical flow. For example, a fish market could use FIFO because it would want to sell its old inventory first. Note that during inflation, FIFO produces a higher income than other methods. So companies using FIFO during this time must pay more taxes.

We conclude this unit by using the LIFO method to value Blue Company's inventory.

LIFO—Last-In, First-Out Method

If Blue Company chooses the **last-in, first-out (LIFO)** method of inventory valuation, then the goods sold by Blue would be the last goods brought into the store. The ending inventory would consist of the old goods that Blue bought earlier.

You can calculate inventory with the LIFO method by using the steps that follow.

Steps for Calculating the LIFO Inventory
Step 1. List units and their costs to be included in ending inventory.
Step 2. Calculate cost of ending inventory.
Step 3. Calculate cost of goods sold.

Now we use these steps to calculate LIFO for Blue.

LIFO (top down)	Number of units purchased	Cost per unit	Total cost
Beginning inventory	40	$ 8	$ 320
First purchase (April 1)	20	9	180
Second purchase (May 1)	20	10	200
Third purchase (October 1)	20	12	240
Fourth purchase (December 1)	20	13	260
Goods (merchandise) available for sale	120		$1,200
Units sold	72		
Units in ending inventory	48		

40 units of beginning inventory at $8 ← Step 1 → $320
8 units from April at $9 — 72 — Step 2
48 units result in an ending inventory cost of $392

Cost of goods available for sale − Cost of ending inventory = Cost of goods sold

↑ $1,200 ↑ $392 ↑ $808 ← Step 3

Although LIFO doesn't always match the physical flow of goods, companies do still use it to calculate the flow of costs. Also, during inflation, LIFO produces lower income than other methods. This results in less taxes for companies using LIFO.

Before we conclude this unit, let's make the following summary for the cost of ending inventory and cost of goods sold under weighted average, FIFO, and LIFO:

	Weighted average	FIFO	LIFO
Cost of ending inventory	$480	$580	$392
Cost of goods sold	720	620	808

From this summary, you can see that in times of rising prices, LIFO gives the highest cost of goods sold ($808). This results in a tax savings for Blue. The weighted-average method tends to smooth out the fluctuations between LIFO and FIFO and falls in the middle.

The key to this discussion on inventory valuation is that different costing methods produce different results. This means that management, investors, and potential investors should understand the different inventory costing methods and know which method a particular company uses.

Let's check your understanding of this unit with a Practice Quiz.

LU 18–1 PRACTICE QUIZ

From the following, calculate (**a**) the cost of ending inventory, and (**b**) the cost of goods sold under the assumption of (1) weighted-average method, (2) FIFO, and (3) LIFO (ending inventory shows 72 units):

	Number of books purchased for resale	Cost per unit	Total
January 1 inventory	30	$3	$ 90
March 1	50	2	100
April 1	20	4	80
November 1	60	6	360

SOLUTIONS TO LU 18–1 PRACTICE QUIZ

1. a. 72 units of ending inventory × $3.94 = $283.68 cost of ending inventory
($630 ÷ 160)

b. Cost of goods available for sale − Cost of ending inventory = Cost of goods sold

$630 − $283.68 = $346.32

2. a. 60 units from November 1 purchased at $6 $360
12 units from April 1 purchased at $4 48
72 units Cost of ending inventory $408

b. Cost of goods available for sale − Cost of ending inventory = Cost of goods sold

$630 − $408 = $222

3. a. 30 units from January 1 purchased at $3 $ 90
42 units from March 1 purchased at $2 84
72 Cost of ending inventory $174

b. Cost of goods available for sale − Cost of ending inventory = Cost of goods sold

$630 − $174 = $456

LEARNING UNIT 18–2 RETAIL METHOD; GROSS PROFIT METHOD; INVENTORY TURNOVER; DISTRIBUTION OF OVERHEAD

Taking a physical inventory can be time-consuming and expensive. Some stores make monthly financial reports but do not want to spend the time or money to take a monthly physical inventory. These stores estimate the amount of inventory on hand. Stores may also have to estimate their inventories when they have a loss of goods due to fire, theft, flood, and the like. This unit begins with two methods of estimating the value of ending inventory—the retail method and the gross profit method.

Retail Method

Many chain stores, department stores, and so on, use the **retail method** to estimate their inventory. As shown in Figure 18–2, this method does not require that a company calculate an inventory cost for each item. To calculate the $3,500 ending inventory in Figure 18–2, Green Company used the steps that follow.

Steps for Calculating the Retail Method

Step 1. Calculate cost of goods available for sale at cost and retail: $6,300; $9,000.

Step 2. Calculate a cost ratio using:

$$\frac{\text{Cost of goods available for sale at cost}}{\text{Cost of goods available for sale at retail}} = \frac{\$6,300}{\$9,000} = .70$$

Step 3. Deduct net sales from cost of goods available for sale at retail: $9,000 − $4,000.

Step 4. Multiply cost ratio times ending inventory at retail: .70 × $5,000.

Now let's look at the gross profit method.

FIGURE 18–2
Estimating Inventory with the Retail Method

	Cost	Retail	
Beginning inventory	$4,000	$6,000	
Net purchases during the month	2,300	3,000	
Cost of goods available for sale **(Step 1)**	$6,300	$9,000	
Less net sales for the month		4,000	**(Step 3)**
Ending inventory at retail		$5,000	
Cost ratio ($6,300 ÷ $9,000) **(Step 2)**		70%	
Ending inventory at cost (.70 × $5,000) **(Step 4)**		$3,500	

Gross Profit Method

You can use the following steps to calculate the **gross profit method** to estimate inventory.

> **Steps for Calculating the Gross Profit Method**
>
> **Step 1.** Calculate cost of goods available for sale (Beginning inventory + Net purchases).
>
> **Step 2.** Multiply net sales at retail times complement of gross profit rate. This is the estimated cost of goods sold.
>
> **Step 3.** Calculate cost of estimated inventory (Step 1 − Step 2).

To use the gross profit method, the company must keep track of (1) average gross profit rate, (2) net sales at retail, (3) beginning inventory, and (4) net purchases.

EXAMPLE Assume Radar Company has the following information in its records:

Gross profit on sales	30%
Beginning inventory, January 1, 1994	$20,000
Net purchases	8,000
Net sales at retail for January	12,000

If you use the gross profit method, what is the company's estimated inventory?

The gross profit method calculates Radar's estimated cost of ending inventory at the end of January as follows:

Goods available for sale			
Inventory, January 1, 1994		$20,000	
Net purchases		8,000	
Cost of goods available for sale		$28,000	← **Step 1**
Less: Estimated cost of goods sold:			
Net sales at retail	$12,000		
Cost percentage (100% − 30%) **Step 2** →	.70		
Estimated cost of goods sold		8,400	
Estimated inventory, January 31, 1994		$19,600	← **Step 3**

Note that the cost of goods available for sale less the estimated cost of goods sold gives the estimated cost of ending inventory.

Since this chapter has looked at inventory flow, let's discuss inventory turnover—a key business ratio.

Inventory Turnover (Stock Turnover)

Inventory turnover is the number of times the company replaces inventory during a specific period of time. Companies use the following two formulas to calculate inventory turnover:

$$\text{Inventory turnover at retail} = \frac{\text{Net sales}}{\text{Average inventory at retail}}$$

$$\text{Inventory turnover at cost} = \frac{\text{Cost of goods sold}}{\text{Average inventory at cost}}$$

You should note that inventory turnover at retail is usually lower than inventory turnover at cost. This is due to theft, markdowns, spoilage, and so on. Also, retail outlets and grocery stores usually have a high turnover, but jewelry and appliance stores have a low turnover.

Now let's use an example to calculate the inventory turnover at retail and at cost. The following facts are for the Abby Company, a local sporting goods store (rounded to nearest hundredth):

Net sales	$32,000
Beginning inventory at retail	11,000
Ending inventory at retail	8,900
Cost of goods sold	22,000
Beginning inventory at cost	7,500
Ending inventory at cost	5,600

With these facts, we can make the following calculations:

$$\textbf{Average inventory} = \frac{\text{Beginning inventory} + \text{Ending inventory}}{2}$$

$$\text{At retail: } \frac{\$32{,}000}{\frac{\$11{,}000 + \$8{,}900}{2}} = \frac{\$32{,}000}{\$9{,}950} = 3.22$$

$$\text{At cost: } \frac{\$22{,}000}{\frac{\$7{,}500 + \$5{,}600}{2}} = \frac{\$22{,}000}{\$6{,}550} = 3.36$$

What Turnover Means

Inventory is often a company's most expensive asset. The turnover of inventory can have important implications. Too much inventory results in the use of needed space, extra insurance coverage, and so on. A slow inventory turnover could indicate customer dissatisfaction, too much tied up capital, and possible product obsolescence. A high inventory turnover might mean insufficient amounts of inventory causing stockouts that may lead to future lost sales. If inventory is moving out fast, it may be that the company's selling price is too low in relation to that of its competitors. Companies should compare their inventory turnover with competitors, industry standards, past turnovers, and so on. Before concluding this unit, let's see how companies distribute overhead.

Distribution of Overhead

In Chapter 16, we studied cost of goods sold and operating expenses on the income statement. The operating expenses included **overhead expenses,** expenses that are *not* directly associated with a specific department or product but that contribute indirectly to the running of the business. Examples of such overhead expenses are rent, taxes, and insurance. Companies must allocate these expenses to various departments in the company. The two common methods of calculating the **distribution of overhead** are by (1) floor space (square feet) or (2) sales volume.

Distribution of Overhead by Floor Space

To calculate the distribution of overhead by floor space, use the steps that follow.

Steps for Calculating the Distribution of Overhead by Floor Space

Step 1. Calculate total square feet in all departments.

Step 2. Calculate ratio for each department based on floor space.

Step 3. Multiply each department's floor space ratio times the total overhead.

Roy Company has three departments with the following floor space:

Department A	6,000 square feet
Department B	3,000 square feet
Department C	1,000 square feet

The accountant's job is to allocate the $90,000 of overhead expenses to the three departments.

To allocate this overhead by floor space:

	Floor space in square feet	**Ratio**	
Department A	6,000	$\frac{6{,}000}{10{,}000} = 60\%$	← Steps 1 and 2
Department B	3,000	$\frac{3{,}000}{10{,}000} = 30\%$	
Department C	1,000	$\frac{1{,}000}{10{,}000} = 10\%$	
	10,000 total square feet		

Department A	.60 × $90,000 =	$54,000	← Step 3
Department B	.30 × $90,000 =	27,000	
Department C	.10 × $90,000 =	9,000	
		$90,000	

Distribution of Overhead by Sales

To calculate the distribution of overhead by sales, use the steps that follow.

Steps for Calculating the Distribution of Overhead by Sales

Step 1. Calculate total sales in all departments.

Step 2. Calculate ratio for each department based on sales.

Step 3. Multiply each department's sales ratios times the total overhead.

Morse Company distributes its overhead expenses based on the sales of its departments. For example, last year Morse's overhead expenses were $60,000. Sales of its two departments were as follows along with its ratio calculation.

Since Department A makes 80% of the sales, it is allocated 80% of the overhead expenses.

	Sales	Ratio	
Department A	$ 80,000	$80,000 / $100,000 = .80	← **Steps 1 and 2**
Department B	20,000	$20,000 / $100,000 = .20	
Total sales	$100,000		

These ratios are then multiplied times the overhead expense to be allocated.

Department A	.80 × $60,000 =	$48,000
Department B	.20 × $60,000 =	12,000 ← **Step 3**
		$60,000

Its time to try another Practice Quiz.

LU 18-2 PRACTICE QUIZ

1. From the following facts calculate cost of ending inventory using the retail method (round cost ratio to nearest tenth percent):

January 1—inventory at cost	$ 18,000
January 1—inventory at retail	58,000
Net purchases at cost	220,000
Net purchases at retail	376,000
Net sales at retail	364,000

2. Given the following, calculate the estimated cost of ending inventory using the gross profit method:

Gross profit on sales	40%
Beginning inventory, January 1, 1994	$27,000
Net purchases	7,500
Net sales at retail for January	15,000

3. Calculate the inventory turnover at cost and at retail from the following (round turnover to nearest hundredth):

Average inventory at cost	Average inventory at retail	Net sales	Cost of goods sold
$10,590	$19,180	$109,890	$60,990

4. From the following, calculate the distribution of overhead to Departments A and B based on floor space.

Amount of overhead expense to be allocated	Square footage
$70,000	10,000 Department A
	30,000 Department B

SOLUTIONS TO LU 18-2 PRACTICE QUIZ

1.	Cost	Retail
Beginning inventory	$ 18,000	$ 58,000
Net purchases during the month	220,000	376,000
Cost of goods available for sale	$238,000	$434,000
Less net sales for the month		364,000
Ending inventory at retail		$ 70,000
Cost ratio ($238,000 ÷ $434,000)		54.8%
Ending inventory at cost .548 × $70,000		$ 38,360

2. Goods available for sale

Inventory, January 1, 1994		$27,000
Net purchases		7,500
Cost of goods available for sale		$34,500
Less: Estimated cost of goods sold:		
Net sales at retail	$15,000	
Cost percentage (100% − 40%)	.60	
Estimated cost of goods sold		9,000
Estimated inventory, January 31, 1994		$25,500

3. $$\text{Inventory turnover at cost} = \frac{\text{Cost of goods sold}}{\text{Average inventory at cost}} = \frac{\$60,990}{\$10,590} = 5.76$$

$$\text{Inventory turnover at retail} = \frac{\text{Net sales}}{\text{Average inventory at retail}} = \frac{\$109,890}{\$19,180} = 5.73$$

4.

		Ratio		
Department A	10,000	$\frac{10,000}{40,000}$	= .25 × $70,000 =	$17,500
Department B	30,000	$\frac{30,000}{40,000}$	= .75 × $70,000 =	$52,500
	40,000	40,000		$70,000

CHAPTER ORGANIZER: A REFERENCE GUIDE

Page	Topic	Key point, procedure, formula	Example(s) to illustrate situation
401	Specific identification method	Identification could be by serial number, physical description, or coding. The flow of goods and flow of costs are the same.	Cost per unit / Total cost Apr. 1, 3 units at $7 — $21 May 5, 4 units at 8 — 32 $53 If 1 unit from each group is left, ending inventory is: 1 × $7 = $ 7 + 1 × 8 = 8 $15 Cost of goods available for sale − Cost of ending inventory = Cost of goods sold $53 − $15 = $38
402	Weighted-average method	$\text{Weighted-average unit cost} = \frac{\text{Total cost of goods available for sale}}{\text{Total number of units available for sale}}$	Cost per unit / Total cost 1/XX, 4 units at $4 — $16 5/XX, 2 units at 5 — 10 8/XX, 3 units at 6 — 18 $44 Unit cost = $\frac{\$44}{9}$ = $4.89 If 5 units left, cost of ending inventory is: 5 units × $4.89 = $24.45
403	FIFO—first-in, first-out method	Sell old inventory first. Ending inventory is made up of "last" merchandise brought into store.	Using example above: 5 units left: ↓ (Last into store) 3 units at $6 — $18 2 units at $5 — 10 Cost of ending inventory — $28

Page	Topic	Key point, procedure, formula	Example(s) to illustrate situation
404	LIFO—last-in, first-out method	Sell last inventory brought into store first. Ending inventory is made up of oldest merchandise in store.	Using weighted-average example: 5 units left: ↓ (First into store) 4 units at $4 $16 1 unit at $5 5 Cost of ending inventory $21
405	Retail method	Ending inventory at cost equals: $\frac{\text{Cost of goods available at cost}}{\text{Cost of goods available at retail}} \times \text{Ending inventory at retail}$ (This is cost ratio.)	Cost / Retail Beginning inventory $52,000 $ 83,000 Net purchases 28,000 37,000 Cost of goods available for sale $80,000 $120,000 Less net sales for month 80,000 Ending inventory at retail $ 40,000 Cost ratio $= \frac{\$80{,}000}{\$120{,}000} = .67 = 67\%$ Rounded to nearest percent. Ending inventory at cost, $26,800 (.67 × $40,000)
406	Gross profit method	Beginning inventory + Net purchases − Estimated cost of goods sold = Estimated ending inventory	**Goods available for sale** Beginning inventory $30,000 Net purchases 3,000 Cost of goods available for sale $33,000 Less: Estimated cost of goods sold: Net sales at retail $18,000 Cost percentage (100% − 30%) .70 Estimated cost of goods sold 12,600 Estimated ending inventory $20,400
406	Inventory turnover at retail and cost	$\frac{\text{Net sales}}{\text{Average inventory at retail}}$ or $\frac{\text{Cost of goods sold}}{\text{Average inventory at cost}}$	Inventory, Jan. 1 at cost $20,000 Inventory, Dec. 31 at cost 48,000 Cost of goods sold 62,000 At cost: $\frac{\$62{,}000}{\frac{\$20{,}000 + \$48{,}000}{2}} = 1.82$ (inventory turnover at cost)
407	Distribution of overhead	Based on floor space or sales volume calculate: 1. Ratios of department floor space or sales to the total. 2. Multiply ratios times total amount of overhead to be distributed.	Total overhead to be distributed, $10,000 **Floor space** Department A 6,000 sq. ft. Department B 2,000 sq. ft. 8,000 sq. ft. Ratio A $= \frac{6{,}000}{8{,}000} = .75$ Ratio B $= \frac{2{,}000}{8{,}000} = .25$ Dept. A = .75 × $10,000 = $7,500 Dept. B = .25 × $10,000 = $2,500
	Key terms	Average inventory, *p. 406* Distribution of overhead, *p. 407* First-in, first-out method (FIFO), *p. 402* Gross profit method, *p. 406* Inventory turnover, *p. 406* Last-in, first-out method (LIFO), *p. 404*	Overhead expenses, *p. 407* Periodic inventory system, *p. 400* Perpetual inventory system, *p. 400* Retail method, *p. 405* Specific identification method, *p. 401* Weighted-average method, *p. 402*

END-OF-CHAPTER PROBLEMS

Drill Problems

Additional homework assignments by learning unit are at the end of text in Appendix I p. I–80). Solutions to odd problems are at the end of text in Appendix II.

18–1. Using the specific identification method, calculate (**a**) the cost of ending inventory and (**b**) cost of goods sold given the following:

Date	Units purchased	Cost per can		Ending inventory
May 1	40 cans	$6	$ 240	2 cans from May 1
July 1	60 cans	7	420	6 cans from July 1
August 1	50 cans	8	400	11 cans from August 1
			$1,060	

May 1	2 cans × $6 =	$ 12
July 1	6 cans × $7 =	42
August 1	11 cans × $8 =	88
		$142

$1,060 cost of goods available for sale
− 142 (**a**) cost of ending inventory
$ 918 (**b**) cost of goods sold

From the following, calculate cost of ending inventory (round average unit cost to nearest cent) and cost of goods sold using the weighted-average method, FIFO, and LIFO (ending inventory shows 61 units).

	Number purchased	Cost per unit	Total
January 1 inventory	40	$4	$ 160
April 1	60	7	420
June 1	50	8	400
November 1	55	9	495
	205		$1,475

18–2. Weighted average:

$\frac{\$1,475}{205} = \$7.20$ per unit × 61 = $439.20 (cost of ending inventory)

$1,475	−	$439.20	=	$1,035.80
Cost of goods available for sale		Ending inventory		Cost of goods sold

FIFO—old sold first.

18–3. FIFO:

55 × $9 =	$495
6 × 8 =	48
Cost of ending inventory	$543
Cost of goods available for sale	$1,475
Ending inventory	− 543
Cost of goods sold	$ 932

LIFO—new sold first.

18–4. LIFO:

40 × $4 =	$160
21 × 7 =	147
Cost of ending inventory	$307
Cost of goods available for sale	$1,475
Ending inventory	− 307
Cost of goods sold	$1,168

From the following, calculate the cost of ending inventory and cost of goods sold for LIFO, FIFO, and weighted average (make sure to first find total cost to complete the table); ending inventory is 49 units:

	Beginning inventory and purchases	Units	Unit cost	Total dollar cost
18–5.	Beginning inventory, January 1	5	$2.00	$ 10.00
18–6.	April 10	10	2.50	25.00
18–7.	May 15	12	3.00	36.00
18–8.	July 22	15	3.25	48.75
18–9.	August 19	18	4.00	72.00
18–10.	September 30	20	4.20	84.00
18–11.	November 10	32	4.40	140.80
18–12.	December 15	16	4.80	76.80
		128		$493.35

18–13. LIFO:

Cost of ending inventory		**Cost of goods sold**
5 at \$2.00 =	\$ 10.00	\$493.35
10 at \$2.50 =	25.00	− 147.75
12 at \$3.00 =	36.00	\$345.60
15 at \$3.25 =	48.75	
7 at \$4.00 =	28.00	
Cost of ending inventory =	\$147.75	

18–14. FIFO:

Cost of ending inventory		**Cost of goods sold**
16 at \$4.80 =	\$ 76.80	\$493.35
32 at \$4.40 =	140.80	− 221.80
1 at \$4.20 =	4.20	\$271.55
	\$221.80	

18–15. Weighted average:

Cost of ending inventory

$$\frac{\$493.35}{128} = \$\ 3.85$$

49 × \$3.85 = \$188.65

Cost of goods sold

\$493.35
− 188.65
\$304.70

18–16. Calculate the cost ratio (round to nearest hundredth percent) and the cost of ending inventory to nearest cent under the retail method from the following:

Net sales at retail for year	\$40,000	Purchases—cost	\$14,000
Beginning inventory—cost	27,000	Purchases—retail	19,000
Beginning inventory—retail	49,000		

	Cost	**Retail**
Beginning inventory	\$27,000	\$49,000
Net purchases	14,000	19,000
Cost of goods available for sale	\$41,000	\$68,000
Less net sales at retail		40,000
Ending inventory at retail		\$28,000
Cost ratio (\$41,000 ÷ \$68,000)		60.29%
Ending inventory at cost .6029 × \$28,000		\$16,881.20

18–17. Complete the following (round answers to nearest hundredth):

a. Average inventory at cost	**b.** Average inventory at retail	**c.** Net sales	**d.** Cost of goods sold	**e.** Inventory turnover at cost	**f.** Inventory turnover at retail
\$14,000	\$21,540	\$70,000	\$49,800	3.56	3.25

e. $= \dfrac{\$49{,}800\ (\mathbf{d})}{\$14{,}000\ (\mathbf{a})} = 3.56$

f. $= \dfrac{\$70{,}000\ (\mathbf{c})}{\$21{,}540\ (\mathbf{b})} = 3.25$

Complete the following (assume \$70,000 of overhead to be distributed):

		Square feet	**Ratio**	**Amount of overhead allocated**
18–18.	Department A	5,000	.25 (5,000 ÷ 20,000)	\$17,500 (.25 × \$70,000)
18–19.	Department B	15,000	.75 (15,000 ÷ 20,000)	\$52,500 (.75 × \$70,000)

18–20. Given the following, calculate the estimated cost of ending inventory using the gross profit method.

Gross profit on sales	55%	Net purchases	$ 3,900
Beginning inventory	$29,000	Net sales at retail	17,000

Goods available for sale

Beginning inventory		$29,000
Net purchases		3,900
Cost of goods available for sale		$32,900
Less: Estimated cost of goods sold:		
Net sales at retail	$17,000	
Cost percentage (100% − 55%)	.45	
Estimated cost of goods sold		7,650
Estimated ending inventory		$25,250

Word Problems

18–21. The Sneaker Den made the following wholesale purchases of new Nike running shoes: 10 pairs at $42; 16 pairs at $49.50; and 7 pairs at $55. An inventory taken last week indicates that 12 pairs are still in stock. Calculate the cost of ending inventory by FIFO and calculate cost of goods sold.

10 × $42.00 = $420.00
16 × $49.50 = 792.00
7 × $55.00 = 385.00
$1,597.00

7 × $55.00 = $385.00
5 × $49.50 = 247.50
$632.50 (cost of ending inventory)

$1,597.00 − $632.50 = $964.50

18–22. Marvin Company has beginning inventory of 12 sets of paints at a cost of $1.50 each. During the year, the store purchased 4 at $1.60, 6 at $2.20, 6 at $2.50, and 10 at $3.00. By the end of the year, 25 sets were sold. Calculate (1) the number of paint sets in stock and (2) the cost of ending inventory under LIFO, FIFO, and weighted average. Round to nearest cent for the weighted average.

12 at $1.50 = $18.00
4 at $1.60 = 6.40
6 at $2.20 = 13.20
6 at $2.50 = 15.00
10 at $3.00 = 30.00
38 $82.60

LIFO

38 sets
− 25 sets sold
13 inventory

12 × $1.50 = $18.00
1 × $1.60 = + 1.60
$19.60 (cost of ending inventory)

FIFO 10 × $3.00 = $30.00
3 × $2.50 = + 7.50
$37.50 (cost of ending inventory)

Weighted average $\frac{\$82.60}{38} = \$2.17 \times 13 = \$28.21$ (cost of ending inventory)

18–23. Jeffrey Company allocated overhead expenses to all departments on the basis of floor space (square feet) occupied by each department. The total overhead expenses for a recent year amounted to $70,000. Department A occupied 14,800 square feet; Department B, 4,900 square feet; Department C, 8,000 square feet. What is the amount of the overhead allocated to Department C? Round ratio to nearest whole percent.

14,800 + 4,900 + 8,000 = 27,700 square feet

Department C $= \frac{8{,}000}{27{,}700} = 29\%$ $.29 \times \$70{,}000 = \$20{,}300$

18–24. Moose Company has a beginning inventory at a cost of $77,000 and an ending inventory costing $84,000. Sales were $302,000. Assume Moose's markup rate is 37%. Based on the selling price, what is the inventory turnover at cost? Round to nearest hundredth.

Cost of goods sold = .63 × $302,000 = $190,260

$$\frac{\$190{,}260}{\frac{\$77{,}000 + \$84{,}000}{2}} = \frac{\$190{,}260}{\$80{,}500} = 2.36$$

18–25. May's Dress Shop's inventory at cost on January 1 was $39,000. Its retail value is $59,000. During the year, May purchased additional merchandise at a cost of

$195,000 with a retail value of $395,000. The net sales at retail for the year was $348,000. Could you calculate May's inventory at cost by the retail method? Round cost ratio to nearest whole percent.

	Cost	Retail
Beginning inventory	$ 39,000	$ 59,000
Purchases	195,000	395,000
Cost of goods available for sale	$234,000	$454,000
Less net sales for year		348,000
Ending inventory at retail		$106,000
Cost ratio ($234,000 ÷ $454,000)		52%
Ending inventory at cost (.52 × $106,000)		$55,120

18–26. A sneaker shop has made the following wholesale purchases of new running shoes: 11 pairs at $24, 20 pairs at $2.50, and 16 pairs at $26.50. An inventory taken last week indicates that 17 pairs are still in stock. Calculate the cost of this inventory by FIFO.

11 at $24.00 = $264
20 at $ 2.50 = 50
16 at $26.50 = 424
47 $738

FIFO 16 × $26.50 = $424.00
1 × $2.50 = + $ 2.50
$426.50 (cost of ending inventory)

18–27. Over the past three years, the gross profit rate for Jini Company was 35%. Last week a fire destroyed all of Jini's inventory. Using the gross profit method, estimate the cost of inventory destroyed in the fire given the following facts that were recorded in a fireproof safe:

Beginning inventory	$ 6,000
Net purchases	64,000
Net sales at retail	49,000

Goods available for sale

Beginning inventory		$ 6,000
Net purchases		64,000
Cost of goods available for sale		$70,000
Less: Estimated cost of goods sold:		
Net sales at retail	$49,000	
Cost percentage (100% − 35%)	.65	
Estimated cost of goods sold		31,850
Estimated ending inventory		$38,150

Challenge Problem
Calculating Sales When Inventory Markup Known

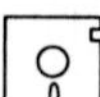

18–28. Monroe Company had a beginning inventory of 350 cans of paint at $12 each on January 1 at a cost of $4,200. During the year, the following purchases were made:

February 15	280 cans at $14.00
April 30	110 cans at $14.50
July 1	100 cans at $15.00

Monroe marks up its goods at 40% on cost. At the end of the year, ending inventory showed 105 units remaining. Calculate the amount of sales assuming a FIFO flow of inventory.

Beginning inventory	350 at $12.00 =	$ 4,200
February 15	280 at $14.00 =	3,920
April 30	110 at $14.50 =	1,595
July 1	100 at $15.00 =	1,500
	840 cans	$11,215 (total cost)

840 cans
− 105 cans (end. inv.)
735 sold

Sold: 350 cans at retail = $4,200 × 1.4 = $ 5,880.00
(cost + 40%)
280 cans at $14 = $3,920.00 × 1.4 = 5,488.00
105 cans at $14.50 = $1,522.50 × 1.4 = 2,131.50
$13,499.50

Summary Practice Test

Solutions are at end of text in Appendix II.

Quick Reference

If you get any wrong answers, study the page numbers given for each problem.

1. Pp. 400–404.

8 at $1.25 =	*$10.00*
3 at $1.50 =	*4.50*
5 at $2.00 =	*10.00*
6 at $2.50 =	*15.00*
10 at $3.00 =	*30.00*
32	*$69.50*

1. A toy store has beginning inventory of 8 sets of paints at a cost of $1.25 each. During the year, the toy store purchased 3 at $1.50; 5 at $2.00; 6 at $2.50, and 10 at $3.00. By the end of the year, 21 sets were sold. Calculate (**a**) the number of paint sets in stock and (**b**) the cost of ending inventory under LIFO, FIFO, and weighted average.

a. Ending inventory = 32 − 21 = 11

b.

LIFO		FIFO		Weighted average
8 at $1.25 =	$10.00	10 at $3.00 =	$30.00	$\frac{\$69.50}{32} = \$\ 2.17$
3 at $1.50 =	4.50	1 at $2.50 =	2.50	
Ending inv.	$14.50		$32.50	11 × $2.17 = $23.87

2. Pp. 407–8.

2. Janson Company allocates overhead expenses to all departments on the basis of floor space (square feet) occupied by each department. The total overhead expenses for a recent year amounted to $60,000. Department A occupied 13,200 square feet; Department B, 6,800 square feet; and Department C, 5,000 square feet. What is the amount of the overhead allocated to Department C?

13,200
6,800
5,000
25,000 square feet

$$\text{Dept. C} = \frac{5{,}000}{25{,}000} = .20 \qquad .20 \times \$60{,}000 = \$12{,}000$$

3. P. 406.

3. Johnson Company has a beginning inventory at a cost of $66,900 and an ending inventory costing $80,400. Sales were $294,000. Assume Johnson's markup rate on selling price is 35%. Based on the selling price, what is the inventory turnover at cost? Round to nearest hundredth.

Cost of goods is .65 × $294,000 = $191,100

$$\frac{\$191{,}100}{\frac{\$66{,}900 + \$80{,}400}{2}} = \frac{\$191{,}100}{\$73{,}650} = 2.59$$

4. P. 405.

4. Johnson Dress Shop's inventory at cost on January 1 was $28,700. Its retail value is $47,000. During the year, Johnson purchased additional merchandise at a cost of $185,000 with a retail value of $380,000. The net sales at retail for the year was $308,000. Could you calculate Johnson's inventory at cost by the retail method? Round cost ratio to nearest whole percent.

	Cost	Retail
Beginning inventory	$ 28,700	$ 47,000
Purchases	185,000	380,000
Cost of goods available for sale	$213,700	$427,000
Less net sales for year		308,000
Ending inventory at retail		$119,000
Cost ratio ($213,700 ÷ $427,000)		50%
Ending inventory at cost .50 × $119,000		$ 59,500

5. P. 406.

5. Janet Company on January 1 had inventory costing $40,000 and during January had net purchases of $112,000. Over recent years, Janet's gross profit has averaged 35% on sales. Given that the company has net sales of $170,000, calculate the estimated cost of ending inventory using the gross profit method:

Goods available for sale		
Inventory, January 1		$ 40,000
Net purchases		112,000
Cost of goods available for sale		$152,000
Less: Estimated cost of goods sold:		
Net sales at retail	$170,000	
Cost percentage (100% − 35%)	.65	
Estimated cost of goods sold		110,500
Estimated inventory, January 31		$ 41,500

BUSINESS MATH SCRAPBOOK

Project A

LIFO INVENTORIES hit by disasters may raise tax liabilities, a CPA says.

Last-in, first-out accounting is a popular way to offset inflation. A concern with a supply of a product that has risen in cost over time, say to $5 from $1, writes off the new $5 item first against sales income, to hold down taxable profit. But companies that lose and replace fully insured LIFO inventories as the result of an earthquake or other disaster may provide Uncle Sam with an unexpected tax windfall, Thomas Ochsenschlager of Grant Thornton says.

If the inventory can't be replaced in full by the end of the tax year, the individual items are valued differently. Instead of ranging from $1 to $5 as before, replacement costs are averaged; each item is valued at, say, $3. If sales exceed additions to inventory, the first item sold from inventory has a deductible cost of $3 instead of $5, Ochsenschlager says; that increases the taxable profit and leaves the company worse off than before. Ochsenschlager favors a law change to prevent that effect.

Visit a local store and find out how they value their inventory.

Project B

Given an overhead of $120,000, please allocate to the departments based on square footage.

Fresh produce	20%
Meat	25
Bakery	10
Grocery	30
Dairy	15

Fresh produce	.20 × $120,000 =	$ 24,000
Meat	.25 × 120,000 =	30,000
Bakery	.10 × 120,000 =	12,000
Grocery	.30 × 120,000 =	36,000
Dairy	.15 × 120,000 =	18,000
		$120,000

Fresh-Food Era Leaves Tin Can Lacking Luster

By Robert Johnson
Staff Reporter of The Wall Street Journal

Industry observers feel the toughest competition facing canned foods is coming from supermarket fresh-produce departments, which currently occupy about 20% of a store's floor space. "We recently asked 2,000 consumers to draw their ideal supermarket and it was 80% fresh produce," says Faith Popcorn, owner of BrainReserve, a New York advertising and marketing firm.

NOTES

INTRODUCING THE MOST EXTRAORDINARY NEW TIRE YOU'VE EVER SEEN.

AQUATRED. ONLY FROM GOODYEAR.

THAT WAS THEN . . .
. . . THIS IS NOW

Unlike the person during the Depression in 1934 who bought the "G-3" tire in the ad, today in most states when you buy tires, as well as other "luxury" goods, you will pay an excise tax and a sales tax on them.

19

Sales, Excise, and Property Tax

LEARNING UNIT OBJECTIVES

LU 19–1: Sales and Excise Taxes

1. Compute sales tax on goods sold involving trade and cash discounts and shipping charges. *pp. 420–21.*
2. Explain and calculate excise tax. *p. 422.*

LU 19–2: Property Tax

1. Define assessed valuation and mills. *p. 423.*
2. Calculate the tax rate in decimal. *p. 423.*
3. Convert tax rate in decimal to percent, per $100 of assessed valuation, per $1,000 of assessed valuation, and in mills. *p. 423.*
4. Compute property tax due. *p. 424.*

Did you know that:

1. A .25% temporary sales tax for earthquake repairs in California raised $767 million?
2. Coupon holders still pay sales tax on certain items?
3. Usually a rebate on a car doesn't cover the price that is subject to sales tax?
4. Merchants pay fees to credit card companies like MasterCard based on their *total* sales (including sales tax)?

Learning Unit 19–1 should make these facts more meaningful as you study the calculation of sales taxes.

LEARNING UNIT 19–1 SALES AND EXCISE TAXES

Today, many states have been raising their sales and excise taxes. Also, states have been gradually dropping some of their sales tax exemptions. In Connecticut, a 6% sales tax was imposed on newspapers sold at newsstands but not through subscriptions. Connecticut also imposed a 6% sales tax at vending machines. State sales and excise taxes will probably remain with us always.

Sales Tax

In many cities, counties, and states, sellers of certain goods and services collect **sales tax** and forward it to the appropriate government agency. Forty-five states have a sales tax. Sales taxes vary from 4% to 10%. Residents of New Orleans pay a 4% state sales tax and a 5% local sales tax. Due to the special taxing district, the sales tax at New Orleans International is 10%—the highest in the United States. The list of items not taxed varies from state to state. Of the 45 states with sales tax, 28 and the District of Columbia exempt food; 44 and the District of Columbia exempt prescription drugs.

Before sellers compute sales tax, they subtract all trade discounts from the original selling price. The cost of shipping, handling, and so on, are not subject to sales tax. Sellers add these costs after they calculate the tax. Sellers also take cash discounts on the base price before adding the sales tax. Figure 19–1 shows how sellers tax cold cups and paper plates at 5% but exempt edible foods.

To show how sellers calculate sales tax manually and with a table, let's look at the following example of a car battery.

EXAMPLE

Selling price of a Sears battery	$32.00
Trade discount	10.50
Shipping charge	3.50
Sales tax	5%

Manual calculation

$32.00 (selling price)	−	$10.50 (trade discount)	=	$21.50	taxable
				× 1.05	← 100% is base; 5% is tax; 105% is total
				$22.58	
				+ 3.50	shipping
				$26.08	

In decimal, 105% is 1.05.

Table calculation

Now let's use Table 19–1 to calculate the car battery's sales tax. This table is used by a state with a 5% sales tax. Note that Table 19–1 goes up to $30.09. After this, sellers calculate the tax at 5%. Also note that Table 19–1 states that sellers must compute the tax on the *total sale* and not on the prices of individual items included in the sale. Using Table 19–1, we calculate the sales tax of the battery as follows:

$32.00 (selling price)	−	$10.50 (trade discount)	=	$21.50	taxable
				+ 1.08	sales tax by Table 19–1
				$22.58	
				+ 3.50	shipping
				$26.08	

FIGURE 19–1
Taxing of Paper Products but Not Food

```
S&S COLD CUP80CT        1.53 TX
FLEISH MARGARINE        1.19*
   4.76LB @ .99/ LB        T
CHILL FLMD GRAPE        4.71*
SG PLT 9IN 100CT         .91 TX
BREAK TEMPTEE12Z        1.51*
X LRGE CANTELOPE        1.29*
LNDR ONION BAGEL         .79*
          TOTAL   $    12.05
          CASH TEND    20.05

          SUBTOTAL     11.93
          TAX PAID  →    .12

        8.00 CHANGE
```

$1.53
+ .91
$2.44
× .05
.122 = 12¢

TABLE 19–1
Tax Table

MASSACHUSETTS DEPARTMENT OF REVENUE
5% SALES TAX SCHEDULE
INCLUDING MEALS, PREPARED FOOD AND/OR ALCOHOLIC BEVERAGES,

AMOUNT OF SALE	TAX	AMOUNT OF SALE	TAX
$.10 - $.29	$.01	$7.70 - $7.89	$.39
.30 - .49	.02	7.90 - 8.09	.40
.50 - .69	.03	8.10 - 8.29	.41
.70 - .89	.04	8.30 - 8.49	.42
.90 - 1.09	.05	8.50 - 8.69	.43
1.10 - 1.29	.06	8.70 - 8.89	.44
1.30 - 1.49	.07	8.90 - 9.09	.45
1.50 - 1.69	.08	9.10 - 9.29	.46
1.70 - 1.89	.09	9.30 - 9.49	.47
1.90 - 2.09	.10	9.50 - 9.69	.48
2.10 - 2.29	.11	9.70 - 9.89	.49
2.30 - 2.49	.12	9.90 - 10.09	.50
2.50 - 2.69	.13	10.10 - 10.29	.51
2.70 - 2.89	.14	10.30 - 10.49	.52
2.90 - 3.09	.15	10.50 - 10.69	.53
3.10 - 3.29	.16	10.70 - 10.89	.54
3.30 - 3.49	.17	10.90 - 11.09	.55
3.50 - 3.69	.18	11.10 - 11.29	.56
3.70 - 3.89	.19	11.30 - 11.49	.57
3.90 - 4.09	.20	11.50 - 11.69	.58
4.10 - 4.29	.21	11.70 - 11.89	.59
4.30 - 4.49	.22	11.90 - 12.09	.60
4.50 - 4.69	.23	12.10 - 12.29	.61
4.70 - 4.89	.24	12.30 - 12.49	.62
4.90 - 5.09	.25	12.50 - 12.69	.63
5.10 - 5.29	.26	12.70 - 12.89	.64
5.30 - 5.49	.27	12.90 - 13.09	.65
5.50 - 5.69	.28	13.10 - 13.29	.66
5.70 - 5.89	.29	13.30 - 13.49	.67
5.90 - 6.09	.30	13.50 - 13.69	.68
6.10 - 6.29	.31	13.70 - 13.89	.69
6.30 - 6.49	.32	13.90 - 14.09	.70
6.50 - 6.69	.33	14.10 - 14.29	.71
6.70 - 6.89	.34	14.30 - 14.49	.72
6.90 - 7.09	.35	14.50 - 14.69	.73
7.10 - 7.29	.36	14.70 - 14.89	.74
7.30 - 7.49	.37	14.90 - 15.09	.75
7.50 - 7.69	.38	15.10 - 15.29	.76

CONTINUED ON REVERSE →

SC/NH-775

SC/NH/775B

AMOUNT OF SALE	TAX	AMOUNT OF SALE	TAX
$15.30 - $15.49	$ .77	$22.70 - $22.89	$1.14
15.50 - 15.69	.78	22.90 - 23.09	1.15
15.70 - 15.89	.79	23.10 - 23.29	1.16
15.90 - 16.09	.80	23.30 - 23.49	1.17
16.10 - 16.29	.81	23.50 - 23.69	1.18
16.30 - 16.49	.82	23.70 - 23.89	1.19
16.50 - 16.69	.83	23.90 - 24.09	1.20
16.70 - 16.89	.84	24.10 - 24.29	1.21
16.90 - 17.09	.85	24.30 - 24.49	1.22
17.10 - 17.29	.86	24.50 - 24.69	1.23
17.30 - 17.49	.87	24.70 - 24.89	1.24
17.50 - 17.69	.88	24.90 - 25.09	1.25
17.70 - 17.89	.89	25.10 - 25.29	1.26
17.90 - 18.09	.90	25.30 - 25.49	1.27
18.10 - 18.29	.91	25.50 - 25.69	1.28
18.30 - 18.49	.92	25.70 - 25.89	1.29
18.50 - 18.69	.93	25.90 - 26.09	1.30
18.70 - 18.89	.94	26.10 - 26.29	1.31
18.90 - 19.09	.95	26.30 - 26.49	1.32
19.10 - 19.29	.96	26.50 - 26.69	1.33
19.30 - 19.49	.97	26.70 - 26.89	1.34
19.50 - 19.69	.98	26.90 - 27.09	1.35
19.70 - 19.89	.99	27.10 - 27.29	1.36
19.90 - 20.09	1.00	27.30 - 27.49	1.37
20.10 - 20.29	1.01	27.50 - 27.69	1.38
20.30 - 20.49	1.02	27.70 - 27.89	1.39
20.50 - 20.69	1.03	27.90 - 28.09	1.40
20.70 - 20.89	1.04	28.10 - 28.29	1.41
20.90 - 21.09	1.05	28.30 - 28.49	1.42
21.10 - 21.29	1.06	28.50 - 28.69	1.43
21.30 - 21.49	1.07	28.70 - 28.89	1.44
21.50 - 21.69	1.08	28.90 - 29.09	1.45
21.70 - 21.89	1.09	29.10 - 29.29	1.46
21.90 - 22.09	1.10	29.30 - 29.49	1.47
22.10 - 22.29	1.11	29.50 - 29.69	1.48
22.30 - 22.49	1.12	29.70 - 29.89	1.49
22.50 - 22.69	1.13	29.90 - 30.09	1.50

ON ANY CHARGE OVER $30.09, ADAPT ABOVE AMOUNTS OR MULTIPLY BY .05.
THE TAX MUST BE COMPUTED ON THE TOTAL SALE AND NOT ON PRICES OF INDIVIDUAL ITEMS INCLUDED IN THE SALE.
ST-3, 5% Rate COMMISSIONER OF REVENUE

In this example, if the buyer is entitled to a 6% cash discount, the seller first calculates the amount and discount:

$$.06 \times \$21.50 = \$1.29$$

Remember we do not take cash discounts on the sales tax or shipping charges.

Calculating Actual Sales

Hint: $40,000 is 107% of actual sales.

Managers often use the cash register to get a summary of total sales for the day. The total sales figure includes the sales tax. So the sales tax must be deducted from the total sales. To illustrate this, let's assume the total sales for the day were $40,000, which included a 7% sales tax. What were the actual sales?

$$\text{Actual sales} = \frac{\text{Total sales}}{1 + \text{Tax}}$$

Total sales

$$\text{Actual sales} = \frac{\$40{,}000}{1.07} = \$37{,}383.18$$

100%	sales
7%	tax
107% → 1.07	

Thus, the store's actual sales are $37,383.18. The actual sales plus the tax equals the $40,000.

Check

$37,383.18 × .07 =	$ 2,616.82	sales tax
	+ 37,383.18	actual sales
	$40,000.00	total sales including sales tax

Excise Tax

Howard Davis/FPG International, Inc.

Governments (local, federal, and state) levy **excise tax** on particular products and services. Effective 1991, higher excise tax will result in an extra $66 billion over the next five years.

Consumers pay the excise tax in addition to the sales tax. The excise tax is based on a percent of the *retail* price of a product or service. This tax, which varies in different states, is imposed on luxury items or nonessentials. Examples of products or services subject to the excise tax include airline travel, telephone service, alcoholic beverages, jewelry, furs, fishing rods, tobacco products, motor vehicles, and so on. Although excise tax is often calculated as a percentage of the selling price, the tax can be stated as a fixed amount per item sold. The following example calculates excise tax as a percentage of the selling price.[1]

EXAMPLE On June 1, Angel Rowe bought a fur coat for a retail price of $5,000. Sales tax is 7% with an excise tax of 8%. Her total cost is as follows:

$5,000	
+ 350	sales tax (.07 × $5,000)
+ 400	excise tax (.08 × $5,000)
$5,750	

Let's check your progress with a Practice Quiz.

LU 19–1 PRACTICE QUIZ

From the following shopping list, calculate the total sales tax (food items are excluded from sales tax, which is 8%):

Chicken	$6.10	Orange juice	$1.29
Lettuce	.75	Laundry detergent	3.65
Shampoo	4.10		

SOLUTION TO LU 19–1 PRACTICE QUIZ

Shampoo	$4.10
Laundry detergent	+ 3.65
	$7.75 × .08 = $.62

[1] If excise tax were a stated fixed amount per item it would have to be added to cost of goods or services before any sales tax were taken. For example, a $100 truck tire with a $4 excise tax would be $104 before calculating sales tax.

LEARNING UNIT 19–2 PROPERTY TAX

You cannot own property without paying property tax. In this unit, we listen in to a conversation between a property owner and a tax assessor.

Defining Assessed Valuation

Bill Adams became upset when he read in his local paper that his property tax rate had increased. Bill realizes that the revenue the town receives from his tax helps supply the funds for fire and police protection, schools, and other public services. However, Bill wants to know how his town set the new rate and what his new property tax will be.

Bill went to the town assessor's office to get specific details. The assessor is a local official who estimates the fair market value of a house. Before you read the summary of Bill's discussion, note the following formula:

$$\text{Assessed valuation} = \text{Assessment rate} \times \text{Market value}$$

Property Can Have Two Meanings

Both subject to property tax
1. ***Real property***—*land, buildings, etc.*
2. ***Personal property***—*possessions like jewelry, autos, furniture, etc.*

Bill What does **assessed valuation** mean?

Assessor *Assessed value* is the value of property for purposes of computing property taxes. We estimated the market value of your home at $210,000. In our town, we assess property at 30% of the market value. Thus, your home has an assessed value of $63,000 ($210,000 × .30). Usually, assessed value is rounded to the nearest dollar.

Bill I know that the **tax rate** times my assessed value ($63,000) determines the amount of my property tax. What I would like to know now is how did you set the new tax rate?

Determining Tax Rate

Assessor In our town, we estimate the total amount of revenue needed to meet our budget. We divide the total of all assessed property into this figure to get the *tax rate*. The formula looks like this:

$$\text{Tax rate} = \frac{\text{Budget needed}^{2}}{\text{Total assessed value}}$$

Our town budget is $125,000, and we have total assessed property value of $1,930,000. Using the formula, we have:

$$\frac{\$125{,}000}{\$1{,}930{,}000} = \$.0647668 = .0648 \text{ tax rate per dollar}$$

Note that the rate should be rounded up to the indicated digit, *even if less than 5*. Here we rounded to nearest ten thousandth.

How the Tax Rate Is Expressed

Assessor We can express the $.0648 tax rate in the following forms:

By percent	Per $100 of assessed valuation	Per $1,000 of assessed valuation	In mills
6.48% (Move decimal two places to right.)	$6.48 (.0648 × 100)	$64.80 (.0648 × 1,000)	64.80 $\left(\frac{.0648}{.001}\right)$

[2] Keep in mind that exemptions include land and buildings used for educational and religious purposes and the like.

In the problems in this text, we round the mills per dollar to nearest hundredth.

A **mill** is an amount that represents $\frac{1}{10}$ of a cent or $\frac{1}{1,000}$ of a dollar (.001). To represent the number of mills as a tax rate per dollar, we divide the tax rate in decimal by .001. Rounding practices vary from state to state. An alternative to finding the rate in mills is to multiply the rate per dollars by 1,000 since there are 1,000 mills in a dollar.

How to Calculate Property Tax Due[3]

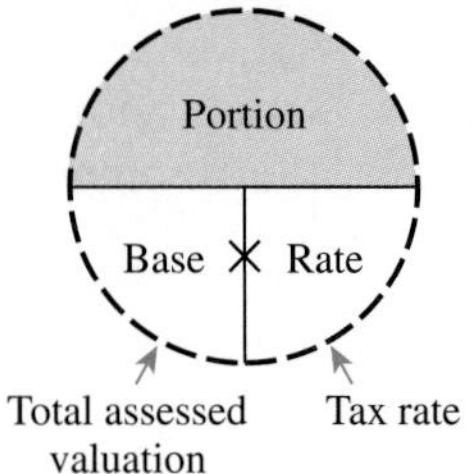

Assessor The following formula will show you how we arrive at your **property tax:**

Total property tax due (Portion)	=	Tax rate (Rate)	×	Total assessed valuation (Base)
↑		↑		↑
$4,082.40	=	.0648	×	$63,000

We can use the other forms of the decimal tax rate to show you how the property tax will not change even when expressed in various forms:

By percent	Per $100	Per $1,000	Mills
6.48% × $63,000 = $4,082.40	$\frac{\$63,000}{\$100} = 630$ 630 × $6.48 = $4,082.40	$\frac{\$63,000}{\$1,000} = 63$ 63 × $64.80 = $4,082.40	Property tax due = Mills × .001 × Assessed value = 64.80 × .001 × $63,000 = $4,082.40

What Is the Estimated Annual Property Tax on a $100,000 Home?

State	Annual bill	State	Annual bill	State	Annual bill	State	Annual bill
Alabama	$ 380	Indiana	$1,130	Nebraska	$2,310	Rhode Island	$1,930
Alaska	1,350	Iowa	1,750	Nevada	1,130	South Carolina	840
Arizona	740	Kansas	930	New Hampshire	1,730	South Dakota	1,690
Arkansas	1,420	Kentucky	1,140	New Jersey	2,530	Tennessee	1,420
California	1,040	Louisiana	280	New Mexico	1,140	Texas	1,680
Colorado	1,010	Maine	1,420	New York	2,750	Utah	1,030
Connecticut	1,530	Maryland	1,250	North Carolina	1,070	Vermont	1,600
Delaware	790	Massachusetts	2,430	North Dakota	1,010	Virginia	1,390
Florida	920	Michigan	2,740	Ohio	1,070	Washington	950
Georgia	1,210	Minnesota	790	Oklahoma	820	West Virginia	370
Hawaii	360	Mississippi	860	Oregon	1,560	Wisconsin	1,750
Idaho	940	Missouri	950	Pennsylvania	1,500	Wyoming	470
Illinois	1,470	Montana	1,080				

Now it's time to try the Practice Quiz.

[3] Some states have credits available to reduce what the homeowner actually pays. For example, 42 out of 50 states give tax breaks to people over 65. In Alaska, $150,000 of assessed value is excluded from property tax for senior citizens.

LU 19–2 PRACTICE QUIZ

From the following facts: (1) calculate assessed value of Bill's home; (2) calculate the tax rate for the community in decimal (to nearest ten thousandths); (3) convert the decimal to (**a**) %, (**b**) per $100 of assessed valuation, (**c**) per $1,000 of assessed valuation, and (**d**) in mills (to nearest hundredth); and (4) calculate the property tax due on Bill's home in decimal, per $100, per $1,000, and in mills.

Given

Assessed market value	40%	Total budget needed	$ 176,000
Market value of Bill's home	$ 210,000	Total assessed value	1,910,000

SOLUTIONS TO LU 19–2 PRACTICE QUIZ

1. .40 × $210,000 = $84,000

2. $\frac{\$176,000}{\$1,910,000} = .0922$

3. a. .0922 = 9.22%

b. .0922 × 100 = $9.22

c. .0922 × 1,000 = $92.20

d. $\frac{.0922}{.001}$ = 92.20 mills (or .0922 × 1,000)

4. .0922 × $84,000 = $7,744.80
$9.22 × 840 = $7,744.80
$92.20 × 84 = $7,744.80
92.20 × .001 × $84,000 = $7,744.80

CHAPTER ORGANIZER: A REFERENCE GUIDE

Page	Topic	Key point, procedure, formula	Example(s) to illustrate situation
420	Sales tax	Sales tax is not calculated on trade discounts. Shipping charges, etc., also not subject to sales tax. $\text{Actual sales} = \frac{\text{Total sales}}{1 + \text{Tax}}$ Cash discounts are calculated on sale price before sales tax is added on.	Calculate sales tax: Purchased 12 bags of mulch at $59.40; 10% trade discount; 5% sales tax. $59.40 − $5.94 = $53.46 $53.46 × .05 $2.67 sales tax Any cash discount would be calculated on $53.46.
422	Excise tax	Excise tax is calculated separately from sales tax and is an additional tax. It is based as a percent of the selling price. It could be stated as a fixed amount per item sold. In that case, the excise tax would be added to cost of item before any sales tax calculations. Rate for excise tax will vary.	Jewelry $4,000 retail price Sales tax 7% Excise tax 10% $4,000 + 280 sales tax + 400 excise tax $4,680
423	Assessed valuation	Assessment rate × Market value	$100,000 house; rate, 30%; $30,000 assessed value.
423	Tax rate	$\frac{\text{Budget needed}}{\text{Total assessed value}} = \text{Tax rate}$ (Round rate up to indicated digit even if less than 5.)	$\frac{\$800,000}{\$9,200,000}$ = $.08695 = $.0870 tax rate per $1
423	Expressing tax rate in other forms	1. Percent: Move decimal two places to right. Add % sign. 2. Per $100: Multiply by 100. 3. Per $1,000: Multiply by 1,000 4. Mills: Divide by .001.	1. .0870 = 8.7% 2. $.0870 × 100 = $8.70 3. $.0870 × 1,000 = $87 4. $\frac{.0870}{.001}$ = 87 mills

Page	Topic	Key point, procedure, formula	Example(s) to illustrate situation
424	Calculating property tax	Total property tax due = Tax rate × Total assessed valuation Various forms: 1. Percent × Assessed value 2. Per \$100: $\frac{\text{Assessed value}}{\$100} \times \text{Rate}$ 3. Per \$1,000: $\frac{\text{Assessed value}}{\$1{,}000} \times \text{Rate}$ 4. Mills: Mills × .001 × Assessed value	*Example:* Rate \$.0870 per \$1; \$30,000 assessed value 1. (.087) 8.7% × \$30,000 = \$2,610 2. $\frac{\$30{,}000}{\$100} = 300 \times \$8.70 = \$2{,}610$ 3. $\frac{\$30{,}000}{\$1{,}000} = 30 \times \$87 = \$2{,}610$ 4. $\frac{.0870}{.001} = 87$ mills 87 mills × .001 × \$30,000 = \$2,610
	Key terms	Assessed valuation, *p. 423* Excise tax, *p. 422* Mill, *p. 424* Personal property, *p. 423*	Property tax, *p. 424* Real property, *p. 423* Sales tax, *p. 420* Tax rate, *p. 423*

END-OF-CHAPTER PROBLEMS

Drill Problems

Additional homework assignments by learning unit are at the end of text in Appendix I (p. I–84). Solutions to odd problems are at the end of text in Appendix II.

Calculate the following without sales tax table:

	Retail selling price		Sales tax (6%)		Excise tax (8%)	Total price including taxes
19–1.	$ 800	+	$48 ($800 × .06)	+	$64 ($800 × .08)	$ 912
19–2.	$1,200	+	$72 ($1,200 × .06)	+	$96 ($1,200 × .08)	$1,368

Calculate sales tax by Table 19–1 and final total purchase price:

19–3. $17.95 laundry detergent, $2.50 trade discount, and $1.00 shipping charge.

$17.95 − $2.50 = $15.45

By Table 19–1, tax is $.77

$15.45
+ .77
$16.22
+ 1.00 shipping
$17.22

Calculate the actual sales since the sales and sales tax were rung up together; assume a 6% sales tax (round answer to nearest cent):

19–4. $\frac{\$28{,}000}{1.06} = \$26{,}415.09$

19–5. $\frac{\$26{,}000}{1.06} = \$24{,}528.30$

Calculate the assessed valuation of the following pieces of property:

	Assessment rate		Market value		Assessed valuation
19–6.	40%	×	$105,000	=	$ 42,000
19–7.	80%	×	$210,000	=	$168,000

Calculate the tax rate in decimal form to nearest ten thousandth:

	Required budget		Total assessed value		Tax rate per dollar
19–8.	$920,000	÷	$39,500,000	=	$.0233

Complete the following:

	Tax rate per dollar	In percent	Per $100	Per $1,000	
19–9.	$.0956	9.56% (.0956)	$9.56 ($.0956 × 100)	$95.60 ($.0956 × 1,000)	95.60 $\left(\frac{.0956}{.001}\right)$
19–10.	$.0699	6.99% (.0699)	$6.99 ($.0699 × 100)	$69.90 ($.0699 × 1,000)	69.90 $\left(\frac{.0699}{.001}\right)$

Complete the amount of property tax due to nearest cent for each situation:

	Tax rate	Assessed valuation	Amount of property tax due
19–11.	30 mills × .001 ×	$ 90,000	= $ 2,700
19–12.	$42.50 per $1,000	($105,000 ÷ $1,000) × $42.50	= $ 4,462.50
19–13.	$8.75 per $100	($125,000 ÷ $100) × $8.75	= $10,937.50
19–14.	$94.10 per $1,000	($180,500 ÷ $1,000) × $94.10	= $16,985.05

Word Problems

19–15. Tom Fall bought a \$60 fishing rod that is subject to a 5% sales tax and a 10% excise tax. What is the total amount Tom paid for the rod?

\$60 + \$3 + \$6 = \$69
(\$60 × .05) (\$60 × .10)

19–16. Don Chather bought a new computer for \$1,995. This included a 6% sales tax. What is the amount of sales tax and the selling price before the tax?

$\frac{\$1{,}995}{1.06}$ = \$1,882.08 actual sale \$1,995 − \$1,882.08 = \$112.92 sales tax

19–17. Al's warehouse has a market value of \$212,000. The property in Al's area is assessed at 30% of the market value. The tax rate is \$105.40 per \$1,000 of assessed valuation. What is Al's property tax?

$\$212{,}000 \times .30 = \frac{\$63{,}600}{\$1{,}000} = 63.6 \times \$105.40 = \$6{,}703.44$

19–18. In the community of Ross, the market value of a home is \$200,000. The assessment rate is 40%. What is the assessed value?

.40 × \$200,000 = \$80,000

19–19. Moe Blunt bought a hammer from Jan's Hardware Store for \$14.55 plus tax. Jan rang up the sale and looked at her sales tax chart (use Table 19–1). How much is the total of the sale?

\$14.55 + \$.73 = \$15.28
(from Table 19–1)

19–20. Sheri Missan bought a ring for \$6,000. She must still pay a 5% sales tax and a 10% excise tax. The jeweler is shipping the ring so Sheri must also pay a \$40 shipping charge. What is the total purchase price of Sheri's ring?

\$6,000
300 (.05 × \$6,000) sales tax
600 (.10 × \$6,000) excise tax
40 shipping
\$6,940

19–21. Blunt County needs \$700,000 from property tax to meet its budget. The total value of assessed property in Blunt is \$110,000,000. What is the tax rate of Blunt? Round to nearest ten thousandths. Express the rate in mills.

$\frac{\$700{,}000}{\$110{,}000{,}000} = .0064 \quad \frac{.0064}{.001} = 6.40 \text{ mills}$

19–22. Bill Shass pays a property tax of \$3,200. In his community, the tax rate is 50 mills. What is Bill's assessed valuation?

$\text{Mills} \times .001 \times A = \$3{,}200$
$50 \times .001 \times A = \$3{,}200$
$.05A = \$3{,}200$
$A = \$64{,}000$

19–23. The home of Bill Burton is assessed at \$80,000. The tax rate is 18.50 mills. What is the tax on Bill's home?

18.50 × .001 × \$80,000 = \$1,480

19–24. The building of Bill's Hardware is assessed at \$105,000. The tax rate is \$88.95 per \$1,000 of assessed valuation. What is the tax due?

$\frac{\$105{,}000}{\$1{,}000} = 105 \times \$88.95 = \$9{,}339.75$

19–25. Bill Blake pays a property tax of \$2,500. In his community, the tax rate is 55 mills. What is Bill's assessed valuation? Round to the nearest dollar.

$\text{Mills} \times .001 \times A = \$2{,}500$
$55 \times .001 \times A = \$2{,}500$
$.055\,A = \$2{,}500$
$A = \$45{,}455$

19–26. Ginny Fieg expanded her beauty salon by increasing her space by 20%. Ginny paid property taxes of \$2,800 at 22 mills. The new rate is now 24 mills. As Ginny's accountant, estimate what she may have to pay for property taxes this year. Round

Hint: Calculate assessed valuation (round to nearest dollar) before expansion and multiply by 1.2 for new assessed valuation after addition.

final answer to nearest dollar. In calculation, round assessed value to nearest dollar.

$22 \times .001 \times A = \$2,800; A = \frac{\$2,800}{.022} = \$127,272.72$

$\$127,273 \times 1.2 = \$152,728$

$24 \text{ mills} \times .001 \times \$152,728 = \$3,665.47 = \$3,665$

Challenge Problem
Real Estate Rental

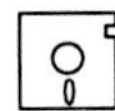

19–27. Art Neuner, an investor in real estate, bought an office condominium. The market value of the condo was $250,000 with a 70% assessment rate. Art feels that his return should be 12% per month on his investment after all expenses. The tax rate is $31.50 per thousand. Art estimates it will cost $275 per month to cover general repairs, insurance, and so on. He pays a $140 condo fee per month. All utilities and heat are the responsibility of the tenant. Could you calculate monthly rent for Art? Round to nearest dollar (at intermediate stages).

$250,000 × .70 = $175,000 assessed value

Tax = 175 × $31.50 =	$5,512.50	Tax	
	+ 3,300.00	($275 × 12)	Repairs and insurance
	+ 1,680.00	($140 × 12)	Condo fee
	$10,492.50 ÷ 12 = $874		

$874 × 1.12 = $978.88 = $979

Summary Practice Test

Solutions are at end of text in Appendix II.

Quick Reference
If you get any wrong answers study the page numbers given for each problem.

1. John Morris bought a new IBM computer for $2,600. This price included 8% sales tax. What is the sales tax and the selling price before the tax?

1. P. 421.

$\frac{\$2,600}{1.08} = \$2,407.41$ actual sale

$2,600.00
− 2,407.41
$ 192.59 sales tax

2. Daniel Miller bought a ring for $6,400. He must pay a 6% sales tax and a 10% excise tax. The jeweler is shipping the ring so Daniel must also pay a $20 shipping charge. What is the total purchase price of Daniel's ring?

2. P. 422.

$6,400
+ 384 (.06 × $6,400) sales tax
+ 640 (.10 × $6,400) excise tax
+ 20 shipping charge
$7,444

3. P. 423.

3. In the community of Straus, the market value of a home is $180,000. The assessment rate is 35%. What is the assessed value?

.35 × $180,000 = $63,000

4. P. 423.

4. Blunt County needs $825,000 from property tax to meet its budget. The total value of assessed property in Blunt is $160,000,000. What is the tax rate of Blunt? Round to nearest ten thousandths. Express the rate in mills (to one tenth).

$\frac{\$825,000}{\$160,000,000} = \$.0051562 = \$.0052 \qquad \frac{.0052}{.001} = 5.2 \text{ mills}$

5. P. 423.

5. The home of Jim Burton is assessed at $60,000. The tax rate is 15.10 mills. What is the tax on Jim's home?

15.10 mills × .001 × $60,000 = $906

6. P. 424.

6. Mike's Warehouse has a market value of $6,000,000. The property in Mike's area is assessed at 30% of the market value. The tax rate is $151.50 per $1,000 of assessed valuation. What is Mike's property tax?

$\$6,000,000 \times .30 = \frac{\$1,800,000}{\$1,000}$

$= 1,800 \times \$151.50$

$= \$272,700$

Project A

1. Check the total tax.

2. Check the assessed value of $265,900.

3. Check the tax rate of $10.94 per $1,000.

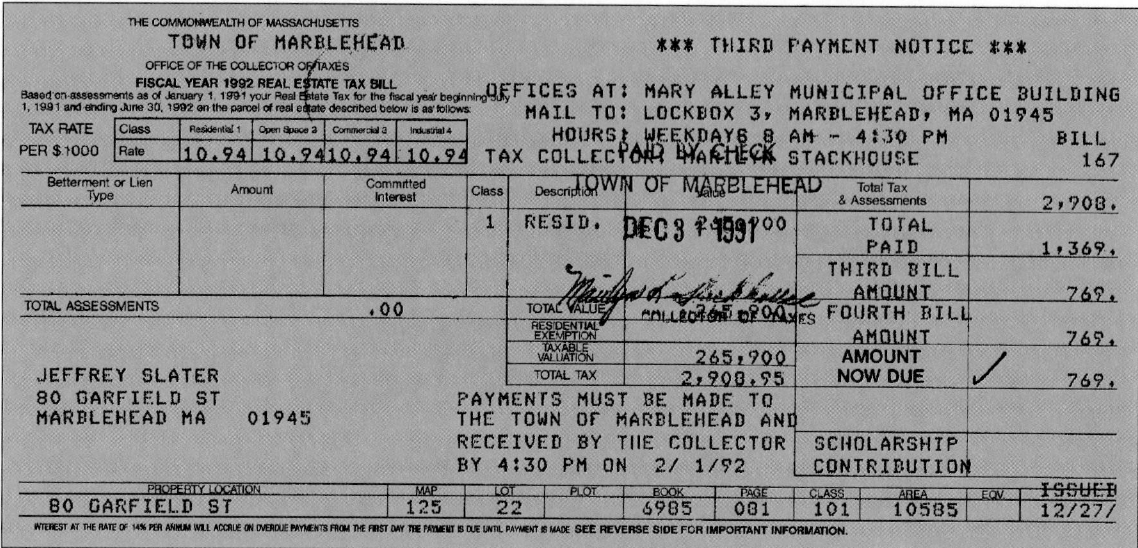

THE COMMONWEALTH OF MASSACHUSETTS
TOWN OF MARBLEHEAD
OFFICE OF THE COLLECTOR OF TAXES
FISCAL YEAR 1992 REAL ESTATE TAX BILL
Based on assessments as of January 1, 1991 your Real Estate Tax for the fiscal year beginning July 1, 1991 and ending June 30, 1992 on the parcel of real estate described below is as follows:

TAX RATE	Class	Residential 1	Open Space 3	Commercial 3	Industrial 4
PER $1000	Rate	10.94	10.94	10.94	10.94

*** THIRD PAYMENT NOTICE ***
OFFICES AT: MARY ALLEY MUNICIPAL OFFICE BUILDING
MAIL TO: LOCKBOX 3, MARBLEHEAD, MA 01945
HOURS: WEEKDAYS 8 AM - 4:30 PM
TAX COLLECTOR: MARILYN STACKHOUSE
BILL 167

PAID BY CHECK
TOWN OF MARBLEHEAD
DEC 3 1991
COLLECTOR OF TAXES

Betterment or Lien Type	Amount	Committed Interest	Class	Description	Value	Total Tax & Assessments	2,908.
			1	RESID.	265,900	TOTAL PAID	1,369.
						THIRD BILL AMOUNT	769.
TOTAL ASSESSMENTS		.00		TOTAL VALUE	265,900	FOURTH BILL AMOUNT	769.
				RESIDENTIAL EXEMPTION			
				TAXABLE VALUATION	265,900	AMOUNT NOW DUE	769.
				TOTAL TAX	2,908.95		

JEFFREY SLATER
80 GARFIELD ST
MARBLEHEAD MA 01945

PAYMENTS MUST BE MADE TO THE TOWN OF MARBLEHEAD AND RECEIVED BY THE COLLECTOR BY 4:30 PM ON 2/ 1/92

SCHOLARSHIP CONTRIBUTION

PROPERTY LOCATION	MAP	LOT	PLOT	BOOK	PAGE	CLASS	AREA	EQV.	ISSUED
80 GARFIELD ST	125	22		6985	081	101	10585		12/27/

INTEREST AT THE RATE OF 14% PER ANNUM WILL ACCRUE ON OVERDUE PAYMENTS FROM THE FIRST DAY THE PAYMENT IS DUE UNTIL PAYMENT IS MADE. SEE REVERSE SIDE FOR IMPORTANT INFORMATION.

1. $\frac{\$265{,}900}{\$1{,}000} = 265.9 \times \$10.94 = \$2{,}908.95$

2. $\frac{\$2{,}908.95}{\$10.94} = 265.9 \times \$1{,}000 = \$265{,}900$

3. $\frac{\$2{,}908.95}{\$265{,}900} = .01094 \times \$1{,}000 = \$10.94$

NOTES

IN A CHANGING WORLD,
ONE THING REMAINS ROCK SOLID.

THAT WAS THEN . . .
. . . THIS IS NOW

Whether in 1929 (as in the old ad) or the 1990s, Prudential uses the rock to represent protection and stability. Today there are many new types of insurance, such as universal life, that you as the consumer need to evaluate.

20

Life, Fire, and Auto Insurance

LEARNING UNIT OBJECTIVES

LU 20–1: Life Insurance

1. Define and calculate life insurance premiums and discuss the advantages and disadvantages of term, straight life, 20-payment life, 20-year endowment, and universal life. *pp. 434–37.*
2. Explain and calculate cash value and other nonforfeiture options if the insured stops paying or cancels straight life, 20-payment life, or 20-year endowment. *p. 436.*

LU 20–2: Fire Insurance

1. Explain and calculate premiums for fire insurance of buildings and their contents. *pp. 438–39.*
2. Calculate cost of premium and refund to be received using the short-rate table when insured cancels. *pp. 438–39.*
3. Explain and calculate insurance loss when coinsurance is not met. *pp. 439–40.*

LU 20–3: Auto Insurance

1. Explain some of the factors that an insurance company considers in setting its auto insurance rates. *p. 441.*
2. Compare and contrast bodily injury, comprehensive, and collision. *pp. 442–43.*
3. Calculate the annual premium cost of auto insurance for a typical driver. *p. 444.*

What is the best type of life insurance for you? If a serious fire occurs in your home or your parents' home, will there be enough insurance to rebuild? Do you have enough collision coverage on your car?

This chapter should answer many of your questions about life insurance, fire insurance, and auto insurance. We begin by studying life insurance.

LEARNING UNIT 20–1 LIFE INSURANCE

Bob Brady owns Bob's Deli, Bob is 40 years of age, married, and has three children. He wants to know what type of life insurance protection will best meet his needs. The following is a discussion between an insurance agent, Rick Jones, and Bob.

Bob I would like to buy a life insurance policy that would pay my wife $200,000 in the event of my death. The problem is that I don't have much cash. You know, bills, bills, bills. Could you explain some types of insurance and their costs?

Rick Let's first explain some life insurance terminology. The **insured** is the one receiving coverage. The **insurer** is the company selling the insurance policy. Your wife would be the **beneficiary.** As the beneficiary, she is the person named in the policy to receive the insurance proceeds at the death of the insured (that's you, Bob). The amount stated in the policy, say, $200,000, is the **face amount** of the policy. The **premium** is the periodic payments you agree to make for the cost of the insurance policy. You can pay premiums annually, semiannually, quarterly, or monthly. The more frequent the payment, the higher the total cost due to increased paperwork, billing, and so on. Now let's look at the different types of insurance.

Types of Insurance

In this section, Rick discusses term insurance, straight life (ordinary life), 20-payment life, 20-year endowment, and universal life insurance.

Term Insurance

Rick **Term insurance** is the cheapest type of insurance, but it only provides *temporary* protection. This type of insurance pays the face amount to your wife (beneficiary) only if you die within the period of the insurance (1, 5, 10 years, and so on). For example, let's say you take out a 5-year term policy. The company automatically allows you to renew the policy at increased rates until age 70. A new policy called **level premium term** may be less expensive than an annual term policy since each year for 50 years, and so on, the premium would be fixed.

The policy of my company lets you convert to other insurance types without a medical examination. To determine your rates under 5-year term insurance, check this table (Table 20–1). The annual premium at 40 years per $1,000 of insurance is $352. We can calculate the total yearly premium as follows:

> **Steps for Calculating Annual Life Insurance Premium**
>
> **Step 1.** Look up age and type of insurance in table (for females, subtract 3 years). This gives premium cost per $1,000.
>
> **Step 2.** Divide amount of coverage by $1,000 and multiply times premium cost per $1,000.

$$\frac{\$200{,}000 \text{ (coverage)}}{\$1{,}000} = 200 \times \$3.52 = \$704$$

(200: Number of thousands; $3.52: Cost per thousand for age 40; $704: Annual premium)

Buying flight insurance at an airport is a type of term insurance. After the flight, there is no protection or cash value.

From this formula, you can see that for $704 per year for the next 5 years, we offer to pay your wife $200,000 in case of your death. At the end of the 5th year, you are not entitled to any cash from your paid premiums. If you do not renew your policy (at a higher rate) and die on the 6th year, we would not pay your wife anything. Term insurance provides protection for only a specific period of time.

TABLE 20–1
Life Insurance Rates*

For females, subtract three years off age.

Age	Five-year term	Age	Straight life	Age	Twenty-payment life	Age	Twenty-year endowment
20	1.85	20	5.90	20	8.28	20	13.85
21	1.85	21	6.13	21	8.61	21	14.35
22	1.85	22	6.35	22	8.91	22	14.92
23	1.85	23	6.60	23	9.23	23	15.54
24	1.85	24	6.85	24	9.56	24	16.05
25	1.85	25	7.13	25	9.91	25	17.55
26	1.85	26	7.43	26	10.29	26	17.66
27	1.86	27	7.75	27	10.70	27	18.33
28	1.86	28	8.08	28	11.12	28	19.12
29	1.87	29	8.46	29	11.58	29	20.00
30	1.87	30	8.85	30	12.05	30	20.90
31	1.87	31	9.27	31	12.57	31	21.88
32	1.88	32	9.71	32	13.10	32	22.89
33	1.95	33	10.20	33	13.67	33	23.98
34	2.08	34	10.71	34	14.28	34	25.13
35	2.23	35	11.26	35	14.92	35	26.35
36	2.44	36	11.84	36	15.60	36	27.64
37	2.67	37	12.46	37	16.30	37	28.97
38	2.95	38	13.12	38	17.04	38	30.38
39	3.24	39	13.81	39	17.81	39	31.84
40	3.52	40	14.54	40	18.61	40	33.36
41	3.79	41	15.30	41	19.44	41	34.94
42	4.04	42	16.11	42	20.31	42	36.59
43	4.26	43	16.96	43	21.21	43	38.29
44	4.50	44	17.86	44	22.15	44	40.09

* Note these tables are a sampling of age groups, premium costs, and insurance coverage that are available under 45 years of age.

Bob Are you telling me that my premium does not build up any cash savings you call **cash value?**

Rick The term insurance policy does not build up cash savings. Let me show you a policy that does build up cash value. This policy is straight life.

Straight Life (Ordinary Life)

***Face value** is usually amount paid to beneficiary at time of insured's death.*

Rick **Straight life insurance** provides *permanent* protection rather than the temporary protection provided by term insurance. The insured pays the same premium each year or until death.[1] The premium for straight life is higher than for term insurance because straight life provides both protection and a built-in cash savings feature. According to our table (Table 20–1), your annual premium, Bob, would be:

$$\frac{\$200{,}000}{\$1{,}000} = 200 \times \$14.54 = \boxed{\$2{,}908} \text{ annual premium}$$

Bob Compared to term, straight life is quite expensive.

Rick Remember that term has no cash value accumulating like straight life. Let me show you another type of insurance that builds up cash value, called 20-payment life.

Twenty-Payment Life

Rick A **20-payment life** policy is similar to straight life in that it provides permanent protection and cash value but you only pay premiums for the first 20 years, after which you own **paid-up insurance.** According to my table (Table 20–1), your annual premium would be:

$$\frac{\$200{,}000}{\$1{,}000} = 200 \times \$18.61 = \boxed{\$3{,}722} \text{ annual premium}$$

[1] In the section on nonforfeiture values, we show how a policyholder in later years can stop making payments and still be covered by using the accumulated cash value built up.

Bob The 20-payment life policy is more expensive than straight life.

Rick This is because you are only paying for 20 years. The shorter period of time does result in increased yearly costs. Remember that in straight life you pay premiums over your entire life. Let me show you another alternative we call 20-year endowment.

Twenty-Year Endowment

Rick The **20-year endowment** insurance policy is the most expensive. It is a combination of term insurance and cash value. For example, from age 40 to 60, you receive term insurance protection in that your wife would receive $200,000 should you die. At age 60, your protection *ends* and you receive the face value of the policy which equals the $200,000 cash value. Let's use my table again (Table 20–1) to see how expensive the 20-year endowment is:

$$\frac{\$200{,}000}{\$1{,}000} = 200 \times \$33.36 = \$6{,}672 \text{ annual premium}$$

In summary, Bob here is a review of the costs for the various types of insurance we have talked about:

	5-year term	Straight life	20-payment life	20-year endowment
Premium cost per year	$704	$2,908	$3,722	$6,672

Before we proceed, I have another policy that may interest you—universal life.

Universal Life Insurance

Rick **Universal life** is basically a whole life insurance plan with flexible premium schedules and death benefits. Under whole life, the premiums and death benefits are fixed. Universal has limited guarantees with more risk on the holder of the policy. For example, if interest rates fall, the policyholder must pay higher premiums, increase the number of payments, or switch to smaller death benefits in the future.

Bob That policy is not for me—too much risk. I'd prefer fixed premiums and death benefits.

Rick Ok, let's look at how straight life, 20-payment life, and 20-year endowment can build up cash value and provide an opportunity for insurance coverage without paying additional premiums. We call these options **nonforfeiture values.**

Nonforfeiture Values

Rick Except for term insurance, the other types of life insurance build up cash value as you pay premiums. These policies provide three options should you, the **policyholder,** ever want to cancel your policy, stop paying premiums, or collect the cash value. My company lists these options here (Figure 20–1).

For example, Bob, Let's assume that at age 40 we sell you a $200,000 straight life policy. Assume that at age 55, after the policy has been in force for 15 years, you want to stop paying premiums. From this table (Table 20–2), I can show you the options that are available.

Insight into Business Insurance

Although we have concentrated on personal life insurance in this unit, you should be aware of some key types of business insurance that you may need in your business life. These could include fire insurance, business interruption insurance (business loss until physical damages are fixed), casualty insurance (insurance against a customer's suing your business due to an accident on company property), workers' compensation (insurance against injuries or sickness from being on the job), and group insurance (health and accident insurance). Should you need any of these types of insurance, be sure you shop around for the best price versus the desired coverage. In our next unit, we will look specifically at fire insurance.

Let's check your understanding of this unit with a Practice Quiz.

FIGURE 20–1
Nonforfeiture Options

Option 1: Cash value (cash surrender value)
a. Receive cash value of policy.
b. Policy is terminated.
The longer the policy has been in effect, the higher the cash value because more premiums have been paid in.

Option 2: Reduced paid-up insurance
a. Cash value buys protection without paying new premiums.
b. Face amount of policy is related to cash value buildup and age of insured. The **face amount is less than original policy.**
c. Policy continues for life (at a reduced face amount).

Option 3: Extended term insurance
a. Original face amount of policy continues for a certain period of time.
b. Length of policy depends on cash value built up and on insured's age.
c. This option results automatically if policyholder doesn't pay premiums and fails to elect another option.

TABLE 20–2 Nonforfeiture Options Based on $1,000 Face Value

Years insurance policy in force	Straight life				20-payment life				20-year endowment			
	Cash value	Amount of paid-up insurance	Extended term		Cash value	Amount of paid-up insurance	Extended term		Cash value	Amount of paid-up insurance	Extended term	
			Years	Day			Years	Day			Years	Day
5	29	86	9	91	71	220	19	190	92	229	23	140
10	96	259	18	76	186	521	28	195	319	520	30	160
15	148	371	20	165	317	781	32	176	610	790	35	300
20	265	550	21	300	475	1,000	Life		1,000	1,000	Life	

Option 1: Cash value
$$\frac{\$200,000}{\$1,000} = 200 \times \$148 = \$29,600$$
Option 2: Reduced paid-up insurance
$$\frac{\$200,000}{\$1,000} = 200 \times \$371 = \$74,200$$
Option 3: Extended term insurance
Bob could continue this $200,000 policy for 20 years and 165 days.

LU 20–1 PRACTICE QUIZ

1. Bill Boot, age 39, purchased a $60,000, 5-year term life insurance policy. Calculate his annual premium from Table 20–1. After 4 years, what is his cash value?
2. Ginny Katz, age 32, purchased a $78,000, straight life policy. Calculate her annual premium. If after 10 years she wants to surrender her policy, what options and what amounts are available to her?

SOLUTIONS TO LU 20–1 PRACTICE QUIZ

1. $\frac{\$60,000}{\$1,000} = 60 \times \$3.24 = \$194.40$ No cash value in term insurance.
2. $\frac{\$78,000}{\$1,000} = 78 \times \$8.46^{*} = \$659.88$

Option 1:	Cash value	78 × $ 96 = $7,488
Option 2:	Paid up	78 × $259 = $20,202
Option 3:	Extended term	18 years and 76 days

* For females we subtract 3 years.

LEARNING UNIT 20–2 FIRE INSURANCE

When a tragedy like Hurricane Andrew occurs, insurance companies must pay heavy damages. The following *Wall Street Journal* clipping states that Allstate's large payout for Hurricane Andrew damages means bad news for Sears' near-term bottom line.

Sears Is Likely To Report Loss From Hurricane

Andrew's Damage Claims At Firm's Allstate Unit May Reach $1.2 Billion

By JAMES P. MILLER
Staff Reporter of THE WALL STREET JOURNAL

CHICAGO – **Sears, Roebuck** & Co. will likely report a third-quarter loss after its Allstate Insurance Co. unit said it expects policyholders to file about $1.2 billion in claims for damage wrought by Hurricane Andrew.

Even with Allstate's reinsurers picking up a modest portion of the storm's cost, the remaining tab will drag down earnings at the nation's second-largest insurance concern by about $700 million after taxes.

Disclosure of the big expected cost didn't come as a shock for investors, given the still-tentative status of estimates of Andrew's overall damage and Allstate's 20% share of the property/casualty market in Florida.

The hurricane's effects still spell bad news for its parent's near-term bottom line, however.

Prior to the storm, the surging insurance group had been Sears's biggest moneymaker, providing a much-needed boost to its parent's recent results. In the latest quarter, for example, Allstate's $235.3 mil

Adequate **fire insurance** is very important. Let's look at Alice Swan and how she discusses her fire insurance needs for her new dress shop at 4 Park Plaza with her insurance agent. (Alice owns the building.)

Fire insurance premium equals premium for building and premium for contents.

Alice What is "extended coverage"?

Bob Your basic fire insurance policy provides financial protection if fire or lightning damages your property. However, the extended coverage protects you from smoke, chemicals, water, or other damages that firemen may cause to control the fire. We have many options available.

Alice What is the cost of a fire insurance policy?

Bob Years ago, if you bought a policy for 2, 3, 5, or more years, reduced rates were available. Today, with rising costs of reimbursing losses from fires, most insurance companies write policies for 1 to 3 years. The cost of a 3-year policy premium is three times the annual premium. Because of rising insurance premiums, total costs are cheaper to buy a 3-year policy rather than three 1-year policies.

Alice For my purpose, I will need coverage for 1 year. Before you give me the premium rates, what factors affect the cost of my premium?

Bob In your case, you have several factors in your favor that will result in a lower premium. For example, (1) your building is brick, (2) the roof is fire resistant, (3) the building is located near a fire hydrant, (4) the building is in a good location (not next to a gas station) with easy access for the fire department, and (5) the goods within your store are not as flammable as, say, a paint store. I have a table here (Table 20–3) that gives an example of typical fire insurance rates for buildings and contents (furniture, fixtures, etc.).

Let's assume your building has an insured value of $190,000, is rated Class B, Area No. 2, and we insure your contents for $80,000. Then we calculate your total annual premium for building and contents as follows:

For our purpose, we round all premiums to nearest cent. In practice, the premium is rounded to the nearest dollar.

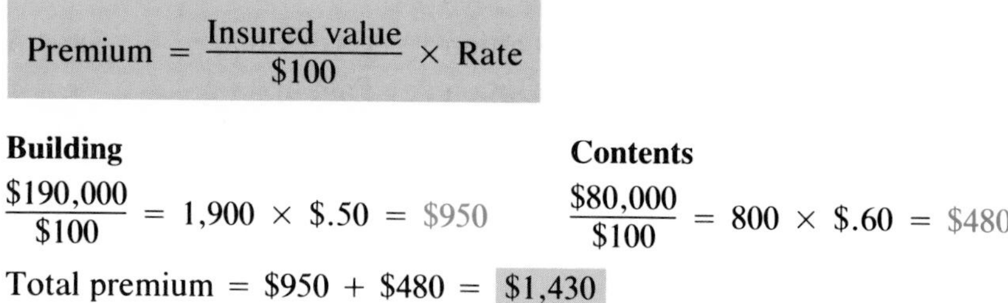

$$\text{Premium} = \frac{\text{Insured value}}{\$100} \times \text{Rate}$$

Building

$$\frac{\$190{,}000}{\$100} = 1{,}900 \times \$.50 = \$950$$

Contents

$$\frac{\$80{,}000}{\$100} = 800 \times \$.60 = \$480$$

Total premium = $950 + $480 = $1,430

TABLE 20–3
Fire Insurance Rates per $100 of Coverage for Buildings and Contents

Rating of area	Classification of building: Class A Building	Class A Contents	Class B Building	Class B Contents
1	.28	.35	.41	.54
2	.33	.47	.50	.60
3	.41	.50	.61	.65

TABLE 20–4
Fire Insurance Short-Rate and Cancellation Table

Time policy is in force		Percent of annual rate to be charged	Time policy is in force		Percent of annual rate to be charged
Days:	5	8%	Months:	5	52
	10	10		6	61
	20	15		7	67
	25	17		8	74
Months:	1	19		9	81
	2	27		10	87
	3	35		11	96
	4	44		12	100

Canceling of Fire Insurance by Insured or Insurance Company

Alice What if my business fails in seven months? Do I get back any portion of my premium when I cancel?

Bob If the insured—that's you, Alice—cancels or wants a policy for less than one year, we use this **short-rate table** (Table 20–4). The rates in the short-rate table will cost you more. For example, if you cancel at the end of 7 months, the premium cost is 67% of the annual premium. These rates are higher because it is more expensive to process a policy for a short time. We would calculate your refund as follows:

Short-rate premium = Annual premium × Short rate
↑ $958.10 ↑ $1,430 ↑ .67

Refund = Annual premium − Short-rate premium
↑ $471.90 = ↑ $1,430 − ↑ $958.10

Alice Let's say that I don't pay my premium or follow the fire codes. What happens if your insurance company cancels me?

Bob If the insurance company cancels you, the company is *not* allowed to use the short-rate table. To calculate what part of the premium the company may keep,[2] you can prorate the premium based on the actual days that have elapsed. We can illustrate the amount of your refund by assuming you are canceled after 7 months:

Note that when the insurance company cancels the policy, the refund ($595.83) is greater than if the insured cancels ($471.90).

For insurance company: Charge = $1,430 annual premium × $\frac{\text{7 months elapsed}}{12}$
→ Charge = $834.17

For insured: Refund = $1,430 annual premium − $834.17 charge
↘ Refund = $595.83

[2] Many companies use $\frac{\text{Exact time}}{365}$

Coinsurance

Alice My friend tells me that I should meet the coinsurance clause. What is coinsurance?

Bob Usually, fire does not destroy the entire property. **Coinsurance** means that you and the insurance company *share* the risk. The reason for this coinsurance clause[3] is to encourage property owners to purchase adequate coverage.

Alice What is adequate coverage?

Bob In the industry, the usual rate for coinsurance is 80% of the current replacement cost. This cost equals the value to replace what was destroyed. If your insurance coverage is 80% of the current value, the insurance company will pay all damages up to the face value of the policy.

If the insurance you carry is not 80% of the replacement value, you will have to share a portion of the loss.

Alice Hold it Bob! Will you please show me how this coinsurance is figured?

Bob Yes, Alice, I'll be happy to show you how we figure coinsurance. Let's begin by looking at the following steps so you can see what amount insurance the company will pay?

Steps for Calculating What Insurance Company Pays with Coinsurance Clause

Step 1. Set up a fraction. Numerator is actual amount of insurance on property carried. Denominator is amount of insurance on property you should be carrying to meet coinsurance (80% times the replacement value).

Step 2. Multiply fraction times amount of loss (up to the face value of the policy).

Let's say you carry $60,000 of insurance. To replace it would cost $100,000. If the coinsurance clause is 80% and you suffer a loss of $20,000, the following would show what the insurance company would pay.

$$\textbf{Step 1} \rightarrow \frac{\$60{,}000}{\$80{,}000} \times \$20{,}000 = \$15{,}000^{4}$$

Step 2 (points to $20,000)

(\$100,000 × .80) (points to $80,000)

If you had actual insurance coverage of $80,000, then the insurance company would have paid $20,000. Remember, the most an insurance company will pay is up to the face value of the policy if the coinsurance clause is met.

LU 20–2 PRACTICE QUIZ

1. Calculate the total annual premium of a warehouse that has an area rating of 2 with a building classification of B. The value of the warehouse is $90,000 with contents valued at $30,000.
2. If insured cancels in Problem 1 at the end of month 9, what is the cost of the premium and the refund?
3. Jones insures a building for $120,000 with an 80% coinsurance clause. The replacement value is $200,000. Assume a loss of $60,000 from fire. What will the insurance company pay? If the loss was $160,000 and coinsurance *was* met, what would the insurance company pay?

SOLUTIONS TO LU 20–2 PRACTICE QUIZ

1. $\frac{\$90{,}000}{100} = 900 \times \$.50 = \$450$

   $\frac{\$30{,}000}{100} = 300 \times \$.60 = \underline{180}$ total premium

   $\$630$

2. $\$630 \times .81 = \$510.30$ $\quad \$630 - \$510.30 = \$119.70$

3. $\frac{\$120{,}000}{\$160{,}000} = \frac{3}{4} \times \$60{,}000 = \$45{,}000$

   (.80 × $200,000) (points to $160,000) $\quad$ $160,000 never more than face value

[3] In some states (including Wisconsin), the clause is not in effect for losses under $1,000.

[4] This kind of limited insurance payment for a loss is often called an **indemnity**.

LEARNING UNIT 20–3 AUTO INSURANCE

Shirley, who just bought a new car, has never before purchased auto insurance. So Shirley called her insurance agent, Bob Long, who agreed to meet her for lunch. We will listen in on their conversation.

Liability Insurance Includes

***Bodily injury**—injury or death to people in passenger car or other cars, etc.*

***Property damage**—injury to other people's autos, trees, buildings, hydrants, etc.*

Shirley Bob, where do I start?

Bob Our state has two kinds of **liability insurance,** or **compulsory insurance,** that by law you must buy (regulations and requirements vary among states). Liability insurance covers any physical damages that you inflict on someone or their property. You must buy liability insurance for:

1. **Bodily injury** to others: 10/20. This means the insurance company will pay damages to people injured or killed by your auto up to $10,000 for injury to one person per accident or a total of $20,000 for injuries to two or more people per accident.
2. Damage to someone else's property: 5 (**property damage**). The insurance company will pay up to $5,000 for damages that you have caused to the property of others.

Now we leave Shirley and Bob for a few moments as we calculate Shirley's premium for compulsory insurance.

Calculating Shirley's Premium for Compulsory Insurance[5]

The tables we use in this unit are for Territory 5. Other tables are available for different territories. A congested area would have higher premiums than a quiet residential area.

In case of lawsuits, the minimum coverage may not be adequate. Some states add surcharges to the premium if the person has a poor driving record.

Insurance companies base auto insurance rates on the territory you live in, the class of driver (class 10 is experienced driver with driver training), whether auto is for business use, how much you drive the car, the age of the car, and the make of car (symbol). Shirley lives in Territory 5 (suburbia). She is classified as 17 because she is an inexperienced operator licensed less than 6 years. Her car is age 3 and symbol 4 (make of car). Using Table 20–5, we calculate Shirley's compulsory insurance as follows:

Bodily	$ 98
+ Property	160
	$258

Remember that the $258 premium represents minimum coverage. Assume Shirley hits two people, and the courts award them $13,000 and $5,000, respectively. Shirley would be responsible for $3,000 because the insurance company only pays up to $10,000 per person and a total of $20,000 per accident:

TABLE 20–5
Compulsory Insurance (Based on Class of Driver)

Bodily injury to others		Damage to someone else's property	
Class	10/20	Class	5M*
10	$ 55	10	129
17	98	17	160
18	80	18	160
20	116	20	186

Explanation of 10/20 and 5

10 /	20 /	5
Most paid to one person per accident for bodily injury	Most paid for total bodily injury per accident	Most paid for property damage per accident

* M means thousands.

[5] Some states may offer medical payment insurance (a supplement to policyholders' health and accident insurance) as well as personal injury protection caused by uninsured or underinsured motorists.

Although total damages of $18,000 are less than $20,000 the insurance company only pays $15,000.

	(1)		(2)		
	$13,000	+	$5,000	=	$18,000
Paid by insurance company ⟶	− 10,000	−	5,000	=	− 15,000
Paid by Shirley ⟶	$ 3,000	+	$ 0	=	$ 3,000

We return to Shirley and Bob again. Bob now shows Shirley how to calculate her optional insurance coverage.

Calculating Shirley's Optional Insurance Coverage

Superstock, Inc.

Bob In our state, you can add optional bodily injury in addition to the compulsory amount. If you finance your car, the lender may require specific amounts of optional insurance to protect its investment. I have two tables (Tables 20–6 and 20–7) here that we use to calculate the option of 250/500/50. This means that in an accident the insurance company would pay $250,000 per person, up to $500,000 per accident, and up to $50,000 for property damage. (Bob then explains the tables to Shirley. By studying the tables, you can see how insurance companies figure bodily injury and damage to someone else's property.)

Shirley is Class 17:

Bodily
250/500 = $228

Property
50M = + 168
$396 premium for optional bodily injury and property damage

Shirley Is that all I need?

Collision and comprehensive are optional insurance that only pay the insured. Note that Tables 20–8 and 20–9 are based on territory, age, and car symbol. The higher the symbol, the more expensive the car.

Bob No, I would recommned two more types of optional coverage: **collision** and **comprehensive.** Collision provides protection against damages to your car caused by a moving vehicle. It covers the cost of repairs less **deductibles** (amount of repair you cover first before the insurance company pays the rest) and depreciation.[6] In collision, insurance companies pay the resale or book value. So as the car gets older, after 5 or more years, it might make sense to drop the collision. The decision depends on how much risk you are willing to assume. Comprehensive covers damages resulting from theft, fire, falling objects, and so on. Now let's calculate

TABLE 20–6 Bodily Injury

Class	15/30	20/40	20/50	25/50	25/60	50/100	100/300	250/500	500/1000
10	27	37	40	44	47	69	94	144	187
17	37	52	58	63	69	104	146	228	298
18	33	46	50	55	60	89	124	193	251
20	41	59	65	72	78	119	168	263	344

TABLE 20–7 Damage to Someone Else's Property

Class	5M	10M	25M	50M	100M
10	129	132	134	135	136
17	160	164	166	168	169
18	160	164	166	168	169
20	180	191	193	195	197

[6] In some states, repair to glass has no deductible and many insurance companies now use a $500 deductible instead of the $300.

the cost of these two types of coverage—assuming a $100 deductible for collision and a $200 deductible for comprehensive—with some more of my tables (Tables 20–8) and 20–9).

	Class	Age	Symbol	Premium
Collision	17	3	4	$191 ($148 + $43)
Comprehensive	17	3	4	+ 56 ($52 + $4)
				$247

Cost to reduce deductible from $300 to $100

Total premium for collision and comprehensive

Shirley Anything else?

Bob I would also recommend that you buy towing and substitute transportation coverage. The insurance company will pay up to $25 for each tow. Under substitute transportation, the insurance company will pay you $12 a day for renting a car, up to $300 total. Again, from another table (Table 20–10), we find the additional premium for towing and substitute transportation is $20 ($16 + $4).

We leave Shirley and Bob now as we make a summary of Shirley's total auto premium in Table 20–11.

TABLE 20–8 Collision

Classes	Age group	Symbols 1–3 $300 ded.	Symbol 4 $300 ded.	Symbol 5 $300 ded.	Symbol 6 $300 ded.	Symbol 7 $300 ded.	Symbol 8 $300 ded.	Symbol 10 $300 ded.
10–20	1	180	180	187	194	214	264	279
	2	160	160	166	172	190	233	246
	3	148	148	154	166	183	221	233
	4	136	136	142	160	176	208	221
	5	124	124	130	154	169	196	208

These classes would use this table and the one below.

To find premium, use the age and symbol only.

Class	Additional cost to reduce deductible: From $300 to $200	From $300 to $100
10	13	27
17	20	43
18	16	33
20	26	55

TABLE 20–9 Comprehensive

Classes	Age group	Symbols 1–3 $300 ded.	Symbol 4 $300 ded.	Symbol 5 $300 ded.	Symbol 6 $300 ded.	Symbol 7 $300 ded.	Symbol 8 $300 ded.	Symbol 10 $300 ded.
10–25	1	61	61	65	85	123	157	211
	2	55	55	58	75	108	138	185
	3	52	52	55	73	104	131	178
	4	49	49	52	70	99	124	170
	5	47	47	49	67	94	116	163

Additional cost to reduce deductible: From $300 to $200 add $4.

TABLE 20–10
Transportation and Towing

Substitute transportation	$16
Towing and labor	4

TABLE 20–11
Worksheet for Calculating Shirley's Auto Premium

Compulsory insurance	Limits	Deductible	Premium
Bodily injury to others	$10,000 per person $20,000 per accident	None	$98 (Table 20–5)
Damage to someone else's property	$5,000 per accident	None	$160 (Table 20–5)
Options			
Optional bodily injury to others	$250,000 per person $500,000 per accident	None	$228 (Table 20–6)
Optional property damage	$50,000 per accident	None	$168 (Table 20–7)
Collision	Actual cash value	$100	$191 (Table 20–8) ($148 + $43)
Comprehensive	Actual cash value	$200	$ 56 (Table 20–9) ($52 + $4)
Substitute transportation	Up to $12 per day or $300 total	None	$16 (Table 20–10)
Towing and labor	$25 per tow	None	$4 (Table 20–10) $921 Total premium

Premiums for collision, property damage, and comprehensive are not reduced by no fault.

No-Fault Insurance

Some states have **no-fault insurance,** a type of auto insurance that was intended to reduce premium costs on bodily injury. With no fault, one forfeits the right to sue for *small* claims involving medical expense and loss of wages, and so on. Each person would collect the bodily injury from their own insurance company no matter who is at fault. In reality, no fault has not reduced premium costs, due to large lawsuits, fraud, and operating costs of insurance companies. Many states that were once considering no fault are no longer pursuing its adoption. It should be noted that states with no fault require the purchase of *personal-injury protection* (PIP). The most successful no-fault law seems to be in Michigan since it has tough restrictions on the right to sue along with unlimited medical and rehabilitation benefits.

It's time to take your final Practice Quiz in this chapter.

LU 20–3 PRACTICE QUIZ

Calculate the annual auto premium for Mel Jones who lives in Territory 5, is a classified driver 18, has a car with age 4 and symbol 7. His state has compulsory insurance, and Mel wants to add the following options:

1. Bodily injury, 100/300
2. Damage to someone else's property, 10M
3. Collision, $200 deductible
4. Comprehensive, $200 deductible
5. Towing

SOLUTIONS TO LU 20-3 PRACTICE QUIZ

Compulsory			
Bodily	$ 80		(Table 20–5)
Property	160		(Table 20–5)
Options			
Bodily	124		(Table 20–6)
Property	164		(Table 20–7)
Collision	192	(\$176 + \$16)	(Table 20–8)
Comprehensive	103	(\$99 + \$4)	(Table 20–9)
Towing	4		(Table 20–10)
Total annual premium	$827		

CHAPTER ORGANIZER: A REFERENCE GUIDE

Page	Topic	Key point, procedure, formula	Example(s) to illustrate situation
434	Life insurance	Using Table 20–1, per \$1,000: $\frac{\text{Coverage desired}}{\$1,000} \times \text{Rate}$ For females, subtract three years.	**Given** \$80,000 of insurance desired; age 34; male. 1. Five-year term: $\frac{\$80,000}{\$1,000} = 80 \times \$2.08 = \$166.40$ 2. Straight life: $\frac{\$80,000}{\$1,000} = 80 \times \$10.71 = \$856.80$ 3. Twenty-payment life: $\frac{\$80,000}{\$1,000} = 80 \times \$14.28 = \$1,142.40$ 4. Twenty-year endowment: $\frac{\$80,000}{\$1,000} = 80 \times \$25.13 = \$2,010.40$
436	Nonforfeiture values	**By Table 20–2** Option 1: Cash surrender value. Option 2: Reduced paid-up insurance policy continues for life at reduced face amount. Option 3: Extended term—original face policy continued for a certain period of time.	A \$50,000 straight-life policy was issued to Jim Rose at age 28. At age 48 Jim wants to stop paying premiums. What are his nonforfeiture options? Option 1: $\frac{\$50,000}{\$1,000} = 50 \times \$265$ $= \$13,250$ Option 2: 50 × \$550 = \$27,500 Option 3: 21 years 300 days
438	Fire insurance	Per \$100 $\text{Premium} = \frac{\text{Insurance value}}{\$100} \times \text{Rate}$ Rate can be for buildings or contents.	**Given** Area 3; Class B; building insured for \$90,000; contents, \$30,000 Building: $\frac{\$90,000}{\$100} = 900 \times \$.61 = \$549$ Contents: $\frac{\$30,000}{\$100} = 300 \times \$.65 = \$195$ Total: \$549 + \$195 = \$744
439	Canceling fire insurance—short-rate Table 20–4 (canceling by policyholder)	$\text{Annual premium} \times \text{Short rate} = \text{Short-rate premium}$ $\text{Refund} = \text{Annual premium} - \text{Short-rate premium}$ If insurance company cancels, do not use Table 20–4.	Annual premium is \$400. Short rate is .35 (cancel end of 3 months). \$400 × .35 = \$140 Refund = \$400 − \$140 = \$260

Page	Topic	Key point, procedure, formula	Example(s) to illustrate situation
439	Canceling by insurance company	Annual premium $\times \frac{\text{Months elapsed}}{12}$ (Refund is higher since company cancels.)	Using example above but if insurance company cancels at end of 3 months: $\$400 \times \frac{1}{4} = \$100$ Refund = \$400 − \$100 = \$300
440	Coinsurance	Amount insurance company pays: $\frac{\text{Actual insurance} \rightarrow \text{Insurance carried (face value)}}{\text{What coverage should have been} \rightarrow \text{Insurance required to meet coinsurance (Rate} \times \text{Replacement value)}} \times \text{Loss}$ Insurance company never pays more than the face value.	**Given** Face value, \$30,000; replacement value, \$50,000; coinsurance rate, 80%; loss, \$10,000; insurance to meet required coinsurance, \$40,000. $\frac{\$30{,}000}{\$40{,}000} \times \$10{,}000 = \$7{,}500$ paid by insurance company (\$40,000 = \$50,000 × .80)
441	Auto insurance	**Compulsory** Required insurance. **Optional** Bodily—pays for injury to person caused by insured. Property damage—pays for property damage (not for insured auto). Collision—pays for damages to insured auto. Comprehensive—pays for damage to insured auto for fire, theft, etc. Towing. Substitute transportation.	Calculate the annual premium: Driver class 10; compulsory 10/20/5. **Optional** Bodily—100/300 Property—10M Collision—age 3, symbol 10, \$100 deductible Comprehensive—\$300 deductible 10/20/5 \$184 Table 20–5 (\$55 + \$129) Bodily 94 Table 20–6 Property 132 Table 20–7 Collision 260 Table 20–8 (\$233 + \$27) Comprehensive 178 Table 20–9 Total premium \$848
	Key terms	Beneficiary, *p. 434* Bodily injury, *p. 441* Cash value, *p. 435* Coinsurance, *p. 440* Collision, *p. 442* Comprehensive insurance, *p. 442* Compulsory insurance, *p. 441* Deductibles, *p. 442* Extended term insurance, *p. 438* Face amount, *p. 435* Fire insurance, *p. 438* Indemnity, *p. 440* Insured, *p. 434* Insurer, *p. 434* Level premium term, *p. 434*	Liability insurance, *p. 441* No-fault insurance, *p. 444* Nonforfeiture values, *p. 436* Paid-up insurance, *p. 435* Policyholder, *p. 436* Premium, *p. 434* Property damage, *p. 441* Reduced paid-up insurance, *p. 437* Short-rate table, *p. 439* Straight life insurance, *p. 435* Term insurance, *p. 434* 20-payment life, *p. 435* 20-year endowment, *p. 436* Universal life, *p. 436* Whole life, *p. 436*

END-OF-CHAPTER PROBLEMS

Drill Problems

Additional homework assignments by learning unit are at the end of text in Appendix I (p. I–87). Solutions to odd problems are at the end of text in Appendix II.

Calculate the annual premium for the following policies (for females subtract 3 years off the table) using Table 20–1:

	Amount of coverage (face value of policy)	Age and sex of insured	Type of insurance policy	Annual premium
20–1.	$65,000	29F	Straight life	65 × $7.43 = $482.95
20–2.	$80,000	40M	20-payment life	80 × $18.61 = $1,488.80
20–3.	$75,000	38M	5-year term	75 × $2.95 = $221.25
20–4.	$50,000	27F	20-year endowment	50 × $16.05 = $802.50

Calculate the nonforfeiture options given the following: Al Jones, age 35—purchased $200,000 straight life policy. At end of year 15, Al stopped paying premiums.

20–5. Option 1: Cash surrender value

$$\frac{\$200{,}000}{\$1{,}000} = 200 \times \$148 = \$29{,}600$$

20–6. Option 2: Reduced paid-up insurance

200 × $371 = $74,200

20–7. Option 3: Extended term insurance

20 years 165 days

Calculate total cost of premium for fire insurance for building and contents given the following (round to nearest cent):

20–8.

Rating of area	Class	Building	Contents	Total premium cost
2	B	$70,000	$30,000	$530 ($350 + $180)

$$\text{Building: } \frac{\$70{,}000}{\$100} = 700 \times \$.50 = \$350$$

$$\text{Contents: } \frac{\$30{,}000}{100} = 300 \times \$.60 = \$180$$

Calculate the short-rate premium and refund:

	Annual premium	Canceled after	Short-rate premium	Refund
20–9.	$700	8 months by insured	$518 (.74 × $700)	$182 ($700 − $518)
20–10.	$360	4 months by insurance company	$120 $\left(\frac{4}{12} \times 360\right)$	$240 ($360 − $120)

Complete the following:

	Replacement value of property	Amount of insurance	Kind of policy	Actual fire loss	Amount insurance company will pay
20–11.	$100,000	$60,000	80% coinsurance	$22,000	$16,500

$$(\$100{,}000 \times .80) \longrightarrow \frac{\$60{,}000}{\$80{,}000} = \frac{3}{4} \times \$22{,}000 = \$16{,}500$$

	Replacement value of property	Amount of insurance	Kind of policy	Actual fire loss	Amount insurance company will pay
20–12.	$ 60,000	$40,000	80% coinsurance	$42,000	$35,000

$$(\$60{,}000 \times .80) \longrightarrow \frac{\$40{,}000}{\$48{,}000} = \frac{5}{6} \times \$42{,}000 = \$35{,}000$$

Calculate annual auto insurance premium:

20–13. Bill Burns, Territory 5
Class 17 operator
Compulsory, 10/20/5 — $ 258 ($98 + $160)

Optional

a. Bodily injury, 500/1,000 — $ 298
b. Property damage, 25M — $ 166
c. Collision, $100 deductible — $ 233 ($190 + $43)
Age of car is 2; symbol of car is 7
d. Comprehensive, $200 deductible — $ 112 ($108 + $4)
Total annual premium — $1,067

Word Problems

20–14. Bill Jones, age 40, saw a Prudential Life Insurance advertisement stating that their $100,000 term policy would cost $173 per year. Compare this to Table 20–1 in the text; how much would he save by going with Prudential?

Text $352 $\left(\frac{\$100{,}000}{\$1{,}000} \times 100 \times \$3.52\right)$
Prudential 173
$179 cheaper—it pays to shop around!

20–15. Margie Rale, age 38, a well-known actress, decided to take out a limited-payment life policy. She chose this since she expects her income to decline in future years. Margie decided to take out a 20-year payment life policy with a coverage amount of $90,000. Could you advise Margie about what her annual premium will be? If she decides to stop paying premiums after 15 years, what would be her cash value?

$$\frac{\$90{,}000}{\$1{,}000} = 90 \times \$14.92 = \$1{,}342.80$$

Cash value = 90 × $317 = $28,530

20–16. Joyce Gail has two young children and wants to take out an additional $400,000 of 5-year term insurance. Joyce is 34 years old. What will her additional annual premium be? In 3 years, what cash value would have been built up?

$$\frac{\$400{,}000}{\$1{,}000} = 400 \times \$1.87 = \$748$$

No cash value for term.

20–17. Roger's office building has a $320,000 value, a 2 rating, and a B building classification. The contents in the building are valued at $105,000. Could you help Roger calculate his total annual premium?

$$\text{Building: } \frac{\$320{,}000}{\$100} = 3{,}200 \times \$.50 = \$1{,}600$$

$$\text{Contents: } \frac{\$105{,}000}{\$100} = 1{,}050 \times \$.60 = \$630$$

Total premium = $1,600 + $630 = $2,230

20–18. Abby Ellen's toy store is worth $400,000 and is insured for $200,000. Assume an 80% coinsurance clause and that a fire caused $190,000 damage. What is the liability of the insurance company?

$\frac{\$200{,}000}{\$320{,}000} \times \$190{,}000 = \$118{,}750$ (.80 × $400,000)

20–19. Property of Al's Garage is worth $500,000. Al has a fire insurance policy of $225,000 that contains an 80% coinsurance clause. What will the insurance company pay on a fire that causes $200,000 damage?

$\frac{\$225{,}000}{\$400{,}000} \times \$200{,}000 = \$112{,}500$ (.80 × $500,000)

20–20. Pete Williams had taken out a $75,000 fire insurance policy for his new restaurant at a rate of $.83 per $100. Seven months later, Pete canceled the policy and decided to move his store to a new location. What was the cost of the premium to Pete?

$\frac{\$75{,}000}{\$100} = 750 \times \$.83 = \$622.50$

$\$622.50 \times .67 = \$417.08$

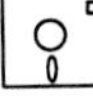

20–21. Earl Miller insured his pizza shop for $100,000 for fire insurance at an annual rate per $100 of $.66. At the end of 11 months, Earl canceled the policy since his pizza shop went out of business. What was the cost of Earl's premium and his refund?

$\frac{\$100{,}000}{\$100} = 1{,}000 \times \$.66 = \$660$

Cost of premium = .96 × $660 = $633.60

Refund = .04 × $660 = $26.40

20–22. Ron Tagney insured his real estate office with a fire insurance policy for $95,000 at a cost of $.59 per $100. Eight months later his insurance company canceled his policy because of a failure to correct a fire hazard. What did Ron have to pay for the 8 months of coverage? Round to nearest cent.

$\frac{\$95{,}000}{\$100} = 950 \times \$.59 = \$560.50$

$\frac{8}{12} = \frac{2}{3} \times \$560.50 = \$373.67$

20–23. Jim Smith, who lives in Territory 5, carries 10/20/5 compulsory liability insurance along with optional collision that has a $500 deductible. Jim was at fault in an accident that caused $2,400 damage to the other auto and $800 damage to his own. Also, the courts awarded $14,000 and $9,000, respectively, to the two passengers in the other car for personal injuries. How much will the insurance company pay, and what is Jim's share of the responsibility?

Insurance company pays		**Jim**
Property damage	$ 2,400	$ 500 deductible
Collision ($800 − $500)	300	4,000 bodily
Bodily	10,000	
	9,000	
Total	$21,700	$4,500

20–24. Marion Sloan bought a new jeep and insured it with only 10/20/5 compulsory insurance. Driving up to her ski chalet one snowy evening, Marion hit a parked van and injured the couple inside. Marion's car had damage of $4,200, and the van she struck had damage of $5,500. After a lengthy court suit, the injured persons were awarded personal injury judgments of $16,000 and $7,900, respectively. What will the insurance company pay for this accident, and what is Marion's responsibility?

Insurance company pays		**Marion pays**
Bodily	$10,000 + $7,900	$ 6,000
Property	5,000	4,200 no collision
		500 of property damage not covered by compulsory
Total	$22,900	$10,700

Challenge Problem
How Much Insurance Coverage Can You Afford?

20–25. Bill, who understands the types of insurance that are available, is planning his life insurance needs. At this stage of his life (age 35), he has budgeted $200 a year for life insurance premiums. Could you calculate for Bill the amount of coverage that is available under straight life and for a 5-year term? Could you also show Bill that if he were to die at age 40, how much more his beneficiary would receive if he'd been covered under the 5-year term? Round to nearest thousand.

Straight life

$200 ÷ $11.26 = 17.762 × $1,000 = $17,762 = $18,000

Five-year term

$200 ÷ $2.23 = 89.686 × $1,000 = $89,686 = $90,000

$90,000
− 18,000
$72,000

Summary Practice Test

Solutions are at end of text in Appendix II.

Quick Reference
If you get any wrong answers, study the page numbers given for each problem.

1. Pp. 434–36.
2. Pp.434–36.

1. Jennefer Brown, age 31, a well-known actress, decided to take out a limited-payment life policy. She chose this since she expects her income to decline in future years. Jennefer decided to take out a 20-year payment life policy with a coverage amount of $70,000. Could you advise Jennefer of what her annual premium will be? If she decides to stop paying premiums after 15 years, what would be her cash value?

$\frac{\$70{,}000}{\$1{,}000} = 70 \times \$11.12 = \$778.40$

Cash value = 70 × $317 = $22,190

2. Roy Small, age 28, bought a straight life insurance policy for $95,000. Calculate his annual premium. If after 20 years he no longer pays in premiums, what nonforfeiture options are available to him?

$\frac{\$95{,}000}{\$1{,}000} = 95 \times \$8.08 = \$767.60$

Option 1: Cash value
95 × $265 = $25,175

Option 2: Paid-up insurance
95 × $550 = $52,250

Option 3: Extended term
21 years, 300 days

3. Pp. 439–40.

3. The property of Al's Garage is worth $300,000. Al has a fire insurance policy of $180,000 that contains an 80% coinsurance clause. What will the insurance company pay on a fire that causes $210,000 damage? If Al met the coinsurance, how much would the insurance company have paid?

$\frac{\$180{,}000}{\$240{,}000} \times \$210{,}000 = \$157{,}500$

($300,000 × .80)

If coinsurance is met, the insurance company would have paid up to face value of $210,000.

4. Pp. 438–39.

4. Earl Miller insured his pizza shop for $90,000 for fire insurance at an annual rate per $100 of $.59. At the end of 11 months, Earl canceled the policy since his pizza shop went out of business. What was the cost of Earl's premium and his refund?

900 × $.59 = $531 $531 × .96 = $509.76

$531.00
− 509.76
$ 21.24 refund

5. Pp. 438–39.

5. Ron Tagney insured his real estate office with a fire insurance policy for $60,000 at a cost of $.48 per $100. Ten months later his insurance company canceled his policy because of a failure to correct a fire hazard. What did Ron have to pay for the 10 months of coverage?

600 × $.48 = $288 $\frac{10}{12} \times \$288 = \$240$ premium cost

6. Pp. 441–44.

6. Jim Smith, who lives in Territory 5, carries 10/20/5 compulsory liability insurance along with optional collision that has a $200 deductible. Jim was at fault in an accident that caused $1,800 damage to the other auto and $600 damage to his own. Also, the courts awarded $13,000 and $8,000, respectively, to the two passengers in the other car for personal injuries. How much does insurance company pay, and what is Jim's share of responsibility?

Insurance company pays		Jim pays
Property damage ($5,000)	$ 1,800	
Collision ($600 − $200 deductible)	$ 400	
Bodily (10/20)	$10,000	$3,000
(most is $10,000		($13,000 − $10,000)
to one person)		$ 200 on deductible
	$ 8,000	$3,200
Total	$20,200	

Project A

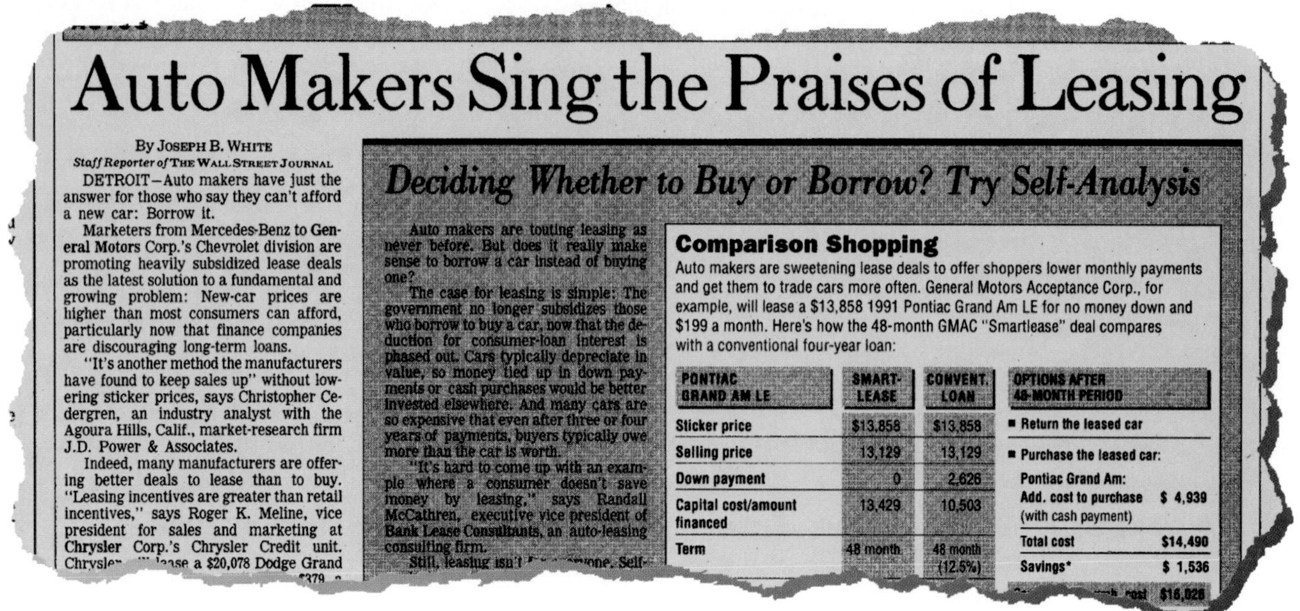

Auto Makers Sing the Praises of Leasing

By JOSEPH B. WHITE
Staff Reporter of THE WALL STREET JOURNAL

DETROIT—Auto makers have just the answer for those who say they can't afford a new car: Borrow it.

Marketers from Mercedes-Benz to General Motors Corp.'s Chevrolet division are promoting heavily subsidized lease deals as the latest solution to a fundamental and growing problem: New-car prices are higher than most consumers can afford, particularly now that finance companies are discouraging long-term loans.

"It's another method the manufacturers have found to keep sales up" without lowering sticker prices, says Christopher Cedergren, an industry analyst with the Agoura Hills, Calif., market-research firm J.D. Power & Associates.

Indeed, many manufacturers are offering better deals to lease than to buy. "Leasing incentives are greater than retail incentives," says Roger K. Meline, vice president for sales and marketing at Chrysler Corp.'s Chrysler Credit unit. Chrysler [illegible] lease a $20,078 Dodge Grand [illegible]

Deciding Whether to Buy or Borrow? Try Self-Analysis

Auto makers are touting leasing as never before. But does it really make sense to borrow a car instead of buying one?

The case for leasing is simple: The government no longer subsidizes those who borrow to buy a car, now that the deduction for consumer-loan interest is phased out. Cars typically depreciate in value, so money tied up in down payments or cash purchases would be better invested elsewhere. And many cars are so expensive that even after three or four years of payments, buyers typically owe more than the car is worth.

"It's hard to come up with an example where a consumer doesn't save money by leasing," says Randall McCathren, executive vice president of Bank Lease Consultants, an auto-leasing consulting firm.

Still, leasing isn't [illegible] one. Self- [illegible]

Comparison Shopping

Auto makers are sweetening lease deals to offer shoppers lower monthly payments and get them to trade cars more often. General Motors Acceptance Corp., for example, will lease a $13,858 1991 Pontiac Grand Am LE for no money down and $199 a month. Here's how the 48-month GMAC "Smartlease" deal compares with a conventional four-year loan:

PONTIAC GRAND AM LE	SMART-LEASE	CONVENT. LOAN
Sticker price	$13,858	$13,858
Selling price	13,129	13,129
Down payment	0	2,626
Capital cost/amount financed	13,429	10,503
Term	48 month	48 month (12.5%)

OPTIONS AFTER 48-MONTH PERIOD	
■ Return the leased car	
■ Purchase the leased car:	
Pontiac Grand Am: Add. cost to purchase (with cash payment)	$ 4,939
Total cost	$14,490
Savings*	$ 1,536
[illegible] cost	$16,026

Visit a local car dealer to see what's new in leasing versus buying.

NOTES

THAT WAS THEN . . .
. . . THIS IS NOW

The New York Stock Exchange of 1853 and of today represents an auction-type market. In the financial section of your newspaper, stock information lists activity completed on the floor of the exchange.

21

Stocks and Bonds

LEARNING UNIT OBJECTIVES

LU 21–1: Stocks

1. Read and explain stock quotations. *p. 457.*
2. Explain the difference between round and odd lots. *p. 458.*
3. Calculate dividends on preferred (cumulative) and common stock and calculate return on investments. *p. 459.*

LU 21–2: Bonds

1. Read and explain bond quotations. *p. 461.*
2. Compare and contrast bond yields versus bond premiums and bond discounts. *pp. 461–63.*

Note: There is a special supplement on the inside front cover of your text on how to read financial data in *The Wall Street Journal.*

The heading in the following *Wall Street Journal* clipping announces that Colgate-Palmolive raised its quarterly dividend by 18%. Investors reacted favorably, and Colgate stock rose to $76.375.

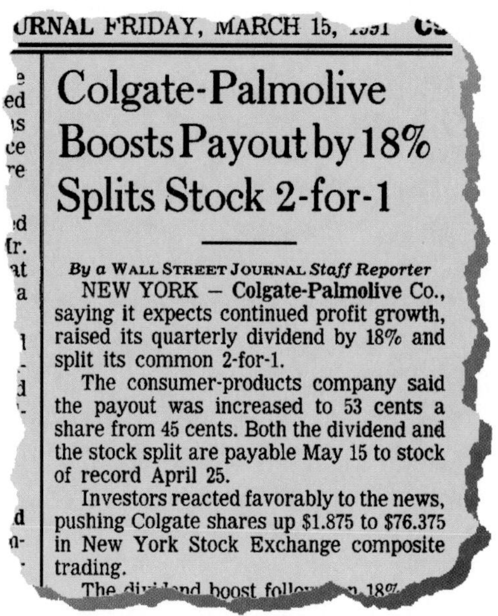

JOURNAL FRIDAY, MARCH 15, 1991

Colgate-Palmolive Boosts Payout by 18% Splits Stock 2-for-1

By a WALL STREET JOURNAL *Staff Reporter*

NEW YORK – Colgate-Palmolive Co., saying it expects continued profit growth, raised its quarterly dividend by 18% and split its common 2-for-1.

The consumer-products company said the payout was increased to 53 cents a share from 45 cents. Both the dividend and the stock split are payable May 15 to stock of record April 25.

Investors reacted favorably to the news, pushing Colgate shares up $1.875 to $76.375 in New York Stock Exchange composite trading.

If you are not familiar with the stock terms in the clipping, this chapter will explain them. You will also learn about bonds.

LEARNING UNIT 21–1 STOCKS

This unit begins with an introduction to basic stock terms. Then you will learn about buying stocks, how to read stock quotations in the newspaper, dividends, and calculating investment return.

Introduction to Basic Stock Terms

Companies sell shares of ownership in their company to raise money to finance operations, plan expansion, and so on. These ownership shares are called **stocks.** The buyers of the stock **(stockholders)** receive **stock certificates** (Figure 21–1) verifying the number of shares of stock they own. In the Business Math Scrapbook (p. 468), you will see how stock certificates are being phased out.

If you own 50 shares of common stock, you would be entitled to 50 votes in company elections. Preferred stockholders would not have this right.

The two basic types of stock are **common** and **preferred.** Common stockholders have voting rights. Preferred stockholders do not have voting rights but they receive preference over common stockholders in **dividends** (payments from profit). If the company goes bankrupt, preferred stockholders also have preference over common stockholders to the company's assets. **Cumulative preferred stock** entitles its owners to a specific amount of dividends in a year. If the company fails to pay these dividends, the **dividends in arrears** accumulate. The company pays no dividends to common stockholders until the company brings the preferred dividend payments up-to-date.

Why Buy Stocks?

Some investors own stock because they think the stock will become more valuable, for example, if the company makes more profit, new discoveries, and the like. Other investors own stock to share in the profit distributed by the company in **dividends** (cash or stock).

For various reasons, investors at different times want to sell their stock or buy more stock. Strikes, inflation, or technological changes may cause some investors to think their stock will decline in value. These investors may decide to sell. Then the laws of

FIGURE 21-1
Stock Certificate

Stockholders
↓
elect
↓
board of directors
↓
elect
↓
officers of corporation

supply and demand takes over. As more people want to sell, the stock price goes down. Should more people want to buy, the stock price would go up.

How Are Stocks Traded?

Stock exchanges provide an orderly trading place for stock. You can think of these exchanges as an auction place. Only **stockbrokers** are allowed on the floor of the exchange. They act as middlemen and do the trading. Stockbrokers charge commissions for the buying and selling of stock.

How to Read Stock Quotations in the Newspaper Financial Section

The following table on fractional stock amounts will be helpful since stocks are traded in eighths of a dollar.

Fractional Stock Amounts			
$\frac{1}{8}$ of a dollar	\$.125	$\frac{5}{8}$ of a dollar	\$.625
$\frac{1}{4}$ of a dollar	.25	$\frac{3}{4}$ of a dollar	.75
$\frac{3}{8}$ of a dollar	.375	$\frac{7}{8}$ of a dollar	.875
$\frac{1}{2}$ of a dollar	.50		

We will use Disney stock to learn how to read stock quotations found in your newspaper. Note the following newspaper listing of Disney stock.

High	Low	Stock	SYM	Div.	Yld. %	P-E ratio	Vol. 100s	High	Low	Close	Net change
$129\frac{3}{4}$	$93\frac{5}{8}$	Disney	DIS	.70	.6	26	11397	$123\frac{3}{8}$	$119\frac{1}{2}$	$122\frac{1}{2}$	$+2\frac{1}{2}$

High, $129\frac{3}{4}$

The highest price at which Disney stock traded during the year was \$129.75 per share. This means that during the year someone was willing to pay \$129.75 for a share of stock.

Low, $93\frac{5}{8}$

The lowest price at which the Disney stock traded during the year was $93.625 per share.

Stock, Disney
SYM DIS
Div., .70

The newspaper lists the company name. The symbol of Disney used for trading is DIS. Disney paid $.70 per share to stock owners last year. So if you owned 100 shares, you received a **cash dividend** of $70 (100 shares × $.70).

Yld. %, .6

The **stock yield** tells the stockholder that the dividend per share is returning a rate of .6% to the investor. This .6% is based on the closing price. The calculation is:

$$\text{Stock yield} = \frac{\text{Annual dividend per share}}{\text{Today's closing price per share}} = \frac{\$.70}{\$122.50} = .571\% \text{ or } .6\% \text{ (rounded to nearest tenth percent)}$$

Last trade of the day

The .6% return may seem low to people who could earn a better return on their money elsewhere. Remember that if the stock price rises and you sell, your investment may result in a high rate of return. For example, 3 years ago from this date Disney stock was selling at $63. In 3 years, people doubled their money.

P-E ratio, 26

The Disney stock is selling at $122.50; it is selling at 26 times its **earnings per share.**

$$\text{Earnings per share} = \text{Annual earnings} \div \text{Total number of shares outstanding}$$

The **price-earning ratio** will often vary in a range from 0 to 50, depending on quality, future expectations, economic conditions, and so on. So if a company is pioneering a *new* project and has little earnings, the price of the stock could be high (a high P-E ratio). For Disney, we calculate the following price-earnings ratio. (Assume Disney earns $4.71 per share. This is not listed in the newspaper.)

$$\text{P-E ratio} = \frac{\text{Closing price per share of stock}}{\text{Annual earnings per share}} = \frac{\$122.50}{\$4.71} = 26$$

Vol 100s, 11397

If the P-E ratio column shows ". . .," it means the company has no earnings. To the volume number, add two zeros. This indicates that 1,139,700 shares (rounded to the nearest hundred) were traded on this day. Remember that shares of stock need a buyer and a seller to trade.

High, $123\frac{3}{8}$

The highest selling price per share of Disney stock during the day was $123\frac{3}{8}$. (Someone was willing to pay $123.375, and someone was willing to sell for $123.375.)

Low, $119\frac{1}{2}$

The lowest selling price per share of Disney stock during the day was $119\frac{1}{2}$, or $119.50.

Close, $122\frac{1}{2}$

The last trade of the day was at $122.50 per share.

Net change, + $2\frac{1}{2}$

Since the *previous day,* the last closing price was $120 (not given). The *new* close is $122.50. The end result is that the closing price is up $2\frac{1}{2}$, or $2.50 from the *previous day.* The $2.50 increase is from yesterday's close.

Round and Odd Lots

For the varying costs of trading stocks, see the clipping in the Business Math Scrapbook.

Let's look at what it would cost to buy 200 shares of Disney. To keep it simple, assume the commission of the stockbroker is 2% of the purchase (or selling price). If the order is in multiples of 100 (200, 300, and so on), it is a **round lot.** If the order is an odd lot (fewer than 100 shares), the commission is an *additional* 1% on the **odd lot** portion. Keep in mind that whether you *buy* or *sell,* a commission charge results.

Courtesy of Charles Schwab & Company

If you bought the 200 shares at market (going price) for \$122.50 per share, you would use the following steps to calculate your total cost.

Step 1. Calculate trading cost:	200 shares × \$122.50 =	\$24,500	
Step 2. Calculate commission on trading cost:	.02 × \$24,500 =	+ 490	
		\$24,990	total cost to buy 200 shares of stock

If you bought 240 shares, the 40 shares is an odd lot. The steps to calculate the commission are:

Step 1. Calculate trading cost:	240 shares × \$122.50 =	\$29,400
Step 2. Calculate commission:	.02 × \$29,400 =	588
Step 3. Calculate additional commission on odd lot:	.01 × \$4,900 =	+ 49
	(40 shares × \$122.50)	\$30,037

Dividends on Preferred and Common Stock

As we stated earlier, cumulative preferred stockholders must be paid all past and present dividends before common stockholders can receive any dividends. Let's use an example to illustrate the calculation of dividends on preferred and common stock for 1994 and 1995.

EXAMPLE The stock records of Jason Corporation show the following:

Preferred stock issued: 20,000 shares.
Preferred stock cumulative at \$.80 per share.
Common stock issued: 400,000 shares.
In 1994, paid no dividends.
In 1995, paid \$512,000 in dividends.

Remember that common stockholders do not have the cumulative feature like preferred.

Since the company declared no dividends in 1994, the company has \$16,000 dividends in arrears to preferred (20,000 shares × \$.80 = \$16,000). The dividend of \$512,000 in 1995 is divided between preferred and common stock as follows:

To preferred[1]

20,000 shares × \$.80 =	\$16,000	dividend in arrears for 1994
20,000 shares × \$.80 =	16,000	dividend for 1995
	\$32,000	total dividend to preferred

To common

\$512,000	Total dividend	Since preferred doesn't participate in any dividend beyond the \$.80 per share that is cumulative
− 32,000	To preferred	
\$480,000	To common	

$$\frac{\$480{,}000}{400{,}000 \text{ shares}} = \$1.20 \text{ per share}$$

[1] For a discussion of par value (arbitrary value placed on stock for accounting purposes) and cash and stock dividend distribution, check your accounting text.

Calculating Return on Investment

Now let's learn how to calculate a return on your investment of Disney stock assuming the following:

Bought 300 shares at $122.50
Sold at end of 1 year 300 shares at $140
3% commission rate on buying and selling stock
Current $.70 dividend per share in effect

Bought		**Sold**	
300 shares at $122.50	$36,750.00	300 shares at $140	$42,000
+ Broker's commission		− Broker's commission	
(.03 × $36,750)	+ 1,102.50	(.03 × $42,000)	− 1,260
Total cost	$37,852.50	Total receipt	$40,740

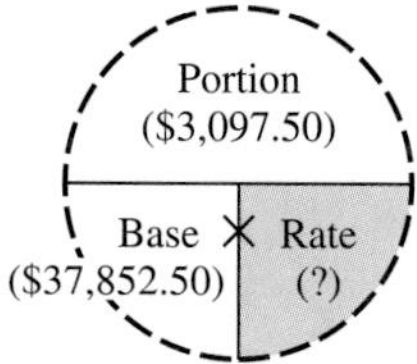

Note: A commission is charged on both the buying and selling.

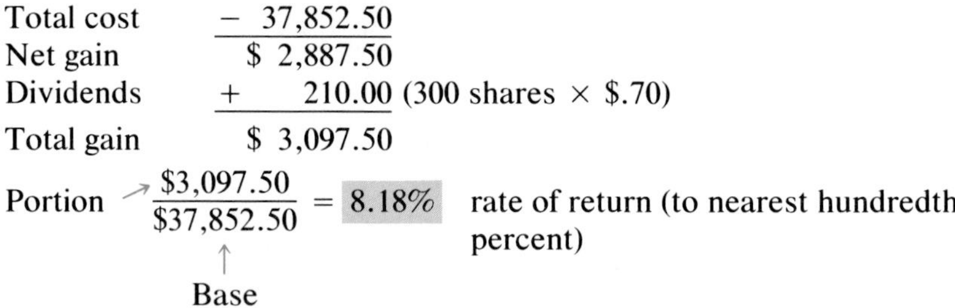

Total receipt	$40,740.00
Total cost	− 37,852.50
Net gain	$ 2,887.50
Dividends	+ 210.00 (300 shares × $.70)
Total gain	$ 3,097.50

$$\text{Portion} \rightarrow \frac{\$3,097.50}{\$37,852.50} = 8.18\%$$ rate of return (to nearest hundredth percent)

↑ Base

It's time for another Practice Quiz.

LU 21-1 PRACTICE QUIZ

1. From the following **(a)** explain the letters, **(b)** estimate the company's earnings per share, and **(c)** show how "Yld. %" was calculated.

High	Low	Stock	SYM	Div.	Yld. %	P-E ratio	Vol. 100s	High	Low	Close	Net change
$56\frac{1}{8}$	$28\frac{1}{8}$	Gillette	G.	.62	1.2	28	6268	$53\frac{7}{8}$	$52\frac{3}{8}$	$53\frac{3}{8}$	$+\frac{1}{4}$
(A)	(B)	(C)	(D)	(E)	(F)	(G)	(H)	(I)	(J)	(K)	(L)

2. **Given:** 30,000 shares of preferred cumulative stock at $.70 per share; 200,000 shares of common; 1994, no dividend; 1995, $109,000. How much is paid to each in 1995?

SOLUTIONS TO LU 21-1 PRACTICE QUIZ

1. **a.** (A) Highest price traded for year is $56.125.
(B) Lowest price traded for year is $28.125.
(C) Name of corporation is Gillette.
(D) Symbol is G.
(E) Dividend per share per year is $.62.
(F) Yield for year is 1.2%.
(G) Stock of Gillette sells at 28 times its earnings.
(H) Sale volume for day is 626,800 shares.
(I) Highest price for the day is $53.875.
(J) Lowest price for the day is $52.375.
(K) The last trade (closing price for the day) is $53.375.
(L) Stock is up $.25 from closing price yesterday.

b. EPS $= \frac{\$53.375}{28}$ $= \$1.91$ per share

c. $\frac{\$.62}{\$53.375} = 1.2\%$

2. Preferred: 30,000 × \$.70 = \$21,000 Arrears 1994
+ 21,000 1995
\$42,000

Common: \$67,000 (\$109,000 − \$42,000)

LEARNING UNIT 21–2 BONDS

This unit shows you how to read bond quotations and calculate bond yields.

Reading Bond Quotations

Bond quotes are stated in percents of face value of bond and not in dollars like stock.

Sometimes companies raise money by selling bonds instead of stock. When you buy stock, you become a part owner in the company. But company management may not want to dilute the ownership of the current stock owners by selling more stock. So to raise money, they sell bonds. **Bonds** represent a promise from the company to pay the face amount to the bond owner at a future date, along with interest payments at a stated rate. Once a company issues bonds, they are traded like stock. If a company goes bankrupt, bondholders have the first claim to the assets of the corporation—before stockholders. As with stock, changes in bond prices are the result of supply and demand. Brokers also charge commissions on bond trading. These commissions vary.

How to Read the Bond Section of the Newspaper

The bond section of the newspaper shows the bonds that are traded on the American Stock Exchange that day. The information given on bonds differs from the information given on stocks. The newspaper states bond prices in *percent of face amount and not in dollar amounts* like stock prices. Also, bonds are usually in denominations of \$1,000 (the face amount).

When a bond sells at a price below its face value, the bond is sold at a discount. Why? The interest that the bond pays may not be as high as the current market rate. When this happens, the bond is not as attractive to investors and it sells for a **discount**. The opposite could, of course, also occur. The bond may sell at a **premium**, which means that the bond sells for more than its face value or the bond interest is higher than the current market rate. Let's look at this newspaper information given for Mattel bonds:

Bonds	Current yield	Vol.	High	Low	Close	Net change
Mattel $11\frac{5}{8}$ 03	12.6	5	$93\frac{1}{2}$	$91\frac{3}{4}$	92	+3

Note: Bond prices stated as a percent of face amount.

Bonds, Mattel $11\frac{5}{8}$ 03

The name of the company is Mattel. It produces a wide range of children's toys. The interest on the bond is $11\frac{5}{8}\%$. The company pays the interest semiannually. The bond matures (comes due) in 2003. The total interest for the year is \$116.25 (.11625 × \$1,000). Remember that the face value of the bond is \$1,000. Now let's show this with the following formula:

$$\text{Yearly interest} = \text{Face value of bond} \times \text{Stated yearly interest rate}$$

$$\$116.25 = \$1,000 \times .11625$$

Current yield, 12.6

We calculate the 12.6% yield by dividing the total annual interest of the bond by the total cost of the bond. (For our purposes, we will omit the commission cost.) All bond yields are rounded to nearest tenth percent.

Note this bond is selling for less than $1,000 since its interest is not as attractive as some of the other new offerings.

$$\frac{\text{Yearly interest}}{\text{Cost of bond at closing}} = \frac{\$116.25}{\$920} \quad \begin{array}{l}(.11625 \times \$1{,}000)\\(.92 \times \$1{,}000)\end{array}$$

$$= 12.6\%$$

Volume, 5

Five $1,000 bonds were traded. Note that we do *not* add two zeros like we did to the sales volume of stock.

High, $93\frac{1}{2}$

Bond quotations are expressed as a percent of face value (not as a dollar amount like stock). The highest bond traded on this day was $93\frac{1}{2}\%$ of face value. To calculate this in dollars, we use the following steps:

Step 1. Change fraction percent to decimal equivalent percent: $93\frac{1}{2}\% = 93.50\%$.

Step 2. Convert to a decimal: .9350.

Step 3. Multiply times $1,000 (face value): .9350 × $1,000 = $935.

Low, $91\frac{3}{4}$

The lowest the bond traded on this day was $91\frac{3}{4}\%$ of face value. We calculate this in dollars using these steps:

Step 1. $91\frac{3}{4}\% = 91.75\%$.

Step 2. 91.75% = .9175.

Step 3. .9175 × $1,000 = $917.50.

Close, 92

The last bond traded on this day was 92% of face value, or in dollars, $920 (92% = .92 × $1,000).

Net change, +3

The last trade of the day was up 3% of the face value from the last trade of yesterday. In dollars this is: 3% = $30.

$$3\% = .03 \times \$1{,}000 = \$30$$

Thus, the closing price on this day, 92% − 3%, equals yesterday's close of 89% ($890). Note that *yesterday's close is not listed in today's quotations.*

Calculating Bond Yields

Let's look at why the Mattel bond (selling at a discount) pays $11\frac{5}{8}\%$ interest when it is yielding investors 12.6%.

$$\text{Bond yield} = \frac{\text{Total annual interest of bond}}{\text{Total current cost of bond at closing}^{2}}$$

The following example will show us how to calculate **bond yields.**

EXAMPLE Jim Smith bought 5 bonds of Mattel at the closing price of 92 (remember that in dollars 92% is $920). Jim's total cost excluding commission is:

$$5 \times \$920 = \$4{,}600$$

What is Jim's interest?

The yield is 12.6% since Jim paid less for the bonds and still receives $11\frac{5}{8}\%$ of the face value.

No matter what Jim pays for the bonds, he will still receive interest of $116.25 per bond (.11625 × $1,000). Jim bought the bonds at $920 each, resulting in a bond yield of 12.64%. Let's calculate Jim's yield to the nearest tenth percent:

(5 bonds × $116.25 interest per bond per year)

$$\frac{\$581.25}{\$4{,}600} = 12.64\% = 12.6\%$$

Now let's try another Practice Quiz.

[2] We assume this to be the buyer's purchase price.

LU 21-2 PRACTICE QUIZ

Bonds	Yield	Sales	High	Low	Close	Net change
AMR Air $16\frac{1}{8}$ 02	15.5	74	$104\frac{1}{4}$	$103\frac{5}{8}$	$104\frac{1}{4}$	. . .

From the above bond quotation for AMR Airlines, (1) calculate cost of 5 bonds at closing (disregard commissions) and (2) check current yield of 15.5%.

SOLUTIONS TO LU 21-2 PRACTICE QUIZ

1. $104\frac{1}{4}\% = 104.25\% = 1.0425 \times \$1{,}000 = \$1{,}042.50 \times 5 = \$5{,}212.50$
2. $16.125\% = .16125 \times \$1{,}000 = \$161.25$ annual interest

   $\frac{\$161.25}{\$1{,}042.50} = 15.47\% = 15.5\%$

CHAPTER ORGANIZER: A REFERENCE GUIDE

Page	Topic	Key point, procedure, formula	Example(s) to illustrate situation
458	Stock yield	$\frac{\text{Annual dividend per share}}{\text{Today's closing price per share}}$ (Round yield to nearest tenth percent.)	Annual dividend, \$.72 Today's closing price, $42\frac{3}{8}$ $\frac{\$.72}{\$42.375} = 1.7\%$
458	Price-earnings ratio	$\text{P-E} = \frac{\text{Closing price per share of stock}}{\text{Annual earnings per share}}$ (Round answer to nearest whole number.)	From example above: Closing price, $42\frac{3}{8}$ Annual earnings per share, \$4.24 $\frac{\$42.375}{\$4.24} = 9.99 = 10$
459	Dividends with cumulative preferred	Cumulative preferred stock is entitled to all dividends in arrears before common stock receives dividend.	1994 dividend omitted; in 1995, \$400,000 in dividends paid out. Preferred is cumulative at \$.90 per share; 20,000 shares of preferred issued and 100,000 shares of common issued. To preferred: 20,000 shares × \$.90 = \$18,000 In arrears 1994: 20,000 shares × .90 = 18,000 Dividend to preferred \$36,000 To common: \$364,000 (\$400,000 − \$36,000) $\frac{\$364{,}000}{100{,}000 \text{ shares}}$ = \$3.64 dividend to common per share
462	Cost of a bond	Bond prices are stated as a percent of the face value. Bonds selling for less than face result in bond discounts. Bonds selling for more than face result in bond premiums.	Bill purchases 5 \$1,000, 12% bonds at closing price of $103\frac{1}{4}$. What is his cost (omitting commissions)? $103\frac{1}{4}\% = 103.25\% = 1.0325$ in decimal $1.0325 \times \frac{\$1{,}000}{\text{bond}} = \frac{\$1{,}032.50}{\text{per bond}}$ 5 bonds × \$1,032.50 = \$5,162.50

Page	Topic	Key point, procedure, formula	Example(s) to illustrate situation
462	Bond yield	$\frac{\text{Total annual interest of bond}}{\text{Total current cost of bond at closing}}$ (Round to nearest tenth percent.)	Calculate bond yield from last example on one bond. ($1,000 × .12) $\frac{\$120}{\$1,032.50} = 11.6\%$
	Key terms	Bonds, *p. 461* Bond yield, *p. 462* Cash dividend, *p. 458* Common stocks, *p. 456* Cumulative preferred stock, *p. 456* Discount, *p. 461* Dividends, *p. 456* Dividends in arrears, *p. 456* Earnings per share, *p. 458* Odd lot, *p. 458*	Preferred stock, *p. 459* Premium, *p. 461* Price-earnings ratio, *p. 458* Round lot, *p. 458* Stockbrokers, *p. 457* Stock certificate, *p. 456* Stockholders, *p. 456* Stocks, *p. 456* Stock yield, *p. 458*

END-OF-CHAPTER PROBLEMS

Drill Problems

Additional homework assignments by learning unit are at the end of text in Appendix I (p. I–91). Solutions to odd problems are at the end of text in Appendix II.

Calculate the cost (omit commission) of buying the following shares of stock:

21–1. 300 shares of Quaker Oats at $70\frac{1}{8}$ $21,037.50 300 × $70.125 = $21,037.50

21–2. 400 shares of Tootsie Roll at $77\frac{1}{4}$ $30,900 400 × $77.25 = $30,900

Calculate the yield of each of the following stocks (round to nearest tenth percent):

	Company		Yearly dividend	Closing price per share	Yield
21–3.	McDonalds	$\left(\frac{\$.37}{\$41.125}\right)$	$.37	$41\frac{1}{8}$	.9%
21–4.	Lowes Corp.	$\left(\frac{\$.75}{\$15.50}\right)$	$.75	$15\frac{1}{2}$	4.8%

Calculate the earnings per share, price-earnings ratio, or stock price as needed:

	Company	Earnings per share	Closing price per share		Price-earnings ratio
21–5.	Digital	$1.80	$29\frac{1}{2}$	$\frac{\$29.50}{\$1.80}$	16
21–6.	ATT	$4.50	$54.00 (12 × $4.50)		12

21–7. Calculate the total cost of buying 350 shares of Good Year at $54\frac{3}{4}$. Assume a 2% commission with an additional 1% commission on odd lots.

350 shares × $54.75 = $19,162.50
.02 × $19,162.50 = 383.25
.01 × 2,737.50 = 27.38
(50 shares × $54.75) $19,573.13

21–8. Disregarding commission, if in Problem 21–1 the 300 shares of Quaker Oats were sold at $65\frac{1}{4}$, what would be the loss?

Buy: 300 shares × $70.125 = $21,037.50
Sell: 300 shares × $65.25 = − 19,575.00
$ 1,462.50 loss

21–9. **Given:** 20,000 shares of cumulative preferred ($2.25 dividend per share); 40,000 shares of common. Dividend paid: 1994, $8,000; 1995, 0; 1996, $160,000. How much will preferred and common receive each year?

1994 Preferred $ 8,000 ($45,000 − $8,000 = $37,000 in arrears)
1995 0 to both
1996 Preferred 127,000 ($37,000 + $45,000 + $45,000)
Common 33,000 ($160,000 − $127,000)

For each of these bonds, calculate the total dollar amount you would pay at the quoted price (disregard commission or any interest that may have accrued):

	Company	Bond price	Number of bonds purchased	Dollar amount of purchase price
21–10.	Petro	$87\frac{3}{4}$	3	$2,632.50
21–11.	Wang	114	2	$2,280

21–10: $87\frac{3}{4}\%$ = 87.75% = .8775 × $1,000 = $877.50 × 3 = $2,632.50

21–11: 114% = 1.14 × $1,000 = $1,140 × 2 = $2,280

From the following bonds calculate the total annual interest, total cost, and current yield (to nearest tenth percent):

	Bond	Number of bonds purchased	Selling price	Total annual interest	Total cost	Current yield
21–12.	Sharn $11\frac{3}{4}$ 99	2	115	$235.00	$2,300	10.2%
21–13.	Wang $6\frac{1}{2}$ 98	4	$68\frac{1}{8}$	$260.00	$2,725	9.5%

21–12: .1175 × $1,000 = $117.50 interest per bond; $\frac{\$117.50}{\$1,150}$ ← (115% = 1.15 × $1,000)

21–13: .065 × $1,000 = $65 interest per bond; $\frac{\$65}{\$681.25}$ ← $\left(68\frac{1}{8}\% = 68.125\% = .68125 \times \$1,000\right)$

Word Problems

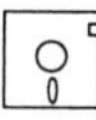

21–14. Norm Dorian bought 300 shares of CBS at $\$52\frac{1}{2}$ per share. Assume a commission of 2% of the purchase price. What is the total cost to Norm?

300 × \$52.50 = \$15,750 × 1.02 = \$16,065

21–15. Assume in Problem 21–14 that Norm sells the stock for $\$69\frac{1}{4}$ with the same 2% commission rate. What is the bottom line for Norm?

300 × \$69.25 = \$20,775 × .98 = \$20,359.50

Sell	\$20,359.50
Buy	− 16,065.00
Gain	\$ 4,294.50

21–16. Jim Corporation pays its cumulative preferred stockholders \$1.60 per share. Jim has 30,000 shares of preferred and 75,000 shares of common. In 1992, 1993, and 1994, due to slowdowns in the economy, Jim paid no dividends. Now in 1995, the board of directors has decided to pay out \$500,000 in dividends. How much of the \$500,000 does each class of stock receive as dividends?

Preferred 30,000 shares × \$1.60 = \$ 48,000 per year
× 4 (current + 3 years in arrears)
\$192,000

Common \$500,000 − \$192,000 = \$308,000

21–17. Roger Company earns \$4.80 per share. Today the stock is trading at $\$59\frac{1}{4}$. The company pays an annual dividend of \$1.40. Could you calculate **(a)** the price-earnings ratio (round to nearest whole number) and **(b)** the yield on the stock (to nearest tenth percent)?

a. $\text{P-E} = \frac{\$59.25}{\$4.80} = 12$ **b.** $\text{Yield} = \frac{\$1.40}{\$59.25} = 2.4\%$

21–18. The stock of VIC Corporation is trading at $\$61\frac{1}{2}$. The price-earnings ratio is 12 times earnings. Could you calculate the earnings per share for VIC Corporation?

$\text{EPS} = \frac{\$61.50}{12} = \$5.13$

21–19. Jerry Ryan bought the 5 bonds of Mort Company $12\frac{3}{4}$ 96 at $82\frac{1}{2}$ and 4 bonds of Inst. System 12x99 for $90\frac{1}{4}$. If the commission on the bonds is \$2.50 per bond, what was the total cost of all the purchases?

$82\frac{1}{2}\% = .825 \times \$1{,}000 = \$825 \quad \times 5 = \$4{,}125.00$

$90\frac{1}{4}\% = .9025 \times \$1{,}000 = \$902.50 \times 4 = 3{,}610.00$

$\$2.50 \times 9 = 22.50$

\$7,757.50 total cost

21–20. Melyon Company sells its bonds at $107\frac{3}{4}$. What is the amount of premium or discount the bond is selling for?

$107\frac{3}{4}\% = 107.75\% = 1.0775 \times \$1{,}000 = \$1{,}077.50$ per bond
\$1,077.50 − \$1,000 = \$77.50 Premium of \$77.50

21–21. Ron bought a bond for $79\frac{1}{4}$ of Bee Company. The original bond was $5\frac{3}{4}$ 96. Ron wanted to know the current yield (to nearest tenth percent). Please help Ron with the calculation.

$79\frac{1}{4}\% = 79.25\% = .7925 \times \$1{,}000 = \$792.50$

$\frac{\$57.50}{\$792.50} = 7.3\%$ $\left(5\frac{3}{4}\% = 5.75\% = .0575 \times \$1{,}000 = \$57.50\right)$

21–22. Abby Sane decided to buy corporate bonds instead of stock. She desired to have the fixed-interest payments. She purchased 5 bonds of Meg Corporation $11\frac{3}{4}$ 99 at $88\frac{1}{4}$. As the stockbroker for Abby (assume you charge her a \$5 commission per bond), please provide her with the following: (1) the total cost of the purchase, (2) total annual interest to be received, and (3) current yield (to nearest tenth percent).

1. $88\frac{1}{4}\% = 88.25\% = .8825 \times \$1{,}000 = \$882.50$
× 5
\$4,412.50
+ 25.00
\$4,437.50

2. .1175 × \$1,000 = \$117.50 × 5 = \$587.50

3. $\frac{\$117.50}{\$882.50} = 13.3\%$

21–23. Mary Blake is considering whether to buy stocks or bonds. She has a good understanding of the pros and cons of both. The stock she is looking at is trading at $59\frac{1}{4}$, with an annual dividend of $3.99. Meanwhile, the bond is trading at $96\frac{1}{4}$, with an annual interest rate of $11\frac{1}{2}\%$. Calculate for Mary her yield (tenth percent) for the stock and the bond.

Stock: $\frac{\$3.99}{\$59.25} = 6.7\%$

$96\frac{1}{4}\% = 96.25\% = .9625 \times \$1{,}000 = \$962.50$

$.115 \times \$1{,}000 = \$115$

$\frac{\$115}{\$962.50} = 11.9\%$

Challenge Problem
Buying a Bond

Hint: Final cost = Cost of bond + Accrued interest + Brokerage fee. Calculate time for accrued interest.

21–24. On September 6, Irene Westing purchased one bond of Mick Corporation at $98\frac{1}{2}$. The bond pays $8\frac{3}{4}$ interest on June 1 and December 1. The stockbroker told Irene that she would have to pay the accrued interest and the market price of the bond and a $6 brokerage fee. What was the total purchase price for Irene. Assume a 360-day year (each month is 30 days) in calculating accrued interest.

1. Cost of bond: $1,000 × .985 = $985
2. Time for accrued interest:

June	30 days
July	30 days
Aug	30 days
Sept	6 days
	96 days

Interest: $1,000 × .0875 = $87.50

$\frac{\$87.50}{360} = \$.2430555$ per day
× 96
$23.33

3. Final cost of bond

Final cost of bond	$ 985.00
Accrued interest	23.33
Brokerage fee	6.00
	$1,014.33

Summary Practice Test

Solutions are at end of text in Appendix II.

Quick Reference
If you get any wrong answers, study the page numbers given for each problem.

1. P. 459.

1. Jean O'Brien bought 300 shares of Tandy Corp stock at $28\frac{1}{8}$ per share. Assume a commission of 4% of the purchase price. What is the total cost to Jean?
300 × $28.125 = $8,437.50 × 1.04 = $8,775

2. P. 458.

2. Blue Company earns $5 per share. Today, the stock is trading at $45. The company pays an annual dividend of $.65. Could you calculate the (**a**) price-earnings ratio, and (**b**) the yield on the stock (to the nearest tenth percent)?

a. $\frac{\$45}{\$5} = 9$ **b.** $\frac{\$.65}{\$45} = 1.4\%$

3. P. 458.

3. The stock of Morris Company is trading at $44\frac{1}{4}$. The price-earnings ratio is 16 times earnings. Could you calculate the earnings per share (to nearest cent) for Morris Company?

$\text{EPS} = \frac{\$44.25}{16} = \$2.77$

4. P. 462.

4. Denise Royal bought 6 bonds of BLT Company $9\frac{3}{4}$ 99 at 79 and 6 bonds of RT Company $10\frac{3}{4}$ 98 at 81. Assume the commission on the bonds is $3 per bond. What was the total cost of all the purchases?
6 × $790 = $4,740
6 × $810 = + 4,860
$9,600 + $36 = $9,636

5. P. 462.

5. Jeff Bass bought one bond of Blue Company for 135. The original bond was $7\frac{3}{4}$ 98. Jeff wanted to know the current yield to the nearest tenth percent. Could you help Jeff with the calculation?

(.0775 × $1,000) $\frac{\$77.50}{\$1{,}350} = 5.7\%$

6. P. 459.

6. Cumulative preferred stockholders receive $.85 per share. There are 60,000 shares. For the last 3 years no dividends have been paid. This year $189,000 is paid out in dividends. How much dividends to preferred is still in arrears?
60,000 × $.85 = $51,000
× 4
$204,000 − 189,000 = $15,000 in arrears

How Discount Brokerage Commissions Compare

Commission charges quoted by several discounters for buying or selling various amounts of a $26 stock, and charges at two full-service firms. (Prices to nearest dollar.)

BROKERAGE FIRM	NUMBER OF SHARES TRADED 100	200	400	1,000	2,500
Fidelity Investments					
Brokerage Account	$51	$86	$106	$151	$216
FidelityPlus	48	82	100	143	206
Spartan Brokerage	44	44	52	94	192
Andrew Peck	50	56	72	90	140
Quick & Reilly	49	61	85	121	175
Charles Schwab[1]	49	82	100	143	206
Waterhouse Securities	35	35	60	128	240
Jack White & Co.	48	71	89	132	210
York Securities	35	35	53	75	125
Merrill Lynch	**80**	**132**	**226**	**418**	**728**
Shearson Lehman	**75**	**139**	**241**	**497**	**878**

[1]Schwab says it is actively considering a commission increase that would add about $5 to the charge for the average trade. Schwab customers who use the firm's computerized trading systems or its Tele-Broker telephone service receive a 10% discount.

NOTE: Many firms offer additional discounts or rebates for active traders, with the amount linked to trading activity.

Project A

How much commission would you save if you bought 1,000 shares from Waterhouse Securities rather than from Merrill Lynch?

Merrill Lynch	$418
Waterhouse Securities	− 128
	$290

Project B

Visit a local securities firm to see what fees they might charge for certificates.

Stock Certificates Move a Step Closer to the Scrap Pile

YOUR MONEY MATTERS

By WILLIAM POWER
And MICHAEL SICONOLFI
Staff Reporters of THE WALL STREET JOURNAL

The good ol' stock certificate is rapidly marching to the graveyard.

Merrill Lynch & Co., in letters mailed out this month, is telling investors that it will institute a $15-a-security fee for the privilege of holding a stock or bond certificate, starting in September.

"Most of the rest of the industry will follow suit," predicts Guy Moszkowski, brokerage-industry analyst at Sanford C. Bernstein & Co. "It's something that most of the firms have wanted to do away with for quite some time."

But the introduction of fees will be only the latest move by Wall Street to discourage the time-honored use of certificates to confirm the purchase or sale of investments. Stocks, mutual funds, and even certificates of deposit are all being converted to computerized "book-entry" form, whether small investors like it or not.

"The other capital markets of the world, particularly Japan, have been moving toward the certificate-less society," says Frank G. Zarb, chairman of Primerica Corp.'s Smith Barney, Harris Upham & Co. securities unit. Smith Barney doesn't rule out following Merrill's lead.

Until certificates have entirely departed, a growing number of investors will have to weigh the costs and benefits of holding certificates vs. opting for book entry (in which investors' holdings are confirmed only on account statements).

For example, investors can face problems if they try to transfer accounts from a brokerage firm without having a stock certificate in hand. Phillip Goldstein, a New York investor, tried to get his stock certificates from Thomson McKinnon Securities Inc. after the firm was absorbed into Prudential Securities Inc. in 1989. "I was sent a transfer form [for the stock certificates], but it got fouled up, and I never got them transferred out of" Thomson, Mr. Goldstein says.

There are other reasons to hold stock certificates, says Mr. Goldste... chooses book entr... sometimes buys... traded, "c... correspon... wouldn...

NOTES

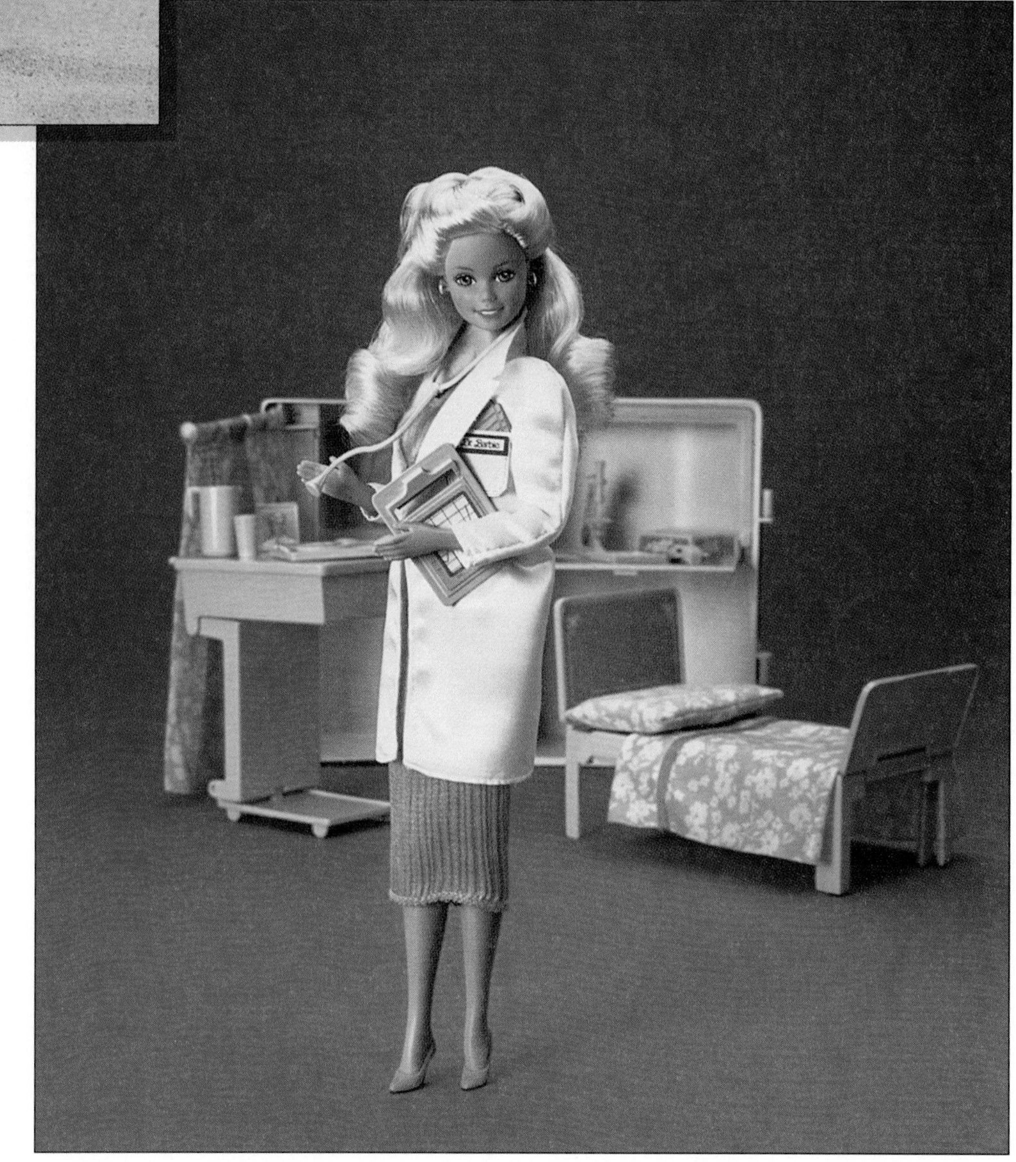

THAT WAS THEN . . .
. . . THIS IS NOW

In 1959 the Barbie fashion doll was introduced. Since then more than 500 million dolls have been sold. Mattel feels that 9 of 10 girls age 3 to 11 will own one or more Barbies. We could easily show sales on bar or line graphs.

22

Business Statistics

LEARNING UNIT OBJECTIVES

LU 22–1: Mean, Median, and Mode

1. Define and calculate the mean. *p. 472.*
2. Explain and calculate a weighted mean. *pp. 472–73.*
3. Define and calculate the median. *p. 473.*
4. Define and identify the mode. *p. 474.*

LU 22–2: Frequency Distributions and Graphs

1. Prepare a frequency distribution. *p. 475.*
2. Prepare bar, line, and circle graphs. *pp. 476–78.*

Courtesy of Nike

Businesses are surrounded by all kinds of raw data. For example, Reebok has a 24% market share compared to a 30% share for Nike. To solve problems and gain knowledge, businesses take raw data, organize it, and study the results. Today, computer graphics can automatically show these results in meaningful graphs. Business statistics plays an important role in achieving successful business operations.

In this chapter, we look at various techniques to analyze and graphically represent business statistics. We begin by using the mean, median, and mode to find averages of raw data.

LEARNING UNIT 22–1 MEAN, MEDIAN, AND MODE

Companies frequently use averages to guide their business decisions. This unit discusses the three most common averages that businesses use to indicate a single value that represents an entire group of numbers.

Mean

The accountant of Bill's Sport Shop told Bill, the owner, that the average daily sales for the week were \$150.14. The accountant stressed that \$150.14 was an average and did not represent specific daily sales. Bill wanted to know how the accountant arrived at \$150.14.

The accountant went on to explain that he used an arithmetic average, or **mean** (a measurement), to arrive at \$150.14 (rounded to the nearest hundredth). He showed Bill the following formula:

$$\text{Mean} = \frac{\text{Sum of all values}}{\text{Number of values}}$$

The data the accountant used was:

	Sun.	Mon.	Tues.	Wed.	Thur.	Fri.	Sat.
Sport shop sales	\$400	\$100	\$68	\$115	\$120	\$68	\$180

The accountant used this data to compute the mean:

$$\text{Mean} = \frac{\$400 + \$100 + \$68 + \$115 + \$120 + \$68 + \$180}{7} = \$150.14$$

When values appear more than once, businesses often look for a **weighted mean.** The format for the weighted mean is slightly different from the mean. The concept, however, is the same except that you weight each value by how often it occurs (its frequency). Thus, considering the frequency of the occurrence of each value allows a weighting of each day's sales in proper importance. The formula for the weighted mean is:

$$\text{Weighted mean} = \frac{\text{Sum of products}}{\text{Sum of frequencies}}$$

Let's change the sales data for Bill's Sport Shop and see how we would calculate a weighted mean:

	Sun.	Mon.	Tues.	Wed.	Thur.	Fri.	Sat.
Sport shop sales	\$400	\$100	\$100	\$80	\$80	\$100	\$400

Value	Frequency	Product
$400	2	$ 800
100	3	300
80	2	160
		$1,260

The weighted mean is $\frac{\$1,260}{7} = \$180$

Note how we multiply each value by its frequency of occurrence to arrive at the product. Then we divide the sum of the products by the sum of the frequencies.

When you calculate your grade point average, you are using a weighted average. Let's show how Jill Rivers calculated her G.P.A. to the nearest tenth.

Given A = 4; B = 3; C = 2; D = 1; F = 0

Courses attempted	Credits	Grade	Units × Grade
Introduction to Computers	4	A	16 (4 × 4)
Psychology	3	B	9 (3 × 3)
English Composition	3	B	9 (3 × 3)
Business Law	3	C	6 (2 × 3)
Business Math	3	B	9 (3 × 3)
	16		49

$$\frac{49}{16} = 3.1$$

When high or low numbers do not significantly affect a list of numbers, the mean is a good indicator of where the center of the data occurs. If high or low numbers do have an effect, the median may be a better indicator to use.

Median

The **median** is another measurement that indicates where the center of the data occurs. The median does not distort an average that has one or more extreme values. For example, let's look at the yearly salaries of the employees of Rusty's Clothing Shop:

Alice Knight	$95,000	Jane Wang	$67,000
Jane Hess	27,000	Bill Joy	40,000
Joe Floyd	32,000		

Note how Alice's salary of $95,000 will distort an averge calculated by the mean:

$$\frac{\$95,000 + \$27,000 + \$32,000 + \$67,000 + \$40,000}{5} = \$52,200$$

The $52,200 average salary is considerably more than the salary of three of the employees. So it is not a good representation of the store's average salary. Let's see what we get by using the median.

We find the median by:

1. Orderly arranging values from the smallest to the largest.
2. a. **Odd number of values:** Median is the middle value. You find this by first dividing the total number of numbers by 2. The next higher number is the median.
   b. **Even number of values:** Median is the average of the two middle values.

For Rusty's Clothing Shop, we find the median by:

1. Arranging values from smallest to largest:

   \$27,000; \$32,000; **\$40,000;** \$67,000; \$95,000

2. Since the middle value is an odd number, **\$40,000** is the median. Note that half of the salaries fall below the median and half fall above ($5 \div 2 = 2\frac{1}{2}$—next number is the median).

If Jane Hess (\$27,000) were not on the payroll, we would find the median as follows:

1. Arrange values from smallest to largest:

   \$32,000; \$40,000; \$67,000; \$95,000

2. Average of two middle values:

$$\frac{\$40{,}000 + \$67{,}000}{2} = \$53{,}500$$

Note that the median results in two salaries below and two salaries above the average.
Now we'll look at another measurement tool—the mode.

Mode

The **mode** is a measurement that also records values. In a series of numbers, the value that occurs most often is the mode. If all the values are different, there is no mode. If two or more numbers appear most often, you may have two or more modes. Note that we do not have to arrange the numbers in the lowest to highest order, although this could make it easier to find the mode.

EXAMPLE 3, 4, 5, 6, 3, 8, 9, 3, 5, 3
3 is the mode since it is listed 4 times.

Now let's check your progress with a Practice Quiz.

LU 22-1 PRACTICE QUIZ

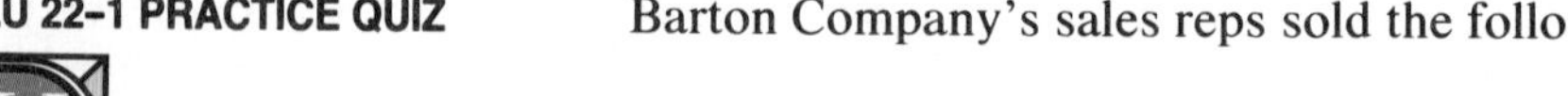

Barton Company's sales reps sold the following last month:

Sales rep	Sales volume
A	\$16,500
B	15,000
C	12,000
D	48,900

Calculate the mean and the median. Which is the better indicator of where the center of the data occurs? Is there a mode?

SOLUTIONS TO LU 22-1 PRACTICE QUIZ

$$\text{Mean} = \frac{\$16{,}500 + \$15{,}000 + \$12{,}000 + \$48{,}900}{4}$$

$$= \$23{,}100$$

$$\text{Median} = \frac{\$15{,}000 + \$16{,}500}{2}$$

$$= \$15{,}750$$

\$12,000, \$15,000, \$16,500, \$48,900. Note how we arrange numbers from smallest to highest to calculate median.

Median is the better indicator since in calculating the mean, the \$48,900 puts the average of \$23,100 much too high. There is no mode.

LEARNING UNIT 22-2 FREQUENCY DISTRIBUTIONS AND GRAPHS

In this unit, we learn how to gather information and show it visually. Today, computer software programs can make beautiful color graphics. For example, note how the following graphic shows how Japanese auto makers are targeting purchasing U.S. parts.

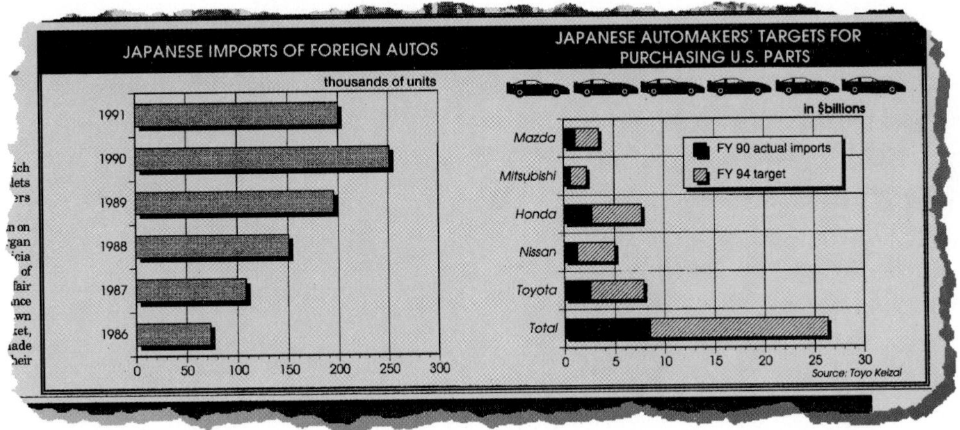

A computer industry consultant wants to know how much college freshmen are willing to spend to set up a computer in their dormitory rooms. After visiting a local college dorm, the consultant gathered the following data on the amount of money 20 students spent on computers:

$1,000	$7,000	$ 4,000	$1,000
5,000	1,000	3,000	5,000
2,000	3,000	3,000	3,000
8,000	9,000	3,000	6,000
6,000	1,000	10,000	1,000

Note that this raw data is not arranged in any order. To make the data more meaningful, the consultant made the following **frequency distribution** table. Think of this distribution table as a way to organize a list of numbers to show the patterns that may exist.

Price of computer	Tally	Frequency
$ 1,000	𝍸	5
2,000	|	1
3,000	𝍸	5
4,000	|	1
5,000	||	2
6,000	||	2
7,000	|	1
8,000	|	1
9,000	|	1
10,000	|	1

As you can see, 25% ($\frac{5}{20} = \frac{1}{4} = 25\%$) of the students spent $1,000 and another 25% spent $3,000. Only four students spent $7,000 or more.

Now let's see how we can use bar graphs.

Bar Graph

We can make a visual presentation of the computer purchases data collected by the consultant on the following graph. This is a **bar graph.** Note that the height of the bar represents the frequency of each purchase. Bar graphs can be vertical or horizontal.

Courtesy of Apple Computer, Inc.

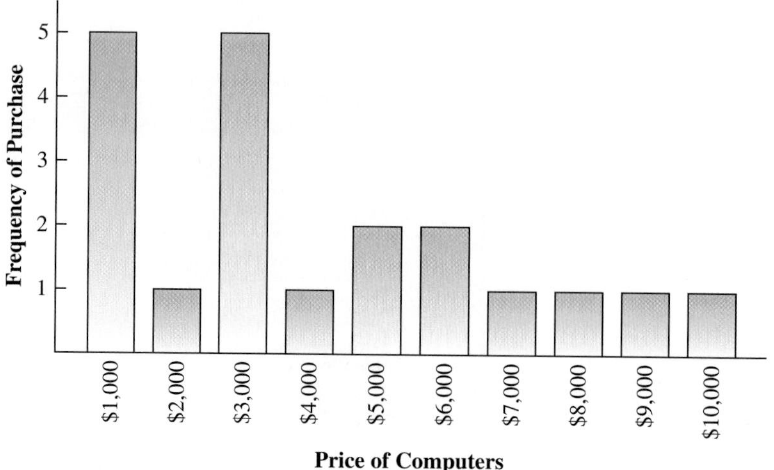

We can simplify this bar graph by grouping the prices of the computers. The grouping, or *intervals,* should be of equal sizes.

Class	Frequency
$1,000–$ 3,000.99	11
3,001– 5,000.99	3
5,001– 7,000.99	3
7,001– 9,000.99	2
9,001– 11,000.99	1

A bar graph for the grouped data follows.

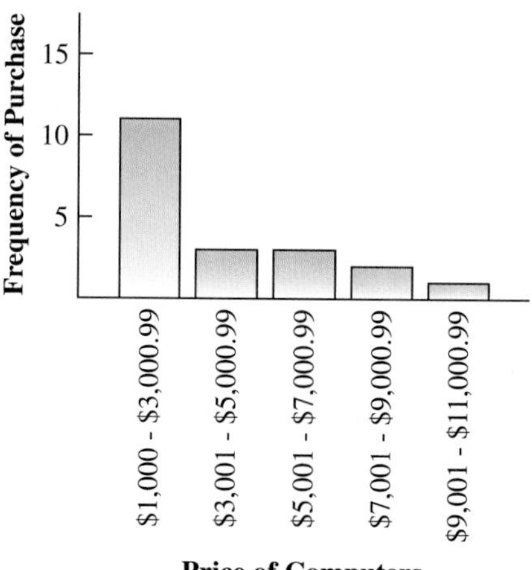

Here is an example of a bar graph that shows existing jobs versus jobs expected in the year 2,000.

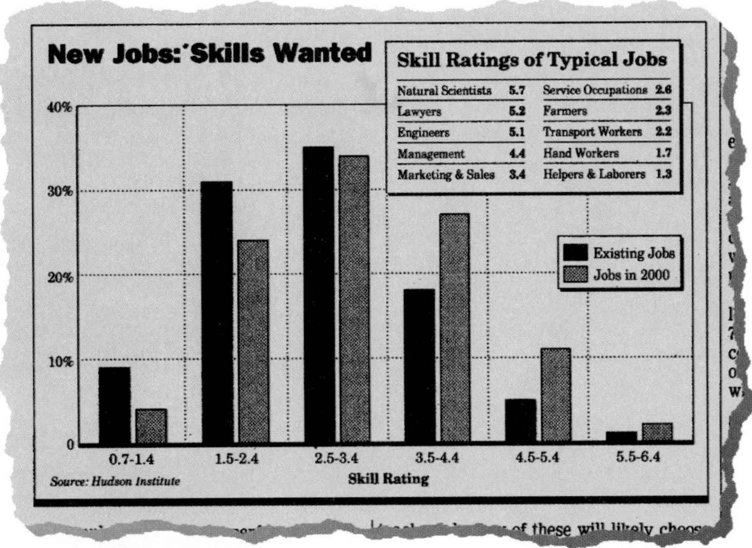

Now let's see how we use line graphs.

Line Graphs

Another type of graph that we can use to show trends is the **line graph.** In the following line graph, note how term insurance is compared to cash value policies.

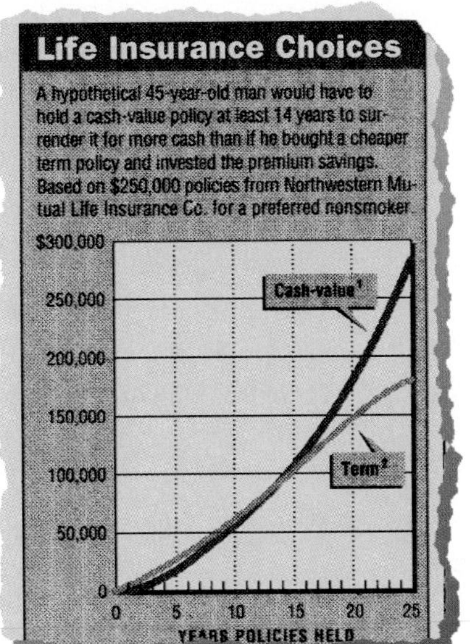

We conclude the unit with the use of circle graphs.

Circle Graphs

We often refer to **circle graphs** as pie charts. In a pie chart, the total circle represents 100%, or 360°. Note in the pie chart how a pepperoni pizza has 39% cheese while a cheese pizza has 52%.

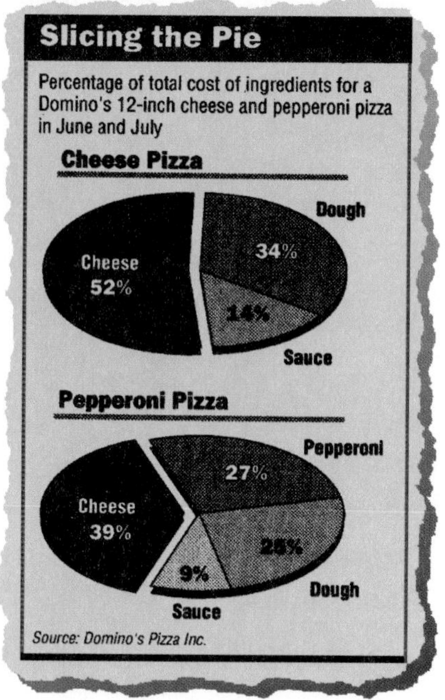

Reprinted by permission of *The Wall Street Journal*, © 1991 Dow Jones & Company, Inc. All Rights Reserved Worldwide.

To draw a pie chart, or circle graph, you begin by drawing a circle. Then you take the percentages and convert each percentage to degrees, fill in the pie chart with the percentages (they must total 360°), and label the sections. Let's show how we could construct the Slicing the Pie pie chart above.

$$\begin{aligned} 34\% &= .34 \times 360° = 122.4° \\ 52\% &= .52 \times 360° = 187.2° \\ 14\% &= .14 \times 360° = \underline{50.4°} \\ & \qquad\qquad\qquad\quad 360° \end{aligned}$$

Once again, we complete the unit with a Practice Quiz.

LU 22-2 PRACTICE QUIZ

1. The following is the number of sales made by 20 salespeople on a given day. Prepare a frequency distribution and a bar graph. Do not use intervals for this example.

5	8	9	1	4	4	0	3	2	8
8	9	5	1	9	6	7	5	9	10

2. Assuming the following market shares for diapers five years ago, prepare a pie chart:

Pampers	32%	Huggies	24%
Luvs	20%	Others	24%

SOLUTIONS TO LU 22-2 PRACTICE QUIZ

1.

Number of sales	Tally	Frequency
0	|	1
1	||	2
2	|	1
3	|	1
4	||	2
5	|||	3
6	|	1
7	|	1
8	|||	3
9	||||	4
10	|	1

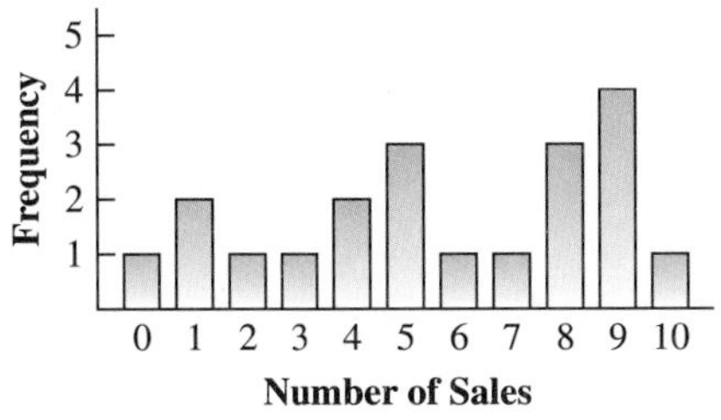

2.

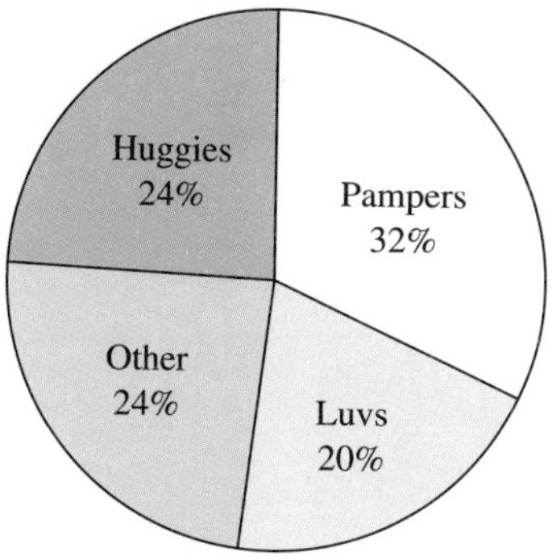

$.32 \times 360° = 115.20°$
$.20 \times 360° = 72.00°$
$.24 \times 360° = 86.40°$
$.24 \times 360° = 86.40°$

CHAPTER ORGANIZER: A REFERENCE GUIDE

Page	Topic	Key point, procedure, formula	Example(s) to illustrate situation
472	Mean	$\frac{\text{Sum of all values}}{\text{Number of values}}$	Age of basketball team: 22, 28, 31, 19, 15 $\text{Mean} = \frac{22 + 28 + 31 + 19 + 15}{5}$ $= 23$
472	Weighted mean	$\frac{\text{Sum of products}}{\text{Sum of frequencies}}$	S. M. T. W. Th. F. S. Sales $90 $75 $80 $75 $80 $90 $90 **Value** **Frequency** **Product** $90 3 $270 75 2 150 80 2 160 7 $580 $\text{Mean} = \frac{\$580}{7} = \$82.86$
473	Median	**1.** Arrange values from smallest to largest. **2. a. Odd number of values:** median is middle value. $\left(\frac{\text{Total number of numbers}}{2}\right)$ Next higher number is median. **b. Even number of values:** average of two middle values.	12, 15, 8, 6, 3 **1.** 3 6 8 12 15 **2.** $\frac{5}{2} = 2.5$ Median is third number, 8.

Page	Topic	Key point, procedure, formula	Example(s) to illustrate situation
475	Frequency distribution	Method of listing numbers or amounts not arranged in any particular way by columns for numbers (amounts), tally, and frequency	Number of sodas consumed in one day: 1, 5, 4, 3, 4, 2, 2, 3, 2, 0 **Number of sodas** / **Tally** / **Frequency** 0 / | / 1 1 / | / 1 2 / ||| / 3 3 / || / 2 4 / || / 2 5 / | / 1
476	Bar graph	Height of bar represents frequency. Bar graph used for grouped data. Bar graphs can be vertical or horizontal.	From soda example above: 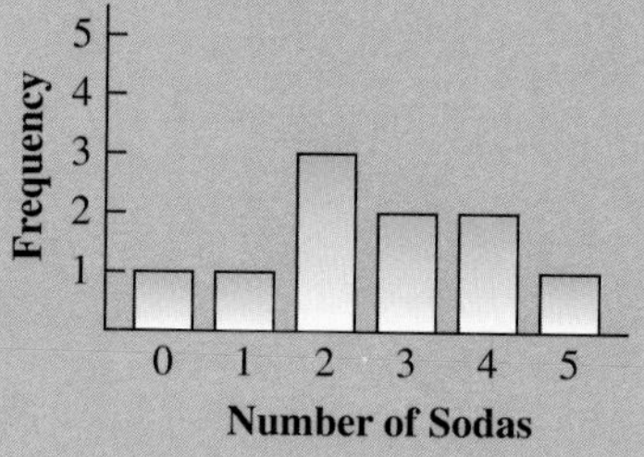 Frequency: 1, 2, 3, 4, 5 0 1 2 3 4 5 **Number of Sodas**
477	Line graph	Shows trend. Helps to put numbers in order.	**Sales** 1993 $1,000 1994 2,000 1995 3,000 3,000 2,000 1,000 1993 1994 1995
478	Circle graph	Circle = 360° % × 360° = Degrees of pie to represent percent Total should = 360°	60% favor diet soda 40% favor sugared soda 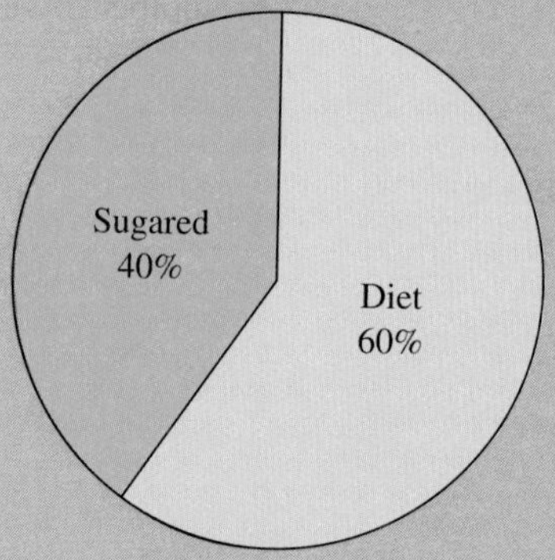 Sugared 40% Diet 60% .60 × 360° = 216° .40 × 360° = 144° 360°
	Key terms	Bar graph, *pp. 475–76* Circle graph, *p. 478* Frequency distribution, *p. 475* Line graph, *p. 477*	Mean, *p. 472* Median, *p. 472* Mode, *p. 474* Weighted mean, *p. 472*

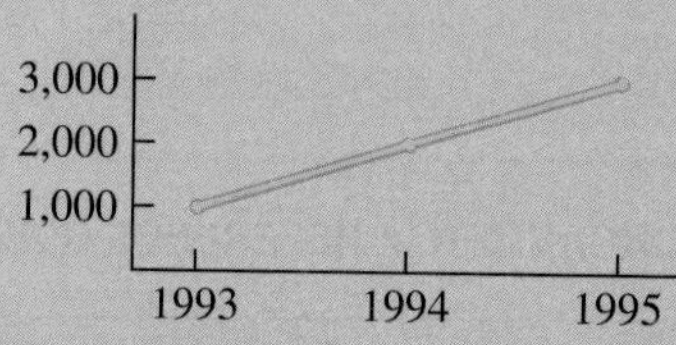

END-OF-CHAPTER PROBLEMS

Drill Problems

Additional homework assignments by learning unit are at the end of text in Appendix I (p. I–94). Solutions to odd problems are at the end of text in Appendix II.

Calculate the mean (to the nearest hundredth):

22–1. 7, 9, 3, 6 $= \frac{25}{4} = 6.25$

22–2. 9, 3, 8, 6, 5, 4 $= \frac{35}{6} = 5.83$

22–3. \$55.83, \$66.92, \$108.93 $= \frac{\$231.68}{3} = \$77.23$

22–4. \$1,001, \$68.50, \$33.82, \$581.95 $= \frac{\$1,685.27}{4} = \$421.32$

22–5. Calculate the grade point average: A = 4, B = 3, C = 2, D = 1, F = 0 (to nearest tenth).

Courses attempted	Credits	Grade	Units × Grade	
Computer Principles	3	B	9 (3 × 3)	
Business Law	3	C	6 (3 × 2)	
Logic	3	D	3 (3 × 1)	$\frac{43}{16} = 2.7$
Biology	4	A	16 (4 × 4)	
Marketing	3	B	9 (3 × 3)	
	16		43	

22–6. Find the weighted mean (to nearest tenth):

Value	Frequency	Product	
4	7	28	
8	3	24	$\frac{78}{21} = 3.7$
2	9	18	
4	2	8	
	21	78	

Find the median:

22–7. 55, 10, 19, 38, 100, 25 $\frac{25 + 38}{2} = 31.5$
10, 19, 25, 38, 55, 100

22–8. 95, 103, 98, 62, 31, 15, 82
15, 31, 62, 82, 95, 98, 103
↑

Find the mode:

22–9. 8, 9, 3, 4, 12, 8, 8, 9 — 8

22–10. 22, 19, 15, 16, 18, 18, 5, 18 — 18

22–11. 5, 3, 9, 1, 2, 10 — No mode

22–12. Given the following sales of Lowe Corporation, prepare a line graph (run sales from \$5,000 to \$20,000).

1994	\$ 8,000
1995	11,000
1996	13,000
1997	18,000

22–13. Prepare a frequency distribution from the following weekly salaries of teachers at Moore Community College. Use intervals of:

\$200–\$299.99
300–399.99
400–499.99
500–599.99

\$210	\$505	\$310	\$380	\$275
290	480	550	490	200
286	410	305	444	368

Salaries	Tally	Frequency
\$200–\$299.99	~~IIII~~	5
300–399.99	IIII	4
400–499.99	IIII	4
500–599.99	II	2

22–14. Prepare a bar graph from frequency distribution in Problem 22–13.

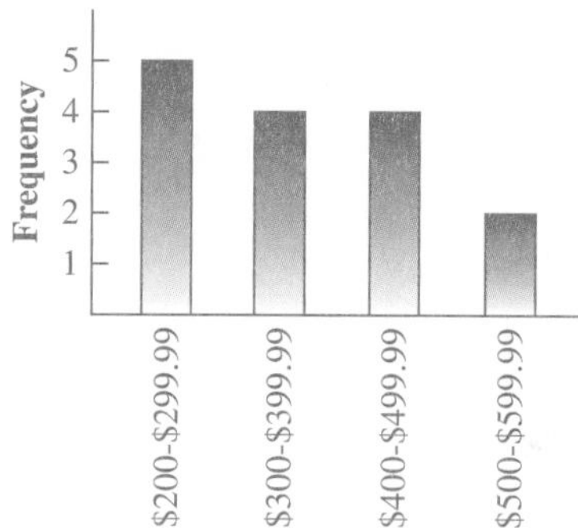

22–15. How many degrees on a pie chart would each be given from the following:

Wear digital watch	42%	$.42 \times 360° = 151.2°$
Wear traditional watch	51%	$.51 \times 360° = 183.6°$
Wear no watch	7%	$.07 \times 360° = 25.2°$
		360°

Word Problems

22–16. The four leading camcorders weighed the following: 4 pounds, 3 pounds, 2 pounds, 1 pound. What would be the **(a)** mean, **(b)** median, and **(c)** mode.

a. Mean $= \frac{4 + 3 + 2 + 1}{4} = \frac{10}{4} = 2.5$ pounds

b. Median = 1, 2, 3, 4 $\quad \frac{2 + 3}{2} = 2.5$

c. No mode

22–17. Neil Keefe recorded the cost of a Diet Coke at five different locations as follows: \$.90, \$.55, \$.60, \$.65, \$.85. What would be the median price?
\$.55, \$.60, \$.65, \$.85, \$.90
↑

22–18. Moe's garage received the following number of Sears Die Hard batteries each day:

M.	T.	W.	Th.	F.	Sat.
14	5	6	14	6	6

What is the mode? 6

22–19. Bill Small, a travel agent, provided Alice Hall the following information regarding the cost of her upcoming vacation:

Transportation	35%
Hotel	28%
Food and entertainment	20%
Miscellaneous	17%

Construct a circle graph for Alice.

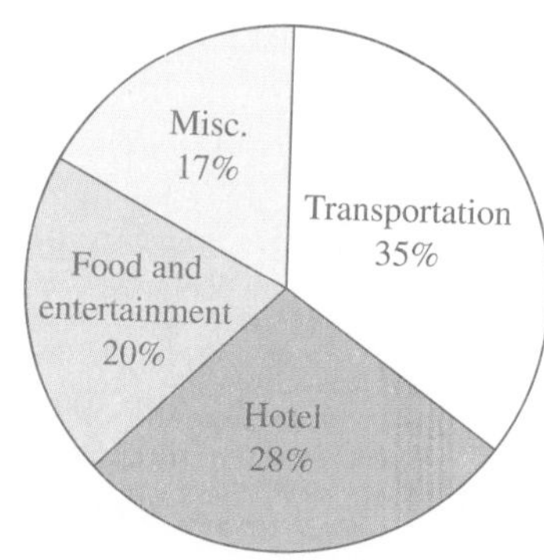

$.35 \times 360° = 126°$
$.28 \times 360° = 100.8°$
$.20 \times 360° = 72°$
$.17 \times 360° = 61.2°$

22–20. Jim Smith, a marketing student, observed how much each customer spent in a local convenience store. Based on the following results, prepare (**a**) a frequency distribution and (**b**) a bar graph. Use intervals of $0–$5.99, $6.00–$11.99, $12.00–$17.99 and $18.00–$23.99.

$18.50	$18.24	$ 6.88	$9.95
16.10	3.55	14.10	6.80
12.11	3.82	2.10	
15.88	3.95	5.50	

Intervals	Tally	Frequency
$0–$5.99	𝍸	5
$6.00–$11.99	|||	3
$12.00–$17.99	||||	4
$18.00–$23.99	||	2

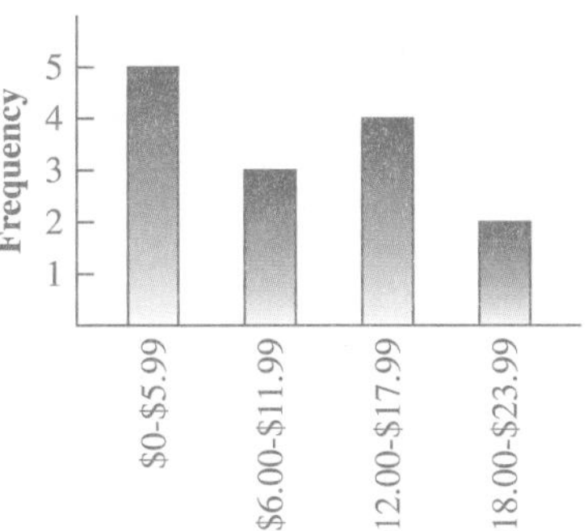

22–21. Angie's Bakery bakes bagels. Find the weighted mean (to nearest whole) given the following daily production for June:

200	150	200	150	200
150	190	360	360	150
190	190	190	200	150
360	400	400	150	200
400	360	150	400	360
400	400	200	150	150

	Tally	Day	× Bagels	= Product
150	𝍸 ||||	9	× 150	= 1,350
190	||||	4	× 190	= 760
200	𝍸 |	6	× 200	= 1,200
360	𝍸	5	× 360	= 1,800
400	𝍸 |	6	× 400	= 2,400
				7,510

$$\frac{7{,}510}{30} = 250.33 = 250 \text{ bagels}$$

22–22. Melvin Company reported sales in 1995 of $300,000. This compared to sales of $150,000 in 1994 and $100,000 in 1993. Please construct a line graph for Melvin Company.

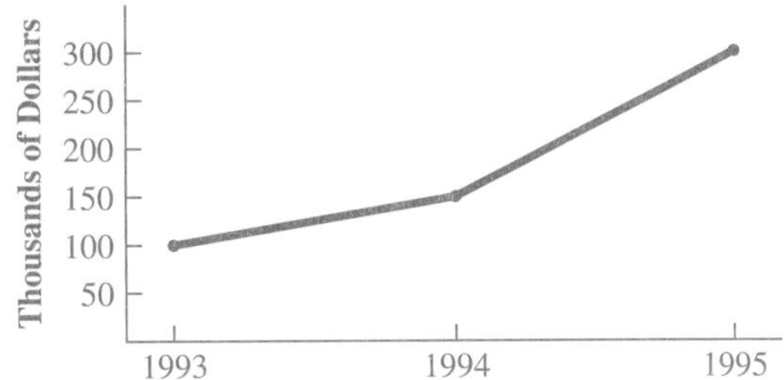

Challenge Problem

Calculate Circle Graph Percents and Degrees

22–23. The following circle graph is a suggested budget for Ron Rye and his family for a month:

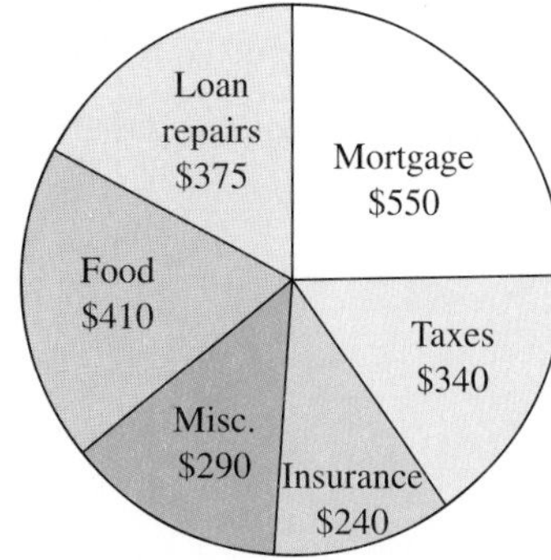

Ron would like you to calculate the percent (to hundredth) for each part of the circle graph along with the appropriate number of degrees.

$\$550 + \$340 + \$240 + \$290 + \$410 + \$375 = \$2,205$

$\frac{\$550}{\$2,205} = 24.94\%$ $\frac{\$340}{\$2,205} = 15.42\%$ $\frac{\$240}{\$2,205} = 10.88\%$

$\frac{\$290}{\$2,205} = 13.15\%$ $\frac{\$410}{\$2,205} = 18.59\%$ $\frac{\$375}{\$2,205} = 17.01\%$

$.2494 \times 360° = 89.78°$
$.1542 \times 360° = 55.51°$
$.1088 \times 360° = 39.17°$
$.1315 \times 360° = 47.34°$
$.1859 \times 360° = 66.92°$
$.1701 \times 360° = \underline{61.24°}$
$359.96°$ (due to rounding)

Summary Practice Test

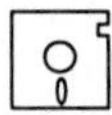

Solutions are at end of text in Appendix II.

Quick Reference
If you get any wrong answers, study the page numbers given for each problem.

1. P. 472–73.

1. Sales at Sullivan Realty totaled 10 homes for the month. They were as follows: \$182,900; \$189,000; \$160,000; \$210,000; \$175,000; \$158,000; \$99,000; \$126,000; \$185,000; \$109,000. Calculate the mean and the median.

Mean

$$\frac{\$182,900 + \$189,000 + \$160,000 + \$210,000 + \$175,000 + \$158,000 + \$99,000 + \$126,000 + \$185,000 + \$109,000}{10}$$

$= \$159,390$

Median \$99,000; \$109,000; \$126,000; \$158,000; \$160,000; \$175,000; \$182,900; \$185,000; \$189,000; \$210,000.

$$\frac{\$160,000 + \$175,000}{2} = \$167,500$$

2. P. 474.

2. Jones Department Store counted the number of customers entering the store for a week. The results: 1,008, 1,009, 850, 750, 1,009, 899, 1,009. What is the mode?
1,009

3. P. 473.

3. This semester Mary Black took four 3-credit courses at River Community College. She received an A in Accounting and three Bs (History, Logic, Math). What is her cumulative grade point average (assume A = 4, B = 3) to nearest hundredth?

Accounting	$3 \times 4 = 12$	
History	$3 \times 3 = 9$	$\frac{39}{12} = 3.25$
Logic	$3 \times 3 = 9$	
Math	$3 \times 3 = 9$	
	12 39	

4. P. 475.

4. Moe's Hardware reported the following sales for the first 20 days of October:

\$400	\$600	\$400	\$400	\$600
300	500	500	300	100
200	700	300	300	200
500	500	200	700	200

Prepare a frequency distribution for Moe.

Sales	Tally	Frequency
\$100	|	1
200	||||	4
300	||||	4
400	|||	3
500	||||	4
600	||	2
700	||	2

5. P. 476.

5. Jones Printing Company produced the following number of bound books during the first 5 weeks of last year. Prepare a bar graph.

Week	Books bound
1	500
2	600
3	800
4	300
5	400

Bound Books
800
700
600
500
400
300
200
100
1 2 3 4 5
Weeks

6. P. 478.

6. McGiven Corporation reported record profits of 15%. It stated in the report that cost of sales were 55% with expenses of 30%. Prepare a pie graph for McGiven.

$.15 \times 360° = 54°$
$.55 \times 360° = 198°$
$.30 \times 360° = 108°$

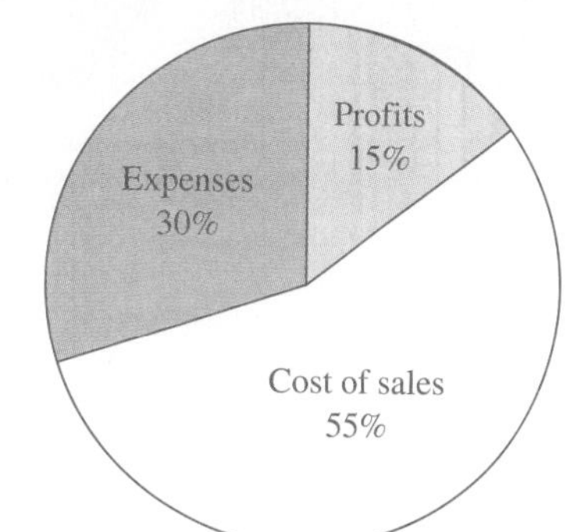

Project A

The cereal market is a $7.5 billion a year business. Based on the pie chart, what are the sales for each company?

General Mills	.28 × $7.5 = $2.10
Post	.11 × 7.5 = $ .83
Quaker	.07 × 7.5 = $ .53
Ralston	.06 × 7.5 = $ .45
Nabisco	.04 × 7.5 = $ .30
Private label	.05 × 7.5 = $ .38
Other	.01 × 7.5 = $ .08
Kellogg	.38 × 7.5 = $2.85

Appendixes

LIST OF APPENDIXES

I

Additional Homework Assignments by Learning Unit

Date ____________ Name ________________________________

LU 1-1: Writing Whole Numbers; Rounding Whole Numbers

Drill Problems

1. Express the following numbers in verbal form:

a. 3,875 Three thousand, eight hundred seventy-five

b. 160,501 One hundred sixty thousand, five hundred one

c. 2,098,767 Two million, ninety-eight thousand, seven hundred sixty-seven

d. 58,003 Fifty-eight thousand, three

e. 50,025,212,015 Fifty billion, twenty-five million, two hundred twelve thousand, fifteen

2. Write in numeric form:

a. Seventy thousand, one hundred eighty-two 70,182

b. Fifty-eight thousand, three 58,003

c. Two hundred eighty thousand, five 280,005

d. Three million, ten 3,000,010

e. Sixty-seven thousand, seven hundred sixty 67,760

3. Round off the following numbers:

a. To the nearest ten:

42 40 379 380 855 860 5,981 5,980 206 210

b. To the nearest hundred:

9,664 9,700 2,074 2,100 888 900 271 300 75 100

c. To the nearest thousand:

21,486 21,000 621 1,000 3,504 4,000 9,735 10,000

4. Round off each number to the nearest ten, nearest hundred, nearest thousand, and round all the way. (Remember that you are rounding the original number each time.)

		Nearest ten	Nearest hundred	Nearest thousand	Round all the way
a.	4,752	4,750	4,800	5,000	5,000
b.	70,351	70,350	70,400	70,000	70,000
c.	9,386	9,390	9,400	9,000	9,000
d.	4,983	4,980	5,000	5,000	5,000
e.	408,119	408,120	408,100	408,000	400,000
f.	30,051	30,050	30,100	30,000	30,000

5. Name the place position (place value) of the underlined digit.

a. 8,348 hundreds place

b. 9,734 thousands place

c. 347,107 ten thousands place

d. 723 tens place

e. 28,200,000,121 billions place

f. 706,359,005 ten millions place

g. 27,563,530 hundred thousands place

Word Problems

6. Ken Lawler was shopping for a computer. He went to three different stores and found the computer he wanted at three different prices. At Store A the price was $2,115, at Store B the price was $1,990, and at Store C the price was $2,050. What is the approximate price Ken will have to pay for the computer? Round to the nearest thousand. (Just one price.)

Approximately $2,000

7. Amy Parker had to write a check at the bookstore when she purchased her books for the new semester. The total cost of the books was $384. How will she write this amount in verbal form on her check?
   Three hundred eighty-four
8. Matt Schaeffer was listening to the news and heard that steel production last week was one million, five hundred eighty-seven thousand tons. Express this amount in numeric form.
   1,587,000 tons
9. Jackie Martin is the city clerk and must go to the alderman's meetings and take notes on what is discussed. At last night's meeting, they were discussing repairs for the public library, which will cost three hundred seventy-five thousand, nine hundred eighty-five dollars. Write this in numeric form as Jackie would.
   $375,985
10. A government survey revealed that 25,963,400 people are employed as office workers. To show the approximate number of office workers, round the number all the way.
    30,000,000 office workers
11. Bob Donaldson wished to present his top student with a certificate of achievement at the end of the school year in 1995. To make it appear more official, he wanted to write the year in verbal form. How will he write the year?
    One thousand, nine hundred ninety-five
12. Nancy Morrissey has a problem reading large numbers and determining place value. She asked her brother to name the place value of the 4 in the number 13,542,966. Can you tell Nancy the place value of the 4? What is the place value of the 3?
    The 4 is in the ___ten thousands___ place
    The 3 is in the ___millions___ place

Date ____________ Name ____________________________

LU 1-2: Whole Numbers—Addition and Subtraction

Drill Problems

1. Add by totaling each separate column:

a.	b.	c.	d.	e.	f.	g.	h.
776	43	493	36	716	535	751	75,730
185	58	826	76	458	107	378	48,531
11	96	9	43	397	778	135	15,797
15	17	11	24	139	215	747	8
8	18	1 2	19	478	391	368	15
961	197	1,319	16	38	26	29	1 9
			179	25	20	25	18
				1 9	1 8	2 1	12
				2,188	2,026	2,379	140,058

2. Estimate by rounding all the way, then add the actual numbers:

a.		b.		c.	
580	600	1,470	1,000	475	500
971	1,000	7,631	8,000	837	800
548	500	4,383	4,000	213	200
430	400	13,484	13,000	775	800
506	500			432	400
3,035	3,000			2,732	2,700

d.		e.		f.	
442	400	2,571	3,000	10,928	10,000
609	600	3,625	4,000	9,321	9,000
766	800	4,091	4,000	12,654	10,000
410	400	928	1,000	15,492	20,000
128	100	11,215	12,000	48,395	49,000
2,355	2,300				

3. Estimate by rounding all the way, then subtract the actual numbers:

a.		b.		c.	
81	80	91	90	68	70
− 42	− 40	− 33	− 30	− 59	− 60
39	40	58	60	9	10

d.		e.		f.	
981	1,000	622	600	1,125	1,000
− 283	−300	− 328	− 300	− 913	− 900
698	700	294	300	212	100

4. Subtract and check:

a.		b.		c.	
4,947	585	3,724	1,586	474,820	388,973
− 4,362	+ 4,362	− 2,138	+ 2,138	− 85,847	+ 85,847
585	4,947	1,586	3,724	388,973	474,820

d.		e.		f.	
50,000	28,238	65,003	40,016	15,715	12,212
− 21,762	+ 21,762	− 24,987	+ 24,987	− 3,503	+ 3,503
28,238	50,000	40,016	65,003	12,212	15,715

5. In the following sales report, total the rows and the columns, then check that the grand total is the same both horizontally and vertically.

	Salesman	Region 1	Region 2	Region 3	Total
a.	Becker	$ 5,692	$ 7,403	$ 3,591	$16,686
b.	Edwards	7,652	7,590	3,021	18,263
c.	Graff	6,545	6,738	4,545	17,828
d.	Jackson	6,937	6,950	4,913	18,800
e.	Total	$26,826	$28,681	$16,070	$71,577

Word Problems

6. Tom Griffin owes $4,921 on his car loan, plus interest of $541. How much will it cost him to pay off this loan?

   $4,921 + $541 = $5,462 to pay off loan

7. Sales at Rich's Convenience Store were $3,587 on Monday, $3,944 on Tuesday, $4,007 on Wednesday, $3,890 on Thursday, and $4,545 on Friday. What were the total sales for the week?

```
$ 3,587
  3,944
  4,007
  3,890
  4,545
$19,973 total sales
```

8. Poor's Variety Store sold $5,000 worth of lottery tickets in the first week of August; they sold $289 less in the second week. How much were the lottery ticket sales in the second week of August?

$5,000 − $289 = $4,711 in lottery ticket sales

9. A truck weighed 9,550 pounds when it was empty. After being filled with rubbish, it was driven to the dump where it was weighed in at 22,347 pounds. How much did the rubbish weigh?

22,347 − 9,550 = 12,797 pounds of rubbish

10. Lynn Jackson had $549 in her checking account when she went to the bookstore. Lynn purchased an accounting book for $62, the working papers for $28, a study guide for $25, and a mechanical pencil for $5. After Lynn writes a check for the entire purchase, how much money will remain in her checking account?

```
$ 62                      $549
  28                     − 120
  25                      $429 remaining balance
   5
$120 total of purchase
```

11. A new hard-body truck is advertised with a base price of $6,986 delivered. However, the window sticker on the truck reads as follows: tinted glass, $210; automatic transmission, $650; power steering, $210; power brakes, $215; safety locks, $95; air conditioning, $1,056. Estimate the total price, including the accessories, by rounding all the way, *then* calculate the exact price.

```
$7,000      $6,986
   200         210
   700         650
   200         210
   200         215
   100          95
 1,000       1,056
$9,400      $9,422
```

12. Four different stores are offering the same make and model of camcorder:

Store A	Store B	Store C	Store D
$1,285	$1,380	$1,440	$1,355

Find the difference between the highest price and the lowest price. (Check your answer.)

Check

```
 $1,440          $ 155
− 1,285        + 1,285
 $  155         $1,440
```

Date ____________ Name ____________

LU 1-3: Whole Numbers—Multiplication and Division

Drill Problems

1. In the following problems, first estimate by rounding all the way, then work the actual problems, and check:

	Actual	Estimate	Check
a.	175 × 14 = 700 + 175 = 2,450	200 × 10 = 2,000	4 × 175 = 700 10 × 175 = 1,750 2,450
b.	4,216 × 45 = 21080 + 16864 = 189,720	4,000 × 50 = 200,000	5 × 4,216 = 21,080 40 × 4,216 = 168,640 189,720
c.	52,376 × 309 = 471384 + 1571280 = 16,184,184	50,000 × 300 = 15,000,000	9 × 52,376 = 471,384 300 × 52,376 = 15,712,800 16,184,184
d.	3,106 × 28 = 24848 + 6212 = 86,968	3,000 × 30 = 90,000	8 × 3,106 = 24,848 20 × 3,106 = 62,120 86,968

2. Multiply (use the shortcut when applicable):

a. 4,072 × 100 = 407,200

1 × 4,072 + 2 zeros = 407,200

b. 5,100 × 40 = 204,000

4 × 51 + 3 zeros = 204,000

c. 76,000 × 1,200 = 91,200,000

12 × 76 + 5 zeros = 91,200,000

d. 93 × 100,000 = 9,300,000

93 × 1 + 5 zeros = 9,300,000

3. Divide by rounding all the way, then do the actual calculation and check showing the remainder as a whole number.

	Actual	Estimate	Check
a.	8)7,709 = 963 R5 72 50 48 29 24 5	8)8,000 = 1,000	8 × 963 = 7,704 + 5 7,709
b.	26)5,910 = 227 R8 52 71 52 190 182 8	30)6,000 = 200	26 × 227 = 5,902 + 8 5,910

	Actual	Estimate	Check
c.	$\begin{array}{r} 25 \text{ R8} \\ 151\overline{)3,783} \\ \underline{302} \\ 763 \\ \underline{755} \\ 8 \end{array}$	$\begin{array}{r} 20 \\ 200\overline{)4,000} \end{array}$	$151 \times 25 = 3,775$ $+ 8$ $3,783$
d.	$\begin{array}{r} 425 \\ 46\overline{)19,550} \\ \underline{184} \\ 115 \\ \underline{92} \\ 230 \\ \underline{230} \end{array}$	$\begin{array}{r} 400 \\ 50\overline{)20,000} \end{array}$	$46 \times 425 = 19,550$

4. Divide by the shortcut method:

a. $200\overline{)5,400}$ = 27
Drop 2 zeros: 54 ÷ 2 = 27

b. $50\overline{)5,650}$ = 113
Drop 1 zero: 565 ÷ 5 = 113

c. $1,200\overline{)43,200}$ = 36
Drop 2 zeros: 432 ÷ 12 = 36

d. $17,000\overline{)510,000}$ = 30
Drop 3 zeros: 510 ÷ 17 = 30

Word Problems

5. Jeanne Francis sells state lottery tickets in her variety store. If Jeanne's Variety Store sells 385 lottery tickets per day, how many tickets will be sold in a 7-day period?
385 × 7 = 2,695 lottery tickets

6. Arlex Oil Corporation employs 100 people who are eligible for profit sharing. The financial manager has announced that the profits to be shared amount to $64,000. How much will each employee receive?
$64,000 ÷ 100 = $640 per employee

7. John Duncan's employer withheld $4,056 in federal taxes from his pay for the year. If equal deductions are made each week, what is John's weekly deduction?
$4,056 ÷ 52 = $78 weekly withholding

8. Anne Domingoes drives a Volvo that gets 32 miles per gallon of gasoline. How many miles can she travel on 25 gallons of gas?
32 × 25 = 800 miles

9. How many 8-inch pieces of yellow ribbon can be cut from a spool of ribbon that contains 6 yards? (1 yard = 36 inches)
6 × 36 = 216 total inches of ribbon   216 ÷ 8 = 27 pieces of ribbon

10. The number of commercials aired per day on a local television station is 672. How many commercials are aired in a year?
672 × 365 = 245,280 commercials per year

11. The computer department at City College purchased 18 computers at a cost of $2,400 each. What was the total price for the computer purchase?
$2,400 × 18 = $43,200 total price

12. Net income for the Goodwin's Partnership was $64,500. The five partners share profits and losses equally. What was each partner's share?
$64,500 ÷ 5 = $12,900 per partner

13. Ben Krenshaw's supervisor at the construction site told Ben to divide a load of 1,423 bricks into stacks containing 35 bricks each. How many stacks will there be when Ben has finished the job? How many "extra" bricks will there be?

$$\begin{array}{r} 40 \text{ R23} \\ 35\overline{)1,423} \\ \underline{1\ 40} \\ 23 \end{array}$$

40 stacks, and 23 "extra" bricks

Date ____________ Name ____________________________

LU 2-1: Types of Fractions and Conversion Procedures

Drill Problems

1. Identify the type of fraction—proper, improper, or mixed:

a. $\frac{1}{10}$ Proper **b.** $\frac{27}{29}$ Proper **c.** $\frac{29}{27}$ Improper

d. $9\frac{3}{11}$ Mixed number **e.** $\frac{18}{5}$ Improper **f.** $\frac{30}{37}$ Proper

2. Convert to a mixed number:

a. $\frac{29}{4}$

$4\overline{)29}$ = $7\frac{1}{4}$; 28; 1

b. $\frac{137}{8}$

$8\overline{)137}$ = $17\frac{1}{8}$; 8; 57; 56; 1

c. $\frac{27}{5}$

$5\overline{)27}$ = $5\frac{2}{5}$; 25; 2

d. $\frac{29}{9}$

$9\overline{)29}$ = $3\frac{2}{9}$; 27; 2

e. $\frac{71}{8}$

$8\overline{)71}$ = $8\frac{7}{8}$; 64; 7

f. $\frac{43}{6}$

$6\overline{)43}$ = $7\frac{1}{6}$; 42; 1

3. Convert mixed number to an improper fraction:

a. $7\frac{1}{5} = \frac{(5 \times 7) + 1}{5} = \frac{36}{5}$ **b.** $12\frac{3}{11} = \frac{(11 \times 12) + 3}{11} = \frac{135}{11}$

c. $4\frac{3}{7} = \frac{(7 \times 4) + 3}{7} = \frac{31}{7}$ **d.** $20\frac{4}{9} = \frac{(9 \times 20) + 4}{9} = \frac{184}{9}$

e. $10\frac{11}{12} = \frac{(12 \times 10) + 11}{12} = \frac{131}{12}$ **f.** $17\frac{2}{3} = \frac{(3 \times 17) + 2}{3} = \frac{53}{3}$

4. Tell whether the fractions in each pair are equivalent or not:

a. $\frac{3}{4}$ $\frac{9}{12}$ Yes **b.** $\frac{2}{3}$ $\frac{12}{18}$ Yes **c.** $\frac{7}{8}$ $\frac{15}{16}$ No

d. $\frac{4}{5}$ $\frac{12}{15}$ Yes **e.** $\frac{3}{2}$ $\frac{9}{4}$ No **f.** $\frac{5}{8}$ $\frac{7}{11}$ No

g. $\frac{7}{12}$ $\frac{7}{24}$ No **h.** $\frac{5}{4}$ $\frac{30}{24}$ Yes **i.** $\frac{10}{26}$ $\frac{12}{26}$ No

5. Find the greatest common divisor by the step approach and reduce to lowest terms:

a. $\frac{36}{42}$

$36\overline{)42}$ = 1; 36; 6 → $6\overline{)36}$ = 6; 36; 0

$\frac{36 \div 6}{42 \div 6} = \frac{6}{7}$

b. $\frac{30}{75}$

$30\overline{)75}$ = 2; 60; 15 → $15\overline{)30}$ = 2; 30; 0

$\frac{30 \div 15}{75 \div 15} = \frac{2}{5}$

c. $\frac{74}{148}$

$74\overline{)148}$ = 2; 148; 0

$\frac{74 \div 74}{148 \div 74} = \frac{1}{2}$

d. $\frac{15}{600}$

$15\overline{)600}$ = 40; 60; 00

$\frac{15 \div 15}{600 \div 15} = \frac{1}{40}$

e. $\frac{96}{132}$

$96\overline{)132}$ = 1; 96; 36 → $36\overline{)96}$ = 2; 72; 24 → $24\overline{)36}$ = 1; 24; 12 → $12\overline{)24}$ = 2; 24; 0

$\frac{96 \div 12}{132 \div 12} = \frac{8}{11}$

f. $\frac{84}{154}$

$84\overline{)154}$ = 1; 84; 70 $70\overline{)84}$ = 1; 70; 14 $14\overline{)70}$ = 5; 70; 0

$\frac{84 \div 14}{154 \div 14} = \frac{6}{11}$

6. Convert to higher terms:

a. $\frac{8}{10} = \frac{}{70}$	$10\overline{)70}$ quotient 7	$7 \times 8 = 56$	$\frac{8}{10} = \frac{56}{70}$
b. $\frac{2}{15} = \frac{}{30}$	$15\overline{)30}$ quotient 2	$2 \times 2 = 4$	$\frac{2}{15} = \frac{4}{30}$
c. $\frac{6}{11} = \frac{}{132}$	$11\overline{)132}$ quotient 12	$12 \times 6 = 72$	$\frac{6}{11} = \frac{72}{132}$
d. $\frac{4}{9} = \frac{}{36}$	$9\overline{)36}$ quotient 4	$4 \times 4 = 16$	$\frac{4}{9} = \frac{16}{36}$
e. $\frac{7}{20} = \frac{}{100}$	$20\overline{)100}$ quotient 5	$7 \times 5 = 35$	$\frac{7}{20} = \frac{35}{100}$
f. $\frac{7}{8} = \frac{}{560}$	$8\overline{)560}$ quotient 70	$7 \times 70 = 490$	$\frac{7}{8} = \frac{490}{560}$

Word Problems

7. Ken drove to college in $3\frac{1}{4}$ hours. How many quarter hours is that? (Show as an improper fraction.)

$3\frac{1}{4} = \frac{(4 \times 3) + 1}{4} = \frac{13}{4}$ hours

8. Mary looked in the refrigerator for a dozen eggs. When she found the box, only 5 eggs were left. What fractional part of the box of eggs were left?

$\frac{5}{12}$ of the box

9. At a recent meeting of a local Boosters Club, 17 out of the 25 members attending were men. What fraction of those in attendance were men?

$\frac{17}{25}$ men

10. By weight, water is two parts out of three parts of the human body. What fraction is water?

$\frac{2}{3}$ of the body is water

11. Three out of 5 students who begin college will continue until they receive their degree. Show in fractional form how many out of 100 beginning students will graduate.

$\frac{3}{5} = \frac{60}{100}$

12. Tina and her friends came in late to a party and found only $\frac{3}{4}$ of an uncut pizza remaining. In order for everyone to get some pizza, she wanted to divide it into smaller pieces. If she divides the pizza into twelfths, how many pieces will she have? Show your answer in fractional form.

$\frac{3}{4} = \frac{9}{12}$

13. Sharon and Spunky noted that it took them 35 minutes to do their exercise routine. What fractional part of an hour is that? (Show your answer in lowest terms.)

$\frac{35}{60} = \frac{35 \div 5}{60 \div 5} = \frac{7}{12}$

14. Norman and his friend ordered several pizzas, which were all cut into eighths. The group ate 43 pieces of pizza. How many pizzas did they eat? (Show your answer as a mixed number.)

$\frac{43}{8} = 5\frac{3}{8}$

$8\overline{)43}$ = 5 R3; 40; 3

Date ____________ Name ______________________________________

LU 2-2: Fractions—Addition and Subtraction

Drill Problems

1. Find the least common denominator (LCD) for each of the following groups of denominators using the prime numbers.

a. 12, 15, 30

$$\begin{array}{r|rrr} 2 & 12 & 15 & 30 \\ 3 & 6 & 15 & 15 \\ 5 & 2 & 5 & 5 \\ & 2 & 1 & 1 \end{array}$$

$2 \times 3 \times 5 \times 2 = 60$

b. 9, 15, 20

$$\begin{array}{r|rrr} 3 & 9 & 15 & 20 \\ 5 & 3 & 5 & 20 \\ & 3 & 1 & 4 \end{array}$$

$3 \times 5 \times 3 \times 1 \times 4 = 180$

c. 12, 15, 32

$$\begin{array}{r|rrr} 2 & 12 & 15 & 32 \\ 2 & 6 & 15 & 16 \\ 3 & 3 & 15 & 8 \\ & 1 & 5 & 8 \end{array}$$

$2 \times 2 \times 3 \times 1 \times 5 \times 8 = 480$

d. 7, 9, 14, 28

$$\begin{array}{r|rrrr} 2 & 7 & 9 & 14 & 28 \\ 7 & 7 & 9 & 7 & 14 \\ & 1 & 9 & 1 & 2 \end{array}$$

$2 \times 7 \times 1 \times 9 \times 1 \times 2 = 252$

2. Add and reduce to lowest terms or change to mixed number if needed.

a. $\frac{2}{7} + \frac{3}{7} = \frac{5}{7}$

b. $\frac{5}{12} + \frac{8}{15} = \frac{25}{60} + \frac{32}{60} = \frac{57}{60} = \frac{19}{20}$

$\frac{5}{12} = \frac{?}{60} = \frac{25}{60} \quad \frac{8}{15} = \frac{?}{60} = \frac{32}{60}$

c. $\frac{7}{8} + \frac{5}{12} = 1\frac{7}{24}$

$\frac{21}{24} + \frac{10}{24} = \frac{31}{24} \quad \frac{7}{8} = \frac{?}{24} = \frac{21}{24} \quad \frac{5}{12} = \frac{?}{24} = \frac{10}{24}$

$\frac{31}{24} = 24\overline{)31}$ 1 R7 $= 1\frac{7}{24}$

$$\begin{array}{r} 24 \\ \hline 7 \end{array}$$

d. $7\frac{2}{3} + 5\frac{1}{4} = 12\frac{11}{12}$

$$\begin{array}{rr} 7\frac{2}{3} & 7\frac{8}{12} \\ +\,5\frac{1}{4} & +\,5\frac{3}{12} \\ \hline & 12\frac{11}{12} \end{array}$$

$\frac{2}{3} = \frac{?}{12} = \frac{8}{12} \quad \frac{1}{4} = \frac{?}{12} = \frac{3}{12}$

e. $\frac{2}{3} + \frac{4}{9} + \frac{1}{4} = 1\frac{13}{36} \quad \frac{24}{36} + \frac{16}{36} + \frac{9}{36} = \frac{49}{36} = 36\overline{)49}$ 1 R13 $= 1\frac{13}{36}$

$$\begin{array}{r} 36 \\ \hline 13 \end{array}$$

$\frac{2}{3} = \frac{?}{36} = \frac{24}{36} \quad \frac{4}{9} = \frac{?}{36} = \frac{16}{36} \quad \frac{1}{4} = \frac{?}{36} = \frac{9}{36}$

3. Subtract and reduce to lowest terms:

a. $\frac{5}{9} - \frac{2}{9} = \frac{3}{9} = \frac{1}{3}$

b. $\frac{14}{15} - \frac{4}{15} = \frac{10}{15} = \frac{2}{3}$

c. $\frac{8}{9} - \frac{5}{6} = \frac{1}{18}$

$\frac{16}{18} - \frac{15}{18} = \frac{1}{18}$

d. $\frac{7}{12} - \frac{9}{16} = \frac{1}{48}$

$\frac{28}{48} - \frac{27}{48} = \frac{1}{48}$

e. $33\frac{5}{8} - 27\frac{1}{2} = 6\frac{1}{8}$

$$\begin{array}{rr} 33\frac{5}{8} & 33\frac{5}{8} \\ -\,27\frac{1}{2} & -\,27\frac{4}{8} \\ \hline & 6\frac{1}{8} \end{array}$$

f. $9 - 2\frac{3}{7} = 6\frac{4}{7}$

$$\begin{array}{rr} 9 & 8\frac{7}{7} \\ -\,2\frac{3}{7} & -\,2\frac{3}{7} \\ \hline & 6\frac{4}{7} \end{array}$$

g. $15\frac{1}{3} - 9\frac{7}{12} = 5\frac{3}{4}$

$$\begin{array}{rrr} 15\frac{1}{3} & 15\frac{4}{12} & 14\frac{16}{12} \\ -\,9\frac{7}{12} & -\,9\frac{7}{12} & -\,9\frac{7}{12} \\ \hline & & 5\frac{9}{12} = 5\frac{3}{4} \end{array}$$

h. $92\frac{3}{10} - 35\frac{7}{15} = 56\frac{5}{6}$

$$\begin{array}{rrr} 92\frac{3}{10} & 92\frac{9}{30} & 91\frac{39}{30} \\ -\,35\frac{7}{15} & -\,35\frac{14}{30} & -\,35\frac{14}{30} \\ \hline & & 56\frac{25}{30} = 56\frac{5}{6} \end{array}$$

i. $93 - 57\frac{5}{12} = 35\frac{7}{12}$

$$\begin{array}{rr} 93 & 92\frac{12}{12} \\ -\,57\frac{5}{12} & -\,57\frac{5}{12} \\ \hline & 35\frac{7}{12} \end{array}$$

j. $22\frac{5}{8} - 17\frac{1}{4} = 5\frac{3}{8}$

$$\begin{array}{rr} 22\frac{5}{8} & 22\frac{5}{8} \\ -\,17\frac{1}{4} & -\,17\frac{2}{8} \\ \hline & 5\frac{3}{8} \end{array}$$

Word Problems

4. Dan Lund took a cross-country trip. He drove $5\frac{3}{8}$ hours on Monday, $6\frac{1}{2}$ hours on Tuesday, $9\frac{3}{4}$ hours on Wednesday, $6\frac{3}{8}$ hours on Thursday, and $10\frac{1}{4}$ hours on Friday. Find the total number of hours Dan drove in the first five days of his trip.

$$\begin{array}{rr} 5\frac{3}{8} & 5\frac{3}{8} \\ 6\frac{1}{2} & 6\frac{4}{8} \\ 9\frac{3}{4} & 9\frac{6}{8} \\ 6\frac{3}{8} & 6\frac{3}{8} \\ +\ 10\frac{1}{4} & +\ 10\frac{2}{8} \\ \hline & 36\frac{18}{8} \end{array}$$

$36\frac{18}{8} = 36 + 2\frac{2}{8} = 38\frac{2}{8} = 38\frac{1}{4}$ hours driven

5. Sharon Parker bought 20 yards of material to make curtains. She used $4\frac{1}{2}$ yards for one bedroom window, $8\frac{3}{5}$ yards for another bedroom window, and $3\frac{7}{8}$ yards for a hall window. How much material did she have left?

$$\begin{array}{rr} 4\frac{1}{2} & 4\frac{20}{40} \\ 8\frac{3}{5} & 8\frac{24}{40} \\ +\ 3\frac{7}{8} & +\ 3\frac{35}{40} \\ \hline & 15\frac{79}{40} \end{array}$$

$15\frac{79}{40} = 15 + 1\frac{39}{40} = 16\frac{39}{40}$ material used

$$\begin{array}{rr} 20 & 19\frac{40}{40} \\ -\ 16\frac{39}{40} & -\ 16\frac{39}{40} \\ \hline & 3\frac{1}{40} \end{array}$$

$3\frac{1}{40}$ yards of material left

6. On Friday, the opening stock price of MYCO Corporation was $43\frac{7}{8}$. The stock closed at $43\frac{1}{2}$. What was the amount of the increase in price?

$$\begin{array}{rrr} \$47\frac{1}{2} & \$47\frac{4}{8} & \$46\frac{12}{8} \\ -\ 43\frac{7}{8} & -\ 43\frac{7}{8} & -\ 43\frac{7}{8} \\ \hline & & \$\ 3\frac{5}{8} \end{array}$$

$\$\ 3\frac{5}{8}$ increase

7. Bill Williams had to drive $46\frac{1}{4}$ miles to work. After driving $28\frac{5}{6}$ miles he noticed he was low on gas and had to decide if he should stop to fill the gas tank. How many more miles does Bill have to drive to get to work?

$$\begin{array}{rrr} 46\frac{1}{4} & 46\frac{3}{12} & 45\frac{15}{12} \\ -\ 28\frac{5}{6} & -\ 28\frac{10}{12} & -\ 28\frac{10}{12} \\ \hline & & 17\frac{5}{12} \end{array}$$

$17\frac{5}{12}$ miles remaining

8. Albert's Lumber Yard purchased $52\frac{1}{2}$ cords of lumber on Monday and $48\frac{3}{4}$ cords on Tuesday. They sold $21\frac{3}{8}$ cords on Friday. How many cords of lumber remain at Albert's Lumber Yard?

$$\begin{array}{rr} 52\frac{1}{2} & 52\frac{2}{4} \\ +\ 48\frac{3}{4} & +\ 48\frac{3}{4} \\ \hline & 100\frac{5}{4} \end{array}$$

$100\frac{5}{4} = 101\frac{1}{4}$ cords purchased

$$\begin{array}{rrr} 101\frac{1}{4} & 101\frac{2}{8} & 100\frac{10}{8} \\ -\ 21\frac{3}{8} & -\ 21\frac{3}{8} & -\ 21\frac{3}{8} \\ \hline & & 79\frac{7}{8} \end{array}$$

$79\frac{7}{8}$ cords remain

9. At Arlen Oil Company, where Dave Bursett is the service manager, it took $42\frac{1}{3}$ hours to clean five boilers. After a new cleaning tool was purchased, the time for cleaning five boilers was reduced to $37\frac{4}{9}$ hours. How much time was saved?

$$\begin{array}{rrr} 42\frac{1}{3} & 42\frac{3}{9} & 41\frac{12}{9} \\ -\ 37\frac{4}{9} & -\ 37\frac{4}{9} & -\ 37\frac{4}{9} \\ \hline & & 4\frac{8}{9} \end{array}$$

$4\frac{8}{9}$ hours saved

Date ______________________ Name ____

LU 2-3: Fractions—Multiplication and Division

Drill Problems

1. Multiply (use cancellation technique)

a. $\frac{7}{11} \times \frac{6}{14} = \frac{\overset{1}{\cancel{7}}}{11} \times \frac{\overset{3}{\cancel{6}}}{\underset{\underset{1}{\cancel{2}}}{\cancel{14}}} = \frac{3}{11}$

b. $\frac{3}{8} \times \frac{2}{3} = \frac{\overset{1}{\cancel{3}}}{\underset{4}{\cancel{8}}} \times \frac{\overset{1}{\cancel{2}}}{\underset{1}{\cancel{3}}} = \frac{1}{4}$

c. $\frac{5}{7} \times \frac{9}{10} = \frac{\overset{1}{\cancel{5}}}{7} \times \frac{9}{\underset{2}{\cancel{10}}} = \frac{9}{14}$

d. $\frac{3}{4} \times \frac{9}{13} \times \frac{26}{27} = \frac{\overset{1}{\cancel{3}}}{\underset{2}{\cancel{4}}} \times \frac{\overset{1}{\cancel{9}}}{13} \times \frac{\overset{\overset{1}{\cancel{2}}}{\cancel{26}}}{\underset{\underset{1}{\cancel{3}}}{\cancel{27}}} = \frac{1}{2}$

e. $6\frac{2}{5} \times 3\frac{1}{8}$

$\frac{\overset{4}{\cancel{32}}}{\underset{1}{\cancel{5}}} \times \frac{\overset{5}{\cancel{25}}}{\underset{1}{\cancel{8}}} = \frac{20}{1} = 20$

f. $2\frac{2}{3} \times 2\frac{7}{10} = 7\frac{1}{5}$

$\frac{\overset{4}{\cancel{8}}}{\underset{1}{\cancel{3}}} \times \frac{\overset{9}{\cancel{27}}}{\underset{5}{\cancel{10}}} = \frac{36}{5} = 7\frac{1}{5}$

g. $45 \times \frac{7}{9} = 35$

$\overset{5}{\cancel{45}} \times \frac{7}{\underset{1}{\cancel{9}}} = 35$

h. $3\frac{1}{9} \times 1\frac{2}{7} \times \frac{3}{4} = 3$

$\frac{\overset{\overset{1}{\cancel{4}}}{\cancel{28}}}{\underset{1}{\cancel{9}}} \times \frac{\overset{1}{\cancel{9}}}{\underset{1}{\cancel{7}}} \times \frac{3}{\underset{1}{\cancel{4}}} = 3$

i. $\frac{3}{4} \times \frac{7}{9} \times 3\frac{1}{3} = 1\frac{17}{18}$

$\frac{\overset{1}{\cancel{3}}}{\underset{2}{\cancel{4}}} \times \frac{7}{9} \times \frac{\overset{5}{\cancel{10}}}{\underset{1}{\cancel{3}}} = \frac{35}{18} = 1\frac{17}{18}$

j. $\frac{1}{8} \times 6\frac{2}{3} \times \frac{1}{10} = \frac{1}{12}$

$\frac{1}{\underset{4}{\cancel{8}}} \times \frac{\overset{\overset{1}{\cancel{2}}}{\cancel{20}}}{3} \times \frac{1}{\underset{1}{\cancel{10}}} = \frac{1}{12}$

2. Multiply (do not use canceling; reduce by finding greatest common divisor):

a. $\frac{3}{4} \times \frac{8}{9} = \frac{24 \div 12}{36 \div 12} = \frac{2}{3}$

$\begin{array}{r} 1 \\ 24\overline{)36} \\ 24 \\ \hline 12 \end{array} \nearrow \begin{array}{r} 2 \\ 12\overline{)24} \\ 24 \\ \hline 0 \end{array}$

b. $\frac{7}{16} \times \frac{8}{13} = \frac{56 \div 8}{208 \div 8} = \frac{7}{26}$

$\begin{array}{r} 3 \\ 56\overline{)208} \\ 168 \\ \hline 40 \end{array} \nearrow \begin{array}{r} 1 \\ 40\overline{)56} \\ 40 \\ \hline 16 \end{array} \nearrow \begin{array}{r} 2 \\ 16\overline{)40} \\ 32 \\ \hline 8 \end{array} \nearrow \begin{array}{r} 2 \\ 8\overline{)16} \\ 16 \\ \hline 0 \end{array}$

3. Multiply or divide as indicated:

a. $\frac{25}{36} \div \frac{5}{9} = \frac{\overset{5}{\cancel{25}}}{\underset{4}{\cancel{36}}} \times \frac{\overset{1}{\cancel{9}}}{\underset{1}{\cancel{5}}} = \frac{5}{4} = 1\frac{1}{4}$

b. $\frac{18}{8} \div \frac{12}{16} = \frac{\overset{3}{\cancel{18}}}{\underset{1}{\cancel{8}}} \times \frac{\overset{\overset{1}{\cancel{2}}}{\cancel{16}}}{\underset{\underset{1}{\cancel{2}}}{\cancel{12}}} = 3$

c. $2\frac{6}{7} \div 2\frac{2}{5} = 1\frac{4}{21}$

$\frac{20}{7} \div \frac{12}{5} = \frac{\overset{5}{\cancel{20}}}{7} \times \frac{5}{\underset{3}{\cancel{12}}} = \frac{25}{21} = 1\frac{4}{21}$

d. $3\frac{1}{4} \div 16 = \frac{13}{64}$

$\frac{13}{4} \div \frac{16}{1} = \frac{13}{4} \times \frac{1}{16} = \frac{13}{64}$

e. $24 \div 1\frac{1}{3} = 18$

$\frac{24}{1} \div \frac{4}{3} = \frac{\overset{6}{\cancel{24}}}{1} \times \frac{3}{\underset{1}{\cancel{4}}} = 18$

f. $6 \times \frac{3}{2} = 9$

$\frac{\overset{3}{\cancel{6}}}{1} \times \frac{3}{\underset{1}{\cancel{2}}} = 9$

g. $3\frac{1}{5} \times 7\frac{1}{2} = 24$

$\frac{\overset{8}{\cancel{16}}}{\underset{1}{\cancel{5}}} \times \frac{\overset{3}{\cancel{15}}}{\underset{1}{\cancel{2}}} = 24$

h. $\frac{3}{8} \div \frac{7}{4} = \frac{3}{14}$

$\frac{3}{\underset{2}{\cancel{8}}} \times \frac{\overset{1}{\cancel{4}}}{7} = \frac{3}{14}$

i. $9 \div 3\frac{3}{4} = 2\frac{2}{5}$

$$\frac{9}{1} \div \frac{15}{4} = \frac{\overset{3}{\cancel{9}}}{1} \times \frac{4}{\underset{5}{\cancel{15}}} = \frac{12}{5} = 2\frac{2}{5}$$

j. $\frac{11}{24} \times \frac{24}{33} = \frac{1}{3}$

$$\frac{\overset{1}{\cancel{11}}}{\underset{1}{\cancel{24}}} \times \frac{\overset{1}{\cancel{24}}}{\underset{3}{\cancel{33}}} = \frac{1}{3}$$

k. $\frac{12}{14} \div 27 = \frac{2}{63}$

$$\frac{12}{14} \div \frac{27}{1} = \frac{\overset{2}{\overset{\cancel{4}}{\cancel{12}}}}{\underset{7}{\cancel{14}}} \times \frac{1}{\underset{9}{\cancel{27}}} = \frac{2}{63}$$

l. $\frac{3}{5} \times \frac{2}{7} \div \frac{3}{10} = \frac{4}{7}$

$$\frac{\overset{1}{\cancel{3}}}{\underset{1}{\cancel{5}}} \times \frac{2}{7} \times \frac{\overset{2}{\cancel{10}}}{\underset{1}{\cancel{3}}} = \frac{4}{7}$$

Word Problems

4. Mary Smith plans to make 12 meatloafs to store in her freezer. Each meatloaf requires $2\frac{1}{4}$ pounds of ground beef. How much ground beef does Mary need?

$$12 \times 2\frac{1}{4} = \overset{3}{\cancel{12}} \times \frac{9}{\underset{1}{\cancel{4}}} = 27 \text{ pounds}$$

5. Judy Carter purchased a real estate lot for \$24,000. She sold it two years later for $1\frac{5}{8}$ times as much as she had paid for it. What was the selling price?

$$\$24{,}000 \times 1\frac{5}{8} = \overset{3{,}000}{\cancel{24{,}000}} \times \frac{13}{\underset{1}{\cancel{8}}} = \$39{,}000$$

6. Lynn Clarkson saw an ad for a camcorder that cost \$980. She knew of a discount store that would sell it to her for a markdown of $\frac{3}{20}$ off the advertised price. How much is the discount she can get?

$$\overset{49}{\cancel{\$980}} \times \frac{3}{\underset{1}{\cancel{20}}} = \$147 \text{ discount}$$

7. In order to raise money for their club, the Marketing Club purchased 68 bushels of popcorn to resell. They plan to repackage the popcorn in bags that hold $\frac{2}{21}$ of a bushel each. How many bags of popcorn will they be able to fill?

$$68 \div \frac{2}{21} = \overset{34}{\cancel{68}} \times \frac{21}{\underset{1}{\cancel{2}}} = 714 \text{ bags}$$

8. Richard Tracy paid a total \$375 for stocks costing $\$9\frac{3}{8}$ per share. How many shares did he purchase?

$$\$375 \div \$9\frac{3}{8} = 375 \div \frac{75}{8} = \overset{5}{\cancel{375}} \times \frac{8}{\underset{1}{\cancel{75}}} = 40 \text{ shares}$$

9. While training for a marathon, Kristin Woods jogged $7\frac{3}{4}$ miles per hour for $2\frac{2}{3}$ hours. How many miles did Kristen jog?

$$7\frac{3}{4} \times 2\frac{2}{3} = \frac{31}{\underset{1}{\cancel{4}}} \times \frac{\overset{2}{\cancel{8}}}{3} = \frac{62}{3} = 20\frac{2}{3} \text{ miles}$$

10. On a map, one inch represents 240 miles. How many miles are represented by $\frac{3}{8}$ of an inch?

$$\overset{30}{\cancel{240}} \times \frac{3}{\underset{1}{\cancel{8}}} = 90 \text{ miles}$$

11. In Massachusetts, the governor wants to allot $\frac{1}{6}$ of the total sales tax collections to public education. The total sales tax collected is \$2,472,000; how much will go to education?

$$\overset{412{,}000}{\cancel{\$2{,}472{,}000}} \times \frac{1}{\underset{1}{\cancel{6}}} = \$412{,}000 \text{ to education}$$

Date ______________ Name ______________________________

LU 3–1: Rounding; Fractions and Decimal Conversions

Drill Problems

1. Write in decimal form:
   a. Forty-seven hundredths .47
   b. Three tenths .3
   c. Nine hundred fifty-three thousandths .953
   d. Four hundred one thousandths .401
   e. Six hundredths .06
2. Round each decimal to the place indicated:
   a. .4326 to the nearest thousandth .433
   b. .051 to the nearest tenth .1
   c. 8.207 to the nearest hundredth 8.21
   d. 2.094 to the nearest hundredth 2.09
   e. .511172 to the nearest ten thousandth .5112
3. Name the place position of the underlined digit:
   a. .8<u>2</u>6 Hundredths place
   b. .91<u>4</u> Thousandths place
   c. 3.<u>1</u>169 Tenths place
   d. 53.17<u>5</u> Thousandths place
   e. 1.017<u>4</u> Ten thousandths place
4. Convert to fractions (do not reduce):
   a. .83 $\frac{83}{100}$ b. .426 $\frac{426}{1,000}$ c. 2.516 $2\frac{516}{1,000}$
   d. $.62\frac{1}{2}$ $\frac{625}{1,000}$ e. 13.007 $13\frac{7}{1,000}$ f. $5.03\frac{1}{4}$ $5\frac{325}{10,000}$
5. Convert to fractions and reduce to lowest terms:
   a. $.4 = \frac{4}{10} = \frac{2}{5}$ b. $.44 = \frac{44}{100} = \frac{11}{25}$
   c. $.53 = \frac{53}{100}$ d. $.336 = \frac{336}{1,000} = \frac{42}{125}$
   e. $.096 = \frac{96}{1,000} = \frac{12}{125}$ f. $.125 = \frac{125}{1,000} = \frac{1}{8}$
   g. $.3125 = \frac{3,125}{10,000} = \frac{5}{16}$ h. $.008 = \frac{8}{1,000} = \frac{1}{125}$
   i. $2.625 = 2\frac{625}{1,000} = 2\frac{5}{8}$ j. $5.75 = 5\frac{75}{100} = 5\frac{3}{4}$
   k. $3.375 = 3\frac{375}{1,000} = 3\frac{3}{8}$ l. $9.04 = 9\frac{4}{100} = 9\frac{1}{25}$
6. Convert the following fractions to decimals and round answer to the nearest hundredth:
   a. $\frac{1}{8} = .125 = .13$ b. $\frac{7}{16} = .4375 = .44$
   c. $\frac{2}{3} = .6666 = .67$ d. $\frac{3}{4} = .75$
   e. $\frac{9}{16} = .5625 = .56$ f. $\frac{5}{6} = .8333 = .83$
   g. $\frac{7}{9} = .7777 = .78$ h. $\frac{38}{79} = .4810 = .48$
   i. $2\frac{3}{8} = 2 + .375 = 2.38$ j. $9\frac{1}{3} = 9 + .3333 = 9.33$
   k. $11\frac{19}{50} = 11 + .38 = 11.38$ l. $6\frac{21}{32} = 6 + .6562 = 6.66$

m. $4\frac{83}{97} = 4 + .8556 = 4.86$

n. $1\frac{2}{5} = 1 + .40 = 1.40$

o. $2\frac{2}{11} = 2 + .1818 = 2.18$

p. $13\frac{30}{42} = 13 + .7142 = 13.71$

Word Problems

7. Alan Angel got 2 hits in his first 7 times at bat. What is his average to the nearest thousandths place?

$\frac{2}{7} = .2857 = .286$

8. Bill Breen earned $1,555, and his employer calculated that his total FICA deduction should be $118.9575. Round this deduction to the nearest cent.

$118.9575 = $118.96

9. At the local college, .566 of the students are men. Convert to a fraction. (Do not reduce.)

$.566 = \frac{566}{1{,}000}$

10. The average television set is watched 2,400 hours a year. If there are 8,760 hours in a year, what fractional part of the year is spent watching television? (Reduce to lowest terms.)

$\frac{\overset{20}{\cancel{2{,}400}}}{\underset{73}{\cancel{8{,}760}}} = \frac{20}{73}$

11. On Saturday, the employees at the Empire Fish Co. work only $\frac{1}{3}$ of a day. How would this be expressed as a decimal to nearest thousandths?

$\frac{1}{3} = .333$

12. The North Shore Cinema has 610 seats. At a recent film screening there were 55 vacant seats. Show as a fraction the number of filled seats. (Reduce as needed.)

$610 - 55 = 555$

$\frac{555}{610} = \frac{111}{122}$

13. Michael Sullivan was planning his marketing strategy for a new product his company had produced. He was fascinated to discover that Rhode Island, the smallest state in the United States, was only twenty thousand, five hundred seven ten millionths the size of the largest state, Alaska. Write this in decimal form.

.0020507

14. Bull Moose Co. purchased a new manufacturing plant, located on an acre of land, for a total price of $2,250,000. The accountant determined that $\frac{3}{7}$ of the total price should be allocated as the price of the building. What decimal portion is the price of the building? Round to the nearest thousandth.

$\frac{3}{7} = .4285 = .429$

Date ____________ Name ____________

LU 3–2: Decimal Addition, Subtraction, Multiplication, and Division; Shortcuts

Drill Problems

1. Rearrange vertically and add:

a. 3.68 + 7.4 + 11.007 + 1.82

```
  3.680
  7.400
 11.007
+ 1.820
 23.907
```

b. 1.0625 + 4.0881 + .0775

```
 1.0625
 4.0881
+ .0775
 5.2281
```

c. .903 + .078 + .17 + .1 + .96

```
  .903
  .078
  .170
  .100
+ .960
 2.211
```

d. 3.38 + .175 + .0186 + .2

```
 3.3800
  .1750
  .0186
+ .2000
 3.7736
```

2. Rearrange and subtract:

a. .86 − .43

```
  .86
− .43
  .43
```

b. .885 − .069

```
  .885
− .069
  .816
```

c. 11.67 − .935

```
 11.670
−   .935
 10.735
```

d. 261.2 − 8.08

```
 261.20
−  8.08
 253.12
```

3. Multiply and round to the nearest tenth:

a. 13.6 × .02

```
 13.6
× .02
 .272 = .3
```

b. 1.73 × .069

```
   1.73
  ×.069
   1557
  1038
 .11937 = .1
```

c. 400 × 3.7

```
  400
× 3.7
 2800
1 200
1,480 = 1,480.0
```

d. 0.025 × 5.6

```
 0.025
×  5.6
   150
  125
 .1400 = .1
```

4. Divide and round to the nearest hundredth:

a. 13.869 ÷ .6

```
     23.115 = 23.12
.6)13.8690
   12
    18
    18
     06
      6
     09
      6
      30
      30
```

b. 1.0088 ÷ .14

```
      7.205 = 7.21
.14)1.00880
      98
       28
       28
        080
         70
```

c. 18.7 ÷ 2.16

```
         8.657 = 8.66
2.16)18.70000
     1728
      1420
      1296
       1240
       1080
        1600
        1512
```

d. 15.64 ÷ .34

```
      46. = 46.00
.34)15.64
    136
     204
     204
```

5. Complete by the shortcut method:

a.	6.87 × 1,000 = 6,870	**b.**	927,530 ÷ 100 = 9,275.3
c.	27.2 ÷ 1,000 = .0272	**d.**	.21 × 1,000 = 210
e.	347 × 100 = 34,700	**f.**	347 ÷ 100 = 3.47
g.	.0021 ÷ 10 = .00021	**h.**	85.44 × 10,000 = 854,400
i.	83.298 × 100 = 8,329.8	**j.**	23.0109 ÷ 100 = .230109

Word Problems

6. John Sampson noted his odometer reading of 17,629.3 at the beginning of his vacation. At the end of his vacation the reading was 20,545.1. How many miles did he drive during his vacation?

```
  20,545.1
− 17,629.3
   2,915.8 miles
```

7. Jeanne Allyn purchased 12.25 yards of ribbon for a craft project. The ribbon cost 37¢ per yard. What was the total cost of the ribbon?

```
   12.25
 × $.37
   8575
  3675
$4.5325 = $4.53
```

8. Leo Green wanted to find out the gas mileage for his company truck. When he filled the gas tank he wrote down the odometer reading of 9,650.7. The next time he filled the gas tank the odometer reading was 10,112.2. He looked at the gas pump and saw that he had taken 18.5 gallons of gas. Find the gas mileage per gallon for Leo's truck. (Round to the nearest tenth.)

```
  10,112.2                              24.94 = 24.9 mpg
−  9,650.7                     18.5)461.500
     461.5 miles traveled            370
                                      915
                                      740
                                      1750
                                      1665
                                        850
                                        740
```

9. At Halley's Rent-a-Car the cost-per-day to rent a medium-size car is $35.25 plus 37¢ a mile. What would be the charge to rent this car for one day if you drove 205.4 miles?

```
   205.4                 $ 76.00
 ×  $.37                 +35.25
   14378                 $111.25 charge
   6162
 $75.998 = $76.00
```

10. Emily Abbott earned $320.58 at the regular pay rate, $24.20 at the overtime rate, and $36.09 at the holiday rate. What was her total gross pay?

```
$320.58
  24.20
 +36.09
$380.87 total gross pay
```

11. If a commemorative gold coin weighs 7.842 grams, find the number of coins that can be produced from 116 grams of gold. (Round to the nearest whole number.)

```
               14.7 = 15 coins
7.842)116.0000
        7842
        37580
        31368
         62120
         54894
          7226
```

Date ____________ Name ____________________________

LU 4-1: The Checking Account; Credit Card Transactions

1. The following is a deposit slip made out by Fred Young of the F. W. Young Company.
   a. How much cash did Young deposit? $527.64
   b. How many checks did Young deposit? 3
   c. What was the total amount deposited? $910.32

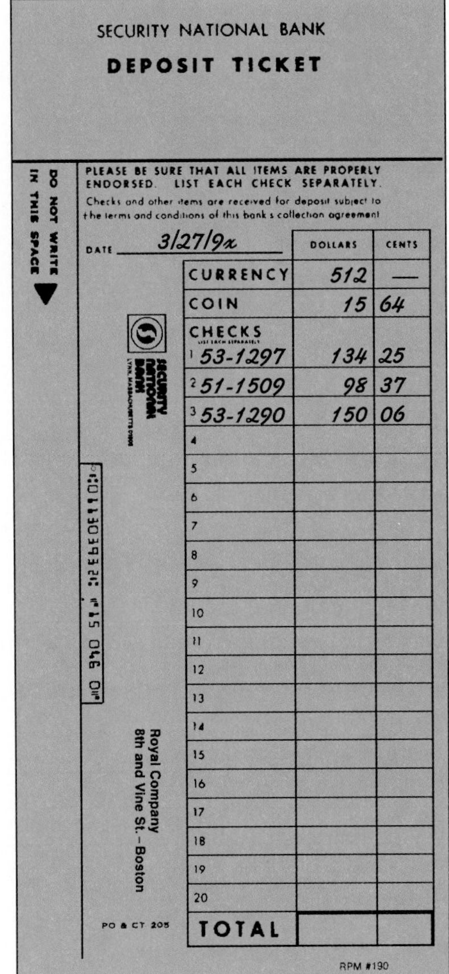

SECURITY NATIONAL BANK

DEPOSIT TICKET

DO NOT WRITE IN THIS SPACE

PLEASE BE SURE THAT ALL ITEMS ARE PROPERLY ENDORSED. LIST EACH CHECK SEPARATELY.

Checks and other items are received for deposit subject to the terms and conditions of this bank's collection agreement.

DATE 3/27/9x

	DOLLARS	CENTS
CURRENCY	512	—
COIN	15	64
CHECKS		
1 53-1297	134	25
2 51-1509	98	37
3 53-1290	150	06
4		
5		
6		
7		
8		
9		
10		
11		
12		
13		
14		
15		
16		
17		
18		
19		
20		
TOTAL		

Royal Company
8th and Vine St. - Boston

PO & CT 205

RPM #190

2. The Blackstone Company had a balance of $2,173.18 in its checking account. Henry James, Blackstone's accountant, made a deposit that consisted of 2 fifty-dollar bills, 120 ten-dollar bills, 6 five-dollar bills, 14 one-dollar bills, $9.54 in change, plus two checks they had accepted, one for $16.38 and the other for $102.50. Find the amount of the deposit and the new balance in Blackstone's checking account.

$ 100.00	$2,173.18
1,200.00	+ 1,472.42
30.00	$3,645.60 new balance
14.00	
9.54	
16.38	
+ 102.50	
$1,472.42 deposit	

3. Answer the following questions using the illustration.

No. 113 $ 750 00/100
October 4 19 XX
To Neuner Realty
For real estate

	DOLLARS	CENTS
BALANCE	1,020	93
AMT. DEPOSITED	2,756	80
TOTAL	3,777	73
AMT. THIS CHECK	750	00
BALANCE FORWARD	3,027	73

Jones Company
22 Aster Road
Salem, MA 01970

No. 113

October 4 19 XX 5-13/110

PAY TO THE ORDER OF Neuner Realty Company $ 750 00/100

Seven Hundred Fifty and 00/100 DOLLARS

Fleet Bank FLEET BANK OF MASSACHUSETTS, NATIONAL ASSOCIATION BOSTON, MASSACHUSETTS

MEMO real estate

Kevin Jones

⑆0110001381⑆ 14 0380 113

a. Who is the payee? Neuner Realty Company
b. Who is the drawer? Kevin Jones
c. Who is the drawee? Fleet Bank
d. What is the bank's identification number? 5-13/110
e. What is Jones Company account number? 14 0380
f. What was the balance in the account on Sept. 30? $1,020.93
g. For how much did Jones write check No. 113? $750.00
h. How much was deposited on Oct. 1? $2,756.80
i. How much was left after check No. 113 was written? $3,027.73

4. Write each of the following amounts in verbal form as you would on a check:
a. $25 Twenty five and XX/100 ---------------- DOLLARS
b. $245.75 Two hundred forty-five and 75/100 ---------------- DOLLARS
c. $3.98 Three and 98/100 ---------------- DOLLARS
d. $1,205.05 One thousand, two hundred five and 05/100 ---------------- DOLLARS
e. $3,013 Three thousand, thirteen and XX/100 ---------------- DOLLARS
f. $510.10 Five hundred ten and 10/100 ---------------- DOLLARS

5. From the following credit card transactions, calculate the net deposit that would be recorded on the merchant batch summary slip for the day.

MasterCard sales	Returns
$22.95	$ 4.09
18.51	16.50
16.92	

$22.95 + $18.51 + $16.92 = $58.38
− 20.59
$37.79 net deposit

Date ________________ Name ________________________________

LU 4–2: Bank Statement and Reconciliation Process: Insight into Current Trends

1. Find the bank balance on January 31.

Date	Checks and payments			Deposits	Balance
Jan. 1					401.17
Jan. 2	108.64				292.53
Jan. 5	116.50			432.16	608.19
Jan. 6	14.92	150.00	10.00		433.27
Jan. 11	12.29			633.89	1,054.87
Jan. 18	108.64	18.60			927.63
Jan. 25	43.91	23.77		657.22	1,517.17
Jan. 26	75.00				1,442.17
Jan. 31	6.75 sc				1,435.42

2. Joe Madruga, of Madruga's Taxi Service, received a bank statement for the month of May showing a balance of $932.36. His records show that the bank had not yet recorded two of his deposits, one for $521.50 and the other for $98.46. There are outstanding checks in the amounts of $41.67, $135.18, and $25.30. The statement also shows a service charge of $3.38. The balance in the check register is $1,353.55. Prepare a bank reconciliation for Madruga's as of May 31.

Madruga's Taxi Service
Bank Reconciliation as of May 31, 199x

Checkbook balance		Bank statement balance	
Checkbook balance	$1,353.55	Bank statement balance	$ 932.36
Less: Service charge	3.38	Add: Deposits in transit	521.50
			98.46
			$1,552.32
		Less: Outstanding checks	41.67
			135.18
			25.30
Reconciled balance	$1,350.17	Reconciled balance	$1,350.17

3. In reconciling the checking account for Nasser Enterprises, Beth Accomando found that the bank had collected a $3,000 promissory note on the company's behalf and had charged a $15.00 collection fee. There was also a service charge of $7.25. What amount should be added/subtracted from the checkbook balance to bring it up to date?
   Add: $3,000 Deduct: $22.25
   $15.00 collection fee
   7.25 service fee
   $22.25

4. In reconciling the checking account for Colonial Cleaners, Steve Papa found that a check for $34.50 had been recorded in the check register as $43.50. The bank returned an NSF check in the amount of $62.55. Interest income of $8.25 was earned and a service charge of $10.32 was assessed. What amount should be added/subtracted from the checkbook balance to bring it up to date?
   Add: $17.25
   $ 9.00 recording error
   8.25 interest earned
   $17.25
   Deduct: $72.87
   $62.55 returned check
   10.32 service charge
   $72.87

5. Matthew Stokes was completing the bank reconciliation for Parker's Tool and Die Company. The check register balance was $1,503.67. Matthew found that a $76.00 check had been recorded in the check register as $67.00, that a note for $1,500 had been collected by the bank for Parker's and the collection fee was $12.00, that $15.60 interest was earned on the account, and that an $8.35 service charge had been assessed. What should the check register balance be after Matthew updates it with the bank reconciliation information?

$1,503.67	beginning balance	$1,500.00	note	$ 9.00	error
+ 1,515.60		15.60	interest	12.00	fee
− 29.35		$1,515.60	(add)	8.35	service charge
$2,989.92	ending balance			$29.35	(deduct)

6. Long's Video Shop had the following MasterCard sales: $44.18, $66.10, $12.50, $24.95. Returns for the day were $13.88 and $12.99. What would be the amount of the net deposit for Long's Video Shop on the merchant batch summary slip?

$44.18 + $66.10 + $12.50 + $24.95 = $147.73
− 26.87 ($13.88 + $12.99)
$120.86 net deposit

Date ______________ Name ______________________________

LU 5–1: Solving Equations for the Unknown

1. Write equations for the following. Use N for the unknown number. Do not solve the equations.

   a. Five times a number is 60.
   $5N = 60$

   b. A number increased by 13 equals 25.
   $N + 13 = 25$

   c. Seven less than a number is 5.
   $N - 7 = 5$

   d. Fifty-seven decreased by 3 times a number is 21.
   $57 - 3N = 21$

   e. Fourteen added to one third of a number is 18.
   $14 + \frac{N}{3} = 18$

   f. Twice the sum of a number and 4 is 32.
   $2(N + 4) = 32$

   g. Three fourths of a number is 9.
   $\frac{3}{4}N = 9$

   h. Two times a number plus 3 times the same number plus 8 is 68.
   $2N + 3N + 8 = 68$

2. Solve for the unknown number:

   a.
$$\begin{aligned} B + 12 &= 38 \\ -12 &\quad -12 \\ B &= 26 \end{aligned}$$

   b.
$$\begin{aligned} 29 + M &= 44 \\ -29 &\quad -29 \\ M &= 15 \end{aligned}$$

   c.
$$\begin{aligned} D - 77 &= 98 \\ +77 &\quad +77 \\ D &= 175 \end{aligned}$$

   d.
$$\begin{aligned} 7N &= 63 \\ \frac{\cancel{7}N}{\cancel{7}} &= \frac{63}{7} \\ N &= 9 \end{aligned}$$

   e.
$$\begin{aligned} \frac{X}{12} &= 11 \\ (\cancel{12})\frac{X}{\cancel{12}} &= 11(12) \\ X &= 132 \end{aligned}$$

   f.
$$\begin{aligned} 3Q + 4Q + 2Q &= 108 \\ \frac{\cancel{9}Q}{\cancel{9}} &= \frac{108}{9} \\ Q &= 12 \end{aligned}$$

   g.
$$\begin{aligned} H + 5H + 3 &= 57 \\ 6H + 3 &= 57 \\ -3 &\quad -3 \\ \frac{\cancel{6}H}{\cancel{6}} &= \frac{54}{6} \\ H &= 9 \end{aligned}$$

   h.
$$\begin{aligned} 2(N - 3) &= 62 \\ 2N - 6 &= 62 \\ +6 &\quad +6 \\ \frac{\cancel{2}N}{\cancel{2}} &= \frac{68}{2} \\ N &= 34 \end{aligned}$$

   i.
$$\begin{aligned} \frac{3R}{4} &= 27 \\ \cancel{4}\left(\frac{3R}{\cancel{4}}\right) &= 27(4) \\ \frac{\cancel{3}R}{\cancel{3}} &= \frac{108}{3} \\ R &= 36 \end{aligned}$$

   j.
$$\begin{aligned} E - 32 &= 41 \\ +32 &\quad +32 \\ E &= 73 \end{aligned}$$

   k.
$$\begin{aligned} 5(2T - 2) &= 120 \\ 10T - 10 &= 120 \\ +10 &\quad +10 \\ \frac{\cancel{10}T}{\cancel{10}} &= \frac{130}{10} \\ T &= 13 \end{aligned}$$

   l.
$$\begin{aligned} 12W - 5W &= 98 \\ \frac{\cancel{7}W}{\cancel{7}} &= \frac{98}{7} \\ W &= 14 \end{aligned}$$

m.

$$
\begin{array}{rcl}
49 - X & = & 37 \\
+ X & & + X \\
\hline
49 & = & 37 + X \\
- 37 & & - 37 \\
\hline
12 & = & X
\end{array}
$$

n.

$$
\begin{array}{rcl}
12(V + 2) & = & 84 \\
12V + 24 & = & 84 \\
- 24 & & - 24 \\
\hline
\frac{\cancel{12}V}{\cancel{12}} & = & \frac{60}{12} \\
V & = & 5
\end{array}
$$

o.

$$
\begin{array}{rcl}
7D + 4 & = & 5D + 14 \\
- 5D & & - 5D \\
\hline
2D + 4 & = & 14 \\
- 4 & & - 4 \\
\hline
\frac{\cancel{2}D}{\cancel{2}} & = & \frac{10}{2} \\
D & = & 5
\end{array}
$$

p.

$$
\begin{array}{rcl}
7(T - 2) & = & 2T - 9 \\
7T - 14 & = & 2T - 9 \\
- 2T & & - 2T \\
\hline
5T - 14 & = & - 9 \\
+ 14 & & + 14 \\
\hline
\frac{\cancel{5}T}{\cancel{5}} & = & \frac{5}{5} \\
T & = & 1
\end{array}
$$

Date ______________ Name ______________________________

LU 5–2: Solving Word Problems for the Unknown

Word Problems

1. A blue denim shirt at the Lodge was marked down \$15. The sale price was \$21. What was the original price?

Unknown(s)	Variable(s)	Relationship
Original price	P	$P - \$15 =$ Sale price Sale price $= \$21$

$$P - \$15 = \$21$$
$$+\ 15 \qquad +\ 15$$
$$P = \$36 \text{ original price of shirt}$$

2. Goodwin's Corporation found that $\frac{2}{3}$ of its employees were vested in their retirement plan. If 124 employees are vested, what is the total number of employees at Goodwin's?

Unknown(s)	Variable(s)	Relationship
Total number of employees	E	$\frac{2}{3}E =$ Vested employees Vested employees $= 124$

$$\frac{2}{3}E = 124$$
$$\not{3}\left(\frac{2E}{\not{3}}\right) = 124(3)$$
$$\frac{\not{2}E}{\not{2}} = \frac{372}{2}$$
$$E = 186 \text{ employees}$$

3. Eileen Haskin's utility and telephone bills for the month totaled \$180. The utility bill was 3 times as much as the telephone bill. How much was each bill?

Unknown(s)	Variable(s)	Relationship
Telephone bill Utility bill	B $3B$	$B + 3B =$ total bill Total bill $= \$180$

$$B + 3B = \$180$$
$$\frac{\not{4}B}{\not{4}} = \frac{\$180}{4}$$
$$B = \$45 \text{ telephone bill; } 3B = \$135 \text{ utility bill}$$

4. Ryan and his friends went to the golf course to hunt for golf balls. Ryan found 15 more than $\frac{1}{3}$ of the total number of golf balls that were found. How many golf balls were found if Ryan found 75 golf balls?

Unknown(s)	Variable(s)	Relationship
Total golf balls found	G	$\frac{1}{3}G + 15 =$ Ryan found Ryan found $= 75$

$$\frac{1}{3}G + 15 = 75$$
$$-\ 15 = -\ 15$$
$$\not{3}\left(\frac{G}{\not{3}}\right) = 60\ (3)$$
$$G = 180 \text{ total golf balls found}$$

5. Linda Mills and Sherry Somers sold 459 tickets for the Advertising Club's raffle. If Linda sold 8 times as many tickets as Sherry, how many tickets did each one sell?

Unknown(s)	Variable(s)	Relationship
Linda Sherry	$8T$ T	$8T + T =$ total tickets Total tickets $= 459$

$$8T + T = 459$$
$$\frac{\not{9}T}{\not{9}} = \frac{459}{9}$$
$$T = 51 \text{ tickets Sherry sold; } 8 \times 51 = 408 \text{ tickets Linda sold}$$

6. Jason Mazzola wanted to buy a suit at Giblee's. Jason did not have enough money with him, so Mr. Giblee told him he would hold the suit if Jason gave him a deposit of $\frac{1}{5}$ of the cost of the suit. Jason agreed, and gave Mr. Giblee \$79. What was the price of the suit?

Unknown(s)	Variable(s)	Relationship
Price of suit	S	$\frac{1}{5}S =$ Jason's payment Jason's payment $= \$79$

$$\frac{1}{5}S = \$79$$
$$\not{5}\left(\frac{S}{\not{5}}\right) = 79(5)$$
$$S = \$395 \text{ price of suit}$$

7. Peter sold watches ($7) and necklaces ($4) at a flea market. Total sales were $300. People bought 3 times as many watches as necklaces. How many of each did Peter sell? What was the total dollar sales of each?

Unknown(s)	Variable(s)	Price	Relationship
Watches Necklaces	$3N$ N	$7 4	$21N$ $+ 4N$ $300

$$21N + 4N = 300$$
$$\frac{25N}{25} = \frac{300}{25}$$
$$N = 12$$
$$12(\$4) + 36(\$7) = \$300$$
$$\$48 + \$252 = \$300$$
$$\$300 = \$300$$

12 necklaces
36 watches

8. Peter sold watches ($7) and necklaces ($4) at a flea market. Total sales for 48 watches and necklaces were $300. How many of each did Pete sell? What was the total dollar sales of each?

Unknown(s)	Variable(s)	Price	Relationship
Watches Necklaces	W $48 - W$	$7 4	$7W$ $4(48 - W)$ $300

$$7W + 4(48 - W) = 300$$
$$7W + 192 - 4W = 300$$
$$3W + 192 = 300$$
$$-192 \quad -192$$
$$\frac{3W}{3} = \frac{108}{3}$$
$$W = 36$$
$$36(\$7) + 12(\$4) = \$300$$
$$\$252 + \$48 = \$300$$
$$\$300 = \$300$$

36 watches
48 − 36 = 12 necklaces

Date ____________ Name ____________

LU 6-1: Conversions

Drill Problems

1. Convert the following to percents (round to the nearest tenth of a percent if needed):

a.	.04	4 %	b.	.875	87.5 %
c.	.002	.2 %	d.	8.3	830 %
e.	5.26	526 %	f.	6	600 %
g.	.0105	1.1 %	h.	.1180	11.8 %
i.	5.0375	503.8 %	j.	.862	86.2 %
k.	.2615	26.2 %	l.	.8	80 %
m.	.025	2.5 %	n.	.06	6 %

2. Convert the following to decimals (do not round):

a.	37%	.37	b.	.09%	.0009
c.	4.7%	.047	d.	9.67%	.0967
e.	.2%	.002	f.	$\frac{1}{4}$%	.0025
g.	.76%	.0076	h.	110%	1.1
i.	$12\frac{1}{2}$%	.125	j.	5%	.05
k.	.004%	.00004	l.	$7\frac{5}{10}$%	.075
m.	$\frac{3}{4}$%	.0075	n.	1%	.01

3. Convert the following to percents (round to the nearest tenth of a percent if needed):

a.	$\frac{7}{10}$	70 %	b.	$\frac{1}{5}$	20 %
c.	$1\frac{5}{8}$	162.5 %	d.	$\frac{2}{7}$	28.6 %
e.	2	200 %	f.	$\frac{14}{100}$	14 %
g.	$\frac{1}{6}$	16.7 %	h.	$\frac{1}{2}$	50 %
i.	$\frac{3}{5}$	60 %	j.	$\frac{3}{25}$	12 %
k.	$\frac{5}{16}$	31.3 %	l.	$\frac{11}{50}$	22 %
m.	$4\frac{3}{4}$	475 %	n.	$\frac{3}{200}$	1.5 %

4. Convert the following to fractions in simplest form:

a.	40%	$\frac{2}{5}$	b.	15%	$\frac{3}{20}$
c.	50%	$\frac{1}{2}$	d.	75%	$\frac{3}{4}$
e.	35%	$\frac{7}{20}$	f.	85%	$\frac{17}{20}$
g.	$12\frac{1}{2}$%	$\frac{1}{8}$	h.	$37\frac{1}{2}$%	$\frac{3}{8}$
i.	$33\frac{1}{3}$%	$\frac{1}{3}$	j.	3%	$\frac{3}{100}$
k.	8.5%	$\frac{17}{200}$	l.	$5\frac{3}{4}$%	$\frac{23}{400}$
m.	100%	1	n.	10%	$\frac{1}{10}$

5. Complete the following table by finding the missing fraction, decimal, or percent equivalent:

	Fraction	Decimal	Percent		Fraction	Decimal	Percent
a.	$\frac{1}{4}$	.25	25%	h.	$\frac{1}{6}$	$.1\overline{6}\overline{6}$	$16\frac{2}{3}\%$
b.	$\frac{3}{8}$	.375	$37\frac{1}{2}\%$	i.	$\frac{1}{12}$	$.083\overline{3}$	$8\frac{1}{3}\%$
c.	$\frac{1}{2}$	.5	50%	j.	$\frac{1}{9}$	$.11\overline{1}$	$11\frac{1}{9}\%$
d.	$\frac{2}{3}$	$.66\overline{6}$	$66\frac{2}{3}\%$	k.	$\frac{5}{16}$	.3125	$31\frac{1}{4}\%$
e.	$\frac{2}{5}$	.4	40%	l.	$\frac{3}{40}$	.075	$7\frac{1}{2}\%$
f.	$\frac{3}{5}$	.6	60%	m.	$\frac{1}{4}$	.25	25%
g.	$\frac{7}{10}$	.7	70%	n.	$1\frac{1}{8}$	1.125	$112\frac{1}{2}\%$

Word Problems

6. In 1994, Mutual of New York reported an overwhelming 70% of their new sales came from existing clients. What fractional part of their new sales came from existing clients? (Reduce to simplest form.)

$70\% = \frac{70}{100} = \frac{7}{10}$

7. Six hundred ninety corporations and design firms competed for the Industrial Design Excellence Award (IDEA) in 1995. Twenty were selected as the year's best and received gold awards. Show the gold award winners as a fraction, then show what percent of the entrants received gold awards? (Round to the nearest tenth of a percent.)

$\frac{20}{690} = \frac{2}{69}$

$$\begin{array}{r} .0289 = 2.9\% \\ 69\overline{)2.0000} \\ 1\,38 \\ \hline 620 \\ 552 \\ \hline 680 \\ 621 \\ \hline 59 \end{array}$$

8. In the first half of 1994, stock prices in the Standard & Poor's 500-stock index rose 17.5%. Show the increase in decimal form.

17.5% = .175

9. In the recent banking crisis, many banks were unable to cover their bad loans. Citicorp, the nation's largest real estate lender, was reported as having only enough reserves to cover 39% of its bad loans. What fractional part of their loan losses were covered?

$39\% = \frac{39}{100}$

10. Dave Mattera spent his vacation in Las Vegas. He ordered breakfast in his room, and when he went downstairs to the coffee shop he discovered that the same breakfast was much less expensive. He had paid 1.884 times as much for the breakfast in his room. What was the percent of increase for the breakfast in his room?

1.884 = 188.4%

11. Putnam Management Co. of Boston recently increased its management fee by .09%. What is the increase as a decimal? What is the same increase as a fraction?

.09% = .0009 $\qquad$ $.09\% = .0009 = \frac{9}{10{,}000}$

12. Joel Black and Karen Whyte formed a partnership and drew up a partnership agreement with profits and losses to be divided equally after each partner receives a $7\frac{1}{2}\%$ return on his or her capital contribution. Show their return on investment as a decimal and as a fraction. (Reduce)

$7\frac{1}{2}\% = 7.5\% = .075$ $\qquad$ $7\frac{1}{2}\% = 7.5\% = .075 = \frac{75}{1{,}000} = \frac{3}{40}$

Date ____________ Name ____________

LU 6–2: Application of Percents—Portion Formula

Drill Problems

1. Fill in the amount of the base, rate, and portion in each of the following statements:
   a. The Johnson's spend $480 a month on food, which is 10% of their monthly income of $4,800.
   Base $4,800 Rate 10% Portion $480
   b. Rocky Norman got a $15 discount when he purchased a new camera. This was 20% off the sticker price of $75.
   Base $75 Rate 20% Portion $15
   c. Mary Burns got a 12% senior citizens discount when she bought a $7.00 movie ticket. She saved $0.84.
   Base $7.00 Rate 12% Portion $0.84
   d. Arthur Bogey received a commission of $13,500 when he sold the Brown's house for $225,000. His commission rate is 6%.
   Base $225,000 Rate 6% Portion $13,500
   e. Leo Davis deposited $5,000 in a certificate of deposit (CD). A year later he received an interest payment of $450 which was a yield of 9%.
   Base $5,000 Rate 9% Portion $450
   f. Grace Tremblay is on a diet that allows her to eat 1,600 calories per day. For breakfast she had 600 calories, which is $37\frac{1}{2}$% of her allowance.
   Base 1,600 Rate $37\frac{1}{2}$% Portion 600

2. Find the portion; round to the nearest hundredth if necessary:

a. 7% of 74	5.18 (74 × .07)	b. 12% of 205	24.60	c. 16% of 630	100.8
d. 7.5% of 920	69	e. 25% of 1,004	251	f. 10% of 79	7.90
g. 103% of 44	45.32	h. 30% of 78	23.40	i. .2% of 50	.10
j. 1% of 5,622	56.22	k. $6\frac{1}{4}$% of 480	30	l. 150% of 10	15
m. 100% of 34	34	n. $\frac{1}{2}$% of 27	.14		

3. Find the rate; round to the nearest tenth of a percent as needed:

a. 30 is what percent of 90?	33.3% $\left(\frac{30}{90}\right)$	b. 6 is what percent of 200?	3%
c. 275 is what percent of 1,000?	27.5%	d. .8 is what percent of 44?	1.8%
e. 67 is what percent of 2,010?	3.3%	f. 550 is what percent of 250?	220%
g. 13 is what percent of 650?	2%	h. $15 is what percent of $455?	3.3%
i. .05 is what percent of 100?	.1%	j. $6.25 is what percent of $10	62.5%

4. Find the base, round to the nearest tenth as needed:

a. 63 is 30% of	210 $\left(\frac{63}{.30}\right)$	b. 60 is 33% of	181.8	c. 150 is 25% of	600
d. 47 is 1% of	4,700	e. $21 is 120% of	$17.50	f. 2.26 is 40% of	5.7
g. 75 is $12\frac{1}{2}$% of	600	h. 18 is 22.2% of	81.1	i. $37.50 is 50% of	$75.00
j. 250 is 100% of	250				

5. Find the percent of increase or decrease. Round to nearest tenth percent as needed:

	Last year	This year	Amount of change	Percent of change
a.	5,962	4,378	−1,584	−26.6% $\left(\frac{1,584}{5,962}\right)$
b.	$10,995	$12,250	1,255	11.4%
c.	120,000	140,000	20,000	16.7%
d.	120,000	100,000	- 20,000	−16.7%

Word Problems

6. A machine that originally cost $2,400 was sold for $600 at the end of five years. What percent of the original cost is the selling price?

$$\frac{\$600}{\$2,400} = .25 = 25\%$$

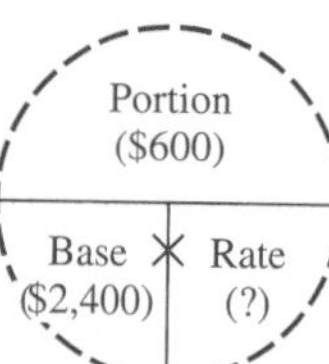

7. Joanne Byrne invested $75,000 into a candy shop, and is making 12% per year on her investment. How much money per year is she making on her investment?

$\$75,000 \times .12 = \$9,000$

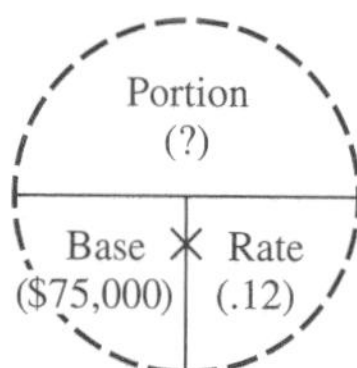

8. There was a fire in Bill Porper's store that caused 2,780 inventory items to be destroyed. Before the fire, 9,565 inventory items were in the store. What percent of inventory was destroyed? (Round to nearest tenth percent.)

$$\frac{2,780}{9,565} = 29.1\%$$

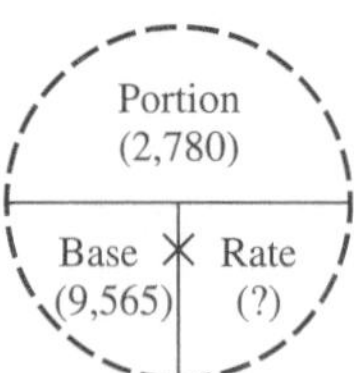

9. Elyse's Dress Shoppe makes 25% of their sales for cash. If the cash receipts on January 21 were $799, what were the total sales for the day?

$$\frac{\$799}{.25} = \$3,196$$

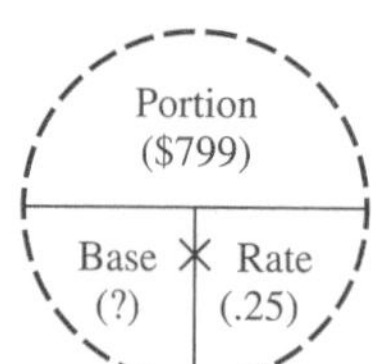

10. The YMCA is holding a fund-raiser to collect money for a new gym floor. So far they have collected $7,875, which is 63% of their goal. What is the amount of their goal? And how much more money must they collect?

$$\frac{\$7,875}{.63} = \$12,500 \text{ goal}$$

$\$12,500 - \$7,875 = \$4,625$

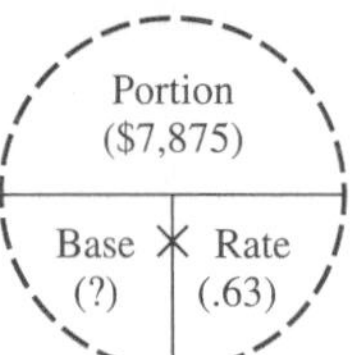

11. Leslie Tracey purchased her home for $51,500. She sold it last year for $221,200. What percent profit did she make on the sale? (Round to nearest tenth percent.)

$$\begin{array}{r} \$221,200 \\ -\ 51,500 \\ \hline \$169,700 \end{array}$$

$$\frac{\$169,700}{\$51,500} = 329.5\%$$

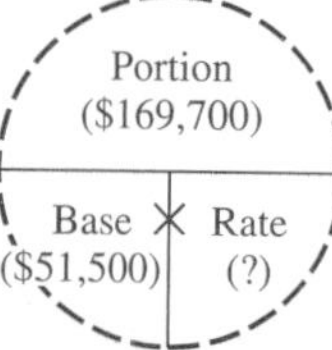

12. Maplewood Park Tool & Die had an annual production of 375,165 units this year. This is 140% of the annual production last year. What was last year's annual production?

$$\frac{375,165}{1.40} = 267,975 \text{ units}$$

Portion
(375,165)
Base
(?)
Rate
(1.40)

Date ____________ Name ____________________________

LU 7-1: Trade Discounts—Single and Chain

Drill Problems

1. Calculate the trade discount amount for each of the following items:

Item	List price	Trade discount	Trade discount amount
a. Computer	$2,500	25%	$625
b. Sofa	1,200	30%	$360
c. Suit	500	10%	$50
d. Bicycle	800	$12\frac{1}{2}\%$	$100
e. Television	950	40%	$380

a. $2,500 × .25 = $625
b. $1,200 × .30 = $360
c. $500 × .10 = $50
d. $800 × .125 = $100
e. $950 × .40 = $380

2. Calculate the net price for each of the following items:

Item	List price	Trade discount amount	Net price
a. Table	$600	$250	$350
b. Bookcase	525	129	$396
c. Rocking chair	480	95	$385

a. $600 − $250 = $350
b. $525 − $129 = $396
c. $480 − $95 = $385

3. Fill in the missing amount for each of the following items:

Item	List price	Trade discount amount	Net price
a. Electric saw	$75	$19	$56
b. Electric drill	$90	$21.50	$68.50
c. Ladder	$56	$15.25	$40.75

a. $56 + $19 = $75
b. $90 − $68.50 = $21.50
c. $56 − $15.25 = $40.75

4. For each of the following, find the percent paid (complement of trade discount) and the net price.

List price	Trade discount	Percent paid	Net price
a. $45	15%	85%	$38.25
b. $195	12.2%	87.8%	$171.21
c. $325	50%	50%	$162.50
d. $120	18%	82%	$98.40

a. 100% − 15% = 85%
$45 × .85 = $38.25
b. 100% − 12.2% = 87.8%
$195 × .878 = $171.21
c. 100% − 50% = 50%
$325 × .5 = $162.50
d. 100% − 18% = 82%
$120 × .82 = $98.40

5. In each of the following examples, find the net price equivalent rate and the single equivalent discount rate:

Chain discount	Net price equivalent rate	Single equivalent discount rate
a. 25/5	.7125	.2875
b. 15/15	.7225	.2775
c. 15/10/5	.72675	.27325
d. 12/12/6	.727936	.272064

a. .75 × .95 = .7125
1 − .7125 = .2875
b. .85 × .85 = .7225
1 − .7225 = .2775
c. .85 × .9 × .95 = .72675
1 − .72675 = .27325
d. .88 × .88 × .94 = .727936
1 − .727936 = .272064

6. In each of the following examples, find the net price and the trade discount:

	List price	Chain discount	Net price	Trade discount	
a.	$5,000	10/10/5	$3,847.50	$1,152.50	
b.	$7,500	9/6/3	$6,223.04	$1,276.97	(total is off 1¢ due to rounding)
c.	$ 898	20/7/2	$654.75	$243.25	
d.	$1,500	25/10	$1,012.50	$487.50	

a. (.9 × .9 × .95) × $5,000 = $3,847.50 $5,000 × (1 − .7695) = $1,152.50

b. (.91 × .94 × .97) × $7,500 = $6,223.035 $7,500 × (1 − .829738) = $1,276.965

c. (.8 × .93 × .98) × $898 = $654.74976 $898 × (1 − .72912) = $243.25

d. (.75 × .9) × $1,500 = $1,012.50 $1,500 × (1 − .675) = $487.50

7. The list price of a hand-held calculator is $19.50, and the trade discount is 18%. Find the trade discount amount.

$$\begin{array}{r} \$19.50 \\ \times\ .18 \\ \hline 15600 \\ 1950 \\ \hline 3.5100 \end{array} = \$3.51$$

8. The list price of a silver picture frame is $29.95, and the trade discount is 15%. Find the trade discount amount and the net price.

$$\begin{array}{r} \$29.95 \\ \times\ .15 \\ \hline 14975 \\ 2995 \\ \hline 4.4925 \end{array} = \$4.49 \text{ trade discount amount}$$

$$\begin{array}{r} \$29.95 \\ -\ 4.49 \\ \hline \$25.46 \end{array} \text{ net price}$$

or $29.95 × .85 = $25.46

9. The net price of a set of pots and pans is $65.00, and the trade discount is 20%. What is the list price?

$$\frac{\$65}{1 - .20} = \frac{\$65}{.80} = \$81.25$$

10. Jennie's Variety Store has the opportunity to purchase candy from three different wholesalers; each of the wholesalers offers a different chain discount. Co. A offers 25/5/5, Co. B offers 20/10/5, and Co. C offers 15/20. Which company should Jennie deal with? (*Hint:* choose the company with the highest single equivalent discount rate.)

Co. A: .75 × .95 × .95 = .676875   1 − .676875 = .323125 = 32.31%

Co. B: .8 × .9 × .95 = .684   1 − .684 = .316 = 31.6%

Co. C: .85 × .8 = .68   1 − .68 = .32 = 32%

Choose Co. A for the 32.31% discount.

11. The list price of a television set is $625. Find the net price after a series discount of 30/20/10.

(.7 × .8 × .9) × $625 = $315 net price

12. Mandy's Accessories Shop purchased 12 purses with a total list price of $726. What was the net price of each purse if the wholesaler offered a chain discount of 25/20?

(.75 × .8) × $726 = $435.60 $435.60 ÷ 12 = $36.30 net price/purse

13. Kransberg Furniture Store purchased a bedroom set for $1,097.25 from Furniture Wholesalers. The list price of the set was $1,995. What trade discount rate did Kransberg receive?

List price − Net price = Trade discount amount $\frac{\$1,995 - \$1,097.25}{\$1,995} = .45 = 45\%$

14. Susan Monk teaches second grade and receives a discount at the local art supply store. Recently she paid $47.25 for art supplies after receiving a chain discount of 30/10. What was the regular price of the art supplies?

.7 × .9 = .63 net price equivalent rate $\frac{\$47.25}{.63} = \$75$

Date ____________ Name ____________

LU 7–2: Cash Discounts, Credit Terms, and Partial Payments

Drill Problems

1. Complete the following table:

	Date of invoice	Date goods received	Terms	Last day of discount period	End of credit period
a.	Feb. 12		2/10, n/30	Feb. 22	Mar. 14
b.	Aug. 26		2/10, n/30	Sept. 5	Sept. 25
c.	Oct. 17		3/10, n/60	Oct. 27	Dec. 16
d.	Mar. 11	May 10	3/10, n/30, ROG	May 20	June 9
e.	Sept. 14		2/10, EOM	Oct. 10	Oct. 30
f.	May 31		2/10, EOM	July 10	July 30

2. Calculate the cash discount and the net amount paid.

	Invoice amount	Cash discount rate	Discount amount	Net amount paid
a.	$75	3%	$2.25 ($75 × .03)	$72.75 ($75 × .97)
b.	$1,559	2%	$31.18	$1,527.82
c.	$546.25	2%	$10.93	$535.33 (rounded)
d.	$9,788.75	1%	$97.89	$9,690.86

3. Use the complement of the cash discount to calculate the net amount paid. Assume all invoices are paid within the discount period.

	Terms of invoice	Amount of invoice		Complement		Net amount paid
a.	2/10, n/30	$1,125	×	.98	=	$1,102.50
b.	3/10, n/30 ROG	$4,500		.97		$4,365
c.	2/10, EOM	$375.50		.98		$367.99
d.	1/15, n/45	$3,998		.99		$3,958.02

4. Calculate the amount of cash discount and the net amount paid.

	Date of invoice	Terms of invoice	Amount of invoice	Date paid	Cash discount	Amount paid
a.	Jan. 12	2/10, n/30	$5,320	Jan. 22	$106.40	$5,213.60
b.	May 28	2/10, n/30	$975	June 7	$19.50	$955.50
c.	Aug. 15	2/10, n/30	$7,700	Aug. 26	0	$7,700
d.	Mar. 8	2/10, EOM	$480	Apr. 10	$9.60	$470.40
e.	Jan. 24	3/10, n/60	$1,225	Feb. 3	$36.75	$1,188.25

5. Complete the following table:

	Total invoice	Freight charges included in invoice total	Date of invoice	Terms of invoice	Date of payment	Cash discount	Amount paid
a.	$852	$12.50	3/19	2/10, n/30	3/29	$16.79	$835.21
	[($852 − $12.50) × .02 = $16.79], ($822.71 + $12.50 = $835.21)						
b.	$669.57	$15.63	7/28	3/10, EOM	9/10	$19.62	$649.95
	[($669.57 − $15.63) × .03 = $19.62], ($634.32 + $15.63 = $649.95)						
c.	$500	$11.50	4/25	2/10, n/60	6/5	0	$500.00
	no discount, pay total invoice						
d.	$188	$9.70	1/12	2/10, EOM	2/10	$3.57	$184.43
	[($188 − $9.70) × .02 = $3.57], ($174.73 + $9.70 = $184.43)						

6. In the following table, assume that all of the partial payments were made within the discount period.

	Amount of invoice	Terms of invoice	Partial payment	Amount to be credited	Balance outstanding
a.	$481.90	2/10, n/30	$90.00	$91.84	$390.06
	($90 ÷ .98 = $91.84), ($481.90 − $91.84 = $390.06)				
b.	$1,000	2/10, EOM	$500.00	$510.20	$489.80
	($500 ÷ .98 = $510.20), ($1,000 − $510.20 = $489.80)				
c.	$782.88	3/10, n/30, ROG	$275.00	$283.51	$499.37
	($275 ÷ .97 = $283.51), ($782.88 − $283.51 = $499.37)				
d.	$318.80	2/15, n/60	$200.00	$204.08	$114.72
	($200 ÷ .98 = $204.08), ($318.80 − $204.08 = $114.72)				

Word Problems

7. Northwest Chemical Company received an invoice for $12,480, dated March 12, with terms of 2/10, n/30. If the invoice was paid March 22, what was the amount due?
   100% − 2% = 98% $12,480 × .98 = $12,230.40

8. On May 27, Trotter Hardware Store received an invoice for trash barrels purchased for $13,650 with terms of 3/10, EOM; the freight charge, which is included in the price, is $412. What is **(a)** the last day of the discount period, and **(b)** the amount of the payment due on this date?
   a. Last discount date is July 10   **b.**
   $13,650
   − 412 freight
   13,238
   × .97 complement (100% − 3% = 97%)
   12,840.86
   + 412.00 freight
   $13,252.86 total due in discount period

9. The Glass Sailboat received an invoice for $930.50 with terms 2/10, n/30 on April 19. On April 29 they sent a payment of $430.50. **(a)** How much credit will be given on the total due? **(b)** What is the new balance due?
   100% − 2% = 98%   **a.** $430.50 ÷ .98 = $439.29 credit given
   b. $930.50 − $439.29 = $491.21 balance due

10. Dallas Ductworks offers cash discounts of 2/10, 1/15, n/30 on all purchases. If an invoice for $544 dated July 18 is paid on August 2, what is the amount due?
    July 18 to August 2 = 15 days
    100% − 1% = 99%
    $544 × .99 = $538.56 amount due

11. The list price of a compact disc player is $299.90 with trade discounts of 10/20 and terms of 3/10, n/30. If a retailer pays the invoice within the discount period, what amount must the retailer pay?
    .9 × .8 = .72   100% − 3% = 97%
    $299.90 × .72 = $215.928 = $215.93 net price $215.93 × .97 = $209.45 payment

12. The invoice of sneaker supplier totaled $2,488.50, was dated February 7, and offered terms 2/10, ROG. The shipment of sneakers was received on March 7. What is **(a)** the last date of the discount period and **(b)** the amount of the discount that will be lost if the invoice is paid after that date?
    a. Last discount date is March 17.
    b. $2,488.50 × .02 = $49.77 discount lost after March 17

13. Starburst Toy Company receives an invoice amounting to $1,152.30 with terms of 2/10, EOM and dated November 6. If a partial payment of $750 is made on December 8, what is **(a)** the credit given for the partial payment and **(b)** the balance due on the invoice?
    100% − 2% = 98%   **a.** $750 ÷ .98 = $765.31 (rounded)
    b. $1,152.30 − $765.31 = $386.99 balance due

14. Todd's Sporting Goods received an invoice for soccer equipment dated July 26 with terms 3/10, 1/15, n/30 in the amount of $3,225.83, which included shipping charges of $375.50. If this bill is paid on August 5, what amount must be paid?
    $3,225.83 − $375.50 = $2,850.33 $2,850.33 × .97 = $2,764.82 (rounded)
    100% − 3% = 97% $2,764.82 + $375.50 = $3,140.32

Date ______________ Name ______________________________________

LU 8–1: Markups Based on Cost (100%)

Drill Problems

1. Fill in the missing numbers:

	Cost	Markup	Selling price	
a.	$5.50	$1.35	$6.85	
	S = C + M	S = $5.50 + $1.35		
b.	$8.32	$2.72	$11.04	($11.04 − $8.32 = $2.72)
c.	$25.27	$4.35	$29.62	($29.62 − $25.27 = $4.35)
d.	$90.00	$75.00	$165.00	($165 − $75 = $90)
e.	$86.54	$29.77	$116.31	($86.54 + $29.77 = $116.31)

2. Calculate the markup based on cost (round to the nearest cent):

	Cost	Markup (percent of cost)	Markup amount	
a.	$425.00	30%	$127.50	($425 × .30 = $127.50)
b.	$1.52	20%	$0.30	($1.52 × .20 = $.304)
c.	$9.90	$12\frac{1}{2}$%	$1.24	($9.90 × .125 = $1.24)
d.	$298.10	50%	$149.05	($298.10 × .50 = $149.05)
e.	$74.25	38%	$28.22	($74.25 × .38 = $28.22)
f.	$552.25	100%	$552.25	($552.25 × 1 = $552.25)

3. Calculate the markup amount and rate of the markup as a percent of cost (round percents to nearest tenth percent). Verify your result, which may be slightly off due to rounding.

	Cost	Selling price	Markup amount	Markup (percent of cost)	Verify
a.	$2.50	$4.50	$2.00	80%	$\frac{\$2.00}{.80} = \$2.50$
	($4.50 − $2.50 = $2.00); ($2 ÷ $2.50 = .8 = 80%)				
b.	$12.50	$19.00	$6.50	52%	$\frac{\$6.50}{.52} = \$12.50$
	($19.00 − $12.50 = $6.50); ($6.50 ÷ $12.50 = .52 = 52%)				
c.	$0.97	$1.25	$0.28	28.9%	$\frac{\$.28}{.289} = \$.97$
	($1.25 − $.97 = $0.28); ($.28 ÷ $.97 = .2886 = 28.9%)				
d.	$132.25	$175.00	$42.75	32.3%	$\frac{\$42.75}{.323} = \$132.35$
	($175 − $132.25 = $42.75); ($42.75 ÷ $132.25 = .3232 = 32.3%)				
e.	$65.00	$89.99	$24.99	38.4%	$\frac{\$24.99}{.384} = \$65.08$
	($89.99 − $65 = $24.99); ($24.99 ÷ $65 = .3844 = 38.4%)				

4. Calculate the markup and the selling price:

	Cost	Markup (percent of cost)	Markup amount	Selling price	
a.	$2.20	40%	$0.88	$3.08	$S = C + M$
	($2.20 × .40 = $.88); ($2.20 + $.88 = $3.08)				$S = \$2.20 + .40\ (\$2.20)$
b.	$2.80	16%	$0.45	$3.25	
	($2.80 × .16 = .448 = $0.45); ($2.80 + $.45 = $3.25)				
c.	$840.00	$12\frac{1}{2}$%	$105.00	$945.00	
	($840 × .125 = $105); ($840 + $105 = $945)				
d.	$24.36	30%	$7.31	$31.67	
	($24.36 × .30 = $7.31); ($24.36 + $7.31 = $31.67)				

5. Calculate the cost (round to nearest cent):

	Selling price	Rate of markup based on cost	Cost	
a.	$1.98	30%	$1.52	$S = C + M$
	($1.98 ÷ 1.30 = $1.52)			$\$1.98 = C + .30C$
b.	$360.00	60%	$225.00	$S = C + M$
	($360 ÷ 1.60 = $225)			$\$360 = C + .60C$
c.	$447.50	20%	$372.92	
	($447.50 ÷ 1.20 = $372.92)			
d.	$1,250.00	100%	$625.00	
	($1,250 ÷ 2 = $625)			

6. Find the missing numbers. Round money to nearest cent, and percents to the nearest tenth percent.

	Cost	Markup amount	Percent markup on cost	Selling price	
a.	$72.00	$28.80	40%	$100.80	$S = C + M$
	($72 × .40 = $28.80); ($72.00 + $28.80 = $100.80)				$S = \$72 + .40\ (\$72)$
b.	$28.00	$7.00	25%	$35.00	$S = C + M$
	($35 − $7 = $28); ($7 ÷ $28 = .25 = 25%)				$\$35 = C + \$7$
c.	$8.80	$1.10	12.5%	$9.90	
	($1.10 ÷ $8.80 = .125 = 12.5%); ($8.80 + $1.10 = $9.90)				
d.	$15.50	$4.34	28%	$19.84	$S = C + M$
	($19.84 ÷ 1.28 = $15.50); ($19.84 − $15.50 = $4.34)				$\$19.84 = C + .28C$
e.	$175.00	$61.25	35%	$236.25	
	($236.25 − $175 = $61.25); ($61.25 ÷ $175 = .35 = 35%)				

Word Problems

7. The cost of an office chair is $159.00 and the markup rate is 24% of the cost. What is **(a)** the markup and **(b)** the selling price?
   a. $159 × .24 = $38.16 markup — $S = C + M$
   b. $159 + $38.16 = $197.16 selling price — $S = \$159 + .24\ (\$159)$

8. If Barry's Furniture Store purchased a floor lamp for $120 and plans to add a markup of $90, **(a)** what will the selling price be and **(b)** what is the markup as a percent of cost?
   a. $120 + $90 = $210 selling price — $S = C + M$
   b. $90 ÷ $120 = .75 = 75% — $S = \$120 + \$90$

9. If Lesjardin's Jewelry Store is selling a gold bracelet for $349, which includes a markup of 35% on cost, what is **(a)** Lesjardin's cost and **(b)** the amount of the markup?
   a. $349 ÷ 1.35 = $258.518 = $258.52 cost — $S = C + M$
   b. $349 − $258.52 = $90.48 markup — $\$349 = C + .35C$

10. Toll's Variety Store sells an alarm clock for $14.75. The alarm clock cost Toll's $9.90. What is the markup amount as a percent of cost? (Round to nearest whole percent.)
    $14.75 − $9.90 = $4.85 $4.85 ÷ $9.90 = .4898 = 49% markup

11. Swanson's Audio Supply marks up its merchandise by 40% on cost. If the markup on a cassette player is $85, what is **(a)** the cost of the cassette player and **(b)** the selling price?
    a. $85 ÷ .40 = $212.50 cost
    b. $212.50 + $85 = $297.50 selling price

    $$C = \frac{\text{Markup amount}}{\text{Percent markup on cost}} \qquad C = \frac{\$85}{.40}$$

    $S = C + M$
    $S = \$212.50 + 85$

12. Brown's Department Store is selling a shirt for $55. If the markup is 70% on cost, what is Brown's cost (to the nearest cent)?
    $55 ÷ 1.70 = $32.35

    $$\text{Cost} = \frac{\text{Markup amount}}{\text{Percent markup on cost}}$$

13. Ward's Greenhouse purchased tomato flats for $5.75 each. Ward's has decided to use a markup of 42% on cost. Find the selling price.
    $5.75 × .42 = $2.415 = $2.42 — $S = C + M$
    $5.75 + $2.42 = $8.17 selling price — $S = \$5.75 + .42\ (\$5.75)$

Date ______________ Name ______________________________

LU 8-2: Markups Based on Selling Price (100%)

Drill Problems

1. Calculate the markup based on the selling price:

	Selling price	Markup (percent of selling price)	Markup amount	
a.	$4.50	20%	$0.90	($4.50 × .20 = $.90)
b.	$230.00	25%	$57.50	($230 × .25 = $57.50)
c.	$81.00	42.5%	$34.43	($81 × .425 = 34.425 = $34.43)
d.	$72.88	$37\frac{1}{2}$%	$27.33	($72.88 × .375 = $27.33)
e.	$1.98	$7\frac{1}{2}$%	$0.15	($1.98 × .075 = $.148 = $0.15)

2. Calculate the markup amount and the markup as a percent of selling price (to the nearest tenth percent). Verify your answer, which may be slightly off due to rounding.

	Cost	Selling price	Markup amount	Markup (percent of selling price)	Verify
a.	$2.50	$4.25	$1.75	41.2%	$\frac{\$1.75}{.412} = \$4.25$
	($4.25 − $2.50 = $1.75); ($1.75 ÷ $4.25 = .4117 = 41.2%)				
b.	$16.00	$24.00	$8.00	33.3%	$\frac{\$8.00}{.333} = \$24.02$
	($24 − $16 = $8); ($8 ÷ $24 = .3333)				
c.	$45.25	$85.00	$39.75	46.8%	$\frac{\$39.75}{.468} = \$84.94$
	($85 − $45.25 = $39.75); ($39.75 ÷ $85 = .4676 = 46.8%)				
d.	$0.19	$0.25	$0.06	24%	$\frac{\$.06}{.24} = \$.25$
	($.25 − $.19 = $.06); ($.06 ÷ $.25 = .24 = 24%)				
e.	$5.50	$8.98	$3.48	38.8%	$\frac{\$3.48}{.388} = \$8.97$
	($8.98 − $5.50 = $3.48); ($3.48 ÷ $8.98 = .3875 = 38.8%)				

3. Given the *cost* and the markup as a percent of *selling price*, calculate the selling price:

	Cost	Markup (percent of selling price)	Selling price	
a.	$5.90	15%	$6.94	$S = C + M$
	[$5.90 ÷ (1 − .15) = $5.90 ÷ .85 = $6.941 = $6.94]			$S = \$5.90 + .15S$
b.	$600	32%	$882.35	$S = C + M$
	[$600 ÷ (1 − .32) = $600 ÷ .68 = $882.352 = $882.35]			$S = \$600 + .32S$
c.	$15	50%	$30	$S = C + M$
	[$15 ÷ (1 − .50) = $15 ÷ .50 = $30]			$S = \$15 + .50(S)$
d.	$120	30%	$171.43	$S = C + M$
	[$120 ÷ (1 − .30) = $120 ÷ .70 = $171.43]			$S = \$120 + .30(S)$
e.	$0.29	20%	$0.36	$S = C + M$
	[$.29 ÷ (1 − .20) = $.29 ÷ .8 = $0.362 = $0.36]			$S = \$.29 + .20(S)$

4. Given the selling price and the percent markup on selling price, calculate the cost:

	Cost	Markup (percent of selling price)	Selling price	
a.	$3.75	40%	$6.25	$S = C + M$
	[$6.25 × (1 − .40) = $6.25 × .60 = $3.75]			$\$6.25 = C + .40(\$6.25)$
b.	$13.00	20%	$16.25	$S = C + M$
	[$16.25 × (1 − .20) = $16.25 × .80 = $13]			$\$16.25 = C + .20(\$16.25)$
c.	$51.75	19%	$63.89	$S = C + M$
	[$63.89 × (1 − .19) = $63.89 × .81 = $51.75]			$\$63.89 = C + .19(\$63.89)$
d.	$16.50	$62\frac{1}{2}$%	$44.00	$S = C + M$
	[$44 × (1 − .625) = $44 × .375 = $16.50]			$\$44 = C + .625(\$44)$

5. Calculate the equivalent rate of markup (round to the nearest hundredth percent):

	Markup on cost	Markup on selling price		Markup on cost	Markup on selling price
a.	40%	$28.57%	b.	50%	33.33%
	(.40 ÷ 1.40 = .28571 = 28.57%)			(.50 ÷ 1.50 = .33333 = 33.33%)	
c.	100%	50%	d.	53.85%	35%
	(.50 ÷ .50 = 1 = 100%)			(.35 ÷ .65 = .53846 = 53.85%)	
e.	66.67%	40%			
	(.40 ÷ .60 = .66666 = 66.67%)				

Word Problems

6. Fisher Equipment is selling a Wet/Dry Shop Vac for $49.97. If Fisher's markup is 40% of the selling price, what is the cost of the Shop Vac?

$\$49.97 = C + .40(\$49.97)$
$\$49.97 = C + \$19.99$ or $\$49.97 \times (1 - .40)$
$-19.99 \qquad -19.99$
$\$29.98 = C$

7. Gove Lumber Company purchased a 10-inch table saw for $225 and will mark up the price 35% on the selling price. What will the selling price be?

$S = \$225 + .35S$
$-.35S \qquad -.35S$ or $\dfrac{\$225}{1 - .35}$
$\dfrac{.65S}{.65} = \dfrac{\$225}{.65}$
$S = \$346.153 = \$346.15$

8. In order to realize a sufficient gross margin, City Paint and Supply Company marks up its paint 27% on the selling price. If a gallon of Latex Semi-Gloss Enamel has a markup of $4.02, find **(a)** the selling price, and **(b)** the cost.

a. $\dfrac{\$4.02}{.27} = \$14.89$ **b.** $\$14.89 - \$4.02 = C$, $\$10.87 = C$ $\qquad S = \dfrac{\text{Markup amount}}{\text{Percent markup on selling price}}$

9. A Magnavox 20-inch color TV cost $180 and sells for $297. What is the markup based on the selling price? (Round to nearest hundredth percent.)

$297 − $180 = $117 markup $\qquad$ $117 ÷ $297 = .39393 = 39.39%

10. Bargain Furniture sells a five-piece country maple bedroom set for $1,299. The cost of this set is $700. What is **(a)** the markup on the bedroom set, **(b)** the markup percent on cost, and **(c)** the markup percent on the selling price. (Round to nearest hundredth percent.)

a. $1,299 − $700 = $599 **b.** $\dfrac{\$599}{\$700} = 85.57\%$ **c.** $\dfrac{\$599}{\$1{,}299} = 46.11\%$

11. Robert's Department Store marks up its sundries by 28% on the selling price. If a 6.4-ounce tube of toothpaste cost $1.65, what will the selling price be?

$S = \$1.65 + .28S$
$-.28S \qquad -.28S$ or $\dfrac{\$1.65}{1 - .28}$
$\dfrac{.72S}{.72} = \dfrac{\$1.65}{.72}$
$S = \$2.291 = \$2.29$ selling price

12. In order to be competitive, Tinker Toys must sell the Nintendo Control Deck for $89.99. To meet expenses and make a sufficient profit, Tinker Toys must add a markup on selling price of 23%. What is the maximum amount that Tinker Toys can afford to pay a wholesaler for Nintendo?

$\$89.99 = C + .23(\$89.99)$ or $\$89.99 \times (1 - .23)$
$\$89.99 = C + \$20.70$
$-20.70 \qquad -20.70$
$\$69.29 = C$ (maximum cost)

13. Nicole's Restaurant charges $7.50 for a linguini dinner that cost $2.75 for the ingredients. What rate of markup is earned on the selling price? (Round to nearest hundredth percent.)

$7.50 − $2.75 = $4.75 $\qquad$ $4.75 ÷ $7.50 = .63333 = 63.33% on selling price

Date ______________ Name ______________________________

LU 8–3: Markdowns and Perishables

Drill Problems

1. Find the markdown and the sale price:

	Original selling price	Markdown percent	Markdown amount	Sale price
a.	$56	10%	$5.60	$50.40
	($56 × .10 = $5.60), ($56 − $5.60 = $50.40)			
b.	$2,099.98	25%	$525	$1,574.98
	($2,099.98 × .25 = $524.995 = $525) ($2,099.98 − $525 = $1,574.98)			
c.	$729	30%	$218.70	$510.30
	(729 × .30 = $218.70), ($729 − $218.70 = $510.30)			

2. Find the markdown amount and the markdown percent on original selling price:

	Original selling price	Sale price	Markdown amount	Markdown percent
a.	$19.50	$9.75	$9.75	50%
	$19.50 − $9.75 = $9.75)	$\left(\frac{\$9.75}{\$19.50} = 0.50 = 50\%\right)$		
b.	$250	$175	$75	30%
	($250 − $175 = $75)	$\left(\frac{\$75}{\$250} = 30\%\right)$		
c.	$39.95	$29.96	$9.99	25%
	($39.95 − $29.96 = $9.99)	$\left(\frac{\$9.99}{\$39.95} = 25\%\right)$		

3. Find the original selling price:

	Sale price	Markdown percent	Original selling price
a.	$328	20%	$410
	(100% − 20% = 80%)	$\left(\frac{\$328}{.80} = \$410\right)$	
b.	$15.85	15%	$18.65
	(100% − 15% = 85%)	$\left(\frac{\$15.85}{.85} = \$18.65\right)$	

$\frac{P}{B \times R} \quad \frac{\$328}{.80}$

4. Calculate the final selling price:

	Original selling price	First markdown	Second markdown	Final markup	Final selling price
a.	$4.96	25%	8%	5%	$3.59
	[$4.96 × (1 − .25) = $3.72] [$3.72 × (1 − .08) = $3.42] [$3.42 × (1 + .05) = $3.59]				
b.	$130	30%	10%	20%	$98.28
	[$130 × (1 − .30) = $91] [$91 × (1 − .10) = $81.90] [$81.90 × (1 + .20) = $98.28]				

5. Find the missing amounts:

	Number of units	Unit cost	Total cost	Estimated* spoilage	Desired markup (percent of cost)	Total selling price	Selling price per unit
a.	72	$3	$216	12%	50%	$324	$5.14
	(72 × $3 = $216); [$216 + ($216 × .50) = $324] (72 × .12 = 8.64 = 9 units) $TS = TC + TM$ [$324/(72 − 9) = $5.14]						
b.	50	$0.90	$45	16%	42%	$63.90	$1.52
	(50 × $0.90 = $45), [$45 + ($45 × .42) = $63.90] (50 × .16 = 8 units) [$63.90/(50 − 8) = $1.52]						

* Round to nearest whole unit as needed.

Word Problems

6. Windom's is having a 30% off sale on their box springs and mattresses. A queen-size, back-supporter mattress is priced at $325. What is the sale price of the mattress?
$325 × .30 = $97.50 or $325 × .70 = $227.50
$325 − $97.50 = $227.50

7. Murray and Sons sell a personal fax machine for $602.27. They are having a sale, and the fax machine is marked down to $499.88. What is the percent of the markdown?
$602.27 − $499.88 = $102.39 $\frac{\$102.39}{\$602.27} = 17\%$

8. Coleman's is having a clearance sale. A lamp with an original selling price of $249 is now selling for $198. Find the percent of the markdown. (Round to nearest hundredth percent.)
$249 − $198 = $51 $\frac{\$51}{\$249} = 20.48\%$

9. Johnny's Sports Shop has advertised markdowns on certain items of 22%. A soccer ball is marked with a sale price of $16.50. What was the original price of the soccer ball?
100% − 22% = 78% $\frac{\$16.50}{.78} = \$21.15$ $\frac{P\ \$16.50}{B \times R}$? .78

10. Sam Grillo sells seasonal furnishings. Near the end of the summer a five-piece patio set that was priced $349.99 had not been sold, so he marked it down by 12%. As Labor Day approached, he still had not sold the patio set, so he marked it down an additional 18%. What was the final selling price of the patio set?
$349.99 × .88 = $307.99 × .82 = $252.55

11. Calsey's Department Store sells their down comforters for a regular price of $325. During their white sale the comforters were marked down 22%. Then, at the end of the sale, they held a special promotion and gave a second markdown of 10%. When the sale was over, the remaining comforters were marked up 20%. What was the final selling price of the remaining comforters?
$325 × .78 = $253.50 $253.50 × .90 = $228.15 $228.15 × 1.2 = $273.78

12. The New Howard Bakery wants to make a 60% profit on the cost of its pies. In order to calculate the price of their pies, they have estimated that the usual amount of spoilage they have is 5 pies. Calculate the selling price for each pie if the number of pies baked each day is 24 and the cost of the ingredients for each pie is $1.80.
24 × $1.80 = $43.20 total cost
$43.20 × 1.60 = $69.12 total selling price $TS = TC + TM$
24 − 5 = 19
$\frac{\$69.12}{19} = \$3.64$ per pie

13. Sunshine Bakery bakes 660 loaves of bread each day and estimates that 10% of the bread will go stale before it is sold and have to be discarded. The owner of the bakery wishes to realize a 55% markup on cost on his bread. If his cost to make a loaf of bread is $0.46, what should he sell each loaf for?
660 × $.46 = $303.60 total cost $470.58/(660 − 66) = $.79
$303.60 × 1.55 = $470.58 total selling price
660 × .10 = 66 units spoilage

Date ____________ Name ____________

LU 9-1: Calculating Various Types of Employees' Gross Pay

Drill Problems

1. Fill in the missing amounts for each of the following employees: Do not round overtime rate in your calculations and round final answers to nearest cent.

	Employee	Total hours	Rate per hour	Regular pay	Overtime pay	Gross pay
a.	Ben Badger	40	$ 6.50	$260.00	$ 0.00	$260.00
b.	Casey Guitare	43	9.00	360.00	40.50	400.50
c.	Norma Harris	37	7.50	277.50	0.00	277.50
d.	Ed Jackson	45	12.25	490.00	91.88	581.88

a. 40 × $6.50 = $260.00
b. (40 × $9.00 = $360.00) + (3 × $13.50 = $40.50) = $400.50
c. 37 × $7.50 = $277.50
d. (40 × $12.25 = $490.00) + (5 × $18.375 = $91.875) = $581.88

2. Calculate each employee's gross from the following date. Do not round overtime rate in your calculation, and round final answer to nearest cent.

	Employee	S	M	T	W	T	F	S	Total hours	Rate per hour	Regular pay	Overtime pay	Gross pay
a.	L. Adams	0	8	8	8	8	8	0	40	$ 8.10	$324.00	$ 0.00	$324.00
b.	M. Card	0	9	8	9	8	8	4	46	11.35	454.00	102.15	556.15
c.	P. Kline	2	$7\frac{1}{2}$	$8\frac{1}{4}$	8	$10\frac{3}{4}$	9	2	$47\frac{1}{2}$	10.60	424.00	119.25	543.25
d.	J. Mack	0	$9\frac{1}{2}$	$9\frac{3}{4}$	$9\frac{1}{2}$	10	10	4	$52\frac{3}{4}$	9.95	398.00	190.29	588.29

a. 40 × $8.10 = $324.00
b. (40 × $11.35 = $454.00) + (6 × $17.025 = $102.15) = $556.15
c. (40 × $10.60 = $424.00) + $\left(7\frac{1}{2} \times \$15.90 = \$119.25\right)$ = $543.25
d. (40 × $9.95 = $398.00) + $\left(12\frac{3}{4} \times \$14.925 = \$190.29\right)$ = $588.29

3. Calculate the gross wages of the following production workers:

	Employee	Rate per unit	Number of units produced	Gross pay	
a.	A. Bossie	$0.67	655	$438.85	$0.67 × 655 = $438.85
b.	J. Carson	0.87\frac{1}{2}$	703	$615.13	$0.875 × 703 = $615.125 = $615.13

4. Using the given differential scale, calculate the gross wages of the following production workers:

Units produced	Amount per unit
1–50	$.55
51–100	.65
101–200	.72
Over 200	.95

	Employee	Units produced	Gross pay
a.	F. Burns	190	$124.80
b.	B. English	210	141.50
c.	E. Jackson	200	132.00

a. (50 × $0.55) + (50 × $0.65) + (90 × $0.72) = $124.80
b. (50 × $0.55) + (50 × $0.65) + (100 × $0.72) + (10 × $0.95) = $141.50
c. (50 × $0.55) + (50 × $0.65) + (100 × .72) = $132.00

5. Calculate the following salespersons' gross wages:

a. Straight commission:

Employee	Net sales	Commission	Gross pay
M. Salley	$40,000	13%	$5,200

$40,000 × .13 = $5,200

b. Straight commission with Draw:

Employee	Net sales	Commission	Draw	Gross pay
G. Gorsbeck	$38,000	12%	$600	$3,960

($38,000 × .12) − $600 = $3,960

c. Variable commission scale:

Up to $25,000	8%
Excess of $25,000 to $40,000	10%
Over $40,000	12%

Employee	Net sales	Gross pay
H. Lloyd	$42,000	$3,740

($25,000 × .08) + ($15,000 × .10) + ($2,000 × .12) = $3,740

d. Salary plus commission:

Employee	Salary	Commission	Quota	Net sales	Gross pay
P. Floyd	$2,500	3%	$400,000	$475,000	$4,750

($475,000 − $400,000) × .03 + $2,500 = $4,750

Word Problems

For all problems with overtime, be sure to round only the final answer.

6. In the first week of December, Dana Robinson worked 52 hours. His regular rate of pay is $11.25 per hour. What will Dana's gross pay for the week be?
52 − 40 = 12 hours overtime $652.50 gross pay
(40 × $11.25) + (12 × $16.875)
$450 + $202.50

7. Davis Fisheries pays its workers for each box of fish they pack. Sunny Melanson receives $0.30 per box. During the third week of July, Sunny packed 2,410 boxes of fish. What is Sunny's gross pay?
2,410 × $.30 = $723.00 gross pay

8. Maye George is a real estate broker who receives a straight commission of 6%. What would her commission be for a house that sold for $197,500?
$197,500 × .06 = $11,850 commission

9. Devon Company pays Eileen Haskins a straight commission of $12\frac{1}{2}$% on her net sales. In January, Devon gave Eileen a draw of $600. She had net sales that month of $35,570. What is Eileen's gross pay?
$35,570 × .125 = $4,446.25
− 600.00
$3,846.25 gross pay

10. Parker and Company pays Selma Stokes on a variable commission scale. In a month when Selma had net sales of $155,000, what was her gross pay based on the following schedule?

Net sales	Commission rate
Up to $40,000	5%
Excess of $40,000 to $75,000	5.5%
Excess of $75,000 to $100,000	6%
Over $100,000	7%

($40,000 × .05) + ($35,000 × .055) + ($25,000 × .06) + ($55,000 × .07) $9,275 gross pay
$2,000 + $1,925 + $1,500 + $3,850

11. Marsh Furniture Company pays Joshua Charles a montly salary of $1,900 plus a commission of $2\frac{1}{2}$% on sales over $12,500. Last month, Joshua had net sales of $17,799. What is Joshua's gross pay for the month?
$1,900 + [($17,799 − $12,500) × .025] $2,032.48 gross pay
$1,900 + $132.48

12. Amy McWha works at the Lamplighter Bookstore where she earns $7.75 per hour plus a commission of 2% on her weekly sales in excess of $1,500. Last week, Amy worked 39 hours and had total sales of $2,250. What is Amy's gross pay for the week?
($7.75 × 39) + [($2,250 − $1,500) × .02] $317.25 gross pay
$302.25 + $15.00

Date ______________ Name ______________________________

LU 9-2: Computing Payroll Deductions for Employees' Pay; Insight into Employer Responsibilities

Drill Problems

Use tables in the Business Math Handbook (assume FICA rates in text).

Complete	Allowances and marital status	Cumulative earnings	Salary per week	Taxable earnings S.S.	Taxable earnings Medicare
1. Pete Small	M–3	55,000	$ 780	a. $500	b. $780
2. Alice Hall	M–1	55,500	1,100	c. 0	d. $1,100
3. Jean Rose	M–2	130,000	990	e. 0	f. $200

a. $55,500 − 55,000 = $500   b. $780   c. 0   d. 1,100   e. 0   f. $130,200 − 30,000 = $200

4. What is the FIT for Pete Small by wage bracket table?
   $87
5. What is the tax for Social Security and Medicare for Pete in Problem 1.
   Social Security .062 × $500 = $31.00
   Medicare .0145 × $780 = $11.31
6. Calculate Pete's FIT by the percentage method.
   $780.00
   − 132.69 (3 × $44.23)
   $647.31
   − 71.00
   $576.31 × .15 = $86.45
7. What would employees contribute for this week's payroll for SUTA and FUTA?
   0; wages over $7,000 are exempt

Word Problems

8. Cynthia Pratt has earned $54,000 thus far this year. This week she earned $1,050. Find her total FICA tax deduction (Social Security and Medicare).
   $54,000
   + 1,050
   $55,050 Still not over base of $55,500 for Social Security or $130,200 for Medicare.
   FICA: Social Security .062 × $1,050 = $65.10
   Medicare .0145 × $1,050 = 15.23
   $80.33 total FICA
   Or: .0765 × $1,050 = $80.33 (We can do this since no base has been broken yet.)
9. If Cynthia (Problem 8) earns $1,050 the following week, what will her total FICA tax deduction be?
   Cynthia is over base for Social Security $55,500 base
   55,050 cumulative earning before payroll
   $ 450 was taxed for Social Security
   Social Security .062 × $450 = $27.90 All wages still taxed for Medicare.
   Medicare .0145 × $1,050 = 15.23
   $43.13
10. The next week, Cynthia (Problems 8 and 9) again earned $1,050. What will her total FICA deduction be this week?
    No tax for Social Security
    $1,050 × .0145 = $15.23 Medicare
11. Martin Hartley is single and claims no withholding allowances. Use the proper wage bracket table to find his federal withholding tax if he earns $4,166.67 for the month of May.
    $908 Single Monthly Table 9–2

12. Roger Alley, a service dispatcher, has weekly earnings of $685. He claimed four allowances on his W-4 form and is married. Besides his FIT and FICA deductions, he also has deductions of $35.16 for medical insurance and $17.25 for union dues. Calculate his net earnings for the third week in February. (Use the wage bracket tables.)

FIT = $ 66.00
FICA = $ 52.40 (Social Security .062 × $685 Medicare .0145 × $685)
Note: Here we could multiply 0.0765 × $685 since the base for Social Security and Medicare were not reached.

Medical insurance =	35.16
Union dues =	17.25
Total deductions	$170.81

$685 − $170.81 = $514.19

13. Nicole Mariotte is unmarried and claimed one withholding allowance on her W-4 Form. In the second week of February, she earned $707.35. Deductions from her pay included federal withholding, FICA, health insurance for $47.75, and $30 for the company meal plan. What is Nicole's net pay for the week? (Use the percentage method.)

$707.35 − $44.23 = $663.12
[($663.12 − $438) × .28] + $61.95
$63.03 + $61.95 = $124.98 FIT

FIT	$124.98	
FICA (S.S. + Medicare)	54.11	($707.35 × .0765)
Health insurance	47.75	
Meal plan	30.00	
Total deductions	$256.84	

$707.35 − $256.84 = $450.51 net pay

14. Gerard Knowlton had total gross earnings of $54,700 in the last week of November. His earnings for the first week in December were $804.70. His employer uses the percentage method to calculate federal withholding. If Gerard is married, claims two allowances and has medical insurance of $52.25 deducted each week from his pay, what is his net pay for the week?

$804.70 − ($44.23 × 2) = $716.24
FIT = .15 × ($716.24 − $71) = $96.79

FIT	$ 96.79
FICA	61.27
Medical insurance	52.25
Total deductions	$210.31

$804.70
− 210.31
$594.39 net pay

$55,500
54,700
$ 800 Only $800 can be taxed for Social Security; full amount is taxable for Medicare.

Social Security:	$800 × .062 = $49.60
Medicare:	$804.70 × .0145 = 11.67
Total FICA	$61.27

Date ______________ Name ______________________________

LU 10–1: Calculation of Simple Interest

Drill Problems

1. Find the simple interest for each of the following loans:

	Principal	Rate	Time	Interest
a.	$ 2,000	9%	1 year	$180
b.	3,000	12%	3 years	$1,080
c.	18,000	$8\frac{1}{2}\%$	10 months	$1,275

a. $2,000 × .09 × 1 = $180
b. $3,000 × .12 × 3 = $1,080
c. $\$18{,}000 \times .085 \times \frac{10}{12} = \$1{,}275$

2. Find the simple interest for each of the following loans; use the exact time, exact interest method. (Use the days-in-a-year calendar in the text when needed.)

	Principal	Rate	Time	Interest
a.	$ 700	14%	30 days	$8.05
b.	4,290	8%	250 days	$235.07
c.	1,500	8%	Made March 11 Due July 11	$40.11

July 11 192
March 11 − 70
122

a. $\$700 \times .14 \times \frac{30}{365} = \$8.05$ b. $\$4{,}290 \times .08 \times \frac{250}{365} = \$235.07$ c. $\$1{,}500 \times .08 \times \frac{122}{365} = \$40.11$

3. Find the simple interest for each of the following loans using the exact time, ordinary interest method (Banker's Rule).

	Principal	Rate	Time	Interest
a.	$ 5,250	$7\frac{1}{2}\%$	120 days	$131.25
b.	700	12%	70 days	$16.33
c.	2,600	11%	Made on June 15 Due October 17	$98.51

October 17 290
June 15 − 166
124

a. $\$5{,}250 \times .075 \times \frac{120}{360} = \$131.25$ b. $\$700 \times .12 \times \frac{70}{360} = \$16.33$ c. $\$2{,}600 \times .11 \times \frac{124}{360} = \$98.51$

4. For each of the following invoices, calculate the savings, if any, from taking out a loan to pay within the discount period. (Use 360 days.)

	Invoice amount	Invoice terms	Bank interest rate	Cash discount	Interest on loan	Savings
a.	$ 1,200	2/10, n/60	10%	$24	$16.33	$7.67
b.	9,675	3/10, n/60	9%	$290.25	$117.31	$172.94

a. $1,200 × .02 = $24 cash discount, $1,200 − $24 = $1,176 borrowing amount
$\$1{,}176 \times .10 \times \frac{50}{360} = \$16.33$ interest, $24 − $16.33 = $7.67 savings

b. $9,675 × .03 = $290.25 cash discount, $9,675 − $290.25 = $9,384.75 borrowing amount
$\$9{,}384.75 \times .09 \times \frac{50}{360} = \$117.31$ interest, $290.25 − $117.31 = $172.94 savings

Word Problems

5. On October 17, Nina Verga borrowed $3,136 at a rate of 12%. She promised to repay the loan in 10 months. What is **(a)** the amount of the simple interest and **(b)** the total amount owed upon maturity?

a. $\$3{,}136 \times .12 \times \frac{10}{12} = \$313.60$ interest b. $3,136 + $313.60 = $3,449.60 maturity value

6. Marjorie Folsom borrowed $5,500 to purchase a computer. The loan was for nine months at an annual interest rate of $12\frac{1}{2}\%$. What is **(a)** the amount of interest Marjorie must pay and **(b)** the maturity value of the loan?

a. $\$5{,}500 \times .125 \times \frac{9}{12} = \$515.63$ interest b. $5,500 + $515.63 = $6,015.63 maturity value

7. Eric has a loan for $1,200 at an ordinary interest rate of 9.5% for 80 days. Julie has a loan for $1,200 at an exact interest rate of 9.5% for 80 days. Calculate (**a**) the total amount due on Eric's loan and (**b**) the total amount due on Julie's loan.

a. $\$1{,}200 \times .095 \times \frac{80}{360} = \$25.33$ interest $\$1{,}200 + \$25.33 = \$1{,}225.33$ maturity value of Eric's loan

b. $\$1{,}200 \times .095 \times \frac{80}{365} = \$24.99$ interest $\$1{,}200 + \$24.99 = \$1{,}224.99$ maturity value of Julie's loan

8. Roger Lee borrowed $5,280 at $13\frac{1}{2}\%$ on May 24, and agreed to repay the loan on August 24. The lender calculates interest using the exact time, exact interest method. How much will Roger be required to pay on August 24?

August 24 − May 24
236 − 144 = 92 days

$\$5{,}280 \times .135 \times \frac{92}{365} = \$179.66$ interest

$\$5{,}280 + \$179.66 = \$5{,}459.66$ maturity value, due August 24

9. On March 8, Jack Faltin borrowed $10,225 at $9\frac{3}{4}\%$. He signed a note agreeing to repay the loan and interest on November 8. If the lender calculates interest using the exact time, ordinary interest method, what will Jack's repayment be?

November 8 − March 8
312 − 67 = 245 days

$\$10{,}225 \times .0975 \times \frac{245}{360} = \$678.47$ interest

$\$10{,}225 + \$678.47 = \$10{,}903.47$ maturity value, due November 8

10. Dianne Smith's real estate taxes of $641.49 were due on November 1, 1994. Due to financial difficulties, Dianne was unable to pay her tax bill until January 15, 1995. The penalty for late payment is $13\frac{3}{8}\%$ ordinary interest. What is the penalty Dianne will have to pay and what is Dianne's total payment on January 15?

December 31 − November 1 + January 15
365 − 305 = 60 + 15 = 75 days

$\$641.49 \times .13375 \times \frac{75}{360} = \$17.87$ penalty

$\$641.49 + \$17.87 = \$659.36$ total due on January 15

11. On August 8, Rex Eason had a credit card balance of $550, but he was unable to pay his bill. The credit card company charges interest of $18\frac{1}{2}\%$ annually on late payments. What amount will Rex have to pay if he pays his bill one month late?

$\$550 + \left(\$550 \times .185 \times \frac{1}{12}\right) = \$558.48$ (principal + interest)

12. The Waltrude sisters received an invoice on May 18 for jewelry and cosmetics that totaled $5,238 including $35 for shipping charges. The terms of the invoice were 3/15, n/90. The Waltrudes want to know if they should take out a short term loan at a rate of 13% in order to pay the invoice within the discount period. Show the calculations that will help them to decide.

$\$5{,}238 - \$35 = \$5{,}203$, $\$5{,}203 \times .03 = \$156.09$ discount
$\$5{,}238 - \$156.09 = \$5{,}081.91$ borrowing amount

$\$5{,}081.91 \times .13 \times \frac{75}{360} = \$137.64$ interest

$\$156.09 - \$137.64 = \$18.45$ savings

Date ____________ Name ____________

LU 10-2: Finding Unknown in Simple Interest Formula

Drill Problems

1. Find the principal in each of the following. (Round to the nearest cent. Assume 360 days.) *Calculator hint: Do denominator calculation first, do not round; when answer is displayed, save it in memory by pressing [M+]. Now key in the numerator (interest amount), [÷], [MR], [=] for the answer. Be sure to clear memory after each problem by pressing [MR] again so that the M is no longer in the display.*

	Rate	Time	Interest	Principal
a.	8%	70 days	$68	$4,371.44
b.	11%	90 days	$125	4,545.45
c.	9%	120 days	$103	3,433.33
d.	$8\frac{1}{2}$%	60 days	$150	10,588.29

a. $\dfrac{\$68}{.08 \times \frac{70}{360}} = \dfrac{\$68}{.0155555} = \$4{,}371.44$ b. $\dfrac{\$125}{.11 \times \frac{90}{360}} = \dfrac{\$125}{.0275} = \$4{,}545.45$

c. $\dfrac{\$103}{.09 \times \frac{120}{360}} = \dfrac{\$103}{.03} = \$3{,}433.33$ d. $\dfrac{\$150}{.085 \times \frac{60}{360}} = \dfrac{\$150}{.0141666} = \$10{,}588.29$

2. Find the rate in each of the following. (Assume 360 days. Round to the nearest tenth of a percent.)

	Principal	Time	Interest	Rate
a.	$7,500	120 days	$350	14%
b.	$975	60 days	$25	15.4%
c.	$20,800	220 days	$910	7.2%
d.	$150	30 days	$2.10	16.8%

a. $\dfrac{\$350}{\$7{,}500 \times \frac{120}{360}} = \dfrac{\$350}{\$2{,}500} = .14$ b. $\dfrac{\$25}{\$975 \times \frac{60}{360}} = \dfrac{\$25}{\$162.5} = .1538$

c. $\dfrac{\$910}{\$20{,}800 \times \frac{220}{360}} = \dfrac{\$910}{\$12{,}711.111} = .0715$ d. $\dfrac{\$2.10}{\$150 \times \frac{30}{360}} = \dfrac{\$2.10}{\$12.5} = .168$

3. Find the time (to nearest day) in each of the following. (Assuming ordinary interest use 360 days.)

	Principal	Rate	Interest	Time(days)
a.	$400	11%	$7.33	60
b.	$7,000	12.5%	$292	120
c.	$1,550	9.2%	$106.95	270
d.	$157,000	10.75%	$6,797.88	145

a. $\dfrac{\$7.33}{\$400 \times .11} = \dfrac{\$7.33}{\$44} \times 360 = 59.9$ b. $\dfrac{\$292}{\$7{,}000 \times .125} = \dfrac{\$292}{\$875} \times 360 = 120.1$

c. $\dfrac{\$106.95}{\$1{,}550 \times .092} = \dfrac{\$106.95}{\$142.6} \times 360 = 270$ d. $\dfrac{\$6{,}797.88}{\$157{,}000 \times .1075} = \dfrac{\$6{,}797.88}{\$16{,}877.50} \times 360 = 144.9$

4. Complete the following. (Assume 360 days for all examples.)

	Principal	Rate (nearest tenth percent)	Time (nearest day)	Simple interest
a.	$345	10%	150 days	$14.38
b.	$1,500.16	12.5%	90 days	$46.88
c.	$750	12.2%	75 days	$19.06
d.	$20,260	16.7%	110 days	$1,033.82

a. $\dfrac{\$14.38}{\$345 \times \frac{150}{360}} = \dfrac{\$14.38}{\$143.75} = .1000$ b. $\dfrac{\$46.88}{.125 \times \frac{90}{360}} = \dfrac{\$46.88}{.03125} = \$1{,}500.16$

c. $\dfrac{\$19.06}{\$750 \times .122} = \dfrac{\$19.06}{\$91.5} \times 360 = 74.9$ d. $\$20{,}260 \times .167 \times \frac{110}{360} = \$1{,}033.822$

Word Problems

Use 360 days.

5. Lannon Supply is going to invest $21,000 at 11%. How long will it take to earn $770 in interest?

$$\frac{\$770}{\$21{,}000 \times .11} = \frac{\$770}{\$2{,}310} \times 360 = 119.9 = 120 \text{ days}$$

6. Dr. Vaccarro invested his money at $12\frac{1}{2}\%$ for 175 days and earned interest of $760. How much money did Dr. Vaccarro invest?

$$\frac{\$760}{.125 \times \frac{175}{360}} = \frac{\$760}{.0607638} = \$12{,}507.446 = \$12{,}507.45 \text{ principal}$$

7. Carolyn Ryan invested $2,225 for 90 days and earned $59.52 in interest. What rate of interest was she paid?

$$\frac{\$59.52}{\$2{,}225 \times \frac{90}{360}} = \frac{\$59.52}{556.25} = 10.7\%$$

8. Thomas Kyrouz opened a savings account and deposited $750 in a bank that was paying 7.2% simple interest. How much are his savings worth in 200 days?

$$\$750 \times .072 \times \frac{200}{360} = \$30 \qquad \$750 + \$30 = \$780$$

9. Mary Millitello paid the bank $53.90 in interest on a 66-day loan at 9.8%. How much money did Mary borrow? (Round to nearest dollar.)

$$\frac{\$53.90}{.098 \times \frac{66}{360}} = \frac{\$53.90}{.0179666} = \$3{,}000$$

10. If Anthony Lucido deposits $2,400 for 66 days and makes $60.72 in interest, what interest rate is he receiving?

$$\frac{\$60.72}{\$2{,}400 \times \frac{66}{360}} = \frac{\$60.72}{\$440} = .138 = 13.8\%$$

11. Find how long in days David Wong must invest $23,500 of his company's cash at 8.4% in order to earn $652.50 in interest.

$$\frac{\$652.50}{\$23{,}500 \times .084} = \frac{\$652.50}{\$1{,}974} \times 360 = 118.99 = 119 \text{ days}$$

12. Harry McDougall invested some of his money at 10.5% for 95 days and earned $457.19 in interest. How much did Harry invest?

$$\frac{\$457.19}{.105 \times \frac{95}{360}} = \frac{\$457.19}{.0277083} = \$16{,}500.11$$

13. Gaspar's Variety Store deposited $4,000 at 6.25% and received $154.17 in interest. Find the length of time in days the money was deposited.

$$\frac{\$154.17}{\$4{,}000 \times .0625} = \frac{\$154.17}{\$250} \times 360 = 222.0 = 222 \text{ days}$$

14. Joel Michealson made $364 on a deposit of $8,375 for 200 days. What was the rate of interest he received? (Round to nearest tenth percent.)

$$\frac{\$364}{\$8{,}375 \times \frac{200}{360}} = \frac{\$364}{\$4{,}652.7777} = 7.8\%$$

Date ____________ Name ____________

LU 10–3: U.S. Rule versus Merchant's Rule in Making Partial Note Payments before Due Date

Drill Problems

1. A merchant borrowed $3,000 for 320 days at 11% (assume a 360-day year).

   a. Use the **U.S. Rule** to complete the following table:

Payment number	Payment day	Amount paid	Interest to date	Principal payment	Adjusted balance
					$3,000
1	75	$ 500	$68.75	$431.25	$2,568.75
2	160	750	66.72	683.28	$1,885.47
3	220	1,000	34.57	965.43	$ 920.04
4	320	948.15	28.11	920.04	0

1. $\$3{,}000 \times .11 \times \frac{75}{360} = \$68.75$; $\$500 - \$68.75 = \$431.25$
   $\$3{,}000 - \$431.25 = \$2{,}568.75$

2. $160 - 75 = 85$ days
   $\$2{,}568.75 \times .11 \times \frac{85}{360} = \$66.72$; $\$750 - \$66.72 = \$683.28$
   $\$2{,}568.75 - \$683.28 = \$1{,}885.47$

3. $220 - 160 = 60$ days
   $\$1{,}885.47 \times .11 \times \frac{60}{360} = \$34.57$; $\$1{,}000 - \$34.57 = \$965.43$
   $\$1{,}885.47 - \$965.43 = \$920.04$

4. $320 - 220 = 100$ days
   $\$920.04 \times .11 \times \frac{100}{360} = \$28.11$; $\$920.04 + \$28.11 = \$948.15$

   b. Use the **Merchant's Rule** to complete the following table from part **a**:

Payment number	Payment day	Amount paid	Interest to due date	Interest + payment	Adjusted balance	
					$3,293.33	total amt. of loan
1	75	$ 500	$37.43	$ 537.43	$2,755.83	
2	160	750	$36.67	$ 786.67	$1,969.16	
3	220	1,000	$30.56	$1,030.56	$ 938.60	
4	320	$938.60			0	

$\$3{,}000 \times .11 \times \frac{320}{360} = \$293.33$ interest

$\$3{,}000 + \$293.33 = \$3{,}293.33$ amount

1. $320 - 75 = 245$ days left
   $\$500 \times .11 \times \frac{245}{360} = \$37.43$; $\$500 + \$37.43 = \$537.43$
   $\$3{,}293.33 - \$537.50 = \$2{,}755.83$

2. $320 - 160 = 160$ days left
   $\$750 \times .11 \times \frac{160}{360} = \$36.67$; $\$750 + \$36.67 = \$786.67$
   $\$2{,}755.83 - \$786.67 = \$1{,}969.16$

3. $320 - 220 = 100$ days left
   $\$1{,}000 \times .11 \times \frac{100}{360} = \$30.56$: $\$1{,}000 + \$30.56 = \$1{,}030.56$
   $\$1{,}969.16 - \$1{,}030.56 = \$938.60$

Word Problems

2. John Joseph borrowed \$10,800 for one year at 14%. After 60 days he paid \$2,500 on the note. On the 200th day, he paid an additional \$5,000. Use the U.S. Rule and ordinary interest to find the final balance due.

$\$10{,}800 \times .14 \times \frac{60}{360} = \$252; \$2{,}500 - \$252 = \$2{,}248; \$10{,}800 - \$2{,}248 = \$8{,}552$

$200 - 60 = 140$ days; $\$8{,}552 \times .14 \times \frac{140}{360} = \$465.61; \$5{,}000 - \$465.61 = \$4{,}534.39;$

$\$8{,}552 - \$4{,}534.39 = \$4{,}017.61$

$360 - 200 = 160; \$4{,}017.61 \times .14 \times \frac{160}{360} = \$249.98;$

$\$4{,}017.61 + \$249.98 = \$4{,}267.59$ final balance due

3. John (Problem 2) would like to know what the final balance due would be if you used the Merchant's Rule. (Use ordinary interest again.)

$\$10{,}800 \times .14 \times 1 = \$1{,}512 + \$10{,}800 = \$12{,}312$

$360 - 60 = 300$ days left

$\$2{,}500 \times .14 \times \frac{300}{360} = \$291.67 + \$2{,}500 = \$2{,}791.67;$

$\$12{,}312 - \$2{,}791.67 = \$9{,}520.33$

$360 - 200 = 160$ days left

$\$5{,}000 \times .14 \times \frac{160}{360} = \$311.11 + \$5{,}000 = \$5{,}311.11;$

$\$9{,}520.33 - \$5{,}311.11 = \$4{,}209.22$ final balance due

4. Doris Davis borrowed \$8,200 on March 5 for 90 days at $8\frac{3}{4}\%$. After 32 days Doris made a payment on the loan of \$2,700. On the 65th day she made another payment of \$2,500. What is her final payment if you use the U.S. Rule with ordinary interest?

$\$8{,}200 \times .0875 \times \frac{32}{360} = \$63.78; \$2{,}700 - \$63.78 = \$2{,}636.22$

$\$8{,}200 - \$2{,}636.22 = \$5{,}563.78$

$65 - 32 = 33$ days; $\$5{,}563.78 \times .0875 \times \frac{33}{360} = \$44.63;$

$\$2{,}500 - \$44.63 = \$2{,}455.37; \$5{,}563.70 - \$2{,}455.37 = \$3{,}108.33$

$90 - 65 = 25$ days; $\$3{,}108.33 \times .0875 \times \frac{25}{360} = \$18.89;$

$\$3{,}108.33 + \$18.89 = \$3{,}127.22$ final payment

5. What should Doris's final payment be using the Merchant's Rule with ordinary interest?

$\$8{,}200 \times .0875 \times \frac{90}{360} = \$179.38; \$8{,}200 + \$179.38 = \$8{,}379.38$

$90 - 32 = 58$ days left

$\$2{,}700 \times .0875 \times \frac{58}{360} = \$38.06 + \$2{,}700 = \$2{,}738.06;$

$\$8{,}379.38 - \$2{,}738.06 = \$5{,}641.32$

$90 - 65 = 25$ days left

$\$2{,}500 \times .0875 \times \frac{25}{360} = \$15.19 + \$2{,}500 = \$2{,}515.19;$

$\$5{,}641.32 - \$2{,}515.19 = \$3{,}126.13$ final payment due

Date ______________ Name ______________________________

LU 11–1: Structure of Promissory Notes; The Simple Discount Note

Drill Problems

1. Identify each of the following characteristics of promissory notes with an **I** for simple interest note, a **D** for simple discount note, or a **B** if it is true for both.

   I __ Interest is computed on face value, or what is actually borrowed.
   B __ A promissory note for a loan usually less than one year.
   D __ Borrower receives proceeds = Face value − Bank discount.
   I __ Maturity value = Face value + Interest.
   D __ Maturity value = Face value.
   I __ Borrower receives the face value.
   B __ Paid back by one payment at maturity.
   D __ Interest computed on maturity value, or what will be repaid, and not on actual amount borrowed.

2. Find the bank discount and the proceeds for the following (assume 360 days):

	Maturity value	Discount rate	Time (days)	Bank discount	Proceeds
a.	$7,000	9%	60	$105	$6,895
b.	$4,550	8.1%	110	$112.61	$4,437.39
c.	$19,350	12.7%	55	$375.44	$18,974.56
d.	$63,400	10%	90	$1,585	$61,815
e.	$13,490	7.9%	200	$592.06	$12,897.94
f.	$780	$12\frac{1}{2}\%$	65	$17.60	$762.40

a. $\$7,000 \times .09 \times \frac{60}{360} = \$105; \$7,000 - \$105 = \$6,895$

b. $\$4,550 \times .081 \times \frac{110}{360} = \$112.61; \$4,550 - \$112.61 = \$4,437.39$

c. $\$19,350 \times .127 \times \frac{55}{360} = \$375.44; \$19,350 - \$375.44 = \$18,974.56$

d. $\$63,400 \times .10 \times \frac{90}{360} = \$1,585; \$63,400 - \$1,585 = \$61,815$

e. $\$13,490 \times .079 \times \frac{200}{360} = \$592.06; \$13,490 - \$592.06 = \$12,897.94$

f. $\$780 \times .125 \times \frac{65}{360} = \$17.60; \$780 - \$17.60 = \$762.40$

3. Find the effective rate of interest for each of the loans in Problem 2. Use the answers you calculated in Problem 2 to solve these problems (round to nearest tenth percent):

	Maturity value	Discount rate	Time (days)	Effective rate
a.	$7,000	9%	60	9.1%
b.	$4,550	8.1%	110	8.3%
c.	$19,350	12.7%	55	13%
d.	$63,400	10%	90	10.3%
e.	$13,490	7.9%	200	8.3%
f.	$780	$12\frac{1}{2}\%$	65	12.8%

a. $\dfrac{\$105}{\$6,895 \times \frac{60}{360}} = .0913 = 9.1\%$

b. $\dfrac{\$112.61}{\$4,437.39 \times \frac{110}{360}} = .0830 = 8.3\%$

c. $\dfrac{\$375.44}{\$18,974.56 \times \frac{55}{360}} = .1295 = 13\%$

d. $\dfrac{\$1,585}{\$61,815 \times \frac{90}{360}} = .1026 = 10.3\%$

e. $\dfrac{\$592.06}{\$12,897.94 \times \frac{200}{360}} = .0826 = 8.3\%$

f. $\dfrac{\$17.60}{\$762.40 \times \frac{65}{360}} = .1279 = 12.8\%$

Word Problems

Assume 360 days.

4. Mary Smith signed a $7,500 note for 135 days at a discount rate of 13%. Find the discount and the proceeds Mary received.

$\$7{,}500 \times .13 \times \frac{135}{360} = \$365.63$ discount

$\$7{,}500 - \$365.63 = \$7{,}134.37$ proceeds

5. The Salem Cooperative Bank charges an $8\frac{3}{4}\%$ discount rate. What is the discount and the proceeds for a $16,200 note for 60 days?

$\$16{,}200 \times .0875 \times \frac{60}{360} = \$236.25$ discount

$\$16{,}200 - \$236.25 = \$15{,}963.75$ proceeds

6. Bill Jackson is planning to buy a second-hand car. He went to the City Credit Union to take out a loan for $6,400 for 300 days. If the credit union charges a discount rate of $11\frac{1}{2}\%$, what will the proceeds of this loan be?

$\$6{,}400 \times .115 \times \frac{300}{360} = \$613.33$; $\$6{,}400 - \$613.33 = \$5{,}786.67$ proceeds

7. Mike Drislane goes to the bank and signs a note for $9,700. The bank charges a 15% discount rate. Find the discount and the proceeds if the loan is for 210 days.

$\$9{,}700 \times .15 \times \frac{210}{360} = \$848.75$ discount

$\$9{,}700 - \$848.75 = \$8{,}851.25$ proceeds

8. Flora Foley plans to have a deck built on the back of her house. She decides to take out a loan at the bank for $14,300. She signs a note promising to pay back the loan in 280 days. If the note was discounted at 9.2%, how much money will Flora receive from the bank?

$\$14{,}300 \times .092 \times \frac{280}{360} = \$1{,}023.24$

$\$14{,}300 - \$1{,}023.24 = \$13{,}276.76$ proceeds Flora receives

9. At the end of 280 days, Flora (Problem 8) must pay back the loan. What is the maturity value of the loan?
$14,300 maturity value

10. Dave Cassidy signed a $7,855 note at a bank that charges a 14.2% discount rate. If the loan is for 190 days find (**a**) the proceeds and (**b**) the effective rate charged by the bank (to nearest tenth percent).

a. $\$7{,}855 \times .142 \times \frac{190}{360} = \$588.69$

$\$7{,}855 - \$588.69 = \$7{,}266.31$ proceeds

b. $\dfrac{\$588.69}{\$7{,}266.31 \times \frac{190}{360}} = .1535 = 15.4\%$ effective rate

11. How much money must Dave (Problem 10) pay back to the bank?
Dave pays back $7,855.

Date ______________ Name ______________________________

LU 11-2: Discounting an Interest-Bearing Note before Maturity

Drill Problems

1. Calculate the maturity value for each of the following promissory notes (use 360 days):

	Date of note	Principal of note	Length of note (days)	Interest rate	Maturity value
a.	April 12	$4,800	135	10%	$4,980
b.	August 23	$15,990	85	13%	$16,480.80
c.	Dec. 10	$985	30	11.5%	$994.44

a. $\$4{,}800 \times .10 \times \frac{135}{360} = \$180 + \$4{,}800 = \$4{,}980$

b. $\$15{,}990 \times .13 \times \frac{85}{360} = \$490.80 + \$15{,}990 = \$16{,}480.80$

c. $\$985 \times .115 \times \frac{30}{360} = \$9.44 + \$985 = \$994.44$

2. Find the maturity date and the discount period for the following; assume no leap years. *Hint:* Exact Days-in-a-Year Calendar, Chapter 7.

	Date of note	Length of note (days)	Date of discount	Maturity date	Discount period
a.	March 11	200	June 28	September 27	91 days
b.	Jan. 22	60	March 2	March 23	21 days
c.	April 19	85	June 6	July 13	37 days
d.	Nov. 17	120	Feb. 15	March 17	30 days

a. 70 + 200 = 270 = Sept. 27; 270 − 179 = 91 days or 200 − (20 + 30 + 31 + 28) = 91
b. 22 + 60 = 82 = March 23; 82 − 61 = 21 days or 60 − (9 + 28 + 2) = 21
c. 109 + 85 = 194 = July 13; 194 − 157 = 37 days or 85 − (11 + 31 + 6) = 37
d. 365 − 321 = 44; 120 − 44 = 76 = March 17; 76 − 46 = 30 days or 120 − (13 + 31 + 31 + 15) = 30

3. Find the bank discount for each of the following (use 360 days):

	Date of note	Principal of note	Length of note	Interest rate	Bank discount rate	Date of discount	Bank discount
a.	Oct. 5	$2,475	88 days	11%	9.5%	December 10	$14.76
b.	June 13	$9,055	112 days	15%	16%	August 11	$223.25
c.	March 20	$1,065	75 days	12%	11.5%	May 24	$3.49

a. Maturity value $= \$2{,}475 \times .11 \times \frac{88}{360} = \$66.55 + \$2{,}475 = \$2{,}541.55$

Discount period = 88 − (26 + 30 + 10) = 22 days

Bank discount $= \$2{,}541.55 \times .095 \times \frac{22}{360} = \$14.76$

b. Maturity value $= \$9{,}055 \times .15 \times \frac{112}{360} = \$422.57 + \$9{,}055 = \$9{,}477.57$

Discount period = 112 − (17 + 31 + 11) = 53 days

Bank discount $= \$9{,}477.57 \times .16 \times \frac{53}{360} = \$223.25$

c. Maturity value $= \$1{,}065 \times .12 \times \frac{75}{360} = \$26.63 + \$1{,}065 = \$1{,}091.63$

Discount period = 75 − (11 + 30 + 24) = 10 days

Bank discount $= \$1{,}091.63 \times .115 \times \frac{10}{360} = \$3.49$

4. Find the proceeds for each of the discounted notes in Problem 3.

a. $2,526.79 a. $2,541.55 − $14.76 = $2,526.79
b. $9,254.32 b. $9,477.57 − $223.25 = $9,254.32
c. $1,088.14 c. $1,091.63 − $3.49 = $1,088.14

Word Problems

5. Connors Company received a $4,000, 90-day, 10% note dated April 6 from one of its customers. Connors Company held the note until May 16, when they discounted it at a bank at a discount rate of 12%. What were the proceeds Connors Company received?

$\$4{,}000 \times .10 \times \frac{90}{360} = \$100 + \$4{,}000 = \$4{,}100$

$90 - (24 + 16) = 50$ days $\quad \$4{,}100 \times .12 \times \frac{50}{360} = \$68.33$; $\$4{,}100 - \$68.33 = \$4{,}031.67$

6. Souza & Sons accepted a 9%, $22,000, 120-day note from one of their customers on July 22. On October 2, they discounted the note at the Cooperative Bank. The discount rate was 12%. What was **(a)** the bank discount and **(b)** the proceeds?

$\$22{,}000 \times .09 \times \frac{120}{360} = \$660 + \$22{,}000 = \$22{,}660$ $\quad \$22{,}660 \times .12 \times \frac{48}{360} = \$362.56$ bank discount **(a)**

$120 - (9 + 31 + 30 + 2) = 48$ days $\quad \$22{,}660 - \$362.56 = \$22{,}297.44$ proceeds **(b)**

7. The Fargate Store accepted an $8,250, 75-day, 9% note from one of its customers on March 18. Fargate's discounted the note at Parkside National Bank at $9\frac{1}{2}$%, on March 29. What proceeds did Fargate receive?

$\$8{,}250 \times .09 \times \frac{75}{360} = \$154.69 + \$8{,}250 = \$8{,}404.69$

$75 - 11 = 64$ days $\quad \$8{,}404.69 \times .095 \times \frac{64}{360} = \$141.95$; $\$8{,}404.69 - \$141.95 = \$8{,}262.74$

8. On November 1, Majorie's Clothing Store accepted a $5,200, $8\frac{1}{2}$%, 90-day note from Mary Rose in granting her a time extension on her bill. On January 13, Marjorie discounted the note at the Seawater Bank, which charged a 10% discount rate. What were the proceeds that Marjorie received?

$\$5{,}200 \times .085 \times \frac{90}{360} = \$110.50 + \$5{,}200 = \$5{,}310.50$

$90 - (29 + 31 + 13) = 17$ $\quad \$5{,}310.50 \times .10 \times \frac{17}{360} = \$25.08$; $\$5{,}310.50 - \$25.08 = \$5{,}285.42$

9. On December 3, Duncan's Company accepted a $5,000, 90-day, 12% note from Al Finney in exchange for a $5,000 bill that was past due. On January 29, Duncan discounted the note at The Sidwell Bank at 13.1%. What were the proceeds from the note?

$\$5{,}000 \times .12 \times \frac{90}{360} = \$150 + \$5{,}000 = \$5{,}150$

$90 - (28 + 29) = 33$ days $\quad \$5{,}150 \times .131 \times \frac{33}{360} = \$61.84$; $\$5{,}150 - \$61.84 = \$5{,}088.16$

10. On February 26, the Sullivan Company accepted a 60-day, 10% note in exchange for a $1,500 past-due bill from Tabot Company. On March 28, the Sullivan Company discounted at the National Bank the note received from Tabot Company. The bank discount rate was 12%. What are **(a)** the bank discount and **(b)** the proceeds?

$\$1{,}500 \times .10 \times \frac{60}{360} = \$25 + \$1{,}500 = \$1{,}525$ $\quad$ **a.** $\$1{,}525 \times .12 \times \frac{30}{360} = \$15.25$ bank discount

$60 - (2 + 28) = 30$ days $\quad$ **b.** $\$1{,}525 - \$15.25 = \$1{,}509.75$ proceeds

11. On June 4, Johnson Company received from Marty Russo a 30-day, 11% note for $720 to settle Russo's debt. On June 17, Johnson discounted the note at the Eastern Bank whose discount rate was 15%. What proceeds did Johnson receive?

$\$720 \times .11 \times \frac{30}{360} = \$6.60 + \$720 = \$726.60$

$30 - 13 = 17$ days $\quad \$726.60 \times .15 \times \frac{17}{360} = \$5.15$; $\$726.60 - \$5.15 = \$721.45$

12. On December 15 at the bank, Lawlers Company discounted a 10%, 90-day, $14,000 note dated October 21. The bank charged a discount rate of 12%. What were the proceeds of the note?

$\$14{,}000 \times .10 \times \frac{90}{360} = \$350 + \$14{,}000 = \$14{,}350$

$90 - (10 + 30 + 15) = 35$ days $\quad \$14{,}350 \times .12 \times \frac{35}{360} = \$167.42$; $\$14{,}350 - \$167.42 = \$14{,}182.58$

Date ____________ Name ____________

LU 12-1: Compound Interest (Future Value)—The Big Picture and Specific Calculations

Drill Problems

1. In the following examples, calculate manually the amount at year-end for each of the deposits assuming that interest is compounded annually. (Round to the nearest cent each year.)

	Principal	Rate	Number of years	Year 1	Year 2	Year 3	Year 4
a.	$530	8%	2	$572.40	$618.19		
b.	$1,980	12%	4	$2,217.60	$2,483.71	$2,781.76	$3,115.57

a. $530 × 1.08 = $572.40; $572.40 × 1.08 = $618.19
b. $1,980 × 1.12 = $2,217.60; $2,217.60 × 1.12 = $2,483.71; $2,483.71 × 1.12 = $2,781.76; $2,781.76 × 1.12 = $3,115.57

2. In the following examples, calculate the simple interest, the compound interest, and the difference between the two. (Round to the nearest cent; do not use tables.)

	Principal	Rate	Number of years	Simple interest	Compound interest	Difference
a.	$4,600	10%	2	$920	$966	$46
b.	$18,400	9%	4	$6,624	$7,573.10	$949.10
c.	$855	$7\frac{1}{5}\%$	3	$184.68	$198.30	$13.62

a. $4,600 × .10 × 2 = $920; $4,600 × 1.1 × 1.1 = $5,566; $5,566 − $4,600 = $966; $966 − $920 = $46
b. $18,400 × .09 × 4 = $6,624; $18,400 × 1.09 × 1.09 × 1.09 × 1.09 = $25,973.10; $25,973.10 − $18,400 = $7,573.10; $7,573.10 − $6,624 = $949.10
c. $855 × .072 × 3 = $184.68; $855 × 1.072 × 1.072 × 1.072 = $1,053.30; $1,053.30 − $855 = $198.30; $198.30 − $184.68 = $13.62

3. Find the future value and the compound interest using the Future Value of $1 at Compound Interest table or Compound Daily table. (Round to the nearest cent.)

	Principal	Investment terms	Future value	Compound interest
a.	$10,000	6 years at 8% Compounded annually	$15,869	$5,869
b.	$10,000	6 years at 8% Compounded quarterly	$16,084	$6,084
c.	$8,400	7 years at 12% Compounded semiannually	$18,991.56	$10,591.56
d.	$2,500	15 years at 10% Compounded daily	$11,202	$8,702
e.	$9,600	5 years at 6% Compounded quarterly	$12,930.24	$3,330.24

a. $10,000 × 1.5869 = $15,869 − $10,000 = $5,869 (8%, 6 periods)
b. $10,000 × 1.6084 = $16,084; $16,084 − $10,000 = $6,084 (2%, 24 periods)
c. $8,400 × 2.2609 = $18,991.56; $18,991.56 − $8,400 = $10,591.56 (6%, 14 periods)
d. $2,500 × 4.4808 = $11,202; $11,202 − $2,500 = $8,702
e. $9,600 × 1.3469 = $12,930.24; $12,930.24 − $9,600 = $3,330.24

4. Calculate the effective rate of interest using the Future Value of $1 at Compound Interest table:

	Investment terms	Effective rate
a.	12% compounded quarterly	12.55%
b.	12% compounded semiannually	12.36%
c.	6% compounded quarterly	6.14%

a. $\frac{12\%}{4}$ = 3% for 4 periods; 1.1255 − 1.0000 = .1255 = 12.55% $\left(\frac{\$.1255}{\$1.000} = \frac{\text{int. per/year}}{\text{principal}}\right)$

b. $\frac{12\%}{2}$ = 6% for 2 periods; 1.1236 − 1.0000 = .1236 = 12.36%

c. $\frac{6\%}{4}$ = $1\frac{1}{2}$% for 4 periods; 1.0614 − 1.0000 = .0614 = 6.14%

Word Problems

5. John Mackey deposited $5,000 in his savings account at the Salem Savings Bank. If the bank pays 6% interest compounded quarterly, what will be the balance of his account at the end of 3 years?
   $5,000 × 1.1960 = $5,980 (1.5%, 12 periods)

6. The Pine Valley Savings Bank offers a certificate of deposit at 12% interest, compounded quarterly. What is the effective rate of interest?
   1.1255 − 1.0000 = .1255 = 12.55% (3%, 4 periods)

7. Jack Billings loaned $6,000 to his brother-in-law Dan, who was opening a new business. Dan promised to repay the loan at the end of 5 years, with interest of 8% compounded semiannually. How much will Dan pay to Jack at the end of the 5 years?
   $6,000 × 1.4802 = $8,881.20 (4%, 10 periods)

8. Eileen Hogarty deposits $5,630 in the City Bank, which pays 12% interest, compounded quarterly. How much money will Eileen have in her account at the end of 7 years?
   $5,630 × 2.2879 = $12,880.88 (3%, 28 periods)

9. If Kevin Bassage deposits $3,500 in the Scarsdale Savings Bank, which pays 8% interest, compounded quarterly, what will be in his account at the end of 6 years? How much interest will he have earned at this time?
   $3,500 × 1.6084 = $5,629.40 amount
   $5,629.40 − $3,500 = $2,129.40 interest (2%, 24 periods)

10. Arlington Trust pays 6% compounded semiannually. How much interest would be earned on $7,200 for one year?
    $7,200 × 1.0609 = $7,638.48 (3%, 2 periods) $7,638.48 − $7,200 = $438.48 interest

11. The Paladium Savings Bank pays 9% compounded quarterly. Find the amount and the interest on $3,000 after three quarters. (Do not use a table.)
    $3,000 × 1.0225 = $3,067.50; $3,067.50 × 1.0225 = $3,136.52; $3,136.52 × 1.0225 = $3,207.09 amount
    $3,207.09 − $3,000 = $207.09 interest $\frac{9\%}{4} = 2\frac{1}{4}\%$

12. David Siderski bought a $7,500 bank certificate paying 16% compounded semiannually. How much money did he obtain upon cashing in the certificate three years later?
    $7,500 × 1.5869 = $11,901.75 (8%, 6 periods)

Date ____________ Name ____________

LU 12-2: Present Value—The Big Picture and Specific Calculations

Drill Problems

1. Use Table 12-3 or the Business Math Handbook to find the table factor for each of the following:

	Future value	Rate	Number of years	Compounded	Table value
a.	$1.00	10%	5	Annually	.6209
b.	$1.00	12%	8	Semiannually	.3936
c.	$1.00	6%	10	Quarterly	.5513
d.	$1.00	12%	2	Monthly	.7876
e.	$1.00	8%	15	Semiannually	.3083

a. 10%, 5 periods; .6209 **b.** 6%, 16 periods; .3936

c. $1\frac{1}{2}$%, 40 periods; .5513 **d.** 1%, 24 periods; .7876

e. 4%, 30 periods; .3083

2. Use Table 12-3 or the Business Math Handbook to find the table factor and the present value for each of the following:

	Future value	Rate	Number of years	Compounded	Table value	Present value
a.	$1,000	14%	6	Semiannually	.4440	$444.00
b.	$1,000	16%	7	Quarterly	.3335	$333.50
c.	$1,000	8%	7	Quarterly	.5744	$574.40
d.	$1,000	8%	7	Semiannually	.5775	$577.50
e.	$1,000	8%	7	Annually	.5835	$583.50

a. 7%, 12 periods; .4440 × 1,000 = $444.00 **b.** 4%, 28 periods; .3335 × 1,000 = $333.50
c. 2%, 28 periods; .5744 × 1,000 = $574.40 **d.** 4%, 14 periods; .5775 × 1,000 = $577.50
e. 8%, 7 periods; .5835 × 1,000 = $583.50

3. Find the present value and the interest earned for the following:

	Future value	Numbers of years	Rate	Compounded	Present value	Interest earned
a.	$2,500	6	8%	Annually	$1,575.50	$924.50
b.	$4,600	10	6%	Semiannually	$2,547.02	$2,052.98
c.	$12,800	8	10%	Semiannually	$5,863.68	$6,936.32
d.	$28,400	7	8%	Quarterly	$16,312.96	$12,087.04
e.	$53,050	1	12%	Monthly	$47,076.57	$5,973.43

a. 8%, 6; .6302 × $2,500 = $1,575.50; $2,500 − $1,575.50 = $924.50
b. 3%, 20; .5537 × $4,600 = $2,547.02; $4,600 − $2,547.02 = $2,052.98
c. 5%, 16; .4581 × $12,800 = $5,863.68; $12,800 − $5,863.68 = $6,936.32
d. 2%, 28; .5744 × $28,400 = $16,312.96; $28,400 − $16,312.96 = $12,087.04
e. 1%, 12; .8874 × $53,050 = $47,076.57; $53,050 − $47,076.57 = $5,973.43

4. Find the missing amount (present value or future value) for each of the following:

	Present value	Investment terms	Future value
a.	$ 3,500	5 years at 8% Compounded annually	$ 5,142.55
b.	$ 4,473	6 years at 12% Compounded semiannually	$ 9,000
c.	$ 4,700	9 years at 14% Compounded semiannually	$15,885.53

a. 8%, 5; 1.4693 × $3,500 = $5,142.55 **b.** 6%, 12; .4970 × $9,000 = $4,473
c. 7%, 18; 3.3799 × $4,700 = $15,885.53

Word Problems

Solve for future value or present value.

5. Paul Palumbo assumes that he will need to have a new roof put on his house in 4 years. He estimates that the roof will cost him $18,000 at that time. What amount of money should Paul invest today at 8%, compounded semiannually, to be able to pay for the roof?
   4%, 8 periods; .7307 × $18,000 = $13,152.60
6. Tilton the pharmacist rents his store and has signed a lease that will expire in 3 years. When the lease expires, Tilton wants to buy his own store. He wants to have a down payment of $35,000 at that time. How much money should Tilton invest today at 6% compounded quarterly to yield $35,000?
   $1\frac{1}{2}$%, 12 periods; .8364 × $35,000 = $29,274
7. Brad Morrissey loans $8,200 to his brother-in-law. He will be repaid at the end of 5 years, with interest at 10% compounded semiannually. Find out how much he will be repaid.
   5%, 10 periods; 1.6289 × $8,200 = $13,356.98
8. The owner of Waverly Sheet Metal Company plans to buy some new machinery in 6 years. He estimates that the machines he wishes to purchase will cost $39,700 at that time. What must he invest today at 8% compounded semiannually, in order to have sufficient money to purchase the new machines?
   4%, 12 periods; .6246 × $39,700 = $24,796.62
9. Paul Stevens' grandparents want to buy him a car when he graduates from college in 4 years. They feel that they should have $27,000 in the bank at that time. How much should they invest at 12% compounded quarterly in order to reach their goal?
   3%, 16 periods; .6232 × $27,000 = $16,826.40
10. Gilda Nardi deposits $5,325 in a bank that pays 12% interest, compounded quarterly. Find the amount she will have at the end of 7 years.
    3%, 28 periods; 2.2879 × $5,325 = $12,183.07
11. Mary Wilson wants to buy a new set of golf clubs in 2 years. They will cost $775. How much money should she invest today at 9% compounded annually so that she will have enough money to buy the new clubs?
    9%, 2 periods; .8417 × $775 = $652.32
12. Jack Beggs plans to invest $30,000 at 10% compounded semiannually, for 5 years. What is the future value of the investment?
    5%, 10 periods; 1.6289 × $30,000 = $48,867

Date ________________ Name ________________________________

LU 13-1: Annuities: Ordinary Annuity and Annuity Due

Note to instructor: All worked-out solutions for Chapters 13–22 are located in your file folders by chapter.

Drill Problems

1. Find the value of the following ordinary annuities (calculate manually):

	Amount of each annual deposit	Rate	Value at end of year 1	Value at end of year 2	Value at end of year 3
a.	$1,000	8%	$1,000	$2,080	$3,246.40
b.	$2,500	12%	$2,500	$5,300	$8,436
c.	$7,200	10%	$7,200	$15,120	$23,832

2. Use the Ordinary Annuity Table: Compound Sum of an Annuity of $1 to find the value of the following ordinary annuities:

	Annuity payment	Payment period	Terms of Annuity	Rate	Value of annuity
a.	$650	Semiannually	5 years	6%	$7,451.54
b.	$3,790	Annually	13 years	12%	$106,230.28
c.	$500	Quarterly	1 year	8%	$2,060.80

3. Find the annuity due (deposits are made at beginning of period) for each of the following using the Ordinary Annuity Table:

	Amount of payment	Payment period	Rate	Time (years)	Amount of annuity
a.	$900	Annually	7%	6	$6,888.60
b.	$1,200	Annually	11%	4	$6,273.36
c.	$550	Semiannually	10%	9	$16,246.40

4. Find the amount of each annuity:

	Amount of payment	Payment period	Rate	Time (years)	Type of annuity	Amount of annuity
a.	$600	Semiannually	12%	8	Ordinary	$15,403.50
b.	$600	Semiannually	12%	8	Due	$16,327.68
c.	$1,100	Annually	9%	7	Ordinary	$10,120.44

Word Problems

5. At the end of each year for the next 9 years, the D'Aldo Company will deposit $25,000 in an ordinary annuity account paying 9% interest compounded annually. Find the value of the annuity at the end of the 9 years.
$325,525

6. David McCarthy is a professional baseball player who expects to play in the major leagues for 10 years. To save for the future, he will deposit $50,000 at the beginning of each year into an account that pays 11% interest compounded annually. How much will he have in this account at the end of 10 years?
$928,070

7. Tom and Sue plan to get married soon. Because they hope to have a large wedding, they are going to deposit $1,000 at the end of each month into an account that pays 24% compounded monthly. How much will they have in this account at the end of one year?
$13,412

8. Chris Dennen deposits $15,000 at the end of each year for 13 years into an account paying 7% interest compounded annually. What is the value of her annuity at the end of 13 years? How much interest will she have earned?
$302,109 value $107,109 interest

9. Amanda Blinn is 52 years old today, and has just opened an IRA. She plans to deposit $500 at the end of each quarter into her account. If Amanda retires on her 62nd birthday, what amount will she have in her account if the account pays 8% interest compounded quarterly?
$30,200.85

10. Jerry Davis won the citywide sweepstakes and will receive a check for $2,000 at the beginning of each six months for the next 5 years. If Larry deposits each check in an account that pays 8% compounded semiannually, how much will he have at the end of the 5 years?
$24,972.60

11. Mary Hynes purchased an ordinary annuity from an investment broker at 8% interest compounded semiannually. If her semiannual deposit is $600, what will be the value of the annuity at the end of 15 years?
$33,650.94

LU 13-2: Present Value of an Ordinary Annuity (Finds Present Worth)

Drill Problems

1. Use the Present Value of an Annuity of $1 table to find the amount to be invested today to receive a stream of payments for a given number of years in the future. Show the manual check of your answer. (Check may be a few pennies off due to rounding.)

	Amount of expected payments	Payment period	Rate	Term of annuity	Present value of annuity
a.	$1,500	Yearly	9%	2 years	$2,638.65
b.	$2,700	Yearly	13%	3 years	$6,375.24
c.	$2,700	Yearly	6%	3 years	$7,217.10

2. Find the present value of the following annuities. Use the Present Value of an Annuity of $1 table.

	Amount of each payment	Payment period	Rate	Time (years)	Compounded	Present value of annuity
a.	$2,000	Year	7%	25	Annually	$23,307.20
b.	$7,000	Year	11%	12	Annually	$45,446.80
c.	$850	6 months	12%	5	Semiannually	$6,256.09
d.	$1,950	6 months	14%	9	Semiannually	$19,615.25
e.	$500	Quarter	12%	10	Quarterly	$11,557.40

Word Problems

3. Tom Hanson would like to receive $200 each quarter for the 4 years he is in college. If his banking account pays 8% compounded quarterly, how much must he have in his account when he begins college?
$2,715.54

4. Jean Reith has just retired, and will receive a retirement check every six months of $12,500 for the next 20 years. If her employer can invest money at 12% compounded semiannually, what amount must he invest today to make the semiannual payments to Jean?
$188,078.75

5. Tom Herrick will pay $4,500 at the end of each year for the next 7 years to pay the balance of his college loans. If Tom can invest his money at 7% compounded annually, how much must he invest today to make the annual payments?
$24,251.85

6. Helen Grahan is planning an extended sabbatical for the next three years. She would like to invest a lump sum of money at 10% interest so that she can withdraw $6,000 every 6 months while on sabbatical. What is the amount of the lump sum that Helen must invest?
$30,454.20

7. Linda Rudd has signed a rental contract for office equipment agreeing to pay $3,200 at the end of each quarter for the next 5 years. If Linda can invest money at 12% compounded quarterly, find the lump sum she can deposit today to make the payments for the length of the contract.
$47,608

8. Sam Adams is considering lending his brother John $6,000. John said that he would repay Sam $775 every six months for the 4 years. If money can be invested at 8%, calculate the equivalent cash value of the offer today. Should Sam go ahead with the loan?
$5,217.84 Sam should not take the deal.

9. The State Lotto Game offers a grand prize of $1,000,000 paid in 20 yearly payments of $50,000. If the State Treasurer can invest money at 9% compounded annually, how much must he invest today in order to make the payments to the grand prize winner?
$456,425

10. Thomas Martin's uncle has promised him a graduation gift of $20,000 in cash or $2,000 every quarter for the next 3 years. If money can be invested at 8%, which offer will Thomas accept? (Thomas is a business major.)
$21,150.60 Choose annuity.

11. Paul Sasso is selling a piece of land. He has received two solid offers. Jason Smith has offered a $60,000 down payment and $50,000 a year for the next 5 years. Kevin Bassage offered $35,000 down and $55,000 a year for the next 5 years. If money can be invested at 7% compounded annually, which offer should Paul accept? (To make the comparison, find the equivalent cash price of each offer.)
Paul should accept Jason's offer. $265,010

12. Abe Hoster decided to retire to Spain in 10 years. What amount should Abe invest today so that he will be able to withdraw $30,000 at the end of each year for 20 years after he retires? Assume he can invest money at 8% interest compounded annually.
$136,432.31

LU 13-3: Sinking Funds (Finds Payment Amount)

Drill Problems

1. Given the number of years and the interest rate, use the Sinking Fund Table Based on $1 to calculate the amount of the periodic payment.

	Frequency of payment	Length of time	Interest rate	Future amount	Sinking fund payment
a.	Annually	19 years	5%	$125,000	$4,087.50
b.	Annually	7 years	10%	$205,000	$21,607.00
c.	Semiannually	10 years	6%	$37,500	$1,395.00
d.	Quarterly	9 years	12%	$12,750	$201.45
e.	Quarterly	6 years	8%	$25,600	$842.24

2. Find the amount of each payment into the sinking fund and the amount of interest earned.

	Maturity value	Interest rate	Term (years)	Frequency of payment	Sinking fund payment	Interest earned
a.	$45,500	5%	13	Annually	$2,570.75	$12,080.25
b.	$8,500	10%	20	Semiannually	$70.55	$5,678.00
c.	$11,000	8%	5	Quarterly	$453.20	$1,936.00
d.	$66,600	12%	$7\frac{1}{2}$	Semiannually	$2,863.80	$23,643.00

Word Problems

3. In order to finance a new police station, the town of Pine Valley issued bonds totaling $600,000. The town treasurer set up a sinking fund at 8% compounded quarterly in order to redeem the bonds in 7 years. What is the quarterly payment that must be deposited into the fund?
$16,200 quarterly payment

4. Arlex Oil Corporation plans to build a new garage in 6 years. The financial manager established a $250,000 sinking fund at 6% compounded semiannually in order to finance the project. Find the semiannual payment required for the fund.
$17,625

5. The City Fisheries Corporation sold $300,000 worth of bonds that must be redeemed in 9 years. The corporation agreed to set up a sinking fund to accumulate the $300,000. Find the amount of the periodic payments made into the fund if payments are made annually and the fund earns 8% compounded annually.
$24,030 annual payment

6. Gregory Mines Corporation wishes to purchase a new piece of equipment in 4 years. The estimated price of the equipment is $100,000. If the corporation makes periodic payments into a sinking fund with 12% interest compounded quarterly, find the amount of the periodic payments.
$4,960 quarterly payments

7. The Best Corporation must buy a new piece of machinery in $4\frac{1}{2}$ years that will cost $350,000. If the firm sets up a sinking fund to finance this new machine, what will the quarterly deposits be assuming the fund earns 8% interest compounded quarterly?
$16,345 quarterly payments

8. The Lowest-Price-in-Town Company needs $75,500 in 6 years to pay off a debt. The company makes a decision to set up a sinking fund and make semiannual deposits. What will their payments be if the fund pays 10% interest compounded semiannually?
$4,741.40 semiannual payment

9. The WIR Company plans to renovate their offices in 5 years. They estimate that the cost will be $235,000. If they set up a sinking fund that pays 12% quarterly, what will their quarterly payments be?
$8,742 quarterly payment

Date ______________ Name ______________________________

LU 14–1: Cost of Installment Buying: The Cost of Buying a Pickup Truck

Drill Problems

1. For the following installment purchases, find the amount financed and the finance charge.

	Sale price	Down payment	Number of monthly payments	Monthly payment	Amount financed	Finance charge
a.	$1,500	$300	24	$58	$1,200	$192
b.	$12,000	$3,000	30	$340	$9,000	$1,200
c.	$62,500	$4,700	48	$1,500	$57,800	$14,200
d.	$4,975	$620	18	$272	$4,355	$541
e.	$825	$82.50	12	$67.45	$742.50	$66.90

2. For each of the above purchases, find the **deferred payment price.**

	Sale price	Down payment	Monthly payments	Monthly payment	Deferred payment price
a.	$1,500	$300	24	$58	$1,692
b.	$12,000	$3,000	30	$340	$13,200
c.	$62,500	$4,700	48	$1,500	$76,700
d.	$4,975	$620	18	$272	$5,516
e.	$825	$82.50	12	$67.45	$891.90

3. For each of the purchases in Problem 1, use the formula to calculate the estimated annual percentage rate (APR). Round to nearest hundredth percent.

	Sale price	Down payment	Monthly payments	Monthly payment	Annual percentage rate (APR)
a.	$1,500	$300	24	$58	15.36%
b.	$12,000	$3,000	30	$340	10.32%
c.	$62,500	$4,700	48	$1,500	12.03%
d.	$4,975	$620	18	$272	15.69%
e.	$825	$82.50	12	$67.45	16.63%

4. Use the Annual Percentage Rate Table per $100 to calculate the estimated APR for each of the previous purchases.

	Sale price	Down payment	Monthly payments	Monthly payment	Annual percentage rate
a.	$1,500	$300	24	$58	14.75%
b.	$12,000	$3,000	30	$340	10%
c.	$62,500	$4,700	48	$1,500	11.25%
d.	$4,975	$620	18	$272	15.25%
e.	$825	$82.50	12	$67.45	16.25%

5. Given the following information, calculate the monthly payment by the loan amortization table.

	Amount financed	Rate	Number of months of loan	Monthly payment
a.	$12,000	10%	18	$720.72
b.	$18,000	11%	36	$589.32
c.	$25,500	13.50%	54	$632.66

Word Problems

6. Jill Walsh purchased a bedroom set with a cash price of $3,920. The down payment is $392, and the monthly installment payment is $176 for 24 months. Find **(a)** the amount financed, **(b)** the finance charge, and **(c)** the deferred payment price.

a. $3,528 b. $696 c. $4,616

7. Jason Mazzola purchased a motorcycle with a sticker price of $5,500. He had to make a down payment of $412.50. He is obligated to make monthly payments of $171 for 36 months. Use the formula to calculate the estimated APR Jason is being charged. Round to nearest hundredth percent.
   APR = 13.62%

8. David Nason purchased a recreational vehicle for $25,000. David went to City Bank to finance the purchase. The bank required David to make a 10% down payment and make monthly payments of $571.50 for 4 years. Find **(a)** the amount financed, **(b)** the finance charge, and **(c)** the deferred payment price that David paid.
   a. $22,500 b. $4,932 c. $29,932

9. Calculate the estimated APR that David (Problem 8) was charged using **(a)** the formula (to the nearest hundredth percent) and using **(b)** the Annual Percentage Rate Table per $100.
   a. 10.74% b. Approximately 10%

10. Young's Motors advertised a new car for $16,720. They offered an installment plan of 5% down and 42 monthly payments of $470. What is **(a)** the deferred payment price and **(b)** the estimated APR for this car (use the table)?
    a. $20,576 b. 12.75%

11. Angie French bought a used car for $9,000. Angie put down $2,000 and financed the balance at 11.50% for 36 months. What is her monthly payment? (Use the loan amortization table.)
    $230.86

LU 14-2: Paying Off Installment Loan before Due Date

Drill Problems

1. Find the balance of each loan outstanding and the total finance charge:

	Amount financed	Monthly payment	Number of payments	Payments to date	Balance of loan outstanding	Finance charge
a.	$1,500	$125	15	10	$625	$375
b.	$21,090	$600	40	24	$9,600	$2,910
c.	$895	$60	18	10	$480	$185
d.	$4,850	$150	42	30	$1,800	$1,450

2. For the loans in Problem 1, find the number of payments remaining, and calculate the rebate amount of the finance charge (use Rebate Fraction Table Based on Rule of 78):

	Amount financed	Monthly payment	Number of payments	Payments to date	Number of payments remaining	Finance charge rebate
a.	$1,500	$125	15	10	5	$46.88
b.	$21,090	$600	40	24	16	$482.63
c.	$895	$60	18	10	8	$38.95
d.	$4,850	$150	42	30	12	$125.25

3. For the loans in Problems 1 and 2, show the remaining balance of the loan and calculate the payoff amount to retire the loan at this time:

	Amount financed	Monthly payment	Number of payments	Payments to date	Balance of loan outstanding	Final payoff
a.	$1,500	$125	15	10	$625	$578.12
b.	$21,090	$600	40	24	$9,600	$9,117.37
c.	$895	$60	18	10	$480	$441.05
d.	$4,850	$150	42	30	$1,800	$1,674.75

4. Complete the following; show all of the steps:

	Loan	Months of loan	Monthly payment	End of month loan is repaid	Final payoff
a.	$6,200	36	$219	24	$2,430.77
b.	$960	12	$99	8	$366.77

Word Problems

5. Maryjane Hannon took out a loan for $5,600 to have a swimming pool installed in her back yard. The note she signed required 21 monthly payments of $293. At the end of 15 months, Maryjane wants to know the balance of her loan outstanding and what the total finance charge is.
   $1,758 balance of loan outstanding $553 total finance charge
6. After calculating the above data (Problem 5), Maryjane is considering paying off the rest of the loan. In order to make her decision, Maryjane wants to know the finance charge rebate she will receive, and what the final payoff amount will be.
   $50.27 rebate amount $1,707.73 final payoff
7. Ben Casey decided to buy a used car for $7,200. He agreed to make monthly payments of $225 for 36 months. What is Ben's total finance charge?
   $900
8. After making 20 payments, Ben (Problem 7) wants to pay off the rest of the loan. What will be the amount of Ben's final payoff?
   $3,416.22
9. Jeremy Vagos took out a loan to buy a new boat that cost $12,440. He agreed to pay $350 a month for 48 months. After 24 monthly payments, he calculates that he has paid $8,400 on his loan, and has 24 payments remaining. Jeremy's friend Luke tells Jeremy that he will pay off the rest of the loan (in a single payment) if he can be half owner of the boat. What is the amount that Luke will have to pay?
   $7,287.76

LU 14-3: Revolving Charge and Credit Cards

Drill Problems

1. Use the U.S. Rule to calculate the outstanding balance due for each of the following independent situations:

	Monthly payment number	Outstanding balance due	$1\frac{1}{2}\%$ interest payment	Amount of monthly payment	Reduction in balance due	Outstanding balance due
a.	1	$9,000.00	$135	$600	$465	$8,535
b.	5	$5,625.00	$84.38	$1,000	$915.62	$4,709.38
c.	4	$926.50	$13.90	$250	$236.10	$690.40
d.	12	$62,391.28	$935.87	$1,200	$264.13	$62,127.15
e.	8	$3,255.19	$48.83	$325	$276.17	$2,979.02

2. Complete the missing data for a $6,500 purchase made on credit. The annual interest charge on this revolving charge account is 18% or $1\frac{1}{2}\%$ interest on previous month's balance. Use the U.S. Rule.

Monthly payment number	Outstanding balance due	$1\frac{1}{2}\%$ interest payment	Amount of monthly payment	Reduction in balance due	Outstanding balance due
1	$6,500	$97.50	$700	$602.50	$5,897.50
2	$5,897.50	$88.46	$700	$611.54	$5,285.96
3	$5,285.96	$79.29	$700	$620.71	$4,665.25

3. Calculate the average daily balance for each of the monthly statements for these revolving credit accounts (assume a 30-day billing cycle):

	Billing date	Previous balance	Payment date	Payment amount	Charge date(s)	Charge amount(s)	Average daily balance
a.	4/10	$329	4/25	$35	4/29	$56	$332.03
b.	6/15	$573	6/25	$60	6/26 6/30	$25 $72	$584.83
c.	9/15	$335.50	9/20	$33.55	9/25 9/26	$12.50 $108	$384.28

4. Find the finance charge for each monthly statement (Problem 3) if the annual percentage rate is 15%.
   a. $4.15 b. $7.31 c. $4.80

Word Problems

5. Niki Marshall is going to buy a new bedroom set at Scottie's Furniture Store, where she has a revolving charge account. The cost of the bedroom set is $5,500. Niki does not plan to charge anything else to her account until she has completely paid for the bedroom set. Scottie's Furniture Store charges an annual percentage rate of 18%, or $1\frac{1}{2}$% per month. Niki plans to pay $1,000 per month until she has paid for the bedroom set. Set up a schedule for Niki to show her outstanding balance at the end of each month after her $1,000 payment, and also what the amount of her final payment will be. Use the U.S. Rule.
   $784.39

6. Frances Dollof received her monthly statement from Brown's Department Store. The following is part of the information contained on that statement. Finance charge is calculated on the average daily balance.

DATE	REFERENCE	DEPT.	DESCRIPTION	AMOUNT
DEC 15	5921	359	PETITE SPORTSWEAR	84.98
DEC 15	9612	432	FOOTWEAR	55.99
DEC 15	2600	126	WOMENS FRAGRANCE	35.18
DEC 23	6247	61	RALPH LAUREN TOWELS	20.99
DEC 24	0129	998	PAYMENT RECEIVED-THANK YOU	100.00CR

PREVIOUS BALANCE		ANNUAL PERCENTAGE RATE	BILLING DATE
719.04	12/13	18%	JAN 13

BROWN'S CHARGE ACCOUNT TERMS

Payment is required in monthly installments upon receipt of monthly statement in accordance with Brown's payment terms.

When My New Balance Is:	My Minimum Required Payment Is:	When My New Balance Is:	My Minimum Required Payment Is:
Up to $20.00	New Balance	$350.01 to $400.00	$40.00
$ 20.01 to $200.00	$20.00	$400.01 to $450.00	$45.00
$200.01 to $250.00	$25.00	$450.01 to $500.00	$50.00
$250.01 to $300.00	$30.00	Over $500.00	$50.00 plus $10.00 for each $50.00 (or fraction thereof) of New Balance over $500.00
$300.01 to $350.00	$35.00		

   a. Calculate the average daily balance for the month.
      $833.53
   b. What is Ms. Dollof's finance charge?
      $12.50
   c. What is the new balance for Ms. Dollof's account?
      $828.68
   d. What is the minimum payment Frances is required to pay according to Brown's payment terms?
      $120

7. What would the finance charge be for a Brown's customer that has an average daily balance of $3,422.67?
   $51.34

8. What would be the minimum payment for a Brown's customer with a new balance of $522.00?
   $60

9. What would be the minimum payment for a Brown's customer with a new balance of $325.01?
   $35

10. What is the new balance for a Brown's customer with a previous balance of $309.35, the purchases totaled $213.00, the customer made a payment of $75.00, and the finance charge was $4.65?
    $452.00

Date ____________ Name ____________

LU 15-1: Types of Mortgages and the Monthly Mortgage Payment

Drill Problems

1. Use the table in the Business Math Handbook to calculate the monthly payment for principal and interest for the following mortgages:

	Price of home	Down payment	Interest rate	Term in years	Monthly payment
a.	$200,000	15%	$10\frac{1}{2}\%$	25	$1,606.50
b.	$200,000	15%	$10\frac{1}{2}\%$	30	$1,555.50
c.	$450,000	10%	$11\frac{3}{4}\%$	30	$4,090.50
d.	$450,000	10%	11%	30	$3,859.65

2. For each of the mortgages in Problem 1, calculate the amount of interest that will be paid over the life of the loan.

	Price of home	Down payment	Interest rate	Term in years	Total interest paid
a.	$200,000	15%	$10\frac{1}{2}\%$	25	$281,950
b.	$200,000	15%	$10\frac{1}{2}\%$	30	$359,980
c.	$450,000	10%	$11\frac{3}{4}\%$	30	$1,022,580
d.	$450,000	10%	11%	30	$939,474

3. Calculate the increase in the monthly mortgage payments for each of the rate increases in the following mortgages. Also calculate what percent of change the increase represents (round to a tenth percent):

	Mortgage amount	Term in years	Interest rate	Increase in interest rate	Increase in monthly payment	Percent change
a.	$175,000	22	9%	1%	$117.25	7.7%
b.	$300,000	30	$11\frac{3}{4}\%$	$\frac{3}{4}\%$	$174	5.7%

4. Calculate the increase in total interest paid for the increase in interest rates in Problem 3.

	Mortgage amount	Term in years	Interest rate	Increase in interest rate	Increase in total interest paid
a.	$175,000	22	9%	1%	$30,954
b.	$300,000	30	$11\frac{3}{4}\%$	$\frac{3}{4}\%$	$62,640

Word Problems

5. The Counties are planning to purchase a new home that costs $329,000. The bank is charging them $10\frac{1}{2}\%$ interest and requires a 20% down payment. The Counties are planning to take a 25-year mortgage. How much will their monthly payment be for principal and interest?
$2,487.24

6. The MacEacherns wish to buy a new house that costs $299,000. The bank requires a 15% down payment, and charges $11\frac{1}{2}\%$ interest. If the MacEacherns take out a 15-year mortgage, what will their monthly payment for principal and interest be?
$2,971.01

7. Because the monthly payments are so high, the MacEacherns (Problem 6) want to know what the monthly payments would be for **(a)** a 25-year mortgage and **(b)** a 30-year mortgage. Calculate these two payments.
a. $2,584.71 **b.** $2,518.63

8. If the MacEacherns choose a 30-year mortgage instead of a 15-year mortgage, **(a)** how much money will they "save" monthly and **(b)** how much more interest will they pay over the life of the loan?
   a. $452.38 b. $371,925

9. If the MacEacherns choose the 25-year mortgage instead of the 30-year mortgage, **(a)** how much more will they pay monthly and **(b)** how much less interest will they pay over the life of the loan?
   a. $66.08 b. $131,293.80

10. Larry and Doris Davis plan to purchase a new home that costs $415,000. The bank that they are dealing with requires a 20% down payment and charges $12\frac{3}{4}$%. The Davises are planning to take a 25-year mortgage. What will the monthly payments be?
    $3,685.20

11. How much interest will the Davises (Problem 10) pay over the life of the loan?
    $773,560

LU 15-2: Amortization Schedule—Breaking Down the Monthly Payment

Drill Problems

1. In the following, calculate the monthly payment for each mortgage, the portion of the first monthly payment that goes to interest, and the portion of the payment that is paid towards the principal.

	Amount of mortgage	Interest rate	Term in years	Monthly payment	Portion to interest	Portion to principal
a.	$170,000	8%	22	$1,371.90	$1,133.33	$238.57
b.	$222,000	$11\frac{3}{4}$%	30	$2,242.20	$2,173.75	$68.45
c.	$167,000	$10\frac{1}{2}$%	25	$1,578.15	$1,461.25	$116.90
d.	$307,000	13%	15	$3,886.62	$3,325.83	$560.79
e.	$409,500	$12\frac{1}{2}$%	20	$4,656.02	$4,265.63	$390.39

2. Prepare an amortization schedule for the first three months for a 25-year, 12% mortgage on $265,000.

Payment number	Monthly payment	Portion to interest	Portion to principal	Balance of loan outstanding
1	$2,793.10	$2,650.00	$143.10	$264,856.90
2	$2,793.10	$2,648.57	$144.53	$264,712.37
3	$2,793.10	$2,647.12	$145.98	$264,566.39

3. Prepare an amortization schedule for the first four months for a 30-year, $10\frac{1}{2}$% mortgage on $195,500.

Payment number	Monthly payment	Portion to interest	Portion to principal	Balance of loan outstanding
1	$1,788.83	$1,710.63	$78.20	$195,421.80
2	$1,788.83	$1,709.94	$78.89	$195,342.91
3	$1,788.83	$1,709.25	$79.58	$195,263.33
4	$1,788.83	$1,708.55	$80.28	$195,183.05

Word Problems

4. Jim and Janice Hurst are buying a new home for $235,000. The bank where they are financing the home requires a 20% down payment and charges a $13\frac{1}{2}$% interest rate. Janice wants to know **(a)** what the monthly payment for the principal and interest will be if they take out a 30-year mortgage, and **(b)** how much of the first payment will be for interest on the loan.
   a. $2,154.48
   b. $2,115

5. The Hursts (Problem 4) thought that a lot of their money was going to interest. They asked the banker just how much they would be paying for interest over the life of the loan. Calculate the total amount of interest that the Hursts will have to pay.
   $587,612.80
6. The banker told the Hursts (Problem 4) that they could, of course, save on the interest payments if they took out a loan for a shorter period of time. Jim and Janice decided to see if they could afford a 15-year mortgage Calculate how much more the Hursts would have to pay each month for principal and interest if they take a 15-year mortgage for their loan.
   $287.64
7. The Hursts (Problem 4) thought that they might be able to afford this, but first wanted to see **(a)** how much of the first payment would go to the principal, and **(b)** how much total interest they would be paying with a 15-year mortgage.
   a. $327.12 principal payment
   b. $251,581.60

Date ____________ Name ______________________________

LU 16–1: Balance Sheet: Report as of a Particular Date

Drill Problems

1. Complete the balance sheet for David Harrison, Attorney, and show that:

   Assets = Liabilities + Owner's Equity

   Account totals are as follows: Accounts Receivable is $4,800, Office Supplies is $375, Building (net) is $130,000, Accounts Payable is $1,200, Notes Payable is $137,200, Cash is $2,250, Prepaid Insurance is $1,050, Office Equipment (net) is $11,250, Land is $75,000, Capital is $85,900, and Salaries Payable is $425.

DAVID HARRISON, ATTORNEY
Balance Sheet
December 31, 1995

Assets			
Current assets:			
Cash	$ 2,250		
Accounts receivable	4,800		
Prepaid insurance	1,050		
Office supplies	375		
Total current assets		$ 8,475	
Plant and equipment:			
Office equipment (net)	$ 11,250		
Building (net)	130,000		
Land	75,000		
Total plant and equipment		216,250	
Total assets			$224,725
Liabilities			
Current liabilities:			
Accounts payable	$ 1,200		
Salaries payable	425		
Total current liabilities		$ 1,625	
Long-term liabilities:			
Notes payable		137,200	
Total liabilities			$138,825
Owner's Equity			
David Harrison, capital, December 31, 1995			85,900
Total liabilities and owner's equity			$224,725

2. Given the amounts in each of the accounts of Fisher-George Electric Corp., fill in these amounts on the balance sheet to show that:

   Assets = Liabilities + Stockholders' Equity

   Account totals are as follows: Cash is $2,500, Merchandise Inventory is $1,325, Automobiles (net) is $9,250, Common Stock is $10,000, Accounts Payable is $275, Office Equipment (net) is $5,065, Accounts Receivable is $300, Retained Earnings is $6,895, Prepaid Insurance is $1,075, Salaries Payable is $175, and Mortgage Payable is $2,170.

FISHER-GEORGE ELECTRIC CORP.
Balance Sheet
December 31, 1995

Assets			
Current assets:			
Cash	$2,500		
Accounts receivable	300		
Merchandise inventory	1,325		
Prepaid insurance	1,075		
Total current assets		$ 5,200	
Plant and equipment:			
Office equipment (net)	$5,065		
Automobiles (net)	9,250		
Total plant and equipment		14,315	
Total assets			$19,515
Liabilities			
Current liabilities:			
Accounts payable	$ 275		
Salaries payable	175		
Total current liabilities		$ 450	
Long-term liabilities:			
Mortgage payable		2,170	
Total liabilities			$ 2,620
Stockholders' Equity			
Common stock		$10,000	
Retained earnings		6,895	
Total stockholders' equity			16,895
Total liabilities and stockholders' equity			$19,515

3. Complete a vertical analysis of the following partial balance sheet (round all percents to the nearest hundredth percent):

THREEMAX, INC.
Comparative Balance Sheet Vertical Analysis
At December 31, 1994 and 1995

	1995		1994	
	Amount	**Percent**	**Amount**	**Percent**
Assets				
Cash	$ 8,500	2.13	$ 10,200	2.84%
Accounts receivable (net)	11,750	2.95	15,300	4.26
Merchandise inventory	55,430	13.90	54,370	15.12
Store supplies	700	0.18	532	0.15
Office supplies	650	0.16	640	0.18
Prepaid insurance	2,450	0.61	2,675	0.74
Office equipment (net)	12,000	3.01	14,300	3.98
Store equipment (net)	32,000	8.02	31,000	8.62
Building (net)	75,400	18.90	80,500	22.39
Land	200.000	50.14	150,000	41.72
Total assets	$398,880	100.00	$359,517	100.00

4. Complete a horizontal analysis of the following partial balance sheet (round all percents to the nearest hundredth percent):

THREEMAX, INC.
Comparative Balance Sheet Horizontal Analysis
At December 31, 1994 and 1995

	1995	1994	Change	Percent
Assets				
Cash	$ 8,500	$ 10,200	$ − 1,700	− 16.67%
Accounts receivable (net)	11,750	15,300	− 3,550	− 23.20
Merchandise inventory	55,430	54,370	1,060	1.95
Store supplies	700	532	168	31.58
Office supplies	650	640	10	1.56
Prepaid insurance	2,450	2,675	− 225	− 8.41
Office equipment (net)	12,000	14,300	− 2,300	− 16.08
Store equipment (net)	32,000	31,000	1,000	3.23
Building (net)	75,400	80,500	− 5,100	− 6.34
Land	200.000	150,000	50,000	33.33
Total assets	$398,880	$359,517		

LU 16–2: Income Statement: Report for a Specific Period of Time

Drill Problems

1. Complete the income statement for Foley Realty doing all the necessary addition. Office salaries expense is $15,255, advertising expense is $2,400, rent expense is $18,000, telephone expense is $650, insurance expense is $1,550, office supplies is $980, depreciation expense, office equipment is $990, depreciation expense, automobile is $2,100, sales commissions earned is $98,400, and management fees earned is $1,260.

FOLEY REALTY
Income Statement
For the Year Ended December 31, 1994

Revenues:		
Sales commissions earned	$98,400	
Management fees earned	1,260	
Total revenues		$99,660
Operating expenses:		
Office salaries expense	$15,225	
Advertising expense	2,400	
Rent expense	18,000	
Telephone expense	650	
Insurance expense	1,550	
Office supplies expense	980	
Depreciation expense, office equipment	990	
Depreciation expense, automobile	2,100	
Total operating expenses		41,895
Net income		$57,765

2. Complete the income statement for Toll's Inc., a merchandising concern, doing all the necessary addition and subtraction. Sales were $250,000, sales returns and allowances were $1,400, sales discounts were $2,100, merchandise inventory, December 31, 1994, was $42,000, purchases were $156,000, purchases returns and allowances were $1,100, purchases discounts were $3,000, merchandise inventory, December 31, 1995, was $47,000, selling expenses were $37,000, and general and administrative expenses were $29,000.

TOLL'S, INCORPORATED
Income Statement
For the Year Ended December 31, 1995

Revenues:				
Sales				$250,000
Less: Sales returns and allowances			$ 1,400	
Sales discounts			2,100	3,500
Net sales				$246,500
Cost of goods sold:				
Merchandise inventory, December 31, 1994			$ 42,000	
Purchases		$156,000		
Less: Purchases returns and allowances	$1,100			
Purchase discounts	3,000	4,100		
Cost of net purchases			151,900	
Goods available for sale			$193,900	
Merchandise inventory, December 31, 1995			47,000	
Total cost of goods sold				146,900
Gross profit from sales				$ 99,600
Operating expenses:				
Selling expenses			$ 37,000	
General and administrative expenses			29,000	
Total operating expenses				66,000
Net income				$ 33,600

3. Complete a vertical analysis of the following partial income statement (round all percents to the nearest hundredth percent): Note net sales is 100%.

THREEMAX, INC.
Comparative Income Statement Vertical Analysis
For Periods Ended December 31, 1994 and 1995

	1995		1994	
	Amount	**Percent**	**Amount**	**Percent**
Sales	$795,450	101.63	$665,532	101.60
Sales returns and allowances	− 6,250	− 0.80	− 5,340	− 0.82
Sales discounts	− 6,470	− 0.83	− 5,125	− 0.78
Net sales	$782,730	100.00	$655,067	100.00
Cost of goods sold:				
Beginning inventory	$ 75,394	9.63	$ 81,083	12.38
Purchases	575,980	73.59	467,920	71.43
Purchases discounts	− 4,976	− 0.64	− 2,290	− 0.35
Goods available for sale	$646,398	82.58	$546,713	83.46
Less ending inventory	− 66,254	− 8.46	− 65,712	− 10.03
Total costs of good sold	$580,144	74.12	$481,001	73.43
Gross profit	$202,586	25.88	$174,066	26.57

4. Complete a horizontal analysis of the following partial income statement (round all percents to the nearest hundredth percent):

THREEMAX, INC.
Comparative Income Statement Horizontal Analysis
For Periods Ended December 31, 1994 and 1995

	1995	1994	Change	Percent
Sales	$795,450	$665,532	129,918	19.52
Sales returns and allowances	– 6,250	– 5,340	– 910	17.04
Sales discounts	– 6,470	– 5,125	– 1,345	26.24
Net sales	$782,730	$655,067	127,663	19.49
Cost of goods sold:				
Beginning inventory	$ 75,394	$ 81,083	– 5,689	– 7.02
Purchases	575,980	467,920	108,060	23.09
Purchases discounts	– 4,976	– 2,290	– 2,686	117.29
Goods available for sale	$646,398	$546,713	99,685	18.23
Less ending inventory	– 66,254	– 65,712	– 542	0.82
Total costs of good sold	$580,144	$481,001	99,143	20.61
Gross profit	$202,586	$174,066	28,520	16.38

LU 16–3: Trend and Ratio Analysis

Drill Problems

1. Express each amount as a percent of the base year (1992) amount. Round to the nearest tenth percent.

	1995	1994	1993	1992
Sales	$562,791	$560,776	$588,096	$601,982
Percent	93.5%	93.2%	97.7%	100.0%
Gross profit	$168,837	$196,271	$235,238	$270,891
Percent	62.3%	72.5%	86.8%	100.0%
Net income	$ 67,934	$ 65,927	$ 56,737	$ 62,762
Percent	108.2%	105.0%	90.4%	100.0%

2. If current assets = $42,500, and current liabilities = $56,400, what is the current ratio (to the nearest hundredth)?
0.75

3. In Problem 2, if inventory = $20,500, and prepaid expenses = $9,750, what is the quick ratio, or acid test (to the nearest hundredth)?
0.22

4. If accounts receivable = $36,720, and net sales = $249,700, what is the average day's collection (to the nearest whole day)?
53 days

5. If total liabilities = $243,000, and total assets = $409,870, what is the total debt to total assets (to the nearest hundredth percent)?
59.29%

6. If net income = $55,970, and total stockholders' equity = $440,780, what is the return on equity (to the nearest hundredth percent)?
12.70%

7. If net sales = $900,000, and total assets = $1,090,000, what is the asset turnover (to the nearest hundredth)?
.83

8. In Problem 7, if the net income is $36,600, what is the profit margin on net sales (to the nearest hundredth percent)?
4.07%

Word Problems

9. Calculate trend percentages for the following items using 1992 as the base year. Round to the nearest hundredth percent.

	1995	1994	1993	1992
Sales	$298,000	$280,000	$264,000	$249,250
Cost of goods sold	187,085	175,227	164,687	156,785
Accounts receivable	29,820	28,850	27,300	26,250

Sales: 119.56%, 112.34%, 105.92%
Cost of goods sold: 119.33%, 111.76%, 105.04%
Accounts receivable: 113.60%, 109.90%, 104.00%

10. According to the balance sheet for Ralph's Market, current assets = $165,500, and current liabilities = $70,500. Find the current ratio (to the nearest hundredth).
2.35

11. On the balance sheet for Ralph's Market (Problem 10), merchandise inventory = $102,000. Find the quick ratio (acid test).
.90

12. The balance sheet of Moses Contractors shows cash of $5,500, accounts receivable of $64,500, an inventory of $42,500, and current liabilities of $57,500. Find Moses' current ratio, and acid test ratio (both to nearest hundredth).
1.96 current ratio 1.22 acid test

13. Moses' income statement shows gross sales of $413,000, sales returns of $8,600, and net income of $22,300. Find the profit margin on net sales (to the nearest hundredth percent).
5.51%

14. Given:

Cash	$ 39,000	Retained earnings	$194,000
Accounts receivable	109,000	Net sales	825,000
Inventory	150,000	Cost of goods sold	528,000
Prepaid expenses	48,000	Operating expense	209,300
Plant & equipment (net)	487,000	Interest expense	13,500
Accounts payable	46,000	Income taxes	32,400
Other current liabilities	43,000	Net income	41,800
Long-term liabilities	225,000		
Common stock	325,000		

Calculate (to nearest hundredth or hundredth percent as needed):

a. Current ratio.
3.89

b. Quick ratio
1.66

c. Average day's collection.
47.56 days

d. Total debt to total assets.
37.70%

e. Return on equity.
8.05%

f. Asset turnover.
$0.99

g. Profit margin on net sales.
5.07%

Date ____________ Name ____________

LU 17–1: Concepts of Depreciation and the Straight-Line Method

Drill Problems

1. Find the annual straight-line rate of depreciation, given the following estimated lives.

	Life	Annual rate		Life	Annual rate
a.	25 years	4%	**b.**	4 years	25%
c.	10 years	10%	**d.**	5 years	20%
e.	8 years	$12\frac{1}{2}\%$	**f.**	30 years	$3\frac{1}{3}\%$

2. Find the annual depreciation amount using the straight-line depreciation method (round to the nearest whole dollar).

	Cost of asset	Residual value	Useful life	Annual depreciation
a.	$2,460	$400	4 years	$515
b.	$24,300	$2,000	6 years	$3,717
c.	$350,000	$42,500	12 years	$25,625
d.	$17,325	$5,000	5 years	$2,465
e.	$2,550,000	$75,000	30 years	$82,500

3. Find the annual depreciation, and ending book value for the first year using the straight-line depreciation method. Round to the nearest dollar.

	Cost	Residual value	Useful life	Annual depreciation	Ending book value
a.	$6,700	$600	3 years	$2,033	$4,667
b.	$11,600	$500	6 years	$1,850	$9,750
c.	$9,980	0	5 years	$1,996	$7,984
d.	$36,950	$2,500	12 years	$2,871	$34,079
e.	$101,690	$3,600	27 years	$3,633	$98,057

4. Find the first year depreciation to nearest dollar for the following assets which were only owned for part of a year. (Round to the nearest whole dollar annual depreciation for in between calculations).

	Date of purchase	Cost of asset	Residual value	Useful life	First year depreciation
a.	April 8	$10,500	$1,200	4 years	$1,744
b.	July 12	$23,900	$3,200	6 years	$1,725
c.	June 19	$8,880	$800	3 years	$1,347
d.	November 2	$125,675	$6,000	17 years	$1,173
e.	May 25	$44,050	0	9 years	$2,855

Word Problems

5. North Shore Grinding purchased a lathe for $37,500. This machine has a residual value of $3,000 and an expected useful life of four years. Prepare a depreciation schedule for the lathe using the straight-line depreciation method.
$8,625 annual depreciation

6. Colby Wayne paid $7,750 for a photocopy machine with an estimated life of six years and a residual value of $900. Prepare a depreciation schedule using the straight-line depreciation method. Round to nearest whole dollar. (Last year depreciation may have to be adjusted due to rounding.)
$1,142 annual depreciation

7. The Leo Brothers purchased a machine for $8,400 that has an estimated life of three years. At the end of three years the machine will have no value. Prepare a depreciation schedule for this machine.
$2,800 annual depreciation

8. Fox Realty bought a computer table for $1,700. The estimated useful life of the table is seven years. The residual value at the end of seven years is $370. Find (**a**) the annual rate of depreciation to the nearest hundredth percent, **(b)** the annual amount of depreciation, and **(c)** the book value of the table at the end of the third year using the straight-line depreciation method.

a. 14.29% b. $190 c. $1,130

9. Cashman Inc. purchased an overhead projector for $560. It has an estimated useful life of six years at which time it will have no remaining value. Find the book value at the end of five years using the straight-line depreciation method. Round annual depreciation to nearest whole dollar.

$95

10. The Shelley Corporation purchased a new machine for $15,000. The estimated life of the machine is 12 years, with a residual value of $2,400. Find **(a)** the annual rate of depreciation to the nearest hundredth percent, **(b)** the annual amount of depreciation, **(c)** the accumulated depreciation at the end of seven years, and **(d)** the book value at the end of nine years.

a. 8.33% b. $1,050 c. $7,350 d. $5,550

11. Wolfe Ltd. purchased a super computer for $75,000 on July 7, 1994. The computer has an estimated life of five years and will have a residual value of $15,000. Find **(a)** the annual depreciation amount, **(b)** the depreciation amount for 1994, **(c)** the accumulated depreciation at the end of 1995, and **(d)** the book value at the end of 1996.

a. $12,000 b. $6,000 c. $18,000 d. $45,000

LU 17–2: Units-of-Production Method

Drill Problems

1. Find the depreciation per unit for each of the following assets. Round to three decimal places.

	Cost of asset	Residual value	Estimated production	Depreciation per unit
a.	$3,500	$800	9,000 units	$0.30
b.	$309,560	$22,000	1,500,000 units	$0.192
c.	$54,890	$6,500	275,000 units	$0.176

2. Find the annual depreciation expense for each of the assets in Problem 1.

	Cost of asset	Residual value	Estimated production	Depreciation per unit	Units produced	Amount of depreciation
a.	$3,500	$800	9,000 units	$0.30	3,000	$900
b.	$309,560	$22,000	1,500,000 units	$0.192	45,500	$8,736
c.	$54,890	$6,500	275,000 units	$0.176	4,788	$842.69

3. Find the book value at the end of the first year for each of the assets in Problems 1 and 2.

	Cost of asset	Residual value	Estimated production	Depreciation per unit	Units produced	Book value
a.	$3,500	$800	9,000 units	$0.30	3,000	$2,600
b.	$309,560	$22,000	1,500,000 units	$0.192	45,500	$300,824
c.	$54,890	$6,500	275,000 units	$0.176	4,788	$54,047.31

4. Calculate the accumulated depreciation at the end of year 2 for each of the following machines. Carry out unit depreciation to three decimal places.

	Cost of machine	Residual value	Estimated life	Hours used during year 1	Hours used during year 2	Accumulated depreciation
a.	$67,900	$4,300	19,000 hours	5,430	4,856	$34,427.24
b.	$3,810	$600	33,000 hours	10,500	9,330	$1,923.51
c.	$25,000	$4,900	80,000 hours	7,000	12,600	$4,919.60

Word Problems

5. Prepare a depreciation schedule for the following machine: The machine cost $63,400, has an estimated residual value of $5,300, and expected life of 290,500 units. The units produced were:

Year 1	95,000 units	
Year 2	80,000 units	
Year 3	50,000 units	$5,300 book value at the end of year 5
Year 4	35,500 units	
Year 5	30,000 units	

6. Forsmann & Smythe purchased a new machine that cost $46,030. The machine has a residual value of $2,200, and estimated output of 430,000 hours. Prepare a units-of-production depreciation schedule for this machine (round unit depreciation to three decimal places). The hours of use were:

Year 1	90,000 hours	
Year 2	150,000 hours	$2,200 book value at the end of year 4
Year 3	105,000 hours	
Year 4	90,000 hours	

7. The Young Electrical Company depreciates their vans using the units-of-production method. The cost of their new van was $24,600, the useful life is 125,000 miles, and the trade-in value is $5,250. What is **(a)** depreciation expense per mile (to three decimal places), and **(b)** the book value at the end of the first year if they drive 29,667 miles?

   a. $0.155 **b.** $20,001.61

8. The Tremblay Manufacturing Company purchased a new machine for $52,000. The machine has an estimated useful life of 185,000 hours and a residual value of $10,000. The machine was used for 51,200 hours the first year. Find **(a)** the depreciation rate per hour (round to three decimal places), **(b)** the depreciation expense for the first year, and **(c)** the book value of the machine at the end of the first year.

   a. $0.227 **b.** $11,622.40 **c.** $40,377.60

LU 17–3: Sum-of-the-Years'-Digits Method

Drill Problems

1. Find the sum-of-the-years'-digits depreciation rate as a fraction for each year of life for the following assets.

Useful life	Year 1	Year 2	Year 3	Year 4	Year 5	Year 6	Year 7	Year 8
a. 5 years	$\frac{5}{15}$	$\frac{4}{15}$	$\frac{3}{15}$	$\frac{2}{15}$	$\frac{1}{15}$			
b. 3 years	$\frac{3}{6}$	$\frac{2}{6}$	$\frac{1}{6}$					
c. 8 years	$\frac{8}{36}$	$\frac{7}{36}$	$\frac{6}{36}$	$\frac{5}{36}$	$\frac{4}{36}$	$\frac{3}{36}$	$\frac{2}{36}$	$\frac{1}{36}$

2. Find the first year depreciation amount for the following assets using the sum-of-the-years'-digits depreciation method. (Round to the nearest whole dollar.)

Cost of asset	Residual value	Useful life	First year depreciation
a. $2,460	$400	4 years	$824
b. $24,300	$2,000	6 years	$6,371
c. $350,000	$42,500	12 years	$47,308
d. $17,325	$5,000	5 years	$4,108
e. $2,550,000	$75,000	30 years	$159,677

3. Find the depreciation expense, and ending book value for the first year using the sum-of-the-years'-digits depreciation method. Round to the nearest dollar (depreciation expense as well as ending book value).

	Cost	Residual value	Useful life	First year depreciation	Ending book value
a.	$6,700	$600	3 years	$3,050	$3,650
b.	$11,600	$500	6 years	$3,171	$8,429
c.	$9,980	0	5 years	$3,327	$6,653
d.	$36,950	$2,500	12 years	$5,300	$31,650
e.	$101,690	$3,600	27 years	$7,006	$94,684

Word Problem

4. North Shore Grinding purchased a lathe for $37,500. This machine has a residual value of $3,000 and an expected useful life of four years. Prepare a depreciation schedule for the lathe using the sum-of-the-years'-digits depreciation method.
$3,000 book value at end of year 4
5. Colby Wayne paid $7,750 for a photocopy machine with an estimated life of six years and a residual value of $900. Prepare a depreciation schedule using the sum-of-the-years'-digits depreciation method. Round all amounts to the nearest whole dollar.
$900 book value at the end of year 6
6. The Leo Brothers purchased a machine for $8,400 that has an estimated life of three years. At the end of three years, the machine will have no value. Prepare a depreciation schedule for this machine.
0 book value at the end of year 3
7. Fox Realty bought a computer table for $1,700. The estimated useful life of the table is seven years. The residual value at the end of seven years is $370. Find **(a)** the sum-of-the-years' denominator, **(b)** the amount of depreciation at the end of the *third* year, and **(c)** the book value of the table at the end of the *third* year using the sum-of-the-years'-digits depreciation method.
a. 28 b. $237.50 c. $845
8. Cashman Inc. purchased an overhead projector for $560. It has an estimated useful life of six years at which time it will have no remaining value. Find the book value at the end of five years using the sum-of-the-years'-digits depreciation method. Round to nearest whole dollar.
$27

LU 17-4: Declining-Balance Method

Drill Problems

1. Find the declining-balance rate of depreciation, given the following estimated lives.

	Life	Double-declining rate
a.	25 years	8% $\left(\frac{1}{25} \times 2 = \frac{2}{25}\right)$
b.	10 years	20% $\left(\frac{1}{10} \times 2 = \frac{2}{10}\right)$
c.	8 years	25% $\left(\frac{1}{8} \times 2 = \frac{2}{8}\right)$

2. Find the first year depreciation amount for the following assets using the double-declining-balance depreciation method. (Round to the nearest whole dollar.)

	Cost of asset	Residual value	Useful life	First year depreciation
a.	$2,460	$400	4 years	$1,230
b.	$24,300	$2,000	6 years	$8,100
c.	$350,000	$42,500	12 years	$58,333
d.	$17,325	$5,000	5 years	$6,930
e.	$2,550,000	$75,000	30 years	$170,000

3. Find the depreciation expense, and ending book value for the first year using the double-declining-balance depreciation method. Round to the nearest dollar.

	Cost	Residual value	Useful life	First year depreciation	Ending book value
a.	$6,700	$600	3 years	$4,467	$2,233
b.	$11,600	$500	6 years	$3,867	$7,733
c.	$9,980	0	5 years	$3,992	$5,988
d.	$36,950	$2,500	12 years	$6,158	$30,792
e.	$101,690	$3,600	27 years	$7,533	$94,157

Word Problems

4. North Shore Grinding purchased a lathe for $37,500. This machine has a residual value of $3,000 and an expected useful life of four years. Prepare a depreciation schedule for the lathe using the double-declining-balance depreciation method. Round to nearest whole dollar.
   Depreciation in year 4, $1,687
5. Colby Wayne paid $7,750 for a photocopy machine with an estimated life of six years and a residual value of $900. Prepare a depreciation schedule using the double-declining-balance depreciation method. Round to nearest whole dollar.
   Depreciation in year 6, $121
6. The Leo Brothers purchased a machine for $8,400 that has an estimated life of three years. At the end of three years, the machine will have no value. Prepare a depreciation schedule for this machine. Round to nearest whole dollar.
   Depreciation in year 3, $933
7. Fox Realty bought a computer table for $1,700. The estimated useful life of the table is seven years. The residual value at the end of seven years is $370. Find **(a)** the double-declining depreciation rate (to nearest hundredth percent), **(b)** the amount of depreciation at the end of the *third* year, and **(c)** the book value of the table at the end of the *third* year using the double-declining-balance depreciation method. Round to nearest whole dollar.
   a. 28.57% b. $248 c. $619
8. Cashman Inc. purchased an overhead projector for $560. It has an estimated useful life of six years, at which time it will have no remaining value. Find the book value at the end of five years using the double-declining-balance depreciation method. Round to nearest whole dollar.
   $74
9. The Shelley Corporation purchased a new machine for $15,000. The estimated life of the machine is 12 years, with a residual value of $2,400. Find **(a)** the double-declining-balance depreciation rate as a fraction and as a percent (hundredth percent), **(b)** the amount of depreciation at the end of the first year, **(c)** the accumulated depreciation at the end of seven years, and **(d)** the book value at the end of nine years. (Round to the nearest dollar.)
   a. $\frac{1}{6}$; 16.67% b. $2,500 c. $10,814 d. $2,907

LU 17–5: Modified Accelerated Cost Recovery System (MACRS)

Drill Problems

1. Using the MACRS method of depreciation, find the recovery rate, first-year depreciation expense, and the book value of the asset at the end of the first year. (Round to nearest whole dollar.)

	Cost of asset	Recovery period	Recovery rate	Depreciation expense	End-of-year book value
a.	$2,500	3 years	33%	$825	$1,675
b.	$52,980	3 years	33%	$17,483	$35,497
c.	$4,250	5 years	20%	$850	$3,400
d.	$128,950	10 years	10%	$12,895	$116,055
e.	$13,775	5 years	20%	$2,755	$11,020

2. Find the accumulated depreciation at the end of the second year for each of the following assets. (Round to the nearest whole dollar.)

	Cost of asset	Recovery period	Accumulated depreciation end of 2nd year using MACRS	Book value, end of 2nd year using MACRS
a.	$2,500	3 years	$1,950	$550
b.	$52,980	3 years	$41,324	$11,656
c.	$4,250	5 years	$2,210	$2,040
d.	$128,950	10 years	$36,106	$92,844
e.	$13,775	5 years	$7,163	$6,612

Word Problems

3. Colby Wayne paid $7,750 for a photocopy machine which is classified as equipment and has a residual value of $900. Prepare a depreciation schedule using the MACRS depreciation method. Round all calculations to the nearest whole dollar.
   Depreciation in year 8, $346

4. Fox Realty bought a computer table for $1,700. The table is classified as furniture. The residual value at the end of its useful life is $370. Using the MACRS depreciation method, find **(a)** the amount of depreciation at the end of the *third* year, **(b)** the total accumulated depreciation at the end of year 3, and **(c)** the book value of the table at the end of the *third* year. Round all calculations to the nearest dollar.
   a. $297 b. $956 c. $744

5. Cashman Inc. purchased an overhead projector for $560. It is classified as office equipment and will have no residual value. Find the book value at the end of five years using the MACRS depreciation method. Round to nearest whole dollar.
   $125

6. The Shelley Corporation purchased a new machine for $15,000. The machine is comparable to equipment used for two-way exchange of voice and data, with a residual value of $2,400. Find **(a)** the amount of depreciation at the end of the first year, **(b)** the accumulated depreciation at the end of seven years, and **(c)** the book value at the end of nine years. (Round to the nearest dollar.)
   a. $750 b. $7,470 c. $5,760

7. Wolfe Ltd. purchased a supercomputer for $75,000 at the beginning of 1994. The computer is classified as a five-year asset and will have a residual value of $15,000. Using MACRS, find **(a)** the depreciation amount for 1994, **(b)** the accumulated depreciation at the end of 1995, **(c)** the book value at the end of 1996, and **(d)** the last year that the asset will be depreciated.
   a. $15,000 b. $39,000 c. $21,600 d. 1999

Date ____________ Name ____________________

LU 18-1: Assigning Costs to Ending Inventory: Specific Identification; Weighted Average; FIFO; LIFO

Drill Problems

1. Given the value of the beginning inventory, purchases for the year, and the ending inventory, find the cost of goods available for sale, and the cost of goods sold.

	Beginning inventory	Purchases	Ending inventory	Cost of goods available for sale	Cost of goods sold
a.	$1,000	$4,120	$2,100	$5,120	$3,020
b.	$52,400	$270,846	$49,700	$323,246	$273,546
c.	$205	$48,445	$376	$48,650	$48,274
d.	$78,470	$2,788,560	$100,600	$2,867,030	$2,766,430
e.	$965	$53,799	$2,876	$54,764	$51,888

2. Find the missing amounts, then calculate the number of units available for sale, and the cost of the goods available for sale.

Date	Category	Quantity	Unit cost	Total cost
January 1	Beginning inventory	1,207	$45	$ 54,315
February 7	Purchase	850	$46	39,100
April 19	Purchase	700	$47	32,900
July 5	Purchase	1,050	$49	51,450
November 2	Purchase	450	$52	23,400
Goods available for sale		4,257		$201,165

3. Use the *specific identification* method to find the ending inventory and cost of goods sold for the merchandising concern in Problem 2.

Remaining inventory	Unit cost	Total cost
20 units from beginning inventory	$45	$ 900
35 units from February 7	$46	$ 1,610
257 units from July 5	$49	$ 12,593
400 units from November 2	$52	$ 20,800
Cost of ending inventory		$ 35,903
Cost of goods sold		$165,262

4. Using the *weighted-average* method, find the average cost per unit (to the nearest cent) and cost of the ending inventory.

	Units available for sale	Cost of goods available for sale	Units in ending inventory	Weighted average unit cost	Cost of ending inventory
a.	2,350	$120,320	1,265	$51.20	$64,768
b.	7,090	$151,017	1,876	$21.30	$39,958.80
c.	855	$12,790	989	$14.96	$14,795.44
d.	12,964	$125,970	9,542	$ 9.72	$92,748.24
e.	235,780	$507,398	239,013	$ 2.15	$513,877.95

5. Use the *FIFO* method of inventory valuation to determine the value of the ending inventory, which consists of 40 units, and the cost of goods sold.

Date	Category	Quantity	Unit cost	Total cost
January 1	Beginning inventory	37	$219.00	$ 8,103.00
March 5	Purchases	18	230.60	4,150.80
June 17	Purchases	22	255.70	5,625.40
October 18	Purchases	34	264.00	8,976.00
Goods available for sale		111		$26,855.20

Ending inventory = $10,510.20 Cost of goods sold = $16,345

6. Use the *LIFO* method of inventory valuation to determine the value of the ending inventory, which consists of 40 units, and the cost of goods sold.

Date	Category	Quantity	Unit cost	Total cost
January 1	Beginning inventory	37	$219.00	$ 8,103.00
March 5	Purchases	18	230.60	4,150.80
June 17	Purchases	22	255.70	5,625.40
October 18	Purchases	34	264.00	8,976.00
Goods available for sale		111		$26,855.20

Ending inventory = $8,794.80 Cost of goods sold = $18,060.40

Word Problems

7. At the beginning of September, Green's of Gloucester had an inventory of 13 yellow raincoats in stock. These raincoats cost $36.80 each. During the month, Green's purchased 14 raincoats for $37.50 each, 16 for $38.40 each, and they sold 26 raincoats. Calculate **(a)** the average unit cost (round to nearest cent) and **(b)** the ending inventory value using the weighted-average method.

   a. $37.62 b. $639.54

8. If Green's of Gloucester (Problem 7) used the FIFO method, what would the value of the ending inventory be?

   $651.90

9. If Green's of Gloucester (Problem 7) used the LIFO method, what would the value of the ending inventory be?

   $628.40

10. Hobby Caterers purchased recycled paper sketch pads during the year as follows:

January	350 pads for $0.27 each
March	400 pads for $0.31 each
July	200 pads for $0.36 each
October	850 pads for $0.26 each
November	400 pads for $0.31 each

At the end of the year, they had 775 of these sketch pads in stock. Find the ending inventory value using **(a)** the weighted-average method (round to nearest cent), **(b)** the FIFO method, and **(c)** the LIFO method.

a. $224.75 b. $221.50 c. $227.50

11. On March 1, Sandler's Shoe Store had the following sports shoes in stock:

13 pairs running shoes for $33 pair
22 pairs walking shoes for $29 pair
35 pairs aerobic shoes for $26 pair
21 pairs cross-trainers for $52 pair

During the month they sold 10 pairs of running shoes, 15 pairs of walking shoes, 28 pairs of aerobic shoes, and 12 pairs of cross-trainers. Use the specific identification method to find **(a)** the cost of the goods available for sale, **(b)** the value of the ending inventory, and **(c)** the cost of goods sold.

a. $3,069 b. $952 c. $2,117

LU 18-2: Retail Method; Gross Profit Method; Inventory Turnover; Distribution of Overhead

Drill Problems

1. Given the following information, calculate **(a)** the goods available for sale at cost and retail, **(b)** the cost ratio (to the nearest thousandth), **(c)** the ending inventory at retail, and **(d)** the cost of the March 31 inventory (to the nearest dollar) by the retail inventory method:

	Cost	Retail
Beginning inventory, March 1	$57,300	$95,500
Purchases during March	28,400	48,000
Sales during March		79,000

a. $85,700; $143,500
b. 0.597
c. $64,500
d. $38,507

2. Given the following information, use the gross profit method to calculate (**a**) cost of goods available for sale, (**b**) the cost percentage, (**c**) estimated cost of goods sold, and (**d**) estimated cost of the inventory as of April 30.

Beginning inventory, April 1	$30,000		a. $111,800
Net purchases during April	81,800		b. 60%
Sales during April	98,000		c. $58,800
Average gross profit on sales	40%		d. $53,000
Inventory, April 1		$ 30,000	
Net purchases		81,800	

3. Given the following information find the average inventory:

Merchandise inventory, January 1, 199A	$82,000	$85,000
Merchandise inventory, December 31, 199A	$88,000	

4. Given the following information, find the inventory turnover for the company in Problem 3 to the nearest hundredth:
Cost of goods sold (12/31/9A) $625,000 7.35

5. Given the following information, calculate (**a**) average inventory at retail, (**b**) average inventory at cost, (**c**) inventory turnover at retail, and (**d**) inventory turnover at cost. (Round to the nearest hundredth.)

	Cost	**Retail**	
Merchandise inventory, January 1	$ 250,000	$ 355,000	a. $342,000
Merchandise inventory, December 31	$ 235,000	$ 329,000	b. $242,500
Cost of goods sold	$1,525,000		c. 5.85
Sales		$2,001,000	d. 6.29

6. Given the floor space for the following departments, find the entire floor space and the percent each department represents:

		Percent of floor space
Department A	15,000 square feet	30%
Department B	25,000 square feet	50%
Department C	10,000 square feet	20%
Total floor space	50,000 square feet	100%

7. If the total overhead for all of the departments (Problem 6) is $200,000, how much of the overhead expense should be allocated to each department?

	Overhead/department
Department A	$ 60,000
Department B	100,000
Department C	40,000

Word Problems

8. During the accounting period, Ward's Greenery sold $290,000 of merchandise at marked retail prices. At the end of the period, the following information was available from Ward's records:

	Cost	**Retail**
Beginning inventory	$ 53,000	$ 79,000
Net purchases	204,000	280,000

Use the retail method to estimate Ward's ending inventory at cost. Round cost ratio to the nearest thousandth.
$49,404

9. On January 1, Benny's Retail Mart had a $49,000 inventory at cost. During the first quarter of the year, Benny's made net purchases of $199,900. Benny's records show that during the past several years the store's gross profit on sales has averaged 35%. If Benny's records show $275,000 in sales for the quarter, estimate the ending inventory for the first quarter using the gross profit method.
$70,150

10. On April 4, there was a big fire and the entire inventory of the R. W. Wilson Company was destroyed. The company records were salvaged, and showed the following information:

Sales (January 1 through April 4)	$127,000
Merchandise inventory, January 1	16,000
Net purchases	71,250

On January 1, the inventory was priced to sell for $38,000, and additional items bought during the period were priced to sell for $102,000. Calculate the cost of the inventory that was destroyed by the fire using the retail method. Round cost ratio to the nearest thousandth.
$8,099

11. During the past four years, the average gross margin on sales for the R. W. Wilson Company was 36% of net sales. Using the data in Problem 10, calculate the cost of the ending inventory destroyed by fire using the gross profit method.
$5,970

12. The Chase Bank has to make a decision on whether to grant a loan to the Sally's Furniture Store. The lending officer is interested in how often Sally's inventory is turned over. Using selected information from Sally's income statement, calculate the inventory turnover for Sally's Furniture Store (to nearest hundredth).

Merchandise inventory, January 1, 199A	$ 43,000
Merchandise inventory, December 31, 199A	55,000
Cost of goods sold	128,000

2.61 times

13. Wanting to know more about a business he was considering buying, Jake Paige studied the business's books. He found that beginning inventory for the previous year was $51,000 at cost and $91,800 at retail, ending inventory was $44,000 at cost and $72,600 at retail, sales were $251,000, and cost of goods sold was $154,000. Using this information, calculate for Jake the inventory turnover at cost and the inventory turnover at retail.
3.24 times (at cost)
3.05 times (at retail)

14. Ralph's Retail Outlet has calculated its expenses for the year. Total overhead expenses are $147,000. Ralph's accountant must allocate this overhead to four different departments. Given the following information regarding the floor space occupied by each department, calculate how much overhead expense should be allocated to each department.

Department W	12,000 square feet	$42,000
Department X	9,000 square feet	31,500
Department Y	14,000 square feet	49,000
Department Z	7,000 square feet	24,500

15. How much overhead would be allocated to each department of Ralph's Retail Outlet (Problem 14) if the basis of allocation was the sales of each department? Sales for each of the departments were:

Department W	$110,000	$32,340
Department X	$120,000	$35,280
Department Y	$170,000	$49,980
Department Z	$100,000	$29,400

Date ____________ Name ____________

LU 19–1: Sales and Excise Taxes

Drill Problems

1. Calculate the sales tax and the total amount due for each of the following:

	Total sales	Sales tax rate	Sales tax	Total amount due
a.	$536	5%	$26.80	$562.80
b.	$11,980	6%	$718.80	$12,698.80
c.	$3,090	$8\frac{1}{4}\%$	$254.93	$3,344.93
d.	$17.65	$5\frac{1}{2}\%$	$0.97	$18.62
e.	$294	7.42%	$21.81	$315.81

2. Find the amount of actual sales and amount of sales tax on the following total receipts.

	Total receipts	Sales tax rate	Actual sales	Sales tax
a.	$27,932.15	5.5%	$26,475.97	$1,456.18
b.	$35,911.53	7%	$33,562.18	$2,349.35
c.	$115,677.06	$6\frac{1}{2}\%$	$108,616.95	$7,060.11
d.	$142.96	$5\frac{1}{4}\%$	$135.83	$7.13
e.	$5,799.24	4.75%	$5,536.27	$262.97

3. Find the sales tax, excise tax, and the total cost for each of the following items:

	Retail price	Sales tax, 5.2%	Excise tax, 11%	Total cost
a.	$399	$20.75	$43.89	$463.64
b.	$22,684	$1,179.57	$2,495.24	$26,358.81
c.	$7,703	$400.56	$847.33	$8,950.89

4. For each of the following sales amounts, use Table 19–1 to show the amount-of-sale range and the sales tax amount.

	Total sales	Amount of sale range	Sales tax amount
a.	$28.75	28.70–28.89	$1.44
b.	$7.39	7.30–7.49	$.37
c.	$14.00	13.90–14.09	$0.70
d.	$11.30	11.30–11.49	$0.57
e.	$24.89	24.70–24.89	$1.24

5. Calculate the amount, subtotal, sales tax, and total amount due:

Quantity	Description	Unit price	Amount
3	Taxable item	$4.30	$12.90
2	Taxable item	5.23	10.46
4	Taxable item	1.20	4.80
		subtotal	$28.16
		5% sales tax	1.41
		Total	$29.57

6. Given the sales tax rate and the amount of the sales tax, calculate the price of the purchase (before tax was added).

	Tax rate	Tax amount	Price of purchase
a.	7%	$71.61	$1,023
b.	$5\frac{1}{2}\%$	$ 3.22	$58.55

7. Given the sales tax rate and the total price (including tax), calculate the price of the purchase (before the tax was added).

	Tax rate	Total price	Price of purchase
a.	5%	$ 340.20	$ 324
b.	6%	$1,224.30	$1,155

Word Problems

8. In a state with a 4.75% sales tax, what would be the sales tax and the total price of a video game marked $110?
$5.23 sales tax $115.23 total price

9. Browning's invoice included a sales tax of $38.15. If the sales tax rate is 6%, what was the total cost of the taxable goods on the invoice?
$635.83

10. David Bowan paid a total of $2,763 for a new computer. If this includes a sales tax of 5.3%, what was the marked price of the computer?
$2,623.93

11. After a 5% sales tax and a 12% excise tax, the total cost of a leather jacket was $972. What was the selling price of the jacket?
$830.77

12. A customer at the RDM Discount Store purchased four tubes of toothpaste priced at $1.88 each, six toothbrushes for $1.69 each, and three bottles of shampoo for $2.39 each. What did the customer have to pay, if the sales tax is $5\frac{1}{2}$%?
$26.20

13. Bill Harrington purchased a mountain bike for $875. Bill had to pay a sales tax of 6% and an excise tax of 11%. What was the total amount Bill had to pay for his mountain bike?
$1,023.75

14. Donna DeCoff received a bill for $754 for a new chair she had purchased. The bill included a 6.2% sales tax, and a delivery charge of $26. What was the selling price of the chair?
$685.50

LU 19-2: Property Tax

Drill Problems

1. Find the assessed valuation of the following properties (round to the nearest whole dollar).

	Market value	Assessment rate	Assessed valuation
a.	$195,000	35%	$68,250
b.	1,550,900	50%	775,450
c.	75,000	75%	56,250
d.	2,585,400	65%	1,680,510
e.	349,500	85%	297,075

2. Find the tax rate for each of the following municipalities (round to the nearest tenth of a percent).

	Budget needed	Total assessed value	Tax rate
a.	$2,594,000	$44,392,000	5.8%
b.	17,989,000	221,900,000	8.1%
c.	6,750,000	47,635,000	14.2%
d.	13,540,000	143,555,500	9.4%
e.	1,099,000	12,687,000	8.7%

3. Express each of the following tax rates in all of the indicated forms:

	By percent	Per $100 of assessed valuation	Per $1,000 of assessed valuation	In mills
a.	7.45%	$7.45	$74.50	74.50
b.	14.24%	$14.24	$142.40	142.40
c.	9.08%	$9.08	$90.80	90.8
d.	6.2%	$6.20	$62.00	62

4. Calculate the property tax due for each of the following:

	Total assessed valuation	Tax rate	Total property tax due
a.	$12,900	$6.60 per $100	$851.40
b.	$175,400	43 mills	$7,542.20
c.	$320,500	2.7%	$8,653.50
d.	$2,480,000	$17.85 per $1,000	$44,268.00
e.	$78,900	59 mills	$4,655.10
f.	$225,550	$11.39 per $1,000	$2,569.01
g.	$198,750	$2.63 per $100	$5,227.13

Word Problems

5. The county of Chelsea approved a budget of $3,450,000, which would have to be raised through property taxation. If the total assessed value of properties in the county of Chelsea is $37,923,854, what will the tax rate be? The tax rate is stated per $100 of assessed valuation.
   $9.10

6. Linda Tawse lives in Camden and her home has a market value of $235,000. Property in Camden is assessed at 55% of its market value and the tax rate for the current year is $64.75 per $1,000. What is the assessed valuation of Linda's home?
   $129,250

7. Using the information in Problem 6 find the amount of property tax that Linda will have to pay.
   $8,368.94

8. Mary Faye Souza has property with a fair market value of $219,500. Property in Mary Faye's city is assessed at 65% of its market value and the tax rate is $3.64 per $100. How much is Mary Faye's property tax due?
   $5,193.37

9. Cagney's Greenhouse has a fair market value of $1,880,000. Property is assessed at 35% by the city. The tax rate is 6.4%. What is the property tax due for Cagney's Greenhouse?
   $42,112

10. In Chester County, property is assessed at 40% of its market value; the residential tax rate is $12.30 per $1,000, and the commercial tax rate is $13.85 per $1,000. What is the property tax due on a home that has a market value of $205,000?
    $1,008.60

11. Using the information in Problem 10, find the property tax due on a grocery store with a market value of $5,875,000.
    $32,547.50

12. Bob Rose's home is assessed at $195,900. Last year the tax rate was 11.8 mills and this year it was raised to 13.2 mills. How much more will Bob have to pay in taxes this year?
    $274.26

Date ______________ Name ______________

LU 20–1: Life Insurance

Drill Problems

1. Use the table in the Business Math Handbook to find the annual premium per $1,000 of life insurance and calculate the annual premiums for each policy listed. (Assume insured are males.)

	Face value of policy	Type of insurance	Age at issue	Annual premium per $1,000	Number of $1,000's in face value	Annual premium
a.	$25,000	Straight	31	$9.27	25	$231.75
b.	$40,500	20-year endowment	40	$33.36	40.5	$1,351.08
c.	$200,000	Straight	44	$17.86	200	$3,572
d.	$62,500	20-payment	25	$9.91	62.5	$619.38
e.	$12,250	5-year term	35	$2.23	12.25	$27.32
f.	$42,500	20-year endowment	42	$36.59	42.5	$1,555.08

2. Use Table 20–1 to find the annual premium for each of the following life insurance policies. Assume the insured is a 30-year old male.

	Face value of policy	Five-year term policy	Straight life policy	Twenty-payment life policy	Twenty-year endowment
a.	$50,000	$93.50	$442.50	$602.50	$1,045.00
b.	$1,000,000	$1,870.00	$8,850.00	$12,050.00	$20,900.00
c.	$250,000	$467.50	$2,212.50	$3,012.50	$5,225.00
d.	$72,500	$135.58	$641.63	$873.63	$1,515.25

3. Use the table in the Business Math Handbook to find the annual premium for each of the following life insurance policies. Assume the insured is a 30-year old female.

	Face value of policy	Five-year term policy	Straight life policy	Twenty-payment life policy	Twenty-year endowment
a.	$50,000	$93.00	$387.50	$535.00	$916.50
b.	$1,000,000	$1,860.00	$7,750.00	$10,700.00	$18,330.00
c.	$250,000	$465.00	$1,937.50	$2,675.00	$4,582.50
d.	$72,500	$134.85	$561.88	$775.75	$1,328.93

4. Use the table in the Business Math Handbook to find the nonforfeiture options for the following policies:

	Years policy in force	Type of policy	Face value	Cash value	Amount of paid-up insurance	Extended term
a.	10	Straight life	$25,000	$2,400	$6,475	18 yrs 76 dy
b.	20	20-year endow.	500,000	$500,000	$500,000	Life
c.	5	20-payment life	2,000,000	$142,000	$440,000	19 yrs 190 dy
d.	15	Straight life	750,000	$111,000	$278,250	20 yrs 165 dy
e.	5	20-year endow.	93,500	$8,602	$21,411.50	23 yrs 140 dy

Word Problems

5. If Mr. Davis, aged 39, buys a $90,000 straight life insurance policy, what is the amount of his annual premium?
$1,242.90

6. If Miss Jennie McDonald, age 27, takes out a $65,000 20-year endowment policy, what premium amount will she pay each year?
$1,043.25

7. If Gary Thomas decides to cash in his $45,000 20-payment life insurance policy after 15 years, what cash surrender value will he receive?
$14,265

8. Mary Allyn purchased a $70,000 20-year endowment policy when she was 26 years old. Ten years later, she decided that she could no longer afford the premiums. If Mary decides to convert her policy to paid-up insurance, what amount of paid-up insurance coverage will she have?
$36,400

9. Peter and Jane Rizzo are both 28 years old and are both planning to take out $50,000 straight life insurance policies. What is the difference in the annual premiums they will have to pay?
$47.50

10. Paul Nasser purchased a $125,000 straight life policy when he was 30 years old. He is now 50 years old. Two months ago, he slipped in the bath tub and injured his back; he will not be able to return to his regular job for several months. Due to a lack of income, he feels that he can no longer continue paying the premiums on his life insurance policy. If Mr. Nasser decides to surrender his policy for cash, how much cash will he receive?
$33,125

11. If Mr. Nasser (Problem 10) chooses to convert his policy to paid-up insurance, what will the face value of his new policy be?
$68,750

LU 20–2: Fire Insurance

Drill Problems

1. Use the tables in the Business Math Handbook to find the premium for each of the following:

	Rating of area	Building class	Building value	Contents value	Total annual premium
a.	3	A	$80,000	$32,000	$488
b.	2	B	$340,000	$202,000	$2,912
c.	2	A	$221,700	$190,000	$1,624.61
d.	1	B	$96,400	$23,400	$521.60
e.	3	B	$65,780	$62,000	$804.26

2. Use the tables in the Business Math Handbook to find the amount of refund due if insured cancels:

	Annual premium	Months of coverage	Short-term premium	Refund due
a.	$1,860	3	$651	$1,209
b.	$650	7	$435.50	$214.50
c.	$1,200	10	$1,044	$156
d.	$341	12	$341	None
e.	$1,051	4	$462.44	$588.56

3. Find the amount to be paid for each of the following losses:

	Property value	Coinsurance clause	Insurance required	Insurance carried	Amount of loss	Insurance company pays (indemnity)
a.	$85,000	80%	$68,000	$70,000	$60,000	$60,000
b.	$52,000	80%	$41,600	$45,000	$50,000	$45,000
c.	$44,000	80%	$35,200	$33,000	$33,000	$30,937.50
d.	$182,000	80%	$145,600	$127,400	$61,000	$53,375

Word Problems

4. Mary Rose wants to purchase fire insurance for her building, which is rated as Class B; the rating of the area is 2. If her building is worth $225,000, and the contents are worth $70,000, what will her annual premium be?
$1,545

5. Janet Ambrose owns a Class A building valued at $180,000. The contents of the building are valued at $145,000. The territorial rating is 3. What is her annual fire insurance premium?
$1,463

6. Jack Altshuler owns a building worth $355,500. The contents are worth $120,000. The classification of the building is B, and the rating of the area is 1. What annual premium must Jack pay for his fire insurance?
$2,105.55

7. Jay Viola owns a store valued at $460,000. His fire insurance policy (which has an 80% coinsurance clause) has a face value of $345,000. A recent fire resulted in a loss of $125,000. How much will the insurance company pay?
$117,187.50

8. The building which is owned by Tally's Garage is valued at $275,000 and is insured for $225,000. The policy has an 80% coinsurance clause. If there was a fire in the building and the damages amount to $175,000, how much of the loss will be paid for by the insurance company?
$220,000

9. Michael Dannon owns a building worth $420,000. He has a fire insurance policy with a face value of $336,000 (there is an 80% coinsurance clause). There was recently a fire which resulted in a $400,000 loss. How much money will he receive from the insurance company?
$336,000

10. Rice's Rent-A-Center business is worth $375,000. He has purchased a $250,000 fire insurance policy. The policy has an 80% coinsurance clause. What will Rice's reimbursement be **(a)** after a $150,000 fire? and **(b)** after a $330,000 fire?
a. $125,000 b. $250,000

11. If Maria's Pizza Shop is valued at $210,000 and is insured for $147,000 with a policy that contains an 80% coinsurance clause, what settlement is due after a fire that causes **(a)** $150,000 in damages? and **(b)** $175,000 in damages?
a. $131,250 b. $147,000

LU 20-3: Auto Insurance

Drill Problems

1. Calculate the annual premium for compulsory coverage for each of the following:

Driver classification	Bodily	Property	Total premium
a. 17	$98	$160	$258
b. 20	$116	$186	$302
c. 10	$55	$129	$184

2. Calculate the amount of money the insurance company and the driver should pay for each of the following accidents assuming the driver carries compulsory insurance only.

Accident and court award	Insurance company pays	Driver pays
a. Driver hit one person and court awarded $15,000	$10,000	$5,000
b. Driver hit one person and court awarded $12,000 for personal injury	$10,000	$2,000
c. Driver hit two people; court awarded first person $9,000 and the second person $12,000	$19,000	$2,000

3. Calculate the additional premium payment for each of the following options:

Optional insurance coverage	Addition to premium
a. Bodily injury 50/100/25, driver class 20	$312
b. Bodily injury 25/60/5, driver class 17	$229
c. Collision insurance, driver class 10, age group 3, symbol 5, deductible $100	$181
d. Comprehensive insurance, driver class 10, age group 3, symbol 5, deductible $200	$59
e. Substitute transportation, towing and labor driver class 10, age group 3, symbol 5	$20

4. Compute the annual premium for compulsory insurance with optional liability coverage for bodily injury and damage to someone else's property.

	Driver classification	Bodily coverage	Premium
a.	17	50/100/25	$528
b.	20	100/300/10	$661
c.	10	25/60/25	$365
d.	18	250/500/50	$601
e.	20	25/50/5	$554

5. Calculate the annual premium for each of the following drivers with the indicated options. All drivers must carry compulsory insurance.

	Driver classification	Car age	Car symbol	Bodily injury	Collision	Comprehensive	Transportation and towing	Annual premium
a.	10	2	4	50/100/10	$100 deductible	$300 deductible	yes	$647
b.	18	3	2	25/60/25	$200 deductible	$200 deductible	yes	$706

Word Problems

6. Ann Centerino's driver classification is 10. She carries only compulsory insurance coverage. What annual insurance premium must she pay?
$184

7. Gary Hines is a class 18 driver. He wants to add optional bodily injury and property damage of 250/500/50 to his compulsory insurance coverage. What is Gary's total annual premium?
$601

8. Sara Goldberg wants optional bodily injury coverage of 50/100/25 and collision coverage with a deductible of $300 in addition to the compulsory coverage her state requires. Sara is a class 17 driver and has a symbol 4 car that is 2 years old. What annual premium must Sara pay?
$688

9. Karen Babson has just purchased a new car with a symbol of 8. She wants bodily injury and property liability of 500/1,000/100, comprehensive and collision insurance with a $200 deductible, and transportation and towing coverage. If Karen is a class 10 driver, what is her annual insurance premium? There is no compulsory insurance requirement in her state. Assume age group 1.
$781

10. Craig Haberland is a class 18 driver. He has a 5-year old car with a symbol of 4. His state requires compulsory insurance coverage. In addition to this, he wishes to purchase collision and comprehensive coverage with the maximum deductible. He also wants towing insurance. What will Craig's annual insurance premium be?
$415

11. Nancy Poland has an insurance policy with limits of 10/20. If Nancy injures a pedestrian and the judge awards damages of $18,000, **(a)** how much will the insurance company pay? and **(b)** how much will Nancy pay?
a. $10,000 b. $8,000

12. Peter Bell carries insurance with bodily injury limits of 25/60. Peter is in an accident and is charged with injuring four people. The judge awards damages of $10,000 to each of the injured parties. How much will the insurance company pay? How much will Peter pay?
Company pays $40,000. Peter pays $0.

13. Jerry Greeley carries an insurance policy with bodily injury limits of 25/60. Jerry is in an accident and is charged with injuring four people. If the judge awards damages of $20,000 to each of the injured parties, **(a)** how much will the insurance company pay? and **(b)** how much will Jerry pay?
a. $60,000 b. $20,000

Date ____________ Name ____________

LU 21-1: Stocks

Drill Problems

52 weeks Hi	Lo	Stocks	Sym	Div	Yld %	PE	Vol 100s	High	Low	Close	Net chg
$20\frac{7}{8}$	16	BostCelts	BOS	2.25	11.0	14	13	$20\frac{5}{8}$	$20\frac{1}{4}$	$20\frac{1}{2}$	$+\frac{1}{8}$

1. From the listed information for the Boston Celtics, complete the following:

   a. $20.875 was the highest price at which the Boston Celtics stock traded during the year.
   b. $16.00 was the lowest price at which the Boston Celtics stock traded during the year.
   c. $2.25 was the amount of the dividend the Boston Celtics paid to their shareholders last year.
   d. $225.00 is the amount a shareholder with 100 shares would receive.
   e. $11.0% is the rate of return the stock yielded to its stockholders.
   f. 14 is how many times the earnings per share the stock is selling for.
   g. 1,300 is the number of shares traded on the day of this stock quote.
   h. $20.625 is the highest price paid for Celtics stock on this day.
   i. $20.25 is the lowest price paid for Celtics stock on this day.
   j. $.125 inc is the change in price from yesterday's closing price.

2. Use the Celtics information to show how the yield percent was calculated.
   11.0%
3. Use the listing information to calculate the earnings per share for the Boston Celtics stock.
   $1.46
4. What was the price of the last trade of Boston Celtics stock yesterday?
   $20.375

Word Problems

5. Assume a stockbroker commission of 2% for round lots plus 1% extra on odd lots. What will it cost **(a)** to purchase 400 shares of Boston Celtics stock at $20\frac{1}{2}$ and **(b)** to purchase 350 shares at the same market price?
   a. $8,364 b. $7,328.75
6. In Problem 5, the stockbroker's commission for selling stock is the same as for buying stock. If the customer who purchased the 400 shares at $20\frac{1}{2}$ sells the 400 shares of stock at the end of the year at 27, what will be the return on the investment (to the nearest tenth percent)? The dividend was the same this year as last.
   37.3%
7. Holtz Corporation's records show 80,000 shares of preferred stock issued. The preferred dividend is $2 per share, which is cumulative. The records show 750,000 shares of common stock issued. In 1994, no dividends were paid. In 1995, the board of directors declared a dividend of $582,500. What is **(a)** the total amount of dividends paid to preferred stockholders? **(b)** the total amount of dividends paid to common stockholders? and **(c)** the amount of the common dividend per share?
   a. $320,000 b. $262,500 c. $0.35
8. Melissa Tucker bought 300 shares of Delta Air Lines stock listed at $59\frac{5}{8}$ per share. What is the total amount she paid if the stockbroker's commission is 2.5%?
   $18,334.69
9. A year later, Melissa (Problem 8) sold the stock she had purchased. The market price of the stock at this time was $77\frac{3}{8}$. Delta Air Lines had paid its shareholders a dividend of $1.20 per share. If the stockbroker's commission to sell stock is 2.5%, what rate of return did Melissa earn on her stock?
   25.4%
10. The board of directors of Parker Electronics Inc. declared a $539,000 dividend. If the corporation has 70,000 shares of common stock outstanding, what is the dividend per share?
    $7.70

LU 21-2: Bonds

Drill Problems

Bond	Current yield	Sales	High	Low	Close	Net change
IBM $10\frac{1}{4}$95	10.0	11	103	$101\frac{3}{4}$	$102\frac{1}{2}$	$+\frac{1}{8}$

1. From the bond listing above complete the following:
   a. IBM is the name of the company.
   b. $10\frac{1}{4}$ is the percent of interest paid on the bond.
   c. 1995 is the year the bond matures.
   d. $102.50 is the total interest for the year. (.1025 × $1,000 = $102.50)
   e. $102\frac{3}{8}$ was yesterday's close on the IBM bond.
2. Show how to calculate the current yield of 10.0% for IBM. (Trade commissions have been omitted.)
   10.0%
3. Use the information for the IBM bonds to calculate **(a)** the amount the highest bond was traded for on this day, **(b)** the amount the lowest bond traded for on this day, **(c)** the amount the last bond traded for on this day, and **(d)** the amount the last bond traded for yesterday.
   a. $1,030 b. $1,017.50 c. $1,025 d. $1,023.75
4. What will be the annual interest payment **(a)** to the bondholder who purchased the lowest bond ($101\frac{3}{4}$)? and **(b)** to the bondholder who purchased the last bond ($102\frac{1}{2}$)?
   a. $102.50 b. $102.50
5. If Terry Gambol purchased three IBM bonds at this day's closing price, **(a)** what would be her total cost excluding commission and **(b)** how much interest will she receive for the year?
   a. $3,075 b. $307.50
6. Calculate the bond yield (to the nearest tenth percent) for each of the following:

	Bond interest rate	Purchase price	Bond yield
a.	7%	97	7.2%
b.	$9\frac{1}{2}$%	$101\frac{5}{8}$	9.3%
c.	$13\frac{1}{4}$%	$104\frac{1}{4}$	12.7%

7. For each of the following, state whether the bond sold at a premium or a discount and give the amount of the premium or discount.

	Bond interest rate	Purchase price	Premium/discount
a.	7%	97	$30 discount
b.	$9\frac{1}{2}$%	$101\frac{5}{8}$	$16.25 premium
c.	$13\frac{1}{4}$%	$104\frac{1}{4}$	$42.50 premium

Word Problems

8. If Rob Morrissey purchased a $1,000 bond that was quoted at $102\frac{1}{4}$ and paying $8\frac{7}{8}$% interest, **(a)** how much did Rob pay for the bond? **(b)** what was the premium or discount? **(c)** how much annual interest will he receive?
   a. $1,022.50 b. $22.50 c. $88.75
9. If Jackie Anderson purchased a bond that was quoted at $62\frac{1}{2}$ and paying interest of $10\frac{1}{2}$%, **(a)** how much did Jackie pay for the bond? **(b)** what was the premium or discount? **(c)** what is the interest Jackie will receive annually? and **(d)** what is the bond's current annual yield (to the nearest tenth percent)?
   a. $625 b. $375 c. $105 d. 16.8%

10. The Swartz Company issued bonds totaling $2,000,000 in order to purchase updated equipment. If the bonds pay interest of 11%, what is the total amount of interest the Swartz Company must pay semiannually?
$110,000

11. The RJR and ACyan companies have both issued bonds that are paying $7\frac{3}{8}$% interest. The quoted price of the RJR bond is $94\frac{1}{8}$ and the quoted price of the ACyan bond is $102\frac{7}{8}$. Find the current annual yield on each (to the nearest tenth percent).
7.8% yield for RJR bond 7.2% yield for ACyan

12. Mary Rowe purchased 25 bonds of Chrysler Corporation $8\frac{3}{8}$% bonds of 1997. The bonds closed at $93\frac{1}{4}$. Find **(a)** the total purchase price and **(b)** the amount of the first semiannual interest payment Mary will receive.
a. $23,312.50 **b.** $1,046.88

13. What is the annual yield (to the nearest hundredth percent) of the bonds Mary Rowe purchased?
8.98%

14. Mary Rowe purchased a $1,000 bond listed as ARch $10\frac{7}{8}$05 for $122\frac{3}{4}$. What is the annual yield of this bond (to the nearest tenth percent)?
8.9%

Date ____________ Name ____________

LU 22-1: Mean, Median, and Mode

Drill Problems

1. Find the mean for the following lists of numbers. Round to the nearest hundredth.
   a. 12, 16, 20, 25, 29 Mean 20.4
   b. 80, 91, 98, 82, 68, 82, 79, 90 Mean 83.75
   c. 9.5, 12.3, 10.5, 7.5, 10.1, 18.4, 9.8, 6.2, 11.1, 4.8, 10.6 Mean 10.07
2. Find the weighted mean of the following. Round to the nearest hundredth.
   a. 4, 4, 6, 8, 8, 13, 4, 6, 8 Weighted mean 6.78
   b. 82, 85, 87, 82, 82, 90, 87, 63, 100, 85, 87 Weighted mean 84.55
3. Find the median for the following.
   a. 56, 89, 47, 36, 90, 63, 55, 82, 46, 81 Median 59.5
   b. 59, 22, 39, 47, 33, 98, 50, 73, 54, 46, 99 Median 50
4. Find the mode for the following.
   24, 35, 49, 35, 52, 35, 52 Mode 35
5. Find the mean, median, and mode for each of the following:
   a. 72, 48, 62, 54, 73, 62, 75, 57, 62, 58, 78
      Mean 63.7 Median 62 Mode 62
   b. $0.50, $1.19, $0.58, $1.19, $2.83, $1.71, $2.21, $0.58, $1.29, $0.58
      Mean $1.27 Median $1.19 Mode $0.58
   c. $92, $113, $99, $117, $99, $105, $119, $112, $95, $116, $102, $120
      Mean $107.42 Median $108.50 Mode $99
   d. 88, 105, 120, 119, 105, 128, 160, 151, 90, 153, 107, 119, 105
      Mean 119.23 Median 119 Mode 105

Word Problems

6. The sales for the year at the 8 Bed and Linen Stores were $1,442,897, $1,556,793, $1,703,767, $1,093,320, $1,443,984, $1,665,308, $1,197,692, and $1,880,433. Find the mean earnings for a Bed and Linen Store for the year.
   $1,498,025.20
7. In order to avoid having an extreme number effect the average, the manager of the Bed and Linen Stores (Problem 6) would like you to find the median earnings for the 8 stores.
   $1,500,388.50
8. The Bed and Linen Store in Salem sells many different towels. Following are the prices of all of the towels that were sold on Wednesday: $7.98, $9.98, $9.98, $11.49, $11.98, $7.98, $12.49, $12.49, $11.49, $9.98, $9.98, $16.00, and $7.98. Find the mean price of a towel.
   $10.75
9. Looking at the towel prices, the Salem manager (Problem 8) decided that he should have calculated a weighted mean. Find the weighted mean price of a towel.
   $10.75
10. The manager of the Salem Bed and Linen Store above would like to find another measure of the central tendency called the median. Find the median price for the towels sold.
    $9.98
11. The manager at the Salem Bed and Linen Store would like to know the most popular towel among the group of towels sold on Wednesday. Find the mode for the towel prices for Wednesday.
    $9.98

LU 22-2: Frequency Distributions and Graphs

Drill Problems

1. A local dairy distributor wants to know many containers of yogurt health club members consume in a month. The distributor gathered the following data:

17	17	22	14	26	23	23	15	18	16
18	15	23	18	29	20	24	17	12	15
18	19	18	20	28	21	25	21	26	14
16	18	15	19	27	15	22	19	19	13
20	17	13	24	28	18	28	20	17	16

Construct a frequency distribution table to organize this data.

18   卌 ||

2. Construct a bar graph for the Problem 1 data. The height of each bar should represent the frequency of each amount consumed.

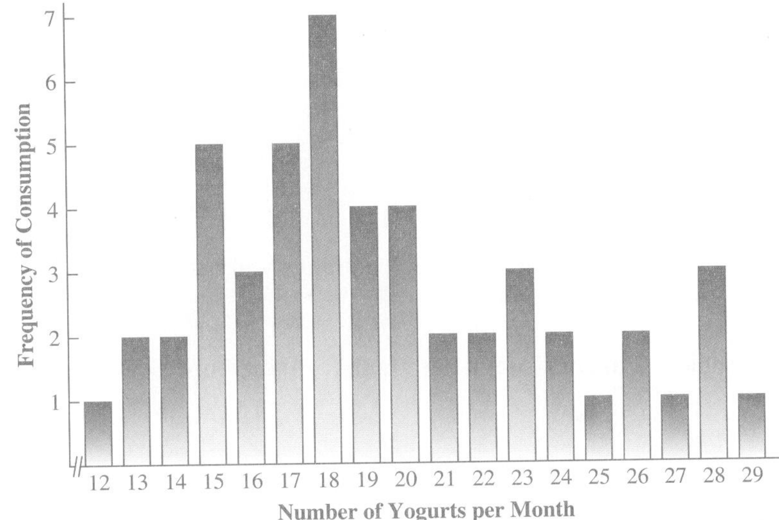

3. To simplify the amount of data concerning yogurt consumption, construct a relative frequency distribution table. The range will be from 1 to 30 with five class intervals: 1–6, 7–12, 13–18, 19–24, and 25–30.

25–30   卌 ||| 8

4. Construct a bar graph for the grouped data.

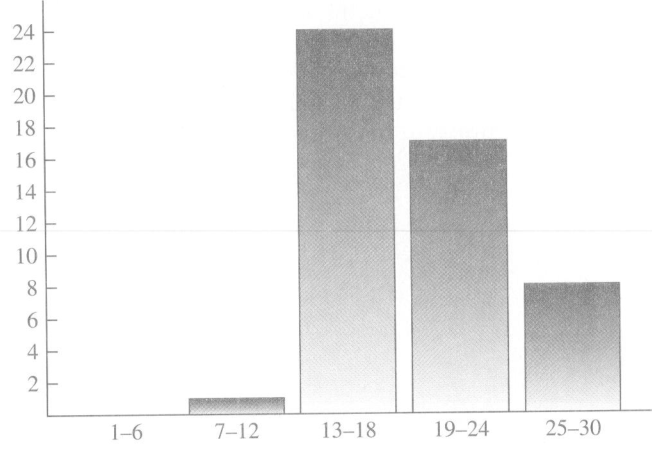

5. Prepare a pie chart to represent the above data.

7–12 $\frac{1}{50} \times 360° = 7.2°$

Word Problems

6. The women's department of a local department store lists its total sales for the year: January $39,800, February $22,400, March $32,500, April $33,000, May $30,000, June $29,200, July $26,400, August $24,800, September $34,000, October $34,200, November $38,400, December $41,100. Draw a line graph to represent the monthly sales of the women's department for the year. The vertical axis should represent the dollar amount of the sales.

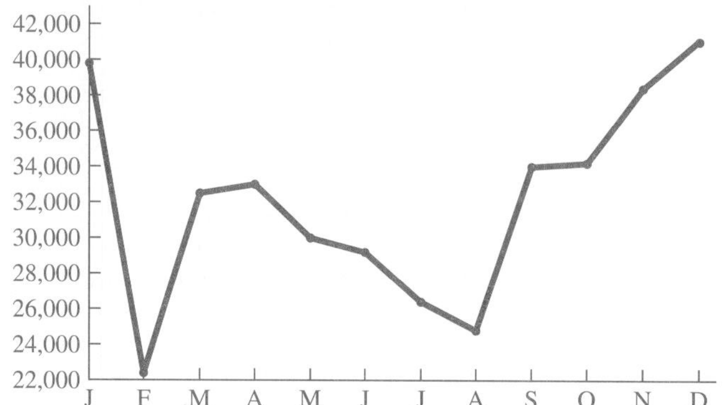

7. The following list shows the number of television sets sold in a year by the sales associates at Sousa's TV and Appliance Store.

115	125	139	127	142	153	169	126	141
130	137	150	169	157	146	173	168	156
140	146	134	123	142	129	141	122	141

Construct a relative frequency distribution table to represent the data. The range will be from 115 to 174 with intervals of 10.

145–154 |||| 4

8. Use the data in the distribution table for Problem 7 to construct a bar graph for the grouped data.

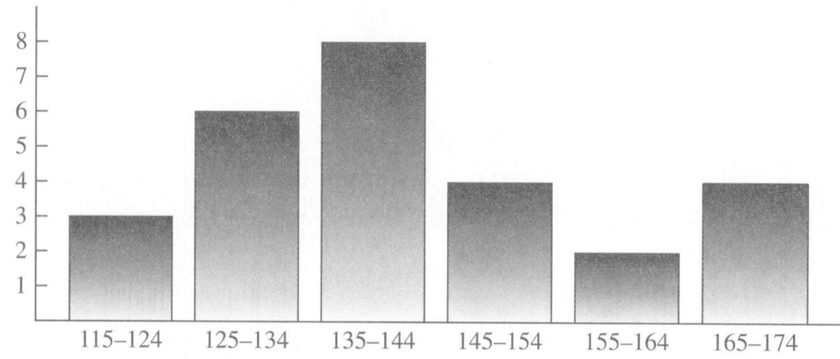

9. Expenses for the Flora Foley Real Estate Agency for the month of June were as follows: salaries expense $2,790, utilities expense $280, rent expense $2,000, commissions expense $4,800, other expenses $340. Present this data in a circle graph. (First calculate the percent relationship between each item and the total, then determine the number of degrees that represent each item.)

98.4° 9.9° 70.5° 169.2° 11.9°

Check Figures

CHECK FIGURES FOR:

1. **Odd Drill and Word Problems (includes Additional Sets and Challenge Problem).**
2. **Summary Practice Tests (all).**
3. **Cumulative Reviews (all).**
4. **Odd Additional Assignments by Learning Unit.**

Check Figures to Drill and Word Problems (Odds), Summary Practice Tests, and Cumulative Reviews

Chapter 1
End-of-Chapter Problems

1–1. 103
1–3. 194
1–5. 14,201
1–7. 101,484
1–9. 52
1–11. 1,700
1–13. 1,074
1–15. 31,110
1–17. 177,576
1–19. 126,000
1–21. 80
1–23. 45R1
1–25. 202
1–27. 1,616
1–29. 24,816
1–31. 18,000; 17,989
1–33. 80
1–35. 105
1–37. 216
1–39. 19 R21
1–41. 842
1–43. 2,526
1–45. 7,690; 6,990
1–47. 63,000; 66,740
1–49. 700
1–51. $75 for week
1–53. 2,050 shares
1–55. $1,060
1–57. $19,780
1–59. 3,445 shares; $62,010
1–61. 84
1–63. 1 mile per gallon
1–65. 1,312; $57,728
1–67. 93,000 cans; $1,116,000
1–69. 410 customers, $2,870 week; $149,240 year
1–71. $114,000
1–73. $18,388
1–75. $2,595; $519
1–77. $24,086
1–79. $137,900
1–81. $72; $272
1–83. No; $33
1–85. Buy at Sears $85
1–87. $21 per square yard
1–89. $12,000 difference

Summary Practice Test

1. 8,022,346
2. Six million, eight hundred fifteen thousand, five hundred sixty-nine
3. **a.** 50 **b.** 700 **c.** 8,000 **d.** 10,000
4. 15,000; 14,484
5. 3,000,000; 3,182,760
6. 751,810,000
7. 225 R6
8. 10
9. $91
10. $875
11. 31 houses
12. $400

Chapter 2
End-of-Chapter Problems

2–1. P
2–3. I
2–5. $66\frac{1}{4}$
2–7. $\frac{115}{8}$
2–9. $\frac{11}{13}$
2–11. 72 $(2 \times 3 \times 3 \times 4)$
2–13. 60 $(2 \times 2 \times 3 \times 5)$
2–15. $\frac{7}{9}$
2–17. $15\frac{5}{12}$
2–19. $\frac{5}{9}$
2–21. $7\frac{4}{9}$
2–23. $\frac{5}{16}$
2–25. $\frac{3}{25}$
2–27. $\frac{11}{24}$
2–29. $\frac{7}{18}$
2–31. $1\frac{173}{275}$
2–33. $300\frac{11}{24}$ gallons more
2–35. $4\frac{3}{8}$ pounds
2–37. $32\frac{1}{4}$ hours
2–39. $\frac{3}{8}$ cup margarine; 1 egg; $\frac{1}{2}$ teaspoon vanilla; $1\frac{1}{8}$ cups flour $\frac{1}{2}$ teaspoon soda; $\frac{2}{3}$ cup brown sugar; $\frac{1}{4}$ teaspoon salt; $\frac{1}{2}$ cup M&M's®; $\frac{1}{4}$ cup nuts
2–41. $398\frac{1}{8}$ feet
2–43. $\frac{21}{40}$ of a ton
2–45. $193,750
2–47. 60 guests
2–49. $54
2–51. $60
2–53. $3\frac{3}{4}$ pounds of apples; $8\frac{1}{8}$ cups flour; $\frac{5}{8}$ cup margarine; $5\frac{15}{16}$ cups sugar; 5 tsp. of cinnamon
2–55. $79\frac{3}{8}$ gallons less
2–57. $16,500
2–59. 275 gloves
2–61. $2\frac{37}{40}$ hours over
2–63. $\$51\frac{1}{8}$
2–65. $4\frac{1}{2}$ pounds
2–67. 4,960 bags
2–69. 900 people
2–71. $7\frac{1}{2}$ ounces chocolate chips; $6\frac{3}{4}$ cups flour; $\frac{3}{5}$ cup margarine; $3\frac{3}{4}$ cups of sugar; 12 eggs
2–73. $12,000
2–75. **a.** 400 homes; **b.** $320,000; **c.** 3,000 people; 2,500 people; **d.** $112.50 **e.** $8,800,000

Summary Practice Test

1. M
2. P
3. I
4. $17\frac{1}{7}$
5. $\frac{33}{4}$
6. $\frac{19}{32}$
7. 126
8. 40 $(2 \times 2 \times 5 \times 1 \times 1 \times 1 \times 2)$
9. $4\frac{11}{16}$
10. $\frac{5}{26}$
11. $3\frac{69}{76}$
12. $\frac{1}{9}$
13. 3 hours

14. $364\frac{1}{2}$ widgets

15. **a.** 10,500 people; **b.** 7,000 people

16. $36\frac{1}{4}$ hours

17. $\$26\frac{7}{8}$

Chapter 3
End-of-Chapter Problems

3–1. Hundredths
3–3. .5; .46; .458
3–5. 5.9; 5.89; 5.893
3–7. 6.6; 6.56; 6.556
3–9. $1,822.58
3–11. .03
3–13. .08
3–15. .84
3–17. 16.82
3–19. $\frac{33}{100}$
3–21. $\frac{125}{10,000}$
3–23. $\frac{825}{1,000}$
3–25. $\frac{7,065}{10,000}$
3–27. $28\frac{48}{100}$
3–29. .003
3–31. .0065
3–33. 713.8763
3–35. 1.2
3–37. 2.32
3–39. 1.2; 1.26791
3–41. 4; 4.0425
3–43. 24,526.67
3–45. 161.29
3–47. 6,824.15
3–49. .04
3–51. .63
3–53. 2.585
3–55. .0086
3–57. 486
3–59. 3.950
3–61. 7,913.2
3–63. .444
3–65. $5.99
3–67. 4.23 degrees
3–69. $.185 cheaper
3–71. $119.47
3–73. $30.52
3–75. $4,231.64
3–77. $6,650.28
3–79. Laundry A, $.05
Mustard B, $.13
Tuna B, $.15
3–81. 10.662 lbs No room for refrig.
3–83. 285.25 gallons
3–85. $4,666.67
3–87. $10.55
3–89. $.016 or 2 cents
3–91. 4.27 degrees
3–93. $560.45

Summary Practice Test

1. 785.705
2. .9
3. .09
4. .009
5. $\frac{8}{10}$
6. $2\frac{66}{100}$
7. $\frac{951}{1,000}$
8. .71
9. .60
10. 6.88
11. .50
12. 273.8951
13. 11.1
14. 100.97
15. 60,104.9
16. 54,650
17. 401,111,932.50
18. $83.41
19. $214.66
20. $163.60
21. Fruit A $.154

Cumulative Review 1, 2, 3

1. $245
2. 200,000
3. 50,560,000
4. $10
5. $225,000 savings from Boston
6. 1¢: $500
$1\frac{1}{2}$¢: $750
7. $369.56
8. $130,000,000
9. $47.73; $15.91; $63.64
10. $178,900; $200,000; $36,137

Chapter 4
End-of-Chapter Problems

4–1. $866.18
4–3. $449.85
4–5. $10,955.64
4–7. $289.62
4–9. $11,133.63
4–11. $2,637.66
4–13. $8,677.20
4–15. $1,701
4–16. $3,061.67 (challenge)

Summary Practice Test

1. $211.60
2. $1,167.71
3. $3,140
4. $759.75
5. 7,736.82

Chapter 5
End-of-Chapter Problems

5–1. $V = 26$
5–3. $N = 120$
5–5. $Y = 15$
5–7. $Y = 12$
5–9. $P = 25$
5–11. $P = \$355$
5–13. 30 Hubert 120 Soo
5–15. 50 shorts; 200 t-shirts
5–17. $Y = 11$
5–19. $N = 63$
5–21. $Y = 7$
5–23. $P = \$214$
5–25. Pete = 90; Bill = 450
5–27. 48 boxes paper; 240 diskettes
5–29. $D = 47$
5–31. $M = 60$
5–33. $1,250
5–35. 129
5–37. Shift 1 3,360; shift 2 2,240
5–39. 22 cartons hammers
18 cartons wrenches
5–40. **a.** 2.5 **b.** 15 miles
c. 6 hours

Summary Practice Test

1. $189
2. $174
3. Solly 32; TriCity 128
4. Rita 100; Alice 300
5. 20 dishes; 60 pots
6. 300 hamburgers; 200 pizzas

Chapter 6
End-of-Chapter Problems

6–1. 85%
6–3. 60%
6–5. 214.5%
6–7. .04
6–9. .459
6–11. 1.04
6–13. 6.7%
6–15. 62.5%

6–17. $\frac{1}{20}$
6–19. $\frac{19}{60}$
6–21. $\frac{27}{400}$
6–23. 7.2
6–25. 102.5
6–27. 156.6
6–29. 114.88
6–31. 12
6–33. 76.67
6–35. 10,000
6–37. 17,777.78
6–39. 108.2%
6–41. 110%
6–43. 400%
6–45. 59.40
6–47. 1,100
6–49. 40%
6–51. −48.28%
6–53. 10%
6–55. $10,000
6–57. 1,260,000
6–59. $1,111.11
6–61. 80%
6–63. $4,000
6–65. 39.94%
6–67. 12.8%
6–69. 1,000
6–71. $400
6–73. 25%
6–75. $3,000
6–77. 43.27%
6–79. 13.3%
6–81. 40%
6–83. $1,160,000
6–85. $24,000
6–87. 12%
6–89. $41,176
6–91. 40%
6–93. 585,000
6–94. 68%; 125%; $749,028; $20; 7

Summary Practice Test

1. 16.9%
2. 60%
3. 1,631%
4. 600%
5. .19
6. .0414
7. 2.0
8. .0020
9. 12.5%
10. 77.8%
11. $\frac{37}{150}$
12. $\frac{129}{1,000}$
13. $32,500
14. $750,000
15. 60%
16. 7.14%
17. $521.74
18. $390
19. $240,000

Chapter 7
End-of-Chapter Problems

7–1. .855; .145; $94.25; $555.75
7–3. .817516; .182484; $27.37; $122.63
7–5. $369.70; $80.30
7–7. $1,392.59; $457.41
7–9. June 24; July 14
7–11. June 15; July 5
7–13. July 10; July 30
7–15. $118; $5,882
7–17. $2; $198
7–19. $112.24; $337.76
7–21. $5.99; $33.96
7–23. $160; $240
7–25. $576.06; $48.94
7–27. $5,100; $5,250
7–29. $967.98; $82.02
7–31. 25%
7–33. $6,174
7–35. $244.44; $805.56
7–37. A; .32
7–39. $170; $255
7–41. $5,344
7–43. $5,970; $6,090
7–45. $5,459.25
7–47. $4,794.99

Summary Practice Test

1. $360
2. $800
3. $331.20; $68.80
4. **a.** July 25; Aug. 14 **b.** June 13, 1995; July 3, 1995 **c.** May 10; May 30 **d.** July 10; July 30
5. $272; $528
6. $6,900
7. A; .3034
8. $2,080.81
9. $2,228.60

Chapter 8
End-of-Chapter Problems

8–1. $90; $240
8–3. $4,285.71
8–5. $6.90; 45.70%
8–7. $130; $195
8–9. $110.83
8–11. $34.20; 69.8%
8–13. 11%
8–15. $3,830.40; $1,169.60; 23.39%
8–17. $35; 87.5%
8–19. $14.29
8–21. $2,000
8–23. $84
8–25. 42.86%
8–27. $3.56
8–29. $1,108.89
8–31. $30; 75.09%
8–33. $22.19
8–35. $439.45
8–37. $2.31
8–38. $135.69; $20.36; loss

Summary Practice Test

1. $340.80
2. 135.37%
3. $325; $325
4. $40; 62.5%
5. $195.56
6. $374.96
7. 33.33%
8. $96
9. 33.3%
10. $2.59

Chapter 9
End-of-Chapter Problems

9–1. $173.25
9–3. $9.30; $331.70
9–5. $661.50
9–7. $60
9–9. $13,000
9–11. $4,500
9–13. $11,900; $6,900; $138; $388
9–15. $6.20; $23.20
9–17. $105; $52.70; $12.33; $679.97
9–19. $317.01; $105.40; $24.65; $1,252.94
9–21. $273.40
9–23. $376.50
9–25. $3,120
9–27. $5,200
9–29. $6,900 Social Security
9–31. $201.39
9–33. $946.40; $135.20; 0 for week 30
9–35. $1,463.46 net pay; difference $2.99 too low; $52

Summary Practice Test

1. 46.5; $323.38
2. $323

3. $4,800
4. $341; $232
5. $222.78
6. $700.06 SUTA; $96.56 FUTA
   $111.94 SUTA; $15.44 FUTA

Chapter 10
End-of-Chapter Problems

10–1. $247.50; $3,247.50
10–3. $32.38; $632.38
10–5. $28.23; $613.23
10–7. $20.38; $1,020.38
10–9. $73.78; $1,273.78
10–11. 2 years
10–13. 12%
10–15. $525; $12,525
10–17. $2,377.70
10–19. 4.7 years
10–21. $12,892.50
10–23. $714.87; $44.87; $714.21; $44.21
10–25. $2,610.16
10–27. 5.8 years
10–29. $11,610.02; $610.02
10–31. $7.82; $275.33

Summary Practice Test

1. $16.80; $811.98
2. $127,500
3. $5,239.90
4. $5,236.61
5. $18,782.67
6. $4,715.30; $115.30
7. $4,714.47; $114.47

Chapter 11
End-of-Chapter Problems

11–1. $107.43; $6,892.57
11–3. 3 days
11–5. $41,600; $613.60; $40,986.40
11–7. 10.26%
11–9. $60; $4,060; $4,000; $4,000; $3,940
11–11. $9,081.31
11–13. $5,061.46 proceeds
11–15. $171.67 save
11–16. $2,127.66; 9.57%

Summary Practice Test

1. $200,000
2. $146.67; $5,853.33; $6,000; 11.3%
3. $8,172.09
4. $18,251.08
5. $7,371.35; 6.6%

Chapter 12
End-of-Chapter Problems

12–1. 8; 4%; $1,094.86; $294.86
12–3. $10,404; $404
12–5. 12.55%
12–7. 8; 2%; .8535; $768.15
12–9. 28; 3%; .4371; $7,692.96
12–11. 2.2879 × $7,692.96
12–13. $17,762.40
12–15. Mystic $4,775
12–17. $21,673.20
12–19. $15,244.65
12–21. $37,644
12–23. $17,908 yes
12–25. $3,739.20
12–27. $13,883.30
12–28. 6.14%; 8.24%

Summary Practice Test

1. $18,206.40
2. $52,605
3. $98,500.70
4. $316.20 shortage
5. 8.16%
6. $1,749.60
7. $8,684
8. $37,826.40

Chapter 13
End-of-Chapter Problems

13–1. $24,188.28
13–3. $24,913.92
13–5. $1,546.26
13–7. End of first year $1,069.96
13–9. $1,410
13–11. $3,248.70
13–13. $900,655
13–15. $33,444
13–17. $6,809.25
13–19. Annuity $12,219.93
13–21. $3,625.60
13–23. $111,013.29
13–25. $199.29

Summary Practice Test

1. $22,071.30
2. $15,073.32
3. $21,680.40
4. $1,878
5. $1,510
6. $31,512.50
7. $14,305.68
8. $17,723.34
9. $342,858.25

Cumulative Review 10, 11, 12, 13

1. Annuity $2,058.62
2. $5,118.70
3. $116,963.02
4. $3,113.92
5. $5,797.92
6. $18,465.20
7. $29,632.35
8. $55,251

Chapter 14
End-of-Chapter Problems

14–1. FC $940
14–3. FC $1,279.76; 14.09%
14–5. 12.75% to 13%
14–7. $119.39; $119.37
14–9. $43.64
14–11. $119.23; $2,430.77
14–13. $2,741
14–15. **a.** $3,889 **b.** $1,457.60 **c.** $5,441.60 **d.** 13.25% to 13.50% **e.** $89.11 **f.** 14.75%
14–17. $32.20; $297.80
14–19. 14% to 14.25%
14–21. $218.31 outstanding balance
14–22. $1.53, not $1.75

Summary Practice Test

1. $13,000; $2,000
2. $77.55
3. $6,611.40; 15.76%; 14%–14.25%
4. $7,660.03
5. $770.20; $6,249.80
6. $534.48

Chapter 15
End-of-Chapter Problems

15–1. $1,544
15–3. $1,764
15–5. $173,141.60
15–7. $1,679.04; $1,656.25; $22.79; $158,977.21
15–9. $1,874
15–11. $771.93; $196,894.80
15–13. Payment 3, $119,857.38
15–15. $1,284.74; $179,971.36; $1,061.33
15–16. $1,690.15; $415,954

Summary Practice Test

1. $1,478.40; $1,458.33; $20.07; $139,979.93
2. $260,224
3. **a.** $610.20; $123,060
   b. $654.60; $136,380

c. $699.60; $149,880
d. $768.60; $170,580
4. $1,713.84
5. $292,152

Chapter 16
End-of-Chapter Problems

16–1. Total assets $18,000
16–3. Inventory −16.67%; mortgage note +13.79%
16–5. Depreciation .77; .66
16–7. Depreciation $100; +16.67%
16–9. 1.43; 1.79
16–11. .20; .23
16–13. .06; .08
16–15. $255,000
16–17. $298,200
16–19. $15,991.47
16–21. 1.4
16–22. Net income $431

Summary Practice Test

1. a. $44,000 b. $10,000 c. $34,000 d. $29,500
2. Acc. receiv. 21.05%; 15.22%
3. Cash $5,000; + 62.50%
4. 1994 88%
5. Total assets $127,000
6. a. 1.33 b. 1.13 c. 36 days d. 1.33 e. .13

Chapter 17
End-of-Chapter Problems

17–1. Book value (end of year) $6,560
17–3. Book value (end of year) $3,680
17–5. Book value (end of year) $800
17–7. Book value (end of year) $4,000
17–9. Book value (end of year) $1,000
17–11. Book value (end of year) $9,000
17–13. Book value (end of year) $5,000
17–15. $2,240
17–17. $54,000; $13,500
17–19. $37,600; $22,560
17–21. $3,750
17–23. $4,750; $9,500
17–25. $23,040
17–27. St. Line $5,000 per year sum of the years' digits $8,333.33; depreciation expense year 1; Dec. Bal. $3,822; depreciation expense year 3
17–28. 1994, $17,500; 1995, $66,500; 1996, $52,500

Summary Practice Test

1. Book value end of year 3: $2,125
2. $1,142.40
3. Depreciation expense, $6,000; $4,000; $2,000
4. $5,000 difference
5. $1,800 difference

Chapter 18
End-of-Chapter Problems

18–1. $142; $918
18–3. $543; $932
18–5. $10
18–7. $36
18–9. $72
18–11. $140.80
18–13. $147.75; $345.60
18–15. $188.65; $304.70
18–17. 3.56; 3.25
18–19. .75; $52,500
18–21. $632.50; $964.50
18–23. $20,300
18–25. $55,120
18–27. $38,150
18–28. $13,499.50

Summary Practice Test

1. a. 11 b. $14.50 c. $32.50 d. $23.87
2. $12,000
3. 2.59
4. $59,500
5. $41,500

Chapter 19
End-of-Chapter Problems

19–1. $912
19–3. $17.22
19–5. $24,528.30
19–7. $168,000
19–9. 9.56%; $9.56; $95.60: 95.60
19–11. $2,700
19–13. $10,937.50
19–15. $69
19–17. $6,703.44
19–19. $15.28
19–21. 6.40 mills
19–23. $1,480
19–25. $45,455
19–27. $979

Summary Practice Test

1. $192.59
2. $7,444
3. $63,000
4. 5.2 mills
5. $906
6. $272,700

Chapter 20
End-of-Chapter Problems

20–1. $482.95
20–3. $221.25
20–5. $29,600
20–7. 20 years, 165 days
20–9. $518; $182
20–11. $22,000; $16,500
20–13. $1,067
20–15. $1,342.80; $28,530
20–17. $2,230
20–19. $112,500
20–21. $633.60; $26.40
20–23. Insurance company pays $21,700; Jim pays $4,500
20–25. Straight life $18,000; Term $90,000

Summary Practice Test

1. $778.40; $22,190
2. $767.60; $25,175; $52,250; 21 years, 300 days
3. $157,500; $210,000
4. $531; $21.24
5. $240
6. Insurance company pays $20,200; Jim pays $3,200

Chapter 21
End-of-Chapter Problems

21–1. $21,037.50
21–3. .9%
21–5. 16
21–7. $19,573.13
21–9. 1994 preferred $8,000
1995 0
1996 preferred $127,000
common $33,000
21–11. $2,280
21–13. $260; $2,725; 9.5%
21–15. $4,294.50
21–17. 12; 2.4%
21–19. $7,757.50
21–21. 7.3%
21–23. Stock 6.7%; Bond 11.9%
21–24. $1,014.33

Summary Practice Test

1. $8,775
2. 9; 1.4%

3. $2.77
4. $9,636
5. 5.7%
6. $15,000

Chapter 22
End-of-Chapter Problems

22–1. 6.25
22–3. $77.23
22–5. 2.7
22–7. 31.5
22–9. 8
22–11. No mode
22–13. $200–$299.99 卌|
22–15. Traditional watch 183.6°
22–17. $.65
22–19. Transportation 126°
Hotel 100.8°
Food 72°
Miscellaneous 61.2°

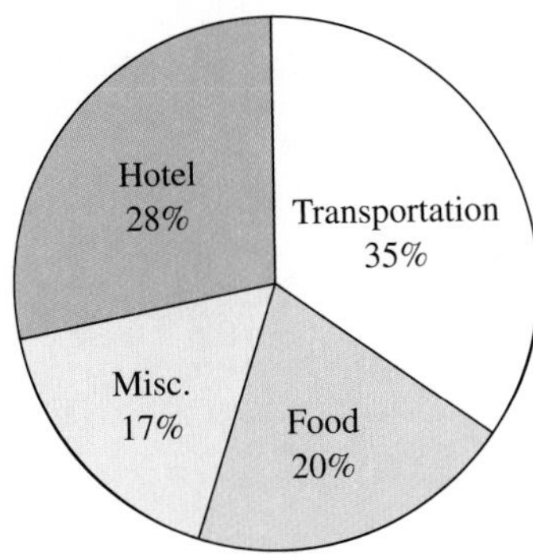

22–21. 250
22–23. Food; 18.59%; 66.92°

Summary Practice Test

1. $159,390; $167,500
2. 1,009
3. 3.25
4. 400; 111; 3
5. Bar 3 on horizontal axis goes up to 800 on vertical axis
6. Profits 54°
Cost of sales 198°
Expense 108°

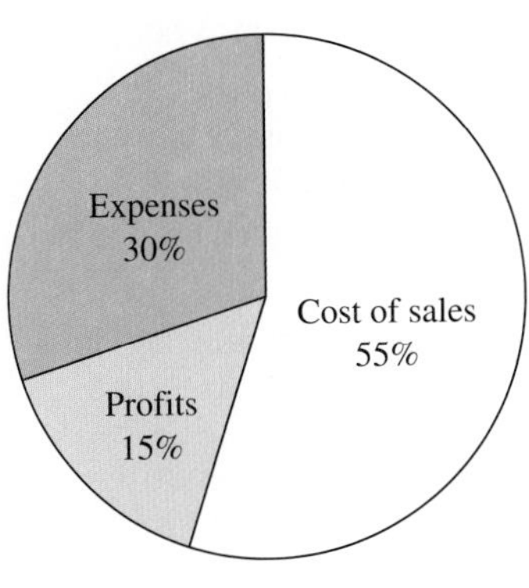

Check Figures (Odds) to Additional Assignments by Learning Unit

LU 1-1

1. **a.** Three thousand, eight hundred seventy-five
d. Fifty-eight thousand, three
3. **a.** 40; 380; 860; 5,980; 210
c. 21,000; 1,000; 4,000; 10,000
5. **a.** Hundreds place
c. Ten thousands place
e. Billions place
7. Three hundred eighty-four
9. $375,985
11. One thousand, nine hundred ninety-five

LU 1-2

1. **a.** 961 **c.** 1,319 **d.** 179
3. **a.** Estimated 40; 39
c. Estimated 10; 9
5. $71,577
7. $19,973
9. 12,797
11. Estimated $9,400; $9,422

LU 1-3

1. **a.** Estimated 2,000; actual 2,450
c. Estimated 15,000,000; actual 16,184,184
3. **a.** Estimated 1,000; actual 963 R5
c. Estimated 20; actual 25 R8
5. 2,695
7. $78
9. 27
11. $43,200
13. 40 stacks and 23 "extra" bricks

LU 2-1

1. **a.** P **b.** P **c.** I **d.** M
e. I **f.** P.
3. **a.** $\frac{36}{5}$ **c.** $\frac{31}{7}$ **f.** $\frac{53}{3}$
5. **a.** $6; \frac{6}{7}$ **b.** $15; \frac{2}{5}$ **e.** $12; \frac{8}{11}$
7. $\frac{13}{4}$
9. $\frac{17}{25}$
11. $\frac{60}{100}$
13. $\frac{7}{12}$

LU 2-2

1. **a.** 60 **b.** 180 **c.** 480
d. 252
3. **a.** $\frac{1}{3}$ **b.** $\frac{2}{3}$ **e.** $6\frac{1}{8}$ **h.** $56\frac{5}{6}$
5. $3\frac{1}{40}$ yards
7. $17\frac{5}{12}$ miles
9. $4\frac{8}{9}$ hours

LU 2-3

1. **a.** $\frac{\overset{1}{\cancel{7}}}{11} \times \frac{\overset{3}{\cancel{6}}}{\underset{\underset{1}{\cancel{2}}}{\cancel{14}}} = \frac{3}{11}$
3. **a.** $1\frac{1}{4}$ **b.** 3 **g.** 24 **l.** $\frac{4}{7}$
5. $39,000
7. 714
9. $20\frac{2}{3}$ miles
11. $412,000

LU 3-1

1. **a.** .47 **b.** .3 **c.** .953
d. .401 **e.** .06
3. **a.** hundredths place
d. thousandths place
5. **a.** $\frac{2}{5}$ **b.** $\frac{11}{25}$
g. $\frac{5}{16}$ **l.** $9\frac{1}{25}$
7. .286
9. $\frac{566}{1,000}$
11. .333
13. .0020507

LU 3-2

1. **a.** 23.907 **b.** 5.2281
d. 3.7736
3. **a.** .3 **b.** .1 **c.** 1,480.0
d. .1
5. **a.** 6,870 **c.** .0272
e. 34,700 **i** 8,329.8
7. $4.53
9. $111.25
11. 15

LU 4-1

1. **a.** $527.64 **b.** 3
c. $910.32
3. **a.** Neuner Realty Co.
b. Kevin Jones
h. $2,756.80
5. $37.79

LU 4-2

1. $1,435.42
3. Add $3,000; deduct $22.25
5. $2,989.92

LU 5-1

1. **a.** $5N = 60$ **e.** $14 + \frac{N}{3} = 18$
h. $2N + 3N + 8 = 68$

LU 5-2

1. $36
3. $45 telephone; $135 utility
5. 51 tickets—Sherry; 408 tickets—Linda
7. 12 necklaces ($48); 36 watches ($252)

LU 6-1

1. **a.** 4% **b.** 87.5%
i. 503.8% **l.** 80%
3. **a.** 70% **c.** 162.5%
h. 50% **n.** 1.5%
5. **a.** $\frac{1}{4}$ **b.** .375 **c.** 50%
d. $.66\overline{6}$ **n.** $1\frac{1}{8}$
7. 2.9%
9. $\frac{39}{100}$
11. $\frac{9}{10,000}$

LU 6-2

1. **a.** $4,800; 10%; $480
c. $7.00; 12%; $.84
3. **a.** 33.3% **b.** 3% **c.** 27.5%
5. **a.** −1,584; −26.6%
d. −20,000; −16.7%
7. $9,000
9. $3,196
11. 329.5%

LU 7-1

1. **a.** $625 **b.** $360 **c.** $50
d. $100 **e.** $380
3. **a.** $75 **b.** $21.50; $40.75
5. **a.** .7125; .2875 **b.** .7225; .2775
7. $3.51
9. $81.25
11. $315
13. 45%

LU 7–2

1. a. February 22; March 14
   d. May 20; June 9
   e. October 10; October 30
3. a. .98; $1,102.50
   c. .98; $367.99
5. a. $16.79; $835.21
7. $12,230.40
9. a. $439.29; b. $491.21
11. $209.45
13. a. $765.31 b. $386.99

LU 8–1

1. a. $6.85 b. $2.72
   c. $4.35 d. $90 e. $116.31
3. a. $2; 80% b. $6.50; 52%
   c. $.28; 28.9%
5. a. $1.52 b. $225
   c. $372.92 d. $625
7. a. $38.16 b. $197.16
9. a. $258.52 b. $90.48
11. a. $212.50 b. $297.50
13. $8.17

LU 8–2

1. a. $.90 b. $57.50
   c. $34.43 d. $27.33 e. $.15
3. a. $6.94 b. $882.35 c. $30
   d. $171.43
5. a. 28.57% b. 33.33%
   d. 53.85%
7. $346.15
9. 39.39%
11. $2.29
13. 63.33%

LU 8–3

1. a. $5.60; $50.40 b. $525;
   $1,574.98
3. a. $410; b. $18.65
5. a. $216; $324; $5.14
   b. $45; $63.90; $1.52
7. 17%
9. $21.15
11. $273.78
13. $.79

LU 9–1

1. a. $260; 0; $260 b. $360;
   $40.50; $400.50
3. a. $438.85 b. $615.13
5. a. $5,200 b. $3,960
   c. $3,740 d. $4,750
7. $723.00
9. $3,846.25
11. $2,032.48

LU 9–2

1. a. $500; $780
3. 0; $200
5. $31.00; $11.31 medical
7. -0-
9. $43.13
11. $908
13. $450.51

LU 10–1

1. a. $180 b. $1,080
   c. $1,275
3. a. $131.25 b. $16.33
   c. $98.51
5. a. $313.60 b. $3,449.60
7. a. $1,225.33
9. $10,903.47
11. $558.48

LU 10–2

1. a. $4,371.44 b. $4,545.45
   c. $3,433.33
3. a. 60 b. 120 c. 270
   d. 145
5. 120 days
7. 10.7%
9. $3,000
11. 119 days
13. 222 days

LU 10–3

1. a. $2,568.75; $1,885.47;
   $920.04 b. $3,293.33;
   $2,755.83; $1,969.16; $938.60
3. $4,209.22
5. $3,126.13

LU 11–1

1. I; B; D; I; D; I; B; D
3. a. 9.1% c. 13%
5. $15,963.75
7. $848.75; $8,851.25
9. $14,300
11. $7,855

LU 11–2

1. a. $4,980 b. $16,480.80
   c. $994.44
3. a. $14.76 b. $223.25
   c. $3.49
5. $4,031.67
7. $8,262.74
9. $5,088.16
11. $721.45

LU 12–1

1. a. $618.19 yr. 2
   b. $3,115.57 yr. 4
3. a. $15,869; $5,869
   b. $16,084; $6,084
5. $5,980
7. $8,881.20
9. $2,129.40
11. $3,207.09; $207.09

LU 12–2

1. a. .6209 b. .3936 c. .5513
3. a. $1,575.50; $924.50
   b. $2,547.02; $2,052.98
5. $13,152.60
7. $13,356.98
9. $16,826.40
11. $652.32

LU 13–1

1. a. $1,000; $2,080; $3,246.40
3. a. $6,888.60 b. $6,273.36
5. $325,525
7. $13,412
9. $30,200.85
11. $33,650.94

LU 13–2

1. a. $2,638.65 b. $6,375.24;
   $7,217.10
3. $2,715.54
5. $24,251.85
7. $47,608
9. $456,425
11. Accept Jason $265,010

LU 13–3

1. a. $4,087.50
3. $16,200
5. $24,030
7. $16,345
9. $8,742

LU 14–1

1. a. $1,200; $192 b. $9,000;
   $1,200
3. a. 15.36% b. 10.32%
   c. 12.03%
5. a. $720.72 b. $589.32
   c. $632.66
7. 13.62%
9. a. 10.74% b. 10%
11. $230.86

LU 14–2

1. a. $625; $375
b. $9,600; $2,910
3. a. 625; $578.12
5. $1,758; $553
7. $900
9. $7,287.76

LU 14–3

1. a. $465; $8,535
b. $915.62; $4,709.38
3. a. $332.03 b. $584.83
c. $384.28
5. Final payment $784.39
7. $51.34
9. $35

LU 15–1

1. a. $1,606.50 b. $1,555.50; $4,090.50; $3,859.65
3. a. $117.25, 7.7% b. $174, 5.7%
5. $2,487.24
7. $2,584.71; $2,518.63
9. a. $66.08 b. $131,293.80
11. $773,560

LU 15–2

1. a. $1,371.90; $1,133.33; $238.57
3. #4 balance outstanding $195,183.05
5. $587,612.80
7. $327.12; $251,581.60

LU 16–1

1. Total assets $224,725
3. Merch. inventory 13.90% 15.12%

LU 16–2

1. Net income $57,765
3. Purchases 73.59%; 71.43%

LU 16–3

1. Sales 1995 93.5%; 1994 93.2%
3. .22
5. 59.29%
7. .83
9. COGS 119.33%; 111.76%; 105.04%
11. .90
13. 5.51%

LU 17–1

1. a. 4% b. 25% c. 10%
d. 20%
3. a. $2,033; $4,667 b. $1,850; $9,750
5. $8,625 depreciation per year
7. $2,800 depreciation per year
9. $95
11. a. $12,000 b. $6,000
c. $18,000 d. $45,000

LU 17–2

1. a. $.30 b. $.192 c. $.176
3. a. $.30, $2,600 b. $.192, $300,824
5. $5,300 book value end of year 5
7. a. $.155 b. $20,001.61

LU 17–3

1. a. $\frac{5}{15}, \frac{4}{15}, \frac{3}{15}, \frac{2}{15}, \frac{1}{15}$
3. a. $3,050; $3,650
b. $3,171; $8,429
5. $900 book value end of year 6
7. a. 28 b. $237.50 c. $845

LU 17–4

1. a. 8% b. 20% c. 25%
3. a. $4,467; $2,233
b. $3,867; $7,733
5. $121, year 6
7. a. 28.57% b. $248 c. $619
9. a. 16.67% b. $2,500
c. $10,814 d. $2,907

LU 17–5

1. a. 33%; $825; $1,675
3. Depreciation year 8, $346
5. $125
7. a. $15,000 b. $39,000
c. $21,600 d. 1999

LU 18–1

1. a. $5,120; $3,020
b. $323,246; $273,546
3. $35,903; $165,262
5. $10,510.20; $16,345
7. $37.62; $639.54
9. $628.40
11. $3,069; $952; $2,117

LU 18–2

1. a. $85,700; $143,500; .597; $64,500; $38,507
3. $85,000
5. $342,000; $242,500; 5.85; 6.29
7. $60,000; $100,000; $40,000
9. $70,150
11. $5,970
13. 3.24; 3.05
15. $32,340; $35,280; $49,980; $29,400

LU 19–1

1. a. $26.80; $562.80
b. $718.80; $12,698.80
3. a. $20.75; $43.89; $463.64
5. Total is $29.57
7. a. $324 b. $1,155
9. $635.83
11. $830.77
13. $1,023.75

LU 19–2

1. a. $68,250 b. $775,450
3. a. $7.45; $74.50; 74.50
5. $9.10
7. $8,368.94
9. $42,112
11. $32,547.50

LU 20–1

1. a. $9.27; 25; $231.75
3. a. $93.00; $387.50; $535.00; $916.50
5. $1,242.90
7. $14,265
9. $47.50 more
11. $68,750

LU 20–2

1. a. $488 b. $2,912
3. a. $68,000; $60,000
b. $41,600; $45,000
5. $1,463
7. $117,187.50
9. $336,000
11. a. $131,250
b. $147,000

LU 20–3

1. a. $98; $160; $258
3. a. $312 b. $229 c. $181
d. $59; $20
5. a. $647 b. $706
7. $601
9. $781
11. $10,000; $8,000
13. $60,000; $20,000

LU 21-1

1. **a.** $20.875 **f.** 14
3. $1.46
5. **a.** $8,364; $7,328.75
7. **a.** $320,000; $262,500; $.35
9. 25.4%

LU 21-2

1. **a.** IBM **b.** $10\frac{1}{4}$ **c.** 1995 **d.** $102.50 **e.** $102\frac{3}{8}$
3. **a.** $1,030 **b.** $1,017.50 **c.** $1,025 **d.** $1,023.75
5. **a.** $3,075 **b.** $307.50
7. **a.** $30 discount **b.** $16.25 premium **c.** $42.50 premium
9. **a.** $625 **b.** $375 discount **c.** $105 **d.** 16.8%
11. 7.8%; 7.2%
13. 8.98%

LU 22-1

1. **a.** 20.4 **b.** 83.75 **c.** 10.07
3. **a.** 59.5 **b.** 50
5. **a.** 63.7; 62; 62
7. 1,500,388.50
9. $10.75
11. $9.98

LU 22-2

1. 18 ~~||||~~ || 7
3. 25–30 ~~||||~~ ||| 8
5. 7.2°; 172.8°; 122.4°; 57.6°
7. 145–154 |||| 4
9. 98.4°; 9.9°; 70.5°; 169.2°; 11.9°

Glossary

Accelerated method Computes more depreciation expense in the early years of the asset's life than in the later years.

Accounts payable Amounts owed to creditors for services or items purchased.

Accounts receivable Amount owed by customers to a business from previous sales.

Accumulated depreciation Amount of depreciation that has accumulated on plant and equipment assets.

Acid test Current assets less inventory less prepaid expenses divided by current liabilities.

Addends Numbers that are combined in the addition process. *Example:* 8 + 9 = 17, of which 8 and 9 are the addends.

Adjustable rate mortgage Rate of mortgage is lower than a fixed rate mortgage. Rates adjusted without refinancing. Caps available to limit how high rate can go for each adjustment period over term of loan.

Adjusted bank balance Current balance of checkbook after reconciliation process.

Amortization Process of paying back a loan (principal plus interest) by equal periodic payments (see **amortization schedule**).

Amortization schedule Shows monthly payment to pay back loan at maturity. Payment also includes interest. Note payment is fixed at same amount each month.

Amount financed Cash price less down payment.

Annual percentage rate (APR) True or effective annual interest rate charged by sellers. Required to be stated by Truth in Lending Act.

Annual percentage rate (APR) table Effective annual rate of interest on a loan or installment purchase as shown by table lookup.

Annuities certain Annuities that have stated beginning and ending dates.

Annuity Stream of equal payments made at periodic times.

Annuity due Annuity that is paid (or received) at the beginning of the time period.

Assessed valuation Value of a property that an assessor sets (usually a percent of property's market value) that is used in calculating property taxes.

Asset cost Amount company paid for the asset.

Assets Things of value owned by a business.

Asset turnover Net sales divided by total assets.

ATM Automatic teller machine that allows customers of a bank to transfer funds and make deposits or withdrawals.

Average daily balance Sum of daily balances divided by number of days in billing cycle.

Average inventory Total of all inventories divided by number of times inventory taken.

Balance sheet Financial report that lists assets, liabilities, and equity. Report reflects the financial position of the company as of a particular date.

Bank discount (Maturity value × Bank discount rate × Number of days bank holds note) ÷ 360.

Banker's Rule Time is exact time/360 in calculating simple interest.

Bank reconciliation Process of comparing the bank balance to the checkbook balance so adjustments can be made regarding checks outstanding, deposits in transit, and the like.

Bank statement Report sent by the bank to the owner of the checking account indicating checks processed, deposits made, and so on, along with beginning and ending balance.

Bar graph Visual representation using horizontal or vertical bars to make comparison or to show relationships on item of similar makeup.

Base Number that represents the whole 100%. It is the whole to which something is being compared. Usually follows word *of.*

Beneficiary Person(s) designated to receive the face value of the life insurance when insured dies.

Biweekly Every two weeks (26 times in a year).

Biweekly mortgage Mortgage payments made every two weeks rather than monthly. This payment method takes years off the life of the mortgage and substantially reduces cost of interest.

Blank endorsement Current owner of check signs name on back. Whoever presents checks for payment receives the money.

Bodily injury Auto insurance that pays damages to people injured or killed by your auto.

Bond discount Bond selling for less than the face value.

Bond premium Bond selling for more than the face value.

Bonds Written promise by a company that borrows money usually with fixed-interest payment until maturity (repayment time).

Bond yield Total annual interest divided by total cost.

Book value Cost less accumulated depreciation.

Cancellation Reducing process that is used to simplify the multiplication and division of fractions. *Example:*

$$\frac{\overset{1}{\cancel{4}}}{8} \times \frac{1}{\underset{1}{\cancel{4}}}$$

Capital Owners' investment in the business.

Cash advance Money borrowed by holder of credit card. It is recorded as another purchase and is used in the calculation of the average daily balance.

Cash discount Savings that result from early payment by taking advantage of discounts offered by the seller; discount is not taken on freight or taxes.

Cash dividend Cash distribution of company's profit to owners of stock.

Cash value Except for term insurance, this indicates the value of the policy when terminated. Options fall under the heading of nonforfeiture values.

Centi- Prefix indicates .01 of a basic metric unit.

Chain discount Two or more trade discounts that are applied to the balance remaining after the previous discount is taken. Often called a **series discount.**

Check register Recordkeeping device that records checks paid and deposits made by companies using a checking account.

Checks Written documents signed by appropriate person that directs the bank to pay a specific amount of money to a particular person or company.

Check stub Provides a record of checks written. It is attached to the check.

Circle graph A visual representation of the parts to the whole.

CM Abbreviation for **credit memorandum.** The bank is adding to your account. The CM is found on the bank statement. *Example:* Bank collects a note for you.

Coinsurance Type of fire insurance in which the insurer and insured share the risk. Usually 80% coinsurance clause.

Collision Optional auto insurance that pays for the repairs to your auto from an accident after deductible is met. Insurance company will only pay for repairs up to the value of the auto (less deductible).

Commissions Payments based on established performance criteria.

Common stocks Units of ownership called shares.

Comparative statement Statement showing data from two or more periods side by side.

Complement 100% less the stated percent. *Example:* 18% → 82% is the complement (100% − 18%).

Compounding (FV) Calculating the interest periodically over the life of the loan and adding it to the principal.

Compound interest The interest that is calculated periodically and then added to the principal. The next period the interest is calculated on the adjusted principal (old principal plus interest).

Comprehensive insurance Optional auto insurance that pays for damages to the auto caused by factors other than from collision (fire, vandalism, theft, and the like).

Compulsory insurance Insurance required by law—standard coverage.

Constants Numbers such as 3 or −7. Placed on right side of equation.

Contingent annuities Beginning and ending dates of the annuity are uncertain (not fixed).

Conversion periods How often (a period of time) the interest is calculated in the compounding process. *Example:* Daily—each day; monthly—12 times a year; quarterly—every 3 months; semiannually—every 6 months.

Cost Price paid to supplier to bring merchandise into store.

Cost of goods (merchandise) sold Beginning inventory + Net purchases − Ending inventory.

Credit period (end) Credit days are counted from date of invoice. Has no relationship to the discount period.

Cumulative preferred stock Holders of preferred stock must receive current year and any dividends in arrears before any dividends are paid out to the holders of common stock.

Current assets Assets that are used up or converted into cash within one year or operating cycle.

Current liabilities Obligations of a company due within one year.

Current ratio Current assets divided by current liabilities.

Daily balance Calculated to determine customer's finance charge: Previous balance + Any cash advances + Purchases − Payments.

Daily compounding Interest calculated on balance each day.

Deca- Prefix indicates 10 times basic metric unit.

Deci- Prefix indicates .1 of basic metric unit.

Decimal equivalent Decimal represents the same value of the fraction. *Example:*

$$.05 = \frac{5}{100}$$

Decimal fraction Decimal representing a fraction; the denominator has a power of ten.

Decimal point Position located between units and tenths.

Decimals Numbers written with a decimal point. *Example:* 5.3, 18.22.

Declining-balance method Accelerated method of depreciation. The depreciation each year is calculated by book value beginning each year times the rate.

Deductibles Amount insured pays before insurance company pays. Usually the higher the deductible, the lower the premium will be.

Deductions Amounts deducted from gross earnings to arrive at net pay.

Deferred payment price Total of all monthly payments plus down payment.

Denominator The number of a common fraction below the division line (bar). *Example:*

$\frac{8}{9}$, of which 9 is the denominator

Deposits in transit Deposits not received or processed by bank at the time bank statement is prepared.

Deposit ticket Document that shows date, name, account number, and items making up a deposit.

Depreciation Process of allocating the cost of an asset (less residual value) over the asset's estimated life.

Depreciation causes Normal use, product obsolesence, aging, and so on.

Depreciation expense Process involving asset cost, estimated useful life, and residual value (salvage or trade-in value).

Depreciation schedule Table showing amount of depreciation expense, accumulated depreciation, and book value for each period of time for a plant asset.

Difference The resulting answer from a subtraction problem. *Example:* Minuend less subtrahend equals difference.

215 − 15 = 200

Differential pay schedule Pay rate is based on a schedule of units completed.

Digit Our decimal number system of 10 characters from 0 to 9.

Discounting a note Receiving cash from selling a note to a bank before the due date of a note. Steps to discount include: (1) find maturity value, (2) calculate number of days bank waits for money, (3) calculate bank discount, and (4) find proceeds.

Discount period Amount of time to take advantage of a cash discount.

Distribution of overhead Companies distribute overhead by floor space or sales volume.

Dividend Number in the division process that is being divided by another. *Example:* $5\overline{)15}$, in which 15 is the dividend.

Dividends Distribution of company's profit in cash or stock to owners of stock.

Dividends in arrears Dividends that accumulate when a company fails to pay dividends to cumulative preferred stockholders.

Divisor Number in the division process that is dividing into another. *Example:* $5\overline{)15}$, in which 5 is the divisor.

DM Abbreviation for **debit memorandum.** The bank is charging your account. The DM is found on the bank statement. *Example:* NSF.

Down payment Amount of initial cash payment made when item is purchased.

Drawee One ordered to pay the check.

Drawer One who writes the check.

Drawing account The receiving of advance wages to cover business or personal expenses. Once wages are earned, drawing amount reduces actual amount received.

Due date Maturity date or when the note will be repaid.

Earnings per share Annual earnings ÷ Total number of shares outstanding.

Effective rate True rate of interest. The more frequent the compounding, the higher the effective rate.

Electronic funds transfer (EFT) A computerized operation that electronically transfers funds among parties without the use of paper checks.

Employee's Withholding Allowance Certificate (W-4) Completed by employee to indicate allowance claimed to determine amount of FIT that is deducted.

End of month—EOM (also **Proximo**) Cash discount period begins at the end of the month invoice is dated. After the 25th discount period, one additional month results.

Endorsements Signing the back of the check; thus ownership is transferred to another party.

Endowment life Form of insurance that pays at maturity a fixed amount of money to insured or the beneficiary. Insurance coverage would terminate when paid—similar to term.

Equation Math statement that shows equality for expressions or numbers, or both.

Equivalent (fractional) Two or more fractions equivalent in value.

Estimated APR by formula

$$\frac{2 \times \text{Number of payment periods in one year} \times \text{Finance charge}}{\text{Amount of loan} \times (\text{Number of payments} + 1)}$$

Exact interest Calculating simple interest using 365 days per year in time.

Exact time Exact number of days used in time when calculating simple interest.

Exact time, exact interest

$$T = \frac{\text{Exact number of days}}{365}$$

Exact time, ordinary interest

$$T = \frac{\text{Exact number of days}}{360}$$

Excise tax Tax that government levies on particular products and services. Tax on specific luxury items or nonessentials.

Extended term insurance Resulting from nonforfeiture, it keeps the policy for the full face value going without further premium payments for a specific period of time.

Face value Amount of insurance that is stated on the policy. It is usually the maximum amount for which the insurance company is liable.

Fair Credit and Charge Card Act of 1988 Act tightens controls on credit card companies soliciting new business.

Fair Labor Standards Act Federal law has minimum wage standards and the requirement of overtime pay. There are many exemptions for administrative personnel and for others.

Federal income tax withholding (FIT) Federal tax withheld from paycheck.

Federal Insurance Contribution Act (FICA) Percent on base amount of each employee's salary. FICA taxes used to fund retirement, disabled workers, Medicare, and so on. FICA is now broken down into Social Security and Medicare.

Federal Unemployment Tax Act (FUTA) Tax paid by employer. Current rate is .8% on first $7,000 of earnings.

Federal withholding tax See **Income tax.**

Finance charge Total payments − Actual loan cost.

Fire insurance Stipulated percent (normally 80%) of value that is required for insurance company to pay to reimburse one's losses.

First-in, first-out method (FIFO) This method assumes the first inventory brought into the store will be the first sold. Ending inventory is made up of goods most recently purchased.

FOB destination Seller pays cost of freight in getting goods to buyer's location.

FOB shipping point Buyer pays cost of freight in getting goods to his location.

Fraction Expresses a part of a whole number. *Example:*

$\frac{5}{6}$ expresses 5 parts out of 6

Frequency distribution Shows by table the number of times event(s) occurs.

Full endorsement This endorsement identifies the next person or company to whom the check is to be transferred.

Graduated-payment mortgage Borrower pays less at beginning of mortgage. As years go on, the payments increase.

Graduated plans In beginning years, mortgage payment is less. As years go on, monthly payments rise.

Gram Basic unit of weight in metric system. An ounce equals about 28 grams.

Greatest common divisor The largest possible number that will divide evenly into both the numerator and denominator.

Gross pay Wages before deductions.

Gross profit from sales Net sales − Cost of goods sold.

Gross profit method A method for estimating the value of ending inventory.

Hecto- Prefix indicates 100 times basic metric unit.

Higher terms Expressing a fraction with a new numerator and denominator that is equivalent to the original. *Example:*

$$\frac{2}{9} \rightarrow \frac{6}{27}$$

Home equity loan Cheap and readily accessible lines of credit backed by equity in your home; tax deductible; rates can be locked in.

Horizontal analysis Method of analyzing financial reports where each total this period is compared by amount of percent to the same total last period.

Improper fraction Type of fraction when numerator is equal to or greater than the denominator. *Example:*

$$\frac{6}{6}, \frac{14}{9}$$

Income statement Financial report that lists the revenues and expenses for a specific period of time. It reflects how well the company is performing.

Income tax or FIT Tax depends on allowances claimed, marital status, and wages earned.

Indemnity Insurance company's payment to insured for loss.

Individual retirement account (IRA) An account established for retirement planning.

Installment buyers Purchase of an item(s) that requires periodic payments for a specific period of time with usually a high rate of interest.

Installment cost Down payment + (Number of payments × Monthly payment). Also called deferred payment.

Insured Customer or policyholder.

Insurer The insurance company that issues the policy.

Interest Principal × Rate × Time.

Interest-bearing note Maturity value of note is greater than amount borrowed since interest is added on.

Inventory turnover Ratio that indicates how quickly inventory turns:
$$\frac{\text{Cost of goods sold}}{\text{Average inventory at cost}}$$

Invoice Document recording purchase and sales transactions.

Kilo- Prefix indicates 1,000 times basic metric unit.

Last-in, first-out method (LIFO) This method assumes the last inventory brought into the store will be the first sold. Ending inventory is made up of the oldest goods purchased.

Least common denominator (LCD) Smallest whole number into which denominators of two or more fractions will divide evenly. *Example:*

$\frac{2}{3}$ and $\frac{1}{4}$ LCD = 12

Liabilities Amount business owes to creditors.

Liability insurance Insurance for bodily injury to others and damage to someone else's property.

Like fractions Proper fractions with the same denominators.

Like terms Terms that are made up with the same variable:
$A + 2A + 3A = 6A$

Limited payment life (20-payment life) Premiums are for 20 years (a fixed period) and provide paid-up insurance for the full face value of the policy.

Line graphs Graphical presentation that involves a time element. Shows trends, failures, backlogs, and the like.

Line of credit Provides immediate financing up to an approved limit.

Liquid assets Cash or other assets that can be converted quickly into cash.

List price Suggested retail price paid by customers.

Liter Basic unit of measure in metric, for volume.

Long-term liabilities Debts or obligations that company does not have to pay within one year.

Lowest terms Expressing a fraction when no number divides evenly into the numerator and denominator except the number 1. *Example:*

$\frac{5}{10} \rightarrow \frac{1}{2}$

Maker One who writes the note.

Markdown amount Original selling price less the reduction to price. Markdown may be stated as a percent of the original selling price. *Example:*
$$\frac{\text{Markdown amount}}{\text{Original selling price}}$$

Markup amount Selling price less cost. Difference is the amount of the markup.

Markup percent calculation (see markup amount) Markup percent on cost × Cost = Markup amount; or Markup percent on selling price × Selling price = Markup amount.

Maturity date Date the principal and interest are due.

Maturity value Principal plus interest (if interest is charged). Represents amount due on the due date.

Maturity value of note Amount of cash paid on the due date. If interest-bearing maturity value is greater than amount borrowed.

Mean Statistical term that is found by:
$$\frac{\text{Sum of all figures}}{\text{Number of figures}}$$

Median Statistical term that represents the central or midpoint of a series of numbers.

Merchandise inventory Cost of goods for resale.

Merchant's Rule Method that allows the borrower to receive proper interest credits when paying off a loan in more than one payment before the maturity date. Also see **U.S. Rule.**

Meter Basic unit of length in metric system. A meter is a little longer than a yard.

Metric system A decimal system of weights and measures. The basic units are meters, grams, and liters.

Mill $\frac{1}{10}$ of a cent or $\frac{1}{1,000}$ of a dollar.

In decimal, it is .001. *In application:*
Property tax due = Mills × .001 × Assessed valuation

Milli- Prefix indicates .001 of basic metric unit.

Minuend In a subtraction problem, the larger number from which another is subtracted. *Example:*
$50 - 40 = 10$

Mixed decimal Combination of a whole number and decimal, such as 59.8, 810.85.

Mixed numbers Number written as a whole number and a proper fraction:

$2\frac{1}{4}$, $3\frac{8}{9}$

Mode Value that occurs most often in a series of numbers.

Modified accelerated cost recovery system (MACRS) Part of Tax Reform Act of 1986 which revised depreciation schedules of ACRS. Tax Bill of 1989 updates MACRS.

Monthly Some employers pay employees monthly.

Mortgage Cost of home less down payment.

Multiplicand The first or top number being multiplied in a multiplication problem. *Example:*

Product	=	Multiplicand	×	Multiplier
40	=	20	×	2

Multiplier The second or bottom number doing the multiplication in a problem. *Example:*

Product	=	Multiplicand	×	Multiplier
40	=	20	×	2

Negative numbers A collection of numbers with negative signs.

$-5, -\frac{1}{2}$

Net deposits Credit card sales less returns.

Net income (net profit) Gross profit − Operating expenses.

Net pay See **Net wages.**

Net price List price less amount of trade discount. The net price is before any cash discount.

Net price equivalent rate When multiplied times the list price, this rate or factor produces the actual cost to the buyer. Rate is found by taking the complement of each term in the discount and multiplying them together (do not round off).

Net proceeds Maturity value less bank discount.

Net purchases Purchases − Purchase discounts − Purchase returns and allowances.

Net sales Gross sales − Sales discounts − Sales returns and allowances.

Net wages Gross pay less deductions.

Net worth Assets less liabilities.

No-fault insurance Involves bodily injury. Damage (before a certain level) that is paid by an insurance company no matter who is to blame.

Nominal rate Stated rate.

Nonforfeiture values When a life insurance policy is terminated (except term), it represents (1) the available cash value, (2) additional extended term, or (3) additional paid-up insurance.

Noninterest-bearing note Note where the maturity value will be equal to the amount of money borrowed since no additional interest is charged.

NSF (nonsufficient funds) Drawer's account lacked sufficient funds to pay written amount of check.

Numerator Number of a common fraction above the division line (bar). *Example:*

$\frac{8}{9}$, in which 8 is the numerator

Odd lot Fewer than 100 shares.

Open-end credit Set payment period. Also, additional credit amounts can be added up to a set limit. It is a revolving charge account.

Operating expenses Regular expenses of doing business. These are not costs.

Ordinary annuities Annuity that is paid (or received) at end of the time period.

Ordinary dating Cash discount is available within the discount period. Full amount due by end of credit period if discount is missed.

Ordinary interest Calculating simple interest using 360 days per year in time.

Ordinary life insurance See **Straight life insurance.**

Outstanding balance Amount left to be paid on a loan.

Outstanding checks Checks written but not yet processed by the bank before bank statement preparation.

Overhead expenses Operating expenses *not* directly associated with a specific department or product.

Override. Commission managers receive due to sales by people that they supervise.

Overtime Time-and-a-half pay for more than 40 hours of work.

Owner's equity See **Capital.**

Paid-up insurance A certain level of insurance can continue, although the premiums are terminated. This results from the nonforfeiture value (except term). Result is a reduced paid-up policy until death.

Partial products Numbers between multiplier and product.

Payee One who is named to receive the amount of the check.

Payroll register Multicolumn form to record payroll data.

Percent Stands for hundredths. *Example:*

4% is 4 parts of a hundred, or $\frac{4}{100}$

Percentage method A method to calculate withholdings. Opposite of wage bracket method.

Percent decrease Calculated by decrease in price over original amount.

Percent increase Calculated by increase in price over original amount.

Percent markup on cost Markup amount divided by the cost; thus, markup is a percent of the cost.

Percent markup on selling price Markup amount divided by the selling price; thus, markup is a percent of the selling price.

Periodic inventory system Physical count of inventory taken at end of a time period. Inventory records are not continually updated.

Periods Number of years times the number of times compounded per year (see **Conversion period**).

Perishables Goods or services with a limited life.

Perpetual inventory system Inventory records are continually updated; opposite of periodic.

Personal property Items of possession, like cars, home, furnishings, jewelry, and so on. These are taxed by the property tax (don't forget real property is also taxed).

Piecework Compensation based on per item produced or completed.

Place value The digit value that results from its position in a number.

Plant and equipment Assets that will last longer than one year.

Point of sale Terminal that accepts cards (like those used at ATMs) to purchase items at retail outlets. No cash would be physically exchanged.

Points Percentage(s) of mortgage that represents an additional cost of borrowing. It is a one-time payment made at closing.

Policy Written insurance contract.

Policyholder The insured.

Portion Amount, part, or portion that results from multiplying the base times the rate. Not expressed as a percent, it is expressed as a number.

Positive numbers Collection of numbers with a positive sign. *Examples:*

$+\frac{5}{7}, +9$

Preferred stock Type of stock that has a preference regarding a corporation's profits and assets.

Premium Periodic payments that one makes for various kinds of insurance protection.

Premium rates (payroll) Higher rates based on a quota system.

Prepaid expenses Items a company buys that have not been used are shown as assets.

Prepaid rent Rent paid in advance.

Present value of annuity Amount of money needed today to receive a specified stream (annuity) of money in the future.

Present value (PV) How much money will have to be deposited today (or at some date) to reach a specific amount of maturity (in the future).

Price-earnings ratio (P-E) Closing price per share of stock divided by earnings per share.

Prime numbers Number (larger than 1) that is only divisible by itself and 1. *Examples:* 2, 3, 5.

Principal Amount of money that is originally borrowed, loaned, or deposited.

Proceeds Maturity value less the bank charge.

Product Answer of a multiplication process, such as:

Product	=	Multiplicand	×	Multiplier
50	=	5	×	10

Promissory note Written unconditional promise to pay a certain sum (with or without interest) at a fixed time in the future.

Proper fractions Fractions with numerator less than denominator, such as $\frac{5}{9}$.

Property damage Auto insurance covering damages that are caused to the property of others.

Property tax Tax that raises revenue for school districts, cities, counties, and the like.

Property tax due Tax rate × Assessed valuation

Proximo (prox) Same as end of month.

Quick assets Current assets − Inventory − Prepaid expenses.

Quick ratio (Current assets − Inventory − Prepaid expenses) ÷ Current liabilities.

Quotient The answer of a division problem.

Rate Percent that is multiplied times the base that indicates what part of the base we are trying to compare to. Rate is not a whole number.

Rate of interest Percent of interest that is used to compute the interest charge on a loan for a specific time.

Ratio analysis Relationship of one number to another.

Real property Land, buildings, and so on, which are taxed by the property tax.

Rebate Finance charge customer receives for paying off a loan early.

Rebate fraction Sum of digits based on number of months to go divided by sum of digits based on total number of months of loan.

Receipt of goods (ROG) Used in calculating the cash discount period; begins the day that the goods are received.

Reciprocal of a fraction The interchanging of the numerator and the denominator. *Example:*

$$\frac{6}{7} \rightarrow \frac{7}{6}$$

Reduced paid-up insurance Insurance that uses cash value to buy protection, face amount is less than original policy, and policy continues for life.

Remainder Leftover amount in division.

Repeating decimals Decimal numbers that repeat themselves continuously and thus do not end.

Residual value Estimated value of a plant asset after depreciation is taken (or end of useful life).

Restrictive endorsement Check must be deposited to the payee's account. This restricts one from cashing it.

Retail method Method to estimate cost of ending inventory. The cost ratio times ending inventory at retail equals the ending cost of inventory.

Retained earnings Amount of earnings that is kept in the business.

Return on equity Net income divided by stockholders' equity.

Revenues Total earned sales (cash or credit) less any sales discounts, returns, or allowances.

Revolving charge account Charges for a customer are allowed up to a specified maximum and a minimum monthly payment is required and interest is charged on balance outstanding.

ROG Receipt of goods; cash discount period begins when goods are received, not ordered.

Rounding decimals Reducing the number of decimals to an indicated position, such as 59.59—59.6 to nearest tenth.

Rounding whole numbers all the way Process to estimate actual answer. When rounding all the way, only one nonzero digit is left. Rounding all the way gives the least degree of accuracy. *Example:* 1,251 to 1,000; 2,995 to 3,000.

Round lot One hundred shares of stock or multiples of a hundred.

Rule of 78 Method to compute rebates on consumer finance loans. How much of finance charge you are entitled to? Formula or table lookup may be used.

Safekeeping Bank procedure whereby a bank does not return checks. Canceled checks are photocopied.

Sales tax Tax levied on consumers for certain sales of merchandise or services by states, counties, or various local governments.

Salvage value Cost less accumulated depreciation.

Selling price Cost plus markup equals selling price.

Semiannually Twice a year.

Semimonthly Some employees are paid twice a month.

Series discount See **chain discount.**

Short-rate table Fire insurance rate table used when insured cancels the policy.

Short-term policy Fire insurance policy for less than one year.

Signature card Information card signed by person opening a checking account.

Simple discount note A note in which bank deducts interest in advance.

Simple interest Interest is only calculated on the principal. In $I = P \times R \times T$, the interest plus original principal equals the maturity value of an interest-bearing note.

Simple interest formula

$$\text{Interest} = \text{Principal} \times \text{Rate} \times \text{Time}$$

$$\text{Principal} = \frac{\text{Interest}}{\text{Rate} \times \text{Time}}$$

$$\text{Rate} = \frac{\text{Interest}}{\text{Principal} \times \text{Time}}$$

$$\text{Time} = \frac{\text{Interest}}{\text{Principal} \times \text{Rate}}$$

Single equivalent discount rate Rate or factor as a single discount that calculates the amount of the trade discount by multiplying the rate times the list price. This single equivalent discount replaces a series of chain discounts. The single equivalent rate is (1 − Net price equivalent rate).

Sinking fund An annuity in which the stream of deposits with appropriate interest will equal a specified amount in the future.

Sliding scale commissions Different commision. Rates depend on different levels of sales.

Specific identification method This method calculates the cost of ending inventory by identifying each item remaining to invoice price.

State unemployment tax (SUTA) Tax paid by employer. Rate varies depending on amount of unemployment the company experiences.

Stock certificate Piece of paper that shows certificate of ownership in a company.

Stockholder One who owns stock in a company.

Stockholders' equity Assets less liabilities.

Stocks Ownership shares in the company sold to buyers, who receive stock certificates.

Stock yield percent Dividend per share divided by the closing price per share.

Straight commission Wages are based as a percent of the value of goods sold.

Straight life insurance (whole or ordinary) Protection (full value of policy) results from continual payment of premiums by insured. Until death or retirement, nonforfeiture values exist for straight life.

Straight-line method Method of depreciation that spreads an equal amount of depreciation each year over the life of the assets.

Straight-line rate (rate of depreciation) One divided by number of years of expected life.

Subtrahend In a subtraction problem smaller number that is being subtracted from another. *Example:* 30 in 150 − 30 = 120

Sum Total in the adding process.

Sum-of-the years'-digits method Accelerated method of depreciation. Depreciation each year is calculated by multiplying cost (less residual value) times a fraction. Numerator is number of years of useful life remaining. Denominator is the sum of the years of estimated life.

Tax rate $\frac{\text{Budget needed}}{\text{Total assessed value}}$

Term life insurance Inexpensive life insurance that provides protection for a specific period of time. No nonforfeiture values exist for term.

Term policy Period of time that the policy is in effect.

Terms of the sale Criteria on invoice showing when cash discounts are available, such as rate and time period.

Time Expressed as years or fractional years, used to calculate the simple interest.

Trade discount amount List price less net price.

Trade-in (scrap) Estimated value of a plant asset after depreciation is taken (or end of useful life).

Trend analysis Analyzing each number as a percentage of a base year.

Truth in Lending Act Federal law that requires sellers to inform buyers, in writing, of (1) the finance charge and (2) the annual percentage rate. The law doesn't dictate what can be charged.

Twenty-year endowment Most expensive life insurance policy. It is a combination of term insurance and cash value.

Unemployment tax Tax paid by the employer that is used to aid unemployed persons.

Units-of-production method Depreciation method that estimates amount of depreciation based on usage.

Universal life Whole life insurance plan with flexible premium and death benefits. This life plan has limited guarantees.

Unknown The variable we are solving for.

Unlike fractions Proper fractions with different denominators.

Useful life Estimated number of years the plant asset is used.

U.S. Rule Method that allows the borrower to receive proper interest credits when paying off a loan in more than one payment before the maturity date.

U.S. Treasury bill A note issued by federal government to investors.

Value of an annuity Sum of series of payments and interest (think of this as like the maturity value of compounding).

Variable commission scale Company pays different commission rates for different levels of net sales.

Variable rate Home mortgage rate is not fixed over its lifetime.

Variables Letters or symbols that represent unknowns.

Vertical analysis Method of analyzing financial reports where each total is compared to one total. *Example:* Cash is a percent of total assets.

W-4 See **Employee's Withholding Allowance Certificate.**

Wage bracket method Tables used in Circular E to compute FIT withholdings.

Weighted-average method Calculates the cost of ending inventory by applying an average unit cost to items remaining in inventory for that period of time.

Weighted mean Used to find an average when values appear more than once.

Whole life insurance See **Straight life insurance.**

Whole number Number that is 0 or larger, which doesn't contain a decimal or fraction, such as 10, 55, 92.

Withholding Amount of deduction from one's paycheck.

Workers' compensation Business insurance covering sickness or accidental injuries to employees that result from on-the-job activities.

Word Problem Blueprint Aid

For your convenience, on the following pages are blank Blueprint Aids to use as masters for making multiple copies.

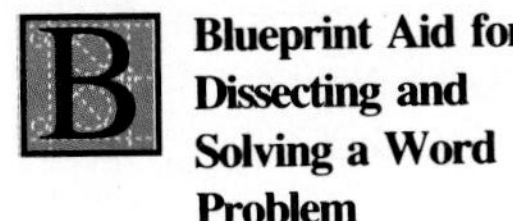

Blueprint Aid for Dissecting and Solving a Word Problem

A. Gather the facts	B. What am I solving for?	C. What must I know or calculate before solving problem?	D. Key points to remember

Steps to Solving Problem

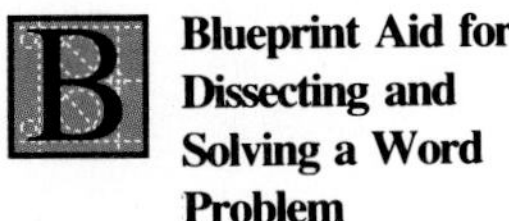

Blueprint Aid for Dissecting and Solving a Word Problem

A. Gather the facts	B. What am I solving for?	C. What must I know or calculate before solving problem?	D. Key points to remember

Steps to Solving Problem

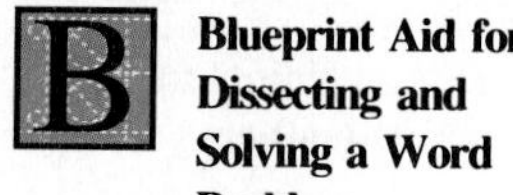

Blueprint Aid for Dissecting and Solving a Word Problem

A. Gather the facts	B. What am I solving for?	C. What must I know or calculate before solving problem?	D. Key points to remember

Steps to Solving Problem

V

Metric System

THE MOVE TO METRIC gets a boost from new laws and trade pressures.

The U.S.'s voluntary switch to metric measurements–legislated in 1975–fell flat. But international trade pressures, combined with a 1988 law requiring federal agencies to buy metric products by 1992 unless impractical or inefficient, are expected to move metric into the mainstream with many U.S. manufacturers. "I think it is going to be the turning point for the U.S. to go metric," says Valerie Antoine of the U.S. Metric Association, Northridge, Calif., noting government buying carries lots of clout.

Companies are already starting to plan conversions. Last month, Parker Hannifin Corp., Cleveland, held a "metric summit conference" with mobile-equipment makers to start developing new metric standards. The switch to metric will help U.S. companies compete in the coming European Economic Community and in South America, where Pacific-rim nations have gained market share, says G.T. Underwood of the U.S. Office of Metric Programs.

Not everyone will convert. Local dairies, for example, probably won't change bottles, Mr. Underwood says.

John Sullivan Angie, I drove into the gas station last night to fill the tank up. Did I get upset! The pumps were not in gallons but in liters. This country (U.S.) going to metric is sure making it confusing.

Angie Smith Don't get upset. Let me first explain the key units of measure in metric, and then I'll show you a convenient table I keep in my purse to convert metric to U.S. (also called customary system), and U.S. to metric. Let's go on.

The metric system is really a decimal system in which each unit of measure is exactly 10 times as large as the unit just smaller. In a moment, we will see how this aids in conversions. First, look at the middle column (Units) of this to see the basic units of measure:

U.S.	Thousands	Hundreds	Tens	Units	Tenths	Hundredths	Thousandths
Metric	Kilo- 1,000	Hecto- 100	Deka- 10	Gram Meter Liter 1	Deci- .1	Centi- .01	Milli- .001

Weight: Gram (think of it as $\frac{1}{30}$ of an ounce).
Length: Meter (think of it for now as a little more than a yard).
Volume: Liter (little more than a quart).

To aid you in looking at this, think of a decimeter, a centimeter, or a millimeter as being "shorter" (smaller) than a meter. Whereas a dekameter, hectometer, and kilometer are "larger" than a meter. For example:

1 centimeter = $\frac{1}{100}$ of a meter; or 100 centimeters equal 1 meter.
1 millimeter = $\frac{1}{1,000}$ meter; or 1,000 millimeters equal 1 meter.
1 hectometer = 100 meters.
1 kilometer = 1,000 meters.

Remember we could have used the same set up for grams or liters. Note the summary here.

Length	Volume	Mass
1 meter: = 10 decimeters = 100 centimeters = 1,000 millimeters = .1 dekameter = .01 hectometer = .001 kilometer	1 liter: = 10 deciliters = 100 centiliters = 1,000 milliliters = .1 dekaliter = .01 hectoliter = .001 kiloliter	1 gram: = 10 decigrams = 100 centigrams = 1,000 milligrams = .1 dekagram = .01 hectogram = .001 kilogram

Practice these conversions and check solutions.

PRACTICE QUIZ 1

V

Convert the following:

1. 7.2 m to cm
2. .89 m to mm
3. 64 cm to m
4. 350 g to kg
5. 7.4 L to cl
6. 2,500 mg to g

SOLUTIONS TO PRACTICE QUIZ 1

1. 7.2 m = 7.2 × 100 = 720 cm (remember 1 meter = 100 cm)
2. .89 m = .89 × 1,000 = 890 mm (remember 1 meter = 1,000 mm)
3. 64 cm = $\frac{64}{100}$ = .64 m (remember 1 meter = 100 cm)
4. 350 g = $\frac{350}{1,000}$ = .35 kg (remember 1 kg = 1,000 grams)

5. 7.4 L = 7.4 × 100 = 740 cl (remember 1 liter = 100 cl)

6. 2,500 mg = $\frac{2,500}{1,000}$ = 2.5 g (remember 1 gram = 1,000 mg)

Angie Look at the table of conversions and I'll show you how easy it is. Note how we can convert liters to gallons. Using the conversion from meters to U.S. (liters to gallons), we see that you multiply numbers of liters times .26, or 37.85 × .26 = 9.84 gallons.

Common conversion factors for English/metric

A. To convert from English	**to Metric**	**Multiply by**	**B. To convert from metric**	**to English**	**Multiply by**
Length:			*Length:*		
Inches	Meters	.025	Meters	Inches	39.37
Feet	Meters	.31	Meters	Feet	3.28
Yards	Meters	.91	Meters	Yards	1.1
Miles	Kilometers	1.6	Kilometers	Miles	.62
Weight:			*Weight:*		
Ounces	Grams	28	Grams	Ounces	.035
Pounds	Grams	454	Grams	Pounds	.0022
Pounds	Kilograms	.45	Kilograms	Pounds	2.2
Volume or capacity:			*Volume or capacity:*		
Pints	Liters	.47	Liters	Pints	2.1
Quarts	Liters	.95	Liters	Quarts	1.06
Gallons	Liters	3.8	Liters	Gallons	.26

John How would I convert 6 miles into kilometers?

Angie Take the number of miles times 1.6, thus 6 miles × 1.6 = 9.6 kilometers.

John If I weigh 120 pounds, what would be my weight in kilograms?

Angie 120 times .45 (use the conversion table) equals 54 kilograms.

John OK. Last night, when I bought 16.6 liters of gas, I really bought 4.3 gallons (16.6 liters times .26)

PRACTICE QUIZ 2

V

Convert the following:

1. 10 meters to yards
2. 110 quarts to liters
3. 78 kilometers to miles
4. 52 yards to meters
5. 82 meters to inches
6. 292 miles to kilometers

SOLUTIONS TO PRACTICE QUIZ 2

1. 10 meters × 1.1 = 11 yards
2. 110 quarts × .95 = 104.5 liters
3. 78 kilometers × .62 = 48.36 miles
4. 52 yards × .91 = 47.32 meters
5. 82 meters × 39.37 = 3,228.34 inches
6. 292 miles × 1.6 = 467.20 kilometers

APPENDIX V PROBLEMS

Drill Problems

Convert:

1. 65 cm to m .65 m $\left(\frac{65}{100}\right)$
2. 7.85 m to cm 785 cm (7.85 × 100)
3. 44 cl to L .44 liter $\left(\frac{44}{100}\right)$
4. 1,500 g to kg 1.5 kg $\left(\frac{1{,}500}{1{,}000}\right)$
5. 842 mm to m .842 m $\left(\frac{842}{1{,}000}\right)$
6. 9.4 kg to g 9,400 g (9.4 × 1,000)
7. .854 kg to g 854 g (.854 × 1,000)
8. 5.9 m to mm 5,900 mm (5.9 × 1,000)
9. 8.91 kg to g 8,910 g (8.91 × 1,000)
10. 2.3 m to mm 2,300 mm (2.3 × 1,000)

Convert (round off to nearest tenth):

11. 50.9 kg to pounds 111.98 lb (50.9 × 2.2)
12. 8.9 pounds to g 4,040.6 g (8.9 × 454)
13. 395 km to miles 244.9 mi (395 × .62)
14. 33 yards to m 30.03 m (33 × .91)
15. 13.9 pounds to g 6,310 g (13.9 × 454)
16. 594 miles to km 950.4 km (594 × 1.6)
17. 4.9 feet to m 1.5 m (4.9 ft × .31)
18. 9.9 feet to m 3.1 m (9.9 × .31)
19. 100 yards to m 91 m (100 × .91)
20. 40.9 kg to pounds 90 lbs (40.9 × 2.2)
21. 895 miles to km 1,432 km (895 × 1.6)
22. 1,000 grams to pounds 2.2 lbs (1,000 × .0022)
23. 79.1 m to yards 87 yards (79.1 × 1.1)
24. 12 liters to quarts 12.720 (12 × 1.06)
25. 2.92 m to feet 9.6 ft (2.92 × 3.28)
26. 5 liters to gallons 1.3 gal (5 × .26)
27. 8.7 m to feet 28.5 ft (8.7 × 3.28)
28. 8 gallons to liters 30.4 L (8 × 3.8)
29. 1,600 g to pounds 3.52 lbs (1,600 × .0022)
30. 310 m to yards 341 yards (310 × 1.1)

Word Problem

31. **Given:** A metric ton is 39.4 bushels of corn. Calculate number of bushels purchased from metric tons to bushels of corn.

    Problem: Soviets bought 450,000 metric tons of U.S. corn, valued at $58 million, for delivery after September 30.
    450,000 × 39.4 = 17,730,000 bushels of corn

Index

NOTES

NOTES

NOTES

NOTES

NOTES

NOTES

NOTES

NOTES